THE OXFORD HANDBOOK OF
LATIN AMERICAN SOCIAL MOVEMENTS

Advance Praise for *The Oxford Handbook of Latin American Social Movements*

"A 'must book' for anyone interested in social movements in general and in Latin America in particular. Contributors address a range of theoretical perspectives, and provide rich analyses of a wide variety of social movements. The most comprehensive book!"
—Susan Eckstein, Boston University

"Pervaded by inequalities of all sorts, Latin America has been a fertile terrain for the emergence of social movements and, therefore, of a remarkable production of analyses of their role and characteristics. In addition to an impressive and exhaustive array of different themes and analytical perspectives, this book has the crucial merit of opening space for significant theoretical contributions from Latin American scholarship on social movements, so often ignored by the English-language academia."
—Evelina Dagnino, Universidade Estadual de Campinas

"Latin America is as belligerent as it is unequal. The notable group of scholars assembled in this important volume tells us how and why social movements emerge and persist, offering students of contentious politics a vast array of insightful theoretical tools and empirical lessons."
—Javier Auyero, University of Texas at Austin

"*The Oxford Handbook of Latin American Social Movements* constitutes a major contribution to the field. It brings together in an interconnected way an important number of chapters, which cover a vast range of topics and problems, all of them of importance for the study of Latin American social movements. Recognizing the diversity of approaches applied to the study of social movements, it shows conceptual articulation and, in its full reading, offers an excellent overview of the field. This book is a significant contribution to the diffusion and debate of Latin American social and political sciences, the international circulation of the region's research and specific issues, while it contributes to the global debate on social movement studies."
—Federico Schuster, Universidad de Buenos Aires

THE OXFORD HANDBOOK OF

LATIN AMERICAN SOCIAL MOVEMENTS

Edited by
FEDERICO M. ROSSI

OXFORD
UNIVERSITY PRESS

Oxford University Press is a department of the University of Oxford. It furthers the University's objective of excellence in research, scholarship, and education by publishing worldwide. Oxford is a registered trade mark of Oxford University Press in the UK and certain other countries.

Published in the United States of America by Oxford University Press
198 Madison Avenue, New York, NY 10016, United States of America.

© Oxford University Press 2023

All rights reserved. No part of this publication may be reproduced, stored in a retrieval system, or transmitted, in any form or by any means, without the prior permission in writing of Oxford University Press, or as expressly permitted by law, by license, or under terms agreed with the appropriate reproduction rights organization. Inquiries concerning reproduction outside the scope of the above should be sent to the Rights Department, Oxford University Press, at the address above.

You must not circulate this work in any other form
and you must impose this same condition on any acquirer.

CIP data is on file at the Library of Congress
ISBN 978-0-19-087036-2

DOI: 10.1093/oxfordhb/9780190870362.001.0001

1 3 5 7 9 8 6 4 2

Printed by Marquis, Canada

*A te, Marco,
che adesso capirai il perché del tuo nome.*

Contents

About the Editor   xiii
About the Contributors   xv

INTRODUCTION

1. Multiple Paradigms for Understanding a Mobilized Region   3
   FEDERICO M. ROSSI

PART I: THEORETICAL PERSPECTIVES

2. Marxist Theories of Latin American Social Movements   17
   JEFFERY R. WEBBER

3. Resource Mobilization and Political Process Theories in Latin America   35
   NICOLÁS M. SOMMA

4. New Social Movements in Latin America and the Changing Socio-Political Matrix   54
   MANUEL ANTONIO GARRETÓN AND NICOLÁS SELAMÉ

5. Relational Approaches to Social Movements in (and beyond) Latin America   70
   SAM HALVORSEN AND FEDERICO M. ROSSI

6. Network Approaches to Latin America Social Movements   87
   ROSE J. SPALDING

7. Feminist and Queer Perspectives on Latin American Social Movements   107
   NIKI JOHNSON AND DIEGO SEMPOL

8. Decolonizing Approaches to Latin American Social Movements   123
   MARÍA JULIANA FLÓREZ-FLÓREZ AND MARÍA CAROLINA OLARTE-OLARTE

PART II: MAIN PROCESSES AND DYNAMICS

9. Protest Waves in Latin America: Facilitating Conditions and Outcomes — 143
   PAUL ALMEIDA

10. Social Movements and Nationalism in Latin America — 162
    MATTHIAS VOM HAU

11. Social Movements and Revolutions in Latin America: A Complex Relationship — 180
    SALVADOR MARTÍ I PUIG AND ALBERTO MARTÍN ÁLVAREZ

12. Social Movements under Authoritarian Regimes in Latin America — 196
    CHARLES D. BROCKETT

13. Social Movements and Democratization Processes in Latin America — 213
    MARÍA INCLÁN

14. Social Movements and Capitalist Models of Development in Latin America — 229
    FEDERICO M. ROSSI

15. Social Movements and Globalization in Latin America — 249
    DANIEL BURRIDGE AND JOHN MARKOFF

16. Movements and Territorial Conflicts in Latin America — 266
    BERNARDO MANÇANO FERNANDES AND CLIFF WELCH

17. Demobilization Processes in Latin America — 283
    PABLO LAPEGNA, RENATA MOTTA, AND MARITZA PAREDES

PART III: MAIN SOCIAL MOVEMENTS

18. Transformations of Workers' Mobilization in Latin America — 303
    FRANKLIN RAMÍREZ GALLEGOS AND SOLEDAD STOESSEL

19. Peasant Movements in Recent Latin American History — 320
    CLIFF WELCH

20. Women's Movements in Latin America: From Elite Organizing to Intersectional Mass Mobilization — 336
    CHRISTINA EWIG AND ELISABETH JAY FRIEDMAN

21. Indigenous Movements in Latin America: Characteristics and
Contributions 354
ROBERTA RICE

22. Afro-Social Movements and the Struggle for Racial Equality in Latin
America 370
KWAME DIXON AND KIA LILLY CALDWELL

23. Student Movements in Latin America: Pushing the Education
Agenda and Beyond 389
SOFIA DONOSO

24. Lesbian and Gay Social Movements in Latin America 406
JORDI DÍEZ

25. Human Rights Movements across Latin America 422
JONAS WOLFF

26. Environmental Mobilization in Latin America: Beyond the Lenses of
Social Movements 439
LUCAS G. CHRISTEL AND RICARDO A. GUTIÉRREZ

27. Urban Social Movements and the Politics of Inclusion in Latin
America 455
PHILIP OXHORN

28. Anti-Corruption Social Mobilization in Latin America 471
SEBASTIÁN PEREYRA, TOMÁS GOLD, AND MARÍA SOLEDAD GATTONI

29. Consumer (Rights) Movements in Latin America 488
SYBIL RHODES

30. Autonomist Movements in Latin America 505
MARCELO LOPES DE SOUZA

31. Transnational Social Movements in Latin America 521
MARISA VON BÜLOW

32. Right-Wing Movements in Latin America 537
LEIGH A. PAYNE

33. Revolutionary Movements and Guerrillas in Latin America: From
Revolutions to revolutions 556
LEONIDAS OIKONOMAKIS

PART IV: IDEATIONAL AND STRATEGIC DIMENSIONS OF SOCIAL MOVEMENTS

34. Social Movements in Latin America: The Cultural Dimension   573
    TON SALMAN

35. Identity in Latin American Social Movements   590
    LORENZA B. FONTANA

36. Ideas, Ideology, and Citizenship of Social Movements   607
    ANTHONY PETROS SPANAKOS AND MISHELLA ROMO RIVAS

37. Religious Groups and Social Movements in Latin America   625
    ROBERT SEAN MACKIN

38. Education, Pedagogy, and Social Movements in Latin America   643
    REBECCA TARLAU

39. Repertoires of Contention across Latin America   660
    TAKESHI WADA

40. Shifting Geographies of Activism and the Spatial Logics of Latin American Social Movements   678
    DIANE E. DAVIS AND TAYLOR DAVEY

41. Strengths and Blind Spots of Digital Activism in Latin America: Mapping Actors, Tools, and Theories   696
    EMILIANO TRERÉ AND SUMMER HARLOW

PART V: INSTITUTIONAL POLITICS AND SOCIAL MOVEMENTS

42. Social Movements and Party Politics: Popular Mobilization and the Reciprocal Structuring of Political Representation in Latin America   715
    KENNETH M. ROBERTS

43. Social Movement Activism, Informal Politics, and Clientelism in Latin America   731
    HÉLÈNE COMBES AND JULIETA QUIRÓS

44. Legal Mobilization: Social Movements and the Judicial System across Latin America 746
 ALBA RUIBAL

45. Social Movements and Participatory Institutions in Latin America 761
 ROCÍO ANNUNZIATA AND BENJAMIN GOLDFRANK

46. Social Movements and Modes of Institutionalization 777
 ADRIAN GURZA LAVALLE AND JOSÉ SZWAKO

Index 795

About the Editor

FEDERICO M. Rossi (PhD, European University Institute, Florence) is a Profesor-Investigador of the Consejo Nacional de Investigaciones Científicas y Técnicas (CONICET) at the Universidad Nacional de San Martín in Buenos Aires, and a Senior Fellow of the Humboldt Stiftung at the German Institute for Global and Area Studies (GIGA) in Hamburg. He has published *The Poor's Struggle for Political Incorporation: The Piquetero Movement in Argentina* (Cambridge University Press), *Reshaping the Political Arena in Latin America: From Resisting Neoliberalism to the Second Incorporation* (University of Pittsburgh Press), *Social Movement Dynamics: New Perspectives on Theory and Research from Latin America* (Routledge), and *La participación de las juventudes hoy: la condición juvenil y la redefinición del involucramiento político y social* (Prometeo).

About the Contributors

Paul Almeida, University of California, Merced, United States

Alberto Martín Álvarez, Universitat de Girona, Spain

Rocío Annunziata, Consejo Nacional de Investigaciones Científicas y Técnicas (CONICET)—Universidad Nacional de San Martín, Argentina

Charles D. Brockett, Sewanee: The University of the South, United States

Daniel Burridge, University of Pittsburgh, United States

Kia Lilly Caldwell, Washington University in St. Louis, United States

Lucas G. Christel, Consejo Nacional de Investigaciones Científicas y Técnicas (CONICET)—Universidad Nacional de San Martín, Argentina

Hélène Combes, Centre national de la recherche scientifique (CNRS)—Centre de recherches internationale (CERI) of Sciences Po, France

Taylor Davey, Harvard University, United States

Diane E. Davis, Harvard University, United States

Jordi Díez, University of Guelph, Canada

Kwame Dixon, Howard University, United States

Sofia Donoso, Universidad de Chile and Centro de Estudios de Conflicto y Cohesión Social (COES), Chile

Christina Ewig, University of Minnesota, United States

Bernardo Mançano Fernandes, Universidade Estadual Paulista "Júlio de Mesquita Filho" (UNESP), Brazil

María Juliana Flórez-Flórez, Pontificia Universidad Javeriana, Colombia

Lorenza B. Fontana, University of Glasgow, United Kingdom

Elisabeth Jay Friedman, University of San Francisco, United States

Manuel Antonio Garretón, Universidad de Chile, Chile

María Soledad Gattoni, Universidad Nacional de San Martín (UNSAM), Argentina

Tomás Gold, University of Notre Dame, United States

Benjamin Goldfrank, Seton Hall University, United States

Adrian Gurza Lavalle, Universidade de São Paulo and Centro de Estudos da Metrópole (CEM)—Centro Brasileiro de Análise e Planejamento (CEBRAP), Brazil

Ricardo A. Gutiérrez, Consejo Nacional de Investigaciones Científicas y Técnicas (CONICET)—Universidad Nacional de San Martín, Argentina

Sam Halvorsen, Queen Mary University of London, United Kingdom

Summer Harlow, University of Houston, United States

María Inclán, Centro de Investigación y Docencia Económicas (CIDE), Mexico

Niki Johnson, Universidad de la República, Uruguay

Pablo Lapegna, University of Georgia, United States

Robert Sean Mackin, Texas A&M University, United States

John Markoff, University of Pittsburgh, United States

Salvador Martí i Puig, Universitat de Girona, Spain

Renata Motta, Heidelberg University, Germany

Leonidas Oikonomakis, University of Crete (Πανεπιστήμιο Κρήτης), Greece

María Carolina Olarte-Olarte, Universidad de Los Andes, Colombia

Philip Oxhorn, Vancouver Island University, Canada

Maritza Paredes, Pontificia Universidad Católica del Perú, Peru

Leigh A. Payne, University of Oxford, United Kingdom

Sebastián Pereyra, Consejo Nacional de Investigaciones Científicas y Técnicas (CONICET)—Universidad Nacional de San Martín, Argentina

Julieta Quirós, Consejo Nacional de Investigaciones Científicas y Técnicas (CONICET)—Instituto de Antropología de Córdoba, Argentina

Franklin Ramírez Gallegos, Facultad Latinoamericana de Ciencias Sociales (FLACSO), Ecuador

Sybil Rhodes, Universidad del Centro de Estudios Macroeconómicos de Argentina (UCEMA), Argentina

Roberta Rice, University of Calgary, Canada

Kenneth M. Roberts, Cornell University, Unites States

Mishella Romo Rivas, Princeton University, United States

Alba Ruibal, Consejo Nacional de Investigaciones Científicas y Técnicas (CONICET)—Universidad Nacional de Córdoba, Argentina

Ton Salman, Vrije Universiteit Amsterdam, Netherlands

Nicolás Selamé, Facultad Latinoamericana de Ciencias Sociales (FLACSO), Chile

Diego Sempol, Universidad de la República, Uruguay

Nicolás M. Somma, Pontificia Universidad Católica de Chile and Centro de Estudios de Conflicto y Cohesión Social (COES), Chile

Marcelo Lopes de Souza, Universidade Federal de Rio de Janeiro, Brazil

Rose J. Spalding, DePaul University, United States

Anthony Petros Spanakos, Montclair State University, United States

Soledad Stoessel, Consejo Nacional de Investigaciones Científicas y Técnicas (CONICET)—Universidad Nacional de La Plata, Argentina

José Szwako, Instituto de Estudos Sociais e Politicos, Universidade do Estado do Rio de Janeiro, Brazil

Rebecca Tarlau, Pennsylvania State University, United States

Emiliano Treré, Cardiff University, United Kingdom

Matthias vom Hau, Institut Barcelona d'Estudis Internacionals, Spain

Marisa von Bülow, Universidade de Brasília, Brazil

Takeshi Wada, The University of Tokyo (東京大学), Japan

Jeffery R. Webber, York University, Canada

Cliff Welch, Universidade Federal de São Paulo, Brazil

Jonas Wolff, Goethe University Frankfurt and Peace Research Institute Frankfurt (PRIF), Germany

INTRODUCTION

CHAPTER 1

MULTIPLE PARADIGMS FOR UNDERSTANDING A MOBILIZED REGION

FEDERICO M. ROSSI

Introduction

When humans get involved in the making of history, collective action is an essential component in the struggle for or against social change. The fate of societies is not written in stone but rather is made through a process of disputing contending ideas and interests about how we will live together. Social movements, as informal networks of conflict-oriented interactions composed of individuals, groups, and/or organizations that, based on shared solidarities, are provided with a collective political identity and use protest as one means—among others—of presenting themselves in the public arena, are crucial actors in the battle to define what Latin America is and should be. Latin America is a region as diverse as it is immense, with a multiplicity of experiences and grievances and tied together by a shared Luso-Hispanic colonial legacy. The question of how to understand the struggles that have defined Latin American history since independence has produced very intense theoretical debate and the development of several ways of identifying the role of social movements. The multiplicity of movements that have been in constant struggle is fertile ground for theoretical innovation and interdisciplinary research, as this introduction will reveal in its presentation of the contributions to *The Oxford Handbook of Latin American Social Movements*.

Theoretical Perspectives

In such a huge territory as Latin America is not possible to expect a unified or hegemonic theoretical approach, as can happen in a single country. Thus, the development in

Latin America of social movement studies as a subdiscipline has been characterized by a great diversity of theoretical approaches and a pragmatic combination of perspectives in empirical studies. This volume reflects this wide variety of viewpoints. Its first section covers the main theoretical perspectives in the debate on social movements in Latin America, something that has never been done before. In this sense, this book is the first to present all the main theoretical approaches with some systematic application to Latin American social movements that have been developed in or applied to the region.

Much older than social movement studies and originally not focused on movements, the pioneering approach in the study of social conflicts has been Marxism. In past decades, many changes were seen within the realm of Marxist approaches in Latin America, emphasizing capitalism, totality, and class for the study of social movements. Studying the decisive influence of José Carlos Mariátegui, Antonio Gramsci, dependency theory and the contemporary contributions to the commons, autonomy, and social movement–state relations is at the core of Jeffery R. Webber's chapter. The critical dialogue with Marxism provides the fuel for other main approaches. Resource mobilization theory and the political process approach emerged in the 1970s in the United States as a critique of modernization theories and Marxism, quickly becoming one of the most influential approaches for studying social movements. As Nicolás M. Somma shows, scholars of Latin American movements have long noted the relevance of resources, strategies, organizations, and political contexts, providing a promising setting for expanding and refining mainstream approaches. In the 1980s, there was no sign of change in the economic or class structure in Latin America, as seems to have taken place in Europe according to the New Social Movements approach. Instead, as argued by Manuel Antonio Garretón and Nicolás Selamé, the disintegration of the socio-political matrix and the traditional developmentalist state is more relevant to explain the emergence of New Social Movements in Latin America as an influential approach to social movements.

In the 2000s, relationality emerged as a crucial perspective in the study of social movements. However, there are different ways of understanding what relational means in social movement studies, according to Sam Halvorsen and Federico M. Rossi. Schematically, this depends on the main dimension(s) studied as the focus of research. Intersectional approaches examine relations across core categories of identity. Historical approaches examine relations between movements and other actors across time. Spatial approaches explore the co-constitution of the social and the spatial in social movements. Finally, ecological approaches focus on the relations between movements and nature. Among these relational approaches, prominent are network approaches on Latin American social movements. Rose Spalding's chapter identifies two dominant ones: formal network analysis involving quantitative analysis of large-n data sets in which relationships are depicted in matrices, sociogram visualizations, and graphs; and informal, small-n comparative studies of network structures found in specific movements, often analyzed across an extended period of time using process tracing techniques. Network analysis in Latin America draws attention to ways in which activists interconnect across the region, and the consequences in terms of movement strength and impact.

The key theories and concepts informing feminist and queer perspectives on Latin American social movements are the focus of Niki Johnson's and Diego Sempol's chapter. They argue that these result from processes of translation and contestation of theories produced by academic research in the Global North, and from the development of locally grounded theoretical perspectives. The chapter discusses how feminist and queer perspectives in research have opened up avenues for analyzing the complexities of collective identity construction and the tensions within as well as among social movements. New developments in feminist and queer social and political theorizing and epistemological reflection in the region seek to decolonize knowledge production. Decolonizing approaches is precisely the topic of the last theoretical approach covered. Juliana Flórez-Flórez and María Carolina Olarte-Olarte show that the theories on social movements mentioned above are colonial despite being critical of modernity. They argue that it is dialogue with movements—as opposed to discussion about movements—that makes it possible to evaluate collective action.

Within this rich diversity in theoretical approaches, common to them all has been that they have been built on a double dialogue *within* the region and *with* Europe or the United States (even the decolonizing critique implies a dialogue *against* the core). Yet if not all approaches are equally positivist, they are all historically rooted theoretical contributions that reflect Latin American social movements. In this sense, theoretical eclecticism dominates in pragmatic applications of literature and approaches. This obviously does not come without difficulties, creating an increasing multiplicity of studies that do not dialogue among themselves. Language barriers have been historically very relevant, and are still present, with three main language-confined debates (Portuguese, Spanish, and English) which are gradually merging into a regional debate. This publication is offered in English because the less established dialogue is the one this handbook aims to promote. Here many important contributions that are ignored by English-language academia can be accessed in a synthetic fashion across the chapters. However, this will not resolve a huge problem that exists beyond social movement studies in Latin America, which is the relative isolation of certain smaller or weaker national academic spaces. Beyond differences and problems, a common basic trend of all the literature in and about the region is the centrality of grievances, the economy, and a radical/revolutionary horizon in the actors studied and (sometimes also) in the scholars involved in the analysis of these movements.

Main Processes and Dynamics

As social movements are inserted in, are constituted by, and mold the key processes and contentious dynamics that define the history of Latin America, the second section examines each of the main macro-dynamics and the role played by social movements in them. These dynamics are parallel and simultaneous, with movements dealing with them partially and—in a very few cases—intersectionally. The hegemon of each historical period of Latin American history (the Iberian Peninsula, Britain, the United States, and—soon–China) is one of the unifiers of so many struggles but, still, cross-grievance battles are extremely difficult if seen in relational terms. Not all approaches are relational, though, and the analysis of the macro-dynamics reflects the richness of Latin American social movement studies.

Among the multiple waves that intersect in Latin American history, protest waves are crucial for understanding periods of widespread popular mobilization by multiple sectors across the national territory, as Paul Almeida argues and demonstrates in his chapter. Protest waves and other mobilizational dynamics since the postcolonial era intersect with nationalism. As Matthias vom Hau argues, nationalism and social movements emerged during the early nineteenth-century struggles for the formation of independent national states, followed by the mid-twentieth-century decline of oligarchic rule and the emergence of mass societies, and since the late twentieth century due to the adoption of neoliberalism and the rise of multiculturalism and indigenous movements.

Throughout the twentieth century, successful revolutions in Latin America were engineered by broad inter-class, urban–rural coalitions led by insurgent elites. Salvador Martí i Puig and Alberto Martín Álvarez study the different types of relationships established between social movements and the revolutionary vanguard in the analyses of revolutionary dynamics across Latin America. Many revolutionary ambitions were stopped by coups or turned into authoritarianism. Charles D. Brockett's chapter analyzes the vast and varied Latin American experience with confrontations between social movements and authoritarian regimes in a typology of personal dictatorships, military regimes, and competitive authoritarianism. The one constant found between cases and across regime types is that when an authoritarian regime possesses both the capacity and propensity to repress social movements it will almost always succeed. The transition from authoritarianism to democracy has been one of the main Latin American regional dynamics. María Inclán offers a review of the most salient cases of social movements and democratization processes in Latin America, evaluating the role that social movements have played in triggering democratizing processes in the region and exploring the movements that have emerged as democracy has deepened in the region.

Political dynamics are intertwined with economic dynamics. The capitalist models of development that predominated across Latin American history is the topic of Federico M. Rossi's chapter. A political economy of social movements reveals multiple struggles for the expansion of the socio-political arena and the resistance to this expansion with plutocratic retrenchment periods that contract the socio-political arena. Globalization has been the central capitalist transformation of Latin America in the 1990s and beyond. As Daniel Burridge and John Markoff argue, the policies of globalized neoliberal capitalism coincided with regional democratization, new technologies of communication, and changing ideas on the left to both generate a number of grievances and facilitate varied forms of social movement resistance. In addition, the main long-term dynamic against and within capitalism is the intense struggle for land across Latin America. Indigenous peoples, peasants, and the descendants of fugitive slaves have resisted the expropriation of their territories for five centuries. As Bernardo Mançano Fernandes and Cliff Welch argue, territorial clashes are also disputing divergent models of development.

All these processes and dynamics may produce enduring results and sustain protracted struggles across decades, which tend to go through some periods of increased disruption—as protest waves and revolutionary dynamics show—and others of latency and demobilization. As Pablo Lapegna, Renata Motta, and Maritza Paredes argue, demobilization is not simply the absence of mobilization, as it assumes the previous organization of contentious actions of organizations that are still active. The study of demobilization requires focusing on the role of agency and strategy to better understand how social movements refrain from mobilizing to advance their claims and achieve their goals.

The interconnection of processes and dynamics and the different roles of movements within them becomes evident as the chapters gradually add one after another new layers to the multidimensional process of social change. Social movements struggle within, against, and in favor of and constitute these processes and dynamics as much as they are constituted by them, as the centuries of history analyzed in this section show. However, to fully comprehend these contentious dynamics we need to understand the main social movements contending for the definition of grievances and the prefiguration of alternatives.

Main Social Movements

When observing the main social movements as the central focus of scrutiny we can perceive how the historical construction of struggles and their interconnection has produced paths that reflect specific theoretical debates that have dominated the Latin American scholarship. Even though is impossible to cover all types of movements that exist, the collection of movements studied in the third section allows for a quite clear understanding of the social movement field in Latin America from the mid-nineteenth to the early twenty-first century.

Labor movements, given their centrality in Latin American politics, are analyzed in the opening chapter. Franklin Gallegos Ramírez and Soledad Stoessel observe the link between changing economic contexts, state–society relations, and workers' collective action to show that union dynamics for extending workers' rights do not fully explain labor movements. Instead, successive waves of politicization of the "worker question" are a result of interactions of class, ethnicity, gender, and territory. If in the urban realm labor movements have been the central actors, in the rural one peasant movements have been the defining popular movement. As Cliff Welch argues, overlapping developments in diverse locations that are generally determined by the intensity of the penetration of capitalist relations of production have marked peasant movements in Latin America.

As can be seen in the case of women's movements, which have evolved from elite efforts into intersectional mass movements, not all movements have always been popular-based in Latin America. In the construction of a mass movement, Christina Ewig and Elisabeth Jay Friedman claim that women mobilized in response to a contradictory assortment of political opportunities, including the modernizing patriarchies of early states; the conservative gendered discourses and repression of authoritarian governments; the androcentric processes of democracy and neoliberal reform; and the ideals of revolutionary and left-leaning movements and parties across the twentieth century.

Race, ethnicity, and land are the historical roots of indigenous dispossession, and the characteristics and contributions of indigenous struggles for identity, territory, and autonomy help understand social movement theory and practice, according to Roberta Rice. The struggle for racial justice and human rights and the rise of Afro-Latin social movements, Black consciousness, and Afro civil society is analyzed by Kwame Dixon and Kia Lilly Caldwell. In both movements, the chapters show how the accumulation of efforts led to important multicultural and constitutional reforms in Latin America.

Among the two more mobilized middle-class actors are students and LGBTIQ+ movements. The role that student movements have played in Latin America's political development is the topic of Sofía Donoso's chapter. It examines their impact both in the field of education and in broader political reforms. Student movements have constituted a space of ideological renewal of and resistance to the various socio-political and economic inequalities that historically have characterized the region. In this renewal of ideas, lesbian and gay movements, despite their significantly smaller size compared to other movements, appear to be one of the most successful in the region given the speed with which they have emerged and strengthened as well as the scope of their political victories. As Jordi Díez explains, historically oppressed and marginalized, not only have gays and lesbians forced national debates on the regulation of sexuality, but, in several countries, their mobilization has resulted in the attainment of numerous rights, all in a relatively short period of time.

Many of these transformations are directly or indirectly related to the development of a human rights agenda that reaches beyond citizenship rights to social rights. Jonas Wolff eloquently shows how the narrow focus on a rather minimalist conception of human rights that had characterized the first generation of human rights movements has been replaced by a much broader human rights agenda, which encompasses social, economic, and cultural rights, as well as by more specific demands based on issue- or group-specific rights. As the rights agenda expanded and connected with the questioning of models of development and the struggle for land, environmental issues have produced—as shown by Lucas G. Christel and Ricardo A. Gutiérrez—an increased mobilization aiming to influence decisions regarding the political and economic regulation of the interactions between human beings and their environment. While the environmental question is global and quite recent, its contentious dynamics have been overwhelmingly performed in rural areas and on the margins of urban areas. The urban question, instead, has been a central topic for much longer—as Philip Oxhorn argues in his chapter—leading to the emergence of a growing number of urban social movements and a focus on democratic politics and citizenship rights associated with a new model of citizenship in the region: citizenship as agency. The region's commitment to relatively free and fair elections based on universal suffrage creates a unique opportunity for the mobilization of urban movements demanding improved collective consumption, respect for community culture, and political self-governance.

The double transition to liberal democratic politics and market-based economies has been as much an opportunity for mobilization as a trigger for abrupt dislocation in Latin American societies. This huge transformation has favored the proliferation of movements and claims from both the left and the right that attempt to regulate the new status quo by making representatives accountable and controlling patterns of consumption, transforming how things stand with the prefiguration of alternative social practices, interconnecting actors and struggles across scales, and resisting transformations of all kinds. Sebastián Pereyra, Tomás Gold, and María Soledad Gattoni show how corruption as a social problem was progressively incorporated into the frame of social mobilization as a significant element of criticism and confrontation with party politics. Sybil Rhodes outlines the history of consumption and consumer mobilization in Latin America, showing how consumption differences between haves and have-nots remain as a fundamental point of tension. Marcelo Lopes de Souza argues that autonomist movements have emerged from the crisis of Marxism-Leninism, the rise of neoliberalism, and the reinvigoration/rediscovering of left-libertarian ideas and tactics such as self-management, horizontality, and decentralization. Autonomists sometimes resemble urban movements, while also participating in transnational networks. Latin America has been an important cradle for transnational social movements since the beginning of the twentieth century, as Marisa von Bülow explores. These movements not only launched reactive campaigns to counter threats but also built new organizational fora and events to think about policy alternatives in innovative ways. Novelty and change have been increasingly resisted by right-wing movements that have emerged in the region with a profound impact on Latin American social and political life. Leigh A. Payne proposes to deepen our understanding of this important global phenomenon with a typology of right-wing movements in the region: counter-movements, uncivil movements, and neoliberal militarized movements.

There has been plenty of innovation, as well as continuity, in social movement dynamics. In this sense, the armed struggle option of Latin American social movements has never disappeared, although it has metamorphosed in important ways. Leonidas Oikonomakis analyzes revolutionary movements in contemporary Latin America, arguing that while it seems that the age of Latin American Revolutions with a capital R is coming to an end, we may be entering an age of revolutions (with a small r, following John Holloway) in which Revolution has changed meaning, becoming more of a political process and less of a political event.

As the chapters in this section show in their cumulative analysis of the transformations of social movements and their struggles, we cannot fully understand movements without studying their ideational and strategic dimensions and the relationship of movements with institutional politics. The two last sections focus on the crucial theoretical debates in social movement studies that Latin American scholarship has quite thoroughly developed in these regards.

Ideational and Strategic Dimensions of Social Movements

The fourth section deals with ideational and strategic dimensions of social movements, both central components of any struggle for or against social change. The diversity of scholarship on Latin American social movements has produced interesting debates on topics that are now classical, such as the role of religion, identity, and ideology in movements, and on new ones, such as those involving spatial analysis or examining the party system and the internet.

Ton Salman starts these studies with an exploration of the three modes in which he proposes culture should be studied in social movement research: culture as an overarching, partially shared, and partially subconscious set of practices and routines that orient both contenders and authorities; culture as the issue social movements are addressing and criticizing; and the culture the movements attempt to embody and broadcast in their forms and operations.

Equally important to culture are identity, ideology, and religious beliefs on movements. Lorenza B. Fontana examines the origins of identity as a key concept in socio-political analysis and illustrates the role it has played both in making sense of social and political transformations and in influencing the very processes of collective mobilization in Latin America. Anthony Petros Spanakos and Mishella Romo Rivas examine how ideology and ideas about popular sovereignty highlight important nuances between movements that might otherwise be grouped together. While many social movements share left-wing roots, anti-neoliberal politics, and the making of demands for recognition of marginal groups as part of a process of a thick form of citizenship, they differ considerably on how and where they rule. The common beliefs and values of mobilized actors are sometimes composed of religious ideas, too. Thus, the historical role of Roman Catholicism and the more recent Pentecostalization of religion has been crucial for both the struggle for social justice and the mobilization of conservative movements to denounce so-called "morality" issues (such as birth control, abortion, or marriage equality).

For constituting the desired transformations in society, ideational components are as essential to social movements as strategic dimensions. The cultural battle has been at the core of all social movement strategies, and the role of education has been crucial within

Latin American social movements. Rebecca Tarlau's chapter gives an overview of political education starting from the first half of the twentieth century, with a focus on the Communist Party and anarchists. She analyzes the impact, from the mid-1960s to the early 1980s, of Paulo Freire, and for the period after the re-democratization of the region focuses on non-formal education as well as the movement's transformation of and co-governance with public education.

The idea of repertoires of contention has become an integral part of the study of protest strategy in Latin American social movements. To explain the reasons why new and innovative forms of contention emerge in Latin America, Takeshi Wada looks for some of the main causal factors suggested in the repertoire literature including, among others, regime characteristics, material resources, cultural schemas, and collective identities. Expanding the repertoire of contention debate, according to Diane E. Davis and Taylor Davey, the repertoire has undergone historical changes in its geography and spatiality in Latin America. The authors identify new repertoires of mobilization, link them to changing social, political, and economic conditions, and assess the significance of these shifts for both the theory and practice of social mobilization in contemporary Latin America. Among the most radical changes in the repertoire has been the emergence of digital activism. However, according to Emiliano Treré and Summer Harlow, this trend has not yet produced a unified scholarly debate and is dominated by the propensity to adopt conceptual lenses from the Global North, displaying both methodological and conceptual shortcomings governing the Latin American literature.

The ideational and strategic dimensions of social movements are integrated in this section. Each chapter looks at one dimension in depth, which tends to leave no space for exploring in detail the interconnection between the ideational and strategic dimensions that all contributors to this section systematically assert. When all the layers added are interrelated, it becomes clear that in the formation of a movement and its repertoire, ideas and strategies are co-constituted through contentious dynamics. Consequently, ideas and strategies are all performed throughout the processes explored in the second section, evolving in the specific paths for each movement analyzed in the third section. All of this happens within the realm and in confrontation with an institutional context that is the topic of the last section.

INSTITUTIONAL POLITICS AND SOCIAL MOVEMENTS

The book's last section deals with the interaction of social movements with the institutional arena, analyzing its formal as well as informal fields of struggle. The institutional realm is conceived as more than the rules and actors of the state (omnipresent across all the book in direct or indirect ways). Social movements strive to change or reinforce a preexisting institutional apparatus, and, in this battle, there are important theoretical debates that the scholarship on Latin American social movements has produced and which are examined here.

Movements and parties are both collective actors that offer citizens a space in the public sphere to express interests and values. As Kenneth M. Roberts argues, movements and parties can be mutually constitutive, and they reciprocally structure, and sometimes de-structure, mass political representation. Understanding political representation in the region requires close attention to the interaction between parties and movements and their mutual role in the building of popular collective subjects. In this sense, the overlaps between social movement activism, informal party politics, and the dispute over state resources is the focus of Hélène Combes and Julieta Quirós's chapter. The nature of contentious politics, in which the popular sectors in Latin America have played a leading role, has been shaped by the close relationship that exists between processes of politicization and the reproduction of life of these subaltern segments of society.

These formal and informal links have not prevented movements from developing rapports with the judiciary, executive, and legislative. As eloquently shown by Alba Ruibal, the use of law and courts has become part of the repertoire of collective action by social movements in Latin America. After democratic transitions, the rights discourse set out to permeate political claims, social actors started framing their grievances and goals in terms of legal and constitutional rights, and constitutional and judicial reforms brought about new legal opportunities for social actors in different Latin American countries. In this setting, legal mobilization became part of social movements' work and strategies, and movements began to take on a relevant role in constitutional politics. Concerning the executive and the legislative, Rocío Annunziata and Benjamin Goldfrank show that while research on social movements rarely pays attention to participatory institutions, since they tend to be introduced by government authorities from the top down and oriented towards consensus, the literature on participatory institutions has been interested in social movements as key promoters, supporters, or participants. However, the role of social movements in participatory institutions is not always and not necessarily related to more inclusionary participation.

Finally, the influence of social movements on public policy has become increasingly relevant in Latin America. Adrian Gurza Lavalle and José Szwako examine the modes of institutionalization of social movements, proposing four modes: programmatic, positional, symbolic, and practical. The programmatic mode refers to a form of institutionalization of public policies and institutional arenas. The positional mode can be understood as a form of institutionalization in which official positions within the state apparatus are linked to social movements and occupied by activists. The symbolic mode concerns the internalization of symbolic and cognitive categories of social actors by the state. Finally, the practical mode of institutionalization refers to what are often understood as "merely technical" aspects or "minor details" of public policy.

This section introduces the main avenues for the study of the interactions of social movements with institutional politics, giving a general and—at the same time—detailed idea of the main debates to which the Latin American scholarship has mostly contributed. If this section is linked back to the previous one, many topics become intertwined, as the debate on repertoires reappears in the discussion of judicial mobilization and the institutional apparatus was crucial for the analysis of educational projects in social movements. Institutionalization and demobilization are alternative ways of observing non-contentious strategies of movements if agency is kept at the core of the relational construction of social movement paths and contentious dynamics. The interconnections and dialogue between chapters are limitless—seeming pieces of a kinetic puzzle that is always moving as the collection of actors that are the focus of this volume constantly change.

Conclusion

This book offers the most complete analysis to date of the debates that dominate social movement studies in Latin America. The collective effort of the contributors mentioned in these pages show how, in order to understand such a mobilized region, we need to open the discussion to the situated analysis of explorations that can deal with theoretically driven questions while also inquiring into Latin American history without theoretical dogmatisms. The scholarship on Latin American social movements offers to the general social movement literature—as well as to core disciplinary debates in social sciences and the humanities—multiple answers to theoretical gaps. The reader is invited to dive into the pages that follow to understand the contention of Latin American social movements to influence the course of history.

PART I
THEORETICAL PERSPECTIVES

CHAPTER 2

MARXIST THEORIES OF LATIN AMERICAN SOCIAL MOVEMENTS

JEFFERY R. WEBBER

Introduction

How have general Marxist areas of inquiry informed, and how have they been informed by, the study of social movements in Latin America? To begin, the influence of Marx and Marxism in Latin America dates back to at least a century before the formal concept of "social movements" becomes widely used in the region in the 1980s and 1990s. Indeed, it is only with the crisis of Marxism in the latter period, and Marxism's attendant decline as an analytical and political project, that the terminology of social movements, as borrowed and adapted from American and European social sciences, gains ascendancy in Latin America (Modonesi and Iglesias 2016: 119). This chapter provides both a conceptual introduction to Marxism and social movements and a chronological survey of the development of Marxism in the region with special attention to its implications for the conceptualization and politicization of social movements.

Marxism and Social Movements

In the collected works of Karl Marx and Friedrich Engels one often encounters the notion of "movement," and less frequently "social movement," but not "social movements." What is more, even when movement or social movement appear as terms they are not theorized as concepts in anything approximating a full elaboration. "An account of Marxism's approach to social movements must therefore involve a degree of selection and reconstruction, and must hold in mind that Marxism is itself both a *contested* and a *developing* tradition" (Barker 2013).

With this caveat noted, I will nonetheless argue that, to date, three areas of focus distinguish Marxist approaches from other perspectives on social movements: *capitalism*, *totality*, and *class*. If identity or New Social Movement (NSM) theorists replaced capitalism and class with culture, meaning, and constructed identities in the 1980s and 1990s (see Garretón and Selamé in this volume), strategy theorists of resource mobilization and political opportunity structures over time abandoned an early interest in capitalism and class, in the 1960s and 1970s, in favor of ostensibly autonomous realms of politics, institutions, and opportunities, in more recent decades (see Somma in this volume). A Marxist approach to social movements reintroduces the enabling and inhibiting features of capitalism in its relationship to social movements, highlights the class dynamics of all social movements, and, through the concept of totality (and "unity of the diverse"), draws connections between seemingly disparate social movements, including those of labor, ecology, gender, ethnicity, sexuality, and nation (Barker et al. 2013; Silver and Karatasli 2015; Webber 2019). Precisely to indicate the connectivity across movements some Marxist theorists suggest that perhaps a return to discussion of the "social movement" in singular, with different sectional struggles constituting distinct parts of the complex whole, is in order (Barker 2012). Others suggest putting an accent on the notion of *subaltern political action*, rather than *social movements*, where political action from below is understood as a vector for the politicization of subaltern classes, with the experience of struggle, insubordination, and antagonism constituting the basis for political subjectivity (Modonesi 2016: 12, 23).

Capitalism, Class, and Totality

Why capitalism? First, because the commodification of labor is inherent in capitalism, and because human beings grieve and resist their reduction to commodities, labor struggle is a necessary and perpetual feature of capitalism, leading to variegated forms and scales of political contestation depending on the situation. Second, because the historical development of capitalism introduces recurring organizational transformations of production and consumption, working classes are perpetually made, unmade, and remade across the globe. Such creative and destructive processes vis-à-vis the working classes help to produce different forms of class struggle. Third, class struggle, broadly understood, is not reducible to the workplace. Rather, unrest associated with labor occurs in the workplace, the labor market, the community, and in national and international politics. Fourth, there is interpenetration between labor movements and status-based movements. The historical development of capitalism has involved the mobilization by capitalists, states, and/or workers themselves of status-based distinctions among the working class—gender, race, ethnicity, and/or citizenship—to foment division or to gain advantage or protection in the marketplace (Silver and Karatasli 2015). *Pace* NSM theory, struggle around status and struggle around class have been and will continue to be irrevocably interconnected. Because concrete and historical capitalism is always gendered and racialized, so too are all concrete and historical manifestations of class struggle. In the Latin American context, an important recent collection of essays on the role of the region's twentieth-century Left in struggles against gender and racial oppression demonstrates this kind of connectedness through analyses of Bolivian indigenous communities' constitutive relations with the Left in the 1920s, the role of revolutionary women in El Salvador's guerrilla movements of the 1980s, and the complexity of the "ethnic question" within Guatemala's guerrilla insurgencies (Young 2019). Bringing capitalism back into our study of social movements reorients our entire outlook and draws otherwise invisible connections between superficially disparate local movements (see Rossi in this volume). The logic of capitalist accumulation infuses the dynamics of all these movements and sets limits on their myriad hopes and aspirations.

A Marxist approach to social movements also has to involve the concept of totality. One of the weaknesses of social movement studies in recent decades—with the partial exception of recent work in "contentious politics" (see Almeida, Wada in this volume)—has been a fragmentation of subject matter. This or that particular social movement is studied in desolate isolation from other movements, opponents, and the wider environment. Likewise, there is a ruthless division of labor and territorial policing of borders across the myriad academic disciplines; for example, the hiving off of labor studies into a separate area of inquiry from social movements, or the separation of the study of revolution from the study of social movement.

The concept of totality can help overcome this fragmentation and enhance our understanding of movements, just as it can inform activists' strategy and tactics with regard to connecting existing commonalities, and forging new ones, across seemingly disparate local or sectional conflicts. Totality allows Marxists to name the capitalist system as an overarching enemy that helps to determine the parameters of seemingly fragmented contestations over power in capitalist society (Barker et al. 2013: 13). This is perhaps particularly true of the complex social structures underlying dependent-capitalist societies in Latin America.

Totality involves a recovery of interest in, and attention to, the relationship between the whole and its internally related parts (Lukács 1972). This implies more than the truism that everything is interrelated; it is rather to stress how the conditions of existence of each component part of the whole are a part of—are interior to—the component itself (Ollman 1977: 26–39). To be part of a totality is to be a constitutive element in a total situation that is subject to processes of social change. This throws light on the complex of determinations of each particular moment, as distinct from seeing each moment in artificial isolation (Davidson 2012: 28). The notion of totality allows us to capture the multi-layered complexity of capitalism as a mode of production, and therefore the multi-layered complexity of movements that arise within and against that mode of production.

To the factors of capitalism and totality, finally, we need to add social class and class struggle. The fact that Marxism, at its best, offers a multidimensional, historical, and processual approach to class struggle means that it can make a central contribution to social movement studies more generally. It points to the need to identify *class dynamics* in *every* movement, as distinct from sometimes thinking in class terms, and otherwise not so much, or not at all. "We know that class division is not the exclusive terrain of the constitution of power, even though in class societies all power bears a class significance" (Poulantzas 1978: 43). Such a theory of class struggle offers a way of tackling the complexly organized, mediated, and articulated social relations of oppression and exploitation under capitalism, and the forms of resistance they engender. Such a conception of social class is simultaneously attentive to objective determinations of evolving class structures and the subjective processes of political identity formation.

The Opening Phases of Latin American Marxism: 1870–1910, 1910–1932, 1932–1959

An initial gestation of Latin American Marxism (1870–1910) involved the dissemination of the writings of Marx and Engels in the region, alongside the organization of the first Latin American sections of the Communist International, and initial elaboration of socialist programs in places like Cuba, Mexico, Uruguay, and Argentina (Vitale 1983).

The second, revolutionary phase (1910–1932) kicked off with the Mexican Revolution of 1910, and brought to the surface the problems of land, indigenous liberation, the unity of Latin American peoples from the new vantage point of the popular classes and oppressed groups, the role of national and anti-imperialist struggle, and the socialist character of envisaged revolutions on the horizon. In the wake of the Russian Revolution of 1917, the first Communist Parties were formed: Argentina (1918), Uruguay (1920), Chile (1922), Mexico (1919), and Brazil (1922). This was the era of giants, like Cuban revolutionary Julio Antonio Mella, and, most decisively, Peru's José Carlos Mariátegui, to this day Latin America's most original theoretician (Aricó 1980).

In the work of Mariátegui, a utopian-revolutionary dialectic borrows selectively from the indigenous precapitalist past to fortify a forward-looking vision of socialist emancipation. Strategically, the revolutionary subjects are workers and peasants, oriented in opposition not just against foreign capital but vis-à-vis class enemies at home. Mariátegui's vision struck simultaneously at the core of Comintern orthodoxy—he was denounced as a populist for his particular appeals to the indigenous peasantry, as well as his stubborn resistance to anti-imperialist alliances led by the bourgeoisie or petty bourgeoisie—and the reigning nationalism of his country, as captured in the ideology of the Alianza Popular Revolucionaria Americana (APRA).

According to Acha and D'Antonio (2010: 229),

> Mariátegui conceives of the revolutionary capacity of the indigenous masses and the liberation from the yoke of the landowner in the manner of [Georges] Sorel;

that is, in connection with the formation of myths and hopes of redemption that propel the oppressed classes toward socialist revolution. The myths are not arbitrary representations, or imaginary constructions, because they respond to historical experiences and material situations. In the case of the urban proletariat, Mariátegui conceives their revolutionary potentiality in classical Marxist terms; that is to say, considering their position in the productive system and their objective confrontation with the capitalist class. With respect to the peasantry, the revolutionary mythology is rooted in real communities, and its traditions are embodied in the *ayllus*, where Mariátegui discerns social relations similar to socialist relations. That inheritance makes possible a transition to socialism on such bases, but in a sense of surpassing [them].

Mariátegui's meticulous study of the history of colonialism, Peru's integration into the world market, and the ongoing imperialist character of the global capitalist system in the early twentieth century, led him to develop a thoroughgoing and original anti-imperialist perspective. With the unity and simultaneity of anti-imperialism and revolutionary socialist politics at its core, this optic finds its clearest expression in the document, "Anti-Imperialist Point of View," submitted to the First Latin American Communist Conference in Buenos Aires in June 1929. Here Mariátegui savages the complicit role played by Latin American national bourgeoisies in the perpetuation of imperialism, which they saw as "the best source" of their own profits and the continuity of their own political power (Mariátegui 2011a: 265–66). Any coherent anti-imperialist alliance could not therefore be led by bourgeois or petty bourgeois forces under the banner of nationalism—under such leaders there would be no rupture with imperialism. Instead, the only possible winning alliance would have to be forged and led by workers and peasants, in a combined movement of anti-imperialism and commitment to revolutionary socialism at home (Mariátegui 2011a: 272).[1]

Thus in Mariátegui we find the Marxist trilogy of capitalism, totality, and class. With regard to the first two elements, Mariátegui painstakingly analyses the uneven development of global capitalism and Peru's specific subordinated position as a constituent part of that global totality. With regard to class, he is concerned above all with identifying the principal antagonisms between popular and bourgeois classes, precisely in order to better forge the necessary class alliances to build a successful socialist and anti-imperialist movement suitable to the particularities of the Latin American context. He also connects the political subjectivity of classes-in-motion, or how classes come to understand themselves and their activities in political terms, with the material, structural realities of the Peruvian economy. If these are the universalist components of Mariátegui's work, his simultaneous attentiveness to the centrality of indigenous oppression, and therefore of the necessity of indigenous liberation, is indicative of his equal stress on the concrete and particular within the Latin American setting.

This second, revolutionary phase of Latin American Marxism beginning in 1910, to which Mariátegui contributed so significantly in theoretical and practical terms, was brought to a tragic conclusion in 1932 in El Salvador. In January of that year, thousands of indigenous and *ladino* (non-indigenous) rural laborers made waves in protest against electoral fraud and the repression of strikes. Rebels seized control of a number of municipalities in central and western El Salvador. The uprising was organized by Communists, many of whom were themselves indigenous rural laborers and union militants of the coffee plantations. The Salvadoran military and allied paramilitary militias quickly won back the towns and massacred thousands of mainly indigenous rural activists (Lauria-Santiago and Gould 2008). The leaders of the Communist Party in El Salvador—Farabundo Martí, Alfonso Luna, Mario Zapata, and Miguel Mármol—had been imprisoned prior to the insurrection, in a preventive crackdown orchestrated by the state. Party documents of the period demonstrate that the aim of the upheaval was nothing short of socialist transformation of Salvadoran society, and that the initiative was born independently of any directives emanating from the Kremlin (Löwy 2007: 23).

In the decades following the Salvadoran massacre, the third phase of Latin American Marxism (1932–1959), the main currents of Marxist movement and thought lost such independence and audacity. Communist Parties throughout the region were systematically brought under the thumb of Stalinism, in what was to be a painfully sclerotic period of regional Marxism, lasting until the Cuban Revolution. For the bulk of the 1930s, 1940s, and 1950s, the dogma of Stalinist development-by-stages prevailed, with any revolutions in Latin America to be contained within the boundaries of the national-democratic type, in accordance with the region's presumed feudal phase of development. On this view, a long period of industrial capitalist development was the next step in progress, necessitating political alliances in the short and medium term between the popular classes and "progressive" national bourgeoisies. Socialist revolution would only be possible sometime in the distant future, once productive forces had been sufficiently advanced (Löwy 2007: 9–10).

Marxist Renewals: 1959–1980

A fourth phase of revolutionary experimentation in the history of Latin American Marxism (1959–1980) begins with the Cuban Revolution, passes through Salvador Allende's Chile, takes a last breath in Sandinista Nicaragua, and is quickly eclipsed by the neoliberal counter-reformation of the 1980s and 1990s. The many internal threads and currents of dependency theory, as well as Latin America's encounter with the work of Italian Marxist Antonio Gramsci, were a central part of this intellectual and political tumult. Each of these areas of thought and action would have significant implications for how intellectuals and activists understood social movements and popular political alliances. It was the dawn of a period of creativity and experimentation in political struggle, as distinct from the preceding era where mechanistic Stalinist frameworks were dominant.

In her important recent study of Latin American social theory of the twentieth and early twenty-first centuries, Svampa (2016: chapter 3) treats the span from 1965 to 1979—the apogee of dependency theory—as one of Latin America's most intellectually fertile periods. The political context was one of expanding authoritarian rule, with successive coups from the mid-1960s to mid-1970s in Brazil, Bolivia, Uruguay, Chile, and Argentina. Brazil, Chile, and Mexico take pride of place in this telling of dependency's history, the first as the country of origin of many of the classical theorists—Fernando Henrique Cardoso, Theotonio Dos Santos, Ruy Mauro Marini, and Vânia Bambirra—and the latter two as uniquely fecund habitats of exile.

Probably the most influential single text of dependency was *Dependencia y desarrollo en América Latina*, by Cardoso and Faletto (1978), which provided a sophisticated sociological foundation to the particularity of Latin American class structures and state forms and thus the structural parameters within which, and out of which, specific kinds of social movements would be likely to emerge. Strategies of social movement struggle would need to be attentive both to the specificity of social structure in dependent-capitalist societies and how it differed from the class structure of societies in the advanced capitalist core, as well as to the differentiation of class structures between different Latin American societies depending upon the varied historical paths through which they were subordinately incorporated into the world market. Marini's version of dependency theory was in many ways developed in contradistinction to Cardoso and Faletto, and was more expressly revolutionary in its political and analytical aspirations. Marini's *Subdesarrollo y revolución* (1969), and in particular *Dialéctica de la dependencia* (1973), was to become his most lasting contribution (Marini 1975, 1982). Marini's innovative conceptualizations of "super-exploitation" and "sub-imperialism" continue to inform current Latin American debates in the critical social sciences.

On the one hand, dependency marked an epistemological break with the economic structuralism of mainstream institutions such as the United Nations Economic Commission for Latin America and the Caribbean (ECLAC); at the same time, and more important for the question of socio-political movements, it represented a visceral riposte to the stodgy theoretical dogmas, political pragmatism, and stagist determinism of Stalinized Communist Parties throughout the region in that era. Eclectic points of political reference for *dependentistas* were instead the Cuban Revolution, widening guerrilla movements, and Chile's road to socialism under Allende. The scope for political voluntarism, at times woefully exaggerated, was in many ways the paradoxical political mirror to dependency theory's somewhat rigid economic analyses. Many of the urban and rural guerrilla formations they supported in various Latin American countries in the decades following the Cuban revolution were systematically and decisively repressed by state forces (Wickham-Crowley 1992). Dependency theory's attentiveness to Latin America's particular, subordinate incorporation into the world capitalist system highlighted both the structural foundations of the specific expressions of capitalism in the region and therefore the structural terrain of socio-political struggle within which movements found themselves.

Parallel to the growth of dependency theory in the fields of sociology and economics, the terrain of Marxist political theory, as well as the praxis of social movements—particularly in Brazil and Argentina—were increasingly informed by the region's encounter with Gramsci. Gramsci's reception in Latin America in this period became a powerful source of insights. Latin American theorists adapted Gramsci's notions of the national-popular, socialism, and democracy to the Latin American context, and developed his ideas further in conversation with regional debates on the phenomenon of populism. Gramscian approaches to the national-popular as a complex field of struggle undermined the early functionalist theses crafted by the Argentine modernization sociologists Germani and Di Tella, who had depicted the manipulation of the masses by authoritarian charismatic leadership as the quintessence of populism (Di Tella, Germani, and Graciarena 1965).

Carlos Nelson Coutinho translated Gramsci into Portuguese in the 1960s and later published a series of influential Gramscian interventions that helped to shape critical Brazilian social theory in the 1980s and 1990s (Coutinho 1980, 1985, 1991; Coutinho and Aurélio 1987; Freeland 2014), with a significant impact on, among other things, the early ideological orientation of the Partido de Trabalhadores (PT) and associated social movements (Burgos 2002). In Argentina, Juan Carlos Portantiero authored one of the most influential Latin American treatments of Gramsci, *Los usos de Gramsci*, and edited the Gramscian-inflected Marxist journal *Pasado y Presente*, together with Jose Aricó, also of Argentina (Portantiero 1981). These Latin American theorists, responsible for the initial reception of Gramsci in Latin America from the 1960s to the 1980s, overcame some of the more stultified versions of Stalinized Marxism (Caballero 1989). The Gramscian renaissance took seriously the co-constitutive dialectical unity of base and superstructure, managing to "examine [simultaneously] the relational formation of political subjectivity, the transformation of economic relations of state forms, and the evolution of competing ideologies vying for common-sense status" (Grandin 2010: 43). Susan Stokes' seminal *Cultures in Conflict: Social Movements and the State in Peru*, and in particular her use of Gramsci to theorize Peruvian social movements of the urban poor, contests for hegemony, political culture, and state power, is but one expression of the ways in which Gramsci's initial reception in Latin American thought would be expanded upon, elaborated, and refined in coming decades to better deal with the specific domain of social movement studies (Stokes 1995).

A Long Neoliberal Night: 1980–1998

If the rough periodization of Latin American Marxism offered so far suggests an initial set of four stages, a fifth (1980–1998) maps onto the regional reign of neoliberal orthodoxy, and is unsurprisingly characterized by retraction, defeat, and self-criticism, although also by renovation at the margins. This was the era of abandoned revolutionary strategy, the fall of the Soviet Union and its client states, the transition to capitalism in China, the isolation of the Cuban Revolution, and the defeat of the Nicaraguan Revolution. Most Latin American Marxist intellectuals decamped, opting for post-structuralism or straightforward liberalism (Acha and D'Antonio 2010: 224).

Neoliberal restructuring radically transformed class structures in the region, decomposing old-Left social bases in trade unions and peasant associations. Left-wing parties went the way of most Marxist intellectuals—adapting to the parameters of debate proscribed by the new liberal epoch. The right-wing dictatorships of the 1960s and 1970s had been transformed into electoral regimes, but the legacy of their dirty work lingered like a nightmare. Dictatorships of the Southern Cone, and the counter-insurgencies of Central America, had murdered hundreds of thousands. Along with lasting effects of collective psychological terror, the socio-political roots of the Left in these societies had been annihilated. Few of the usual conveyor belts of collective memory in the history of the twentieth-century Left—experienced cadre, formal associations, and informal cultural infrastructures—remained to pass on lessons to a new generation; and besides, Latin American social structures had been so deeply transformed by state terror, imperial intervention, and capitalist counter-reform that any new Left to emerge at this stage would necessarily look much different than what had come before, even if it would have to draw—as all new Lefts must—on critical investigation of the past (Webber 2017: chapter 2).

Latin American social movement studies as a formal area of inquiry first emerged in the 1980s and 1990s in an intellectual and political climate which was distinctly hostile to Marxism. This field of inquiry immediately favored the "identity" approach of NSM, often uncritically applying the European lens to the Latin American setting (Foweraker 1995). Despite some incorporation of strategy, economy, formal politics, and the state, the emphasis remained on NSM themes of analysis in Latin American social movement studies for most of these two decades (Alvarez, Dagnino and Escobar 1998). From the vantage point of NSM critique, Marxist theory had always been reductionist in two senses: (1) economic, because an economic logic determines social formations and political and ideological processes, such that politics and ideology are epiphenomena of the economic realm; and (2) in terms of class, given that the identity of social actors is derived primarily from their class-position (Canel 1997: 190). NSM theorists, by contrast, believed that the heterogeneity of the "new" movements were concerned more with the "process of symbolic production and the redefinition of social roles than the economy" (Canel 1997). Culture, meaning, constructed identities, civil society, and newness were the watchwords of choice, set against class, the economy, the state, and ostensibly traditional social actors, like the working class (Canel 1997: 189). The NSM paradigm had critical cross-disciplinary influence throughout the 1980s and 1990s (see Garretón and Selamé in this volume).

Davis (1999: 586–88) points out that, in addition to the positive appeal of the civil-society focus of the NSM perspective, the "strategy-oriented" paradigm was often seen as state-centered by Latin-American scholars. She argues this was essentially a "kiss of death" for the paradigm in a region where the state was generally conceived of as the enemy, given the proliferation of authoritarian regimes in the 1960s and 1970s.

Moreover, she suggests, the role of "anti-Americanism" among Latin American social movement scholars/activists, and (at that time) a pervasive intellectual Eurocentrism, may also have played some role in determining the hegemonic status of the "identity" school (Davis 1999). Given the authoritarian setting of much of Latin America during this period, it was difficult for many to think of "political opportunities," so central to the strategy school, as important variables (Edelman 2001: 292). Following the transition to electoral democracies throughout the 1980s, however, mainstream studies of social movements have increasingly drawn from the strategy-oriented theoretical frameworks (see Somma in this volume).

NEOLIBERAL CRISIS AND MARXIST RETURNS: 1998–PRESENT

The light of a new dawn for Marxism arrived in the late 1990s. Between 1998 and 2002, South America experienced the worst recession since the height of the debt crisis in the 1980s. The economic crisis of neoliberalism—with earlier utterances in Mexico in 1994, Southeast Asia in 1997, and Russia in 1998—had made its bold entrance into South American markets. Poverty, inequality, unemployment, and peasant dispossession—all of which had steadily worsened through the two preceding decades in which Latin America was transformed into a Hayekian laboratory—experienced a sharp spike. The answer of ruling conservative and liberal governments was to increase the dosage of the same medicine. While this had had some appeal to popular classes in Latin America suffering under the weight of hyperinflation and stagnation in the early 1980s, after twenty years of firsthand participation in the failed drug trial of neoclassical economics, the promise of more of the same rang hollow.

A new extra-parliamentary Left erupted in different colors across the subcontinent. In Argentina, unemployed workers led the way; in Bolivia novel Left-indigenous, rural, and urban coalitions of social struggle, and the Confederación de Nacionalidades Indígenas del Ecuador (CONAIE), followed by the militant public sectors of the labor movement. Neoliberal governments were toppled as the economic crisis of neoliberalism matured into an organic crisis of political rule. By the mid-2000s, as recession turned to dynamism with the onset of a Chinese-driven world commodities boom, the extra-parliamentary Left found muted expression on the electoral terrain as Centre-Left and Left governments took power nearly everywhere in South America.

The richness of the extra-parliamentary cycle of revolt, and the contradictions of subsequent Left-government rule, unsurprisingly spurred a new period of Latin American Marxism (2000–). It is perhaps imprudent to make summative judgements on key features of the theory and praxis generated thus far. But some tentative conclusions might be hazarded with regard to the theorization of social movements within the latest season of Latin American Marxism.

Following Modonesi and Iglesias (2016), we can identify four key areas which dominated debate on social movements in early twenty-first-century Latin America, and in each area there have been specific contributions made by Marxist theoreticians: the territoriality of socio-political conflict; the political emergence of indigenous communal struggles and the ascendancy of the communal form; the construction of autonomies as both the collective self-governing practices of popular movements and as an emancipatory horizon beyond the liberal capitalist state; and, finally, the contested relationship between social movements and the state (Bruckmann and Dos Santos 2005; Ceceña 2002; Iglesias 2011; Modonesi and Iglesias 2016: 100; Parra 2011; Rebón and Modonesi 2014). Let us deal with each of these in turn.

First, the territorialization of socio-political conflict has been identified by a number of Latin American social movement analysts as one of the most important elements characterizing the resurgence of popular collective action beginning in the mid-to-late 1990s (see Fernandes and Welch, Davis and Davey in this volume). In both urban and rural settings, social movements are said to be reclaiming territory as spaces of resistance, meaning, and new social relations which prefigure non-capitalist forms of collective life (Svampa 2008, 2016; Zibechi 2011). Prominent urban examples include the Argentine unemployed workers' movement (Rossi 2017) and Venezuelan experimentations with workers' control, communal councils, and communes (Azzellini 2018), while rural manifestations include indigenous and peasant resistance to mining expansion (Gordon and Webber 2016) and indigenous communities' "counter spaces of resistance" in Oaxaca and Chiapas, Mexico (Hesketh 2017; Vergara-Camus 2014). The specifically Marxist contribution to this analysis has mainly been the link made between these territorial struggles and the political economy of urban and rural restructuring associated with the specific neoliberal phase of capitalism, whether it be through the privatization of urban services and processes of gentrification in the neoliberal Latin American city, or socio-ecological resistance to the expansion of extractive capitalism—mining, natural gas and oil, agro-industrial mono-cropping, and large-scale infrastructural projects, such as hydroelectric dams—in the Latin American countryside (Composto and Navarro 2014; Seoane, Taddei, and Algranati 2013).

Second, Marxists have been at the forefront of theoretical contributions attempting to explain how some Latin American movements are rooted in a defense of various forms of "commons"—territories and communities organized as much as possible on non-capitalist premises of cooperation—as against the enclosure of every more aspects of everyday life by the imperatives of capitalist markets under neoliberal capitalism. Overlapping with the question of territory, Marxists have emphasized the centrality in the recent movement wave of popular struggles to reclaim the rural and urban "commons" against recurring processes and pressures of expropriation and dispossession by private capital, backed by the capitalist state (Gutiérrez Aguilar 2013). At the forefront of such struggle has been the resurgence of indigenous liberation movements, drawing on very long histories of resistance to colonial conquest and the expansion of capitalist relations in the region, which run into conflict with foreign and domestic capitalists seeking to profit from the privatization and intensified exploitation of natural resources in the region. Indigenous mobilization in this sense combines dimensions of identity and economic demands, and is irreducible to either one of these two components (Modonesi and Iglesias 2016: 104; Webber 2012). "Crucially, this demand is not *just* for *land* but for territory ... the right to continue collective forms of land ownership and in this way challenging head-on the capitalist form of property and the neoliberal logic of the spread of markets in land.... Indigenous struggles spearhead popular class demands; these are *struggles against (transnational) capital* and for a transformation of property relations" (Robinson 2008: 302–3; emphasis in original).

Third, with regard to the issue of autonomy and Latin American social movements, different Marxist currents have developed quite distinct positions. Marxist enthusiasts of autonomy see in it a combination of means and ends, a way of building counter-power or anti-power in the "cracks" of capitalism and the capitalist state (Holloway 2010a, 2010b), while prefiguring self-governing collective practices outside of and against capital and the state. Autonomous movements as a means and as an end are a way of avoiding, in this view, the exaggerated hierarchies and rigidities of classical revolutionary parties, as well as the corrupting and bureaucratizing influence of the traditional revolutionary strategy of "taking state power" (Holloway 2010a, 2010b; Zibechi 2007; Sousa in this volume). Dinerstein (2015) argues that an emphasis on autonomy runs through social movements as varied as the neighborhood assemblies, road blocks, factory seizures and workers' cooperatives during the Argentine crisis of 2001–2002, the Zapatista uprising and forms of autonomous self-governance since their explosive emergence from years of clandestine organizing in January 1994, Left-indigenous movements in the countryside and cities of Bolivia between 2000 and 2005, and the landless rural workers' movement in Brazil. For Marxist critics of "autonomism," attention to such social movements on their own is insufficient. There must also be, in this view, an attentiveness to the terrain of politics and strategic orientation which autonomism neglects (Katz 2005; Webber and Carr 2013: 11–12). The terrain of politics, furthermore, requires a relationship between movements and parties as "two modes of popular organization": "Movements sustain the immediate social struggle, and parties fuel a more fully developed political activity. Both are necessary for facilitating direct action and electoral participation. But this complementarity is frequently questioned by exclusivist advocates of movement or party" (Katz 2007: 45).

Finally, and relatedly, there is the issue of the relationship between social movements and the state. Those stressing the means and ends of autonomy within contemporary Latin American social movements have unsurprisingly exalted also the ostensible horizontalism of movements and stressed their independence from and even antagonism toward the state, whether or not the state in question is occupied by a leftist government (Machado and Zibechi 2017). In contrast, and perhaps the dominant Marxist current as the twenty-first century entered its second decade, stressed what they took to be the dynamic and positive synergy between social movements and the progressive governments of the "pink tide" (Borón 2014; Dussel 2006; García Linera 2011; Harnecker 2015; Sader 2011).

However, perhaps the most innovative theorizations on the state and social movements within Latin American Marxism in the twenty-first century have taken place within what might be called the region's second season of Gramsci, and in particular the application of Gramsci's concept of "passive revolution" as a framework for understanding the rise and decline of progressive governments in the last couple of decades (Modonesi 2013). As Thomas (2013: 30) has shown, Gramsci's concept of passive revolution was developed across three principal moments in the *Prison Notebooks*, which together comprise a "strategic or partial theory" of the "specific organizational form of bourgeois hegemony." Most relevant to our discussion here is the way in which passive revolution refers "to instances in which aspects of the social relations of capitalist development are either instituted and/or expanded, resulting in both "revolutionary" rupture and a "restitution" of social relations" (Morton 2011: 18). This is the sense in which, as Morton (ibid.) notes, the concept captures "progressive aspects of historical change during revolutionary upheaval that become undermined resulting in the reconstitution of social relations but within *new forms* of capitalist order."

In the work of Modonesi (2017), for example, the South American passive revolution of the twenty-first century involved a process of modernization pushed forward by progressive governments from above, which partially and carefully recognized demands issued forth from movements from below. Through this process, state managers guaranteed the increasing passivity and reduced autonomy of popular movements over time. New state-society relations were built up by progressive governments, creating precarious but surprisingly lasting equilibriums that functioned to reproduce a system of governance based, on the one hand, on compensatory redistributive social policies and, on the other, the intensification of extractivism in a context of high commodity prices. At the top of these new configurations of power rested charismatic populist figures, alongside institutional mechanisms of bureaucratization. Once the commodity prices dropped, these governments increasingly entered into crisis and the reduced capacities for mobilization on the part of bureaucratized popular movements partially explains the subsequent ascendancy of the political Right (Modonesi 2017; Webber 2017).

Conclusion

This chapter has sought to convey both the central distinguishing characteristics of Marxist approaches to social movements relative to competing perspectives, and the particular way in which Latin American Marxism has theorized social movements over its various chronological phases. Regarding the specificity of Marxist approaches to social movements, it was argued that capitalism, totality, and class are the foremost distinctive categories of this perspective. Concerning the phases of Latin American Marxism, the chapter began with a survey of the opening three historical phases, stretching from 1870 to 1959. Particular attention was paid to the highly innovative period of Latin American Marxism between 1910 and 1932, and specifically the work of Mariátegui. Following the interregnum of Stalinist orthodoxy from 1932 to 1959, the chapter turned its attention to the renewal of innovation between 1959 and 1980, with particular attentiveness to dependency theory and Latin America's first season of Gramscian studies. It was then argued that the subsequent period of neoliberal ascent and consolidation, between 1980 and 1998, was an epoch in which the analytical and political project of Marxism entered into crisis. Not coincidentally, the same period witnessed the rise of the social scientific terminology of "social movements" in the region, as borrowed and adapted from North American and European sociology. The NSM perspective which stressed "identity" was the favored lens through which to view Latin American social movements in the 1980s and 1990s, although the strategy perspective has gained increasing currency since then. Finally, the chapter examined the crisis of neoliberalism and the rise of the Pink Tide in Latin America. This period witnessed a return to critical Marxist theory in the region, with specific contributions made by Marxists to the most vibrant areas of inquiry into social movements of the period: territoriality, indigenous struggle and the commons, autonomy and autonomies, and social movement–state relations.

Note

1. There are links here between these reflections and Mariátegui's reading of the limited social achievements flowing out of the War of Independence between 1811 and 1821. While formal independence from Spain was achieved, the internal hierarchies of class and racial stratification remained intact, and new forms of economic subordination to different dominant powers emerged on an international scale as Peru was inserted ever more thoroughly into the machinations of the world market. The independence revolution, Mariátegui is at pains to point out, was carried forward for the benefit of *creoles* (descendants of Spanish colonialists born in Peru), and expressly against the indigenous peasant majority, even if the indigenous masses were enlisted in the battles. The Peruvian independence revolution "did not bring in a new ruling class.... The colony's landholding aristocracy, the owner of power, retained their feudal rights over land and, therefore, over the Indians" (Mariátegui 2011b: 147).

References

Acha, Omar and Débora D'Antonio (2010), "Cartografía y perspectivas del 'marxismo latinoamericano,'" *A contra corriente* 7(2), 210–56.
Alvarez, Sonia, Evelina Dagnino, and Arturo Escobar (eds.) (1998), *Cultures of Politics, Politics of Culture: Re-Visioning the Latin American Social Movements* (Boulder, CO: Westview).
Aricó, José (1980), *Marx y América Latina* (Mexico: Folio Ediciones).
Azzellini, Dario (2018), *Communes and Workers' Control in Venezuela: Building 21st Century Socialism from Below* (Chicago: Haymarket).
Barker, Colin (2012), "'Not Drowning but Waving': Mapping the Movement?" Paper presented at the 17th International Conference on Alternative Futures and Popular Protest, University

of Manchester. Available at https://drive.google.com/file/d/0Bz3wUg3e6r_4dDFFZVVm RV81WlU/view.

Barker, Colin (2013), "Class Struggle and Social Movements," in Colin Barker, Laurence Cox, John Krinsky, and Alf Gunvald Nilsen (eds.), *Marxism and Social Movements*, 41–61 (Leiden: Brill).

Barker, Colin, Laurence Cox, John Krinsky, and Alf Gunvald Nilsen (2013), "Marxism and Social Movements: An Introduction," in Colin Barker, Laurence Cox, John Krinsky, and Alf Gunvald Nilsen (eds.), *Marxism and Social Movements*, 1–37 (Leiden: Brill).

Borón, Atilio (2014), *Socialismo siglo XXI: ¿Hay vida después del neoliberalismo?* (Buenos Aires: Luxemburgo Editores).

Bruckmann, Mónica and Theotonio Dos Santos (2005), *Los movimientos sociales en América Latina: Un balance histórico* (Buenos Aires: CLACSO).

Burgos, Raúl (2002), "The Gramscian Intervention in the Theoretical and Political Production of the Latin American Left," *Latin American Perspectives* 29(1), 9–37.

Caballero, Manuel (1989), *Latin America and the Comintern, 1919–1943* (Cambridge: Cambridge University Press).

Canel, Eduardo (1997), "New Social-Movement Theory and Resource-Mobilisation Theory: The Need for Integration," in Michael Kaufman and Haroldo Dilla Alfonso (eds.), *Community Power and Grassroots Democracy: The Transformation of Social Life*, 189–221 (London: Zed).

Cardoso, Fernando Henrique and Enzo Faletto (1978), *Dependencia y desarrollo en América Latina* (Mexico: Siglo XXI).

Ceceña, Ana Esther (2002), "Rebeldías sociales y movimientos ciudadanos," *OSAL* (6), 11–16.

Composto, Claudia and Mina Lorena Navarro (eds.) (2014), *Territorios en disputa: despojo capitalista, luchas en defensa de los bienes comunes naturales y alternativas emancipatorias para América Latina* (Mexico: Bajo Tierra Ediciones).

Coutinho, Carlos Nelson (1980), *A democracia como valor universal: notas sobre a questão democrática no Brasil* (São Paulo: Editora Ciências Humanas).

Coutinho, Carlos Nelson (1985), *A dualidade de poderes: introdução à teoria marxista de estado e revolução* (São Paulo: Brasiliense).

Coutinho, Carlos Nelson (1991), "Brasil y Gramsci: variadas lecturas de un pensamiento," *Nueva Sociedad* (115), 104–13.

Coutinho, Carlos Nelson and Marco Aurélio (eds.) (1987), *Gramsci e a América Latina* (Rio de Janeiro: Paz e Terra).

Davidson, Neil (2012), "The Necessity of Multiple Nation-States for Capital," *Rethinking Marxism* 24(1), 26–46.

Davis, Diane E. (1999), "The Power of Distance: Re-Theorizing Social Movements in Latin America," *Theory and Society* 28(4), 585–638.

Dinerstein, Ana (2015), *The Politics of Autonomy in Latin America: The Art of Organizing Hope* (New York: Palgrave).

Di Tella, Torcuato, Gino Germani, and Jorge Graciarena (eds.) (1965), *Argentina, sociedad de masas* (Buenos Aires: EUDEBA).

Dussel, Enrique (2006), *20 Tesis de política* (Mexico: Siglo XXI).

Edelman, Marc (2001), "Social Movements: Changing Paradigms and Forms of Politics," *Annual Review of Anthropology* 30(1), 285–317.

Foweraker, Joe (1995), *Theorizing Social Movements: Latin American Perspectives* (London: Pluto).

Freeland, Anne (2014), "The Gramscian Turn: Readings from Brazil, Argentina, and Bolivia," *A Contracorriente: una revista de estudios latinoamericanos* 11(2), 278–301.

García Linera, Álvaro (2011), *Las tensiones creativas de la revolución: La quinta fase del proceso de cambio* (La Paz: Vicepresidencia del Estado).

Gordon, Todd and Jeffery R. Webber (2016), *Blood of Extraction: Canadian Imperialism in Latin America* (Halifax: Fernwood).

Grandin, Greg (2010), "Living in Revolutionary Time: Coming to Terms with the Violence of Latin America's Long Cold War," in Greg Grandin and Gilbert M. Joseph (eds.), *A Century of Revolution: Insurgent and Counterinsurgent Violence during Latin America's Long Cold War*, 1–43 (Durham, NC: Duke University Press).

Gutiérrez Aguilar, Raquel (2013), *Horizontes comunitario-populares: Producción de lo común más allá de las políticas estado-céntricas* (Madrid: Traficantes de Sueños).

Harnecker, Marta (2015), *A World to Build: New Paths toward Twenty-First Century Socialism* (New York: Monthly Review Press).

Hesketh, Chris (2017), *Spaces of Capital/Spaces of Resistance* (Athens: University of Georgia Press).

Holloway, John (2010a), *Change the World without Taking Power—New Edition: The Meaning of Revolution Today* (London: Pluto).

Holloway, John (2010b), *Crack Capitalism* (London: Pluto).

Iglesias, Mónica (2011) "Teoría en movimiento: más de una década de pensamiento crítico," *OSAL* 12(30), 25–42.

Katz, Claudio (2005), "Problems of Autonomism: Strategies for the Latin American Left," *International Socialist Review* 44(November–December). Available at https://isreview.org/issues/44/autonomism/.

Katz, Claudio (2007), "Socialist Strategies in Latin America," *Monthly Review* 59(4). Available at https://monthlyreview.org/2007/09/01/socialist-strategies-in-latin-america/.

Lauria-Santiago, Aldo A. and Jeffrey Gould (2008), *To Rise in Darkness: Revolution, Repression, and Memory in El Salvador, 1920–1932* (Durham, NC: Duke University Press).

Löwy, Michael (2007), "Introducción: puntos de referencia para una historia del marxismo en América Latina," in Michael Löwy, *El marxismo en América Latina: antología, desde 1909 hasta nuestros días*, 9–67 (Santiago: LOM).

Lukács, Georg (1972), *History and Class Consciousness: Studies in Marxist Dialectics* (Cambridge, MA: The MIT Press).

Machado, Decio and Raúl Zibechi (2017), *Cambiar el mundo desde arriba: Los límites del progresismo* (Granada: Zambra / Baladre).

Mariátegui, José Carlos (2011a), "Anti-Imperialist Point of View," in Harry. E. Vanden and Marc Becker (eds.), *José Carlos Mariátegui: An Anthology*, 265–74 (New York: Monthly Review Press).

Mariátegui, José Carlos (2011b), "On the Indigenous Problem: A Brief Historical Overview," in Harry. E. Vanden and Marc Becker (eds.), *José Carlos Mariátegui: An Anthology*, 145–50 (New York: Monthly Review Press).

Marini, Ruy Mauro (1975), *Subdesarrollo y revolución* (Mexico: Siglo XXI).

Marini, Ruy Mauro (1982), *Dialéctica de la dependencia* (Mexico: Editorial Era).

Modonesi, Massimo (ed.) (2013), *Horizontes gramscianos. Estudios en torno al pensamiento de Antonio Gramsci* (Mexico: FCPyS-UNAM).

Modonesi, Massimo (2016), *El principio antagonista: Marxismo y acción política* (Mexico: Itaca / UNAM).

Modonesi, Massimo (2017), *Revoluciones pasivas en América* (Mexico: Itaca/UAM-A).
Modonesi, Massimo and Mónica Iglesias (2016), "Perspectivas teóricas para el estudio de los movimientos sociopolíticos en América Latina: ¿cambio de época o década perdida?" *Del Raíz Diversa* 3(5), 95–124.
Morton, Adam (2011), *Revolution and State in Modern Mexico: The Political Economy of Uneven Development* (Lanham, MD: Rowman & Littlefield).
Ollman, Bertell (1977), *Alienation: Marx's Conception of Man in a Capitalist Society* (Cambridge: Cambridge University Press).
Parra, Marcela Alejandra (2011), "Características actuales de la movilización social en América Latina," *OSAL* 12(30), 43–64.
Portantiero, Juan Carlos (1981), *Los usos de Gramsci* (Mexico: Folios).
Poulantzas, Nicos (1978), *State, Power, Socialism* (London: Verso).
Rebón, Julián and Massimo Modonesi (eds.) (2014), *Una década en movimiento: Luchas populares en América Latina en el amanecer del siglo XXI* (Buenos Aires: CLACSO).
Robinson, William I. (2008), *Latin America and Global Capitalism: A Critical Globalization Perspective* (Baltimore, MD: Johns Hopkins University Press).
Rossi, Federico M. (2017), *The Poor's Struggle for Political Incorporation: The Piquetero Movement in Argentina* (Cambridge: Cambridge University Press).
Sader, Emir (2011), *The New Mole: Paths of the Latin American Left* (London: Verso).
Seoane, José, Emilio Taddei, and Clara Algranati (2013), *Extractivismo, despojo y crisis climática: desafíos para los movimientos sociales y los proyectos emancipatorios de Nuestra América* (Buenos Aires: Ediciones Herramienta).
Silver, Beverly J. and Sahan Savas Karatasli (2015), "Historical Dynamics of Capitalism and Labor Movements," in Donatella Della Porta and Mario Diani (eds.), *The Oxford Handbook of Social Movements*, 133–45 (Oxford: Oxford University Press).
Stokes, Susan C. (1995), *Cultures in Conflict: Social Movements and the State in Peru* (Berkeley and Los Angeles: University of California Press).
Svampa, Maristella (2008), *Cambio de época. Movimientos sociales y poder político* (Buenos Aires: Siglo XXI - CLACSO).
Svampa, Maristella (2016), *Debates latinoamericanos: indianismo, desarrollo, dependencia y populismo* (Buenos Aires: Edhasa).
Thomas, Peter (2013), "Hegemony, Passive Revolution, and the Modern Prince," *Thesis Eleven* 117(1), 20–39.
Vergara-Camus, Leandro (2014), *Land and Freedom: The MST, the Zapatistas and Peasant Alternatives to Neoliberalism* (London: Zed).
Vitale, Luis (1983), "El marxismo latinoamericano ante dos desafíos: feminismo y crisis ecológica," *Nueva Sociedad* 66, 90–98.
Webber, Jeffery R. (2012), *Red October: Left-Indigenous Struggles in Modern Bolivia* (Chicago: Haymarket).
Webber, Jeffery R. (2017), *The Last Day of Oppression, and the First Day of the Same: The Politics and Economics of the New Latin American Left* (Chicago: Haymarket).
Webber, Jeffery R. (2019), "Resurrection of the Dead, Exaltation of the New Struggles: Marxism, Class Conflict, and Social Movement," *Historical Materialism* 27(1), 1–51.
Webber, Jeffery R. and Barry Carr (2013), "Introduction: The Latin American Left in Theory and Practice," in Jeffery R. Webber and Barry Carr (eds.), *The New Latin American Left: Cracks in the Empire*, 1–29 (Lanham, MD: Rowman & Littlefield).

Wickham-Crowley, Timothy P. (1992), *Guerrillas and Revolution in Latin America: A Comparative Study of Insurgents and Regimes since 1956* (Princeton, NJ: Princeton University Press).

Young, Kevin A. (2019) *Making the Revolution: Histories of the Latin American Left* (Cambridge: Cambridge University Press).

Zibechi, Raúl (2007), *Dispersar el poder: los movimientos como poderes antiestatales* (Barcelona: Virus Editorial).

Zibechi, Raúl (2011), *Territorios en resistencia: cartografía política de las periferias urbanas latinoamericanas* (Granada: Zambra).

CHAPTER 3

RESOURCE MOBILIZATION AND POLITICAL PROCESS THEORIES IN LATIN AMERICA

NICOLÁS M. SOMMA

Introduction

Resource mobilization theory and political process theory emerged in the 1970s and 1980s, mainly in the United States, as alternatives to strain theories for the study of social movements (McAdam 1999; Useem 1998). Relativizing the role of grievances and discontent, they emphasized the relevance of resources, organization, strategy, and the political context for explaining movement activity. They have become among the predominant approaches in the field, transcending their geographic origins and being employed for examining social movements across the world including Latin America. This chapter explores Latin American social movements from the lenses of resource mobilization theory (RMT hereinafter) and political process theory (PPT). I address several questions. Can RMT and PPT be fruitfully used for analyzing Latin American social movements? Are their assumptions plausible? Are their concepts useful? Is existing research on Latin American social movements consistent with their tenets and hypotheses?

RMT and PPT comprise several interrelated yet distinct claims operating at the macro, meso, and even micro-levels of analysis. It is perfectly possible that some of these claims work while others do not. Also, because Latin American social movements are varied, it is possible that these theories are more useful for some movements than for others. Thus, it is unproductive to ask whether RMT and PPT serve for Latin American social movements as a whole. Rather, the question should be what parts of these theories are useful (if any), and for which classes of movements.

I develop three broad arguments. First, RMT and PPT provide a unique and powerful perspective for understanding Latin American social movements. Second, given the contextual differences between the United States and Latin America, careless use of these theories may lead to the conclusion that "they work" at the cost of ignoring any specificity of Latin American social movements. Third, precisely given these differences (which I discuss below), Latin America provides an interesting setting for expanding and refining RMT and PPT. I start with RMT and continue with PPT.

RESOURCE MOBILIZATION THEORY AND LATIN AMERICAN SOCIAL MOVEMENTS

RMT challenged the prevailing notion in mid-twentieth-century sociology that social movements are outbursts of irrational, aggrieved massess reacting to structural changes like modernization or war (Jenkins 1983). Mostly developed by United States scholars permeated by the activist atmosphere of the 1970s, RMT held that the emergence and decline of movements depend not on grievances but on people's ability to develop organizational structures and mobilize material, social, and human resources (McCarthy and Zald 1973, 1977; Tilly 1978). Additionally, RMT opened new debates regarding the repertoires of collective action and the determinants of movement outcomes and success (Gamson 1975). RMT is not a unified theory. It has several versions that emphasize different aspects (such as the role of movement entrepreneurs, or the relative relevance of internal vs. external resources; see, e.g. Morris 1981, 1984). Their proponents disagree in some respects, such as whether moderate or radical tactics and goals benefit movements (see Jenkins 1983 for an early review and Edwards and Kane 2014; Edwards and McCarthy 2004; and McCarthy and Zald 2001 for recent developments).

The classic works in RMT hardly refer to Latin American movements, and studies about the latter explicitly referring to resource mobilization theory do not abound either, as already noted by Gohn (1997: 216). Foweraker's claim more than two decades ago that "resource mobilization theory has been almost entirely ignored" (1995: 1) in Latin American social movements studies is not completely accurate now but still has some truth. Nevertheless, the interesting point is that many of such studies do develop arguments consistent with RMT. This section discusses research about Latin American social movements through the lenses of RMT. Specifically, I address four key issues: the scope conditions of RMT and its applicability to Latin America, the types of movements conceptualized, the role of organizations, and the sources and types of resources mobilized.

Scope Conditions

RMT was developed having in mind the United States of the 1960s and 1970s. While not always explicit about the scope conditions of the theory—as McCarthy and Zald

(2001: 535) acknowledge—RMT scholars had in mind advanced industrial societies with a strong tradition of voluntary associations, with civil and political rights promoted and protected, and with a mass media complex that spreads the grievances of organized groups. Until recently few Latin American countries could be portrayed in such terms, a fact that probably discouraged a wider use of RMT among scholars of Latin American social movements. But does this render RMT useless? My answer is "no."

First, RMT assumes a minimum level of societal wealth so that material resources not devoted to subsistence activities can be channeled to social movements. Of course, this makes sense for a rich country like the United States more than for Latin America. Yet nowadays some Latin American countries are approaching the level of wealth (as measured by per capita GDP) that the United States had in the 1960s, when the RMT was based on thrived.[1] And because inequality in Latin America is high, some segments of Latin American societies may mobilize enough material resources to sustain movements across time. This is the case for university student movements in the richest Latin American countries (e.g., Chile), where upper-middle class youngsters abound (Disi 2017; Donoso 2016). Of course, this is not the case for many peasant and indigenous movements as well as movements of the urban poor in previous decades (Calderón 1985; Calderón and Jelin 1987). But movements which are poor in material resources may be rich in human or social resources, as demonstrated by the Water Wars in Bolivia (Simmons 2016).

Second, RMT hinges upon the existence of a dense network of civic associations—an enduring feature that De Tocqueville (2003) found in the United States already in the 1830s, and which combined the traditions of political liberalism and protestantism. Specifically, RMT emphasized the relevance of the kind of single-issue organizations that were flourishing in the 1970s (Skocpol 2003), which resemble lobby organizations more than grassroots social movements. Although Latin America did not develop a liberal-protestant tradition of associations (Valenzuela and Cousiño 2000; see Mackin in this volume), since the nineteenth century it has developed vibrant Western-style organizations of urban workers, peasants, and students. And although the military dictatorships of the 1970s and 1980s suppressed much of such associational life, it resumed with democratic transitions to nurture movement activity (see the following; see also Brockett, Inclán in this volume).

It is important to note that while the associational sector in the United States developed to a large extent as a reaction to the state, its Latin American counterpart relied more heavily upon the actions of populist governments and clientelistic state policies (see Combes and Quirós in this volume). Especially during the import substitution period, Latin American governments helped structuring associations of workers and peasants as a means of incorporating them in ordered ways into the polity (Collier and Collier 1991; see also Rossi in this volume). This may explain why, during the 1980s and 1990s, some Latin American social movements emphasized the need of gaining "autonomy" from state and party actors (Escobar and Alvarez 1992; see also Garretón and Selamé in this volume), a goal that is less common in US movements.

Which Kinds of Activists and Movements?

Mass society and strain theories of the 1950s and 1960s assumed that movement activists were pathologic, anomic individuals. An important breakthrough of both RMT and PPT was the assertion that movement activity is rather "normal" politics carried out by people integrated to mainstream institutions, and therefore comparable to institutional actions like voting. This seems consistent with much research on Latin American social movements, which implicitly conceive social movements as legitimate actors arousing from organized communities. While such communities may be economically and politically marginalized, scholars recognize their potential for positive contributions to social change (see Roberts 1997).

But this affinity was not enough to install RMT within studies of Latin American social movements. In their attempt to break with strain theories, resource mobilization theorists made the controversial assertion that grievances and discontent were not the central drives of social movements (McCarthy and Zald 1977; Tilly 1978). This assertion does not fit accounts of Latin American social movements, which often emphasize the enormous pain and grievances driving movements in a region historically marked by poverty, inequality, authoritarianism, and repression (Eckstein 1989). The many scholars who participated in such movements suffered from state repression, or were acquainted with the rural and urban poor, so a theory downplaying the role of grievances was a hard pill to swallow.

A further complication for adopting RMT in Latin America was the very conception of social movements. The influential "entrepreneurial" version of RMT developed by McCarthy and Zald (1973, 1977) has at its very heart a conception of social movements and social movement organizations (or "SMOs") that differs from usual conceptions of Latin American social movements. Entrepreneurial RMT conceptualizes movement organizations almost as nonprofit organizations, to the point of speaking of a "nonprofit/social movement sector" (McCarthy and Zald 2001: 537) and asserting that, "SMOs are a subset of nonprofit organizations in the United States" (ibid.: 539). SMOs specialize in gathering information, providing legal services, and engaging in lobby activities rather than mobilizing grassroots communities. They work on issues such as consumer rights, anti-drunk driving, anti-smoking, or governmental accountability. Few would argue that this characterization fits influential Latin American social movements such as Brazil's *Movimento dos Trabalhadores Rurais Sem Terra* (MST) (Ondetti 2010), Argentina's *piquetero* movement (Rossi 2017), or Bolivia's coca growers (Anria 2018)—let alone hundreds of small urban movements struggling for getting basic services (Oxhorn in this volume) or territorial movements (Svampa 2008; Davis and Davey in this volume).

Another variant of RMT developed by Morris (1981, 1984), which treats movements as grassroots organized action developed by local communities, is more consistent with conventional approaches to Latin American social movements. Still, a few recent studies seem to conceive them closer to non-profit organizations. Two examples are von Bülow's (2010) study on organizations working against free trade agreements, and Rhodes' (2012) study of consumer organizations (see also Rhodes in this volume).

Organizations

RMT is known for emphasizing the relevance of organizations for the development of social movements. But organizations may vary in their characteristics—from bureaucratic and formal ones, to networks of like-minded people adopting a name for becoming visible to the world. Also, organizations relevant to social movements can either predate social movements—such as Black churches and colleges for the American Civil Rights movement (McAdam 1999)—or can be built from scratch for pursuing movement goals (Morris 1984).

Consistent with RMT, studies on Latin American social movements have shown the relevance of organizations of different kinds. Regarding formal, preexisting organizations, labor unions built during the nineteenth century for representing the interests of workers often form the basis of contemporary protest campaigns. Peasant organizations were reinvigorated in the 1950s (Scully 1992; Welch in this volume) and indigenous organizations strenghtened since the 1990s (Van Cott 2010; Rice in this volume), providing the basis of peasant and indigenous movements later on (see also Zibechi 2007). As Rice (2012) shows, countries where indigenous groups were mobilized by populist parties during the 1960s and 1970s (for example, Ecuador and Bolivia), autonomous indigenous organizations appeared from the 1990s onwards. Yet countries in which they were mobilized around socialist lines (for example, Chile and Peru) left little space for the development of autonomous and powerful indigenous movements once democracy was restored. Likewise, student organizations built one century ago form the organizational basis for launching important contemporary mobilizations—as is usual in Mexico, Chile, Peru, or Uruguay (Disi 2017). This differs from the more fragmented student movement of the United States, strongly articulated around campus activities.

The organizations supporting international movements are often created with the explicit purpose of promoting social change. Keck and Sikkink (1998) argued that transnational advocacy networks on issues such as human rights and the environment influenced domestic governments only in those countries having a previous tradition of domestic mobilization on such issues. Also, issues which by definition result from interactions among national governments—such as free trade agreements in the Americas—can be contested by strong coalitions of organizations from different countries (von Bülow 2010). As globalization boosts the relevance of transnational issues such as climate change and migration, transnational coalitions of movement organizations become more relevant (see Burridge and Markoff, von Bülow in this volume).

The relevance of organizations for collective protest in Latin America has also been documented by studies using survey data. As in other regions, Latin Americans more embedded in organizational networks protest more than the rest (Moseley 2015; Valenzuela et al. 2016). While RMT was pitched at the macro and organizational level and not at the individual level, this finding is consistent with the theory's assertion that movements recruit protesters among people already organized for other purposes (Oberschall 1973). Such studies also show that Latin Americans with more socioeconomic resources protest more (Moseley 2015; Valenzuela et al. 2016), which is also consistent with RMT's emphasis on resources.

Yet not all social movement activity in Latin America is channeled through formal organizations. The culturalist approach (Escobar and Alvarez 1992; Alvarez et al. 1998; see Salman in this volume) noted the informal and flexible nature of much movement activity during the 1980s, when authoritarian regimes repressed civil society organizations. Resistance was often found in communities, neighborhoods, or informal networks of aggrieved people. The arrival of the internet in social movements in the 1990s, in Latin America and abroad, also dispensed collective action from the need of extensive organization. The Mexican Zapatistas was probably the first Latin American movement to use the internet to spread its message across the globe and gain decisive international support (Inclán 2018; Olesen 2006), and Indymedia soon followed suit supporting several causes. Thus, Latin Americans using the internet for political purposes are more likely to protest than the rest, and internet use even reduces protest gaps resulting from individual differences in age and gender (Valenzuela et al. 2016). The internet provides protest opportunities to people who may otherwise remain passive.

Still, the internet is also heavily used by movement organizations. For instance, von Bülow's (2018) study of the Chilean student movement shows that the adoption of new digital technologies such as Twitter, while expanding the movement's external reach, can reinforce preexisting asymmetries within movement organizations, leading to reactions aimed at moderating them. Rather than counterposing traditional organizational work versus the internet as alternative means for mobilization, it is more useful to study how activists combine them and how they interact. Classical RMT obviously lags behind in this discussion for the simple reason that internet did not exist when it was formulated, yet recent developments have incorporated it in convincing ways (Earl and Kimport 2011; see Treré and Summer in this volume).

Resources

An important question since the origins of RMT revolved around the source of the resources being mobilized. Do resources come from the aggrieved constituencies on behalf of which the movement acts, or from external providers such as governments, NGOs, or other elites? This is a consequential point: movements funded by external sources may be more easily coopted by authorities, and tamed in their goals and tactics, than those resorting to internal resources (McAdam 1999; Morris 1984).

The predominant views on Latin American social movements often portray them as based on internal resources. Indigenous communities struggling against timber or mining companies, LGBTIQ+ communities combating discrimination, or workers mobilized against wage cuts, are more common characters in movement accounts than international donors or government programs supporting aggrieved groups (Almeida and Cordero 2015; Calderón 1985; Díez in this volume; Franklin and Stoessel in this volume; Silva 2009; Rice in this volume), although the point merits systematic research. The predominance of "internalist" accounts makes sense for the 1970s and 1980s, when most movements faced authoritarian regimes—dictators would hardly provide resources to movements challenging them. It also makes sense for a relatively poor region such as Latin America and especially for its poorest countries, where few surplus resources could exist (especially monetary ones) to be channeled to movement activities. However, during the 2000s sustained economic growth, better transportation and communication infrastructures, and state programs on issues relevant for movements—such as the environment, gender relations, indigenous issues, or political reforms—may have boosted external resources channeled to movements.

The types of resources RMT deemed relevant broadened as the theory evolved, from an initial emphasis in monetary and social resources to cultural and moral resources (Edwards and McCarthy 2004). The relevance of money makes sense in a fully capitalist economy such as that of the United States. Yet in poorer regions of Latin America, social and human resources (emphasized by the "internalist" version of RMT) may be comparatively more relevant to movements' fate, as attested by the massive actions of landless workers in Brazil (see Fernandes and Welch, Welch in this volume) or poor women organizing soup kitchens during the "lost decade" of the 1980s (Calderón 1985; Ewig and Friedman in this volume).

Some Pending Issues

RMT is a complex theory that has evolved across the last four decades. It is not surprising that some of its more interesting recent developments have been barely considered in studies of Latin American social movements. I mention three. First, several scholars have combined RMT with organizational ecology theory—a multi-disciplinary approach exploring how populations of organizations (SMOs in this case) emerge, adapt to their contexts and survive (or not). Such scholars have explored processes of goal and tactical differentiation in SMOs and movement industries in the United States (see Soule 2013 for a review). This approach has infused vitality to RM studies but has rarely been pursued in Latin America, possibly because it requires protest event data—which is not abundant in the region—and due to the lack of familiarity of scholars with organizational ecology theory (but see Spalding in this volume).

A second topic, which is central to RMT, revolves around recruitment efforts by movement leaders for gaining adherents to their cause. RMT has noted that participation should not be taken for granted and that activists often have to make considerable efforts to persuade people to participate and contribute resources. Research on Latin American social movements, however, has paid little attention to how people overcome participation costs and how activists provide selective incentives for reducing them. Recent studies on Latin American demonstrators following the Caught in the Act of

Protest methodology, which maps the motivations and mobilization trajectories of participants in major demonstrations, promise to start addressing this important gap (Inclán 2019; Inclán and Almeida 2017; Somma, Rossi, and Donoso 2020).

Finally, RMT noted early the relevance of the mass media for movement development and success. Movements gaining positive attention from the media may have won half of the battle in terms of recruiting sympathizers and influencing political authorities. A few studies have noted this for the MST (Ondetti 2010) and the Zapatistas (Bob 2005; Olesen 2006), but the topic certainly merits more research.

Political Process Theory and Latin American Social Movements

Since the seminal works of McAdam (1999) and Tilly (1978), political process theory (PPT) became one of the most influential approaches for the study of social movements. PPT holds that movement activity depends on the conditions of the broader political and economic context in which movements develop (see Meyer 2004 for a review). The political context shapes not only the types of grievances but also the choice of goals, tactics, and strategies of activists, who never act in a vacuum. Protest increases when the political context opens "political opportunities" such as the presence of influential allies, elite divisions, political instability or liberalization, or a softening of state repression (Tarrow 1998). Tilly (1978) noted that threats, and not only opportunities, serve as incentives for mobilization (see also Goodwin 2001). PPT also emphasizes the role of mobilizing structures, to the point it sometimes fuses with RMT. In the last two decades, some of the main PPT scholars responded to earlier criticisms that the theory was too rigid and structural (Goodwin and Jasper 1999) by developing the "contentious politics approach" (McAdam, Tarrow, and Tilly 2001), focused on how a wide array of contentious activities in different historical settings results from the combination of mechanisms such as brokerage or polarization.

During the 1990s, Latin American social movements scholarship was heavily influenced by culturalist approaches that explored their potential for cultural change (see Gohn 1997; Garretón and Selamé, Salman in this volume). Redemocratization processes motivated scholars to address questions related to the extent to which the political environment shapes movements (Inclán in this volume). It became clear that many movements prefer to seek resources and alliances with institutional actors rather than create distance from them (Abers and von Bülow 2011; Davis 1999; Foweraker 1995; Gurza Lavalle and Szwako in this volume; Rossi 2017; Somma 2020; Roberts in this volume). Additionally, during the last two decades a growing number of scholars raised new questions about the rise and decline of social movements, movement outcomes and success, and the adoption of different protest tactics. These political and academic changes boosted the influence of PPT and made it a major approach in the study of Latin

American social movements, as attested by the works of Almeida (2008), Yashar (2005), Silva (2009), and Ondetti (2010), to name a few.

Below I discuss whether key assumptions of PPT make sense in Latin America. Then I explore the role of four of its central concepts in research on Latin American social movements: the openness of the polity, influential allies, political instability, and state repression. I note the ambiguities of the theory and contradictory research findings. I conclude noting a few areas that merit further research within the PPT framework.

Some Assumptions

The considerable influence of PPT partially results from the plausibility of its assumptions in Latin America. While democracy is far from consolidated wholesale, democratic regimes prevail and elections capable of destabilizing political alignments are frequent. Latin American congresses typically harbor opposition parties and coalitions which can side with movements and act as "tribunes of the people" (Almeida 2010; Tarrow 1998). Movements are attentive to political dynamics and there is considerable ideological variation among institutional actors as to represent threats for some movements and opportunities for other ones if reaching power. Moreover, many Latin American countries have transitioned to democracy in recent decades, which heavily changed its collective actions patterns as suggested by Garretón (2001, 2002). Thus, the region is more useful than the United States—with a lasting consolidated democracy—for exploring how major variations in the level of democracy shape movements. This helps us understand why Tarrow's (1998) path-breaking book makes several references to Latin American examples to illustrate PPT. Of course, this does not negate the differences between Latin America's political trajectories and political culture, and those of the developed countries of the Northern hemisphere, aptly summarized by Gohn (1997: chapter 6).

Likewise, Latin America provides a panoply of events and processes that may "undermine the calculations and assumptions on which the political establishment is structured"—McAdam's (1999: xi) influential definition of political opportunities. Democratic transitions, the economic crisis of the 1980s, the "left turn" of the 2000s, and the globalization of human rights policies could all be interpreted as political opportunities as long as they challenge directly or indirectly the political establishment (see Calderón 2012: chapter 3 for a review). It is more difficult, however, to assert whether the impact of these changes on movements happens because they increase strain and discontent, as previous strain theories would suggest, or because they alter political power relations and mobilization costs, as PPT would expect. McAdam's definition is pretty broad and disparate things may fit in.

Two additional aspects that contributed to PPT's reception among scholars of Latin American social movements are the claims that activists choose strategically their action paths and tactics, and that movements are oriented towards political-institutional goals. The strategic dimension made sense when looking at movements in authoritarian regimes, which had to calibrate carefully their actions to avoid fatal repression (see Brockett in this volume). The political orientation was inescapable for movements protesting against the evils of authoritarianism, such as human rights violations or lack of elections. In democratic times some movements flirted with institutional politics or set the basis for new political parties (Anria 2018), reaffirming the connection between protest politics and institutional politics. This is consistent with survey research showing that Latin American movement activists are more likely to vote and participate institutionally than non-activists (Moseley 2015; Valenzuela et al. 2016).

Likewise, in an influential article Davis (1999) reacted to the New Social Movements perspective by noting that many Latin American social movements, rather than seeking autonomy, tried to approach the state to influence it and access state resources. Consistent with PPT, she argues that movement's distance to the state (geographic, institutional, cultural, and socioeconomic) shapes their objectives and strategies: more distant movements should be more violent and radical than movements closer to the state.

Next, I discuss key dimensions of political opportunities in relation to Latin American social movements.

Openness of the Polity

PPT holds that the degree of openness or closure of the institutionalized political system affects movement activity (McAdam 1999; Tarrow 1998). Political oppenness often occurs when national governments are sympathetic to movements and espouse a political ideology consistent with movement goals. This should promote collective protest, as movements perceive protest is more effective for obtaining governmental concessions. This partially explains the protest wave of the 1960s in the United States, which took place under sympathetic Democratic administrations (McAdam and Tarrow 2010). Likewise, Ondetti (2010) found that the intensity of the protest of Brazil's MST across three decades depended on the national government's openness to the movement, with progressive governments stimulating movement activity and conservative governments weakening it.

But PPT also considers, perhaps bafflingly, an alternative prediction: that governments with an ideology *contrary* to a movement create a sense of threat that spurs protest (Tilly 1978). An adverse government also provides a common enemy that helps unifying variegated groups. A common explanation of the 2011 student mobilizations in Chile takes this path: it was in 2010, when the center-right came to power, that student organizations felt threatened and coalesced around a powerful movement (Donoso 2016). Following this logic, one should expect that governments sympathetic to movements *depress* protest. Eckstein (1989) notes that worker protest was rare in Mexico under the Partido Revolucionario Institucional (PRI), which coopted workers through corporatist arrangements, or in the early days of presidents Alan García (Peru) and Raúl Alfonsín (Argentina), which displayed populist discourses broadly sympathetic to social movements.

Alternatively, the oppeness of the polity can refer to the extent to which it provides democratic mechanisms for allowing people's preferences to influence political decisions—for example, via elections. Thus, Latin American redemocratizations should be followed by increased movement activity (see Inclán in this volume). The new democracies certainly opened associational spaces that permitted all sorts of movements to flourish (Almeida and Johnston 2006; Silva 2009). Yet in some countries redemocratization seems to have depressed collective protest (Roberts 1998). Transitions often led to low-intensity democracies (Kruit 2001) with extensive powers in the executive and technocratic dominance (O'Donnell 1994), all of which may discourage movement activity. Moreover, as noted in Inclán's (2018) fascinating study of the Mexican Zapatista movement, while democratization may create a political atmosphere that facilitates mobilization and movement survival across time, it may also conspire against movement's achievement of political goals.

Influential Allies

Infuential political allies can be an important source of opportunities for social movements. By defending movements in courts, negotiating on their behalf, or softening repression, allies can stimulate mobilization and contribute to movement success (Tarrow 1998). In Latin America movements allies usually come from the ranks of leftist parties. This stands in contrast with the United States, which never had strong leftist parties of socialist or Marxist inspiration. This makes Latin America (and continental Europe for that matter) a fruitful ground for expanding PPT formulations.

Success of some Latin American movements can be credited to their alliances. For Díez (2015), one of the reasons why Argentina and Mexico adopted gay marriage has to do with the political alliances built by LGTBIQ+ movements with leftist parties in these countries. Sympathetic leftist politicians were key in launching and promoting gay marriage projects in congress. The Chilean LGTBIQ+ movement did not fare as well because Chilean leftist parties, long-time coalition partners with the Christian Democrats (which opposed gay marriage), did not want to endanger the coalition for an issue that was marginal to their platforms (see also Somma, Rossi, and Donoso 2020).

In a similar vein, Almeida (2010) explores variegated cases of alliances between movements opposed to neoliberalism and leftist oppositional parties in Bolivia, Ecuador, El Salvador, Nicaragua, and Uruguay. He finds that parties are more likely to ally with movements when the public opinion supports movement goals and when there is substantial organizational overlap between party members and movements. Such alliances, expressed in protest campaigns against governmental reforms, are more likely to succeed when parties have gained electoral power and can influence the policymaking process (see Roberts in this volume). Yet leftist parties can be a double-edged sword for movements. The decline of collective protest in Chile and Peru after redemocratization resulted, in part, from divisions within the Left among moderates and radicals (Roberts 1998), weakening movements' connections to the political establishment (Somma and Medel 2017).

While the United States has a pretty stable and institutionalized party competition, Latin American countries show important variability—both among countries and within countries across time—in their degree of party system institutionalization (Mainwaring 2018). These differences may determine whether fruitful movement-party alliances are viable or not. Again, this offers a novel terrain for exploring the role of movement allies. For instance, as Arce's (2014) subnational analysis in Peru shows, due to the extreme volatility and personalistic nature of Peruvian parties, collective protest is more intense in regions with more political fragmentation (i.e., more parties). More parties mean worse representation of popular interests, which leads to stronger movement activity. Machado, Scartascini, and Tommasi (2011) show a negative association between the strength of political institutions and the level of protest participation in seventeen Latin American countries—protest flourishes when institutions are weak. Rice (2012) reaches a similar conclusion in her study of indigenous movements in four Latin American countries. Challenging PPT expectations, this suggests that protest increases when movements seem *unable* to find well-structured and reliable institutional allies.

Political Instability

PPT argues that events creating instability in the political status quo open opportunities for social movements. Democratization processes mean not only increased openness, as noted above, but also major instability since by definition they imply regime changes. For instance, Alvarez-Rivadulla (2017) argues that the heightened activity of the Uruguayan squatter movement after the transition by mid-1980s resulted from political parties attempting to mobilize poor voters in a new and uncertain electoral scenario. And yet Latin American redemocratization did not foster movement activity across the board. In some cases, elites threatened by authoritarian reversals rather tried to demobilize organized popular sectors (Garretón 2004). Elections in general can increase instability since they anticipate realignments between voters and parties, shifts the structure of political coalitions, and the possibility of a rotation of power holders. Yet more political competition weakened protest in Peru (Arce 2014).

Repression

PPT asserts that state repression depresses protest by increasing the costs of mobilization, although too much repression may spur protest—the relationship may be curvilinear (Tarrow 1998; Tilly 1978). Latin America provides an interesting scenario for examining this issue. Historically, states have reacted to social movements through repression, especially in the early stages of labor movements and during military dictatorships. Movements' reactions have in turn shaped states' ways of approaching them (Ortiz 2015). Although Svampa (2008) highlights that the "criminalization of protest" persists under current democratic regimes, Latin America during the last four decades likely shows more empirical variation in the levels of repression than the United States and Europe, from the extremely repressive Central American states of the 1970s (Goodwin 2001), to the less repressive democracies of the Southern Cone (Ortiz 2015).

Extreme repression is obviously relevant for explaining low movement activity during authoritarian periods. Authoritarian regimes made strenuous efforts for dismantling political parties and civil society organizations and exterminating its most "threatening" leaders (Calderón and Jelin 1987). Yet repression is full of unintended consequences. First, if massive and indiscriminate, it can backfire and stimulate popular support to revolutionary movements, as Goodwin (2001) shows for Central America. According to Foweraker (1995), state violence also promoted guerrilla movements in Argentina, Brazil, Colombia, and Peru from the 1960s to the 1990s. Almeida (2008) shows that in El Salvador democratic regimes fostered the creation of civic organizations that pushed for moderate goals and choose nonviolent tactics, yet they radicalized when state repression increased. Second, repression can indirectly favor movements in the long run. For instance, the repression of parties by Augusto Pinochet's military regime in Chile created a space that allowed the emergence of autonomous popular organizations (Oxhorn 2010). Likewise, in democratic settings, police repression involving killings and widespread media coverage can turn the public opinion to the side of movements and force governments to meet their demands, as shown in Ondetti's (2010) analysis of the MST in Brazil.

Future Research

As with RMT, scholars are far from having exhausted the potential of PPT for the study of Latin American social movements. PPT is a complex and sometimes even ambiguous theory. It can be explored using different research designs such as qualitative case studies, small-n comparisons, and longitudinal analyses of single or varied movement industries across time. Its main concepts can be operationalized in many ways (Meyer 2004). While a considerable number of case studies on Latin American movements use explicitly PPT, a robust assessment requires more research. Below I present three potential topics.

First, the "dynamics of contention" approach (McAdam, Tarrow, and Tilly 2001) has influenced recent research that emphasizes the mechanisms through which Latin Americans stage collective contention (Hanson and Lapegna 2018; Rossi and von Bülow 2015; von Bülow 2010; Halvorsen and Rossi in this volume). This is a much needed complement to the static views that pervaded the field in the 1970s under the auspices of structuralism and Marxism (see Bringel 2012; Webber in this volume). Second, as Latin American social movements are increasingly coordinating actions across national borders (Silva 2013), it is important to explore how the international political context provides opportunities, constraints, and threats to Latin American movements, as well as how movements from different countries provide opportunities to each other (von Bülow in this volume). Finally, as noted above, the impact of democracy and democratization processes on Latin American movements is far from being settled and likely occurs through several mechanisms that need to be disentangled.

Conclusions

For about four decades, resource mobilization and political process theories have shaped social movement research across the globe. In Latin America they have become increasingly relevant during the 2000s and 2010s. Using variegated vocabularies, scholars have long noted the relevance of resources, strategies, organizations, and the political context in Latin America without necessarily referring to RMT and PPT (e.g., Calderón 1985; see Somma 2020 for a review). Yet these theories provide a core set of concepts and claims that facilitate dialogue both among scholars of Latin American social movements, and with scholars studying other regions.

I briefly mention two points before concluding. First, it makes little sense to ask whether RMT and PPT as a whole are useful or not for studying Latin American social movements. As I have tried to show across the chapter, some of their concepts and claims seem more plausible than others, and for some movements more than for other ones. Things get even more complex since neither RMT nor PPT are unified theories—different interpretations of them may lead to contradictory empirical expectations. Thus, a toolkit approach to RMT and PPT is preferable to a holy grail one. For instance, within RMT, Morris' "indigenous resources" variant may serve for studying peasant movements in the Andes (Rice 2012). Yet McCarthy and Zald's "entreprenurial" variant may be adequate for studying consumer movements in Buenos Aires (see Rhodes in this volume). Within PPT, a focus on state structures might explain why Bolivian workers use more disruptive strategies than their Chilean counterparts (Silva 2009). Yet shifting political opportunities may better explain why movements increase their public visibility across time (Ondetti 2010).

The second point is that Latin America provides an interesting terrain for exploring and eventually refining RMT and PPT. Compared to the United States, it expands the variance of some of the factors that in theory shape movements. Consider this quick list: authoritarianisms and redemocratization processes; cases of indiscriminate repression; massive poverty in countries hosting some of the richest people in the world; considerable regions weakly connected to the global capitalist economy; successful presidential impeachments, and presidents removed after protest waves; guerrilla movements turning into legal players; varied developmental models (from twenty-first-century socialism to neoliberalism imposed by shock); and left turns and (more recently) right turns via elections. Such variety allows not only an expansion of RMT and PPT but also the development of *sui generis* theoretical arguments that may travel beyond the region (Rossi and von Bülow 2015).

Acknowledgements

I appreciate the support of the Agencia Nacional de Investigación y Desarrollo de Chile (ANID) through a FONDECYT Regular grant (#1200190) and the Centre for Social Conflict and Cohesion Studies (COES) (CONICYT/FONDAP/15130009).

Note

1. The per capita GDP in the United States during the 1960s averaged about US$21,000. This is similar to the current figures for Argentina, Chile, Panama, and Uruguay (see the Maddison Project Database 2018, available at www.rug.nl/ggdc/historicaldevelopment/maddison/. Retrieved July 26, 2019).

References

Abers, Rebeca, and Marisa von Bülow (2011), "Movimentos sociais na teoria e na prática: como estudar o ativismo através da fronteira entre estado e sociedade?" *Sociologias* 13(28), 52–84.

Almeida, Paul D. (2008), *Waves of Protest: Popular Struggle in El Salvador, 1925–2005* (Minneapolis: University of Minnesota Press).

Almeida, Paul D. (2010), "Social Movement Partyism: Collective Action and Political Parties," in Nella Van Dyke and Holly J. McCammon (eds.), *Strategic Alliances: New Studies of Social Movement Coalitions*, 170–96 (Minneapolis: University of Minnesota Press).

Almeida, Paul D. and Allen Cordero Ulate (eds.) (2015), *Handbook of Social Movements across Latin America* (New York: Springer).

Alvarez, Sonia, Evelina Dagnino, and Arturo Escobar (eds.) (1998), *Cultures of Politics/Politics of Cultures: Re-Visioning Latin American Social Movements* (Boulder, CO: Westview Press).

Álvarez-Rivadulla, María José (2017), *Squatters and the Politics of Marginality in Uruguay* (Basingstoke: Palgrave-Macmillan).

Anria, Santiago (2018), *When Movements Become Parties: The Bolivian MAS in Comparative Perspective* (Cambridge: Cambridge University Press).

Arce, Moisés (2014), *Resource Extraction and Protest in Peru* (Pittsburgh: University of Pittsburgh Press).

Bob, Clifford (2005), *The Marketing of Rebellion: Insurgents, Media, and International Activism* (Cambridge: Cambridge University Press).

Bringel, Breno (2012), "Com, contra e para além de Charles Tilly: mudanças teóricas no estudo das ações coletivas e dos movimentos sociais," *Sociologia & Antropologia* 2(3), 43–67.

Calderón, Fernando (1985), *Los movimientos sociales ante la crisis* (Buenos Aires: CLACSO).

Calderón, Fernando (ed.) (2012), *La protesta social en América Latina*. Cuaderno de Prospectiva Política 1 - PAPEP-PNUD (Mexico: Siglo XXI).

Calderón, Fernando and Elizabeth Jelin (1987), *Clases y movimientos sociales en América Latina: perspectivas y realidades* (Buenos Aires: Centro de Estudios de Estado y Sociedad).

Collier, Ruth Berins and David Collier (1991), *Shaping the Political Arena: Critical Junctures, the Labor Movement, and Regime Dynamics in Latin America* (Princeton, NJ: Princeton University Press).

Davis, Diane E. (1999), "The Power of Distance: re-Theorizing Social Movements in Latin America," *Theory and Society* 28(4), 585–638.
De Tocqueville, Alexis (2003), *Democracy in America* (Washington: Regnery Publishing).
Díez, Jordi (2015), *The Politics of Gay Marriage in Latin America: Argentina, Chile, and Mexico* (Cambridge: Cambridge University Press).
Disi, Rodolfo (2017), "Policies, Politics, and Protests: Explaining Student Mobilization in Latin America," PhD diss., University of Texas at Austin.
Donoso, Sofía (2016), "When Social Movements Become a Democratizing Force: The Political Impact of the Student Movement in Chile," in Thomas Davies, Holly Eva Ryan, Alejandro Milcíades Peña (eds.), *Protest, Social Movements and Global Democracy Since 2011: New Perspectives*, 167–96 (Bingley: Emerald).
Earl, Jennifer and Katrina Kimport (2011), *Digitally Enabled Social Change: Activism in the Internet Age* (Cambridge, MA: MIT Press).
Eckstein, Susan (1989), "Power and Popular Protest in Latin America," in Susan Eckstein (ed.), *Power and Popular Protest: Latin American Social Movements*, 1–60 (Berkeley and Los Angeles: University of California Press).
Edwards, Bob and Melinda Kane (2014), "Resource Mobilization and Social and Political Movements," in Hein-Anton van der Heijden (ed.), *Handbook of Political Citizenship and Social Movements*, 205–32 (Cheltenham: Edward Elgar).
Edwards, Bob and John D. McCarthy (2004), "Resources and Social Movement Mobilization," in David Snow, Sarah Soule and Hanspeter Kriesi (eds.), *The Blackwell Companion to Social Movements*, 116–52 (London: Blackwell).
Escobar, Arturo and Sonia Alvarez (eds.) (1992), *The Making of Social Movements in Latin America: Identity, Strategy, and Democracy* (Boulder, CO: Westview Press).
Foweraker, Joe (1995), *Theorizing Social Movements* (London: Pluto Press).
Gamson, William (1975), *The Strategy of Social Protest* (Homewood: The Dorsey Press).
Garretón, Manuel Antonio (2004), *Incomplete Democracy: Political Democratization in Chile and Latin America* (Chapel Hill: University of North Carolina Press).
Garretón, Manuel Antonio (2001), *Cambios sociales, actores y acción colectiva en América Latina* (Santiago: CEPAL, División de Desarrollo Social).
Garretón, Manuel Antonio (2002), "La transformación de la acción colectiva en América Latina," *CEPAL Review* 76(1), 7–24.
Gohn, Maria da Glória (1997), *Teorias dos movimentos sociais: paradigmas clássicos e contemporâneos* (São Paulo: Edições Loyola).
Goodwin, Jeff (2001), *No Other Way Out: States and Revolutionary Movements, 1945–1991* (Cambridge: Cambridge University Press).
Goodwin, Jeff and James Jasper (1999), "Caught in a Winding, Snarling Vine: The Structural Bias of Political Process Theory," *Sociological Forum* 14(1), 27–54.
Hanson, Rebecca and Pablo Lapegna (2018), "Popular Participation and Governance in the Kirchners' Argentina and Chávez's Venezuela: Recognition, Incorporation and Supportive Mobilisation," *Journal of Latin American Studies* 50(1), 153–82.
Inclán, María (2018), *The Zapatista Movement and Mexico's Democratic Transition: Mobilization, Success, and Survival* (Oxford: Oxford University Press).
Inclán, María (2019), "Mexican Movers and Shakers: Protest Mobilization and Political Attitudes in Mexico City," *Latin American Politics and Society* 61(1), 78–100.

Inclán, María and Paul D. Almeida (2017), "Ritual Demonstrations versus Reactive Protests: Participation Across Mobilizing Contexts in Mexico City," *Latin American Politics and Society* 59(4), 47–74.

Jenkins, J. Craig (1983), "Resource Mobilization Theory and the Study of Social Movements," *Annual Review of Sociology* 9(1), 527–53.

Johnston, Hank and Paul D. Almeida (eds.) (2006), *Latin American Social Movements: Globalization, Democratization, and Transnational Networks* (Lanham, MD: Rowman & Littlefield).

Keck, Margaret and Kathryn Sikkink (1998), *Activists Beyond Borders: Transnational Activist Networks in International Politics* (New York: Cornell University Press).

Kruit, Dirk (2001), "Low Intensity Democracies: Latin America in the Post-dictatorial Era," *Bulletin of Latin American Research* 20(4), 409–30.

Machado, Fabiana, Carlos Scartascini, and Mariano Tommasi (2011), "Political Institutions and Street Protests in Latin America," *Journal of Conflict Resolution* 55(3), 340–65.

Mainwaring, Scott (ed.) (2018), *Party Systems in Latin America: Institutionalization, Decay, and Collapse* (Cambridge: Cambridge University Press).

McAdam, Doug (1999), *Political Process and the Development of Black Insurgency, 1930–1970* (Chicago: University of Chicago Press).

McAdam, Doug and Sidney Tarrow (2010), "Ballots and Barricades: On the Reciprocal Relationship between Elections and Social Movements," *Perspectives on Politics* 8(2), 529–42.

McAdam, Doug, Sidney Tarrow, and Charles Tilly (2001), *Dynamics of Contention* (Cambridge: Cambridge University Press).

McCarthy, John D. and Mayer N. Zald (1973), *The Trend of Social Movements in America: Professionalization and Resource Mobilization* (Morristown: General Learning Press).

McCarthy, John D. and Mayer N. Zald (1977), "Resource Mobilization and Social Movements: A Partial Theory," *American Journal of Sociology* 82(6), 1212–41.

McCarthy, John D. and Mayer N. Zald (2001), "The Enduring Vitality of the Resource Mobilization Theory of Social Movements," in Jonathan Turner (ed.), *Handbook of Sociological Theory*, 533–65 (New York: Springer).

Meyer, David (2004), "Protest and Political Opportunities," *Annual Review of Sociology* 30, 125–45.

Morris, Aldon (1981), "Black Southern Student Sit-in Movement: An Analysis of Internal Organization," *American Sociological Review* 46(6), 744–67.

Morris, Aldon (1984), *The Origin of the Civil Rights Movement: Black Communities Organizing for Change* (New York: The Free Press).

Moseley, Mason W. (2015), "Contentious Engagement: Understanding Protest Participation in Latin American Democracies," *Journal of Politics in Latin America* 7(3), 3–48.

Oberschall, Anthony (1973), *Social Conflict and Social Movements* (Englewood Cliffs, NJ: Prentice-Hall).

O'Donnell, Guillermo A. (1994), "Delegative Democracy," *Journal of Democracy* 5(1), 55–69.

Olesen, Thomas (2006), "The Zapatistas and Transnational Framing," in Hank Johnston and Paul Almeida (eds.), *Latin American Social Movements: Globalization, Democratization, and Transnational Networks*, 179–96 (Lanham, MD: Rowman & Littlefield).

Ondetti, Gabriel (2010), *Land, Protest, and Politics: The Landless Movement and the Struggle for Agrarian Reform in Brazil* (University Park, PA: Penn State Press).

Ortiz, David (2015), "State Repression and Mobilization in Latin America," in Paul Almeida and Allen Cordero Ulate (eds.), *Handbook of Social Movements across Latin America*, 43–59 (New York: Springer).

Oxhorn, Philip D. (2010), *Organizing Civil Society: The Popular Sectors and the Struggle for Democracy in Chile* (University Park, PA: Penn State Press).

Rhodes, Sybil (2012), *Social Movements and Free-Market Capitalism in Latin America: Telecommunications Privatization and the Rise of Consumer Protest* (New York: SUNY Press).

Rice, Roberta (2012), *The New Politics of Protest: Indigenous Mobilization in Latin America's Neoliberal Era* (Tucson: University of Arizona Press).

Roberts, Kenneth M. (1997), "Beyond Romanticism: Social Movements and the Study of Political Change in Latin America," *Latin American Research Review* 32(2), 137–51.

Roberts, Kenneth. M. (1998), *Deepening Democracy? The Modern Left and Social Movements in Chile and Peru* (Stanford, CA: Stanford University Press).

Rossi, Federico M. (2017), *The Poor's Struggle for Political Incorporation: The Piquetero Movement in Argentina* (Cambridge: Cambridge University Press).

Rossi, Federico M. and Marisa von Bülow (2015), *Social Movement Dynamics: New Perspectives on Theory and Research from Latin America* (Abingdon: Routledge).

Scully, Timothy R. (1992), *Rethinking the Center: Party Politics in Nineteenth and Twentieth-Century Chile* (Stanford, CA: Stanford University Press).

Silva, Eduardo (2009), *Challenging Neoliberalism in Latin America* (Cambridge: Cambridge University Press).

Silva, Eduardo (ed.) (2013), *Transnational Activism and National Movements in Latin America: Bridging the Divide* (London: Routledge).

Simmons, Erica S. (2016), *Meaningful Resistance: Market Reforms and the Roots of Social Protest in Latin America* (Cambridge: Cambridge University Press).

Skocpol, Theda (2003), *Diminished Democracy: From Membership to Management in American Civic Life* (Norman: University of Oklahoma Press).

Somma, Nicolás M. and Rodrigo Medel (2017), "Shifting Relationships between Social Movements and Institutional Politics," in Marisa vön Bulow and Sofía Donoso (eds.), *Social Movements in Chile: Organization, Trajectories, and Political Consequences*, 29–61 (Basingstoke: Palgrave-Macmillan).

Somma, Nicolás M. (2020) "Social Movements in Latin America: Mapping the Literature," in Xóchitl Bada and Liliana Rivera (eds.), *The Oxford Handbook of the Sociology of Latin America*, 304–24 (New York: Oxford University Press).

Somma, Nicolás M., Federico M. Rossi, and Sofía Donoso (2020), "The Attachment of Demonstrators to Institutional Politics: Comparing LGBTIQ Pride Marches in Argentina and Chile," *Bulletin of Latin American Research* 39(3), 380–97.

Soule, Sarah A. (2013), "Bringing Organizational Studies Back Into Social Movement Scholarship," in Jacquelien van Stekelenburg, Conny Roggeband and Bert Klandermans (eds.) *The Future of Social Movement Research: Dynamics, Mechanisms, and Processes*, 107–24 (Minneapolis: University of Minnesota Press).

Svampa, Maristella (2008), *Cambio de época. Movimientos sociales y poder político* (Buenos Aires: Siglo XXI - CLACSO).

Tarrow, Sidney (1998), *Power in Movement: Social Movements and Contentious Politics* (Cambridge: Cambridge University Press).

Tilly, Charles (1978), *From Mobilization to Revolution* (Boston, MA: Addison-Wesley Publishing).

Useem, Bert (1998), "Breakdown Theories of Collective Action," *Annual Review of Sociology* 24(1), 215–38.

Valenzuela, Eduardo and Carlos Cousiño (2000), "Sociabilidad y asociatividad," *Estudios Públicos* 77, 322–39.

Valenzuela, Sebastián, Nicolás M. Somma, Andrés Scherman, and Arturo Arriagada (2016), "Social Media in Latin America: Deepening or Bridging Gaps in Protest Participation?" *Online Information Review* 40(5), 695–711.

Van Cott, Donna Lee (2010), "Indigenous Peoples' Politics in Latin America," *Annual Review of Political Science* 13, 385–405.

von Bülow, Marisa (2010), *Building Transnational Networks: Civil Society and the Politics of Trade in the Americas* (Cambridge: Cambridge University Press).

von Bülow, Marisa (2018), "The Survival of Leaders and Organizations in the Digital Age: Lessons from the Chilean Student Movement," *Mobilization: An International Quarterly* 23(1), 45–64.

Yashar, Denorah J. (2005), *Contesting Citizenship in Latin America: The Rise of Indigenous Movements and the Postliberal Challenge* (Cambridge: Cambridge University Press).

Zibechi, Raúl (2007), *Autonomías y emancipaciones. América Latina en movimiento* (Lima: Universidad Nacional Mayor de San Marcos).

CHAPTER 4

NEW SOCIAL MOVEMENTS IN LATIN AMERICA AND THE CHANGING SOCIO-POLITICAL MATRIX

MANUEL ANTONIO GARRETÓN AND
NICOLÁS SELAMÉ

Introduction

During the 1960s, Europe and the United States saw the rise of new types of social actors and movements not directly linked to traditional social classes or political parties, such as the feminist, anti-nuclear or environmentalist, among others, giving way to the first approaches of what was called "New Social Movements" (NSMs). In Latin America, social scientists started to use this concept especially to refer to movements that arose during the military dictatorships (Boschi 1983; O'Donnell 1978). These two elements were at the origins of the elaborations about NSMs. The object of this chapter will be to explain what changes in collective action motivates NSMs theories in Europe and North America, and the specificities of this theoretical framework in Latin America in the face of particularities of the region that were not anticipated by First World scholars of the NSMs approach.

The new characteristics that social movements exhibited after the 1960s in Europe and North America opened a debate about how these emerging movements should be studied. Although the debate is still open six decades later, it inaugurated a new theory, a field of study, and a sociological concept. Its primary understanding is in opposition to what were considered *traditional* social movements. While the latter used to coalesce mainly around material demands and highly cohesive groups (such as social class or strong territorial communities), the former put their focus on identity or cultural demands and laxer inner ties (Habermas 1981; Melucci 1985; Touraine 1997).

When reviewing the European and North American debate, one of the leading causes of the emergence of NSMs theories is related to the insufficiency of structural-determinist theories (such as Marxism) to explain the nature of a broader diversity of movements, especially those that were not class-based (Buechler 1995). Disagreements linger in discussions around how much collective action effectively changes when faced by these theories and how much the theoretical shift is better explained by a change of perspective in researchers who started to consider aspects of the problem that were previously underestimated (Escobar and Álvarez 1992: 6). However, empirical studies tend to prove, at least, a massification of the new forms of collective action that NSMs researchers studied during the 1980s (Kriesi 1989).

Beyond the debate about what is essentially new in NSMs, a discussion developed about contemporary tendencies in social movements under the NSMs concept's umbrella. Minimum consensus relied on the material sphere's limited relevance to explaining social movements, but there were several disagreements regarding the movement's internal dynamics. According to Habermas, the specificity of NSMs is that conflicts jump from the material reproduction problem to the cultural reproduction one, with the solution to their demands taking place in the cultural dimension of social life (Habermas 1981). Melucci's (1985) reply to this argument is that the main difference between NSMs and traditional movements lies in the transition of conflicts from the political field to the cultural one.

As can be seen, Habermas and Melucci disagree about the social sphere in which traditional movements constitute themselves. However, in reference to NSMs, they agree in pointing out the centrality of cultural dynamics as the main explicative factor. In this sense, theirs can be classified as "cultural interpretations" of NSMs, opposed to political interpretations, such as that of Castells (2001), which are oriented towards an understanding of the dispute as state-centered and related to macro-social projects (Buechler 1995: 457). In addition, Touraine (1997: 112) defines as a particular characteristic of social movements "the fact that an specific category of actors gets involved in a conflict with an adversary to dispute the management of the main means of action that society has to act over itself," or in more simple words, the conflict for power; this, in opposition to "cultural movements" which tend to focus in the transformation of the notion of the subject, is the reason why the idea of an adversary can be absent or be vague and diffuse. For Touraine, the subject's problem and the way society conceives it is the primary object around which NSMs coalesce and struggle. However, at the same time, NSMs emerge because subjects start to get in conflict with the social order, making it a goal for these movements. Castells (2001) has a similar understanding in the centrality he gives to politics in the dispute raised by NSMs, as politics is the space in which social life is organized.

Despite NSM theories' rejection of structural determination, the structure is still present in NSMs' theorizations of movements, but with a reconceptualization of the role it plays in agency configuration. For example, many authors share the suspicion that not all social sectors are equally prone to participate in NSM actions (Offe 1985). The role of structure generating the conditions for this new type of movement to emerge is still a problem: the consensus around a shift in the content of NSMs' demands centers on the cultural sphere and it simultaneously tends to problematize post-materialist issues (Inglehart 1990). Such is the case of identity, which becomes a central topic not only for the articulation of NSMs but also as one of their claims (see Fontana in this volume).

The discussion of NSMs has also pointed to their tendency to keep themselves outside institutional channels of political representation, pursuing their goals through influencing public opinion, disruptive actions in social life, and other outsider tactics (Tarrow 1994). Although this is also present in traditional social movements, the exclusion from channels of political representation tends to be central in NSMs, being more a characteristic of their nature than a circumstantial condition. For example, for NSMs, it would be almost unthinkable to sustain a relationship like the one that led to the creation of Britain's Labor Party as a branch of the trade union movement (Duverger 2012: 45) or other means of party linkage with similar strength. This particularity generates more unstable organizations and new ways of more extended solidarity and participation, beyond the most compromised members (Melucci 1985).

The case of Latin America introduces more variance and complexity to the discussion of NSMs, starting from two break points in the region's reality that launched the use of the NSMs concept into the Latin American debate: the crisis of the national-popular, developmentalist, or in some cases oligarchic state (Cardoso and Faletto 1977; Germani 1968) that had been a crucial trait in the region since the 1930s; and the crisis of political parties' mechanism of representation (Escobar and Álvarez 1992: 4). This last issue has also been referred to as the collapse of the traditional socio-political matrix, as seen later (Garretón et al. 2003). In contrast to the central NSM thesis previously described, the Latin American version of this debate sees a structural change in the explanation of the causes of these movements not only in the degree of economic development or the emergence of a new class (Kriesi 1989) but also in the type of link that they can produce with the political sphere due to the already mentioned reconfigurations of society.

The latter has two implications of great importance for social movements in the region. In the first place, movements maintain a structural class determination (although they do not necessarily configure themselves as a class-based movement), since materialistic social unrest persists and still articulates demands emerging from the economic sphere (Boschi 1983; de la Maza and Garcés 1985). Second, besides material solutions, demands for a political regime change, respect for human rights, and non-material demands emerge (Jelin and Calderón 1987). We use "non-material" instead of "post-material" due to the latter's association with a state of economic development where material problems lose importance, which is not the case for Latin American movements. Demands for human rights or political regime change can be understood as "non-material" in some literature, due to contextual differences, such as in the First World, in which the ascription to them is done by value options, in opposition to what happened in Latin America in the 1980s, under dictatorships that made human rights claims a matter of life or death. However, in a certain way these demands do represent a novelty for Latin American social movements.

Besides the complexity of the debate about NSMs and the persistent irresolution of the elements defining this field of study, the use of the NSM concept in Latin America introduces an additional problematic dimension. It not only puts in tension the original hypotheses about the causes of these movements' origins, but it also tends to blend the most traditional components of social movements with those attributed to the new ones. For example, a structural articulation of mobilized groups, typical of traditional social movements, is compatible with identity-based or non-material demands. Further, while Latin American NSMs may become distant from political parties, as happens with First World NSMs, this appears to be a product of the repressive context in Latin America rather than an intrinsic characteristic of NSMs as it is in Europe or the United States. Such was it, at least, when the discussions started during the 1980s, a specific moment for social movements in Latin America and their study.

New Social Movements in Latin America: Concept and Debates

The development of traditional social movements in Latin America has two breakpoints that must be considered in understanding the emergence of new social movements. The first one refers to the impact of the Cuban Revolution in the region. The second, to the advent of dictatorships (Brockett in this volume).

The Cuban Revolution changed how social movements related to the "reformist" politics of institutionalized left-wing parties (notwithstanding the several links that were sustained by movements, like clientelism and personalism in the Argentine case; or in Brazil, where the state and the local authorities were stronger than social movements; or in Chile and Uruguay, which presented a strong intertwining of parties and movements [Garretón et al. 2003: 23–25]). The Cuban Revolution's ideological impact penetrated with diverse intensity in every case, generating a radicalization of certain parties that tried to guide social movements to an armed revolutionary socialist project (see Martí i Puig and Álvarez in this volume). In this sense, authoritarianism in the region will emerge as a violent reaction to that radicalization to reestablish the order for capitalist accumulation (O'Donnell 1978).

In the following decades, authoritarian regimes dismantled developmentalist states and introduced neoliberal reforms, generating particular conditions for social mobilizations in what will later be called "the new social movements in Latin America" (NSMLA) and the consequent academic debate. During the authoritarian regimes, repression over movements turned self-defense and, therefore, the fight for human rights into a main goal. The foundational dimension of the dictatorships—understood as the political and economic restructuration of the countries they ruled—generated new ways of expressions for these movements, which combined cultural, material and political dimensions. All of them, linked to the struggle against repression, perspectives of changing the regime and conditions for the transitions to democracy (Garretón 2014). This is what happened, for example, in the case of "*ollas comunes*," the name given to neighbor gatherings and collaboration during times of increased unemployment and stern repression against popular sectors, or "*peñas*," the popular musical meetings (Bravo and González 2009). Beyond specific demands or activities, these spaces became a way for marginalized popular identities to acquire visibility in a public imaginary from which they were increasingly erased (Hardy 1986). With many others, these spaces became natural points of both propaganda and articulation in opposition to dictatorships, making them explicitly politicized. Another example is the case of the Madres de la Plaza de Mayo, a movement generated around a politicized demand—truth and justice in the cases of human rights violations—which in this way was from the beginning a movement with a transformational horizon (Navarro 1989).

As a component of the developmentalist state's dismantling, the Washington Consensus emerges as another issue of importance for NSMLA. This consensus consists mainly of a neoliberal agenda expressed in a list of reforms promoted by the monetary institutions based on debates that took place in Washington, inspired by a market-social-order conception of politics (Martínez and Soto 2012). Despite the formal democratic context in which it tries to work, the Washington Consensus advocates for a closure of the state against movements and atomized politics, promoting the disarticulation of civil society groups, with an evident impact on the previous traditional social movements and their participation in politics. The end of authoritarianism and beginning of transitions to democracy also tended to weaken social movements, because it blurred a clear collective enemy. This induced a loss of strength that isolated movements to particularistic struggles, producing a theoretical shift to cope with context change.[1]

This changing context led to a theoretical shift in order to solve three conceptions that showed inadequate for understanding the new circumstance. First, the neoliberal approach, which conceives social movements as distortions of individual market relations that must prevail. Second, the Marxist view, which presumes predominant class struggle dynamics in every social movement. Third, the postmodernist perspective, which considers that the logic of culturally-centered movements is non-reducible to contingent politics (Eckstein 2001: 365).

In place of these pre-shaped comprehensions, the theoretical shift proposed by the NSMs approach led to the consideration of some variables highlighted as critical for the understanding of social movements. These are: (1) the political, cultural, and economic conditions bequeathed by transitions to democracy in which movements unfold; (2) their social background (specifying their gender, class, or territorial composition, among other aspects); and (3) the specific way in which movements tended to relate with politics (Eckstein 2001).

The NSMs approach can help explore how neoliberal politics in each country are recepted in the population. This, by locating these politics in the field of conflict between different agents, with special attention to the role that NSMs play in those conflicts. This also carries a revalorization of democracy as the normative orientation where NSMs unfolds, as it looks at the decisions that social movements make—and not theoretically pre-conceived responses—as the key for understanding their political behavior, in which democracy is a requirement for expression. This perspective is opposed to the political closure promoted by the Washington Consensus described before, proposing a reconsideration for the limits that democracy presupposes for social movements, while simultaneously relativizing the revolutionary horizon given the acceptance for pluralism and diverse demands in a constant re-elaboration.

In the 1990s, a shift in the dynamics and studies of new social movements, mainly explained by the Chiapas Zapatista uprising in 1994, stirred the tension between movements, formal democracy, and the Washington Consensus in the struggle for substantive democracy. That gave way to a new boost for movements to confront neoliberalism and globalization, outlining a social opposition agenda. In that sense, Chiapas implied for the 1990s social movements' struggles what the human rights movements (such as the Madres of the Plaza de Mayo in Argentina) had done during the dictatorships' period: they gave a horizon of social transformation to the immediate social demands for which the context urges NSMs to fight (Garretón 2014). That horizon will be central in social conflict and political debate during the next two decades in Latin America, just as are citizenship equality, social justice, and cultural diversity. In this sense, the uprising is the first expression of a new sociohistorical *problematique*.[2] That *problematique* can be synthesized by the idea of a multidimensional struggle for equality (CEPAL 2010), which will nourish progressive governments and the region's most politicized movements.

The consideration for these dimensions in NSMLA also opens the possibility for understanding the interrelation of movements with other societal problems and the region's historical course. In this way, for example, it can be said that the left turn that took place at the beginning of this century in Latin America cannot be understood without the role of NSMLA. The most interesting fact at this respect is that in these processes, social movements play diverse roles, from the rise of political alternatives towards the Left, like in Bolivia and Brazil, to their external articulation from the state in populist projects (Levitsky and Roberts 2011). In some cases, the politicization that affected movements during the "left turn" put into tension the original definition of NSMs, in which a relative autonomy from politics tends to be one of the predominant characteristics. NSMLA studies around shifts towards the Left should try to understand how the linkage of these autonomous movements with politics began and what happened to them during this shift and their possible disaggregation in specific topics because of their distance from politics.[3]

Because of this relation with national development projects, the discussion around NSMLA has been intimately related to the debate about the quality of democracy (O'Donnell et al. 2003) and the limits and potentials that it imposes on collective actors. For example, feminist movements have discussed the limits to the promise of equality that democracy supposes (Molyneux 2001). At the same time, these studies have shown the need that democracy has of social movements, predominantly for understanding the transitions to democracy (Hipsher 1998).

During the 2010s, new social processes emerged from outside the limits of the left-turn governments, or even surpassing them. These processes have been marked by a lower degree of classic politicization, a weaker connection with political parties that challenge their capacity of representation, a more spontaneous organization, a component of violence, and a tendency towards material-oriented demands (Bringel and Pleyers 2017). The so called "outbreaks" in Brazil (2015), Chile (2019), and Ecuador (2019) are some examples of these new kinds of mobilizations and potential re-politicizations. However, due to their recent emergence, it is too early to classify them as a type of NSMs or only as a new wave of mobilizations. From a theoretical and analytical point of view, there are two main questions: first, it must be discerned if these revolts only emerged as reactions to critical junctures or are the birth of a NSMs that will sustain over time. Second, it must be discussed in which conditions an outbreak can become a social movement.

Economic, Social, Cultural, and Political Dimensions

For a long time, the study of social phenomena has evolved in a tension between agency and structure as a central explanatory factor. That tension can partially be solved by approaches that consider both social structures and agents, and the mutual affectations between them to explain social life (Archer 2003). The cultural, economic, social, and political dimensions of NSMLA can be understood by taking this perspective. In these dimensions, the contemporary social movements' emergence is within a context that becomes relevant to the modernity model that movements relate to, the terms in which globalization and neoliberalism are installed, subjectivation and identity, and the crisis of politics and democracy. All these contextual dimensions are interconnected.

In what is called the model of modernity, the first assumption is that "a" single modernity does not exist, but rather different types of modernity are sustained on how a society combines its historical rationality, subjectivation, and memory in the constitution of its subjects. The model of modernity is crucial for understanding NSMLA since it becomes one of their objects of dispute (Garreton 2014; 2015). The dispute of "models of modernity" conditions how social movements and their specific demands are inscribed in society. In this sense, NSMLA are part of the construction of the modernity of their societies, and this is especially relevant in the case of ethnic movements like, for example, the Bolivian one. In the same way, the convergence of struggles against patriarchalism, capitalism, and colonialism gives NSMLA different characteristics in contexts where institutions have been inherited from other models of modernity. This is why, among other things, the meaning of democracy in the context of globalization in Latin America must be considered as the background in which NSMs unfold and, as it has been said, its definition is an object of dispute (Touraine 1997).

Another dimension of NSMs' context, which connects strongly with the previous one, is neoliberal globalization (Calderón 2004) as the global experience of the modern social condition (Martuccelli 2017). For example, communication beyond the traditional mass media, and the global neoliberal agenda that imposes on resistance movements the necessity or the desire to articulate their struggles beyond borders (Pleyers 2010). In this way the double meaning of globalization can be understood: while it acts in the cultural sphere (mainly through the role of networks and media), it is also a structural condition for movements, as today's political economy is explained by the insertion of countries in the dynamics of globalization (see Burridge and Markoff in this volume). Several social movements have had to confront this problem. In the case of the already mentioned paradigmatic case of the Chiapas movement, they had developed ways of "trans-locality" for movement's survival, which means that the defense of their common identity requires alliances and knowledge that transcend the local origin, combining its initial radical opposition to globalization to struggle specifically against the dangers of neoliberal globalization (Ayora 2008). Thus, the distinction between neoliberalism and globalization was a learning process for NSMLA. In the beginning, many of them struggled as "anti-globalization" movements while now the object of struggle has changed to "alter-globalization" against a particular type of globalization, betting for global relations as an alternative to the neoliberal hegemonic path.[4]

Subjectivation is understood as how individuals insert and unfold themselves in social relations and has always been a relevant issue in the study of social movements. The same happens with the identity that individuals develop due to processes of subjectivation since it establishes differences between social groups that can even become a reason for conflicts. As stated in the introduction to this chapter, both subjectivation and identity are central to NSMs. First, identity plays a critical role in articulating these movements, to the point that some of them are classified as mainly identitarian movements. Second, the insertion of conflicts into the cultural sphere creates an area in which the process of subjectivation becomes a "leitmotiv" for the mobilization of individuals. In this sense, the problem of how societies generate individuals under specific processes of subjectivation, with degrees of autonomous existence from the community, acquires renewed importance (Martuccelli 2010). One of the best examples of the identity dimension is the feminist movement. Here, identity becomes a major topic of configuration. Because of that, some authors have pointed out that as one of the problematic issues to sustain their struggle, given the difficulties to stabilize a particular identity within a relation of gender and power that is in constant transformation (Alcoff 1988; see Ewig and Friedman in this volume).

Identity and subjectivation are not only present in non-materially oriented movements. This is shown by the diverse cases in the region that, while they configure themselves around material demands, also contest subjectivation and cultural issues. Moreover, this is very patent in approaching topics like inequality, central to the current sociohistorical *problematique* of Latin America. Inequality, which is undeniably linked to substantial necessities that mobilize popular sectors, is a problem that is expressed through a discourse of civil rights, surpassing the material problem and relating to the issues of "dignity" or "well-being" that have been key terms in many movements and massive mobilizations since the 1990s (Calderón 2017).

Last but not least, the political context, as we have mentioned, is one of the main factors in the analysis of social movements. In Latin America, the main change in this regard has to do with the decomposition of the links between the social and the political sphere that characterized the region's society during the national-popular period. This phase was marked by a close relation between the different dimensions of social life, usually articulated by a strong party system, several social groups or a personalized leader who mobilized interest in the state (Garretón et al. 2003). The erosion of this relation led the late democratic governments to look for a re-construction of some type of sociopolitical links, mainly marked by two factors: the left turn and the diverse conflictive ways in which they deal with the neoliberal global cycle (Ruiz and Boccardo 2014). The diversity shown from case to case illustrates how politics can potentiate, determine, or guide social movements (Roberts 2014), and debilitate them or limit them programmatically through clientelism, exclusion from political power, or depoliticization. In twenty-first-century Latin America, almost all these types of state-society relations have been present, obviously as a result of conditions that exceed the mere will of political agents. Theoretically, it is important to understand the relation of the political sphere with movements as one of mutual influence, with multiple possibilities for articulation that give space to specific types of democracy, and particular agendas that are confronted. We will refer to this in the next section.

The Changing Socio-political Matrix and New Social Movements in Latin America

The "socio-political matrix" concept compares the configuration of Latin-American societies between different countries and historical periods. This is possible by defining societies as the relations that they generate between their central constituent elements: the state, the representation system, the socioeconomic order, and specific cultural orientations (Garretón et al. 2003). In this way, a country is analyzed by looking at how those elements interrelate in a specific social formation. During the twentieth century, these components linked themselves in Latin American society in a particular configuration called the "statist-national-popular" type of matrix, based usually in a model of development called import substitution industrialization, with some remnants of oligarchic elements, especially in the countryside. This matrix fused the constituent elements of the socio-political matrix: state, political parties, and social actors. Although Latin American societies inspire the socio-political matrix approach, it can also comprehend First-World articulations between movements and politics.

Within this approach—connected to Touraine (1997)—a distinction must be established between social movements (in plural and lower cases) and the Central Social Movement of a society (in singular and capital letters) (Garretón 2014). The latter is charged with a core meaning and a transformational project, encompassing and directing the particular movements mobilized by their diverse demands[5] with ideological content and conflicts printed in the articulations of a specific socio-political matrix. In this perspective, material and non-material demands become articulated in a global framework sense in which the factual claims of each movement are inscribed. The most evident example of this Central Social Movement is how left-wing parties and social movements used to claim a global transformation of society while also struggling for particular reforms for material needs during the twentieth century. Therefore, the dichotomy between material and non-material demands, expressed in the NSMs debate about the post-material epochal change (Melucci 1985; Offe 1985), is replaced by a comprehension of the connection of the cultural and material that can conceive a dialogue between both spheres when necessary.

Up to a certain extent, these movements' nature tends to change as their relationship with politics does: through parties or by a direct link with the state. This last difference is not trivial. How particular socio-political matrixes are configured, and the preponderance of some elements over others, can explain important courses of history, and how the same matrixes change. For example, during the dominant period of the national-popular matrix in Chile, it was impossible to understand social movements without the influence that political parties exercised over them, to the point that the repression of the last dictatorship over parties also caused a halt of movements. Different is the case of Argentina, where social movements enjoy greater importance and autonomy to make themselves heard in the political sphere, which explains the immediate opposition that they could articulate against the dictatorship, despite the fierce political persecution that parties suffered during that regime (Garretón et al. 2003).

Even though the authoritarian regimes put an abrupt end to the previous socio-political matrix in Latin American, a new one did not emerge in every national case. The diversity of factors that configured the new socio-political matrixes in Latin America during the twenty-first century gives way to several different national cases that make possible only a general overview.

The emergence of neoliberal politics became one of the most critical factors in the decomposition of more traditional Latin American social movements due to the rupture introduced in the link of movements with politics (Garretón 2015). The empire of neoliberal politics encompasses the most crucial contextual dimensions that affect social movements: it constructs a type of modernity, inserts society into the globalization process in a determined condition, and establishes specific means of individualization, subjectivation, and linking between the political sphere and movements. In this sense, the importance of social movements lies to a good extent in their contribution to reconstruct the socio-political matrixes in their countries, as a way of recompose national communities. On one side, we find Evo Morales' Bolivia, where the social movement grassroots rebuilds a socio-political matrix. On the opposite side, we find the difficulties of the democratic governments after the dictatorship in Chile to overcome the neo-liberal socio-political matrix, leading to an increasing distance between the political system and mobilizations and social movements (Garretón et al. 2003).

However, despite the contextual variance that the different socio-political matrixes in the region impose on social movements, some general characteristics of this period are present in most countries. First, almost all of them have been crossed by "the new historical *problematique*" of Latin America, in which Chiapas' Zapatista movement was a pioneer. In the cases where movements have upgraded their struggles, they have also tended to oppose neoliberal politics, since it marginalizes them from decision making.

Nevertheless, internal problems can also be seen in the NSMLA. Under the value of equality lies a tension between the need for articulation between a concrete perception of problems that motivate movements and a more comprehensive transformative project to overcome these problems. This is explained by Habermas (1981) as the difficulty that NSMs face transcending the "life-worlds" in which they are embedded. In other words, the reaction against the immediate conditions to promote an effective political solution to NSMLA "life-worlds" requires a new relation with politics, from which NSMLA tend to be excluded.

The tension between concrete requests and major transformations has also been theorized as the need for a utopian horizon to sustain and project movements' aspirations (Touraine 1997). In its development lies the possibility for movements to exist beyond a first brief moment of clash and to aspire for a solution to social problems and enter into dialogue with other groups and social spheres that can be questioned from the NSMLA horizon. This problem, related to the increasing difficulty to transcend the immediacy of isolation, can be traced to the first developments in the NSM debate described at the beginning of this chapter, and in several historical cases in Latin America. It is one of the common characteristics between NSMs and NSMLA, justifying the shared use of this concept.

Conclusion

During the 1970s and 1980s, collective action showed several new traits that generated a debate around how to study social movements. These are the distance that social movements were having with the political system, the importance of normative claims and non-material demands, the middle-class social composition, and the centrality of identity, among others. Around these characteristics emerged the concept and study of "New Social Movements," and the attempts not only to understand their ways of action, but also the changes in society that could explain their emergence in contraposition to "traditional movements."

Beyond this consensus around these movements' new characteristics, the NSMs approach was also crossed by polemics that confronted scholars with diverse thesis.

Among them can be mentioned different understandings of the role of politics in and for NSMs, the transformational horizon NSMs can aspire to, their relation to capitalism, and, especially, their relation to democracy. This gave birth to NSMs theorizations in a double way. First, as a middle-range theory of collective action, with some basic agreements and diverse debates. Second, as a concept that, while wrought under the NSMs theory, was also linked to other theoretical frameworks in a flexible use.

In Latin America, the use of the concept was due to a new political context, mainly explained by the rise of dictatorships and the new links promoted between state and society. This represents a different cause than that which started the discussion in Europe and North America. During the 1980s, when the discussion started in the region, there were no signals of change in the economic or class structure as seemed to happen in the First World. The new characteristics of social structure, where a new illustrated class gathers interest, and the consequent importance of the cultural sphere over the economic context, were not present in Latin America's social reality. Instead, more relevant for explaining the causes for the emergence of NSMLA are the authoritarian regimes, the decomposition of the socio-political matrix and the traditional or developmentalist state.

These causes received more or less attention depending on the scholar, but these and not the advanced development of capitalism viewed in the First World are what changed social movements in Latin America. For the same reason, the new characteristics of the NSMLA were not the same as those reported by European and North American studies. The historical specificities and the diverse ways in which the debate about NSMs has been approached—whether as a whole theory or as a flexible concept—led to an even more heterodox approach for their study in Latin America.

The disengagement between social movements and political representation in Latin America was mainly caused by the changes in the socio-political matrix provoked by the new forms of authoritarianism of the 1970s. This has important implications for the comparison of NSMs in Latin America and the First World. In Europe, the prevalence of the cultural sphere in post-materialist societies was subtracting weight from material demands and, because of that, moving movements away from politics. Instead, in Latin America, the lack of political representation gave more autonomy to movements but without removing them from the materialistic demands. On the other side, the 1980s non-materialistic demands of NSMLA are explained in most cases by a repressive context of dictatorships that made a priority to call for regime change and the defense for human rights (see Brockett, Wolff in this volume), but not because of new material conditions that prioritized cultural concerns over other dimensions of life. There is, then, a contextual explanation that sustains the different emergence of NSMLA.

The narrated dynamics explain why, in the 1990s, with the democratization process (see Inclán in this volume), a regional-specific turning point exists for the development of NSMLA. The repressive context agglutinated several demands, material, and non-material ones, from diverse movements that found in the dictatorships a common enemy. Instead, the transition to democracy gave place to a dispersion of these demands and a less clear common enemy. The persistence of most of the common traits of NSMLA despite this change of context forced it to look for another reason for articulating these movements.

In this chapter, we have argued that the dismantling of the socio-political matrix in Latin America refers not only to the context of repressive dictatorships but also to the neoliberalization of the economy, the insertion of societies in the globalization process, and the dispute with the model of modernity. Alongside subjectivation and identity, all these elements within the context of democratic political crises have shaped NSMLA.

Even if this chapter has made an effort to unify the study of NSMLA, and although some general lines have been postulated, the attempt has obvious difficulties given the internal diversity of Latin America. A pessimistic vision could even reject the possibility of reaching a general state of the art in studying Latin American social movements. However, we think it worthwhile to do this mainly in contraposition to the First World's approaches. This chapter must be understood as an introduction to significant attempts to highlight this region's uniqueness concerning the NSMs debate, rather than an approach for a detailed study of social movements in a particular country.

Among the key questions, emerges the one for the direction that social movements take with the reflux of the progressist cycle lived in the region from the 2000s until 2019 (Levitsky and Roberts 2011; Ruiz and Boccardo 2014). The development of NSMLA during the first two decades of the twenty-first century finds its explanation—partially—in the influence that constituted the left turn. The left-turn end presents the question about the future of movements and the possibilities for the emergence of a new Central Social Movement. Here must be highlighted, on the one hand, the new kind of mobilizations that have been called "*estallidos sociales*," and their capacity to transform themselves in real social movements; and on the other hand, the new wave of feminist and environmentalist movements that emerged with cultural goals and attempts to link themselves to other struggles (Carosio 2017). Both tendencies lead us to ask whether NSMLA should be interpreted under the frames used until now, or rather they shall be pushed to new theoretical frontiers.

Notes

1. This theoretical shift and also the described context is condensed in Eckstein (2001, especially the Epilogue), and in Garretón (1996, especially the general framework; and 2014).
2. The sociohistorical *problematique* refers to the central topics around which societies in their main spheres (the state, party systems, and civil society) will focus their interests and conflicts during a specific period (Garretón 2014: 93).
3. In this respect, Escobar and Álvarez (1992) try to mark out the break points of Latin American history that launch NSMLA studies in the end of national-populist states; Rossi and von Bülow (2015) articulate the analysis of diverse cases of social movements in the region considering as their main analytical axis the interactions between routine and contentious politics; and the work of Almeida and Cordero (2017) aims to draw a context for NSMLA that considers material and non-material social basis for mobilization, and the several differences that can be seen in each national case.

4. This is clearly expressed by their turn to the motto "globalize the struggle, globalize the hope," associated with the emergence of several social forums that demanded an "alter-globalization" (Thwaites 2010).
5. For example, the human rights or democratic movement under the dictatorships was a Central Sócial Movement, and the Madres de Plaza de Mayo are a concrete expression of it.

References

Alcoff, Linda (1988), "Cultural Feminism Versus Post-Structuralism: The Identity Crisis in Feminist Theory," *Journal of Woman in Culture and Society* 13(3), 405–36.

Almeida, Paul, and Allen Cordero (2017), "Movimientos sociales en América Latina," in Paul Almeida and Allen Cordero (eds.), *Movimientos sociales en América Latina: perspectivas, tendencias y casos*, 13–26 (Buenos Aires: CLACSO).

Archer, Margaret (2003), *Structure, Agency and the Internal Conversation* (Cambridge: Cambridge University Press).

Ayora, Steffan (2008), "Translocalidad y la antropología de los procesos globales: saber y poder en Chiapas y Yucatán," *Journal of Latin American and Caribbean Anthropology* 12(1), 134–63.

Boschi, Renato Raul (1983), *Movimientos coletivos no Brasil urbano* (Rio de Janeiro: Zahar Editores).

Bravo, Gabriela. and Cristián González (2009), *Ecos del tiempo subterráneo* (Santiago: LOM).

Bringel, Breno and Geoffrey Pleyers (eds.) (2017), *Protesta e indignación global: los movimientos sociales en el nuevo orden mundial* (Buenos Aires: CLACSO).

Buechler, Steven (1995), "New Social Movement Theories," *The Sociological Quarterly*, 36(3), 441–464.

Calderón, Fernando (2004), *¿Es sostenible la globalización en América Latina?* (Santiago: Fondo de Cultura Económica).

Calderón, Fernando (2017), "Cultura de igualdad, deliberación y desarrollo humano," in Fernando Calderón (ed.), *La construcción social de los derechos y la cuestión social del desarrollo*, 565–626 (Buenos Aires: CLACSO).

Cardoso, Fernando Henrique and Enzo Faletto (1977), *Dependencia y desarrollo en América Latina* (Buenos Aires: Siglo XXI).

Carosio, Alba (2017), "Perspectivas feministas para ampliar horizontes del pensamiento crítico latinoamericano," in Montserrat Sagot (ed.), *Feminismos, pensamiento crítico y propuestas alternativas en América Latina*, 17–42 (Buenos Aires: CLACSO).

Castells, Manuel (2001), *La era de la información: economía, sociedad y cultura, volumen II: el poder de la identidad* (Mexico: Siglo XXI).

CEPAL (2010), *La hora de la igualdad: brechas por cerrar, caminos por abrir* (Santiago: CEPAL).

de la Maza, Gonzalo and Mario Garcés (1985), *La explosión de las mayorías* (Santiago: Educación y Comunicaciones).

Duverger, Maurice (2012), *Los partidos políticos* (Mexico: Fondo de Cultura Económica).

Eckstein, Susan (2001), "Epílogo," in Susan Eckstein (ed.), *Poder y protesta popular: movimientos sociales latinoamericanos*, 363–413 (Mexico: Siglo XXI).

Escobar, Arturo and Sonia Álvarez (1992), "Introduction: Theory and Protest in Latin America Today," in Arturo Escobar and Sonia Álvarez (eds.), *The Making of Social Movements in Latin America*, 1–15 (Boulder, CO: Westview Press).

Garretón, Manuel Antonio (2014), *Las ciencias sociales en la trama de Chile y América Latina* (Santiago: LOM Editores).

Garretón, Manuel Antonio (2015), "Political Modernity, Democracy and State-Society Relations in Latin America: A New Socio-Historical Problématique?" in Gerard Rosich, and Peter Wagner (eds.), *The Trouble with Democracy*, 121–47 (Oxford: Oxford University Press).

Garretón, Manuel Antonio (1996), "Social Movements and the Process of Democratization. A General Framework," *International Review of Sociology* 6(1), 39–49.

Garretón, Manuel Antonio, Marcelo Cavarozzi, Peter Cleaves, Gary Gereffi, and Jonathan Hartlyn (2003), *Latin America in the 21st Century: Toward a New Sociopolitical Matrix* (Miami: North-South Center Press).

Germani, Gino (1968), *Política y sociedad en una época de transición; de la sociedad tradicional a la sociedad de masas* (Buenos Aires: Paidós).

Habermas, Jurgen (1981), "New Social Movements," *Telos* 49, 33–37.

Hardy, Clarisa (1986), *Hambre + dignidad = ollas comunes* (Santiago: PET).

Hipsher, Patricia (1998), "Democratic Transitions as Protest Cycles: Social Movement Dynamics in Democratizing Latin America," in David Meyer and Sidney Tarrow (eds.), *Social Movement Society*, 153–72 (Oxford: Rowman and Littlefield).

Inglehart, Ronald (1990), "Values, Ideology, and Cognitive Mobilization in New Social Movements," in Dalton Russell and Manfred Kuechler (eds.), *Challenging the Political Order: New Social and Political Movements in Western Democracies*, 43–66 (Cambridge: Polity).

Jelin, Elizabeth and Fernando Calderón (1987), "Clases sociales y movimientos en américa latina," *Revista Brasileira de Ciencias Sociais* 2(5), 173–89.

Kriesi, Hanspeter (1989), "New Social Movements and the New Class in the Netherlands" *American Journal of Sociology* 94(5), 1078–116.

Levitsky, Steven and Kenneth Roberts (2011), "Latin America's 'Left Turn'," in Steven Levitsky and Kenneth Roberts (eds.), *The Resurgence of the Latin American Left*, 1–30 (Baltimore, MD: Johns Hopkins University Press).

Martínez, Rubí and Ernesto Soto (2012), "El consenso de Washington: La instauración de las políticas neoliberales en América Latina," *Política y Cultura* 37, 35–64.

Martuccelli, Danilo (2010), *¿Existen individuos en el sur?* (Santiago: LOM).

Martuccelli, Danilo (2017), "La nueva dinámica de la condición social moderna," *Revista de Sociología* 32, 89–105.

Melucci, Alberto (1985), "The Symbolic Challenge of Contemporary Movement," *Social Research* 52(4), 789–816.

Molyneux, Maxine (2001), "Género y ciudadanía en América Latina: Cuestiones históricas y contemporáneas," *Debate Feminista* 23, 3–66.

Navarro, Marysa (1989), "The Personal is Political: Las Madres De Plaza De Mayo," in Susan Eckstein (ed), *Power and Popular Protest: Latin American Social Movements*, 241–258 (Berkeley: University of California Press).

O'Donnell, Guillermo (1978), "Reflections on the Patterns of Change in the Bureaucratic Authoritarian State in Latin America," *Latin American Research Review* 13(1), 3–38.

O'Donnell, Guillermo, Osvaldo Iazzetta, and Jorge Vargas (eds.) (2003), *Democracia, desarrollo humano y ciudadanía: reflexiones sobre la calidad de la democracia en América Latina* (Buenos Aires: Homo Sapiens-PNUD).

Offe, Claus (1985), "New Social Movements: Challenging the Boundaries of Institutional Politics," *Social Research* 52(4), 817–68.

Pleyers, Geoffrey (2010), *Alter-Globalization: Becoming Actors in a Global Age* (Cambridge: Polity).

Roberts, Kenneth (2014), *Changing Course in Latin America* (Cambridge: Cambridge University Press).

Rossi, Federico M. and Marisa von Bülow (2015) "Theory-Building Beyond Borders," in Federico M. Rossi and Marisa von Bülow (eds), *Social Movements Dynamics: New Perspectives on Theory and Research from Latin America*, 1–14 (Farnham: Ashgate).

Ruiz, Carlos and Giorgio Boccardo (2014), "¿América Latina ante una nueva encrucijada?" *Anuario Del Conflicto Social* 4, 765–83.

Tarrow, Sidney (1994), *Power in Movement* (Cambridge: Cambridge University Press).

Thwaites, Mabel (2010), "Después de la globalización neoliberal: ¿qué Estado en América Latina?" *Observatorio Social de América Latina* 11(27), 19–43.

Touraine, Alain (1997), *¿Podremos Vivir Juntos?* (Mexico: Fondo de Cultura Económica).

CHAPTER 5

RELATIONAL APPROACHES TO SOCIAL MOVEMENTS IN (AND BEYOND) LATIN AMERICA

SAM HALVORSEN AND FEDERICO M. ROSSI

Introduction

Social movements are inherently relational phenomena yet rarely are they explicitly theorized as such. This chapter aims to pull together different strands of relational literature on Latin American social movements as a first step in setting the agenda for future studies.

Relational approaches often start from the perspective that social relations are primordial and that individuals and collectives are merely historical crystallizations of social relations at a specific point in time (Corcuff 2013: 27). From a sociological perspective, Emirbayer (1997: 287) defined it as follows: "In this point of view, which I shall also label 'relational,' the very terms or units involved in a transaction derive their meaning, significance, and identity from the (changing) functional roles they play within that transaction. The latter, seen as a dynamic, unfolding process, becomes the primary unit of analysis rather than the constituent elements themselves." Other disciplines have developed specific understandings of relationality, such as geography where it usually refers to the stretching of social relations beyond place-based fixity and towards extra local flows and networks. However, beyond these basic definitions there is no unified "relational approach" in the social sciences, and social movement studies have reproduced some of the divisions of the general literature.

There are different ways of understanding what relational means in social movement studies. Schematically, this would depend on the main dimension(s) studied as the focus of research. When the question is the *how* of social conflict, a historical viewpoint dominates. When the question is the *where* of social conflict, a geographical vantage point comes to the fore. An ecological perspective tends to respond to questions over our relation to *what we are not*, and when the question is on *who* is mobilized, an intersectional perspective tends to dominate.

Another pattern that seems to exist among relational perspectives in social movement studies is that those scholars interested in the historical analysis of social movements are mostly linked to the political process and contentious politics approaches, while those with a geographical viewpoint to the new social movements approach. Moreover, the ecological approach is often linked to decolonial theories and the intersectional, to a certain degree, to all four. These perspectives are synthesized in Table 5.1.

We identify these four perspectives on relationality in social movement studies (in Latin America) because they are the ones which have developed an explicit understanding of the relational study of social movements. This is not an exhaustive list but is what we consider as the core and most promising foci for social movement studies. Even though, as we will show, there is no common understanding of what the relational is, there are interesting developments in each perspective that could potentially be used

Table 5.1 Main relational approaches to social movements

	Main dimension studied	Understanding of relational	Social movement perspective that developed it further
Intersectional	Identities	*Who?* The relations across core categories of collective identities—such as class, gender, and ethnicity—as constitutive of the mobilized actors.	To an extent, all social movement perspectives
Historical	Time	*How?* The position of mobilized actors and sequence of events establishes social dynamics, sometimes understood as mechanisms.	Political process and contentious politics
Geographical	Space	*Where?* The co-constitution of the social and spatial in social movements as well as the (dis)continuities in movements across space.	New Social Movements
Ecological	Nature	*What we are (not)?* The relations between humans and nature, understood as socio-natural relations, often framed as struggles of political ontology.	Decolonial

in eclectic combinations to study social movements. Our aim is to show that the study of Latin American social movements can provide an interesting context for relational studies of social movements in and beyond the region.

Intersectional

The importance of identities in social movement studies is crucial given that movements are a collection of actors. The most influential definition of social movements is intrinsically relational due to the interactive constitution of what we call a social movement. In Diani's (1992: 13) words: "A social movement is a network of informal interactions between a plurality of individuals, groups and/or organizations, engaged in a political or cultural conflict, on the basis of a shared collective identity." In this definition there is a crucial component: *a collective identity*. Intersectional approaches examine exactly that—the relations across core categories of collective identities, such as class, gender, and ethnicity—and the ensuing mobilization dynamics.

In a relational approach, identities are not considered as a substance of the actors but instead seen as a configuration of relationships in the course of social conflicts, as such they are mutable and dependent on the position of the contenders in the dynamics studied (McAdam, Tarrow, and Tilly 2001). This is as much an individual as a collective process (Melucci 1996; Pizzorno 1994). Identities are also communication strategies, as Mische (2015) proposes in a relational-pragmatic model to challenge the divide between instrumental and communicative action. She explores how people perform varied identities in particular relational settings. Mische (2008, 2015) analyzes how student activists in Brazil suppress or reinforce multiple identities as styles of communication linking partisan and civic spaces in their communication in public.

In a networked understanding of social movements, such as social network analysis (Scherer-Warren, 1993; Spalding in this volume), White's (1992, 2008 [1965]) concept of "catnets" (i.e., "category + network," meaning the relationship between common characteristics and linking ties), is central to defining a social movement (Diani 1992; Tilly 1978). Understanding movements as networks also allows us to identify the difference between the social movement organizations (SMOs), allies, and the full catnet of a social movement. For instance, the landless peasants movement in Brazil is composed of around 110 SMOs, even though its dominant SMO, the Movimento dos Trabalhadores Rurais Sem Terra (MST), is often conflated with the full movement (Feliciano 2011: 34–36; Rossi 2017a: 263). Boundary definition is a typical problem in social movement studies in Latin America and in relational analysis in general (Emirbayer 1997).

Intersectional approaches to Latin American social movements came to the fore in parallel to debates elsewhere on the limitations of class as the over-riding identity for mobilization and, in particular, with the growth of visibility around women's (and women-led) movements (Alvarez, Dagnino, and Escobar 1997; Radcliffe and Westwood 1993; Johnson and Sempol in this volume). The Argentine Madres de Plaza de Mayo are a paradigmatic case that gives prominence to the demands of women in relation to a growing human rights movement in the region (Jelin 1990; Wolff in this volume). At the same time, the explosion of popular urban movements in the region gave a prominent role to the organizational capacity of women who were often at the frontline of coordinating community responses to the crises of an accelerating neoliberal mode of development across the region (Lazar 2008; Schönwälder 2002; Velasco 2015; Ewig and Friedman in this volume). Intersectional, relational approaches bring to the forefront grievances over social reproduction in addition to more traditionally framed classist approaches.

Moreover, since the 1990s there has been a huge interest into multiple intersections, including sexuality and gender together with a resurgence of strategic focus on ethnicity in social movements across Latin America (Muteba Rahierm 2012; see Spanakos and Romo, Rice, Fontana in this volume). Intersectionality has provided a sharp-edge analytical approach for understanding the complex and inter-connected forms of mobilization across the region, from the role of women in indigenous movements (Rousseau and Hudon 2017), to race in urban poor activism (Carril 2006) through to the intersection of sexuality and class in popular movements, as the LGBTIQ+ and Peronist SMO Agrupación Nacional Putos Peronistas show in their combination of gender and ideology with popular sectors' definition of their claims for recognition (Médica and Villegas 2012).

One theoretical framework for making sense of these intersections has been the renewed efforts to understand autonomy as a the central objective of Latin American social movements (Dinerstein 2015; Reyes 2012; Zibechi 2012; Sousa in this volume), which deliberately forces analyses to break away from pre-conceived "single issue" foci (such as class or gender). Nevertheless, autonomous approaches to intersectionality can fall prey to their own boundedness, whether it be in the search for an "outside" to dominant categories such as capital and the state or through an insufficiently relational reading of the historical and geographical dynamics of mobilization.

Historical

The importance of time for Latin American social movements is essential if we intend to understand how dynamics of conflictive social relations develop into transformation or reproduction. Historical relational approaches examine transactions between movements and other actors across time.

The relational turn in social movement studies was proposed in the 2000s by McAdam, Tarrow, and Tilly (2001), suggesting a move away from a static movement-centric view to an understanding of contentious politics as "episodic, public, collective interaction among makers of claims and their objects when (a) at least one government is a claimant, an object of claim, or a party to the claims, and (b) the claims would, if realized, affect the interests of at least one of the claimants" (ibid.: 5). This perspective intends to replace the study of social movements with that of recurrent social mechanisms that produce different or similar outcomes depending on the way in which they are causally interconnected (ibid.: 37). The intention is to turn all the key concepts of the political process and the resource mobilization approaches into relational mechanisms (see Somma in this volume), which were previously considered too static (McAdam, Tarrow, and Tilly 2001: 18, 43–45).

Tilly's (1978, 1984) processual social history is the driving force behind the contentious politics agenda proposed by McAdam, Tarrow, and Tilly (2001). Tilly (1984) is a crucial reference point for all the later work of the relationalists in social movement studies. His work is intrinsically relational, as he combines White's (1992, 2008 [1965]) concept of "catnets," the relational perspective of Georg Simmel (Tilly 1978: 62–63, 1984: 28–29) and the historical understanding of social dynamics of Karl Marx (Tilly 1984: 78–79). He postulates that we need to study social relations historically in "well-defined processes, and in recognizing from the outset that time matters—that when things happen within a sequence affects how they happen, that every structure or process constitutes a series of choice points. Outcomes at a given point in time constrain possible outcomes at later points in time" (ibid.: 14). In other words, a diachronic analysis of processual conflictive relations defines the historical relational approach.

Latin American scholarship on movements tends to use different elements from this historical relational approach (Rossi and von Bülow 2015). Overall, in Latin America the dynamic relational turn in social movement studies has influenced—explicitly or implicitly—protest studies rather than other dimensions of social movements (for example, Almeida 2008; Ancelovici and Guzmán-Concha 2019; Auyero 2002; and see Almeida, Wada in this volume for reviews). Among relational scholars of Latin American social movements, network analyses prevail (for example, Gurza Lavalle and Bueno 2011; Spalding 2015; von Bülow 2010; and see Spalding in this volume for a review). As such, duration, tempo, timing, sequencing, paths, and social mechanisms of social movement dynamics have been generally disregarded, with a tendency for static single-case or comparative studies.

Among those scholars of Latin American movements that have adopted the relational historical approach, the call to replace social movements with contentious politics as suggested by McAdam, Tarrow, and Tilly (2001) was not taken up (a common tendency elsewhere, too). Instead, movements were introduced into the interactive, dynamic, mechanisms of causal construction of sequences that build processes such as the study of the struggle for reincorporation of the *piquetero* movement in Argentina (Rossi 2017a) or eventful analysis such as the research of the earthquake victims movement in Mexico City by Tavera Fenollosa (2015). In relational terms, this is quite logical, if social movements are understood following Diani (1992), because they are already a dynamic set of interactions and not a unified actor. This seems coherent even with the proposal that nation-states are not context (in opposition to what the political opportunity structure concept implied in its original formulations, see Somma in this volume), but rather a contender in the disruptive dynamics studied (McAdam, Tarrow, and Tilly 2001: 74).

Social mechanisms have been further explored by several scholars studying Latin American movements. Hanson and Lapegna (2018) developed a combination of the political economy of social movements (see Rossi in this volume) and social mechanisms to analyze the mediating mechanisms of *incorporation*, *recognition*, and *supportive mobilization* between social movements and governments in Argentina and Venezuela. Rossi (2017b) unpacked two types of compulsion mechanisms: *compulsive support* and *compulsive control*. In both types, without using physical repression, the state's institutions reinforced the assemblies movement of Buenos Aires identities while also prompting it to adapt its repertoire of strategies to the state institutions' requirements. In addition, Ancelovici and Guzmán-Concha (2019) comparatively studied the dynamics of student protests in Chile and Quebec, identifying three parallel processes: *mediation* in coalition making and creation of new groups, *polarization* as radicalization, and *spillover* in the spiraling of new claims and mobilizations. These processes condition each other, showing that similar mechanisms can generate relatively similar effects in different contexts.

The networked version of the relational approaches has also been applied to the study of brokerage and intermediation. Gurza Lavalle and von Bülow (2015) developed a typology of institutionalized brokers with the aim of understanding the dynamics of institutionalization of collective action intermediation in Mexico and Brazil. Using the metaphor of the "brokerage ladder," the three types of institutionalized brokers identified are classified according to their internal and external complexity in intermediation tasks. *Peak associations* have rigid boundaries with affiliated members with coordinator/articulator/representative roles. *Associational hubs* are more flexible and open to wider actors with the same roles as the former, plus that of translator. Finally, *multisectoral bodies* have no clear boundaries and are as open as associational hubs but have a differentiated brokerage role: externally as translators and internally as both coordinators and articulators. This promising research agenda was later expanded in Zaremberg, Guarneros-Meza, and Gurza Lavalle (2017).

At the transnational level, Spalding (2015) studied coalition formation and brokerage in El Salvador's anti-mining movement, conceptualizing two transnational mobilization processes. First, there is a *domestic loop*, which maps the intersection between domestic coalition partners and transnational allies and, second, a *deleveraging hook*, meaning the shifts made by domestic movements when they add a second dimension as a result of their transnational alliances. These processes of transnationalism help explain social movement reconfigurations across scales (see also Spalding, von Bülow in this volume).

Nevertheless, in Latin America, as elsewhere, a shift towards the historical relational approach to analyzing social movements has not necessarily been accompanied by an explicit recognition of a crucial dimension to relationality: space. In response, geographically sensitive scholars have increasingly sought to counter the trend towards historicity by emphasizing the relationally constitutive role of spatiality in all processes of social movement mobilization.

Geographical

The importance of space for Latin American social movements is profound, emphasizing the inseparability of *place*, *territory*, *scale*, and other geographical categories from the ideas and practices of mobilization in the region (for one overview, see Perreault 2008). Relational geographical approaches explore the co-constitution of the social and spatial in movements as well as the (dis)continuities in movements across space.

Although Anglophone debates within the discipline of geography have emphasized the significance of a "relational turn" since the 1990s, in which the ontologies of fixity and boundedness came to be replaced by inter-connectedness, flows, and networks (Jones 2009; Massey 1991), geography is an inherently relational discipline. The significance of the spatial, in addition to the historical, as a constitutive dimension of social life has been slowly acknowledged across the social sciences, but the argument has been led by pioneering geographers and spatially minded scholars, notably from Western Europe and South America (in particular, Brazil).

Building on heterodox Marxist approaches, a range of scholars in the 1970s and 1980s sought to (re)define spatiality as the product of social relations, rather than static interpretations of space as a container of social life that had long prevailed (Harvey 1996; Lefebvre 1991; Soja 1989). Rather than space and society existing external to each other, they are better understood as dialectically interrelated (Soja 1980), always embedded in historical specificity. The scholarship of Brazilian geographers, alongside other colleagues across the region (Lindón and Hiernaux 2011), constructed a bridge between European critical theory and the lived realities of Latin America. Santos (1994, 1996) referred to the "indissolubility" of systems of actions and objects that constitute space, leaving an important legacy on ideas of space, place and territory across Latin America. Santos' (1996) relational theory of space sought to directly intervene in society (see Santos et al. 2000) and was always directed to understanding the political implications of socially produced space, what he termed "used territory," and the possibilities for our transformations of it. In the 1990s a debate was opened up by Brazilian geographers grappling with territory and territoriality at time of globalization and increasing mobility (Haesbaert 2004; Souza 1995), which had implications for social movements. As Porto-Gonçalves (2001) put it, social movements actors were, since the 1980s, increasingly mobilizing a "new territoriality" that emerged as a response to structural transformations in a de-industrializing region. His landmark study of the Amazonian *seringueiros*, who resisted extractive industries, examined their struggle to self-affirm their own identities and values in and through their organization and political appropriation of space.

A relational, sociospatial understanding of social movements in Latin America has slowly come to prominence since the 1990s due to both the spatial turn in the social sciences, that started to make its way into social movement studies (see Davis 1999; Davis and Davey in this volume), and also due to the explicit geographical framing of movement identities and repertoires across the region (see Fernandes 2000; Porto-Gonçalves 2001; Souza 2015; Fernandes and Welch in this volume). This can be seen in literatures on diverse movements, including mobilizations over public space in an ever-urbanizing region (Irazábal 2008) or the geographies of Black movements in Brazil (dos Santos 2011). The global resonances of the 1994 Zapatista uprising, alongside the increasing mobility provided by new technologies and transport, also saw a more explicit attempt to grapple with the transnationalization of socio-spatial mobilization, involving both the building of alliances across borders and the scaling up of demands from local to national and international arenas (Olesen 2004; Perreault 2003; see Oikonomakis in this volume). Relational approaches to geography have not only emphasized the inseparability of space and society but also the (dis)continuities across networks, scales, places and territories.

Social movement scholars working with geographical perspectives have sought to identify the connections between spatialities, including place, territory, scale, positionality and networks, in order to examine the multiple, intersecting and overlapping spatial dimensions through which activists mobilize (Nicholls, Miller, and Beaumont 2013), with some interesting applications to Latin American social movements (Blank 2016; Bosco 2001; Bringel and Cabezas 2014), although a unified approach is yet to be consolidated. Relational perspectives on the spatialities of mobilization in Latin American have been particularly developed within a large body of literature examining the role of territory and territoriality (Halvorsen 2019; Porto-Gonçalves 2012; Sandoval, Robertsdotter, and Paredes 2016; Tobío 2012; Zibechi 2012) which examine territory from its intersections with multi-scalar, networked and place-based struggles. For example, Ulloa's (2011) work on indigenous movements in Colombia emphasizes how their territorial activism necessarily brings about internal relations between different actors such as NGOs, paramilitaries and guerilla movements, operating across scales and places.

Building on Fernandes (2005) long-standing work with the MST, Halvorsen, Fernandes, and Torres (2019) recently outlined an explicitly relational approach to what they term *socioterritorial movements*, defined as those movements for whom the political control of space is a central objective of their mobilizational strategy. They identify four relational axes across which socioterritorial movements mobilize. First, movement strategies are developed in and through territory, with the realization of objectives dependent on the appropriation of a demarcated space. Second, identity is often constructed in relation to the appropriated territory through which movements mobilize, such that their political subjectivities are necessarily geographical. Third, the political socialization of Latin American social movements, through which they frame contention (Snow and Benford 1992) and the bonds and ties that sustain their activist networks (Bosco 2001), takes place in and through appropriated territories. Finally, social movement institutionalization (see Gurza Lavalle and Szwako in this volume), understood as the creation of sets of rules and regularized patterns that structure social activity, takes place through a relational process of territorialization, deterritorialization and reterritorialization (TDR). The process of TDR often involves moving across scales as movements see new political opportunities.

While promising, the above approaches also suffer from limitations from a relational perspective. On the one hand, by emphasizing spatiality there is a creeping tendency to sideline the relationality of history, thus downplaying key relational dynamics of mobilization. On the other hand, the strong emphasis given to territory risks downplaying the relationality of other spatialities. Most challenging, however, are suggestions that all the above approaches remain trapped within an anthropocentric epistemology that erases the underlying ontological struggles from which social movements, especially indigenous, have mobilized in recent decades.

Ecological

The importance of nature for Latin American social movements has been appreciated from several vantage points although is often just associated with the identities and grievances of indigenous social movements as well as anti-extractivist mobilizations (see Svampa 2017; Christel and Gutiérrez in this volume). For an ecological approach, the social and natural are not conceived as separate entities but as inter-related realms, that is, *socionatural relations*, and this inter-relationality has important implications on the identities, strategies and objectives of social movements. Put simply, the ecological approach focuses on the relations between movements and nature. This, in turn, opens up an ontological level of politics that challenges the framing of relationality in the above approaches.

Theoretically, this approach has been most developed by scholars such as Blaser (2014), de la Cadena (2015) and Escobar (2016, 2018) who, among other concepts, have pioneered understandings into *political ontology*, which challenges pre-conceived barriers between culture and nature, humans and non-humans. By mobilizing within the realm of ontology, some social movements raise fundamental challenges towards how demands are perceived and met in the context of the (post)colonial state in Latin America (Blaser 2014; Escobar 2016; see Flórez-Flórez and Olarte-Olarte in this volume). They also pose a direct challenge to Western theories of social movements, which tend to fall back on binaries, and instead emerge through what Santos (2014) terms the *epistemologies of the South*. As Escobar (2018) emphasizes, these epistemologies provide fundamental challenges to dualist notions of development and economy, and instead demand a recognition that there are multiple *relational worlds*—that is, assemblages of co-existing, always emerging human and non-human entities—which constitute the field through which social movements mobilize.

Acknowledging the coexistence of multiple worlds, sometimes referred to as the *pluriverse* (de la Cadena and Blaser 2018; Escobar 2018), has led scholars to confront the ontological assumptions of Western knowledge production, instead paying closer attention to the strategies and imaginations of Latin American activists (Ogden and

Gutiérrez 2018). This has been particularly emphasized in the context of indigenous and afro-descendent activism (see Di Giminiani 2018; Radcliffe 2016; Dixon and Caldwell in this volume). A range of ethnographically rich studies emphasize the relationality of humans and more-than-humans, in dialogue with post-structural approaches such as Actor-network theory and "assemblage," referring to the provisional coming together of human and more-than-human elements, as well as decolonial thought (Escobar 2008; Oslender 2016). Indigenous concepts such as Pachamama, which has become a central discourse of Andean social movements since the 1980s, well exemplifies the relational ontology that defies society-nature distinctions (de la Cadena 2015; Jackson and Warren 2005; Jenkins 2015, Radcliffe 2019; see Rice in this volume).

The *aquatic spaces* (Oslender 2004) where Afro-Colombian social movements have formed on the country's Pacific coast are a good example of *relational worlds* (Escobar 2016). Tidal rhythms of estuaries, the moon, mangroves, diverse life forms including humans, chants, rituals, and spiritualities, all provide the assemblage of life worlds (Escobar 2018) that informs the political organization strategies that Oslender (2016) elaborates through his ethnographic study of movements of Black communities on Colombia's Pacific. The river basin both structures how movements organize across space (in harmony with tidal rhythms and mangrove landscapes) but also the identities, values and objectives of mobilization, such as the reformulation of how land titles are defined, by including mangrove areas.

Elsewhere, the socio-natural assemblages of indigenous social movements played a key role in the mobilization in support of the progressive governments of Bolivia (2005–2019) and Ecuador (2007–2016) as well as their ongoing linkages, and subsequent tensions, with social actors. This has been examined with reference to social movements' roles in the drafting of new constitutions and the insertion of a core set of rights under the idea of "living well" (*buen vivir/vivir bien/sumak kawsay*), which recognizes nature as an active subject, co-existing in relational worlds with other human and non-human subjects (Escobar 2018). The Bolivian and Ecuadorian constitutions are an outcome of years of indigenous struggle and present a direct challenge to the formulation of the (post-)colonial state in Latin America (Altmann 2013; Becker 2011; Deneulin 2012). At the same time, the entry into electoral politics by indigenous movements (on that, see Van Cott 2005) also presents a tension with regards the entanglement of strategies based on *epistemologies of the South* with Western political and legal frameworks (Lizárraga and Rivero 2014; Walsh 2010). The challenge here is thus to avoid the dualist (non-relational) approach dominant to much social movement literature and appreciate the co-existence of different political ontologies within and between struggles (Escobar 2016).

The ontological challenge to studying social movements in Latin America presented by ecological approaches is significant and deliberately eschews providing a "one size fits all" analysis that can be replicated across cases. Nevertheless, central to the relational critique made by scholars such as Escobar, de la Cadena, and others is the need to avoid reductionist dualisms, most centrally that of culture–nature, and to appreciate the relational worlds through which social movements mobilize. In Latin America, taking seriously the ontological starting points of indigenous and afro-descendent movements has forced scholars to re-assess some of their epistemological frameworks of analysis, recently coalescing with a turn towards decolonial thought (Castro-Gómez and Grosfoguel 2007; Rivera Cusicanqui 2010; Flórez-Flórez and Olarte-Olarte in this volume). As such, ecological relational approaches bring us back full circle to the significance of taking multiple identities seriously and suggest promise for developing a more integrated relational approach.

Conclusion

We have identified four main relational approaches to social movements, all with applications in Latin American studies. Intersectional approaches examine the relations across core categories of identity. Historical approaches examine relations between movements and other actors across time. Spatial approaches explore (dis)continuities in movements across space. Finally, ecological approaches focus on the relations between movements and nature.

Relationality can provide a powerful tool for the analysis of social movements in Latin America, yet it also risks closing down alternative perspectives if not realized in an integrated way. For example, there remain issues with regards to how to define boundaries of social movements and this poses challenges for the relationality of any empirical work—what Emirbayer (1997) calls the nominalists versus realists discussion. However, the catnet avenue is a powerful tool for building networked relational analyses.

Moreover, it could be argued that the growing emphasis on space (and territory in particular) is detracting from temporality, which is crucial for understanding Latin American social movements, from the relational analysis. However, if combined with the identification of mobilization dynamics across time we could build an integrated perspective that unifies the tempo-spatial location of events in diachronic analyses that avoid the agency–structure dilemma as suggested by Rossi (2017a: chapter 2).

In addition, relationality, as posited by some advocates of political ontology, risks leading towards a relativism which in turn can direct attention away from (indeed at times it may explicitly deny) the identification of causality in mobilization. However, the pluriverse does not entail a lack of connection between events but rather a different one that transcends the anthropocentric ontology of the social sciences. A relational diachronic and spatial approach to studying social movements requires us to both identify the construction-deconstruction-reconstruction dynamics of human (individual and collective) identities as well as relocate ourselves in a non-extractivist relationship with nature.

An integrated relational approach presents a compelling agenda yet is likely to be some way off. On the one hand, specific calls for relational frameworks within the above approaches (e.g. McAdam, Tarrow, and Tilly 2001; Nicholls, Miller, and Beaumont

2013) remain to be taken up with any consistency in studies of Latin American social movements, and we are thus still in the preliminary phases of an integrated relational turn. On the other hand, as we have identified, there are significant ontological and epistemological divergences (and clashes) across the four approaches that pose challenges for how to operationalize an integrated analysis in practice.

Building on a rich tradition of militant and engaged research (e.g., Colectivo Situaciones 2002; Fals Borda 2012; Freire 1970), an integrated approach can also be positioned in relation to the protagonists of struggles themselves and the positionality of differently situated actors, inside and beyond social movements. At stake is taking seriously the ethical and political implications of moving across different relational vantage points, while—as argued by Halvorsen (2018)—also finding tactics to avoid falling into a (neo)colonial and extractivist approach to knowledge production.

References

Almeida, Paul D. (2008), *Waves of Protest: Popular Struggle in El Salvador, 1925–2005* (Minneapolis: University of Minnesota Press).

Altmann, Philipp (2013), "Good Life as a Social Movement Proposal for Natural Resource Use: The Indigenous Movement in Ecuador," *Consilience: The Journal of Sustainable Development* 10(1), 59–71.

Alvarez, Sonia, Evalina Dagnino, and Arturo Escobar (eds.), (1997), *Cultures of Politics/Politics of Cultures: Revisioning Latin American Social Movements* (Boulder, CO: Westview Press).

Ancelovici, Marcos and César Guzmán-Concha (2019), "Struggling for Education: The Dynamics of Student Protests in Chile and Quebec," *Current Sociology* 67(7), 978–96.

Auyero, Javier (2002), "Los cambios en el repertorio de la protesta social en la Argentina," *Desarrollo Económico* 42 (166), 187–210.

Becker, Marc (2011), "Correa, Indigenous Movements and the Writing of a New Constitution in Ecuador," *Latin American Perspectives* 38(1), 47–62.

Blank, Martina (2016), "De-Fetishizing the Analysis of Spatial Movement Strategies: Polymorphy and *Trabajo Territorial* in Argentina," *Political Geography* 50: 1–9.

Blaser Mario (2014), "Ontology and Indigeneity: On the Political Ontology of Heterogeneous Assemblages," *Cultural Geographies* 21(1), 49–58.

Bosco, Fernando (2001), "Place, Space, Networks, and the Sustainability of Collective Action: the Madres de Plaza e Mayo," *Global Networks* 1(4): 307–29.

Bringel, Breno and Almudena Cabezas González (2014), "Geopolítica de los movimientos sociales latinoamericanos: espacialidades, ciclos de contestación y horizonte de posibilidades," in Jaime Preciado Coronado (ed.), *Anuario de integración latinoamericana y caribeña 2011*, 323–42 (Guadalajara: Universidad de Guadalajara).

Carril, Lourdes (2006), *Quilombo, favela e periferia: A longa busca da cidadania* (São Paulo: FASEP).

Castro-Gómez, Santiago, and Ramón Grosfoguel (2007), *El giro decolonial: Reflexiones para una diversidad epistémica más allá del capitalismo global* (Bogotá: Siglo del Hombre editores).

Colectivo Situaciones (2002), *19 y 20. Apuntes para el nuevo protagonismo social* (Buenos Aires: De mano en mano).

Corcuff, Philippe (2013), *Las nuevas sociologías. Principales corrientes y debates, 1980-2010* (Buenos Aires: Siglo XXI).

Davis, Diane (1999), "The Power of Distance: Re-theorizing Social Movements in Latin America," *Theory and Society* 28(4), 585-638.

De la Cadena, Marisol (2015), *Earth Beings: Ecologies of Practice Across Andean Worlds* (Durham, NC: Duke University Press).

De la Cadena, Marisol and Mario Blaser (eds.) (2018), *A World of Many Worlds* (Durham, NC: Duke University Press).

Deneulin, Severine (2012), "Justice and Deliberation about the Good Life: The Contribution of Latin American Buen Vivir Social Movements to the Idea of Justice," *Bath Papers in International Development and Well-Being*, 17 (Bath: University of Bath).

Di Giminiani, Piergorgio (2018), "Indigenous Activism in Latin America," in Julie Cupples, Marcela Palomino-Schalscha, and Manuel Prieto (eds.), *The Routledge Handbook of Latin American Development*, 225-35 (London: Routledge).

Diani, Mario (1992), "The Concept of Social Movements," *The Sociological Review* 40, 1-25.

Dinerstein, Ana (2015), *The Politics of Autonomy in Latin America* (Basingstoke: Palgrave-Macmillan).

dos Santos, Renato Emerson (2011) *Movimentos sociais e geografia: sobre a(s) espacialidade(s) da ação social* (Rio de Janeiro: Consequência).

Emirbayer, Mustafa (1997), "Manifesto for a Relational Sociology," *American Journal of Sociology* 103(2), 281-317.

Escobar, Arturo (2008), *Territories of Difference: Place, Movements, Life, Redes* (Durham, NC: Duke University Press).

Escobar, Arturo (2016), "Thinking-Feeling with the Earth: Territorial Struggles and the Ontological Dimensions of the Epistemologies of the South," *Revista de Antropología Iberoamericana* 11(1), 11-32.

Escobar, Arturo (2018), *Designs for the Pluriverse: Radical Interdependence, Autonomy, and the Making of Worlds* (Durham, NC: Duke University Press).

Fals Borda, Orlando (2012), *Ciencia, compromiso y cambio social* (Buenos Aires: Editorial el Colectivo).

Feliciano, Carlos Alberto (ed.) (2011), *DATALUTA—Banco de dados da luta pela terra: relatório 2010* (Presidente Prudente: NERA—Núcleo de Estudos, Pesquisas e Projetos de Reforma Agrária).

Fernandes, Bernardo Mançano (2005), "Movimentos socioterritoriais e movimentos socioespaciais: contribução teórica para uma leitura geográfica dos movimentos sociais," *Revista Nera* 8(6), 14-34.

Fernandes, Bernardo Mançano (2000), "Movimento social como categoria geográfica," *Revista Terra Livre* 15, 59-85.

Freire, Paulo (1970), *Pedagogy of the Oppressed* (London: Continuum).

Gurza Lavalle, Adrian Gurza and Natália S. Bueno (2011), "Waves of Change Within Civil Society in Latin America," *Politics & Society* 39(3), 415-50.

Gurza Lavalle, Adrian Gurza and Marisa von Bülow (2015), "Institutionalized Brokers and Collective Actors: Different Types, Similar Challenges," in Federico M. Rossi and Marisa von Bülow (eds.), *Social Movement Dynamics: New Perspectives on Theory and Research from Latin America*, 157-80 (Farnham: Ashgate).

Haesbaert, Rogério (2004), *O mito da desterritorializaçãao: do "fim dos territorios" a multiterritorialidade* (Rio de Janeiro: Bertrand).

Halvorsen, Sam, Bernardo Mançano Fernandes, and Fernanda Torres (2019), "Mobilizing Territory: Socioterritorial Movements in Comparative Perspective," *Annals of the Association of American Geographers* 109(5), 1454-70.

Halvorsen, Sam (2018), "Cartographies of Epistemic Expropriation: Critical Reflections on Learning from The South," *Geoforum* 95, 11-20.

Halvorsen, Sam (2019), "Decolonising Territory: Dialogues with Latin American Knowledges and Grassroots Politics," *Progress in Human Geography* 43(5), 790-814.

Hanson, Rebecca and Pablo Lapegna (2018), "Popular Participation and Governance in the Kirchners' Argentina and Chávez's Venezuela: Recognition, Incorporation and Supportive Mobilisation," *Journal of Latin American Studies* 50(1), 153-82.

Harvey, David (1996), *Justice, Nature & the Geography of Difference* (Oxford: Blackwell).

Irazábal, Clara (ed.) (2008), *Ordinary Places, Extraordinary Events: Citizenship, Democracy, and Public Space in Latin America* (London: Routledge).

Jackson, Jean and Kay Warren (2005), "Indigenous Movements in Latin America, 1992-2004: Controversies, Ironies, New Directions," *Annual Review of Anthropology* 34(5), 49-73.

Jelin, Elizabeth (1990), *Women and Social Change in Latin America* (London: Zed Books).

Jenkins, Katy (2015), "Unearthing Women's Anti-Mining Activism in the Andes: Pachamama and the Mad Old Women," *Antipode* 47 (2), 442-60.

Jones, Martin (2009), "Phase Space: Geography, Relational Thinking, and Beyond," *Progress in Human Geography* 33(4), 802-22.

Lazar, Sian (2008), *El Alto, Rebel City: Self and Citizenship in Andean Bolivia* (Durham, NC: Duke University Press).

Lefebvre, Henri (1991), *The Production of Space* (Oxford: Blackwell).

Lindón, Alicia and Daniel Hiernaux (2011), *Los giros de la geografía humana. Desafíos y horizontes* (Mexico: Anthropos).

Lizárraga, Pilar and Carlos Rivero (2014) "La descolonización del territorio: Luchas y resistencias campesinas e indígenas en Bolivia," in Guillermo Almeyra, Luciano Cocheiro Bórquez, João Márcio Mendes Pereira, and Carlos Walter Porto-Gonçalves (eds.), *Capitalismo: Tierra y poder en América Latina (1982-2012)*, 2:17-60 (Buenos Aires: CLACSO).

Massey, Doreen (1991), "A Global Sense of Place," *Marxism Today* 38(June), 24-29.

McAdam, Doug, Sidney Tarrow, and Charles Tilly (2001), *Dynamics of Contention* (New York: Cambridge University Press).

Médica, Gerardo and Viviana Villegas (2012), "A la vera de la Ruta 3 'la gloriosa doble P': Una aproximación a los 'Putos Peronistas' de La Matanza," *Oral History Forum d'histoire orale* 32, 1-18.

Melucci, Antonio (1996), *Challenging Codes. Collective Action in the Information Age* (New York: Cambridge University Press).

Mische, Ann (2008), *Partisan Publics: Communication and Contention across Brazilian Youth Activist Networks* (Princeton, NJ: Princeton University Press).

Mische, Ann (2015), "Partisan Performances: The Relational Construction of Brazilian Youth Activist Publics," in Federico M. Rossi and Marisa von Bülow (eds.), *Social Movement Dynamics: New Perspectives on Theory and Research from Latin America*, 43-71 (Farnham: Ashgate).

Muteba Rahier, Jean (2012), *Black Social Movements in Latin America. From Monocultural Mestizaje to Multiculturalism* (New York: Palgrave).

Nicholls, Walter, Byron Miller, and Justin Beaumont (eds.) (2013), *Spaces of Contention: Spatialities and Social Movements* (Farnham: Ashgate).

Ogden, Laura and Grant Gutierrez (2018), "More-Than-Human Politics," in Julie Cupples, Marcela Palomino-Schalscha, and Manuel Prieto (eds.), *The Routledge Handbook of Latin American Development*, 205–12 (London: Routledge).

Olesen, Thomas (2004), "The Transnational Zapatista Solidarity Network: An Infrastructure Analysis," *Global Networks* 4(1), 89–107.

Oslender, Ulrich (2016), *The Geographies of Social Movements: Afro-Colombian Mobilization and the Aquatic Space* (Durham, NC: Duke University Press).

Oslender, Ulrich (2004), "Fleshing out the Geographies of Social Movements: Colombia's Pacific Coast Black Communities and the 'Aquatic Space'," *Political Geography* 23(8), 957–85.

Perreault Thomas (2003), "Changing Places: Transnational Networks, Ethnic Politics, and Community Development in the Ecuadorian Amazon," *Political Geography* 22(1), 61–88.

Perreault Thomas (2008), "Latin American Social Movements: A Review and Critique of the Geographical Literature," *Geography Compass* 2(5), 1363–85.

Pizzorno, Alessandro (1994), "Identidad e interés," *Zona Abierta* 69, 135–52.

Porto-Gonçalves, Carlos Walter (2012, May), *A reinvenção dos territorios na América Latina/ Abya Yala* (Universidad Autónoma de México). Available at: http://conceptos.sociales.unam.mx/conceptos_final/505trabajo.pdf.

Porto-Gonçalves, Carlos Walter (2001), *Geo-grafías: Movimientos sociales, nuevas territorialidades y sustentabilidad* (Mexico: Siglo XXI).

Radcliffe, Sarah (2016), "The Difference Indigeneity Makes: Socio-Natures, Knowledges and Contested Policy," in Michela Coletta and Malanya Raftopoulos (eds.), *Provincializing Nature: Multidisciplinary Approaches to the Politics of the Environment in Latin America*, 161–86 (London: Institute of Latin American Studies).

Radcliffe, Sarah and Sallie Westwood (eds.) (1993), *"Viva": Women and Popular Protest in Latin America* (New York: Routledge).

Radcliffe, Sarah (2019), "Pachamama, Subaltern Geographies, and Decolonial Projects in Andean Ecuador," in Tariq Jazeel and Stephen Legg (eds.), *Subaltern Geographies*, 119–41 (Athens: University of Georgia Press).

Reyes, Álvaro (ed.) (2012), "Autonomy and Emancipation in Latin America," Special issue, *South Atlantic Quarterly* 111(1).

Rivera Cusicanqui, Silvia (2010), *Ch'ixinakax utxiwa: Una reflexión sobre prácticas y discursos descolonizadores* (Buenos Aires: Tinta Limón).

Rossi, Federico M. (2017a), *The Poor's Struggle for Political Incorporation: The Piquetero Movement in Argentina* (New York: Cambridge University Press).

Rossi, Federico M. (2017b), "Compulsion Mechanisms: State-Movement Dynamics in Buenos Aires," *Social Movement Studies* 16(5), 578–94.

Rossi, Federico M. and Marisa von Bülow (eds.) (2015), *Social Movement Dynamics: New Perspectives on Theory and Research from Latin America* (Farnham: Ashgate).

Rousseau, Stéphanie and Anahi Hudon (2017), *Indigenous Women's Movements in Latin America: Gender and Ethnicity in Peru, Mexico, and Bolivia* (New York: Palgrave-Macmillan).

Sandoval, Maria, Andrea Robertsdotter, and Myriam Paredes (2016), "Space, Power and Locality: The Contemporary use of Territorio in Latin American Geography," *Journal of Latin American Geography* 16(1), 43–67.

Santos, Boaventura de Sousa (2014), *Epistemologies of the South: Justice against Epistemicide* (London: Routledge).

Santos, Boaventura de Sousa (2018), *The End of the Cognitive Empire: The Coming of Age of Epistemologies of the South* (Durham, NC: Duke University Press).

Santos, Milton (1994), "O retorno do território," in Milton Santos, Maria Adelia Souza, and María Laura Silviera (eds.), *Territorio, globalização e fragmentação*, 251–61 (São Paulo: Editora JUCITEC).

Santos, Milton (1996), *A natureza do espaço: técnica e tempo, razão e emoção* (São Paulo: Edusp—Editora da Universidade de São Paulo).

Santos, Milton with Adriana Bernardes, Adriano Zerbini, Cilene Gomes, Edison Bicudo, Eliza Almeida, Flávia Contel, Flávia Grimm, Gustavo Nobre, Lídia Antongiovanni, María Bueno Pinheiro, Marcos Xavier, María Laura Silveria, Marina Montenegro, Marisa Ferreira da Rocha, Mónica Arroyo, Paula Borin, Soraia Ramos, and Vanir de Lima Belo (2000), "O papel ativo da geografia: Um manifesto," *Revista Território* 5 (9), 103–9.

Scherer-Warren, Ilse (1993), *Redes de Movimentos Sociais* (Loyola: São Paulo).

Schönwälder, Gerd (2002), *Linking Civil Society and the State: Urban Popular Movements, the Left and Local Government in Peru, 1980–1992* (University Park: Pennsylvania State University Press).

Snow, David and Robert Benford (1992), "Master Frames and Cycles of Protest," in Aldon Morris and Carol McClurg Mueller (eds.), *Frontiers in Social Movement Theory*, 133–55 (New Haven, CT: Yale University Press).

Soja, Edward (1980), "The Socio-Spatial Dialectic," *Annals of the Association of American Geographers* 70(2), 207–25.

Soja, Edward (1989), *Postmodern Geographies: The Reassertion of Space in Critical Social Theory* (London: Verso).

Souza, Marcelo Lopes de (1995), "O territorio: Sobre espaço e poder, autonomia e desenvolvimento," in Iná Elias de Castro, Paulo Cesar da Costa Gomes, and Roberto Lobato Correa, (eds.), *Geografia: Conceitos e temas*, 77–116 (Rio de Janeiro: Bertrand).

Souza, Marcelo Lopes de (2015), "Lessons from Praxis: Autonomy and Spatiality in Contemporary Latin American Social Movements," *Antipode* 48(5), 1292–316.

Spalding, Rose (2015), "Domestic Loops and Deleveraging Hooks: Transnational Social Movements and the Politics of Scale Shift," in Federico M. Rossi and Marisa von Bülow (eds.), *Social Movement Dynamics: New Perspectives on Theory and Research from Latin America*, 181–211 (Farnham: Ashgate).

Svampa, Maristella (2017), *Del cambio de época al fin del ciclo: Gobiernos progresistas, extractivismo y movimientos sociales en América Latina* (Buenos Aires: Edhasa).

Tavera Fenollosa, Ligia (2015), "Eventful Temporality and the Unintended Outcomes of Mexico's Earthquake Victims Movement," in Federico M. Rossi and Marisa von Bülow (eds.), *Social Movement Dynamics: New Perspectives on Theory and Research from Latin America*, 127–54 (Farnham: Ashgate).

Tilly, Charles (1978), *From Mobilization to Revolution* (New York: Random House).

Tilly, Charles (1984), *Big Structures, Large Processes, Huge Comparisons* (New York: Russell Sage Foundation).

Tobío, Omar (2012), *Territorios de la incertidumbre: Apuntes para una geografía social* (Buenos Aires: UNSAM Edita).

Ulloa, Astrid (2011), "The Politics of Autonomy of Indigenous Peoples of the Sierra Nevada de Santa Marta, Colombia: A Process of Relational Indigenous Autonomy," *Latin American and Caribbean Ethnic Studies* 6(1), 79–107

Van Cott, Donna (2005), *From Movements to Parties in Latin America: The Evolution of Ethnic Politics* (Cambridge: Cambridge University Press).

Velasco, Alejandro (2015), *Barrio Rising: Urban Popular Politics and the Making of Modern Venezuela* (Berkley and Los Angeles: University of California Press).

von Bülow, Marisa (2010), *Building Transnational Networks: Civil Society and the Politics of Trade in the Americas* (Cambridge: Cambridge University Press).

Walsh, Catherine (2010), "Development as Buen Vivir: Institutional Arrangements and (De)colonial Entanglements," *Development* 53(1), 15–21.

White, Harrison C. (1992), *Identity and Control: A Structural Theory of Social Action* (Princeton, NJ: Princeton University Press).

White, Harrison C. (2008 [1965]), "Notes on the Constituents of Social Structure. Soc. Rel. 10 - Spring '65," *Sociologica* 1(May–June), 1–15.

Zaremberg, Gisela, Valeria Guarneros-Meza, and Adrian Gurza Gurza Lavalle (eds.) (2017), *Intermediation and Representation in Latin America: Actors and Roles beyond Elections* (London: Palgrave-Macmillan).

Zibechi, Raúl (2012), *Territories in Resistance: A Cartography of Latin American Social Movements* (Oakland: AK Press).

CHAPTER 6

NETWORK APPROACHES TO LATIN AMERICA SOCIAL MOVEMENTS

ROSE J. SPALDING

Introduction

Networks are relational mechanisms that connect segments of social movements and facilitate collaboration. They involve structures and flows through which movement actors interact, disseminate information, distribute resources, frame grievances, recruit affiliates, collaborate on tasks, and identify formal and informal leaders. As della Porta and Diani (2006: 159) observe, "Social movement action on a large scale has always been organized in network forms."

The underlying reticular character of social movement networks typically includes identifiable building blocks connected through links in a fibrous structure. These connections give network analysis an engineering dimension that is commonly described with spatial metaphors and construction terminology (Diani 2015). Yet networks are not simply static substructures operating within fixed parameters. They also reconfigure in response to fluid dynamics, including shifting identities, membership fluctuations, and changing contextual features (McAdam, Tarrow, and Tilly 2001). In terms of durability, networks occupy an intermediate space between the relative solidity of institutions and the fluidity of campaigns. This combination of durable and flexible elements makes network analysis a complex area of inquiry.

Network mechanisms and processes play a significant role in putting social movements into motion. Describing the "mobilizing structures" of contentious politics, Tarrow (1998: 124) notes that "the most effective forms of organization are based on partly autonomous and contextually rooted local units linked by connective structures and coordinated by formal organizations." Network connections foster the diffusion of novel ideas, facilitate internal frame alignment, and support co-construction of master frames. Networks also provide mechanisms through which activities and repertoires may become modular, and channel recruitment efforts that may animate broad clusters of previously unmobilized groups and individuals (Crossley and Diani 2018; della Porta and Diani 2006; Givan, Roberts and Soule 2010; McAdam, Tarrow, and Tilly 2001; Tarrow 1998). Networks contribute to intensity through organizational density and coordination, and they foster recrudescence following periods of abeyance, drawing on the accumulation of personal and collective experience and intentional strategies of memory keeping (Almeida 2014; McAdam 1986; Rossi 2017).

Although networks are critical to processes of mobilization and change, they also circumscribe and contain movement operations. They may reinforce formal and informal power hierarchies and undermine innovation by congealing repertoires and frames. They may also truncate alignments by failing to include potential actors in a field and by separating affiliated groups from their potential allies. The formal organizational structure of a network may "imperfectly reflect the informal connective tissue of a movement" (Tarrow 1998: 124). In that sense, networks and movements are not coterminous, nor are they necessarily consistently reinforcing. Movement recruitment does not always occur through network mechanisms, as alternative forms of information diffusion may also be at work. Although underlying networks of communication and collaboration are critical features of sustained social movements, and affect their internal dynamics and capacity for persistence, they remain vulnerable to manipulation by powerful actors and are potentially disruptive to movement re-composition and change (della Porta and Diani 2006: 121–26).

As a field of inquiry, network analysis employs a variety of methodologies and research techniques. This field did not evolve out of a single discipline; instead, it emerged simultaneously in areas as varied as mathematics, computer science, psychology, sociology, communications studies, political science, and marketing. Network analysis does not, consequently, adhere to a coherent theoretical framework or embrace a single, canonical research method. Instead, two trends have emerged simultaneously: large-n quantitative studies using formal network modeling and visualizations; and small-n, in-depth studies using comparative historical analysis and process tracing methods.

The formal modeling approach renders networks in architectural terms and promotes the use of quantitative measures and techniques. In this version, networks are interpreted using concepts like nodes, ties, brokers, scales, and directional flows. Nodes are constituted by individuals, organizations, or categories, which are joined together through either direct ties, when connections and interactions are explicit, or indirect ties, when nodal actors share an activity, identity, or resource but do not have personal or face-to-face interactions (Diani 2015).

This approach to network analysis often employs modeling to examine the particular position of a node in a social network (Diani 2015; Krinsky and Crossley 2014). This process can be used to assess a node's "centrality" to the grid and to determine the directionality of communication flows. Concepts like eigenvector centrality, used in mathematical social network analysis, attempt to determine the relative influence of a specific node by measuring the density of its links. This calculation assesses not simply the number of links a particular node has with other nodes, but also how connected it is to other influential (well-connected) nodes. Some formal analysts also use *blockmodeling*, which takes raw data and clusters "structurally equivalent" actors, events, and frames into categories (Tilly and Wood 2003; Wada 2014). This approach permits the reduction of a potentially incoherent mass of information into a streamlined model that can be more readily interpreted to reveal trends and interactions within and between conceptually meaningful categories.

Formal network analysis has been used to identify the roles played by particular organizations within the broader whole (Crossley and Diani 2018; Diani 2015; Gurza Lavalle and von Bülow 2015; Krinsky and Crossley 2014). This assessment may be based on calculations of membership overlaps or frequency of involvement in collaborative activities. Role assessment may also be conducted using statistical analysis of questionnaire responses provided by organizational leaders. Associated literature includes discussion of organizational ecologies, in which relationships among constituent parts are closely mapped. This approach introduces refined concepts of brokerage and coalition formation. Often drawing on measurable information about formal organizational characteristics, membership intersections, resource sharing, and joint actions, this approach lends itself to large-n research.

An alternative approach to social movement networks explores these linkages in a more intuitive way as processes that connect people and groups for a wide array of relational performances (Alvarez, Dagnino, and Escobar 1998; McAdam, Tarrow, and Tilly 2001; Mische 2008; Rossi 2017; Tarrow 1998; Wood 2003; Halvorsen and Rossi in this volume). In this variant, network concepts are employed to study different forms of shared meaning making, including in the shaping of identities, values, and beliefs. This approach to networks emphasizes their function as purposeful and emotive bonds of connection that can attract and mobilize people for a common purpose. Network formation is understood as a process that builds and maps interpersonal and inter-group relationships. Analyzed in psychological, sociological, and historical terms, network participation may impact collective attitudes about empowerment and exclusion and influence the subsequent choices and lives of activists.

Networks here are understood to be continuously negotiated webs of interaction leading to the creation and transformation of actors themselves, as well as for the coordination of resources for purposes of political or policy change. This variant of network analysis, which often uses process tracing to identify patterns in within-case or across-case small-n comparisons, helps to clarify currents and eddies within underlying organizational substructures and to ferret out identities in formation as well as internal legacies, rivalries, and competition.

Both large scale quantitative analyses employing statistical techniques and qualitative case studies tracing network formation and reconfiguration have been used productively in the study of Latin American social movements, often in creative and distinctive ways. This literature is quite varied, with research methods ranging from first person accounts reporting on activist network experiences (Kohl, Farthing, and Muruchi 2011), to innovative theoretical accounts by academic analysts who are constructing new models of political communication (Mische 2008; von Bülow 2010).

Network concepts explored in this body of work include new assessments of the impact of close and weak ties; appraisals of bridging, bonding, and brokerage mechanisms; and studies of organizational density and intensity, centralization and decentralization, hierarchical and horizontal connections, and institutionalization and informality (Mische 2008; Olesen 2004; Rossi and von Bülow 2015; Spalding 2023; Stahler-Sholk, Vanden, and Becker 2014). Beyond simply employing the established conceptual vocabulary of movement studies, research in Latin America offers new insights into network dynamics and introduces innovative forms of network mapping. This work also facilitates analysis of the complex intersections of social movement organizing across local, national and transnational scales (Hochstetler and Keck 2007; Silva 2013; Thayer 2010; von Bülow 2010).

Network Elements and Arguments

Networks may be built on linkages of both "bonding" and "bridging" varieties (Putnam 2000). These variations parallel the distinction between "close" and "weak" ties observed in the study of social capital and movement organization (Granovetter 1973, 1982). Networks built on bonding or close ties, in which participants have frequent, routine, and often organic (based on family, friendship and neighborhood) connections, are imbued with familiarity and permit a ready flow of interaction and communication. These mechanisms produce closed-circuit patterns of information diffusion that tend to reinforce message content through repetition and trust-based validation.

Bridging, in contrast, builds on weak ties, which link actors beyond their primary groups and provide more distinctive and less predictable flows of information. As the literature on the strength of weak ties indicates (Granovetter 1982; Levin and Cross 2004; Marsden and Campbell 2012), these connections allow networks to extend beyond the clusters of redundant communication that characterize close-tie alliances, and kindle new linkages that can both broaden and accelerate the diffusion of mobilizing ideas and information. The cultivation of weak ties can also facilitate and expand multisectoralism, and permit greater functional specialization in keeping with the variation in resources and experience that the broadened networks mobilize. For social movement actors, bridging may encourage repertoire diversification by connecting those who, for example, have different kinds of expertise with regard to lobbying, media access, legal strategies, and political party ties (see Ruibal, Roberts in this volume).

In terms of social movement dynamics, close ties built on pre-existing relationships and bonding connections can stoke attitudinal cohesion and facilitate recurring mobilization, including bloc recruitment,[1] passion-driven protest, and risk taking (Biggs and Andrews 2015; McAdams 1986). By providing emotional support and validation, multiple close ties may contribute to organizational density, which has been linked to participatory intensity. Weak ties, in contrast, may be characterized by less frequent or emotionally resonant communication. Demonstrating their own forms of strength, however, these thinner connections can extend the network beyond its historical reach, encourage broader awareness of issues, and support detectable shifts in public opinion. Although weak ties increase the risk of internal tensions and network fragmentation, they may also provide the leverage needed to affect a broader swath of public attitudes and policy outcomes (Putnam 2000).

The character and quality of network ties may affect their impact on multisectoral alliances, processes of diffusion, and brokerage. Analysts of Latin American social movements have called attention to an underlying pattern of multisectoralism that frequently emerges as movements gain traction, and fails to emerge when they do not (Almeida 2014, 2019; Rossi 2017; Silva 2009; Spalding 2023). Multisectoral networking allows activists to mobilize the complementary resources available in different segments of society and to achieve the breadth required to secure visibility. Multisectoralism also facilitates diffusion, a complex set of transfer and translation processes permitting "the spread of some innovation through direct or indirect channels across members of a social system" (Givan, Roberts, and Soule 2010: 1). Effective multisectoralism and diffusion may advance through brokerage, "the linking of two or more previously unconnected social sites by a unit that mediates their relations with one another and/or with yet other sites" (McAdam, Tarrow, and Tilly 2001: 26).

To improve our understanding of brokerage, Gurza Lavalle and von Bülow (2015) developed the concept of a "brokerage ladder," in which these processes are broken into hierarchically ranked subcategories. Drawing on organizational survey data compiled for their research on civil society networks in Mexico and Brazil, their brokerage ladder begins by identifying simple "translator" roles, which involve receiving, decoding and diffusing information across the network. The ladder then advances through "coordinator" and "articulator" roles, and culminates with the role of "representative," which is played by high profile brokers who serve as network spokespeople and are tasked with harmonizing interests across the network. Analyzing variation in the degree of broker formality and institutionalization, Gurza Lavalle and von Bülow go on to excavate a hierarchy of network clusters in descending order from formal and institutionalized "peak associations" to "associational hubs." At the lowest level, they place loosely articulated "multisectoral bodies" characterized by greater organizational informality. This conceptual map helps to disentangle network threads and permits more refined analysis of network infrastructure.

Network Participation and Recruitment

Research about social movement networks in Latin America has both expanded on and challenged conventional theories. Studies of the United States civil rights movement, for example, pointed to the power of close ties to mobilize participation and encourage risk taking and innovation (Biggs and Andrews 2015; McAdam 1986). Holzner's (2004) comparison of two squatter networks in Oaxaca, in contrast, shows how "strong" ties within well-established communities reinforced the system of clientelism on which the population had long depended, and slowed the process of political change in this Mexican community. Risky behavior involving shifts in political loyalty and voting for opposition parties advanced more rapidly in newer settlements, where thin and weak ties were more prevalent.

Network analysis in Latin America also steps beyond the civic mainstream to examine the mobilization of non-conventional movements, including insurgencies and revolutionary forces. Viterna's (2006, 2013) work on the recruitment of women into the Frente Farabundo Martí para la Liberación Nacional (FMLN) guerrilla army in El Salvador identified three affiliation pathways. Based on interviews with randomly selected women and men in former war zones in rural El Salvador, Viterna's analysis of the "micro-processes of mobilization" found that women's decisions to join the FMLN were not well explained by simple close tie claims. Theories suggesting that female recruits enrolled because they had family members in the FMLN were only partially supported by her evidence; while guerrillas in the war zone often had family ties to other rebels, so did those who declined to join. Other factors, including FMLN recruitment targeting practices and living as a displaced person in a refugee camp, especially in the absence of an intact family, provided a more nuanced explanation for women's pathways into the rebel army (see Oikonomakis in this volume).

Wood's (2003) ethnographic study of insurgent collective action in El Salvador also mapped rebel recruitment pathways. This work, based on interviews with peasant participants and non-participants in the FMLN in contested areas between 1987 and 1996, allowed her to delineate organizational affiliations that shaped the mobilization of FMLN rebel army factions and their associated support networks. Wood's analysis pointed to the significant organizational roles played by activist leaders in the Catholic Church.

At the local and diocesan levels, Catholic clergy often serve as agglutinative agents in Latin American movement networks (see Mackin in this volume). By providing "space for protected contention" (Rossi 2017: 87), they offer organizational resources that are critical to movement advancement. Arellano-Yanguas's (2014) research on the role of the Church in mining protests in Peru finds that activist clergy eschewed leadership roles in the network, opting instead for "accompaniment" based on pastoral norms. Sánchez's (2017) work on anti-mining mobilization in Nicaragua calls attention to the networks constructed at the intersection of Church-led and peasant ecologism. Trejo (2009) documents Catholic Church support for indigenous movements in Mexico, finding that it was a "membership retention strategy" during an era of increasing religious competition. Spalding's (2018) research on the national anti-mining network in El Salvador calls attention to the multilayered brokerage role played by Catholic Church leaders, who connected supporters across territorial and partisan divisions and were prominently involved in drafting the national mining ban. Catholic Church leadership in movements to prohibit abortion and criminalize sodomy, at the same time, demonstrates the divergent roles played by this powerful network node (Howe 2013; Kampwirth 2013).

Finally, the role of networks in mobilizing participation and the construction of identities has drawn a wave of scholarly attention (Arce, Hendricks, and Polizzi 2022; Goett 2017; Velásquez 2022; see Fontana in this volume). Mische (2008) offers an innovative analysis of the intersecting networks through which young activists in Brazil construct their political lives. Building on in-depth interviews, questionnaire responses, and ethnographic observations, Mische tracked multiple forms of young adult engagement across student, religious, NGO, antidiscrimination, professional, business, and partisan organizations. Mapping changes in the composition of activist networks between 1977 and 1997, she identifies four leadership types, classified as bridging leaders, entrenched leaders, explorers, and focused activists. Using the algebraic technique of Galois lattice analysis, Mische mapped the structure of overlapping organizational and institutional affiliations, and traced shifting patterns across five sub-periods of political transition (opening, reconstructing, rethinking, "new face," and globalizing). Coding respondent involvement annually by level (total number of groups they participated in), depth (number of involvements within a sector) and span (number of involvements across sectors), Mische explores the ways in which the resulting permutations of network engagement impacted participatory styles, communication strategies, and leadership development for young adult activists during this critical era of political change.

Networks in "Old" and "New" Social Movements

As social mobilization around identity issues became increasingly common in the 1990s, a literature emerged that attempted to differentiate "old" and "new" social movements in Latin America (Alvarez, Dagnino, and Escobar 1998; Laraña, Johnston, and Gusfield 1994; see Garretón and Selamé in this volume). Old social movements, which focused on issues of workers' rights, social class, land access, and concerns about material goods, were found to prioritize economic matters and follow a vertical and centralized network design. These networks were grounded in unions and labor organizations, and focused on formal sector workers and peasant federations. Thickly institutionalized through legal codes and state-designated corporatist spaces, these networks were denounced by their critics as rigid and exclusionary, if not corrupted through subservience to political elites and party apparatchiks.

Old social movement networks were contrasted with new ones developing around cultural markers and identity claims, where mobilization was thought to emerge from below. Analysts identified a broad range of new movements concerned with historically marginalized communities and intersectional identities, including networks of activists affirming gender, race, ethnic, and indigenous rights. These networks were depicted as embracing a loose, horizontal, and decentralized shape. Informal and intentionally autonomous from established institutional actors, these movements were often perceived as operating against and beyond the state (Alvarez, Dagnino, and Escobar 1998; Alvarez et al. 2003; Juris and Khasnabish 2013; Laraña, Johnston, and Gusfield 1994; Sitrin and Azzelini 2014; Stahler-Sholk, Vanden, and Becker 2014; see Garretón and Selamé in this volume).

Subsequent analysis suggests that old-new distinctions may have been overdrawn (Silva 2009; Wickham-Crowley and Eckstein 2015). Fuller assessment revealed more substantial thematic and organizational continuities across periods and network types. Rather than diverging along a stark divide, both kinds of movements registered concerns about material needs, and they both contained notable organizational interlayering. Adopting a Polanyian framework, Silva (2009) traces the way that "concatenations of new and old social movements" shaped a countermovement against neoliberal commodification that aligned broad sectors of society in a movement for self-protection. Neoliberal economics "dethroned" but did not abolish organized labor, while simultaneously inspiring a host of resistance movements advocating decommodification, including many subaltern social groups that employed identity framing and rhetoric (see Rossi in this volume). Analyzing anti-neoliberal mass mobilization in Latin America, Silva found that the networks that emerged in this struggle connected established and emerging identities in broad, if impermanent, alliances. Where framing and brokerage mechanisms served to link protest groups in reformist coalitions, as in Argentina, Bolivia, Ecuador, and Venezuela, they played a critical role in regime transition; where they did not, as in Peru and Chile, regimes committed to significant market reform failed to consolidate (Silva 2009: 47–48).

Rossi's (2017) analysis of the *piquetero* movement in Argentina also leapt the old-new movement divide. This "poor people's movement," which emerged following an era of neoliberal disincorporation, pursued recognition and rule reformulation that would permit a new round of inclusion in the body politic, this time of a non-corporatist variety. Meticulously tracing movement development over a twenty-year period and pinpointing the strategic choices made by actors in different corners of the network, Rossi showed how key sectors adapted organizational scripts derived from two analytically distinct points of departure—either left-wing parties and political organizations, or clusters of the country's trade union movement. Through laborious historical reconstruction, Rossi shows how currents within the movement grew from their early enclave settings in the 1990s, spread through processes of emulation and diffusion, and drew on brokerage mechanisms to scale shift upward from the peripheral provinces to Buenos Aires, where they ultimately formed the "largest movement of unemployed people in the contemporary world" (Rossi 2017: 5). He introduces two new concepts—"repertoire of strategies" and "stock of legacies"—to describe how the agentic decisions of activists drew on accumulated historical experiences while also creating space for adaptations.

Rossi's findings about how prior experiences of struggle affect network dynamics recall Almeida's (2014) observations about the significance of "strategic capital" as a catalyst for subsequent mobilization and protest. Almeida (ibid.: 25) defines strategic capital as "stockpiles of valuable information and experience in how to launch local mobilization campaigns by exploiting local infrastructural assets". Drawing on records of over 4,000 protest events geocoded to the municipal level in five Central American countries over a thirty-year period, he concluded that protest was more likely to occur in communities where high levels of strategic capital combine with a propitious physical (roads) and organizational (universities, unions, NGOs, oppositional political parties) infrastructure. These longitudinal studies of social mobilization, which trace movement development across multiple decades, allow us to see how network structures and legacies leave a durable trace that can affect subsequent movement recrudescence, reconfiguration, and renewal.

Transnational Networks

Latin American movement networks transnationalized with the emergence of international human rights campaigns and movements against neoliberal globalization (Cisneros 2016; Keck and Sikkink 1998; Silva 2013; Smith 2008; Stahler-Sholk, Vanden, and Becker 2014; von Bülow, Wolff in this volume). Transnational networks organized in response to a wide variety of threats and opportunities, including in opposition to megaproject development, extractivism, and trade deals, and in favor of democracy, environmental protection, and identity rights. Research on transnational networks expanded rapidly in Latin America as cross-national alliances multiplied in the 1990s and 2000s.

This research has been both creative and contested. Keck and Sikkink (1998) sparked new thinking about transnational advocacy networks, identifying the ways in which domestic activists who faced an unresponsive national government could align with external allies to bring increased pressure from the outside. This "boomerang" pattern has been found effective in getting even authoritarian regimes to act based on formal international obligations and to improve their human rights performance, in spite of the inability of local activists to influence their government directly.

Significant advances in understanding of transnational network development, operation, and contraction emerge from von Bülow's (2010) study of the movement against the Free Trade Area of the Americas (FTAA). A pioneer in the use of survey-based network mapping in the Americas, von Bülow traces the linkages among local, national, and hemispheric networks that mobilized against the FTAA in the 1990s and early 2000s. Tracking two decades of trade-related collective action in Latin America and the United States, she documents shifts in network configurations across time and scale. Data from two rounds of interviews and surveys in Brazil, Chile, Mexico, and the United States mapped six kinds of organizational nodes (labor, rural, environmental, faith-based, business, and other NGOs), each with their own domestic and international alliance structure. Asking questions about "closest allies" and histories of organization connections, she identified the central actors in each of these networks, pinpointing areas of communication density and locating network brokers. This research revealed areas of tension and distrust along with episodes of successful collaboration.

As political opportunities for local activists improved in Latin America following the transition to electoral democracy, researchers explored the ways internationally connected activists pursued change at home (Silva 2013). Kay (2011) analyzes the construction of cross-national labor alliances in the wake of the North American Free Trade Agreement (NAFTA), pointing to the ways in which the agreement fostered the development of new institutions that promoted transnational labor organizing across the US–Mexican border. International conventions such as the Indigenous and Tribal Peoples Convention 1989 (ILO 169)[2] also fostered regional and international networking to promote the consultation rights of indigenous communities faced with encroachment and dispossession. An emerging literature on indigenous social movements examines activist efforts to build political and juridical mechanisms to enhance rights enforcement in the face of state resistance and manipulation (Couso, Huneeus, and Sieder 2010; Eisenstadt and West 2019; Fontana and Grugel 2016; Jaskoski 2022; Walter and Urkidi 2016; Yashar 2005; Ruibal in this volume).

Although transnational linkages can generate resources that support social mobilization, Latin American analysts have raised pointed questions about power hierarchies embedded within these networks and the way these asymmetries amplify and distort the positions of local network participants. These analysts call attention to the extent to which organizations from the Global North dominate these networks and undermine organizational efforts of "partners" in the Global South. Better resourced, and often even serving as primary funders, northern allies have been found to set agendas, define rules, appropriate messages, and control decision-making (Andrews 2010; Lewis 2016; Petras 1997; Thayer 2010).

The story of the Zapatista movement in Mexico reveals the tensions and risks inherent in transnational networking. The Zapatistas garnered a high level of international attention in the wake of their 1994 Chiapas uprising, and their 1996 Encounter for Humanity and Against Neoliberalism drew more than 3,000 supporters to Chiapas for global reflection and networking (Juris and Khasnabish 2013). According to Olesen (2004), the global Zapatista solidarity network that emerged in the following decade operated at five levels. Building from ground zero in the Zapatista indigenous communities in Chiapas, it expanded outward to a layer of Mexican NGOs, whose role was primarily information gathering, processing, and distribution. Level three extended to non-Mexican organizations that translated and disseminated information to mobilize international support using managed websites ("Basta Ya") and listservs (Chiapas95, Chiapas-L). The fourth level consisted of a "periphery" of more distant information recipients, and the fifth was a "transitory" level composed of a lightly connected international audience that engaged only occasionally. Subnetworks linked nodes and ties in various combinations, including star form (single broker connecting all pieces) and polycephalous design (loosely connected networks combining multiple direct and indirect ties).

Concerns about how outsiders were appropriating their struggle led to a sharp Zapatista critique of neocolonial practices embedded in this transnational network and a shift in network dynamics in 2003. Zapatista communities began screening external proposals and taxing donations to better control the impact of outsiders and promote the development of local autonomy practices (Andrews 2010; Stahler-Sholk 2019). The "Sixth Declaration of the Lacandón Jungle" in 2005 called for the formation of a new kind of international solidarity coalition, which would operate within parameters defined by the communities. Research on this case illustrates the struggle to find an appropriate balance between local actors and their transnational allies.

Even when transnational actors avoid overtly hegemonic practices, they may still dominate communication flows, leaving their counterparts in the Global South struggling to exercise voice. Recent network analysis of transnational communication flows within the international women's movement found that organizations in the Global North continued to dominate, even though membership in women's organizations in parts of the Global South increased notably in the 1980s and 1990s. Using longitudinal network data for 447 women's international nongovernmental organizations (WINGOs) and testing for changes in density, network correlations, and eigenvector centrality between 1978 and 2008, Hughes and colleagues (2018) found that even in parts of the Global South where women's organizations had become relatively well developed (Brazil, Argentina), their participation in international communications flows remained peripheral to the global network (see Ewig and Friedman in this volume).

In other cases, however, power sharing between external and domestic components of the network permitted more fluid and successful collaboration, including vernacularization of the message frame and empowerment of local voices. Research on how transnational networks operate under different structures of opportunity and threat points to significant variation (von Bülow in this volume). Case studies exploring these intersections in Latin America have introduced new concepts, typologies, and trends, including innovative discussion of alternative forms of connection, such as lateral transnationalism, horizontalism, solidarity, and international networking to counter hegemonic practices.

Lateral transnationalism connects similarly situated actors, often in neighboring countries, and permits relatively fluid flows of locally-relevant information, with fewer hierarchical costs (Spalding 2015). *Horizontalism*, as defined by Stahler-Sholk, Vanden, and Becker (2014, 8), involves "the rejection of hierarchical relations of power that are created and reproduced through vanguardism, political and economic elitism, and the goal of seizing rather than transforming state power." Networks that embrace principles of horizontalism are designed to be decentralized and flattened, and are characterized by a high degree of unit autonomy. Solidarity networks are typically built to promote people-to-people connections and may be particularly intentional regarding power balances (Nepstad 2004). My research on solidarity networks in Central America (Spalding 2015) explores the concept of organizational *domestication*, an assimilationist tendency which can emerge in a foreign-funded NGO over a long process of sustained engagement. In this variant of transnational networking, external allies endorse horizontality and deference, and adopt local staffing and decision-making structures that are designed to reduce external imposition.

Solidarity networks can help local allies build a *deleveraging hook* (Spalding 2015), a process through which domestic groups pressure external actors to disengage, thereby creating more latitude for internal decision-making. Network dynamics that serve to hold back or constrict external pressures may be of particular interest in Latin America, where social movements often seek greater local control. Perla's (2017) research on asymmetrical bargaining in the international arena takes up this question. His work focuses on the construction of an international solidarity network in opposition to the "Contra" war against the Sandinista government in Nicaragua during the 1980s. He traces the way Nicaraguan leaders and activists, drawing on the mobilizing capacity of United States solidarity and church groups, promoted the construction of an international network in which directionality flowed from Nicaragua back into the United States, with the goal of challenging the discourse of the Ronald Reagan administration about the regime's repressiveness and Soviet alignment. This research points to ongoing theorizing about the internal dynamics of transnational networks in Latin America and the circumstances under which variation emerges.

Network Fragmentation and Internal Competition

Research using discourse analysis and tracing movement dynamics frequently identifies seams and rivalries that fracture social movement networks (della Porta and Diani 2006: 156–61). Differences in the extent of change pursued by "reformative" and "transformative" social movements (McAdam and Snow 1997: xix–xx) or in strategies deployed by "rule-conforming" and "rule-violating" collective actors (Piven and Cloward 1995) frame recurring variations in network cohesion. Network analysis helps to identify lines of organizational cleavage and fragmentation as well as systems of brokerage and agglutination. As transnational campaigns emerged in opposition to neoliberal reform, for example, debate sometimes erupted between movement "insiders" and "outsiders," with each group aligned in separate network structures (Smith and Korzeniewicz 2007). Movement insiders generally adopted mainstream or reformist positions and used the modest openings offered by the regime to push for piecemeal change. Outsiders, in contrast, typically rejected the parameters of the existing system and pushed for more radical change, including a search for alternative concepts of development, new international alliances, and local level decentralization and autonomy.

The network bifurcation that Smith and Korzeniewicz (2007) identified in the FTAA debate has been noted in other disputes in Latin America, including the debate over the Central American Free Trade Agreement (CAFTA) and organizing by environmental activists. Based on interviews with over 200 participants, Spalding (2014) identified two distinct opposition networks that alternately competed and collaborated during the CAFTA ratification process. "Critic negotiators" pursued treaty modifications and complementary measures, while accepting the overall trade negotiation framework. "Transgressive resisters," on the other hand, sought to block negotiations and pursue alternative development strategies. Each group formed a separate national network and aligned with a different regional bloc, reinforcing cross-regional fissures.

Additional cleavages have been identified in Lewis's (2016) analysis of the Ecuadorian environmental movement. Using the tools of environmental sociology to trace organizing across the 1978–2015 period, she described interactions between "ecoimperialists," who hailed from the Global North and sought to impose an external agenda, and locally based "ecodependents," who were obligated by their foreign funders to adhere to that protocol. A third group, composed of "ecoresisters," in contrast, opted for greater organizational autonomy and pursued a more radical form of environmentalism, while a fourth, the "ecoentrepreneurs," pursued business opportunities associated with sustainable environmental management. Each organizational cluster operated according to a distinct logic and drew on different kinds of resources, with their fortunes rising and falling across political regimes.

Oppositional tendencies within a social movement can give rise to decertification campaigns in which adversaries attempt to deny the legitimacy of their rivals. Under some circumstances, however, it may be possible for fissures to contract. Attempting to explain how broad-based and consequential movements developed to defend water rights in Bolivia and maize production in Mexico, Simmons (2016) focused on the catalytic role of certain types of grievances, particularly those that arise from subsistence threats and that call founding ideas about community identity into question. Simmons' analysis depicts a dynamic in which pre-existing organizations, which had previously failed to construct a cohesive network, moved to do so when livelihoods and identities were at stake, and, in the process, melted away layers of structural rigidities that previously separated them.

Networks and Social Media

As elsewhere, social movement analysts in Latin America have undertaken research on the role of virtual networks in mobilizing collective action. New media analysts ask whether computer mediated communication competes with or complements face-to-face networking. They attempt to understand the quality of the social ties that emerge through those connections and the consequences for movement durability and success (Earl 2016; Masías, Hecking, and Hoppe 2018; Tarrow 1998). Social media use in protest behavior is reportedly less common in Latin America than in the United States, but it has become more widely available over time, with theorizing following sluggishly behind (Treré and Harlow in this volume). Sierra Caballero and Gravante (2018) examine the growth in Latin America of "grassroots communication" and "citizen media" via web portals and hashtags. Following Castells (2012), they envision an expanding terrain characterized by self-renewing and horizontal connections.

Targeted research on the Chilean case, where social media use is common and student protests have been frequent, identifies significant network patterns and issues for future research. Valenzuela, Correa, and Gil de Zúñiga (2018) analyze the impact of social media tie strength on protest behavior in Chile. Using data from a 2014 survey of 1,000 young adults in three urban areas, they identified different protest pathways for Facebook and Twitter users. Facebook, a medium that requires mutual approval for tie construction, was found to deploy "strong ties," whereas Twitter, where "following" does not require mutual approval, was classified by the authors as generating "weak ties." They found that Facebook, where politically mobilizing information came from people known personally to the respondent, was more likely to influence protest participation; Twitter messages, in contrast, were more influential as a source of novel information and were less closely connected to protest behavior. This study, which supports the general finding in the literature that social media use enhances political engagement, calls for more nuanced understanding of the ways that network participation impacts behavior, differentiating by type of social media and digital pathway.

Von Bülow (2018) also explores the use of social media in Chilean student protests. Asking whether self-mobilization through use of digital tools diminishes the role of formal leaders and organizations, she concludes that both processes remain salient. Analyzing 255,910 retweets from 270 Twitter accounts of student leaders and organizations in 2011–2013, she found massive asymmetries in forwarded information, with a handful of prominent leaders, all based in Santiago, dominating the network. Although compensatory actions by other organizational actors helped to keep the movement message coherent and constrained directorial control by movement leader-pioneers, communication imbalances pointed to hierarchical risks in social media-driven mobilizations.

Conclusion

This chapter points to theories that interpret the way networks operate in Latin American social movements and identifies themes that call for further analysis. Researchers in this politically dynamic region provide insight into the interplay between networks operating in conventional and contentious settings, and in highly varied national contexts. They introduce debates about horizontalism and alternative modes of resistance, adding to established studies of alliance behavior. Seminal work in this region examines the operation of transnational advocacy networks, producing innovative theories about interactions between domestic and international allies as they seek to promote human rights, contest neoliberal policy reform, and define new forms of participatory democracy. Documentation of Latin American social movements as they rise and retreat across the decades generates new thinking about network legacies and their long-term impacts on social struggles. Recent research contributes to a growing body of literature on protest cycles, including those organized through social media networks.

This research introduces original theories about how social relationships link to purposive political action, and how organizational islands preserve a measure of autonomy in increasingly connected societies. It offers new ideas about the processes through which network roles and responsibilities are assigned; the circumstances under which networks function as unitary and comprehensive mechanisms as opposed to partial and competitive ones; and the complex intersections between social movements and the state. This work adds to established research on multisectoralism and brokerage, helping to refine core concepts used in the field. It also tests claims about social networks made in research conducted elsewhere and challenges several generalizations. Significantly, Latin America network research also demonstrates the need for long-term analysis by revealing the dynamic interplay of organizational layers, scale shifting, and abeyance structures as social mobilizations wax and wane across the decades.

Although this work has generated significant results, network analysis in Latin America suffers from several limitations, some specific to the region and some that are common to the field. Databases needed to track network development are still under construction and are not widely shared. Some of the metrics used to measure network roles and centrality are still rudimentary. The findings advanced are generally not replicated or even replicable, given the challenges of teasing results out of time-sensitive ethnographic and survey data. When follow-up research is completed, lack of agreement about appropriate questions and methods can yield findings that are inconsistent or contradictory. Some trends in network analysis elsewhere have not resonated broadly in Latin American research, including innovative spatial visualizations of network patterns, which may require more data and expertise than are currently available outside a handful of leading universities in the region.

In spite of the challenges, network analysis remains a significant area of inquiry for analysts of Latin American social movements. Since political institutions are not well-consolidated in parts of the region, and political life is often volatile, social movements in Latin America may be more consequential than those in the United States and Europe. To the extent that network analysis in this region can reveal underlying structures of communication and connection, it can provide an important counterpoint to the study of formal institutional processes. Social movements are a critical mechanism through which ordinary people attempt to protect and promote community welfare; the networks that underpin them provide dynamic channels through which movement energies and interconnections flow.

Notes

1. Bloc recruitment involves recruitment of whole groups based on a shared affiliation (members of a congregation, for example) rather than recruitment of single individuals who join one-by-one.
2. International Labor Organization 169 is an agreement that commits signatory states to protect the rights of indigenous people to decide on their own priorities.

References

Almeida, Paul D. (2014), *Mobilizing Democracy: Globalization and Citizen Protest* (Baltimore, MD: Johns Hopkins University Press).

Almeida, Paul D. (2019), *Social Movements: The Structure of Collective Mobilization* (Oakland, CA: University of California Press).

Alvarez, Sonia E., Elisabeth Jay Friedman, Ericka Beckman, Maylei Blackwell, Norma Stoltz Chinchilla, Nathalie Lebon, Marysa Navarro, and Marcela Ríos Tobar (2003), "Encountering Latin American and Caribbean Feminisms," *Signs* 28(2), 537–79.

Alvarez, Sonia E., Evelina Dagnino, and Arturo Escobar (eds.) (1998), *Cultures of Politics, Politics of Cultures: Re-visioning Latin American Social Movements* (Boulder, CO: Westview).

Andrews, Abigail (2010), "Constructing Mutuality: The Zapatistas' Transformation of Transnational Activist Power," *Latin American Politics and Society* 52(1), 89–120.

Arce, Moisés, Michael S. Hendricks, and Marc S. Polizzi (2022), *The Roots of Engagement: Understanding Opposition and Support for Resource Extraction* (New York: Oxford University Press).

Arellano-Yanguas, Javier (2014), "Religion and Resistance to Extraction in Rural Peru: Is the Catholic Church Following the People?," *Latin American Research Review* 49, 61–80.

Biggs, Michael and Kenneth T. Andrews (2015), "Protest Campaigns and Movement Success: Desegregating the U.S. South in the Early 1960s," *American Sociological Review* 80(2), 416–43.

Castells, Manuel (2012), *Networks of Outrage and Hope: Social Movements in the Internet Age* (Cambridge: Polity Press).

Cisneros, Paúl, (ed.) (2016), *Política minera y sociedad civil en América Latina* (Quito: Instituto de Altos Estudios Nacionales).

Couso, Javier, Alexandra Huneeus, and Rachel Sieder (2010), *Cultures of Legality: Judicialization and Political Activism in Latin America* (Cambridge: Cambridge University Press).

Crossley, Nick and Mario Diani (2018), "Networks and Fields," in David A. Snow, Sarah A. Soule, Hanspeter Kreisi, and Holly J. McCammon (eds.), *Wiley Blackwell Companion to Social Movements*, 151–66 (Hoboken: Wiley).

della Porta, Donatella and Mario Diani (2006), *Social Movements: An Introduction*, 2nd ed. (Malden: Blackwell).

Diani, Mario (2015), *The Cement of Civil Society: Studying Networks in Localities* (Cambridge: Cambridge University Press).

Earl, Jennifer (2016), "Protest Online: Theorizing the Consequences of Online Engagement," in Lorenzo Bosi, Marco Giugni and Katrin Uba (eds.), *The Consequences of Social Movements*, 363–400 (Cambridge: Cambridge University Press).

Eisenstadt, Todd A. and Karleen Jones West (2019), *Who Speaks for Nature? Indigenous Movements, Public Opinion, and the Petro-State in Ecuador* (New York: Oxford University Press).

Fontana, Lorenza B. and Jean Grugel (2016), "The Politics of Indigenous Participation through 'Free Prior Informed Consent': Reflections from the Bolivian Case," *World Development* 77, 249–61.

Givan, Rebecca Kolins, Kenneth M. Roberts, and Sarah A. Soule (eds.) (2010), *The Diffusion of Social Movements: Actors, Mechanisms, and Political Effects* (Cambridge: Cambridge University Press).

Goett, Jennifer (2017), *Black Autonomy: Race, Gender, and Afro-Nicaraguan Activism* (Stanford: Stanford University Press).

Granovetter, Mark S. (1973), "The Strength of Weak Ties," *American Journal of Sociology* 78(6), 1360–80.

Granovetter, Mark S. (1982), "The Strength of Weak Ties: A Network Theory Revisited," in Peter V. Marsden and Nan Lin (eds.), *Social Structure and Network Analysis*, 105–30 (Thousand Oaks, CA: SAGE).

Gurza Lavalle, Adrian and Marisa von Bülow (2015), "Institutionalized Brokers and Collective Actors: Different Types, Similar Challenges," in Federico M. Rossi and Marisa von Bülow (eds.), *Social Movement Dynamics: New Perspectives on Theory and Research from Latin America*, 157–80 (Farnham: Ashgate).

Hochstetler, Kathryn and Margaret E. Keck (2007), *Greening Brazil: Environmental Activism in State and Society* (Durham, NC: Duke University Press).

Holzner, Claudio A. (2004), "The End of Clientelism? Strong and Weak Networks in a Mexican Squatter Movement," *Mobilization* 9(3), 223–40.

Howe, Cymene (2013), *Intimate Activism: The Struggle for Sexual Rights in Postrevolutionary Nicaragua* (Durham, NC: Duke University Press).

Hughes, Melanie M., Pamela Poxton, Sharon Quinsaat, and Nicholas Reith (2018), "Does the Global North Still Dominate Women's International Organizing? A Network Analysis from 1978 to 2008," *Mobilization* 23(1), 1–21.

Jaskoski, Maiah (2022), *The Politics of Extraction: Territorial Rights, Participatory Institutions, and Conflict in Latin America* (New York: Oxford University Press).

Juris, Jeffrey S. and Alex Khasnabish (eds.) (2013), *Insurgent Encounters: Transnational Activism, Ethnography and the Political* (Durham, NC: Duke University Press).

Kampwirth, Karen (2014), "Organising the *Hombre Nuevo Gay*: LGBT Politics and the Second Sandinista Revolution," *Bulletin of Latin American Research* 33(3), 319–33.

Kay, Tamara (2011), *NAFTA and the Politics of Labor Transnationalism* (Cambridge: Cambridge University Press).

Keck, Margaret and Kathryn Sikkink (1998), *Activists Beyond Borders* (Ithaca, NY: Cornell University Press).

Kohl, Benjamin and Linda C. Farthing, with Félix Muruchi (2011), *From the Mines to the Streets: A Bolivian Activist's Life* (Austin: University of Texas Press).

Krinsky, John and Nick Crossley (2014), "Social Movements and Social Networks: Introduction," *Social Movement Studies* 13(1), 1–21.

Laraña, Enrique, Hank Johnston, and Joseph R. Gusfield (eds.) (1994), *New Social Movements: From Ideology to Identity* (Philadelphia, PA: Temple University Press).

Levin, Daniel Z. and Rob Cross (2004), "The Strength of Weak Ties You Can Trust: The Mediating Role of Trust in Effective Knowledge Transfer," *Management Science* 50(11), 1477–90.

Lewis, Tammy L. (2016), *Ecuador's Environmental Revolutions: Ecoimperialists, Ecodependents, and Ecoresisters* (Cambridge, MA: MIT Press).

Marsden, Peter V. and Karen E. Campbell (2012), "Reflections on Conceptualizing and Measuring Tie Strength," *Social Forces* 91(1), 17–23.

Masías, Víctor Hugo, Tobias Hecking, and Ulrich Hoppe (2018), "Social Networking Site Usage and Participation in Protest Activities in 17 Latin American Countries," *Telematics and Informatics* 35, 1809–31.

McAdam, Doug (1986), "Recruitment to High Risk Activism: The Case of Freedom Summer," *American Journal of Sociology* 92, 64–90.

McAdam, Doug and David A. Snow (eds.) (1997), *Readings on Social Movements: Origins, Dynamics and Outcomes* (New York: Oxford University Press).
McAdam, Doug, Sidney Tarrow, and Charles Tilly (2001), *Dynamics of Contention* (Cambridge: Cambridge University Press).
Mische, Ann (2008), *Partisan Publics: Communication and Contention across Brazilian Youth Activist Networks* (Princeton, NJ: Princeton University Press).
Nepstad, Sharon Erickson (2004), *Convictions of the Soul: Religion, Culture, and Agency in the Central American Solidarity Movement* (New York: Oxford University Press).
Olesen, Thomas (2004), "The Transnational Zapatista Solidarity Network: An Infrastructure Analysis," *Global Networks* 4(1), 89–107.
Perla, Hector, Jr. (2017), *Sandinista Nicaragua's Resistance to U.S. Coercion: Revolutionary Deterrence in Asymmetric Conflict* (Cambridge: Cambridge University Press).
Petras, James (1997), "Imperialism and NGOs in Latin America," *Monthly Review* 49(7), https://monthlyreview.org/1997/12/01/imperialism-and-ngos-in-latin-america/.
Piven, Frances Fox, and Richard A. Cloward (1995), "Collective Protest: A Critique of Resource-Mobilization Theory," in Stanford M. Lyman (ed.), *Social Movements: Critiques, Concepts, Case-Studies*, 137–67 (New York: NYU Press).
Putnam, Robert (2000), *Bowling Alone: The Collapse and Revival of American Community* (New York: Simon and Schuster).
Rossi, Federico M. (2017), *The Poor's Struggle for Political Incorporation: The Piquetero Movement in Argentina* (Cambridge: Cambridge University Press).
Rossi, Federico M. and Marisa von Bülow (eds.) 2015, *Social Movement Dynamics: New Perspectives on Theory and Research from Latin America* (Farnham: Ashgate).
Sánchez, Mario (2017), *Extractivismo y lucha campesina en Rancho Grande* (Managua: Universidad Centroamericana).
Sierra Caballero, Francisco and Tommaso Gravante (2018), "Digital Media Practices and Social Movements. A Theoretical Framework from Latin America," in Francisco Sierra Caballero and Tommaso Gravante (eds.), *Networks, Movements and Technopolitics in Latin America: Critical Analysis and Current Challenges*, 17–41 (New York: Palgrave).
Silva, Eduardo (2009), *Challenging Neoliberalism in Latin America* (Cambridge: Cambridge University Press).
Silva, Eduardo (ed.) (2013), *Transnational Activism and National Movements in Latin America: Bridging the Divide* (New York: Routledge).
Simmons, Erica (2016), *Meaningful Resistance: Market Reforms and the Roots of Social Protest in Latin America* (Cambridge: Cambridge University Press).
Sitrin, Marina and Dario Azzelini (2014), *They Can't Represent Us! Reinventing Democracy from Greece to Occupy* (New York: Verso).
Smith, Jackie (2008), *Social Movements for Global Democracy* (Baltimore: Johns Hopkins University Press).
Smith, William C. and Roberto Patricio Korzeniewicz (2007), "Insiders, Outsiders and the Politics of Civil Society," in Gordon Mace, Jean-Philippe Thérien, and Paul Haslam (eds.), *Governing the Americas: Assessing Multilateral Institutions* (Boulder: Lynne Rienner), 151–174.
Spalding, Rose J. (2014), *Contesting Trade in Central America: Market Reform and Resistance* (Austin: University of Texas Press).

Spalding, Rose J. (2015), "Domestic Loops and Deleveraging Hooks: Transnational Social Movements and the Politics of Scale Shift," in Federico M. Rossi and Marisa von Bülow (eds.), *Social Movement Dynamics: New Perspectives on Theory and Research from Latin America*, 181–214 (Farnham: Ashgate).

Spalding, Rose J. (2018), "From the Streets to the Chamber: Social Movements and the Mining Ban in El Salvador," *European Review of Latin American and Caribbean Studies* 106, 47–74.

Spalding, Rose J. (2023), *Breaking Ground: From Extraction Booms to Mining Bans in Latin America* (New York: Oxford University Press).

Stahler-Sholk, Richard (2019), "The Zapatistas and New Ways of Doing Politics," *Oxford Research Encyclopedia of Politics*. Available at: https://oxfordre.com/politics/abstract/10.1093/acrefore/9780190228637.001.0001/acrefore-9780190228637-e-1724?rskey=aMsLDT&result=6.

Stahler-Sholk, Richard, Harry E. Vanden, and Marc Becker (eds.) (2014), *Rethinking Latin American Social Movements: Radical Action from Below* (Lanham, MD: Rowman and Littlefield).

Tarrow, Sidney (1998), *Power in Movement*, 2nd ed. (Cambridge: Cambridge University Press).

Thayer, Millie (2010), *Making Transnational Feminism: Rural Women, NGO Activists, and Northern Donors in Brazil* (New York: Routledge).

Tilly, Charles and Lesley Wood (2003), "Contentious Connections in Great Britain, 1828-1834," in Mario Diani and Doug McAdam (eds.), *Social Movements and Networks: Relational Approaches in Collective Action*, 147–72 (New York: Oxford University Press).

Trejo, Guillermo (2009), "Religious Competition and Ethnic Mobilization in Latin America: Why the Catholic Church Promotes Indigenous Movements in Mexico," *American Political Science Review* 103(3), 323–42.

Valenzuela, Sebastián, Teresa Correa, and Homero Gil de Zúñiga (2018), "Ties, Likes, and Tweets: Using Strong and Weak Ties to Explain Differences in Protest Participation across Facebook and Twitter Use," *Journal of Political Communication* 35(1), 117–34.

Velásquez, Teresa A. (2022), *Pachamama Politics: Campesino Water Defenders and the Anti-Mining Movement in Andean Ecuador* (Tucson, AZ: University of Arizona Press).

Viterna, Jocelyn (2006), "Pulled, Pushed and Persuaded: Explaining Women's Mobilization into the Salvadoran Guerrilla Army," *American Journal of Sociology* 112(1), 1–45.

Viterna, Jocelyn (2013), *Women in War: The Micro-Processes of Mobilization in El Salvador* (New York: Oxford University Press).

von Bülow, Marisa (2010), *Building Transnational Networks: Civil Society and the Politics of Trade in the Americas* (Cambridge: Cambridge University Press).

von Bülow, Marisa (2018), "The Survival of Leaders and Organizations in the Digital Age: Lessons from the Chilean Student Movement," *Mobilization* 23(1), 45–64.

Wada, Takeshi (2014), "Who Are the Active and Central Actors in the 'Rising Civil Society' in Mexico?" *Social Movement Studies* 13(1), 127–57.

Walter, Mariana and Leire Urkidi (2016), "Community Consultations: Local Response to Large-Scale Mining in Latin America," in Fabio de Castro, Barbara Hogenboom, and Michiel Baud (eds.), *Environmental Governance in Latin America*, 287–325 (New York: Palgrave Macmillan).

Wickham-Crowley, Timothy and Susan Eva Eckstein (2015) "'There and Back Again': Latin American Social Movements and Reasserting the Powers of Structural Theories," in Paul

Almeida and Allen Cordero Ulate (eds.), *Handbook of Social Movements across Latin America*, 25–42 (New York: Springer).

Wood, Elisabeth Jean (2003), *Insurgent Collective Action and Civil War in El Salvador* (Cambridge: Cambridge University Press).

Yashar, Deborah J. (2005), *Contesting Citizenship in Latin America: The Rise of Indigenous Movements and the Postliberal Challenge* (Cambridge: Cambridge University Press).

CHAPTER 7

FEMINIST AND QUEER PERSPECTIVES ON LATIN AMERICAN SOCIAL MOVEMENTS

NIKI JOHNSON AND DIEGO SEMPOL

INTRODUCTION

This chapter reviews and discusses some of the key theories and concepts informing feminist and queer perspectives on Latin American social movements, focusing on the post-authoritarian period (1980s onwards). Such a review must start from a recognition of the diversity of influences—both endogenous and exogenous to the region—that have contributed to the development of these perspectives over the past forty years. While social movement theory originated in the analysis of European or North American contexts, the spread of social movement studies to Latin America did not simply entail the transfer and replication of theories, models, and concepts developed in the North but a process of translation and contestation whereby researchers of Latin American social movements resignified those theoretical perspectives in the light of local realities.

Similarly, while Latin American feminist and queer theoretical perspectives on social movements share common conceptual ground with their counterparts in the North, they also question and challenge the relevance of certain concepts for understanding social activism in the South. It should also be noted that the development in Latin America of feminist and queer theoretical perspectives on social movements is often very closely linked to actual social and political activism. It is not just that the links between theory and action are explored in studies of women's and lesbian, gay, bisexual, transgender, and intersex (LGBTI) movements in the region (see Ewig and Friedman, Díez in this volume), but rather that much of the theory in this field emerges from the ground up. As a result, to review such perspectives on social movements in Latin America necessarily implies referencing cases of social movement activism in the region.

The main body of this chapter is divided into three sections. The first reviews some of the principal debates and concepts developed in feminist and queer theory around critiques of the public/private divide and the resulting narrowly institutionalist conceptions of the political, which constitute challenges and contributions to mainstream theorizing of social movements. The second section reviews how feminist and queer perspectives in research have opened up avenues for analyzing the complexities of collective identity construction and the tensions within as well as among social movements. The third section highlights new developments in feminist and queer social and political theorizing and epistemological reflection in the region that seek to "decolonize" knowledge production. Finally, the chapter concludes by offering some reflections on the significance of these perspectives for understanding and resisting the growing conservative and religious antifeminist and homo-lesbo-transphobic backlash across Latin America.

Feminist and Queer Challenges to Mainstream Social Movement Theory

As various authors have signaled (Van Dyke, Soule, and Taylor 2004; Wulff, Bernstein, and Taylor 2015), the policy process approach to the study of social movements is based on a conception of power and politics that privileges the state and economic relations as the target and site of contentious politics and collective action. This focus means that what are considered social movements is restricted to those that direct their demands at the state. This perspective has been both critiqued and enriched by the theoretical contributions emerging from empirical studies of new social movements in Europe and Latin America (Escobar and Alvarez 1992; Jelin 1985, 1987; Melucci 1985; see Garretón and Selamé in this volume), and by feminist theory and contemporary cultural studies (Jasper 2010; see Salman in this volume).

A first dimension of these debates highlights the masculinist assumptions underpinning the theoretical division between public and private spheres that is central to both the concept of the political in the liberal tradition and to Western knowledge production in general, and which was succinctly challenged from the 1960s by the feminist slogan "the personal is political."[1] The "superimposition of three dichotomies: political/apolitical, public/private, and male/female" (Siltanen and Stanworth 1984: 101) so central to Western political thought was also reproduced in early social movement theory, leading to women's organizing at community level being overlooked or dismissed as a- or pre-political.

In the face of this theoretical erasing of women as social agents, certain key tenets of feminist theory and research methodologies have proved central for rendering visible women's activism within social movements and revealing the gendered dynamics of their organization and strategies, as well as for constituting identity-based movements and non-traditional forms of collective action as legitimate objects of study. In particular, experiential grounding implies taking the everyday lives of women and experiences of those marginalized by conventional sex/gender structures as the starting point for research in order to focus on aspects of social life and perspectives that typically are rendered invisible by the normatively masculinist focus of conventional social science research (Harding 1991; Taylor 1998).

However, feminist approaches to social movement research not only rendered women's activism visible and revealed the gender power relations embedded in social movement organizations and practices, but also showed that political opportunity structures themselves could be seen to be gendered. As Ferree and Mueller (2004: 589) point out, blindness to the political nature of women's domestic-based activism "may provide protective coloration in a wide variety of dictatorships and other conditions of marginal opportunity for male mobilization". In other words, from this feminist perspective political opportunity structures are not solely determined by factors relating to regime change, the party system, or characteristics of the political elite, but also shaped by the gendered norms regulating social life, which may in specific cultural contexts open up or close off gender-differentiated spaces for political activism.

By questioning the conceptualization of politics and state-centric models of domination and activism, feminist scholars expanded the conceptual boundaries of what constitutes political action as well as the very definition of social movements. Furthermore, the uncovering of gendered inequalities and power dynamics within social movements raised questions regarding the accountability and political commitment of these purportedly progressive collectives to the principles of justice and equality that they publicly espouse (Horn 2013: 12).

The notion that "the personal is political" has been reinscribed by feminist scholarship on women's activism in the Latin American context at different moments in the period under study, to describe the politicization of the private/domestic sphere as a site of political struggle. Early feminist studies of women's participation in social movements that emerged during the period of authoritarian rule in South America, for example, revealed how activities that to androcentric visions of social activism were merely an extension of women's domestic or mothering roles, such as community soup kitchens or organizations like the Madres de Plaza de Mayo, were in fact crucial nodes in the resistance to authoritarian regimes (Jaquette 1989; Jelin 1987, 1990). More recently, feminist ethnographies of the Argentine *piquetero* movement have revealed gender divisions of labor and power that are largely ignored by mainstream studies (and media reporting) but which are essential to understanding how these movements work and their repertoire of contention (Andújar 2014; Cross and Freytes 2007).

In a similar way, Michel Foucault's (1984) theorizing on sexual identities allowed sexuality to be reconsidered as an integral part of culture and politics, a perspective that helped visualize identities as forms of social control and the product of language and specific knowledge discourses. This resulted in an expansion of what is understood by politics and the construction of new analytical tools to understand sex-gender movements and their struggle for sexual and reproductive rights in both Europe and Latin America.

From these critical perspectives a multi-dimensional idea of power was developed that included both symbolic and material aspects (Alvarez, Dagnino, and Escobar 1998; Wulff, Bernstein, and Taylor 2015) and implied redefining in a more inclusive manner what social movements are. Within this approach, the term "social movement" is understood to encompass collective action that seeks to challenge and transform cultural norms or social representations, by working at the level of social imaginaries, public opinion, or knowledge systems, as well as collective action that promotes political institutional change. In addition, this multi-dimensional vision of power and politics implies rethinking who are considered to be activists, what strategy means and how social movement outputs should be evaluated (Wulff, Bernstein, and Taylor 2015).

In this sense, feminist and LGBTI movements are key for researching the relationship between social movements and cultural change. Analyses of the strategies developed by such movements to introduce controversial topics and visions that challenge hegemonic paradigms allow researchers to explore the articulation between movement objectives that aim to achieve material changes at normative or institutional levels, and those that seek to bring about transformations in the production of meanings at the social and cultural levels (see Halvorsen and Rossi, Salman, Díez in this volume).

The public/private division has also been the object of queer theorizing. According to Clarke (2000), the public sphere is not so much a space or the institutions themselves, but rather the tense relation between Enlightenment ideals of democratic polity and their material realization. This author traces the relationship between bourgeois morality, politics and economy—which historically limited many groups' access to the public sphere—and points out the unfulfilled promise that such limitations would imply. Queerness thus faces two obstacles in its advance into the public sphere: first, the erotic experience is a constitutive part of identity and of the sphere of intimacy; and second, the universal norm of humanity that regulates the public arena is defined with reference to values associated with the bourgeois heterosexual family. In this way, as Plummer (2001) points out, the concept of sexual citizenship introduces two contradictions into the notion of the public, by politicizing a new area of social life: it brings intimacy into the public, while at the same time it aims to protect the private lives of individuals.

As a result, the relation and division between public and private spheres—a problem central to both feminist and queer theory—reflects the fact that the organization of public institutionality, as the terrain of control and disciplinary production of bodies, reflects a power regime that is also sexed and gendered. From this perspective, many of the discourses, strategies, and actions of Latin American social movements can be thought of as practices that defy disciplinary technologies and combat the hegemonic discourses that underpin the regulatory measures and ideas about order that determine where bodies may circulate, become visible, and are afforded recognition at societal level.

Foucault's (1984) work on the history of sexuality was key for querying liberal humanist narratives that celebrated the emergence of gay and lesbian movements against oppressive regimes. One critique was that these narratives frequently ignored the challenges that the gay agenda introduces in the state, as well as the ideas of "family" and "decency" that the organizations often reproduced in their discourses and practices (Halperin 1995). The Foucauldian perspective lays the ground for an alternative, more complex approach, centered on concepts such as "reverse discourse,"[2] which enable researchers to explore the multiple genealogies of LGBTI movements. These, in turn, reveal differences between movements or social organizations that work in conjunction with radical and transformative projects and those that primarily reproduce hegemonic notions of masculinity and family that are racialized and heterosexist, and thus perpetuate the traditional division between what is considered public or private in terms of social norms.

Another significant dimension of cultural processes that feminist and queer perspectives have highlighted is the role played by emotions in mobilizing collective action. This represents another layer of the dichotomous distinction between public-political-man and private-apolitical-woman. That is, men's participation in collective action was traditionally interpreted as a rational, strategic response to opportunities or threats, while women's "natural" emotionality limited their capacity for rational thought and by extension for strategic decision-making in collective action (Jaggar 1989). In contrast, feminist theorists refuted this clear-cut counterposition of emotionality/rationality and signaled the pervasiveness and relevance of emotions to political action, thus encouraging the expansion of "the model of the social movement actor from a narrowly cognitive rational actor to a more historically and biographically situated person with attachments and emotions that can be intrinsically motivating" (Ferree and Mueller 2004: 497).

In the Latin American context, social movement research has thrown light on how emotions are part of the framing process for collective identity formation and action, certainly within women's movements but also beyond. The archetypical "emotional" frame of organizations of mothers searching for their disappeared or detained loved ones under dictatorships in the Southern Cone and Central America, was simultaneously strategically effective in that it used emotionally charged gendered norms as a protective measure against possible retaliation by the military. Likewise, the impact of the HIV/AIDS pandemic and the forms of activism that developed to confront its consequences became a key issue for the study of how emotions—anger, indignation, pride, fear, and loss—impact on collective action, shaping gays' and lesbians' responses to the pandemic. Emotions were seen to impel people to activism and to foster commitment to political action; they were also regarded as instrumental in the development of strategies for achieving political visibility in countries where the LGBTI community was not mobilized (on Argentina, see Pecheny 2001; on Brazil, see Parker 1994).

Feminist and Queer Perspectives on Collective Identity Formation

Studies of the struggles and internal divisions both in the feminist movement and in LGBTI movements have also contributed to understanding how collective identities are constructed. This is because identity formation depends directly on processes of socialization and mechanisms of internalization of certain beliefs, which take place, among others, in day-to-day intimate interactions (Jasper 2007). Studies of different forms of feminist and LGBTI organizing in the region highlight the theoretical value of interrogating the multiple and shifting identities that inform the composition of all types of social movements and the dynamics of power that flow from them, as well as the need to acknowledge and explore the implications of the diversity contained within broad brush terms such as "feminist" or "gay" movement.

Butler (1993), building on the Foucauldian idea that sexuality is produced discursively, argues that gender is performative, a daily reiteration regulated by gender norms, which is experienced by individuals as an essential and natural identity. The concept of heteronormativity[3] links identity and gender expressions to desire, revealing the political order that propagates compulsory heterosexuality and a classification of bodies that identifies cisgender heterosexuality as something natural and given, while all other possible alternatives are regarded as abject bodies, mere copies or forms at odds with what is socially understood to be "human." This critique of the expressive theories of gender, and the de-essentialization of the category of "sex" that it entails, leads Butler to argue against feminist politics being based on the gender identity category "woman," since it renders invisible the multiple expressions of corporeality that exist, and because it is implicitly based on binary norms of sex-gender relations.

A similarly de-essentializing perspective has been proposed by intersectional theory which developed initially from critiques made by African American feminist activists (Crenshaw 1991; Davis 1983) of single-axis frameworks for understanding the dynamics of social relations of domination. The single-axis perspective treats, for example, racism as a totally separate phenomenon from gender-based discrimination or homophobia. As intersectional theorists (Collins 2000; Yuval-Davis 2006) have argued, such an approach renders invisible subjects' simultaneous location in multiple socially constructed categories such as gender, race, class, sexuality, and so on. This in turn generates at the micro-level interlocking patterns of privilege/power and marginalization/discrimination that cannot simply be seen as the sum of different experiences of social inequality, but a specific outcome of the interaction between multiple axes of inequality. This perspective, then, challenges the homogenizing tendency to assign people to mutually exclusive social categories, and relocates the focus of analysis on how discrimination is experienced differently by individuals who may share a common group identity but not necessarily the same social positioning.

Both the intersectional framework and the notion of gender as non-binary and performative have opened up theoretical avenues of great importance for analyzing both how identity formation takes place in social movements, as well as how identity is used for different purposes in the realm of collective action. These theories provide useful tools for exploring the complex interaction between cultural identities and social class in Latin American social movement frames, as has been explored in empirical studies of women's organizing in mixed-gender movements in Latin America, such as in the Via Campesina peasant movement (Desmarais 2003), or the urban *piquetero* movement in Argentina (Andújar 2014).

Applying an intersectional lens to the mechanisms of "boundary-making," identified in mainstream social movement theory as the delineation of an oppositional relationship between social movements and dominant groups in society at large (Tarrow 2011; Tilly 2004), can help visualize internal movement dynamics. Tracing internal patterns of boundary-making along the lines of diverse social positioning within what is externally presented as a unified collective highlights the inequalities that are reproduced in the interior of social movements. Intersectional analyses can therefore be used to explore the power dynamics that determine which social positioning markers are reflected in the construction and public expression of the movements' collective identity and reveal how that identity may perpetuate ethnocentric or heteronormative cosmovisions, rendering invisible the specific problems, interests and needs of different social groups within the movement (Bastian Duarte 2012; de la Dehesa 2010; Rousseau and Hudon 2017; Halvorsen and Rossi in this volume).

For example, the comparative and intersectional analysis of indigenous women's organizing in Latin America undertaken by Rousseau and Hudon (2017) reveals the importance of distinguishing between social positioning—class and gender—and group identity—indigeneity—present within indigenous movements. As this research shows, "the articulation of gender and indigeneity in women's collective identity formation has positioned them in complex situations of negotiation of the boundaries and the framing of the indigenous movement's discourse and agendas" (Rousseau and Hudon 2017: 198). How these complex negotiations work out has implications for indigenous women's mobilization: continued exclusion from leadership or silencing of their agendas within mixed-gender indigenous movements leads them to create autonomous organizational structures outside the movement; their articulation of gender and ethnicity may be given partial recognition within the movement and allocated organizational and discursive spaces, which may enjoy a greater or lesser degree of autonomy; or their agendas and presence may be fully integrated, reconfiguring the movement's wider group identity in gendered terms. Moreover, this study shows that boundary negotiation is also relevant to indigenous women activists outside their mixed-gender movements, in their interaction with the broader women's movement and feminism. In this sense, indigenous women activists have challenged the ethnic and class-based power relations that are seen to permeate urban, white, middle-class feminist movements. Finally, Rousseau and Hudon (2017) show how these processes of boundary negotiation, internally within mixed-gender indigenous movements and externally with other women's or feminist movements, are also shaped by the gendered political opportunity structures and culturally-specific country contexts within which they are located.

Critiques of feminism's use of gender as a universal, stable, and decontextualized category of analysis which leads to homogenizing and essentialist constructions of "womanhood" have also come from Afro-descendant women activists, who voice similar charges of ethnocentric and classist exclusionary practices and discourses in mainstream Latin American feminist movements (Curiel 2007, 2010; Werneck 2005). Sueli Carneiro (2005), a Brazilian Afro-descendant feminist, has signaled the need to "blacken" feminism and "feminize" the struggle against racism in order to reveal the intersections between sexism and racism that shape specific experiences of discrimination for Afro-Latin American women (see Dixon and Caldwell in this volume). As Townsend-Bell (2007) has shown in the case of the Uruguayan feminist movement, a discursive acknowledgement of the relevance of the intersectional frame for a deeper understanding of women's subordination does not necessarily translate into intersectional praxis on the ground, in organizing and agenda building. Similar critiques have been directed at Latin American feminist movements by lesbian and transgender activists (Bastian Duarte 2012), and resulted in the emergence of transfeminist movements in countries like Argentina and Brazil and to a lesser degree in other parts of the region (Berkins 2003; Berkins and Fernández 2005; Fernández and Araneta 2014).

The anti-essentialist critiques of identity politics have had different implications for LGBTI movements in Latin America. Early on Gamson (2002) discussed the dilemmas that such critiques created for collective action. This discussion was taken up to a greater or lesser extent in Latin America depending on the trajectories of the LGBTI movements and the contexts in which they were operating. As de la Dehesa (2010) points out in his comparative analysis of Brazilian and Mexican LGBT movements, in Brazil the movement adopted an identitarian discourse in its actions directed at the state, defining a clearly demarcated homosexual community as the subject of rights, in the same way as any other minority group. By contrast, in the Mexican case the movement constructed collective political identities centered on notions such as "sexual diversity" which allowed it to forge broader legislative alliances in support of its demands. In de la Dehesa's (ibid.) view these differences reflect how each local movement related to a shared repertoire of transnational activism, selecting from it certain elements in accordance with its own needs and timing. Additionally, in Mexico the presence of greater barriers to the movement accessing institutional politics forced it to adopt a more flexible construction of collective identity. This strong identitarian turn in the Brazilian movement has also been noted by other authors (Facchini 2005; Green 1999; MacRae 1990), most of whom in turn relate the emergence of this kind of activism with the development of urban, middle-class homosexual sub-cultures in major Brazilian cities.

As Figari (2016) points out, the contributions from queer theory were often read from a political practice closely linked to intersectionality or articulation, as formulated by Laclau and Mouffe (1985), whereby a radical democracy requires the articulation of different social movement struggles through the construction of a "we" that allows these struggles to be linked without erasing their plurality or difference. In this respect, the Uruguayan sexual diversity movement is probably one of the least identity-bound in the region. This is partly the result of the development of a political culture that creates barriers which prevent social identities from being able to generate mass-mobilization in public space; it is also due in part to the post-identity tradition that characterizes the Uruguayan movement (Sempol 2013a), by which political mobilization does not center on social identities nor seeks to essentialize them, but rather emphasizes a political project that involves various groups and identities while at the same time transcending them. In instances of great political and media exposure, such as the annual "diversity march" in Uruguay, feminist, Afro-descendant, student, and union movements participated together with LGBTI organizations in support of a broad agenda, drawing points of intersection between issues such as the decriminalization of abortion, the regulation of marijuana, legal rights for transgender people, same-sex marriage, and opposition to the lowering of the age of criminal liability in the Penal Code.

But in general, Figari (2016) shows, the degree to which queer theory was incorporated in theorizing on political activism in the region varied in both extent and intensity according to each local context, with its impact being greater within Latin American academic circles,[4] and much more limited within social movements. This is because, in the first place, unlike in Uruguay, most Latin American LGBTI movements have been strongly identity-based, hence queer theory's critique of identity was regarded as demobilizing and depoliticizing, or simply as another identity to be absorbed into the movement, as in the addition of the "Q." In the second place, the disruptive critique of queer theory proved difficult to translate into political practice at a moment when opportunities for dialogue were opening up with political parties and the state, leading to the consecration in law and public policies of rights for the LGBTI population in the region. There have also been aesthetic-political experiences, such as the *Revista El Teje: Primer Periódico Travesti Latinoamericano*, published in Argentina, which seeks to publicize alternative visions of sex-gender dissidence. Similarly, in Uruguay, *Ojo T* is a political transgender poetry project which led to the emergence of transfeminist political reflection and action at local level, and in Ecuador the *Wankavika Trans* and *Ballet Folklórico Ñuca Trans* projects seek to destabilize sexual normativity through racial destabilization (Castellanos 2016).

Decolonizing Feminist and Queer Theory in Latin America

The multiple challenges to the political identity category of "woman" and "feminist" in Latin America have also been linked to lesbian antiracist decolonial critiques (Curiel 2007, 2010). There is a growing body of both academic and grassroots theoretical reflection on "decolonial feminism" (Schutte 2011), which analyzes how hegemonic urban, white, middle-class feminism operates in Latin America, pursuing agendas, strategies, and priorities that are defined by the North and ignoring the claims, forms of struggle, and perspectives of subaltern Latin American women. Some theorists see mainstream Latin American feminism as reproducing a "salvationist" rhetoric imbued with teleological visions of modernity and the colonial episteme (Bidaseca 2011) and call for a new language of decolonial feminism that acknowledges the multiple identities and cosmovisions of women on the continent (Segato 2011). Other studies use ethnographic methods to explore points of encounter and dissent between locally-sited indigenous constructions of gender relations and institutionalized feminist claims, and the nuanced implications that these have for women's organizing on the ground (Burman 2011).

Decolonial perspectives thus offer a different take on how ideas and discourses travel at transnational level and the imperialist impact of global forms of activism (see Flórez-Flórez and Orlate-Orlate in this volume). While diverse studies of regional-level feminist and women's networks in Latin America around issues such as sexual and reproductive rights and violence against women have shown the importance of transnational activism for advancing movement claims at national level, there are also critical analyses of the "civilizing forces" that the reproduction of transnational strategies may generate, such as the position known as "the right to silence," which disputes the "coming out of the closet" narrative as the only way to achieve liberation for non-heterosexuals (Guzmán 2006). The emergence of LGBT political identities in Latin American public spheres has been seen by some authors, such as Santiago (2002), as an example of alienated or colonized politics, arguing that these global sexual identities are associated with teleological narratives of progress linked to Eurocentric ideas of modernization and development, whereas local sexual identities are seen as a sign of backwardness and stagnation. This perspective has been criticized by other scholars such as de la Dehesa (2010: 127–28) in that it ignores the long history of mass circulation of political traditions of all types between the core and Latin American countries, as well as the multiple ways in which these traditions were appropriated over time.

In recent years, Civil Code reforms legalizing same-sex marriages (Argentina, Mexico City, and Uruguay), as well as common law precedents that remove obstacles for the celebration of such marriages (Brazil and Colombia), have placed at the center of discussions on Latin American LGBTI movements questions about the process of normalization and its effects in both the short and long term on sex-gender politics. This discussion often imports arguments and critiques produced by exponents of queer theory in Anglo-Saxon contexts (United States, Canada), and bypasses a contextualized analysis of the factors that explain the emergence of this type of demand in the Latin American context. In this sense, some organizations have argued that these reforms were normalizing and assimilationist (Cuello 2014), a view that renders invisible their democratizing impact in political, legal, and social terms (Díez 2018; Pecheny et al. 2010; Sempol 2013a, 2013b), as well as denying the variety in the content of these reforms across the region.[5] This perspective also ignores the contexts in which these claims were being made: the debate in the recently recovered Latin American democracies around accepting and implementing a regulatory policy with a radical base that articulates human rights and an emancipatory vision, versus a neoliberal multicultural model that naturalizes and depoliticizes differences, seeking their integration via segregationist policy measures or legal solutions (Corrales and Pecheny 2010).

The discussion also often precludes analyzing the strategy of Latin American LGBTI movements as an attempt to convert collective action into a "symbolic multiplier" (Melucci 2002: 104). This possible reading stems from the fact that, rather than defining their strategy in terms of efficacy, the movements' aim is to compel the political system and society in general to reveal their logic and the weakness of their arguments on certain issues. The strategic objective is to render visible the power dynamics and the ways in which conservative forces reason and operate. This in itself is an important political achievement, focused on targeting hegemonic visions of LGBTI sex-gender identities and their positioning within society. In both Argentina and Uruguay, the demand for same-sex marriage originated in this way. Moreover, those positions critical of same-sex marriage reforms ignore the fact that this was never the only claim being made by the LGBTI movement in Argentina, Chile, Mexico, and Uruguay, and that its prioritization at certain moments in time was linked to strategic decisions relating to the political opportunity structure (Díez 2018: 391; see Díez in this volume).

Without going so far as to make a localist claim, it is essential to consider the conditions of production of all theory, as well as exploring the possible avenues to decolonizing its episteme (Flórez-Flórez and Orlate-Orlate in this volume). The proliferation of terms such as "cuir," "kuir," "cuier," or "cuiar" reflect the transition between different contexts and the plurality of readings of queer theory that took place in Latin America (Delfino and Rapisard 2010). For some authors, such as Epps (2008), the globalization of queer theory beyond the English-speaking world is problematic because the particular contexts that give the term specific disruptive meanings are lost to view. Similarly, Rivas (2010) points out that queer theory became in Latin America the hegemonic parameter for classifying—including retroactively—Latin American authors and aesthetic political interventions as pre-queer theory. This in turn eliminates the possibility of visualizing other local genealogies and creates static one-directional channels through which knowledge circulates between territories crossed by disparate power relations. It is in this way that often the works and critiques made by Néstor Perlongher (2008) of the Argentine gay movement in the 1980s are read and interpreted (Rapisardi and Modarelli 2001; Sempol 2013b), or the Chilean Pedro Lemebel's texts and his performative interventions with the group Yeguas del Apocalipsis (Maristany 2008), or even the works of the philosopher Nelly Richard in the context of the return to democracy in Chile (Rivas 2010). In the Southern Cone the movement has also contributed an important critique of the forms of production and uses of the term "queer" in local contexts. Cabral (2016: 17) has highlighted the existence of mechanisms of "academic para-inclusion," referring to how trans and intersex people are invited to participate in different spaces or research projects to provide testimonies, but never as subjects and theory producers in their own right.

Conclusions

In one of the most violent regions of the world and with high indices of gender-based and homo-lesbo-transphobic violence, one current concern stimulating reflection and dialogue within feminist and queer theory on Latin American social movements is the need to rethink and critically analyze the processes of assimilation and normalization suffered by social movements in the local context. The deconstructivism that queer interventions often propose, while a powerful and necessary theoretical tool, must be placed in context in order to avoid formulations that reify liberal individualistic ideas and turn queerness into yet another object of consumption of neoliberal global capitalism. However, this must be done while avoiding displacing meanings that end up promoting anti-rights visions, which facilitate the processes of appropriation of the human rights paradigm by conservative actors and the roll-back of the normative and institutional gains that have been achieved thus far. The extreme right-wing mobilizations in the region threaten progressive social movements of all kinds, but the particular ferocity of their hate-speech directed at what they term "gender ideology" and "unnatural" sexualities and gender identities will make the theoretical debates discussed in this chapter all the more relevant for the study of social movements in Latin America in coming years.

Notes

1. For a review and discussion of these critiques, see Squires (2003).
2. Foucault (1984: 111) states: "There is no question that the appearance in nineteenth-century psychiatry, jurisprudence, and literature of a whole series of discourses on the species and subspecies of homosexuality, inversion, pederasty, and 'psychic hermaphrodism' made possible a strong advance of social controls into this area of 'perversity'; but it also made possible the formation of a 'reverse' discourse: homosexuality began to speak in its own behalf, to demand that its legitimacy or 'naturality' be acknowledged, often in the same vocabulary, using the same categories by which it was medically disqualified."
3. The concept of heteronormativity was first coined by Warren (1991) and later adopted and reworked by Butler and many other exponents of queer theory.
4. Among the former is the appearance in 1996 of the Área de Estudios Queer at the Universidad de Buenos Aires, which sought to link research and activism by articulating anti-discrimination and anti-repression perspectives. Other examples are the Área Académica Queer at the Universidad de la República (Uruguay), which since 2007 has developed a close dialogue with local social movements and a form of "academic activism"; and the spaces affiliated to the Coordinadora Universitaria de Disidencia Sexual in Chile.
5. In this respect, while same-sex marriage legislation passed in Argentina only modified those articles of the Civil Code that preventing same-sex couples from getting married, the Uruguayan law included many other significant changes which also affected different-sex couples. These included the possibility of changing the order of the surnames of children

of both same-sex and different-sex couples in order to avoid the historical appropriation by men of women's reproductive labor within different-sex couples.

References

Alvarez, Sonia E., Evangelina Dagnino, and Arturo Escobar (eds.) (1998), *Cultures of Politics, Politics of Cultures. Re-visioning Latin American Social Movements* (Boulder, CO: Westview Press).

Andújar, Andrea (2014), *Rutas argentinas hasta el fin: Mujeres, política y piquetes, 1996–2001* (Buenos Aires: Luxemburgo Ediciones).

Bastian Duarte, Ángela Ixkic (2012), "From the Margins of Latin American Feminism: Indigenous and Lesbian Feminisms," *Journal of Women in Culture and Society* 38(1), 153–78.

Berkins, Lohana (2003), "Un itinerario político del travestismo," in Diana Maffía (ed.), *Sexualidades migrantes. Género y transgénero*, 127–37 (Buenos Aires: Feminaria Editora).

Berkins, Lohana and Josefina Fernández (eds.) (2005), *La gesta del nombre propio* (Buenos Aires: Ediciones Madres de Plaza de Mayo).

Bidaseca, Karina (2011), "Mujeres blancas buscando salvar a las mujeres color café de los hombres color café. O reflexiones sobre desigualdad y colonialismo jurídico desde el feminismo poscolonial," in Karina Bidaseca and Vanesa Vazquez Laba (eds.), *Feminismo y poscolonialidad. Descolonizando el feminismo desde y en América Latina*, 95–118 (Buenos Aires: Ediciones Godot).

Burman, Anders (2011), "Chachawarmi: Silence and Rival Voices on Decolonisation and Gender Politics in Andean Bolivia," *Journal of Latin American Studies* 43(1), 65–91.

Butler, Judith (1993), *Bodies that Matters. On the Discursive Limits of Sex* (New York: Routledge).

Cabral, Mauro (2016), "Prologo," in Martín De Mauro Rucovsky, *Cuerpos en escena. Materialidad y cuerpo sexuado en Judith Butler y Paul B. Preciado*, 11–18 (Barcelona: Egales).

Carneiro, Sueli (2005), "Ennegrecer al feminismo. La situación de la mujer negra en América Latina desde una perspectiva de género," *Nouvelles questions féministes* 24(2), 21–26.

Castellanos, Santiago (2016), "Sexualidades no-normativas, diferencia racial y la erótica del poder: escenarios de deseo queer en el Ecuador del siglo XXI," in Diego Falconi, Santiago Castellanos and María Amelia Viteri (eds.), *Resentir lo queer en América Latina: diálogos desde/con el sur*, 195–214 (Barcelona: Egales).

Clarke, Eric (2000), *Virtuous Vice. Homoeroticism and the Public Sphere* (Durham, NC: Duke University Press).

Collins, Patricia Hill (2000), *Black Feminist Thought: Knowledge, Consciousness, and the Politics of Empowerment* (New York: Routledge).

Corrales, Javier and Mario Pecheny (eds.) (2010), *The Politics of Sexuality in Latin America. A Reader on Lesbian, Gay, Bisexual and Transgender Rights* (Pittsburgh, PA: Pittsburgh University Press).

Crenshaw, Kimberlé (1991), "Mapping the Margins: Intersectionality, Identity Politics, and Violence Against Women of Color," *Stanford Law Review* 43(6), 1241–99.

Cross, Cecilia and Ada Cora Freytes Frey (2007), "Movimientos piqueteros: Tensiones de género en la definición del liderazgo," *Argumentos* 20(55), 77–94.

Cuello, Nicolás (2014), "Flujos, roces y derrames del activismo artístico en Argentina 2003-2013. Políticas sexuales y comunidades de resistencia sexo-afectiva," *Errata revista de artes visuales* 12, 70–95.

Curiel, Ochy (2007), "Crítica poscolonial desde las prácticas políticas del feminismo antirracista," *Nómadas* 26, 92–101.
Curiel, Ochy (2010), "Hacia la construcción de un feminismo descolonizado. A propósito de la realización del Encuentro Feminista Autónomo: haciendo comunidad en la Casa de las Diferencias," in Yuderkys Espinosa Miñosa (ed.), *Aproximaciones críticas a las prácticas teórico-políticas del feminismo latinoamericano*, 69–77 (Buenos Aires: En la Frontera).
Davis, Angela (1983), *Women, Race and Class* (New York: Vintage).
de la Dehesa, Rafael (2010), *Queering the Public Sphere in Mexico and Brazil: Sexual Rights in Emerging Democracies* (Durham, NC: Duke University Press).
Delfino, Silvia and Flavio Rapisard (2010), "Cuirizando la cultura argentina desde La Queerencia," *Ramona* 99, 10–14.
Desmarais, Annette Aurélie (2003), "The Via Campesina: Peasant Women at the Frontiers of Food Sovereignty," *Canadian Women's Studies* 23(1), 140–45.
Díez, Jordi (2018), *La política del matrimonio gay en América Latina: Argentina, Chile y México* (Mexico: Fondo Cultura Económica).
Epps, Brad (2008), "Retos, riesgos, pautas y promesas de la teoría queer," *Revista iberoamericana* 225(74), 897–920.
Escobar, Arturo and Sonia E. Alvarez (1992), *The Making of Social Movements in Latin America: Identity, Strategy, and Democracy* (Boulder, CO: Westview Press).
Facchini, Regina (2005), *Sopa de letrinhas: Movimento homossexual e produçao de identidades colectivas nos anos 90* (Rio de Janeiro: Garamond Universitaria).
Fernández, Sandra and Aitzole Araneta (2014), "Genealogías trans(feministas)," in Miriam Solá and Elena Urko (eds.), *Transfeminismos. Epistemes, fricciones y flujos*, 45–59 (Bilbao: Editorial Txalaparta).
Ferree, Myra Marx and Carol McClurg Mueller (2004), "Feminism and the Women's Movement," in David A. Snow, Sarah A. Soule, and Hanspeter Kriesi (eds.), *The Blackwell Companion to Social Movements*, 576–607 (Oxford: Blackwell).
Figari, Carlos (2016), "Fagocitando lo queer en el Cono Sur," in Diego Falconi, Santiago Castellanos, and María Amelia Viteri (eds.), *Resentir lo queer en América Latina: diálogos desde/con el sur*, 63–80 (Barcelona: Egales).
Foucault, Michel (1984), *The History of Sexuality: An Introduction* (Penguin: Harmondsworth).
Gamson, Joshua (2002), "¿Deben autodestruirse los movimientos identitarios? Un extraño dilema," in Rafael Mérida Jiménez (ed.), *Sexualidades transgresoras*, 141–72 (Barcelona: Icaria).
Green, James (1999), *Beyond Carnival: Male Homosexuality in Twentieth-Century Brazil* (Chicago: University of Chicago Press).
Guzmán, Manolo (2006), *Gay Hegemonies/Latino Homosexualities* (New York: Routledge).
Halperin, David (1995), *Saint Foucault: Towards a Gay Hagiography* (Oxford: Oxford University Press).
Harding, Sandra (1991), *Whose Science? Whose Knowledge? Thinking from Women's Lives* (Ithaca, NY: Cornell University Press).
Horn, Jessica (2013), *Gender and Social Movements. Overview Report* (Brighton: Institute of Development Studies-Bridge).
Jaggar, Alison M. (1989), "Love and Knowledge: Emotion in Feminist Epistemology," *Inquiry* 32(2), 151–76.
Jaquette, Jane (ed.) (1989), *The Women's Movement in Latin America: Feminism and the Transition to Democracy* (Boulder, CO: Westview Press).

Jasper, James (2007), "Cultural Approaches in the Sociology of Social Movements," in Bert Klandermans and Conny Roggeband (eds.), *Handbook of Social Movement Across Disciplines*, 59–109 (New York: Springer).
Jasper, James M. (2010), "Social Movement Theory Today: Toward a Theory of Action?" *Sociology Compass* 4(11), 965–76.
Jelin, Elizabeth (ed.) (1985), *Los nuevos movimientos sociales* (Buenos Aires: CEAL).
Jelin, Elizabeth (ed.) (1987), *Ciudadanía e identidad: Las mujeres en los movimientos sociales latinoamericanos* (Geneva: UNRISD).
Jelin, Elizabeth (ed.) (1990), *Women and Social Change in Latin America* (London: Zed Books).
Laclau, Ernesto and Chantal Mouffe (1985), *Hegemony and Socialist Strategy: Towards a Radical Democratic Politics* (London: Verso).
MacRae, Edward (1990), *A construçao da igualdade: Identidad sexual e politica no Brasil do Abertura* (Campinas: UNICAMP).
Maristany, José Javier (2008), "¿Una teoría queer latinoamericana? Postestructuralismo y políticas desde el Cono Sur," *Lectures du genre*, 4: Lecturas queer desde el Cono Sur, 17–25.
Melucci, Alberto (1985), "The Symbolic Challenge of Contemporary Movements," *Social Research*, 52, 789–816.
Melucci, Alberto (2002), *Acción colectiva, vida cotidiana y democracia* (Mexico City: El Colegio de México).
Parker, Richard (1994), *A construçao da solidariedade: AIDS, sexualidade e política no Brasil* (Rio de Janeiro: Abia, IMS-UERJ, Relume Dumará).
Pecheny, Mario (2001), *La construction de l'avortement et du sida en tant que questions politiques: Le cas de l'Argentine* (Villeneuve d'Ascq: Presses Universitaires du Septentrion).
Pecheny, Mario, Rafaeil de la Dehesa, Ernesto Meccia, Renata Hiller, Roberto Gargarella, Laura Clérico, Martín Aldao, Mariano Fernández, and Laura Clérico (eds.) (2010), *Matrimonio igualitario: Perspectivas sociales, políticas y jurídicas* (Buenos Aires: Eudeba).
Perlongher, Néstor (2008), *Prosa plebeya: Ensayos 1980–1992* (Buenos Aires: Colihue).
Plummer, Ken (2001), "The Square of Intimate Citizenship: Some Preliminary Proposals," *Citizenship Studies* 5(3), 237–53.
Rapisardi, Flavio and Alejandro Modarelli (2001), *Fiestas, baños y exilio: Los gay porteños en la última dictadura* (Buenos Aires: Sudamericana).
Rivas, Felipe (2010), "Diga queer con la lengua afuera: sobre la confusión del debate latinoamericano," in Coordinadora Universitaria por la Disidencia Sexual (ed.), *Por un feminismo sin mujeres*, 59–75 (Santiago de Chile: Territorios Sexuales Ediciones).
Rousseau, Stéphanie and Anahi Morales Hudon (2017), *Indigenous Women's Movements in Latin America. Crossing Boundaries of Gender and Politics in the Global South* (New York: Palgrave Macmillan).
Santiago, Silviano (2002), "The Wily Homosexual (First—and Necessarily Hasty— Notes)," in Arnaldo Cruz Malavé y Martín Manalansan (eds.), *Queer Globalizations: Citizenship and the Afterlife of Colonialism*, 13–19 (New York: New York Press).
Schutte, Ofelia (2011), "Engaging Latin American Feminisms Today: Methods, Theory, Practice," *Hypatia* 26(4), 783–803.
Segato, Rita Laura (2011), "Género y colonialidad: En busca de claves de lectura y de un vocabulario estratégico descolonial," in Karina Bidaseca and Vanesa Vazquez Laba (eds.), *Feminismo y poscolonialidad. Descolonizando el feminismo desde y en América Latina* (Buenos Aires: Ediciones Godot), 17–47.

Sempol, Diego (2013a), *De los baños a la calle. Historia del movimiento lésbico gay trans uruguayo 1984-2013* (Montevideo: Debate).

Sempol, Diego (2013b), "Violence and the Emergence of Gay and Lesbian Activism in Argentina, 1983-90," in Saskia Wieringa and Horacio Sívori (eds.), *The Sexual History of the Global South: Sexual Politics in Africa, Asia and Latin America* (New York: Zed), 99–120.

Siltanen, Janet and Michelle Stanworth (1984), "The Politics of Private Woman and Public Man," *Theory and Society* 13, 91–118.

Squires, Judith (2003), "Public and Private," in Richard Bellamy and Andrew Mason (eds.), *Political Concepts*, 131–44 (Manchester: Manchester University Press).

Tarrow, Sidney G. (2011), *Power in Movement: Social Movements and Contentious Politics* (Cambridge: Cambridge University Press).

Taylor, Verta (1998), "Feminist Methodology in Social Movements Research," *Qualitative Sociology* 21(4), 357–79.

Tilly, Charles (2004), "Social Boundary Mechanisms," *Philosophy of the Social Sciences* 34(2), 211–36.

Townsend-Bell, Erica E. (2007), "Identities Matter: Identity Politics, Coalition Possibilities, and Feminist Organizing"(PhD thesis, Washington University).

Van Dyke, Nella, Sarah Soule, and Verta Taylor (2004), "The Targets of Social Movements: Beyond a Focus on the State," *Research in Social Movements, Conflicts and Change* 25, 27–51.

Warren, Michel (1991), "Introduction: Fear of a Queer Planet," *Social Text* 19, 3–17.

Werneck, Jurema (2005), "De ialodês y feministas. Reflexiones sobre la acción política de las mujeres negras en América Latina y el Caribe," *Nouvelles questions féministes* 24(2), 27–40.

Wulff, Stephen, Mary Bernstein, and Verta Taylor (2015), "New Theoretical Directions from the Study of Gender and Sexuality Movements: Collective Identity, Multi-institutional Politics, and Emotions," in Donatella Della Porta and Mario Diani (eds.), *The Oxford Handbook of Social Movements*, 108–30 (Oxford: Oxford University Press).

Yuval-Davis, Nira (2006), "Intersectionality and Feminist Politics," *The European Journal of Women's Studies* 13(3), 193–209.

CHAPTER 8

DECOLONIZING APPROACHES TO LATIN AMERICAN SOCIAL MOVEMENTS

MARÍA JULIANA FLÓREZ-FLÓREZ AND MARÍA CAROLINA OLARTE-OLARTE

INTRODUCTION

The literature on social movements has conventionally recognized two turning points in the study of these collective actors. The first involves a long period of around 100 years, beginning in the middle of the nineteenth century when von Stein (1850) coins the term "social movement." Key contributions of the time were made at the end of the century by the classical theories (LeBon 1895; Tarde 1901), and subsequently by the United States functionalist theories (Smelser 1962), followed by symbolic interactionism (Gurr 1970). The contributions of Robert Owen through cooperativism and those brought by Marxism are, in contrast, rarely cited despite their highly formative role for social movements (see Webber in this volume). The second turning point occurs in the 1980s when movements are no longer associated with irrational actions or behaviors that deviate from the norm (Mendiola 2002). Instead, they begin to be regarded as rational actors that can denounce modernity crises and propose alternatives to them (see Somma; Garretón and Selamé in this volume).

This chapter introduces a different perspective: *decolonizing approaches* (from now on DA) to study Latin American social movements. Following Flórez-Flórez (2005, 2014), DA allow us to surpass the disheartening diagnoses of a significant part of social movement theories that argue, intensely or not, that Latin American movements had little *potentia* to denounce the crises of modernity and even less so to offer alternatives to it. The DA show that the theories mentioned above on social movements are colonial despite being critical of modernity. Thus, while this inflection was fundamental in recognizing that movements were able to question the crisis of modernity and propose alternatives to it, vis-à-vis Latin American struggles, such recognition seemed to be unceasingly pending further requirements.

The purpose of this chapter is to show how the DA provide key elements and debates to understand and resist basic colonial premises and enable a change of terms under which knowledge on social movements is produced, evaluated, and stratified. It is the dialogue *with* movements—as opposed to *about* movements—that makes it possible to evaluate collective action.

Decolonizing Approaches

On the verge of the millennium, many authors' concerns converged in a renewed interest in colonial processes. Part of the reason for this greater interest involved the collective actions that, during the 1990s, orbited around what the Zapatistas called "the long night of 500 years." The interest in making such topics more visible and questioning how knowledge about colonization was produced was not entirely novel; it had already appeared in Latin American social sciences and other parts of the Global South (Mbembe 1996; Tuhiwai 1999). The emphasis on the critical role that colonial processes continue to play in modernity construction was the novelty. Such an emphasis brings to the fore two challenges that today permeate any renewed interest in the colonial question. First, the desire to avoid anachronisms that might obliterate the transformations that have emerged over two centuries of independence. Second, the aim was to identify and resist colonial domination's continuity, ranging from renewed attempts to exterminate ancestral communities, the inherited colonial power of elite families, and the self-censorship of body aesthetics hinging on colonial ideals of whiteness.

This renewed interest in the colonial question consolidated an approach that emerged about forty years ago. In the 1980s, Silvia Rivera-Cusicanqui's *Taller de Historia Oral Andina* was one of the first alternative academic spaces committed to decolonizing objectives and methodologies. In the 1990s, decolonial approaches were popularized by the Modernity/Coloniality network and the work of Boaventura de Sousa Santos, thus gaining attention beyond the social sciences—the arts, law, health sciences, among others. More recently, feminists have enhanced these approaches with a reflexive turn, which includes, for instance, a critique of the reproduction of colonial practices in academia.

A defining feature of the DA is that they do not constitute a unified theory. On the one hand, the decolonizing literature deploys a whole range of terms: "research program" (Escobar 2003), "network turn" (Castro and Grosfoguel 2007), "political intervention projects" (Carvalho 2010), "paradigm other" (Mignolo 2003), "inflection" (Restrepo and Rojas 2010), "praxis" (Rivera-Cusicanqui 2015), "a trend within Latin American cultural studies" (Beverley 2002), among others. On the other, their influence comes from a wide range of inspirational trajectories and interlocutors: *transdisciplinary fields of study* (postcolonial, subaltern, cultural, and critical development studies); *critical theories of modernity* (Frankfurt school, the Modern World-System); *Latin American critical thought* (popular education, dependency theory, liberation theology, participatory action-research); *Indigenous and Afro-diasporic trajectories* (diverse practices and modes of self-representation); *feminism* (Marxist, Chicano, African-American, and cyber); *emancipatory horizons of the European left* (heterodox Marxism, anarchism, and communal struggles). Rather than undermining these approaches, the dispersion within the DA, and the heterogeneous trajectories and interlocutors, has given rise to ongoing theoretical tensions.

However, despite their differences, the DA authors have several practices and concerns in common. First is the creation of links between academia and movements, such as the *Grupo Latinoamericano de Estudio, Formación y Acción Feminista* since 2007. Second is the redesign of university curriculums programs, such as the *Encuentro de Saberes* project (Carvalho 2010) involving *masters* of ancestral knowledge as regular professors (Brazil, since 2010). Last is the expansion of research centers with different political perspectives, like *El Tambo*, where manual and intellectual work are reconnected through the body (Bolivia, since 2013).

Today, the DA are both embraced and flagrantly criticized, further confirming that they have reached a consolidation point. Three scenarios are indicative of their extensive reception. First, the DA have been recognized as an interlocutor in several alternative universities where social movements have a powerful presence, as in the Universidad de la Tierra de Oaxaca (Mexico). Second, state institutions have co-opted decolonizing language. For instance, the Bolivian Viceministerio de Descolonización was created in 2009. Third, the DA have entered into other disciplines' agendas even beyond the region, such as in the 2017 Annual Conference of the Royal Geographical Society, whose main topic was "Decolonising Geographical Knowledges" (2017). Among those that reject it, DA has been criticized for several aspects, ranging from being excessively postmodern, anti-revolutionary, and bourgeois reformist (Artavia 2005), to being regarded as a backward trend of low intellectual quality that re-awakens racism and that is more ideological than it is scientific (Le Point 2018).

Contribution of the Decolonizing Approaches: Changing the Terms of the Debate on Social Movements in Latin America

Most social movement theories assume that Latin American struggles do not fully challenge the crisis of modernity and do not even offer alternatives to it. The basis for these arguments is colonial in itself. Three issues in this regard are telling.

A first colonial issue is the study of struggles in terms of what they lack. For instance, the political process approach refers to a twofold deficiency. Latin American social movements are devoid of autonomy vis-à-vis the state (Foweraker 1995) and symbolic claims (but see Somma in this volume). Such an assessment of movements reductively simplifies state-movement relations in state co-optation and uncritically subordinates material claims to symbolic ones. This interpretation also implies that material claims—such as access to water, land, or transport—are mere essential services claims (Mainwaring and Viola 1984). They are not, under this perspective, new social movements but archaic struggles.

Second, there are classifications of social movements that stratify struggles according to pre-established requirements. For instance, Touraine (1987, 1988) argued that in Latin America, due to the dependency of the regional economies and the high level of state intervention, struggles have been incapable of producing their historicity. As a result, they are not Social Movements but rather socio-historical movements. Also, Laclau and Mouffe (1985) argued that actors in the periphery of the capitalist system tend to build a division of the political space into two opposing fields, in contrast to those in the center who tend to build a plurality of political spaces with multiple fields of antagonism. Consequently, the periphery's struggles are not democratic but popular, as they have not crossed a "certain" democratic threshold.

A third and last colonial issue is the subordination of cultural differences in the study of Latin American struggles. For instance, Giddens' (2002) analysis of the changes from pre-modernity to modernity would imply an inescapable abandonment of traditional practices. When this analysis is extrapolated to current indigenous, Afro, and peasant struggles in Latin America, such a premise would neutralize the agency of these struggles as their non-modern practices are constitutive of their modes of resistance. Finally, although Melucci (2001) argues that ethnic struggles should not be subordinated to class ones, he exceptionally concedes such subordination to more economically backward contexts. Although all these theories are critical to modernity, paradoxically, when it comes to formally evaluating Latin American movements or where the categories are extrapolated, they—as suggested by Escobar (1997)—resort to modern hierarchies: autonomy-dependency, advanced-backward, development-underdevelopment, center-periphery, and so on. By doing so, they end up paving the way for a scheme in which the South's movements must follow the path traced by those of the North.

So, *what do the DA contribute to the study of social movements?* They provide alternative analyses to the colonial issues such as those described above. However, rather than attempting to provide one correct conclusion, they offer a series of conceptual tools that can *change* the debate's terms, as expressed by Mignolo (2003). Specifically, the DA enable a change of relationship under which knowledge on social movements is produced in dialogue *with* social movements, instead of theorizing *about* social movements.

The DA contribute to change the terms of the debate in social movement studies in three ways. A first DA contribution is *to expand the temporal scales*, questioning the continuities and ruptures of colonial processes as something that is still alive in the region's construction of its modernity. This contribution is not limited to specifying that colonial temporality in Latin America (fifteenth to nineteenth centuries) is different from the one explored by postcolonial studies (nineteenth and twentieth centuries). What is argued is for a different way of relating to the past and the future by acknowledging other temporalities underlying both colonial processes and the struggles against them, which challenges the linear and progressive understanding of time.

Concerning the past, the DA seek to enable analyses that, without anachronistically rejecting changes, trace prevailing colonial structures, dynamics, and practices. Here, Rivera-Cusicanqui's (2010b) analysis is essential, as she examines the place of the indigenous in Bolivian society in what she refers to as the *colonial wound*. A reading of the entire region through the lens of this wound would consist in this simultaneity of being both white and non-white; a burden that—as Rivera-Cusicanqui explains—may be present in the blood but also in practices, landscapes, languages, food, knowledge, objects, corporal attitudes, and elsewhere. Rooted in subjectivity, these dimensions have been denied, despised, and criminalized, not only by the official histories of the region but also by family and autobiographic narratives, and even in terms of self-censorship. With regard to the future, the DA aim to rediscover and create concrete scenarios in which alternatives to colonial burdens could arise (Escobar 2016a).

Concerning the study of social movements, expanding the temporal scales pinpoints the conceptual limits of the category of "social movement," a concern present in the literature (Mires 1993). As pointed out by Gutiérrez (2008) and Rivera-Cusicanqui (2014), the category might fall short of accounting for the complexity of the struggles in the region. As explained by Rivera-Cusicanqui, the category "social movement" falls short of capturing the complexity of the long-term processes of resistance to colonialism in times of world crisis. She adds that the indigenous worlds do not conceive history linearly and, thus, their present struggles contain past and future, and each one involves regression or progression and the repetition or overcoming of the past. Hence, the author proposes the term *anti-colonial struggles* as a much broader category than social movement.

A second DA contribution is *to enrich the geopolitical dimension of knowledge*, with a commitment to positioning the region not as an object or study area. Instead, it is a place of enunciation, which is autonomous and valid for producing knowledge. It is not just a matter of recognizing authors from the South writing in the North. Above all, it requires breaking away from colonial tutelage as maintained by the region's universities since their foundation (Carvalho 2010; Castro 2005b). Thus, Latin America is substituted by other terms such as *Americas* (Marcos 2010); *Nuestramérica*—inspired by José Martí (Gargallo 2012; Segato 2015); *Améfrica*—inspired by the Afro-Brazilian Lélia Gonzalez (1988); *Abya Yala*—the Kuna name for the region (Escobar 2018a; Espinoza, Gómez and Ochoa 2014; Walsh 2006).

When it comes to the study of social movements, all these different practices proposed by DA might lead to conceiving social movement activists as authors. From this perspective, social movements not only provide mere testimonies of activism, but they also actually construct the region's theoretical thought (Curiel 2010). Furthermore, authorship is conceived of as collective and inseparable from embodied practices, such as celebrating, working, dancing, and desiring (Zibechi 2015).

Finally, for some DA scholars, *a situated and close relationship to social movements is fundamental*. Therefore, it is not enough to recognize social movements as producers of knowledge—instead, pedagogical and research processes are developed *with* them. In such cases, there is a deliberate attempt to dilute the distance between theorization and its modes and reception sites. Following Segato (2015), to recognize the conditions that restrict and permit the peoples to *weave* their own historicity. This process might activate scenarios of an apparent dispute relating to the relationship between academia and social movements, and requires—not always without tensions—a negotiation of research practices such as: sharing the space of expertise in academic events, forgoing the use of cryptic scientific language in community events, and negotiating non-academic authorships with editorials. In doing so, in line with the concept of *cognitive territories* (Eyerman and Jamison 1991), the DA recognize social movements' capacity to produce knowledge. But the DA, closer to Cultural Studies, also recognize movements as producers of *extra-academic intellectual practices* (Mato 2002).

With these three contributions, the DA are changing the terms of the debate on the production of knowledge about and with social movements. The DA have opened a window in academia to connect it with the resistance to colonization that social movements had been carrying on for a long time before.

Concepts and Perspectives for Social Movement Studies

This section outlines some of the concepts and perspectives that are especially useful in decolonizing social movements' readings. They are formulated by DA authors and the social movements themselves. They are grouped into four sets, indicating their aims, the decolonizing possibilities each one opens, and the sense in which these concepts change the terms of the debate on Latin American movements.

Some concepts *extend the temporality of struggles*, subverting Latin American social movements' location in a linear narrative with respect to those of the North. It expands modern temporality by considering that colonial processes are constitutive of modernity—considering these two processes as inseparable. For example, the *Modernity/Coloniality* duo (Quijano 2000), the idea of colonialism as not additive but *substantive* to capitalism (Castro, 2005a), and the distinction between *first* and *second modernity* (Dussel 2000). These concepts question both the confinement of social movements' study to the second modernity and the meaning and scope of colonial resistance in the first modernity. The category of *anti-colonial struggles* (Rivera-Cusicanqui 2014) is also relevant here as it shows the continuity between current movements and the long-term resistances forged since colonial times. Notions of this kind destabilize the Eurocentric vision of modernity dominant in the specialized literature and according to which the actors in the region are passive in waiting for the arrival of modernity to their territories. Also, from the perspectives opened by these concepts, neither the forms of oppression persistent in the region nor their resistance are confined to isolated and dehistoricized narratives. In doing so, these concepts challenge diagnoses according to which Latin American social movements have not fully consolidated, and they make explicit how anti-colonial struggles have been challenging modernity for a very long time.

Besides the lineal, DA *recognize other temporalities* such as *cyclic, spiraling,* and *rhythmic.* As Rivera-Cusicanqui (2010a: 55) points out regarding Bolivian indigenous struggles, history is neither linear nor teleological. The past and future are contained in the present, and therefore: "in every situation, the repetition and overcoming of the past are at stake, and they depend more on our words than our actions." As stated by Acossatto (2017), this type of temporal reading does not focus solely on the moments of intensification of popular rebellions. Instead, it attempts to understand the connection, articulation, and even the historical significance between one cycle and another. Gutiérrez (2008), referring to the Bolivian struggles in Chapare, Cochabamba, and El Alto between 2000 and 2005, highlights the importance of looking at the rhythms—rather than just cycles—of protests to avoid prescriptive analyses of them. These ideas complement and, at the same time, challenge the temporal assumptions underlying social movement theories—such as Klandermans' (1998) "protest cycles" or Melucci's (1988) "submerged networks."

DA also warns against the *irreversibility of time.* Movements such as the Colombian indigenous Nasa[1] have been warning against the possibility of a point of no return due to, among other things, extractive economies. In doing so, social movements are showing not yet another crisis of modernity but a crisis of no return. Accordingly, the alternatives they set forth cannot be read as just *new political paradigms* (Offe 1988); they are designing alternative worlds with a future possibilities (Escobar 2016a).

Some *concepts and perspectives that go beyond and counterpoise the state,* which includes three decolonizing initiatives. First, those that show that social movements' demands cannot be spatially circumscribed to nation-states due to the *cross-border nature of struggles.* Such is the case of movements that defend the Amazon (i.e., the Foro Social Panamazónico, which articulates organizations and activists from nine countries within that territory) and the Mapuche struggles at the Chile-Argentina border. Second, there are the *inter-relational and entanglement perspectives* (Escobar 2016b, 2018b) that show that the territories under dispute are unconceivable without their interconnection with the rest of the planet. In this sense, the nation-state cannot be the exclusive interlocutor of movements, as reflected in the Colombian Nasa's demand for the liberation of Mother Earth or the Brazilian *quilombos* movement for which the Earth is not ours, we are the Earth (Bispo 2015). These perspectives resonate with theories that consider the global connections underlying some movements (for instance, Giddens 2002), yet they go beyond, as they reveal the many interdependencies whose concealment has been vital for the centrality of nation-state during modernity. Finally, concepts of *autonomy from the nation-state* recognize that movements develop strategies that depend partially on the state, but also that defending their autonomy vis-à-vis the state is a key element of how they organize themselves. For example, Glagys Tzul-Tzul (2018), referring to the Ixil women's movement in Guatemala, resisting mining and water explorations in an area where they were looking for their disappeared relatives, speaks of *autonomous communal rebuilding* to highlight how communities affected by war have autonomously rebuilt themselves against the state. These concepts help to explain how movements' processes and actions go beyond and counterpoise the state, undermining the supposed lack of autonomy attributed to Latin American movements by some theories. As they focus on the communal, they also extend the function of social movements beyond mediating between civil society and the state, as argued by the political process theory.

Other DA concepts propose an epistemic diversity in which two contrasting types of concepts can be included. The first of them concerns *epistemic reductionism*, which helps to question the tendency to study movements from a supposedly superior scientific, moral, and political locus of enunciation. They include, among others: *coloniality of knowledge* (Lander 2000), *Eurocentrism* (Dussel 2000), *Occidentalism* (Mignolo 2000), *imperialism* (Slater 2008), *Euroexclusivism* (Carvalho 2018), *ecogenoethnocide* (Arboleda 2018), and *sociology of absences* (Sousa Santos 2009). The second group includes concepts that opt for an *affirmative epistemology*. They account for independent thought produced on and from social movements in: *epistemic diversity* (Castro 2005b) and *epistemic pluriversity* (Carvalho 2010), *epistemologies of the South* (Sousa-Santos 2009), *Chí'xi thought* (Rivera-Cusicanqui 2010a, 2018), *afro-epistemology* (García 2006), and *Afro-diasporic thought* (Lao 2007), among others. Both types of concept make it possible to analyze decolonizing processes that encompass, as suggested by Michael Hardt when referring to Bolivian social movements, elements of critique and dismantling, but also of creation (mentioned in Santiesteban Ramírez 2008).

Finally, some concepts *expand the meanings of struggles* in two ways. First, by incorporating diverse systems of oppression and related identities to the analysis of modernity's colonial character. These include the *coloniality of power* (Quijano 2000), which rejects the orthodox Marxist reading of racism as a smokescreen for the "real" struggle of the workers' movement; the *coloniality of being* (Maldonado 2007), which widens the discussion on the ontological dimensions of coloniality; and feminist concepts that problematize colonial critiques: *coloniality of gender* (Lugones 2008), *gender-based violence* (Segato 2016), *patriarchal junction* (Paredes 2013), and *ancestral origin patriarchy* (Cabnal 2010), among others (see Johnson and Sempol in this volume). In resonance with the intersectionality of Black feminism in the United States, these contributions resist a certain tendency to confine movements to a compartmentalized identity.

A second set of DA contributions decenter the human as the defining axis of how movements understand the world and, therefore, how they articulate demands. Among others, these include *relational ontologies* (Cadena 2015) and *analysis of spirituality* (Marcos 2010). From different perspectives, these concepts highlight the heterogeneous nature of the political subjects around which the struggles are articulated. For instance, Afro and indigenous claims exceed how the concept of *new social movements* has situated ethnic struggles. Further, they contribute to the contemporary debates of environmental and animalist movements. These decolonial concepts resonate with Haraway's (1995) and Braidotti's (2009) cyborg feminism, questioning the binary humans and non-humans, in dialogue with Anzaldúa's (2002) Chicano feminism, highlighting the spiritual dimension underlying social struggles.

Decolonizing Readings of the Struggles for the Territory

Many Latin American movements have been involved in disputes concerning the materiality, meaning, and scope of *territory*. The expansion of development projects (agribusiness and mining, among others) has increased the global demand for land and resources (see Christel and Gutiérrez in this volume). These conflicts' implications include overlapping demands on the same geographic areas, the displacement and dispossession of peasants, indigenous people, Black communities, and city and peri-urban inhabitants. Many claims are related to a plurality of issues that are today reconfiguring social disputes around the territory. They include, among others, demands for independence and self-determination, demands that require the identification and visualization of the temporal and spatial scales of the damages caused by development, disputes regarding physical access to portions of land and their elements (water, subsoil, minerals), and disputes for the control of their use and representation (Olarte-Olarte 2019). Thus, the meaning of territory for many social movements is polysemous, as are the multiple practices and strategies for its defense. This is why territories are under dispute in Latin America (Sandoval et al. 2017; Svampa 2008) and being reinvented (Porto-Gonçalves 2009, 2015).

The territorially based struggles in Latin America significantly contribute to the recent discussions on the meaning and scope of the term (Sandoval et al. 2017) even outside the region (Halvorsen 2018), and they manifest some of the region's contributions to a decolonizing understanding of the environment, its resources, and their collective use and management. They question institutional notions of territorial development, the construction of ideas regarding fertility and productivity, and the corporate representations of the physical space to promote investment. In so doing, they destabilize the most orthodox notions of territory that reduce it to an element of state sovereignty (see Halvorsen and Rossi in this volume).

In what follows, we present three decolonizing readings of social struggles for the meaning, use, experience, and representation of the territory. A first perspective on territorial struggles questions the positioning of Latin America as a space that is subaltern (Alimonda 2011; Alimonda, Toro, and Martín 2017; Machado, 2012) and subordinated (Quijano 2000), and therefore can be *exploited, devastated,* and *reconfigured* (Alimonda 2011) according to global economic demands. This perspective invites us to trace the continuities and connections between colonial forms of exploitation and contemporary practices of extraction, confinement, and deprivation of the common use of resources (such as water and soil), as well as certain forms of conservation and tourism. For instance, violence associated to territories that were once created as *quilombos* in Brazil—territories of freedom for Afros in resistance against colonial slavery—are considered today strategic areas that have triggered renewed forms of violence (Bispo 2015; Porto-Gonçalves 2009: 62). Another example is the continuity between forms of colonial mining and contemporary domination by mining companies in Peru, which today are resisted by, among others, the Coordinadora Nacional de Comunidades Afectadas por la Minería and the Asociación Interétnica de Desarrollo de la Selva Peruana (Alimonda 2015). Such perspectives help to render visible the relationship between knowledge and space, identifying the knowledge and modes of life that have been eliminated, excluded, or subordinated (Porto-Gonçalves 2009). Subalternization brings with it a certain *epistemic reductionism*, which geopolitically relocates Latin America as a producer, of course, of raw material, but also of readily available territory-based knowledge.

Besides, as some elites and institutions in the region promote large-scale extractive practices despite the rights of collective territories and alternative views to development, manifestations of internal colonization persist in the region. Examples include supporting the monopoly of seed production and trade, and aggressive forms of labor reconversion of the agricultural sector against food self-sufficiency economies. Reports of social movements in and Costa Rica, Nicaragua, and Panama resisting monocultures of banana, pineapple, and oil palm, offer essential clues of how to analyze this phenomenon's consequences.

A second decolonial reading highlights the *relational nature of territory*, referring to the *sense of place* shared by multiple social movements in the region. This sense of place includes symbolic-cultural dimensions, transgenerational experiences, and an interdependent understanding of land and its elements. Escobar (2016b: 18) described the relational nature of the territory as a "dense network of interrelations," highlighting the links between humans and non-humans. When referring to the mangroves of the Colombian Pacific, Escobar (2015: 348) argues that there is "an infinite set of practices carried out by all kinds of beings and life forms, involving a complex organic and inorganic materiality of water, minerals, degrees of salinity, forms of energy (sun, tides, moon, relations of force), and so forth." The relationality implies that "things and beings are their relations; they do not exist prior to them" and that, therefore: "living beings of all kinds constitute each other's conditions for existence" (Escobar 2016b: 18). This relational perspective reveals notions of territory that exceed the local to expose how their exploitation and use can endanger the planet's survival and its species (Porto-Gonçalves 2015). It also sheds light on the complex connections between humans and incorporating non-human entities (e.g., mountains or rivers) in political spaces (Cadena 2010). This relationality is reflected in many Latin American movements. For example, the Coordinadora de Comunidades Mapuche Williche por la Defensa del Territorio Willi Lafken Weychan has mobilized to defend the territory linked to an ancestral worldview and the promotion of *kume felen* (good living). Here, the notion of territory is based on "reciprocity among the community and the *itrofill mongen* or biodiversity" (Comunicaciones OC

2018). This reciprocity plays a central role in examining colonization processes and their relationship to the territory and goes beyond any state representation. It can also be read in cross-generational terms to ensure that future generations can continue to enjoy biodiversity in their territories.

Another example can be found in the *Liberación de la Madre Tierra* Project implemented by part of the Nasa peoples in the Colombian Southwest. For them, an understanding of the territory is inseparable from a dispute for food autonomy, protection from soil depletion, and the Nasa people's permanence in their region (Olarte-Olarte 2019). Liberation, as the struggle to recover ancestral territories now occupied by sugarcane monocultures, is based on a notion and experience of nature where there is no break between the human and the non-human. Therefore, nature expands, as described by Escobar (2018b), through a continuous universe where everything is alive.

A last example of a relational view of the territory is expressed by the peasant and Maya indigenous struggles against deforestation and its effects on beekeeping in Mexico's Chenes region. Their claim against increasing deforestation to make way for the agro-industrial cultivation of genetically modified soybean reveals the fluidity of the territory and the limitations of understanding this, based on a notion of property that conceives it as divisible.

By highlighting the relational nature of the territory underlying the struggles, the DA contribute to transdisciplinary discussions (from critical geography, anthropology, and political ecology, among others) that challenge the limited and fragmented understandings of land, its elements, and the multiple manners in which people relate to them (see Halvorsen and Rossi in this volume). This perspective potentiates the movements' politics of place, regarding, in particular, their connection to a colonial past, contemporary manifestations of coloniality, global processes, and internal colonialism.

Finally, we have the links between the meaning of territory and the intensification of communalizing practices and knowledge, such as *communing, the commons, communalization, community*, and *the communal*. From the perspective these practices and knowledge promote, the control, use, management, and access to water, air, soil, or intangible goods such as traditional knowledge or communal work, cannot be subject to confinement, encroachment, and privatization, suppression or depletion. They seek to avoid or resist forms of excludability and subtractability. Instances of communalization include cases of community-based water management initiatives, such as the Honduran Consejo Cívico de Organizaciones Populares e Indígenas; peasant struggles for the defense of the commons, such as the Coordinadora Latinoamericana de Organizaciones; the defense of food autonomy as established by the Comité de Unidad Campesina de Guatemala and the Venezuelan Cecosesola Network; and struggles for the preservation, freedom, and exchange of seeds such as the Red de Mujeres Rurales of Costa Rica or the Red de Semillas Libres in Colombia.

These communalizing practices and knowledge of Latin American movements could give rise to three axes of decolonizing the territory's interpretations. First, the renewed interest in understanding, naming, and attaining the *communal and the communitarian* (Escobar 2016a; Gutiérrez 2015). There is an ongoing effort to record and theorize the initiatives of multiple social movements to rethink and mobilize the communal (Paredes 2013). In this sense, as argued by Escobar (2016a: 208), a community must be understood "in profoundly historical terms that are open and nonessential" and as a constant result of autonomy understood as a process that enables the preservation of "its capacity for self-creation." In this respect, Rivera-Cusicanqui (2015: 145) highlights the creation of a community that underlies food production in the Andes: "a community of human and non-human beings, between human and non-human subjects, between humans and the products of human work, between humans and the products of the work of other species."

The second axis is the *resistance to considering nature an economic resource*. This interpretation articulates communalizing practices and knowledge of social movements with a broad critique of how the orthodox economy excludes developmental projects' socio-environmental consequences. Svampa (2011), in her analysis of what she calls the eco-territorial turn of Latin American movements, refers to the tension between their practices of the *commoning*, vis-à-vis the goals of the extractive industries. While extractivism treats and intervenes natural resources as commodities, movements consider natural elements inseparable from territorial dispossession processes.

The third and last axis concerns the *translation of communalizing practices and knowledge as alternatives to development*—something many struggles have done in the past. In following these processes, DA have contributed to the movements' current study in two main ways. On the one hand, DA have contributed to identifying the developmental logic behind the exploitation of nature as resource to the capitalist economy. On the other hand, DA have contributed to movements' demands to remain in a specific place (*permanecer en el Territorio*), something at the core of movements' alternative proposals to dominant developmental projects. In Latin America, this is not just another demand among many. Remaining in a place is deeply linked to the survival of the multiple livelihoods that constitute the region's rich diversity and the continuity of many solidarity and communitarian economies. This struggle is subject to increasingly lethal threats and attacks to social activists. Last, the participation of the DA in the practices of food autonomy is opening a promising agenda. The production of alternatives to the dominant developmental projects redefines movements' struggles as more than mere survival strategies.

Conclusions for a Research Agenda

In contrast to most of the literature on social movements, a decolonizing approach to Latin American movements vindicates movements as actors that denounce modernity limits and offer alternatives to it. A decolonizing reading of struggles provides new research agendas and analytical avenues concerning colonial oppression's continuities and transformations. Incorporating the notion of *long-term, anti-colonial struggles* demand the temporal and spatial expansion of collective action analyses and, with it, a problematization of the same category of social movements. Besides, the DA critique of different epistemic reductionism forms in the region contributes to understanding and approaching Latin American movements as producers of knowledge while continuously challenging academic practices to make research possible *with* social movements.

Rather than undermining this approach, the variety of perspectives and work agendas in the DA account for the tensions and complexities of the colonial wound, turning it into a suitable place for a dynamic reflection committed to Latin American movements' demands. Nevertheless, there is still work to be done by the DA regarding the study of and with social movements. One challenge is to further consider the manifold character of the colonial trajectories throughout the region to decenter the Spanish ruling period as the main point of reference. Another challenge would be to undertake a more detailed analysis of colonial processes' role for contemporary capitalist dynamics that constitute the target of multiple struggles. However, another challenge concerns the need for a self-critique regarding two demanding issues. First, the gap that the DA jargon open between academia and social movements and, second, the clouding of dissenting positions within DA itself regarding authoritarian rulers that conceived themselves as progressive. Besides, to follow the increasing exchanges among movements—particularly artistic practices—more closely constitutes a fourth challenge. A fifth is to recognize the contributions of feminist intellectuals more explicitly and give more weight to the cross-generational dimension of struggles, as suggested by territorial movements.

Finally, in virtue of the growing centrality of territorial struggles for the region, DA might contribute to a research program on communalizing practices and knowledge crucial for Latin America movements. Beyond the region, this agenda would likely give rise to new alternatives to hegemonic forms of production while expanding the so-called commons' scope and theorization.

Note

1. Asociación de Cabildos Indígenas del Norte del Cauca (ACIN), https://nasaacin.org/, accessed August 16, 2019.

References

Accossatto, Romina (2017), "Colonialismo interno y memoria colectiva. Aportes de Silvia Rivera-Cusicanqui al estudio de los movimientos sociales y las identificaciones políticas," *Economía y Sociedad* 21(36), 167–81.

Alimonda, Héctor (2011), "La colonialidad de la naturaleza. Una aproximación a la Ecología Política Latinoamericana," in Héctor Alimonda (eds.), *La naturaleza colonizada: Ecología política y minería en América Latina*, 21–60 (Buenos Aires: CLACSO).

Alimonda, Héctor (2015), "Ecología política latinoamericana y pensamiento crítico: vanguardias arraigadas," *Desenvolvimento e Meio Ambiente* 35, 161–68.

Alimonda, Héctor, Catalina Toro and Facundo Martín (eds.) (2017), *Ecología política latinoamericana* (Buenos Aires: CLACSO).
Anzaldúa, Gloria E. (2002), "now let us shift ... the path of Conocimiento ... inner work, public acts," in Gloria E. Anzaldúa and AnneLouise Keating (eds.), *This Bridge We Call Home: Radical Visions for Transformation*, 540–78 (London: Routledge).
Arboleda, Santiago (2018), "Defensa ambiental, derechos humanos y ecogenoetnocidio afrocolombiano," *Pesquisa em Educação Ambiental* 13(1), 10–27.
Artavia, Víctor (2005), "Crítica al giro decolonial: entre el anticomunismo y el populismo reformista," *Revista SoB* (29), 337–81.
Braidotti, Rosi (2009) *Transposiciones: Sobre la ética nómada* (Barcelona: Gedisa).
Beverley, John (2002), "La persistencia del subalterno," *Revista Nómadas* 17, 48–56.
Bispo Dos Santos, Antônio (2015), *Colonizaçao, quilomobos e significados* (Brasilia: INCTI).
Cabnal, Lorena (2010), "Acercamiento a la construcción de la propuesta de pensamiento epistémico de las mujeres indígenas feministas comunitarias de Abya Yala," in ACSUR-Las Segovias (eds.) *Feminismos diversos: el feminismo comunitario*, 11–25 (Madrid: Asociación para la Cooperación con el Sur).
Cadena, Marisol (2010), "Indigenous Cosmopolitics in the Andes: Conceptual Reflections beyond 'Politics'," *Cultural Anthropology* 25(2), 334–70.
Cadena, Marisol (2015), *Earth Beings: Ecologies of Practice across Andean Worlds* (Durham, NC: Duke University Press).
Carvalho, José (2010), "Los estudios culturales en América Latina: interculturalidad, acciones afirmativas y encuentro de saberes," *Tabula Rasa* (12) 229–51.
Carvalho, José (2018), "Encontro de saberes e cotas epistêmicas: um movimento de descolonização do mundo acadêmico brasileiro," in Joaze Costa, Nelson Maldonado-Torres, and Ramón Grosfoguel (eds.) *Decolonialidade e pensamento afrodiaspórico*, 79–106 (Belo Horizonte: Autêntica).
Castro, Santiago (2005a), *La poscolonialidad explicada a los niños* (Bogotá: Instituto Pensar-PUJ).
Castro, Santiago (2005b), *La hybris del punto cero: ciencia, raza e Ilustración en la Nueva Granada (1750–1816)* (Bogotá: Editorial PUJ).
Castro, Santiago and Ramón Grosfoguel (eds.) (2007), *El giro decolonial. Reflexiones para una diversidad epistémica más allá del capitalismo global* (Bogotá: SHE).
Comunicaciones OC (2018). "Declaración pública: Coordinadora de comunidades Mapuche williche por la defensa del territorio willi lafken weychan." Available at: https://observatorio.cl/declaracion-publica-coordinadora-de-comunidades-mapuche-williche-por-la-defensa-del-territorio-willi-lafken-weychan/.
Curiel, Ochy (2010), "Hacia la construcción de un feminismo descolonizado," in Yuderkys Espinosa, Diana Gómez, and Karina Ochoa (eds.) (2014), *Tejiendo de otro modo: feminismo, epistemología y apuestas descoloniales en Abya Yala*, 325–54 (Popayán: UniCauca).
Dussel, Enrique (2000), "Europa, modernidad y eurocentrismo," in Edgardo Lander (ed.), *La colonialidad del saber: eurocentrismo y ciencias sociales. Perspectivas latinoamericanas*, 41–53 (Buenos Aires: CLACSO).
Escobar, Arturo (1997), "Imaginando un futuro: pensamiento crítico, desarrollo y movimientos sociales," in López Maya, Margarita (ed.) *Desarrollo y Democracia*, 135–72 (Caracas: Nueva Sociedad).
Escobar, Arturo (2003), "Mundos y conocimientos de otro modo: El programa de investigación de modernidad/colonialidad latinoamericano," *Tabula Rasa* 1, 51–86.

Escobar, Arturo (2015), "Commons in the Pluriverse," in David Bollier and Silke Helfrich (eds.), *Patterns of Commoning*, 348–60 (Amherst, MA: The Commons Strategies Group).

Escobar, Arturo (2016a), *Autonomía y diseño: La realización de lo comunal* (Popayán: Editorial UC).

Escobar, Arturo (2016b), "Thinking-feeling with the Earth: Territorial Struggles and the Ontological Dimension of the Epistemologies of the South," *Revista de Antropología Iberoamericana* 11(1), 11–32.

Escobar, Arturo (2018a), *Otro posible es posible. Caminando hacia las transiciones desde Abya Yala/Afro/Latino-América* (Bogotá: Ediciones desde Abajo).

Escobar, Arturo (2018b), *Designs for the Pluriverse: Radical Interdependence, Autonomy, and the Making of Worlds* (Durham, NC: Duke University Press).

Espinosa, Yuderkys, Diana Gómez, and Karina Ochoa (eds.) (2014), *Tejiendo de otro modo: feminismo, epistemología y apuestas descoloniales en Abya Yala* (Popayán: UniCauca).

Eyerman, Ron and Andrew Jamison (1991), *Social Movements: A Cognitive Approach* (Cambridge: Polity).

Flórez-Flórez, Juliana (2005), "Aportes postcoloniales (latinoamericanos) al estudio de los movimientos sociales," *Tabula Rasa* 3, 73–96.

Flórez-Flórez, Juliana (2014), *Lecturas emergentes. El giro decolonial en los movimientos sociales* (Bogotá: Editorial PUJ).

Foweraker, Joe (1995), *Theorizing Social Movements* (London: Pluto Press).

García, Jesús (2006), *Caribeñidad: afroespiritualidad y afroepistemología* (Caracas: Editorial El Perro y la Rana).

Gargallo, Francesca (2012), *Feminismos desde Abya Yala. Ideas y proposiciones de las mujeres de 607 pueblos en nuestra América* (Bogotá: Ediciones desde abajo).

Giddens, Anthony [1990] (2002), *Las consecuencias de la modernidad* (Madrid: Alianza).

Gurr, Ted (1970), *Why Men Rebel* (Princeton, NJ: Princeton University Press).

Gutiérrez, Raquel (2008), *Los ritmos del Pachakuti: movilización y levantamiento indígena-popular en Bolivia (2000–2005)* (Buenos Aires: Tinta Limón).

Gutiérrez, Raquel (2015), *Horizontes comunitario-populares. Producción de lo común más allá de las políticas estado-céntricas* (Madrid: Traficantes de Sueños).

Halvorsen, Sam (2018), "Decolonising Territory: Dialogues with Latin American Knowledges and Grassroots Strategies," *Progress in Human Geography* 43(5), 790–814.

Haraway, Donna (1995), *Ciencia, cyborgs y mujeres. La reinvención de la naturaleza* (Madrid: Cátedra).

Klandermans, Bert (1998), "La necesidad de un estudio longitudinal de la participación en movimientos sociales," in Benjamín Tejerina and Pedro Ibarra (eds.), *Los movimientos sociales: transformaciones políticas y cambio cultural*, 271–90 (Madrid: Trotta).

Laclau, Ernesto and Chantal Mouffe [1985] (1997), *Hegemonía y estrategia socialista: hacia una radicalización de la democracia* (Madrid: Siglo XXI).

Lander, Edgardo (2000), "Ciencias sociales: saberes coloniales y eurocéntricos," in Edgardo Lander (ed.), *La colonialidad del saber: eurocentrismo y ciencias sociales. Perspectivas latinoamericanas*, 11–42 (Buenos Aires: CLACSO).

Lao, Agustín (2007), "Hilos descoloniales. Trans-localizando los espacios de la diáspora Africana," *Tabula Rasa* 7, 47–79.

Le Point (2018), "Le 'décolonialisme', une stratégie hégémonique: L'appel de 80 intellectuels," *Le point* (November 28), https://www.lepoint.fr/politique/le-decolonialisme-une-strategie-hegemonique-l-appel-de-80-intellectuels-28-11-2018-2275104_20.php.

LeBon, Gustave (1895), *Psicología de las masas. Estudio sobre la psicología de las multitudes* (Madrid: Morata).

Lugones, María (2008), "Colonialidad y género," *Tabula Rasa* 9, 73–101.

Machado, Horacio (2012), "Los dolores de Nuestra América y la condición neocolonial. Extractivismo y biopolítica de la expropiación," *Observatorio Latinoamericano de Ciencias Sociales* 32, 51–66.

Mainwaring, Scott and Eduardo Viola, "New Social Movements, Political Culture and Democracy: Brazil and Argentina in the 1980s," *Telos* 61, 17–54.

Maldonado-Torres, Nelson (2007), "Sobre la colonialidad del ser: Contribuciones al desarrollo de un concepto," in Santiago Castro and Ramón Grosfoguel (eds.), *El giro decolonial, reflexiones para una diversidad epistémica más allá del capitalismo global*, 127–68 (Bogotá: IESCO-UC and Instituto Pensar-PUJ).

Marcos, Sylvia (2010), *Cruzando fronteras: mujeres indígenas y feminismos abajo y a la izquierda* (San Cristóbal de Las Casas: CIDECI-Universidad de la Tierra).

Mato, Daniel (2002) *Estudios y otras prácticas intelectuales latinoamericanas en cultura y poder* (Buenos Aires: CLACSO).

Mbembe, Achille (1996), *La naissance du maquis dans le Sud-Cameroun (1920–1960)* (Paris: Karthala).

Melucci, Alberto (1988), "Social Movements and the Democratization of Everyday Life," in John Keane (ed.), *Civil Society and the State: New European Perspectives*, 245–60 (London: Verso).

Melucci, Alberto (2001), *Vivencia y Convivencia: Teoría social para una era de la información* (Madrid: Trota).

Mendiola, Ignacio (2002), *Movimientos sociales: Definición y teoría* (Barcelona: UOC).

Mignolo, Walter [2000] (2003), *Historias locales/diseños globales: Colonialidad, conocimientos subalternos y pensamiento fronterizo* (Madrid: Akal).

Mires, Fernando (1993), *El discurso de la miseria o la crisis de la sociología en América Latina* (Caracas: Nueva Sociedad).

Offe, Claus (1988), *Partidos políticos y nuevos movimientos sociales* (Madrid: Sistema).

Olarte-Olarte, María Carolina (2019), "From Territorial Peace to Territorial Pacification: Anti-Riot Police Powers and Socio-Environmental Dissent in the Implementation of Colombia's Peace Agreement," *Revista de Estudios Sociales* 67, 26–39.

Paredes, Julieta [2010] (2013), *Hilando Fino. Desde el feminismo comunitario* (Mexico: Comunidad Mujeres Creando Comunidad).

Porto-Gonçalves, Carlos (2009), *Territorialidades y lucha por el territorio en América Latina: geografía de los movimientos sociales en América Latina* (Caracas: IVIC).

Porto-Gonçalves, Carlos (2015), "Del desarrollo a la autonomía: la reinvención de los territorios. El desarrollo como noción colonial," *Kavilando* 2, 157–61.

Quijano, Aníbal (2000), "Colonialidad del poder, eurocentrismo y América Latina," in Edgardo Lander (ed.), *La colonialidad del saber: eurocentrismo y ciencias sociales. Perspectivas latinoamericanas*, 201–46 (Buenos Aires: CLACSO).

Santiesteban Ramírez, Héctor (2008), "Introducción," in Toni Negri, Michael Hardt, Judith Revel, Giuseppe Cocco, Álvaro García Linera, and Luis Tapia (ed.), *Imperio, multitud y sociedad abigarrada*, 7–9 (La Paz: CLACSO—Muela del Diablo—Comuna—Vicepresidencia de la República).

Restrepo, Eduardo and Axel Rojas (2010). *Inflexión decolonial: Fuentes, conceptos y cuestionamientos* (Popayán: Editorial Universidad del Cauca).

Rivera-Cusicanqui, Silvia (2010a), *Ch'ixinakax utxiwa: Una reflexión sobre prácticas y discursos descolonizadores* (Buenos Aires: Tinta Limón).

Rivera-Cusicanqui, Silvia [1984] (2010b), *Oprimidos, pero no vencidos: Luchas del campesinado aymara y qhechwa 1900–1980* (Querétaro: La Mirada Salvaje).

Rivera-Cusicanqui, Silvia (2014), *Hambre de huelga: Ch'ixinakax Utxiwa y otros textos* (Querétaro: La Mirada Salvaje).

Rivera-Cusicanqui, Silvia (2015), *Sociología de la imagen: Miradas ch'ixi desde la historia andina* (Buenos Aires: Tinta Limón).

Rivera-Cusicanqui, Silvia (2018), *Un mundo Ch'ixi es posible: Ensayos desde un presente en crisis* (Buenos Aires: Tinta Limón).

Sandoval, María, Robertsdotter, Andrea and Paredes, Myriam (2017), "Space, Power and Locality: The Contemporary Use of Territorio in Latin American Geography," *Journal of Latin American Geography* 16(1), 43–67.

Segato, Rita (2015), *La crítica de la colonialidad en ocho ensayos: Y una antropología por demanda* (Buenos Aires, Prometeo).

Segato, Rita (2016), *La guerra contra las mujeres* (Madrid: Traficantes de sueños).

Slater, David (2008), "Repensando la geopolítica del conocimiento," *Tabula Rasa* 8, 335–58.

Smelser, Neil (1962), *Theory of Collective Behavior* (New York: The Free Press).

Sousa-Santos, Boaventura (2009), *Una epistemología de sur: La reinvención del conocimiento y la emancipación social* (México: Siglo XXI—CLACSO).

Svampa, Maristella (2008), *Cambio de época: Movimientos sociales y poder político* (Buenos Aires: Siglo XXI—CLACSO).

Svampa, Maritsella (2011), "Extractivismo neodesarrollista y movimientos sociales ¿un giro ecoterritorial hacia nuevas alternativas? Más allá del desarrollo," in Miriam Lang and Dunia Mokrani (eds.), *Más allá del desarrollo. Grupo permanente de trabajo sobre alternativas al desarrollo*, 185–218 (Quito: Abya Yala and Fundación Rosa Luxemburgo).

Tarde, Gabriel [1901] (1986), *La opinión y la multitud* (Madrid: Taurus).

Touraine, Alan (1987), *Actores sociales y sistemas políticos en América Latina*. (Santiago de Chile: PREALC/OIT).

Touraine, Alain (1988), *La parole et le sang: Politique et societé en Ameriqué Latine* (Paris: Edition Odile).

Tuhiwai, Linda (1999), *Decolonizing Methodologies: Research and Indigenous Peoples* (London: Zed Books).

Tzul-Tzul, Gladys (2018), *Sistemas de gobierno comunales indígenas: Mujeres y tramas de parentesco Chuimeq'ena'* (México: Libertad bajo palabra).

Von Stein, Lorenz [1850] (1981), *Movimientos sociales y monarquía* (Madrid: CEPC).

Walsh, Catherine (2006), *Interculturalidad, descolonización del estado y del conocimiento* (Buenos Aires: Del Signo).

Zibechi, Raúl (2015), *Descolonializar el pensamiento crítico y las prácticas emancipatorias* (Bogotá: Ediciones desde abajo).

PART II

MAIN PROCESSES AND DYNAMICS

CHAPTER 9

PROTEST WAVES IN LATIN AMERICA
Facilitating Conditions and Outcomes

PAUL ALMEIDA

Introduction

This chapter highlights the dynamics of waves of protest in Latin America. Although protest waves occur under special circumstances and are relatively infrequent, they have transformed the political landscape of the Americas. Protest waves have led to a variety of results, including revolutionary mobilizations (see Martí i Puig and Álvarez in this volume), leftist electoral triumphs, backlash state repression reaching near genocidal proportions (see Brockett in this volume), and more moderate policy reforms. Activists and popular organizations also emulate and locally adopt the idioms and ideologies in world society to provide unity and cohesion to sustain a cycle of contention over the long run. To date, scholars have largely discussed protest waves in terms of transnational processes or national level processes (Beck 2014; Weyland 2014). This chapter covers *national level protest waves* where the bulk of existing studies have focused and developed the concept of a protest wave or cycle. At the national level, precipitating conditions and outcomes of protest waves are analyzed.

Basic Dynamics of National Waves of Protest

During cycles or waves of protest, many sectors of society participate (e.g., NGOs, students, civil servants, indigenous people, informal sector workers, peasants, etc.)

and often employ increasingly confrontational tactics. Thus, a protest wave is a rapid expansion of social movement action in geographical scale, diversity of participating social classes and sectors, and amount of disruptive activity. Scholars also interchange the concept of a cycle of protest with "protest cycles" and "protest waves." Such waves are examined in a variety of contexts including advanced capitalist industrialized democracies, repressive regimes, lesser developed countries, and earlier historical settings. Protest cycle research focuses on the emergence of protest waves, internal dynamics and the spread of actions within a cycle, and the political and cultural outcomes left in the aftermath of such large-scale contention. Tarrow (1989: 14–15) states, "Protest becomes a protest cycle when it is diffused to several sectors of the population, is highly organized, and is widely used as the instrument to put forward demands." Tarrow also hypothesizes that cycles of protest have a parabolic pattern. That is, political institutions open and resources expand in such a way that encourage protest activity to increase for one or a few social movements, such as student movements in universities, and quickly spread to other groups (such as urban labor, rural workers, and public employees) by providing them with new occasions to act and highlighting the vulnerability of particular state and economic agencies and political elites.

Facilitating Conditions of Latin American Protest Waves

There are at least five facilitating conditions that lead to a widespread outbreak of protest or series of campaigns from multiple sectors eventuating in a wave of contention. These conditions include: (1) an elaborate organizational infrastructure, (2) periods of political liberalization and widening political opportunities, (3) ongoing acts of state repression, (4) widespread economic threats attributed to the state, and (5) unifying narratives. An extensive organizational infrastructure is a necessary but insufficient condition for a protest wave to develop. Other motivating conditions such as political liberalization, state repression, or economic threats must also enter the national environment on a large-scale. A unifying narrative or master frame provides meaning to the diverse sectors participating in the wave.

Organizational Infrastructures

Associational ties and solidarity networks need to be established on a wide scale in order for a protest wave to ascend. These social bonds generally derive from already mobilized groups as well as everyday organizations. Already mobilized sectors include civic associations, labor unions, unemployed workers' organizations, militant political parties, indigenous people's federations, and rural cooperatives (Rossi 2017). Everyday organizations include religious bodies, educational institutions, NGOs, soup kitchens, soccer leagues, and neighborhood associations, to name a few (Bobea 1999). Protest waves begin by activating both sets of organizations. The social sectors with mobilization potential also vary by time period of economic development and across demographic and cultural characteristics of individual countries (see Rossi in this volume).

Prior to World War II, agricultural and mineral exports dominated the economic activities of the region. Hence, rural labor, including indigenous peoples, along with urban craft unions, and smaller but influential groups (such as students, teachers, middle class professionals, and civil servants) were the key protagonists participating in protest waves (Almeida 2016). At times, oppositional leftist parties aided by linking these groups together, especially socialist and communist parties (Becker 2008). The above groups were active in the protest waves in El Salvador (1930–1932); Cuba (1930–1935); and Guatemala (1944–1954) (Ching, López Bernal, and Tilley 2011).

After World War II, Latin America entered the era of state-led economic development with a rapid expansion of the public and social infrastructure. This increased the mobilization potential for waves of protest by generating a larger set of organizations and social institutions from which collective action could emerge on a much broader scale in terms of the number of participants and geographical reach. These state-led development changes between the 1940s and 1980s included the massive buildup of public schools, administrative offices, universities, hospitals and clinics, industrial manufacturing, highways, public utilities, and overall urbanization. Between the 1950s and 1980s, we see the leading sectors in protest waves or attempted waves emerging from these state-development institutions such as university students and manufacturing workers in Argentina in the late 1960s (e.g., the *Cordobazo*) and similar sectors in the Bolivian nationalist-populist Revolution of 1952, as well as students, public school teachers, transport workers, and manufacturing workers in El Salvador's non-violent protest wave between 1967 and 1972 (Almeida 2008). Similar coalitions of groups, with labor unions in the vanguard, participated in the protest wave against austerity cuts in Peru between 1976 and 1978 (Roberts 1998).

The state-development sector also lives on in the neoliberal period (between the 1980s and 2010s) in terms of providing the organizational infrastructure for oppositional protest waves to economic liberalization policies (Almeida 2015). There are two main rationales for the critical role of the state infrastructure as the organizational backbone to protest waves in the neoliberal era. First, with the weakening of traditional labor unions and peasant cooperatives, the state infrastructure offers some of the few remaining institutions to launch a protest wave. This would include public schools, universities, hospitals, and other components of the state first developed in the post-World War II period. Such institutions group large numbers of people and are distributed across the national territory. Second, these same institutions are often faced with economic threats under neoliberal policies via potential cutbacks in funding, wages, and even privatization. These economic threats create the motivations for public sector institutions and groups to serve in vanguard roles in protest waves in the neoliberal period. Sosa (2013) has shown such a pattern in two separate protest waves in Honduras

(1990–1993 and 1999–2004) whereby public school teachers and public hospital workers participated with the highest frequency in the protest cycles. In another comparative study of anti-neoliberal protest waves across six Central American countries, public school teachers, university students, and public sector employees served as core actors in all major campaigns (Almeida 2014).

Also in the neoliberal period, NGOs and oppositional political parties play fundamental roles within the organizational infrastructure. The actions and duties of NGOs in terms of collective action have mixed findings. Some view them as de-mobilizing agents often tied to foreign interests (Bretón 2001). Others have empirically established NGOs increasing the rate of protest (Boulding 2014). While NGOs act as a broad category that ranges from Alcoholics' Anonymous groups to rural women's cooperatives, they offer a potential everyday organization that can be appropriated for social movement campaigns. In the neoliberal period as the state continues to withdraw from its obligations to social welfare and social citizenship, NGOs are some of the only organizational units that engage in routine interaction with marginalized urban and rural communities. Hence, in major waves of anti-neoliberal protest in the early 2000s in Guatemala, El Salvador, and Nicaragua (Almeida 2014) as well as Bolivia (Boulding 2014), a variety of NGOs have mobilized subaltern populations to participate (Yashar 2005).

Oppositional political parties provided coordinating resources in earlier protest waves in the 1930s in Costa Rica, Cuba, and El Salvador, especially communist and socialist parties. In the neoliberal era with democratization, oppositional parties are a common feature in consolidating protest waves. Opposition parties are organized in many regions within a country. In order to remain competitive and to grow in electoral strength they need to take on issues with public opinion support. One avenue to garner mass appeal for left-of-center parties that lack the financial resources of traditional and elite parties involves engaging in social movement campaigns. By taking on unfavorable privatization policies, free trade agreements, or subsidy cuts by mobilizing party members and others in the streets, opposition parties build support for the next electoral cycle.

Examples abound of small and large leftist and populist parties playing major coordinating roles in protest waves against neoliberal policies and structural adjustment between 1990 and the 2010s. This list includes: the Frente Sandinista de Liberación Nacional (FSLN) in Nicaragua in the early 1990s, Frente País Solidario (FREPASO), local Peronist chapters, and smaller leftist parties in Argentina between 1997 and 2000 (Arce and Mangonnet 2013; Silva 2009); Pachakutik in Ecuador in the late 1990s (Becker 2010); Movimiento al Socialismo (MAS) and Movimiento Indígena Pachakuti (MIP) in Bolivia between 1999 and 2005 (Postero 2017); the Frente Farabundo Martí para la Liberación Nacional (FMLN) in El Salvador in the early 2000s; and the Libertad y Refundación (LIBRE) party in Honduras in the 2010s. Often, the protest wave begins by the oppositional party supporting a particular campaign against a specific neoliberal policy measure such as the MORENA party's resistance to PEMEX privatization and the fuel price hikes in Mexico in 2016 and 2017 (the *gasolinazo*). If multiple campaigns occur close together in time, momentum may build into a full-blown protest wave (della Porta 2013).

Another feature of the organizational infrastructure that is often associated with protest waves is a multi-sectoral structure or coalition of popular organizations that survives from campaign to campaign contributing to sustaining large-scale contention over time and across the nation. These multi-sectoral coalitions often include the types of organizations mentioned above. A loosely coupled federation of civil society groups enhances the scale of "associational power" (Silva 2009).

Multi-sectoral coalitions were behind protest waves in earlier historical periods such as the Bloque Popular Revolucionario (BPR), Frente de Acción Popular Unificado (FAPU), and the Coordinadora Revolucionaria de las Masas (CRM) in El Salvador (between 1974 and 1980) and the Movimiento Popular Unificado (MPU) in Nicaragua (Camacho and Menjívar 1985). Such coalitions are even more commonplace in the more recent waves of protest against economic liberalization in the region over the past twenty years (Almeida and Pérez Martín 2022). These examples include: the Bloque Popular, the Coordinadora Nacional de Resistencia Popular (CNRP), and the Frente Nacional de Resistencia Popular (FNRP) in Honduras; the Central de Trabajadores de la Argentina (CTA) and the Corriente Clasista Combativa (CCC) in Argentina; the Coordinadora de Movimientos Sociales in Ecuador; the Frente Nacional por la Defensa de los Derechos Económicos y Sociales (Frenadeso) in Panama; the Red Nacional de Defensa de los Consumidores (RNDC) and the Coordinadora Social in Nicaragua; the Estado Mayor in Bolivia; the Frente Nacional de Lucha (FNL) in Guatemala; the Alianza Ciudadana contra la Privatización (ACCP) and the Movimiento de Resistencia—12 de Octubre in El Salvador; and Frente Nacional de Defensa de los Bienes Públicos y el Patrimonio Nacional in Paraguay.

In the second decade of the twenty-first century, internet communication technologies (ICTs) and social media have added another layer to the organizational infrastructure (see Treré and Harlow in this volume). Castells (2013) contends that new ICT and social media platforms open up a historically unprecedented ability for "mass self-communication" by less powerful groups. Since the tremendous growth in access by ordinary citizens to the internet in the 2010s, the technologies have played a significant part in every major wave of protest in Latin America, including Central American countries with relatively less ICT access than their more powerful neighbors to the south and north. For example, the wave of protest that began over transit fares in Brazil in 2013 tapped into ICTs and social media. As Penna, Rosa, and Pereyra (2017: 105) state, "the 2013 demonstrations were organized mainly through social media, such as Twitter, Facebook and WhatsApp, and within two months they reached national scale, mobilizing millions of people in different cities." Von Bülow (2018) found that the majority of student federations in the Chilean cycle of education protest from 2011 to 2016 maintained Twitter accounts and websites, but that social media communication within the wave also reproduced traditional organizational hierarchies between movement leaders and the mass base (see also von Bülow, Vilaça, and Abelin 2018; Donoso in this volume).

In protest waves against government corruption in Honduras and Guatemala between 2015 and 2019, WhatsApp emerged as a major means of connecting people to locations of protest events and information about ongoing fraud (Solis Miranda 2016; Sosa 2017). The wave of popular unrest in Nicaragua against the repression of the Ortega regime since March of 2018 also is largely mobilized via WhatsApp including the sharing of outrageous acts of state violence and new protest songs written about martyrs to motivate continued high-risk protest. As in other parts of the globe, social media and ICTs will likely continue to create the potential for large-scale mobilization by simultaneously and instantly reaching multitudes with similar grievances. It remains an open question if internet and social media-based activism has the ability to sustain opposition in the same way traditional face-to-face organizing does through long term solidarity relationships and membership in popular organizations.

In summary, the organizational infrastructure that undergirds protest waves derives from a combination of state institutions, civil society organizations, oppositional political parties, religious institutions, and increasingly ICTs and social media. The associational power of the organizational infrastructure reaches greater mobilization potential when activists establish multi-sectoral coalitions across a wide variety of groups (Van Dyke and Amos 2017). The activation of the organizational infrastructure and multi-sectoral coalitions into a protest wave becomes more likely via incentives of political liberalization, state repression, or economic threats.

Political Liberalization

In the past, when Latin American regimes changed from authoritarian rule and began to allow basic freedoms such as rights to association and public assembly as well as competitive elections, they signaled to civil society that the costs of mobilization had been greatly reduced. The legalization of civic associations provides an added incentive for subaltern groups to launch collective action campaigns. These favorable changes are consistent with what political process scholars refer to as political opportunities (McAdam and Tarrow 2018).

The political liberalization pathway to a protest wave can be observed in several Latin American countries. In the 1927–1930 period, El Salvador experienced an unprecedented political liberalization after several decades of authoritarian and dynastic rule. The new government of Pio Romero Bosque legalized labor unions, formed a Ministry of Labor, shortened the working day to eight hours and convoked competitive elections at the municipal level (Ching 2014). Upon taking power, Romero Bosque also lifted a state of siege that had been in place since the early 1920s. The lifting of the state of emergency first allowed groups to form organizations and strengthen existing solidarity relationships such as fraternal religious groupings in indigenous communities. Already by 1928 there were clear signs El Salvador had entered a protest wave. Over the entire period between 1927 and 1930, several sectors of society mobilized (González Marquez 2017). These sectors included university students, anti-imperial movements against

United States intervention in Nicaragua, urban artisanal labor movements, urban consumers organizing over public transportation and electricity prices, and even indigenous rural labor groups at the end of the era.

In Guatemala, following the Jorge Ubico dictatorship, a wave a protest took place between 1945 and 1954, during the decade of democratic opening (Yagenova 2006). Bolivia also experienced a protest wave under the democratically elected government of Hernán Siles Zuazo (1956–1960). The post-revolutionary government that overthrew the military junta, created institutional access by incorporating workers' representatives into several branches of government, including cabinet ministries. The labor movement and other groups used this unprecedented political liberalization to launch a massive number of labor strikes and other actions against MNR's inflation stabilization plan and other economic measures between 1956 and 1960 (Alexander 2005; Morales 2003). With the advent of the slow political liberalization and democratization process in Brazil in the 1980s, a wave of protest took off led by unions, student groups, women's organizations, environmentalists, and the Partido dos Trabalhadores (Keck 1992; Seidman 1994).

Once democratic practices stabilize after several rounds of competitive elections, as is the case for most of Latin America since the 1980s (Markoff 2015), political opportunities in the form of new positive signals from the state or an opening in institutional access may also motivate a wave of protest (Inclán in this volume). Competing political parties in democratic Chile between the mid-1960s and early 1970s also opened space for a reformist wave of protest with the rapid organization and mobilization of peasants, urban squatters, and unions (Roberts 1998; Schneider 1995).

State Repression

Violent acts by the state may also trigger a cycle of protest. Although state repressive measures appear as the opposite behavior of political liberalization, both sets of conditions affect large numbers of groups creating the potential for a full-blown protest wave. When repressive state actions become extremely violent, in the form of multiple human rights abuses such as torture, assassination, disappearances, and mass arrests, they likely radicalize the tactics and ideologies of the opposition. Scholars of revolution and repression find that *indiscriminate* repression against civil society is especially potent in creating mobilizing grievances (Goodwin 2001). In this perspective, individuals calculate they have nothing to lose by engaging in high-risk protest activities, since the state might harm them no matter what action they take. Others contend that state repression against organized actors creates backlash mobilization because such groups already have the capacity to mobilize (Almeida 2008).

Latin America witnessed several state repression-induced protest waves in the late twentieth century (Wickham-Crowley 2014). The popular mobilizations prior to the Cuban Revolution between 1953 and 1958 can be considered a wave of protest against the repressive actions of the Batista dictatorship (García Pérez 1998; Pérez Martín 2019). Large-scale protest waves against repressive regimes in El Salvador, Guatemala, and Nicaragua also broke out in the late 1970s (Torres-Rivas 2011; Vela Castañeda 2011; Viterna 2013). In the Cuban and Central American cases, the opposition united across several sectors and social classes (peasants, teachers, students, labor unions, Catholic youth groups) because of the brutality of the regimes they confronted (Foran 2005; Goodwin 2001).

In the twenty-first century, the region continues to experience protest waves driven by state repression. Honduras and Nicaragua offer the most prominent examples. In June of 2009, the Honduran military overthrew the popularly elected government of Manuel Zelaya in a coup and immediately unleashed repressive actions against Zelaya's supporters. A multi-sectoral coalition that had mobilized in the preceding years against neoliberal policies (CAFTA, privatizations, etc.), the Coordinadora Nacional de Resistencia Popular (CNRP), transformed into the Frente Nacional de Resistencia Popular (FNRP). The FNRP mobilized a protest wave against the military coup and state repression for two years, sustaining weekly protests (if not daily) across the national territory (Sosa 2012).

In Nicaragua, in 2017 and the beginning of 2018, a series of protests had occurred over foreign mining, plans for the construction of a trans-oceanic canal, and a forest fire that threatened a tropical reserve. In April of 2018 the government of Daniel Ortega announced an International Monetary Fund (IMF)-suggested policy of making severe cuts and changes to the state social security program. Students and social security beneficiaries responded with street protests that were met with police violence way out of proportion to the popular demands. Nearly two dozen protesters were killed by security forces in April of 2018 when the social security measures were announced. The brutal response by the Ortega regime set off a cycle of protest as continued acts of state repression were met with popular resistance (Cabrales 2019). Oppositional groups drew on the Nicaraguan repertoire of contention that had been used in past waves of protest including the legendary erection of barricades of the revolutionary wave of the late 1970s as well as dozens of road blocks (called "tranques" in Nicaragua) used to battle austerity policies in protest campaigns of the 1990s (Almeida 2014). The anti-repression wave also included massive street marches in the capital reaching several hundred thousand participants, possibly the largest single demonstrations in the country's modern history. Between April and August of 2018 alone, about 2,000 protest events were registered (Cabrales 2019). Nonetheless, the ongoing state repression has been effective with nearly 400 civilian deaths and 1,000 arrests since April 2018, and a drastic reduction in protest events since August of 2018.

Economic Threats

Another major catalyst of protest waves involves economic threats, especially when the state is unable to ameliorate widespread economic crisis (Almeida 2019). Two major economic crises associated with economic threat-induced protest waves include (1) the worldwide Depression in the early 1930s and (2) the 1980s debt crisis in the global South.

Both sets of economic crises unleashed a number of protest waves around the globe, including Latin America (see Rossi in this volume).

The global Depression that commenced at the end of 1929 set off multiple protest waves in Latin America. The world market crash in basic commodity prices for crops such as bananas, sugarcane, and coffee severely impacted the agro-export economies of the region. Perhaps the best documented cases include Costa Rica, Cuba, and El Salvador. In Costa Rica, the Depression led to a series of urban strikes and unemployed workers' marches and peaked with the 1934 banana strike on the Atlantic coast with the solidarity of urban labor and the coordination of the Costa Rican Communist Party. In Cuba, the Depression not only affected the local economy with falling sugar prices but also occurred during the repressive government of Gerardo Machado and his successors. Between 1930 and 1935, a series of general strikes, marches, and occupations occurred with the participation of a broad cross-section of civil society. One high point of the protest wave beyond the impressive general strikes of 1933 and 1935, occurred with the worker occupations of dozens of sugar mills and sugar plantations in 1933 with the support of the Cuban Communist Party (Carr 1996). El Salvador also faced a serious economic crisis in 1930 as coffee accounted for about 90% of exports. An economic-induced protest wave began with a series of marches by unemployed rural and urban workers. The protests were met with violent repression from the state in 1930 and 1931, which radicalized the protest wave into a violent insurrection in 1932 (Gould and Lauria-Santiago 2009).

The major economic threat of the late twentieth and the early twenty-first centuries involves the policies associated with neoliberalism, including privatization, austerity and subsidy cuts, consumer price increases, mass layoffs, free trade treaties, and labor flexibility laws (Almeida and Pérez Martín 2022). This family of policies began with the debt crisis in the global South. Between 1980 and the present, the implementation of the economic liberalization policies have at times initiated waves of protest in countries throughout the region (Roberts 2008; Seoane, Taddei, and Algranati 2006). Between 1980 and 2008 alone, most Latin American countries have been under an IMF or World Bank structural adjustment loan for at least ten years (Abouharb and Cingranelli 2007; Almeida and Pérez Martín 2021). Such economic development policies create deep grievances by breaking culturally embedded moral and social contracts (Auyero 2006; Simmons 2016; Almeida and Chase-Dunn 2018).

In this context, neoliberal-induced protest waves have now become commonplace in the region. Such protest waves include Peru 1977–1978, Costa Rica 1978–1983, Chile 1983–1986, Nicaragua 1990–1993, Honduras 1990–1993, Bolivia 1999–2005, Costa Rica 2000–2007, Panama 1998–2005, Paraguay 2000–2003, Argentina 1997–2003, Honduras 1999–2005, and Ecuador 1997–2001. The economic threats of neoliberalism take away social citizenship rights established in the previous period of state-led development and populist regimes (Almeida 2007; Silva 2009). Most recently, several massive campaigns against economic policies have emerged in Chile (2019); Colombia (2019 and 2021); Cuba (2021); Ecuador (2019 and 2022); Costa Rica (2020); Honduras (2019); and Panama (2022).

Privatization of the public infrastructure that threatens multiple societal groups is especially powerful for mobilization in that many sectors of society benefit from low-cost access to water, sewage, electricity, healthcare, and telecommunications. Privatization promoted protest waves include natural resources such as natural gas, petroleum, and water; public utilities such as electricity and telecommunications; and key social services such as education, health care, and pensions/social security (Spronk and Terhorst 2012). Free trade agreements also create widespread discontent because they often incorporate multiple neoliberal measures in a single accord (Raventós Vorst 2018; Silva 2013).

Unifying Frames

A final feature often consolidating a protest wave is some kind of collective action frame or narrative in the ideological sphere of political life. Snow and Benford (1992) refer to such narratives that unify something as widespread as a cycle of protest as a "master frame." Often the master frame may exist at the transnational level as an ideational concept in world society (Beck 2014). Domestic actors may adopt the frame in world society and add local elements so it resonates with large numbers of subaltern groups (Sohrabi 2011). For example, local socialist and communist parties used ideas and slogans from the Comintern in the early 1930s such as diagnosing the final demise of capitalism and the importance of worker and peasant alliances in the protest waves in Costa Rica, Cuba, and El Salvador discussed above. The international frames were transmitted through written literature and propaganda, and attendance at international labor and socialist conferences.

The international trend toward democratization in the immediate post World War II period (Markoff 2015), quickly turned into a call for de-colonization and national liberation by the 1950s and 1960s. Protest waves in Latin America that were radicalized via state repression drew heavily from the ideas of national liberation and anti-neocolonialism, especially in Cuba, El Salvador, Guatemala, and Nicaragua. Several other attempts using a national liberation discourse to generate a revolutionary wave of protest failed to materialize between the 1960s and 1980s in Argentina, Brazil, Colombia, Honduras, Mexico, Peru, Uruguay, and Venezuela (Wickham-Crowley 2014). Such sentiments of anti-neocolonialism were diffused and reinforced via written works and international conferences featuring struggles in the global South such as Bandung, the Non-Aligned Movement, and the Tri-Continental Conference (Prashad 2007). They eventually combined with local "oppositional cultures of resistance" with the conjuring up of past national martyrs and struggles against foreign domination (Foran 2005).

Another influential ideational force in world society shaping protest waves in Latin America was Catholic Social Doctrine, namely Vatican II reforms in the 1960s and Liberation Theology in the 1970s (Mackin in this volume). This dramatic shift in Church doctrine gave priority to working with the poor and alleviating poverty and inequality. These beliefs led to the founding of a wide variety of new Catholic organizations such as peasant cooperatives, urban youth and student groups, and Christian Base

Communities that played indispensable roles in laying the ground work of consciousness raising and community organizing for protest waves in the 1960s and 1970s in El Salvador, Guatemala, and Nicaragua (Vega 1994; Vela Casteñada 2011).

In the neoliberal era an anti-neoliberal frame slowly emerged in the region by the late 1990s (López Maya 1999). Even though the debt crisis already produced a series of short-term protest waves by the mid-1980s, protest cycles occurred with greater frequency in the late 1990s and 2000s. As an abstract economic philosophy of economic deregulation, it would take time and experience before neoliberalism became a stigmatized term on the streets in the Americas. In the 1990s, unions facing structural adjustment cuts began using the term neoliberalism in a pejorative sense. A major boost to anti-neoliberal discourse came from the Zapatista struggle in Mexico, inaugurated by an uprising against free trade and then sustained with a nonviolent protest wave for a decade in Chiapas (Inclán 2018; see Oikonomakis in this volume). Equally important in this era for nations with substantial indigenous populations is the consolidation of a language and ideology of rights and citizenship (Dagnino 2001) associated with multicultural and plurinational frames (Simbaña 2005; see Rice in this volume).

As a second generation of structural adjustment policies in the late 1990s and early 2000s took shape, that often included plans for the privatization of the public infrastructure, a stronger anti-neoliberal master frame began to unify the major protest waves in both South and Central America. The anti-neoliberal protest waves of the late 1990s and early 2000s in Argentina, Bolivia, Costa Rica, Ecuador, El Salvador, Honduras, Panama, and Paraguay also benefited from the regional and international conferences and organizations battling against neoliberalism at the transnational level such as the Foro Mesoamericano, World Social Forum, São Paulo Forum, and the Alianza Social Continental (Bidaseca and Rossi 2008; Rossi 2013; von Bülow 2010). In these spaces, a discourse developed to diagnose neoliberalism and how it was sponsored and implemented to the benefit of global capital and local segments of the transnational financial elite (Robinson 2014). By this time, major political leaders in the region, such as Hugo Chávez, Carlos "Perro" Santillán, and Evo Morales were referring to neoliberalism as a savage form of capitalism. The trend continues in the late 2010s with the newly elected president of Mexico, Andrés Manuel López Obrador, also denouncing neoliberalism in his inaugural address.

Table 9.1 synthesizes the main facilitating conditions of protest waves. Organizational infrastructures explain the "how" of protest waves. In order to move from shorter-term protest campaigns and individual social movements, elaborate building blocks of organizational and institutional resources must be in place. The composition of the infrastructure varies across regions and time. For example, the coordinating structures of indigenous communities are much more prominent in regions with large native populations such as in Guatemala, Mexico, Panama, and the Andes (Gutiérrez and Escárzaga 2006). As we observe protest waves in the 2010s and beyond, ICT and social media technologies become essential in bringing large crowds into cities and plazas. Political liberalization, opportunities, state repression, and economic threats offer some of the main motivations for a wave of protest to materialize.

Table 9.1 Summary of facilitating conditions of protest waves in Latin America

Type of Facilitating Condition	Examples
Organizational infrastructures	Civil society associations, labor unions, peasant confederations, teachers' associations, student groups, multi-sectoral coalitions, feminist collectives, state institutions, public schools, everyday organizations, NGOs, oppositional political parties, federations of indigenous peoples, religious institutions, ICT and social media technologies.
Political liberalization	Political openings following authoritarian rule such as competitive elections, freedom of assembly and association, and legalization of civil society organizations. In more stable democratic contexts, political opportunities such as widespread institutional access and positive signaling from the state (e.g., wage hikes, agrarian reform, etc.).
Repressive threats	Martial law, states of siege, military coup, repeated acts of state violence including legal repression, harassment, arrest, torture, disappearance, homicide, and other human rights violations.
Economic threats	Global depression, mass unemployment, economic austerity, structural adjustment, public sector privatization, free trade agreements, subsidy cuts, price hikes, labor flexibility laws.
Unifying frames	Comintern strategies; national liberation/de-colonization, Vatican II, Catholic social doctrine, liberation theology, democratization, anti-neoliberal frames.

It is important to acknowledge that economic and repressive threats may occur simultaneously as consumer inflation and state violence both catalyzed protest waves in El Salvador, Guatemala, and Nicaragua in the 1970s. The protest waves against neoliberalism over the past three decades have also occurred under relatively more democratic regimes allowing political space to organize and coordinate actions against economic threats (Silva 2009). Finally, in the ideational sphere, a protest wave is likely maintained with a unifying frame or narrative.

Outcomes of Latin American Protest Waves

In Tarrow's (2011) original conceptualization of protest cycles he focused on the outcomes of reform, exhaustion, and repression. Because protest waves are such large outpourings of social discontent, it is likely that political and economic elites will attempt to respond in order to end such large-scale social disruption. The reform response occurs when political and economic institutions are altered in reaction to a protest cycle. Moderate reforms take place when the government responds to a particular phase or campaign within a protest wave, such as when oppositional groups in El Salvador halted attempts at the privatization of health care on two separate occasions within a larger anti-neoliberal wave. Similar victories in the 2000s against water privatization in Bolivia, Panama, and Uruguay; electricity and telecommunications privatization in Costa Rica; or a free trade agreement with the United States in Ecuador offer other examples.

Another deeper level outcome associated with protest waves in the twenty-first century involves converting the cycle of protest into a victorious *electoral struggle* and the taking of state power (Almeida and Pérez Martín 2022). Silva (2009) documented such patterns in his comparison of six countries and their corresponding anti-neoliberal episodes of contention in South America. He found that activists in Argentina, Bolivia, Ecuador, and Venezuela successfully transferred popular protests against economic liberalization into the election of neo-Polanyist regimes that implemented social policies and programs that attempted overcome the most exclusive forms of neoliberal measures. One may be able to add the victory of the Alianza Patriótica para el Cambio in Paraguay in 2008 and the FMLN in El Salvador in 2009 to this same pattern of left-leaning parties elected in the aftermath of major anti-neoliberal protest waves (along with other similar electoral triumphs in Brazil and Uruguay in the 2000s as part of the overall Pink Tide). This conversion from a protest wave to an electoral triumph was partially made possible by the prior participation of oppositional political parties in coordinating the protest wave and building electoral support—a process referred to as *social movement partyism* (Almeida 2006, 2010). Most recently, anti-neoliberal protest waves in Honduras, Chile, and Colombia resulted in the electoral triumph of leftist parties in 2021 and 2022.

Another outcome of a protest wave is *movement exhaustion*. Protest waves are constituted by ordinary people with limited means who volunteer their time and resources to participate in organizing and attending social movement activities. Political and economic elites are aware of these realities and often do not respond to the major demands proposed within a protest wave. This scenario is common under conditions such as an impending implementation of a major austerity or structural adjustment program. If the protest wave fails to halt the neoliberal measures and they are implemented, it is often difficult to continue the momentum of the wave and it likely fizzles out at this point (Svampa 2017). Such a scenario occurred in Honduras in the early 1990s, despite massive opposition to the country's first major structural adjustment plan (Sosa 2013). This was also the case for the protest waves in Central America against CAFTA between 2003 and 2007. In country after country once the free trade treaty was ratified and implemented popular mobilization rapidly declined, even in Costa Rica, where the opposition held general strikes, roadblocks, and multiple street demonstrations of over 100,000 participants (Raventós Vorst 2018).

Another crucial outcome to explore is the function of state repression once the protest wave begins to peak. While the role of state repression was discussed above as a facilitating condition or pathway in creating a protest cycle, governments (especially non-democratic regimes) will continue to use force to suppress a full-blown protest wave. In some cases, the repressive actions by the state radicalize the movement even further into a revolutionary movement that seeks to overthrow the government. This protest cycle radicalization occurred in Cuba in the 1950s, and in El Salvador, Guatemala, and Nicaragua in the 1970s (Brockett 2005; Goodwin 2001). In the cases of Cuba and Nicaragua it led to a social revolution (Foran 2005; see Brockett; Martí i Puig and Álvarez, Oikonomakis in this volume).

In El Salvador and Guatemala, the military regimes of the 1970s and early 1980s unleashed genocidal levels of repression against the protest waves, which prevented a revolutionary triumph at the cost of prolonged civil war and the deaths of over two hundred thousand people (largely poor, rural, and indigenous). The social disintegration of the "Northern Triangle" Central American states and the current migrant refugee crisis directly relates back to the massive state violence to suppress these protest waves with substantial military funding, sponsorship, and training provided by the Reagan administration (Crandall 2016).

The outcomes of protest waves transform the societies in which they take place. Even waves that end in exhaustion have left valuable experiences, skills, and memories in the minds of the participants. Those lessons may be used in the next round of contention and passed on to new generations (Morris 1984).

Conclusion

These dynamics of protest cycle radicalization, repression, and revolution in Latin America also offer lessons to other world regions such as the outcomes of the Arab Spring uprisings and the current conflicts in Egypt, Syria, Libya, and Yemen (Alimi 2016). Perhaps more analytical power of the outcomes of protest cycles can come from more systematic comparisons between countries as undertaken by Brockett (2005) for Central America and Silva (2009) for South America. Protest cycles are also a critical feature in interpreting major historical events such as genocide, terrorism, civil war, revolutions, social disintegration, and mass out-migration since a substantial portion of society is organized during such an episode, the stakes are high in how states and elites respond as well as the international community.

Acknowledgements

The author appreciates the detailed comments provided by Amalia Pérez Martín and Federico Rossi on this chapter.

REFERENCES

Abouharb, M. Rodwan, and David L. Cingranelli (2007), *Human Rights and Structural Adjustment* (Cambridge: Cambridge University Press).

Alexander, Robert J. (2005), *A History of Organized Labor in Bolivia* (New York: Praeger).

Alimi, Eitan Y. (2016), "Introduction: Popular Contention, Regime, and Transition: A Comparative Perspective," in Eitan Alimi, Avraham Sela, and Mario Sznajder (eds.), *Popular Contention, Regime, and Transition: The Arab Revolts in Comparative*, 1–24 Global Perspective (Oxford: Oxford University Press).

Almeida, Paul (2006), "Social Movement Unionism, Social Movement Partyism, and Policy Outcomes: Health Care Privatization in El Salvador," in Hank Johnston and Paul Almeida (eds.), *Latin American Social Movements: Globalization, Democratization, and Transnational Networks*, 57–76 (Lanham, MD: Rowman and Littlefield).

Almeida Paul (2007), "Defensive Mobilization: Popular Movements against Economic Adjustment Policies in Latin America," *Latin American Perspectives* 34(3), 123–39.

Almeida, Paul (2008), *Waves of Protest: Popular Struggle in El Salvador, 1925–2005* (Minneapolis: University of Minnesota Press).

Almeida, Paul (2010), "Social Movement Partyism: Collective Action and Political Parties," in Nella Van Dyke and Holly McCammon (eds.), *Strategic Alliances: New Studies of Social Movement Coalitions*, 170–96 (Minneapolis: University of Minnesota Press).

Almeida, Paul (2014), *Mobilizing Democracy: Globalization and Citizen Protest* (Baltimore, MD: Johns Hopkins University Press).

Almeida, Paul (2015), "Unintended Consequences of State-Led Development: A Theory of Mobilized Opposition to Neoliberalism," *Sociology of Development* 1(2), 259–76.

Almeida, Paul (2016), "Social Movements and Economic Development," in Greg Hooks, Paul Almeida, David Brown, Sam Cohn, Sara Curran, Rebecca Emigh, Ho-fung Hung, Andrew K. Jorgenson, Richard Lachmann, Linda Lobao, and Valentine Moghadam (eds.), *The Sociology of Development Handbook*, 528–50 (Berkeley and Los Angeles: University of California Press).

Almeida, Paul (2019), "The Role of Threat in Collective Action," in David Snow, Sara Soule, Hansperter Kriesi, and Holly McCammon (eds.), *Wiley-Blackwell Companion to Social Movements*, 43–62 (Oxford: Wiley-Blackwell).

Almeida, Paul and Christopher Chase-Dunn (2018), "Globalization and Social Movements," *Annual Review of Sociology* 44, 189–211.

Almeida, Paul and Amalia Pérez Martín (2021), "Economic Globalization and Social Movements in Latin America," in Xóchitl Bada and Liliana Rivera (eds.), *The Oxford Handbook of the Sociology of Latin America*, 391–414 (Oxford: Oxford University Press).

Almeida, Paul and Amalia Pérez Martín. (2022). *Collective Resistance to Neoliberalism*. Cambridge: Cambridge University Press.

Arce, Moisés and Jorge Mangonnet (2013), "Competitiveness, Partisanship, And Subnational Protest in Argentina," *Comparative Political Studies* 46(8), 895–919.

Auyero, Javier (2006), "The Moral Politics of Argentine Crowds," in Hank Johnston and Paul Almeida (eds.), *Latin American Social Movements: Globalization, Democratization, and Transnational Networks*, 147–62 (Lanham, MD: Rowman and Littlefield).

Beck, Colin J. (2014), "Reflections on the Revolutionary Wave in 2011," *Theory and Society* 43, 197–223.

Becker, Mark (2008), *Indians and Leftists in the Making of Ecuador's Modern Indigenous Movements* (Durham, NC: Duke University Press).
Becker, Mark (2010), *Pachakutik: Indigenous Movements and Electoral Politics in Ecuador* (Lanham, MD: Rowman and Littlefield).
Bidaseca, Karina and Federico M. Rossi (2008), "Coaliciones nacionales contra procesos continentales de liberalización comercial: la Autoconvocatoria No al ALCA," in Alejandro Grimson and Sebastián Pereyra (eds.), *Conflictos globales, voces locales: Movilización y activismo en clave transnacional*, 51–89 (Buenos Aires: UNRISD-Prometeo).
Bobea, Lilian (1999), "De la protesta a la propuesta: Articulaciones entre los movimientos populares y el Estado en República Dominicana," in Margarita López Maya (ed.), *Lucha popular, democracia, neoliberalismo: Protesta popular en América Latina en los años de ajuste*, 179–208 (Caracas: Nueva Sociedad).
Boulding, Carew (2014), *NGOs, Political Protest, and Civil Society* (Cambridge: University Press).
Bretón, Víctor (2001), *Cooperación al desarrollo y Demandas étnicas en los Andes Ecuatorianos. Ensayos sobre indigenismo, desarrollo rural y neoindigenismo* (Quito: FLACSO Ecuador).
Brockett, Charles (2005), *Political Movements and Violence in Central America* (Cambridge: Cambridge University Press).
Cabrales, Sergio (2019), "Terremoto sociopolítico en Nicaragua: Procesos, mecanismos y resultados de la inesperada oleada de protestas de 2018," Working Paper (Pittsburg: University of Pittsburgh).
Camacho, Daniel and Rafael Menjívar (1985), "El movimiento popular en Centroamérica: 1970-1983. Síntesis y perspectivas," in Daniel Camacho and Rafael Menjívar (eds). *Movimientos populares en Centroamérica*, 9–61 (San José: EDUCA).
Carr, Barry (1996), "The Mobilisation of Sugar Workers in Cuba, 1917–1933," *Journal of Latin American Studies* 28(1), 129–58.
Castells. Manuel. (2013). *Communication Power*. Oxford: Oxford University Press.
Ching, Erik, Carlos Gregorio López Bernal, and Virginia Tilley (2011), *Las masas, la matanza y el martinato en El Salvador* (San Salvador: UCA Editores).
Ching, Erik (2014), *Authoritarian El Salvador: Politics and the Origins of the Military Regimes* (South Bend, IN: University of Notre Dame Press).
Crandall, Russell (2016), *The Salvador Option: The United States in El Salvador, 1977–1992* (Cambridge: Cambridge University Press).
Dagnino, Evelina (2001), "Cultura, ciudadanía y democracia: Los discursos y prácticas cambiantes de la izquierda latinoamericana," in Arturo Escobar, Sonia Álvarez, and Evelina Dagnino (eds.), *Política cultural y cultura política. Una nueva mirada sobre los movimientos sociales latinoamericanos*, 72–77 (Bogotá: Taurus-ICANH).
della Porta, Donatella (2013), "Protest Cycles and Waves," in David Snow, Donatella della Porta, Bert Klandermans, and Doug McAdam (eds.), *The Wiley-Blackwell Encyclopedia of Social and Political Movements*, 1014–19 (Oxford: Wiley).
Foran, John (2005), *Taking Power: On the Origins of Third World Revolutions* (Cambridge: Cambridge University Press).
García-Pérez, Gladys Marel (1998), *Insurrection and Revolution: Armed Struggle in Cuba, 1952–1959* (Boulder, CO: Lynne Rienner).
Goodwin, Jeff (2001), *No Other Way Out: States and Revolutionary Movements, 1945–1991* (Cambridge: Cambridge University Press).

González Márquez, Luis Rubén (2017), "Política popular contenciosa: movilización social y hegemonía en El Salvador, 1919–1932" (MA thesis in Sociology FLACSO, Ecuador).

Gould, Jeffrey and Aldo Lauria-Santiago (2009), *To Rise in Darkness: Revolution, Repression, and Memory in El Salvador, 1920–1932* (Durham, NC: Duke University Press).

Gutiérrez, Raquel and Fabiola Escázaga (2006), *Movimiento indígena en América Latina: Resistencia y Proyecto alternativo*, 3 (Mexico: Casa Juan Pablos).

Inclán María (2018), *The Zapatista Movement and Mexico's Democratic Transition: Mobilization, Success, and Survival* (Oxford: Oxford University Press).

Keck, Margaret (1992), *The Workers' Party and Democratization in Brazil* (New Haven, CT: Yale University Press).

López Maya, Margarita (1999), "La protesta popular venezolana entre 1989 y 1993 (en el umbral del neoliberalismo)," in Margarita López Maya (ed.), *Lucha popular, democracia, neoliberalismo: Protesta popular en América Latina en los años de ajuste*, 209–35 (Caracas: Nueva Sociedad).

Markoff, John (2015), *Waves of Democracy: Social Movements and Political Change* (Thousand Oaks, CA: Sage).

McAdam, Doug and Sidney G. Tarrow (2018), "The Political Context of Social Movements," in David Snow, Sara Soule, Hansperter Kriesi, and Holly McCammon (eds.), *The Wiley-Blackwell Companion to Social Movements*, 19–42 (Oxford: Wiley-Blackwell).

Morales, Antonio (2003), "The National Revolution and its Legacy," in Merilee S. Grindle and Pilar Domingo (eds.), *Proclaiming Revolution: Bolivia in Comparative Perspective*, 213–31 (London: Institute of Latin American Studies).

Morris, Aldon (1984), *The Origins of the Civil Rights Movement: Black Communities Organizing for Change* (New York: Free Press).

Penna, Camila, Marcelo Carvalho Rosa, and Sebastián Pereyra (2017), "Vote and Protest in Argentina and Brazil: Contemporary Research Based Reflections on Political Participation," *Sociologies in Dialogue* 3(2), 96–117.

Pérez Martín, Amalia (2019), "Revisiting the History of the 1959 Revolutionary Triumph in Cuba: Movement Frames and Legal Repression in Authoritarian Regimes," (MA paper, University of California).

Postero, Nancy (2017), *The Indigenous State: Race, Politics, and Performance in Plurinational Bolivia* (Berkeley and Los Angeles: University of California Press).

Prashad Vijay (2007), *The Darker Nations: A People's History of the Third World* (New York: New Press).

Raventós Vorst, Ciska (2018), *Mi corazón dice no: el movimiento de oposición del TLC en Costa Rica* (San Jose: Editorial Universidad de Costa Rica).

Roberts, Kenneth (2008), "The Mobilization of Opposition to Economic Liberalization," *Annual Review of Political Science* 11, 327–49.

Roberts, Kenneth (1998), *Deepening Democracy? The Modern Left and Social Movements in Chile and Peru* (Stanford, CA: Stanford University Press).

Robinson, William (2014), *Capitalism and the Crisis of Humanity* (Cambridge: Cambridge University Press).

Rossi, Federico M. (2017), *The Poor's Struggle for Political Incorporation: The Piquetero Movement in Argentina* (Cambridge: Cambridge University Press).

Rossi, Federico M. (2013), "Juggling Multiple Agendas: The Struggle of Trade Unions against National, Continental, and International Neoliberalism in Argentina," in Eduardo Silva (ed.), *Transnational Activism and National Movements in Latin America*, 157–76 (New York: Routledge).

Schneider, Cathy Lisa (1996), *Shantytown Protest in Pinochet's Chile* (Philadelphia: Temple University Press).

Seidman, Gay W. (1994), *Manufacturing Militance: Workers' Movements in Brazil and South Africa, 1970–1985* (Berkeley and Los Angeles: University of California Press).

Seoane, José, Emilio Taddei, and Clara Algranati (2006), "Las nuevas configuraciones de los movimientos populares en América Latina," in Atilio A. Borón and Gladys Lechini (eds.), *Política y movimientos sociales en un mundo hegemónico. Lecciones desde África, Asia y América Latina*, 227–50 (Buenos Aires: CLACSO).

Silva, Eduardo (2009), *Challenging Neoliberalism in Latin America* (Cambridge: Cambridge University Press).

Silva, Eduardo (2013), "Transnational Activism and National Movements in Latin America: Concepts, Theories, and Expectations," in Eduardo Silva, (ed.), *Transnational Activism and National Movements in Latin America: Bridging the Divide*, 1–22 (New York: Routledge).

Simbaña, Floresmilo (2005), "Plurinacionalidad y derechos colectivos: El caso ecuatoriano," in Pablo Dávalos (ed.), *Pueblos indígenas, Estado y democracia*, 197–215 (Buenos Aires: CLACSO).

Simmons, Erica (2016), *Meaningful Mobilization: Market Reforms and the Roots of Social Protest in Latin America* (Cambridge: Cambridge University Press).

Snow, David A. and Robert D. Benford (1992), "Master Frames and Cycles of Protest," in Aldon D. Morris and Carol McClurg Mueller (eds.), *Frontiers of Social Movement Theory*, 133–55 (New Haven, CT: Yale University Press).

Sohrabi, Nader (2011), *Revolution and Constitutionalism in the Ottoman Empire and Iran* (Cambridge: Cambridge University Press).

Solis Miranda, R. (2016), *La fuerza de las plazas, bitácora de la indignación ciudadana en 2015* (Guatemala City: Fundación Friedrich Ebert).

Sosa, Eugenio (2012). "La contienda política tras el golpe de estado oligárquico: de la resistencia en las calles hacia la disputa político electoral," *Bajo el Volcán* 11(17), 21–42.

Sosa, Eugenio (2013), *Dinámica de la protesta social en Honduras* (Tegucigalpa: Editorial Guaymuras).

Sosa, Eugenio (2017), *Democracia y movimientos sociales en Honduras: De la transición política a la ciudadanía indignada* (Tegucigalpa: Editorial Guaymuras).

Spronk, Susan and Philipp Terhorst (2012), "Social Movement Struggles for Public Services," in David McDonald and Greg Ruiters (eds.), *Alternatives to Privatization in the Global South*, 133–56 (New York: Routledge).

Svampa, Maristela (2017), "Cuatro claves para entender América Latina," *Nueva Sociedad* 268, 50–64.

Tarrow, Sidney (1989), *Democracy and Disorder: Protest and Politics in Italy, 1965–1975* (Oxford: Oxford University Press).

Tarrow Sidney (2011), *Power in Movement* (Cambridge: Cambridge University Press).

Torres-Rivas, Edelberto (2011), *Revoluciones sin cambios revolucionarios* (Guatemala City: F&G Editores).

Van Dyke, Nella and Bryan Amos (2017), "Social Movement Coalitions: Formation, Longevity, and Success," *Sociology Compass* 11(7), 1–17.

Vega, Juan Ramon (1994), *Las comunidades cristianas de base en América Central: Estudio sociológico* (San Salvador: Publicaciones del Arzobispado).

Vela Castañeda, Manolo (2011), *Guatemala, la infinita historia de las resistencias* (Guatemala City: Secretaría de la Paz de la Presidencia de la República de Guatemala).

Viterna, Jocelyn (2013), *Women in War: The Micro-processes of Mobilization in El Salvador* (Oxford: Oxford University Press).

von Bülow, Marisa (2010), *Building Transnational Networks: Civil Society and the Politics of Trade in the Americas* (Cambridge: Cambridge University Press).

von Bülow, Marisa (2018), "The Survival of Leaders and Organizations in the Digital Age: Lessons from the Chilean Student Movement," *Mobilization* 23(1), 45–64.

von Bülow, Marisa, Luiz Vilaça, and Pedro Henrique Abelin (2018), "Varieties of Digital Activist Practices: Students and Mobilization in Chile," *Information, Communication & Society* 22(12), 1770–88.

Weyland, Kurt (2014), *Making Waves: Democratic Contention in Europe and Latin America since the Revolutions of 1848* (Cambridge: Cambridge University Press).

Wickham-Crowley, Timothy (2014), "Two "Waves" of Guerrilla-Movement Organizing in Latin America, 1956–1990," *Comparative Studies in Society and History* 56(1), 215–42.

Yagenova, Simona Violetta (2006), *Los maestros y la revolución de octubre (1944–1954)* (Guatemala City: Editorial de Ciencias Sociales).

Yashar, Deborah (2005), *Contesting Citizenship in Latin America: The Rise of Indigenous Movements and the Postliberal Challenge* (Cambridge: Cambridge University Press).

CHAPTER 10

SOCIAL MOVEMENTS AND NATIONALISM IN LATIN AMERICA

MATTHIAS VOM HAU

Introduction

Students of social movements in Latin America have employed the concept of nationalism rather loosely, using it to describe phenomena as diverse as regimes, policies, civil society organizations, ideologies, rhetorical styles, stereotypes, collective emotions, and patterns of self-identification (e.g., Mallon 1995; Silva 2009). In turn, scholars of nationalism in the region primarily focus on the role of the state (e.g., Anderson 1991; Centeno 2002; Hobsbawm 1995; López-Alves 2000) and, if at all, deal with social movements in a largely descriptive manner, thereby ignoring recent advances in social movement theory.

This chapter seeks to bring these two distinct bodies of work into conversation with each other and explore the relationship between nationalism and social movements in Latin America in a more systematic manner. I will start by identifying three major approaches to the conceptualization of nationalism: as (1) a set of political behaviors, (2) a collective sentiment, or (3) a form of ideology or discourse. Each of them leads to different ideas about how nationalism affects or is affected by social movements. The chapter will further illustrate that the three conceptual approaches shed new light on important historical developments in the region, namely independence from colonial rule and the formation of national states during the nineteenth century, the political incorporation of popular sectors and the rise of mass society during the early and mid-twentieth century, the growing relevance of ethnic-based mobilization in the region more recently, and the relative absence of separatist nationalism in Latin America.

The overall aspiration of the chapter is to identify broad patterns that characterize nationalism and social movements across Latin America. Yet many of the illustrative examples are derived from the cases of Argentina, Mexico, and Peru. These three countries were chosen because they represent likely extreme points in the region with respect to the relevant macrohistorical context. As the former centers of Spanish colonialism, Mexico and Peru are broadly similar in their colonial legacies and levels of ethnic diversity, while Argentina provides a sharp contrast. Yet in both postcolonial Argentina and Peru political development was characterized by instability and repeated transitions from authoritarianism to democracy (Collier and Collier 1991; Klarén 2000; Knight 1992; Mahoney 2010; Rock 1987).

The literature covered in this chapter is eclectic and interdisciplinary. Given the relative scarcity of studies that approach nationalism in Latin America from an explicitly articulated social movements/contentious politics perspective, I draw on a wider scholarship in history, anthropology, comparative historical sociology, comparative politics, and political geography. What connects these studies is that they touch on various aspects of the relationship between nationalism and social movements in the region, yet without being directly engaged with social movements research. My discussion of this body of work then selectively brings in arguments and more general debates from social movement theory and theories of nationalism.

NATIONALISM AND SOCIAL MOVEMENTS: CONCEPTUAL AND THEORETICAL CONSIDERATIONS

Nationalism is a notoriously slippery concept, its meaning hotly debated. In this section I will distinguish between three major approaches. Some scholars take a *cognitive* approach and treat nationalism as a shared mental and discursive framework that supplies particular ways to imagine community and experience social relations (Anderson 1991; Brubaker 2004; Calhoun 1997). In this perspective the basic underpinning of nationalism is the idea that a political unit, the state (or polity), is or ought to be congruent with a cultural community of nationals (Gellner 1983). Others take an *affective* approach and conceptualize nationalism as a form of social solidarity infusing with passion ties to the nation and establishing a sense of belonging (Guibernau 1996; Marx 2003). According to this body of work, nationalism varies with respect to the intensity of identification with and attachment to the nation. Still others subscribe to a *behavioral* approach and treat nationalism as collective action that is oriented towards advancing the interests or claiming to speak in the name of a particular national community (Beissinger 2002; Hechter 2000; Tilly 1994). This perspective thus identifies nationalism as a political activity that both states and social movements may engage in, either to legitimate or challenge the boundaries of state power.

Each of the three approaches has distinct implications for how to think about the relationship between nationalism and social movements. The behavioral perspective suggests a focus on protest and mobilization itself. This means to distinguish nationalist from non-nationalist movements—or collective action characterized by demands for or the defense of the autonomous political status or even separate statehood of a particular nation from collective action advancing other types of claims.

By contrast, a focus on cognition urges us to abstain from treating (some) movements as nationalist but instead draw a sharp analytical distinction between collective action and nationalism. For one thing, because of their "framing work" (Gamson 1992; Snow et al. 1986), social movements are important *producers* of nationalism. The national ideologies advanced by movements represent demands as indicative of "national interest" while portraying the claims of contending social actors as antagonistic to national well-being. Simultaneously, social movements are also *consumers* of nationalism and draw on already widely shared understandings of nationhood in order to achieve wider resonance for their claims.

By treating nationalism as an emotion, the affective approach also implies a dual perspective. On the one hand, movements are involved in the creation of national identifications and sentiments. Research has shown that social movements play a central role in generating affective loyalties to the national community they claim to speak for, for example by transforming shame into pride or by (performatively, rhetorically, or even physically) humbling those perceived as enemies of the nation (Berezin 2001; Scheff 1994). At the same time, social movements are also facilitated or constrained by existing national attachments. For example, the desire for the recognition of one's identity can bring people in and out of collective mobilization efforts (Goodwin et al. 2000).

These three approaches to nationalism (and the relationship between nationalism and social movements) have different strengths and weaknesses. The behavioral approach has the advantage of providing a concise definition that focuses on nationalist mobilization as a rare but highly consequential phenomenon. But restricting nationalism to collective action bears the danger of ignoring cultural practices and expressions. Moreover, without tracing the framing strategies of social movements—and thus having the cognitive approach entering through the backdoor—it is largely impossible to discern empirically what distinguishes nationalist from non-nationalist mobilization.

A significant strength of the affective approach is that it is able to address one of the central puzzles in the study of nationalism, namely the disposition of many ordinary people to make dramatic sacrifices for their nations. It also draws attention to affective loyalties as one of possible drivers behind nationalist mobilization. The main drawback of this approach is measurement. Collective emotions are notoriously difficult to trace empirically in a systematic manner.

The strength of the cognitive approach is to bring the political and the cultural together. Moreover, this perspective helps to distinguish the contents of particular nationalisms and the collective actions involved in producing and diffusing them. Yet, and in a mirror image to the behavioral approach, the focus on nationalism as cognition also bears the danger of concept stretching and turning it into a vague and all-encompassing concept.

When taken in conjunction, these three different approaches provide a useful backdrop to explore the relationship between nationalism and social movements in Latin America. Specifically, they allow investigating the role of social movements in the origins of nationalism, the transformations of national ideologies and attachments over time, and the peculiar nature of nationalist mobilization in the region.

Creating Nationalism? Social Movements and the Formation of National States

The rise of nationalism in Latin America is closely entwined with the implosion of the Spanish colonial empire and the formation of independent states across the region in the early nineteenth century. The regime protests of Creoles—the American-born offspring of peninsular Spaniards—gradually turned into anticolonial mobilization for political and economic independence from Spain. Yet, even though the importance of social movements in driving this transition from colonial empire to postcolonial national states is widely acknowledged (e.g., Guerra 2000; Hobsbawm 1995; Lynch 1973), social movement studies has largely ignored this critical historical epoch. To the best of my knowledge, there are no studies that approach Latin American independence from a contentious politics perspective/social movement theory. This is even more surprising, given that comparable historical turning points in Europe and other world regions have received ample attention within social movement studies and in fact have been crucial for more general theory-building on contentious politics (e.g., Sewell 1996; Slater 2010; Tilly 1964). Consequently, current research on nationalism and social movements during this period is dominated by historians, primarily focuses on individual countries or even subnational regions within a country, and tends to draw on a variety of (often left implicit) conceptual and theoretical frameworks.

Contributors to this body of work agree that nationalism as ideological form played an important role in Latin American independence struggles and the formation of national states. Creole insurgents envisioned distinct national identities to justify their claims for self-determination; these elites also highlighted certain cultural traits to distinguish themselves from Spain. Their discourses emphasized distinct origins narratives, religious symbols, linguistic patterns, and literary traditions, and celebrated a vague sense of regional belonging (Brading 1985; Shumway 1991; Thurner 1997). There is also agreement on the class composition of these movements. The actors at the center of anti-colonial mobilization were Creoles, who usually stood at the top of the socioeconomic ladder and the ethnoracial hierarchy, only eclipsed by the status of peninsular

Spaniards who circulated through the upper echelons of the colonial administrative apparatus (Anderson 1991; Brading 1991). Subordinate sectors were less central to Latin American independence, even though in some cases, most importantly in Mexico, they became important allies for Creole elites in their challenge of the established colonial order (Thurner 1997; Van Young 2001).

What remains a matter of debate, however, is the precise relationship between different aspects of nationalism during the transition from colonial empire to independent national states. Some scholars emphasize the collective mobilization and framing work of insurgent movements in creating new national ideologies and attachments. In order to legitimate their claims and bridge inequalities among constituencies, Creole elites promoted, if not invented, politically and culturally distinct nations as bearers of sovereignty (Hobsbawm 1995; Shumway 1991). Benedict Anderson (1991) even goes as far to suggest that nationalism was invented by insurgent Creoles and subsequently established a "blueprint" to be copied around the globe (though this claim has been met with significant skepticism by Latin Americanists, see Lomnitz 2001). Other scholars reverse the causal arrow and argue that preexisting (proto-national) ideological forms and collective attachments set the boundaries of what kinds of national projects could subsequently be imagined and thus shaped how nationalist mobilization unfolded. In this perspective, the possibility for insurgents to invent nations and mobilize people under their banner was preconfigured by established understandings of political community and cultural sameness. For example, in late colonial Mexico "Creole patriotism" already imagined a *patria* that was distinct from Spain and other colonial administrative units. This discourse locates Mexico's mythical roots in the Aztec Empire and embraces the Virgin of Guadalupe as an encompassing symbol shared by both elites and popular sectors (Brading 1991). In late colonial Peru, Creole patriotism was less powerful, to an important extent because of the geographical distance between the colonial capital (Lima) and the capital of the precolonial Inca Empire (Cuzco), but also because of still recent memories of dramatic subordinate uprisings, most prominently the Túpac Amaru rebellion during the 1780s (Mallon 1995; Walker 1999). Accordingly, Peruvian insurgents followed the example of their Argentine counterparts and celebrated the natural beauty of specific landscapes as the basis for national identity (Gutiérrez 1990; Shumway 1991)—probably a less compelling framing to garner popular support.

Another debate concerns the extent to which the new understandings of nationhood embraced by Creole insurgents resonated among the wider population. Some scholars argue that the struggles for independence—and the political and economic crises of the new postcolonial states immediately thereafter—led wide sectors of the population to see themselves as part of a larger national community that transcended their local lived experience. According to these works, the growing national identification among subordinate sectors had an important strategic component (Di Meglio 2006; Guardino 1996; Thurner 1997). Peasants as well as the urban poor learned quickly that identifying as Mexicans, Colombians, or Peruvians allowed them to frame their own political demands as being of "national interest" and thus provided them with a power resource in their own mobilizations for the extension of social and political rights to them in the newly formed national states (see Kastoryano 2002). Yet others remain skeptical about the wider resonance of nationalism during the independence struggles and the immediate postcolonial era. In this perspective, rural people were mostly concerned about maintaining their village identities and lifeways intact, and their collective mobilizations took a largely defensive posture towards the national(izing) projects advanced by Creole elites (Van Young 2001).

Seen in this light, more systematic comparative research on Latin American independence struggles from a social movement/contentious politics perspective is warranted. This is particularly pertinent given that the discussions surrounding the rise of nationalism in early nineteenth-century Latin America ultimately echo broader debates in the fields of nationalism and social movement studies. The study of nationalism has long been marked by controversy about whether nationalism (as an ideology and/or political movement) requires or precedes some wider national consciousness (see Gellner 1983; Gorski 2000; Greenfeld 1992; Hobsbawm 1990; Smith 1986). Yet most of the participants in this debate draw almost exclusively on case studies from the European context. In social movement studies the issue of frame resonance remains contested. The debate centers on the ways and extent to which the framing activities of social movements are bound by and can transcend the wider cultural resource base in a given context (Benford and Snow 2000; Goodwin and Jaspers 1999; McDonnell et al. 2017), as exemplified by the contradictory interpretations of Creole insurgents and their framing work.

Transforming Nationalism? Social Movements and the Rise of Mass Society

During the late nineteenth and early twentieth centuries the official nationalism advanced by most, if not all Latin American states combined civic with highly exclusionary and hierarchical visions of the nation (Itzigsohn and vom Hau 2006; Miller 2006). State-sponsored national ideologies stressed the political underpinnings of the national community, celebrating the respective constitutional framework in each country as a major source of attachment and pride. At the same time, these national ideologies were also deeply influenced by ideas about biologically determined social hierarchies and the efficient management of society from above. The spread of "civilization"—a category associated with whiteness, economic modernization, and an urban European culture—appeared as the ideal path for achieving national unity and progress (Quijada 2000). In fact, the indigenous population appeared as the main manifestation of "barbarism," to be overcome through education, European migration, or even outright extermination campaigns. Accordingly, national history represented an evolution through different stages, moving towards greater degrees of civilization. Benevolent elites were at the center stage of this process, and accounts of national history focused on major political leaders, whether Aztec or Inca rulers, colonial viceroys, or postcolonial presidents (vom Hau 2009).

This liberal-elitist nationalism was contested. During the late nineteenth century various social movements challenged this official national ideology. Growing and increasingly politicized middle sectors demanded their political and symbolic inclusion. These collective actors and their political organizations sought to counter the social Darwinist underpinnings of official national ideologies by advancing alternative nationalisms that put greater emphasis on the cultural essence of the respective national community (Florescano 1999; Rock 1993; Sábato 2000). Similarly, regional elites that felt threatened by the rising power of the central state disseminated contending nationalisms that envisioned an alternative geographical ordering of the nation (e.g., by treating Cuzco as the cradle of the Peruvian nation) (de la Cadena 2000; Rénique 1987). Finally, political Catholics protested the expanding "ideological work" of states by designating the Catholic faith as the most important national identity marker (Klaiber 1996; Meyer 1974).

From the early twentieth century onwards, in a context marked by the growing mobilization of subordinate sectors, labor and peasant movements pushed for their political inclusion and advanced class-based visions of nationhood that depicted peasants and workers as "true" nationals (Córdova 1973; Cotler 2005; Knight 1994; Mallon 1995). Specific movements varied in their framing strategies, movement infrastructure, and constituencies, yet they reconceived of established notions about national history and identity and infused them with different political meanings. These challenges also drew inspiration from transnational trends. From the late nineteenth century onward nationalist mobilization intensified around the globe, and national ideologies increasingly built on the ideal of a culturally homogeneous nation and stressed the principle of popular sovereignty and self-determination (Goswami 2002).

Yet, the wider resonance of these alternative nationalisms in official national ideologies and public discourse varied (vom Hau 2008). In some countries, for example Mexico, cultural-assimilationist and class-based conceptions of the national community became a regular product of state organizations and also reverberated in public culture. In other countries, most prominently Argentina, this new popular nationalism became official national ideology, but it remained fiercely contested and did not gain hegemonic status (Kyriazi and vom Hau 2020).

This poses the question: when did alternative nationalisms promoted by social movements gain wider resonance in official national ideologies and public discourse? The major theories of nationalism and their "developmentalist" approach (Brubaker 1996) ultimately do not offer a satisfactory answer. The distinct patterns of transformation found in Mexico and Argentina neither map onto differences in urbanization and industrialization (e.g., Gellner 1983), cultural modernization (e.g., Anderson 1991; Deutsch 1966), nor political modernization (e.g., Hobsbawn 1990; Mann 1993). Similarly, theories of social movement consequences that solely focus on movement infrastructure and resources (e.g., Andrews 2001) as well as inter- and intra-movement conflicts (e.g., Shelef 2010) have only limited explanatory power for the puzzle at hand. For example, both early twentieth-century Mexico and Argentina had well-organized labor movements and witnessed intense competition among rival movements and struggles between hardliners and tacticians within the same movement (Carr 1976; Hamilton 1982; Horowitz 1990; Suriano 2001; see Ramírez Gallegos and Stoessel in this volume).

More promising are approaches that combine attention to movement infrastructure—composed of the organizational structure, resources, and leadership of movements (Andrews 2001)—and the wider political opportunities and constraints confronted by those movements (Amenta 2006). Specifically, I argue that the wider resonance of movement-promoted nationalisms requires *intrastate* support (vom Hau 2018). Seen in this light, the most dramatic transformations of nationalism in Latin America unfolded when subordinate movements gained in political weight and when local state officials who were tasked with socializing citizens or otherwise disseminating official ideological projects embraced their national narratives. During the 1930s in post-revolutionary Mexico an alliance consolidated between organized labor, peasants, and post-revolutionary state elites (Knight 2002). Artists associated with the labor movement, such as the Mexican muralist Diego Rivera, found themselves on the government's payroll, while activists of the Communist Party were appointed to posts in the Secretaría de Educación Pública (SEP) (Vaughan 1997). Moreover, the majority of public school teachers active during the 1930s largely followed suit and embraced class-based understandings of national identity and history. During the 1940s and 1950s in Peronist Argentina, organized labor similarly formed part of the ruling coalition. Yet local state officials such as teachers opposed movement-promoted understandings of nationhood. In their own understandings of national identity and history Argentine teachers tended to follow cultural and highly elitist projections of nationhood (Cucuzza and Somoza 2001; Gvirtz 1999; vom Hau 2009).

Rejecting Nationalism? Social Movements in the Postnational Age

Nationalism in Latin America remains contested and changing (Itzigsohn and vom Hau 2006). This section takes stock of the scholarship on recent challenges of state-sponsored national ideologies, the main focus being indigenous movements (see Rice in this volume).

During recent decades indigenous peoples became a formidable political force in their own right, something unthinkable even a generation ago (Isla 2002; Lucero 2008; Stavenhagen 2002; Van Cott 2005). Their movements demand equal rights to overcome longstanding socioeconomic inequalities and they push for special rights to secure more political and territorial autonomy. The causes behind the rise of indigenous mobilization are multi-faceted and associated with major changes in global and national *opportunity structures*—most prominently the emergence of a global human rights regime (Risse and Sikkink 1999; Van Cott 2000; see Wolff in this volume). They are also linked to new *mobilizing resources*—most importantly the expansion of secondary and higher education and the rise of a new generation of indigenous activists (Gutierrez 1999; Wimmer 2002), and a decline of class politics in structuring interest mediation between states and their citizens (Castells 1997; Sieder 2002; Yashar 2005; see Rossi in this volume). A major *motivation* for local activists to make use of these new opportunities and resources, however, is recent economic changes linked to trade liberalization and the (re-)emergence of national development models focused on raw material extraction (Bebbington et al. 2008; Burchardt and Dietz 2014; Zoomers 2000). Export-oriented agriculture (e.g., wine, soybeans) and the expansion of extractive industries (e.g., mining) have put pressures on established landholding patterns, instigating new forms of conflict, especially because rural indigenous communities often lack tenure rights and do not have the title of the lands they live on and use.

From a nationalism perspective, the demands of indigenous movements for land and territorial rights and their pressures to address durable legacies of marginalization and discrimination are embedded in alternative understandings of nationhood. Indigenous movements seek recognition of the inherently multiethnic character of Latin American nations. Activists aspire more inclusive Latin American nations (de la Peña 2006; Gutiérrez 1999; Itzigsohn and vom Hau 2006; Paschel 2016), and this *multicultural nationalism* defines itself against the assimilationist tendencies of the cultural and class-based understandings of nationhood that prevailed in the region during the twentieth century. It treats citizenship (and not ethnicity) as the basic criterion of inclusion into the national community and envisions national unity to be achieved through the recognition of cultural and ethnic differences among co-nationals.

Yet it bears emphasis that the rise of multicultural nationalism in Latin America is not a direct result of indigenous mobilization. In fact, the relationship between the two should best be treated as a two-way street, with multicultural nationalism also facilitating the formation of indigenous movements: from the 1980s and 1990s onwards global and regional models of nationalism changed. Assimilationist nation-building lost normative purchasing power, while calls for the recognition of multiethnic nations started to provide local actors with a template for legitimate political action (see Meyer et al. 1997). Most prominently, in Latin America constitutional multiculturalism spread, leading most countries in the region to adopt new group rights that specifically apply to those among their citizens who identify as indigenous and/or Black (Paschel 2016; Van Cott 2000). Moreover, multicultural nationalism also found its way into official national ideologies. In Mexico, Peru, and Argentina, for instance, school curricula and textbooks started to embrace the imagery of a multiethnic nation and emphasized the recognition of cultural differences as integral part of the national project (García 2005; Gutiérrez 1999; Romero 2004).

Given the obvious articulation between the two, it is curious that the relationship between nationalism and indigenous movements has so far only received scarce attention in the literature. Much of the existing research on the emergence of indigenous movements emphasizes their transnational nature, especially with regards to newly available mobilizing resources and political opportunities such as international advocacy networks and funding sources (e.g., Brysk 2000; Keck and Sikkink 1998; Paschel 2016). What has received comparatively less airtime is how differences in the wider resonance of the old assimilationist nationalisms might have affected the nature of challenges launched by indigenous and Black movements (see Marx 1998; Dixon and Caldwell in this volume). A similar gap is variations in the extent to which the new multicultural nationalism has gained hold in public culture, and how this might be driven by differences in indigenous mobilization across Latin American countries.

STATE-SEEKING NATIONALISM? THE RELATIVE ABSENCE OF SEPARATIST MOBILIZATION

A final puzzle explored in this chapter is the paucity of state-seeking nationalism in Latin America (so far). While many indigenous movements strive to redefine official national ideologies and their criteria of inclusion and recognition (see Fontana in this volume), they do not seek their own state. In fact, when compared to other world regions, Latin America has only rarely seen the emergence of nationalist movements that claim separate statehood for a national community that currently does not have state control. This absence of state-seeking nationalism is nothing novel but has become an even more pronounced characteristic of the region since the second half of the twentieth century. For example, according to the *Correlates of War* database eight secessionist wars took place in Latin America during the nineteenth century, and only one secessionist conflict (Paulistas vs. Brazil 1932) during the twentieth century (see Wimmer and Min 2009). While separatist war is obviously only one possible manifestation of state-seeking nationalism, it is nonetheless illustrative of the "Latin American exceptionalism" in this regard.

What then explains the relative absence of state-seeking nationalist mobilization in the region? Surprisingly, this question has to this stage—with one working paper (Ross 2010) as the notable exception—not elicited any systematic research. This is even more puzzling, given that the current scholarship on separatism is not particularly well-equipped to provide a convincing answer. Studies on the political economy of secession (Balton and Roland 1997; Collier and Hoeffler 2011) usually emphasize a wealth maximization rationale, arguing that state-seeking nationalism is more likely where distinct groups (or regions within states) perceive secession as economically advantageous to them. This can cut both ways. Economically better-off groups (or regions) mobilize for secession because they want to avoid subsidizing less prosperous ones in a state, while economically disadvantaged groups (or regions) seek their own state because this would reduce competition over public goods and employment (Jenne et al. 2007). But following the argument set out by this body of work, state-seeking nationalism should be much more frequent in Latin America than it actually is. Stark socioeconomic differences between indigenous and non-indigenous groups prevail, even after three decades of indigenous mobilization for greater equity, and within-country differences in wealth and public goods provision are rampant, as for example illustrated by regional contrasts in Mexico (e.g., Chiapas vs. Nuevo León) or Argentina (e.g., Chaco vs. Santa Cruz).

Other studies emphasize political demography to account for the rise of secessionist movements. In this perspective, state-seeking nationalism is more likely when ethnic groups are geographically concentrated in a territory they perceive as their homeland, thereby facilitating claims for separate statehood (Tuft 2003). Analogously, separatist mobilization is more likely to occur in countries with comparatively large populations that make state control over marginalized groups more difficult (Wimmer et al. 2009). But again, these arguments do not hold up well for Latin America. Bolivia, Ecuador, Guatemala, Mexico, and Peru all have large and geographically-concentrated indigenous populations that—according to these studies—should have been predestined to fight for independence, while population size as such also appears to have limited explanatory power (Ross 2010).

Yet another body of research brings politics to the analytical forefront and draws—at least implicitly—inspiration from a contentious politics/social movement theory approach (Cederman et al. 2010; Salehyan 2007; Wimmer et al. 2009). In this perspective, the wider political context and mobilization resources matter to explain instances of state-seeking nationalism. Specifically, separatist mobilization is more likely when ethnic groups and their political representatives are excluded from national government and/or when they have experienced only a short history of independence (and are therefore not used to be governed directly). Moreover, following these authors, separatism is more likely to occur when ethnic groups (or regions) can draw on resources that facilitate mobilization, for example their relative group size or transnational networks to ethnic kin groups in neighboring countries. How do these factors play out to account for the relative absence of state-seeking nationalism in Latin America? As discussed in the previous section, indigenous groups have been politically marginalized until very recently. There is also no shortage of transnational connections between indigenous kin groups such as the Mapuche in Argentina and Chile or the Mbya Guarani in Argentina, Brazil, and Paraguay, whose historical sphere of influence spans across the territorial boundaries of those neighboring countries (vom Hau and Wilde 2010; Warren 2013).

In light of the rather limited explanatory power the scholarship on secessionism offers, what other factors might help to explain the Latin American puzzle? A possible way forward is to focus on individual cases that—while not resembling full-blown separatist nationalism—come at least reasonably close and then work backwards from their enabling conditions. The obvious case to start with is Santa Cruz in lowland Bolivia. In recent years this region has experienced rising mobilization around a radical project of autonomy that would, if realized, include control over its natural resources and most tax revenues as well as policy authority over every matter except defense and foreign policy (Eaton 2007; Gustafson 2006). Some see Santa Cruz's ambitions as a response of regional economic elites to indigenous mobilization and the ascendance of indigenous Bolivians to political power. This backlash was facilitated by the spatial disjuncture between political power (La Paz) and economic power (Santa Cruz) in the country, and the absence of a strong national party representing the interest of economic elites (Eaton 2007). Others emphasize the overlap between spatial and racial divisions—Santa Cruz remains dominated by whites—and the formation of tactical alliances between Cruceño elites and lowland indigenous peoples (Lowrey 2006). Either way, these enabling conditions for the radical autonomy project pursued by Santa Cruz may not be present in other Latin American cases and therefore help to provide a springboard for gaining a better understanding of the relative absence of separatist mobilization in other countries.

Conclusion

This chapter has focused on nationalism and its relationship to the causes, processes, and consequences of social movements in Latin America. To do so, it has unpacked the concept by distinguishing between three major approaches—namely nationalism as (1) a particular form of collective action, (2) a sense of attachment and identification, and (3) a cognitive and discursive framework that supplies particular ways to imagine a community. Equipped with this conceptual lens, the chapter has explored crucial turning points in the region's postcolonial history and examined the intersection between nationalism and social movements during the early nineteenth-century struggles for the formation of independent national states; the mid-twentieth-century decline of oligarchic rule and the emergence of mass societies; and the late twentieth-century adoption of neoliberalism and the rise of multiculturalism. Another issue covered was a Latin American peculiarity, namely the striking lack—from a cross-regional comparative perspective—of nationalist mobilization for secession and a separate state.

For each of these historical turning points and/or issues the chapter has discussed the major points of convergence and debate found in the relevant scholarship. It has also identified important gaps that require further attention and more systematic research from a social movement/contentious politics perspective. Specifically, the chapter suggests more cross-regional comparative research on Creole insurgents and their framing work, and the ways and extent to which the new understandings of nationhood promoted by them were bound by or transcended the wider cultural resource base. The chapter further argued for the need to develop theoretically informed accounts of when movement-promoted nationalisms achieve wider public resonance and gain entry into official national ideologies. More work is also needed on the role of nationalism in the recent intensification of ethnic-based mobilization in Latin America, both as a potential cause and an outcome of indigenous movements. Finally, the relative absence of state-seeking nationalism in Latin America remains a puzzle *and* an understudied subject— even more so in light of the fact that not only the existing scholarship on secessionism, but also the literatures on separatist conflict and contentious politics/social movements, appear unable to solve it.

References

Amenta, Edwin (2006), *When Movements Matter: The Townsend Plan and the Rise of Social Security* (Princeton, NJ: Princeton University Press).

Anderson, Benedict (1991), *Imagined Communities: Reflections on the Origins and Spread of Nationalism* (New York: Verso).

Andrews, Kenneth T. (2001), "Social Movements and Policy Implementation: The Mississippi Civil Rights Movement and the War on Poverty, 1965 to 1971," *American Sociological Review* 66(1), 71–95.

Bolton, Patrick and Gérard Roland (1997), "The Breakup of Nations: A Political Economy Analysis," *The Quarterly Journal of Economics* 112 (4), 1057–90.

Bebbington, Anthony, Denise Humphreys Bebbington, Jeffrey Buryc, Jeannet Lingand, Juan Pablo Muñoz, and Martin Scurrah (2008), "Mining and Social Movements: Struggles Over Livelihood and Rural Territorial Development in the Andes," *World Development* 36(12), 2888–905.

Beissinger, Mark R. (2002), *Nationalist Mobilization and the Collapse of the Soviet State* (New York: Cambridge University Press).

Benford, Robert D. and David A. Snow (2000), "Framing Processes and Social Movements. An Overview and Assessment," *Annual Review of Sociology* 26(1), 611–39.

Berezin, Mabel (2001), "Emotions and Political Identity: Mobilizing Affection for the Polity," in Jeff Goodwin, James M. Jasper, and Francesca Polletta (eds.), *Passionate Politics: Emotions and Social Movements*, 83–98 (Chicago, IL: The University of Chicago Press).

Brading, David A. (1985), *The Origins of Mexican Nationalism* (Cambridge: Center for Latin American Studies, University of Cambridge).

Brading, David A. (1991), *The First America: The Spanish Monarchy, Creole Patriots, and the Liberal State 1492–1867* (Cambridge: Cambridge University Press).

Brubaker, Rogers (1996), *Nationalism Reframed: Nationhood and the National Question in the New Europe* (Cambridge: Cambridge University Press).

Brubaker, Rogers (2004), *Ethnicity without Groups* (Cambridge, MA: Harvard University Press).

Brysk, Alison (2000), *From Tribal Village to Global Village: Indian Rights and International Relations in Latin America* (Stanford, CA: Stanford University Press).

Burchardt, Hans-Jürgen and Kristina Dietz (2014), "(Neo-)extractivism—A New Challenge for Development Theory from Latin America," *Third World Quarterly* 35, 468–86.

Calhoun, Craig (1997), *Nationalism* (Minneapolis: University of Minnesota Press).

Carr, Barry (1976), *El movimiento obrero y la política en México, 1910–1929* (Mexico: Secretaría de Educación Pública).

Castells, Manuel (1997), *The Power of Identity* (Malden: Blackwell).

Cederman, Lars, Andreas Wimmer, and Brian Min (2010). "Why Do Ethnic Groups Rebel? New Data and Analysis," *World Politics* 62(1), 87–119.

Centeno, Miguel Angel (2002), *Blood and Debt: War and the Nation-State in Latin America* (University Park: Pennsylvania State University Press).

Collier, David and Ruth Berins Collier (1991), *Shaping the Political Arena: Critical Junctures, the Labor Movement, and Regime Dynamics in Latin America* (Princeton, NJ: Princeton University Press).

Collier, Paul and Anke Hoeffler (2011), "The Political Economy of Secession," in Hurst Hannum (ed.), *Autonomy, Sovereignty, and Self-Determination: The Accommodation of Conflicting Rights*, 37–59 (Philadelphia: University of Philadelphia Press).

Córdova, Arnaldo (1973), *La ideología de la Revolución Mexicana* (Mexico: Ediciones Era).

Cotler, Julio (2005) [1978], *Clases, estado y nación en el Perú* (Lima: Instituto de Estudios Peruanos).

Cucuzza, Héctor and Miguel Somoza (2001), "Representaciones sociales en los libros escolares peronistas: una pedagogía para una nueva hegemonía," in Gabriela Ossenbach and Miguel Somoza (eds.), *Los manuales escolares como fuente para la historia de la educación en América Latina* (Madrid: Universidad Nacional de Educación a Distancia), 209–58.

de la Cadena, Marisol (2000), *Indigenous Mestizos: Race and the Politics of Representation in Cuzco, 1919–1991* (Durham, NC: Duke University Press).

de la Peña, Guillermo (2006), "A New Mexican Nationalism? Indigenous Rights, Constitutional Reform and the Conflicting Meanings of Multiculturalism," *Nations and Nationalism* 12, 279–302.

Deutsch, Karl (1966), *Nationalism and Social Communication: An Inquiry into the Formation of Nationality* (Cambridge, MA: MIT Press).

Di Meglio, Gabriel (2006), *¡Viva el bajo pueblo!: La plebe urbana de Buenos Aires y la política entre la Revolución de Mayo y el Rosismo (1810–1829)* (Buenos Aires: Prometeo).

Eaton, Kent (2007), "Backlash in Bolivia: Regional Autonomy as a Reaction against Indigenous Mobilization," *Politics & Society* 35, 71–102.

Florescano, Enrique (1999), *Memoria indígena* (Mexico: Taurus).

Gamson, William (1992), *Talking Politics* (Cambridge: Cambridge University Press).

García, María Elena (2005), *Making Indigenous Citizens: Identities, Education, and Multicultural Development in Peru* (Stanford, CA: Stanford University Press).

Gellner, Ernest (1983), *Nations and Nationalism* (Oxford: Oxford University Press).

Goodwin, Jeff and James Jasper (1999), "Caught in a Winding, Snarling Vine: The Structural Bias of Political Process Theory," *Sociological Forum* 14(1), 27–54.

Goodwin, Jeff, James Jasper, and Francesca Polletta (2000), "The Return of The Repressed: The Fall and Rise of Emotions in Social Movement Theory," *Mobilization* 5(1), 65–83.

Gorski, Philip S. (2000), "The Mosaic Moment: An Early Modernist Critique of Modernist Theories of Nationalism," *American Journal of Sociology* 105(5), 1428–68.

Goswami, Manu (2002), "Rethinking the Modular Nation Form: Toward a Sociohistorical Conception of Nationalism," *Comparative Studies in Society and History* 44(4), 770–99.

Greenfeld, Liah (1992), *Nationalism: Five Roads to Modernity* (Cambridge: Harvard University Press).

Guardino, Peter (1996), *Peasants, Politics and the Formation of Mexico's National State: Guerrero, 1800–1857* (Stanford, CA: Stanford University Press).

Guerra, Francisco-Xavier (2000), "The Implosion of the Spanish Empire: Emerging Statehood and Collective Identities," in Luis Roniger and Tamar Herzog (eds.), *The Collective and the*

Public in Latin America: Cultural Identities and Political Order (Brighton: Sussex Academic Press), 71–94.
Guibernau, Montserrat (1996), Nationalism: The Nation-State and Nationalism in the Twentieth Century (Cambridge: Polity).
Gutiérrez, Natividad (1990), "Memoria indígena en el nacionalismo precursor de México y Perú en el siglo XVIII," Estudios Interdisciplinarios de América Latina y el Caribe 1(2), 55–70.
Gutiérrez, Natividad (1999), Nationalist Myths and Ethnic Identities: Indigenous Intellectuals and the Mexican State (Lincoln: University of Nebraska Press).
Gustafson, Bret (2006), "Spectacles of Autonomy and Crisis: Or, What Bulls and Beauty Queens have to do with Regionalism in Eastern Bolivia," Journal of Latin American Anthropology 11, 351–79.
Gvirtz, Silvina (1999), El discurso escolar a través de los cuadernos de clase, Argentina 1930–1970 (Buenos Aires: EUDEBA).
Hamilton, Nora (1982), The Limits of State Autonomy: Post-revolutionary Mexico (Princeton, NJ: Princeton University Press).
Hechter, Michael (2000), Containing Nationalism (Oxford: Oxford University Press).
Hobsbawn, Eric J. (1990), Nations and Nationalism since 1780: Programme, Myth, Reality (Cambridge: Cambridge University Press).
Hobsbawm, Eric (1995), "Nationalism and National Identity in Latin America," in Bouda Etemad, Jean Baton, and Thomas David (eds.), Pour Une histoire Economique et Sociale Internationale: Melanges Offerts a Paul Bairoch (Geneva: Editions Passe Present), 313–23.
Horowitz, Joel (1990), Argentine Unions: The State and the Rise of Perón (Berkeley and Los Angeles: Institute of International Studies, University of California).
Isla, Alejandro (2002), Los usos politicos de la identidad: Indigenismo y Estado (Buenos Aires: Editorial de las Ciencias).
Itzigsohn, José and Matthias vom Hau (2006), "Unfinished Imagined Communities: States, Social Movements, and Nationalism in Latin America," Theory and Society 35, 193–212.
Jenne, Erin K., Stephen M. Saideman, and Will Lowe (2007), "Separatism as a Bargaining Posture: The Role of Leverage in Minority Radicalization." Journal of Peace Research 44(5), 539–58.
Kastoryano, Riva (2002), Negotiating Identities (Princeton, NJ: Princeton University Press).
Keck, Margaret E., and Kathryn Sikkink (1998), Activists Beyond Borders: Advocacy Networks in International Politics (Ithaca, NY: Cornell University Press).
Klaiber, Jeffrey (1996), La Iglesia en el Perú (Lima: Pontificia Universidad Católica del Perú).
Klarén, Peter Flindell (2000), Peru: Society and Nationhood in the Andes (Oxford: Oxford University Press).
Knight, Alan (1992), "The Peculiarities of Mexican History: Mexico Compared to Latin America, 1821–1992," Journal of Latin American Studies 24(1), 99–144.
Knight, Alan (1994), "Peasants into Patriots: Thoughts on the Making of the Mexican Nation," Mexican Studies 10(1), 135–62.
Knight, Alan (2002), "The Weight of the State in Modern Mexico," in James Dunkerley (ed.), Studies in the Formation of the Nation-State in Latin America, 212–53 (London: Institute of Latin American Studies).
Kyriazi, Anna and Matthias vom Hau (2020), "Textbooks, Postcards, and the Public Consolidation of Nationalism in Latin America," Qualitative Sociology 43(4), 515–42.
Lomnitz, Claudio (2001), "Nationalism as Practical System: Benedict Anderson's Theory of Nationalism from the Vantage Point of Spanish America," in Miguel Angel Centeno and

Fernando Lopez-Alves (eds.), *The Other Mirror: Grand Theory through the Lens of Latin America* (Princeton, NJ: Princeton University Press), 329–59.

López-Alves, Fernando (2000), *State Formation and Democracy in Latin America, 1810–1900* (Durham, NC: Duke University Press).

Lowrey, Kathleen (2006), "Bolivia Multiétnico y Pluricultural, Ten Years Later: White Separatism in the Bolivian Lowlands," *Latin American and Caribbean Ethnic Studies* 1(1), 63–84.

Lucero, José Antonio (2008), *Struggles of Voice: The Politics of Indigenous Representation in the Andes* (Pittsburgh, PA: University of Pittsburgh Press).

Lynch, John (1973), *Latin American Revolutions, 1808–1826: Old and New World Origins* (Oklahoma City: University of Oklahoma Press).

Mahoney, James (2010), *Colonialism and Postcolonial Development: Spanish American in Comparative Perspective* (New York: Cambridge University Press).

Mallon, Florencia (1995), *Peasant and Nation: The Making of Postcolonial Mexico and Peru* (Berkeley and Los Angeles: University of California Press).

Mann, Michael (1993), *The Sources of Social Power.* Vol. 2, *The Rise of Classes and Nation States 1760–1914* (Cambridge: Cambridge University Press).

Marx, Anthony (1998), *Making Race and Nation: A Comparison of South Africa, the United States, and Brazil* (Cambridge: Cambridge University Press).

Marx, Anthony (2003), *Faith in Nation: Exclusionary Origins of Nationalism* (New York: Oxford University Press).

McDonnell, Terrence. E., Christopher. A. Bail, and Iddo Tavory (2017), "A Theory of Resonance," *Sociological Theory* 35(1), 1–14.

Meyer, Jean. (1974), *La Cristiada* (Mexico: Siglo XXI).

Meyer, John W., John Boli, George Thomas, and Francisco O. Ramirez (1997), "World Society and the Nation-State," *American Journal of Sociology* 103(1), 144–81.

Miller, Nicola (2006), "The Historiography of Nationalism and National Identity in Latin America," *Nations and Nationalism* 12, 201–21.

Paschel, Tianna S. (2016), *Becoming Black Political Subjects: Movements and Ethno-Racial Rights in Colombia and Brazil* (Princeton, NJ: Princeton University Press).

Quijada, Mónica (2000), "El paradigma de la homogeneidad," in Mónica Quijada, Carmen Bernand, and Arnd Schneider (eds.), *Homogeneidad y Nación* (Madrid: Consejo Superior de Investigaciones Científicas), 15–55.

Rénique, José Luis (1987), "De la iber el progreso al mito andino," *Márgenes* 1, 9–33.

Risse, Thomas and Kathryn Sikkink (1999), "The Socialization of International Human Rights Norms into Domestic Practices: Introduction," in Thomas Risse, Stephen C. Ropp, and Kathryn Sikkink (eds.), *The Power of Human Rights International Norms and Domestic Change* (New York: Cambridge University Press), 1–38.

Rock, David (1987), *Argentina, 1516–1982: From Spanish Colonization to the Falklands War* (Berkeley and Los Angeles: University of California Press).

Rock, David (1993), *Authoritarian Argentina: The Nationalist Movement, Its History and Its Impact* (Berkeley and Los Angeles: University of California Press).

Romero, Luis Alberto (ed.) (2004), *La Argentina en la escuela: La idea de Nación en los textos escolares* (Buenos Aires: Siglo XXI).

Ross, Michael (2010), *Latin America's Missing Oil Wars.* Working paper, Department of Political Science, University of California, Los Angeles. http://www.michaelross.info/papers/working/Latin%20America's%20Missing%20Oil%20Wars.pdf

Sábato, Hilda (2000), *Ciudadanía política y formación de las naciones: perspectivas históricas de América Latina* (Mexico: Fondo de Cultura Económica).
Salehyan, Idean (2007), "Transnational Rebels: Neighboring States as Sanctuary for Rebel Groups," *World Politics* 59(2), 217–42.
Scheff, Thomas. J. (1994), *Bloody Revenge: Emotions, Nationalism, and War* (Boulder, CO, Westview Press).
Sewell, William H. (1996), "Historical Events as Transformations of Structures: Inventing Revolution at the Bastille," *Theory and Society* 25(6), 841–81.
Shelef, Nadav G. (2010), *Evolving Nationalism. Homeland, Identity, and Religion in Israel, 1925–2005* (Ithaca, NY: Cornell University Press).
Shumway, Nicolas (1991), *The Invention of Argentina* (Berkeley and Los Angeles: University of California Press).
Sieder, Rachel (2002), "Introduction," in Rachel Sieder (ed.), *Multiculturalism in Latin America: Indigenous Rights, Diversity, and Democracy*, 1–23 (New York: Palgrave Macmillan).
Silva, Eduardo (2009), *Challenging Neoliberalism in Latin America* (New York: Cambridge University Press).
Slater, Dan (2010), *Ordering Power. Contentious Politics and Authoritarian Leviathans in Southeast Asia* (New York: Cambridge University Press).
Smith, Anthony (1986), *The Ethnic Origins of Nations* (Oxford: Blackwell).
Snow, David A., E. Burke Rochford, Jr., Steven K. Worden, and Robert D. Benford (1986), "Frame Alignment Processes, Micromobilization, and Movement Participation," *American Sociological Review* 51, 464–81.
Stavenhagen, Rodolfo (2002), "Indigenous Peoples and the State in Latin America: An Ongoing Debate," in Rachel Sieder (ed.), *Multiculturalism in Latin America: Indigenous Rights, Diversity, and Democracy*, 24–44 (New York: Palgrave Macmillan).
Suriano, Juan (2001), *Anarquistas: Cultura y política libertaria en Buenos Aires, 1890–1910* (Buenos Aires: Manantial).
Thurner, Mark (1997), *From Two Republics to One Divided* (Durham, NC: Duke University Press).
Tilly, Charles (1964), *The Vendée* (Cambridge: Harvard University Press).
Tilly, Charles (1994), "States and Nationalism in Europe 1492–1992," *Theory and Society* 26(2/3), 131–46.
Van Cott, Donna Lee (2000), *The Friendly Liquidation of the Past: The Politics of Diversity in Latin America* (Pittsburgh: University of Pittsburgh Press).
Van Cott, Donna (2005), *From Movements to Parties in Latin America: The Evolution of Ethnic Politics* (New York: Cambridge University Press).
Van Young, Eric (2001), *The Other Rebellion: Popular Violence, Ideology, and the Mexican Struggle for Independence, 1810–1821* (Stanford, CA: Stanford University Press).
Vaughan, Mary Kay (1997), *Cultural Politics in Revolution: Teachers, Peasants, and Schools in Mexico, 1930–1940* (Tucson: University of Arizona Press).
vom Hau, Matthias (2008), "State Infrastructural Power and Nationalism: Comparative Lessons from Mexico and Argentina," *Studies in Comparative International Development* 43(3–4), 334–54.
vom Hau, Matthias (2009), "Unpacking the School: Textbooks, Teachers, and the Construction of Nationhood in Mexico, Argentina, and Peru," *Latin American Research Review* 44(3), 127–54.

vom Hau, Matthias (2018), "The Developmental State and the Rise of Popular Nationalism: Cause, Coincidence, or Elective Affinity?" in Miguel Centeno and Agustín Ferraro (eds.), *State and Nation Making in Latin America and Spain*. Vol. 2, *Rise & Fall of the Developmental State*, 317–45 (New York: Cambridge University Press).

vom Hau, Matthias and Guillermo Wilde (2010), "We Have Always Lived Here: Indigenous Movements, Citizenship, and Poverty in Argentina," *Journal of Development Studies* 46(7), 1283–303.

Walker, Charles F. (1999), *Smoldering Ashes. Cuzco and the Creation or Republican Peru, 1780–1840* (Durham, NC: Duke University Press).

Warren, Sarah (2013), "A Nation Divided: Building the Cross-Border Mapuche Nation in Chile and Argentina," *Journal of Latin American Studies*, 45 (2), 235–264.

Wimmer, Andreas (2002), *Nationalist Exclusion and Ethnic Conflict: Shadows of Modernity* (Cambridge: Cambridge University Press).

Wimmer, Andreas and Brian Min (2009), "The Location and Purpose of Wars Around the World: A New Global Dataset, 1816–2001," *International Interactions* 35(4), 390–417.

Wimmer, Andreas, Lars Cederman, and Brian Min (2009), "Ethnic Politics and Armed Conflict: A Configurational Analysis of a New Global Data Set," *American Sociological Review* 74(2), 316–37.

Yashar, Deborah (2005), *Contesting Citizenship in Latin America: The Rise of Indigenous Movements and the Postliberal Challenge* (Cambridge: Cambridge University Press).

Zoomers, Annelies (2000), *Current Land Policy in Latin America: Regulating Land Tenure under Neoliberalism* (Amsterdam: Royal Tropical Institute).

CHAPTER 11

SOCIAL MOVEMENTS AND REVOLUTIONS IN LATIN AMERICA

A Complex Relationship

SALVADOR MARTÍ I PUIG AND
ALBERTO MARTÍN ÁLVAREZ

Introduction

The concept of political and social revolution, in contrast to other concepts such as uprisings, rebellions, riots, or coups, implies a profound and lasting transformation of society. Based on the definition proposed by Selbin (1993: 11–13), social revolution can be understood as "the overthrowing of a ruling elite by an insurgent elite (or revolutionary vanguard), which has managed to capitalize on broad popular support, and which, once in power, seeks to change the social, economic and political structures of society." Thus, a revolution implies a dialectical process in which the will to destroy the "previous order" is linked to the aspiration to restructure a new social, economic and political reality. Throughout this process, the relationship among the stakeholders that drive (or restrict) change may be conflictive and tortuous.

Throughout the last decades of the twentieth century and in the first few years of the twenty-first, the debate surrounding the causes of revolutions was both intense and fruitful. A large part of this academic output has highlighted the vulnerability of certain types of political regimes to revolutionary challenges. For example, Skocpol (1984) pointed out that social revolution originated in the inability of some states—partially bureaucratized authoritarian monarchies—to deal with military challenges from foreign powers and to extract resources from the ruling class in order to respond to such challenges. For his part, Goodwin (2001) argued that revolutionary movements in the

Global South generally arose in the face of politically exclusive, repressive regimes with little military and police strength. Moreover, when faced with corrupt, personalist regimes, these movements had the chance to succeed.

Recent studies on revolutions in Global South societies have adopted a multi-causal approach made up of diverse factors (contingency, agency, and socio-economic and discursive factors). Thus, for example, Wickham-Crowley (1992: 320) posited that in Latin America after 1959 certain patrimonial praetorian regimes collapsed when faced with guerrilla movements with strong peasant support and significant military strength. In these cases (Cuba and Nicaragua), the guerrillas were able to create a broad inter-class alliance against patrimonial dictators that lacked social bases of support and were finally defeated by national resistance movements. In turn, in a larger study, Foran (2005) pinpointed five factors, which, occurring in conjunction, were necessary for a successful revolution: dependent development; a repressive exclusionary, personalist state; effective and powerful political cultures of resistance; an economic downturn; and a world-systemic opening. The combination of these factors would enable a "multi-class, cross-racial and all-gendered coalition of aggrieved social forces" to surface (Foran 2005: 23).

Successful revolutions in twentieth-century Latin America were also the work of broad inter-class, urban-rural coalitions led by insurgent elites. However, little discussion has been held on the importance of the relationship between social movements in a broad sense—where mobilizations, organizational density, and critical social capital are included—and guerrilla organizations, considered as armed insurgent elites. Similarly, how the efforts of the revolutionaries enabled different revolutionary coalitions to emerge, or how their strategies were able to provide greater or lesser breadth and keep the coalitions united (or not) have received little in-depth analysis.

Despite not overlooking the importance of the repressive capacity of the state, the type of regime, or the international situation, in this chapter we maintain that the "agency" of revolutionary movements plays a key role in the success of a revolutionary struggle. Our objective is to contribute to exploring the effects that the degree of cohesion of the armed insurgent elites have had as well as the different forms of relationship between these elites and social movements in the revolutionary conflicts of Latin America; that is, to explore the relationship between social movements, the vanguard and the outcomes of revolutions. To do so, we will start by mentioning briefly three classic revolutions that took place in the subcontinent—in Bolivia, Cuba, and Mexico— in order to shed some light on the differences among them in terms of the interaction between leaders and movements. We will then point out the dynamics that existed in the relationship between the guerrilla vanguard and social movements in the 1959–1989 period, which spanned the first and second wave of guerrilla warfare. In the following section, we will analyze the change in logic that the Zapatista uprising represented and its repercussions in transnational solidarity movements and the resistance to neoliberalism. Finally, by way of conclusion, we will present the tentative findings provided by this chapter.

The Revolutionary Tradition in Latin America and the "Victorious" Revolutions: Mexico, Bolivia, and Cuba

The role played by social movements in these three revolutionary processes differed considerably. In Mexico, the peasant movements far exceeded the plans conceived by the elites to replace Porfirio Díaz's government. In contrast, in Bolivia, the revolutionary elites were successful in controlling the aspirations of the worker's movements to strengthen the revolution. Meanwhile, in Cuba, the vanguard exercised remarkable control over popular movements in both the insurrectionary period and in the subsequent organization of the new revolutionary regime.

The great Latin American revolution of the first half of the twentieth century was the one that took place in Mexico. Originating in 1910 in the context of the re-election of Porfirio Díaz, it was based on the struggle to democratize the regime (Knight 2010; Silva Herzog 2010). A new power elite led by the president, Francisco I. Madero, and embodied in the middle classes, was established as a new historical bloc. However, in the end, the revolutionary whirlwind favored diversity within its ranks, the consolidation of different projects, and the establishment of revolutionary leaders who flew the flag for the ambitions of other social groups, calling into question the hegemony of the middle classes. The coordination of the different factions was carried out through charismatic political-military leadership embodied in Emiliano Zapata and Pancho Villa (Katz 2002; Womack 2004).

From 1917, with the drafting of the new constitution, the revolution launched some fundamental changes. These included the agrarian reform, which became state policy until the middle of the twentieth century, the consolidation of a framework to guarantee labor rights, and the establishment of clear rules for the political game. Thus, the institutionalization of the new regime became a reality, exemplified by a single party, a renewed economy, a powerful state, boosted industrialization, class conciliation, and a revolutionary-oriented, anti-imperialist nationalist ideology (see vom Hau in this volume).

The revolutionary leaders built the foundations to stabilize the post-revolutionary regime and not only planned orderly economic growth but also guaranteed social peace. However, despite their achievements, in the period from 1917 to 1930, a strict control over trade unionism was maintained, the agrarian reform was timidly developed, militant anti-clericalism existed, and foreign capital was present in the mining and oil sectors. Moreover, this period was marked by the assassination of the main revolutionary leaders, who represented the popular sectors, and by the rise of regional military leaders and *caudillos* through the single party. The institutionalized revolution finally imposed itself and enabled the peasant and proletarian movements, which had presided over the revolutionary momentum, to develop. In the mid-1940s, with the end of the

Second World War and the prolegomena to the Cold War, the revolutionary process was brought to a close.

The Bolivian revolution is impossible to understand without taking into account the disaster of the Chaco War (1932–1935), which shook the foundations of Bolivian society and had a strong impact on intellectuals and urban youth (Gotkowitz 2007; Klein 2003). The result of the conflict led to the emergence of a radical critique of the racist and classist foundations of the society and the oligarchic nature of its economic structures (Klein 2003: 202). Against this backdrop, the Partido Obrero Revolucionario (POR), of Trotskyist tendency, was founded in exile, and in 1942, the more reformist Movimiento Nacional Revolucionario (MNR), led by Víctor Paz Estenssoro and Hernán Siles Suazo, was founded. This party became part of the government after the 1943 coup led by Gualberto Villarroel (1943–1946). During this period, the MNR sought to get closer to the indigenous masses and mine workers organized by the POR. In 1944, the collaboration between the MNR and the POR enabled a federation of mine workers, the Federación Sindical de Trabajadores Mineros de Bolivia (FSTMB), to be created. It became the most powerful trade union movement in the country. The alliance forged between the MNR and the workers organized in the FSTMB contributed to the ideological re-configuration of the party and laid the foundations for the revolutionary coalition that would come to power in 1952. The violence and repression of these years would mean an increase in social mobilization that the MNR sought to channel through the electoral route in 1951, proposing Paz Estenssoro and Siles Suazo as presidential candidates. The party won the elections, but before it could take over the presidency, the armed forces intervened by canceling the election results and outlawing the MNR. Against this backdrop, and together with a severe crisis in the price of tin, increasing unrest was generated among the ranks of organized miners and the MNR by the actions of the FSTMB and the leadership of the MNR itself. After several attempts, the final revolt took place on April 9, 1952. In just three days, the state collapsed, its military and police forces outnumbered by the armed population grouped into urban and rural militia led by the FSTMB and the MNR. The arming of the people and the disappearance of state institutions led to a social revolution that brought the MNR to power.

The revolutionary regime immediately established universal suffrage, purged army officers, and reduced the number of military forces. However, the MNR did everything in its power to control the most radical property redistribution measures demanded by both miners and peasants.

With regard to Cuba, the Movimiento 26 de Julio (M26-J) was created in hiding in 1955 by the survivors of the assault on the Moncada barracks and was led by Fidel Castro. This group joined forces with the MNR, founded by Rafael García Bárcenas, the Juventud Ortodoxa, and the Acción Nacional Revolucionaria led by Frank País, thus bringing together nationalists, social democrats, socialists, and Partido Ortodoxo militants in one group (Sweig 2002: 15). The movement's initial strategy to seize power rapidly was intended to combine the landing of a small band of guerrillas in the province of Oriente with a popular uprising in the province's capital, Santiago de Cuba, on November 30, 1956. The failure of this strategy led the M26-J to raise the need for strengthening the guerrilla front in the mountains and the formation of an urban militia and a civilian front was proposed. From then on, the strategy used to overthrow Fulgencio Batista's government would be the general strike backed by armed struggle. The movement organized a national Directorate, led by Frank País (until his death), and by Léster Rodríguez.

The M26-J managed to lead the opposition against Batista, displacing Blas Roca's Partido Socialista Popular (PSP). The PSP was hindered by having collaborated with the dictatorship since the 1930s and was skeptical about the strategy of armed struggle proposed by M26-J. It was not until the end of 1957 when the PSP would sign a collaboration agreement with the M26-J, building the Frente Nacional Obrero, which would back clandestine guerrilla support activities.

In March 1957, the Directorio Revolucionario 13 de Marzo, together with the Organización Auténtica (OA) launched an assault on the Presidential palace with the hope that the regime would collapse after the dictator had been physically eliminated. This action, in which the M26-J did not participate, was a failure that resulted in the loss of forty militants from the organizations involved and the arrest of another four hundred, considerably weakening both organizations. Nor was the relation between the M26-J and the OA exempt from tensions and rivalries. At the time of the Granma landing, the OA did not support the M26-J in Santiago de Cuba as initially promised. After the failed assault on the Presidential Palace, the OA leaders went into exile and trained to land in Cuba again. This landing took place in May 1957 and was again a resounding failure. The M26-J benefitted politically from the defeats suffered by the Directorio and the OA in the course of 1957. From then on, the forces led by Castro and País became the only viable insurgent force. As of December 1958, with the Pact of Pedrero, the M26-J and the Directorio agreed on unity of action. In this context, the M26-J became the vanguard of the revolution, displacing the rest of the organizations.

In the Cuban insurrectionary process (1956–1959), the revolutionary movement was led by an alliance of clandestine organizations, whose leadership was mainly composed of middle-class militants united under the banner of nationalism, anti-imperialism, and the anti-dictatorial struggle. The most distinctive feature of the Cuban case, compared to the two previous cases, is that the leadership of the revolutionary movement was located in a small armed contingent of the M26-J, which deployed guerrilla warfare against the armed forces. After just over two years of armed struggle, the Cuban rebels managed to seize power and establish a new regime that has declared itself socialist since 1961. Although the repertoire of actions carried out by the revolutionaries during the period of the struggle against Batista's dictatorship was not restricted to rural guerrilla warfare, the new regime constructed a narrative of its own struggle based on this strategy.

In each of these successful revolutions, the relationship between movements and the vanguard has clearly differed. In the case of Mexico, insurgent peasant movements far exceeded the limits of the plans conceived by the revolutionary elites, which had initially been aimed only at ending the *Porfiriato* and establishing agreements allowing them to alternate in the exercise of state power. In Bolivia, the vanguard held back the labor movement when it threatened to become more radical and extend the scope of the revolutionary project, ending in a state of implosion. In the Cuban revolution, the vanguard gained advantage and exercised remarkable control over the people's movements, contributing to their victory. Subsequently, it organized and supervised the movements from the government, turning these movements into mass organizations that were later to play a role in the actions and objectives of the socialist project, albeit with little autonomy and within the framework of party discipline.

THE REVOLUTIONARY WAVE (1960S-1980S)

The Cuban revolution was a *catalyst movement* (McAdam 1995). As Minkoff (1997: 2) points out, a successful movement usually produces an increase in the density of social movement organizations and, in turn, this organizational infrastructure contributes to spreading the protest and, if conditions are favorable, triggering cycles of protest. In the case of Cuba, combined with the demonstration effect of the Cuban victory was the active policy of support shown by the new revolutionary government to the revolutionary movements formed in its wake throughout Latin America, which provided greater impetus and a longer duration to the revolutionary wave begun in the 1960s.

This wave ebbed and flowed for over three decades. Analysis reveals that at least two waves of activity can be distinguished in the founding of these organizations (Martín Álvarez and Rey Tristán 2018), whose development is associated with the incorporation of different cohorts of militants in revolutionary movements against a backdrop of intense political mobilization (Figure 11.1).[1]

In the first wave of activity, which encompasses the revolutionary groups that emerged between 1960 and 1967, a strategy inspired by the *foco* theory was developed. This centered on introducing small military contingents in mountain or forest areas away from state control. It must be said that the *foco* theory was an *ex post facto* theoretical creation, which had been disseminated in the writings of Che Guevara and Regis

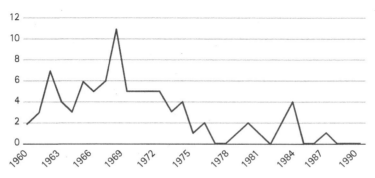

FIGURE 11.1 Latin American emergence of armed revolutionary groups by year (1960–1990)

Source: Martín Álvarez and Rey Tristán (2018)

Debray since the mid-1960s (Childs 1995). The Cuban victory was actually the work of a broad revolutionary coalition of urban and rural organizations and not merely that of a heroic group of mountain-based guerrillas, as subsequent theory elaboration was aimed at demonstrating. These armed vanguard movements were mainly composed of young dissidents from left-wing (or center-Left) parties, university students, ex-military, and a strikingly low proportion of manual laborers and peasants (Martín Álvarez 2017).

At this stage, the armed vanguards were considerably cut off from the people's movements. In almost all cases, the armed groups resorted to creating student support organizations or sought to forge links with the unions or opposition parties. However, the geographical isolation of the guerrilla fighters, the clandestine nature of the majority of their militants, and the almost exclusive focus on development and military confrontation, made it difficult to create an organizational infrastructure for a social movement connected with the revolutionaries' strategy. Moreover, it should be noted that the level of cohesion among the armed vanguard groups was in itself low. Highly significant political and strategic differences existed among the different organizations, making a unified strategy of confrontation with the state impossible (Kruijt, Rey Tristán, and Martín Álvarez 2020).

Some cases in which left-wing armed groups acquired greater relative development during this stage serve to illustrate the above. Between 1960 and 1962, the Movimiento Revolucionario 13 de Noviembre (MR-13) and the Fuerzas Armadas Rebeldes (FAR) emerged in Guatemala. In turn, their appearance on the scene was related with the cycle of authoritarianism begun after overthrowing Jacobo Arbenz, with the support provided by the government of General Ydígoras Fuentes to the training of anti-Castro forces in Guatemalan territory, and with the repression of student protests in 1962 (Gott 2008; Martín Álvarez 2017; see Brockett in this volume). The revolutionary vanguard, strongly influenced by the *foco* theory, was mainly composed of students, a small group of former nationalist military and the Partido Guatemalteco del Trabajo (PGT communist). From 1962 to 1970, period in which the FAR and the MR-13 remained active, the focus was on developing military activities in rural areas and on maintaining a clandestine rearguard in the capital for logistic purposes. Their geographical isolation in mountain areas, where they had no previous social connections, and their clandestine situation in cities hindered their ability to build a broad social support environment in a context of general demobilization motivated by state repression. To this must be added the lack of cohesion of the revolutionary vanguard itself, especially due to ideological differences. Therefore, the first wave of revolutionary activity in Guatemala ended with an outright military defeat.

In Nicaragua, the armed struggle had been part of the confrontation repertoire of the opposition forces since Somoza's rise to power. To be precise, the extermination of a guerrilla column, made up of militants of the traditional parties, triggered a series of student mobilizations in León in 1959. The ensuing repression led to the radicalization of a small group of students who called themselves the Juventud Revolucionaria Nicaragüense (JRN). This group was joined by a small organization made up of students and some workers that went on to form the Frente Sandinista de Liberación Nacional (FSLN) between 1961 and 1963. Throughout the 1960s, this organization adopted a repertoire based on the *foco* theory, introducing small armed contingents in isolated mountain areas where they did not have pre-existing networks of organized militants. The defeat of this first attempt did not mark the end of the FSLN. The organization persisted in its strategy and created a new guerrilla base in the Matagalpa department, which was also decimated by the armed forces in 1967. This second disaster, which led to the death of two of its leaders, brought the first stage of the development of the Frente Sandinista to an end. Throughout this first period, the Sandinismo was unable to build a broad supportive social environment apart from clandestine networks. Its strategy, focused almost exclusively on the rural armed struggle, led to the isolation of its militancy, and resulted in its inability to expand its urban support bases (Martín Álvarez 2017).

During this first period, revolutionary organizations in other countries of the region met a similar fate. The Ejército de Liberación Nacional (ELN) and the Movimiento de la Izquierda Revolucionaria (MIR) of Peru (1962–1965) and the Fuerzas Armadas de Liberación Nacional (FALN) of Venezuela (1962–1969) were guerrilla groups deployed in isolated mountain areas. They were unable to build significant alliances with opposition parties (except in the case of the FALN whose presence in cities was linked to the Partido Comunista de Venezuela—PCV). Lack of cohesion was also a constant feature of the revolutionary elites, and they were wiped out by the military in a few years. In Peru, the MIR and the ELN failed to reach an agreement to coordinate their actions, while, in Venezuela, the PCV left the FALN in 1965, undermining its ability to become linked to communist-inspired social movements.

It should also be mentioned that almost all the armed organizations of this period received support in the form of training or arms from the Cuban government (Kruijt 2017). However, this support decreased considerably after Cuban policy towards Latin America was reoriented in 1968. This reorientation was caused by the Cuban-Soviet rapprochement, Che Guevara's failed operation in Bolivia and a new approach in Cuban leadership towards possible alliances with national-revolutionary Latin American governments (Harmer 2013). The death of Che Guevara in Bolivia in October 1967 marked the symbolic closure of the wave of activity carried out by revolutionary movements inspired by, and under the influence of, the Cuban *foco* strategy.

Since the mid-1960s, other innovations had been taking shape in armed struggle repertoires among opposition groups in some countries with the aim of adapting them to the conditions present in highly urbanized societies. This was the case, for example, of the Movimiento de Liberación Nacional Tupamaros in Uruguay, which saw an increase in its ranks following the 1968 student protests in this country, but whose origins were actually linked to the demonstration effect of Cuba's successful victory (Rey Tristán, 2005). There were also cases in which armed organizations tried to construct popular war strategies,[2] but were unable to develop them for different reasons, so they focused their fundamental activities in urban environments. Such was the case of the Ejército Revolucionario del Pueblo (ERP) in Argentina between 1970 and 1976.

New Ripples in the Revolutionary Wave

In the early 1970s, new organizations emerged, encouraged by cohorts of younger militants motivated and inspired not only by the example of Cuba, but also by other successful revolutionary processes, including the struggle of the Vietnamese National Liberation Front. This second ripple of activity had its own origins in each country but clear patterns of similarities also existed between them. The repression of the cycle of student and labor protests that occurred in the region between 1967 and 1969 had contributed to the radicalization of new cohorts of activists, who, in some cases, founded new armed left-wing groups or were incorporated into the survivors of previous groups. In cases like Guatemala, Nicaragua, Colombia, or Peru, the cohort of founders of armed organizations in the early 1960s either worked on rebuilding these organizations or founding new ones, but this time according to new strategic foundations (Martín Álvarez, 2017). People's war as a strategy—in its different variants inspired by the writings of Mao Tse Tung, Ho-Chi Minh, and Nguyen Giap—was one of the main sources of inspiration.

Regardless of its loyalty to the original models, the adaptation of this strategy resulted in considering revolutionary mobilization in a broad sense, going well beyond military aspects and, by necessity, involving the organized masses. This involvement saw the creation of social formations (unions, student organizations, and peasants from marginalized regions) who ended up collaborating with, or joining, a revolutionary coalition. In these cases, the social movements maintained different degrees of autonomy with respect to the armed vanguard and occasionally ended up becoming a part of the guerrilla structure itself through clandestine links. Evidence would suggest that the type of links between the guerrilla groups and these movements, and the degree of autonomy of one with respect to the other, had a significant impact in terms of the consistency of the strategy and the magnitude of the challenge to which the respective states were subjected.[3]

Second-wave guerrilla groups were better able to challenge the status quo than those of the first wave because of their capacity for establishing links with subordinate social groups and their demands, and especially with grassroots ecclesial communities and urban popular movements (see Mackin, Oxhorn in this volume). In addition, second-wave organizations generally developed a clear strategy for creating supportive social environments in both urban and rural settings. An example of this is the FSLN, which survived the transition from first to second wave and largely fits the pattern described above. In the first wave, the FSLN was an organization concentrated in rural areas, with weak links to social movements composed mainly of students, However, in the second wave, the FSLN was split up into three factions, each linked to different movements: the FSLN Prolonged People's War among the peasantry, the FSLN Proletarian Tendency among rural and urban unions, and the FSLN Third Party among students and middle-class intellectuals. At the same time, the FSLN created movements (for women, students, workers, and intellectuals) in which new militants could be recruited (Martí i Puig

1997). Following the victory of the revolution, the new Nicaraguan revolutionary regime based the mechanisms of popular representation on incorporating the organizational infrastructure of people's movements into the structures of the state.

This strategy was very different from the one developed by other revolutionary groups, where supportive social environments were stronger than military structures. This was the case, for example, in Guatemala and El Salvador during the second half of the 1970s (Martín Álvarez and Cortina Orero 2014; Vázquez Olivera and Campos Hernández 2020). Moreover, in these cases, revolutionary organizations were unable to bridge their differences and build unified revolutionary movements. As a result, the revolutionaries failed to develop a coherent anti-state strategy, and on many occasions, competed with one another for the recruitment of militants, the direction of the movement or for resources from abroad. In this sense, the Nicaraguan example clearly contrasts with that of El Salvador, in which the armed vanguard, present since 1970, converged with a popular movement prior to that of the vanguard itself. In contrast to what had occurred in Nicaragua, the Salvadoran people's movements, at least in the early years, enjoyed relative autonomy with respect to the revolutionary elite in terms of strategy development and confrontation repertoire. On the other hand, and more importantly, the revolutionary elites continued to lack unity for almost a decade and were unable to capitalize on the rise in mobilizations among popular movements in the late 1970s. When the armed organizations finally decided to join forces in October 1980 with the formation of the Frente Farabundo Martí para la Liberación Nacional (FMLN), the wave of protest was ebbing due to state repression. The result was that the FMLN was able to count on a strong, stable support base in its confrontation with the state, but was no longer able to trigger sufficient social mobilization for a generalized insurrection that might have led to the victory of the revolution.

Finally, the Nicaraguan victory in 1979 had a strong impact throughout the region and contributed to the recovery of confidence in the armed struggle as a tool for political and social change by opposition sectors throughout the area. This led to some new armed left-wing groups being founded in the early 1980s, mainly in Peru, Chile, and Ecuador (Reyes 2017), and an increase in the activity of pre-existing organizations in Colombia, El Salvador, and Guatemala. However, during this period, there were no notable innovations in terms of the relationships between the vanguard and their supportive environment, and for various reasons, the new armed organizations failed to forge sufficient links with the organizational infrastructure of the social movements.

In summary, it is important to point out two issues. The first is the importance of the ability of the revolutionary vanguard to establish broad alliances (across classes, urban and rural, and with sectors of the political elites) with their environment in the revolutionary struggle. The second is that the vanguard's capacity (or lack thereof) for disciplining its social environment was central to the effectiveness of the insurrectional uprising. This is one of the major differences between first- and second-wave organizations. In the second wave, the guerrilla groups were more organized and connected with like-minded social groups, although their ability to control them was mixed: the FSLN succeeded, while the FMLN could not, since the existing network of social movements in El Salvador—especially at first—had remarkable autonomy.

The Revolution after the Fall of the Berlin Wall: Zapatismo

With the fall of the Berlin Wall, the implosion of the Soviet Union, the Special Period in Cuba, the electoral defeat of the FSLN in Nicaragua, and the signing of peace agreements in El Salvador (1992) and in Guatemala (1996), the revolutionary movements in Latin America began a process of decline. Against this backdrop, the uprising of the Ejército Zapatista de Liberación Nacional (EZLN) in Chiapas in 1994 was an unexpected surprise, while also promoting a radically different revolutionary struggle from previous ones and a new relationship with social movements. Thus, although the EZLN was a movement whose origins dated back to the national liberation movements of the 1970s,[4] it changed its discourse, strategy, and repertoire a few days after the uprising and implemented a new type of insurgency that paved the way for, and foreshadowed, the anti-globalization movements (see Volpi 2004; Oikonomakis, von Bülow in this volume), even though its discourse continued to adhere to the principle of "seizing power and carrying out the revolution" (Rovira 1997).

The relationship between the EZLN and the social movements was novel in two aspects: in the way they organized their bases in "their territory," and in their ability to organize a broad network of national and, above all, transnational solidarity (see Rovira 2009; Davis and Davey in this volume). Regarding the way the bases were organized in Zapatista-controlled territories, it should be noted that, with the Zapatista uprising, many peasants from different communities linked to the EZLN overwhelmed the leadership and occupied land, since for a majority of the population in the area, occupation was the only way to obtain land. The *agrarian distribution* of the Mexican Revolution had arrived only very sporadically in Chiapas and had had practically no impact on the large estates there (De Vos 2002: 323–29). In the end, the occupied territories were the physical space from which the *autonomous municipalities* were created. These became structures for the coordination, representation, and administration of the bases that supported the EZLN (known as *support bases*), and who lived in communities.

This process meant a kind of "re-municipalization" of the north-eastern region of Chiapas, with over thirty autonomous municipalities being created in 1998. According to Van der Haar (1998), this led to the construction of a parallel, rival structure to the official municipality. The autonomous municipalities were a challenge for the government because they had their own laws and representatives, and they managed their own resources. Another characteristic of the autonomous municipalities was that they were not defined geographically but by the affiliation of their bases, a fact that meant the existence of parallel, rival structures of people and resources in the same space. Autonomous municipalities assumed jurisdiction over the Zapatista-affiliated population and over the occupied land, resources, health services, education, and the administration of justice. Yet the municipalities and Zapatista-controlled territories have been changing since 1994. Since the Zapatista uprising the territory had been divided into units called *Aguascalientes*. Later, in 2003, their new designation was *Caracoles*, of which there were five until August 2019, and subsequently eleven.[5] A *Caracol*, in Zapatista terminology, refers to the physical space where the civil administration of the rebel territory is coordinated. The heads of administration are called *Juntas de Buen Gobierno* (Good Government Boards) and are made up of representatives from each of the communities present in the territory. At the beginning of the uprising, these municipalities were places of encounter between the EZLN and the national and international civil society that supported them. These boards held meetings that had a great impact in the world of international revolutionary solidarity and in the political dynamics of Mexico. The two most emblematic cases were the *National Democratic Convention* in Guadalupe Tepeyac in 1994 and the *Intercontinental Encounter for Humanity and against Neoliberalism* held in La Realidad in 1995.

These meetings were the crowning moment in a love relationship between radical social movements and Zapatismo, generating a new capacity to link a revolutionary organization with social movements. This phenomenon has been linked to the media impact that Zapatismo had, since it sparked a great wave of national and international solidarity to the point that the Mexican army had to stop the hostilities and enter into negotiations with the insurgents just a few days after fighting the EZLN. It was at this moment that the EZLN changed tactics: it changed the armed struggle for the symbolic struggle with the aim of seizing the official revolutionary imaginary from the government and the state, while constructing a discourse asserting indigenous identity and calling for transnational solidarity (Rovira 2009).

The negotiations between the EZLN and the state—the San Andres Accords—made clear the Zapatista political project, based mainly on the struggle for the social and political rights of indigenous peoples, and the condemnation of the neoliberal world order. This discourse had a great impact on international solidarity movements and the EZLN had soon garnered the support of a dense network of Mexican civil society and international organizations.

This revolutionary experience was notable, on the one hand, for its determination to give a voice to the indigenous communities and, on the other, for the formation of a transnational solidarity movement connected via the new communication technologies, especially the internet (Castells 2000; Olesen 2005; Rovira 1997). It was through the internet that, for the first time in history, the Mexican and international civil community were made aware of what was happening in Chiapas (Castells 2000). At the same time, in every *Zapatista community* there was always a contingent of internationalists— *civilian camps for peace*—that reported from the Zapatista territories in real time as well as serving as human shields. Also worthy of note in the EZLN was the capacity of its spokesperson—Subcomandante Marcos—for maintaining direct contact with his supporters through his speeches, which were disseminated online (Rovira 2009: 92).

The Zapatista experience changed course in 2002 after a journey in stages by a delegation of Zapatista insurgents through almost the whole of Mexico—a journey known as the Earth's Color March—and the presentation of a law on indigenous autonomy in the National Congress, which was finally rejected by the legislative authority. From then on, the EZLN broke off all contact with the state and decided to start implementing autonomy on its own, constructing it outside the framework of the state. A strategic withdrawal then took place, aimed at creating some kind of administration of Zapatista-controlled territories while expecting nothing from the state with which they had ceased to negotiate and, as a result, international solidarity also diminished. Nowadays, the Zapatista experience continues to have international support because of its will to resist, but with less sermonizing and media visibility. It is worth noting the contribution it has made to alter-globalization and the new wave of transnational mobilization in the twenty-first century (von Bülow in this volume); a new wave of radicalness that cannot be understood without Zapatismo.

Conclusion

The relationships between social movements and revolutionary organizations (guerrilla or armed vanguard groups) are crucial to be able to interpret the outcomes of insurgent and revolutionary projects. However, the dynamics between the vanguard and social movements of the four successful revolutions in Latin America in the twentieth century— Bolivia, Cuba, Mexico, and Nicaragua—were very different. In the case of Mexico, the people's insurgent movements quickly went far beyond the boundaries of the projects conceived by an elite and went on to become a protracted social struggle that lasted a decade and led to the creation of a modernizing state that promoted profound social transformations until the 1940s. In Bolivia, the vanguard always tried to contain the workers', peasants', and miners' movements, which were highly radicalized and intended to bring about great transformations. The tension and distrust between the vanguard and robust, radicalized movements is one of the elements that can help us understand the failure of the Bolivian project. The case of Cuba was different due to the vanguard's ability to control the popular movements that contributed to their victory, even though this control meant later being framed as executing organizations for implementing the revolutionary government's plans. Finally, in the case of Nicaragua, the FSLN—which had spent almost two decades of its existence as a guerrilla group—became fragmented from 1979 onwards and began to organize social groups and create a network of like-minded movements that could be easily controlled. Obviously, the insurrectional victory of the FSLN was not immune to this change in strategy and, therefore, the Sandinistas have been classified as an organization belonging to the second wave of insurgency.

The insurrectional victory of the FLSN is a sign that, since 1959, revolutionary coalitions in Latin America have been made up of a heterogeneous alliance of armed vanguard movements, unions, small parties and different kinds of organizations (Martí i Puig 1997; Martí i Puig and Figueroa Ibarra 2006). The scope of these revolutionary coalitions and the control over them by the vanguard would appear to be key variables for understanding the victories (and failures) of the insurgent groups after the Cuban revolution.

As of 1989, the revolutionary vanguard groups in the region saw how the most dynamic social movements turned their backs on them. Against this backdrop, the Zapatista uprising in 1994 represented a renewal of the revolutionary imaginary, its repertoire, and the solidarity it generated. The EZLN did not gain power, but its presence transformed the national political arena, breaking for good not only with the long-standing hegemony of the Partido Revolucionario Institucional (PRI), but also with the way international solidarity and transnational revolutionary struggles were conceived, giving rise to the anti-globalization movement.

Notes

1. The concept of "wave" is used here as Marc Sageman (2010) used it, highlighting the importance of cohort replacement as a key mechanism in the persistence of a wave of revolutionary mobilization.
2. We use this term to refer to Maoist-inspired strategies that highlighted the need for a protracted war with massive support from an organized population and whose main setting should be rural areas.
3. Here we explore more deeply the line of analysis put forward in pioneering studies by Waldmann (2008) and Malthaner and Waldmann (2014).
4. The EZLN was founded in the framework of the second wave of guerrilla warfare, but once established in the Chiapas highlands, its members quickly discovered that the Mayan population, the agrarian situation and the presence of the Catholic Church (with the Indigenous Pastoral approach) did not allow a traditional organization to be created (see, for example: De Vos 2002, Legorreta 1998; Oikonomakis in this volume).
5. See the news report on the change in territorial organization in Zapatista-controlled territories conducted in August 2019 at: https://www.jornada.com.mx/2019/08/18/politica/008n1pol consultado.

References

Castells, Manuel (2000), *La era de la información*. Vol. 2 (Madrid: Alianza Editorial).
Childs, Matt D. (1995), "An historical critique of the emergence and evolution of Ernesto Che Guevara's Foco Theory," *Journal of Latin American Studies* 27(3), 593–624.
De Vos, Jan (2002), *Una tierra para sembrar sueños. Historia reciente de la Selva Lacandona, 1950–2000* (Mexico: Fondo de Cultura Económica).
Foran, John (2005), *Taking Power. On the Origins of Third World Revolutions* (Cambridge: Cambridge University Press).
Gotkowitz, Laura (2007), *A Revolution of Our Rights: Indigenous Struggles for Land and Justice in Bolivia, 1880–1952* (Durham, NC: Duke University Press).

Gott, Richard W. (2008), *Guerrilla movements in Latin America* (London: Seagull Books).
Goodwin, Jeff (2001), *No Other Way Out. States and Revolutionary Movements, 1945–1991* (Cambridge: Cambridge University Press).
Harmer, Tanya (2013), "Two, Three, Many Revolutions? Cuba and the Prospects for Revolutionary Change in Latin America, 1967–1975," *Journal of Latin American Studies* 45(1), 61–89.
Katz, Friedrich (2002), *Pancho Villa* (Mexico: ERA).
Klein, Herbert. S. (2003), *A Concise History of Bolivia* (Cambridge: Cambridge University Press).
Knight, Alan (2010), *La Revolución Mexicana. Del porfiriato al nuevo régimen constitucional* (México: Fondo de Cultura Económica).
Kruijt, Dirk, Alberto Martín Álvarez, and Eduardo Rey Tristán (2020), "A Balance of the Latin American Guerrilla," in Dirk Kruijt, Eduardo Rey Tristán, and Alberto Martín Álvarez (eds.), *Latin American Guerrilla Movements. Origins, Evolution, Outcomes*, 208–26 (London: Routledge).
Kruijt, Dirk (2017), *Cuba and Revolutionary Latin America: An Oral History* (London: Zed).
Legorreta, María del Carmen (1998), *Religión, política y guerrilla en Las Cañadas de la Selva Lacandona* (Mexico: Cal y Arena).
Malthaner, Stefan, Waldmann, Peter (2014), "The Radical Milieu: Conceptualizing the Supportive Social Environment of Terrorists Groups," *Studies in Conflict and Terrorism* 37(12), 979–98.
Martí i Puig, Salvador (1997), *La revolución enredada. Nicaragua 1979–1990* (Madrid: La Catarata).
Martí i Puig, Salvador; Figueroa Ibarra, Carlos (2006), *La izquierda revolucionaria en Centroamérica: De la lucha armada a la participación electoral* (Madrid: La Catarata).
Martín Álvarez, Alberto (2017), "The Long Wave. The Revolutionary Left in Guatemala, Nicaragua and El Salvador," in Alberto Martín Álvarez and Eduardo Rey Tristán (eds.), *Revolutionary Violence and the New Left. Transnational Perspectives*, 223–45 (London: Routledge).
Martín Álvarez, Alberto, Rey Tristán, Eduardo (2018), "La dimensión transnacional de la izquierda armada," *América Latina Hoy* 80: 9–28.
Martín Álvarez, Alberto and Eduardo Rey Tristán (eds.) (2017), *Revolutionary Violence and the New Left: Transnational Perspectives* (London: Routledge).
Martín Álvarez, Alberto and Eudald Cortina Orero (2014), "The Genesis and Internal Dynamics of the of El Salvador's People's Revolutionary Army (ERP), 1970–1976," *Journal of Latin American Studies* 46(4), 663–89.
McAdam, Dough (1995), "Initiator and Spinoff Movements: Diffusion Processes in Protest Cycles," in Mark Traugott (ed.), *Repertoires and Cycles of Collective Action*, 217–41 (Durham, NC: Duke University Press).
Minkoff, Debra (1997), "The Sequencing of Social Movements," *American Sociological Review* 62(5), 779–99.
Olesen, Thomas (2005), *Internacional Zapatismo: The Construction of Solidarity in the Age of Globalization* (London: Zed Books).
Rey Tristán, Eduardo (2005), *La izquierda revolucionaria uruguaya (1955–1973)* (Madrid: CSIC).
Reyes, Miguel Ángel (2017), "La cultura de la revolución en los Andes: Aproximación a las relaciones trasnacionales entre el M-19 y AVC en la década de 1980," *Estudios Interdisciplinares de América Latina y el Caribe* 28(2), 104–28.

Rovira Sancho, Guiomar (1997), *Las mujeres del maíz* (Mexico: ERA).
Rovira Sancho, Guiomar (2009), *Zapatistas sin fronteras: Las redes de solidaridad con Chiapas y el altermundismo* (Mexico: ERA).
Sageman, Marc (2010), "Ripples in the waves: Fantasies and Fashions," in Jean Rosenfeld (ed.), *Terrorism, Identity and Legitimacy: The Four Waves Theory and Political Violence*, 87–93 (London: Routledge).
Selbin, Eric (1993), *Modern Latin American Revolutions* (Boulder, CO: Westview Press).
Silva Herzog, Jesús (2010), *Breve historia de la revolución Mexicana: Los antecedentes y la etapa maderista* (Mexico: Fondo de Cultura Económica).
Skocpol, Theda (1984), *Los estados y las revoluciones sociales: Un análisis comparativo de Francia, Rusia y China* (Mexico: Fondo de Cultura Económica).
Sweig, Julia E. (2002), *Inside the Cuban Revolution. Fidel Castro and the Urban Underground* (Cambridge, MA: Harvard University Press).
Van der Haar, Gemma (1998), "Levantamiento zapatista, indígenas y municipio en Chiapas, México," in Willem Assies and Hans Gundermann (eds.), *Movimientos indígenas y gobiernos locales en América Latina*, 199–225 (Santiago: Línea Editorial IIAM, Universidad Católica del Norte).
Vázquez Olivera, Mario; Campos Hernández, Fabián (2020), "The Second Cycle of the Guatemalan Insurgency (1970–1996)," in Dirk Kruijt, Eduardo Rey Tristán, and Alberto Martín Álvarez (eds.), *Latin American Guerrilla Movements. Origins, Evolution, Outcomes*, 151–62 (London: Routledge).
Volpi, Jorge (2004), *La guerra y las palabras: Una historia intelectual de 1994* (Mexico: ERA).
Waldmann, Peter (2008), "The Radical Milieu: The Under-Investigated Relationship Between Terrorists and Sympathetic Communities," *Perspectives on Terrorism* 2(9), 25–27.
Whickham-Crowley, Timothy (1992), *Guerrillas and Revolution in Latin America: A Comparative Study of Insurgents and Regimes Since 1956* (Princeton, NJ: Princeton University Press).
Womack, John (2004), *Zapata y la revolución mexicana* (Mexico: Siglo XXI).

CHAPTER 12

SOCIAL MOVEMENTS UNDER AUTHORITARIAN REGIMES IN LATIN AMERICA

CHARLES D. BROCKETT

Introduction

Latin America has had ample experience with authoritarianism across the centuries right up to the present. Social movements are a more recent phenomenon with the last sixty years providing numerous important examples, as did prior decades on occasion. When threatened by social movements, authoritarians have used their full repertoire, from appeasement to cooptation, from soft repression to state terrorism, sometimes successfully but other times not. Conversely, social movement responses to the state have ranged from acquiescence to heightened mobilization, from passivity to radicalized boldness. Amidst the diversity of these responses and the multitude of cases, this chapter provides some order and highlights significant patterns.[1]

The major different types of authoritarian regimes that have governed Latin America during the past six decades organize the chapter. Totalitarian regimes, following Linz's (1975) classic distinction, are not relevant because they proscribe autonomous social movements (which has remained true of Cuba since its revolution). Authoritarian regimes limit political pluralism and control popular mobilization. Following the lead of Linz, along with other scholars (e.g., Geddes, Wright, and Frantz 2018; O'Donnell 1986), Latin American authoritarian regimes are categorized as personal, military, or competitive. For each type, cases featuring prominent social movement activity are discussed, drawing from different decades and regions.[2] This broad cross-section provides ample material for drawing conclusions about the relationship between authoritarianism and social movements, particularly concerning the use of repression (Table 12.1).

Table 12.1 Authoritarian regimes and protest-repression relationship

Type	Illustrative Cases	Scale of Social Movement Activity	Scope of Repression
Personalistic Dictatorship	Haiti (1971–1986) Nicaragua (1967–1979) Panama (1983–1989)	least	
Military Regime	Argentina (1966–1973) Argentina (1976–1983) Brazil (1964–1985) Chile (1973–1990) Uruguay (1973–1985) El Salvador (1967–1992) Guatemala (1970–1996)		
Competitive Authoritarianism	Mexico (1929–2000) Nicaragua (? to ?) Venezuela (? to ?)		least

Personal Dictatorships

Personal dictatorships are based on loyalty gained more by fear and rewards rather than tradition or ideology. There is a direct relationship between increasing personalization and observed repression (Frantz et al. 2019). Classic examples include Rafael Trujillo (Dominican Republic, 1930–1961), François Duvalier (Haiti, 1957–1971), and Fulgencio Batista (Cuba, 1952–1959). Significant social movements have been less likely to develop under such dictators since their countries usually have been at lower levels of socio-economic development with fewer mobilization resources available to potential challengers (Tilly and Tarrow 2015: 11). Furthermore, the dictator's heavy reliance on repression leaves less opportunity for popular mobilization. Nonetheless, there have been some notable examples of social movements under these regimes, even back to 1944 when broad-based movements brought down dictators in El Salvador and Guatemala (Parkman 1988). More recent examples to be discussed here are Nicaragua in the 1970s and Haiti and Panama in the 1980s.

The Somoza family dynasty in Nicaragua is a paradigmatic example of this regime type. Especially under Anastasio Somoza Debayle (1967–1979), state power was concentrated in the dictator's hands. Driven by formidable greed, so too was an increasing amount of the economy (Booth 1982; Brockett 1998). The military had little autonomy, serving instead the desires of the dictator (Brockett 2005).

Somoza faced growing discontent from across society coming into the 1970s. Popular mobilization accelerated further as a devastating earthquake in 1972 brought greater corruption. Students protested; workers went on strike; peasants organized land take-overs, often facilitated overtly by religious activists and covertly by the Frente Sandinista de Liberación Nacional (FSLN) (see Martí i Puig and Álvarez in this volume). Somoza declared martial law in 1974. His repression was severe, and in rural areas especially vicious, gaining the social passivity desired.

Somoza lifted the state of siege after thirty-three months, believing the threat had been eliminated. He also was responding to considerable pressures from Washington. With this liberalization, open mass opposition returned, broadened, grew, and radicalized. Leading opposition figure Pedro Joaquín Chamorro was murdered in January 1978. Large, angry demonstrations followed, in turn followed by urban uprisings in February and September. Another in May 1979 set in motion the final events leading to Somoza's departure in July 1979.

Each uprising provided the FSLN with golden opportunities to broaden its recruitment base, radicalize tactics, and forge stronger alliances with social movement regime opponents. These efforts were only strengthened by the barbarity of Somoza's repressive response, including aerial bombings of urban centers of resistance. His repression and broad-based opposition also drove international actors, including the United States, to seek his departure, which then further emboldened his domestic opposition.

The Haitian case demonstrates many of these same dynamics. With the death of François Duvalier in 1971, Jean-Claude Duvalier (1971–1986) inherited not only the Haitian presidency but also one of the most effective terroristic dictatorships in the Americas. Only nineteen at the time, he lacked his father's intelligence and interest in governing, though perhaps surpassed his greed. The corruption of his small ruling circle, along with many of his policies, increased societal discontent, from the peasantry up to traditional elite circles (Danner 1989; Fatton 2002; Weinstein and Segal 1992).

Jean-Claude gradually lessened repression in the late 1970s in response to pressures from Haitians and the Jimmy Carter administration. When popular mobilization went too far for the dictator, he clamped back down shortly after Ronald Reagan's 1980 victory. Nonetheless, centers of power that his father had subjugated—such as the army, the Catholic Church, economic elites, and intellectuals—remained activated. For the next few years, the most important was the church, particularly its liberationist wing, their efforts invigorated by the Pope's 1983 visit.

Intermittent large protests began the following year amid a continuing economic downturn. The murders of three students during a 1985 demonstration coalesced a movement that had lacked focus, as they "became the martyrs and symbols of the urban revolts" (Weinstein and Segal 1992: 46). Protests intensified, strikes multiplied, and disorder spread. By the end of January 1986, the United States ambassador was actively working with Haitian counterparts to bring a peaceful end to the regime. In this they were greatly aided by Jean-Claude himself. His forces "were eager to crush the revolt" but Duvalier lacked the "stomach for the fight" (Danner November 27, 1989: 58). A week after imposing a state of siege, Duvalier left Haiti.

In Panama the next year another sustained mass mobilization looked like it too would drive its dictator out of power. Following the 1981 death of long-time ruler Omar Torrijos, Manuel Noriega (1983–1989) shared power with several military colleagues, consolidating his dominance within two years. In 1987 he forced rival Roberto Díaz Herrera into retirement. Rather than going quietly, Díaz instead issued a stunning set of charges against Noriega, from his involvement in drug trafficking and electoral fraud to the deaths of Torrijos and Hugo Spadafora. Kidnapped in 1985 and tortured horrifically, Spadafora's murder provoked protests but they eventually dissipated (Arjona and Cambra 2013; Dinges 1990; Nepstad 2011).

With Díaz's charges large street protests renewed. When they were met by repression, rioting resulted. Organization soon followed based on pre-existing ties and networks, including prior anti-Noriega activities. Fortuitously, a number of those who formed the Civic Crusade for Justice and Democracy had already been involved in a United States-assisted effort to create an electoral monitoring organization for the 1989 elections. Headquartered at the Chamber of Commerce, the largely middle-class Crusade called for a campaign of civil disobedience to pressure Noriega to resign.

Through a combination of mass demonstrations, general strikes, labor strikes, and non-payment of bills, Noriega was on the ropes. However, his support within the military held. The regime's repression grew more adroit, substantial enough to break up both marches and the Crusade's leadership but not so excessive as to create a succession of martyrs. When a demonstration drew more troops than marchers, it was clear that the opposition was exhausted. Challengers turned their attention to voting his regime out in the May 1989 elections. However, Noriega nullified the election when the vote went against his candidate. Instead, it was a United States military invasion that ended the dictatorship later that year.

These personalistic dictatorships shared several traits. Each had enjoyed at least US acceptance and at times support. The hegemon's moving to opposition closely interacted with anti-regime mobilization. In each the opposition campaign received support from domestic elite interests as well as widespread middle sector involvement. However, the Panamanian campaign did not include broad rural and urban lower-class participation like in Haiti and Nicaragua. Neither did Noriega face an insurgency, certainly not one that had so penetrated the social movement sector as in Nicaragua. Finally, the cases varied widely in the propensity for repression, with the contrast striking between Somoza on the one hand and Duvalier and Noriega on the other.

Military Regimes

Putnam's (1967: 107) influential quantitative study of Latin America for 1956–1965 concluded that "Social mobilization clearly increases the prospects for civilian rule." The implication was clear—with modernization, dictatorships would disappear and democracies would spread. Ironically, this research was conducted just as the new form of authoritarian rule by the military as an institution appeared. Unlike the many caretaker military interventions of the past, these new regimes intended to govern indefinitely to remake society. Driving their seizure of power and objectives was the perceived threat from contentious social movements. These regimes will be discussed in two sets: the Southern Cone (Argentina, Brazil, Chile, and Uruguay) and Central America (El Salvador and Guatemala).[3]

Southern Cone

Juan Perón was the rising star within Argentina's military government of the mid-1940s when his rivals had him jailed. A huge demonstration by his working-class supporters soon gained his release. Perón won the presidential elections of 1946 and "ensured that he himself should embody the political desires of Argentine workers" (James 1976: 294). Easily re-elected in 1951, in a highly polarized nation the military forced him into exile in 1955. The inability of the Argentine system to find an accommodation between *Peronismo* and its opponents, especially a military purged of his supporters, plagued the country for decades to come.

Civilian administrations that followed did not find the answer. Consequently, there was little opposition when the military seized power in 1966. However, this military intended a "revolution" to move the county beyond its impasse. Political parties were banned, the press controlled, and free market reforms instituted. The archetype of a "bureaucratic-authoritarian" regime resulted, with the military as an institution collaborating with the "transnationalized bourgeoisie," united by their desire to politically exclude "a previously activated popular sector" (O'Donnell 1988: 31–32). How well this model applied to other Southern Cone military regimes in terms of class alliances and economic projects generated debate (Munck 1998; Remmer and Merkz 1982; Schamis 1991). However, they all shared their repressive response to the perceived threat inherent in social movements.[4]

Argentine students bore the brunt of the initial repressive measures. Labor suffered as well, especially when it pushed back through protests and strikes. Nonetheless, protests continued intermittently into May 1969, expanding in size, locations, and intensity. And then came the *Cordobazo*, "the greatest working class protest in postwar Latin America" (Brennan 1994: 138). The major industrial center of Córdoba was placed under martial law enforced by army troops. But the regime's authority was gravely damaged—as much by "impotence in the face of social protest as by the army's vacillation in repressing it" (Romero 2002: 192). It took the military another four years to extricate itself from power, but its transformational project was over.

The final proof of the 1966 regime's failure was Perón's landslide 1973 presidential victory. Prior years had seen high levels of labor and student mobilization, often repressed by security forces (Berrotarán and Pozzi 1994). Several guerrilla organizations were growing in size and boldness, including murdering high-ranking officers. Political deaths from both right and left climbed. Perón died in July 1974, replaced by his vice president and third wife, who possessed neither political experience nor skill.

It was almost another two years before the military returned to power, but its infamous dirty war began during this period. Increasing numbers of social movement activists were slain or disappeared. Guerrillas upped their violence as well but were largely contained by the time of the March 1976 coup and then decimated within the year. Human rights groups usually estimate about 30,000 deaths for the 1974–1983 reign of terror. Seeking to eliminate all political activism, the military regime created "a peace of the tomb" (Romero 2002: 236). Nonetheless, militaries are not unitary actors, containing personal, service, and ideological rivalries. Particularly important differences in Argentina concerned two related issues: what to do about labor and how deep and long to repress. As these conflicts played out, space was created for labor activism, first at the workplace and eventually more broadly (Munck 1998; Novaro and Palermo 2003).

The regime banned any demonstrations. That did not stop one of the best known of all human rights actors, the Madres de Plaza de Mayo. Their silent weekly walk in front of the presidential palace began in April 1977. At first the government ignored them, giving the Madres time to overcome fear and develop organization (Fisher 1989). However, as they grew, they faced harassment and then intermittent repression. Nonetheless, they remained steadfast, playing an important role linking with international human rights organizations (Bouvard 1994; see Wolff in this volume). So too did another set of domestic human rights groups (Brysk 1994).

Argentina was another major target of Carter's human rights policy. An Organization of American States fact-finding missions in 1979 provided global attention while energizing domestic groups. The 1980 Nobel Peace Prize honored human rights activist Adolfo Pérez Esquivel. The global economic recession added economic grievances to the long list endured by Argentines. Strikes spread through 1980 and into the following years. Political parties came back to life, joining labor and human rights organizations in a wave of protests, culminating in a large demonstration in March 1982 demanding a return to democracy. The military responded with intermittent repression and then in April the disastrous invasion of the Islas Malvinas. The end was at hand.

When the Brazilian military took control in 1964 the level of popular mobilization was considerably lower than that of Argentina. Instead, its primary perceived threat was a leftist government. During its first years the dictatorship was not much different in approach and objectives from its 1966 Argentine counterpart. However, this changed in late 1968 as the social movement sector came back to life at new levels of intensity while revolutionaries undertook their first actions. But, with four years of building its repressive apparatus, the military quickly squashed challengers (Alves 1985; O'Donnell 1986, 1988; Skidmore 1998).

Although repression was mild in comparison to what would follow in the 1970s in Chile and Argentina, thousands were detained and some tortured. About 500 political leaders had their political rights removed or suspended while about 10,000 labor leaders were dismissed (Klein and Luna 2017: 54). Of the 434 documented direct political assassinations over the course of the regime to 1985, a quarter was labor activists. Employers killed with impunity another 1,500 or more rural workers while the regime looked the other way, as it did with the murders of some 8,350 indigenous people (Purdy 2016: 302).

Student organizations also were targets, but it was especially students who brought the social movement sector back to life, becoming "the most visible and emblematic symbol of opposition to the regime" (Langland 2013: 108). Tragedy spurred the movement on to new levels. Police killed a student in March 1968 and used violence against those attending the memorial masses. In response, a broad swath of society marched, perhaps some 50,000 in all. That number was doubled at a subsequent march in June. The Catholic Church openly supported the challengers, as did a group of moderate and conservative politicians promoting re-democratization (Alves 1985).

During the second half of 1968 demonstrators grew more contentious and violent. Participation dropped, as did popular support (Valle 1999). Small guerrilla organizations increased their armed actions throughout 1968, largely bank robberies but also assassinations. In December the regime significantly deepened its repression, quickly ending the wave of protests but driving some protestors into the ranks of the insurgents and heightening the commitment of militants (Fico 2001). Nonetheless, the regime soon contained the guerrillas and then eliminated them. State terrorism in Brazil did not rely on the disappearances prevalent in Argentina but instead on the widespread use of torture. Estimates range up to 20,000 citizens tortured during the life of the regime, especially during the worst years of 1969–1973 (Fico 2001: 13). Torture was effective in creating a culture of fear. Alves (1985: 126), in one of the best books on the subject of this chapter, captures well the contradictory effect: "although repression angers the population and turns previously supportive groups or sectors against the government authorities, the great fear of torture effectively prevents actual participation in political activities."

The Brazilian military regime was more successful than any of its counterparts. The worst of its repression corresponded with Brazil's "economic miracle" of annual growth rates averaging 10%. The regime last twenty-one years and was able to extend its disengagement from governing over a longer period and with greater control. The slow liberalization process began in 1974, not because of civilian pressures but due to their absence, along with different preferences within the military (Mainwaring 1986; Philip 1984). Repression still continued as believed necessary but limited liberalization did open space for social movement reactivation. Cautiously and led by elements of the Catholic Church in the beginning (see below), by 1977 a new labor movement had emerged as a political force and an increasingly contentious and effective one through the remainder of the liberalization process (Alves 1985).

Military regimes assuming power in Chile and Uruguay in 1973 can most effectively be brought into this discussion by drawing on Loveman's (1998) comparison of them to Argentina. Repression was no less brutal in Chile in the first trimester following its coup against the elected Marxist government of Salvador Allende than in Argentina. About half of the regime's 3,500 to 4,500 deaths and disappearance occurred during that short period, as did about one-third of its huge number of political detentions (Policzer 2009: 57; Stern 2006: xxi). Yet, significant social movement activity resumed more quickly in Chile than in Argentina and especially Uruguay. Several differences stand out, but the primary reason Loveman highlights was the contrasting role of the Catholic Church in the three. Although not including Brazil in her discussion, it fits into the analysis well (see Mackin in this volume).

Religious institutions have provided the safest spaces for the revitalization of social movements in, or following, highly repressive situations. In highly secularized Uruguay this did not occur. That function was sorely missed because repression was more total than elsewhere, facilitated by the country's very small size. Uruguay relied before and after its coup not on disappearances but rather imprisonment (and torture), giving it the world's highest rate of political prisoners. Consequently, the first meaningful human rights organization did not emerge until 1981 with the regime itself lasting until 1985.

In Chile most Catholic Church leaders initially welcomed the coup, expecting it to be brief and relatively bloodless. Instead, the regime was shockingly brutal and soon made clear its intention to remain in power and remake society. Although publically the hierarchy did not challenge the regime for the first two years, individual leaders soon took steps that would eventually facilitate the return of social movement activism. An ecumenical Comité de Cooperación para la Paz en Chile was established in October to assistant families of the regime's repression. The Comité grew into an important information gathering and disseminating organization. Eventually a whole array of social services was provided. These activities created network ties among activists. They also brought harassment from the regime along with intermittent repression, including murdering several priests. The primary impact was to energize further activism. At the end of 1975 the regime forced the closing of the Comité. Cardinal Raúl Silva Henríquez responded by creating the Vicaría de la Solidarida, which continued with the same functions but now as a legally protected part of the church. Throughout, these church efforts could also draw on substantial moral and financial support from its multiple international ties, which also brought the Chilean case to worldwide attention (Smith 1982).

However, 1977–1980 was the regime's economic boom years, accompanied by continuing repression. Protests were intermittent and small. Then the economy crashed in 1982 and protests escalated (Stern 2006). In May 1983 labor initiated a series of mass protests that continued into late 1984 (Barrera and Valenzuela 1986), particularly in Santiago's shantytowns with historic ties to the Communist Party (Schneider 1995). Finally, a state of siege was enforced in November 1984 but another broad-based protest wave began in April 1986. Needing to justify its Central American policies as pro-democratic, the Reagan administration backed away from Pinochet. Responding to these and other pressures, Pinochet agreed to hold a 1988 referendum on remaining president. Shocking at least himself, he lost and the opposition won the subsequent 1989 elections. He left office in early 1990 (Nepstad 2011).

In great contrast, the Argentine church hierarchy supported their military regime. Finally, Brazil provided a fourth pattern. Befitting its great size and decentralized structures, the role of the Brazilian church varied between regions. By the mid-1960s, progressive bishops in the poor northeast were vocal in denouncing human rights abuses. When the regime took its deeper repressive turn after late 1968, it was the church more than any other actor that denounced abuses and assisted victims despite considerable repression against the church itself. Indeed, repression moved even some of the conservative hierarchy to hold the regime accountable (Mainwaring 1986; Serbin 2000).

Central America

Central America has experienced substantial authoritarian rule. Guatemala was governed by military regimes for all but nine years between 1954 and 1985, and with the military a dominant force when it did not govern. El Salvador was a hybrid for 1948–1982 with the ruling military also utilizing a regime political party. Nonetheless, it is striking how much social movement activity occurred in both, largely during periods of relative liberalization.

El Salvador's first important postwar protest cycle began in 1967 with the historic success of a progressive general strike. Labor strikes continued, accompanied by national teacher strikes in 1968 and 1971 and increasing student mobilization. They joined together in 1972, supporting the first major national electoral challenge to the regime. Believing fraud denied them victory, they protested, attempted a general strike, and then many supported a coup. When it failed, repression followed, ending this protest cycle (Almeida 2008; Brockett 1998, 2005; Montgomery 1995).

Nevertheless, important mobilization efforts soon resumed. Catholic groups continued organizational work with peasants, often assisted by local teachers and urban students. These ties were formalized in mid-decade with the emergence of popular organizations uniting individual associations of peasants, teachers, students, and others for contentious action. There were also strong but covert ties to revolutionary organizations now increasingly active. Although repression still often countered protests, the 1977 elections opened more space for social movements. This election too brought fraud, protest, repression, and radicalization. The regime clamped down in November with its draconian Public Order Law.

Under pressure from the Carter administration, the law was revoked in early February 1979 and contention by the popular organizations exploded into a new protest cycle lasting through 1980. Frequent demonstrations were augmented by occupations of farms, factories, embassies, churches, and public buildings. Guerrillas also stepped up their violent tactics. Repression escalated as well but, encouraged by events in Nicaragua, challengers pushed on, with their peak moment coming in January 1980 as over 100,000 marched. But the repression was unrelenting. The regime and its allies murdered around 500 urban civilians in three of the four quarters beginning at the end of 1979 and then over 1,000 during the final quarter of 1980 (Brockett 2005: 301). The regime eliminated social movements but instigated a twelve-year civil war.

The overthrow in Guatemala of Jacobo Arbenz in 1954 ended ten years of elected progressive government and expanding popular mobilization. If those who followed in power had all been hardline tyrants, there would have been little social movement activity. However, there were two significant periods of liberalization before the military regime ended in 1985, both of which unleashed substantial social movement challenges (Brockett 1998, 2005; Torres-Rivas 2011). The first protest cycle, largely-student driven, occurred in 1962. The president, although a general, had long been out of military service, was elected, and was not the military's candidate. Accordingly, this was not a truly authoritarian regime.

The military did use fraud as necessary to ensure the election of its candidates, all generals, from 1970 on. However, its president elected in 1974 opened political space for popular organizing, notably not using violence against demonstrations in the capital during his tenure. However, death squads tied to other regime figures remained active. This protest cycle began in June 1977 with a large demonstration reacting to the assassination of a key adviser to a reviving labor movement (Levenson-Estrada 1994). Large and contentious demonstrations followed almost monthly, maintained especially by labor and students (Kobrak 1999). The steady assassination of movement leaders by death squads placed ending repression at the forefront of demands, along with social justice objectives. The context drastically changed with a new president in July 1978. Now violence increasingly came directly from the government itself. However, given the high level of mobilization, it would take substantial repression to suppress social movements. Urban contention peaked in late 1978 and then revitalized in early 1980, joined now by substantial peasant mobilization.

The peasant movement had been developing for years (LeBot 1995). As elsewhere, church workers were crucial, with their lengthy efforts helping to develop community groups that later became building blocks for broader and more politicized organizations. The contentious peak for this movement came in February 1980 with the largest strike in Guatemala's history as some 50–80,000 peasants at sugar and cotton estates marched, maintained barricades at critical highways and sugar mills, and invaded numerous farms, destroying substantial amounts of property.

The regime reacted viciously to these urban and rural challenges. The last significant nonviolent protest occurred with the May 1 demonstration. Thirty-two people died. In the next few months, forty-four labor leaders were disappeared in two separate incidents. State terrorism eliminated social movements. Meanwhile, some of the survivors joined the revolutionaries whose ranks and activities had been growing in the countryside for some time. Now the regime focused on them with a scorched earth campaign that would leave tens of thousands dead, primarily noncombatant indigenous peasants.

It is noteworthy that the scholarship on Central American social movements under authoritarianism features more events data studies based on domestic sources than do other parts of Latin America. Brockett (2005), the major source for this section, analyzes the relationship for both El Salvador and Guatemala. Almeida (2008) examines the lengthiest period—eight decades up to 2003, with his events data covering 1962–1981. His study of the 1977–1981 protest wave confirms the analysis here, providing good evidence that while escalating repression eventually smothered non-violent protest it also provoked an increase in violent actions by challengers.

Sullivan (2016a, 2016b) explores Guatemala during 1975–1985. His primary source is both unique and rich. The Guatemalan National Police maintained a thorough archive that has recently been opened to researchers, allowing Sullivan to identify more than 7,000 acts of state and dissident behavior. His quantitative analyses confirm that overt collective challenges, such as demonstrations, were indeed met by increased repression, often provoking further mobilization. More unique are his findings related to mobilization efforts. The behind-the-scenes repression of core activists, uniquely disclosed by the secret police documents, instead undermined challenger capacities and mobilization.

Competitive Authoritarian Regimes

Military presidents in El Salvador and Guatemala often came to office through regular contested elections but that did not make their countries democracies. The same can be true for civilian-led governments. Indeed, the spread of competitive (or electoral) authoritarian regimes is now a disturbing global trend. The classic example, and the focus here, is the regime constructed by the Partido Revolucionario Institucional (PRI) of Mexico (and its predecessors). Brief attention also is given to contemporary Nicaragua and Venezuela.[5]

These are civilian regimes that are competitive because opposition parties "use democratic institutions to contest seriously for power, but they are not democratic because the playing field is heavily skewed in favor of incumbents" (Levitsky and Way 2010: 5). More concisely, "Competition is thus real but unfair" (ibid.). Jorge Castañeda's characterization of Mexico's technically clean 1994 election is apt: "one team included 11 players plus the umpire and the other a mere six or seven players" (Castañeda 1995: 8).

Maintaining the institutional structures identified with democratic governance such as legislatures, political parties, and elections does more for autocrats than provide legitimacy. When dictators need cooperation to secure their objectives and need to mitigate opposition then such institutions can be very useful, especially as instruments of cooptation (Gandhi 2008). These needs were particularly great in Mexico given the comparatively high levels of popular mobilization leading to its revolution of 1910–1917 and then generated by the revolution itself (see Martí i Puig and Álvarez in this volume). The answer developed was a corporatist state with an umbrella political party at its core. That answer was particularly effective, giving Mexico the twentieth century's longest-lasting authoritarian regime until it was voted out of power in 2000 after seventy-one years.

We are reminded not to overstate the regime's dominance. It was "more porous and less absolutist" than often portrayed and with substantial variations between regions in their mix of national, state, and local control (Craig 1990: 280). There also was a long history of social movement challenges, even during the more stable years of the 1950s and early 1960s, from labor, peasant, and civic groups (Knight 1990) as well as by students (Pensado 2013). Still, until the regime's last decades these challenges usually were not to the overall corporatist system but rather to its "clientelistic lines of control" (Foweraker

1990: 16). In a comparative context, then, the PRI regime was notably effective at self-perpetuation through its mix of concessions, co-optation, and intermittent repression.

With its decades of continuous rule, the regime could count on using the public treasury for its own purposes "with virtual impunity," from electoral campaigns to buying off challengers (Greene 2007: 98). The PRI could also increase and strategically target social spending program during times of serious challenges. This capability was essential for presidents like Luis Echeverría in the early 1970s and Carlos Salinas following his fraud-ridden 1988 victory.

Students mobilized in Mexico in 1968 at unprecedented levels and contentiousness. Believing communist subversion was at work on the eve of hosting the Olympic games, the regime struck back with violence. More than 300 protesters were murdered at Mexico City's Tlatelolco Plaza and many more jailed (Keller 2015). Peaceful marchers were attacked again in the Corpus Christi massacre of 1971 with 50 dead. More repression against the left followed in a dirty war that "rose to the level of state-sponsored violence in fully closed authoritarian regimes" with over 500 people disappeared (Greene 2007: 83). However, Echeverría accompanied repression with a substantial increase in social spending. Consequently, although intermittent protests continued, overall social movement activity declined across the next decade (Tamayo 1990).

Nonetheless, the desire for democratization grew, within the PRI itself as well as among social movements. Following a lengthy economic downturn from the early 1980s, the 1988 elections proved a crucial turning point. Leftist social movements often ignored elections as meaningless charades. This election was different. A broad movement supported the candidate of the left (Tamayo 1990). The PRI responded with fraud and repression against the massive protests that followed, including the murders of many activists (Greene 2007; Trevizo 2014). Salinas also responded with strategically targeted social spending. The regime continued on, winning the next two presidential elections, but clearly its days were numbered.

At the same time, Mexico also provides numerous examples of less intense repression energizing social movements to new levels of activity, sometimes even sufficient to gain policy concessions. Prominent examples included human rights organizations (Trevizo 2014) and indigenous movements (Trejos 2012). More broadly, Favela (2006: 100) shows that for 207 social movements between 1946 and 1997, two-thirds of those seeking material benefits received positive regime responses (although only a fifth of the more numerous movements seeking political and civil rights did).

Current competitive authoritarian regimes in Nicaragua and Venezuela demonstrate that it is often the gradual erosion of democracy that creates such regimes (Cameron 2018; Geddes, Wright, and Frantz 2018). Although there might be uncertainty about when to mark either regime's transformation, there is widespread agreement that it has occurred for both. Step by step Daniel Ortega in Nicaragua and Hugo Chávez and Nicolás Maduro in Venezuela tilted the electoral field further to the regime's advantage while reducing checks and balances within the government. As key examples, Ortega remained popular enough that he could probably have won a fair 2016 presidential election but instead drew on a variety of authoritarian measures to ensure a substantial victory (Cruz 2018). After the opposition won control of the Venezuelan National Assembly in 2015, it was neutered by the regime.

Popular protests have been a constant in Venezuela for some years, intermittently on a massive scale. Protesters have been met with harassment and also death. Over 130 protesters were killed between 2014 and 2017 (Naim and Toro 2018). In Nicaragua, protests over policy issues beginning in April 2018 were met by violence, broadening the movement and expanding its demands to ending the regime, which then escalated the repression. Over 300 have been killed and many jailed (Cruz 2018). Later, regime repression successfully contained the social movement challenge in both countries. Still, the latest scholarship indicates that Mexico was the outlier. Competitive authoritarianism is an inherently unstable regime type normally with limited duration (Carothers 2018).

Conclusion

The many cases discussed here demonstrate that when an authoritarian regime has the capacity and willingness to violently repress protesters to whatever the level necessary it usually will succeed. When the social movement sector is broad and highly motivated, that has required extraordinary levels of imprisonment, torture, and death along with the suppression of democratic institutions. Indeed, authoritarian regimes have "responded with ruthless violence that often had no relationship to the original threat" (Klein and Luna 2017: 37).

However, these same cases also demonstrate that protesters have remarkable tenacity. Repression at lower levels has often provoked social movements to greater levels of activity. Even as repression escalates, deterring further activity on the part of many, others recommit to the struggle. It is also notable how quickly social movement activity resumed after so many of these periods of severe repression, often led by the most committed surviving activists from the past (Franklin 2015).

Although these generalizations apply across the regime types used to organize this chapter, there are some differences between them. The scale of social movement activity (breadth and durability) has been least under the personal dictatorships. The scope and severity of repression has been least under competitive authoritarianism (but do note the higher death toll of Mexico's dirty war compared to Brazil's military dictatorship). Otherwise, what stands out is the greater variation between cases within each type—and even within the same country (e.g., the Argentine military regimes of 1966 and 1976 or the first four years of the Brazilian regime compared to the next four years). The constant is the interplay between a regime's perceived threat from popular movements and its capacity and propensity to repress.

Given the frequent brutality of authoritarian regimes, an important topic for further research is the role of self-restraint. A notable comparison was Duvalier's decision *not* to unleash his repressive apparatus in 1986 but to leave Haiti at a point far earlier in the confrontation than did Somoza in Nicaragua. Similarly significant was the decision of the Argentine military not to increase its repression as a response to the social movement reactivation that followed the *Cordobazo* and the similar choice of the Brazilian regime as it embarked on its slow liberalization process. Pinochet might have fought on more like Somoza but was prevented by other top military leaders from rigging or annulling the 1988 plebiscite that moved the Chilean regime toward its end.

Another suggestion concerns approach. Quantitative cross-national analysis tests hypotheses, providing direction for more extensive research, but is constrained by the immense task of developing valid country-specific data. In contrast, well-executed individual case studies are welcomed for their ability to clarify dynamics but are limited by the uncertainty of their generalizability. The rich solution is more comparative works with few enough cases to allow in depth analysis, perhaps even based on events data. A number of the works cited here serve as good models (and Trejos [2012], an excellent study, reminds us that units can be subnational).

Notes

1. For related essays see Johnston (2015) and Ortiz (2015).
2. Space limitations preclude discussion of quantitative cross-national studies of repression and protest (see Almeida, Wada in this volume).
3. Chile does not fit as fully into this category since Augusto Pinochet constructed a more personalistic regime, but it certainly belongs with this group rather than the prior (Policzer 2009; Remmer 1989).
4. In contrast, the Peruvian regime of 1968–1990 was more progressive and less repressive.
5. Alberto Fujimori in Peru was another example.

References

Almeida, Paul (2008), *Waves of Protest: Popular Struggle in El Salvador, 1925–2005* (Minneapolis: University of Minnesota Press).

Alves, Maria Helena Moreira (1985), *State and Opposition in Military Brazil* (Austin: University of Texas).

Arjona, Nadhji and Manuel Cambra (2013), *Cuando la libertad se vistió de blanco: testimonios de lucha y sacrifico* (Panamá: Editorial Libertad Ciudadana).

Barrera, Manuel and J. Samuel Valenzuela (1986), "The Development of Labor Movement Opposition to the Military Regime," in J. Samuel Valenzuela and Arturo Valenzuela (eds.), *Military Rule in Chile: Dictatorship and Oppositions*, 230–69 (Baltimore, MD: Johns Hopkins University Press).

Berrotarán, Patricia and Pablo Pozzi (eds.) (1994), *Estudios inconformistas sobre la clase obrera argentina: 1955–1989* (Buenos Aires: Ediciones Letra Buena).

Booth, John (1982), *The End and the Beginning: The Nicaraguan Revolution* (Boulder, CO: Westview Press).

Bouvard, Marguerite Guzman (1994), *Revolutionizing Motherhood: The Mothers of the Plaza De Mayo* (Wilmington, DE: Scholarly Resources).

Brennan, James (1994), *The Labor Wars in Córdoba, 1955–1976: Ideology, Work, and Labor Politics in an Argentine Industrial City* (Cambridge, MA: Harvard University Press).

Brockett, Charles (1998), *Land, Power, and Poverty: Agrarian Transformation and Political Conflict in Central America* (Boulder, CO: Westview Press).

Brockett, Charles (2005), *Political Movements and Violence in Central America* (New York: Cambridge University Press).

Brysk, Alision (1994), *The Politics of Human Rights in Argentina* (Stanford, CA: Stanford University Press).

Cameron, Maxwell (2018), "Making Sense of Competitive Authoritarianism: Lessons from the Andes," *Latin American Politics and Society* 60(2), 1–22.

Carothers, Christopher (2018), "The Surprising Instability of Competitive Authoritarianism," *Journal of Democracy* 29(4), 129–35.

Castañeda, Jorge G. (1995), *The Mexican Shock: Its Meaning for the United States* (New York: The New Press).

Craig, Ann (1990), "Institutional Context and Popular Strategies," in Joe Foweraker and Ann Craig (eds.), *Popular Movements and Political Change in Mexico* (Boulder, CO: Lynne Rienner), 271–84.

Cruz, Arturo (2018), "How to Understand the Nicaragua Crisis," Latin America Program (Washington DC: Wilson Center).

Danner, Mark (1989), "Beyond the Mountains," *The New Yorker* (November 27, December 4, December 11).

Dinges, John (1990), *Our Man in Panama: How General Noriega Used the United States—and Made Millions in Drugs and Arms* (New York: Random House).

Fatton, Robert (2002), *Haiti's Predatory Republic: The Unending Transition to Democracy* (Boulder, CO: Lynne Rienner).

Favela, Diana Margarita (2006), *Protesta y reforma en México: Interacción entre Estado y sociedad 1946–1997* (Mexico: Universidad Nacional Autónoma de México).

Fico, Carlos (2001), *Como eles agiam: os subterrâneos da Ditadura Militar. Espionagem e polícia política* (Rio de Janeiro: Editora Record).

Fisher, Jo (1989), *Mothers of the Disappeared* (Boston, MA: South End Press).

Foweraker, Joe (1990), "Popular Movements and Political Change in Mexico," in Joe Foweraker and Ann Craig (eds.), *Popular Movements and Political Change in Mexico*, 3–20 (Boulder, CO: Lynne Rienner).

Franklin, James (2015), "Persistent Challengers: Repression, Concessions, Challenger Strength, and Commitment in Latin America," *Mobilization* 20(1), 61–80.

Frantz, Erica, Andrea Kendall-Taylor, Joseph Wrighty, and Xu Xu (2019), "Personalization of Power and Repression in Dictatorships," *Journal of Politics* 82(1), 372–77.

Gandhi, Jennifer (2008), *Political Institutions under Dictatorship* (New York: Cambridge University Press).

Geddes, Barbara, Joseph Wright, and Erica Frantz (2018), *How Dictatorships Work: Power, Personalization, and Collapse* (New York: Cambridge University Press).

Greene, Kenneth (2007), *Why Dominant Parties Lose: Mexico's Democratization in Comparative Perspective* (New York: Cambridge University Press).

James, Daniel (1976), "The Peronist Left: 1955–1975," *Journal of Latin American Studies* 8(2), 273–96.

Johnston, Hank (2015), "'The Game's Afoot': Social Movements in Authoritarian States," in Donatella della Porta and Mario Diani (eds.), *The Oxford Handbook of Social Movements*, 619–33 (Oxford: Oxford University Press).

Keller, Renata (2015), *Mexico's Cold War: Cuba, the United States, and the Legacy of the Mexican Revolution* (New York: Cambridge University Press).

Klein, Herbert and Francisco Vidal Luna (2017), *Brazil, 1964–1985: The Military Regimes of Latin America in the Cold War* (New Haven, CT: Yale University Press).

Kobrak, Paul (1999), *Organizing and Repression in the University of San Carlos, Guatemala, 1944 to 1996* (Washington, DC: American Association for the Advancement of Science).

Knight, Alan (1990), "Historical Continuities in Social Movements," in Joe Foweraker and Ann Craig (eds.), *Popular Movements and Political Change in Mexico*, 78–102 (Boulder, CO: Lynne Rienner).

Langland, Victoria (2013), *Speaking of Flowers: Student Movements and the Making and Remembering of 1968 in Military Brazil* (Durham, NC: Duke).

Le Bot, Yvon (1995), *La guerra en tierras Mayas: comunidad, violencia y modernidad en Guatemala (1970–1992)* (Mexico: Fondo de Cultura Económica).

Levenson-Estrada, Deborah (1994), *Trade Unionists against Terror: Guatemala City, 1954–1985* (Chapel Hill: University of North Carolina Press).

Levitsky, Steven and Lucan Way (2010), *Competitive Authoritarianism: Hybrid Regimes after the Cold War* (New York: Cambridge University Press).

Loveman, Mara (1998), "High-Risk Collective Action: Defending Human Rights in Chile, Uruguay, and Argentina," *American Journal of Sociology* 104(2), 477–525.

Linz, Juan (1975), "Totalitarianism and Authoritarian Regimes," in Fred Greenstein and Nelson Polsby (eds.), *Macropolitical Theory*, 175–411 (Boulder, CO: Lynne Rienner).

Mainwaring, Scott (1986), *The Catholic Church and Politics in Brazil, 1916-1985* (Stanford, CA: Stanford University Press).

Montgomery, Tommie Sue (1995), *Revolution in El Salvador* (Boulder, CO: Westview Press).

Munck, Gerardo (1998), *Authoritarianism and Democratization: Soldiers and Workers in Argentina, 1976–1983* (University Park, PA: Penn State University Press).

Naím, Moisés and Francisco Toro (2018), "Venezuela's Suicide: Lessons for a Failed State," *Foreign Affairs* (November/December), https://www.foreignaffairs.com/articles/south-america/2018-10-15/venezuelas-suicide.

O'Donnell, Guillermo (1986), "Introduction to the Latin American Cases," in Guillermo O'Donnell, Philippe Schmitter, and Laurence Whitehead (eds.), *Transitions from Authoritarian Rule: Latin America* (Baltimore, MD: Johns Hopkins University Press), 3–18.

O'Donnell, Guillermo (1988), *Bureaucratic Authoritarianism: Argentina, 1966–1973, in Comparative Perspective* (Berkeley and Los Angeles: University of California Press).

Ortiz, David (2015), "State Repression and Mobilization in Latin America," in Paul Almeida and Allen Cordero Ulate (eds.), *Handbook of Social Movements across Latin America* (New York: Springer), 43–59.

Nepstad, Sharon Erickson (2011), *Nonviolent Revolutions: Civil Resistance in the Late 20th Century* (New York: Oxford University Press).

Novaro, Marcos and Vicente Palermo (2003), *La dictadura militar, 1976–1983: Del golpe de estado a la restauración democrática* (Buenos Aires: Paidós).

Parkman, Patricia (1988), *Nonviolent Insurrection in El Salvador: The Fall of Maximiliano Hernández Martínez* (Tucson: University of Arizona Press).

Pensado, Jaime (2013), *Rebel Mexico: Student Unrest and Authoritarian Political Culture during the Long Sixties* (Stanford, CA: Stanford University Press).
Philip, George (1984), "Military-Authoritarianism in South America: Brazil, Chile, Uruguay and Argentina," *Political Studies* 32, 10–20.
Policzer, Pablo (2009), *The Rise and Fall of Repression in Chile* (Notre Dame, IN: University of Notre Dame Press).
Purdy, Sean (2016), "Workers and Dictators: Brazilian Labour History 50 Years after the Military Coup (Review Essay)," *Labour/Le Travail* 78(fall), 301–17.
Putnam, Robert (1967), "Toward Explaining Military Intervention in Latin American Politics," *World Politics* 20(1), 83–110.
Remmer, Karen (1989), "Neopatrimonialism: The Politics of Military Rule in Chile, 1973–1987," *Comparative Politics* 21(2), 149–70.
Remmer, Karen and Gilbert Merkx (1982), "Bureaucratic-Authoritarianism Revisited," *Latin American Research Review* 17(2), 3–40.
Romero, Luis (2002), *A History of Argentina in the Twentieth Century* (University Park, PA: Penn State University Press).
Schamis, Hector (1991), "Reconceptualizing Latin American Authoritarianism in the 1970s: From Bureaucratic-Authoritarianism to Neoconservatism," *Comparative Politics* 23(2), 201–20.
Schneider, Cathy (1995), *Shantytown Protest in Pinochet's Chile* (Philadelphia, PA: Temple University Press).
Serbin, Kenneth (2000), *Secret Dialogues: Church-State Relations, Torture, and Social Justice in Authoritarian Brazil* (Pittsburgh, PA: University of Pittsburgh Press).
Skidmore, Thomas (1988), *The Politics of Military Rule in Brazil, 1964–85* (New York: Oxford University Press).
Smith, Brian (1982), *The Church and Politics in Chile: Challenges to Modern Catholicism* (Princeton, NJ: Princeton University Press).
Stern, Steve (2006), *Battling for Hearts and Minds: Memory Struggles in Pinochet's Chile, 1973–1988* (Durham, NC: Duke University Press).
Sullivan, Christopher M. (2016a), "Political Repression and the Destruction of Dissident Organizations: Evidence from the Archives of the Guatemalan National Police," *World Politics* 68(4), 645–76.
Sullivan, Christopher (2016b), "Undermining Resistance: Mobilization, Repression, and the Enforcement of Political Order," *Journal of Conflict Resolution* 60(7), 1163–90.
Tamayo, Jaime (1990), "Neoliberalism Encounters *Neocardenismo*," in Joe Foweraker and Ann Craig (eds.), *Popular Movements and Political Change in Mexico* (Boulder, CO: Lynne Rienner), 121–36.
Tilly, Charles and Sidney Tarrow (2015), *Contentious Politics* (New York: Oxford University Press).
Torres-Rivas, Edelberto (2011), *Revoluciones sin cambios revolucionarios: Ensayos sobre la crisis en Centroamérica*. (Guatemala: F&G Editores).
Trejo, Guillermo (2012), *Popular Movements in Autocracies: Religion, Repression, and Indigenous Collective Action in Mexico* (New York: Cambridge University Press).
Trevizo, Dolores (2014), "Political Repression and the Struggles for Human Rights in Mexico: 1968–1990s," *Social Science History* 38 (winter), 483–511.
Valle, Maria Ribeiro do (1999), *1968: O diálogo é a violência. Movimento estudantil e ditadura militar no Brasil* (Campinas: Editora da Unicamp).
Weinstein, Brian and Aaron Segal (1992), *Haiti: The Failure of Politics* (New York: Praeger).

CHAPTER 13

SOCIAL MOVEMENTS AND DEMOCRATIZATION PROCESSES IN LATIN AMERICA

MARÍA INCLÁN

Introduction

With the exception of El Salvador, which followed an insurgent path to democracy (Wood 2000), democratization processes in Latin America in the late twentieth century kept to different versions of the "transitions from above" model, in which incumbent and opposition elites, together with influential economic players and the military, negotiate pacts to transit towards more inclusive regimes in a stable manner. Still, all Latin American transitions to democracy have been accompanied by salient protest movements. In the case of El Salvador, insurgents became counter-elites sitting at the peace-and-democracy negotiating tables (Wood 2000). In the case of Mexico, the Zapatista uprising in 1994 triggered elite-negotiated democratizing pacts (Inclán 2018; Trejo 2012), even when they did not take part in them. In Argentina, Chile, and Uruguay, unions and human rights movements were crucial for the protection of labor and human rights' provisions after the transition (Collier 1999; Keck and Sikkink 1998; Noonan 1995; see Wolff in this volume), while in Bolivia, Colombia, Costa Rica, Ecuador, Guatemala, and Nicaragua, indigenous movements forced the inclusion of indigenous peoples' rights in the emerging more politically liberal regimes (van Cott 1994, 2005; Yashar 1997, 2005; Rice in this volume). In all cases, democratic transitions also had determining effects in the development and outcomes of social movements in the region. Not only changing political conditions during transitional periods may affect movements' cycles of protest and opportunities to gain political allies in power, but also the new institutional arrangements may influence their fate as these young democracies consolidate. Thus, despite the crucial role that social movements might play during the liberalizing phase of a democratic transition (Collier 1999; Garretón 2003; O'Donnell and Schmitter 1986; Rossi and della Porta 2009), their relative success will depend on concessions granted by democratizing elites during negotiations, as well as on the new institutional settings that may open or close opportunities to advance their interests in the emerging democratic regime. Because of this, in this chapter I present a review of these three types of phenomena. First, I briefly review definitions on democratic transitions: transitions from above, transitions from below, and protracted transitions. Then, I review some of the effects that different transitions had on the outcomes of emblematic democratizing social movements in Latin America. Finally, I discuss some of the social movements emerging as democracy has consolidated in the region.

Social Movements within Transitions from Above, Transitions from Below, and Protracted Processes

Democratic transitions are understood as regime changing processes from authoritarianism that usually comprehend three major longitudinal periods: liberalization, transition, and consolidation or further democratization (O'Donnell and Schmitter 1986; Przeworski 1991; Schedler 1998). As we have witnessed more and different paths towards democracy, scholars have developed more detailed literature, concepts, and assessments to better understand the process and the different types of democratic regimes taking shape (Rossi and della Porta 2009; Schedler 1998). Two paths towards democracy stand out, however, as the most common: transitions from above and transitions from below.

In both types of transition, the role that social movements play is crucial and, as Ruth Berins Collier highlighted back in 1999, it needs to be brought back into our analyses of democratic transitions. Dissenting elites pressing for liberalizing reforms benefit from the legitimizing power of broad social movements contentiously articulating democratizing demands, while social movement actors profit from the instability underlying political elites during a transition to achieve further concessions (McAdam 1996). This link between social movement actors and political elites during a transition is what O'Donnell and Schmitter (1986) called "the moment of civil society." However, for this link to solidify and social movements' interests be represented beyond the democratizing table, a new social pact between political parties and social movement actors (labor, peasants, human rights, professional, and popular sectors) needs to be reached either before (Collier 1999; Wolff in this volume) or after the democratizing pacts take place, so that new legal protections on political, civil, and social rights get institutionalized in the emerging democratic regime.

Social Movements within Transitions from Above

The pattern "from above" begins when authoritarian governments reach an economic or political crisis that threatens their rule (Przeworski 1991). As the crisis deepens and their legitimacy erodes, authoritarian rulers begin to realize they need to soften their grip, if they are to hold on to power and negotiate a gracious exit. The pressure for liberalization may come from within the ruling party, military junta, or bureaucracy, as divisions among authoritarian elites appear. However, liberalizing demands might also come from outside: from dissenting unions whose interests had up until then been represented by authoritarian incumbents; from rebel insurgents fighting for regime change; or from organized victims of the authoritarian repression. Authoritarian rulers tolerate these actions out of fear of further losing legitimacy (Beissinger 2002), and in hope of coopting them. As the pressure mounts, economic interests become compromised, and the legitimacy of the authoritarian regime starts to crumble. Incumbent and emerging opposition elites begin negotiating the characteristic transitional pacts, in which not only exit strategies for the incumbents and new rules of the political game are negotiated, but in the best scenarios, also legal protections of civil liberties and political rights for the emerging regime. Depending on the modes of transition, what actors are involved, and how democratically ambitious their political agendas are, democratizing pacts will be more or less comprehensive, and the emerging political regime may aspire to become not only an electoral democracy, but also a liberal one (Munck and Leff 1997).

Chile represents the paradigmatic Latin American example of democratic transitions from above, within the democratizing wave in the 1980s and 1990s, that began in Southern Europe and had its culminating point with the disintegration of the Soviet Union into fifteen new independent republics (Linz and Stepan 1996; O'Donnell and Schmitter 1986; Przeworski 1991). Through pacts, authoritarian incumbents and opposition elites negotiated the processes by which elections where to take place in the country and incumbent elites were to exit power. Social movements played an important role within the liberalizing stages of the transitions, with strong social mobilization accompanying the processes until negotiations took place (Oxhorn 1995; Schneider 1995). The referendum lost by Augusto Pinochet and the outcome of the transitional negotiations left a large sector of the population not only dissatisfied, but also demobilized, given the prerogatives that the military were able to keep. Still, Chileans continued protesting against authoritarian rulers for failing to address socioeconomic demands, rights, and prerogatives that they had claimed to represent, such as unions striking to defend labor rights, women denouncing the disappearance of their partners and children, popular movements demanding basic public services, and citizens protesting against austerity measures (Garretón 2003). However, once regime change negotiations began, social movements were considered exogenous forces or were plain absent from the democratizing pacts (Collier 1999; Oxhorn 1995; Schneider 1995).

The incorporation of social movement demands, such as the protection of labor human rights, socioeconomic redistribution, and public services, depended not only on the pressure these groups exerted, as the regime began to crumble and the degree to which opposition parties became vulnerable to their interests and articulated them in their platforms (O'Donnell and Schmitter 1986), but also on the political power that the working class and human rights advocating actors had prior to the transition (Collier 1999; Rueschemeyer, Stephens, and Stephens 1992). The stronger their prior political power, the higher the probability they would become influential actors in the new more democratic regime—in the form of working-class political parties, trade unions, civil society organizations (human rights advocacy), and think-tanks (professional associations); and the higher the chances their demands would be institutionalized through legal protections to labor and human rights, civil liberties, and political rights. In the case of Chile, what we witnessed was that their prior political power decreased significantly during and after democratizing negotiations, as military elites were able to retain significant legal protections to face justice for their human rights crimes during the dictatorship. The retention of these protections, together with legislative prerogatives, effectively demobilized social movements up until 2011, when a new generation of students initiated massive protests that progressively moved to point out the inequalities generated by neoliberal reforms in the last forty years. As the cycle of protest and repression grew, protests culminated forcing a referendum call for a constitutional review in 2020. We are still to witness the outcomes of this mobilizing effort.

More important to the consolidation of a more democratic regime, and to a possible evaluation of the role of social movements in achieving it, were the movements' demands for justice and how these demands were addressed after elite pacts. In Munck and Leff's (1997) words, the modes of transition affected policy implementation in the new regime. Social movements' democratizing demands did not only revolve around guaranteeing free and fair elections, civil liberty protections, and equal protections under the law. Demands to bring authoritarian incumbents to justice for their human rights crimes and violations posed significant difficulties for political elites to surpass during negotiations. Still, human rights movements that supported or triggered these transitions were somewhat successful in achieving their goals in Argentina, El Salvador, and Guatemala (Bakiner 2015; Pereyra 2015). The creation of truth commissions, as transitional justice mechanisms, allowed incoming political elites to settle accounts with former military dictators to come to terms with the past without jeopardizing the new regime's stability (Bakiner 2015)—with the Argentine model being emblematic for others to follow in what to do or to avoid (Engstrom and Pereira 2012; Lessa and Druliolle 2011). They recommended reparations in all cases, and in all cases either immediate or delayed courts were created. Except for El Salvador, all truth commissions were officially endorsed and reports were produced, but no follow up-institutions were created, and recommended reparations were only conceded in Guatemala as a result of civil society mobilization (Bakiner 2015: 110). Because of these uneven results, victims, activists, and scholars remain dissatisfied with the results of the truth commissions, as they fall short of bringing human rights violators from the military regime to full justice; and the democratizing process in general, because these transitional justice mechanisms have proven insufficient to establish judicial and security systems capable of containing and processing the current increases in criminal violence in several of these young democracies (Trejo and Ley 2020; Trejo, Albarracín, and Tiscornia 2018). Nevertheless, as democracy has progressed in the region, social movements have also taken advantage of the more open political conditions to launch and sustain their mobilizing campaigns. They have also learned to use the new political and judicial settings to advance citizen's rights through more institutional means and channels (Gallagher 2017).

Social Movements within Transitions from Below

The pattern "from below" is triggered by large and persistent social mobilization, or insurgency, which through a sustained rebellion compromises the interests of the economic elites, which in turn, force political elites to negotiate with the rebels (Bratton and van de Walle 1997; Wood 2000). Such pacts are intended to stabilize the political order and bring certainty to economic elites, while granting political participation to previously disenfranchised sectors of the population, and more free and fair elections. Transitions from below, however, have proven to be unstable democratizing processes that do not lead to a long-lasting new political order. The most recent examples of failed regime-change attempts from below come from the Arab Spring mobilizing efforts. With the exception of the insurgent paths to democracy achieved in El Salvador and South Africa, other transitions from below have not been led by well-organized leaders capable of becoming counter-elites at the transitional negotiating tables (Wood 2000). Political reforms achieved in these cases have included protections for freedom of expression, organization, and contestation; greater competition within one-party regimes, administrative reforms within the existing legal framework; and some checks on executive power. Nevertheless, they have rarely increased political pluralism, because negotiated concessions have been granted through opportunistic coalitions between rebel leaders and authoritarian incumbents, that have been easily reversed (Bratton and van del Walle 1997).

In the case of El Salvador, insurgents became counter-elites with whom political authoritarian incumbents had to negotiate after oligarchic economic elites pressed for such agreements (Wood 2000). As Wood (2000) argues, national economic interests had been compromised by a successfully sustained insurgency over a long period of time. Negotiating the installment of a democratic political regime became the only option for authoritarian incumbents, if they were to achieve political stability and protect economic development in the country. For the insurgents, this meant their inclusion among elites, and the political participation of previously disenfranchised sectors of the population. For economic elites, this meant the protection of their wealth and property rights. For authoritarian incumbents, the importance of negotiating the transition to a more electorally democratic regime with counter-elites rested on the capacity of insurgent leaders to make the achieved accords hold despite infighting among insurgent factions during and as a consequence of democratizing negotiations.

The relative success of the Salvadoran insurgency in becoming counter-elite actors can be attributed to the relative success that social movement organizations had in surviving a highly repressive dictatorial regime (Almeida 2008), which would not have been possible without the resilience and defiance that drove people to join the insurgency and empowered unions, churches, and human rights organizations under high-risk conditions (Brockett, 2005; Viterna 2013; Brockett in this volume). The resilience of organizations during dictatorial regimes was also key in the resurrection of civil society in the southern cone transitions (Almeida 2008; Noonan 1995; O'Donnell and Schmitter 1986). The denser and more diverse the local and transnational organizational networks, the more successful were human rights organizations in challenging the authoritarian regime and seeking justice and retribution (Keck and Sikkink 1998; Loveman 1998).

Being at the negotiating table allowed guerrillas to become formalized political parties. Peace accords also guaranteed amnesty to rebels (Almeida 2008; Wood 2000). These were not minor accomplishments. Through them dissenting voices secured the freedom to organize, mobilize, and articulate their demands through more institutional means. Most of the citizenry's civil liberties and political rights were also ensured. Not only did dissension begin to be tolerated, but contentious politics also became normalized. Civic organizations and political parties could resurge. As such, El Salvador took big steps towards consolidating a more democratic regime. Still, being at the negotiating table did not guarantee the political inclusion or a significant improvement in the socioeconomic conditions of the marginalized, as counter-elite insurgent leaders intended (Wood 2000). The current tragic situation of migrants fleeing extreme violence and poverty in El Salvador has shown that the electoral democracy that emerged after the 1992 Peace Accords was not based on institutional reforms that guaranteed accountability and the rule of law, socioeconomic development, and a process of reconciliation after the war, but only on regulations to make elections more competitive (Moodie 2010). As violence increased and became the norm, encouraged by the social cleansing that a militarized policing strategy entails, implementing a rights-respecting security strategy and the rule of law in the country has proved to be an almost impossible task to accomplish (Zilberg 2011).

Social Movements within Protracted Transitions

The Ejército Zapatista de Liberación Nacional (EZLN) is another example of a relatively successful social movement that was poised to become an influential political actor within a transition from below. However, as we know now and will see why in this section, the EZLN did not take part in Mexico democratizing pacts among political elites, and while the EZLN held peace negotiations with the government they failed to have their demand for autonomy addressed (Martí i Puig and Álvarez in this volume). The relative success of the Zapatista movement in surviving up to these days has more to do with the transnational advocacy networks of solidary movements around the world, than with their ability to sit down at the negotiating table with political elites (Inclán

2018). I argue that this is because the Zapatista movement developed within a protracted transition and because peace negotiations were not part of democratizing negotiations among political elites, but occurred parallel to the reforms that allowed for more competitive elections in the country.

A protracted democratization process is defined as a long transition from either military rule or a one-party regime. It involves a long period of negotiations among political elite actors, that lead to incremental reforms to regulate electoral competition, but do not necessarily liberalize the political system further than guaranteeing free and fair elections (Casper and Taylor 1996; Eisenstadt 2004). Such a protracted path to transition helps authoritarian incumbents channel potential mobilizing actors against the regime into the electoral process, because opposition parties are forced to remain loyal to the quest of regime change first, before they can begin articulating social movement's interests during democratizing pacts and electoral campaigns. As such, a protracted transition allows authoritarian incumbents to prolong their control of the political system and it also prolongs the liberalization process before free and fair elections become the norm. Because of this, a protracted transition can be conceived as within the *from above* type of democratizing processes, as through gradual concessions, authoritarian incumbents are able to control possible insurgencies or dissidents from becoming counter-elites. At the same time, they are able to hold on and off negotiations with opposing political elites. As a consequence, we have yet to witness revolutionary movements succeeding as relevant political players within protracted transitions. Only when peace negotiations between rebels and authorities have been part of democratizing pacts (through alliances or direct negotiations), have opportunities for success slid open for insurgents to achieve their political goals (Gamson 1990; Tilly 1978; Wood 2000). Yet, even in those cases, they have fallen short of being able to transform such opportunities and concessions into socioeconomic improvements for the population sectors they represent. If, however, as in the Mexican case, peace negotiations with insurgents develop parallel to, but separated from, democratizing negotiations among political elites, it is very unlikely that they will even succeed in achieving their political goals, even less improve the well-being of the marginalized (Inclán 2018).

At the time that democratizing reforms were negotiated among legislative elites in 1996, the EZLN was poised to turn into an influential counter-elite actor with whom political forces had to negotiate. The EZLN had even been invited to take part in such negotiations. The EZLN, however, declined such an invitation, arguing against potential co-optation attempts, given the long history of clientelistic practices of political parties. Additionally, given that peace dialogues were still going on between the EZLN and representatives of the federal government, the EZLN felt compelled to focus on those efforts first. Both decisions proved to be unsuccessful for the Zapatistas, as peace negotiations broke down in September 1996, after President Zedillo failed to recognize the San Andres Accords signed in February, while negotiations to regulate the political competition had already passed without incorporating any of the movement's demand to recognize indigenous autonomy. Given the parallel but separate negotiating settings, neither set of elites at the negotiating tables had the necessary incentives to incorporate the agreements elites had reached in the other negotiating process. These negotiating settings also protected incumbents and opposition elites from social pressures to include social movement demands. Elites ended up being relative immune to the vulnerability characteristic of transitional times, in which the political uncertainty that political parties face, forces them to integrate social movements agendas into their platforms. Finally, because Zapatistas did not count with political allies in power, their interests failed to be even articulated, even less represented by the left in power. Nevertheless, despite these relative failures at achieving its political goals, the Zapatista movement has been able to survive up until these days. Mobilizing opportunities during the transition not only opened opportunities for the proliferation of sympathetic non-governmental organizations as well as their cycle of protest, but also for the survival of the movement as the democratization process advanced and advocacy organizations consolidated within the new civil society. While insurgents were excluded from democratizing negotiations, the liberalizing conditions of the transition allowed them to organize the resistance of the movement over time.

Social Movements within Democracy

Even when social movement actors do not take part in democratizing pacts and negotiations, social movements' outcomes depend on the conditions that will prevail once democracy has become the norm for conducting politics, for both mobilizing as well as negotiating. Democratic transitions tend to be conceived as ripe scenarios for social movements to achieve substantive concessions. Nevertheless, because transitions to democracy exacerbate political instability and institutional settings are in flux, the relative success of social movement actors to achieve their political goals depend on the conditions in which democratizing elites negotiate. Hence, the fate of social movements developing amidst democratic transitions tends to be palpable once the new regime begins to consolidate, and their outcomes depend on gradual democratizing reforms that allow social movement leaders to gain office, form part of governing cabinets or advisory boards, and press for the representation of their interests. However, these same democratizing openings may become important obstacles for the advancement of a social movement's goals because as their leaders are appointed or elected, they have to balance the representation of the movement's demands with the interests of the political parties that brought them to power (Yashar 2005). The different fates experienced by indigenous rights movements in the region illustrate this argument better. Indigenous movements have been successful in Bolivia, Colombia, Ecuador, and Nicaragua when they have challenged governments facing legitimacy crises; when they have counted on influential political allies; and when their demands are shared by large sectors of the population (van Cott 2005). In Ecuador and Bolivia, where indigenous leaders have faced less partisan competition and compromise within the governing bodies they formed, they have been better able to serve their movements' interests, while in Peru they have not been able to do so (Yashar 2005). In addition, indigenous communities in Bolivia,

Ecuador, Colombia, and Venezuela have been able to form ethnic political parties where they face less ethnic competition, have a strong network of loyal mobilizing organizations, and have been able to gain significant concessions as social movements (van Cott 2005; Rice in this volume).

As democracy is institutionalized and socialized as the norm to conduct politics, social movements face more open political conditions or opportunities, such as more tolerance for protest mobilization (Bellinger and Arce 2011; Bruhn 2008; Machado, Scartascini and Tommasi 2001; Medel Sierralta and Somma 2016; Somma 2010, 2015, 2016; Valenzuela et al. 2016); incentives for organizational formation, including transnational solidarity networks, given the funding challenges that local advocacy organizations tend to face in young democracies in developing nations (Ewig 1999; Martí i Puig 2010); and the opportunity to begin influencing the agenda-setting and policymaking processes (Donoso 2016; Foweraker 2001). Newer social movements have also emerged and begun using both contentious and more institutionalized means to defend LGBTQ+ rights (de la Dehesa 2010; Díez in this volume), women's rights (Safa 1990; Ewig and Friedman in this volume), students' rights (Disi Pavlic 2018; Donoso 2016; Donoso in this volume), immigrant rights (Gallagher 2017), the environment (Christel and Gutiérrez in this volume), and popular claims (Roberts and Porter 2006). Contentious politics are more likely where these young democratic institutions are weaker, while more conventional forms of political participation are more likely where institutions are more consolidated (Machado, Scartascini, and Tommasi 2001); with weaker institutions protest activity tends to carry higher economic and political costs if social policy concessions are not granted (Zárate 2014). However, keeping up contentious mobilization, while utilizing the courts to advance the protection of migrants' right to physical integrity, has proven a relative successful way to break up pernicious impunity patterns in systems with relatively weaker social institutional safeguards (Gallagher 2017). Movements against the extractive industries have also proven relatively successful in using contentious politics as well judicial opportunities to advance the interests of environmentalists and indigenous populations to protect natural reserves and sacred lands (Arce 2014; Eaton 2011; Eisenstadt and West 2019).

Still, the success and outcomes of social movements are relatively difficult to measure. Social movements' achievements are usually indirect, as most of their influence is more visible in terms of public opinion than on actual policy changes (Banaszak and Ondercin 2016). Even then, the effects of a given social movement over public opinion and policy tend to be indirect, delayed, and/or marginal (Burstein and Sausner 2005; McAdam and Su 2002). In any case, social movements' outcomes need to be addressed in relation to their goals. Social movements goals can go from raising awareness about a given issue, commemorating past struggles and achievements, forming collective identities, to recruiting activists, fundraising, forming advocacy organizations, organizing protest activity, achieving concessions and compensations, and, as mentioned before, influencing public opinion and the policymaking process, or even seeking political change. The study of Latin American social movements' outcomes has not only focused on their relative success in mobilizing and reaching concessions, compensations, and changes in policy (Eaton 2011; Rubin 2004; Roberts and Porter 2006; Silva 2015; Gurza Lavalle and Szwako in this volume). Scholars have also analyzed the role that social movements' play in empowering organizations and collective identities (Arce 2014), and most importantly the role of social movements in reshaping the political arena taking advantage of political conditions granted by the political process of more established democracies in the region (Rossi 2017). As such, social movements in Latin America should be recognized as crucial political players setting the new institutional order of a polity, and not only ephemeral dissident mobilization around specific socioeconomic issues (Rossi in this volume).

Conclusion

As other scholars have already pointed out and this brief review has shown, social movements, as civil society actors, play a crucial role in both democratic transitions, as well as democratic consolidation or further democratization processes (Diamond 1999; Smulovitz and Peruzzotti 2000). Within the transitional period from authoritarianism to democracy, social movements play a pivotal role pushing forward the liberalization of the regime, as well as pressing negotiations among political elites to set the new institutional settings for political competition and participation. Within democratic consolidation, they contribute to the never-ending process of deepening democracy.

Still, neither the literature on Latin American democratic transitions, nor the literature on social movements in the continent have systematically or comparatively analyzed the extent to which social movements' demands have been incorporated into democratization pacts and the extent to which these demands have been addressed in the new constitutions, through public policy or legal processes within the new democratic regimes. This may be because of the tangential and external role social movements have played in transitions from above as well as protracted transitions or due to the fact that so few social movement actors have become influential actors during transitions—only Salvadoran counter-elite insurgents have been able to sit at the negotiating table themselves (Wood 2000). It may also be because conducting such research has proven to be incredibly labor intensive. Thus, it is no wonder that social movement and democratic transition scholars have concentrated their efforts on analyzing small-n or single cases.

For these reasons, I would like to conclude this chapter by offering some suggestions to advance our knowledge of social movement and democratization processes. First, in order to truly measure the role of social movements within transitions, I believe we should begin with a systematic register of the social movement actors mobilizing during the liberalization stage of democratic transitions in the continent. An account of social movements pushing for further liberalization during the first stages of a transition would help us identify these actors and their demands were present and articulated during democratizing pacts. A report of these actors and demands would enable us to pinpoint which were incorporated into new constitutional orders. Second, to assess the extent to which social movements are actively contributing to deepening democracy in the region, another record of social movement actors in the continent could aid a comparative analysis of their current outcomes. Such an inventory would also permit to recognize the number of social movement organizations registered in each country. This evidence would enable scholars and policymakers alike to begin analyzing the size of each country's civil society, its role in policymaking, and by extension, in strengthening democracy in the continent. Not only we could begin to trace the relative success of local civil society organizations, but we could even track the influence of transnational social movements in the region.

Since protest activity has become accepted as just another normal form of political participation, we have witnessed social mobilization around the negative consequences of globalized free-markets and neoliberal development policies. Recent mobilizations in Chile, Bolivia, Ecuador, and Colombia, and a growing body of literature are resuscitating the role that inequality, employment precarity, and economic crises play in mobilizing aggrieved sectors of the population (Almeida 2014; Arce 2006, 2008; Arce and Rice 2009; Silva 2009; Rossi in this volume), as well as the interactions between party politics and social mobilization around elections to set the agenda of incoming administrations (Bruhn 2008; Trejo 2014; Roberts in this volume), and the role that transnational advocacy organizations have on global governance institutions, like the International Monetary Fund and the International Labor Organization (Haarstad and Andersson 2009; Kay 2011; von Bülow in this volume).

Even as more competitive elections have been routinized in the region, many countries still have not been able to guarantee the rule of law. As a consequence, several countries still lag significantly behind on their transparency and accountability records. This would be another interesting area to analyze the relative influence of Latin American social movements. Corruption and impunity have opened the door to organized crime to reign and violence and extreme poverty are nowadays forcing massive migrations and social mobilization of people in Central America, the Caribbean, Brazil, Venezuela, and Mexico. Transnational migrants' movements are gaining force in Central America and Mexico, despite the precarious legal protections that these groups face as they travel from country to country, individually and collectively organized (Gallagher 2017). Domestic movements against the violence generated by organized crime and the war against drug cartels implemented by the Mexican state also operate amidst unsafe conditions (Ley 2022). Under such conditions, the literature predicts that more violent or less conventional ways of protesting could be more likely to develop, as more repressive and unsafe environments (Tarrow 2011), as well as clientelistic political allies, tend to generate the incentives for dissident groups to adopt more radical repertoires of mobilization (Auyero and Moran 2007). Nevertheless, this has not always been the case. While some communities have organized vigilante groups to protect their safety against organized crime (Zizumbo Colunga 2015), violence victims have also been pressing the Mexican state through more conventional and institutional channels to investigate the crimes and human rights violations committed against them by state officials and cartels alike (Ley and Guzmán 2019; Rojo-Mendoza 2013). Both of these types of movements have emerged and developed under high- and double-risk conditions (Ley 2022), generating similar emotive connections and motivations to take part in organizations to those observed during times of war in Central America (Brockett 2005). Nevertheless, instead of expressing their frustration violently, their collective actions have aimed at democratizing the existing justice administrating institutions. As such, they have opened new opportunities for the continuous democratization process in the country.

To analyze how social movements have promoted the socialization of democracy, we need studies on social movement actors and organizations promoting and behaving within civic values and rules, training activist leaders, providing information useful for policy makers and lobbyists, and building trust and cooperation among civil society actors, as well as with authorities to support citizens' civic and political engagement. Studying the influence of social movements in the habituation of democracy is probably the most challenging area of analysis. This is not only because of the lack of social movements records across the region, but also because of the relative difficulty to accessing the internal rules and practices of social movement organizations. The corporatism legacy hindrances access to information, but more importantly it significantly slows the growth of independent civil society organizations. Given the prevalent economic inequalities in the region, civil society organizations have had a difficult time sustaining their causes and existence. Because of this, we have observed not only that they have to rely on transnational financial support, but that the ones that have emerged independently from external support are usually backed by big domestic philanthropists. As such, a great disparity still exists among social movement organizations and causes in terms of their emergence, success, and survival.

References

Almeida, Paul D. (2014), *Mobilizing Democracy: Globalization and Citizen Protest* (Baltimore, MD: Johns Hopkins University Press).

Almeida, Paul D. (2008), *Waves of Protest. Popular Struggle in El Salvador, 1925–2005* (Minneapolis: University of Minnesota Press).

Haarstad, Håvard and Vibeke Andersson (2009), "Backlash Reconsidered: Neoliberalism and Popular Mobilization in Bolivia," *Latin American Politics and Society* 51(4), 1–28.

Arce, Moises (2006), "The Political Consequences of Market Reform in Peru," *Latin American Politics & Society*, 48 (1), 27–54.

Arce, Moises (2008), "The Repoliticization of Collective Action after Neoliberalism in Peru," *Latin American Politics and Society*, 50 (3), 37–62.

Arce, Moises (2014), *Resource Extraction and Protest in Peru* (Pittsburgh, PA: University of Pittsburgh Press).

Arce, Moises and Roberta Rice (2009), "Societal Protest in Post-Stabilization Bolivia," *Latin American Research Review*, 44 (1), 88–101.

Auyero, Javier and Timothy Patrick Moran (2007), "The Dynamics of Collective Violence: Dissecting Food Riots in Contemporary Argentina," *Social Forces*, 85 (3), 1341–1367.

Bakiner, Omar (2015), *Truth Commissions. Memory, Power, and Legitimacy* (Philadelphia: University of Pennsylvania Press).

Banaszak, Lee Ann and Heather L. Ondercin, (2016), "Public Opinion as a Movement Outcome: The Case of the U.S. Women's Movement," *Mobilization*, 21 (3), 361–378.
Beissinger, Mark R. (2002), *Nationalist Mobilization and the Collapse of the Soviet State* (New York: Cambridge University Press).
Bellinger, Paul T. Jr. and Moises Arce (2011), "Protest and Democracy in Latin America's Market Era," *Political Research Quarterly*, 64 (3), 688–704.
Bratton, Michael and Nicholas van de Walle (1997), *Democratic Experiments in Africa: Regime Transitions in Comparative Perspective* (Cambridge: Cambridge University Press).
Brockett, Charles D. (2005), *Political Movements and Violence in Central America* (New York: Cambridge University Press).
Bruhn, Kathleen (2008), *Urban Protest in Mexico and Brazil* (New York: Cambridge University Press).
Burstein, Paul and Sarah Sausner (2005), "The Incidence and Impact of Policy Oriented Collective Action: Competing Views," *Sociological Forum*, 20 (3), 403–419.
Casper, Gretchen and Michelle M. Taylor (1996), *Negotiating Democracy: Transitions form Authoritarian Rule* (Pittsburgh, PA: University of Pittsburgh Press).
Collier, Ruth Berins (1999), *Paths towards Democracy. The Working Class and Elites in Western Europe and South America* (Cambridge: Cambridge University Press).
de la Dehesa, Rafael (2010), *Queering the Public Sphere in Mexico and Brazil: Sexual Rights Movements in Emerging Democracies* (Durham, NC: Duke University Press).
Diamond, Larry (1999). "Civil Society," in Larry Diamond (ed.), *Developing Democracy. Toward Consolidation* (Baltimore: Johns Hopkins University Press), 218–260.
Disi Pavlic, Rodolfo (2018), "Sentenced to Debt: Explaining Student Mobilization in Chile," *Latin American Research Review*, 53 (3), 448–465.
Donoso, Sofia (2016), "When Social Movements Become a Democratizing Force: The Political Impact of the Student Movement in Chile," *Protest, Social Movements and Global Democracy Since 2011: New Perspectives Research in Social Movements, Conflicts and Change*, 39, 167–196.
Eaton, Kent (2011), "Conservative Autonomy Movements: Territorial Dimensions of Ideological Conflict in Bolivia and Ecuador," *Comparative Politics* 43 (3), 291–310.
Eisenstadt, Todd (2004), *Courting Democracy in Mexico: Party Strategies and Electoral Institutions* (Cambridge: Cambridge University Press).
Eisenstadt, Todd and Karleen West (2019), *Who Speaks for Nature? Indigenous Environmental Movements, Public Opinion, and Ecuador's Petro-State* (New York: Oxford University Press).
Engstrom, Par and Gabriel Pereira (2012), "From Amnesty to Accountability: The Ebb and Flow in the Search of Justice in Argentina," in Francesca Lessa and Leigh A. Payne (eds.), *Amnesty in the Age of Human Rights Accountability.* (New York: Cambridge University Press), 97–122.
Ewig, Christina (1999), "The Strengths and Limits of the NGO Women's Movement Model: Shaping Nicaragua's Democratic Institutions," *Latin American Research Review* 34 (3), 75–102.
Foweraker, Joe (2001), "Grassroots Movements and Political Activism in Latin America. A Critical Comparison of Chile and Brazil," *Journal of Latin American Studies,* 33 (4), 839–865.
Gallagher, Janice (2017), "The Last Mile Problem: Activists, Advocates, and the Struggle for Justice in Domestic Courts," *Comparative Political Studies*, 50 (12), 1666–1698.
Gamson, William (1990), *The Strategy of Social Protest* (Belmont, CA: Wadsworth Publishing Company).

Garretón, Manuel Antonio (2003), *Incomplete Democracy: Political Democratization in Chile and Latin America* (Chapel Hill: The University of North Carolina Press).

Inclán, María (2018), *The Zapatista Movement and Mexico's Democratic Transition* (New York: Oxford University Press).

Kay, Tamara (2011), *NAFTA and the Politics of Labor Transnationalism* (New York: Cambridge University Press).

Keck, Margaret E. and Kathryn Sikkink (1998), *Activists beyond Borders* (Ithaca, NY: Cornell University Press).

Lessa, Francesa and Vincent Druliolle (2011), *The Memory of State Terrorism in the Southern Cone* (New York: Palgrave Macmillan).

Ley, Sandra J. and Magdalena Guzmán (2019), "Doing Business and Criminal Violence: Companies and Civil Action in Mexico," in Deborah Avant, Marie Berry, Erica Chenoweth, Rachel Epstein, Cullen Hendrix, Oliver Kaplan, and Timothy Sisk (eds.), *Civil Action and the Dynamics of Violence*, 147–77 (New York: Oxford University Press).

Ley, Sandra J. (2022), "High-risk participation: Demanding peace and justice amid criminal violence." *Journal of Peace Research*, 0(0). https://doi.org/10.1177/00223433221085441

Linz, Juan J. and Alfred Stepan (1996), *Problems of Democratic Transition and Consolidation. Southern Europe, South America, and Post-Communist Europe* (Baltimore, MD: The Johns Hopkins University Press).

Loveman, Mara (1998), "High-Risk Collective Action: Defending Human Rights in Chile, Uruguay, and Argentina," *American Journal of Sociology* 104(2), 477–525.

Machado, Fabiana, Carlos Scartascini, and Mariano Tommasi (2001), "Political Institutions and Street Protests in Latin America," *Journal of Conflict Resolution* 55(3), 340–65.

Martí i Puig, Salvador (2010), "The Emergence of Indigenous Movements in Latin America and their Impact on the Latin American Political Scene: Interpretive Tools at the Local and Global Levels," *Latin American Perspectives* 37(6), 74–92.

McAdam, Doug (1996), "Conceptual Origins, Current Problems, and Future Directions," in Doug McAdam, John D. McCarthy, and Mayer N. Zald (eds.), *Comparative Perspectives on Social Movements* (Cambridge: Cambridge University Press), 23–40.

McAdam, Doug and Su, Yang (2002), "The War at Home: Antiwar Protests and Congressional Voting, 1965-1973," *American Sociological Review* 67(5), 696–721.

Medel Sierralta, Rodrigo and Somma, Nicolás M. (2016), "¿Marchas, ocupaciones o barricadas? Explorando los determinantes de las tácticas de la protesta en Chile," *Política y Gobierno* 23(1), 163–99.

Moodie, Ellen (2010), *El Salvador in the Aftermath of Peace: Crime, Uncertainty, and the Transition to Democracy* (Philadelphia: University of Pennsylvania Press).

Munck, Gerardo L. and Carol Skalnik Leff (1997), "Modes of Transition and Democratization: South American and Eastern Europe in Comparative Perspectives," *Comparative Politics* 29(3), 343–62.

Noonan, Rita K. (1995), "Women against the State: Political Opportunities and Collective Action Frames in Chile's Transition to Democracy," *Sociological Forum* 10(1), 81–111.

O'Donnell, Guillermo, and Philippe C. Schmitter (1986), *Transitions from Authoritarian Rule. Tentative Conclusions about Uncertain Democracies* (Baltimore, MD: The Johns Hopkins University Press).

Oxhorn, Philip (1995), *Organizing Civil Society. The Popular Sectors and the Struggle for Democracy in Chile* (University Park, PA: Penn State University Press).

Pereyra, Sebastián (2015), "Strategies and Mobilization Cycles of the Human Rights Movement in the Democratic Transition in Argentina," in Bert Klandermans and Cornelis Van Stralen (eds.), *Movements in Times of Democratic Transition*, 186–205 (Philadelphia, PA: Temple University Press).

Przeworski, Adam (1991), *Democracy and the Market. Political and Economic Reforms in Eastern Europe and Latin America* (Cambridge: Cambridge University Press).

Roberts, Bryan R. and Alejandro Portes (2006), "Coping with the Free Market City: Collective Action in Six Latin American Cities and the End of the Twentieth Century," *Latin American Research Review* 41(2), 57–83.

Rojo-Mendoza, Reynaldo (2013), "From Victims to Activists: Crime Victimization, Social Support, and Political Participation in Mexico," PhD Dissertation, University of Pittsburgh.

Rossi, Federico M. (2017), *The Poor's Struggle for Political Incorporation: The Piquetero Movement in Argentina* (New York: Cambridge University Press).

Rossi, Federico M., Donatella della Porta (2009), "Social Movement, Trade Unions, and Advocacy Networks," in Christian W. Haerpfer, Patrick Bernhagen, Ronald F. Inglehart, and Christian Welzel (eds.), *Democractization*, 172–85 (New York: Oxford University Press).

Rubin, Jeffrey W. (2004), "Meanings and Mobilizations: A Cultural Politics Approach to Social Movements and States," *Latin American Research Review* 39(3), 106–42.

Rueschemeyer, Dietrich, Evelyne Huber, and John D. Stephens (1992), *Capitalist Development and Democracy* (Chicago: University of Chicago Press).

Safa, Helen I. (1990), "Women's Social Movements in Latin America," *Gender and Society* 4(3), 354–69.

Schedler, Andreas (1998), "What is Democratic Consolidation?' *Journal of Democracy* 9(2), 91–107.

Schneider, Cathy (1995), *Shantytown Protest in Pinochet's Chile* (Philadelphia, PA: Temple University Press).

Silva, Eduardo (2009), *Challenging Neoliberalism in Latin America* (New York: Cambridge University Press).

Silva, Eduardo (2015), "Social Movements, Protest, and Policy," *European Review of Latin American and Caribbean Studies* 100, 27–39.

Smulovitz, Catalina and Enrique Peruzzotti (2000), "Societal Accountability in Latin America," *Journal of Democracy* 11(4), 147–58.

Somma, Nicolás M. (2010), "How Do Voluntary Organizations Foster Protest? The Role of Organizational Involvement on Individual Protest Participation," *Sociological Quarterly* 51(3), 384–407.

Somma, Nicolás M. (2015), "Participación ciudadana y activismo digital en América Latina," in Bernardo Sorj and Sergio Fausto (eds.), *Internet y movilizaciones sociales: Transformaciones del espacio público y de la sociedad civil*, 103–46 (São Paulo: Ediciones Plataforma Democrática).

Somma, Nicolás M. (2016), "How Do Party Systems Shape Insurgency Levels? A Comparison of Four Nineteenth-Century Latin American Republics," *Social Science History* 40(2), 219–45.

Tarrow, Sidney (2011), *Power in Movement. Social Movements and Contentious Politics* (New York: Cambridge University Press).

Tilly, Charles (1978), *From Mobilization to Revolution* (Reading MA: Addison-Wesley).

Trejo, Guillermo (2012), *Popular Movements in Autocracies: Religion, Repression, and Indigenous Collective Action in Mexico* (New York: Cambridge University Press).

Trejo, Guillermo (2014), "The Ballot and the Street: An Electoral Theory on Social Protest in Autocracies," *Perspectives in Politics* 12(2), 332–52.

Trejo, Guillermo, Juan Albarracín, and Lucía Tiscornia (2018), "Breaking State Impunity in Post-Authoritarian Regimes: Why Transitional Justice Processes Deter Criminal Violence in New Democracies," *Journal of Peace Research* 55(6), 787–809.

Valenzuela, Sebastián, Nicolás M. Somma, Andrés Scherman, and Arturo Arriagada (2016), "Social Media in Latin America: Deepening or Bridging Gaps in Protest Participation?," *Online Information Review* 40(5), 695–711.

van Cott, Donna Lee (ed.) (1994), *Indigenous Peoples and Democracy in Latin America* (New York: The Interamerican Dialogue).

van Cott, Donna Lee (2005), *From Movements to Parties in Latin America. The Evolution of Ethnic Politics* (New York: Cambridge University Press).

Viterna, Jocelyn (2013), *Women in War: The Micro-Processes of Mobilization in El Salvador* (New York: Oxford University Press).

Wood, Elisabeth (2000), *Forging Democracy from Below: Insurgent Transitions in South Africa and El Salvador* (New York: Cambridge University Press).

Yashar, Deborah J. (1997), *Demanding Democracy: Reform and Reaction in Costa Rica and Guatemala, 1870s–1950s* (Palo Alto, CA: Stanford University Press).

Yashar, Deborah J. (2005), *Contesting Citizenship in Latin America: The Rise of Indigenous Movements and the Postliberal Challenge* (New York: Cambridge University Press).

Zárate, Bárbara (2014), "Social Spending Responses to Organized Labor and Mass Protests in Latin America, 1970–2007," *Comparative Political Studies* 47(14), 1945–72.

Zilberg, Elana (2011), *Space of Detention: The Making of a Transnational Gang Crisis between Los Angeles and El Salvador* (Durham, NC: Duke University Press).

Zizumbo Colunga, Daniel (2015), "Taking the Law into Our Hands: Trust, Social Capital, and Vigilante Justice," PhD Thesis, Vanderbilt University.

CHAPTER 14

SOCIAL MOVEMENTS AND CAPITALIST MODELS OF DEVELOPMENT IN LATIN AMERICA

FEDERICO M. ROSSI

Introduction

In order to understand social movements and capitalist dynamics in Latin America it is necessary to analyze the specific paths of capitalism in the region. The capitalist experience on which mainstream North Atlantic social movement literature is implicitly built is far from representative of the rest of the world, where most social conflicts happen. Indeed, most social movement struggles around the world—including those in Latin America—are directly or indirectly related to an economic issue (labor rights, land reform, redistribution, social policies, disincorporation, etc.), with movements' claims generally including calls for alternative politico-economic models of development and for social justice broadly conceived.

The goal of this chapter is to analyze social movement dynamics across the capitalist models of development that predominated in Latin America from independence from colonial rule until the early twenty-first century. The analysis is done through the lens of political economy of social movements, understood as the substantive and theoretical recoupling of political and economic spheres in the relational study of social movements and capitalist dynamics. If we avoid an economically determinist approach and the North Atlantic narrative is decentered, a political economy of social movements reveals multiple struggles for the expansion of the socio-political arena and resistance to this expansion with plutocratic retrenchment periods that contract the socio-political arena.

Capitalism and Social Movement Studies in Latin America

In Latin America, the construction of social movement studies did not disregard capitalism as mainstream North Atlantic approaches did (Hetland and Goodwin 2013). As such, *bringing back capitalism* was never needed in Latin America, and the literature could develop more refined theorizations about the economic dimensions of social movement dynamics. In addition, beyond mainstream social movement studies, the focus on the political economy of social conflicts is certainly far from new. Modernization, dependentista, dependency theory, feminist, Marxist, Polanyian, and New Social Movements perspectives have all contributed to our understanding of how capitalism is related to class struggles, intersectional struggles, the construction of a collective popular actor, societal resistance, and post-materialist claims, among other topics (Cardoso and Faletto 1970; Eckstein 1989; Escobar and Álvarez 1992; Germani 1962; Quijano 1976; Silva 2009; Johnson and Sempol, Garretón and Selamé, Webber in this volume, among others). However, none of these complex approaches have developed systematic analyses of how movements and capitalism interact.

In fact, in Latin America there has been always consideration of the embeddedness of politics and economics, with scholars generally producing studies in the political economy of contention that—except for orthodox Marxism—have not dogmatically followed any specific school of thought but rather promoted a syncretical combination of approaches driven by concrete historical events. This means not that a unified approach exists or even that there has been any explicit basic agreement but rather that, as Somma (2020: 5) identified, a political economy of social movements "emphasizes how political actors craft economic institutions that create grievances, which in turn foster protests" without taking a structuralist class-based approach. However, it was not until the 1980s that a social movement scholarship in Latin America could develop as such beyond the functionalist study of labor-based actors.

Political economy in Latin America, as elsewhere, has been predominantly focused on distributive conflicts and thus has mainly emphasized labor-based organizations, such as urban and rural unions (for instance, Collier and Collier 1991; Etchemendy 2011; Welch 1999). These parallel tracks of political economy of labor and social movement studies have only recently begun to converge. In Latin America, this was a result of the double transition to democracy and neoliberalism that led to an acceleration of neopluralist transformations of social life (Oxhorn 1998; Oxhorn in this volume). Only recently has social movement literature gone from a lack of studies on labor movements that were left to class-based studies to move beyond a worker-centric analysis of the political economy of social conflicts.

Recent research on social movements in Latin America has recognized the crucial role of economic conditions (e.g., neoliberalism, commodity prices) and the significance of socioeconomic demands (e.g., reincorporation, social justice) (Almeida 2019;

Roberts 2008; Rossi 2017; Simmons 2016, among others). In some of this scholarship there is already a gradual transformation from the study of mobilizations by "workers" and "peasants" to a general notion of "popular sectors," implying a move from a functionalist understanding of the mobilized actor to viewing it as a question that requires an empirical study (Rossi 2021). This is a crucial theoretical shift that has allowed elements of a political economy of social movements to begin to be developed.

I identify three broad stages in the gradual emergence of a political economy of social movements in Latin America. The first stage is linked to the debt crisis and democratization, which predominate a moral economy of protest (Walton 1989), class-based analysis (Rueschemeyer, Stephens, and Stephens 1992), New Social Movements (Calderón 1986; Garretón 2002), and dependency theory (Eckstein 1989). Neoliberalism and austerity/state reforms policies characterize the second stage, marked by autonomist perspectives (Dinerstein 2003), ethnographers (Auyero 2002; Quirós 2006), protest wave studies (Almeida 2008; Bellinger and Arce 2011), and Durkheimian studies (anomie) (Svampa 2000). The third stage corresponds to the second wave of incorporation, focusing on comparative politics (Rice 2012; Roberts 2008), world system theory (Almeida 2014; Wickham-Crowley and Eckstein 2015), and Polanyian studies (Silva 2009). This period saw a more explicit political economy of social movements and protest and a superseding of the limiting class-based analysis and its functionalist notion of grievance construction and mobilization.

Despite impressive advancements in this area, answers to how social movements are influenced by changes in capitalism, and how movements change capitalist dynamics, remain tentative. If we aim at a political economy of social movements, this can only be achieved through the theoretical and empirical recoupling of the political and economic spheres in social movements dynamics. With this goal in mind, in the rest of this chapter I analyze transformations in the capitalist models of development and social movement dynamics according to the Latin American experience.

Capitalist Models of Development in Latin America

The variety of models of development implemented in Latin America is conducive to the introduction of a comparative historical analysis of paths of capitalism. Central America has relied on a raw-export model with a short period of light industrialization. The economies of Bolivia, Ecuador, and Paraguay have been always rentier, extractivist, and commodity-based (mainly oil, crops, and mining), as have Peru and Venezuela, which also went through light industrialization. For their part, Brazil and Mexico were early adopters of import substitution industrialization (ISI) and pursued an industry-based model with some liberalization. Argentina, Chile, Colombia, and Uruguay migrated from agro-export to ISI and later to market-driven development (Ocampo and Ros 2011).

The central social movement dynamic for each model of development is the contentious construction of the "social question" and the struggles of movements for the expansion of the socio-political arena. This struggle is linked to the pattern of inequality (modified, reinforced, or inherited), the degree of commodification of social relations, and the type of societal stratification produced by each model of development. How the "social question" is expressed and articulated is linked to who the main mobilized actors are and what interest intermediation arrangements are associated with each model of development to legitimate the mobilized actors. These interest intermediation arrangements are an institutional result of the "social question" in the quest to pacify the disruption produced by the organized victims of a model of development (Rossi 2017: 11–13).

Even though contention takes various forms, in political economy terms, each model of development is linked to a dominant form of oppositional collective action (Almeida 2019: 157–58). When protests organize into movements, this collective action is also linked to revolutionary and reformist proposals for the transformation of the path of development. Moreover, coalitions (and winners and losers) are co-constitutive of the models of development, and the political responses of the losers (or victims) of each model are important to understand the paths within and across models. These contentious responses are sustained on inherited infrastructure from previous models of development (Almeida 2014), constituting material and symbolic resources for building a stock of legacies and prefigure alternatives that (dis)favor certain strategies (Rossi 2017).

I will focus on the struggle for dignity (social rights) and freedom (civic rights) that characterized the history of Latin American social movements. In this meso-level analysis of capitalist models of development and social movements, I will briefly explore two crucial questions: What explains the emergence of the quests for dignity and freedom along parallel tracks, with the former mostly pursued by popular-based movements and the latter mainly by elite-based ones? And, how did these become integrated into a politics of multi-sectoral coalitions?

Agro-Monoculture and Raw Material Export Model (1850s–1930s)

Latin America achieved political independence with an inherited model of development that was not planned by local elites and was an expansion of early globalization under Britain hegemon. The agro-monoculture and raw material export model was connected to a period of rapid growth in Latin America. The organization of politics and economics were conflated in elite-based agreements of oligarchic family networks that controlled portions of territory. This created a pattern of inequality that excluded from the socio-political arena all of the rest of society.

In this period social movements strove for socio-political incorporation and the end of oligarchic regimes. The history of Latin America is to a great degree defined by two waves of incorporation (for the first, see Collier and Collier 1991; and for the second, see Rossi 2015, 2017): "Incorporation waves represent major and prolonged historical processes of struggle among socioeconomic and political groups for the expansion or reduction of the socio-political arena" (Rossi 2017: 9).

The 1850s to the 1880s was the formative period for urban labor movements in the most dynamic ports, such as Buenos Aires and Valparaíso (Romero and Sábato 1992). With the migration of ideas and people from Europe also came a class-based identity (Godio 1987), while in less globalized regions peasants and indigenous protests emerged to resist commodification of their lands and workforce. From the 1880s to the 1930s the emergent "social question" was associated with crisis in the liberal model of development. The financial crisis of 1866 damaged the cohesion of some oligarchic regimes and opened the door to destabilization of this model of development. Oligarchic politics was further eroded with increasingly violent local pressure from the bourgeoisie for political liberalization with male universal suffrage in the Southern Cone, and international British pressure for the abolition of slavery in Brazil (granted in 1888).

The Mexican (1910) and Russian (1917) revolutions stimulated the formation of socialist, communist, syndicalist, and anarchist organizations among subaltern groups (Suriano 2001). This period of innovation, one of several in organizational practices, saw the creation of cooperatives and self-help associations by mostly urban immigrants. And in rural areas new and preexisting communal organizations, such as *ejidos* and *ayllus*, sat uneasily alongside *latifundios*. This period was also characterized by a dual tendency in mobilization dynamics, with labor-based movements decoupled from elite-based student movements due to the oligarchic nature of universities and suffragist movements being dominated by white elite women (see Ewig and Friedman, Donoso in this volume). Meanwhile, despite shared claims for the expansion of the socio-political arena, popular movements and elite-based movements were not coordinating their campaigns. In addition, apart from isolated efforts and some theoretical engagements, urban and rural struggles were detached, and peasants and indigenous communities were mutually wary (see Welch, Rice in this volume).

The collapse of the stock market in 1929 and the Great Depression sent agro-export monoculture models of development into a state of crisis. This new cyclical crisis of capitalism expanded and radicalized the struggles that were already underway. From the 1930s, communists were increasingly assuming union leadership roles with a dominant strategy—encouraged by the Soviet Union—that involved forming popular fronts: antifascist coalitions serving to coordinate multiple actors (Tamarin 1985). For these reasons, state elites responded to the "social question" with a gradual institutionalization of social policies on housing, health, and education coupled with advanced repressive tactics, steadily transforming the model of development (Collier and Collier 1991: 93–94).

State-led Development (1930s–1970s)

State-led development was a result of experimentation due to the collapse of raw material prices, while commodity exporters were still powerful political and economic actors. There was a shift into protectionism and a macro policy centered on balance of payments management, industrialization as the engine of growth, and strong state intervention. Through trial and error, these policies and others progressively led to a mixed economic model sustained on economic planning that, decades later, was conceptualized by the Economic Commission for Latin America and the Caribbean (ECLAC).

With the decline of Britain and the closure of global markets, the driver of development came to be the domestic market, with two main currents. Argentina, Brazil, Chile, Colombia, and Mexico moved into ISI, while Peru, Venezuela, and Central America opted for light industrialization and a development strategy based on raw-commodity export. In this way, the core of the previous model was modified, and, with tariff protection and nationalizations, agriculture was primarily defined as provider of cheap food for the cities. The 1940s saw a period of renewed growth and the United States replacing Britain as the new hegemon. This led to change in the types of trade agreements as well as the political organization of struggles.

Rapid industrialization, unplanned urbanization, and population growth (through immigration and increasing birthrates) all had their effect on popular politics in the region. There was a gradual shift from an urban labor minority in a mostly rural society toward a massive portion of society being urban and proletarian. The previously relatively homogeneous working class with a distinctive identity expanded to make up a large proportion of all Latin American societies that became less stratified. This new majority lost homogeneity as it spread across more diverse occupations, working environments, and formal and informal jobs to constitute the so-called popular sectors of society, with social relations increasingly commodified. Like the narrower working class from which it evolved, this broadened segment occupied a subaltern position in society. Therefore, the popular sectors, despite their differences, shared a common societal experience (and set of grievances) that transcended the strictly functional definition of their lives as that of workers (Rossi 2021).

From the 1930s to the 1950s, stabilization of state-led development was reached through a first wave of incorporation of the popular sectors into the socio-political arena through trade unions in a mostly corporatist fashion. Generally concurrent with the full democratization of society with women's suffrage, this first wave of incorporation produced a massive expansion of the socio-political arena across Latin America. Beyond the specificities of each national process, it is important to bear in mind that waves of incorporation should not be equated with the constitution of a more equal society or the creation of a welfare state but rather with the reshaping of the socio-political arena by redefining and expanding the number of legitimate political actors. In Brazil, this incorporation occurred under the Estado Novo government of Getúlio Vargas (1930–1945), who demobilized labor while introducing corporatist arrangements into the country's weak and divided labor movement without producing an improvement in welfare. In Argentina, during the first two governments of Juan Domingo Perón (1946–1952, 1952–1955), incorporation was also corporatist, but with the purpose of mobilizing labor within a combative movement, achieving massive and fast improvement in welfare (Collier and Collier 1991).

The first wave of incorporation saw the development of neo-corporatist interest intermediation arrangements. This type of incorporation is what explains the reduction in the number of relevant popular movements during this period. This is because, "In contrast to the pattern of interest politics based on autonomous, competing groups and to the total suppression of groups, in the case of corporatism the state encourages the formation of a limited number of officially recognized, non-competing, state-supervised groups" (Collier and Collier 1979: 968). For instance, peasants and the indigenous were treated indistinguishably in functional terms as "rural workers" (Yashar 2005). This disconnected corporatist unions from territorialized popular movements of informal workers in a pattern of inequality in segmented welfare states. This pattern favored formal urban workers in coalition with national industrialists until the unfolding of a series of coups aimed at stopping the process of incorporation (O'Donnell 1978).

The dual track of elite-based movements versus popular movements that had characterized the political economy of movements since independence changed in the 1960s. The enfranchisement of women from the 1940s with universal suffrage permanently redefined women's movements (Ewig and Friedman in this volume). The expansion of basic education and the de-eliticization of the universities led to the emergence of massive student movements in the 1960s (Donoso in this volume). Labor movements reemerged in a more contentious form and expanded beyond corporatist unions (Ramírez and Stoessel in this volume). In this period, a growing interconnectedness between grassroots unionism and the broader struggles of urban and student movements demanding socioeconomic wellbeing and redemocratization produced the first sizeable articulation of the quests for dignity and freedom. In this sense, the first massive coalitions were of student movements and grassroots unions with revolutionary hopes in the 1960s–1970s.

The revolutions in Bolivia (1952), Cuba (1959), Chile (1970), and Nicaragua (1978) produced a perception of accelerated historical time to transcend capitalism. The upsurge in insurgency was a result of restrictive corporatist arrangements, the persecution of generally moderate movement leaders, and military dictatorships intervening in and reorganizing unions (Rossi, 2021). These factors created a social space for labor movements to fill beyond the narrow confines of unionism and encouraged the rise of a younger generation inspired by revolutionary ideals (Oikonomakis in this volume). This was also a period of increased territorialization of labor movements; that is, collective action became part of daily life in the popular sectors beyond the factory (Rossi 2019).

Some countries entered spirals of violence while others saw land reforms, popular urban planning, territorialized grassroots organization, vanguardist insurgency, and intensive strategic debates among movements, unions, and guerrillas. In Chile, labor's insurgency was embraced more strongly, in combination with the efforts of Salvador Allende's (1970–1973) democratic revolutionary path to socialism. However, this insurgency was hampered by the acceleration of local conflicts, inflation, and the 1973 coup and mass executions that decimated all social movements (Zapata 1976).

Meanwhile, in most countries, corporatist unionism pushed distributive conflicts into an inflationary dynamic, deteriorating the coalition with national industrialists. And, as agriculture and mining kept their socioeconomic centrality, traditional landowners could develop coalitions with some sectors of the military, dissatisfied industrialists, and the Catholic Church. These reactive coalitions favored even more repressive coups and disincorporation processes to demobilize and atomize the increasingly revolutionary multi-sectoral coalitions and stop distributive conflicts. Subsequent legislation decentralized and depoliticized these burgeoning popular interest arrangements (Etchemendy 2011).

Market-led Development (1970s–2000s)

Market-led development was theoretically and ideologically formulated in the Austrian and Chicago Schools and applied in Latin America several decades later. While social movements in the previous model faced a process of trial and error that was not clearly justified, in this new model the cultural battle against economic orthodoxy was part of the struggle. The World Bank and International Monetary Fund (IMF) played an important role in the diffusion of the reform agenda and in the imposition of the policy conditionalities. Market integration and debt repayment became the main priorities along with privatization, spending cuts, and administrative and fiscal decentralization. This gave the impression of a fully external imposition, compared to the previous model of development, which had emerged as a response from within to external changes. There was a return to some elements of the nineteenth-century model, now conceptualized as development driven by comparative advantages. This meant a reprimarization of the economies and partial liberalization of the labor market to reduce social benefits and the organizational power of first-wave incorporation actors with limited social spending targeted to informal laborers and those otherwise excluded (those not aided by the segmented welfare states). These reforms were applied in three rounds, corresponding with the 1970s (Argentina, Chile, and Uruguay), 1980s (Brazil, Peru, and most countries), and 1990s (consolidation in all countries). Each round of reforms was accompanied by a wave of protests fighting against their consequences.

The authoritarian wave of the 1970s–1980s initiated the massive disincorporation of the popular sectors from the socio-political arena as citizens as well as laborers. Persecutions of active sectors of the labor movement and the left (sometimes even with the support of corporatist union leadership) quickly and violently demobilized all social movements (Brockett in this volume). Clandestine resistance networks emerged to confront the military dictators or juntas throughout the territory, mostly using grassroots-style strategies (Rossi and della Porta 2019). Strikes were another crucial form of resistance against authoritarian regimes. In Brazil, for instance, a wave of strikes (1974–1979) was followed by a cycle of protest (1978–1982), mainly mobilized by urban movements (Sandoval 1998).

Four models for liberalizing ISI economies were applied in Latin America (Etchemendy 2011). The type of previous economic regime along with the degree of power held by the prior ISI actors (for labor: corporatist unions) produced different policy processes, winners, and compensatory measures for the losers. In each model, unions played a different role and underwent a different degree of recommodification of labor relations promoted by the neoliberalization of the economy. In Brazil and Chile, weak unions were either partially compensated (in the former case) or repressed (in the latter). In Argentina and Mexico, however, their strong unions were offered market-share compensation. Regardless, across the four countries, the corporatist popular interest arrangements that had dominated the ISI economies were transformed into a neo-pluralist model that changed the previous political cleavages (Oxhorn 1998; Roberts 2008). These differences modified the antagonists and types of conflict that social movements faced, as well as the coalitions that could be organized.

Disincorporation weakened the functionalist organization of social conflicts (Rossi 2017). This favored the multiplication in the social movement field of holistic and territorially segmented conflicts and actors, modifying the network format of social movements and the resolution of incorporation struggles beyond neo-corporatist distributive tensions and negotiations. Decentralization and fragmentation created several particularistic claims, posing difficulties for coordination (Calderón 1986). Debilitation of class-based action, however, allowed for the activation of other forms of resistance (Rice 2012; Ramírez and Stoessel in this volume), such as identity- and ethnic-based movements (see Ewig and Friedman, Dixon and Caldwell, Díez, Fontana, Rice in this volume).

The territorialization of the popular sectors increased as corporatist arrangements were debilitated or dissolved (Rossi 2019). At the same time, the social structure of Latin America changed with the visible growth in income inequality and labor informality (Portes and Hoffmann 2003). As a result, the experiences of (and conditions faced by) families in the poor neighborhoods and shantytowns took on an unprecedented centrality in the definition of poor people's political strategies (Merklen 2005). The functionalist logics of welfare provision changed: as formal male labor opportunities decreased, so did the centrality of patriarchal family structures. In some cases, these dynamics favored the emergence of women as providers and as crucial grassroots actors in many movements. Strategically, the new unionism adapted to this novel context by emulating territorial movements in their organizational and protest practices—what is called "social movement unionism" (Rossi 2021).

The 1982 Mexican debt crisis put an end to the post-World War II period of economic growth in Latin America, casting doubt on the ISI model of development and increasing the political influence of neoliberal reformers. From 1983 to 1989 a wave of anti-austerity protests against the IMF spread across Latin America. "Austerity led to popular unrest in the times and places that combined economic hardship, external adjustment demands, hyperurbanization, and local traditions of political mobilization" (Walton and Seddon 1994: 99). This unprecedented wave of protest was mainly located in cities in a coalition of the urban poor, public-sector unions, and students. The 1989 Caracazo was the most massive social explosion in this wave. The main consequence of this protest wave was not the end of neoliberal reforms but the acceleration of democratization in most of South America (Walton and Seddon 1994).

Market reforms conflated with liberal democratization in a double transition throughout the 1980s until 1991 changing the opportunities for resistance and organization. The weakening of labor and the annihilation of grassroots organizations and guerrillas had a dual effect. On the one hand, a vacuum of popular leadership was created that took at least a decade to rebuild. On the other hand, a plurality of social movements thus emerged that questioned the previous repertoire of strategies to different degrees (Roberts 1998). Disincorporation was not equally demobilizing everywhere, though. Chile's double transition to democracy and neoliberalism disbanded the popular sectors and detached society from politics until the emergence of massive student movements in 2011 (Donoso in this volume), while in Argentina, Bolivia, and Uruguay popular movements could reorganize, allying and competing with corporatist unionism from the late 1980s.

Even though labor movements played a significant role in the democratization of Latin America (Drake 1996), the declining power of organized labor meant "that labor recaptured its freedom to organize, negotiate, participate, and vote, but within the limits of an economy dedicated to the private sector and a political system dedicated to stability" (Drake 2007: 162). As a result, the double transition allowed for the reemergence of protest and popular organization while at the same time weakening organized labor, causing trade unions to lose their privileged role in articulating and representing popular sector interests (Collier and Handlin 2009; Oxhorn 1998). These transformations produced an even greater variety of groups and demands and placed popular movements at the forefront of the resistance to neoliberalism and the struggle for reincorporation (Roberts 2008; Rossi 2017). Since the 1990s, multi-sectoral coalitions became a common strategy, with a multiplicity of movements emerging and developing all sorts of campaigns. The growth of identity-based movements such as Afro-Latin American movements (Dixon and Caldwell in this volume) and LGBTQI+ movements were favored by these transformations (Díez in this volume). Meanwhile, some elite-based movements metamorphosed into social movements, think tanks, and NGOs, which favored the expansion of policy-based claims such as health and consumers rights (Rich 2019; Rhodes in this volume). In this period, the main multi-sectoral coalitions unified the victims of neoliberalism (Silva 2009).

In 1991, the Soviet Union collapsed and, with it, an alternative to capitalism and liberal democracy. This was a shock for most of the left and many labor movements, which experienced a deep crisis (Carr and Ellner 1993). In addition, because of the trauma produced by the 1970s dictatorships, the stock of legacies of labor and left-wing actors was redefined to encompass both freedom and dignity (Ollier 2009; Roberts 1998). Thus, the experience in the aftermath of the first incorporation process—with coups and exclusion—connected both struggles in the quest for socio-political reincorporation as citizens (freedom) and wage-earners (dignity).

During this period, the repertoire of strategies expanded with several explorations to consolidate the quest for freedom *with* dignity. Pickets, assemblies, and factory occupations spread across Argentina in a domino effect of social explosions (Rossi 2005); anti-sweatshop advocacy coalitions in Central America and Mexico became quite important in the questioning of the modification of industrial practices as a result of trade agreements, mainly with the United States (Nolan García 2013); and the cooperation of elites through specialized NGOs with popular movements increasingly professionalized claims with judicialization strategies that reformulated the role of the judiciary in democratic politics (Ruibal in this volume).

In the exploration of new state–society dynamics, at least two relevant prefigurative strategies emerged. In the attempt to bridge individuals and local governments, participatory institutional mechanisms started in Porto Alegre and spread throughout the region (Annunciata and Goldfrank in this volume). In a quest for autonomous projects to redefine the relationship with the state, in Chiapas a model of revolution emerged that does not have total societal transformation as its aim (Oikonomakis in this volume).

The destabilization stage of the model of development was initiated when a new "social question" emerged as the victims of neoliberalism organized in their quest to be part of (capitalist) society. With the population's recovery of its civic rights during the 1980s, the main objective of the reincorporation struggles during the 1990s–2000s was to reconnect the lives of the popular sectors—as wage-earners entitled to dignity—with the socio-political arena. In Argentina, the struggle for reincorporation was sustained through the coordinated efforts of unions and the *piquetero* movement in a purely urban process. In Brazil, urban and rural unions and landless peasant movements fought to reincorporate the popular sectors using a mix of urban and rural strategies. Having gradually achieved recognition, legitimation, and partial reincorporation in the socio-political arena, popular movements finally generated the conditions for a second wave of incorporation from the 2000s (Rossi 2017).

Mixed Development (2000s–)

The growing organization of social movements pushing for the expansion of the socio-political arena, along with a new cyclical crisis of capitalism (in this case, the 1997 crisis in Southeast Asia) provoked—once more—a pragmatic policy response to stabilize capitalist dynamics. Initially, Latin American governments expanded repression and social policies as a response—within a neoliberal frame—to the new "social question" of disincorporation. Later, a few of them slowly started to apply pragmatic countercyclical policies with the aim of macroeconomic stabilization without affecting the ongoing process of trade liberalization and open regionalism. Scholars have characterized this pragmatism, which I call here mixed development, as neo-structuralism, post-neoliberalism, or neo-developmentalism (Leiva 2008; Rossi and Silva 2018; Ruckert, McDonald, and Prolix 2017).

This is still an ongoing (and disputed) process that aims at the reconstruction of twentieth-century state–business alliances to go beyond raw material production in an industrialization drive based on research and developmentalism. However, in most cases, the transition to a new model has been sustained on neo-extractivism (mainly mining, soy, oil, and gas). In any case, neo-extractivism is *not* a model of development as there are huge differences between extractivism under conservative neoliberal governments and left-wing post-neoliberal ones. In the latter, extractivism is part of a pragmatic approach to development in neo-structuralist terms, including in most cases resource nationalism, while in the former it is part of a general reprimarization of the economy (Ellner 2021). In all cases, the prices of commodities were the main source of dollars to finance the new "social question" as well as being the cause of multiple territorialized environmental protests (Arce 2014; Ellner 2021; Lapegna 2016).

The elections in Venezuela that brought Hugo Chávez to power (1999–2007, 2007–2013) accelerated the reshaping of the socio-political arena in South America. In Argentina, left-wing Peronists won the 2003 elections after the Argentinazo—the massive national revolt of 2001. That same year in Brazil, the Partido dos Trabalhadores came to power after a protracted struggle. Later, Bolivia and Ecuador continued the trend after huge indigenous and peasant mobilizations. During this period, social movements and unions secured relatively important positions in government. When partial reincorporation was achieved in some countries, the socio-political arena expanded with institutional transformations, innovation in social policies, and the consolidation of many movements that transcended functionalist-based organizational principles (for a detailed analysis: Rossi 2017; Silva and Rossi 2018).

The second wave of incorporation that precipitated these political changes was—like the first—a regional process that involved several countries, each at a different pace and intensity. Common characteristics included recognizing the claims of poor people's movements, as well as reformulating rules (formal or informal) and regulations that govern their participation in politics and their connection with the policy process (Rossi 2017: xi). In most countries, union density declined from the first incorporation period, even if the state's regulatory approach partially reversed the deregulatory liberalization policies of the 1970s–1990s (Collier 2018). As a whole, the second wave of incorporation led to a change in interest intermediation arrangements: from the corporatist pattern of relations based on a functionalist logic to a territorially based approach centered on the multidimensional experience of being poor or impoverished (Collier and Handlin 2009; Rossi 2017: 13–15).

What Argentina, Bolivia, Brazil, Ecuador, and Venezuela shared was the creation of a policy domain for territorialized reincorporation movements. The pattern of inequality associated with the mixed model of development is the segmentation of informal and formal labor in policies directed at individuals more than at social organizations. In most cases, the unit is the family (in heteronormative terms), with the woman as a mother as the main beneficiary of a territorially defined locus of needs. The stratification of society is territorial, reinforcing the social ghettos in geographic areas that are dissociated from each other and from the rest of society in social policies that are holistically applied to specific sites, but in parallel tracks rather than universalizing terms (Rossi 2017).

On the movement side, the second incorporation process was built using a predominant repertoire of strategies that transcended contentious politics. In Argentina, this happened within a mostly trade unionist strategy in combination with other strategies from left-wing traditions (Rossi 2017: ch. 2). This period of economic bonanza and growth led to a lessening of inequality and to a push for redistributive polices (Lustig et al. 2012). These policies were resisted by what Mangonnet and Murillo (2020) called "protests of abundance" because of their contentious opposition to redistribution by those economically better positioned. The case they study in Argentina is that of the 2008 protests against taxation of agricultural commodity exports in a context of price booms for raw materials, which—as I argue—posed serious obstacles to the second incorporation process (Rossi 2017: 226–32). Protests of abundance can be considered as the opposite of anti-austerity protests. The development of a moral economy of protests of abundance could be explored to shed light on the perceptions of grievances and how they are articulated as a contentious response from the winners of a model of development.

The 2000s and the 2010s were a period of exploration of alternative models of development. Venezuela promoted a new democratic path to socialism in what was called Socialism of the 21st Century, which was faced with an international boycott resembling that imposed on Allende, major obstacles in its ability to maintain a democratic path after radicalization spiraled between government and opposition following the death of Chávez in 2013, and the impossibility of diversifying a rentier economy based on oil production (Ellner 2018; García-Guadilla 2018; Hellinger 2018). In Bolivia and Ecuador, a different model aiming to surpass market-led development has been promoted under the name of Buen Vivir/Vivir Bien (Acosta and Martínez 2009). In both its variants, Buen Vivir/Vivir Bien means development as composed of an ecological post-development critique sustained on an Andean indigenous cosmovision of human welfare that remains within nature's limits—as opposed to the submission of nature to human plans—integrated with a neo-Marxist critique of modern capitalism (Beling et al. 2021). This proposal has been incorporated into the constitutions of Bolivia and Ecuador, and its application has been contradictory within the policies of each country. These and other proposals were helped by the World Social Forum as a space that strengthened multi-sectoral coordination and the discussion of alternatives to the market-led model of development (von Bülow in this volume).

Meanwhile, the main hegemonic project of the United States in the continent since the double transition was the promotion of free trade agreements and the total liberalization of markets, provoking an unprecedented response of resistance to this plan (Burridge and Markoff in this volume). In the 2000s, unions developed a continental coalition with social movements, the Hemispheric Social Alliance, to resist the Free Trade Area of the Americas and other neoliberal projects that would have reduced labor, social, and environmental rights (Spalding 2014; von Bülow 2010; von Bülow in this volume). In parallel was China's rapid emergence as a potential new hegemon in competition with the United States, offering a novel multilateral scenario for Latin America (Stallings 2020).

The second Great Depression of 2008 prevented many governments from adopting more inclusionary policies because of the abrupt reduction in commodity prices.

Coalitions of conservative, neoliberal, military, and religious groups (mainly Catholic and evangelical) took advantage of this weakening of the governing elites to recover power. In most countries, this new major crisis of capitalism led to increased mobilization, taking two forms: on one hand, popular-based actors organizing to avoid another disincorporation, and on the other, the emergence of right-wing protests resisting incorporation policies (Ferrero, Natalucci, and Tatagiba 2019; Pereyra, Gold and Gattoni, Payne in this volume). In the aftermath of second incorporation, center-right coalitions took power in an attempt to reformulate or stop the ongoing process like it happened during first incorporation. In Argentina and Ecuador this took place through democratic means and in Brazil and Bolivia as a result of massive protests and civic–military coup d'états. Venezuela, for its part, spiraled into a multifaceted state of crisis.

From a long-term historical perspective, this conservative return to power could be also seen as a plutocratic parenthesis in a process of pendular change in the model of development. As with the first wave of incorporation, the second wave happened over several decades, with as after-effects the rise of novel institutions and the legitimation of actors that expanded the socio-political arena beyond governments and regimes. In 2020, Bolivia's authoritarian government failed and the Movimiento al Socialismo returned to power in a redemocratized country. A year earlier, in Argentina, left-wing Peronists won the national elections, and *piqueteros* and human rights movements returned to the governing coalition. In the case of Chile, it has started to consolidate a new "social question" almost two decades after the rest of South America did. The 2019 social explosion in Chile resembled the Caracazo and the Argentinazo, characterized by riots, anti-elitism, and the demand for multidimensional societal change. Chile's delay in initiating the second incorporation can be attributed to the intensity of neoliberal reforms and of the repression of popular organization. The degree of societal transformation produced by Augusto Pinochet's dictatorship has only been disputed by a new generation of Chileans (Donoso and von Bülow 2017; Posner 2008). It could be argued that the more violently neoliberal reforms were applied, the greater the barriers to the constitution of a "social question" and, with it, to the legitimation of actors mobilizing the claim for reincorporation.

The COVID-19 pandemic in early 2020 provoked the collapse of the world economy with devastating consequences for all Latin Americans. Social mobilization was abruptly cut off by the total disruption of life with the accentuation of social uncertainty through multiple crises triggered by the pandemic. Several countries were in the midst of rising mobilization dynamics when the pandemic hit, and measures restricting movement and assembly affected these processes. The politicization of temporal inequality among segments of society and the dispute between the temporality of continuity and of transformation in the quest for repossessing a future (Faure 2020) accelerated historical time, thus enhancing polarization in pre-pandemic Latin America. In this context, social movements had to look for alternative ways of developing strategies that could respond to the new and changing reality and the prefiguration of a post-pandemic model of development for Latin America (Abers, Rossi, and von Bülow 2021). Political responses to the pandemic may reinforce a mixed model or destabilize it definitively.

Conclusion

The role of social movements in changing or stabilizing capitalism is a crucial and underdeveloped topic in social movement studies. The political economy of social movements is not defined by any single path if it is decentered from its North Atlantic mainstream narrative, which "viewed social movements developing in a relatively linear pattern with the expansion of nation-states, parliamentary democracies, urbanization, industrialization" (Almeida 2019: 147). Within the multiple paths of capitalism, analyzing the relationship between models of development and social movement dynamics may be an avenue for the initiation of a systematic political economy of social movements. The struggle of social movements against/for and in/within capitalism is always incomplete and only partially achieved, with periods of acceleration where some practices are suddenly reformulated, and of steady and (sometimes) microscopic sedimentations of contradictory practices. The outcomes are correlations of contending forces that achieve temporary models of development with clear winners and losers, and majorities that get mixed results. Social movements are co-constitutive of these dynamics and are constituted by them as much as they operate with and within them.

In this chapter, I have explored this co-constitution of social movements and models of development as a general trend in Latin America. Fine-grained comparative historical studies are still needed to identify the dynamics within each capitalist path. The region does not feature a lineal development of capitalism but rather a combination of waves, cycles, and pendulums together with a huge portion of *rhapsodic rhythms* that responded chiefly to (weakly planned) elites' reactions to collective disruption. The interests of economic elites often conflict with one another and with those of political elites; these conflicts and the contention (sometimes violent) that they produce may create opportunities for social movements.

In the struggles for dignity (social rights) and freedom (civic rights) explored here, until the aftermath of the first wave of incorporation, these efforts ran along two parallel tracks: one mobilized by popular-based movements and the other by elite-based movements. In the 1960s–1970s, this situation changed as a result of the transformations produced by the expansion of the socio-political arena. In this period were introduced multi-sectoral coalitions that brought together certain actors and agendas. In the 1980s–2010s, after the tragic experience of losing social and civic rights simultaneously, most struggles for reincorporation showed the intertwining of the quests for dignity *and* freedom in multi-sectoral coalitions.

Acknowledgements

I thank John Markoff, Jessica Rich, Amr Adly, Paul Almeida, and Jeff Goodwin for their comments to different versions of this chapter.

References

Abers, Rebecca Neaera, Federico M. Rossi, and Marisa von Bülow (2021), "State–Society Relations in Uncertain Times: Social Movement Strategies, Ideational Contestation and the Pandemic in Brazil and Argentina," *International Political Science Review* 42(3), 333–49.
Acosta, Alberto and Esperanza Martínez (eds.) (2009), *El buen vivir: Una vía para el desarrollo* (Quito: Abya-Yala).
Almeida, Paul (2008), *Waves of Protest: Popular Struggle in El Salvador, 1925–2005* (Minneapolis: University of Minnesota Press).
Almeida, Paul (2014), *Mobilizing Democracy: Globalization and Citizen Protest* (Baltimore, MD: Johns Hopkins University Press).
Almeida, Paul (2019), *Social Movements: The Structure of Collective Mobilization* (Oakland: University of California Press).
Arce, Moisés (2014), *Resource Extraction and Protest in Peru* (Pittsburgh, PA: University of Pittsburgh Press).
Auyero, Javier (2002), *La protesta. Retratos de la beligerancia popular en la Argentina democrática* (Buenos Aires: CCRR–UBA).
Beling, Adrián E., Ana Patricia Cubillo-Guevara, Julien Vanhulst, and Antonio Luis Hidalgo-Capitán (2021), "Buen vivir (Good Living): A 'Glocal' Genealogy of a Latin American Utopia for the World," *Latin American Perspectives* 48(3), 17–34.
Bellinger, Paul T. and Moisés Arce (2011), "Protest and Democracy in Latin America's Market Era," *Political Research Quarterly* 64(3), 688–704.
Calderón, Fernando (ed.), (1986), *Los movimientos sociales ante la crisis* (Buenos Aires: UNU–CLACSO–IISUNAM).
Cardoso, Fernando Henrique and Enzo Falletto (1970), *Dependência e desenvolvimento na América Latina* (Rio de Janeiro: Zahar).
Carr, Barry and Steve Ellner (eds.) (1993), *The Latin American Left: From the Fall of Allende to the Perestroika* (Boulder, CO: Westview Press).
Collier, Ruth Berins (2018), "Labor Unions in Latin America: Incorporation and Reincorporation under the New Left," in Eduardo Silva and Federico M. Rossi (eds.), *Reshaping the Political Arena in Latin America*, 115–28 (Pittsburgh, PA: University of Pittsburgh Press).
Collier, Ruth Berins and David Collier (1979), "Inducements versus Constraints: Disaggregating 'Corporatism'," *American Political Science Review* 73(4), 967–86.
Collier, Ruth Berins and David Collier (1991), *Shaping the Political Arena: Critical Junctures, the Labor Movement, and Regime Dynamics in Latin America* (Princeton, NJ: Princeton University Press).

Collier, Ruth Berins and Samuel Handlin (eds.) (2009), *Reorganizing Popular Politics: Participation and the New Interest Regime in Latin America* (University Park: Penn State University Press).

Dinerstein, Ana C. (2003), "Power or Counter Power?: The Dilemma of the Piquetero Movement in Argentina Post-crisis," *Capital & Class* 27(3), 1–8.

Donoso, Sofia and Marisa von Bülow (eds.) (2017), *Social Movements in Chile: Organization, Trajectories & Political Consequences* (New York: Palgrave-Macmillan).

Drake, Paul W. (1996), *Labor Movements and Dictatorship: The Southern Cone in Comparative Perspective* (Baltimore, MD: Johns Hopkins University Press).

Drake, Paul W. (2007), "Organized Labor's Global Problems and Local Responses," *International Labor and Working-Class History* 72(1), 161–63.

Eckstein, Susan (ed.) (1989), *Power and Popular Protest: Latin American Social Movements* (Berkeley and Los Angeles: University of California Press).

Ellner, Steve (2018), "Conflicting Currents within the Pro-Chávez Labor Movement and the Dynamics of Decision Making," in Eduardo Silva and Federico M. Rossi (eds.), *Reshaping the Political Arena in Latin America*, 157–78 (Pittsburgh, PA: University of Pittsburgh Press).

Ellner, Steve (2021), "Introduction: Rethinking Latin American Extractivism," in Steve Ellner (ed.), *Latin American Extractivism: Dependency, Resource Nationalism, and Resistance in Broad Perspective*, 1–28 (Lanham, MD: Rowman & Littlefield).

Escobar, Arturo and Sonia Álvarez (eds.) (1992), *The Making of Social Movements in Latin America: Identity, Strategy, and Democracy* (Boulder, CO: Westview Press).

Etchemendy, Sebastián (2011), *Models of Economic Liberalization: Business, Workers, and Compensation in Latin America, Spain, and Portugal* (New York: Cambridge University Press).

Faure, Antoine (2020), "¿Se politizó el tiempo? Ensayo sobre las batallas cronopolíticas del octubre chileno," *Universum (Talca)* 35(1), 46–73.

Ferrero, Juan Pablo, Ana Natalucci, and Luciana Tatagiba (eds.) (2019), *Socio-Political Dynamics within the Crisis of the Left: Argentina and Brazil* (Lanham, MD: Rowman & Littlefield).

García-Guadilla, María Pilar (2018), "The Incorporation of Popular Sectors and Social Movements in Venezuelan Twenty-First-Century Socialism," in Eduardo Silva and Federico M. Rossi (eds.), *Reshaping the Political Arena in Latin American*, 60–77 (Pittsburgh, PA: University of Pittsburgh Press).

Garretón, Manuel Antonio (2002), "La transformación de la acción colectiva en América Latina," *Revista de la CEPAL* 76, 7–24.

Germani, Gino (1962), *Política y sociedad en una época de transición* (Buenos Aires: Paidós).

Godio, Julio (1987), *Historia del movimiento obrero latinoamericano: Anarquistas y socialistas, 1850–1918*, Vol .1 (Caracas: Nueva Sociedad).

Hellinger, Daniel (2018), "The Second Wave of Incorporation and Political Parties in the Venezuelan Petrostate," in Eduardo Silva and Federico M. Rossi (eds.), *Reshaping the Political Arena in Latin America*, 251–74 (Pittsburgh, PA: University of Pittsburgh Press).

Hetland, Gabriel and Jeff Goodwin (2013), "The Strange Disappearance of Capitalism from Social Movement Studies," in Colin Barker, Laurence Cox, John Krinsky, and Alf Gunvald Nilsen (eds.), *Marxism and Social Movements*, 83–102 (Chicago: Haymarket).

Lapegna, Pablo (2016), *Soybeans and Power: Genetically Modified Crops, Environmental Politics, and Social Movements in Argentina* (New York: Oxford University Press).

Leiva, Fernando Ignacio (2008), "Toward a Critique of Latin American Neostructuralism," *Latin American Politics and Society* 50(4), 1–25.

Lustig, Nora, George Gray-Molina, Sean Higgins, Miguel Jaramillo, Wilson Jiménez, Verónica Paz, Claudiney Pereira, Carola Pessino, John Scott, and Ernesto Yañez (2012), *The Impact of Taxes and Social Spending on Inequality and Poverty in Argentina, Bolivia, Brazil, Mexico, and Peru: A Synthesis of Results*, CEQ Working Paper 3 (New Orleans: Tulane University).

Mangonnet, Jorge and María Victoria Murillo (2020), "Protests of Abundance: Distributive Conflict Over Agricultural Rents During the Commodities Boom in Argentina, 2003–2013," *Comparative Political Studies* 53(8), 1223–58.

Merklen, Denis (2005), *Pobres Ciudadanos. Las clases populares en la era democrática (Argentina, 1983–2003)* (Buenos Aires: Gorla).

Nolan García, Kimberly A. (2013), "Network Dynamics and Local Labor Rights Movements in Puebla, Mexico," in Eduardo Silva (ed.), *Transnational Activism and National Movements in Latin America: Bridging the Divide*, 106–40 (New York: Routledge).

Ocampo, José Antonio and Jaime Ros (2011), "Shifting Paradigms in Latin America's Economic Development," in José Antonio Ocampo and Jaime Ros (eds.), *The Oxford Handbook of Latin American Economics*, 3–25 (Oxford: Oxford University Press).

O'Donnell, Guillermo (1978), "State and Alliances in Argentina, 1956–1976," *Journal of Development Studies* 15(1), 3–33.

Ollier, María Matilde (2009), *De la revolución a la democracia: cambios privados, públicos y políticos de la izquierda argentina* (Buenos Aires: Siglo XXI).

Oxhorn, Philip (1998), "Is the Century of Corporatism Over? Neoliberalism and the Rise of Neopluralism," in Philip Oxhorn and Graciela Ducatenzeiler (eds.), *What Kind of Democracy? What Kind of Market? Latin America in the Age of Neoliberalism*, 195–217 (University Park: Pennsylvania State University Press).

Portes, Alejandro and Kelly Hoffmann (2003), "Latin American Class Structures: Their Composition and Change during the Neoliberal Era," *Latin American Research Review* 38(1), 41–82.

Posner, Paul W. (2008), *State, Market, and Democracy in Chile: The Constraint of Popular Participation* (London: Palgrave Macmillan).

Quijano, Aníbal (1976), *Clase obrera en América Latina* (San José: Editorial Universitaria Centroamericana).

Quirós, Julieta (2006), *Cruzando la Sarmiento: Una etnografía sobre piqueteros en la trama social sur del Gran Buenos Aires* (Buenos Aires: Antropofagia-IDES).

Rice, Roberta (2012), *The New Politics of Protest: Indigenous Mobilization in Latin America's Neoliberal Era* (Tucson: University of Arizona Press).

Rich, Jessica A.J. (2019), *State-Sponsored Activism: Bureaucrats and Social Movements in Democratic Brazil* (New York: Cambridge University Press).

Roberts, Kenneth M. (1998), *Deepening Democracy? The Modern Left and Social Movements in Chile and Peru* (Stanford, CA: Stanford University Press).

Roberts, Kenneth M. (2008), "The Mobilization of Opposition to Economic Liberalization," *Annual Review of Political Science* 11(1), 327–49.

Romero, Luis Alberto and Hilda Sábato (1992), *Los trabajadores de Buenos Aires: la experiencia del mercado, 1850–1880* (Buenos Aires: Sudamericana).

Rossi, Federico M. (2005), "Aparición, auge y declinación de un movimiento social: las asambleas vecinales y populares de Buenos Aires, 2001–2003," *European Review of Latin American and Caribbean Studies* 78 (April), 67–88.

Rossi, Federico M. (2015), "The Second Wave of Incorporation in Latin America: A Conceptualization of the Quest for Inclusion Applied to Argentina," *Latin American Politics and Society* 57(1), 1–28.

Rossi, Federico M. (2017), *The Poor's Struggle for Political Incorporation: The Piquetero Movement in Argentina* (New York: Cambridge University Press).

Rossi, Federico M. (2019), "Conceptualising and Tracing the Increased Territorialisation of Politics: Insights from Argentina," *Third World Quarterly* 40(4), 815–37.

Rossi, Federico M. (2021), "Labor Movements in Latin America," in Xóchitl Bada and Liliana Rivera Sánchez (eds.), *The Oxford Handbook of Sociology of Latin America*, 325–38 (Oxford: Oxford University Press).

Rossi, Federico M. and Donatella della Porta (2019), "Social Movements and Contention in Democratization Processes," in Christian W. Haerpfer, Patrick Bernhagen, Christian Welzel, and Ronald F. Inglehart (eds.), *Democratization*, 182–94 (Oxford: Oxford University Press).

Rossi, Federico M. and Eduardo Silva (2018), "Reshaping the Political Arena in Latin America," in Eduardo Silva and Federico M. Rossi (eds.), *Reshaping the Political Arena in Latin America*, 3–20 (Pittsburgh, PA: University of Pittsburgh Press).

Ruckert, Arne, Laura Macdonald, and Kristina R. Proulx (2017), "Post-Neoliberalism in Latin America: A Conceptual Review," *Third World Quarterly* 38(7), 1583–602.

Rueschemeyer, Dietrich, Evelyne Huber Stephens, and John D. Stephens (1992), *Capitalist Development and Democracy* (Chicago: University of Chicago Press).

Sandoval, Salvador A. M. (1998), "Social Movements and Democratization: The case of Brazil and the Latin Countries," in Marco Giugni, Doug McAdam, and Charles Tilly (eds.), *From Contention to Democracy*, 169–201 (Lanham: Rowman & Littlefield).

Silva, Eduardo (2009), *Challenging Neoliberalism in Latin America* (New York: Cambridge University Press).

Silva, Eduardo and Federico M. Rossi (eds.) (2018), Reshaping the Political Arena in Latin America: From Resisting Neoliberalism to the Second Incorporation (Pittsburgh, PA: University of Pittsburgh Press).

Simmons, Erica (2016), *Meaningful Resistance: Market Reforms and the Roots of Social Protest in Latin America* (Cambridge: Cambridge University Press).

Somma, Nicolás M. (2020), "Social Movements in Latin America: Mapping the Literature," in Xóchitl Bada and Liliana Rivera Sánchez (eds.), *The Oxford Handbook of the Sociology of Latin America*, 303–24 (Oxford: Oxford University Press).

Spalding, Rose (2014), *Contesting Trade in Central America: Market Reform and Resistance* (Austin: University of Texas Press).

Stallings, Barbara (2020), *Dependency in the Twenty-First Century? The Political Economy of China-Latin America Relations* (Cambridge: Cambridge University Press).

Suriano, Juan (2001), *Anarquistas: Cultura y política libertaria en Buenos Aires, 1890–1910* (Buenos Aires: Manantial).

Svampa, Maristella (ed.), (2000), *Desde abajo: La transformación de las identidades sociales* (Buenos Aires: Biblos).

Tamarin, David (1985), *The Argentine Labor Movement, 1930–1945: A Study in the Origins of Peronism* (Albuquerque: University of New Mexico Press).

von Bülow, Marisa (2010), *Building Transnational Networks: Civil Society and the Politics of Trade in the Americas* (Cambridge: Cambridge University Press).

Walton, John (1989), "Debt, Protest, and the State in Latin America," in Susan Eckstein (ed.), *Power and Popular Protest: Latin American Social Movements*, 299–328 (Berkeley and Los Angeles: University of California Press).

Walton, John and Jonathan Shefner (1994), "Latin America: Popular Protest and the State," in John Walton and David Seddon (eds.), *Free Markets & Food Riots: The Politics of Global Adjustment*, 97–134 (Oxford: Blackwell).

Welch, Cliff (1999), *The Seed Was Planted: The São Paulo Roots of Brazil's Rural Labor Movement, 1924–1964* (University Park: Penn State University Press).

Wickham-Crowley, Timothy and Susan Eckstein (2015), "'There and Back Again': Latin American Social Movements and Reasserting the Powers of Structural Theories," in Paul Almeida and Allen Cordero Ulate (eds.), *Handbook of Social Movements across Latin America*, 25–42 (New York: Springer).

Yashar, Deborah (2005), *Contesting Citizenship in Latin America: The Rise of Indigenous Movements and the Postliberal Challenge* (New York: Cambridge University Press).

Zapata S., Francisco (1976), "The Chilean Labor Movement under Salvador Allende: 1970–1973," *Latin American Perspectives* 3(1), 85–97.

CHAPTER 15

SOCIAL MOVEMENTS AND GLOBALIZATION IN LATIN AMERICA

DANIEL BURRIDGE AND JOHN MARKOFF

Introduction

"Globalization" refers to the growing and increasingly evident web of economic, political, and cultural processes that connect people in significant ways across national borders. This includes flows of trade and investment, cross-border tourism, and movements of people seeking work or fleeing violence; it includes the movement of sounds, images, and ideas generated in one country and received elsewhere in the world; it includes human activity that transcends national frameworks, including interstate organizations, border spanning capitalist enterprises, criminal organizations, or concerted cross-border action by social activists; and it includes cultural shifts towards understanding oneself and one's actions in a larger framework than one's own national state.

Understood as such, globalization has been going on for centuries, though certainly never at present scales. In recent decades, with ever-expanding geographic reach, and an ever-intensifying penetration of our social worlds, globalization constitutes a fundamental context for understanding the demands and practices of social movements operating at all geographic levels. A long-term perspective would show how important were transnational processes of trade, communication, inspiration, and cultural diffusion in fomenting the transformative and near-simultaneous social turbulence in many places in the late eighteenth and early nineteenth centuries, the end of the twentieth century's two world wars, and other iconic moments (see, e.g., Almeida and Chase-Dunn [2018]). In this chapter however, we focus on the recent era of Latin America in which democratization saw military regimes give way to civilian rule and combatants in civil wars return to civilian life (see Brockett, Inclán in this volume), while the widespread adoption of economic policies aimed at inserting the region into transnational circuits of investment, production, and trade saw ostensibly empowered citizens confronting new, global forms of exploitation and dispossession. And while we take the era of "neoliberal democracy" as our context, we will not address here the very big question of whether the historical evolution of capitalism caused neoliberalism and democracy to occur together (Robinson 1996) or whether we need separate explanations of each (Fishman 2018).

A substantial literature shows the many ways neoliberal globalization has dispossessed Latin American populations of economic and social citizenship and thereby impelled them to *react*. Aggrieved groups' reactions drove new rounds of local, national, and transnational organizing that included such contentious tactics as demonstrations, roadblocks, and strikes frequently coupled with demands for social change aimed at states (and increasingly corporations). Many scholars have framed this movement activity as varied forms of resistance. In this chapter, we build on but go beyond such analyses to show how movements have not only resisted the harms of globalization but have also been globalizing actors themselves. Many historically marginalized collective actors increasingly refashion and appropriate specific aspects of globalization according to local needs and knowledge, and subsequently diffuse novel social movement practices and ideas into global arenas.

Our theoretical framework thus combines a world-systemic, critical globalization approach (Robinson 2008) with a movement-state interactionist lens from political sociology (Goldstone 2003), while also incorporating cultural perspectives on Latin American movements that have been so influential among scholars of the region (Alvarez, Dagnino, and Escobar 1998). We provide varied examples of how globalization has shaped movements and how movements have shaped globalization; of how movements have contested some forms of globalization and created others.

We examine the significance of transnational and global processes in relation to social movements under three rubrics. First, we address the harms generated by neoliberal globalization, paying special attention to environmental challenges, the push to privatization, and how particular movement sectors have mobilized to resist. The second section shows how important transnational processes that *don't* fit neatly into a "neoliberal" category have affected movement strategies and tactics, paying particular attention to regional democratization, the increasing significance of NGOs, the ever-newer communications media, and recent transnational trends within the Left. In our third section we argue that the rise of transnational movements, as well as local and national movements, is not just a response to the stimulus of neoliberal globalization but is itself a form of globalization from the periphery and from below in which social activists are attempting to change the world in novel ways.

How Neoliberal Globalization Generates Movement Grievances and Resistance

At the conclusion of the Second World War, the prevailing economic wisdom embraced state spending in wealthy countries to tame the dreaded business cycle; state spending in poorer countries to achieve economic development; welfare measures to dampen class struggle and boost consumer demand; and flows of aid, loans, and investment from wealthier to less wealthy countries for the same broad purposes conceived transnationally. The managed state would improve on the untrammeled market and capitalist developmentalism would ward off the threat posed by the Soviet Union and its emulators with their own forms of state-managed development. In Latin America, tariffs would protect developing industry, subsidized public transportation would get workers to work, government would protect the national patrimony, and economic planning would shift resources towards development projects.

But since the 1980s, on a world scale, including in Latin America, an ongoing process of reversing such policies has been under way. The free flow of goods and investment was claimed to produce superior results, redistributive measures were denounced as both short-sighted and as theft, social welfare measures were said to cost too much and destroy incentives to work, and state efforts to limit the play of market forces were said to be unnatural and counterproductive. The new economic and social policies took hold in many countries, for example, in a United States or Britain cutting back on state investments in transportation or supporting privatization in education, in a China promoting vast enterprises competing for global trade, or in a poorer country supporting corporations in acquiring rights to resources from ore to water. Their many critics summed up these policies as "neoliberalism" and they had varied, complex, and far-reaching manifestations (Almeida and Chase-Dunn 2018; Harvey 2005; Mudge 2008; Silva 2009). These included: increased vulnerabilities to financial crisis; global shifts toward precarious forms of employment; reduction of tariff barriers; liberalization of markets; privatization of previously state-managed or -owned enterprises; and pressure to conform from transnationally organized corporations, powerful states (especially the United States, but increasingly from global competitors like China), and the institutions that to some extent manage global capitalism (especially the International Monetary Fund [IMF], the World Bank, and the World Trade Organization).

Protestors Push Back

The implementation of such far-reaching policies triggered a wave of protests across Latin America (as in other places) as diverse groups perceived threats to their economic wellbeing and rights of social citizenship; that is, dignified participation in a human community (Spronk and Terhorst 2012; see Almeida, Rossi in this volume). In Argentina, Venezuela, Bolivia, and Ecuador, waves of anti-neoliberal contention by movements and election-contesting parties ousted neoliberal governments (Silva 2009). Throughout the region, many workers and peasants were adversely affected by neoliberal transformations and were among some of the most frequently and militantly mobilized (Almeida 2007). Established labor unions, later joined by collectives of informal workers, initiated significant campaigns against attacks on social security systems, unionized public employment, inexpensive transportation, and progressive tax codes. In Bolivia, miners' unions led resistance to economic packages that sold off state-based companies to foreign investors from the mid-1980s and helped end two neoliberal administrations in the early 2000s (Olivera with Lewis 2004), which some scholars see as part of a revolutionary process of national reconstitution (Hylton and Thompson 2007). In Guatemala, a coalition of Mayan peasant associations and multisectoral union federations spearheaded resistance to IMF-mandated sales tax hikes in 2001 and 2004, the country's largest mass protests since the civil war ended in 1996 (Almeida 2014). New policies reversing earlier policies of state-led developmentalism were generating intense movements to defend the established practices of previous decades (Rossi 2017). These, and many other protests contesting neoliberal market extensions, could be understood as instances of the social self-defense that Karl Polanyi (1957 [1944]) in the mid-twentieth century contended were the unsurprising forms of pushback market extremism repeatedly produces.

Workers were at the forefront of resistance to free trade agreements that made it easier for foreign companies to cheaply invest, flexibilize labor regimes, and strong-arm governments into cracking down on the informal markets of pirated and knock-off goods on which many members of lower classes relied. In Central America, both public and private sector unions were particularly influential in broad-based protest campaigns against the Central American Free Trade Agreement (CAFTA) in the early 2000s. Costa Rica saw the largest protests in its history with upwards of 500,000 protestors (Almeida 2014). El Salvador's anti-CAFTA protests were joined by a highly organized movement of informal vendors with jeopardized livelihoods.

Structural adjustment programs based on neoliberal imperatives also drastically transformed rural economies, opening up the countryside to agribusiness investment and speculation, while slashing the public programs and institutions that had provided subsidies and technical assistance to peasants. Such "austerity" programs proved particularly harsh in post-revolutionary Nicaragua, where the state had provided much public sector employment, and had supported many state- or peasant-run cooperatives during the 1980s. The privatization of "agrarian reform" lands by the incoming right-wing government in 1990 in combination with massive public sector layoffs provoked broad-based protests and general strikes. Further structural adjustments that crippled the National Development Bank, raised interest rates on rural agricultural loans, and reduced their availability to small producers, set off two more protest campaigns in 1995 and 1997. As in 1990, peasant organizations participated in coalitions that slowed but did not halt the neoliberalization of the Nicaraguan countryside (Almeida 2014).

Many movements came to understand globalized neoliberalism as their common foe. Brazil's Movimento dos Trabalhadores Rurais Sem Terra (MST) was launched in the 1980s as military withdrawal from government provided an opening for this struggle against large landowners in the context of extreme rural social inequalities (Wright and Wolford 2003; see also Fernandes and Welch, Welch in this volume). In the neoliberal era, the MST has gone beyond combining calls for agrarian reform with land occupations to denunciations of an unjust economic model, calls for housing and education reform, and participation in many contentious protests. Emblematic of this broadening of specific targets was their takeover of a Swiss factory distributing genetically modified seeds (Vanden 2012).

Environmental Challenges

The increasingly damaging human impact on our planet's capacity to sustain decent forms of human existence is a deeply transnational process that includes ongoing poisoning of lands, waters, and sky, the exhaustion of life-sustaining resources, and the multiple malign consequences of ongoing climate change. These consequences include disruption of established ways of livelihood and human cooperation posed by rising temperatures, the reshaping of ecosystems by chemically supported monocultures, and the destruction of arable land and forest by extractive industries. Since with some frequency it is indigenous peoples whose lives, livelihoods, and accustomed practices are threatened, the numerous movements provoked by environmental damage frequently intersect with burgeoning movements on behalf of indigenous rights (see Christel and Gutiérrez, Rice in this volume).

Perhaps the quintessential Latin American example of the struggle between citizens concerned with protecting their control of natural resources and transnational corporate interests was the Water War of Cochabamba, Bolivia in 2000. In response to a World Bank demand to privatize state services, Cochabamba's municipal government leased the rights for water administration for forty years to a multinational consortium led by the US- and Britain-based Bechtel Corporation. The new municipal law governing water guaranteed company profits through exorbitant price hikes and the confiscation of community water systems. In response, some Cochabambans formed the Coordinadora de Defensa del Agua y de la Vida to defend the "natural gift" of water for free public use. City inhabitants laid non-violent siege to Cochabamba, blockading roads and overwhelming security forces. Bechtel was expelled, local people regained control over a vital natural resource, and the Coordinadora proceeded to call for a constituent assembly, a demand that resonated with similar calls throughout the country (Hylton and Thomson 2007; Olivera with Lewis 2004).

Neighboring Peru provides especially clear evidence of how environmental conflicts directly pit indigenous peoples' sovereignty against transnational economic interests. Near Bagua in the Peruvian Amazon, indigenous peoples formed the Asociación Interétnica de Desarrollo de la Selva Peruana (AIDESEP) to halt the activities of the national oil company in the context of a free trade agreement with the United States. In 2009, in what became known as the Baguazo, in quick succession, police were taken hostage, a large force of police attacked a larger number of indigenous blockaders, over twenty police and ten civilians were killed and dozens were wounded, AIDESEP leaders were arrested, the government repealed some of the enabling decrees, and the protestors halted their blockade (Cabel García 2018).

Attempts to extract other natural resources from the Peruvian subsoil have been equally destructive, in terms of both environmental devastation and loss of human life. The "Las Bambas" mine in Apurimac, operated by MMG Limited (whose majority shareholder is a Chinese corporation), has doubled Peru's copper output, but also intensified ecological degradation. Meanwhile, US-based Southern Copper spent over a decade attempting to begin operation of its "Tía María" copper mine in the Arequipa region, where it has been met by massive strikes organized by local famers. From 2011 to 2015 there were fifty-nine deaths and 1,839 injured in "socio-environmental conflicts" as the government tried to provide foreign companies "equitable investment conditions" (Sullivan 2015).

In El Salvador, anti-mining activists were killed in conflicts with Canadian mining companies, but a broad-based, multi-sectoral movement operating at local, national, and transnational scales successfully blocked mining before it started. This coalition included militant community organizations, national-level peasant groups, environmentalist and academic NGOs, members of the leftist Frente Farabundo Martí para la Liberación Nacional (FMLN) political party, feminist organizations, and the Catholic Church. Their implementation of transnational strategies to harness the support of allies in the United States and Canada who could advocate in their home countries and with the International Centre for Shareholder Investment Disputes (ICSID) (which operates under the auspices of the World Bank) was crucial in winning the legal case against the mining company's lawsuit (Spalding 2014). In 2017, societal pressure culminated in the approval of a ban on metal mining in this tiny and ecologically fragile country, though by mid-2019, anti-mining activists feared that renewed electoral ascendance by the right would reopen conflicts around mining.

Transnational Circulation of Ideas

Like goods, financial flows, and people, ideas cross borders, too. Firms copy each other's innovations. Police forces borrow each other's ideas about technologies of repression and the producers of such technologies market their wares across borders. States copy each other's organizational forms. Social movements get ideas from social movements in other countries. What seems common sense gets reshaped as well, and in our transnationalized era does so on a transnational scale (see von Bülow in this volume). The institutions of global finance impose a common template of austerity plans which national governments find difficult to deviate from (Kedar 2013). Downsizing government, developing accounting schemes, stressing efficiency, and other elements of neoliberal imaginaries thus come to be seen as pragmatic good sense (Drori 2008; Schofer et al. 2012). But what is good sense for powerholders and persuaded citizens may provoke significant resistance from those thereby injured and unpersuaded activists.

This means there was a cultural component to neoliberal globalization, the spread of the view that the market is the pivotal institution to which human action must adapt. Three arguments supported this new common sense: first, the market was held to be more efficient in allocating resources and effort than any plan; second, the resultant of the actions of individually deciding humans was held to be morally superior to even well-intentioned decisions for the supposed common good; and third, pro-market practices had become so deeply institutionalized that even those who retained objections would have to conform pragmatically ("there is no alternative" was the much-repeated mantra).

As an instance, consider the remaking of educational systems. By the early twenty-first century, educational privatization was in vogue in many countries alongside moves to privatization in such disparate arenas as economic production, prison construction and management, health care systems, and even military force. But Chilean moves toward privatization of education were widely seen by young people as perpetuating class-based inequalities and triggered two enormous waves of protest by university and secondary school students—one in 2006 and an even larger one in 2011 when students occupied the Casa Central of the University of Chile for seven months. Social movement theorists might be tempted to explain the first protest wave as triggered by the beginning of the receptive presidential administration of Socialist Michelle Bachelet in 2006 and the second as the backfiring of the more repressive approach of the hostile presidential administration of billionaire Sebastián Piñera who took office in 2010. But since both of these very divergent state responses galvanized huge protests, a more promising explanation would take into account the mobilizing actions of the young protestors themselves. They shifted the debate from technical arguments about how best to achieve quality education to questions of social justice and inequality (Chouhy 2021; Cummings 2015; Disi 2018; see Donoso in this volume).

Myriad additional examples reflect the incompatibility of what business-minded policymakers often understand as common sense and what ordinary people understand as essential to their life and dignity. Especially prone to spur broad coalitions including unions, community-based movements, public sector workers, NGOs, and political parties on the Left were moves to privatize previously state-held or community-held resources. Such policies were experienced as a reversal of earlier policies of state-led developmentalism, generating intense movements to defend the established practice of previous decades (Rossi 2017). In Argentina for example, communities previously benefitting from jobs in state-owned firms responded to the privatization of national oil and gas industries in the early 1990s by turning the *piquete* (roadblock) into a national and regional phenomenon (Auyero 2003). In El Salvador, attempts to privatize health care were met with the largest protests the country had seen in forty years, with hundreds of thousands from almost all social sectors participating in "white marches" for "health and life" (Almeida 2014).

How Transnational Processes Affect Movement Strategies and Tactics

While "globalization" is frequently conflated with the neoliberal economic policies and worldviews that provoked the movement dynamics described above, other transnational processes have deeply affected the strategies and tactics of social movements across Latin America from the mid-1980s into the second decade of the twenty-first century. First, in every one of the many countries under military rule at the beginning of the decade, a democratic transition brought different political practices; in most of the countries engaged in civil wars into the 1990s, a "peace process" established democratic party competition in which the Left could participate; and the unique, long-run single-party dominance of Mexico was superseded by a more genuinely competitive political system (Inclán in this volume). Second, nongovernmental organizations (NGOs) became increasingly significant as political actors, altering the resources available to movements and often connecting local processes, including movements, to the transnational networks in which those NGOs were embedded, generating new opportunities for some activists and important challenges for others. Third, the continually innovating new communications technologies altered the ways movements, like many other forms of human organization, worked (see Treré and Harlow in this volume). Fourth, a multicontinental shift in activist cultures on the Left away from what could be called, broadly speaking, socialist ideas towards the prevalence of anarchist ideas, carried with it changes in short-term goals and models of organizing (see Oikonomakis in this volume).

Regional Democratization

Empowering regimes through contested elections, institutionalized protections for speech and association, and limitations on the repressive discretion of the state have always nurtured social movements; these movements have often contested what democracy was, sometimes proposing alternate or superior visions of democracy and sometimes proposing to end it (Markoff 2011, 2019). Whether or not a political system is a democratic one is therefore a fundamental context for the kinds of collective social action in which people engage (including for movements that protest important features of current versions of democracy) (see Brockett, Inclán in this volume), and cross-border diffusion of ideas and practices means that what happens in one political system will have impacts on what happens in others.

A variety of transnational, even global, processes converged by the late twentieth century to democratize, to one degree or another, a larger swathe of human territory than at any previous moment in human history, including almost all of Latin America. We will briefly indicate four of these processes. First of all, dominant elites became less fearful of revolution, especially led by communists, as the Soviet Union settled into bureaucratic ossification. In many countries, including in Latin America, this meant that the right was less afraid of the Left (especially as in some places the Left had been crushed by repression); transnationally it meant that it became harder to convince Washington that anti-Left state violence was essential for US security. Second, transnationally active banks, having lent enormous sums in the 1970s, exerted great pressure on heavily borrowing states to reverse spendthrift ways, a process with huge consequences for Latin America in the 1980s, for Eastern Europe at the end of that decade, and for Africa in the 1990s, and were increasingly open to replacing authoritarian rulers seen as corrupt and wasteful. Third, the successful democratization of Portugal and Spain in the 1970s resonated throughout Latin America, and beyond, in the next decade, with both Iberian instances demonstrating that even decades-old authoritarian regimes could be replaced by democracy without destroying the fundamental interests of capitalists (Fishman 2018). And fourth, the reforms of the Second Vatican Council (1962–1965), opened the way for a far more positive approach to democracy, undercutting parts of Latin America's antidemocratic right that had claimed to be defending Christian civilization, and providing backing for clergy opposing authoritarian rulers.

These profoundly transnational processes played out in the region, which meant not only the flourishing of a rich diversity of movements supporting democracy but also that, with democracy achieved, Latin America saw the ongoing interplay of movement actions and party electoral competition that characterize all democracies; in the 2010s some scholars of social movements in Latin America, like scholars of other places, were taking a close look at this interplay (Almeida 2014; Rossi and von Bülow 2015; see Roberts in this volume). Since the democratization of this historical moment coincided with neoliberal policies (Robinson 2008), the harms thereby engendered provided many of the diverse grievances those movements strove to address.

NGOs as Political Actors

The growth of NGOs as political actors with significant cross-border financing and other kinds of support centered in rich countries and international agencies both enabled certain forms of activism and hindered others. Local and national movements' greater access to funding facilitates their professionalization and the mainstreaming of movement causes. However, pressure to adopt frames and organizational structures that resonate with international agencies may challenge movement autonomy. Clifford Bob (2005) showed how important were the connections forged by the Zapatistas of Chiapas and their media-savvy Subcomandante Marcos with rich-country supporters in furthering their insurgent agenda. Underlining the transnational dimension, Bob shows some very similar processes at work for a Nigerian movement, and myriad additional examples demonstrate movements benefitting from the financial, technical, and political support of international donors as a result of successful self-marketing.

This increasing foreign support of local movements has been called the "NGOization of resistance" (Roy 2014). Its critics emphasize a tendency for grassroots movements to prioritize the rhetorically restrained discourses and technically proficient practices acceptable to their foreign donors. External attempts to foster development and strong civil societies are associated with the neoliberal roll-back of the functioning of states and may come at the expense of the localized struggles of movements' grassroots bases (Alvarez 1999). NGOization may also augment class- and raced-based divisions within movements, particularly between well-educated, transnationally connected, urban-based activists and NGO staff, and their poorer, more working-class, or rural counterparts (Thayer 2017).

Other analyses have highlighted a more dynamic set of relationships between Latin American movements and rich-country-based NGOs. Sonia Alvarez (2009) shows that foreign financing of Latin American movements may both bolster the creation and dissemination of anti-systemic knowledge and radical discourses, and threaten the potential dilution of movement demands and practices. Millie Thayer (2017) traces the segmented relationships that connect Brazilian feminist organizations to Netherlands-based donor agencies along an "international aid chain." She shows how these movements' organizations began to take on "calculative dimensions" as their discursive goods from the South—such as claims of representativeness, movement success, or feminist authenticity—become exchangeable for Dutch financial resources predicated on quantifiable impacts, increased self-reliance, and upward accountability to donors. This dynamic led to the "stealthy incursion" of market-based discourses into movement frameworks in the course of the 1990s. But Thayer argues that feminist movements have been able to work within the shifting contours of international aid markets intentionally and strategically.

And movements evolve. The Zapatistas took note of this downside of the successful marketing strategies analyzed by Bob (2005) for the 1990s and early 2000s. Since then, they have endeavored to explicitly set the terms of interactions with outside actors to ensure that aid is provided according to collective Zapatista "life plans," as opposed to trends in the transnational development industry (Barronet, Mora Bayo, and Stahler-Sholk 2011). Observers judge that they have managed to achieve significant downward accountability.

New Communication Technologies

The new electronic technologies have enabled much ready communication across, as well as within borders. They have facilitated the spread of ideas and activist-to-activist connections across geographies, movements, and social backgrounds. They have permitted effective, short-run mobilizations unmoored from organizational depth and resources. They have been formidable platforms for the widespread dissemination of a tsunami of disinformation, sometimes organized by strategically astute, anonymous trolls with the skills to disguise their points of entry into electronic networks. They have made it easier to spend many hours glued to a screen or mobile phone, keeping up with sources one enjoys, and thereby spending fewer hours in contact with other points of view, making the new media at once a force for cosmopolitanism and provincialism, for inclusion and exclusion. They have empowered individual and collective resistance to established authority and given authorities new tools to monitor dissent (see Treré and Harlow in this volume).

In Latin America, as elsewhere, these contradictory trends were in evidence. Rapid, online-impelled mobilizations have carved out new political spaces and strategies for social change while amplifying frequently marginalized perspectives and making established media themselves targets of protest. In Mexico, the #YoSoy132 movement of 2012 was triggered by the media labeling as paid agitators students who were protesting then-presidential candidate Enrique Peña Nieto. The protestors then uploaded 131 videos to YouTube to show they really were students and called for impartial media coverage of political campaigns as a part of democratic advance. The movement went viral. Supporters in other Mexican universities and in many places beyond Mexico expressed their affinity with the hashtag #YoSoy132 (I am the 132nd). After sponsoring a series of wide-ranging debates during the 2012 presidential campaign, the #YoSoy132 movement dissolved as such, showing the potentially ephemeral nature of online-based organizing (as argued by Earl and Kimport [2011]). The movement's activists, however, have subsequently run for local office as independents, continued to pursue "digital and media justice" in various ways, and lent important support to the ultimately successful presidential candidacy of Andrés Manuel López Obrador in 2018 (Contreras Alcántara 2017).

Online organizing has also been harnessed by rightwing movements to mobilize new constituencies for contentious actions without relying on the symbolic and material capital typically required to sustain contention. An illustrative example was the pro-impeachment campaign of 2015–2016 in Brazil, which led to the ousting of President Dilma Rouseff. Zanini and Tatagiba (2019) demonstrate how savvy social media use by "new right" and anti-corruption activists led to "engaged action" by largely middle-class, politically unaffiliated people who were eager to show up *en masse* for pro-impeachment rallies. This social-media-driven campaign entailed little penetration of grassroots communities but was crucial in providing anti-Partido dos Trabalhadores (PT) politicians with political cover for their impeachment plan.

New Currents on the Left

A transnational cultural shift on the Left away from organizational models and aspirational ideas of organizing commonly associated with "socialism" towards models and ideas that can be associated with "anarchism" is notable in Latin America as in other places. Strongly hierarchical Left organizations devoted to attaining state power by ballot box or revolution, with clear statements of ideological commitments, well-defined memberships, and socialist identities are being to some extent displaced by groups of activists deeply connected to each other across organizational boundaries, disdainful of leaders and rigid hierarchies, committed to internal democratic debate, more inclined to identify as "activists" than as members of some particular organization, acting in local or transnational arenas as much as national ones, and seeking to develop autonomy from established political and economic structures (Thwaites Rey 2011). This seems increasingly prevalent on the radical Left since at least the 1990s, for example, in Latin American indigenous movements (Zibechi 2010). Although many of these activists would disavow the label, their practices share much with avowedly anarchist movements of the past and are infused with what Bamyeh (2009) argues is the core of anarchism, whether thus labeled or not: a striving for freedom that impels collectivities to construct unimposed order in innovative ways in the here and now. We thus follow Wright (2010) in adopting the term as a convenient, but not fully comfortable, shorthand.

The rise of anarchist ideas and practices seems a result of the confluence of several processes: doubts in our global age that national states are effective levers of radical change; more multisided, less top-down forms of communication powerfully enabled by the new technologies that connect across borders as readily as within them; and disappointment or even outrage over the past results both of socialist parties competing in democratic arenas and socialist parties seizing power by revolutionary violence (see Spanakos and Romo, Oikonomakis in this volume). Survey evidence on almost two thousand activists at Social Forums in Brazil, Kenya, and the United States between 2005 and 2010 by Chase-Dunn and colleagues (2019) suggests that although those who identify as "anarchists" are a small minority, their specific ideas about social change have much in common with anarchist traditions. Further, while valuing engagement in local struggles, they experience themselves as part of a transnationally connected activist community.

Many Latin American movements in the early twenty-first century—including feminists, peasants, and urban squatters—have adopted "horizontalist," or nonhierarchical styles, of organization, claiming this prefigures the values they seek to foment in social life, and manifests their disenchantment with such traditional political vehicles as parties, states, and unions, held to generate hierarchy and subject to pressures from global capital (Stahler-Sholk, Vanden, and Becker 2014). Some of the movements mentioned earlier embodied such horizontalism. In Cochabamba, the successful resistance to water privatization was impelled by grassroots assemblies with rotating leaderships housed in already-existing community organizations. This enabled rapid collective decision-making and an effective, citywide mobilization (Olivera with Lewis 2004). The #YoSoy132 movement in Mexico was catalyzed by the spontaneous use of social media to assemble a leaderless network of activists around broad critiques of political institutions which, just as spontaneously, dissolved into atomized and variegated expressions.

Perhaps the quintessential examples of the tendencies toward anarchist practices and visions in Latin American movements in the context of globalization are those of the Zapatistas in Chiapas, Mexico, and the worker-managed factories in Argentina. In Chiapas, the Zapatistas' initial rebellion was a refusal to acquiesce in a neoliberal takeover of the Mexican state. Their subsequent evolution from revolutionary socialist army to media-savvy international aid magnet, and on to globally connected but locally focused self-governance bodies has been characterized by adaptation, flexibility, strategic innovation, and tactical pragmatism; they even endorsed a candidate in the Mexican presidential elections of 2018. The Zapatistas' creation and collective management of social goods such as education, health care, and agroecological initiatives constitute an emblematic effort to construct autonomy from both the state and capital.

In Argentina, the emergence and subsequent consolidation of worker-run factories began during the country's economic collapse of 2001. Part of a broader shift toward horizontalist strategies—noted among neighborhood assemblies, movements for community-based schools (Heidemann 2018), and alternative human rights organizations—the factory takeovers were at first driven by necessity, as owners sought to close up shop amid crisis. Workers in many factories (and other businesses) responded by assuming all aspects of management. This was not the result of planning by an established leadership, but rather by workers' mutual aid and self-activity in a formal power vacuum, which led to the discovery of new forms of collective power. Although there are important linkages to Peronists and Trotskyists, the grassroots organizing principles adopted could reasonably be called "anarchist," whether or not there was an explicit identification as such. The recuperated workplaces have inspired workers' movements throughout the world and have continued to increase in number in Argentina (Sitrin 2014). Across Latin America and across movements, as in other world regions, transnational organizing is a sign that contention increasingly links local and national struggles with border-crossing processes, and that activists are increasingly oriented to multiple geographic scales (Smith and Wiest 2012). The Salvadoran anti-mining movement described in the first section of this chapter is connected transnationally to other environmental movements in the Alianza Centroamericana Frente a la Minería (ACREFEMIN). Transnationally linked indigenous organizations (for whom the nation-state container may not be their most important experience of political and cultural community), such as the Foro Indígena de Abya Yala, the Foro de Comunicación Indígena, and the Coordinadora Andina de Organizaciones Indígenas (CAOI) have contributed to the crystallization of a hemispheric agenda for indigenous peoples' cultural, social, and political revitalization. Feminist movements have also focused on transnational sites of movement building such as participation in the World March of Women, and numerous regional articulations.

Such transnational movements generate transnational diffusion of strategic repertoires (Rossi 2017). But the scale shift towards a transnational arena in which movements might target international financial institutions or address themselves to globally conceived publics also suggests an increasingly resonant critique of the limits of nation-state-based politics, identities, and cultural frameworks. Such transnational linkages should not be understood merely as responses to globalizing processes, but as *sites* of globalization itself.

How Movements across Borders Are Sites of Globalization

Thus far we have largely described how globalizing processes have shaped movements, but border-crossing movements are themselves elements and agents of globalization. These globally linked movements challenge the logics of neoliberal capitalist globalization by posing alternatives that promote climate, racial, and social justice, solidarity-based economies, and new forms of democratic governance. Transnational movements therefore constitute *social sites* where the transnational arena itself is given new form, amounting to building globalization from below and from the periphery. Such transnational links have increased markedly in recent decades (Smith and Wiest 2012). Latin America has produced some of the most globally relevant of such instances.

A prominent example is the World Social Forum (WSF), born in Porto Alegre, Brazil in 2001. Local Brazilian activists (with important support from the PT) convened the WSF as a cross-border, anti-capitalist movement-building space and critical commentary on the elitism of Davos's World Economic Forum. With its guiding frame that "another world is possible," the WSF provided opportunities for individuals and organizations to share information, tactics, and struggles, thereby fostering increased transnational linkages, alter-globalization imaginaries, and concrete experiments in constructing more democratic social relations. Over time and with the emergence of national and regional analogues, the WSF came to be understood as a "world process" that constituted both a "sub-system of world politics" operating "below" the bureaucracies and exclusions of the formal inter-state system (Smith and Wiest 2012), and a tool to democratize global civil society (Teivainen 2002).

In addition to leadership in the construction of global movement processes, Latin American movements have also pioneered specific tactics that have migrated far beyond the region. Argentine *escraches* have been replicated all over Europe, particularly Spain. These are elaborate demonstrations outside the residences of prominent political or economic figures, often preceded by extensive information campaigns about the target's misdeeds, then followed by street theatre, symbolic actions, and public shaming before the malefactor's neighbors (Sitrin 2014: 215–16).

Perhaps the most famous practice that has emerged from Latin America is participatory budgeting. Arising from—yet again—Porto Alegre, participatory budgeting (PB) was impelled by neighborhood association activists and then taken up by PT officials to enable citizens to participate in deliberations about the allocations of a portion of their municipal taxes. PB was remarkably successful in deepening democracy and spread to other Brazilian places by a "national network" of "Worker's Party administrators along with academics and movement and NGO activists." This practice then diffused far beyond Brazil to thousands of cities, although often modified to limit its full emancipatory potential (Baiocchi and Ganuza 2017: 63).

Especially noteworthy as well has been the galvanizing fallout for global activism from the Chiapas mobilizations of the Zapatistas. They appropriated global discourses of human and indigenous rights to bolster their own struggles for autonomy and subsequently formed common cause with global counter-publics in anti-capitalist projects (Speed 2011), inspiring interconnected global justice activism in many sites around the world. Their insistence on the mutually supportive character of many previously separate struggles—compartmentalized by social base, themes, tactics, or geography—was a catalyst to the forging of many links since. Their intersectional, autonomist, and global ethos has helped reshape debates about what is possible, desirable, and effective for changing the world.

Conclusion

Our account of globalization and social movements in Latin America surveyed the ways the transborder connections forged in the era of neoliberal democracy generated both grievances and opportunities for social movements, and indicated as well that some of those movements were themselves actors in developing new forms of transnational connection from below. But there may be an important temporal boundary to this analysis. If the growing authoritarianism so evident in so many places in the second decade of the twenty-first century—in and out of Latin America—erodes that democratic context, it may be that but a few years after we conclude this survey, an entirely new chapter will need to be written.

References

Almeida, Paul (2007), "Defensive Mobilization: Popular Movements against Economic Adjustment Policies in Latin America," *Latin American Perspectives* 34(3), 123–39.

Almeida, Paul (2014), *Mobilizing Democracy: Globalization and Citizen Protest* (Baltimore, MD: John Hopkins University Press).

Almeida, Paul and Christopher Chase-Dunn (2018), "Globalization and Social Movements," *Annual Review of Sociology* 44, 189–211.

Alvarez, Sonia E. (1999), "Advocating Feminism: The Latin American Feminist NGO 'Boom,'" *International Feminist Journal of Politics* 1(2), 181–209.

Alvarez, Sonia E. (2009), "Beyond NGO-ization? Reflections from Latin America," *Development* 52(2), 175–89.

Alvarez, Sonia E., Evelina Dagnino, and Arturo Escobar (eds.) (1998), *Cultures of Politics, Politics of Cultures: Re-Visioning Latin American Social Movements* (Boulder, CO: Westview Press).

Auyero, Javier (2003), *Contentious Lives: Two Argentine Women, Two Protests, and the Quest for Recognition* (Durham, NC: Duke University Press).

Baiocchi, Gianpaolo and Ernesto Ganuza (2017), *Popular Democracy: The Paradox of Participation* (Stanford, CA: Stanford University Press).

Bamyeh, Mohammed (2009), *Anarchy as Order: The History and Future of Civic Humanity* (Lanham, MD: Rowman and Littlefield).

Barronet, Bruno, Mariana Mora Bayo, and Richard Stahler-Sholk (eds.) (2011), *Luchas "muy otras": Zapatismo, autonomia y las comunidades indígenas de Chiapas* (Mexico: UAM-Xochimilco/CIESAS/UNACH).

Bob, Clifford (2005), *The Marketing of Rebellion: Insurgents, Media, and International Activism* (Cambridge: Cambridge University Press).

Cabel García, Andrea (2018), "La desfamiliarización del otro y del uno: para repensar la violencia y la indigeneidad amazónica peruana." PhD dissertation, University of Pittsburgh.

Chase-Dunn, Christopher, John Aldecoa, Ian Breckenridge-Jackson, and Joel Herrera (2019), "Anarchism in the Web of Transnational Social Movements," *Journal of World-Systems Research* 25(2), 373–94.

Chouhy, Gabriel (2021), "The Moral Life of Econometric Equations: Factoring Class Inequality into School Quality Valuations in Chile," *European Journal of Sociology* 62(1), 141–182.

Disi Pavlic, Rodolfo (2018), "Sentenced to Debt: Explaining Student Mobilization in Chile," *Latin American Research Review* 53(3), 448–565.

Drori, Gili S. (2008), "Institutionalism and Globalization Studies," in Royston Greenwood, Christine Oliver, Kerstin Sahlin, and Roy Suddaby (eds.), *The SAGE Handbook of Organizational Institutionalism*, 798–842 (London: SAGE).

Contreras Alcántara, Javier (2017), "#YoSoy132, Social Media, and Political Organization," *Oxford Research Encyclopedias*, https://oxfordre.com/latinamericanhistory/browse?btog=chap&jumpTo=y&page=4&pageSize=20&sort=titlesort&subSite=latinamericanhistory&to=ORE_LAH%3AREFLAH025.

Cummings, Peter (2015), "Democracy and Student Discontent: Chilean Student Protest in the Post-Pinochet Era," *Journal of Politics in Latin America* 7(3), 49–84.

Earl, Jennifer and Katrina Kimport (2011), *Digitally Enabled Social Change: Activism in the Internet Age* (Cambridge, MA: MIT Press).

Fishman, Robert (2018), "What Made the Third Wave Possible? Historical Contingency and Meta-Politics in the Genesis of Worldwide Democratization," *Comparative Politics* 51, 607–26.

Goldstone, Jack (ed.) (2003). *States, Parties, and Social Movements* (Cambridge: Cambridge University Press).

Harvey, David (2005), *A Brief History of Neoliberalism* (New York: Oxford University Press).

Heidemann, Kai (2018), "Crisis, Protest and Democratization from Below: The Rise of a Community-based Schooling Movement in Argentina," in Rebecca Clothey and Kai Heidemann (eds.), *Another Way: Decentralization, Democratization and the Global Politics of Community-based Schooling*, 31–46 (Rotterdam: Brill).

Hylton, Forrest and Sinclair Thomson (2007), *Revolutionary Horizons: Past and Present in Bolivian Politics* (London and New York: Verso).

Kedar, Claudia (2013), *The International Monetary Fund and Latin America: The Argentine Puzzle in Context* (Philadelphia, PA: Temple University Press).

Markoff, John (2011), "A Moving Target: Democracy," *Archives Européennes de Sociologie/ European Journal of Sociology* 52(2), 239–76.

Markoff, John (2019), "How Democracy Never Worked as Planned (and Perhaps a Good Thing It Didn't)," *Sociological Theory* 37(2), 184–208.

Mudge, Stephanie Lee (2008), "What is Neo-liberalism?," *Socio-Economic Review* 6(4), 703–31.

Olivera, Oscar with Tom Lewis (2004), *Cochabamba! Water War in Bolivia* (Cambridge: South End Press).

Polanyi, Karl (1957 [1944]), *The Great Transformation* (Boston, MA: Beacon).

Robinson, William I. (1996), *Promoting Polyarchy: Globalization, US Intervention, and Hegemony* (Cambridge: Cambridge University Press).

Robinson, William I. (2008), *Latin America and Global Capitalism: A Critical Globalization Perspective* (New York: Verso).

Rossi, Federico M. (2017), *The Poor's Struggle for Political Participation: The Piquetero Movement in Argentina* (Cambridge: Cambridge University Press).

Rossi, Federico M. and Marisa von Bülow (2015) (eds.), *Social Movement Dynamics. New Perspectives on Theory and Research from Latin America* (Farnham: Ashgate).

Roy, Arundhati (2014), "The NGOization of Resistance," *Pambazuka News*. https://www.pambazuka.org/governance/ngo-ization-resistance. September 23, 2014.

Schofer, Evan, Ann Hironaka, David John Frank, and Wesley Longhofer (2012), "Sociological Institutionalism and World Society," in Edwin Amenta, Kate Nash, and Alan Scott (eds.), *The Wiley-Blackwell Companion to Political Sociology*, 57–68 (New York: Wiley-Blackwell).

Silva, Eduardo (2009), *Challenging Neoliberalism in Latin America* (Cambridge: Cambridge University Press).

Sitrin, Marina (2014), "Argentina: Against and Beyond the State," in Richard Stahler-Sholk, Harry Vanden, and Mark Becker (eds.), (2014), *Rethinking Latin American Social Movements: Radical Action from Below*, 209–32 (Lanham, MD: Rowman and Littlefield).

Smith, Jackie and Dawn Wiest (2012), *Social Movements in the World System: The Politics of Crisis and Transformation* (New York: Russell Sage Foundation).

Spalding, Rose (2014), "El Salvador: Horizontalism and the Anti-mining Movement," in Richard Stahler-Sholk, Harry Vanden, and Mark Becker (eds.), *Rethinking Latin American Social Movements: Radical Action from Below* (Lanham, MD: Rowman and Littlefield).

Speed, Shannon (2011), "Exercising Rights and Reconfiguring Resistance in the Zapatista Juntas of Good Governance," in Bruno Baronnet, Mariana Mora Bayo, and Richard Stahler-Sholk (eds.), *Luchas "muy otras": Zapatismo, autonomismo, y las comunidades indígenas de Chiapas*, 135–62 (Mexico: UAM-Xochimilco/CIESAS/UNACH).

Spronk, Susan and Phillip Terhorst (2012), "Social Movement Struggles for Public Services," in David McDonald and Greg Ruiters (eds.), *Alternatives to Privatization: Public Options for Essential Services in in the Global South*, 133–56 (New York: Routledge).

Stahler-Sholk, Richard, Harry Vanden, and Mark Becker (eds.) (2014), *Rethinking Latin American Social Movements: Radical Action from Below* (Lanham, MD: Rowman and Littlefield).

Sullivan, Lynda (2015), "Peru's Tia Maria Mining Conflict: Another Mega Imposition," *Upside Down World*, June 11, http://upsidedownworld.org/archives/peru-archives/perus-tia-maria-mining-conflict-another-mega-imposition/.

Teivainen, Teivo (2002), "The World Social Forum and Global Democratization: Learning from Porto Alegre," *Third World Quarterly* 23(4), 621–32.

Thayer, Millie (2017), "The 'Gray Zone' Between Movements and Markets: Brazilian Feminists and the International Aid Chain," in Sonia E. Alvarez, Jeffrey W. Rubin, Millie Thayer, Gianpaolo Baiocchi, and Agustín Laó-Montes (eds.), *Beyond Civil Society: Activism, Participation, and Protest in Latin America*, 156–78 (Durham, NC: Duke University Press).

Thwaites Rey, Mabel (2011), "La autonomía: Entre el mito y la potencia empancipadora," in Jóvenes en Resistencia (eds.), *Pensar las Autonomías*, 151–214 (Mexico: Bajo Tierra/SISIFO Ediciones).

Vanden, Harry E. (2012), "The Landless Rural Workers' Movement and Their Waning Influence on Brazil's Workers Party government," in Gary Prevost, Carlos Oliva-Campos, and Harry Vanden (eds.), *Social Movements and Leftist Governments in Latin America: Confrontation or Cooptation?*, 34–48 (London: Zed Books).

Wright, Erik Olin (2010), *Envisioning Real Utopias* (London: Verso).

Wright, Angus and Wendy Wolford (2003), *To Inherit the Earth: The Landless Movement and the Struggle for a New Brazil* (Oakland, CA: Food First Books).

Zanini, Debora and Luciana Tatagiba (2019), "Between the Streets and Facebook: Engaged Action in the Pro-Impeachment Campaign in Brazil (2014–2016)," in Juan Pablo Ferrero, Ana Natalucci, and Luciana Tatagiba (eds.), *Socio-Political Dynamics within the Crisis of the Left: Brazil and Argentina*, 95–116 (Lanham, MD: Rowman and Littlefield).

Zibechi, Raul (2010), *Dispersing Power: Social Movements as Anti-State Forces* (Oakland, CA: AK Press).

CHAPTER 16

MOVEMENTS AND TERRITORIAL CONFLICTS IN LATIN AMERICA

BERNARDO MANÇANO FERNANDES AND
CLIFF WELCH

INTRODUCTION

To occupy is to gain access to a better future. Groups of landless families use land occupations to fight against inequality and injustice. Land occupation begins a process that transforms reality. It can change the fate of families as the conquest of land creates conditions for improving a family's quality of life through access to permanent shelter, regular work, education, and healthcare. Land occupation is a permanent process of unequal societies that varies in intensity from time to time and place to place. Although little publicized by the media, these struggles are common in most Latin American countries. The concentration of land ownership associated with intense economic and political inequality helps explain the permanence of land occupations. In Brazil and Bolivia, for example, where agrarian reform policies are either weak or insufficient, thousands of families organize themselves into social movements to claim the right to land to work, produce food, and have decent housing. Understanding how occupations occur is fundamental to knowing these popular struggles and how they create productive communities that contribute to the development of a country. Land occupations by peasants, indigenous peoples, and the descendants of enslaved peoples are not intended to access the land to sell it, but rather to form communities, create sustainable livelihoods, and promote development.

Land occupation is associated with a development model based on family and/or communal farming, where forgotten individuals and groups initiate processes of resistance on the land, forming autonomous associations to control production and markets to make them less dependent on markets controlled by large corporations (Lundstrom 2017). Occupations challenge the predominant practice of land concentration, in which an ever-smaller group of powerful individuals and businesses concentrate control over ever larger areas. Contemporary agribusiness firms have only intensified these trends. A permanent state of conflict over Latin American territories has resulted.

Classical and contemporary literature on land use in Latin America documents how occupation has always been a form of access to land (Chonchol 1994; Rubio 2018). But European colonization of Latin America is the starting point for understanding contemporary land occupations. Spain and Portugal, the region's main colonizers, appropriated indigenous territories to exploit natural wealth through conquest, serfdom, and slave labor. Large estates, called haciendas, fincas, and fazendas, were the territorial bases that started the expropriation of indigenous lands (Chonchol 1994). However, the Iberian countries did not control all of the territory they claimed and indigenous groups migrated to areas not yet dominated by the colonizers. They searched for "free lands," in places far from the coasts, in forests, and on high plains where they founded new territories to rebuild their lives. There, they also mingled increasingly with the underclass of colonizers, those who fled colonial labor and military obligations to practice family agriculture distant from authorities. In the administration of colonies such as Brazil and Cuba, enslaved Africans fled the estates and mines to create free territories, which were known as maroon societies in Spanish America and *quilombos* in Portuguese America (Deere and Royce 2009). The self-liberated *quilombolas* of Brazil and *maroons* of Spanish America searched for unsettled lands to freely raise their families. In the twentieth and twenty-first centuries, the history of these resistance struggles became powerful collective memories, inspiring contemporary indigenous populations, peasants, and slave descendants (Dixon and Caldwell in this volume). Recalling the heroes of the past, today's land occupiers carry on the fight for a dignified life (Bowen 2021).

Territorial control in Latin America was built through social relations of slavery, servitude, and the exploitation of family labor and wage labor. In the late nineteenth century, chattel slavery and indentured servitude were officially abolished in Latin America. As neocolonial states and nascent multinational corporations expanded their investments in agricultural and natural resource extraction in Latin America, they initially encouraged wage labor systems. They created commodity "republics", such as the banana republic of Honduras and the sugar cane republic of Cuba. In these areas, they consolidated their territorial acquisitions expropriating lands occupied by peasants and original peoples, who consequently became dependent on the wages paid by these companies (Burbach and Flynn 1980). In the later twentieth century, as economies diversified, labor markets expanded and global competition intensified, landlords turned to forced labor strategies again, attracting workers with false promises, sequestering their documents, locking them into dormitories at night, docking their "salaries" for room and board, leaving them perpetually indebted. Thus, modern slavery established itself in America (Bales 2000). Productive relations analogous to slavery happen when the dispossessed and underprivileged are forced to work without pay in order to have food and shelter. Situations like these motivate land occupations and public policy innovation.

This summary of modern Latin American history helps explain the regional agrarian question, including processes of territorial control through the concentration of land ownership and how these conditions stimulated the land struggle and the fight for redistributive policies, such as agrarian reform.

Regarding land occupations, Hobsbawm (1998) analyzed their revolutionary potential in Peru, Colombia, and Mexico, where civil wars helped people create non-capitalist spaces on the lands they conquered (see Welch in this volume). These experiences show how occupations transform realities and create new places. Land concentration has its genesis in primitive accumulation through the extraction and exploitation of natural resources, which produces expropriation (Veltmeyer 2005). Neoliberal government policies promote accumulation through dispossession (Rincón and Fernandes 2018). Recent studies document three decades of the land concentration/occupation dynamic in Paraguay, Argentina, Brazil, Colombia, Chile, Bolivia, and Mexico (Fernandes, Rincón, and Kretschmer 2018). While land concentration has accelerated, the occupation of public and private lands has resulted in the growth of land redistribution and the establishment of family farm settlements. Land access through struggle and the implementation of agrarian reform laws have contributed to the development of small-scale agriculture.

Social Movements and Land: The Struggle for Territory

Land occupations occur when one or more families take possession of an area, usually areas of small size, which each family can cultivate with their own labor. But social movements lead most successful land occupations (Fernandes 2005). While rare, some occupations are made by solitary families. These are typical of some indigenous peoples, such as the Guarani in Brazil, who combine occupations with calls to recuperate traditional territories—called *tekohá*—for their extended families (Mota 2018). Occupation is a territorial dispute, a contentious act that can spark violent reactions against occupying families, including physical violence, with people wounded or killed, to psychological violence, such as death threats and unsettling legal persecution. During an occupation, the families involved are vulnerable to threats and violence, which is one of the reasons they organize themselves in movements to fight for land. Increased numbers bring increased safety. Also, larger groups tend to attract mainstream media attention, which encourages others to organize similar acts, such that the spread of occupations inhibits violence against families. When organized, larger groups also offer greater agility in negotiating with landlords and governments. A single family has more difficulty making a claim to land than a group of tens, hundreds, or thousands of families. The greater the number of families the better the chances of achieving the land's distribution. Therefore, scale of organization is a fundamental factor to a victorious land struggle. Nationally, organized social movements, such as the Movimento dos Trabalhadores Rurais Sem Terra (MST) in Brazil, get better results from their struggles than organizations that operate on a local or provincial scale.

Landowners often defend violence against land occupations, claiming the right to self-defense against so-called "land invasions." The term "invasion" infuses "occupations" with negative connotations of theft and other forms of illegitimate aggression. The movements struggle to expose the hypocrisy of the term, since colonizers and extraction industries often celebrate their invasion and conquest of native peoples and their territories. Official history often commemorates the creation of colonies, countries, and large enterprises. To commemorate one form of occupation while attempting to criminalize another exposes history's biases. Land occupations by indigenous and peasants today have legitimacy, sometimes in legal terms but nearly always in moral terms, because they promise to use land for the health and wellbeing of citizens, for their subsistence and the benefit of society. In these terms, land occupations are defended as a human right that contributes to minimizing inequality. By occupying land, the landless seek to fulfill rights to individual (III) and family security (XII); property (XVII); work and just compensation (XXIII); and a family's healthy standard of living, including food, clothing, and shelter (XXV), as indicated by the enumerated articles of 1948 Universal Declaration of Human Rights.

Those who already claim property rights to conquered lands try to deny these rights to occupiers by interpreting their acts as misappropriations. Their perspective is also defended as more economic, associating land concentration with good business practices, such as economies of scale. But these arguments have only aggravated conditions of inequality, poverty, homelessness, illiteracy, environmental devastation, and chronic, widespread underemployment. The lack of public policy solutions causes families to migrate in search of sources of sustenance. Searching for land to plant is a traditional response to insecurity. But the search is complicated with so much land occupied by cattle pasture and commodity crops like sugar, soybeans, and corn. On these plantations, genetic and technological innovations have mechanized most production, greatly reducing employment and land availability. The tireless quest for land can also be stymied when family members get jobs in the city. However, increasing the number of underemployed people in the city while reducing their opportunity to make a living in the countryside only helps grow the number of landless families to the detriment of all Latin American society. In the 1970s, agricultural modernization under the green revolution inputs created myths of an uplifted peasantry and an end to hunger, but these outcomes never materialized. Modernization proved more exclusive than inclusive (Burbach and Flynn 1980).

Occupation is a form of popular struggle, making a right of the claim the dispossessed make to change their lives. Occupation is at one and the same time a form of dialogue and a pressure campaign on governments and landowners. Several scientific studies have shown that land occupations create new communities of rural development, not government policies (Carter 2015; Fernandes 2000; Hobsbawm 1998; Veltmeyer 2005). That is, governments rarely take the initiative to carry out agrarian reform. Occupations pressure governments to promote land redistribution policies. Growth in the number of occupations demonstrate popular demands for national agrarian reform policies. Land reform policies in twentieth-century Latin America mostly resulted in enhanced productivity gains for latifundia. When land was distributed to small farmers, it came with few of the necessary supports, such as road construction, water access, subsidized credit, and investment in services such as schools and health care (Fernandes, Rincón, and Kretschmer 2018).

Land occupations are an element of the agrarian question, debated and negotiated in the field of politics, mediated by governments and interested parties, and settled with agreements for the appropriation of latifundia with or without cash payments for the title holder. At the turn of the twenty-first century, the World Bank decided to concoct an economic remedy (World Bank 2003, 2004). In Latin America, in the context of 1990s neoliberal structural adjustment programs, the World Bank developed projects in three countries: Brazil, Colombia, and Guatemala (Pereira 2018). The bank argued that the state-led reform model, based on land expropriation, had failed and proposed a market-led model of agrarian reform based on land purchases. Using its vast financial resources, the bank aimed to substitute state-led agrarian reform with market-assisted land reform, claiming the switch would promote political stability by ending land occupations and territorial disputes.

The results of the World Bank's market-led land reform fell far short of projected outcomes. Land reform as a business raised the price of land. The land marketed tended to be among the worst for agricultural purposes. Market logic meant that World Bank policy favored sellers who sought to unload their least productive areas, turn a profit *and* prevent competitive family farming development. Unaware of these tendencies, many purchasing families became indebted without any possibility to produce an adequate income to pay off loans. Many were forced to abandon their farms. In the end, only 10% of agrarian reform projects arose from the World Bank initiative (Ramos Filho 2018). In fact, the World Bank's model deepened rather than resolved rural poverty. The bank abandoned the project and extricated itself from agrarian reform debate (Pereira 2018).

The World Bank's failure demonstrated that land in Latin America is not a mere commodity but a fundamental part of national territorial development policy. Democracy would seem to require the diversified use of land and its role in service to different social classes. For the land occupation movement, the democratization of land access facilitated by agrarian reform should result in democratizing access to many other societal benefits (CLOC 2020). Policies that only promote commodity monoculture for export run the risk of annihilating other strategic land uses, especially agriculture and livestock production essential to produce food for local markets. Small-scale farming and ranching based mainly on family labor is the source of most of Latin America's food security (Grain 2014). Agrarian reform nurtures this sector.

Latin America is where agricultural and mineral extraction have long been central elements of economic cycles of production. After a short hiatus in the mid-twentieth century, when import-substitution-industrialization pointed toward a different path, the primary sector returned to central stage in the twenty-first century. Dubbed "agroextractivism" (Petras and Veltmeyer 2016), we can see how the resurgence of agribusiness and mining undermine the growth of a healthy, diversified economy by contributing to the near elimination of manufacturing. The extractive characteristic of grain production and mining approximates the economic interests of landowners to national and multinational corporations. While high capital investments are required to launch such operations, long-term labor and maintenance costs are relatively low. The landowner controls the land and the agribusiness corporations control markets and technologies. In these ways, large-scale production of primary resources for export contributes greatly to land concentration. Agroextractivism intensified the agrarian question in the twenty-first century by expanding land conflicts with indigenous peoples, peasants, and *quilombolas* (see Dixon and Caldwell, Rice, Welch in this volume). About 10% of small-scale producers are associated with agroextractivism as contract farmers, producing commodities as part of integrated networks of large agribusiness enterprises.

Since land ownership involves fractions of national territory, disputes over land are territorial disputes. Agroextractivism means that transnational corporations are part and parcel of territorial disputes because they own millions of hectares of land. They also enter the picture due to their control of large-scale production projects, especially the processing of food and energy, such as the transformation of sugarcane into ethanol, soy into cattle feed, corn into high fructose syrup, and wind into electricity. Finally, their operations are linked to logistical systems like highways, railways, waterways, ports, airports, power generation, transmission lines, and internet networks. These megaprojects expropriate the lands of indigenous peoples, peasants, and *quilombolas*, increasing conflicts and resistance.

A Typology of Land Occupations in Latin America

In Brazil, the concept of "landless" farmers first appeared as a political category in the 1940s as the country struggled to recuperate economically in the wake of the Second World War. At that time, the Partido Comunista Brasileiro (PCB) mobilized the landless along with poor family farmers and rural wage workers in Ligas Camponesas (Welch 2009). The expansion of cotton plantations in response to war demands forced many peasants off the land and into sharecropping and piecework arrangements, which collapsed with the market with war's end. The PCB organized these newly unemployed landless peasants to pressure the government to provide them with conditions to earn a living, including the break-up of latifundia and establishment of agrarian reform settlements. Instead, authorities repressed the leagues, but the landless movement reappeared whenever and wherever peasants were expropriated of their land. Brazil's MST was born from this process in the 1980s (Fernandes 2000). Similar patterns produced similar movements in other Latin American countries, such as the Movimiento de los Trabajadores Rurales Sin Tierra of Bolivia (MST-B) and the Unión de los Trabajadores Rurales Sin Tierra of Argentina (UST). In Bolivia, where two-thirds of the population self-identifies as indigenous, the MST-B represents the indigenous peasant movement. The landless concept helps understand the fundamental role of land for the cultural survival of indigenous, *maroon*, and peasant societies. These societies do not exist without land. As a fraction of a nation's territory, the land they fight for is part of that territory. For this reason, societies that struggle for a fraction of territory, whether rural land or urban housing, are *socio-territorial movements*.

Socio-territorial movements, such as landless, indigenous, and homeless movements, have territory as a condition of their existence. When deprived of their territory, they tend to continue to struggle for territory. The landless concept is a translation of "*sin tierra*," which translates as "without land," which can easily be interpreted as "without territory." This understanding gives even more meaning to occupation movements. To occupy is to fight for territory as a condition of existence, as it guarantees the material conditions to obtain shelter, security, education, health, and work. Territorial acquisition is a permanent quality of the struggle to live. Occupations create diverse territories, processes better understood if organized and analyzed according to their different types.

Hobsbawm (1998) studied land occupations by peasants in Latin America in the 1960s and defined a typology of occupations using as references differences in property and conflicts. Fernandes (2005) studied land occupations in the region from the 1990s to 2000s and updated the typology (see Table 16.1). Occupations can take place on public lands, areas that belong to government agencies, on a local, regional, or national scale, such as municipalities, ministries, or departments. They can occur on private lands owned by an individual, a business, or a national or transnational corporation. All

Table 16.1 Land occupation typology

Occupation types	Movement types	Movement organizational scales	Property types	Owner types	Conflict stages
Original entry and/or Reclamation	peasant	local	private	landowners	negotiation
	indigenous	regional	public	agribusiness	expulsion
	quilombola	national	communal	government	settlement

Note: The table presents typologies for the diverse sets of relationships land occupations set in motion. It can be read in all directions: vertically, horizontally, diagonally, from bottom to top, top to bottom, left to right, or right to left.

types of property relations involve different stakeholders, implying that different forms of negotiation are necessary to resolve occupations. On public lands, negotiations involve the landless and the government. On private lands, they involve landowners, state representatives, and the landless. Communal lands are those controlled by indigenous peoples and fugitive slave descendants. In Mexico, for example, agrarian reform law in the country's revolutionary 1917 constitution established communal ownership through the creation of *ejidos*. Free trade negotiations beginning in the 1980s undermined communal rights, permitting the expropriation of many indigenous communities and territorialization by agribusiness corporations (Foley 1995).

In addition to the elements that have already been presented, Table 16.1 refers to two types of land occupation. Original entry onto the land means that families are claiming the right to occupy an area for the first time. The second involves reclaiming lost lands. This type of occupation is also called a "resumption," which means the families intend to resume the use of lost land. These recoveries or reclamations are constant and the families who claim such lands can end up fighting for years and years.

Resolving these conflicts depends on the correlation of forces among the groups involved. As mentioned, the larger the scale of organized socio-territorial movements, the greater their bargaining power. But landowners often use gunmen to intimidate such movements, causing some families to flee in fear for their lives. Meanwhile, agribusiness firms, especially multinational corporations, tend to have enough resources to influence governments to act in their favor. And governments have their own agendas and constituencies. The results of negotiations remain difficult to calculate; they change according to the pressures interested parties can and do apply.

Some countries, like Brazil, Colombia, and Paraguay, have laws that criminalize occupations and laws that determine criteria for land use, classifying properties as productive or unproductive, in order to determine if they fulfill their "social function." Social function is a classification deriving from Catholic social justice theories and used to determine if land should be redistributed. Some laws specify that land can be redistributed when landowners violate its social function by breaking environmental and labor laws. Peasant claims to occupy such land might well include plans to use agroecological production methods on lands where an agribusiness has depleted the soil, poisoned waterways, or enslaved workers. Therefore, any combination of the political, social, cultural, environmental, or economic dimensions of territory can influence the outcome of negotiations. Another important component is the support of mediating institutions, such as churches, schools, non-profit organizations, political parties, and trade unions.

Occupations do not occur spontaneously. They are planned for months or years in advance. Families organize themselves into spaces of political socialization in order to prepare strategies and tactics. The occupation creates a new space and promotes further spatialization in a continuous process of spatial production (see Davis and Davey in this volume). When families get together for the first time, they create a communicative space where they get to know each other by sharing their life stories and brainstorming ways to change their destinies. The communicative space creates common identities because most participants have similar trajectories. They may see themselves as sharecroppers, sugarcane harvesters, migrant laborers, similarly exploited, expelled, and excluded from the social norms broadcast on television. They learn how they need to organize themselves to make collective decisions in order to change their lives.

Territorial occupation offers the surest way forward. For this decision, a new space is created: an interactive space. In this space, families create strategies of popular struggle to occupy private or public property or to reclaim land that once belonged to them. In this second space of political socialization, they begin to construct a space of struggle and resistance. This space is formed when hundreds or thousands of families collaborate in an organized way, make their goals public, occupy the targeted property, and organize an encampment. Occupations can result in immediate violence. Many people have been killed and injured in Honduras, Mexico, Paraguay, and other countries. In Brazil, the Eldorado dos Carajás massacre in 1996 is just one example. On April 16, military police fired on some 1,500 families gathered in peaceful protest at a crossroads in Pará state, killing nineteen peasants and wounding dozens more. Only non-violent government intervention can guarantee secure negotiations in these conflicts. Camped on the property or in the surroundings, the families hold various demonstrations to press for dialogue with landlords. They march to the cities and protest in front of government buildings. If the outcome of the negotiations is favorable to families, they move onto the land and start a new life. If unfavorable, they initiate a new process to occupy another property (Fernandes 2000, 2005).

Examples of original entry occupations are found in the Pontal do Paranapanema, a region of São Paulo state. By the mid-nineteenth century, more than one million hectares of public land had been claimed by two landowners with falsified property titles. They created two large farms and carved them into smaller properties of various sizes to sell to other wealthy families and firms. These land grabbing practices nearly decimated the native Kaingang, Kaiowa, and Xavante peoples, who suffered violent expropriation by the invading title holders. The survivors migrated further west and continued to experience violent expropriation as livestock grazing and soy monoculture expanded westward. From the beginning of the twentieth century, peasant families began to occupy the Pontal's remaining public lands, but their tenure was constantly challenged by title holders (Leite 1998). Despite ample documentation of these landlords' fraudulent claims to the land, the state government repeatedly tried to normalize their possessions. Starting in the 1980s, however, thousands of peasant families banded together in a large landless movement and conquered more than one hundred thousand hectares, forcing the establishment of more than 100 agrarian reform settlements. Conflict is permanent, however, as fake proprietors continue to marshal economic and political power to block the legal consolidation of many settlements. In the meantime, the landless count on support from the Catholic Church and labor unions (Fernandes 2000; Welch 2009).

An example of land reclamation occupations can be found in the Chánguena community in the Costa Rican province of Puntarenas. In the late nineteenth century, the Costa Rican government granted 325,000 hectares to the British-owned Costa Rica Railway Company. Latin American governments accepted such neocolonial relationships because they rarely had enough capital to build infrastructure. Evidently, such a vast portion of Costa Rica's territory was not "empty." While building the railway, the government forced the indigenous and peasant populations to migrate away or go to work for the company. With the 1890 inauguration of the 165-kilometer railroad, export grade coffee and bananas flowed toward the Atlantic port of Matina. In Puntarenas, the United Fruit Company, a United States-based agribusiness corporation, constructed vast plantations tearing from their homes the Terrabas and Guaymíes people, as well as mestizo peasant communities. About a century later, the company stopped production and sold its assets, leaving the landless peasants without work (Barahona 1980). Uncertain they would receive back wages, many workers occupied United Fruit Company properties, including the Chánguena community. For more than twenty years the families persisted in their occupation until the Costa Rican government initiated a land regularization process in 2017.

Peasantry and Land Occupations

How come the Latin American peasantry continues to struggle for land? What prevents Latin America's agrarian question from being resolved as it seems to have been in developed countries? So long as land concentration exists, peasants will continue to organize land occupations. Developed countries have not resolved their agrarian questions, they have merely shifted the problem to developing countries in the Global South where they invade, control and exploit territories for commodity production. Neocolonial systems, like the Costa Rican case above, maintain territorial controls and bar peasant access to land through expropriation and concentration. Land occupations have served as forms of resistance to the control of territory by colonial and neocolonial systems. In colonial times, mother countries exercised nearly absolute territorial and social control through taxation and labor systems that produced for the metropolis. In the neocolonial era, debts and incentives maintained enough territorial and social controls to guarantee the production of mineral and agricultural commodities for the global market, especially the former metropolitan countries of today's developed world.

Relations between colonizers, indigenous peoples, and African-descended peoples formed the peasantry—family farmers who persevere on territory they produce, organizing themselves in communities and socio-territorial movements. Under the colonial system, indigenous and peasant populations struggled to occupy areas distant from the authority of the colonizer. In the neocolonial system, few "virgin lands" remained, so these populations occupied public lands or traded their labor for access to land on plantations. In the early twenty-first century, the international financing of commodity production in Latin America and the Caribbean accelerated. This process intensified the territorialization of soybean and beef cattle in Argentina's Pampa region, sugarcane in Brazil's southeast region, and mineral exploration in Colombia's Caldas region (Rincón and Fernandes 2018). In these places, expropriated populations organized themselves to occupy land, conquering territorial fractions called family farms in Argentina, settlements in Brazil, and peasant reserves in Colombia.

Settlements, reserves, farms, communities, and villages are some of the names used to describe the reclamation or re-territorialization of the peasantry. But between occupation and these conquests, there is another important space that can last for years. This space is called the encampment, a temporary place where families live until negotiations end. Encampments are composed of huts built by families using wood poles, black plastic, or canvas tarps. Most are divided into two parts: a kitchen and a bedroom. Depending on how long the landless remain camped, some build wooden or block houses and install appliances like a gas stove, running water, solar panels, and lights. To help with subsistence, families plant vegetable gardens and fruit trees and raise small animals, especially chickens. Family members seek employment as day laborers in nearby towns or firms, sometimes from the very industries that made them landless, such as sugar and ethanol producers. Families also claim their rights to public services, demanding local governments provide transportation to schools and access to healthcare. These are fights within the fight. Fighting for land and creating a new territory means striving for all dimensions of development. Encampments can last from months to years, depending on the progress of negotiations. Sometimes title holders win repossession of their fake property claims and the police force families to dismantle their encampment. In such cases, alternative locations are identified to start another cycle of land occupation.

Territorial control in the countryside can be complicated. Colombia exemplifies a place with decades of armed confrontation between the government, guerrilla movements, narcotraffickers, and paramilitary groups, not to mention the original occupants. For almost seven decades, civil war victimized more than eight million people and expropriated more than ten thousand families. Indigenous Colombians and peasants faced the problem of land concentration by corporations, governments, guerrillas, and paramilitary groups. Recent peace processes have made land restitution possible. In 2011, for example, laws regarding victims and land restitution provided peasants with a means to reclaim their land (Pertuz, Fernandes, and Rincón 2019; RUV 2019). But land occupations have also made it possible to create peasant land reserves, with community self-government (Garrido 2016).

Even where there is little occupation, agrarian conflict is constant. On the outskirts of Asunción, Paraguay, tens of thousands of peasants live precariously, anxious to return to the lands from which they were expelled (Palau 2007). Palau, a sociologist, called them refugees from the agro-export model, pointing out the negative impact of soybean territorialization on them. Like most Latin Americans, Paraguayans do not eat soybeans; the crops are mostly exported to China. In 2012, some fourteen of these "refugee" families occupied a small triangle of public land called Marina Kué, located next to a large soybean farm in the municipality of Curuguaty. In June, with no judicial order, more than 300 heavily armed police attacked the group with the intention of expelling them from the land. Eleven peasants were murdered before the Paraguayan president intervened to stop the action. In 2019, the encampment included a fully structured Catholic church, a school and community kitchen (Kretschmer 2019).

When a corporation buys and/or expropriates land in a contiguous or even disconnected way, it is territorializing itself through the multiplication of the fractions of territory it controls. Territorialization happens with the expansion of a firm's properties over the territory of a country. The territorialization of national projects and multinational firms defines agricultural frontiers, that swath of land being transformed from native vegetation, such as forests, to deforested pastures and fields ready for agricultural production. The advance of the agricultural frontier means environmental destruction and the expulsion of indigenous peoples, *quilombolas*, and peasants while agribusiness grows its territory. Simultaneously, these social groups resist expropriation and struggle to reclaim territories. In the twenty-first century, with international capital financing technological innovations in genetics and information science, the territorialization of agribusiness proceeds with great urgency and intensity. As the big data accumulates, firms search for ways to beat the competition by lowering costs and raising shareholders dividends. Advanced technology drives everything from land acquisition to shipping logistics. In the meantime, indigenous populations, fugitive slave descendants, and peasants stand in permanent resistance to the threat posed by agribusiness hegemony.

Indigenous People, Land Occupations, and Territory

For indigenous people, the significance of occupying land and its territorialization differs from what it means to peasants and *maroons*. Among the reasons for these differences are the worldviews of original peoples and their modes of territorial production. Ailton Krenak (2012), coordinator of the Rede Povos da Floresta, related an experience of contact with the Yanomami people in the western Brazilian Amazon thirty years ago. The Yanomamis then believed that they were the only people in the world and were curious to know how many other people there were in the world. Krenak related that there were as many as the stars in the sky and the ants in the forest. One-day, he told them, whites would reach the Yanomami. The Yanomani asked Krenak how so many people managed to feed themselves. Krenak recounted the artifices of modern food production. Then, Krenak was asked what they do with all their trash. He took away a key lesson of the indigenous way of life, a way built on balance, on believing the earth has limits and working with it to construct sustainable modes of life. Or, as the Yanomani told him, to learn to walk softly in the world. As Krenak warned, the whites came and today parts of Yanomami territory have been bulldozed, deforested, and strip-mined. The pressure continues to subject them to large-scale agroextraction, especially ranching and gold-mining, threatening their survival as a people (Survival 2020).

An awareness of the earth's limits and the need to follow a sustainable way of life is much clearer for indigenous peoples than for Western Civilization's offspring. Indigenous peoples have a multidimensional understanding of territory. They understand the land as the mother who gives life. Another important notion is to understand the body as territory. Caring for the land is caring for the body because they are inseparable. As people cannot live disconnected from their bodies, no people can live without territory; to retain land is to gain access to territory to guarantee existence. Indigenous peoples undertake occupations to recover their territories throughout Latin America. The occupation of land by indigenous people is much less destructive than the deterritorialization processes that these peoples have so long suffered. In recent years, in some countries, the number of indigenous-led occupations have increased more than land occupations by peasant movements. In Brazil, for example, from 2000 to 2016, indigenous movements jumped from eighth to third position among socio-territorial movements most engaged in occupations (Girardi et al. 2018).

Since the 1990s, the Mapuche in Chile and Argentina, the Quechua and Aymara in Bolivia, and various indigenous peoples of Ecuador and Peru have mobilized to resist the destruction of their territories and their identities (Rice in this volume). The recovery of territories and identities in several countries has strengthened indigenous peoples in the fight against agribusiness (Fernandes 2008). In response to "free trade" globalization, indigenous movements emerged with the creation of autonomous territories of resistance. In southern Mexico, where several indigenous groups formed the Ejército Zapatista de Liberación Nacional (EZLN), popular militias control self-governed territories in a fight against expropriation (Oikonomakis in this volume). In response to extreme state and paramilitary violence, indigenous peoples adopted powerful forms of resistance to defend their cultural survival.

Two key questions prevent contemporary capitalist society from recognizing indigenous territories. The first is the production model that drives corporations to exploit all resources in all territories, walking very heavily upon the earth. The second is a hardnosed refusal of capitalists to comprehend the territorial basis of indigenous production models as better suited for living in harmony with the earth. For capitalist society, territory is the basis of commodity chains that begin with the land itself; for indigenous society, territory is the space of life. More often than not, the state contributes to the vulnerability of indigenous peoples, even though it is the only institution strong enough to protect indigenous territories from the agroextraction threat.

Territorial Disputes, Development, and Occupations

The construction of agribusiness as a producer of commodities and industrially processed food defines it as a capitalist model of agricultural development. Its global territorialization has been built on the expropriation of indigenous people, peasants, and *quilombolas*. Until the 1980s, it was believed that indigenous people and peasants could be integrated into the agribusiness model. At the beginning of the twenty-first century, however, this model had failed to include these people. They have other modes of territorial production, which have been rejuvenated since then through the landless movement. The peasant model of development has taken shape as the antithesis of the agribusiness model. As agribusiness's name implies, this model uses the land for profit. For the peasant model, the land is more than a space to produce goods, it is a living space, where a way of life is reproduced.

In Latin America, land occupations are disputes over development models (Fernandes 2008). From the confrontations between the peasant and agribusiness models, occupations bring new perspectives for the creation of public policies to support the development of peasant and indigenous agriculture (Rubio 2018). Torn asunder by the North American Free Trade Agreement of 1994, Mexican society seeks to regain national control over food production; in Argentina, ceaseless agribusiness territorialization has been countered by the persistence of small-scale family farmers producing healthy food. The production of healthy food is one of the main reasons for the struggle for agrarian reform. By striving to convert all land to commodity production, hegemonic globalized agribusiness strives to gain control of diets in every corner of the earth, accustoming people to eat chemically altered, salt and sugar laden industrialized foods. In the meantime, peasant and indigenous movements struggle for food sovereignty, that is, local control over diets built on agroecologically cultivated fruits, vegetables, grains, and livestock.

The intense concentration of land in Latin America impedes the expansion of agroecology. As shown in Table 16.2, the countries with the most concentrated land

Table 16.2 Gini Index of Land Concentration in Latin America

Country	Year	Index
Brazil	1996	0.85
Chile	1997	0.91
Colombia	2001	0.80
Equator	2000	0.80
Nicaragua	2001	0.72
Panama	2001	0.52
Uruguay	2000	0.79
Venezuela	1997	0.88

Source: Food and Agricultural Organization of the United Nations, http://www.fao.org/fileadmin/templates/ess/documents/publications_studies/statistical_yearbook/FAO_statistical_yearbook_2007-2008/f05.xls.

structures are Chile, Venezuela, Brazil, Colombia, and Ecuador. The Gini Index is an instrument for measuring the degree of land concentration in each county. The closer to 1, the closer a country is to having all its land controlled by one entity.

The great challenge facing Latin American countries is the implementation of agrarian reform. For agrarian capitalism, reform is senseless since its sources of profit are exportable soybeans, corn, and beef products. Agrarian reform only makes sense if governments defend food and territorial sovereignty, reclaim land, and recognize the strategic importance of peasant and indigenous farming for agricultural development. But the concentration of land and wealth by agribusiness corporations means they exercise significant control over governments, making it difficult to imagine an easy transition to an agroecological production model. Environmental impacts, climate change, land and air pollution, water and food laced with toxic chemicals—all of these situations can alert society to the hazards of the agribusiness model. Local subcultures have begun to confront industrialized food, creating popular markets through both physical and digital social networks. Such virtual spaces are new fronts to occupy in the peasantry's continuing struggle for land and territory.

Conclusion

Understanding land occupations is not easy. Some people prefer to avoid the topic. But it will persist until the underlying structural problem—land concentration—is resolved. Only agrarian reform policies built on the development models of indigenous and peasant movements can ameliorate a question that has grown in complexity over the course of the last five centuries. Neoliberalism accelerated the territorialization of agribusiness corporations by intensifying territorial conflicts. Increasingly threatened, the people of the fields and forests create and recreate conditions to sustain their existence by occupying land, producing alternative spaces, and building territories. As they struggle to guarantee basic livelihoods, they face an onslaught of violence, punctuated by brutal massacres. The violence started during colonization and continues in the so-called postcolonial era (see Flórez-Flórez and Orlate-Orlate in this volume).

All over Latin America, a great variety of processes characterize the resistance conflicts of land occupation struggles. In countries such as Argentina, agribusiness predominates, while in countries like Bolivia and Ecuador indigenous peasants are omnipresent. Despite inequities due to land concentration, indigenous peoples, the descendants of enslaved Africans and peasants are creating a new narrative to advance the land occupation movement. It values the lives of working people, the environment, and healthy food for all social classes. These are weak points in an agribusiness narrative that celebrates machines, genetic engineering, toxic chemicals, and not-so-cheap ultra-processed foods for the masses. Occupation as a form of access to land is also a form of access to food. This is a new fact for Latin America, where the struggle for land has become a struggle for inexpensive, healthy food. The indigenous and peasant movements are, more and more, local food movements, as Holt-Gimenez (2011) has called them.

References

Bales, Kevin (2000), *Disposable People: New Slavery in the Global Economy* (Berkeley and Los Angeles: University of California Press).

Barahona, Francisco (1980), *Reforma agraria y poder político: el caso de Costa Rica: Transformación estructural* (San José: Editorial UNED).

Bowen, Merle L. (2021), *For Land and Liberty: Black Struggles in Rural Brazil* (New York: Cambridge University Press).

Burbach, Roger and Patricia Flynn (1980), *Agribusiness in the Americas* (New York: Monthly Review Press).

Carter, Miguel (ed.) (2015), *Changing Social Inequality: The Landless Rural Workers Movements and Agrarian Reform in Brazil* (Durham, NC: Duke University Press).

Chonchol, Jacques (1994), *Sistemas agrarios en América Latina: de la etapa prehispánica a la modernización conservadora* (Santiago: Fondo de Cultura Económica).

CLOC (Coordinadora Latinoamericana de Organizaciones del Campo) (2020), http://www.cloc-viacampesina.net/.

Deere, Carmen D. and Frederick S. Royce (eds.) (2009), *Rural Social Movements in Latin America: Organizing for Sustainable Livelihoods* (Gainesville: University Press of Florida).

Fernandes, Bernardo Mançano (2000), *A formação do MST no Brasil* (Petrópolis: Vozes).

Fernandes, Bernardo Mançano (2005), "The Occupation as a Form of Access to Land in Brazil: A Theoretical and Methodological Contribution," in Sam Moyo and Paris Yeros (eds.), *Reclaiming the Land*, 317–40 (London: Zed).

Fernandes, Bernardo Mançano (ed.) (2008), *Campesinato e agronegócio na América Latina* (São Paulo, Expressão Popular).

Fernandes, Bernardo Mançano, Luis F. Rincón, and Regina Kretschmer (eds.) (2018), *La actualidad de la reforma agraria en América Latina y el Caribe* (São Paulo: CLACSO/FPA).

Foley, Michael W. (1995), "Privatizing the Countryside: The Mexican Peasant Movement and Neoliberal Reform," *Latin American Perspectives* 22(1), 59–76.

Garrido, Hellen C. C. (2016), "Estrategias de territorialización campesina: Encrucijadas entre el reconocimiento político y la autonomía territorial. Estudio de caso comparado en dos zonas de reserva campesina en Colombia," PhD diss. São Paulo State University.

Girardi, Eduardo et al. (2018), *DATALUTA Report Brazil 2017* (Presidente Prudente: NERA).

Grain (2014), *Hungry for Land: Small Farmers Feed the World with Less Than a Quarter of all Farmland*, https://www.grain.org/en/article/4929-hungry-for-land-small-farmers-feed-the-world-with-less-than-a-quarter-of-all-farmland.

Hobsbawm, Eric (1998), *Uncommon People: Resistance, Rebellion, and Jazz* (New York: The New Press).

Holt-Giménez, Eric (ed.) (2011), *Food Movements Unite! Strategies to Transform our Food Systems* (Oakland, CA: Food First Books).

Krenak, Ailton (2012), "20 ideias para girar o mundo," 20 ideias, July 9, YouTube video, https://www.youtube.com/watch?v=f48HAuobNPc.

Kretschmer, Regina (2019), "Transformaciones agrarias y disputas territoriales en el Departamento San Pedro, Paraguay," PhD diss., Universidad Nacional de Córdoba, Argentina.

Leite, José. Ferreira (1998), *A ocupação do Pontal do Paranapanema* (São Paulo: HUCITEC).

Lundstrom, Markus (2017), *The Making of Resistance: Brazil's Landless Movement and Narrative Enactment* (Stockholm: Springer).

Mota, Juliana Grasieli Bueno (2018), *Territórios, multiterritorialidades e memórias dos povos Guarani e Kaiowá: Diferenças geograficas e as lutas pela descolonização na reserva indígena e nos acampamentos Tekoha, em Dourados/MS* (São Paulo: Editora Unesp).

Palau, Tomas (2007), *Los refugiados del modelo agroexportador: Impacto del monocultivo de soja en las comunidades campesinas paraguaya* (Asunción: Base IS).

Pereira, João. Márcio Mendes (2018), "Banco Mundial, política agrária neoliberal e reforma agrária assistida pelo mercado na América Latina," in Bernardo Mançano Fernandes, Luis F. Rincón, and Regina Kretschmer (eds.), *La actualidad de la reforma agraria en América Latina y el Caribe*, 233–49 (São Paulo: CLACSO/FPA).

Pertuz, Marcia A., Bernardo Mançano Fernandes, and Luis F. Rincón (2019), "Territorialidades pós-conflito: Violência no campo e luta pela terra no âmbito da política de restituição de terras e o processo de justiça transicional na Colômbia," *Terra Livre* 52(2), 179–220.

Petras, James and Henry Veltmeyer (2016), *Extractive Imperialism in the Americas: Capitalism's New Frontier* (Chicago: Haymarket).

Ramos Filho and Eraldo S. (2018), "A reforma agrária como território da política e a reforma agrária de mercado como território da economia," in Bernardo Mançano Fernandes, Luis F. Rincón, and Regina Kretschmer (eds.), *La actualidad de la reforma agraria en América Latina y el Caribe*, 41–68 (São Paulo: CLACSO/FPA).

Rincón, Luis F. and Bernardo Mançano Fernandes (2018), "Territorial Dispossession: Dynamics of Capitalist Expansion in Rural Territories in South America," *Third World Quarterly* 39(11), 2085–102.

Rubio, Blanca (2018), *América Latina em la Mirada: Las transformaciones rurales em la transición capitalista* (Mexico: Universidad Nacional Autónoma de México).

RUV (Registro Único de Victimas) (2019), *Banco de dados*, https://www.unidadvictimas.gov.co/es/registro-unico-de-victimas-ruv/37394.

Survival (2020), *The Yanomami*, https://www.survivalinternational.org/tribes/yanomami.

Veltmeyer, Henry (2005), "The Dynamics of Land Occupations in Latin America," in Sam Moyo and Paris Yeros (eds.) *Reclaiming the Land*, 285–316 (London: Zed).

Welch, Cliff (2009), "Camponeses: Brazil's Peasant Movement in Historical Perspective (1946–2004)," *Latin American Perspectives* 36(4), 126–55.

World Bank (2003), *Land Policies for Growth and Poverty Reduction* (Washington, DC: World Bank).

World Bank (2004), *Colombia: Land Policy in Transition* (Washington, DC: World Bank).

CHAPTER 17

DEMOBILIZATION PROCESSES IN LATIN AMERICA

PABLO LAPEGNA, RENATA MOTTA, AND MARITZA PAREDES

Introduction

What political and economic contexts create obstacles for the contentious collective actions of Latin American social movements? In which ways do the political economy, states, and political parties shape patterns of demobilization? When do social movements decide to refrain from mobilizing? Which political structures, strategic alliances, organizational dynamics, types and access to resources, and cultural elements combine to explain processes of demobilization? What are, in summary, the main dynamics and mechanisms of demobilization among Latin American social movements?

In this chapter, we address these interrelated questions by zooming in on contemporary South America. We focus our attention on specific geographical and historical coordinates: Argentina, Bolivia, Brazil, Ecuador, and Peru in the context of neoliberalization in the 1990s and the "commodity boom" of the 2000s. We understand demobilization as a process resulting from interactions within and between social movements, and between social movements and other actors. Demobilization is not simply the absence of mobilization, as it assumes the previous organization of contentious actions of organizations that are still active. This means that the study of demobilization requires focusing on the role of agency and strategy to better understand how social movements *refrain* from mobilizing to advance their claims and achieve their goals.

Mechanisms of Demobilization

In recent years, a relational perspective has gained prominence among social movement studies (see Halvorsen and Rossi in this volume). This perspective identifies relational mechanisms, including how social movements deal with "external" actors (like adversaries and authorities) as well as internal relations, such as the relationships between leaders and constituents, all while adapting to the political context, seeking to seize opportunities and avert threats. Demobilization is not just about refraining from protest or collaborating with state actors, it also includes the social movement's decision to avoid confrontation strategically, in order to achieve its goals through noncontentious means. In this section, we discuss six mechanisms underpinning recent demobilization trends in Latin America: performative governance, institutional recognition, social conformism, dual pressure, taking sides, and glocalization of protest.

Performative governance refers to situations in which authorities react to contention with discourses and actions that create the impression of attending to a movement's claims while actually not addressing the underlying causes of grievances. This concept repurposes Goffman's notion of impression management and applies it to political situations "in which impressions of committed governance are staged and maintained by officials, yet effective inclusion of citizenry in the decision-making process is negligible" (Futrell 1999: 495). Performative governance combines this idea with Austin's (1962) concept of "performative speech acts." Performative speech acts are those discourses that not only describe the world but also reshape it, as they may "bring about or achieve by saying something, such as convincing, persuading, [and] deterring" (Austin 1962: 108). Performative speech acts include the public discourses of charismatic presidents but also the actions of lower-rank public officials "on the ground," when they interact with movements' constituents and/or write public reports addressing their claims. In doing so, authorities can "do things with words" (as Austin famously put it) by deploying performative actions that create an effect for their audience—more concretely, the effect of creating barriers for contentious collective action, thus demobilizing movements.

Institutional recognition played a key role in demobilizing many social movements across Latin America in the context of the "pink tide." Governments created new bureaucratic bodies closely connected to movement's claims or appointed social movement leaders into those agencies and offices. This involves Latin America's "second wave of popular incorporation," that is, "the recognition of the claims of politically active poor people's movements as well as the creation or reformulation of formal and informal rules and regulations that govern their participation in politics and their connection to the polity process" (Rossi 2017: xi).[1] With a quick reading, this may be seen as "cooptation," yet we avoid this label for its patronizing and pejorative connotations (Lapegna 2014). Processes of this kind involve social movements making strategic decisions, rather than being duped. Besides the inclusion at the national level, the international diffusion of participatory institutions through United Nations Conferences (including those related to indigenous peoples), and state reforms promoting decentralization of policy competences to subnational levels, have had similar effects. Given these subnational, national, and international conditions, social movements may opt to channel their strategies into occupying institutional spaces (see Gurza Lavalle and Szwako in this volume). This can pose questions about the effectiveness of contention to achieve their goals and, alternatively, promote strategies that seek to create pressure on authorities through non-contentious means.

Social conformism emerges when public policies alleviate social problems related to poverty while not addressing the movements' particular demands. It captures the difficulties that social movements' leaders encounter to mobilize their bases against governments they perceive as representing their interests. Conditional cash transfer programs, poverty reduction, the rise in income, and expanded access to public services, for instance, curtails the grievances leading to mobilization. Considering poor peoples' pressing survival needs, when a government adopts policies reducing poverty, that government is seen as an ally and thus constraining mobilization efforts (Motta 2016).

Dual pressure happens in contexts where state-society relations have been historically shaped by patronage politics. When social movements are ensnared in the logic of clientelism, they receive pressure from constituents to solve everyday problems and obtain similar material resources as those that patronage networks distribute among their "clients" (Auyero 2000; Combes and Quirós in this volume). To address constituents' pressures "from below" and maintain their support, social movement organizations obtain resources by forging alliances with authorities. This, in turn, can create pressures "from above," when authorities distributing resources convey to movements (either openly or through the subtle expectations of reciprocity), that they should refrain from confrontation. In sum, by managing and distributing resources resulting from political alliances, movements are able to keep their organizations running at the cost of refraining from contention (Lapegna 2016).

Taking sides gains prominence during political polarization, when movements decide to collaborate or tolerate a government that they see aligned with their interests—especially when conservative forces push for its failure. In these cases, movements might even mobilize in support of the government, despite their claims being disregarded. Taking sides thus happened in the region when "disruptive forms of action were increasingly replaced by mobilizations seeking to bolster specific government initiatives, show support when these governments faced a political threat, or demonstrate strength on the eve of elections" (Hanson and Lapegna 2018: 159). Key to this process is the belief that movements' demands would be eventually addressed and the fear of losing ground if a sympathetic government is ousted. This does not necessarily mean that movements are being manipulated or that they undergo a process of oligarchization (Clemens and Minkoff 2004). As Rossi (2017: 26) explains, "There are many other strategic activities performed by social movement as part of their effort to influence political decisions that are not contentious and public".

The glocalization of protest refers to the politics of scale in social mobilization, when actors engage in transnational networks offering new opportunities, discourses, strategies, repertoires, and resources (Keck and Sikkink 1998; Rossi and von Bülow 2015). Transnational networks have an impact through providing global pressure on national states, and also have intended and unintended consequences over national and local actors at different scales (Paredes 2016). Transnational movements may rapidly deliver resources to local activists, but this may be just temporary. Scaling up of movements may occur through intense an exchange of information facilitated by media resources, but less so by the building of alliances or the creation of new and more stable frames. Transnational movements may empower segmented and localized actors by helping to partially and provisionally resolve conflicts without the need to maintain permanent organizations or build identities. In these cases, "glocalization" can have unintended and demobilizing effects through "global" convergence on one side and "local" fragmentation on the other (ibid.).

Demobilization can also be a response to threats increasing the risks or costs of contention, when authorities and opponents act to control or suppress dissidence (Tarrow 2011). Two mechanisms stand out: outright violence (physical coercion, repression, threats, murder) and the criminalization of activism (creating financial, administrative, and legal hurdles to social movement organizations and/or the imprisonment of activists). The criminalization of social movements may also be enacted discursively, through stigmatization in the media. It can also assume legal forms, through laws constraining freedom of speech, association, and manifestation, or by making social movement activity illegal (e.g., so-called "anti-terrorism" laws passed in Chile and Argentina). Governments of the "pink tide" have resorted to these mechanisms, which show the difficulties in assessing these processes of demobilization in Latin America. While these factors are very important to understand demobilization, we have excluded them from this chapter to concentrate on non-violent mechanisms.

Demobilization in South America

Brazil

Social mobilization has pushed for redemocratization and the implementation of new constitutional rights. Since the late 1980s, the Brazilian state has become more and more permeated by environmentalists, feminists, health activists, and Black movements. This long process of social mobilization culminated in the election of Luis Inácio Lula da Silva of the Partido dos Trabalhadores (PT) for president in 2003. PT grew out of unionism and grassroots work with popular movements, who had been campaigning for the party since its inception. PT won three further presidential elections, staying in power for fourteen years. We will focus on mechanisms of demobilization during the period of 2003 to 2013, taking into account that interactions between the state and social movements varied greatly according to the sector analyzed.

Social movements interpreted that there was a new structure of political opportunities: "this is our government, we have an ally in the President." In fact, there was a greater experimentalism in shaping state–society relations (Abers, Serafim, and Tatagiba 2014) and social movements found *institutional recognition* in the creation of the Ministry for Social Development, and the national secretaries for racial equality and women that, together with the secretary of human rights, had a ministerial status. Activists were designated for these high positions, the most prominent of which been Marina Silva as Minister of Environment. There was an expansion of consultative processes through national conferences, preceded by local and regional stages, in most social areas: health, social security, human rights, women's rights, and LGBT rights. Not only were social movements recognized as political subjects and able to access the polity through institutional channels but they also found direct access to the President. Lula officially received leaders from workers' unions and the Movimento dos Trabalhadores Rurais Sem Terra (MST) and came to their events, a prestige that had been reserved for elites. In some cases, such deference translated into political gains for the movements.

This was the case of workers' movements. After historical peaks in 1990 and 1996, strikes had decreased until 2002 and then started to increase again, reaching another peak in 2012. Urban trade unions from private and public sectors achieved many gains (Boito and Marcelino 2010), combining permanent dialogue and the pressure from the streets with good prospects of obtaining gains in a context of high economic growth. Trade unions received state resources to finance some of their activities. Movement leaders, however, disagree with the interpretation that they were indebted to the government and ended up with reduced autonomy, as is the case in mechanisms of *dual pressure*. According to a leader from the Central Única dos Trabalhadores (CUT), public funding "should be seen as a result from social movements' struggles and their right" (Costa and Prado 2017: 5)—emphasizing that, historically, public funding has been directed to the business sector. At the same time, some critics left the union due to CUT's proximity to the government. Therefore, pressure from below for maintaining a certain degree of autonomy from the government was also at play.

However, when Lula promised agrarian movements that he would speed up land reform or that he would not approve genetically modified crops, it functioned as *performative governance*. He did not deliver the promises, but such performances created effects in movements, including giving the government time and support. The economic growth that formed the context for expressive wage gains for urban labor movements relied on commodities exports and infra-structural projects such as dams and roads. Social movements fighting for socio-environmental justice and indigenous and ethnic rights had fewer prospects to advance in their objectives. This did not mean refraining from protest: between 1995 and 2002, 570,000 families were involved in 3,880 occupations, while between 2003 and 2010, 480,000 families were involved in 3,621 land occupations. However, if only occupied land could be expropriated for land reform purposes, what was once a disruptive protest repertoire became a form of interaction, a means for institutional recognition, losing its potential to generate collective power and more emancipatory social change. During the PT governments, the demarcation of indigenous and *quilombola* lands and families that accessed land through land reform hardly differed from the past government (see Fernandes and Welch in this volume). When Marina Silva resigned in 2008, it became evident that environmentalists were not satisfied with acts of *performative governance* and institutional recognition. Indigenous movements, *quilombolas*, and traditional communities decided to abandon negotiations over the national implementation of the ILO 169 convention in 2013, ten years after Brazil ratified it (Schumann 2018).

Despite access to the state, or even because of institutional recognition, the media and the legislative, judiciary, and subnational authorities started a process of *criminalization* of activists and social movements. "The MST was accused of stealing and diverting public money to practice 'vandalism' and 'invade' land and private property. They were accused of being 'a gang', a 'militant group taking advantage of the Lula government'" (2013 interview with MST activist, in Motta 2016: 108). The media selectively silenced murders of indigenous activists while instead covering when indigenous mobilizations culminated in violent acts (Liebgott 2008). In the whole period analyzed, *outright violence* in conflicts over land, water, and environmental resources remained amongst the highest in the world (CPT 2018).

Feminists and Black movements knew that their agenda was secondary to PT in comparison to the fight against poverty; however, it was the only party that has been open to their demands. Feminist are currently assessing their engagement with the state, which some have named state feminism (Matos and Alvarez 2018), and whether it took time and energy away from grassroots organizing that built bases for solidarity against sexist violence. Leaders from popular feminist and Black feminist movements voiced their criticism to the choice for institutionalized participation when this happens in detriment to the legitimacy of protest and other repertoires (Costa and Prado 2017). Surely, institutional recognition was a victory of the Black movement as well as the approval of the Racial Equality Statute. However, the legislative vetoed crucial issues, including a fund to finance the actions required to implement it. Some Black movements withdrew their support to the process at the time, critical of the lack of governmental commitment and support. In addition, in the period analyzed, the levels of violence and victimization of the poor, Black populations, in particular young Black men and Black women in urban centers, increased significantly (IPEA and FBSP 2018), indicating the limitations of institutional recognition of Black and feminist movements.

Social conformism contributed to demobilization. Peasant movements' leaders faced tremendous hurdles in mobilizing their bases against the national government due to the general perception that the government was good to them. Notwithstanding the clarity that it was fundamentally more important to pursue land reform and policies for peasant farming than to increase social security programs (Stédile 2013), the positive impact of social policies during PT's governments alleviated grievances conducive to mobilization. As (extreme) poverty is more concentrated among rural populations, the social policies targeted at the very poor benefited the rural poor in particular. Bringing electricity to rural areas therefore had a huge impact: "[T]hey never had electricity in their lives, and the government takes office and offers you the possibility to watch television at home, to have a refrigerator, wow, this changes the quality of peasant life a thousand times! . . . And this ensured . . . a kind of social conformism" (2012 interview with MPA, São Paulo, in Motta 2016: 109). In part, PT governments shared a conception of development remnant of the old left, defined as economic growth and full employment. Focusing on socioeconomic rights as a key to citizenship is a powerful discourse in a context in which exclusion from the formal market and from consumption has been the rule.

The dynamic of *taking sides* played out at the beginning of the PT presidency to contain pressure and criticism that would weaken the government, as well as in moments of polarization and during election cycles, when many social movements oriented their bases to re-elect PT governments and went to the streets to support the government. Far from being duped by the government, for some movement leaders "the support for legislative candidates is an important political strategy in order for social movements to widen their spaces in the state, inserting their representatives from social movements" (Costa and Prado 2017). The strategic choice to support a government that fell short of many promises is a reasonable decision when the alternative political option was at best a conservative turn. It would be a mistake to interpret that agrarian movements, for instance, were co-opted by PT. They did achieve many victories: the Family Farming Food Acquisition Program (2003), the expansion and diversification of credit, the Family Farming Law (2006), the destination of 30% of government food procurement for public schools to family farming (2009), a national policy for organic farming (2013), and a systematic increase in the budget of the Ministry for Agrarian Development (MAD) (Sauer e Mezáros 2017). When Dilma Rousseff (2011–2014, 2015–2016) was impeached in 2016, the new government of Michel Temer (2016–2018) closed the MAD and cut drastically the budget for policies supporting family farmers, while the number of assassinations of land and environmental activists peaked. In sum, social movements' decision of *taking sides* was based on the calculation that even the marginal gains of institutional recognition, access and dialogue, and some public policies, could be greatly reversed if PT was defeated. Future research agendas should include how mechanisms of demobilization at play paved the way for the increasing dominance of neo-Pentecostal churches in doing grassroots work as well as to the emergence of extreme right movements in Brazil (see Payne, Mackin in this volume).

Argentina

Demobilization trends in Argentina in the time period we cover here followed a previous phase of heightened mobilization. We zoom in on demobilization trends during the administrations of Néstor Kirchner (2003–2007) and Cristina Fernández de Kirchner (2007–2015), focusing on urban and rural actors: the unemployed or *piquetero* movement, and peasant-indigenous organizations.

During the 1990s, Argentina continued the process of democratization initiated in the 1980s while the national government applied a sweeping program of neoliberalization. As these policies negatively impacted popular sectors, social movements reacted contentiously. Unemployed organizations organized roadblocks in the northeast of the country (Barbetta and Lapegna 2001) and in company-towns severely damaged by the privation of the national oil company, Yacimientos Petrolíferos Fiscales (Auyero 2003). This tactic diffused to large cities across Argentina, particularly in Buenos Aires and Córdoba, as unemployment grew and transgressive protests became widespread (Rossi 2017; Svampa and Pereyra 2003). The typical response to roadblocks was the piecemeal distribution of unemployment subsidies (which in 2002 became a more consistent policy as Plan Jefes y Jefas de Hogar Desocupados, PJJHD; see Rossi 2017: 170). In rural areas, a number of peasant and indigenous organizations sprouted across the country, following the dismantling of the agencies regulating agrarian production and the increasing expansion of agribusiness encroaching upon indigenous-peasant territories (Briones 2005; Domínguez 2009).

In 2003, Néstor Kirchner took power in the aftermath of the profound crisis that engulfed Argentina during 2001–2002. His administration and the two periods of Fernández de Kirchner were characterized by the application of Keynesian policies, the implementation of redistributive policies and cash-transfer programs, and a revival of a "national-popular" project that tapped into the ingrained Peronism among popular classes (Lapegna 2017). The political-ideological affinities between these administrations and grassroots organizations created spaces of confluence and collaboration. Popular social movements interpreted that the "defensive" phase of the 1990s was over and that a new "offensive" moment for popular sectors was in the making. Seen from the perspective of many social movements, Kirchner "proposed them to join the 'national project,' which in practical terms meant joining state programs, the articulation of territorial work with the definition and implementation of public policies, and their withdrawal from the streets" (Natalucci 2012: 26). In the words of a prominent *piquetero* leader, "In 2003 we decided to support the government's project . . . and leave aside, let's say, the contentious politics that we had until then" (Luis D'Elía, leader of a large *piquetero* organization, quoted in Gómez and Massetti 2009: 42).

The convergence between the Kirchner administrations and popular social movements resulted in the demobilization of the latter—or, more specifically, the eschewing of contentious mobilizations targeting the national government. Many social movements were prompted to *take sides* and engaged in *supportive mobilizations*. For example, the roadblocks organized by *piqueteros* sharply diminished between 2003 and 2007 (Lapegna 2015; Rossi 2017: 89). In a context of increasing political polarization, many social movements saw the necessity of taking sides and mobilize in support of a national government that, by the mid-2000s, was perceived as an important ally.

Social movements actively and purposely decided to enter a relationship of *mutual support with the government*. In the case of the *piqueteros*, "more and more unemployed organizations concluded that a measure of co-operation with the [Kirchner] government was the most efficient way to assert at least some of their interests and values"

(Wolff 2007: 24). This "bridging with the state" involved "types of collective action that aim to (re)connect excluded segments of society with state institutions to recover—or for the first time gain—access to rights and benefits that the state has failed or cease to secure or provide" (Rossi 2017: 18). In short, this engagement created a situation of *institutional recognition* in which mobilized actors were incorporated into areas of policy, even though the causes underlying their claims were not addressed. This trade-off resulted in the demobilization of social movements or the taming of their contention. Two examples, drawn from the case of *piqueteros* and peasant-indigenous movements, illustrate these trends.

The involvement of *piqueteros* with the Kirchner administrations allowed them to gain access to agencies dealing with the issues that concerned their constituents. This involvement, however, resulted in a displacement of the more radical flanks of the *piquetero* movement and a consolidation of the organizations that were more inclined to negotiate with the government. In other words, "With increasing opportunities to get 'some ideas heard' and 'some things done,' the balance between the conflicting goals of 'global rejection' and 'concrete claims' and the corresponding strategies had to be continuously adjusted. . . . Negotiation and dialogue as well as concrete governmental offers—social plans and support for local projects and micro enterprises- could hardly be rejected" (Wolff 2007: 22–23). These dynamics of institutional recognition (which acknowledge the legitimacy of the claims but does not directly address the underlying problems) are exemplified in the words of D'Elía, a prominent *piquetero* leader. When assessing his participation in a state program to grant land titles, he expressed that this involvement,

> allowed me to accumulate information, make surveys and collect things that later are political power. . . . For us, to gather information, know the territories, get in touch with the organizations of the towns and settlements is a capital, it serves us . . . . Now, for solving things, unfortunately not. (quoted in Gómez and Massetti, 2009: 43)

The *dual pressure* that this engagement between social movements and governments create reinforces the demobilization effects of institutional recognition. Whereas institutional recognition offered leaders access to policy, the access to resources also creates a *social conformism* among rank-and-file members, who sometimes become wary of confronting powerful allies, and instead pressure leaders to obtain benefits through negotiations. In the case of *piqueteros*, the expansion of welfare benefits like the PJJHD created this type of pressure from below. "The program [PJJHD] . . . has impacted on the common sense of those who did not participate directly in these protests, tending to question the legitimacy of the claims of the organizations of unemployed workers: as the idea of plans as a universal policy gained currency, the protests stopped making sense" (Gaitán and Maneiro 2009: 152).

These mechanisms were also at play in the demobilization of peasant movements. The Kirchner administration took a step towards institutional recognition by creating a new Federal Program of Support of Sustainable Rural Development within the Instituto

Nacional de Tecnología Agropecuaria (INTA), and funding regional centers and institutes to support family agriculture (Juárez et al. 2015). An additional step was taken in 2006 when the national government offered peasant organizations the control of the Programa Social Agropecuario (PSA). The Movimiento Nacional Campesino-Indígena (MNCI) was created around 2005 to work as a sort of federation, connecting grassroots peasants and indigenous organizations that are mostly active at the provincial scale. The control of the PSA allowed the MNCI to reinforce their national scope, as the PSA had offices in twenty-one provinces and hired more than 700 agronomists, veterinarians, and other professionals working on the ground. Even though the MNCI eventually lost control of the PSA, this engagement with the Kirchner administrations put them in a difficult position of confronting a government that, for the first time, was recognizing peasants as a valid actor in agricultural policy and rural development.

These tendencies were also reflected in yet another change of policy, the transformation of the PSA into the Secretary of Rural Development and Family Farming (SRDFF) in 2008. This decision furthered the recognition of peasants and family farmers by turning a program (which had to be renewed annually) into a permanent secretary. Yet, in its implementation at the subnational scale, the SRDFF eventually created extra obstacles for contentious mobilization. The Secretary's funds were administered by provincial governments, which are typically at odds with peasant organizations—since the latter dispute the political space with the top-down political machines of governors. In summary, peasant leaders saw their demands recognized with the creation of institutional spaces, yet this resulted in that some saw negotiations as a better strategy than protest.

It is important to highlight, however, that this process of demobilization was not lost to the members of social movements (as the interview quote above suggests). In other words, it would be shortsighted to argue that these social movements were being duped into demobilizing or that they were easily manipulated. We believe that these processes cannot be equated to co-optation since, according to the classic work of Gamson (1990), a social movement is co-opted when it is recognized but does not obtain benefits—a situation that does not apply here, since social movements obtained benefits like access to information and resources. Social movements in Argentina, in short, mobilized their agency creating their own demobilization. This was a result of their members and leaders maneuvering to achieve their goals, in a constraining scenario created by a complex system of alliances.

The Andes

The last democratic wave in the Andean region in the 1990s was characterized by the emergence of indigenous movements (see Rice in this volume). In Bolivia and Ecuador, and with less favorable outcomes in Peru, indigenous mobilizations opposed economic adjustment and liberalization. Paradoxically, the arrival of Evo Morales (a *cocalero* leader of indigenous origin) to the presidency of Bolivia in 2005 represented both the zenith and the fall of this cycle of contention in the Andes. The beginning of the commodity boom in the 2000s and the expansion of the extractive frontier in the Andes transformed the dynamics of mobilization in the region starting in the new century. On the one hand, socio-environmental conflicts emerged in reaction to growing extractive industries investments (Bebbington 2011). On the other, these local conflicts coexisted with processes of demobilization. In this section, the experience of the Andean countries, mainly Peru, but also Bolivia and Ecuador, illustrates how demobilization mechanisms operate.

International Labor Organization Convention 169 (ILO 169) and indigenous prior consultation (IPC) in the Andes illustrate well the demobilizing power of institutional recognition and *performative governance*. The ratification of ILO 169 by most of the Latin American states is the result of indigenous mobilization in the previous century. ILO 169 is an international biding tool for the recognition of indigenous people rights to autonomy and over their territory. In particular, IPC aims to give indigenous power to protect their ancestral land, their culture, and their livelihoods from the spread of global capitalism. Nevertheless, the implementation of IPC had unexpected effects over the capacity of indigenous peoples to participate and mobilize, as governments have used IPC as a way to curb social conflicts.

The application of IPC has been accused of being merely procedural (Rodríguez-Garavito 2011: 292–93) or even performative in several cases (Perreault 2015: 446). ILO 169 does not specify a clear framework on what IPC implies and the outcomes of consultations are not binding on investments and policies decisions in indigenous territories. The Peruvian Law of IPC of 2011 is considered an advanced piece of legislation. However, indigenous leaders and experts denounce that consultations often take place in a process that disempowers indigenous peoples (Flemmer and Schilling-Vacaflor 2016). Problems include lack of proper representation and insufficient time and resources for people of the communities to make informed decisions, and concessions have already been granted when consultations are taking place.

The vague institutionalization of the IPC is also facilitating performative applications of participatory mechanisms. In Ecuador, light formal rules—generally executive decrees—allow IPC processes without effectively listening to the voices of communities. Requirements as "technically valid" opinions or "relevant authority" decisions, in case of opposition from the community, end up demobilizing and dividing communities over the legitimacy of the IPC process and the discourses offered by the government (Falleti and Riofranco 2014).

In the Bolivian Gran Chaco, the hydrocarbon sector has consulted communities to constraint mobilization through compensations aiming at social conformism. Very similarly to what has been observed in Colombia, in Bolivia companies are in control of consultations and the state only formalizes the process later. The problem in both countries is that companies take several prerogatives, such as limiting participation to leaders and preventing them from counting on the support of regional or national indigenous organizations or professional advice (Urteaga-Crovetto 2018: 11). Professional advisers including translators, lawyers, and engineers are important to reduce the vulnerability of these communities to harmful state or company practices (Eichler 2018), which often deteriorate the cohesion within communities and the organizational resources of indigenous organizations to mobilize.

New participatory institutions that assess the environmental impact of mega investment projects follow the same path as the IPC. The limited capacity and will of governments and private actors to discuss environmental processes in an intercultural manner, instead of only with technical and abstract language, deteriorates the possibilities of substantive participation and disempowers communities (Li 2015).

These processes of demobilization do not imply the absence of protest. Demobilization can coexist with mobilization at different scales (Paredes 2017). During the last cycle of high commodity prices (2004–2014), large international companies have faced strong opposition from communities in the Andes. To oppose large mining investments, a growing number of local communities took advantage of transnational alliances in order to work at different scales, disseminate, expand, re-configure, and transnationalize their protests (von Bülow in this volume). The most striking feature of this shift to the global scale is its unintended consequences on other scales of mobilization. As Paredes (2016) shows in her analysis of the *glocalization* of mining conflicts in Peru, this process brought about the emergence of many mobilized but fragmented local movements. Cases of local mobilization, such as Tambogrande, Espinar, Majaz, Tía María, or Conga have transnationalized their campaigns with the support of global networks of activism, but at the same time, these communities have remained limited to the local level, without converging in regional or national social movements with common demands and platforms within their countries (ibid.).

Furthermore, both Peru and Bolivia approved policies of fiscal decentralization that anticipated the super cycle of extractives between the years of 2004–2014. In Peru, this fiscal transference to local governments allocated important public resources to different levels of subnational governments, from where natural resources are extracted (Dargent et al 2017). Nonetheless, the weakness of political actors and a legacy of weak state territorial institutions in Peru explain the disappointment in the use of these resources (Ponce and McClintock 2014). This new policy produced two features of demobilization. On the one hand, the national government shifted the responsibility for the poor results to the lower levels of the state (i.e., regions, provinces, and districts) (ibid.). As a consequence, nationwide and even region-level mobilizations regarding economic and environmental national policy diminished (Dargent et al. 2017). On the other hand, local negotiation spaces have promoted higher *social conformism* of local poor actors, who had been promised public and private investments in local infrastructure and short-term jobs. However, these investments often have not brought development to local communities but have tempered mobilization.

High fiscal rents from the booming prices of commodities have also helped governments in Ecuador, Bolivia, and Peru (during the government of Ollanta Humala, 2011–2016) to tame movements through *social conformism* and *dual pressure*. In Ecuador and Bolivia, indigenous mobilizations of the last decade stopped the advancement of neoliberalism and generated the propitious scenario for the emergence of leftwing governments in both countries. Once in power, both Evo Morales in

Bolivia (2006–2009, 2009–2014, 2014–2019) and Rafael Correa in Ecuador (2007–2009, 2009–2013) have used tax revenues from the extractivist model to fund specific social programs, including pensions and conditional cash transfers.

In Bolivia, the Renta Dignidad (the pension scheme) is financed by around 27% of the Direct Tax on Oil and Gas (Anria and Niedzwiecki 2016). In Ecuador, the Correa government established a direct connection with grassroots organizations in rural and urban areas, providing them with public infrastructure goods, educational facilities, hospitals, and other benefits (Tuaza 2011). *Social conformism* in the mid-level member organizations benefiting from these programs has complicated the work of leaders when mobilizing their organizations. Moreover, in Bolivia, the governments have turned these organizations into their grassroots bases of socio-political support.

In addition, leaders have faced another pressure next to the organizing of their members—*dual pressure*. For instance, in the urban areas of El Alto in Bolivia, the government of Evo Morales has used its access to generous fiscal funds from exports of natural resources to co-op and infiltrate grassroots organizations such as the Federación de Juntas vecinales de la Paz (FEJUVE) and the Central Obrera Regional (COR). The government has offered leaders of these organizations job posts in the state in exchange for the mobilization of large numbers of voters and through that control a highly organized political area in Bolivia (Anria 2013).

Bolivia is also a good example of how the mechanism of *taking sides* worked for the government to empower some social organizations against others. As affected communities protested to stop a road building project planned to go through the TIPNIS, the government used its ties with the *cocalero* organizations in the area to boycott the protest and to undermine the process of dialogue and consultation (McNeish 2013). The government fueled political polarization, accusing oppositional leaders from the TIPNIS of destabilizing the country and destroying the government's campaign for a "process of change" (ibid.: 226). The *cocaleros*, a non-state actor, *took sides* with the government against TIPNIS indigenous groups, unleashing violence against communities opposing the building of the TIPNIS highway and creating divisions between indigenous organizations formerly united in mobilization for their rights.

In Bolivia, demobilization did not mean the deactivation of urban or rural social organizations (Anria 2013), nor has in Peru the glocalization of (fragmented) mining protest meant the absence of significant local conflict (Paredes 2016). As we have mentioned before, demobilization is not the absence of mobilization. It expresses the contexts in which some mechanisms can reduce the opportunities of people to protest and achieve their goals.

Conclusion

In this chapter, we inquired into the mechanisms explaining demobilization processes in contemporary Latin America. Three political and economic structural conditions impinged on social movements: an export-led growth model based on commodities, policies for poverty reduction, and (in some countries) the rise of left-wing governments incorporating popular sectors and their movements. Redistribution policies and the participation of social movements in the government curtailed grievances and created obstacles for confronting governments that had turned into allies. We conceptualized demobilization as a relational process involving strategic decisions shaped by interactions within and between social movements, and between these and other actors. We identified six non-violent mechanisms promoting the demobilization of South American social movements: performative governance, institutional recognition, social conformism, dual pressure, taking sides, and glocalization of protest, and applied them to Argentina, Bolivia, Brazil, Peru, and Ecuador.

Institutional recognition meant that social movements saw no need to protest in order to make demands to the state, which can have demobilizing consequences. Along similar lines, *performative governance* discouraged movements to engage in contention, as authorities signaled that movements' demands were being taken care of (even though the underlying causes were not addressed). In this context, some movements decided "to achieve access to resources and political gains through non-contentious involvement in the public policy process and the political distribution of posts within the [governing] coalition" (Rossi 2017: 208). Movements' issues were transformed from "police matters" to "political matters," something more clearly seen in Argentina and Brazil. In other places, like the Andean region, protest turned into "policy matters," but the poor implementation of these policies and the few state's efforts and resources directed at them produced demobilization. The redistribution of resources by leftist governments (e.g., Argentina, Bolivia, Brazil) also nurtured the mechanism of *dual pressure*.

The mechanisms that shaped the distribution of resources also fed *social conformism*, and their combination resulted in demobilization or the creation of obstacles for contention. Moreover, in the context of extractivism, the redistribution of rents to lower level of governments and the access to money from private actors looking for communities' consent to carry out investments has also diminished the scope of protest and their character, making actors more prompt to short term and local negotiations. On a parallel but connected process, movements were prompted to *take sides* in a context of political polarization. They considered that necessary to maintain or expand the access to resources they already had, in order to support the political actors that made those gains possible.

Note

1. The first incorporation took place during nationalist governments like Juan Domingo Perón in Argentina and Getúlio Vargas in Brazil.

References

Abers, Rebecca, Lizandra Serafim, and Luciana Tatagiba (2014), "Repertórios de interação estado-sociedade em um estado heterogêneo: A experiência na Era Lula," *Dados* 57(2), 325–57.

Anria, Santiago (2013), "Social Movements, Party Organization, and Populism: Insights from the Bolivian MAS," *Latin American Politics and Society* 55(3), 19–46.
Anria, Santiago and Sara Niedzwiecki (2016), "Social Movements and Social Policy: The Bolivian Renta Dignidad," *Studies in Comparative International Development* 51(3), 308–27.
Austin, John Langshaw (1962), *How To Do Things With Words* (Oxford: Clarendon Press).
Auyero, Javier (2000), *Poor People's Politics: Peronist Survival Networks and the Legacy of Evita* (Durham, NC: Duke University Press).
Auyero, Javier (2003), *Contentious Lives: Two Argentine Women, Two Protests, and the Quest for Recognition* (Durham, NC: Duke University Press).
Barbetta, Pablo and Pablo Lapegna (2001), "Cuando la protesta toma forma: los cortes de ruta en el Norte salteño," in Norma Giarracca (ed.), *La protesta social en la Argentina: Transformaciones económicas y crisis social en el interior del país*, 231–57 (Buenos Aires: Alianza).
Bebbington, Anthony (2011), *Social Conflict, Economic Development and the Extractive Industry: Evidence from South America* (London: Routledge).
Boito Jr., Armando and Paula Marcelino (2010), "O sindicalismo deixou a crise para trás? Um novo ciclo de greves na década de 2000," *Caderno CRH* 23(59), 323–38.
Briones, Claudia (ed.) (2005), *Cartografías argentinas: Políticas indigenistas y formaciones provinciales de alteridad* (Buenos Aires: Antropofagia).
Clemens, Elisabeth S. and Debra C. Minkoff (2004), "Beyond the Iron Law: Rethinking the Place of Organizations in Social Movement Research," in David A. Snow, Sarah A. Soule, and Hanspeter Kriesi (eds.), *The Blackwell Companion to Social Movements*, 155–70 (Malden: Blackwell).
Costa, Frederico Alves and Marco Aurélio Máximo Prado (2017), "Artimanhas da hegemonia: obstáculos à radicalização da democracia no Brasil," *Psicologia & Sociedade* 29, e152680.
CPT (2018). *Caderno Conflitos*, https://www.cptnacional.org.br/index.php/downloads/category/3-cadernoconflitos.
Dargent, Eduardo, José Carlos Orihuela, Maritza Paredes, and Maria Eugenia Ulfe (eds.) (2017), *Resource Booms and Institutional Pathways: The Case of the Extractive Industry in Peru* (New York: Palgrave-Macmillan).
Domínguez, Diego (2009), "La lucha por la tierra en Argentina en los albores del siglo XXI: La recreación del campesinado y de los pueblos originarios," PhD diss., Universidad de Buenos Aires.
Eichler, Jessika (2018), "Indigenous Intermediaries in Prior Consultation Processes: Bridge Builders or Silenced Voices?," *The Journal of Latin American and Caribbean Anthropology* 23, 560–78.
Falleti, Tulia and Thea Riofrancos (2014), "New Participatory Institutions in Latin America: A Comparative Analysis of Prior Consultation in Bolivia and Ecuador," paper presented at FLACSO-International Studies Association Conference, July, 24–26, Buenos Aires.
Flemmer, Riccarda and Almut Schilling-Vacaflor (2016), "Unfulfilled Promises of the Consultation Approach: The Limits to Effective Indigenous Participation in Bolivia's and Peru's Extractive Industries," *Third World Quarterly* 37(1), 172–88.
Futrell, Robert (1999), "Performative Governance: Impression Management, Teamwork, and Conflict Containment in City Commission Proceedings," *Journal of Contemporary Ethnography* 27(4), 494–529.
Gaitán, Flavio A. and María Maneiro (2009), "El plan jefes y jefas de hogar desocupados: Sus efectos en la protesta de los movimientos de trabajadores desocupados," *Barbarói* 30, 139–58.
Gamson, William (1990), *The Strategy of Social Protest* (Belmont, CA: Wadsworth).

Gómez, Marcelo and Astor Massetti (2009), *Los movimientos sociales dicen: Conversaciones con dirigentes piqueteros* (Buenos Aires: Nueva Trilce).

Hanson, Rebecca and Pablo Lapegna (2018), "Popular Participation and Governance in the Kirchners' Argentina and Chávez's Venezuela: Recognition, Incorporation and Supportive Mobilisation," *Journal of Latin American Studies* 50(1), 153–82.

IPEA and Forúm Brasileiro de Seguranca Pública (FBSP) (2018), *Atlas da Violência*, http://www.ipea.gov.br/portal/images/stories/PDFs/relatorio_institucional/180604_atlas_da_violencia_2018.pdf.

Juárez, Paula, Marie Gisclard, Frédéric Goulet, Roberto Cittadini, Julio Elverdin, M. Merecedes Patrouilleau, Christophe Albaladejo, and Edgardo González (2015), "Argentina: políticas de agricultura familiar y desarrollo rural," in Eric Sabourin, Mario Samper, and Octavio Sotomayor (eds.), *Políticas públicas y agriculturas familiares en América Latina y el Caribe*, 43–75 (San José: IICA).

Keck, Margaret E. and Kathryn Sikkink (1998), *Activists Beyond Borders: Advocacy Networks in International Politics* (Ithaca, NY: Cornell University Press).

Lapegna, Pablo (2014), "The Problem with 'Cooptation,'" *States, Power, and Societies* 20(1), 7–9.

Lapegna, Pablo (2015), "Popular Demobilization, Agribusiness Mobilization, and the Agrarian Boom in Post-Neoliberal Argentina," *Journal of World-Systems Research* 21(1), 69–87.

Lapegna, Pablo (2016), *Soybeans and Power: Genetically Modified Crops, Environmental Politics, and Social Movements in Argentina* (New York: Oxford University Press).

Lapegna, Pablo (2017), "The Political Economy of the Agro-Export Boom Under the Kirchners: Hegemony and Passive Revolution in Argentina," *Journal of Agrarian Change* 17(2), 313–29.

Li, Fabiana (2015), *Unearthing Conflict: Corporate Mining, Activism, and Expertise in Peru* (Durham, NC: Duke University Press).

Liebgott, Roberto Antonio (2008), "O governo Lula e as notícias da mídia sobre os Povos Indígenas," *Conselho Indigenista Missionário*, May 26, https://cimi.org.br/2008/05/27450/.

Matos, Marlise and Sonia Alvarez (eds.) (2018), *O Feminismo estatal participativo brasileiro* (Porto Alegre: Editora Zouk).

McNeish, John-Andrew (2013), "Extraction, Protest and Indigeneity in Bolivia: The TIPNIS Effect," *Latin American and Caribbean Ethnic Studies* 8(2), 221–42.

Motta, Renata (2016), *Social Mobilization, Global Capitalism and Struggles over Food: A Comparative Study of Social Movements* (London: Routledge).

Natalucci, Ana (2012), "Los dilemas políticos de los movimientos sociales: El caso de las organizaciones kirchneristas (2001–2010)," *Documentos de trabajo del Instituto Interuniversitario de Iberoamérica* (September).

Paredes, Maritza (2016), "The Globalization of Mining Conflict: Cases from Peru," *Extractive Industries and Society* 3(4), 1046–57.

Paredes, Maritza (2017), "Conflictos mineros en el Perú: entre la protesta y la negociación," *Debates en Sociología* 45, 5–32.

Perreault, Tom (2015), "Performing Participation: Mining, Power, and the Limits of Public Consultation in Bolivia," *Journal of Latin American and Caribbean Anthropology* 20, 433–51.

Ponce, Aldo F. and Cynthia McClintock (2014), "The Explosive Combination of Inefficient Local Bureaucracies and Mining Production: Evidence from Localized Societal Protests in Peru," *Latin American Politics and Society* 56(3), 118–40.

Rodríguez-Garavito, César (2011), "Ethnicity.gov: Global Governance, Indigenous Peoples, and the Right to Prior Consultation in Social Minefields," *Indiana Journal of Global Legal Studies* 18(1), 263–305.

Rossi, Federico M. (2017), *The Poor's Struggle for Political Incorporation: The Piquetero Movement in Argentina* (New York: Cambridge University Press).

Rossi, Federico M. and Marisa von Bülow (eds.) (2015), *Social Movements Dynamics: New Perspectives on Theory and Research from Latin America* (Farnham: Ashgate).

Sauer, Sérgio and George Mészaros (2017), "The Political Economy of Land Struggle in Brazil under Workers' Party governments," *Journal of Agrarian Change* 17(2), 397–414.

Schumann, Charlotte (2018), "Competing Meanings: Negotiating Prior Consultation in Brazil," *The Journal of Latin American and Caribbean Anthropology* 23(3), 541–59.

Stédile, João Pedro (2013), "Mensagem a Dilma: a reforma agrária possível," *Carta Capital*, January 7, https://outraspalavras.net/outrasmidias/o-dilema-da-reforma-agraria-no-brasil-do-agronegocio/.

Svampa, Maristella and Sebastián Pereyra (2003), *Entre la ruta y el barrio: La experiencia de las organizaciones piqueteras* (Buenos Aires: Biblos).

Tarrow, Sidney (2011), *Power in Movement: Social Movements and Contentious Politics* (Cambridge: Cambridge University Press).

Tuaza, Luis Alberto (2011), "La relación del gobierno de Rafael Correa y las bases indígenas: Políticas públicas en el medio rural," *Ecuador Debate* 83, 127–50.

Urteaga-Crovetto, Patricia (2018), "Implementation of the Right to Prior Consultation in the Andean Countries. A Comparative Perspective," *The Journal of Legal Pluralism and Unofficial Law* 50(1), 7–30.

Wolff, Jonas (2007), "(De-)Mobilising the Marginalised: A Comparison of the Argentine Piqueteros and Ecuador's Indigenous Movement," *Journal of Latin American Studies* 39(1), 1–29.

PART III
MAIN SOCIAL MOVEMENTS

CHAPTER 18

TRANSFORMATIONS OF WORKERS' MOBILIZATION IN LATIN AMERICA

FRANKLIN RAMÍREZ GALLEGOS AND
SOLEDAD STOESSEL

Introduction

Mutual aid societies, syndicates of artisans and miners at the end of the nineteenth century; manufacturing workers during the import substitution cycle; peasant and indigenous workers proletarianized through the capitalist modernization of agriculture; organizations of the unemployed, which were informal and outsourced as a result of the structural adjustment of the 1980s; and workers in the popular economy, in worker-run factories (a broadened concept of "work") as responses to neoliberal globalization in the twenty-first century, are all categories of the heterogeneous paths that have shaped the "worker question" in Latin America from the end of the nineteenth century.

This heterogeneity has already been highlighted by seminal works such as those by Spalding (1977) and Bergquist (1986). These studies warned against a certain limitation in the analyses of the Latin American workers' movement that tended to confine it to the dichotomy between urban proletariat and rural workers, turning the former into the genuine substratum of the movement. Thus, their mobilization and their social reproduction worlds were seen as one and the same, while the contribution of workers to national development remained hidden. At the same time, this development was understood to be an extension of the logic of global capitalism which, without any further mediation, explained the vicissitudes of the workers' struggle (see Rossi in this volume). In the face of such emphases, these authors proposed a reading focused on the agency of the workers, taking into account the national environments of economic organization and political conflict.

This chapter takes a similar view and reconstructs the *transformations* of workers mobilization, considering the interactions between the means of capitalist domination and the evolution of labor conflicts around better social conditions, rights and political influence. The analysis studies four periods: 1890–1929: the emergence of workers organizations; 1930–1960: the strengthening of labor unions and grassroots incorporation; 1970–1990: neoliberalism and the organizational breakdown; and 1999–2017: the return of the state and the revitalization of labor unions. Beyond the regimes of accumulation, the chapter stresses the dynamics of the mobilization and demobilization of workers based on their forms of organization, repertoires of state-society interaction and ideological frameworks. This outlook enables us to follow the main lines of conflict in each period by contrasting more and less industrialized countries in the region.

Workers' Emergence (1890–1929)

Between the end of the nineteenth century and the early decades of the twentieth, two processes marked out the origins of worker mobilization in Latin America: (1) the passage from mutual aid organizations to collective groupings concerned with the struggle for better working conditions and the purchase of labor power; and (2) the establishment of workers' movements which then took the form of a wave of powerful events of protest that were harshly put down.

The mutualist societies (Argentina, Colombia, Costa Rica, Ecuador, Nicaragua) took the lead in expanding the organization of artisans, textile workers, peasants, miners (saltpeter in Chile), railway workers, and stevedores (Argentina, Brazil and Mexico), from the mid-nineteenth century (Hall and Spalding 1991). Trade corporations (Brazil), relief organizations (Bolivia and from 1825 in Brazil), or charities also fought for the protection of basic aspects of workers' economic reproduction. Beyond such a commitment, however, the defense of professional trade associations and, in some cases the improvement of working conditions, were included among their non-specified objectives. Exhausting working days (up to sixteen hours, seven days a week), low salaries and a lack of rights—typical conditions at the start of industrialization processes—fed the spiral of extremely strong protests in Argentina, Chile, and Mexico before the 1900s. In 1890, Chilean miners and urban workers led the first general strike in Latin America. This strike confirmed the transition from laborer to proletariat and gave rise to the modern Chilean workers' movement (Salazar and Pinto 1999). A similar protest in the Andean countries and in Central America would take a few more years before getting off the ground.

Workers' emergence towards the end of the nineteenth century went hand-in-hand with the development of exporting economies that boosted the growth of the workforce in different sectors of the economy. In particular were those sectors connected to the export of raw materials, such as mining in Bolivia, Chile, Mexico, and Peru; agricultural production in Argentina and Uruguay; coffee in Brazil, Central America, and

Colombia; and oil in Venezuela (Bergquist 1986). The exporting dynamism increased state resources, created an incipient industry, and improved the demand for an urban workforce. Thus, the conditions for workers' organization changed dramatically but at different rates according to each sub-region.

In Central America the agricultural and mono-exporting structure of the economy meant that the base of urban workers was insignificant, and the artisan and rural sector predominated. The intervention of the United States (in Nicaragua between 1909 and 1933 and in Panama between 1906 and 1928) and the alliance of North American capital with conservative oligarchs were, however, obstacles to the configuration of an influential movement as happened in the Southern Cone. Nevertheless, the workers succeeded in organizing themselves in the 1930s, in part thanks to regional solidarity—especially with Mexican support—leading to the creation of the Confederación Obrera Centroamericana in 1921.

The Mexican Revolution in 1910, led by the peasantry and radicalized working-class sectors, was a political-ideological cornerstone for the Latin American labor movement (see Martí i Puig and Álvarez in this volume). The 1917 Constitution was the first in the world to recognize social rights (work, education, and land) and the working class as a "defined group." It also identified the relationship between capital and labor as a fundamental link that required regulation. Thus, the liberal state was entering into a period of crisis just as the social state was emerging (De la Garza and Melgoza 1996: 132).

Beyond Mexico, the oligarchic state, which accompanied the end-of-century exporting boom, reproduced a strongly liberal political environment with regard to the regulation of the labor market, but at the same time it was interventionist and repressive when controlling mobilizations. In fact, until the beginning of the 1940s the elites did not consider workers' organizations as an actor for negotiations. The demands of the workers, who were increasingly branded as communists, were rejected by the employers and governments allied to their interests. In Chile—Valparaiso (1903), Santiago (1905), Santa María de Iquique (1907)—and in Mexico—Veracruz (1907)—workers were massacred in the hundreds and thousands. A decade later in Argentina (1919 and 1921) and in Ecuador (1922), such bloodbaths were repeated. The protests were provoked by the employers' refusal to negotiate relatively modest demands (reduction in daily working hours, improved wages, and regulation of child labor, among others). This incited worker belligerence, but the official deployment of troops dramatically put an end to the riots.

In addition to repression, the mechanisms used to contain unrest included the institutional framework—moralizing campaigns promoted by the Church and the approval of the emerging labor legislation. Argentina and Colombia were pioneers in legislating on making Sunday a rest day (1905) while Chile (1906), Ecuador (1916), and Costa Rica (1920) approved the eight-hour working day. At the same time, the Department of Labor was created in Mexico in 1911 while in Ecuador the Constitution of 1928 gave parliamentary seats to workers' representatives. The employers usually opposed such legislation even if the regulations included clauses to facilitate capital accumulation (Hall and Spalding 1991).

The main repertoires of dispute were strikes, boycotts, and sabotage (see Wada in this volume). The recourse to "direct action" became more intense in places where anarchism was more robust. Towards the beginning of the 1930s, strikes became widespread as a means of struggle across the whole region. Repression against these actions contributed to the weakening of anarchism (De la Garza and Melgoza 1996) and to the increased influx of ideologies like socialism and communism, which had barely been present, except in Argentina, until the 1920s. There is frequent allusion to these "foreign ideologies" in the origins of the movement, as well as the importance of left-wing parties in its organizational development (Hall and Spalding 1991). Bergquist (1986) has noted, however, that despite the low level of European immigration in countries like Chile or Mexico, powerful workers' organizations did develop.

Both immigration (especially from Europe in the Southern Cone) and the hiring of foreign workers (North Americans in Central America and Venezuela) put a strain on the world of work: in the 1930s and 1940s conflicts emerged in Venezuela between national and foreign oil workers, with the latter being viewed as better qualified. The same thing happened in Panama around banana plantations and the construction of the Canal. Transnational companies preferred to hire foreigners, claiming that the Panamanians were useless and unqualified (Bourgois 1994). Racial discrimination both in Central America and in the Andean region divided the working class. However, this issue did not form part of the workers' agenda at the beginning of the twentieth century. The exception was in the Andean countries.

In fact, towards the end of the 1920s debates were already taking place within the Communist International on the connections between the ethnic question and class struggle in countries with a well-defined indigenous presence (Becker 2002). The Peruvian intellectual, José Carlos Mariátegui (1990) suggested that the proletariat in his country and the main revolutionary subject is none other than the indigenous masses. In view of the fact that their fundamental problem has been land ownership (which was expropriated in colonial times), the indigenous question required a class—rather than a racial—perspective that supported agrarian reform and the self-organization of the masses. Socialism—and not a democratic-bourgeois revolution that opened the way for capitalism—was therefore the way to escape from the feudal system, provided that the indigenous communal tradition prevailed as the basis of a collectivist society advocated by Marxism (see Webber in this volume).

Straddling the resistance of rural workers and an indigenous revolt, the uprising in El Salvador in 1932 also shows the complex inter-relationship between ethnicity and class. The rebellion was a result of the pressures in coffee production on land inhabited by the poor peasant workers, who were mostly indigenous and who challenged difficulties over land tenure, labor exploitation, local political abuses, and racism, amidst the fall in coffee prices on account of the international crisis of 1929. Crushed by the slaughter of more than 20,000 people, the uprising—interpreted for a long time through "communist causality"—was resolved according to certain analyses with an effective ethnocide (Lindo-Fuentes et al. 2010). The eruption of workers in the rest of the sub-region was connected to exploitation in banana enclaves: between 1919 and 1932 several strikes occurred on the plantations in Costa Rica and Guatemala.

Meanwhile in the Southern Cone the "social question" was configured around workers' demands regarding better working conditions, wages, and contracts. The most powerful workers at that time were those in the docks, on streetcars, on the railroad, and in the agricultural industries. The Cry (*El Grito*) of Alcorta, the first rebellion in rural Argentina (1912), was about the landowners' exploitation of the small farmers (the *chacareros*) of the Pampas. The small farmers obtained some victories while suffering the assassination of anarchist leaders. In Uruguay, the newly formed Federación Obrera Regional Uruguaya headed the First General Strike of 1911 led by the port workers demanding better working conditions resulting in the employers giving in. The demonstration effect of the European movement, and the Russian and Mexican revolutions, had an influence on the shape of this area of labor dispute.

DEVELOPMENTALISM, HETERONOMY, AND REVOLUTION (1930–1960)

As an effect of the global crisis of 1929 and the stagnation of traditional exports—and later during World War II, in response to the reduction in the import of manufactured goods—a large part of the region channeled its industrialization strategies into import substitution and the creation of national markets. Latin America experienced a cycle of economic development and the growth of the industrial working class with strong state intervention in the processes of capital accumulation.

Such a scenario meant the decline—not without resistance—of the traditional landowning oligarchies (agricultural or mining exporters), who saw the material bases of their political power deteriorate. Hence the expansion of opportunities for the rise in subaltern movements of a nationalist, popular, and worker outlook. As a condition for the corporate interchange with the state, the unions started to group together in larger organizations (fronts and confederations). In 1936 the Confederación de Trabajadores de Chile (CUT) emerged, in which anarcho-syndicalists, socialists, and communists came together. The CUT represented workers' drive into the state, receiving full rights in the Council for the Production of Development. In Argentina the Confederación General del Trabajo (CGT) was formed in 1930; it consisted of unions by activity or branch, a novelty with regard to representation by trade that was more common at that time. The rise of Peronism (1945) granted to the CGT the monopoly of workers' representation and incorporated it into the Peronist political bloc, resulting in the bureaucratization of the union leadership (James 1990). The Confederación de Trabajadores de Colombia (CTC) emerged in 1935 with state recognition restricted to the need of liberal governments to curb revolutionary activism and its threats to landowners' interests.

Workers' activism tended to coincide with a new urban bourgeoisie whose political project rested on industry and services. At the same time, the commitment to industrialization led to rapid urbanization (rural migration to the cities) and changed the social composition, the ideological background and the interests of workers (Murmis and Portantiero 1971; Weffort 1974). Thus, while the growing working class demanded a greater income distribution, the emerging employer class pressed for protectionist policies and the expansion of the internal market. And the middle classes and civil bureaucracy secured improvements in consumer goods and public education. For their part, the military pressed for a national armaments industry and the sovereign control of natural resources (Stavenhagen and Zapata 1974). Such a list of interests favored the strengthening of the state and the stimulus of development processes with greater autonomy from central countries. Power blocks were formed which were opposed to the oligarchical regimes and came to alter the political landscape in the long term: the governments of Lázaro Cardenas (Mexico), Getúlio Vargas (Brazil), and Juan Domingo Perón (Argentina) expressed in their different ways the distinctiveness of the "nationalist industrialist populist" constellations (Ianni 1975), which were committed to the expansion and democratization of Latin American capitalism.

However, the rise of these industrialist blocs did not always happen. During the 1930s in Peru, the organization of workers was led by the Alianza Popular Revolucionaria Americana (APRA) party, with a nationalist and anti-imperialist outlook and stuck in a struggle with communism. The penetration of APRA among the grassroots repeatedly caused a reaction from the elites. The dictatorship of 1933–1939 cracked down on the APRA rank and file through the support of mutual societies and social legislation measures. The struggle on the left favored this line of action, although both forces were committed to the anti-fascist struggle.

In fact, with the emergence in 1938 of the first combined union confederation in Latin America—the Confederación de Trabajadores de América Latina (CTAL)[1]— a considerable part of the workers' movement adopted a "front" strategy as part of an industrialists-workers pact (as stipulated by the Seventh Congress of the Comintern) in support of the anti-fascist struggle and the avoidance of a possible attack by the Axis Powers against the Soviet Union. For Godio (1985), multi-class unity strengthened the local bourgeoisie and weakened revolutionary unionism.

Rather than just a basic problem of class unification, the inclusion, institutionalization and state legalization of workers' mobilization—to control or strengthen it—in exchange for political support, also limited grassroots incorporation throughout institutional channels (Collier and Collier 1991). Collier and Collier (ibid.: 751) identified two kinds of incorporation: (1) Chile and Brazil where grassroots sectors were incorporated through the new liberal-social state to avoid the radicalization of the workers' movement with no active role of political parties; and (2) incorporation via political parties or multi-class movements that promoted the mobilization of workers under their auspices: Argentina and Peru (labor populism), Uruguay and Colombia (traditional party), Mexico and Venezuela (radical populism). Politicized movements were set up in these countries with strong party links. This did not happen in Chile and Brazil in the early stages of the workers' movement (1920–1940). Thus, when in most countries the oligarchic and authoritarian elites returned to power (1955–1970)—and the parties that incorporated the worker masses were persecuted—workers' movements radicalized or established links with communist parties, as in Chile with the Unidad Popular of Salvador Allende (1970–1973).

However, besides institutional interventions and recognizing the demobilizing effects of certain institutions (labor laws, corporate boards), such a display by the state was also endorsed by workers' organizations themselves in securing greater resources, better working conditions, or specific rights and access to power (Middlebrook 1995). Thus, except for Cuba (1984), between 1931 (Chile) and 1961 (Paraguay), all Latin American states adopted wide-ranging labor laws in response to worker mobilization. The length of time that it took for the full institutionalization of workers' interests may have been linked to the organizational and demographic weakness of the working class even in the midst of economic expansion: by 1950 the proportion of unionized workers in the region was between 8% and 9% of the total economically active population (Godio 1985).

This weakness went hand-inhand with the retreat of populist regimes from the 1950s amidst developmental fatigue. The changes in postwar international trade affected the demand and prices in raw materials and had an effect on the strategy of development for the internal market. Business owners aimed to reestablish their links with foreign capital. The national-popular governments thus lost the legitimacy provided by the local bourgeoisie. The demobilization of the working class at the grassroots, caused by the dependency of transformational leadership, also weakened their force-field: during the military uprising against Perón in 1955, the CGT called for the formation of "workers' militias" but ended up asking not to mobilize. The anti-communist crusade driven by the United States grew stronger. The nationalist revolution in Guatemala (1944–1954) was interrupted by an invasion from Honduras financed by the Central Intelligence Agency (CIA) (González Casanova 1990). Over the following decades there was an increase in the number of popular governments that were overthrown. Emmerich (in González Casanova 1993: 92) noted that of the thirty-nine coups that occurred between 1958 and 1983, 75% were of an anti-populist, anti-reformist, and counter-revolutionary character (see Brockett in this volume). Since then, the quest for the reestablishment of democracy took new relevance in the workers' agenda.

Contrary to such trends, in 1952 the Bolivian army was defeated by popular militias and gave rise to the National Revolution. The Movimiento Nacionalista Revolucionario (MNR) came to power together with the la Central Obrera Boliviana (COB) and the support of the indigenous-peasant population. The Bolivian economy, unlike that of the rest of the region, did not undergo a significant process of industrial development and continued to depend on the export of minerals. At that time the Bolivian miners held a strategic place in the economy, and therefore in the COB. In addition, they formed the major part of the Bolivian proletariat. The deployment of the Bolivian workers' movement therefore depended on the resources of a nucleus of miners with terrible living conditions. Its involvement in constant redistributive disputes with the state, which were handled with strong independence and a belligerent attitude, led to a kind of *revolutionary unionism* transversal to all national politics. Although the nationalization of the mines and agrarian reform, led by the MNR under workers pressure, remained incomplete, the process started in 1952 raised awareness of the importance of direct action on the state as a way of generating corporative representation and developing as a revolutionary movement. Bolivia was a singular case of political incorporation: party intervention and autonomous radical politicization. The military coup of 1964, which crushed mining communities, extinguished the last bastion of a revolution that had run out of steam years before.

Democracy, Workers Decline, and Neoliberalism (1970–1999)

Two major fields of conflict dominated the last third of the twentieth century: the struggle for the return to democracy and the resistance to policies of structural adjustment that dissolved the state-centric matrix (or internal development model) prevalent since the 1930–1960 period (Garretón and Selamé in this volume). During the course of this "double transition," the workers' movement was challenged, both in its relationship with authoritarian governments (Drake 2003) and in its influence in the restructuring of democracy (Murillo 2001). In addition, it was dramatically affected by the impacts of pro-market policies on their reorganization process while causing a disciplining of the workforce. Both scenarios brought about substantive changes in the workers' organizations: the "union format" (García Linera 2001), the most successful organizational model in the collective defense of the rights of workers and in their access to state representation, lost legitimacy once it became associated with bureaucratism, prebendalism, and corruption.

The relationship between the workers' movement and dictatorial governments has been the subject of intense debate. Some refer to the demobilization, the passivity, and even the collaborative willingness of workers (Delich 1983). Others highlight the subversive actions of resistance, the appearance of new forms of protest, and the high levels of disputes as indicators of workers' influence in the declining days of dictatorships (Pozzi 1988).

In any case, the nexus between military regimes and the progressive implementation of structural adjustment policies meant a historical setback for the workers' movement. The most representative cases are the dictatorships in Chile and Uruguay in 1973 and in Argentina in 1976. The first of these countries acted as an incubation laboratory for the neoliberal agenda which later would spread across the region. It was made possible through a systematic policy of "terror" towards the political opposition, the left and the workers. Prior to the coup by Augusto Pinochet, the Chilean workers' movement was seen as one of the most dynamic and best organized in the region. In contrast, by 1990 only 11% of the workforce was represented by trade unions, in other words less than half of the record achieved under the Allende government (Drake 2003). In Argentina, given the successive coups from 1955 and the proscription of Peronism (1955–1973), the party system was eroded. The military who seized power in 1976, in collusion with big business, looked for a definitive solution to this instability via a model that institutionalized a policy of terror (disappearances, assassinations, exile) against workers and grassroots sectors, and brought in the structural adjustment of the economy. In Argentina, the civil-military dictatorship destroyed the achievements of the workers' movement and divided it even further—it is estimated that 67% of the disappeared were workers and union leaders (Basualdo 2010).

Even during a military regime, the case of Brazil offered signs of something other than a total disaster for workers. In fact, from the middle of the 1970s in the engineering belt of São Paulo various general strikes broke out, leading to the *novo sindicalismo* (whose foremost figure was Luiz Inácio Lula da Silva). This was the moment when the workers' movement managed to resurface after the coup of 1964 and when for the first time since the Vargas regime, it seemed to be able to detach itself from the auspices of the state (Collier and Collier 1991) and from *peleguismo* (i.e., labor leaders chosen by the state). Thus, out of the grassroots committees in the factories, a *novo sindicalismo* arose in an attempt to democratize union life, empower workers' organizations, and free those organizations from ties with the state and the political parties, entering into direct negotiations with employers. Innovation of *novo sindicalismo*'s repertoire of protests was key to achieving these objectives. Later on, and with the help of student and civic movements and the support of the Catholic Church (the grassroots church communities), *novo sindicalismo* participated in the network of associations that fought for the return to democracy (see Donoso, Inclán, Mackin, Oxhorn in this volume). It is this unionism, based on an assembly format, without any institutional resources but with a strong ability to mobilize, which led to the creation of the Partido dos Trabalhadores (PT) (Bensusán 2001: 48). At its foundation in 1980, the PT unified grassroots unions, new social movements and part of the left-wing intelligentsia, while distancing itself from the Soviet bloc. Later, the Central Única dos Trabalhadores (1983) and the Central General dos Trabalhadores do Brasil (1988) emerged, revitalizing grassroots movements in Brazil.

Beyond this example and despite the democratic transition, the workers' movement lost strength. In one respect, the neoliberal global reorganization was aimed at the recovery of business competitiveness through a weakening of workers' power. Labor markets were deregulated (negotiation by company, conditions of employability and wages defined by management), work became more precarious (reduction in wages, flexible contracts, reduced employer contributions to social security), and unionism was weakened (greater screening for the organization, the end of collective bargaining). Privatizations, de-industrialization, and de-nationalization of the economies completed the picture of pro-market policies. Although resistance was not permanent, the push towards reforms barely slowed down and the workers' movement lost hegemony among the grassroots. As a result, new movements would take up the lead.

Worker decline cannot be separated from union's managerial collaboration in certain countries with former populist parties that implemented state austerity policies (such as the Partido Justicialista [PJ], the Partido Revolucionario Institucional [PRI], APRA, and Acción Democrática [AD], among others). As a result, unions' survival was in doubt. The leaders of the Confederación de Trabajadores de Venezuela (CTV), the divided CGT in Argentina, and the CTM guaranteed neoliberal governments the support for austerity policies and grassroots support in exchange for access to resources, state power or political influence. That contributed to a certain transformation of unions, with some even developing lucrative activities such as the provision of goods and services. In Mexico, the Sindicato Nacional de Trabajadores de la Educación created outlets for the sale of durable consumer goods and the CGT in Argentina got involved in the administration of pension funds and shareholder participation of private companies (Murillo 2001). This kind of corporatism relegated the defense of members' rights to a second level.

Alongside austerity policies, the increase in labor informality and unemployment functioned as mechanisms of social discipline that inhibited confrontational action. Unemployment in 1980 was 2.6% in Argentina, 10% in Colombia, 5.7% in Ecuador, 6% in Venezuela, and 7.4% in Uruguay. In 1998 these figures had gone up to 12.9%, 15.3%, 11.5%, 11.3%, and 10.1%, respectively. In addition, informal labor increased from 41% in 1990 to 46.3% in 1999 (regional average) (Weller 2017). Unemployment affected the ability of unions to demand wage increases and improvements in hiring conditions. In this environment, since the 1980s the social bases of unionism decreased and its role as a vehicle for social change diminished. The loss of mobilization capacity and negotiation power of the workers' movement reached unprecedented levels in 1980s–1990s. If the populist cycle produced an early process of grassroots inclusion, with the neoliberal policies the issue was reversed and what took shape was a process of disincorporation that included the workers (Rossi 2017).

The Return of the State, Unions Reactivation, and New Movements (1999–2017)

The progressive loss of legitimacy of the Washington Consensus in the twenty-first century marked the collapse of several governments and later left-wing hegemony in the region. The "destituent" mobilizations in Ecuador (2000, 2005), Argentina (2001), and Bolivia (2003, 2005) showed signs of classic labor demands combined with disruptive claims (national sovereignty, replacement of the political class, direct democracy, plurinationality). Thereafter, contentious collective action with new organizational formats took shape, in some cases capable of exceeding and including strictly union-types of disputes. They included social movements, cooperatives, neighborhood mass meetings, factory committees, and grassroots organizations (see Davis and Davey, Oxhorn, Wada in this volume).

In Mexico, in the mid-1990s, a new unionism emerged that challenged neoliberalism and the logics that enabled authoritarian unionism.[2] Under a movement-based framework, organizations were created with assembly structures, internal systems of democracy, and a willingness to make common cause with other actors—examples included the Coordinadora Intersindical Primero de Mayo, the Frente Auténtico del Trabajo, and the Unión Nacional de Trabajadores—bringing together autonomist unions that arose in the 1970s. In Buenos Aires, the Central de Trabajadores de la Argentina (CTA), formed in 1992, acted as a nucleus for several organizations—especially state employee unions—which distanced themselves from the CGT's support for pro-market reforms. With a movement-based perspective, the CTA came to represent different social sectors—informal, retired, and domestic workers—linking with organizations of unemployed workers (*piqueteros*) that emerged in the mid-1990s. The latter led the wave of protests between 2000 and 2003, introducing picketing and mass meetings into the repertoire of protests (see Rossi in this volume).

Politically weakened and with little social support, unions had to form part of broader mobilization networks. The Coordinadora de Movimientos Sociales emerged in Ecuador at the end of the 1990s under the hegemony of the indigenous movement and with support of oil-workers unions, public service unions, and other anti-neoliberal organizations. The Cochabamba "Water War" in Bolivia (2000) took shape from the Coordinadora de Defensa del Agua y la Vida, which brought together coca-growers, environmentalists, neighborhood associations, and laborers. The Coordinadora used road blockades against the privatization of natural resources defined as public assets. It thereby managed to defeat the privatization program and overcome the precariousness of the COB as a place for grassroots expression.

The upsurge of new social movements anticipated the progressive wave of the twenty-first century. By 2008 eleven of the eighteen Latin American countries had left-wing governments. The post-neoliberal scope of their programs created popular expectations and breathed life into the workers' movement. In the midst of a commodities boom, the government agenda repositioned the state as a promoter of development, controlling the markets and redistributing wealth. Many previously repressed demands were turned into public action and took the form of rights (Grugel and Riggirozzi 2009). Until 2012 the so-called "pink tide" linked a triangle of economic growth, reduction in inequality, and a decline in poverty: whereas in 1990 48.8% of the Latin American population was defined as poor (including extreme poverty), this figure fell to 28.1% in 2013 (Weller 2017). The former union leader Lula da Silva, twice elected president of Brazil (2002–2010), symbolized the viability of a "Latin American-style capitalism" forged between populism and the reincorporation of the masses into the market and into politics. A "second wave of popular incorporation" (Rossi 2015) took shape, following that of the 1940s and 1950s. Fundamentally, it involved the incorporation of the grassroots that with their mobilization preceded the turn to the left. In this second wave the classic mechanisms of corporate reincorporation of subalterns were also on the agenda in Bolivia, Uruguay, Brazil, and Argentina.

In the field of organized work, the progressive cycle involved processes of revitalization of unions (Senén González and Haidar 2009): wage increases, growing levels of labor unrest, collective bargaining, and so on reflected the dynamism—with national variation—of unions. Such re-empowerment was linked to state interventionism in key economic sectors, including promotion of policies aimed at restoring labor rights and the capacity of unions to profit from political opportunities made available through post-neoliberalism.

From 2002 to 2013, minimum wages in all Latin American countries showed a constant upward trend (Weller 2017). Wages Councils, a classic corporate institution, were reinstated after several years of being frozen. At the same time, between 2004 and 2012 the number of paid employees surpassed the number of self-employed, although in some countries only historical levels were reached—for example, Argentina (1973) and Venezuela (1990). With regard to social security, while in 2002 54.4% of employees were members of the health system, in 2011 the figure had reached 66.4%. One novel factor was that in fourteen out of seventeen countries the gender gap was reduced thanks to the greater participation of women in the workforce, the increase in minimum wages, and policies formalizing domestic work (Weller 2017).

In a context of economic growth and political will on the part of governments, the workers' movement was better positioned to demand wage increases, participation in profits, and involvement in the state. In certain countries its participation in government did not stop conflicts. In Argentina, strikes increased progressively from 1997 (except for 2003–2004), reaching their peak in 2005 during the government of Néstor Kirchner (Etchemendy and Collier 2007). In Chile, conflicts increased during the first government of Michel Bachelet (2006–2010): 2005 saw the lowest level of labor disputes of the twentieth and twenty-first centuries, while from 2006 they increased progressively until 2009, the year which marked the highest level of worker conflict in both centuries (Osorio and Gaudichaud 2018). There was no less strain between the COB and Evo Morales in Bolivia, while the union confederations in Ecuador confronted Rafael Correa's policy of de-corporatization. The loss of union autonomy had its ups and downs in socio-state relations in Brazil under the PT and was sharper in Venezuela.

From the outset, the anti-elite discourse by Hugo Chávez included the leaders of the CTV, who were accused of participating in the neoliberal reform of the 1990s and the coup attempt of 2002 (Ellner 2003). The putsch resulted in the break-up of the CTV and the emergence in 2002 of the Unión Nacional de Trabajadores (UNT) which, with government support, reopened several factories that had closed during the employers' lockout. However, the government did not like its autonomist position and fostered the creation of the pro-government Central Bolivariana Socialista de Trabajadores in 2011. This was the year of greatest unrest between unions and government since the turn of the century. The intra-union struggles were also significant. In 2010 the new Organic Law of Labor, Men and Female Workers was approved by decree without the awareness or participation of any union organization.

The state-workers conflict continued even despite the increase of state participation in worker leadership. In Bolivia, leaders of the mining, haulage, and coca-leaf worker cooperatives were appointed as civil servants or elected as Deputies in the Plurinational Legislative Assembly. By 2010 one third of the seats in Congress were occupied by grassroots representatives and two decades of "democratic pacts" (with the elites in power) had been abandoned. In Argentina, one of the first alliances of the Kirchner governments was with the workers' movement. This coalition was founded on a "segmented corporatism" (Etchemendy 2011) since it was based on three "winners" of neo-developmentalism—transport, construction, and industry—including the management of transport policies held by union leaders until 2011. In Brazil, between 2004 and 2013 around 1,300 posts in the federal administration were occupied by trade unionists (Marcelino 2017). In Uruguay, during the government of Tabaré Vázquez (2005–2010), thirty officials in the executive and legislature came from unions (Lanzaro 2010). By contrast, in neoliberal Mexico, despite a long corporate tradition of unionism, the inclusion of workers' leaders in parliament fell substantially: from 8% in 2000 to 0.8% in 2012 (Observatorio de Elites Parlamentarias de América Latina 2012).

The requirements of the neo-developmentalist model activated by popular governments determined, in part, the nature of their relationship with different players from the working world: some of them were granted greater prominence in political alliances, although in subordinate roles (Argentina, Brazil, Venezuela), while others were weakened as a way of controlling economic processes. In Bolivia, Morales favored the alliance with private mine workers to the detriment of state miners, whereas Correa undertook several labor reforms in the oil industry in order to weaken the "old" unionism that dominated the sector and take back state control of the extraction process. In countries that continued along the pro-market path, such as Colombia and Mexico, some advances occurred thanks to external pressures and not on account of decisions of national policy. Conditions imposed by the United States and the European Union on Colombia to subscribe to free trade agreements made reference to the achievement of minimum standards in worker and human rights for union members (Celis Ospina, Toro Zuleta, and Valero Julio 2014).

Neither the inclusive efforts of progressivism nor neo-developmentalist dynamism prior to the crisis of 2013 could insert the different manifestations of "non-classic work" (De la Garza 2010) into the formal networks of the economy. The explosion of temporary jobs, workers in the informal economy, the *maquiladora* industries, street vendors, call centers, and so on opened up a struggle for state recognition of workers' rights. Mired in informal, precarious, and idiosyncratic labor contexts, these working sectors found great difficulty in forming associations. Traditional unionism had barely concerned itself with them. Thus, the field of opportunity was open for new organizational strategies. The case of the Confederación de Trabajadores de la Economía Popular (CTEP) in Argentina is paradigmatic in this regard. Formed in 2011, CTEP brought together organizations of street sellers, *manteros* (unlicensed street vendors), stallholders, *cartoneros* (cardboard collectors), and people in worker-managed companies. Paradoxically, aware of the effectiveness of the union format in negotiating with the state, the CTEP attempted to emulate such an organizational approach. In addition, it demanded legal recognition and participation in wage negotiations. In 2015, at the end of her government, Cristina Fernández de Kirchner granted CTEP legal status and opened the way for the creation of the Council for the Popular Economy and the Complementary Social Wage. This institutional framework—established during the government of Mauricio Macri (2015–2019) under organizational pressure—had previously appeared in the new Constitutions of Bolivia, Ecuador, and Venezuela which recognized the plural nature of the economy (private, public, communitarian, cooperative, and voluntary), and created state departments specifically concerned with public policies for these types of workers (Coraggio 2014). More than a straight return to formality, part of this organizational sector struggled to maintain and expand non-capitalist approaches to working in the arenas concerned with labor rights. Thus, *sui generis* alternatives became viable in the midst of the turmoil of post-Fordist globalization (see Burridge and Markoff in this volume).

Workers' achievements in the twenty-first century fell apart following the constraints that appeared with the fall in the price of commodities (2013) and the accusations of corruption against progressive governments (see Pereyra, Gold, and Gattoni in this volume). The latter demanded greater loyalty from their allies and/or fell back on the strength of their supporters. Concerning unions, it led to the end of some alliances, such as CGT-Kirchnerism and CUT-Lulism, favoring electoral defeats.

Conclusion

The extent of workers mobilization in Latin America is far from exhausted in union dynamics and their role in the extension of workers' rights. The reconstruction of sinuous politico-organizational developments in the world of work has instead revealed the complex class, ethnic, gender, and territorial connections that have resulted in successive waves of politicization of the "workers' question." The political subjectivation of workers has evolved in contradictory ways in the different spheres of relationship with the left, populism, the church, and political institutions, as well as a product of the historical vicissitudes of the struggles. Between autonomy and heteronomy, between political inclusion and plebeian insubordination, the "formation of the working class" in Latin America cannot be separated from the fragility of the processes of national development, which are always susceptible to restoring the boundaries of exclusion. If in the countries of the Global North workers' condition was once able to function as a fully-incorporated category, in Latin America it has taken the form of an antagonism which, without its activation, leaves "everything as a potential threat." With a predisposition towards conflict—regularly suppressed or neutralized at the top leadership—the workers' movements have been a fundamental force in nation-state building, in the processes of (re)democratization and in the achievement of social rights.

Notes

1. The CTAL was developed under the aegis of the Confederación de Trabajadores de México (CTM) and the promotion of the government of Lázaro Cárdenas.
2. In Mexico, *charrismo* unionism (i.e., union leaders appointed by the government) led to bureaucratism, authoritarianism, and collaborationism between union leadership and the state.

References

Basualdo, Victoria (2010), *Memoria en las aulas No. 13: La clase trabajadora durante la última dictadura militar argentina (1976-1983)* (Buenos Aires: Comisión Provincial por la Memoria).

Becker, Marc (2002), "Mariátegui y el problema de las razas en América Latina," *Revista Andina* 35, 191–220.

Bensusán, Graciela (2001), "El impacto de la reestructuración neoliberal: Comparación de estrategias sindicales en la Argentina, Brasil, México, Canadá y Estados Unidos," *Cuadernos del Cendes* 8(47), 25–56.

Bergquist, Charles (1986), *Los trabajadores en la historia latinoamericana: Estudios comparativos en Chile, Argentina, Venezuela y Colombia* (Bogotá: Siglo XXI).

Bourgois, Philippe (1994), *Banano, etnia y lucha social en Centroamérica* (San José: Editorial Departamento Ecuménico de Investigaciones).

Celis Ospina, Juan Carlos, Rodrigo Toro Zuleta, and Édgar Augusto Valero Julio (2014), "Sindicalismo colombiano: entre la exclusión del sistema político, el paternalismo y la conflictividad en las relaciones laborales", in Juan Carlos Celis Ospina (ed.), *Reconfiguración de las relaciones entre Estado, sindicatos y partidos en América Latina*, 159–207 (Medellín: CLACSO-Escuela Nacional Sindical).

Collier, Ruth and David Collier (1991), *Shaping the Political Arena. Critical Junctures, the Labor Movement, and Regime Dynamics in Latin America* (Princeton, NJ: Princeton University Press).

Coraggio, José Luis (2014), "La presencia de la economía social y solidaria y su institucionalización en América Latina," UNRISD Occasional Paper: Potential and Limits of Social and Solidarity Economy, 7 (Geneva: United Nations Research Institute for Social Development).

De la Garza, Enrique (2010), *Hacia un concepto ampliado de trabajo: Del concepto clásico al no clásico* (Mexico: Anthropos/UAM-Iztapalapa).

De la Garza, Enrique and Javier Melgoza (1996), "Los Ciclos del Movimiento Obrero Mexicano en el Siglo XX," *Revista Latinoamericana de Estudios del Trabajo* 2(2), 127–62.

Delich, Francisco (1983), "Desmovilización social, reestructuración obrera y cambio sindical," in Peter Waldmann and Ernesto Garzón Valdés (eds.), *El Poder militar en la Argentina, 1976-1981*, 101–16 (Buenos Aires: Galerna).

Drake, Paul (2003), "El movimiento obrero en Chile: De la Unidad Popular a la Concertación," *Revista de Ciencia Política* 23(2), 148–58.

Ellner, Steve (2003), "The Contrasting Variants of the Populism of Hugo Chávez and Alberto Fujimori," *Journal of Latin American Studies* 35(1), 139–162.

Etchemendy, Sebastián (2011), "El sindicalismo argentino en la era pos-liberal (2003--2011)," in Andrés Malamud and Miguel De Luca (eds.), *La política en tiempos de los Kirchner*, 155–66 (Buenos Aires: EUDEBA).

Etchemendy, Sebastián and Ruth Collier (2007), "Down but Not Out: Union Resurgence and Segmented Neocorporatism in Argentina (2003-2007)," *Politics & Society* 35(3), 363–401.

García Linera, Álvaro (2001), "Sindicato, multitud y comunidad: Movimientos sociales y formas de autonomía política en Bolivia," in Álvaro García Linera, Felipe Quispe, Raquel Gutiérrez, Raúl Prada, and Luis Tapia (eds.), *Tiempos de rebelión*, 347–420 (La Paz: Comuna y Muela del Diablo).

Godio, Julio (1985), *Historia del movimiento obrero latinoamericano: Socialdemocracia, socialcristianismo y marxismo: 1930-1980* (Costa Rica: Nueva Sociedad).

González Casanova, Pablo (1990), *El Estado en América Latina: Teoría y práctica* (Meexico: Siglo XXI).

González Casanova, Pablo (1993), *Latin America Today* (Tokyo, New York & Paris: The United Nations University).

Grugel, Jean and Pía Riggirozzi (2009), "The End of the Embrace? Neoliberalism and Alternatives to Neoliberalism in Latin America," in Jean Grugel and Pía Riggirozzi (eds.), *Governance after Neoliberalism in Latin America*, 1–23 (New York: Palgrave-Macmillan).

Hall, Michael M. and Hobart A. Spalding, Jr. (1991), "La clase trabajadora urbana y los primeros movimientos obreros de América Latina (1890-1930)," in Leslie Bethell (ed.), *Historia de América Latina*, 7: 281–315 (Madrid: Editorial Crítica/Cambridge University Press).

Ianni, Octavio (1975), *La formación del estado populista en América Latina* (Mexico: Serie Popular Era).

James, Daniel (1990), *Resistencia e integración: El peronismo y la clase trabajadora Argentina 1946-1976* (Buenos Aires: Sudamericana).

Lanzaro, Jorge (2010), "Uruguay: Un Gobierno Social Democrático En América Latina," *Revista Uruguaya de Ciencia Política* 19(1), 45–68.

Lindo-Fuentes, Héctor, Erik Ching, Rafael Martínez, and Knut Walter (2010), *Recordando 1932: La Matanza, Roque Dalton y la política de la memoria histórica* (El Salvador: FLACSO El Salvador).

Marcelino, Paula (2017), "Sindicalismo e neodesenvolvimentismo: Analisando as greves entre 2003 e 2013 no Brasil," *Tempo Social, Revista de Sociologia da USP* 29(3), 201–27.

Mariátegui, Juan Carlos (1990), *Ideología y Política* (Lima: Biblioteca Amauta).

Middlebrook, Kevin (1995), *The Paradox of Revolution: Labor, the State, and Authoritarianism in Mexico* (Baltimore, MD: Johns Hopkins University Press).

Murillo, María Victoria (2001), *Labor Unions, Partisan Coalitions, and Market Reforms in Latin America* (Cambridge: Cambridge University Press).

Murmis, Miguel and Juan Carlos Portantiero (1971), *Estudios sobre los orígenes del peronismo* (Buenos Aires: Siglo XXI).

Observatorio de Elites Parlamentarias de América Latina (2012), "Estudios por país, México 2012-2015," *Universidad de Salamanca*, https://oir.org.es/pela/estudios-por-pais/.

Osorio, Sebastián and Franck Gaudichaud (2018), "Democracy without the Workers: 25 Years of the Labour Movement and Mature Neo-Liberalism in Chile," in James Petras and Henry Veltmeyer (eds.), *The Class Struggle in Latin America. Making History Today*, 134–50 (New York: Routledge).

Pozzi, Pablo (1988), *La oposición obrera a la dictadura (1976-1982)* (Buenos Aires: Editorial Contrapunto).

Rossi, Federico M. (2015), "The Second Wave of Incorporation in Latin America: A Conceptualization of the Quest for Inclusion Applied to Argentina," *Latin American Politics and Society* 57(1), 1–28.

Rossi, Federico M. (2017), *The Poor's Struggle for Political Incorporation: The Piquetero Movement in Argentina* (New York: Cambridge University Press).

Salazar, Gabriel and Julio Pinto (1999), *Historia contemporánea de Chile II: Actores, identidad y movimientos* (Santiago: LOM Ediciones).

Senén González, Cecilia and Julieta Haidar (2009), "Los debates acerca de la revitalización sindical y su aplicación en el análisis sectorial en Argentina," *Revista Latinoamericana de Estudios del Trabajo* 14(22), 5–31.

Spalding, Hobart (1977), *Organized Labor in Latin America: Historical Case Studies of Urban Workers in Dependent Societies* (New York: New York University Press).

Stavenhagen, Rodolfo and Francisco Zapata (1974), *Sistemas de relación obrero-patronales en América Latina* (Mexico: El Colegio de México).

Weffort, Francisco C. (1974), *Los sindicatos en la política (Brasil 1955-1964)*, Cuadernos del CEIL-CONICET, Serie Sindicalismo, 10 (Buenos Aires: Editorial El Coloquio).

Weller, Jürgen (2017), *Empleo en América Latina y el Caribe. Textos seleccionados* (Santiago: ECLAC).

CHAPTER 19

PEASANT MOVEMENTS IN RECENT LATIN AMERICAN HISTORY

CLIFF WELCH

INTRODUCTION

It is impossible to verify the number of peasant movements that have erupted throughout contemporary Latin American history, but their inevitable occurrence has featured in nearly every account of the region. Latin America's land and what is grown on, discovered under it, or taken from its waters has been the target of profiteers and opportunists since 1492. Generations of moneychangers saw the people who live on the land as useful to the extent that they complied with orders to cut, dig, plant, harvest, fish, and act content. Given this situation, indigenous cultivators and peasants of all kinds rose-up often to defend their rural livelihoods.

Using emblematic case studies, this chapter offers a synthesis of twentieth- and twenty-first-century peasant movements in Latin America and the Caribbean. Taking advantage of a recent resurgence in rural social movement studies, the chapter follows a chronology of overlapping developments in diverse locations generally determined by the intensity of the penetration of capitalist relations of production. Capitalist penetration did not follow a predetermined timeline; it occurred when and where opportunities arose. These homogenizing factors facilitated the elaboration of a categorical system for generalizing about the heterogeneous responses of rural people to the transformations demanded by capitalism in different places and times. The chapter combines peasant movements into descriptive categories—restoration, integration, revolution, and alternation—and uses these terms to chronologically advance an analytical narrative.

Restoration movements were typical of the turn of the twentieth century, wherein peasants banded together to halt change and restore conceptions of an earlier, often idealized order. From the 1920s to the 1950s, many peasants banded together in efforts to integrate themselves into national projects, struggling to shape incorporation instruments like political parties, labor unions, and select public policies. Often frustrated in these attempts, some peasants participated in revolutionary movements from the 1950s to 1980s. During the most recent period analyzed, the 1980s to 2000s, a combination of fading socialist icons and neoliberal restructuring fostered peasant movements intent on ensuring their prosperity through the development of autonomous organizations and alternative social formations. Through these instruments, they sought to enhance their control within capitalist political economies (Deere and Royce, 2009).

In consonance with the perspective of many regional scholars, our definition of the peasantry is broad. The United Nations (2018) declaration on the rights of "people working in rural areas" excludes only full-time salaried farmworkers from their definition of peasants as those who rely on the land and its waters for their livelihoods. They depend primarily on family labor and prioritize the reproduction of their way of life over profit maximization. Varied ethnic identities are present among peasants. In some Latin American countries, indigenous peasants predominate, while in others African-descended people do; those of mixed-ethnicities, including European identities, are ubiquitous. Given this diversity, and the increased importance of cultural identity to the cohesion and strength of these movements, they may be better understood today as agrarian social movements that emphasize a search to establish autonomy from market forces for a breadth of rural productive activities and cultural identities (Borras, 2019).

Restoration

Starting in the late nineteenth century, many Latin American countries experienced violent upheavals in the countryside as dominant classes rallied subordinate classes to help them secure control of resources sought by rapidly expanding industrial capitalist nations. In countries with substantial indigenous populations, ambitious neocolonial regimes undermined relatively stable relationships with Amerindian peasant populations in order to commodify land resources, which were often held in trust by community rather than individual property owners (Bauer 1991). These processes stimulated resistance movements that sought to halt the penetration of capitalist market relations and restore the legitimacy of collective over individual rights.

In Bolivia, indigenous Aymara and Quechua warriors joined Partido Liberal elites in a civil war to overthrow the country's long-standing Conservative government. After establishing independence in 1826, Bolivian elites introduced a number of reform laws affecting the majority indigenous population. Especially disturbing was an 1871 law "delinking" the land from community (*ayllu*) proprietorship. Gradually, the state worked to eliminate the *ayllus* and establish individual ownership, a change meant to free up land for purchase and more intensive exploitation. This reform actually facilitated land concentration among a group of ever more powerful landlords (Ticona Alejo 2003).

Indigenous communities empowered the Aymara chief Pablo Zárate Willka (1850–1905) and other leaders to restore old arrangements when war broke out in the 1890s. Historical accounts privilege the experience of leaders. Since most indigenous people lived in near isolation from occidental society, a defining feature of leaders included abilities such as language skills that helped them transit between worlds. Zárate offered support to Liberals in return for promises to restore community land rights according to pre-colonial traditions. Even before declaring victory in April 1899, the Liberals' indigenous allies acted quickly to recuperate land lost to the *hacendados*. A series of actions on their part frightened elites, who quickly replaced a discourse of federalist collaboration with accusations of "race war." Initially honored for their valiant and essential contribution to winning the war, the Liberals treacherously arrested, jailed, and tortured indigenous warriors, including Zárate (Mendieta 2010; Oporto Ordóñez 2011; Rivera Cusicanqui 1985).

In Mexico, in the years leading up to the revolution of 1910–1920, indigenous peasants in diverse parts of the country mobilized against the forced sale or theft of their land, much of it provoked by rising foreign investments and the export of minerals and foodstuffs (see Martí i Puig and Álvarez in this volume). Foreign capitalists vied for favorable relations with the dictator Porfirio Diaz. In 1910, an insurrection blocked his eighth "election" as president and in the succession struggle that ensued, peasants took back their lands. Many land occupations were short-lived, but in the state of Morelos the revolutionary council of Emiliano Zapata (1879–1919) remained steadfast in its struggle to transform social relations by restoring community land tenure systems. As a mestizo, Zapata identified with a large portion of the peasantry (Brunk 1995).

Written in 1911, Zapata's Plan of Ayala emphasized the revolution's agrarian objectives. According to the document, landlords had "usurped . . . the fields, timber and water," which were to be returned to the original users. In addition, villages were to receive a third of the territorial "monopolies of powerful proprietors" in order to establish "ejidos, colonies, and foundations." Landlords who resisted these restorative measures would have all of their holdings seized and used "for indemnifications of war, pensions for widows and orphans of the victims who succumb in the struggle for the present plan" (Womack Jr. 1970: 400–4). These measures and others were defended in Morelos until Zapata's ambush and murder in 1919.

Brazil offers a counterpoint to these examples. While the restoration of ancestral land tenure was strongest where indigenous groups were present, established peasant communities of diverse ethnicity, like those in Brazil, also fought to retain lands they had occupied in the face of capitalist penetration. In 1908, Brazil authorized a US entrepreneur to build 400 kilometers of railway between São Paulo and a town near Brazil's southern border. His railway, lumber, and settlement companies cut a thirty-kilometer-wide swath of destruction through the Atlantic Forest in a region disputed by elites in the states of Paraná and Santa Catarina. The company invaded this contested region (hence, historians remember the conflict as the *Contestado*) with some 8,000 construction workers, forcing peasants off the land with a 300-man private army, creating the region's first industries (lumber and beef), mines, and colonies, legalizing the pillage with false land titles (Milani 2017).

Ever growing groups of peasants uprooted by the railroad project sought solace as followers of a mystical healer named José Maria. Killed in a skirmish with the army in 1912, he was memorialized as a spiritual leader by the displaced peasants. A popular Catholicism characterized peasant culture, imbuing others with the eternal life of the Holy Spirit, upholding righteousness and reinforcing hierarchy. The pilgrims formed refugee camps that grew to include thousands. For their own survival they planted crops and organized armed patrols and hunting expeditions. They negotiated to acquire meat and other provisions. They understood the railroad and lumber company as an enemy that needed to be contained to defend their own survival. Constantly persecuted by private, state, and federal forces, they attacked company properties. They justified their violence as necessary to restore customary rights established over the years to use the land to sustain themselves. With a fondness for King Pedro II, who ruled independent Brazil until overthrown by a republican movement in 1889, they accused the new leaders of "herding Brazilian sons off the land in order to sell it to foreigners," making it necessary for them to fight for their "rights" (Carvalho 2008: 33–34). The peasants of the Contestado resisted bravely and creatively, but ultimately lost the war in 1916.

Integration

For more than a century, a positivist, modernization theory of history prevailed. Accordingly, intellectuals provided dominant elites with narratives of progress toward brighter futures. Communists and capitalists shared similar assumptions about a general climb toward bigger, better, and easier until the end of the twentieth century. By the 1920s, new movements formed to help peasants ride the progressive wave toward modernity. Integration, often referred to as incorporation in the sense of being brought into the body politic, became the objective (see Ramírez Gallegos and Stoessel; Rossi in this volume). In Colombia, some indigenous peasant movements shifted strategies from a struggle to establish autonomous "Indian Republics" to *Lamismo*, named for the historic indigenous rebel leader Manuel Quintín Lame Chantre (1883–1967), who supported a path to gradual integration after his release from prison in 1921 (Marín Abadía 2014). Arrested in 1917, Colombian authorities sparred Lame from execution, unlike many leaders he had mobilized since 1914 in a fight to restore native lands. Once freed, Lame joined a movement supported by the Partido Socialista to implement Law 89 of 1890, which established norms for communal governance of land use on Indian reservations. It provided a roadmap to what Lame called "the civil integration of indigenous peoples" (Espinosa Arango 2005: 88). But their efforts still met with fierce opposition from landlords and authorities (De la Peña 1994).

In Mexico, after the death of Zapata, victorious revolutionary leaders paid attention to peasant concerns. The 1917 Constitution prohibited foreign ownership of Mexico's natural resources and recognized *ejidos*, that is, areas of communal usufruct rights to forests, land, and water. An agrarian law from 1915 required authorities to break up large, unproductive landholdings. In various parts of the country, peasants formed movements to put the law into effect, organizing land occupations, while landlords plotted to recuperate their power. Worried about losing control of the situation, government officials worked to bureaucratize change by compelling peasants to organize into Ligas de Comunidades Agrarias to process their claims. In the first of a series of integration institutions, politicians used the Ligas to channel discontent, slow down the land distribution process, and discourage peasants from supporting radical alternatives. "This legislation substituted bureaucratic procedure for direct popular action," writes De la Peña (1994: 385). From the point of view of Mexican stability, the system channeled peasant movement discontent fairly well until the North American Free Trade Agreement (NAFTA) went into effect in 1994.

In June 1929, delegates from fourteen Latin American countries convened the First Conference of Latin American Communist Parties in Buenos Aires. The conference stemmed from the Soviet Union's 1928 decision to monitor more thoroughly the revolutionary potential of Latin America through the Comintern. Capitalism was in crisis and communism was on the rise. Among those present was Julio Portocarrero, sent to represent the influential Peruvian intellectual José Mariátegui. His arguments about the "indigenous people's question" stimulated discussion about race and class. Comintern policy favored Indian and Black nationalism, proposing the creation of separate but supposedly equal nation-states for each of the diverse races. But Portocarrero presented Mariátegui's contradictory prepared text. It convinced the majority of delegates that "once the Indians have made the socialist ideal their own, they will serve it with a discipline, tenacity, and strength that few proletarians from other milieus will be able to surpass" (Becker 2006: 456; see Webber in this volume). In Latin America, where increased foreign investment provoked dramatic agrarian change, a key challenge for Latin American communists was that of organizing workers of all races in the countryside. While the practical consequences of these debates cannot be determined, abundant evidence points to increased communist party militancy among the peasantry into the 1970s.

In El Salvador in 1932, a group of families reigned due to their control over the coffee export economy. During a coffee boom in the 1920s, the families accepted some middle-class proposals for improving labor conditions on their farms. But when the boom ended with the Great Depression, they sought to pass off the costs of lost business to their resident laborers and part-time harvesters, stimulating the peasants' anger and further eroding the elite's legitimacy. With legislative elections scheduled for 1931, the Partido Comunista Salvadoreño (PCS) anticipated significant victories from the political opportunity this discontent provoked. Concerned over this prospect, a military coup in December ousted El Salvador's reformist president, and the new regime postponed the elections and moved to repress the communist-led peasant movement. Local leaders appealed to soldiers for restraint and support.

In the coffee region, a peasant insurrection was already underway when the PCS officially condoned it. According to Gould (2010), leaders and militants alike shared the perception that machismo, an honor code, and concerns about the party's credibility made it impossible to restrain the peasant movement. Indian and non-Indian peasants and rural workers in the thousands, most armed only with machetes, attacked several state capitals and took over government buildings in many towns in the coffee-growing region of the country, ousting or killing some twenty officials who would probably not have been re-elected, and replacing them with PCS candidates. The peasants sought to contain the damage and establish "soviets" based on their communal practices. Within days, the National Guard began a counter-offensive. During a second phase, the Army and paramilitary groups carried out search and destroy missions in the countryside, killing thousands of males aged twelve and older (Gould 2010).

Two years later in Chile, under similar circumstances, another integrationist peasant movement, supported by the Partido Comunista de Chile (PCCh), was brutally repressed (Klubock 2010). Called the Ránquil revolt, the principal protagonists were members of a rural labor union that successfully united mestizo and indigenous Mapuche peasants in the southern province of Lonquimay. The union was part of a reformist project to incorporate rural workers and regiment their struggle for improved conditions in the cattle and feed industry. The reformist government created a land registry, discovered substantial irregularities, and implemented land reform, settling hundreds of families in what was now denominated as public or Mapuche reservation land. When the government changed hands in 1932, the landowners' influence was restored. The peasant revolt occurred in reaction to the landowners' use of gunmen and police to retake control of the disputed areas. For a short time, the peasants defended themselves and gained control of the area. When the Chilean military stepped in, the peasants fled, some crossing into Argentina. Hunted down, hundreds were detained and a number varying between twenty and 400 were "disappeared" in the freezing BioBio river (Klubock 2010: 152).

Into the 1940s and 1950s, peasant movements continued to struggle in collaboration with reformist politicians and communist militants in countries like Bolivia, Brazil, and Guatemala. In 1944, peasant participation in the overthrow of Guatemalan dictator Jorge Ubico Castañeda (1931–1944) resulted in the production of a labor code that encouraged rural unionization. The unions became spaces where communists could develop their militancy among the Mayan people. Large strikes impacted United Fruit Company plantations toward the end of the decade. Successful strikes helped create momentum for approving an agrarian reform law in 1952 that gave the government power to "expropriate and redistribute landholdings larger than 90 hectares" (De la Peña 1994: 421). Under this law, the state expropriated and distributed about half a million hectares of land to half a million peasants. They formed agrarian committees to administer their land. The measure provided a profound boost to Guatemala's socioeconomic development. Advised by José Manuel Fortuny, a communist party leader, president Jacobo Arbenz (1951–1954) applied the law to United Fruit Company, which had grabbed more than 200,000 hectares of land during Ubico's rule. Company executives enjoyed close ties to United States government officials, who ordered the Central Intelligence Agency (CIA) to orchestrate a coup, ousting Arbenz in 1954 and ushering in years of military rule. Peasants mobilized to fight a civil war that lasted nearly forty years and cost hundreds of thousands of lives (McAllister 2010).

In Brazil, a network of peasant leagues was established by the Partido Comunista do Brasil (PCB) to help organize the countryside and represent the interests of small farmers, rural workers and the landless. In 1947, when the PCB was suppressed in a Cold War crackdown, the leagues were outlawed. But peasant militancy continued to be nurtured by PCB organizations such as the União de Lavradores e Trabalhadores Agrícolas do Brasil (ULTAB), founded in 1954 and in operation until rural unionization was legalized in 1963. ULTAB's officers easily won election to run the government sanctioned Confederação Nacional de Trabalhadores na Agricultura (CONTAG). By that time, the country had several hundred rural labor unions (Welch 2010).

Revolution

Grandin argues that "millions of Latin Americans lived some part of their lives in revolutionary time" since the Mexican Revolution started in 1910 (Grandin and Joseph 2010: 1). Doubtlessly millions of Latin Americas experienced rebellion, revolt, and political instability during the century, but far fewer experienced revolution. Revolution is a "rapid, fundamental and violent change in the dominant values and myths of a society; in its political institutions, social structure, leadership, and government activity and policies" (Huntington 1968: 264). Revolution is not a "time," it is a process—a connected series of events—that results from "broad, rapid and violent expansion of political participation outside the existing structure of political institutions" (ibid.: 267). Certainly, debate over the concept continues; our purpose is merely to present references of analysis (see Oikonomakis in this volume). In these terms, since the Mexican Revolution, Latin Americans have experienced only three additional revolutions: Bolivia in 1952, Cuba in 1959, and Nicaragua in 1979. A number of other insurgencies, like those of Colombia and El Salvador, promised revolutionary change but were not successful (see Martí i Puig and Álvarez in this volume).

In Bolivia, after the ruling oligarchical regime annulled the 1951 national election results, peasants joined with miners to form militias and councils powerful enough to contain the armed forces and replace local legislative bodies. They insisted on delivering the presidency to the MNR, whose candidate Victor Paz Estenssoro (1952–1956, and later) had won the election promising dramatic reforms. Anxious to upend decades of concentrated wealth and power, peasant and worker councils redistributed land, wealth, and power to numerous communities, factories, and mines. Village "cacique networks deluged authorities with petitions to recuperate ancient land titles" (Gotkowitz 2008: 270). The Paz Estenssoro government passed agrarian, labor, and citizenship legislation that essentially recognized the new status quo. But the new laws compensated landlords and mining companies without providing peasants and workers with adequate assistance to guarantee the success of the conquests. The MNR government also rebuilt the army, setting the stage for a resurgence of reactionary forces in the 1960s.

The Bolivian revolution alarmed United States officials at the same time that it indicated the need for reform in order to deal with the challenging dilemmas peasant movements presented to established power during the Cold War. As the United States learned how to express its influence through international institutions like the United Nations, it helped define peasants as a problem to be solved (Long and Roberts 1997). Authorities interpreted their lack of formal education, isolation, and low productivity as a brake on capitalist accumulation. Economic development theory saw agriculture as a consumer of manufactured goods and a source of surplus labor, subordinating the countryside to urban industrial expansion. In order to increase commodity export income and contain industrial worker wages through lower food prices, the countryside had to be more productive. From the perspective of United States policymakers, the arrangement of this package tied land use to geopolitical concerns, for the discontent of peasants was seen as a source of instability, an Achilles heel that communist agitators might manipulate to topple governments.

In 1959, peasants in Cuba played an important role in overthrowing the island nation's dictator, Fulgencio Batista (1944–1959). The new regime in Cuba led by Fidel Castro attracted widespread interest as a nationalist success story and it promoted its experience as a model for other Latin American countries (Castañeda 1993). The revolution heightened U.S. interest in studying and controlling the peasantry (Long and Roberts 1997; Useem 1977; see Martí i Puig and Álvarez in this volume). Washington officials responded with carrot and stick policies, funding reformist projects to modernize agriculture while reinforcing the repressive apparatus of allied states.

Historians have shown that peasant movements took shape throughout Cuba's long colonial period, that they were a part of the struggle for independence from Spain in the nineteenth century, and that they featured prominently in the 1959 revolution (Martín Barrios 1984). In fact, a very specific segment of the peasantry mobilized in response Castro's call to rebel (Swanger 2015; Useem 1977). A long-standing struggle for land with coffee and sugarcane planters already engaged peasants when they heard the rebel call. Nicknamed *precaristas*, due to the precarious nature of their livelihoods, the peasant squatters knew how to organize themselves in "paramilitary self-defense bands" because they lived "in a state of sometimes subdued, but at other times overt, civil war" (Useem 1977: 105). These peasants protected the revolutionaries' base, or *foco*, as Castro's 26th of July Movement grew to become the vanguard of the insurrection. As Castro's followers grew into an effective force of up to 4,000 soldiers, their revolutionary council issued an agrarian reform law in October 1958 that promised "land to the tiller" and the elimination of unproductive estates. The decree encouraged the squatters and "mobilized more intensively the small farmers in order to incorporate them massively in the ranks of the revolution" (Gutelman 1970: 347). After the flight of Batista in January 1959,

Castro consolidated the dominance of his faction and issued a new agrarian reform law in May 1961 that legalized the distribution of more than one million hectares of land to thousands of peasants.

The Cuban revolution inspired other rebel groups to mobilize peasants to rebel against national governments, especially those aligned with the United States. From 1967, the effort was administered by the Havana-based Organización Latinoamerican a de Solidaridad (OLAS). Many peasants experienced declining standards of living in the aftermath of the Second World War. Violence aggravated the situation, especially in Colombia, where the 1948 murder of populist leader Jorge Eliécer Gaitán set off a new civil war characterized by vigilante violence and revenge killings in both town and country. Large landowners and commercial farmers used the confusion to grab peasant land, but peasants mobilized to defend themselves, aided by Partido Comunista de Colombia (PCC) militias. They established what came to be known as independent peasant republics, "veritable redoubts of Communist rule, with their own systems of productions, police, armed forces and administration of justice" (De la Peña 1994: 441). The largest, centered in Marquetalia in the Tolima province, measured 5,000 square kilometers.

Mobilized by Cold War rhetoric after the Cuban Revolution, the United States repeatedly encouraged the Colombian government to repress the rebels. In May 1964, the United States-funded Latin American Security Operation was launched in Tolima with the arrival of 16,000 counter-insurgency troops. The army intimidated peasant communities, imprisoning hundreds and forcing thousands to flee. Faced with daunting odds, the militias, whose recruits numbered in the hundreds, concentrated on defending the peasant refugees as they pushed east, expanding the conflict into new areas. With the goal of coordinating a national agrarian movement with revolutionary intent, the guerrillas held several meetings and "accepted a national military plan and began a prolonged struggle for the seizure of power" (Pizarro 1989: 30). To accomplish these ends, in 1966 the Communist-led peasant movement created the Fuerzas Armadas Revolucionarias de Colombia (FARC), which continued to wage war into the twenty-first century (see Oikonomakis in this volume).

The FARC, like other Cuban-inspired peasant warrior organizations, did not succeed in its revolutionary goals. The same could be said for armed peasant movements seeking revolutionary change in Bolivia, Brazil, El Salvador, and Guatemala. The pressure of these organizations produced not only repression but some initiatives like additional credit and land reform meant to reward peasants for resisting mobilization. Through policies like the Alliance for Progress, entities like the United States Agency for International Development (USAID) and global capitalist institutions like the World Bank specific agrarian reform laws and projects sought to pacify peasant movements. It is possible to see a pattern in which the more alarming the threat of peasant-based revolution, the more violent the repression and the more "generous" the public policy in the countryside.

Supported by Cuba, the 1979 Nicaraguan Revolution depended heavily on the mobilization of peasants. Nicaraguan agriculture became more tightly integrated to the world market during the twentieth century through demands for coffee, cotton, and beef. Each new export-cycle brought disruption to the lives of Nicaraguan peasants, pushing them off the land and into wage labor as seasonal workers. From 1936, the tightening fist of the ruling Somoza family made resistance difficult to sustain (Deere and Marchetti 1981). With Cuban assistance, however, the Frente Sandinista de Liberación Nacional (FSLN) formed in the early 1960s (De la Peña 1994; Prevost 1990). As cattle grazing expanded from 1965, peasants faced new pressures as their forest habitats were burnt down to create pasture, further limiting their access to the land. Into the 1970s, they organized to retake territory through land occupations.

With the rise in influence of liberation theology, peasants received the protection and support of the Catholic Church (see Mackin in this volume). Through grassroots Christian communities, peasants formed committees to build unity and express their needs. Starting in 1974, the FSLN recruited peasants for their guerrilla army. In the north, where export agriculture was concentrated, "some guerrilla forces . . . came to consist almost entirely of members from the rural community" (Luciak 1990, 58). In August 1978, encouraged by the FSLN, the peasant committees founded the Asociación de los Trabajadores del Campo (ATC). The ATC coordinated protests in the cities, occupations on cotton plantations, and strikes for higher wages. As the Sandinistas gained control of certain zones, ATC peasants occupied plantations to grow foodstuffs for the combatants and commercial crops to fund the revolution. After the FSLN victory in July 1979, ATC delegates were intimately involved in designing agrarian reform development policies and projects (Deere and Marchetti 1981; Núñez Soto 1985). But peasant discontent and United States intervention also undermined the Sandinistas, who were voted out of power in 1990.

ALTERNATION

Arising from a period beset by an international debt crisis, collapsing authoritarian regimes, and the promotion of neoliberal decentralization and government cutbacks, agrarian social movements presented alternative visions and solutions for achieving collective ends and struggled to retain their autonomy from political parties, labor organizations, and the state (Zamosc 1994). This autonomy became all the more important in the 1990s with the collapse of the Soviet Union and its satellites, a fact that caused significant ideological confusion for left-leaning groups. These people's power movements agreed on the benefits of collective action and international solidarity, questioned capitalism and imperialism, and favored alternative modes of production, but had difficulty naming the "ism" that best described their societal projects (Deere and Royce 2009).

In 1989, a multi-ethnic peoples' movement formed in Bogotá to plan campaigns to question the commemoration of 500 years of colonialism in America scheduled to take place in 1992. Organizers held follow-up organizational meetings in São Paulo and Quito. The São Paulo meeting included delegates from movements in eight countries, representing four of the five sub-regions designated in Bogotá. It coincided with the Second National Congress of Brazil's Movimento dos Trabalhadores Rurais Sem Terra (MST) (*Jornal Sem Terra*, April/May 1990). Founded in 1984, the MST quickly became one of the world's most vibrant peasant organizations. Its members were often peasant families dispossessed due to huge hydroelectric construction projects, misguided colonization schemes, and land concentration fueled by the expanding influence of financial capital. The MST built a strong internal culture and, protective of its organizational autonomy, rejected formal recognition in corporatist categories. Autonomy permitted the MST to expand the definition of "landless" to include anyone willing to fight for farmland (Welch 2006).

By partnering with the resistance campaign in 1990, MST leaders demonstrated a far-reaching vision for their movement, one grounded in class consciousness, ethnic diversity, and the common cause of rural people threatened by capitalist globalization (see Burridge and Markoff in this volume). A closing announcement emphasized the uniting themes of their campaign, including combatting imperialism, confronting neoliberal policy by uniting "all the progressive forces of the continent," and alerting one and all to defend revolutionary governments like those of Cuba and Nicaragua and to the value of inter-American solidarity as a "space to learn from each other's struggles, work toward organizational unity, involving not only indigenous peoples and peasants, but also workers and other progressive sectors" (*Jornal Sem Terra*, April/May 1990: 22). In fact, products of this vast "*campesindio*" (indigenous peasants) organizing effort (Bartra 2008) included the 1993 founding of the Via Campesina, now an international consortium of more than 180 agrarian social movements in more than eighty countries, and the 1994 creation of the Coordinadora Latinoamericana de Organizaciones del Campo (CLOC), which unites eighty-five agrarian social movements from twenty-one countries (Seibert and Amorim 2019). Both organizations host congresses for exchanging information and tactics among peasant movements and promote pro-peasant policies at regional and world level forums, like meetings of the United Nation's Food and Agriculture Organization (FAO).

The MST took part in all of these international initiatives while fighting for agrarian reform in Brazil. With one foot planted in Catholic social justice theology and another in the communist-inspired rural labor movement, the MST emphasized reviving the peasantry through land occupations and other direct-action militancy intended to make governments and courts implement articles of Brazil's 1988 constitution that specify the state's responsibility to expropriate rural estates that are either unproductive or violate environmental and labor laws (Fernandes and Welch in this volume). Principally because of MST activism, hundreds of thousands of occupations have occurred and more than one million families have been settled on nearly 9,500 agrarian reform settlements, occupying some eighty million hectares of Brazil's national territory. The MST was the most effective of nearly 140 agrarian social movements active in Brazil between 2000 and 2016 (Girardi 2018). The movement's longevity is largely due to the dedication of militants and its support among settlers, whose control of territory generates farm income from which the organization collects tithes.

The Quito meeting in July 1990 introduced internationally the Confederación de Nacionalidades Indígenas del Ecuador (CONAIE). Founded in 1986, CONAIE arose from a long history of peasant and indigenous people's organizations in Ecuador (see Rice in this volume). One such organization was the Federación Ecuatoriana de Indios (FEI), which, aligned with the Partido Comunista Ecuatoriano, has defended indigenous peoples as peasants since its founding in 1944 (Becker 2008). In fact, until the 1970s, most of Ecuador's indigenous population lived and worked on haciendas as *huasipungueros*, exchanging their labor for access to small plots of land and supplementary wages (Andrade, Gonzalo Herrera, and Ospina 2008; Zamosc 1994). CONAIE argued that agrarian reform laws from the 1960s and 1970s had been implemented in ways that consolidated and modernized haciendas to the detriment of peasants. Within Ecuador, CONAIE defended indigenous people in more than 200 land disputes and fought for constitutional recognition of the pluri-national and multicultural character of the country.

No other *campesindio* mobilization so captured the world's attention as the 1994 Zapatistas insurrection in southern Mexico. On the same day that NAFTA was enacted, January 1, the Ejército Zapatista de Liberación Nacional (EZLN) occupied several towns in the state of Chiapas to protest the international accord (see Oikonomakis, Inclán in this volume). Its negotiation had already forced changes to Mexico's revolutionary era constitution, including abandonment of Article 27, which had protected indigenous communal lands from sale by individuals. In fact, NAFTA disrupted Mexican agriculture by exposing it to foreign investment and competition. More than ten million peasants were displaced by an influx of corn from the United States and Canada; "comparative advantage" further dictated the cultivation of specialty vegetable and fruit crops for export (Foley 1995). The success of "free trade" was built on Mexico's loss of control over its food system, a system ostensibly defended by peasant organizations since they were politically incorporated by the 1910 revolution. But rival political parties and politicians constantly manipulated peasant organizations, resulting in a breakdown of the corporatist system that permitted US imperialism to reassert influence over Mexican agriculture (De la Peña 1994; Grammont and Mackinlay 2009). Alert to the cooptation of peasant representation, a sell-out particularly damaging to *campesindio* autonomy, the Zapatistas said no to NAFTA and yes to a future determined by indigenous peasants themselves (Womack Jr. 1999).

Even in the context of an insurrection, the Zapatistas were accompanied by a civic movement that labored to construct municipal, regional, and national autonomy (see Inclán, Souza in this volume). While defending their territory from external attack and internal paramilitary groups, the EZLN promoted a societal project that presented itself as more promising for humanity than that generated by agrarian capitalism. While incorporating new technologies and scientific knowledge, such as agroecological methods of production, the Zapatistas conceptualized and practiced ways of life meant to place people above profits and nature above environmentally destructive artifacts. Zapatista militancy contributed to de-colonial thought and a continental movement to discover an emancipatory epistemology (see Flórez-Flórez and Orlate-Orlate in this volume).

Conclusion

The vitality of peasant movements in the late twentieth and early twenty-first centuries is intimately linked to capitalist globalization in agriculture. In fact, 1992 marked not only the climax of 500 years of resistance and the beginning of institutionalizing solidarity through organizations like the CLOC, but also huge advances for agrarian capitalism. The conclusion that year of an international process of "liberalizing" agriculture through the imposition of new conventions through the Uruguay round of the General Agreement on Tariffs and Trade (GATT) brought profound change to the countryside as restrictions were lifted on foreign land sales, tariffs were lowered on food imports, and intellectual property protections encouraged the spread of genetic manipulation technology (Oyarzun de Laiglesia 1993). These changes contributed to unprecedented land concentration, facilitating the food imperialism of fewer and fewer transnational agribusiness corporations. Their dominance of the latest technologies in genetically modified seed, fertilizers, and pesticides, and their control of transportation logistics and import-export markets led to the universalization of small-scale farmer immiseration in the world.

In the Americas, peasant dispossession was common, but so was peasant reproduction through contract-farming or integration. While the demand for temporary seasonal harvest labor increased dramatically, the market for stable farm labor jobs became scarce, as only a few skilled machine operators were needed on most large production units. Besides worsening rural poverty, increasing the rural exodus, reducing domestic food production, and deepening dependency on food imports, capitalist globalization in agriculture also contributed to the segmentation and fragmentation of the rural working class, undermining its organizations and weakening its capacity to resist.

These factors contributed to the formation of more independent organizations based on ethnic as well as class identity. While some movements from the past had achieved worldwide solidarity through the Communist International, United States-backed free trade union system, and the Catholic Church, an unprecedented number of Latin American peasant organizations have joined together in the CLOC. The principal idea uniting these disparate agrarian social movements is food sovereignty. The concept was elaborated by the Via Campesina in response to the FAO's endorsement of the "food security" doctrine pronounced at the 1996 World Food Summit. While food security emphasized quantity, price, and trade as responsible for facilitating people's "access to sufficient, safe and nutritious food" (FAO 1996), food sovereignty emphasized power and people. Only the people who produced foodstuffs—the vast majority of them peasants and other small-scale farmers—could best guarantee the world's nutritional wellbeing, it is argued (Rosset 2009).

A central idea of capitalist development in agriculture since the late nineteenth century has been the inevitability of the elimination of peasants as a consequence of agricultural modernization. On the contrary, agricultural modernization has reaffirmed the necessity of small-scale, family-labor based production of foodstuffs and the demand for the availability of a flexible, seasonal, migratory workforce. The agricultural marketplace has bifurcated into these two lines: one, highly industrialized large-scale production of commodities like beef, corn, and soybeans; and two, small-scale production of foodstuffs, like fruits, vegetables, and component parts integral to the commodity food system like raising baby chickens. Public policy has favored large-scale export agriculture and left small farmers to fend for themselves. A sign of change in this distorted view of the global food system came in 2018 when the United Nations, under intense pressure from the Via Campesina, issued its Declaration on the Rights of Peasants and Other People Working in Rural Areas (Montón 2019).

References

Andrade, Maria, Stalin Gonzalo Herrera, and Pablo Ospina (2008), "Mapa de movimentos sociales em el Ecuador," *Instituto de Estudios Ecuatorianos*, https://www.iee.org.ec/ejes/inv estigar-para-transformar/mapa-de-movimientos-sociales-en-el-ecuador.html.

Bartra, Armando (2008), "Campesindios: Aproximaciones a los Campesinos de un Continente Colonizado," *Boletín de Antropología Americana* 44, 5–24.

Bauer, Arnold (1991), "La hispanoamérica rural, 1870–1930," in Leslie Bethell (ed.), *Historia de América Latina*. Vol. 7: *América Latina: Economía y sociedad, c. 1870–1930*, 133–62 (Barcelona: Editorial Crítica).

Becker, Marc (2006), "Mariátegui, the Comintern, and the Indigenous Question in Latin America," *Science & Society* 70(4), 450–79.

Becker, Marc (2008), *Indians and Leftists in the Making of Ecuador's Modern Indigenous Movements* (Durham, NC: Duke University Press).

Borras Jr., Saturnino M. (2019), "Agrarian Social Movements: The Absurdly Difficult but Not Impossible Agenda of Defeating Right-wing Populism and Exploring a Socialist Future," *Journal of Agrarian Change* 20(1), 3–36.

Brunk, Samuel (1995), *¡Emiliano Zapata! Revolution and Betrayal in Mexico* (Albuquerque: University of New Mexico Press).

Carvalho, Tarcísio Motta de (2008), "'Nós não tem direito': Costume e direito à terra no Contestado," in Márcia Janete Espig and Paulo Pinheiro Machado (eds.) *A Guerra Santa revisitada: Novos estudos sobre o movimento do Contestado*, 33–71 (Florianópolis: Editora da UFSC).

Castañeda, Jorge (1993), *Unarmed Utopia: The Latin American Left After the Cold War* (New York: Vintage).

Deere, Carmen Diana and Frederick S. Royce (2009), *Rural Social Movements in Latin America: Organizing for Sustainable Livelihoods* (Gainsville: University Press of Florida).

Deere, Carmen Diana and Marchetti, Peter (1981), "The Worker-Peasant Alliance in the First Year of the Nicaraguan Agrarian Reform," *Latin American Perspectives* 8(2), 40–73.

De La Peña, Guillermo (1994), "Rural Mobilizations in Latin America since c. 1920," in Leslie Bethell (ed.), *The Cambridge History of Latin America*, vol. 6 part II, *Politics and Society*, 379–482 (Cambridge: Cambridge University Press).

Espinosa Arango, Mónica (2005), "'De la historia arranca mi derecho': Manuel Quintín Lame, el pensamiento indígena y la historia," *Disonante* 1, 83–92.

FAO (1996), "Rome Declaration on World Food Security, World Food Summit," November 13–17, www.fao.org/3/w3613e/w3613e00.htm.

Foley, Michael W. (1995), "Privatizing the Countryside: The Mexican Peasant Movement and Neoliberal Reform," *Latin American Perspectives* 22(1), 59–76.

Girardi, Eduardo (ed.) (2018), *DATALUTA: Land Struggle Database. Report 2017*. (Presidente Prudente: NERA/UNESP).

Grammont, Hubert C. de and Horacio Mackinlay (2009), "Campesino and Indigenous Social Organizations Facing Democratic Transition in Mexico, 1938–2006," *Latin American Perspectives* 36(4), 21–40.

Grandin, Greg and Gilbert M. Joseph (eds.) (2010), *A Century of Revolution: Insurgent and Counterinsurgent Violence During Latin America's Long Cold War* (Durham, NC: Duke University Press).

Gotkowitz, Laura (2008), *A Revolution for Our Rights: Indigenous Struggles for Land and Justice in Bolivia, 1880–1952* (Durham, NC: Duke University Press).

Gould, Jeffrey L. (2010), "On the Road to 'El Porvenir': Revolutionary and Counterrevolutionary Violence in El Salvador and Nicaragua," in Greg Grandin and Gilbert M. Joseph. Durham (eds.), *A Century of Revolution: Insurgent and Counterinsurgent Violence during Latin America's Long Cold War*, 88–120 (Durham, NC: Duke University Press).

Gutelman, Michel (1970), "The Socialization of the Means of Production in Cuba," in Rodolfo Stavenhagen (ed.), *Agrarian Problems & Peasant Movements in Latin America*, 347–70 (Garden City: Anchor Books).

Huntington, Samuel P. (1968), *Political Order in Changing Societies* (New Haven, CT: Yale University Press).

Klubock, Thomas Millern (2010), "Ránquil: Violence and Peasant Politics on Chile's Southern Frontier," in Greg Grandin and Gilbert M. Joseph (eds.), *A Century of Revolution: Insurgent and Counterinsurgent Violence during Latin America's Long Cold War*, 121–59 (Durham, NC: Duke University Press).

Long, Norman and Bryan Roberts (1997), "Las estructuras agrarias de América Latina, 1930–1990," in Leslie Bethell (ed.), *Historia de América Latina*, vol. 11, *Economía y sociedad desde 1930* (Barcelona: Editorial Crítica), 278–334.

Luciak, Ilja A. (1990), "Democracy in the Nicaraguan Countryside: A Comparative Analysis of Sandinista Grassroots Movements," *Latin American Perspectives* 17(3), 55–75.

McAllister, Carlota (2010), "A Headlong Rush into the Future: Violence and Revolution in a Guatemalan Indigenous Village," in Greg Grandin and Gilbert M. Joseph (eds.), *A Century of Revolution: Insurgent and Counterinsurgent Violence during Latin America's Long Cold War*, 276–308 (Durham, NC: Duke University Press).

Marín Abadía, Yuly Alexandra (2014), "La resistencia indígena de Quintín Lame como una praxis de liberación," Senior Thesis, Universidad del Valle.

Martín Barrios, Adelfo (1984), "Historia política de los campesinos cubanos," in Pablo González Casanova (ed.), *Historia política de los campesinos latinoamericanos*, vol 1. (México DF: Siglo XXI), 40–92.

Mendieta, Pilar (2010), *Entre la alianza y la confrontación: Pablo Zárate Willka y la rebelión indígena de 1899 en Bolivia* (Lima: Instituto Francés de Estudios Andinos/Plural Editores).

Milani, Matinho Camargo (2017), "Percival Farquhar, um homem quase sem nenhum caráter entre oligarcas e nacionalistas de muita saúde (1898–1952)," PhD diss., University of São Paulo.

Montón, Diego (2019), "La Declaración de los Derechos Campesinos em la ONU," *ALAI* 43(2), 4–8.

Núñez Soto, Orlando (1985), "Los campesinos y la política em Nicaragua," in Pablo González Casanova (ed.), *Historia política de los campesinos latinoamericanos*, vol. 2, *Guatemala, Honduras, El Salvador, Nicaragua, Costa Rica, Panamá*, 116–32 (Mexico: Siglo XXI).

Oporto Ordóñez, Luis (2011), "Zarate, el Temible Willka y la rebellion indigena de 1899 de Ramiro Condarco Morales," *Fuentes* 5(15), 56–62.

Oyarzun de Laiglesia, Javier (1993), "GATT, neoproteccionismo y Ronda Uruguay," *Guadernos de Relaciones Laborales* 2, 155–90. Available at https://revistas.ucm.es/index.php/CRLA/article/view/CRLA9393120155A.

Pizarro Leongómez, Eduardo (1989), "Los origenes del movimento armado comunista em Colombia (1949–1966)," *Análisis Político* 7, 7–31.

Prevost, Gary. (1990), "Cuba and Nicaragua: a special relationship?" *Latin American Perspectives* 17(3), 120–137.

Rivera Cusicanqui, Silvia (1985), "Apuntes para una história de las luchas campesinas en Bolivia (1900–1978)," in Pablo González Casanova (ed.), *Historia polítia de los campesinos latinoamericanos*, vol. 3, *Colombia, Venezuela, Ecuador, Perú, Bolivia, Paraguay*, 146–207 (Mexico: Siglo XXI).

Rosset, Peter (2009), "Agrarian Reform and Food Sovereignty: An Alternative Model for the Rural World," in Carmen Diana Deere and Frederick S. Royce (eds), *Rural Social Movements in Latin America: Organizing for Sustainable Livelihoods*, 55–78 (Gainesville: University Press of Florida).

Seibert, Iridiani Graciele and Jaime Amorim (2019), "Rumbo al VII Congresso de la CLOC/LVC," *ALAI* 43(2), 18–19.

Swanger, Joanna (2015), *Rebel Lands of Cuba: The Campesino Struggles of Oriente and Escambray, 1934–1974* (Lanham, MD: Lexington Books).

Ticona Alejo, Esteban (2003), "Pueblos indígenas y Estado boliviano. La larga historia de conflictos," *Gazeta de Antropología*, 19(10). http://hdl.handle.net/10481/7325.

United Nations (2018), *Declaration on the Rights of Peasants and Other People Working in Rural Areas*. Resolution 73/165, December 17 (New York: United Nations).

Useem, Bert (1977), "Peasant involvement in the Cuban revolution," *Journal of Peasant Studies* 5 (1), 99–111.

Welch, Cliff (2006), "Movement Histories: A Preliminary Historiography of Brazil's Landless Laborers' Movement (MST)," *Latin American Research Review* 41(1), 198–210.

Welch, Clifford Andrew (2010), *A semente foi plantada: as raizes paulistas do movimento camponês, 1924–1964* (São Paulo: Expressão Popular).

Womack Jr., John (1970), *Zapata and the Mexican Revolution* (New York: Vintage).

Womack Jr., John (1999), *Rebellion in Chiapas: An Historical Reader* (New York: The New Press).

Zamosc, Leon (1994), "Agrarian protest and the Indian movement in the Ecuadorian highlands," Latin American Research Review 29(3), 37–68.

CHAPTER 20

WOMEN'S MOVEMENTS IN LATIN AMERICA

From Elite Organizing to Intersectional Mass Mobilization

CHRISTINA EWIG AND ELISABETH JAY FRIEDMAN

INTRODUCTION

Latin American women's movements, beginning with mid-nineteenth century elite activism, have evolved over time to become inclusive, interconnected mass movements. This chapter traces this evolution while highlighting several themes. First, women's movements have defied assumptions of what constitutes "political opportunity" by mobilizing under the most inhospitable conditions and encountering setbacks in perceived liberatory contexts. Second, motherhood has been a unifying identity, key strategy, *and* has influenced the breadth of movement demands, which have been as much about distributive issues as about rights (Fontana in this volume). Third, transnational connections have been a source of mobilization. Finally, social, economic, and cultural inclusivity has been a central challenge—and inspiration.

Latin American women's movements have always included feminist movements challenging gendered relations of power as well as movements of women focused on community needs, especially those related to family survival, and other power relations such as race, ethnicity, and class (see Johnson and Sempol in this volume). There are also examples of conservative women seeking to uphold the status quo. No matter their goals, women-led movements filled with female activists inherently challenge gendered norms.

The policy successes of Latin American women's movements are numerous, from early welfare systems in the nineteenth century, to gender parity in positions of decision-making in the twenty-first. But these movements' influence is broader, including their pioneering demand that women's rights be recognized as human rights and, however imperfectly, insisting that intersecting forms of oppression call for multifaceted forms of liberation. Perhaps the greatest evidence of this commitment to intersectional practice is the contemporary massification, which shows the depth and breadth of movements that have matured through well over a century.

Maternal Demands for Social and Civil Rights

The educated, often professional women from urban upper and middle classes who fomented the first women's movements framed their participation according to their "different mission" from men (Miller 1991: 74). Whether advocating for social welfare, women's rights in the family, more access to education and improved working conditions, or, eventually, suffrage, they justified their politics as rooted in maternal and spousal responsibilities and the higher moral and affective sensibilities associated with them (Lavrin 1995; Marino 2019: 8). Although husbands, employers, and state officials utilized motherhood as a justification for controlling women, Latin American activists used maternal identity strategically for political ends.

The restricted liberal states and nationalist dictatorships that followed the struggles for independence from Spain and Portugal were largely governed by elite men of European descent, with formal participation denied to women and those without property or education. Nationalist rhetoric, constitutions, and legal codes enshrined patriarchy (Dore 2000: 9–25). Although "married women in colonial Latin America had greater bargaining power within marriage than did their counterparts in the United States and England," post-independence legal codification "failed to improve" their property rights, curtailed their control over children, and would become a key focus of early activism (Deere and León 2001: 32–33).

Simultaneously, the post-independence push for development included opportunities for women in education and employment that provided conditions for their empowerment. States in the Southern Cone and Mexico began secular single-sex education. Education remained "restricted to the Spanish-speaking upper classes" in the Andean region and Central America, but across the region women began to enter paid employment (Miller 1991: 59). Some elite urban women entered universities and professions, while young women flocked to teacher training schools; these "female schoolteachers . . . formed the nucleus of the first women's groups to articulate . . . a feminist critique of society" (ibid.: 35, 71).

The feminism that emerged advanced a "maternity that would . . . embrace all humanity"—addressing issues of redistribution and regime change as well as women's status (Lavrin 1995: 34). As early as the 1820s, elite women engaged in philanthropic and other activities to develop some of the first child welfare and public health services

(Besse 1996; Ehrick 2005; Guy 2009). "Feminismo Americano" ("American Feminism") also took aim at US imperialism, authoritarianism, fascism, and even white supremacy (Lavrin 1995: 15, 19; Marino 2019). National origin determined the direction of feminist efforts. While prominent suffragist Bertha Lutz asserted a Brazilian "exceptionalism" and saw her country and the United States as leading the region forward, for others, such as Ofelia Domínguez Navarro of Cuba, anti-imperialism was critical (Marino 2019: chs. 1 and 2).

By the early twentieth century, the expansion of party systems and workers' rights movements resulted in further opportunities for activists. Though most were "of European ethnic origins," they were joined by mestiza and Afro-descendant women (Lavrin 1995: 17). Liberal feminists initially focused on the rights of the individual, equality with men in marriage, education, property ownership, and childrearing. Meanwhile, anarchists focused on the conditions of working-class women, and, in Argentina, advanced "a radical critique of the family, machismo, and authoritarianism in general" (Molyneux 1986: 141–42). The socialist ideas and organizing that spread to the Southern Cone integrated "the concept of gender equality" (Lavrin 1995: 20). In the 1920s, liberal and socialist feminists collaborated on demands for women's education, access to work, and public participation.

Not all feminists were convinced that suffrage should be a priority. While socialists argued for universal suffrage, some feminists agreed with male leaders who opposed suffrage based on women's assumed conservatism, given their association with Catholic piety (Miller 1991: 86); yet others saw voting as ineffective given the political restrictions of the period (Marino 2019: 90). But, inspired by international connections, eminent feminists initiated suffrage advocacy. In 1916, the first female doctor in Uruguay, obstetrician Paulina Luisi, founded the first national suffrage organization in the Southern Cone, the Consejo Nacional de Mujeres Uruguayas (National Council of Uruguayan Women) (ibid.: 14). The Panamanian lawyer Clara González, along with "Afro-Panamanian educators" Sara Sotillo and Felicia Santizo, started the pro-suffrage Partido Nacional Feminista (National Feminist Party) in 1923 (ibid.: 42, fn 50).

Although elite women's feminism had a broad agenda, much of it was "steeped in Western, European-looking racial logics," including eugenicism (Marino 2019: 23). It took a "hygienic" and "scientific" approach to issues ranging from prostitution to child development, treating women of lower social status as the objects, rather than the subjects, of advocacy. But in Mexico, organized women sought "revolutionary citizenship" through recognition of both their political protagonism and reproductive labor (Olcott 2006: 22).

The organization and regional connections of women's rights evolved over this period. Initially, intellectual discussion took place in salons and the budding women's press. Excluded from male-dominated newspapers and journals, feminists founded their own, such as *O Sexo Feminino* (The Feminine Sex, Brazil), *La Mujer* (The Woman, Chile), and *El Aguila Mexicana* (The Mexican Eagle, Mexico). After the turn of the century, organizing expanded through mentoring and networking (Marino 2019: 8, 16). Professionals advanced ideas about childcare, motherhood, and equal education at scientific congresses (Miller 1991: 72–73). Such engagement culminated in the 1910 International Feminist Congress in Buenos Aires, where participants focused on problems of industrialization, including women and children's labor conditions, and continued to promote reforms in healthcare, education, childcare, employment, familial relations, and political rights. Despite their differences, participants articulated the need for a region-wide movement (Marino 2019: 16; Miller 1991: 75).

Regional organizations, which gave "political leverage back home," became central to regional feminisms (Miller 1991: 95). Latin Americans initiated the Pan-American Association for the Advancement of Women in 1922. Finding it oriented to Anglo-American feminism and insufficiently anti-imperial, the following year Mexican feminists founded the Liga Internacional de Mujeres Ibéricas e Hispanoamericanas (International League of Iberian and Hispanic American Women), which incorporated educated women in the Caribbean and Central America (Marino 2019: 35; Miller 1991: 86). At the 1928 International Conference of American States in Havana feminists achieved the recognition of the first intergovernmental women's rights organization, the Inter-American Commission of Women (Miller 1991: 95). Through such organizations, they cooperated with United States feminists while asserting their own priorities in the face of an "egalitarian" and suffrage-oriented agenda (Marino 2019).

TENUOUS ALLIANCES WITH THE LEFT: WOMEN AND POPULAR FRONT AND POPULIST POLITICS

From the 1930s through the 1970s, the uniquely Latin American feminism, centered on motherhood and concerned with redistributive issues as much as with equal rights, thrived in women's movements allied with the national communist, socialist, and pacifist forces. Leftist populism also emerged in Argentina, Brazil, Mexico, and Peru, creating a context less amenable to autonomous women's organizing, and sometimes explicitly anti-feminist. Transnational connections continued through international women's and leftist networks. Suffrage slowly spread across the region (from Ecuador in 1929 to Paraguay in 1961), while activism around married women's civil, legal, and property rights continued. Also rooted in earlier decades of mobilization, one major achievement was state institutionalization of welfare programs supporting mothers and children. Pushed by leftist sensibilities, activists began grappling with inclusion through cross-class women's organizations. Despite their ties to and inspiration from left parties and movements, the response by the left was rarely supportive (Miller 1991: 101).

In the inter-war period, tensions flared between leftists (communist and pacifist) and right-wing fascists. While left movements rarely promoted women's rights, fascism—which explicitly sought to deny women any rights—inspired many women to organize anti-fascist feminist movements (Marino 2019: 120–28). Some women, however, were active in fascist movements, such as the "Green Blouses" of the Ação Integralista Brasileira (Brazilian Integralist Action) (Deutsch 2004). In 1934, elite women from Argentina, Chile, Cuba, Mexico, and Uruguay helped found the World Committee of Women Against War and Fascism, which preceded the 1935 Popular Front alliance when the Communist International endorsed an anti-fascist communist-socialist alliance (Marino 2019: 129). Some of them allied with national popular front movements.

Informed by their leftist consciousness, many sought to forge cross-class, intersectional women's movements. In Brazil and Uruguay, feminist organizations incorporated middle-class women—but were less successful with working class women (Besse 1996: 165; Ehrick 2005). Radical left women also faced constraints from their male comrades. In Brazil, they rejected the Marxist writings of Patricia Galvão and María Lacerda seeking recognition of sexism and racism (Miller 1991: 103–4). The Chilean Movimiento pro Emancipación de la Mujer Chilena (Movement for the Emancipation of Chilean Women) (1935), and the Colombian Unión Femenina (Femenine Union) (1944) and Alianza Femenina (Femenine Alliance) (1945) stand out for developing cross-class movements that addressed "general problems" like education, health and housing, and "unjust sex discrimination" (Gonzalez 2000; Rosemblatt 2000: 100–1). The Cuban Federación Democrática de Mujeres Cubanas (Democratic Federation of Cuban Women) (1948), related to the Communist Party, attempted to "simultaneously address hierarchies of race, class and gender" (Chase 2015: 111–12).

Left-leaning populism provided different challenges and opportunities: populist leaders' inclusive rhetoric worked to activists' advantage, yet they preferred top-down control and most viewed feminism with disdain. Populist movements—such as those led by presidents Lázaro Cárdenas of Mexico (1934), Juan Perón of Argentina (1946), Getúlio Vargas (1930), and Juscelino Kubitscheck of Brazil (1956)—expanded democracies by enfranchising the excluded working classes, and in Mexico, peasants. Vargas's commitment to political inclusion made it difficult for him to deny feminists' demands for suffrage, for which they had advocated since the 1920s (Besse 1996: 170). In Mexico, the Consejo de Mujeres (Women's Council) pressured Cárdenas to endorse women's suffrage. Cárdenas conceded, declaring support for suffrage for "working women" (Miller 1991: 100). Suffragists pushed, however, to define "working women" as "not only factory workers and professionals but also store clerks and housewives"(Olcott 2010: 33). Partido Peronista Femenino (Femenine Peronist Party), organized by Juán Perón's first wife Eva, was one of several top-down attempts to organize women as part of populist movements. Scholars debate to what degree these constitute "women's movements" due to their lack of autonomy. Autonomous feminists were viewed by the party as the "enemy" while motherhood was extoled (Grammático 2010; Guy 2009). Others point to the passage of women's suffrage, divorce, and recognition of children born out of wedlock, and that Perón cemented a national welfare policy that was built upon the foundation laid by early women activists (Feijoo and Gogna 1990: 81–2; Guy 2009). Magda Portal, the only women leader in Peru's populist APRA party, also developed a women's arm, but believed "APRA needed to transform women into revolutionaries before they could be allowed to vote" (García-Bryce 2014: 692–702).

MILITANT MOTHERHOOD AND HUMAN RIGHTS

Elites backed by military forces responded, sometimes brutally, to populist governments' strategies to build national economies and redistribute resources to their working-class electoral base (Gallegos and Stoessel in this volume). Latin American history is punctuated by military interventions and, eventually, long-term, right-wing military rule in several countries (Brockett in this volume). This context inspired women's movements—both right and left. Motherhood became a reason to reject government leadership as illegitimate if it could not provide the means for women to fulfill their traditional roles. Right wing women's movements used this reasoning to back military interventions, while under these regimes other women used it to resist authoritarianism. Through that resistance, women would also make human rights central to Latin American women's movements demands (Wolff in this volume). Exposed to feminism while in exile, leftist women returned armed with feminist inspiration.

Right-wing women's mobilization helped to bring to power long-lasting military dictatorships in Brazil (1964) and Chile (1973). In Brazil, the middle-class Campanha da Mulher pela Democracia (Women's Campaign for Democracy) and Liga da Mulher pela Democracia (Women's League for Democracy) opposed the reform-oriented government of João Goulart as putting Brazil on a path towards communism. Allied with conservative parties and the Catholic Church, these self-identified housewives mobilized to protect Brazil's "traditions" through enormous "Marches of the Family for God with Liberty," which were fundamental in bringing the military to power (Starling 1986: 155). The US government had taken note of Brazilian women's success when it supported a similar women's movement against the socialist government of Salvador Allende in Chile (Power 2002: 86). Claiming an inability to carry out their maternal roles amidst shortages of basic goods, the spectacle of well-to-do women banging pots in the streets was a key force in the downfall of Allende and the rise of Augusto Pinochet's dictatorship (Baldez 2002; Power 2002).

Military governance harmed many other mothers. Governments in Argentina, Brazil, Chile, and Uruguay perpetrated significant human rights abuses, often involving the kidnapping and "disappearances" of young leftist activists engaged in student, labor, and popular movements. These violations were especially prevalent in Argentina after its 1976 coup, where members of the military also kidnapped activists' babies and young children and gave them to supporters to raise in their "war against subversion."

Such abuses spurred the mothers of these activists, and other women, to protest despite the extremely dangerous context, bringing the defense of human rights to the fore of politics. The Argentine Madres de Plaza de Mayo (Mothers of the Plaza de Mayo) became famous for their weekly marches around the main square facing the presidential palace. Drawn together by their common identity, they strategically deployed their motherhood to demand the return of their missing children (Bouvard 2002; Navarro 2001). Seen as crazy, but "apolitical," these mothers—later joined by grandmothers—were able to advance their activism for a time. In neighboring Chile, women in the shantytowns of Santiago gathered to stitch "arpilleras," quilted scenes of the lives of adult children disappeared by the Pinochet dictatorship. The use of a traditional "women's" skill allowed this resistance to flourish (Agosín 2008), while other women maintained more overt human rights organizations like the Agrupación de Familiares de Detenidos-Desparacidos (Group of Relatives of the Detained-Disappeared) (Baldez 2002). In Brazil, as well, women's movements for human rights, and those protesting the high cost of living, were at least at first viewed as non-threatening (Alvarez 1990). Feminists engaged in the Chilean democratization movement drew an analogy between patriarchal state and domestic violence (Frohmann and Valdés 1995); Chilean theorist Julieta Kirkwood insisted on "Democracy in the country, in the home, and in the bedroom" (Kirkwood 1990). This call to recognize women's rights as human rights would be globalized during the 1992 United Nations Human Rights Conference process (Friedman 1996).

Popular (from the Spanish "lo popular" meaning "of the people," or grassroots) women also organized in line with their traditional responsibilities against the failed economic policies of military governments. Lack of access to basic goods, sanitation, health, and education drove them to establish collective means of survival through cooperative soup kitchens and local protests (see, e.g., Feijoo and Gogna 1990; Valdés and Weinstein 1993). In Brazil, the influence of Liberation Theology, which preached a commitment to the poor and encouraged greater involvement of lay members in the Catholic Church (Mackin in this volume), inspired popular women in Christian Base Communities to organize as "militant mothers" (Alvarez 1990). Although rarely overtly oppositional, these comprised a form of collective action unsanctioned by the military regimes.

Meanwhile, leftist women forced to flee their home countries often learned from feminists abroad. Inspired by the transnational diffusion of approaches such as feminist consciousness-raising, Southern Cone exiles translated feminist theory and practice to reflect their own positionality. Latin American women living in Paris formed the Grupo Latino-Americano de Mulheres/Mujeres (Latin American Women's Group) in 1972; Brazilian exiles later created the Círculo de Mulheres Brasileiras (Brazilian Women's Circle). Returning home when democratization got underway, they brought explicitly feminist goals. These new approaches received an uneven welcome by comrades often suspicious of what they saw as bourgeois, imperial imports (Abreu 2014).

Not all military regimes were alike. While initially claiming to include the working-class and indigenous peasants and avoiding the extreme repression of their neighbors to the south, Bolivian and Peruvian military governments were still authoritarian. In Bolivia, the military governments' bloody confrontations with well-organized miners galvanized the Housewives Committees. Indigenous leader of the Comité de Amas de Casa del Distro Minero Siglo XX (Housewives Committee of the Siglo XX Mining District), Domitila Barrios de Chungara, viewed women's liberation as intimately tied to throwing off the "yoke of imperialism" and electing "a worker like us" as a leader (Chungara and Viezzer 1978: 41). The Siglo XX housewives staged the 1977 hunger strike that brought down the Banzer government (Lavaud 2015). In Peru, the organizations that the Velasco government established in rural and urban areas served as the launching pad for peasant and urban popular women's protests against the regime (Barrig 1989; Radcliffe 1993).

These three strands of women's organizations—human rights, popular, and feminist—not only came together at the forefront of democratization movements but also sought to place different women's interests on new democratic agendas. In Brazil, for example, while the feminist movement demanded reproductive rights and salary equality, popular women demanded state-sponsored day care and Afro-Brazilian women foregrounded the specific health, employment and education needs of Black women, many of whom were low-income domestic workers (Alvarez 1990; Rodrigues and Prado Aurelio 2012).

From Revolutionaries to Revolutionary Activism

When much of the Southern Cone lived under military regimes, citizens of countries such as Haiti under "Papa doc" Duvalier, Nicaragua under Anastasio Somoza, Cuba under Fulgencio Batista, and Paraguay under Alfredo Stroessner faced personalistic strongmen as leaders. Governments in El Salvador and Guatemala were not personalistic but were alternately led by elites in close alliance with militaries. The 1959 Cuban revolution was the first to topple one of these governments, inspiring leftist armed insurrections and fear of communism across the region (Martí i Puig and Álvarez in this volume). Women joined revolutionary movements in Venezuela, Guatemala, El Salvador, Nicaragua, Colombia, Peru, and eventually in Chiapas, Mexico. The revolutionary movements spawned in Central America, in particular, catalyzed some of the most dynamic feminist movements of Latin America.

Revolutionary women tended not to initially identify as feminist, but they upended traditional gender expectations. Women played vital roles in the Cuban guerrilla forces and made up a significant portion of revolutionaries in other countries: between 25 and 30 percent in El Salvador, Nicaragua, Guatemala, and Chiapas. In Guatemala and Mexico, significant portions of these combatants were also indigenous (Kampwirth 2002: 84; Luciak 2001; Shayne 2004; see also Oikonomakis in this volume).

The contradictions of experiencing sexism within organizations that sought to "revolutionize" societies sparked some to develop feminist consciousness. Many of them faced sexist attitudes from male comrades. Women's "arms" of revolutionary organizations, while designed to harness women's support for the revolution, also provided a propitious organizational context. Vibrant feminist movements resulted in Nicaragua and El Salvador, while in Cuba the revolution spawned women's activism but not feminism (Chase 2015; Kampwirth 2004; Luciak 2001). Unlike its predecessors, in Chiapas, Mexico, the 1994 Zapatista revolutionary movement included women's equality at the end of its original platform and provided a context for indigenous and mestiza women to organize together (Kampwirth 2002: 112–15). Autonomous indigenous women's organizations successfully moved the male Zapatista leadership to oppose indigenous customs that were detrimental to women (Kampwirth 2004).

While revolutionary women tended to be in their 20s and 30s, older women also mobilized—against authoritarian regimes and for and against revolution. Here again, motherhood was a motivator and camouflage for engaging in politics. In Nicaragua, more women organized as mothers against the persecution of youth by the Somoza governments, the high cost of living, and the deaths of their sons in the United States-backed Contra war that followed the Sandinista revolution, than as revolutionaries or feminists (Bayard de Volo 2001). Women in Cuba, El Salvador, and Guatemala also deployed motherhood to resist authoritarian abuses of human rights (Schirmer 1993; Shayne 2004).

Confronting the Simultaneous Transitions of Democracy and Neoliberalism

Despite women's protagonism in authoritarian resistance and revolution, the democratic and peace-building periods that followed were not as favorable for achieving women's demands as many had expected. When male-dominated parties and unions returned along with democratic processes, they viewed these demands—from reproductive rights to the establishments of women's ministries—as too radical or unimportant. Simultaneously, most countries experienced economic transitions from state-centered economic models to "neoliberal" ones as part of efforts to address economic crises. Under these conditions, the return to democratic politics led, paradoxically, to a decline, and reorientation—but far from an end—to women's organizing. Much had been learned from the previous decades of activism and alliance-building.

Among feminist movements, democracy brought to the fore tensions percolating in women's movements between "feministas" (women who organized apart from parties and the state) and "militantes" (those that worked within these). Autonomous, though often leftist-aligned, feminist organizations formed the nucleus of reorganized movements (Franceschet 2005; Kampwirth 2004; Vargas 1992). In the 1980s, many of these organizations professionalized in order to influence policy, while also keeping a foot in movement politics. By the 1990s, however, states and international organizations began to depend on feminist organizations for their expertise, while feminists depended on these sources for their financial sustainability—leading to a feminist "NGO-Boom" (Alvarez 1999). While in some cases the non-governmental model resulted in successful influence, concerns with fiscal solvency and expertise also brought tensions, as educated middle class women were both viewed as the "experts" by funders and had greater access to funding (Ewig 1999; Thayer 2010).

The harsh neoliberal economic adjustment policies of the 1980s pushed the working class into poverty and the poor into misery. Popular women responded to the "lost decade" of development by expanding their consumption-oriented strategies. Initially supported by church donations, women's unpaid labor was welcomed by governments, which directed international food donations towards them; in some countries—such as Peru—parties created competing clubs as part of their electoral strategies (Friedmann et al. 1996). In Chile and elsewhere, these women became interested in issues of gender subordination, though hesitated to call themselves "feminist" (Richards 2004).

Regional and transnational organizing was rejuvenated by the four world conferences on women hosted by the United Nations between 1975 and 1995, and undergirded by communications technology from faxes to the early internet (Friedman 2017: ch. 2). The 1980 United Nations meeting in Copenhagen planted the seed for the first Latin American and Caribbean feminist "Encuentro" (meeting or encounter), held in 1981 in Bogotá and attended by 200 feminists from fifty organizations across the region, while the 1995 United Nations Conference in Beijing inspired two years of regional preparatory organizing (Alvarez et al. 2003: 44; Sternbach et al. 1992: 405). The Encuentros, held at regular intervals to this day, became crucial sites for collaborating and working through challenges from the issue of autonomy versus "double militancy" with leftist parties, to the perennial search to widen the feminist field to include women of different classes, races, and, taking on greater visibility in the 1990s, sexual orientations and gender identities (Alvarez et al. 2003). As United Nations conferences increasingly attracted conservatives, Latin American activists shifted to events such as the World Social Forum and the World Women's March.

The emergence of new types of autonomous movements made alliance-building and inclusion all the more important. Lesbian feminists began collectives in the 1980s in Argentina, Chile, Costa Rica, Honduras, and Mexico (Espinosa Miñoso 2010). Transwomen organized to demand fundamental human rights ranging from housing and healthcare to freedom from violence (Pecheny and Corrales 2010). Building on their past experiences, indigenous women began to create movements in the 1990s. Whether part of the Bartolina Sisa peasant women's organization in Bolivia or the Zapatistas revolutionary movement, indigenous women shared a common vision of gender "complementarity" with men as well as a double militancy between advancing their specific interests and the goals of broader indigenous movements (Hernández Castillo 2001; Rousseau and Hudon 2017). Afro-descendant women's autonomous activism, begun in the 1970s, became more visible and transnational in the 1990s, with the founding of the Network of Afro-Latin American and Caribbean Women in 1992 and organizing around the 2001 United Nations Conference Against Racism. These activists foregrounded intersections among racism, sexism, and poverty (Laó-Montes 2016). Different collectivities—such as Black lesbians and Black domestic workers—soon advanced their own positionalities and alliances (Bairros et al. 2016: 58–9; Dixon and Caldwell, Díez in this volume).

The region-wide articulation of distinct demands provoked heated debate over the priorities and protagonists of feminist activism. Sometimes urban, light-skinned, "NGO feminists" failed miserably in representing the interests of women unlike themselves (Ewig 2006; Thayer 2010). This phenomenon, alongside the emergence of "femocrats"— feminists who entered state bureaucracies—led to a new iteration of the autonomy debate: this time, between the "autónomas," who insisted agitation outside the state was most effective, and the "institucionalizadas," who were willing to work with, and within, the state itself (Alvarez et al. 2003). But the complex national and regional exchanges around diversity and inequality eventually resulted in strategic alliances that would undergird ever-larger mobilizations and numerous legislative successes (see Gurza Lavalle and Szwako, Ruibal in this volume).

One early success of the democratic period was the creation of "women's machineries"—offices, programs, or ministries—to represent women's interests (Franceschet 2005; Rodríguez Gustá et al. 2017). These machineries, in turn, were often useful for the passage of policies that advanced women's rights. Utilizing a pincer strategy, feminist activists would apply pressure from the outside while femocrats worked from the inside to achieve a common goal (Lycklama à Nijeholt et al. 1998). Among the most important achievements in the first decade after democratization were legislation against violence against women, including the first international treaty, the establishment of gender quotas for political offices, and, in the case of Chile, divorce (Piscopo 2015; Roggeband 2016). More morally contentious issues, such as abortion liberalization, meanwhile, saw little change despite advocacy (Htun 2003).

THE POTENTIALS AND PERILS OF THE PINK TIDE

The spread of the "Pink Tide" of leftist leadership into sixteen countries at the turn of the twenty-first century seemed to herald a dramatic shift in political opportunities for women's movements. Parties as diverse as the institutionalized Partido dos Trabalhadores (Workers' Party or PT) in Brazil and Hugo Chávez's populist Partido Socialista Unido de Venezuela (United Socialist Party of Venezuela) promoted a range of political projects from reformist to revolutionary, but all attempted to redress the deleterious impact of neoliberal economic models on human development and rectify longstanding political exclusion. Although they advanced some gender-specific policies and presented openings to their advocates, this "reactive" left—one with "no clear agenda on gender equality issues" (Blofield et al. 2017: 348)—also ignored, instrumentalized, and even repressed deeper challenges to patriarchal norms, harking back to previous left experiences. Ironically, it was often populist-left executives promising dramatic changes who, in alliance with conservative religious forces, postponed or subverted long-standing claims for gender justice (Blofield and Ewig 2017; Elfenbein 2019; Lind 2012). All governments, however, continued a legacy from neoliberal politics in their reliance on popular women's unpaid labor to achieve policy goals and, often, political mobilization (see e.g. Elfenbein 2019). Yet activists took advantage of the ideological opportunities to continue their advocacy on issues of representation, redistribution, reproductive rights, and gender-based violence through a range of repertoires (Friedman and Tabbush 2019).

Constitutional reform processes provided such an opportunity. Feminist coalitions were active during Ecuadoran and Venezuelan constitutional reform processes, with nearly all their demands inserted in the 1998 Venezuelan constitution (Espina 2007; Lind 2012). In Bolivia, feminists and indigenous women collaborated during the 2008 constitutional convention; their demand for quotas resulted in Bolivia having the second-highest percentage of female legislators globally (Ewig 2018; Rousseau 2011).

Left-leaning states with more institutionalized or movement-based party structures proved permeable to feminist and women's organizations (Blofield et al. 2017). The Uruguayan "multi-nodal policy network" of activists, legislators, and femocrats played a central role in achieving abortion liberalization, same-sex marriage, and gender identity legislation, even in the face of presidential recalcitrance (Johnson et al. 2019). In Brazil, feminists' decades of advocacy within the ruling PT resulted in "hybrid relationships," enabling activists to work through personal contacts (Matos 2019). Well-resourced women's machineries headed by feminists proved a key arena for support; similar agencies for Afro-Brazilians also facilitated intersectional policymaking (Bairros et al. 2016; Rodríguez Gustá et al. 2017). In Bolivia, a strong indigenous women's movement with deep connections to the governing party made an impact on politics and policy (Rousseau and Hudon 2017). To be sure, advocacy continued to reveal tensions and contradictions—multi-nodal alliances could be fragile, given the difficulties of mediating priorities, perspectives, subject positions, use of resources, and disparate treatment by elected or appointed officials (Friedman and Tabbush 2019, 35).

Responding to the promises—and failures—of the Pink Tide, and building on the tireless work of veteran activists, a younger generation took to the streets. The resulting upsurge in protest demonstrated an array of demands and repertoires expanding previous boundaries (Larrondo and Ponce Lara 2019). Reflecting the cross-fertilization of movement fields and ideational currents such as decolonial feminism, queer theory, and intersectional analysis (see Johnson and Sempol, Halvorsen and Rossi, Flórez-Flórez and Olarte-Olarte in this volume), these protests decentered maternal demands in often physical embodiment of their claims. The Marcha de Putas/Vadias—regional variations of the "Slut Walk"—offered dramatic demonstrations by thousands of young women, transfeminists, and sex workers who used their bodies "as a canvas" to denounce all forms of gendered violence. During Brazil's "feminist spring," peasant women, Afro-descendant women, and student activists asserted their overlapping agendas in mass marches (Snyder and Wolff 2019: 96–97). In Argentina, a "feminist people" articulated across identities to support a range of women's rights and deeper democratization (Di Marco 2011), while feminists across the region "sidestreamed" their practices and ideas into other progressive movements (Alvarez 2014). Social media publicized and connected more dispersed communities, such as transgender and gender non-binary people (ibid.: 45). In the legislative realm, disparate activist groups forged "intersectional interests" in crucial instances (Ewig 2018).

This intersectional massification would come into full flower as the Pink Tide receded. In the 2010s, Nicaragua and Venezuela veered into authoritarianism and actively repressed or ignored feminists and their demands. At the other end of the political spectrum, the 2019 election of far-right president Jair Bolsonaro in Brazil nearly shuttered the state to feminist demands, illustrated by his supporters' declaration of "gender" as a dangerous leftist "ideology." Across the region, feminists responded. In June 2015, Argentine feminists sparked the anti-femicide #NiUnaMenos protests of hundreds of thousands, which diffused rapidly. On November 25, 2019, the International Day for the Elimination of Violence against Women, hundreds of Chilean women debuted the performance "Un violador en tu camino" ("A rapist in your way") on the streets of Santiago in the midst of a national uprising against economic and political exclusion. The performance spread by viral video to feminists in streets around the region and the world. Beyond the scourge of gender-based violence, these enormous demonstrations invoked other long-standing—and long-postponed—women's rights demands, from reproductive rights to economic incorporation and redistribution (Larrondo and Ponce Lara 2019).

Conclusion

All social movement scholars can learn valuable lessons from Latin American women's movements, not least because they have grappled with intersectionality as a fundamental challenge and inspiration to movement identity, inclusivity, and impact. In so doing, they have created and nurtured innovative practices and theories enabling capacious agendas and links to broader movements seeking to transform delegitimized political and economic models.

This chapter has outlined the history of Latin American women's movements by subverting the narrative of regional political development. For example, it shows that democratic and left-leaning political regimes, not just authoritarian ones, have presented obstacles to women activists and their central demands. To understand women's resistance in all of its complexity, future scholarship should continue to read against the grain by centering the experiences of non-dominant communities, such as indigenous, Afro-descendant, and sexual and gender diversity.

In tracking the regional backlash against intersectional feminist insights and institutions, which helped to motivate the mass mobilizations of the late 2010s, scholars would be well-advised to deploy transnational analysis. This level continues to be critical to both women's movements and their opponents. Given movements' dependence on transnational digital resources, research that delves into the mutual construction of movements and media will be particularly generative.

Acknowledgements

The authors thank Bianet Castellanos, Lisa Hilbink, and Jessica Lopez Lyman for their comments on an early draft of this chapter.

References

Abreu, Maira (2014), *Feminismo no exílio: O Círculo de mulheres Brasileiras em Paris e o grupo Latino-Americano de mulheres em Paris* (São Paulo: Alameda).
Agosín, Marjorie (2008), *Tapestries of Hope, Threads of Love: The Arpillera Movement in Chile* (Lanham, MD: Rowman & Littlefield).
Alvarez, Sonia E. (1990), *Engendering Democracy in Brazil: Women's Movements in Transition Politics* (Princeton, NJ: Princeton University Press).
Alvarez, Sonia E. (1999), "Advocating Feminism: The Latin American Feminist NGO 'Boom,'" *International Feminist Journal of Politics* 1(2), 181–209.
Alvarez, Sonia E. (2014), "Para além da sociedade civil: reflexões sobre o campo feminista," *Cadernos Pagu* 43, 13–56.
Alvarez, Sonia E. et al. (2003), "Encountering Latin American and Caribbean Feminisms," *Signs* 28(2), 537–79.
Bairros, Luiza, Sonia E. Alvarez, and Miriam Adelman (2016), "Feminisms and Anti-Racism: Intersections and Challenges," *Meridians: Feminism, Race, Transnationalism* 14(1), 50–69.
Baldez, Lisa (2002), *Why Women Protest: Women's Movements in Chile* (Cambridge: Cambridge University Press).
Barrig, Maruja (1989), "The Difficult Equilibrium Between Bread and Roses: Women's Organizations and the Transition from Dictatorship to Democracy in Peru," in Jane S. Jaquette (ed.), *The Women's Movement in Latin America: Feminism and the Transition to Democracy*, 114–48 (Boston, MA: Unwin Hyman).
Bayard de Volo, Lorraine (2001), *Mothers of Heroes and Martyrs: Gender Identity Politics in Nicaragua, 1979–1999* (Baltimore, MD: Johns Hopkins University Press).
Besse, Susan K. (1996), *Restructuring Patriarchy: The Modernization of Gender inequality in Brazil, 1914–1940* (Chapel Hill: University of North Carolina Press).
Blofield, Merike and Christina Ewig (2017), "The Left Turn and Abortion Politics in Latin America," *Social Politics: International Studies in Gender, State & Society* 24(4), 481–510.
Blofield, Merike, Christina Ewig, and Jennifer M. Piscopo (2017), "The Reactive Left: Gender Equality and the Latin American Pink Tide," *Social Politics: International Studies in Gender, State & Society* 24(4), 345–69.

Bouvard, Marguerite Guzman (2002), *Revolutionizing Motherhood: The Mothers of the Plaza de Mayo* (Lanham, MD: Rowman & Littlefield Publishers).
Chase, Michelle (2015), *Revolution within the Revolution Women and Gender Politics in Cuba, 1952–1962* (Chapel Hill: The University of North Carolina Press).
Chungara, Domitila B. De, and Moema Viezzer (1978), *Let Me Speak* (New York: New York University Press).
Deere, Carmen Diana and Magdalena León (2001), *Empowering Women: Land and Property Rights in Latin America* (Pittsburgh, PA: University of Pittsburgh Press).
Deutsch, Sandra McGee (2004), "Christians, Homemakers, and Transgressors: Extreme Right-Wing Women in Twentieth-Century Brazil," *Journal of Women's History* 16(3), 124–37.
Di Marco, Graciela (2011), *El pueblo feminista: Movimientos sociales y lucha de las mujeres en torno a la ciudadanía* (Buenos Aires: Biblos).
Dore, Elizabeth (2000), "One Step Forward, Two Steps Back: Gender and the State in the Long Nineteenth Century," in Elizabeth Dore and Maxine Molyneux (eds.), *Hidden Histories of Gender and the State in Latin America*, 3–32 (Durham, NC: Duke University Press).
Ehrick, Christine (2005), *The Shield of the Weak: Feminism and the State in Uruguay, 1903–1933* (Albuquerque: University of New Mexico Press).
Elfenbein, Rachel (2019), *Engendering Revolution Women, Unpaid Labor, and Maternalism in Bolivarian Venezuela* (Austin: University of Texas Press).
Espina, Gioconda (2007), "Beyond Polarization: Organized Venezuelan Women Promote Their 'Minimum Agenda,'" *NACLA Report on the Americas* 40(2), 20–24.
Espinosa Miñoso, Yuderkys (2010), "The Feminism-Lesbian Relationship in Latin America: A Necessary Link," in Mario Pecheny and Javier Corrales (eds.), *The Politics of Sexuality in Latin America: A Reader on Lesbian, Gay, Bisexual, and Transgender Rights*, 401–5 (Pittsburgh, PA: University of Pittsburgh Press).
Ewig, Christina (1999), "The Strengths and Limits of the NGO Women's Movement Model: Shaping Nicaragua's Democratic Institutions," *Latin American Research Review* 34(3), 75–102.
Ewig, Christina (2006), "Hijacking Global Feminism: Feminists, the Catholic Church, and the Family Planning Debacle in Peru," *Feminist Studies* 32(3), 633–59.
Ewig, Christina (2018), "Forging Women's Substantive Representation: Intersectional Interests, Political Parity, and Pensions in Bolivia," *Politics & Gender* 14(3), 433–59.
Feijoo, Maria del Carmen and Mónica Gogna (1990), "Women in the Transition to Democracy," in Elizabeth Jelin (ed.), *Women and Social Change in Latin America*, 79–114 (London: United Nations Research Institute for Social Development, Zed Books).
Franceschet, Susan (2005), *Women and Politics in Chile* (Boulder, CO: Lynne Rienner).
Friedman, Elisabeth J. (1996), "Women's Human Rights: The Emergence of a Movement," in Julie Peters and Andrea Wolper (eds.), *Women's Rights, Human Rights: International Feminist Perspectives*, 18–35 (London: Routledge).
Friedman, Elisabeth J. (2017), *Interpreting the Internet: Feminist and Queer Counterpublics in Latin America* (Oakland: University of California Press).
Friedman, Elisabeth J. and Constanza Tabbush (2019), "Introduction: Contesting the Pink Tide," in Elisabeth J. Friedman (ed.), *Seeking Rights from the Left: Gender, Sexuality, and the Latin American Pink Tide*, 1–47 (Durham, NC: Duke University Press).
Friedmann, John, Rebecca Abers, and Lilian Autler (1996), *Emergences: Women's Struggles for Livelihood in Latin America* (Berkeley and Los Angeles: University of California Press).

Frohmann, Alicia and Teresa Valdés (1995), "Democracy in the Country and in the Home: The Women's Movement in Chile," in Amrita Basu (ed.), *The Challenge of Local Feminisms: Women's Movements in Global Perspective*, 276–301 (Boulder, CO: Westview Press).

García-Bryce, Iñigo (2014), "Transnational Activist: Magda Portal and the American Popular Revolutionary Alliance (APRA), 1926–1950," *The Americas* 70(4), 677–706.

Gonzalez, Charity Coker (2000), "Agitating for their Rights: The Colombian Women's Movement, 1930–1957," *Pacific Historical Review* 64(4), 689–706.

Grammático, Karen (2010), "Populist Continuities in "Revolutionary" Peronism? A Comparative Analysis of the Gender Discourses of the First Peronism (1944–1955) and the Montoneros," in Karen Kampwirth (ed.), *Gender and Populism in Latin America: Passionate Politics*, 122–39 (University Park: Pennsylvania State University Press).

Guy, Donna (2009), *Women Build the Welfare State: Performing Charity and Creating Rights in Argentina, 1880–1955* (Durham, NC: Duke University Press).

Hernández Castillo, R. Aída (2001), "Entre el etnocentrismo feminista y el esencialismo étnico: Las mujeres indígenas y sus demandas de género," *Debate Feminista* 24, 206–29.

Htun, Mala (2003), *Sex and the State: Abortion, Divorce and the Family Under Latin American Dictatorships and Democracy* (Cambridge: Cambridge University Press).

Johnson, Niki, Ana Laura Rodríguez Gustá, and Diego Sempol (2019), "Explaining Advances and Drawbacks in Women's and LGBTIQ Rights in Uruguay: Multisited Pressures, Political Resistance, and Structural Inertias," in Elisabeth J. Friedman (ed.), *Seeking Rights from the Left: Gender, Sexuality, and the Latin American Pink Tide*, 48–81 (Durham, NC: Duke University Press).

Kampwirth, Karen (2002), *Women and Guerrilla Movements: Nicaragua, El Salvador, Chiapas, Cuba* (University Park: Pennsylvania University State Press).

Kampwirth, Karen (2004), *Feminism and the Legacy of Revolution: Nicaragua, El Salvador, Chiapas* (Athens: Ohio University Press).

Kirkwood, Julieta (1990), *Ser política en Chile: Los nudos de la sabiduría feminista—Memoria Chilena* (Santiago: Cuarto Propio).

Laó-Montes, Agustín (2016), "Afro-Latin American Feminisms at the Cutting Edge of Emerging Political-Epistemic Movements," *Meridians: Feminism, Race, Transnationalism* 14(2), 1–24.

Larrondo, Marina and Camila Ponce Lara, eds. (2019), *Activismos feministas jóvenes: Emergencias, actrices y luchas en América Latina* (Buenos Aires: CLACSO).

Lavaud, Jean-Pierre (2015), *La dictadura minada: La huelga de hambre de las mujeres mineras. Bolivia 1977–1978* (Lima: Institut Français d'études Andines).

Lavrin, Asunción (1995), *Women, Feminism and Social Change in Argentina, Chile and Uruguay, 1890–1940* (Lincoln: University of Nebraska Press).

Lind, Amy (2012), "'Revolution with a Woman's Face'? Family Norms, Constitutional Reform, and the Politics of Redistribution in Post-Neoliberal Ecuador," *Rethinking Marxism* 24(4), 536–55.

Luciak, Ilja A. (2001), *After the Revolution: Gender and Democracy in El Salvador, Nicaragua and Guatemala* (Baltimore, MD: Johns Hopkins University Press).

Lycklama à Nijeholt, Geertje, Joke Sweibel, and Virginia Vargas (1998), "The Global Institutional Framework: The Long March to Beijing," in Geertje Lycklama à Nijeholt, Virginia Vargas, and Saskia Wieringa (eds.), *Women's Movements and Public Policy in Europe, Latin America, and the Caribbean*, 25–48 (New York: Garland Publishing).

Marino, Katherine M. (2019), *Feminism for the Americas* (Chapel Hill: University of North Carolina Press).

Matos, Marlise (2019), "Gender and Sexuality in Brazilian Public Policy: Progress and Regression in Depatriarchalizing and Deheteronormalizing the State," in Elisabeth J. Friedman (ed.), *Seeking Rights from the Left: Gender, Sexuality, and the Latin American Pink Tide*, 144–72 (Durham, NC: Duke University Press).

Miller, Francesca (1991), *Latin American Women and the Search for Social Justice* (Hanover, NH: University Press of New England).

Molyneux, Maxine (1986), "No God, No Boss, No Husband: Anarchist Feminism in Nineteenth-Century Argentina," *Latin American Perspectives* 13(1), 119–45.

Navarro, Marysa (2001), "The Personal is Political: Las Madres de Plaza de Mayo," in Susan Eckstein (ed.), *Power and Popular Protest: Latin American Social Movements*, 241–58 (Berkeley and Los Angeles: University of California Press).

Olcott, Jocelyn H. (2006), *Revolutionary Women in Postrevolutionary Mexico* (Durham, NC: Duke University Press).

Olcott, Jocelyn H. (2010), "The Politics of Opportunity: Mexican Populism under Lázaro Cárdenas and Luis Echeverría," in Karen Kampwirth (ed.), *Gender and Populism in Latin America: Passionate Politics*, 25–46 (University Park: Pennsylvania State University Press).

Pecheny, Mario, and Javier Corrales (2010), *The Politics of Sexuality in Latin America: A Reader on Lesbian, Gay, Bisexual, and Transgender Rights* (Pittsburgh, PA: University of Pittsburgh Press).

Piscopo, Jennifer M. (2015), "States as Gender Equality Activists: The Evolution of Quota Laws in Latin America," *Latin American Politics and Society* 57(3), 27–49.

Power, Margaret (2002), *Right-wing Women in Chile: Feminine Power and the Struggle against Allende, 1964–1973* (University Park: Pennsylvania State University Press).

Radcliffe, Sarah A. (1993), "'People Have to Rise Up—Like the Great Women Fighters': The State and Peasant Women in Peru," in Radcliffe, Sarah A. and Westwood, Sallie (eds.), *"Viva": Women and Popular Protest in Latin America*, 197–218 (London: Routledge).

Richards, Patricia (2004), *Pobladoras, Indígenas, and the State: Conflicts Over Women's Rights in Chile* (New Brunswick, NJ: Rutgers University Press).

Rodrigues, Cristiano and Marco Prado Aurelio (2012), "A History of the Black Women's Movement in Brazil: Mobilization, Political Trajectory and Articulations with the State," *Social Movement Studies* 12(2), 158–77.

Rodríguez Gustá, Ana Laura, Nancy Madera, and Mariana Caminotti (2017), "Governance Models of Gender Policy Machineries under Left and Right Governments in Latin America," *Social Politics: International Studies in Gender, State & Society* 24(4), 452–80.

Roggeband, Conny (2016), "Ending Violence against Women in Latin America: Feminist Norm Setting in a Multilevel Context," *Politics & Gender* 12(1), 143–67.

Rosemblatt, Karin Alejandra (2000), *Gendered Compromises: Political Cultures & the State in Chile, 1920–1950* (Chapel Hill: University of North Carolina Press).

Rousseau, Stéphanie (2011), "Indigenous and Feminist Movements at the Constituent Assembly in Bolivia: Locating the Representation of Indigenous Women," *Latin American Research Review* 46(2), 5–28.

Rousseau, Stéphanie and Anahi Morales Hudon (2017), *Indigenous Women's Movements in Latin America: Gender and Ethnicity in Peru, Mexico, and Bolivia* (New York: Palgrave Macmillan).

Schirmer, Jennifer (1993), "The Seeking of Truth and Gendering Consciousness: The CoMadres of El Salvador and the CONAVIGUA widows of Guatemala," in Sarah A. Radcliffe and Sallie Westwood (eds.), *"Viva": Women and Popular Protest in Latin America*, 30–65 (London: Routledge).

Shayne, Julie (2004), *The Revolution Question: Feminisms in El Salvador, Chile and Cuba* (New Brunswick, NJ: Rutgers University Press).

Snyder, Cara K. and Cristina Scheibe Wolff (2019), "The Perfect Misogynist Storm and The Electromagnetic Shape of Feminism: Weathering Brazil's Political Crisis," *Journal of International Women's Studies* 20(8), 87–109.

Starling, Heloisa Maria Murgel (1986), *Os senhores das Gerais: Os novos inconfidentes e o golpe militar de 1964* (Petrópolis: Vozes).

Sternbach, Nancy Saporta, Marysa Navarro-Aranguren, Patricia Chuchryk, and Sonia E. Alvarez (1992), "Feminisms in Latin America: From Bogotá to San Bernardo," *Signs* 17(2), 393–434.

Thayer, Millie (2010), *Making Transnational Feminism: Rural Women, NGO Activists, and Northern Donors in Brazil* (New York: Routledge).

Valdés, Teresa and Marisa Weinstein (1993), *Mujeres que sueñan: Las organizaciones de pobladoras 1973–1989* (Santiago: FLACSO-Chile).

Vargas, Virginia (1992), "Women: Tragic Encounters with The Left," *Report on the Americas* 25(5), 30–44.

CHAPTER 21

INDIGENOUS MOVEMENTS IN LATIN AMERICA
Characteristics and Contributions

ROBERTA RICE

INTRODUCTION

The rise of powerful and effective Indigenous rights movements in Latin America during the region's third wave of democratization caught most analysts and authorities by surprise. Indigenous demands for identity, territory, and autonomy serve as a challenge to the national unity projects in post-colonial Latin American societies. The Indigenous resurgence raises both conceptual and theoretical questions: What are the major characteristics and contributions of Indigenous movements to Latin American politics and society? What can we learn about social movement theory and practice by studying Indigenous movement dynamics? This chapter addresses these questions by reviewing the key approaches and debates in the literature on Indigenous movements in Latin America. The central argument of the chapter is that the emergence of Indigenous movements problematizes many of the conventional theories of social movement formation as well as the established boundaries between institutionalized and extra-systemic politics that is found in the literature (see Gurza Lavalle and Szwako in this volume). The study of Indigenous movements requires not only the crossing of disciplinary divides, but also new conceptualizations of state-society relations.

The chapter is divided into four sections. The first section examines the historical roots of Indigenous dispossession in Latin America. It details how Latin American societies have long suffered from exclusionary state structures and the failure to incorporate, represent, and respond to large segments of the population. The second section of the chapter provides an overview of the theoretical explanations for Indigenous movement formation in the 1990s, including structural, cultural, and rational choice accounts. The third section analyzes the tensions and contributions of Indigenous movement struggles to our understanding of social movement theory and practice. Particular attention is paid in this section to the multiscalar organizational efforts of Indigenous movements and the bridging of protest and electoral coalitions in achieving movement demands. Indigenous movements in Latin America thwart many of the expectations of social movement scholars. The chapter concludes by charting the course ahead for scholarship on Indigenous movements in Latin America.

Historical Roots of Indigenous Dispossession

The process of Indigenous dispossession that began with the arrival of Europeans in the Americas over 500 years ago continues today through the colonial logic that permeates state structures and institutions. At the time of European conquest, between thirty and seventy million people inhabited the Americas. Possibly half of the Indigenous population died during the conquest. Disease, displacement, and forced labor took the lives of millions more (Vanden and Prevost 2009: 82). The estimated number of Indigenous peoples in the region today ranges from twenty-eight million to forty million, divided among some 670 officially recognized nations or peoples (Layton and Patrinos 2006: 25). Indigenous peoples are a marginalized majority in Bolivia and Guatemala, a substantial portion of the population in Ecuador and Peru, and a significant minority in most other Latin American countries. Race, ethnicity, and power continue to overlap in important ways in contemporary Latin American societies, contributing to the ongoing marginalization of Indigenous peoples as well as Afro-descendant populations (Wade 2010).

Political elites in the post-independence period of the early nineteenth century wrestled with the question of what to do about their respective nations' large, unassimilated Indigenous populations. In the words of the former United Nations Special Rapporteur on the Rights of Indigenous Peoples, Rodolfo Stavenhagen (2002: 28–29): "Latin America's ruling classes, unable to wish Indians away, were quite happy to build nations without Indians, and this they have been trying to do for almost two centuries." It is hardly surprising that the countries with the largest Indigenous populations continue to suffer from weak states with fragile party systems, given that their political systems have excluded the majority of their citizens. According to Félix Cárdenas, Bolivia's Vice Minister of Decolonization (2013), states in the region have not just historically excluded Indigenous peoples; they were founded in opposition to or against them. The construction of a nation-state in opposition to pre-existing Indigenous nations does not serve the interests of its citizens, Indigenous or not. Throughout much of Latin America's history, Indigenous demands have been oppressed, ignored, and silenced. Indigenous groups, where they have mobilized at all, have traditionally done so around class, partisan, religious, and revolutionary identities, as opposed to ethnic ones, as a result of their incorporation into the polity as peasants and as workers (Yashar 2005).

In the name of national unity, Latin American states promoted assimilation into the dominant *mestizo* ("mixed race") culture by reconstituting Indigenous peoples as national peasants as part of the corporatist project of the mid-twentieth century. State corporatism served as an important means for the state to structure group representation and regulate official channels for demand making (Collier 1995). It was through agrarian reform that the rural masses in Latin America were first incorporated into the polity (see Welch in this volume). Land reforms were billed as progressive measures to emancipate Indigenous communities from repressive and exploitative forms of labor control in the countryside (see Fernandes and Welch in this volume). The Indigenous peasantry had long been under the social control of the rural elite and remained beyond the reach of urban politics. In return for access to land, credit, and services from the state, Indigenous peoples were obliged to organize and define themselves as peasants. While Indigenous peoples assumed a peasant status before the state, they continued to express their Indigenous identity within their communities (Yashar 2005).

One of the immediate consequences of the region's adoption of the neoliberal economic model in in the 1980s has been the weakening of state corporatist institutions (Oxhorn 1998). Neoliberal discourse advocates the shift from corporatist, class-based integration to more atomized or individuated state-society relations (see Rossi in this volume). In response to this changing economic and political context, Indigenous groups in Latin America increasingly mobilized on the basis of their ethnic identities (Rice 2012). Beginning in the 1990s, Indigenous movements in Latin America assumed greater political importance in the region. In Bolivia and Ecuador, Indigenous peoples organized nationwide strikes and blockades, toppled corrupt politicians, formed their own political parties, and even captured presidencies. Ecuador's National Indigenous Uprising of June 1990, which served as an expression of citizen frustration with the country's political and economic system, established Indigenous peoples as the lead protagonists in the struggle against neoliberalism (Silva 2009). On the other hand, Bolivia's 1990 March for Territory and Dignity, which saw hundreds of Indigenous peoples walk from the city of Trinidad, Beni, to the administrative capital in La Paz to demand territorial rights and protections, represented a broadening of Indigenous mobilization in that country as highland Quechua and Aymara groups joined forces with their Amazonian counterparts (Lucero 2008). Indigenous conflict also broke out in Chiapas, Mexico in the early 1990s. Since appearing as a central protagonist of change on January 1, 1994, the date of Mexico's integration into the North American Free Trade Agreement (NAFTA), the Indigenous-based Ejército Zapatista de Liberación Nacional (EZLN) has shone a spotlight on Indigenous rights issues in the country (Harvey 1998; Nash 2001).

Theoretical Explanations for Indigenous Movement Formation

The literature on Indigenous movements in Latin America is focused primarily on explaining this sudden and unexpected emergence of Indigenous peoples as critical new social and political actors as well as its implications for the quality and stability of democracy. In the context of a hostile political environment, Indigenous peoples have taken their place on the national political stage not through assimilation but by politicizing their ethnic identity. The politicization of ethnic cleavages is widely regarded in studies on ethnic conflict as having a profoundly negative impact on democracy through the way in which ethnic nationalists pit ethnic groups against each other in an attempt to solidify support among co-ethnics (Horowitz 1985; Rabushka and Shepsle 1972). Referring to the case of Bolivia, Mayorga (2006) has suggested that the politicization of Indigenous identity has undermined representative democracy, governmental capacity, and state unity. In Mayorga's (ibid.: 133) view, Indigenous movements "seek to destroy democratic institutions and replace them with utopian ethnic-based, direct democracy and nationalist populism." Andersen (2010) has gone so far as to caution that the rise of Indigenous movements in Latin America could potentially lead to civil war as they contest the region's artificially imposed nation-states. Notwithstanding the literature on ethnic nationalism, most scholars agree that Indigenous mobilization plays a much-needed role in pushing for a more inclusive society and in broadening political agendas (Lucero 2008; Madrid 2012; Van Cott 2005).

The central point of disagreement among Indigenous movement scholars concerns the factors that lead to movement formation. As one of the most vibrant and celebrated social movements of the last few decades, Indigenous movements have been studied by scholars from a variety of disciplines and theoretical orientations. Structuralists, such as Petras and Veltmeyer (2001), see economic and material goals as the catalyst for Indigenous movement formation. From their perspective, class differences, embodied in the struggle for land, are the main driving force behind Indigenous organizing and mobilization. Structuralists argue that in Latin America, Indigenous movements cannot be analyzed as purely ethnic phenomena when the majority of Indigenous peoples occupy a subordinate position in the class structure. Furthermore, the very real conditions of poverty faced by Indigenous peoples in the region shape and constrain the expression of identities and their capacity for collective action (Otero 2003; Zamosc 2004). The classic work of Yashar (2005) provides a structuralist account of Indigenous movement formation in Latin America. In her view, the combination of changing citizenship regimes, transcommunity networks, and political associational space triggered the politicization of Indigenous identity in the region. The shift from corporatist to neoliberal citizenship regimes politicized ethnic identities by threatening Indigenous peoples' cultural, political, and material interests, while pre-existing community ties provided the organizational linkages to forge movements and political liberalization the space for Indigenous peoples to act. In cases where this combination of factors was absent, such as in Peru, Indigenous movements remained fragmented in nature, regional in scope, and ineffectual at the national level.

Scholars of a more institutionalist theoretical orientation have also offered novel insights into Indigenous movement dynamics in the region. For instance, Van Cott (2005) emphasizes domestic political institutions, such as electoral laws and party system features, as central explanatory variables. According to her analysis, the permissiveness of the institutional environment enables Indigenous political movements to emerge and compete in formal politics. Van Cott's extensive body of work in this area adds a new dimension to the literature on Indigenous movements by examining the transformation of social movements into viable political parties. The decision by Indigenous movements in countries such as Bolivia, Colombia, Ecuador, and Nicaragua to form their own partisan vehicles serves as a puzzle for many social movement scholars who tend to view partisan politics as antithetical to social movement agendas (Beck and Mijeski 2001; Pallares 2002; Yashar 2005). These scholars have typically either ignored the subject of electoral competition altogether or chastised the decision by Indigenous movements to enter into formal politics as being detrimental to movement integrity and unity. This divide has produced an unnecessary rift in the literature between studies of Indigenous movements and those of Indigenous-based parties. Bridging this divide, in Rice (2012) I offer a historical institutionalist explanation as to why Indigenous movements and parties have emerged in some countries but not in others. I argue that strong and cohesive political movements are more likely to arise in countries with weak party systems that do not effectively represent popular sector interests and in which Indigenous actors are able to articulate new collective identities that resonate beyond traditional affiliations based on class, union membership, or partisanship owing from their historic pattern of popular political incorporation.

Comparatively fewer works examine Indigenous movements through a rational choice lens. Glidden (2011) provides a compelling agency-oriented account in her assertion that Indigenous groups choose to mobilize along ethnic lines based on rational, strategic calculations. Her analysis centers on the capacity of identity brokers or movement entrepreneurs to convince potential movement members of the utility of promoting Indigenous identity as their public identity. To do so, brokers play on meaningful symbols and engage in consciousness-raising activities among potential members. They also frame issues as threats to group wellbeing, such as cultural or land loss, as a means to activate their new identity. Alternatively, identity brokers can seek validation or endorsement of a new identity by an outside, authoritative source. In the case of Indigenous peoples, the United Nations Special Rapporteur on the Rights of Indigenous Peoples has been a powerful source of certification by signalling a willingness to recognize and support the existence and claims of Indigenous groups. Movement entrepreneurs will use a newly activated identity to link previously unconnected sites, such as communities to one another or Indigenous groups to the political system, as a means of forming a social movement. This line of analysis helps to explain variation in the emergence and consolidation of Indigenous movements in the region based on the capacity of individual actors and organizations.

A number of studies on Indigenous movements in Latin America offer alternative explanations for their emergence. For instance, Brysk (2000) argues that international factors are paramount in explaining Indigenous movement formation. She suggests that the process of globalization fostered the rise of such movements by allowing Indigenous peoples to appeal to international norms, laws, and organizations to advance their cause (see Burridge and Markoff in this volume). Latin American scholars Xavier Albó (2002) and José Bengoa (2000) propose that both domestic and international factors produced the politicization of ethnic identities. Such factors include a positive international human rights framework and harmful policies of neoliberal economic adjustment. Davis (1999) has proposed a spatial model of collective action that focuses on citizen distance from the state as an explanation for social movement formation. The concept of distance relates to an individual's or a group's degree or level of engagement with the political institutions and practices of the state. Citizens can be distanced from or connected to the state in four ways: geographically, institutionally, culturally, and in terms of class. According to Davis (ibid.), citizens who are distanced from the state on all four dimensions, such as Indigenous peoples, are more likely to form social movements (see also Davis and Davey in this volume). Clearly, no single causal factor can explain the rise of Indigenous movements in Latin America. Most likely, the answer lies in a combination of all of these factors.

The dominant theoretical assumption of much of the scholarship on Indigenous movements in Latin America is that they are a type of New Social Movement (NSM). NSMs refer to new actors, values, and forms of collective action resulting from structural changes in society (Foweraker 1995; Garretón and Selamé in this volume). In other words, NSMs are new responses to new grievances. Older or classic social movements are generally perceived to be those based on class locations, such as peasants and organized workers, and to be oriented toward satisfying material demands, including higher wages or access to land. By contrast, NSMs are distinguished by their emphasis on identity or cultural issues, such as gender, ethnicity, the environment, or peace, as well as their horizontal structure and opposition to traditional partisan politics (Alvarez, Dagnino, and Escobar 1998; Hellman 1997). The NSM school of thought is part of the recent turn toward cultural and ideational explanations of dissent. A central assumption of NSM scholars is that contemporary social movements are the product of ideological, political, and cultural processes, as opposed to class conflicts. Instead of viewing Indigenous movements through the lens of new social movement theory, however, it may be more appropriate to see them as anti-colonial struggles in their melding of old and new concerns. In the words of prominent Chilean scholar José Bengoa (2001: 87): "They are discourses of the past, full of ideas of the future." Indigenous movements in Latin America have opened up new spaces for collective action, transformed Indigenous-state relations, and confounded social movement analysts with the success of both their grassroots campaigns and their international advocacy efforts and their capacity to defend both Indigenous and popular sector demands by pressing for change in the streets and in the legislature.

Indigenous Movements and the Struggle for Identity, Territory, and Autonomy

The core demands of Indigenous movements across the Americas are those of identity, territory, and autonomy. Identity-based demands center on the struggle for recognition as distinct peoples with special rights in the constitution and laws of their respective countries (see Fontana in this volume). Demands for identity include official recognition and protection of Indigenous languages, cultures, and traditions as well as special programs such as bilingual intercultural education, Indigenous health, and community development (Reuque Paillalef 1998). The demand for territory centers on the need for the preservation, protection, and recuperation of previously held Indigenous lands (Almeida 2008). Here land represents a space for the spiritual, cultural, and material reproduction of Indigenous peoples, as opposed to simply an element of production (Ticona Alejo 2000: 142–43). Lastly, the demand for autonomy centers on the call for self-determination and self-government within Indigenous territories (see Souza in this volume). However, autonomy is more than just another demand. It is "the demand that allows for the realization of all other demands" (Díaz Polanco 1998: 218). Indigenous struggles for identity, territory, and autonomy represent an opportunity to address the Indigenous question, in much the same way that worker organization and protest in early twentieth-century Latin America prompted ruling elites to respond to the social question (Collier and Collier 1991).

What role do Indigenous movements play in democratic change in Latin America? One of the main tensions within Indigenous movements relates to the strategic dilemma of maintaining an oppositional stance to their respective political systems or trying to bring about change from within via the formation of a political party or support for an existing one. An institutional strategy is conventionally assumed to risk the loss of legitimacy and the power to mobilize the masses. In contrast to political parties, social movements are supposed to break the rules of the game, not play by them. Institutional participation implies that autonomy is no longer a fundamental principle (Massal and Bonilla 2000). Autonomy and institutional participation, however, do not have to be mutually exclusive. By following a strategy of *autonomy in participation* through the formation of their own electoral vehicles, Indigenous movements in a number of countries have successfully combined disruptive tactics with efforts to elect candidates (Rice 2012). In cases such as Ecuador and Bolivia, Indigenous political movements have been able to amplify social protest demands within the walls of their respective congresses while holding governments to account through their mobilizational campaigns (Ospina 2000).

The work of Goldstone (2003) problematizes the rigid boundary that has been established in the social movement literature between institutionalized and non-institutionalized politics. He argues that in the same way that social movements cannot be fully comprehended without an examination of their political context, public policy and the inner workings of government cannot be fully understood without examining social movement pressure tactics (see Gurza Lavalle and Szwako in this volume). Instead of conceptualizing Indigenous movements as shifting from protesting to proposal making, it is more accurate to view them as participating in both types of activities. By moving outside of the formal political arena and relying on social mobilization campaigns to push through desired legislation in congress or block policies they oppose, the actions of Indigenous movements in Latin America suggest that the divide between protest and electoral politics is fluid rather than fixed (Aminzade 1995; Roberts, Ruibal in this volume).

Bolivia and Ecuador are home to Latin America's most successful Indigenous-based parties to date (see Roberts in this volume). Indigenous movements in the two countries stand out for their mobilizational and organizational capacity in uniting diverse sectors of civil society in the struggle against neoliberalism and for launching their own highly successful national political parties. In Ecuador, the Movimiento de Unidad Plurinacional Pachakutik—Nuevo País (MUPP-NP) party was a major organizational force behind the winning electoral coalition in the 2002 presidential race (Becker 2011; Lucas 2000). However, tensions within the governing coalition over the allocation of key ministerial posts and policy directions resulted in the withdrawal of the MUPP-NP from the government after only 204 days in power (Rice 2012). In Bolivia, the Indigenous and worker-based Movimiento al Socialismo (MAS) party led by Evo Morales managed to obtain a majority vote in the presidential election of December 2005, a feat that had not been achieved by any party since the transition to democracy in the early 1980s (Madrid 2012). President Evo Morales (2006–2019) was re-elected by even wider margins in the 2009 and 2014 presidential elections. The key to effectively combining protest politics with electoral competition is timing and sequence. In Bolivia and Ecuador, Indigenous-based parties developed out of established social movement organizations (Van Cott 2005). Such movements, for the most part, entered into the electoral arena from a position of relative strength, as firmly rooted, consolidated movements with a certain measure of organizational and ideological autonomy.

Ecuador's Indigenous movement was once widely regarded as Latin America's strongest social movement. Under the direction of the Confederación de Nacionalidades Indígenas del Ecuador (CONAIE), the movement managed to disrupt the implementation of neoliberal economic reforms throughout the 1990s. In contrast to other countries with a significant Indigenous population, such as Bolivia, Ecuador's Indigenous movement has been able, at least until quite recently, to avoid extensive interethnic conflict and unite diverse interests from the coastal, highland, and Amazonian regions (Lucero 2008; Van Cott 2005; Yashar 2005). The formation of an Indigenous peoples' party marked a sea change in the strategy of the country's Indigenous movement, from the "politics of influence" to the "politics of power" (Zamosc 2004). Since 2003, however, CONAIE and the Indigenous movement have lost much of their power to convoke the masses both in the streets and in the electoral arena. A complex set of factors contributed to the decline of the movement's power to mobilize, including its participation in a military-supported coup, its ill-fated electoral alliances, and its perceived shift to a more radical, ethnicist stance. Nonetheless, Indigenous activism in the country paved the way for an alternative economic and political model, though under the leadership of left-leaning president Rafael Correa (2007–2017). Ecuador's recent Left Turn government introduced a number of important policy measures to address Indigenous demands in the country, albeit without meaningfully including Indigenous peoples in the policy deliberations.

Bolivia became a global Indigenous rights leader when it incorporated the 2007 United Nations Declaration on the Rights of Indigenous Peoples (UNDRIP) into domestic law and later its constitution (Albó 2010; Schilling-Vacaflor and Kuppe 2012). President Morales made Indigenous rights the cornerstone of his administration. In one of his first official acts, Morales disbanded the Ministry of Indigenous and First Peoples Affairs (MAIPO) under the logic that Indigenous peoples' demands are to be incorporated into all facets of government, rather than addressed separately. Democracy in Bolivia has been re-imagined on the basis of Indigenous citizenship (Canessa 2012). Innovative features of the Morales administration included the introduction of elements of direct, participatory, and communitarian democracy; policies to promote the decolonization and depatriarchalization of the state; and constitutional reforms to advance plurinationality and Indigenous autonomy in the country. Some of the mechanisms for direct citizen participation included recall referendums, town councils, citizen-led legislative initiatives, and the legal-political recognition of citizen's associations and Indigenous groups to contest elections (Exeni Rodríguez 2012). These new spaces of citizen engagement were not construed as an alternative to democracy, but are part of an effort to overcome the basic problems associated with representative democracy (Peruzzotti and Selee 2009; Wampler 2012). The government also made an explicit commitment to the Andean Indigenous principle of *buen vivir* or "living well" as an alternative model of development around which state policies were organized. The living well principle is based on the values of harmony, consensus, and respect, the redistribution of wealth, and the elimination of discrimination within a framework that values diversity, community, and the environment (Fischer and Fasol 2013). The incorporation of civil society actors into the structures of the state had produced a deeper, more meaningful form of democracy in Bolivia.

There is, of course, significant variation in the formation and strength of Indigenous movements across the region. The literature on Indigenous movements specifically, and social movements more generally, has focused overwhelmingly on the positive cases of movement formation. The study of the failure of expected movements to emerge can contribute new insights into and understandings of social movement dynamics. Peru, for example, is an anomalous case of Indigenous mobilization. It is home to one of the largest Indigenous populations in Latin America (Deruyttere 1997) and is sandwiched between Ecuador and Bolivia—the region's Indigenous rights pioneers. Yet Peru does not have a nationally visible Indigenous movement. Ethnic identities have remained muted in the country. As Lucero and García (2007) remind us, ethnicity is expressed differently in different countries. Indigenous collective action in Peru has traditionally emphasized class, regional, or sectoral identities much more than ethnic ones. Notwithstanding this, Peru is a country with a tremendous amount of popular collective activity (Arce 2014; Rice 2012). But while Indigenous movements in Ecuador and Bolivia have captured state power, there is little in the way of a sustained Indigenous challenge in Peru. Instead, protests in the country are localized, sporadic and spontaneous in nature, though at times the intensity of the conflicts causes them to resonate at the national level. There are a number of nascent popular movements in the country, including the coca growers' movement in southern Peru (Denissen, Van Dun, and Koonings 2004; Felbab-Brown 2006), the anti-mining movement in the highlands (De Echave 2005; McDonnell 2015), and a regional Indigenous movement in the Amazonian lowlands (Van Cott 2005). Thus far, however, Peru's Indigenous and popular sector groups have been unable to form a cohesive movement to press for social and political change. Studying the factors that lead to movement failure is potentially as important to advancing social movement theory and practice as examining why they succeed.

The transnational dimension of Indigenous activism in the region also pushes the boundaries of social movement theorization (Brysk 1994; see von Bülow in this volume). Even though Indigenous demands for identity, territory, and autonomy are rooted in local issues, Indigenous movements have been effective at using transnational advocacy networks to pressure intransigent governments at home. According to Keck and Sikkink (1998), a transnational advocacy network is most likely to emerge when: (1) channels between domestic groups and their governments are closed; (2) when political entrepreneurs believe that networking will help them advance their campaigns; and (3) when conferences and other contacts create arenas for forming networks. United Nations working groups on Indigenous rights have been the ideal forum for connecting Indigenous movements from across Latin America. Abandoning the local arena to press for change at the global level, however, is fraught with tensions. Post-development thinkers suggest that activists should "think and act locally" rather than attempting to bring about change at the global scale. In the words of Gustavo Esteva and Madhu Suri Prakash (1997: 282): "When local movements or initiatives lose the ground under their feet, moving their struggle into the enemy's territory—the global arena constructed by global thinking—they become minor players in the global game, doomed to lose their battles." Recent work by social movement scholars has problematized this dichotomous understanding of domestic and international arenas (Castells 2015; Silva 2013). A multiscalar approach to social movement analysis incorporates the conceptual elements of space, scale, and place by viewing movements as operating among local, regional, national, and international scales. Instead of moving from the local to the global as part of a process of scale-shifting, Indigenous activists employ scale-jumping tactics that enable them to move between the various scales as political opportunity structures expand or contract. In other words, Indigenous actors do not shift from local to international activism but expand their collective action repertoires to include both.

The transnational dimension of Indigenous organizing is perhaps most evident in the Amazon. For example, the Coodinadora de las Organizaciones Indígenas de la Cuenca Amazónica (COICA) is a transnational social movement organization whose members are exclusively South American Indigenous peoples. Founded in 1984, COICA coordinates the activities of nine Amazonian or lowland confederations from Brazil, Bolivia, Colombia, Ecuador, French Guyana, Guyana, Peru, Suriname, and Venezuela. It claims to represent the interests of over four hundred Indigenous communities in the Amazon basin (Martin 2014: 94). Indigenous organizing in the Amazonian region can be traced back to the 1960s as a response to state-sanctioned colonization and oil-exploration programs that threatened local lands and livelihoods (Yashar 2005).

During this time period, transnational networks began to form between Indigenous communities and anthropologists, missionaries, and environmental activists concerned with developments in the Amazon. The catalyst for COICA's formation came from an international conference of Amazonian countries held in Lima, Peru in 1984 that was sponsored by the United Nations Working Group on Indigenous Populations (WGIP). The purpose of this important international meeting was to construct a common identity and establish a common agenda in defense of the Amazon. The common identity became that of Indigenous peoples, and the master frame that COICA would come to utilize was that of the environment. According to Martin (2014: 96): "The idea behind this decision was their common understanding that all Indigenous peoples of the Amazon were one whole community bound by the commitment to defend their collective lands and rights." This transnational, multiscalar organizational approach has proven effective at allowing Indigenous peoples in the Amazon, who were once invisible to national and international audiences, to amplify their political voice while simultaneously consolidating local communities across the region (Perreault 2003).

Chile's Mapuche movement has also relied extensively on a transnational strategy to advance its agenda in light of the repeated failure of the state to adequately address Indigenous grievances and demands. The semi-clandestine Consejo de Todas las Tierras (CTT) had taken the lead in seeking out international allies to defend the interests of Indigenous peoples before the state. Indigenous representatives from Chile have long been active participants in international human rights forums (Aylwin 2001). In July 2003, the United Nations Special Rapporteur on the Rights of Indigenous Peoples met with Mapuche leaders to investigate allegations of human rights abuses against Indigenous peoples at the hands of the state. The report produced by the reviewer confirmed the abuses and made a list of thirty recommendations for the government to follow. Included among them were to constitutionally recognize the country's Indigenous peoples, to ratify the International Labor Organization's Convention 169 on Indigenous and Tribal Peoples, to decriminalize the Mapuche movement, and to agree to the participation of a third party appointed by the United Nations in dialogues between the Chilean government and Indigenous peoples (Rice 2012). In September 2007, Chile, alongside all Latin American countries with the exception of Colombia—which later came on board—voted in favor of the United Nations Declaration on the Rights of Indigenous Peoples (UNDRIP). Two years later, on September 15, 2009, the Chilean government finally ratified ILO Convention 169.

Conclusion

This chapter set out to highlight the characteristics and contributions of Indigenous movements to Latin American politics and society as well as to social movement theory and practice. Indigenous movement dynamics provide us with a number of instructional lessons. First and foremost, they require us to reconceptualize our theoretical frameworks in order to keep pace with movement developments. Indigenous movements stubbornly cross geographic and institutional boundaries, disobey the structural constraints on collective action, and meld issues of class and culture in new and unexpected ways (see Halvorsen and Rossi, Salman in this volume). Second, Indigenous movements in Latin America force us to re-think dominant conceptualizations of state-society relations. Indigenous movement dynamics question the rigid divide between civil society and the state that has been posited by much of the literature on this topic. Based on liberal norms and expectations, social actors are viewed as either inside or outside of the polity (Davis 1999; Tilly 1978). In contrast, Indigenous movements in Latin America have captured spaces within the state, through top-down as well as bottom-up processes. Finally, Indigenous movements allow us to re-imagine and revitalize democracy by increasing Indigenous participation and representation and including Indigenous perspectives and priorities within the institutions of representative democracy. As such, the study of Indigenous movements is not the domain of anthropologists, geographers, historians, sociologists, or even political scientists, but of those of us who are brave enough to borrow insights and approaches from across these disciplinary divides.

Today, researchers are interested in a bold new array of questions and topics, both internal to Indigenous movement dynamics as well as external to their linkages across colonial borders and boundaries. We know comparatively little about the decision-making processes around movement strategies and tactics as well as the relationships between organizations and communities within Indigenous movements. More recent work on Indigenous women's movements, for instance, is beginning to pry open the black box of social movement dynamics to reveal important insights for social movement theory and practice (Hernández Castillo and Speed 2006; Rousseau and Morales Hudon 2017; Ewig and Friedman, Flórez-Flórez and Olarte-Olarte in this volume). Rousseau and Morales Hudon (2017) provide us with a typology of organizational forms adopted by Indigenous women with regard to Indigenous movements in the cases of Mexico, Bolivia, and Peru. Their findings suggest that we need to pay closer attention to the political opportunity structures that exist, or fail to materialize, within social movements and how they serve to facilitate or inhibit women's participation. Research in this area has also begun to address the pressing topic of the causes and consequences of violence against Indigenous women, including acts of feminicide that occur in a context of social violence and impunity (Sieder 2011; Speed 2016). Violence against Indigenous women is a multifaceted problem that will require a multifaceted solution, including cultural models of dialogue and reparations as a means to guarantee access to justice. More systematic work on Indigenous women's movements and the question of how to reconcile women's individual rights with their collective rights as Indigenous peoples in the context of Indigenous self-determination and self-government in the region is also greatly warranted (see Ewig and Friedman in this volume). This second-generation body of scholarship on Indigenous movements in Latin America will continue to drive social movement studies in new and innovative directions.

References

Albó, Xavier (2002), *Pueblos indios en la política* (La Paz: Centro de Investigación y Promoción del Campesinado).
Albó, Xavier (2010). "Las Flamantes Autonomias Indigenas en Bolivia," in Miguel Gonzalez, Araceli Burguete Cal y Mayor, and T Pablo Ortiz (eds.), *La Autonomia a Debate: Autogobierno Indigena y Estado Plurinacional en America Latina*, 355–387 (Quito: FLACSO).
Almeida, Alfredo Wagner Berno de (2008), *Terra de quilombo, terras indígenas, "babaçuais livres", "castanhais do povo", faxinais e fundos de pastos: terras tradicionalmente ocupadas* (Manaus: PPGSCA-UFAM/Fundação Ford/PPGDA-UEA).
Alvarez, Sonia E., Evelina Dagnino, and Arturo Escobar (eds.) (1998), *Cultures of Politics, Politics of Cultures: Re-visioning Latin American Social Movements* (Boulder, CO: Westview Press).
Aminzade, Ronald (1995), "Between Movement and Party: The Transformation of Mid-Nineteenth Century French Republicanism," in Craig Jenkins and Bert Klandermans (eds.), *The Politics of Social Protest: Comparative Perspectives on States and Social Movements*, 39–62 (Minneapolis: University of Minnesota Press).
Andersen, Martin Edwin (2010), *Peoples of the Earth: Ethnonationalism, Democracy, and the Indigenous Challenge in "Latin" America* (Lanham, MD: Rowman & Littlefield).
Arce, Moisés (2014), *Resource Extraction and Protest in Peru* (Pittsburgh, PA: University of Pittsburgh Press).
Aylwin, José (2001), "Los conflictos en el territorio Mapuche: Antecedentes y perspectivas," in José Aylwin (ed.), *Políticas públicas y pueblo Mapuche*, 25–54 (Concepción: Ediciones Escaparate).
Beck, Scott H. and Kenneth J. Mijeski (2001), "Barricades and Ballots: Ecuador's Indians and the Pachakutik Political Movement," *Ecuadorian Studies* 1, 1–23.
Becker, Marc (2011), *Pachakutik: Indigenous Movements and Electoral Politics in Ecuador* (Lanham, MD: Rowman & Littlefield).
Bengoa, José (2000), *La emergencia indígena en América Latina* (Santiago: Fondo de Cultura Económica).
Bengoa, José (2001), "Políticas públicas y comunidades mapuches: Del indigenismo a la autogestión," in José Aylwin (ed.), *Políticas públicas y Pueblo Mapuche*, 81–126 (Concepción: Ediciones Escaparate).
Brysk, Alison (1994), "Acting Globally: Indian Rights and International Politics in Latin America," in Donna Lee Van Cott (ed.), *Indigenous Peoples and Democracy in Latin America*, 29–54 (New York: St. Martin's Press).
Brysk, Alison (2000), *From Tribal Village to Global Village: Indian Rights and International Relations in Latin America* (Stanford, CA: Stanford University Press).
Canessa, Andrew (2012), "Conflict, Claim and Contradiction in the New Indigenous State of Bolivia," Desigualdades Working Paper Series No. 22, Freie Universität Berlin.
Castells, Manuel (2015), *Networks of Outrage and Hope: Social Movements in the Internet Age* (Cambridge: Polity).
Collier, David (1995), "Trajectory of a Concept: 'Corporatism' in the Study of Latin American Politics," in Peter H. Smith (ed.), *Latin America in Comparative Perspective*, 135–62 (Boulder, CO: Westview Press).

Collier, Ruth Berins and David Collier (1991), *Shaping the Political Arena: Critical Junctures, the Labor Movement, and Regime Dynamics in Latin America* (Princeton, NJ: Princeton University Press).
Davis, Diane E. (1999), "The Power of Distance: Re-theorizing Social Movements in Latin America," *Theory and Society* 28(4), 585–638.
De Echave, José (2005), "Peruvian Peasants Confront the Mining Industry," *Socialism and Democracy* 19(3), 117–27.
Denissen, Marieke, Mirella Van Dun, and Kees Koonings (2004), "Social Protest against Repression and Violence in Present-Day Argentina and Peru," *Revista Europea de Estudios Latinoamericanos y del Caribe* 77, 91–101.
Deruyttere, Anne (1997), *Indigenous Peoples and Sustainable Development: The Role of the Inter-American Development Bank* (Washington: Inter-American Development Bank).
Díaz Polanco, Héctor (1998), "La autonomía, demanda central de los pueblos indígenas: Significado e implicaciones," in Virginia Alta, Diego Iturralde, and M. A. López Bassola (eds.), *Pueblos indígenas y estado en América Latina*, 213–20 (Quito: Editorial Abya Yala).
Esteva, Gustavo and Madhu Suri Prakash (1997), "From Global Thinking to Local Thinking," in Majid Rahnema with Victoria Bawtree (eds.), *The Post Development Reader*, 227–89 (London: Zed Books).
Exeni Rodríguez, José Luis (2012), "Elusive Demodiversity in Bolivia: Between Representation, Participation and Self-Government," in Maxwell A. Cameron, Eric Hershberg, and Kenneth E. Sharpe (eds.), *New Institutions for Participatory Democracy in Latin America*, 207–29 (New York: Palgrave-Macmillan).
Felbab-Brown, Vanda (2006), "Trouble Ahead: The Cocaleros of Peru," *Current History* 105(688), 79–83.
Fischer, Valdi and Marc Fasol (2013), *Las semillas de "buen vivir": La respuesta de los pueblos indígenas del Abya-Yala a la deriva del modelo de desarrollo occidental* (Quito: Ediciones Fondo Indígena).
Foweraker, Joe (1995), *Theorizing Social Movements* (London: Pluto Press).
Glidden, Lisa M. (2011), *Mobilizing Ethnic Identity in the Andes: A Study of Ecuador and Peru* (Lanham, MD: Lexington Books).
Goldstone, Jack A. (ed.) (2003), *States, Parties, and Social Movements* (New York: Cambridge University Press).
Harvey, Neil (1998), *The Chiapas Rebellion: The Struggle for Land and Democracy* (Durham, NC: Duke University Press).
Hellman, Judith (1997), "Social Movements: Revolution, Reform and Reaction," *NACLA Report on the Americas* 30(6), 13–18.
Hernández Castillo, Rosalva Aída, and Shannon Speed (eds.) (2006), *Dissident Women: Gender and Cultural Politics in Chiapas* (Austin: University of Texas Press).
Horowitz, Donald L. (1985), *Ethnic Groups in Conflict* (Berkeley and Los Angeles: University of California Press).
Keck, Margaret E. and Kathryn Sikkink (1998), *Activists beyond Borders: Advocacy Networks in International Politics* (Ithaca, NY: Cornell University Press).
Layton, Heather Marie and Harry Anthony Patrinos (2006), "Estimating the Number of Indigenous Peoples in Latin America," in Gillette Hall and Harry Anthony Patrinos (eds.), *Indigenous Peoples, Poverty, and Human Development in Latin America*, 25–39 (New York: Palgrave-Macmillan).

Lucas, Kintto (2000), *La rebellion de los indios* (Quito: Ediciones Abya Yala).

Lucero, José Antonio (2008), *Struggles of Voice: The Politics of Indigenous Representation in the Andes* (Pittsburgh, PA: University of Pittsburgh Press).

Lucero, José Antonio and María Elena García (2007), "In the Shadow of Success: Indigenous Politics in Peru and Ecuador," in A. Kim Clark and Marc Becker (eds.), *Highland Indians and the State in Modern Ecuador*, 234–47 (Pittsburgh, PA: University of Pittsburgh Press).

Madrid, Raúl L. (2012), *The Rise of Ethnic Politics in Latin America* (New York: Cambridge University Press).

Martin, Pamela (2014), *The Globalization of Contentious Politics: The Amazonian Indigenous Rights Movement* (New York: Routledge).

Massal, Julie and Marcelo Bonilla (eds.) (2000), *Los movimientos sociales en las democracias andinas* (Quito: FLACSO).

Mayorga, Réne A. (2006), "Outsiders and Neopopulism: The Road to Plebiscitary Democracy," in Scott Mainwaring, Ana María Bejarano, and Eduardo Pizarro Leongómez (eds.), *The Crisis of Democratic Representation in the Andes*, 132–67 (Stanford, CA: Stanford University Press).

McDonnell, Emma (2015), "The Co-Constitution of Neoliberalism, Extractive Industries, and Indigeneity: Anti-Mining Protests in Puno, Peru," *The Extractive Industries and Society* 2, 112–23.

Nash, June C. (2001), *Mayan Visions: The Quest for Autonomy in an Age of Globalization* (New York: Routledge).

Ospina, Pablo (2000), "Reflexiones sobre el transformismo: Movilización indígena y regimen político en el Ecuador (1990-1998)," in Julie Massal and Marcelo Bonilla (eds.), *Los movimientos sociales en las democracias andinas*, 125–46 (Quito: FLACSO).

Otero, Gerardo (2003), "The 'Indian Question' in Latin America: Class, State, and Ethnic Identity Construction," *Latin American Research Review* 38(1), 249–66.

Oxhorn, Philip (1998), "Is the Century of Corporatism Over? Neoliberalism and the Rise of Neopluralism," in Philip D. Oxhorn and Graciela Ducatenzeiler (eds.), *What Kind of Democracy? What Kind of Market? Latin America in the Age of Neoliberalism*, 195–217 (University Park: Penn State University Press).

Pallares, Amalia (2002), *From Peasant Struggles to Indian Resistance: The Ecuadorian Andes in the Late Twentieth Century* (Norman: University of Oklahoma Press).

Perreault, Thomas (2003), "Changing Places: Transnational Networks, Ethnic Politics, and Community Development in the Ecuadorian Amazon," *Political Geography* 22, 61–88.

Peruzzotti, Enrique and Andrew Selee (2009), "Participatory Innovation and Representative Democracy in Latin America," in Andrew Selee and Enrique Peruzzotti (eds.), *Participatory Innovation and Representative Democracy in Latin America*, 1–16 (Washington, DC: Woodrow Wilson Centre/The Johns Hopkins University Press).

Petras, James and Henry Veltmeyer (2001), "Are Latin American Peasant Movements Still a Force for Change? Some New Paradigms Revisited," *Journal of Peasant Studies* 28(2), 83–118.

Rabushka, Alvin and Kenneth A. Shepsle (1972), *Politics in Plural Societies* (Columbus, OH: Charles E. Merrill).

Reuque Paillalef, Isolde (1998), "La identidad es un asunto de afirmación de uno mismo," in Virginia Alta, Diego Iturralde, and M.A. López Bassola (eds.), *Pueblos indígenas y estado en América Latina*, 221–38 (Quito: Editorial Abya Yala).

Rice, Roberta (2012), *The New Politics of Protest: Indigenous Mobilization in Latin America's Neoliberal Era* (Tucson: The University of Arizona Press).

Rousseau, Stéphanie and Anahi Morales Hudon (2017), *Indigenous Women's Movements in Latin America: Gender and Ethnicity in Peru, Mexico, and Bolivia* (New York: Palgrave-Macmillan).

Schilling-Vacaflor, Almut and René Kuppe (2012), "Plurinational Constitutionalism: A New Era of Indigenous-State Relations?" in Detlef Nolte and Almut Schilling-Vacaflor (eds.), *New Constitutionalism in Latin America: Promises and Practices*, 347–70 (Burlington, VT: Ashgate).

Silva, Eduardo (2009), *Challenging Neoliberalism in Latin America* (New York: Cambridge University Press).

Silva, Eduardo (ed.) (2013), *Transnational Activism and National Movements in Latin America: Bridging the Divide* (New York: Routledge).

Sieder, Rachel (2011), "Contested Sovereignties: Indigenous Law, Violence and State Effects in Postwar Guatemala," *Critique of Anthropology* 31(3), 161–84.

Speed, Shannon (2016), "States of Violence: Indigenous Women Migrants in the Era of Neoliberal Multicriminalism," *Critique of Anthropology* 36(3), 280–301.

Stavenhagen, Rodolfo (2002), "Indigenous Peoples and the State in Latin America: An Ongoing Debate," in Rachel Sieder (ed.), *Multiculturalism in Latin America: Indigenous Rights, Diversity and Democracy*, 24–44 (New York: Palgrave-Macmillan).

Ticona Alejo, Esteban (2000), *Organización y liderazgo Aymara: La experiencia indígena en la política boliviana, 1979–1996* (La Paz: University of the Cordilleras).

Tilly, Charles (1978), *From Mobilization to Revolution* (Reading, MA: Addison-Wesley).

Van Cott, Donna Lee (2005), *From Movements to Parties in Latin America: The Evolution of Ethnic Politics* (New York: Cambridge University Press).

Vanden, Harry E. and Gary Prevost (2009), *Politics of Latin America: The Power Game* (New York: Oxford University Press).

Vice Minister of Decolonization (2013), *Resoluciones: 1ra cumbre internacional de descolonización, despatriarcalización, lucha contra el racismo y la discriminación* (La Paz: Ministerio de Culturas y Turismo).

Wade, Peter (2010), *Race and Ethnicity in Latin America* (New York: Palgrave-Macmillan).

Wampler, Brian (2012), "Participation, Representation, and Social Justice: Using Participatory Governance to Transform Representative Democracy," *Polity* 44(4), 666–82.

Yashar, Deborah J. (2005), *Contesting Citizenship in Latin America: The Rise of Indigenous Movements and the Postliberal Challenge* (New York: Cambridge University Press).

Zamosc, Leon (2004), "The Indian Movement in Ecuador: From Politics of Influence to Politics of Power," in Nancy Grey Postero and Leon Zamosc (eds.), *The Struggle for Indigenous Rights in Latin America*, 131–57 (Brighton: Sussex Academic Press).

CHAPTER 22

AFRO-SOCIAL MOVEMENTS AND THE STRUGGLE FOR RACIAL EQUALITY IN LATIN AMERICA

KWAME DIXON AND KIA LILLY CALDWELL

Introduction

This chapter examines the rise of contemporary Black social movements in Latin America from the 1970s to the late-2010s. It seeks to understand what factors explain the rise of Black social movements and explores the multidimensional nature of Afro-based social movements. These movements have been overlooked in much of the literature on Latin American social movements, which has contributed to the belief that challenging racism was not a priority for Black communities in the region during the twentieth century. Contrary to popular perception, Afro-Latin social movements are not new; they form part of the long history of Black resistance in the Americas, which includes varied forms of struggle against enslavement and racial oppression (Andrews 2004; Price 1973).

During the twentieth century, social movements originated in Black civil society, often with close ties to grassroots Afro-Latin American cultural and political organizations, as well as Afro-Latin non-governmental organizations. Black mobilization increased during the final decades of the twentieth century, leading to significant changes in legislation, policy, and state discourse related to race, racism, and Black communities. This chapter argues that Black social movements mainly emerged from Afro-civil society as part of a vast network of civil society groups across the Latin American region. Many have demanded the economic, social, and cultural rights long denied to them, while at the same time opening new democratic spaces and calling for counterhegemonic definitions of national belonging that include anti-racist and land rights legislation, and Blackness as a part of national identity (Alberto 2011; Safa 1995).

Over the past thirty years, there has been increasing recognition of racism in many Latin American countries and the development of state entities to address racism and racial discrimination. Recent transformations in the political spheres of many Latin American countries are rooted in concepts such as "cultural" and "new citizenship," which Black activists have used to claim rights, democratic space, and belonging to societies that formerly excluded them (Caldwell 2007; Dagnino 1998). Moving beyond *de jure* notions of constitutional citizenship, new and cultural citizenship underscores Afro-referenced identity and the fight against racial inequality as core elements of citizenship that is more inclusive and democratic. By challenging racialized, gendered, and class-based structures, as well as developing new strategies of empowerment, Black social movements have expanded citizenship and opened new political possibilities which include human rights protections, new forms of citizenship, and democratic structures that respect the rights of Black peoples.

Historical Antecedents

Afro-Latin mobilization for self-defense and against oppression in Latin America and the Caribbean have a long and rich history, including maroon, *palenque*, and *quilombo* communities founded by self-liberated enslaved people; the Haitian Revolution (1791 to 1804); and the Malê revolt in Salvador da Bahia, Brazil (1835). The Malê revolt is one of the least studied, yet most impactful slave revolts in the Americas (Reis 1993). It was a well-planned insurrection led by Muslim enslaved African-descendant people whose main goal was to seize control of the local government. The revolt was suppressed and, in its aftermath, over 500 enslaved people were either executed, sent to prison, whipped, or deported (Reis 1993).

For almost four centuries, maroon, *palenque*, and *quilombo* communities were scattered across the Americas, from Brazil to the region that would become the southwestern United Sates. These autonomous communities challenged the slave system and ranged from small cells that lasted less than a year to powerful states that constituted thousands of members lasting for centuries (Price 1973). A few examples include the Palmares community of Brazil, Palenque de San Basilio on the Caribbean coast of Colombia, the Black Maroons of Esmeraldas, Ecuador, and San Lorenzo de los Negros, in Mexico (the present-day town of Yanga). These self-contained, Black communities defended their sovereignty at all costs. Many of these *quilombos* or *palenques* still exist today, however they are in a constant battle to defend their land and identities as they continue to fight for their right to exist (Farfán-Santos 2016).

Perhaps the most well-known Black social movement to rock the Western hemisphere was the Haitian Revolution, which was one of the largest and most successful social and political revolutions in the colonial era. Toussaint L'Ouverture and his army of self-liberated enslaved people handily defeated the great empires of the day, Britain and France (James 1938). While Saint-Domingue and the Haitian Revolution may be viewed as part of French colonial history, rather than part of Afro-Latin history, the impact of the revolution was felt throughout the Americas. The Revolution produced the intensification of the slave trade and slavery in places such as Cuba and Brazil, as well as affecting enslaved people and their aspirations for freedom throughout the Americas (Geggus 2007).

At the dawn of the twentieth century, the Partido Independiente de Color (PIC) in Cuba was the first Black political party (outside of Haiti) in the Americas. It was founded in 1908, by Evaristo Estenoz, an Afro-Cuban veteran of the 1895 to 1898 War for Cuban Independence (Helg 1995). The PIC was first organized as a mainstream political party to secure basic rights of Afro-Cubans but had to resort to armed struggle in order to defend itself against aggression by the Cuban and United States governments. The party was banned in 1910 and accused of organizing along racial lines; and in 1912, its core members were massacred in the—predominantly Black—Oriente Province by the Cuban government with US support (Helg 1995). From maroon and *quilombo* communities, to slave rebellions and the Haitian Revolution, to the PIC, Afro-Latin American communities have engaged in centuries-long struggles for autonomy and self-determination.

THE RISE OF MODERN BLACK SOCIAL MOVEMENTS IN LATIN AMERICA

Afro-social movements ebbed and flowed throughout the twentieth century. For example, there were Black newspapers, cultural and religious organizations, fraternal clubs, and other Afro-referenced institutions throughout the twentieth century. In addition to the PIC in Cuba (1908), Marcus Garvey's Universal Negro Improvement Association (1917), the Frente Negra Brasileira (1930s), and the Teatro Experimental do Negro (1950s) all made major inroads into challenging racism and valorizing Black identities. During the early twentieth century, Black newspapers in Brazil also played a key role in creating a Black public sphere in which ideas about race and racial equality were discussed and debated (Alberto 2011). But at the start of 1970s new Afro-Latin social movements emerged across the continent. At the transnational level a new generation of grassroots social justice activists in the region would be inspired by the following: African independence (late 1950s to 1970s); the wars of national liberation in the former Portuguese colonies of Angola, Guinea Bissau, and Mozambique (late 1950s to early 1970s); the Cuban Revolution (1959); the United States human rights movement (1950s to early 1970s); and the anti-apartheid struggle in Southern Africa (1970s to 1990s). At the same time in Latin America there was the Soul Movement in Brazil (1970s) and the Cuban Revolution's rhetoric and campaigns of anti-racial discrimination, one of the first and most comprehensive in the hemisphere. These events and others created new forms of transnational identities and connections for Afro-Latin communities and other

Black peoples across the globe. In the late 1970s, a radical new landscape emerged in Latin America as Black activists created new space to advance a racial justice agenda rooted in the notion that Black communities not only deserve full recognition but also deserve economic, social, and cultural rights. Many Black social movements in the region arose within civil society as autonomous agents of change fighting for racial justice within the confines of the liberal democratic state. Moreover, some of these Black social movements share a central feature of contemporary Latin American social movements, "horizontalism," which refers to an organizing method as well as forms of resistance. According to Stahler-Sholk, Vanden, and Becker (2014), horizontalism refers to actors arising from below with participatory structures in movements that do not seek to overthrow the state but, instead, resist and challenge globalization or neoliberal politics. These new social actors, and the networks they create, are sometimes referred to as New Social Movements because they seek to define new relations of power (Stahler-Sholk, Vanden, and Becker, 2014: 2; see Garretón and Selamé in this volume). At the micro-level, Black social movements across the region are far too diverse in scope, style, form, method, and philosophy to classify. However, horizontalism serves as a useful conceptual frame of reference to categorize many of them. These movements, as formulations of activism, contest the region's prevailing political and economic systems, and challenge narrowly constructed definitions of citizenship, democracy, and participation.

The concept of Afro-civil society is also useful in understanding the rise of contemporary Black social movements in the last third of the twentieth century (Dixon 2016). Scholars have theorized civil society as the space between the state and the citizen. In the Latin American context, it forms the conceptual underpinning for understanding democracy, social and cultural citizenship, grassroots mobilization, identity constructions, and human rights (Alvarez, Dagnino, and Escobar 1998; Feinberg, Waisman, and Zamosc 2006; Stahler-Sholk, Vanden, and Becker 2014). Afro-civil society builds on traditional conceptualization of civil society (i.e., the space between the citizen and the state), while contextualizing the activism and mobilization of Afro-Latin Americans within their particular historical and contemporary experiences and struggles. The efforts of Afro-civil society challenge dominant racial hegemonies by seeking to alter historically inscribed forms of discrimination and destabilize racial hierarchies that privilege Europeanness and whiteness. Afro-civil society is therefore central to understanding the rise of these movements and their impact on the region by highlighting their significance as new civic actors whose work is premised on anti-racist strategies, counter-hegemonic grassroots education, and mobilization (Dixon 2016).

In order to theorize Afro-civil society, as well as Afro-social movements and political mobilization, it is crucial to clarify what "being Black" signifies in Latin America. Black, Black identity, and Blackness are socially contested terms with uneven meanings across the region. For much of the twentieth century, scholars from Latin America and other regions debated whether race or racial categories existed in Latin America and a good deal of research promoted the region's image as being "raceless" and "colorblind". During the final decades of the twentieth century, an increasing number of empirical studies began to highlight practices of racial discrimination and inequality against Afro-Latin

Americans (Telles 2004). Much of this research focused on Brazil, the country which has been the focus of most of the scholarship on race, racism, and Black movements in Latin America.

On one level, terms such as "Black" (*negro/a*), "Black identity" (*identidad negra/ identidade negra*) and "Blackness" (*negritude*) refer to a bundle of ideas and meanings about people who are socially defined as "negro," or "Afro-descendant." "Blackness" is also a form of consciousness among Black people, as well as a deliberate project to produce such consciousness and ideas about Blackness held by non-Black people (Hartigan 2010: 117). Throughout the Western hemisphere, consciousness and projects of Blackness cluster around common descent from Africa, a common history of enslavement, and common experiences of social oppression (Wade 2012), while ideas non-Blacks have about Black people often center on notions of racial inferiority and racist stereotypes. Racial projects that have defined Blackness in Latin America, including slavery, racial oppression, and emancipation, as well as Black identity and consciousness movements (to name only a few), vary from country to country in the Americas. Thus, one of the first priorities of Afro-civil society groups has been to reposition Blackness (Dixon and Johnson 2019) and reclaim Blackness and Black identity while calling into question "*blanqueamiento*," the whitening ideology that has championed whiteness and marginalized Black identity, both historically and in the contemporary period. From "Black is Beautiful" campaigns, to wearing thick flowing Afros, to calling into question traditional racial categories (*mulato, café con leche*)—all these represented forms of contestation that challenged and undermined the prevailing racial logic of *blanquemiento*.

In addition to being a space for political mobilization, Afro-civil society is an alternative epistemological site that values Black identity, cultural traditions, and religions; it therefore represents a unique space where the specificity of Black social experiences, Black knowledge, cultural formations and forms of organization unfold and are theorized.

THE ROAD TO CALI, COLOMBIA: THE FLOURISHING OF AFRO-CIVIL SOCIETY

As previously noted, throughout the twentieth century there were important Black social and cultural movements throughout the Americas. However, the literature on modern Black social movements generally points to the 1970s and early 1980s as a pivotal movement because so many new Afro-nongovernmental organizations burst onto the scene at this time (Caldwell 2007; Covin 2006; Dixon 2016 Hanchard 1994; Johnson 2012; Paschel 2016; Wade 1993). The 1970s therefore represented a unique historical juncture for Black social movements in the Americas as Afro-civil society groups and the seeds of civil society were taking root. Afro-civil society groups were now appearing on the scene with raw energy and urgency and their reemergence ushered in a new

Afro-referenced social and cultural renaissance. This Black cultural and social renaissance led to several Congresses on Black Culture in the Americas, organized between 1977 and 1982, which ushered in a new era in regionwide Afro-Latin social and political mobilization. The first Congress, organized under leadership of Manual Zapata Olivella, founder of the Fundación Colombiana para la Investigación de la Cultura Negra and the Asociación Cultural de Jóvenes Peruanos Negros, took place in Cali, Colombia in August 1977. The Second Congress organized by the Centro de Estudios Panameños took place in Panama in March 1980. The Third Congress met in São Paulo in August 1982 and was co-organized by Abdias do Nacimiento and the Instituto de Pesquisas e Estudos Afro-Brasilieros (Olivella 1977). The theme, "African Diaspora: Political Consciousness and African Culture," reflected the new burgeoning social consciousness unfolding across the Americas. Present at these various Congresses were writers, scholars, activists, intellectuals, and individuals from many spheres of Afrocivil society and they came from across the Americas and parts of Africa. While relatively small in scope, these historic congresses foreshadowed the emerging Black social movements and new forms of political mobilization on the horizon. The Congresses on Black Culture in the Americas focused on similar themes like cultural or racial identity and consciousness, celebration of African roots, pursuit of self-esteem programs, denunciation of racism and marginalization, and establishing and reinforcing regional and transnational networks. One of the common threads of these Congresses and main organizing principles was to develop a plan of action and formulate demands for racial and social justice for the Afro-descendants in the region (Davis, Paschel, and Morrison 2012). During the same period the Congresses on Black Culture took place a number of important Afro-civil society groups sprang up in individual countries (Table 22.1). Some were small cultural or study groups while others were more directly political focusing on research and human rights. But the common thread was racial justice and rescuing Black identity from invisibility and erasure.

The Transition to Civilian Rule and the Maturing of Afro-Civil Society

By the 1980s many Latin American countries were transitioning to civilian rule after years of harsh military dictatorships (see Inclán in this volume). Long-term military rule, with changing leadership in most cases, controlled eleven countries for significant periods from 1964 to 1990 (see Brocket in this volume). While there is a wide body of research on military dictatorships and authoritarian rule in Latin America, there is little if any on the relationship between military dictatorships and their impact on the rise of Afro-social movements during this time. But it is generally recognized that civil society groups were inhibited from organizing. Moreover, in many countries, movement leaders, activists, and regular citizens were disappeared, tortured, jailed, or exiled

Table 22.1 Afro-Civil society organizations in Latin America founded between 1970 and the early 1990s

Country	Year	Organization
Brazil	1974	Iyê Aiyê (bloco)
	1978	Movimento Negro Unificado
	1979	Olodum (bloco)
	1983	Nzinga/Coletivo da Mulheres Negras
	1988	Geledès
	1987	Maria Mulher
	1992	Steve Biko
	1992	Criola
	1997	Fala Preta
Colombia	1975	The Center for the Investigation of Black Culture
	1976	Soweto (Asociación Movimiento Nacional por los Derechos Humanos de las Comunidades Afrocolombianas)
	1970s	Centro de Estudios Afro Colombianos
		Fundación Colombiana de Investigación Folklórica
	1984	Asociación Integral de Campesinos del Río Atrato
	1992	Red de Mujeres Negras
	1993	Proceso de Comunidades Negras
	1999	Asociación de Afrocolombianos Desplazados
Ecuador	1979	Centro de Estudios Afroecuatorianos
	1981	Centro Cultural Afroecuatorianos
	1990s	El Proceso de Comunidades Negras del Norte de Ecuador
	2000s	Fundación de Desarrollo Social y Cultural Afroeuatoriana
Honduras	1979	Organización Fraternal Negra Hondureña
	1992	Organización de Desarrollo Étnico Comunitario
Uruguay	1989	Mundo Afro
Peru	1970s	Movimiento Negro Francisco Congo
	1986	Asociación de la Juventud Cultural Negra Peruano
	1991	Asociación Negra de Defensa de Promoción de Derechos Humanos

(Greene 2010). And the prevailing hegemonic discourse was that race was a non-issue and such discussions were not welcomed. Therefore, the return to civilian rule is critical to understanding the rise of Afro-social movements across the region during this time. From the 1980s onward, new organizations were formed by workers, students, indigenous activists, women, and Blacks. This new constellation of forces provided Afro-civil society a new framework and a democratic space to organize and mobilize around issues of racial justice.

Along with many of the groups listed in Table 22.1 there was now a veritable explosion of Black groups focused on social discrimination in the economy, politics, housing, education, health care, policing, prisons, and affirmative action. As these movements matured, the first and perhaps thorniest question they had to confront was the nature of racial oppression faced by Afro descendants in the Americas; the second, what were the most appropriate grassroots strategies of social mobilization to organize their constituents; and the third, the role of culture and politics and how it shaped, limited, undermined, and/or depoliticized Black consciousness. Finally, but equally important, how to link Black consciousness (or lack therefore) to mass based social movements and mobilizations. Broadly speaking the groups mentioned in Table 22.1 sought to do the following: (1) challenge and overturn the notion of racial democracy; (2) place the issue of racial and gender discrimination on the table to be discussed as a serious political matter; (3) challenge the idea prevalent in civil society and many social movements that race relations were neutral; (4) demand equal and fair treatment for Afro-descendant communities as full and equal citizens; (5) recognize the land rights of Afro-descendants, *palenque*, and *quilombo* communities; (6) challenge state sponsored violence and reform the administration of justice (criminal justice reform in policing, prisons, and jails); (7) demand visibility and respect for Black and Afro-referenced identity (not as a racist stereotype) within the broader national identity of Latin American societies; and (8) destabilize and undermine racial categories and hierarchies that marginalize Afro-descendants.

Starting roughly in the early 1970s, racial justice was by the end of the 1990s and early 2000s being rearticulated forcefully as vibrant social movements were spreading across the Americas like wildfire. In *Orpheus and Power*, one of the earlier works on Black social movements in Brazil, Hanchard (1994) asked why in the 1980s–1990s no major national Black social movement existed in Brazil given the precarious status of Afro-Brazilians. However, more current research by scholars like Caldwell (2007), Perry (2013), and Dixon (2016) demonstrates that there were small, regionally vibrant and culturally active movements in Brazil in the 1970s and 1980s. Hanchard (1994) focused on the role of racial hegemony, as manifested in the ideology of racial democracy, in stymying Black activism and the strategic choices made by Black activists with a focus on Rio de Janeiro and São Paulo. Hanchard (1994) argued that Black activists overemphasized Black cultural identity to the neglect of their potential constituents' more direct social, economic, and political needs and concerns. Based on Hanchard's (1994) study and the work of other scholars who examined Brazil's Black movement in the 1980s and early 1990s, the prospects for successfully challenging the country's image as a racial democracy seemed bleak (Andrews 1995). The implementation of race-conscious policies, such as affirmative action, in the early 2000s was largely unforeseen in the early-to-mid 1990s and signaled a major shift in how race and racism were being conceptualized in Brazil.

Recent scholarship has highlighted both successes and challenges in Black activists' efforts to challenge racism in Brazil (Caldwell 2017; Paschel 2016). As we will discuss later, changes in both the domestic and international contexts provided new openings for Black activists to challenge racism and develop racial equality policies during the early 2000s. In addition, recent research has provided a more complex picture of Black activism in Brazil, by looking at race in relation to gender and class (Caldwell 2007; Perry 2013; Santos 2012). This work underscores the importance of Black women's activism and their conceptualizations of Black feminism. Perry's (2013) work, for example, highlights the significance of Black women's resistance to urban displacement in Salvador da Bahia, Brazil, and links grassroots activism by poor and working-class Black women to the broader Black movement. This analysis is particularly insightful, since grassroots activism and the work of Black movement organizations, especially NGOs, are often thought about and studied as separate and distinct.

AFRO-LATIN AMERICAN WOMEN'S ACTIVISM

While racialization and racial discrimination were central points of departure for Black social movements, gender and the leadership of Afro-Latin women were also important features for the early Black social movement's formation and a defining part of the social landscape. While Black feminist activists and scholars, such as Angela Davis, Patricia Hill Collins, and bell hooks, are internationally renowned, Afro-Latin feminist scholars and activists have been less visible on the international stage. However, they have made important contributions to Afro-feminist thought and praxis, as well as larger Black movement thought and praxis (Alvarez and Caldwell 2016; Carneiro 2016; Gonzalez 1988; Ratts 2007; Smith 2016b; Werneck 2007; Johnson and Sempol in this volume).[1] However, until recently much of their written work has been published outside of formal academic spaces. Black women also have been important leaders and theoreticians from the inception of Afro-Latin organizations and social movements, although their contributions have often been overlooked. As a result, rather than separate Black social movements and Black Politics from Afro-Latin feminism, and vice-versa, it is more useful conceptually to think about the confluence of race and gender as mutually reinforcing and intersecting categories with respect to the early formation of Black social movements in the Americas. This is particularly significant, since like other members of Afro-civil society, Black women are part of a regionwide movement to challenge discrimination in its various forms and promote equality and full citizenship. Black women's groups began to be formed in the 1980s and 1990s as a way to focus on gender-specific struggles and issues. Afro-Latin American women often used these groups as a way to challenge sexism in Black organizations and racism in feminist organizations. Black women's organizations are strong and numerous in countries such as Brazil and Colombia, which have the largest Black populations in the region.

Separate organizing by Black women began in Brazil in the mid-1980s as the country returned to democratic rule. NGOs such as Maria Mulher (1987), Geledés (1988), and Criola (1992) were formed during this time and continue to be highly visible and influential. In the Brazilian case, Black women were active in the Black and the women's movements during the 1970s and 1980s, as well as in mobilizing against the military dictatorship in Brazil (Caldwell 2007, 2019). And, between 1986 and 1989, Black women's collectives and groups were formed in the states of Minas Gerais, São Paulo, Maranhão, Espiritu Santo, Rio de Janeiro, and Rio Grande do Sul (Caldwell 2019).

Beatriz Nascimento and Lélia Gonzalez, a founding member of Movimento Negro Unificado (MNU) (Brazil), were both influential early Black Brazilian feminists and leading theoreticians of the race in Brazil (Gonzalez 1988; Ratts 2007; Smith 2016b). Their writings and activism were important interventions that reflected the ways in which Black women in Brazil in the 1970s and 1980s used intersectional analysis which critiqued sexism and racism as interlocking axes of oppression.

In Colombia, Black women began to organize around gender-related issues and concerns following passage of Law 70 and Transitory Article 55 in 1991. This legislation provided new ethnic and cultural rights and legally recognized Black communities. Women's cooperatives were formed in the Pacific region, which has a large Black population. One such cooperative, FundeMujer (Fundación para el Desarrollo de la Mujer de Buenaventura), had 800 members by the mid-1990s (Asher 2009). Women's health was a focus of FundeMujer, but it also supported income-generating activities. Other cooperatives, such as Ser Mujer, brought together women from various occupational associations. In the early 1990s, Afro-Colombian women held meetings around land issues in the Pacific Region leading to the founding of the Red de Mujeres Negras in the city of Guapi (1992) and replicated in the cities of Buenaventura and Bahía Solano (Asher 2009).

In addition to organizing formally, Afro-Colombian women have also enacted practices of resistance centered on their relationship with the environment and land, from which their communities have been violently displaced for decades. As Afro-Colombian feminist Betty Ruth Lozano has argued, "Many of these practices of resistance and insurgence have been realized in the realm of the domestic-communitarian through the knowledge and use of diverse herbs and other natural properties" (Lozano 2016: 26). For many years, Afro-Colombian women have been leaders in efforts to focus national and international attention on issues of racialized violence and displacement in Colombia, where over eight million people had been internally displaced by 2018 (Human Rights Watch 2019). During the 2014 Marcha de los Turbantes (March of the Turbaned Ones), eighty rural Afro-Colombian women marched from the state of Cauca to Bogotá, a journey of 563 kilometers over a ten-day period. Led by Francia Márquez Mina, an internationally recognized human rights and environmental activist, the marchers occupied the Ministry of the Interior and made demands regarding collective land titles, illegal mining on their lands, and death threats and assassinations against Black leaders. In 2018, Márquez was awarded the Goldman Environmental Prize, the equivalent of the Nobel Prize for the environment, and unsuccessfully ran for a seat in the Colombian Congress representing Black communities the same year. And in the hotly contested presidential elections held in June of 2022, Francia Marquez was elected vice president of Colombia becoming the first black woman to hold the position.

Black women's organizations exist throughout Latin America and engage in similar work related to Black women's identities, self-esteem, and gender empowerment, in addition to providing a voice for intersectional issues of gender, race, class, and sexual orientation with respect to policy development (Lao-Montes 2016). Black women have begun to mobilize in greater numbers in countries such as Mexico, Peru, the Dominican

Republic, and Cuba, as attested by the increasing number of websites, Facebook and other social media pages, and publications by and about Black women in these countries (Castillo and Terry 2011; Centro de Desarrollo Étnico 2010; Mayes 2019).

Similarities in Afro-Latin American women's perspectives and mobilization strategies reflect what Black Brazilian feminist Léila Gonzalez (1988) referred to as "Afro-Latin feminism" and "*Amerafricanidade*" during the 1980s. Both concepts highlight the need to recognize the specificities Black women's experiences in the Latin American context and call attention to the need for regionwide interaction and mobilization. The founding of the Red de Mujeres Afrolatinamericanas, Afrocaribeñas y de la Diaspora by women from various countries in Latin America and the Caribbean was an important step in Black women's organizing at the regional level. The Red was formed during the Primer Encuentro de Mujeres Negras, which took place in Santo Domingo during 1992 in response to the 500-year commemorations of Columbus' arrival in the Americas. Three hundred Black women from thirty-two countries attended the encounter and chose July 25 as the Día Internacional de la Mujer Afrolatinamericana y Afrocaribeña, giving further visibility to Black women in the region. Black women in Brazil have made July a month-long celebration of Black womanhood, now known as Julho das Pretas. Since its founding, the name of the Red has changed to incorporate the term "Diaspora" as a way to extend membership and solidarity to Afro-Latin women who live in other regions. In this way, the Red has played a pioneering role in envisioning Afro-civil society beyond the "borders" of Latin America, with its most recent gathering taking place in Cali, Colombia in 2018. Prominent Afro-Latin American women have provided leadership for the Red, including Epsy Campbell, who became the Vice-President of Costa Rica in 2018.

REGIONAL AND TRANSNATIONAL MOBILIZATIONS

For more than two decades, Black Brazilian women have mobilized at the transnational level and provided important leadership for Brazilian and Latin American participation in the 2001 United Nations World Conference against Racism, Racial Discrimination, Xenophobia, and Related Forms of Intolerance, also known as the Durban Conference. They drew upon their previous policy advocacy experiences during the 1994 United Nations World Conference on Population and Development and the 1995 United Nations World Conference on Women, playing a pivotal role (Caldwell 2017; Paschel 2016). In addition to their efficacy in the policy arena, many Black Brazilian women's NGOs have been recognized for their pioneering work on issues such as human rights, domestic violence, HIV/AIDS, and reproductive health (Caldwell 2017).

There are several explicitly transnational Black networks and organizations in Latin America, including the Red Continental de Organizaciones Afroamericanas, the

Organización Negra Centroamericana, the Red Andina de Organizaciones Afro, and the previously mentioned Red de Mujeres Afrolatinoamericanas, Afrocaribeñas y de la Diáspora (Davis 2019). Many of these groups engaged in regionwide mobilization for the 2001 United Nations World Conference against Racism. As a number of scholars have noted, Afro-Latin American activists used the preparatory process for Durban to increase efforts to challenge racism and influence state policy in their home countries (Caldwell 2017; Davis, Paschel, and Morrison 2012; Dzidzienyo 2005; Mullings 2004; Paschel 2016; Silva and Pereira 2013; Telles 2004; Turner 2002). This was particularly important given the widespread denial of racism throughout Latin America.

As a gathering of Afro-civil society organizations and Latin American heads of state held in preparation for the Durban conference, the 2000 Regional Conference of the Americas was an important turning point in efforts to combat racism in the region. There was a marked civil society presence at the 2000 Preparatory Conference for Durban, which took place in Santiago, Chile and had more than 1,700 participants (Dulitzky 2005). The Santiago conference provided a rare opportunity, probably the first, for Afro-Latin Americans to appear "as significant factors functioning in regional groups at the international level" (ibid.: 51). During the conference, government officials signed on to the Santiago Program of Action, which officially recognized the existence of racism in the Latin American region. In addition, the Santiago declaration called for state action to address racism, racial discrimination, and xenophobia, as well as reparations for slavery. As Paschel (2016: 128) has noted, "many Afro-Latin American activists saw, and continue to see the Santiago Declaration as even more important than the Durban Program of Action."

During the Santiago Conference, Black activists began to use the Spanish and Portuguese terms for Afro-descendant, *afro-descendiente* and *afro-descendente*, to describe Afro-Latin American communities. Black Brazilian feminist Sueli Carneiro (2002) has argued that Black women from Brazil proposed use of these terms at the Santiago Conference. Noting the significance of this terminological shift, one Afro-Uruguayan activist remarked, "We came as blacks and left as Afro-descendants ... Santiago forced Afro-descendants of the Americas to place their development within a regional perspective and to articulate their demands along with their sister communities" (cited in Paschel and Sawyer 2009: 28). In the post-Durban period, the terms *afro-descendiente* and *afro-descendente* were increasingly adopted by civil society organizations, governments, and intergovernmental organizations. Use of these terms represented a departure from other racially loaded terms such as "*negro/a*," which were not always embraced by Afro-Latin Americans due to their historical associations with racial inferiority, as well as poverty and slavery. The terms *afro-descendiente* and *afro-descendente* opened new space for Afro-Latin Americans to recognize and embrace their African ancestry and cultural heritage while, in many cases, also acknowledging their European and indigenous ancestry. At the same time, there has also been a marked increase in the number of people who self-identify as *negro/a* in recent decades, in countries such as Brazil, particularly among younger generations. These shifts in terminology and forms of self-identification have had important implications for who feels included as part of various Afro-Latin American communities and their struggles.

As a result of Black activists' strategic regionwide and transnational mobilization, the Durban conference had a far greater impact in Latin America than it did in the United States. The events of September 11, 2001 and the United States' withdrawal from the conference, due to its opposition to discussions of the transatlantic slave trade and Israel's relationship with Palestine, also weakened the impact of the Durban conference in the United States. The regional and transnational mobilization that took place around the Durban conference increased the legitimacy of the demands many Afro-Latin American activists had been making for decades. The Inter-American Democratic Charter was adopted by the Organization of American States General Assembly in Lima, Peru on September 11, 2001, three days after the Durban conference ended. This charter recognized the importance of eliminating "all forms of discrimination, especially gender, ethnic and race discrimination, as well as diverse forms of intolerance" and affirmed that "respect for ethnic, cultural and religious diversity in the Americas contribute to strengthening democracy and citizen participation" (Dulitzky 2005: 53). The charter's acknowledgement of racial discrimination represented a significant departure from most Latin American countries' longstanding failure to adequately recognize or challenge differential treatment on the basis of race, particularly as it affected Afro-Latin Americans (ibid.).

Post-Durban, several Latin American countries created public institutions to address racism and racial discrimination. These include the National Institute against Discrimination, Xenophobia, and Racism in Argentina, the National Council for the Prevention of Racism in Mexico, and the Special Secretariat for the Promotion of Racial Equality Policies in Brazil (Dulitzky 2005). Following the Durban conference, Brazil began to implement affirmative action policies in employment and higher education and became a leader among its Latin American neighbors by beginning to have high-level policy discussions about the health of the Black population (Caldwell 2017; Fundação Nacional de Saúde 2005). These policy changes are best contextualized within the decades-long struggles of Black activists in Brazil and other countries, rather than being seen as benevolent gestures on the part of government officials. As scholars have noted, Black Brazilian activists adeptly utilized the Durban conference process to educate Brazilian officials about racism and bring the conference's impact "back home" when they returned (Caldwell 2017; Paschel 2016; Silva and Mendes 2013).

Black activists' demands for inclusion of race in national censuses also began to be taken more seriously in the post-Durban period. During the twentieth century, the lack of national census data on Afro-Latin populations perpetuated their statistical, as well as social and political invisibility (Telles 2004, 2014). The lack of census data by race was often justified based on the belief that Latin American countries either did not have African-descendant communities, or that these populations had been "absorbed" into the national population via *mestizaje*. Since the early 2000s, an increasing number of Latin American countries have included racial/ethnic categories on their national censuses. This was an important move, since it provided a means to assess the size of various Afro-Latin American communities, as well as their status with respect to social indicators such as income and education (Telles 2014).

Constitutional, Legal, and Social Gains

The struggles waged by Black activists over the past several decades have led to increased visibility, greater cultural recognition, and an uptick in political participation and representation. Moreover, there are more regional and transnational networks across the region working on similar issues (see von Bülow in this volume). But one of the most important achievements has been the implementation of multicultural constitutional reforms and other legal mechanisms (see Rice in this volume). Equally important, Latin American states, as well as global, regional, and local civil society and multilateral institutions, now acknowledged the persistence of racism and racial discrimination in Latin America. The issue of racial discrimination, textually submerged in larger social relations for most of the twentieth century, now became part of the larger discourse. Brazil, the last country in the Western hemisphere to outlaw/abolish slavery, in 1888, and ironically one of the first to claim it had eliminated racial discrimination (i.e., the elimination of slavery equaled no racism), finally admitted in its seventh periodic report to the United Nations Committee on the Elimination of Racial Discrimination that racism and racial discrimination were a social and political reality in the early 2000s (United Nations 2003).

Recent legal gains that Black communities have obtained include multicultural constitutional recognition, collective land rights legislation, affirmative action, and some criminal sanctions on racial discrimination (Hernandez 2019). Countries with robust multicultural rights include Brazil and Colombia, while Ecuador, Nicaragua, Guatemala, Bolivia, and Venezuela have recognized some form of cultural rights for their Black populations. These collective rights won by Afro-descendants can be grouped into two distinct and broad categories. First are rights that allow some access or the right to preserve land and culture; second are rights aimed at remedying effects of racial discrimination.

Conclusion

Afro-civil society is now mature and vibrant across the Latin American region. However, we recognize that although many Afro-Latin communities have gained greater recognition and visibility in recent years, some continue to be invisible and have ongoing challenges in their efforts to make political claims. This is true of Afro-Mexicans, who constitute slightly more than 2% of the population, yet continue to be overlooked and their existence often denied (Hoffman and Millán 2012; Telles 2014). In addition, while there have been major advances in the struggles against racism and racial inequality in Latin America, these advances are always being contested and challenged as new political forces emerge. Challenges include attempts to roll back affirmative action policies in Brazil and ongoing efforts to displace Afro-Colombian communities from their land and territories, among others (Paschel 2016). Further, more country specific studies are urgently needed to evaluate antidiscrimination measures and the new laws granting Afro-descendants land rights. Laws and policies mean very little if they are not fully implemented or if they are slow walked through a stagnant or hostile bureaucracy (Caldwell 2017). On the one hand, Afro-civil society must consolidate these hard-won gains, while on the other, it must deal with new issues looming on the horizon. Despite any gains that have been made, state-sponsored violence (policing, courts, prisons, jails) and para-military violence by so-called non-state actors need urgent attention (Smith 2016a).

Given its growth and development, Afro-civil society across the region is now more polyvocal, diverse, and multidimensional. However, the old Black identity platform traditionally defined around the axis of race, class, gender, and rural/urban now must incorporate and welcome other identity platforms like gay, lesbian, bi-sexual, and transgendered formations (see Díez in this volume). While still marginalized, these emergent voices are now part of a new wave of progressive Black activism across region. Afro-civil society in its diversity can renew its radical grassroots activism while articulating new forms of citizenship. Simultaneously, as Afro-social movements and Afro-civil society becomes more mature and formally imbricated and tied to traditional political structures, they will have to negotiate the temptations of cooptation, as well as manipulation by political parties, top-down state, or corporate-led developmental initiatives. Instead, they must skillfully negotiate and work together with outside funding agencies (both nationally and transnationally) who offer funding and technical assistance. While such assistance is well-meaning, often Black groups must compete against each other for funding, thus creating divisions. These pressures and counter pressures create rivalries and may serve to divide Afro-civil society.

Note

1. See, for example, Alvarez and Caldwell (2016) and essays in the two-part special issue of the journal *Meridians* on African-descendant feminisms in the Americas that was published in 2016 and 2017.

References

Alberto, Paulina (2011), *Terms of Inclusion: Black Intellectuals in the Twentieth Century Brazil* (Chapel Hill: University of North Carolina Press).

Andrews, George Reid (2004), *Afro-Latin America: 1800–2000* (New York: Cambridge University Press).
Andrews, George Reid (1995), "Black Political Mobilization in Brazil, 1975–1990," in George Reid Andrews and Herrick Chapman (eds.), *The Social Construction of Democracy*, 218–41 (New York: New York University Press).
Alvarez, Sonia and Kia Lilly Caldwell (2016), "Promoting Feminist *Amefricanidade*: Bridging Black Feminist Cultures and Politics in the Americas," *Meridians* 14(1), v–xi.
Alvarez, Sonia, Ernesto Dagnino, and Arturo Escobar (eds.) (1998), *Culture of Politics and Politics of Culture: Re-Visioning Latin American Social Movements* (Boulder, CO: Westview Press).
Asher, Kiran (2009), *Black and Green: Afro-Colombia Women's Development and Nature in the Pacific Lowlands* (Durham, NC: Duke University Press).
Caldwell, Kia Lilly (2007), *Negras in Brazil* (New Brunswick, NJ: Rutgers University Press).
Caldwell, Kia Lilly (2009), "Transnational Black Feminism in the Twenty-First Century: Perspectives from Brazil," in Leith Mullings (ed.), *New Social Movements in the African Diaspora: Challenging Global Apartheid*, 105–20 (New York: Palgrave).
Caldwell, Kia Lilly (2017), *Health Equity in Brazil: Intersections of Gender, Race, and Policy* (Urbana: University of Illinois Press).
Caldwell, Kia Lilly (2019), "The Contours and Contexts of Afro-Latin American Women's Activism," in Kwame Dixon and Ollie Johnson (eds.), *Comparative Racial Politics in Latin America*, 247–70 (New York: Routledge).
Carneiro, Sueli (2002), "A Batalha de Durban," *Estudos Feministas* 10(1), 209–14.
Carneiro, Sueli (2016), "Women in Movement," *Meridians: Feminism, Race, Transnationalism* 14(1), 30–49.
Castillo, Daisy Rubiera and Inés María Martiatu Terry (eds.) (2011), *Afrocubanas: historia, pensamiento y prácticas culturales* (La Habana: Editorial de Ciencias Sociales).
Centro de Desarrollo Étnico (2010), *Insumisas: racismo, sexismo, organización, política y desarrollo de la mujer afrodescendiente* (Lima: Centro de Desarrollo Étnico).
Covin, David (2006), *The Unified Black Movement in Brazil, 1978 to 2002* (Jefferson, NC: McFarland).
Dagnino, Evelina (1998), "Culture, Citizenship, and Democracy: Changing Discourses and Practices of the Latin American Left," in Sonia E. Alvarez, Evelina Dagnino, and Arturo Escobar (eds.), *Cultures of Politics, Politics of Cultures: Re-visioning Latin American Social Movements*, 33–63 (Boulder, CO: Westview).
Davis, Darien (2019), "Beyond Representation Rethinking Rights, Alliances, and Migrations: Themes in Afro-Latin Political Engagement in Afro-Latin Political Engagement," in Kwame Dixon and Ollie Johnson (eds.), *Comparative Racial Politics in Latin*, 17–43 (New York: Routledge).
Davis, Darien, Tianna S. Paschel, and Judith Morrison (2012), "Pan Afro-Latin Americanism Revisited: Legacies and Lessons from Transnational Alliances in the New Millennium," in Bernd Reiter and Kimberly Eaton (eds.), *Afro-Descendants, Identity, and the Struggle for Development in the Americas*, 19–48 (East Lansing: Michigan State University Press).
Dixon, Kwame (2016), *Afro-Politics and Civil Society in Salvador da Bahia* (Gainesville: University of Florida Press).
Dixon, Kwame and John Burdick (eds.) (2012), *Comparative Perspectives on Afro-Latin America* (Gainesville: University of Florida Press).

Dixon, Kwame and Ollie Johnson 2019 (eds.) (2019), *Comparative Racial Politics in Latin America* (New York: Routledge).
Dulitzky, Ariel (2005), "A Region in Denial: Racial Discrimination and Racism in Latin America," in Anani Dziedzienyo and Suzanne Oboler (eds.), *Neither Enemies nor Friends: Latinos, Blacks, Afro-Latinos*, 39–59 (New York: Palgrave-Macmillan).
Dzidzienyo, Anani (2005), "The Changing World of Brazilian Race Relations?"," in Anani Dziedzienyo and Suzanne Oboler (eds.), *Neither Enemies nor Friends: Latinos, Blacks, Afro-Latinos*, 137-55 (New York: Palgrave-Macmillan).
Farfán-Santos, Elizabeth (2016), *Black Bodies, Black Rights: The Politics of Quilombismo in Contemporary Brazil* (Austin: University of Texas Press).
Feinberg, Richard, Carlos Waisman, and León Zamosc (eds.) (2006), *Civil Society and Democracy in Latin America* (New York: Palgrave-Macmillan).
Fundação Nacional de Saúde (2005), *Saúde da população negra no brasil: contribuições para a promoção da equidade* (Brasília: Fundação Nacional de Saúde).
Geggus, David (2007), "The Sounds and Echoes of Freedom: The Impact of the Haitian Revolution in Latin America," in Darién J. Davis (ed.), *Beyond Slavery: The Multilayered Legacy of Africans in Latin America and the Caribbean*, 19–36 (Lanham, MD: Rowman & Littlefield).
Gonzalez, Lélia (1988), "For an Afro-Latin American Feminism," in *Confronting the Crisis in Latin America: Women Organizing for Change*, 95–101 (Isis International and DAWN).
Green, James (2010), *We Cannot Remain Silent: Opposition to the Brazilian Military Dictatorship in the US* (Durham, NC: Duke University Press).
Hanchard, Michael (1994), *Orpheus and Power: The Movimento Negro of Rio de Janeiro and São Paulo, Brazil 1945 to 1988* (Princeton, NJ: Princeton University Press).
Hartigan, John (2010), *Race in the 21st Century: Ethnographic Approaches* (New York: Oxford University Press).
Helg, Ann (1995), *Our Rightful Share: The Afro-Cuban Struggle for Equality 1886 to 1912* (Chapel Hill: University of North Carolina Press).
Hernández, Tanya Katerí (2013), *Racial Subordination in Latin: The Role of the State, Customary Law and the New Civil Rights Response* (Cambridge: Cambridge University Press).
Hernández, Tanya Katerí (2019), "Race and the Law in Latin America," Kwame Dixon and Ollie Johnson (eds.), *Comparative Racial Politics in Latin America*, 271-87 (New York: Routledge).
Hoffman, Odile and Gloria Lara Millán (2012), "Reivindicación afromexicana: Formas de organización de la movilización negra en México," in María José Becerra, Diego Buffa, Hamurabi Noufouri, and Mario Ayala (eds.), *Las poblaciones afrodescendientes de América Latina y el Caribe: Pasado, presente y perspectivas desde el siglo XXI*, 25–46 (Córdoba: Universidad Nacional de Córdoba).
Human Rights Watch (2019), *Colombia: Events of 2018*, https://www.hrw.org/world-report/2019/country-chapters/colombia.
Johnson, Ollie (2012), "Black Activism in Ecuador, 1979 to 2000," in Kwame Dixon and John Burdick (eds.), *Comparative Perspectives on Afro Latin America*, 176–97 (Gainesville: University of Florida Press).
Lao-Montes, Agustín (2016), "Afro-Latin American Feminisms at the Cutting Edge of Emerging Political-Epistemic Movements," *Meridians* 14(2), 1–24.
Lozano, Betty Ruth (2016), "Feminismo Negro – Afrocolombiano: ancestral, insurgente y cimarrón. Un feminismo en – lugar," *Intersticios de la política y la cultura* 5(9), 23–48. https://revistas.unc.edu.ar/index.php/intersticios/article/view/14612.

Martínez-Echazábal, Lourdes (1998), "Mestizaje and the Discourse of National/Cultural Identity in Latin America, 1845-1859," *Latin American Perspectives* 25 (3): 21-42.

Mayes, April J. (2019), "Black Feminist Formations in the Dominican Republic since *La Sentencia*," in Kwame Dixon and Ollie Johnson (eds.), *Comparative Racial Politics in Latin America*, 139–60 (New York: Routledge).

Mullings, Leith (2004), "Race and Globalization: Racialization from Below," *Souls* 6 (2): 1-9.

Olivella, Manuel Zapata (1977), "Primer Congreso de la Cultura Negra," *Selected Correspondence of Manuel Zapata Olivella – Vanderbilt University*, http://mzo.library.vanderbilt.edu/correspondence/essay.php?topic=congresses&id=117.

James, C.L.R. (1938), *The Black Jacobins: Toussaint L'Ouverture and the San Domingo Revolution* (New York: Dial Press).

Paschel, Tianna (2016), *Becoming Black Political Subjects: Movements and Ethno-Racial Rights in Colombia and Brazil* (Princeton, NJ: Princeton University Press).

Paschel, Tianna and Mark Q. Sawyer (2009), "Contesting Politics as Usual: Black Social Movements, Globalization, and Race Policy in Latin America," in Leith Mullings (ed.), *New Social Movements in the African Diaspora: Challenging Global Apartheid*, 13–32 (New York: Palgrave-Macmillan).

Perry, Keisha Khan (2013), *Black Women against the Land Grab: The Fight for Racial Justice in Brazil* (Minneapolis: University of Minnesota Press).

Price, Richard (1973), *Maroon Societies: Rebel Slave Communities in the Americas* (Garden City, NY: Anchor Press).

Ratts, Alex (2007), *Eu sou atlântica: Sobre a trajetória de vida de Beatriz Nascimento* (São Paulo: Imprensa Oficial do Estado de São Paulo/Instituto Kuanza).

Reis, João José (1993), *Slave Rebellion in Brazil: The Muslim Uprising of 1835 in Bahia*. (Baltimore, MD: Johns Hopkins University Press).

Safa, Helen (1995), "Race and National Identity in the Americas," *Latin American Perspectives* 25(3), 3–20.

Santos, Sonia (2012), "Controlling Black Women's Reproductive Health Rights: An Impetus to Black Women's Collective Organizing," *Cultural Dynamics* 24(1), 13–30.

Silva, Joselina da and Amauri Mendes Pereira (2013), *Olhares sobre a mobilização brasileira para a III conferência mundial contra o racismo a discriminação racial, a xenofobia e intolerâncias correlatas* (Belo Horizonte: Nandyala).

Smith, Christen (2016a), *Afro-Paradise: Blackness, Violence and Performance in Brazil* (Urbana: University of Illinois Press).

Smith, Christen (2016b), "Towards a Black Feminist Model of Black Atlantic Liberation: Remembering Beatriz Nascimento," *Meridians* 14(2), 71–87.

Stahler-Sholk, Richard, Harry E. Vanden and Marc Becker (eds.). (2014) *Rethinking Latin American Social Movements: Radical Action from Below* (New York:Rowman and Littlefield).

Telles, Edward (2004), *Race in Another America: The Significance of Skin Color in Brazil* (Princeton: Princeton University Press).

Telles, Edward and the Project on Ethnicity and Race in Latin America (2014), *Pigmentocracies: Ethnicity, Race, and Color in Latin America* (Chapel Hill: University of North Carolina Press).

Torres, Carlos and John Antón Sánchez (2019), "Afro-Ecuadorian Politics," in Kwame Dixon and Ollie Johnson (eds.), *Comparative Racial Politics in Latin America*, 163–82 (New York: Routledge).

Turner, J. Michael (2002), "The Road to Durban – and Back," *NACLA Report on the Americas* 35: 31–35.
United Nations Committee on the Elimination of Racial Discrimination (2003), "International Convention on the Elimination of All Forms of Racial Discrimination," CERD/C/431Add.8 16 October (Geneva: United Nations).
Wade, Pete (1993), *Blackness and Race Mixture: The Dynamics of Racial Identity in Colombia* (Baltimore, MD: Johns Hopkins University Press).
Wade, Pete (2012), "Afro-Colombian Social Movements," in Kwame Dixon and John Burdick (eds.), *Comparative Perspectives on Afro-Latin America*, 135–55 (Gainesville: University of Florida Press).
Werneck, Jurema (2007), "Of Ialodes and Feminists: Reflections on Black Women's Political Action in Latin America and the Caribbean," *Cultural Dynamics* 19(1), 99–113.

CHAPTER 23

STUDENT MOVEMENTS IN LATIN AMERICA

Pushing the Education Agenda and Beyond

SOFIA DONOSO

Introduction

On March 15, 2019, students across the world walked out of their schools for a day of protest, calling on their respective governments to declare a climate emergency and take firm actions to address the issue. According to the organizers of the event, there were more than 2,000 protests in 125 countries (The Guardian 2019). Students also played a key role in the global protest wave of 2011–2012. Massive student protests in the United Kingdom, Canada, and Chile, amongst others, placed the right to education at the top of the policy agendas of their respective countries. There are not only contemporary examples of student movements as drivers of social change. Going back to the twentieth century, student movements pushed for the modernization of universities in Latin America, formed part of the independence movements in Africa and Asia, and spawned a cultural revolution in most of Western societies. This chapter departs from a broad definition of student movements as "a relatively organized effort on the part of a large number of students to either bring about or prevent change in any one of the following: policies, institutional personnel, social structure (institutions), or cultural aspects of society involving either institutionalized or non-institutionalized collective actions or both simultaneously" (Gill and DeFronzo 2009: 208). While student movements, like social movements composed of other actors, can have a wide array of consequences, this chapter focuses on their political influence.

Student movements' political importance in the present and the past has inspired a large scholarly debate on their origins, causes, and consequences. The literature is especially abundant on student mobilizations in May 1968 (Guzmán-Concha 2019). Part of this scholarship has explained the rise of student movements as a product of generational conflicts (Gill and DeFronzo 2009). It argues that rapid social change sparked a conflict between dominant traditional values and modern ones. Because of their participation in the education system, students are particularly prone to defend the latter. Others have stressed psychological variables. Lipset (1964: 30), for example, argued that university students "live on the boundary between the last stage of adolescence, with its freedom from the burdens of adult responsibility, and the first stages of adulthood with its complex of pressing tasks and difficult decisions." Lipset (1971) also stressed that students at elite institutions tend to be liberal, and that this fosters activism. Altbach (2006), in turn, contended that universities constitute a particularly favorable environment for the development of organization among movements. For one, they promote critical thinking. Second, they host a large number of people of a similar age who seek a sense of community. A similar reasoning has been recurrent in social movement scholarship. Research has shown that participation in social movements is largely dependent on what has been referred to as biographical availability—the extent into which political engagement is constrained by work, family, or other variables that are characteristic of the life trajectory (e.g., McAdam 1986; Schussman and Soule 2005).

The bulk of empirical research on student movements is focused on Western societies (Gill and DeFronzo 2009). This is a paradox since, as Gill and DeFronzo (ibid.: 206) note, "student movements in developing societies have often had greater political impacts than those in the more technologically advanced nations." The reason for this is that students in developing countries are exposed to knowledge that can pave the way for the questioning of the inequalities that often characterize their societies, and the elaboration of new ideologies that spark mobilization. Latin American student movements, in particular, were for a long time heralded as a reference point worldwide. Throughout the history of the region, they have offered staunch resistance to authoritarianism at the same time as they have constituted a driving force in the development of the university system. Student movements have thus mobilized for both external and internal demands. While their repertoire of action has varied—spawning from street protests, take-overs, and more recently, digital campaigns—they have forged a long tradition of engagement in Latin America's political history. Only in the last decade, mobilizations spearheaded by #YoSoy132 in Mexico and the student movement in Chile have drawn the attention of the international community in their call for freedom of expression and public free education, respectively, and democratization.

In this chapter, I offer an overview of the role that student movements have played in Latin America's political development. Structuring the chapter chronologically, I begin by examining the Córdoba university reform, driven by the Argentine student movement, and its influence across the region. I then depict student movements' role in the intense political development of the late 1960s, and their fate after the democratic breakdown in Latin America from that decade onwards. The final section analyzes some of the most visible contemporary student movements, namely those in Brazil, Chile, Colombia, Mexico, and Venezuela. In the context of both left- and right-wing governments, student movements in these countries have called for education reforms and for the democratization of the political systems in their countries. Throughout the chapter I show that Latin America's student movements have constituted a space of ideological renewal and resistance to the various sociopolitical and economic inequalities that characterize Latin America. In essence, as Guzmán-Concha (2017: 2) puts it, they have constituted "a field of connection between subterranean and mainstream politics."

Student Movements, Education Reforms, and Democratization

The specific focus of this section is the role that student movements have played in the political life of Latin America. Without pretending to offer a comprehensive account of student movements in neither all countries in the region nor in all political moments, I center on their role in the democratization of both universities and their societies. I thus review the intertwined relationship between students' internal and external demands in some crucial junctures.

The Córdoba University Reform Movement and its Regional Impact

When academics and pundits alike refer to student movements throughout the history of Latin America, the Córdoba university reform movement in 1918 is a common starting point. It also constitutes a milestone that subsequent student movements in the region have referred to (Pittelli and Hermo 2011). The movement's key demands were the secularization and democratization of the Universidad Nacional de Córdoba (UNC), Argentina. The students called for the end of the intervention of pressure groups such as the Catholic Church, political parties, and economic groups linked to the country's oligarchy and foreign forces. To achieve this, the movement launched a campaign for university autonomy, co-government (participation of the students), and the institutionalization of mechanisms to protect academic freedom (Moncayo 2008).

Importantly, the students called for a university that was responsive to social demands and the country's democratization process. The Córdoba university reform movement was a reaction to the elitist nature of the university system. The students spearheading the movement subscribed to a libertarian, urban, scientific, and rationalistic modernity. They embodied the political aspirations of the country's emerging bourgeoisie, which was eager to access spaces that until then were exclusively enjoyed by the oligarchy. Hence, the reform movement was inextricably linked to the modernization of Argentina and the rise of the middle class that this process entailed. The main driver of the reform movement was, in sum, the mismatch between an obsolete and authoritarian university structure and the aspirations of a democratic model.

Sensitive to this new scenario and the student demands, the government presided by the Unión Cívica Radical Party responded to the movement by negotiating with the university authorities. In turn, this paved the way for the enactment of the new statutes which comprised most of the movement's petitions (Pittelli and Hermo 2011). Its success sparked similar reform efforts at other universities in Argentina such as the ones in Santa Fe and Buenos Aires. The principles of the movement also spread to other countries in Latin America (van Aken 1971; Landinelli 2008; Pittelli and Hermo 2011). Its impact, however, varied across the region.

Peruvian students were among the first to adhere to the reformist spirit of their Argentine peers. They called for the academic freedom of the faculty, the legalization of students' right to strike, free attendance at lectures, and representation in the university council (Tünnermann 1998). The reform movement also engaged in issues outside the university. Among other things, it created the popular university where students, workers, and intellectuals developed political thinking with a marked anti-imperialist stamp (ibid.).

In Chile, the student federation of the Universidad de Chile promoted the ideals of the Córdoba Reform, such as university autonomy, access to broader segment of society, student representation in the governing bodies, and free access to lectures (Tünnermann 1998). Yet the participation of students in the university governance structure was an idea strongly resisted by the university faculty. Its implementation would therefore not take place until the end of the 1960s (Ruiz 2011).

The struggle to democratize the university was often intertwined with broader demands for democracy in the country. In Colombia, for example, the student movement had formed prior to the 1918 Córdoba movement against the government presided by Rafael Reyes, a conservative military who had dissolved parliament in 1904 (Moncayo 2008). The students defended the autonomy of the university. This was translated into the reforms of Medellín in 1922 and of Bogotá in 1924, which explicitly stated its adherence to the reform movement in Córdoba (Tünnermann 1998). A few years later, in 1928, Gerardo Molina, a former student leader, became rector of the Universidad Nacional de Colombia in 1928 (Moncayo 2008).

In Venezuela, the efforts to modernize the university system came later. What has been referred to as the "generation of 1928" promoted the principles of the Córdoba university reform movement in the midst of authoritarian rule (Rivas 1998). The fate of student leaders was harsh as the dictatorship of Juan Vicente Gómez persecuted, imprisoned, and exiled a large part of the reformist generation (Pérez Perdomo 2007). That year, and on the occasion of the student week, a group of students mobilized on the streets of Caracas calling for freedom and democracy, responded with repression by the state. After the death of Gómez, a new generation of students pushed for an education reform that in 1944 culminated in a new law.

In the case of Brazil, the reformist spirit came later. While important universities such as the Universidade do Rio de Janeiro, the Universidade Federal de Minas Gerais, and the Universidade de São Paulo were founded in 1920, 1927, and 1934, respectively, and the União Nacional dos Estudantes (UNE) was created at the end of the 1930s, the debate on the democratization of university spaces only appeared in a significant way during the 1960s (Azevedo et al. 2018).

The political context in Mexico, marked by the Mexican Revolution, shaped the prospects of the student demands. The call for a public, free, democratic and autonomous university with social vocation was considered necessary to resist authoritarianism. A first initiative in this direction was the foundation of the Universidad Autónoma del Estado de Potosí, endowed with organizational autonomy, and the demand for autonomy of the Universidad Nacional, which was obtained in 1933 (Aboites 2008). Important encounters between Latin American student leaders at the time were also held in Mexico. Examples of the former were the Primer Congreso Internacional de Estudiantes in 1921, where the Federación Internacional de Estudiantes was created, and the Primer Congreso de Estudiantes Iberoamericanos in 1925 (Pittelli and Hermo 2011).

The impact of the Córdoba reform movement in Latin American countries was not only expressed in the implementation of the immediate reforms, but also in subsequent ones as many student leaders later became university authorities and could shape the fate of their institutions (Tünnermann 1998). Student activism also served as a springboard for high political office (Spielmann 2015). Despite the importance of the student movements that followed the principles of the Córdoba university reform, many of them tailed off in subsequent years, especially after the democratic breakdown that most of Latin America countries experienced from the 1960s onwards (Rivas 1998; Ruiz 2011). Yet, still today, the idea that universities should promote and contribute to the country's national and autonomous development remains unquestioned (Guzmán-Concha 2017).

Student Activism in the Struggle against Authoritarian Regimes

The 1960s in Latin America were marked by political turmoil. Brazil pioneered the rise of authoritarianism with the 1964 military coup (see Brockett in this volume). This was followed by strong repression of the student movement in general and UNE in particular (González 2018). Moreover, the dictatorship took measures to limit the autonomy of Brazilian universities. The promulgation of the Lei Suplicy granted the state a set of tools to intervene institutions of higher education. At the same time, it dissolved the UNE (Millán 2012). Faced with this situation, student organizations had to decide whether to participate in the new spaces facilitated by the military regime while maintaining their organizations (González 2018). At the end of 1967, social mobilization gained traction. Students mobilized to end arbitrary dismissal of professors and the constraints posed on their organization. Costa e Silva, leader of the military regime at the time, responded by escalating repression. This meant the end of the few democratic spaces that existed until then (Moraes 2008).

The year 1968 was particularly eventful. A protest was held at a restaurant in Rio de Janeiro that housed low-income students and served as a meeting point for UNE operations (González 2018). The police soon arrived and fired on one student protester. His death was repudiated and sparked a wave of protests across the country, which was joined by large sectors of the middle class, religious groups, and artists, amongst others (Millán 2012). More students joined in. Later, the student movement supported the strikes by metalworkers in Minas Gerais and São Paulo, establishing a strong alliance with workers (ibid.). At the same time, organizations such as the União Metropolitana dos Estudantes and Dissidência employed repertoires of action such as the occupation of public spaces (González 2018). The response to the heightened phase of protest was the prohibition of both student organizations and trade unions (Millán 2012). After constituting a central actor in Brazil's political life for decades, since the late 1970s the student movement declined (Machado 2015). It was only during the political turmoil of the 2010s that the country would witness massive student protest again.

The rebellious spirit of 1968 also gained traction in Mexico where the Partido Revolucionario Institucional (PRI) had ruled uninterruptedly since 1917. In July 1968, a group of students commemorating the Cuban Revolution were repressed by police forces. A few days later, the army stormed several campuses at the Universidad Nacional Autónoma de México and the Instituto Nacional Politécnico, infuriating both the students and the faculty. The student movement not only questioned police intervention at university campuses, but also the PRI's approach to democracy, liberties, and equal distribution of resources. Joined by intellectuals and members of the middle classes, in August 1968 the students gathered more than 400,000 people to march to the Zócalo, the main square in Mexico City (Markarian 2004). During the march, the students grouped under the National Strike Council decided to leave a permanent guard at the square until the government delivered a response to their concerns. Instead, the demonstration was dissolved by the army and the government initiated a repressive offensive against the student movement (Rivas 2018). Violence escalated, and on October 2 military troops shot thousands of protesters at the Plaza de Tlatelolco in Mexico City. The Tlatelolco massacre was followed by a rapid decline of the student movement due to the fear of participating in the student brigades and assemblies (Rivas 2018). At the same time, the legitimacy of the PRI government was strongly put into question both in Mexico and abroad. Until today, the Tlatelolco Massacre is considered a point of inflexion in the long transition towards democracy in Mexico (Loaeza 1989; see Inclán in this volume).

Argentina was also governed by an authoritarian regime in 1968. Two years earlier, General Juan Carlos Onganía came to power in command of a de facto government through a military coup. Once in power, Onganía intervened educational establishments and prohibited political organizations. The advancement of the 1918 reformist movement's petition—autonomy, co-government, academic freedom, and democratization of the universities—was reversed (Califa and Millán 2016). This triggered mobilization among left-wing students at the main universities. Repression escalated and at the end of 1966 a student of the Universitdad Nacional de Córdoba was killed by the police. This constituted a turning point in the country's political development as the Catholic Church withdrew its support for the military regime (Millán 2012). The student movement reemerged in 1968, when the country celebrated the fiftieth anniversary of the 1918 university reform and an alliance with the more radical factions of the Confederación General del Trabajo (CGT), founded in 1930, was formed (ibid.). Students and workers strengthened their relationship and staged joint protests across the country (Califa and Millán 2016). These intensified when another student was murdered in Rosario in 1969. In Córdoba, the CGT called for a general strike—that then evolved into a popular revolt known as the Cordobazo—which was followed by more rallies in other cities and dozens of students killed (ibid.; see Ramírez and Stoessel in this volume).

Argentina's student movement continued to suffer repression until the coming into power of Juan Perón in 1973. During Perón's short period of government—his third—the Peronist youth was the main political force at Argentine universities. Importantly, in 1974 the Perón government passed the law of national universities, which recognized academic autonomy and administrative independence.

The military coup in 1976 abruptly ended the democratization of universities and student participation. Student leaders were disappeared and killed. From 1981 onwards, especially, students from the UNC spearheaded protests that later would spread across the country demanding issues pertaining not only to the internal organization of the universities, but also the clarification of the situation of detainees and missing persons, and the lifting of the state of siege (Vera de Flachs 2015).

The 1960s in Chile were characterized by an intense political discussion and questioning of the legitimacy of the political and social order. While the university reform had started in the mid-1920s—inspired by the Córdoba student movement—its most active phase was between 1967 and 1973 (Garretón and Martínez 1985). Driven by the student movement, with the support of faculty and administrative staff, a discussion about the social role of universities was added to the country's heated political climate. The demand for the democratization of universities and increased access to tertiary education were a way of putting education at the heart of social transformation (Rivera 2018). The coming into power of President Salvador Allende in 1970 only polarized politics further. This was mirrored by student politics at both universities and high schools (Rojas 2009). High school students organized in the Federación de Estudiantes Secundarios (FESES) initially welcomed the Unidad Popular government presided by Allende. Yet Allende's chief education reform, the Escuela Nacional Unificada, divided the FESES. This reform aimed at restructuring the education system in two main levels with a strong focus on practical skills. It raised a debate that went beyond high school students, and it was never implemented. The importance of university students for Allende was expressed by the decision to give his victory speech in 1970 at the headquarters of the Federación de Estudiantes de la Universidad de Chile (FECH). However, Allende also faced the rise of a strong right-wing at universities. The left, in turn, was fragmented by various groups that starred heated debates about the scope of the social and economic reforms that the Unidad Popular government wanted to implement.

A tough period for those social actors who had supported the government of Allende began with the military coup in 1973. The student movement was no exception. Its main leaders were repressed and, in some cases, disappeared and executed. At the same time, the educational system at all levels was subject to a profound neoliberal restructuring without a strong movement that could offer resistance. For a long time, confined to restricted spaces for participation, cultural expressions offered a way to resist the dictatorship (Muñoz Tamayo 2002). Yet the systematic violence exerted by the military junta added to the economic crisis of the mid-1980s spawned a protest wave that the regime presided over by General Pinochet could not contain. Both university and high school students were active during this struggle against the military regime. As repression increased and the political parties withdrew from the streets, elite settlements and moderation paved the way for the transition to democracy (Cavarozzi 1992).

Contemporary Student Mobilizations in Latin America

After being active in the struggle against the military, student movements in Latin America declined once democracy was reinstated. While the introduction of democratic rule undoubtedly offered a more favorable context for mobilization, the legacies of military rule still endured and constrained collective action (Levy 1991). More recently, however, the region has witnessed an increase in student mobilization. The year 2011 was a particularly eventful one. In Chile, for example, students mobilized during most of the year in the largest protest since 1990. Since then—under both left and right-wing governments—student movements have re-emerged as a key social actor. As research shows, the rise of student mobilization is partly related to the gradual expansion of access to college (Disi Pavlic 2019). This multiplies the pool of potential adherents to the issues promoted by student movements. In some countries such as Colombia and Brazil, student protests arose as a way of resisting education reforms. Social mobilization spearheaded by students in Chile, Venezuela, and Mexico, in turn, pushed for pending democratizing reforms. Thus, contemporary student movements in Latin America have articulated extant discontent with both the functioning of the education system and the deficits of the democratic regimes.

Venezuela: Students Struggle for Democratizing the Media and Resisting Authoritarianism

While student movements in Venezuela traditionally have been left-wing, in the last decade the Bolivarian revolution lost its hegemony over university activism (Ivancheva 2017). In May 2007 a series of protests spearheaded by students in Caracas challenged the government of President Hugo Chávez. The protests were triggered by the government's decision to end the license of the private channel Radio Caracas Televisión (Cannon

2014). The students stressed that this put into question the objectivity of the media and the existence of a media independent of the government (Brading 2012). They also rejected the constitutional amendment proposed by Chávez to complete the transition to a socialist republic. Students and the opposition, however, claimed that the changes to the constitution promoted by the government sought to enable an extension of the presidency of Chávez. The movement introduced the notion of "white hands," a symbol used during the rallies as a sign of freedom.

The continuous student protests gained traction and won support by public opinion. Part of the political establishment also backed the students. Podemos, a political party that had withdrawn from the government coalition and joined the opposition, declared its support to the students (ibid.). The movement, however, sought to distance itself from politicians and embrace new issues that could connect with the interests of common citizens. In fact, students referred to the movement as "students for liberty" and rejected being called students of opposition; they intended to become a citizen movement that was independent of political affiliation (García-Guadilla and Mallén 2010).

The student protests were not in vain as the government of Chávez lost the referendum in November 2007 (Cannon 2014). Despite this success, the movement was unable to articulate further and, although several of its leaders were elected congressmen in subsequent elections, it lost organizational density (Brading 2012; Uzcátegui 2014).

In more recent years, student protests have sparked again. In 2010, for example, protesters marched in defence of the private media, and in 2012 for the lack of funds to higher education (Cannon 2014). Nevertheless, it was not until 2014 that the movement would regain strength. This time students rallied over the marked worsening of the quality of life of Venezuelans and the violation of their civil rights (Said-Hung and Valencia-Cobos 2017). Clashes with the police ended with forty-two dead people, 3,120 detainees, and more than 3,400 imprisoned according to official government data (Cannon 2014; Said-Hung and Valencia-Cobos 2017). This fuelled the movement further, and encouraged the use of social media to denounce police abuse (Said-Hung and Valencia-Cobos 2017). Since then, the situation in Venezuela has further deteriorated, and protests against Chávez's successor Nicolás Maduro have intensified and included a wide array of actors. While declining after the peak of protests in 2007, the impact of the student movement prevailed. In early 2019, Juan Guaidó, one of the student leaders of the 2007 protests and current president of the National Assembly, was proclaimed acting president of Venezuela as the 2018 re-election of Nicolás Maduro was declared invalid.

Chile: The Student Movement Questions the Legacy of the Pinochet Regime

Chile's student movement—like the rest of the country's social movements—struggled to reorganize after the reinstatement of democratic rule in 1990 (Donoso and von Bülow

2017). A wary political class in government, and the institutional constraints left by the Constitution drafted by the Pinochet regime, left little space for contesting the neoliberal education model bequeathed by the military and maintained by the center-left. Yet, while the 1990s was marked by the dearth of social mobilization, the student movement gained force throughout several protest waves in the 2000s (Donoso 2017). Protesting the privatized education system, student organizations spearheading the protests became increasingly disappointed with the center-left governments in power between 1990 and 2010 (Somma 2012). The massive demonstrations across the country staged by both high school and university students in 2011 were thus the result of numerous earlier protest events with unsatisfactory outcomes. The fact that the student movement faced a center right-wing government for the first time signified to have a common adversary and helped to unify an otherwise fragmented left.

The lack of response to the student demands also contributed to fuel the movement and continue the rallies during the whole of 2011. At the same time, the high quorums required in Congress to modify organic laws such as the one that defined the education system convinced the students that the struggle for an egalitarian educational system also required a change of political constitution. The latter was enacted during the military regime and "locked in" crucial policy areas along the neoliberal lines that the Pinochet regime promoted. It also shaped politics and restricted the room of maneuver for reforms by establishing the quorums necessary to pursue change and by introducing incentives for broad coalition-building at the cost of smaller political parties. Thus, the 2011 student movement demanded not only a new education system but also political reforms that could deepen democracy and strengthen alternative political forces that could defend their demands in Congress. As Fleet and Guzmán-Concha (2017: 2) note, "[f]rom a long-term perspective, the 2011 mobilisations accelerated the breakdown of the underlying pacts of the transition from a military to a civil regime in the late 1980s."

In addition, former student leaders frustrated with the few gains of the 2011 protests decided to compete for a legislative seat and push for education and political reforms from this space. This strategy proved successful as at least four of them were elected to Congress in 2013. Since then, other student leaders and activists linked to policy areas that go beyond education formed the Frente Amplio, a left-wing political coalition that currently constitutes the third biggest electoral force in Chile. In the 2017 election, this coalition gained twenty legislative seats in the lower chamber and one in the upper chamber, and its presidential candidate almost made it to the second ballot. Four years later, in 2021, the Frente Amplio elected its first President, former student leader Gabriel Boric.

Colombia: Students Mobilize against President Santos' Education Reforms

In March 2011, Colombian President Juan Manuel Santos announced an ambitious proposal to reform the system of higher education. The plan included an increase of the coverage of education and an improvement of its quality by attracting private investment in public universities and introducing profit-making institutions of higher education, which was deemed crucial to cover the financial deficit of public universities (Cruz Rodríguez 2013; Tarazona Acevedo and Correa 2016). However, the proposal received critics from vice-chancellors of public and private universities, student spokespersons, and politicians, who argued that the reform limited the autonomy of universities, while conceiving of education as a market good (Cruz Rodríguez 2013).

Rejecting the proposal, and inspired by the rise of student movements in other parts of the world, the Colombian student movement organized a national gathering where the Mesa Amplia Nacional Estudiantil (MANE) was created (ibid.). This umbrella organization brought together different student organizations from both private and public universities, and became the cornerstone in the construction of programmatic and organizational unity needed to mobilize (Archila 2012; Cruz Rodríguez 2013). With repertoire of action such as rallies and a national strike, the movement mobilized across the country, staging different types of protest events almost weekly (Archila 2012).

By August 2011, student protests had reached most parts of the country and garnered considerable public support. The government was forced to review the idea of allowing profit-making in institutions of higher education (Cruz Rodríguez 2013). However, this was considered insufficient by the students, who also wanted the government to dismiss the rest of the proposal as it was viewed as an entry point for the privatization of education (ibid.). After the Santos government refused to give in to the movement's petition, public universities initiated a strike, gaining the support of a large number of students from private universities. At the same time, the protests continued to spread through several cities in the country, with more than 20,000 participants (Cruz Rodríguez 2013). On October 12, spokespersons of the MANE issued a statement demanding the government comply with their main demand: a free education of quality at the service of the people, and devoted to the generation of equality, inclusion, and opportunities. The students also wanted the government to institute a commission where students could discuss the problems of higher education (Tarazona Acevedo and Correa 2016). On November 16, 2011, the government of Juan Manuel Santos decided to withdraw the reform project and offered the students an active participation in the formation of a new proposal (ibid.). After months of protest and paralysis in the education system, the protests were interrupted.

Mexico: #YoSoy132 and the Quest to Democratize the Media

On May 11, 2012, two months before the presidential elections, the presidential candidate Enrique Peña Nieto visited the Universidad Iberoamericana to give a conference. While students were welcome to attend the talk, many of the seats in the auditorium were occupied by Peña Nieto's team and some students reported that they had been offered money to avoid asking uncomfortable questions (Alonso 2013). Still, a group of students attending managed to ask about Peña Nieto's role as a governor in the harshly repressed protests in Atenco in 2006 (Treré 2015). When the candidate defended his actions, the situation in the auditorium went out of control and Peña Nieto had to be escorted out by his bodyguards (Alonso 2013). The PRI leaders and the Partido Ecologista Verde of Mexico came out in defence of Peña Nieto, denouncing the protesters as not students from the university and declaring that they had been paid by the left (ibid.). Denying these accusations, 131 students of the Universidad Iberoamericana uploaded a video on YouTube in which they exhibited their student credentials, denying the accusations of political leaders and criticizing their actions (Treré 2015). The video was made viral by the social networks and soon other students joined the protest using the hashtag # YoSoy132, a label that remained a global trending topic for six days (Gómez García and Treré 2014).

In the weeks after the incident with Peña Nieto, the movement's rapid success in social networks led to the participation of hundreds of students in marches to the Televisa facilities in protest of this channel's content and censorship (Alonso 2013). The main criticism of the students focused on the lack of democracy in Mexican media, which was characterized by limited transparency, pluralism, and impartiality when it came to informing citizens and generating critical thinking (Treré 2015). In fact, only two channels (Televisa and TV Azteca) control almost 90% of the audience in Mexico (Gómez García and Treré 2014).

During the months prior to the election, the movement carried out a series of actions that sought to symbolize the detrimental influence of what was referred to as "telecracy" on the elections (Treré 2015). In addition, it produced different documents on how to reform the Mexican media, at the same time as it organized the first political debate in the whole history of the country by social organizations and transmitted by social networks and radios (Gómez García and Treré 2014). The days before the election the movement demonstrated that pre-electoral manipulation was taking place, and during election day it collected evidence that showed clear acts of electoral fraud (Alonso 2013). Despite the signs of electoral irregularities, Peña Nieto was proclaimed president. While this spawned new protests across the country and the blockade of Televisa for twenty-four hours, the biggest movement since 1968 was demoralized with the lack of response and soon declined (Cuninghame 2017).

Brazil: Students Defend their Right to Education and Mobilize against Corruption

Brazilian students have a long institutional and cultural tradition of pro-democracy mobilization (Mische 2008; Snider 2017). In recent years, two episodes have marked the Brazilian student movement: the national protests of June–July 2013 and the protests in São Paulo at the end of 2015 (Catini and Mello 2016; Saad-Filho 2013).

In June 2013, Brazil began to experience the largest of its national protests in more than two decades (Alonso and Mische 2017). Detonated by the rise in transport prices in the city of São Paulo, demands quickly expanded to other sectors, such as the improvement of public services like health and education (Saad-Filho 2013; Snider 2017). Although the students represented a good part of the protesters, the demonstrations grouped a series of interest as those of the professional middle classes and the working class (Alonso and Mische 2017).

The protests of 2013 had important consequences. The violence of the police response only triggered new rallies and an outpouring of public support. Public pressure not only forced the authorities to reverse the increase in the prices of transportation tickets, but also to allocate more federal funding to the education and health systems (Saad-Filho 2013; Snider 2017). As Snider (2017) notes, the protests also served as a catalyst to channel disgruntlement with other issues. Importantly, in the context of strong public concern with political corruption, Congress had to drop an amendment that sought to remove the Public Prosecutor Office's ability to investigate crimes to investigate alleged criminal activity among public officials.

While the protests in favor of improvements in education continued after 2013, it was not until 2015 that students regained media attention. During September of that year, the government of São Paulo announced its education reform proposal, which consisted of a restructuring at the educational levels offered by the state schools. Instead of the three levels that organize primary and secondary education in Brazil, the proposal envisioned that schools would focus on one of the levels with the aim of improving the quality of teaching. At the same time, this would allow to close nearly one hundred establishments. Facing this threat, high school students called for a series of protests and took over their schools. Geraldo Alckmin, governor of the state, rapidly lost public support, reaching a record low. The federal government finally had to withdraw the proposal and the state education secretary resigned. Moreover, the protests also served to uncover corruption scandals in other states, such as irregularities in companies that provided educational services in Goiás (Catini and Mello 2016).

Conclusion

In this chapter I set out to describe the main student movements in Latin America. Following a chronological order, I portrayed the Córdoba university reform movement and its regional influence in the early twentieth century, and the role of students during the struggle against authoritarianism and in contemporary Latin America. By doing so, I sought to disentangle the role of student movements vis-à-vis other actors driving political and social change. The chapter also informs a large body of literature on student movements in other parts of the world, which, despite the political importance of student movements in Latin America, rarely considers them in their analysis.

Student movements have been a central actor in Latin America's past and recent history. As shown in this chapter, they have not only pushed for education reforms and the democratization of educational establishments, but also been closely involved in their countries' political development. As one of the Chilean student movement's slogans during the dictatorship expresses—"security to study, liberty to live"—these two dimensions are most often deeply intertwined. Student movements in the region have been influential in both dimensions. Education reforms have been promoted and resisted, and student mobilizations have put pressure on both authoritarian and democratic governments.

Student movements are important not only for the influence that they may have on immediate education and political reforms, but also as spaces of political socialization and training of future political leaders. Student politics play an important role as a launch pad for political careers. Hence, the fate of many student movements also shapes perceptions and ideological preferences of politicians that later will have the power to implement them (see Spanakos and Romo in this volume). The same can be said in relation to the practices that student movements develop when mobilizing. For example, in recent processes of mobilization such as that in Mexico, social media has played a pivotal role. The insight of the utility of social media to spread a political organization's message will presumably mean that it will continue to be used (see Treré and Harlow in this volume). Rivalries and companionship also develop during protest waves. The construction of adversaries and allies will also shape future politics. In sum, then, student movements offer a privileged lens through which to study political and social transformations.

References

Aboites, Hugo (2008), "La autonomía en México. Entre la libertad, el Estado y el interés privado (1921–2008)," in Emir Sader, Hugo Aboites and Pablo Gentili (eds.), *La reforma universitaria. Desafíos y perspectivas noventa años después*, 80–85 (Buenos Aires: CLACSO).

Aken, Marc J. van (1971), "University Reform before Córdoba," *Hispanic American Historical Review* 51(3), 447–62.

Alonso, Jorge (2013), "Cómo escapar de la cárcel de lo electoral: el movimiento #YoSoy132," *Desacatos* 42, 17–40.

Alonso, Jorge and Ann Mische (2017), "Changing Repertoires and Partisan Ambivalence in the New Brazilian Protests," *Bulletin of Latin American Research* 36(2), 144–59.

Altbach, Philip (2006), "Student Politics: Activism and Culture," in James J. Forest and Philip Altbach (eds.), *International Handbook of Higher Education*, 329–45 (Dordrecht: Springer).

Archila, Mauricio (2012), "El movimiento estudiantil en Colombia: Una mirada histórica," *Revista del Observatorio Social de América Latina* 31, 71–103.

Azevedo, Mario L., Ana Karine Braggio, and Afranio M. Catani (2018), "A reforma universitária de Córdoba de 1918 e sua influência no Brasil: um foco no movimento estudantil antes do golpe de 1964," *Revista Latinoamericana de Educación Comparada* 9(13), 37–51.

Brading, Ryan (2012), "The Anti-Bolivarian Student Movement: New Social Actors Challenge the Advancement of Venezuela's Bolivarian Socialism," *Asian Journal of Latin American Studies* 25(3), 23–46.

Califa, Juan Sebastián and Mariano Millán (2016), "La represión a las universidades y al movimiento estudiantil argentino entre los golpes de estado de 1966 y 1976," *Revista de Historia Iberoamericana* 9(2), 10–38.

Cannon, Barry (2014), "As Clear as MUD: Characteristics, Objectives, and Strategies of the Opposition in Bolivarian Venezuela," *Latin American Politics and Society* 56(4), 49–70.

Catini, Carolina and Gustavo M. Mello (2016), "Escolas de luta, educação política," *Educação & Sociedade* 37(137), 1177–202.

Cavarozzi, Marcelo (1992), "Patterns of Elite Negotiation and Confrontation in Argentina and Chile," in John. Higley and Richard Gunther (eds.), *Elites and Democratic Consolidation in Latin America and Southern Europe*, 208–36 (Cambridge: Cambridge University Press).

Cruz Rodríguez, Edwin (2013), "La reforma de la educación superior y las protestas estudiantiles en Colombia," *Revista PostData* 18(1), 51–71.

Cuninghame, Patrick Gun (2017), "#YoSoy132 and the 'Mexican Spring' of 2012: Between Electoral Engagement and Democratisation," *Bulletin of Latin American Research* 36(2), 192–205.

Disi Pavlic, Rodolfo (2019), "Policies, Parties, and Protests: Explaining Student Protest Events in Latin America," *Social Movement Studies*, 19(2), 183–200.

Donoso, Sofia (2017), "'Outsider' and 'Insider' Strategies: Chile's Student Movement, 1990–2014," in Sofia Donoso and Marisa von Bülow (eds.), *Social Movements in Chile Organization, Trajectories, and Political Consequences*, 65–97 (London: Palgrave-Macmillan).

Donoso, Sofia and Marisa von Bülow (2017), *Social Movements in Chile: Organization, Trajectories, and Political Consequences* (London: Palgrave-Macmillan).

Fleet, Nicolas and César Guzmán-Concha (2017), "Mass Higher Education and the 2011 Student Movement in Chile: Material and Ideological Implications," *Bulletin of Latin American Research* 36(2), 160–76.

García-Guadilla, María Pilar and Ana L. Mallén (2010), "El movimiento estudiantil venezolano: narrativas, polarización social y públicos antagónicos," *Cuadernos Del CENDES* 27(73), 71–95.

Garretón, Manuel Antonio and Javier Martínez (1985), *El movimiento estudiantil: conceptos e historia*, vol. 4 (Santiago: Ediciones SUR).

Gill, Jungyun and James DeFronzo (2009), "A Comparative Framework for the Analysis of International Student Movements," *Social Movement Studies*, (8)3, 203–24.

Gómez García, Rodrigo and Emiliano Treré (2014), "The #YoSoy132 Movement and the Struggle for Media Democratization in Mexico," *Convergence: The International Journal of Research into New Media Technologies*, 20(4), 496–510.

González, Juan I. (2018), "El año breve. Los estudiantes brasileños en su 1968," in Mariano Millán (ed.), *Los '68 Latinoamericanos. Movimientos estudiantiles, política y cultura en México, Brasil, Uruguay, Chile, Argentina y Colombia*, 105–42 (Buenos Aires: CLACSO).

Guzmán-Concha, César (2017), "Introduction: Student Movements and Political Change in Contemporary Latin America," *Bulletin of Latin American Research* 36(2), 141–43.

Guzmán-Concha, César (2019), "Introduction to Special Sub-Section: Student Activism in Global Perspective: Issues, Dynamics and Interactions," *Current Sociology* 67(7), 939–41.

Ivancheva, Mariya P. (2017), "The Discreet Charm of University Autonomy: Conflicting Legacies in the Venezuelan Student Movements," *Bulletin of Latin American Research* 36(2), 177–91.
Landinelli, Jorge (2008), "Trazos del movimiento reformista universitario en Uruguay," in Emir Sader, Hugo Aboites, and Pablo Gentili (eds.), *La reforma universitaria. Desafíos y perspectivas noventa años después*, 104–11 (Buenos Aires: CLACSO).
Levy, Daniel C. (1991), "The Decline of Latin American Student Activism," *Higher Education* 22(2), 145–55.
Lipset, Seymour Martin (1964), "University Students and Politics in Underdeveloped Countries," *Minerva* 3(1), 15–56.
Lipset, Seymour Martin (1971), *Rebellion in the University* (Chicago: University of Chicago Press).
Loaeza, Soledad (1989), "México 1968: Los orígenes de la transición," *Foro Internacional* 30(117), 66–92.
Machado, Otávio Luiz (2015), "Un siglo de movimiento estudiantil en Brasil," in Renate Marsiske (ed.), *Movimientos estudiantiles en la historia de América Latina IV*, 57–80 (Mexico: Plaza y Valdés Editores).
Markarian, Vania (2004), "Debating Tlatelolco: Thirty Years of Public Debates about the Mexican Student Movement of 1968," in Jim Downs and Jennifer Manion (eds.), *Taking Back the Academy! History of Activism*, 25–31 (New York: Routledge).
McAdam, Doug (1986), "Recruitment to High-Risk Activism: The Case of Freedom Summer," *American Journal of Sociology* 92, 64–90.
Millán, Mariano (2012), "Movimiento estudiantil y procesos políticos en Argentina y Brasil (1964–1973)," *Século XXI–Revista de Ciências Sociais* 2(2), 73–112.
Mische, Ann (2008), *Partisan Publics. Communication and Contention across Brazilian Youth Activist Networks* (Princeton, NJ: Princeton University Press).
Moncayo, Víctor Manuel (2008), "Permanencia, continuidad y cambio del movimiento universitario," in Emir Sader, Hugo Aboites, and Pablo Gentili (eds.), *La reforma universitaria. Desafíos y perspectivas noventa años después*, 20–28 (Buenos Aires: CLACSO).
Moraes, Silene (2008), "Movimento estudantil no Brasil: Lutas passadas, desafios presentes," *Revista Historia de La Educación Latinoamericana* 11, 131–46.
Muñoz Tamayo, Víctor (2002), "Movimiento social juvenil y eje cultural: dos contextos de reconstrucción organizativa (1976–1982/1989–2002)," *Última Década* 10(17), 41–64.
Pérez Perdomo, Rogelio (2007), "Estado y justicia en tiempos de Gómez (Venezuela 1909–1935)," *Politeia* 30(39), 121–50.
Pittelli, Cecilia and Javier Pablo Hermo (2011), "La Reforma Universitaria de Córdoba de 1918. Su influencia en el renovado pensamiento emancipatorio en América Latina," *Revista Bicentenario* 29(0), 135–56.
Rivas, José R. (2018), "Antecedentes, desarrollo y repercusiones del '68 mexicano," in Mariano Millán (ed.), *Los '68 latinoamericanos. Movimientos estudiantiles, política y cultura en México, Brasil, Uruguay, Chile, Argentina y Colombia*, 53–78 (Buenos Aires: CLACSO).
Rivas, Ricardo A. (1998), "Ecos de la reforma universitaria en Venezuela," *Revista de La Red Intercátedras de Historia de América Latina Contemporánea-Segunda Época* 2(2), 11–20.
Rivera, Francisco (2018), "El '68 chileno: Orígenes universitarios del triunfo y la derrota popular. 1961–1983," in Mariano Millán (ed.), *Los '68 latinoamericanos. Movimientos estudiantiles, política y cultura en México, Brasil, Uruguay, Chile, Argentina y Colombia*, 175–200 (Buenos Aires: CLACSO).

Rojas, Jorge (2009), "Los estudiantes secundarios durante la Unidad Popular, 1970–1973," *Historia* 42(2), 471–504.
Ruiz, Leopoldo M. (2011), "La reforma de Córdoba y el gobierno de las universidades públicas en América Latina: Análisis comparado de cinco universidades," *Ciencia Política* 6(12), 6–40.
Saad-Filho, Alfredo (2013), "Mass Protests under "Left Neoliberalism": Brazil, June–July 2013," *Critical Sociology* 39(5), 657–69.
Said-Hung, Elias and Jorge Valencia-Cobos (2017), "Twitter y movilización social en Venezuela," *Revista Brasileira de Ciências Sociais* 32(94), 1–18.
Schussman, Alan and Sarah A. Soule (2005), "Process and Protest: Accounting for Individual Protest Participation," *Social Forces* 84(2), 1083–108.
Snider, Colin M. (2017), "Student Mobilization, Higher Education, and the 2013 Protests in Brazil in Historical Perspective," *Latin American Research Review* 52(2), 253–68.
Somma, Nicolás (2012), "The Chilean Student Movement of 2011–2012: Challenging the Marketization of Education," *Interface: A Journal for and about Social Movements* 4(2), 296–309.
Spielmann, Ellen (2015), "Introduction," in Renate Marsiske (ed.), *Movimientos estudiantiles en la historia de América Latina IV*, 15–17 (Mexico: Plaza y Valdés Editores).
Tarazona Acevedo, Álvaro and Andrés Correa (2016), "Rapsodias de la indignación: La movilización estudiantil en Colombia durante el año 2011," *Prospectiva. Revista de Trabajo Social e Intervención Social* 22, 93–115.
The Guardian (2019), "Climate Strikes Held around the World—as It Happened," *The Guardian*, https://www.theguardian.com/environment/live/2019/mar/15/climate-strikes-2019-live-latest-climate-change-global-warming.
Treré, Emiliano (2015), "Reclaiming, Proclaiming, and Maintaining Collective Identity in the #YoSoy132 Movement in Mexico: An Examination of Digital Frontstage and Backstage Activism through Social Media and Instant Messaging Platforms," *Information, Communication & Society* 18(8), 901–15.
Tünnermann, Carlos (1998), "La reforma universitaria de Córdoba," *Educación Superior y Sociedad* 9(1), 103–27.
Uzcátegui, Rafael (2014), "Movilizaciones estudiantiles en Venezuela: Del carisma de Chávez al conflicto en redes," *Nueva Sociedad* 251, 153–65.
Vera de Flachs, María C. (2015), "Escarceos estudiantiles en época de dictadura, Argentina (1976–1981)," in Renate Marsiske (ed.), *Movimientos estudiantiles en la historia de América Latina IV*, 23–54 (Mexico: Plaza y Valdés Editores).

CHAPTER 24

LESBIAN AND GAY SOCIAL MOVEMENTS IN LATIN AMERICA

JORDI DÍEZ

INTRODUCTION

As this collection of essays suggests, social mobilization has been central to the Latin American experience. From the independence movements to the several revolutionary attempts of the mid-twentieth century, to the mobilization that has characterized democratization, the region has historically seen successive waves of social mobilization aiming to bring about political change. Despite this history, it was not until very recently that we saw the emergence of gay and lesbian movements.[1] While women and indigenous peoples, for example, have formed (part of) social movements for some time, gays and lesbians have only recently decided to organize, mobilize, and "come out of the closet" to advance socio-political demands on states. Indeed, historically marginalized, socially oppressed, and politically invisible, Latin America's lesbian and gays have emerged as important political actors demanding the expansion of numerous political rights. Rather notably, lesbian and gay mobilization has not only forced important national debates on the regulation of sexuality, but, in several countries, it has resulted in the attainment of concrete policy achievements, all in a relatively short period of time. Latin American lesbian and gay movements appear to be one of the most successful in the region given the speed with which it strengthened and the scope of its victories.

The success of the gay and lesbian movement is quite remarkable given important disadvantages. Not only are gays and lesbians able to hide (not come out and "pass" as heterosexuals) but they are a very small community everywhere, and even a smaller one representing the politically active population (Corrales and Pecheny 2010). They are, as a result, regularly short of resources. Moreover, gays and lesbians have also faced substantial structural obstacles given the historical dominance of the Catholic Church, which was key in the colonial imposition of very rigid ideas around sexuality and gender roles. Homosexuality has historically been seen as social deviation. Yet, despite these obstacles, gays and lesbians have made significant strides toward the fulfilment of sexual citizenship.

This chapter analyzes the evolution of Latin America's gay and lesbian movements by looking at the several factors that contributed to the making of remarkably strong and successful social movements. It opens with a contextualization of the regulation of sexuality in Latin America, which is necessary to understand subsequent struggles. It then looks at the evolution of lesbian and gay mobilization by demarcating its most important historical phases.

Historical and Cultural Context

Contrary to what may be generally assumed, Latin American understandings of sexuality have historically been fluid. The conquest of Latin America during the sixteenth century witnessed an attempt to impose rigid European definitions of gender and sexuality which revolved around ideas of sex, reproduction, and gender relations guided by Natural Law ideas. These ideas, distilled in the writings of Saint Thomas Aquinas, made marriage and procreation central "human goods" and argued that in order for a sexual act to be moral it has to be of the generative kind and performed within the bounds of married life (Díez 2015: 30–31). As such, any type of sexual activity performed outside marriage that cannot result in reproduction is considered immoral. Thomist principles were adopted by the Catholic Church during the Second Spanish Scholasticism and upheld a binary conceptualization of gender roles and viewed sexual relations as having as primary goal the procreation of the species. Same-sex relations consequently violated Natural Law, and "sodomy" was made the worst type of sin (the heinous crime or *pecado nefando*) (Tomás y Valiente 1990).

The prohibition of homosexuality became Church policy in medieval Spain, punishable by death, by the *fuero real*. Colonialism imposed these ideas on the newly conquered lands of the Americas by Spanish conquistadors. In 1497, five years after the conquest, the Spanish Kings reaffirmed the *fuero real* and enacted the death penalty for the commission of "heinous crime against nature" (Nesvig 2001). The Church's official position on homosexuality became colonial policy thereby regulating same-sex relations for centuries. Starting with the prosecuting of the first "sodomite" by Mexico's Inquisition in 1524, same-sex relations were systematically persecuted by civilian and Church authorities in subsequent years (Cardín 1989).

However, the colonial enterprise attempted to impose these views on a continent in which inhabitants possessed widely varied understandings of sexuality. While there exists limited research on pre-Columbian sexuality, we know that some societies did not adhere to uniform norms regulating sexuality that followed dichotomized male-female gender roles based on sexual activity guided by reproduction. In some societies, such as the Mexica, the Zapotec, and the Nahua, hereditary lineage among the political elite was an important mechanism for the maintenance of power, and marriage between a man and a woman played a central role in the process (Buckhart 1997; Sousa 1997). In these cases, binary gender systems built around procreation appear to have been important. However, in what were highly stratified societies, evidence suggests that, outside the ruling classes, the existence of non-dichotomized gender systems among indigenous peoples was common (Williams 1986). Indeed, scholars have pointed to the existence of a variety of gender, sexual and social roles that did not conform to Western understandings of dual male/female-gender systems, and to varied ideas of what constituted appropriate sexual behavior.

Colonialism saw a forceful attempt to impose Natural Law ideas surrounding sexuality, but fluidity in understanding sexuality has survived. Unlike experiences elsewhere, processes of state formation in Latin America were characterized by top-down dynamics which were not completely successful in completely transforming pre-existing social relations. This is most obviously observed in the perseverance of indigenous cultures and languages in many parts of the region (see Rice in this volume): the newly created states were not able to reach down to all areas, and semi-marginal cultural pockets out of the reach of the state have survived (see Davis and Davey in this volume). In many of these culturally autonomous pockets, Natural Law simply did not take hold. A good example of sexual and gender fluidity in contemporary Latin America are the *muxe* of Oaxaca, Mexico. Widely accepted by their societies, *Muxes* are individuals who identify themselves as a third gender and who practice sexual relations with individuals of different sex (Stephen 2002).

Fluidity has also remained in non-marginal societies. The particularities of state formation in Latin America resulted in the establishment of a general gap between expected social norms and their compliance. This attitude is well encapsulated by the Latin American adage of *obedezco pero no cumplo* (I obey but do not comply with). While it is commonly associated with the dualism that exists between legal formalism and compliance with the law, the adage also captures a generalized attitude regarding sexual practices. Despite the separation of Church and state most countries instituted, with varying degrees, during the nineteenth century, the Church continued to play an important role in dictating and upholding social mores (Corrales and Pecheny 2010). However, adherence to these norms has for the most part been limited to the public sphere, and this includes sexual practices. The newly independent republics were importantly influenced by French developments and ideas. The constitutions and subsequent legal frameworks drafted by Liberal leaders in their push to secularize their states where imbued by French Liberalism, and these magna cartas replicated the decriminalization of homosexuality under the drafting of France's Napoloenic code of 1804 criminal code. However, while intimate sexual relations between adults were decriminalized, the provisions criminalizing "indecency" and "scandal" in the public sphere were included in penal codes. Homosexuality may have been decriminalized, but it continued to be socially unacceptable, and any public expression of scandalous homosexual activity was punishable (Green 1999).

Unlike some Western European countries and their colonies elsewhere, the creation of the category of "homosexual" in the 1870s did not come about with an explicit legal regulation (Salessi 1995). The result has been an important dualism between what is socially expected in the public sphere and what individuals practice in private. And this is not a minor point. As Mario Pecheny (2004) has argued, invisibility and discretion have been expected of Latin American homosexuals and social interaction around homosexuality follows a double moral standard that condemns homosexual practices in public. Yet it tolerates them provided they are hidden from view (ibid.). As a result, in Latin America the organization of peoples' lives and the construction of identities around categorized sexualities have historically not been common and many individuals who may engage in same-sex practices do not define themselves as "gay." That is to say, Latin Americans have historically engaged in same-sex sexual activities but, unlike what has happened in North America and Western Europe, these relationships have not formed the bases for the construction of social identities. In other words, engaging in sexual encounters with the same gender does not make one "gay."

Latin American lesbian and gay activism has emerged from within these broader conceptualizations of sexual behavior.

Early Mobilization

The dualism that existed between the public and the private realms in the regulation of sexuality allowed homosexuals to carve up intimate socializing spaces in Latin America's bigger cities in the 1940s and 1950s. Activities such as the *jornais cariocas*, in Rio de Janeiro, associations made up of *felipitos* in Bogotá and the lesbian events of *fiesteras*, in Buenos Aires, allowed for such socialization (Figari 2016). However, these activities did not have political objectives. Political activism did not emerge until the late 1960s and 1970s in Argentina, Brazil, and Mexico within a context of broader sociopolitical processes both domestic and international (Díez 2011a, 2011b; Green 1999). On the domestic front, the bigger countries began a process of industrialization during the post-war years which contributed to the expansion of a middle-class, growing urbanization, higher levels of education, and increased secularization. A new generation of Latin Americans, one that was more critical of established understandings of social and sexual relations, began to adopt more liberal ideas regarding gender relations and sexuality (Belluccii 2010).

This generation began to challenge norms regarding contraception, patriarchy, and traditional values. In several countries of the region several counter-cultural groups emerged. At the same time, Liberation Theology, which called for a new interpretation of Christian scriptures to bring about social change, was adopted by numerous young Catholics (see Mackin in this volume). It spread throughout the region and motivated various sectors of society to mobilize as it rejected passive acceptance of perceived injustices. A new generation of Latin American youths became therefore a lot more receptive to political events taking place abroad as part of a cycle of protest that swept the world by the late 1960s, which expressed itself most notably through the 1968 French student movement, the demonstrations against the Vietnam War and Prague's Spring. This context allowed for the emergence of women's, Black, indigenous, and student movements throughout the region (see Dixon and Caldwell, Rice, Ewig and Friedman, Donoso in this volume), motivating homosexuals to come out of the closet.

Latin American gay and lesbian activism emerged within these larger socio-political processes and as part of generalized mobilization in the region (Brown 2002; Díez 2011a, 2011b). By the late 1960s Argentine and Mexican homosexuals decided to organize to discuss collectively their personal experiences with sexuality and the social stigmatization of homosexuality. The first organizations were thus formed. The Stonewall riots of 1969 of New York are mythically seen as the catalyst for the emergence of the gay and lesbian movement in the world (Duberman 2019). While all social movements need mythical historical points, in Latin American homosexuals began to organize before then. Indeed, the first gay organization in Latin America, Nuestro Mundo, was founded in 1967 in Argentina, two years before those summer riots. Nuestro Mundo was followed by the formation of the Frente de Liberación Homosexual in 1971 in both Mexico and Argentina. Inspired by the development of the first gay liberationist groups in the United States and some Western European countries, and the literature produced by the United States organization the Black Panther, these early groups began to articulate a discourse based on the need to liberate homosexuals from the oppression created by social stigmatization. For example, in August 1970, Black Panther Party leader, Huey P. Newton, published a letter, titled "A Letter from Huey to the Revolutionary Brothers and Sisters about the Women's Liberation and Gay Liberation Movement," in which he acknowledged that homosexuals constitute an oppressed group and that the group members should recognize the legitimacy of the Gay Liberation Movement (Porter 2012). After the publication of the letter, the United States Gay Liberation movement adopted important discursive tools from the Black Panthers (Corrigan 2019), which would subsequently be adopted by some Latin American gays and lesbian pioneer activists.

The early gay and lesbian organizations were formed mostly by leftist students, intellectuals, and activists from union movements, and had a Marxist bent. They were, for the most part, urban, middle-class individuals who adopted anti-establishment positions and called for an end to imperialist oppression from the Global North (Brown 2002; de la Dehesa 2010; Díez 2015; Green 1999). An important characteristic of these early groups was the uneasy relationship they had with the institutional Latin American Left given its traditional understandings of sexuality. Prejudice as well as fear of losing followers meant that Leftist leaders would intentionally alienate gay activists, and male leaders used macho imagery in nation-building efforts, consciousness raising, and guerilla organization, which strengthened homophobia and discrimination on the Left (Friedman and Tabbush 2019: 4). Many of the first activists were not welcomed by established leftist movements and some were actually expelled from Communist Parties which had official positions declaring homosexuality to be a bourgeois practice. In spite of their isolation, Latin American gay activism has since then taken a decidedly leftist position on politics. The same was not true for relationships many activists formed with other social movements as they were able to form strong alliances early on. Indeed, a salient aspect of early gay and lesbian activism in Latin America was the close relationships activists formed with women's groups during the first years of mobilization (Bellucci 2010; Díez 2015). Gay and lesbian activists were heavily influenced by second-wave feminism and forged close relationships with women's organizations (see Johnson and Sempol in this volume). Steeped in feminist debates, some gay and lesbian activists included a broader perspective in their early struggles and argued against patriarchal oppression and for gender equality (Bellucci 2010). Given that the important role students and intellectuals played in early activism, activists were steeped in the theoretical discussions regarding homosexuality that gathered pace at this time in advanced democracies.

In countries in which gay activists organized and mobilized they managed to ignite public debates regarding sexuality in the early 1970s. Through the publication and distribution of bulletins, flyers, and magazines, and in some cases television interviews, they were able to begin national discussions to challenge one of the main obstacles to gay liberation: the medicalization of homosexuality that had been in place since the turn of the nineteenth century. During its period of "order and progress," and influenced by European ideas of positivism and modernity, the region saw the proliferation of medical and psychological explanations for homosexuality. It was seen as a disease, a physiological defect, and, as such, as a social threat (Bao 1993).

Mobilization under Authoritarianism

The evolution of gay and lesbian activism after the first spurts of mobilization varied across countries and it was largely shaped by larger political processes. In some countries, such as Argentina and Chile, the mid-1970s saw the overthrow of civilian governments by military juntas which abruptly ended any possibility for mobilization. Activism therefore came to a sudden end as the military dictatorships undertook campaigns to "cleanse" societies from "subversives," which included homosexuals. The level of repression varied from country to country. In some cases, the military rulers launched explicit campaigns to exterminate homosexuals. As part of preparatory activities for the soccer world cup, which was held in Argentina in 1978, the military regime established a Moral Brigade, part of the Federal Police, with the objective of "cleansing the streets" of homosexuals so as to "not perturb decent people" (Rapisardi and Modarelli 2001: 23). Some accounts point to the killing of up to 400 homosexuals during Argentina's phase of state terror (1976–1983) (Jáuregui 1987). In other cases, such as in Chile, military rulers did not establish explicit extermination campaigns, but the regime's overall plans to suppress any form of social and political activity made it impossible for gays and lesbians to mobilize. Many homosexuals were forced into exile (Díez 2015). In countries in which military repression was harshest, it would take until the end of military rule for gays and lesbians to start organizing again.

In cases in which authoritarian rule was less repressive, such as Brazil and Mexico, activism strengthened despite unfavorable circumstances and, by the end of the 1970s, it "came out of the closet" (de le Dehesa 2010). In both countries 1978 marked a turning point. Following the intensification of protests against the authoritarian regime, which saw strong student mobilization and workers' strikes in the automobile sector in São Paulo in 1977, the two first Brazilian organizations were formed: Lampão da Esquina in São Paolo (as an alternative newspaper) and Somos in Rio de Janeiro. Two years later women split from these organizations and founded the Grupo Autônomo Feminista Lésbico (Figari 2016).

In Mexico, the Frente de Liberación Homosexual operated mostly underground since its formation in 1971. However, 1978 saw the formation of three organizations which took to the streets: the Frente Homosexual de Acción Revolucionaria (FHAR), Lambda (Grupo Lambda de Liberación Homosexual), and Okiabeth[2] (de la Dehesa 2010; Figari 2016). On July 26, 1978, members of FAHR participated in a march commemorating the Cuban revolution and on October 2, 1978, members of the other two groups joined another demonstration to commemorate the tenth anniversary of the 1968 government repression which killed hundreds of students (Díez 2015: 89). These were the first in a series of actions that would allow these incipient movements to attain important visibility in subsequent years. Indeed, emboldened by this experience, Mexican activists held a march on their own the following year in Mexico City, which became the first gay march in Latin America (de la Dehesa 2010).

In democratic Colombia some gay organizations were also established in the 1970s. León Zuleta and Manuel Velandia formed the organization Movimiento de Liberación Gay in Bogotá. The majority of these groups asserted a liberationist discourse and adopted common slogans, such as "there is no political freedom without sexual freedom" and "the personal is political" (Serrano 2018). The main objectives of these organizations were to attract attention, generate visibility, and demonstrate that homosexuality was not a medical condition. In many instances their calls were addressed to police forces demanding the end of harassment and repression.

DIVISIONS

Early gay and lesbian mobilization in Latin America was marked by two important schisms. The first refers to the relationship activists had with women and feminist demands. For members of some organizations, such as the Argentine Nuestro Mundo and the Mexican Lambada, sexual liberation had to include a fight for gender equality and its membership articulated a vision steeped in feminist arguments: sexual and gender oppression shared patriarchy as the culprit. Many of its members were in fact women. Others, such as FHAR, rejected feminism and argued that, because issues faced by gay men were distinct from women's, their struggles could not be fought united. These divisive positions were, of course, paradoxical: as we have seen, FHAR members had been influenced by the discourse calling for cross-movement alliances advanced by the Black Panthers, yet they opted for narrowing their activism to a particular sub-set of demands: men's. Their vision of the groups which were oppressed was evidently limited, which meant a very limited understanding of social liberation.

A second schism regarded the relationship that activists thought had to be established with the state. Given the revolutionary origins of the movement, some sectors refused to collaborate with state institutions and opted for an adversarial approach in the push for rights. These groups called for more fundamental societal changes, changes that included an overthrow of political systems that were evidently incompatible with collaboration (Figari 2016). Others, often referred as the "reformists," took a starkly different approach and decided to work closely with political parties. In Mexico and Brazil these reformists decided to enter the electoral field and worked together with leftist parties which fielded the first openly gay candidates for elections in 1982 (de la Dehesa 2010). While in Mexico reformists coalesced around one political party (Partido Revolucionario de los Trabajadores) for the congressional and presidential elections held that year, in Brazil they approached candidates and parties across the political spectrum for gubernatorial and legislative elections.

Identity Formation

Gay liberation movements gave way during the 1970s to the adoption of a mobilizing frame based on identity politics. From a discourse based on the need to liberate themselves from state and social oppression, activists in Latin America adopted models grounded on the notion that members of disadvantaged groups needed to organize and place directly on the state particularistic policy demands. As university students and intellectuals, the leaders of these organizations were influenced by global debates of the time during this transition. The writings of philosophers such as Michel Foucault (1977), whose *History of Sexuality* was translated into Spanish in the late 1970s, were fundamental in their understandings of sexuality. Foucault reminded his audience that the term "homosexual" was a relatively new invention (coined in Germany in 1871), brought about by the medicalization of sexuality, and, as such, a socially constructed idea that rendered it a pathology. The term homosexual was as a result replaced with a post-liberationist term "gay" by some activists (Bazán 2010; Figari 2016). Foucault's work, for example, helped many activists deconstruct contemporary ideas of sexuality: they relied on it to articulate arguments that attempted to demonstrate that same-sex relations were natural forms of sexual expression and bases upon which to build legitimate identities. The best example of this development is the work of the iconic Argentine activist Carlos Jáuregui. In one of the first non-fictional works published on homosexuality in Latin America, Jáuregui (1987), a history professor trained in France, relied partly on Foucault to argue for the need to accept same-sex relations as a legitimate form of sexual expression and as a variant of human sexuality. Jáuregui rejected the previous revolutionary approach and adopted a "reformist" view that began to articulate a discourse based in human rights and civil liberties (Brown 2002). In addition, Latin American gay activism began thus to adopt traits and symbols of their northern counterparts, such as the notion of being "proud" of one's sexuality and the now-famous rainbow flag. For these "assimilationist" groups the struggle was not capitalism but, rather, about fighting social stigmatization of homosexuality.

Nevertheless, the adoption of a "gay identity" was not generalized. For some of the more radical sectors, the assumption of an identity-politics frame amounted to a capitulation to the capitalist system and an abdication of the commitment to push for wider social change. It also remained limited to the larger urban sectors. While some gay organizations sprung in other cities, such as Guadalajara in Mexico and Rosario in Argentina, activism continued to be concentrated in the main cities and did not reach much beyond. Indeed, scholarly work points to the failure of these frames to reach homosexuals outside the big metropolises. For example, Guillermo Nuñez Noriega's (2000) work shows that, in northern Mexico, men are able to distinguish between their sexual attractions and practices and their daily lives, and men that have sex with men do not always see themselves as homosexual, nor do they attempt to build a lifestyle around their sexual practices. In certain places, then, the Latin American historical tradition of separating the public expressions from private practices appears not to have adopted a gay identity frame. The formation of gay identities also emerged differently than in some parts of the Global North: whereas the 1980s saw the establishment of gay neighborhoods in many of the larger cities in the United States, this did not happen in Latin America. Some commercial establishments allowing gay men and lesbians socializing spaces sprouted during the 1980s and 1990s, and numerous bars, restaurants, and clubs opened in the bigger cities, even in authoritarian Chile. But gay ghettos were not established, and, to this day, in some of the most vibrant gay cities in Latin America, such as Buenos Aires, gay "villages" do not exist.

The Onset of HIV/AIDS and Its Impact on Mobilization

The onset of the HIV/AIDS crisis in the mid 1980s had important effects on gay and lesbian activism in Latin America. Upon the report of the first cases, a moral panic emerged and conservative sectors, led by the Catholic Church leadership, mounted accusatory campaigns blaming the unnatural behavior of homosexuals for the spread of the "gay cancer" or "pink plague" (Díez 2011b). These campaigns had a destabilizing effect on some activists as without much knowledge about the virus, they were forced to turn inward to look for answers. In several countries the spread of the pandemic had a negative effect on the leadership of many organizations as numerous male leaders succumbed to the disease. In Mexico, for example, activism lost strength and public visibility.

In several countries the spread of the disease significantly shaped activism and changed the relationship it had maintained with the state in important ways, marking a new phase in its evolution. While, prior to the onset of crisis some activists had established a relatively confrontational approach with the governments demanding the end of police harassment and repression, they began to collaborate with them out of necessity. In effect, the HIV/AIDS crisis in Latin America was used by many activists as an opportunity to establish a more institutionalized relationship with the state (Biagni 2009; de la Dehesa 2010; Pecheny 2003). Never before had questions regarding homosexuality been as visible as it became an issue of public health. Numerous organizations devoted much of their energies to the development and implementation of prevention programs financed by governments and international organizations, such as UNAIDS. Groups such as Brazil's Grupo Gay da Bahia and Triângulo Rosa assumed significant visibility as their resources and influence increased (de le Dehesa 2010). In some countries, the new collaborative relationships contributed to the formation of important national and international networks among government officials, practitioners from international organizations, and activists that have lasted for decades and which have been fundamental in the expansion of healthcare services to HIV-positive individuals (Torres-Ruiz 2011).

Another important change regards the articulation of a rights-based discourse. In several countries of the region HIV/AIDS allowed many activists to begin to frame their demands as an issue of rights. In effect, some scholarship points to Latin American gay and lesbian mobilization as the first one to have framed access to health care as a basic human right. Diego Sempol (2013: 101–08), for example, shows that Argentine gay activists were pioneers in articulating a discourse that connected human rights to sexuality. As the diseased ravaged on, (mostly) gay men began to mobilize around the concept of the right to healthcare and to transform a victimization discourse into one that placed the responsibility for the containment of the disease on the state (Magis 2000; Torres-Ruiz 2011).

Nonetheless, the ability of gay activists to bring about policy change varied across the region. In cases such as Argentina, activists managed to force the government to pass legislation fairly early on (1991) to fight the epidemic, which became central for the distribution of anti-retroviral drugs when they became available in the mid-1990s (Pecheny 2003; Sempol 2013). In Brazil and Mexico legislative change in the mid-1990s made the drugs universally available (de la Dehesa 2010). In other cases, such as Chile, it would not be until 2001 that the government would enact legislation, but, even then, they were not distributed universally (Díez 2015).

Globalization and Economic Liberalism

Lesbian and gay activism assumed significant visibility and vigor by the turn of the twentieth century. As Latin American democracies began to consolidate, organizations proliferated in the region and, for the first time, activism in the smaller, less urbanized countries gained public visibility. By 2000 all countries in the region, including authoritarian Cuba, had some form of gay and lesbian mobilization.

An important characteristic of this phase was the adoption of a global discourse around the idea of "sexual diversity." Whereas demands had previously focused on the end to repression and access to healthcare, activism began to adopt the global discourse of equal citizenship rights for a variety of non-conforming sexual identities and expressions (de la Dehesa 2010; Encarnación 2015). Activism thus expanded to include numerous groups which had been invisible, such as transgender individuals. Organized transgender activism attracted public attention for the first time in several countries of the region and very active and well-organized associations were formed, such as Argentina's Asociación por la Identidad Trasvesti Transexual and the Asociación de Trasvestis, Transexuales y Transgenérico. The adoption of a new discourse was partly influenced by Queer Theory (see Johnson and Sempol in this volume). In many countries of the region some university gender programs expanded their curricula to include Queer Studies and, by the late 1990s, numerous activists and academics began to deploy the discursive tools the new theoretical approach offered (Fiol-Matta 2016).

Mobilization was also influenced by global debates on multiculturalism. During the 1990s discussions regarding the protection of cultural minorities gathered pace and countries around the world enacted a variety of measures to protect ethnic, indigenous, and cultural minorities (Kymlicka 2007). In Latin America these international debates coincided with the strengthening of indigenous mobilization in some countries, which sought to renegotiate contemporary understandings of national identity and which demanded the recognition of the multiethnic character of these societies (Yashar 2005; Rice, Fontana in this volume). The diversity called for by Queer theorists therefore found a receptive audience. Queer Theory took hold among many activists in the region and, given the region's rather fluid understandings of sexuality, it resonated deeply in countries that are highly culturally diverse, such as Mexico (Monsiváis 2004). As a result, the categorization of identities based on separate (medical-legal) sexualities lost force. Hybridity therefore continued to characterize Latin American gay and lesbian activism (de le Dehesa 2010).

Economic liberalization has also had an impact on activism. The adoption of market-friendly economic programs contributed to the "commercialization" of lesbian and gay movements. In the main capitals of the region, as unprecedented freedoms began to be enjoyed, a new generation of gays and lesbians began to emulate consumerist lifestyles marketed in advanced democracies, especially the United States. Unsurprisingly, debates among activists on the marketization of gay identities ensued. Strong criticisms, introduced to activism by intellectuals such as Néstor Perlongher (1996) in Argentina, Herbert Daniel and Leila Míccolis (1983) in Brazil, and Carlos Monsiváis (2004) in Mexico, were formulated about the emergence of a new commercialized identity in some quarters which was characterized by white, middle-class men. In a part of the world with the highest socio-economic inequalities, the new class-based identities are seen by some as being highly exclusionary for it they are unattainable for the majority of the population.

State-Directed Activism

Since the early 2000s gay and lesbian activism has mostly focused on the pursuit of anti-discrimination legislation, the expansion of socioeconomic benefits to same-sex couples, and, more recently, on the formal recognition of same-sex relations, such as civil unions and marriage. The demand for same-sex relationship recognition began in some countries, such as Argentina, in the mid-1990s as activists asked for the extension of public socioeconomic benefits, usually those provided to civil servants. It accelerated in the early 2000s in Argentina, Brazil, and Mexico, all federal states, at the subnational level, as well as in Colombia. In Argentina and Mexico, activists decided to push for non-gender specific civil unions in Buenos Aires and Mexico City, cities that had acquired significant policymaking independence as a result of constitutional reforms undertaken in 1994 in both countries. After heated debates, civil unions were approved in Buenos Aires (2002) and Mexico City (2006) (Díez 2013), placing the issue of same-sex relationship recognition on the region's national debates. In the case of Brazil, given that family law is administered by the states, gay and lesbian activists began to demand the enactment of civil unions at the subnational level, primarily looking for the extension of socioeconomic rights. Once activists were able to have civil unions enacted in Buenos Aires and Mexico City, they began to push for same-sex marriage recognition. The first jurisdiction was Mexico City in 2009, followed by Argentina in 2010, and Uruguay and Brazil in 2013. These efforts provided activists with necessary political and discursive tools to pursue same-sex relationship recognition at the national level, through both legislatures and the courts.

Activists' success in the attainment of policy reform has varied widely across the region. Table 24.1 shows the Latin American landscape on sexual rights (countries are accorded a full point if the entire population enjoys full access to rights, half point if some sectors of society and/or jurisdictions do, and a zero if the right does not exist). By looking at the total points scored by each country on the various categories, it becomes obvious that there exists a great deal of variance, from countries such as Panama and Paraguay which score a total of one point each, to Uruguay, which has afforded all its citizens the full expansion of sexual rights.

The factors behind the ability of Latin American gay and lesbian activists to attain policy reform evidently vary across the region, and there is a lively debate among scholars regarding which are most important. However, this scholarship has identified a variety of factors which have been central to pursue and bring about policy change. These include: the formation of alliances with other movements and state actors (Díez 2015); working together with sympathizing political parties, mostly leftists, and taking advantage of liberal openings in government institutions (de la Dehesa 2010); working with bureaucracies closely in the development of programs (Matos 2019); framing their demands in ways that resonate with larger social debates (Díez 2015); electing openly out gay and lesbian candidates (Corrales and Pecheny 2010; Piatti-Crocker and Schulenberg

Table 24.1 Lesbian, gay, transgender, and bisexual rights index

	Sexual activity	Anti-discrimination legislation	Hate crimes legislation	Gender identity	Civil unions	Marriage	Adoption	Total
Argentina	1	0.5	0	1	0.5	1	1	5
Brazil	1	0.5	0	1	1	1	1	4.5
Bolivia	1	1	1	1	0	0	0	4
Chile	1	1	1	1	1	0	0	5
Colombia	1	1	1	1	1	0	1	6
Costa Rica	1	1	0	0	0	0	0	2
Ecuador	1	1	1	1	1	0	0	5
El Salvador	1	1	0	0	0	0	0	2
Guatemala	1	1	0	0	0	0	0	2
Honduras	1	0	1	0	0	0	0	2
Mexico	1	1	.5	1	.5	1	1	6
Nicaragua	1	1	1	0	0	0	0	3
Panama	1	0	0	0	0	0	0	1
Paraguay	1	0	0	0	0	0	0	1
Peru	1	1	0	1	0	0	0	2
Uruguay	1	1	1	1	1	1	1	7
Venezuela	1	.5	0	0	0	0	0	1.5

Source: Adapted from Corrales 2015.

2012); and relying on social media (Friedman 2016). As with most social phenomena, a confluence of different factors depending on the social and political context is likely the answer.

Conclusion

It is not an exaggeration to suggest that the gay and lesbian movements in Latin America have been among the most successful in the region. Historically oppressed, and facing enormous resource and structural obstacles, gays and lesbians have come out of the political closet, organized, mobilized, and begun to advance a series of demands. Not only have they forced important social debates around the regulation of sexuality, which at times have been central to the national politics of some countries, but they have also enjoyed unprecedented success in achieving a variety of policy objectives. This has transpired in a relatively short period of time. Academics and activists looking at examples of successful social mobilization would do well to look closely at Latin American gay and lesbian movements.

The main challenge facing these movements is not only whether they can continue to mobilize so that we can see scores of 7 down the last column of Table 24.1, but whether the already conquered rights can be sustained, given the recent conservative backlash against sexual and reproductive rights. This countermovement, characterized by an importance alliance between Catholic and Evangelical leaders and conservative political parties in several countries of the region, is not surprising: a reading of Latin American history suggests that conservative backlashes tend to follow liberal change. However, armed with an effective frame mounted around the idea of "gender ideology," they are proving to be very successful in obtaining support from various sectors of society, and in achieving political victories. Whether we can continue to qualify Latin America's gay and lesbian movements as successful will no doubt depend on whether they can counteract the strength of this countermovement.

Notes

1. The analysis in this chapter will be limited to gay and lesbian mobilization and will therefore not use the acronym LGTBIQ+, which refers to lesbian, gay, trans, bisexual, intersexual, and allies. This is because, while at times these groups have formed alliances and worked together in mobilization efforts in Latin America, that is not always the case: often they work independently given their specific priorities. Placing all of them into one category would erase important differences among them.
2. Okiabeth derives from the Mayan phrase *LLing Iskan Katunat Babet Tkot*, which in Spanish means "warrior women who make way spreading flowers."

References

Bao, Daniel (1993), "Invertidos sexuales, tortilleras and maricas machos: The Construction of Homosexuality in Argentina, 1900–1950," *Journal of Homosexuality* 24(3–4), 183–219.
Bellucci, Maribel (2010), *Orgullo: Carlos Jáuregui, una biografía política* (Buenos Aires: Emecé).
Biahni, Graciela (2009), *Sociedad Civil y VIH-SIDA: de la acción colectiva a la fragmentación de intereses?* (Buenos Aires: Paidós).
Brown, Stephen (2002), "'Con Discriminación y Represión No Hay Democracia': The Lesbian and Gay Movement in Argentina," *Latin American Perspectives* 29(2), 119–38.
Buckhart, Louise (1997) "Mexica Women on the Home Front: Housework and Religion in Aztec Mexico," in Susan Schroeder, Stephanie Wood, and Robert Kaskett (eds.), *Indian Women of Early Mexico*, 25–43 (Norman: University of Oklahoma Press).
Cardín, Alberto (1989), *Guerreros, chamanes y travestis: Indicios de la homsexualidad en los exóticos* (Barcelona: Tusquets).
Corrales, Javier (2015), "The Politics of LGTB Rights in Latin America and the Caribbean: Research Agendas," *European Review of Latin American and Caribbean Studies* 100, 53–62.
____ . and Mario Pecheny (2010), "Introduction: The Comparative Politics of Sexuality in Latin America," in Javier Corrales and Mario Pecheny (eds.), *The Politics of Sexuality in Latin America*, 1–30 (Pittsburgh, PA: University of Pittsburgh Press).
Corrigan, Lisa M. (2019), "Queering the Panthers: Rhetorical Agency and Black/Queer Liberation Politics," *QED: A Journal in GLBTQ Worldmaking* 6(2), 1–25.

Daniel, Herbert and Míccolis Leila (1983), *Jacarés e Lobisomens: dos Ensaios sobre a Homossexualidade* (Rio de Janeiro: Achiamé).

De la Dehesa, Rafael (2010), *Queering the Public Space in Mexico and Brazil: Sexual Rights Movements in Emerging Democracies* (Durham, NC: Duke University Press).

Díez, Jordi (2011a), "Argentina: A Queer Tango between the LG Movement and the State," in Carol Johnson, David Paternotte, and Manon Tremblay (eds.), *The Gay Movement and the State: Comparative Insights into a Transformed Relationship*, 19–38 (Surrey: Ashgate).

Díez, Jordi (2011b), "La trayectoria política del movimiento lésbico-gayen México," *Estudios Sociológicos* 29(86), 687–712.

Díez, Jordi (2013), "Explaining Policy Outcomes: The Adoption of Same-Sex Unions in Buenos Aires and Mexico City," *Comparative Political Studies* 46(2), 1–24.

Díez, Jordi (2015), *The Politics of Gay Marriage in Latin America: Argentina, Chile and Mexico* (New York: Cambridge University Press).

Duberman, Martin B. (2019), *Stonewall: The Definitive Story of the LGTBQ Uprising that Changed America* (New York: Penguin Random House).

Encarnación, Omar (2015), *Out in the Periphery* (New York: Oxford University Press).

Figari, Calros (2016), "Queer Articulations," in Yolanda Martínez-San Miguel, Ben Sifuentes-Jáuregi, and Marisa Belausteguigoitia (eds.), *Critical Terms in Caribbean and Latin American Thought: Historical and Institutional Trajectories*, 231–8 (New York: Palgrave).

Fiol-Mata, Licia (2016), "Queer/Sexualities," in Yolanda Martínez-San Miguel, Ben Sifuentes-Jáuregi, and Marisa Belausteguigoitia (eds.), *Critical Terms in Caribbean and Latin American Thought: Historical and Institutional Trajectories*, 217–30 (New York: Palgrave).

Foucault, Michel (1977), *La historia de la sexualidad* (Buenos Aires: Siglo XXI).

Friedman, Elisabeth (2016), *Interpreting the Internet: Feminist and Queer Counterpublics in Latin America*. Berkeley, CA: The Univesity of California Press.

___. and Constanza Tabbush (2019), "Contesting the Pink Tide," in Elisabeth Friedman and Constanza Tabbush (eds.), *Seeking Rights from the Left: Gender, Sexuality and the Latin American Pink Tide*, 1–47 (Durham, NC: Duke University Press).

Green, James (1999), *Beyond Carnival: Male Homosexuality in Twentieth-Century Brazil* (Chicago: Chicago University Press).

Jáuregui, Carlos (1987). *La homosexualidad en la Argentina* (Buenos Aires: Terso).

Kymlicka, Will (2007), *Multicultural Odysseys: Navigating the New International Politics of Diversity* (Oxford: Oxford University Press).

Johnson, Lyman and Sonya Lipsett-Rovera (eds.) (1998), *The Faces of Honor: Sex, Shame and Violence in Colonial Latin America* (Alburquerque: University of New Mexico Press).

Magis, Carlos (2000), "Enlace entre polítcas e investoigación. El caso del sida," in Mario Bronfman, Ana Langer Glass, and James Trostle (eds.), *De la investigación a la salud pública: La difícil traducción*, 91–118 (Mexico: El Manual Moderno).

Matos, Marlise (2019), "Gender and Sexuality in Brazilian Public Policy: Progress and Regression in Depatriarcalizing and Deheteronormalizing the State," in Elisabeth J. Friedman (ed.), *Seeking Rights from the Left: Gender, Sexuality and the Latin American Pink Tide*, 144–98 (Durham, NC: Duke University Press).

Monisváis, Carlos (2004), "La emergencia de la Diversidad: Las comunidades marginales y sus batallas por la visibilidad," *Debate Feminista* 15(29), 187–205.

Nesvig, Martin (2001), "The Complicated Terrain of Latin American Homosexuality," *Hispanic American Historical Review* 81, 3–4.

Núñez Noriega, Guillermo (2000), *Sexo entre Varones: Poder y resistencia en el campo sexual* (Mexico: Universidad Nacional Autónoma de México).

Pecheny, Mario (2003), "Sexual Orientation, AIDS, and Human Rights in Argentina: The Paradox of Social Advance amid Health Crisis," in Susan Eckstein and Timothy Wickham-Crowley (eds.), *Struggles for Social Rights in Latin America*, 253–71 (London: Routledge).

Pecheny, Mario (2004), "Lógicas de acción colectiva de los movimientos por los derechos sexuales: Un análisis con aires abstractos de experiencias bien concretas," in Carlos Cáceres, Tim Frasca, Mario Pecheny, and Veriano Treto (eds.) *Ciudadanía sexual en América Latina: Abriendo el debate*, 203–15 (Lima: Universidad Peruana Cayetano Heredia).

Perlongher, Néstor (1996), *Prosa plebeya: Ensayos, 1980–1992* (Buenos Aires: Colihue).

Pierceson, Jason, Adriana Piatti-Crocker, and Shawn Schulenberg (2012), *Same-Sex Marriage in Latin America: Promise and Resistance* (Lanham, MD: Lexington Books).

Porter, Ronald K. (2012), "A Rainbow in Black: The Gay Politics of the Black Panther Party," *Counterpoints* 367, 364–75.

Rapisardi, Flavio and Alejandro Modarelli (2001), *Fiestas, baños y exilio en la última dictadura*. (Buenos Aires: Sudamericana).

Salessi, Jorge (1995), *Médicos, maleantes y maricas* (Rosario: Beatriz Viterbo).

Sempol, Diego (2013), "Violence and the Emergence of Gay and Lesbian Activism in Argentina, 1983–1990," in Saskia Wieringa and Horacio Sívori (eds.), *The Sexual History of the Global South: Sexual Politics in Africa, Asia and Latin America*, 99–120 (New York: Zed Books).

Serrano-Anaya, José Fernando (2018), *Homophobic Violence in Armed Conflict and Political Transition* (New York: Palgrave).

Sousa, Lisa Mary (1997), "Women and Crime in Colonial Oaxaca: Evidence of Complementary Gender Roles in Mixtec and Zapotec Soceties," in Susan Schroeder, Stephanie Wood, and Robert Kaskett (eds.), *Indian Women in Early Mexico*, 199–216 (Norman: University of Oklahoma Press).

Stephen, Lynn (2002), "Sexualities and Genders in Zapotec Oaxaca," *Latin American Perspectives* 29(2), 41–59.

Tomás y Valiente, Francisco (1990), *Sexo barroco y otras transgresiones premodernas* (Madrid: Alianza).

Torres-Ruiz, Antonio (2011), "HIV/ AIDS and Sexual Minorities in Mexico: A Globalized Struggle for the Protection of Human Rights," *Latin American Research Review* 46(1), 30–53.

Williams, Walter (1986), *The Spirit and the Flesh: Sexual Diversity in American Indian Culture* (Boston, MA: Beacon Press).

Yashar, Deborah (2005), *Contesting Citizenship in Latin America: The Rise of Indigenous Movements and the Postliberal Challenge* (Cambridge: Cambridge University Press).

CHAPTER 25

HUMAN RIGHTS MOVEMENTS ACROSS LATIN AMERICA

JONAS WOLFF

INTRODUCTION

When research on social movements in Latin America started to take off in the 1980s, human rights movements were an important topic reliably dealt with in the scholarly work of that time (Calderón 1986a; Eckstein 1989; Jelin 1985; Mainwaring and Viola 1984). This reflected the legacy of the military dictatorships, which had shaped (and, in cases such as Chile, continued to shape) the structures and dynamics of social organization and mobilization as they evolved during the 1980s. On the one hand, the experience of brutal state repression meant that the protection of basic civil rights became a central concern for social activists and movements across Latin America (Foweraker 1995: 28). On the other, in quite a few countries in the region, human rights movements were key actors that opened up spaces for other civil society groups (Calderón 1986b: 374) and contributed to the delegitimization and eventual end of military rule (Brysk 1994; Cleary 1997; Keck and Sikkink 1998; Orellana and Hutchinson 1991; see Inclán in this volume).

Throughout the 1990s, Latin American human rights movements continued to receive scholarly attention.[1] Contributions on the human rights movements in the region also shaped global academic debates, while Latin American experiences of human rights activism diffused to other world regions (Keck and Sikkink 1998; Kelly 2018; Moyn 2010). Key examples include the role of the Madres de Plaza de Mayo and other human rights organizations in challenging the military dictatorship in Argentina (Brysk 1994; Keck and Sikkink 1998) as well as the push of human rights activists for transitional justice following the establishment of democratic regimes in several countries (Barahona de Brito 2001; Bickford 2002; Cleary 1997: ch. 3; Sieder 2001; Zunino 2019).

In contrast to the 1980s and 1990s, recent publications reveal a different picture. Current edited volumes and handbooks that deal with social movements in the region do not contain entries that explicitly discuss human rights movements in the region (see Almeida and Cordero 2015; Alvarez et al. 2017; Rossi and von Bülow 2015; Stahler-Sholk et al. 2014). Why is that? Have human rights movements disappeared from the map of contentious mobilization in Latin America? What has happened to human rights activism in recent years? In reviewing the development of, and the existing research on, human rights movements across Latin America, this chapter also develops some tentative answers to these questions.

More specifically, I will suggest that the relative silence on human rights movements in contemporary academic debates on Latin American social movements is due to two related trends. First, Latin America's traditional human rights movements, and the key organizations sustaining them, have clearly lost in relative importance. In the struggle against the military dictatorships and, following their exit, for comprehensive policies of dealing with the crimes committed under military rule, the explicit claim to a narrow set of human rights played a key role in framing societal mobilization. With a view to the issue of transitional justice, this type of human rights agenda has continued to mobilize people in countries such as Argentina, Chile, or Guatemala well beyond the early 1990s. But, in general, the waves of contentious mobilization that the region has experienced since the late 1990s have been characterized by different collective action frames (such as an "anti-neoliberalism" or "social justice" frame).

Second, however, this does not reflect a diminishing relevance of human rights claims in the struggles of social movements, but rather a broadening and differentiation of the human rights agenda and, correspondingly, of the field of movements and movement organizations that make human rights-oriented claims. Today, many—if not most—social movements across Latin America can be considered as, in one way or another, part of a (heterogeneous) struggle for human rights. Yet, with this expansion and diversification of the human rights agenda of social movements, the common, explicit, and universalist emphasis on a narrow set of physical integrity rights has tended to be replaced: on the one hand, by claims to a much broader human rights agenda that goes beyond liberal and individualist conception and encompasses social, economic, and cultural rights; on the other, by more specific, and at times explicitly particular, discourses that focus on issue- or group-specific rights.

In sum, more traditional human rights organizations and activists do certainly persist and continue to play important roles in many countries of the region—reflecting the still lingering legacies of the military regimes of the past century as well as the continuing, and partially worsening, violations of core physical integrity rights by state, para-and non-state actors in the current context. But today, with some partial exceptions (such as Argentina and Mexico), it is much more difficult to identify "human rights movements" as specific and somehow delimited networks of activists, groups, and organizations that engage in contentious action on explicit behalf of human rights.

The chapter starts with a brief history of the human rights movement in Latin America, focusing on its emergence under authoritarian rule. Then, I will revisit key general elements of human rights movements in Latin America (and beyond), before I turn to developments after the end of the dictatorships. In an overview of the evolution of human rights activism in the region since the 1990s, I trace the expansion of the human rights agenda in terms of issues and actors, discussing two major trends: from human rights towards citizenship rights, as well as towards social rights. The chapter concludes with some final reflections.

THE EMERGENCE OF THE HUMAN RIGHTS MOVEMENT IN LATIN AMERICA

While individual human rights organizations have existed before (Sikkink 1996: 152–54),[2] "movements to defend human rights began to appear in Latin America in the 1970s" (Cleary 1997: 66). As Edward Cleary (1997: 1) puts it in his *The Struggle for Human Rights in Latin America*, the "human rights era" in Latin America began with the military coup in Chile on September 11, 1973 and the repressive Pinochet dictatorship that followed it. In a nutshell, he argues that it was the societal response to the military dictatorships of the 1970s that led to the emergence of a broadening array of human rights organizations in the region. As Kathryn Sikkink summarizes: "Although these norms already existed prior to the 1970s, the term *human rights* was not used frequently by social movements to frame their concerns or demands. Essentially, human rights was 'created' in the 1970s as an important and shared issue" (Sikkink 1996: 153–54).

Argentina and Chile are certainly the most prominent cases in this regard, which correspondingly have also received most scholarly attention (Franklin 2014: 142).[3] But, from the mid-1980s onwards, "human rights organizations also began appearing in countries that had not experienced military rule" (Cleary 1997: 25). In Mexico, for instance, a turn to explicitly human rights-oriented mobilization started in the second half of the 1980s: "In 1984 only four human rights NGOs existed in Mexico; seven years later there were sixty, and by 1993 there were more than two hundred" (Keck and Sikkink 1998: 111; see also Álvarez Izaca 2010: 118–33). In countries that experienced internal armed conflict, it was mainly the severe human rights violations committed by both state and non-state actors in the context of armed struggle that triggered the emergence of human rights movements. In these cases, which include Colombia (Romero 2001), Peru (Bueno-Hansen 2015: 38–42), and Central America (Sieder 2001), the persistence of armed conflicts throughout the 1980s generally meant that human rights groups remained relatively weak as they "had a more difficult time mobilizing and forging transnational alliances" (Cárdenas 2010: 143).

Despite these differences in country contexts, scholars have noted that an "international 'demonstration effect' was at work in Latin America during the decade of the 1980s, as the activities and successes of early human rights organizations inspired others to follow their example" (Keck and Sikkink 1998: 92). While the number and strength of domestic human rights groups continued to vary enormously, the 1980s were generally characterized by a significant growth in domestic human rights organizations across Latin America (Keck and Sikkink 1998: 92). According to a study from 1989, there were 241 human rights organizations in the region, with Chile (fifty-two), Brazil (fifty), Argentina (twenty-four), and Mexico (twenty) displaying the highest numbers (Cleary 1997: 17). In addition, by 1990, "more than 200 NGOs based outside the region worked specifically on human rights in Latin America, Central America, and the Caribbean, while 140 international organizations were identified as being concerned with human rights in Latin America" (Sikkink 1996: 156).

The overall context in which Latin America's human rights movements emerged meant that their initial emphasis was very much focused on a narrow set of core human rights norms, basically related to the "traditional 'rights of the person': life, liberty and personal security" (Brysk 1994: 7; see also Sikkink 1996: 155). Rooted in a liberal and individualist conception of civil and political rights, this "minimalist" agenda (Kelly 2018) not only reflected the specific grievances that drove mobilization at that time, but also proved strategically useful. First, it meant that activists articulated basic moral and legal claims, which were harder to delegitimize by the military dictatorship as compared to outright political or partisan demands.[4] Second, this agenda enabled alliances of individuals, organizations, and movements that were quite heterogeneous in terms of political ideology and strategy (see Moyn 2010: 144; Orellana and Hutchinson 1991: 38–40; Sonderéguer 1985: 10–11). Third, it also "found sympathy in the liberal ideological tradition of Western countries, where the [transnational] human rights movement had the bulk of its members" (Sikkink 1996: 155; see also Bickford 2002: 18–19).

This context-driven focus on basic political and civil rights also meant that, during the emergence of the human rights movement in Latin America, its main concern was with one particular group: "with victims of political repression, often political leaders, students, and union leaders, and likely to be male and middle class" (Sikkink 1996: 160). Furthermore, the target of mobilization was equally clear-cut: it was authoritarian regimes, and more specifically military dictatorships that blatantly violated core human rights (Bickford 2002: 18–20).

Key Elements of Human Rights Movements across Latin America

Human rights movements can be defined as sustained, noninstitutionalized networks of activists, groups and organizations that engage in contentious action on explicit behalf of human rights. This is broadly in line with Alison Brysk's (2013: 570) definition of human rights movements as "organizations, campaigns, and issue-networks that seek to enact the fundamental rights inscribed in the Universal Declaration of Human Rights." Yet, in contrast to Brysk, my definition emphasizes that (a) human rights movements are a subcategory of social movements (that is, of sustained, nonstitutionalized networks that engage in contentious action), and that (b) human rights movements are such because their claim-making is characterized by explicit references to the concept of "human rights" (however they chose to define, justify, and defend human rights).

Human rights *movements* usually comprise human rights *organizations*, but these two types of actors are not the same. While some individual human rights organizations may "combine the qualities of a social movement with that of an NGO," most human rights organizations "fit most clearly into the NGO category" (Sikkink 1996: 151). In fact, a quantitative analysis of human rights contention in seven Latin American countries (Argentina, Brazil, Chile, Guatemala, Mexico, Nicaragua, and Venezuela) between 1981 and 1995 found that the number of human rights organizations does not correlate with the number of contentious challenges on behalf of human rights.[5] The existence of many human rights organizations in and of itself, therefore, does not signal the existence of a human rights movement (Franklin 2014).

According to Alison Brysk, human rights movements usually consist of four overlapping clusters of collective actors. First, there are "institutional reformers," professional organizations, which "are often founded by or comprised of lawyers and usually play a critical role in gathering data and documenting evidence and patterns of abuse" (Brysk 2013: 572). Argentina's Centro de Estudios Legales y Sociales (CELS) is a case in point (Jelin 1994: 40–41). Second, advocacy organizations, which operate based on a logic of solidarity, speak, protest, and lobby on behalf of "victims who cannot speak for themselves" (Brysk 2013: 572). In several Latin American countries, for instance, Church-based organizations played a role in this regard given that they benefited from a certain protection vis-á-vis the military regimes. A prominent example is the Vicaría de la Solidaridad, an office directly associated with the Catholic Church that played a critical role in the emergence of the Chilean human rights movement (Cleary 1997: ch. 1; Orellana and Hutchinson 1991: 21–23).

The third key type of actors concerns groups or movements established by the affected populations themselves. In the case of Latin America, "campaigns by relatives of victims," and most importantly by relatives of the forcefully disappeared, were a crucial element in the emergence and consolidation of human rights movements, which also established "a protest repertoire that diffused worldwide" (Brysk 2013: 571). The Argentine Madres de Plaza de Mayo are certainly the most prominent example, but similar groups emerged all across the region, including in Chile, Colombia, Guatemala, Honduras, El Salvador, and Peru (see Barahona de Brito 2001; Sieder 2001). Fourth and finally, "cutting across these traditional genres but with some distinctive identity and mode of operations, there are normative constituencies organized around religious or professional identity that come to mobilize as human rights movements" (Brysk 2013: 572). At the regional level, this category includes the liberation theology-inspired Servicio de Paz y Justicia en América Latina (SERPAJ) (Brysk 1994: 49–51). SERPAJ, for instance, responded to the repression that followed the series of military coups in the early 1970s by initiating, in 1975, a region-wide human rights campaign that explicitly drew on the Universal Declaration of Human Rights (Veiga 1985: 129).

The example of SERPAJ also indicates that the human rights movements that have emerged in individual Latin American countries since the early 1970s were also shaped by regional and international dynamics. Most importantly, from the very beginning, they were embedded in and supported by what Keck and Sikkink (1998) later termed "transnational advocacy networks" (see also Cárdenas 2010: ch. 4; von Bülow in this volume).[6] In addition to regional and global organizations and networks, United States-based human rights organizations as well as United States-based funders were important in the spread and consolidation of human rights movements across Latin America. The former include organizations such as such as "Americas Watch, the International Human Rights Law Group, the Lawyers Committee for Human Rights, and the Washington Office on Latin America" (Sikkink 1996: 154). A key funding organizations engaging in financing human rights work in the region was the Ford Foundation (Keck and Sikkink 1998: 98–99).

Human Rights Mobilization after the End of the Dictatorships

The context in which human rights movements had emerged across the region changed dramatically between the late 1970s and the early 1990s, when almost all Latin American countries saw the end of military rule and the establishment of democratic regimes (see Brocket, Inclán in this volume). As a consequence, "many observers expected human rights to diminish as an issue" (Cleary 1997: 62). This, however, is not what happened. Yet the new context did pose important challenges to the pre-existing human rights movements.

Generally speaking, the transitions to democracy meant that institutional politics and political parties gained in relevance, at the expense of social movements (Wolff 2020: 177). More specifically, with the military regimes the main target of human rights activism disappeared, while post-transition governments officially incorporated many of the demands of the human rights movements into their policy agenda (Bickford 2002: 22–23; Jelin 1998: 410; Sikkink 1996: 158). Furthermore, with the end of military rule across Latin America, the domestic and international support for human rights movements also subsided. In Chile, for instance, the Catholic Church, which had played a key role in the emergence and rise of the human rights movement after the 1973 coup (see Orellana and Hutchinson 1991), "judged that its direct work in human rights was finished" and, in 1992, closed the Vicariate, the church office that had been responsible for the human rights work (Cleary 1997: 20).[7] Also, in the United States, many groups that had worked on human rights in Latin America and had supported local organizations on these issues, "closed their doors or turned to other issues" (Cleary 1997: 62). Generally, human rights groups in the Southern Cone "experienced a significant decrease in external funding in the late 1980s and early 1990s" (Sikkink 1996: 159; see also Bickford 2002: 20).

Focusing on human rights NGOs in Latin America, Kathryn Sikkink (1996: 153) in the mid-1990s described the years since 1991 as "a time of refocusing and retrenchment, as human rights NGOs struggle to respond, in a changing global context, to new forms of human rights violations in the hemisphere." With a view to those cases in which strong human rights movement emerged under authoritarian rule, scholars have viewed the 1990s as a period of weakening or even of "abeyance" (Pereyra 2015: 192–95). As Elizabeth Jelin summarized in the late 1990s, "the issues raised by these movements [referring to the women's and the human rights movements] expanded significantly and became generalized in the population, which is a clear indication of success." Yet, as their themes were "appropriated by society at large," the movements themselves "became weak and conflict-ridden" (Jelin 1998: 410).

For the case of Argentina, Jelin has argued that the human rights movement, with the transition to democracy, "gradually lost its central political position, entering a phase of internal debate about its role under a democratic regime and revealing its internal cleavages and heterogeneities" (Jelin 1994: 38). Once the human rights movement had "won the initial phase of human rights struggle for 'the right to have rights,'" Brysk observed, "the determination of the *content* of human rights introduced a politicized and ideological dimension that restricted the movement's appeal" (Brysk 1994: 214; italics in original). While some Argentine human rights organizations "concentrated on documenting and addressing specific past and current human rights violations," others "adopted a more radical ideological perspective on human rights violations, which dictated their broader political stances and forms of political action" (Brysk 1994: 124).[8]

In Chile, the 1990s have been even characterized as "a period of relative inactivity" of the human rights movement," in particular when "compared to its famously vibrant period in the 1970s and 1980s" (Bickford 2002: 10):

> For the past ten years, from an organizational point of view, the eight or nine largest human rights organizations (HROs) in Chile—not to mention dozens of smaller groups, including neighborhood and regional HROs—have been weak, underfunded, and minimally staffed; they have garnered low levels of popular enthusiasm and been practically invisible as agenda setters or influential voices in Chilean society (except, perhaps, on the specific issue of Pinochet's possible prosecution) (ibid.).

In the post-transition context, the established collective action frame of the human rights movement—which had directly associated the struggle for human rights (understood in a narrow sense) with the fight against authoritarian rule—was no longer viable and had to be adapted. One option, taken by the Chilean human rights movement, was to hold on to the previous mission but now focus on dealing with the past (ibid.: 24). Another option, represented by Argentina's *Madres de Plaza de Mayo*, consisted in embracing "broad goals that address neoliberalism" and enabled building "bridges with other activists" (Borland 2006: 116)—but at the expense of creating divisions within the national human rights movement (Brysk 1994: 124).

And yet it would be wrong to conclude that the new democratic context was simply adverse for human rights-based mobilization. Generally speaking, the almost region-wide establishment of democratic regimes (and the ending of most civil wars) meant that the political opportunity structure became much more conducive to human rights movements. At the same time, the mission of the human rights movement was not simply fulfilled with the transition to democratic regimes. Persisting human rights issues, first, concerned the crucial task of dealing with the human rights violations committed under military rule and/or during armed conflict. Many human rights organizations across the region, therefore, "turned their attention toward accountability and punishment" (Zunino 2019: 182). Given that the processes of clarifying, investigating, and prosecuting past human rights violations were mostly slow and partial, the mobilization and advocacy for transitional justice became a vibrant field of human rights activism. With varying strength and degrees of success, throughout the 1980s, 1990s, and—in many cases—until today, human rights organizations and activists across the region have pushed for truth and reparation for the victims as well as for prosecution and punishment of the perpetrators (Barahona de Brito 2001; Bickford 2002; Brysk 1994: 63–88; Cleary 1997: ch. 4; Sieder 2001). By and large, this mobilization in the name of transitional justice has continued the minimalist agenda focused on an individualist and liberal conception of human rights (see Zunino 2019: 232).

Second, as human rights violations have generally persisted under democratic rule, the struggle for human rights in the new context was far from a backward-looking activity only. In contrast to the idealized image of democracy theory, according to which the role of social movements in democratic regimes is about "vindicating or protecting particular, delimited and specific sets of rights (since universal rights are guaranteed by the liberal polity)," social movements across Latin America still "have had to press for universal rights," including for "common civil liberties" (Foweraker 1995: 6). These persisting human rights issues included authoritarian legacies and corresponding continuities in terms of physical integrity right violations and impunity as well as a broader (partial) lack on the part of the state to respect and actively protect and promote human rights, including women's and indigenous, social, and economic rights (Braig 2012; Brysk 1994: chs. 6–9; Cleary 1997: ch. 3, 2007; Sikkink 1996: 159–60; Terto Neto 2017). In this context, the traditional type of physical integrity rights-oriented activism has also remained of utmost relevance. Until today, relatives of "detained-disappeared" do not only continue to mobilize with a view to an increasingly distant authoritarian past, but in cases such as Mexico they also respond to contemporary cases (Cárdenas 2010: 112–14).[9] More generally, state repression—including police violence—remains an important topic for human rights activism (Cleary 2007: ch. 6–7). And, unfortunately, it is the very physical integrity of such activists that has become a key concern in many countries of the region as "[h]uman rights defenders have in fact come to constitute one of the principal targets of human rights abuse in Latin America" (Cárdenas 2010: 109).

As a consequence, in terms of quantity, human rights-based activism has continued to spread with democratization. Between 1989 and 1994, the number of human rights organizations in Latin America was estimated to have increased from 241 to 640 (Cleary 1997: 63). And more recent data suggests that this number has continued to increase across the region, more than doubling in most Latin American countries between 1993 and 2007 (Cárdenas 2010: 111). In sum, therefore, the picture is decidedly ambivalent. While national human rights movements were generally weakened in the new context, human rights activism broadly speaking experienced a process of mainstreaming, differentiation, and professionalization. As a result, while many human rights organizations continued to engage in contentious action, they tended to do so not as part of a human rights movement but rather as participants in social movements or protest waves that were held together by different collective action frames. This will be discussed in the following section.

The Expansion of the Human Rights Agenda

The establishment of democratic regimes across the region "brought two streams of activity for human rights advocates": mobilization aimed at pushing for what came to be called "transitional justice"; and human rights advocacy that "expanded into areas beyond death and disappearance" (Cleary 2007: xi–xii). As I will argue in this section, it was the latter process—the broadening of the human rights agenda—that helps explain the paradoxical observation outlined in the beginning of this chapter: the fact that the struggle for human rights continues to be a crucial dimension of contentious politics in contemporary Latin America, but that human rights movements in a strict sense have clearly lost in relevance.

In order to grasp the expansion and diversification of human rights-oriented struggles, the scholarship on social movements in Latin America has identified two related shifts in human-rights-centered claim-making: first, towards a citizenship rights discourse and, second, towards a social rights/justice frame.

From Human Rights to Citizenship Rights

Reviewing the evolving scholarship on social movements in Latin America during the 1990s, Philip Oxhorn (2001) observed a discursive shift from human rights to citizenship rights. Under authoritarian rule, the core idea of human rights claims was that they referred to internationally established, incontestable, universal obligations. In the democratic context, "the very determination of the meaning of 'right' and the assertion of some value or ideal as a 'right' are themselves objects of political struggle," which includes "the invention and creation of *new* rights" (Dagnino 1998: 50). This is not to say that such claims to citizenship rights refer to something other than human rights; in fact, citizenship rights are mostly also understood as human rights. The notion of a shift rather refers to a change from a struggle *for* (human) rights that are assumed to be given to a struggle *over* (citizenship) rights that concerns the very question of "what it means to be a citizen" (Oxhorn 2001: 180).

As a consequence, "groups promoting citizens' rights have opened up a wide field of rights," making spaces "for rights long ignored within Latin American societies" (Cleary 2007: 11, note 10). The human rights movements studied in Cleary's *Mobilizing for Human Rights in Latin America*, therefore, include women's (rights) movements and mobilization by and in the name of (the rights of) street children as well as indigenous rights and landless movements (ibid: chs. 2–5; see Ewig and Friedman, Rice, Welch in this volume). On the one hand, this meant that an expanding range of social groups, organizations and movements were now considered as "local human rights groups": "women's groups, indigenous advocates, relatives of human rights victims, legal aid agencies, religious or social justice organizations, or those fighting on behalf of lesbian, gay, bisexual, and transgender people" (Cárdenas 2010: 108). On the other, "the human rights movement" itself turned its attention to "new themes," including "rights violations of specially vulnerable groups," as well as to the specific rights of "new groups" (Sikkink 1996: 159–60). For the case of Mexico, for instance, Álvarez Izaca (2010: 127) has noted a "diversification" of the human rights agenda, including with a view to "women, sexually diverse people, children, indigenous communities and persons with disabilities."

The most important (human) rights-oriented social movements that are discussed in the literature are women's (rights) movements and indigenous (rights) movements (see Cleary 2007; Eckstein and Wickham-Crowley 2003; Kelly 2018: 272–304). Women had played key roles in the emergence of the human rights movement in Latin America during authoritarian rule, but, as said, human rights at that time had been primarily defined in terms of basic physical integrity rights (Cleary 2007: 16–17; Jelin 2007: 31–34; Orellana and Hutchinson 1991: 46–47). Under democratic regimes, women's movements continued to make human rights-based claims, but the agenda was now characterized by an expanding agenda of women's rights (see Cleary 2007: ch. 2; Jelin 2007: 34–39; Ewig and Friedman in this volume).

Since the early 1990s, the mobilization of indigenous people in several Latin American countries brought indigenous rights to "the top of the human rights agenda" (Cleary 2007: 51; see also Cárdenas 2010: 117–20). To an important extent, the mobilization of indigenous people has been a struggle about indigenous rights (Brysk 2000; Postero and Zamosc 2004). But indigenous movements emerged independent of the classical human rights organizations. In fact, the "juridical model of individual complaints against state agents for the denial of civil liberties," which had been pursued by traditional human rights activists, was "singularly inappropriate for indigenous peoples' concerns" (Brysk 2000: 202). Yet, while indigenous movements themselves broadened the human rights agenda to include an expanding array of indigenous collective rights, human rights organizations increased attention on the specific concerns of indigenous peoples (see ibid.: 202–05; Rice in this volume).

From Human Rights to Social Rights

The second shift in the (human) rights discourse that has shaped social mobilization since the 1990s can be described as a (re-)turn to a focus on social rights (see, for instance, Eckstein and Wickham-Crowley 2003). In a way, this expansion of the human rights agenda from a narrow focus on individual civil and political rights to a broad conception that also encompasses economic, social, and cultural rights, including collective ones, connects the historical struggles for social justice of previous decades with the relatively recent human rights activism (see Kelly 2018: 272–304). This articulation, generally speaking, reflects the contradictory combination of political democratization with neoliberal restructuring across Latin America, which meant that improvements in civil and political rights were accompanied by a curtailment in certain, previously established social and economic rights (see Oxhorn and Starr 1999; Wolff 2020).

A broad range of social movements that have thrived in recent decades make social rights claims, including the women's and indigenous movements discussed in the previous section (Kelly 2018: 272–304). In the context of austerity policies and neoliberal reforms, mobilization in the name of subsistence rights has become an important area of social contention (see Eckstein and Wickham-Crowley 2003; Simmons 2016). Also, rural social movements, including landless movements have adopted a social rights agenda, including claims to territorial rights, food sovereignty rights, or collective indigenous rights (see Cleary 2007: ch. 5; Deere and Royce 2009; Davis and Davey, Fernandes and Welch, Fontana, Welch in this volume). In the context of the commodities boom of the early 2000s, the defense of environmental rights as well as of social and economic rights directly affected by environmental degradation has recently become a particularly important topic driving protests against projects of resource extraction (Segarra 2013).[10] Finally, to be sure, also mobilization in the name of labor rights—certainly not a new phenomenon in Latin America—has persisted throughout the region (see Eckstein and Wickham-Crowley 2003; Ramírez and Stoessel in this volume). Important examples, in this area, have been protests in defense of labor rights threatened by free trade negotiations or openly denied in the context of the *maquiladora* industry (Cárdenas 2010: 120–22; von Bülow in this volume).

In the context of the wave of anti-neoliberal protest movements that swept the region since the mid-1990s, demands and grievances were, in part, justified in terms of human rights (violations) (see Cárdenas 2010: 116). Yet, while the mobilization "against neoliberalism" across the region included claims to social and economic rights, these were not embedded in an explicitly human rights-centered collective action frame but were rather integrated into an "anti-neoliberal" or a "social justice" frame (Almeida 2007; Eckstein and Wickham-Crowley 2003; Silva 2009). The overall agenda of these multifaceted protest movements that prepared the ground for the election of left-wing presidents in countries such as Argentina (2003), Bolivia (2005), or Ecuador (2006) was not anti-liberal, and certainly not anti-human rights. However, it was "postliberal" in the sense of aiming at going beyond narrow liberal notions of procedural democracy and individual human rights (Wolff 2013). The relative absence of explicit human rights claims in this context is thus plausibly related, amongst other things, to the ambivalent relationship between human rights and the neoliberal ideology: on the one hand, human rights claims could be used to challenge, for example, neoliberalism's denial of the state's responsibility to guarantee universal social and economic rights; on the other, the hegemonic human rights discourse with its liberal emphasis on individual, political, and civil rights also shares a common logic with neoliberal thinking (Chambers 2017; Jelin 2007: 39–41; Fontana in this volume).

Against this background, it is probably not by chance that human rights organizations "have perhaps had the most difficulty figuring out how to be relevant in the area of economic and social rights," even if, since the end of the 1990s, "many human rights groups have made a concerted effort to build on their successes in the realm of civil and political rights to address economic, social and cultural rights" (Vivanco and Wilkinson 2010: 221; see also Turner and Popovski 2010: 238).

Conclusion

In the early 2000s, Louis Bickford (2002: 9) articulated doubts whether it still made sense to talk about a human rights *movement* in Chile strictly speaking, even if "a smaller but still committed group of activists and HROs [human rights organizations]" remained active (Bickford 2002: 24). The review of the existing scholarship suggests that the current situation across Latin America is more complex. On the one hand, the numbers of human rights organizations have continued to increase under democratic rule and are today certainly higher than they were in the 1980s. Also, a broad range of most different social organizations and movements make use of human rights-based claims, as—by the way—do political parties, governments, and international organizations. On the other hand, with some partial exceptions, it is hard to identify a human rights movement that would unite a broader set of individuals and collective actors under a common, human rights-centered collective action frame.

This is not simply bad news for human rights, however. As Marianne Braig (2012) has argued, a key role of the human rights discourse in contemporary Latin America (and beyond) is that "the human rights establish a document of authorization that enables the subaltern to express experiences of injustice, which are diverse and relate to a multitude of cultural expressions of subversion (including in the private sphere)" (ibid.: 67). Understood in this way, the role of human rights runs counter to the idea that there are specific human rights movements that can be identified as such. Under certain circumstances, such as in response to particularly gross human rights violations, individual activists, organizations, and social movements may still coalesce in explicit human rights campaigns. The overall trend across Latin America, however, seems to be clear-cut: human rights claims constitute a key element in the collective action frames of many if not most social movements in the region. But, for the time being, the times of vibrant human rights movements strictly speaking are most probably over.

Acknowledgements

The author would like to thank Francy Köllner and Babette Ullemeyer for research assistance as well as Federico Rossi and an anonymous reviewer for helpful comments and suggestions.

Notes

1. For just a few books, see Brysk (1994), Cleary (1997), Keck and Sikkink (1998), as well as Orellana and Hutchinson (1991).
2. Examples include the Liga Argentina por los Derechos del Hombre, which was established in 1937, and Servicio de Paz y Justicia en América Latina (SERPAJ), which initiated its activities in countries across the region in the 1950s (see Veiga 1985).
3. On the Argentine human rights movement, see, for instance, Brysk (1994), Jelin (1994), Pereyra (2015), and Sonderéguer (1985). On Chile, see Bickford (2002), Cleary (1997: ch. 1), and Orellana and Hutchinson (1991). A contrasting case is Brazil, where the human rights movement remained relatively weak (see Barahona de Brito 2001; Terto Neto 2017).
4. To be sure, military regimes did try to delegitimize human rights organizations, if with limited success, as Brysk (1994: 56–58) recounts for the case of Argentina.
5. Franklin (2014:145–46), for instance, found that Brazil had the highest average number of human rights organizations (HROs) (approximately forty-two), but the lowest number of human rights-related challenges (eight), while Argentina had less than half the average number of HROs (approximately eighteen), but experienced more than four times as many challenges (thirty-six) (Franklin 2014: 145–46).
6. See Brysk (1994: 46–50, 169–70) for the case of Argentina and Terto Neto (2017) on Brazil. For comparative studies, see Keck and Sikkink (1999: ch. 3) on Argentina and Mexico, Ropp and Sikkink (1999) on Chile and Guatemala, as well as Sieder (2001) on Central America.
7. Tellingly, Chile's Catholic Church reportedly opened "a new office to work on issues of poverty" instead (Sikkink 1996: 159).
8. On the post-transition evolution of the Madres and the Argentine human rights movement in general, see Borland (2006) and Pereyra (2015).
9. In Mexico, the dramatic increase in the levels of violence against civilians in the last decade has given rise to important processes of social mobilization in which human rights claims have been crucial. Still, it is interesting to note that one of the most important movements that emerged in this context framed its mission as "for peace with justice and dignity" (see Alonso Reynoso and Alonso 2015).
10. In the context of natural resource extraction, a whole range of rights is frequently violated, including indigenous rights—in particular, the collective right to prior, informed consultation (or consent)—subsistence rights, broader social, and environmental rights as well

as, all too often, the physical integrity rights of those that resist extractive projects (see Christel and Gutiérrez in this volume).

References

Almeida, Paul D. (2007), "Defensive Mobilization: Popular Movements against Economic Adjustment Policies in Latin America," *Latin American Perspectives* 34(3), 123–39.
Almeida, Paul and Allen Cordero Ulate (eds.) (2015), *Handbook of Social Movements across Latin America* (New York: Springer).
Alonso Reynoso, Carlos and Jorge Alonso (2015), *Una fuerte indignación que se convirtió en movimiento: Ayotzinapa* (Guadalajara: Universidad de Guadalajara).
Álvarez Icaza, Emilio (2010), "La institucionalización de los derechos humanos: Reflexiones en torno a la sociedad civil y los organismos públicos de derechos humanos," in Roberto Blancarte (ed.), *Los grandes problemas de México XVI: Culturas e Identidades*, 115–47 (Mexico: El Colegio de México).
Alvarez, Sonia E., Jeffrey W. Rubin, Millie Thayer, Gianpaolo Baiocchi, and Agustín Laó-Montes (eds.) (2017), *Beyond Civil Society. Activism, Participation, and Protest in Latin America* (Durham, NC: Duke University Press).
Barahona de Brito, Alexandra (2001), "Truth, Justice, Memory, and Democratization in the Southern Cone," in Alexandra Barahona de Brito, Carmen González-Enríquez, and Paloma Aguilar (eds.), *The Politics of Memory: Transitional Justice in Democratizing Societies*, 119–60 (Oxford: Oxford University Press).
Bickford, Louis N. (2002), "Preserving Memory: The Past and the Human Rights Movement in Chile," in Richard S. Hillman, John A. Peeler, and Elsa Cardozo Da Silva (eds.), *Democracy and Human Rights in Latin America*, 9–30 (Westport, CT: Praeger).
Borland, Elizabeth (2006), "The Mature Resistance of Argentina's Madres de Plaza de Mayo," in Hank Johnston and Paul Almeida (eds.), *Latin American Social Movements. Globalization, Democratization, and Transnational Networks*, 115–30 (Lanham, MD: Rowman & Littlefield).
Braig, Marianne (2012), "Los derechos humanos como autorización para hablar. Metatexto universal y experiencias particulares," in Stefanie Kron, Sérgio Costa, and Marianne Braig (eds.), *Democracia y reconfiguraciones contemporáneas del derecho en América Latina*, 61–72 (Frankfurt: Vervuert).
Brysk, Alison (1994), *The Politics of Human Rights in Argentina: Protest, Change, and Democratization* (Stanford, CA: Stanford University Press).
Brysk, Alison (2000), *From Tribal Village to Global Village: Indian Rights and International Relations in Latin America* (Stanford, CA: Stanford University Press).
Brysk, Alison (2013), "Human Rights Movements," in David A. Snow, Donatella della Porta, Bert Klandermans, and Doug McAdam (eds.), *The Wiley-Blackwell Encyclopedia of Social and Political Movements*, 570–75 (Oxford: Blackwell).
Bueno-Hansen, Pascha (2015), *Feminist and Human Rights Struggles in Peru: Decolonizing Transitional Justice* (Urbana: University of Illinois Press).
Calderón G., Fernando (ed.) (1986a), *Los movimientos sociales ante la crisis* (Buenos Aires: Universidad de las Naciones Unidas).
Calderón G., Fernando (1986b), "Los movimientos sociales frente a la crisis," in Fernando Calderón G. (ed.), *Los movimientos sociales ante la crisis*, 327–98 (Buenos Aires: Universidad de las Naciones Unidas).

Cárdenas, Sonia (2010), *Human Rights in Latin America. A Politics of Terror and Hope* (Philadelphia, PA: University of Pennsylvania Press).

Chambers, Paul A. (2017), "Resisting Neoliberalism in Colombia: The Role of Human Rights," *Latin American Perspectives* 44(5), 127–44.

Cleary, Edward L. (1997), *The Struggle for Human Rights in Latin America* (Westport, CT: Praeger).

Cleary, Edward L. (2007), *Mobilizing for Human Rights in Latin America* (Bloomfield, CT: Kumarian Press).

Dagnino, Evalina (1998), "Culture, Citizenship, and Democracy: Changing Discourses and Practices of the Latin American Left," in Sonia E. Alvarez, Evelina Dagnino, and Arturo Escobar (eds.), *Cultures of Politics/Politics of Cultures. Re-Visioning Latin American Social Movements* (Boulder, CT: Westview Press), 33–63.

Deere, Carmen Diana and Frederick S. Royce (2009), *Rural Social Movements in Latin America: Organizing for Sustainable Livelihoods* (Gainesville: University Press of Florida).

Eckstein, Susan (ed.) (1989), *Power and Popular Protest. Latin American Social Movements* (Berkeley and Los Angeles: University of California Press).

Eckstein, Susan E. and Timothy P. Wickham-Crowley (eds.) (2003), *Struggles for Social Rights in Latin America* (New York: Routledge).

Foweraker, Joe (1995), *Theorizing Social Movements* (London: Pluto Press).

Franklin, James C. (2014), "Human Rights Contention in Latin America: A Comparative Study," *Human Rights Review* 15(2), 139–58.

Jelin, Elizabeth (ed.) (1985), *Los nuevos movimientos sociales*, vol. 2, *Derechos humanos: Obreros, Barrios* (Buenos Aires: Centro Editor de América Latina).

Jelin, Elizabeth (1994). "The Politics of Memory: The Human Rights Movement and the Construction of Democracy in Argentina," *Latin American Perspectives* 81(2), 38–58.

Jelin, Elizabeth (1998). "Toward a Culture of Participation and Citizenship: Challenges for a More Equitable World," in Sonia E. Alvarez, Evelina Dagnino, and Arturo Escobar (eds.), *Cultures of Politics/Politics of Cultures. Re-Visioning Latin American Social Movements* (Boulder, CT: Westview Press), 405–21.

Jelin, Elizabeth (2007), "Trayectorias entrecruzadas: Los Derechos Humanos y el género en el desarrollo de las ciencias sociales latinoamericanas," *Revista Colombiana de Sociología* 28, 27–45.

Keck, Margaret E. and Kathryn Sikkink (1998), *Activists beyond Borders: Advocacy Networks in International Politics* (Ithaca, NY: Cornell University Press).

Kelly, Patrick W. (2018), *Sovereign Emergencies: Latin America and the Making of Global Human Rights Politics* (Cambridge: Cambridge University Press).

Mainwaring, Scott and Eduardo Viola (1984), "New Social Movements, Political Culture, and Democracy: Brazil and Argentina in the 1980s," *Telos* 61, 17–52.

Moyn, Samuel (2010), *The Last Utopia: Human Rights in History* (Cambridge, MA: Belknap Press).

Orellana, Patricio and Elizabetih Q. Hutchinson (1991), *El movimiento de derechos humanos en Chile, 1973–1990* (Santiago: Centro de Estudios Políticos Latinoamericanos Simón Bolívar).

Oxhorn, Philip (2001), "From Human Rights to Citizenship Rights? Recent Trends in the Study of Latin American Social Movements," *Latin American Research Review* 36(3), 163–82.

Oxhorn, Philip and Pamela K. Starr (eds.) (1999), *Markets and Democracy in Latin America: Conflict or Convergence?* (Boulder, CO: Lynne Rienner).

Pereyra, Sebastián (2015), "Strategies and Mobilization Cycles of the Human Rights Movement in the Democratic Transition in Argentina," in Bert Klandermans and Cornelis Van Stralen (eds.), *Movements in Times of Democratic Transition*, 186–205 (Philadelphia, PA: Temple University Press).

Postero, Nancy Grey and Leon Zamosc (eds.) (2004), *The Struggle for Indigenous Rights in Latin America* (Brighton: Sussex Academic Press).

Romero, Flor Alba (2001), "El movimiento de derechos humanos en Colombia. Movimientos sociales," in Mauricio Archila and Mauricio Pardo (eds.), *Movimientos sociales: Estado y democracia en Colombia*, 441–72 (Bogotá: Universidad Nacional de Colombia).

Ropp, Stephen C. and Kathryn Sikkink (1999), "International Norms and Domestic Politics in Chile and Guatemala," in Thomas Risse, Ropp, Steve C. Risse, and Kathryn Sikkink (eds.), *The Power of Human Rights. International Norms and Domestic Change*, 172–204 (Cambridge: Cambridge University Press).

Rossi, Federico M. and Marisa von Bülow (eds.) (2015), *Social Movement Dynamics: New Perspectives on Theory and Research from Latin America* (Farnham: Ashgate).

Segarra, Monique (2013), "Challenging Neoliberalism and Development: Human Rights and the Environment in Latin America," in Katherine Hite and Mark Ungar (eds.), *Sustaining Human Rights in the Twenty-First Century: Strategies from Latin America*, 303–40 (Washington, DC: Woodrow Wilson Center Press).

Sieder, Rachel (2001), "War, Peace, and Memory Politics in Central America," in Alexandra Barahona de Brito, Carmen González-Enríquez, and Paloma Aguilar (eds.), *The Politics of Memory: Transitional Justice in Democratizing Societies*, 161–89 (Oxford: Oxford University Press).

Sikkink, Kathryn A. (1996), "Nongovernmental Organizations, Democracy, and Human Rights in Latin America," in Tom Farer (ed.), *Beyond Sovereignty: Collectively Defending Democracy in the Americas*, 150–68 (Baltimore, MD: The Johns Hopkins University Press).

Silva, Eduardo (2009), *Challenging Neoliberalism in Latin America* (Cambridge: Cambridge University Press).

Simmons, Erica S. (2016), *Meaningful Resistance: Market Reforms and the Roots of Social Protest in Latin America* (Cambridge: Cambridge University Press).

Sonderéguer, María (1985), "Aparición con vida. El movimiento de derechos humanos en la Argentina," in Elizabeth Jelin (ed.), *Los nuevos movimientos sociales*, vol. 2, *Derechos humanos: Obreros, Barrios*, 7–32 (Buenos Aires: Centro Editor de América Latina).

Stahler-Sholk, Richard, Harry E. Vanden, and Marc Becker (eds.) (2014), *Rethinking Latin American Social Movements. Radical Action from Below* (Lanham, MD: Rowman & Littlefield).

Terto Neto, Ulisses (2017), "From Military Authoritarian Rule to Constitutional Democracy: An Overview of the Politics of Human Rights Through the Brazilian Re-democratization," *Revista Direitos Fundamentais & Democracia* 22(3), 215–52.

Turner, Nicholas and Vesselin Popovski (2010), "Human Rights in the Americas: Progress, Challenges and Prospects," in Mónica Serrano and Vesselin Popovski (eds.), *Human Rights Regimes in the Americas*, 228–43 (Tokyo: United Nations University Press).

Veiga, Raúl (1985), *Las organizaciones de derechos humanos* (Buenos Aires: Centro Editor de América Latina).

Vivanco, José Miguel and Daniel Wilkinson (2010), "Battling against the Odds: Human Rights in Hard Times," in Mónica Serrano and Vesselin Popovski (eds.), *Human Rights Regimes in the Americas*, 207–27 (Tokyo: United Nations University Press).

Wolff, Jonas (2013), "Towards Post-Liberal Democracy in Latin America? A Conceptual Framework Applied to Bolivia," *Journal of Latin American Studies* 45(1), 31–59.

Wolff, Jonas (2020), "Contention by Marginalized Groups and Political Change in Latin America: An Overview," in Irene Weipert-Fenner and Jonas Wolff (eds.), *Socioeconomic Protests in MENA and Latin America. Egypt and Tunisia in Interregional Comparison*, 171–93 (Basingstoke: Palgrave Macmillan).

Zunino, Marcos (2019), *Justice Framed: A Genealogy of Transitional Justice* (Cambridge: Cambridge University Press).

CHAPTER 26

ENVIRONMENTAL MOBILIZATION IN LATIN AMERICA

Beyond the Lenses of Social Movements

LUCAS G. CHRISTEL AND RICARDO A. GUTIÉRREZ

Introduction

A large part of the world's natural resources is found in Latin America and the Caribbean, including about a quarter of the planet's arable land and just over a fifth of its forest area, as well as considerable fossil fuel reserves. Since the 1980s, the region has undergone three parallel processes: (1) the expansion of extractive and primary industries, (2) a growing social mobilization over environmental issues, and (3) the emergence of new state regulations on environmental protection. Environmental mobilization in Latin America and the Caribbean has thus occurred and grown as part of complex and often contradictory interactions with both economic reprimarization and state environmentalism. Upon the third wave of democratization, environmental mobilization and participation increased all across Latin America and the Caribbean, encompassing disparate groups, issues, claims, and forms of action.

This chapter reviews and discusses the vast literature on environmental mobilization in the region from the 1980s on. Reviewing this literature is challenging given not only the diversity of the phenomena studied but also the plurality of the disciplines and approaches underlining the studies. We will address this challenge by undertaking a wide examination of works that reflects, as much as possible, the plurality of views and voices on environmental mobilization.

There is a tendency in the literature to use the term environmental "movement" as tantamount to "mobilization" or "organization," while only a few studies elaborate what an environmental movement is and what the conditions for its existence are. Given this lack of precision in using the term movement and the fact that several studies do not use it at all, we seek to answer to what extent the concept of social movement is appropriate to understand environmental mobilization in Latin America and the Caribbean. In order to do so, we undertake a twofold analysis. In next section we summarize the general trends of environmental mobilization in the region and examine the way in which different approaches and case studies analyze key dimensions of mobilization. In the following section we review the way scholars use or not the concept of social movement and discuss the analytical scope of the concept in the study of environmental mobilization. In the closing section we offer some suggestions as to how the conceptual analysis of environmental mobilization can be improved.

Our starting point is the conceptual distinction between environmental mobilization and environmental movement. Building upon Tilly's (1978) classic definition of mobilization as active participation in public life, we understand environmental mobilization as the collective action aiming to influence (in either contentious or institutionalized ways) the decisions regarding the political and economic regulation of the interactions between human beings and their environment. This definition is flexible enough as to capture the complex and multiple ways in which disparate actors with different resources mobilize and interact around environmental issues of all sorts, frame them in different manners, operate at multiple scales, and resort to diverse modes of action, as we examine in the first section.

According to Diani's (1992) definition, a social movement presents three key components: involvement in a given conflict; informal networks of interaction among a plurality of actors; and a shared collective identity. Following this definition, in the second section we analyze how these three key components are considered by the vast literature reviewed in this chapter. We find that only the involvement in an environmental conflict is a regular finding in the literature while the observation of a shared identity and the rigorous analysis of network exchange are minor concerns for the academic works under review. Based on these findings, we contend that the concept of environmental mobilization is better equipped than the notion of social movement to grasp the singularities of Latin American and Caribbean environmentalism.

General Trends of Environmental Mobilization

Given the social, political, economic, and environmental singularities of Latin American and Caribbean countries, it is not easy to identify a general trend that can encompass the manifold experiences and disputes over the environment. As Christen and colleagues (1998) point out, the Latin American environmentalism is too diverse and changing—not only cross-nationally but also within a single country—to be reduced to a unilineal narrative.

Nevertheless, some common features can be found. Conflicts over the environments have multiplied over the last decades. There has been a process of increasing environmental mobilization that started with minor or isolated concerns over very specific issues and has advanced towards more complex and conflictive scenarios where a wide range of environmental issues have been at stake and more actors have been involved.

The environment was not present in the public or government agenda until the mid-twentieth century. The early environmental activism was related to specific sectors such as the conservation of wildlands and biodiversity preservation. The emergence of environmentalism in countries like Costa Rica or Venezuela between the 1960s and the 1980s, for instance, centered on the preservation of forest lands (Christen et al. 1998). Early environmental advocacy was led by elite conservationist groups, that is, middle class people with access to state resources and links to international NGOs with capacity to fund conservation projects. Conservationist and middle-class groups that formed during this first wave of environmentalism would remain central to the environmental arena during the following decades.

A second wave of environmentalism emerged by the end of the 1980s, when manifold grassroots and local organizations started to question and dispute the costs and benefits of the use of the environment, mostly through contentious actions (Carruthers 2008). Local environmental conflicts multiplied all over the region, and different views on the economic activities and the value and protection of the environment increasingly antagonized each other. This outbreak of grassroots organizations is no doubt an element that dominates the current stage of environmental mobilization in Latin America and the Caribbean, either because of their individual actions or because of their participation in wider networks or coalitions.

According to some authors (Svampa 2012; Viola 1992), a third wave or form of environmentalism seems to have been taking place since the 1990s or the turn of the twenty-first century. This third wave would be characterized by the merging of environmental mobilization and groups with other social movements, especially peasant and indigenous movements (see Rice, Welch in this volume). For instance, Viola (1992) distinguishes social movements from what he calls historical movements as different expressions of Brazilian environmentalism. Environmentally oriented historical movements entail the appropriation of environmental ideas and concerns by preexisting social movements (such as the indigenous and the women's movements). In a similar vein, Svampa (2012) speaks of socio-environmentalism to refer to the "environmentalization" of indigenous and peasant movements that occurred towards the late 1990s and the turn of the twenty-first century as a consequence of the advance of extractive activities and large infrastructure projects.

The three waves of environmentalism that have emerged in Latin America actually reflect different approaches to environmental mobilization in the region. As we will see in the following subsections, each approach renders a different view on the key dimensions of environmental mobilization: types of groups involved and resources mobilized, issues in question and frames deployed, modes of action and participation, scales of mobilization, relations to the state, influence of political and economic contexts.

Types of Actors Involved and Resources Mobilized

Consistent with the three waves of environmentalism presented above, the literature on environmental mobilization in Latin America and the Caribbean identifies three main types of actors: professional organizations, grassroots groups, and environmental movements. The main differences among the works reviewed lie on how the actors and the interactions among them are conceived.

Some authors (e.g., Baver and Lynch 2006; Bull and Aguilar-Støen 2015; Christen et al. 1998; Lewis 2016) portray an environmental field made up of two very distinctive and opposing types of groups: elite organizations versus grassroots groups (cf. Gutiérrez and Isuani 2014 on the distinction between professional and grassroots organizations). Different labels are used for each type. Elite, professional, or non-governmental organizations have paid an important role in environmental activism in cases such as Brazil, Costa Rica, Ecuador, México, Venezuela, and the Caribbean countries (Baver and Lynch 2006; Christen et al. 1998; Lewis 2016). Grassroots groups typically (but not only) include indigenous and peasant communities and are identified as local populations (Bull and Aguilar-Støen 2015), grassroots environmentalists (Christen et al. 1998), or community groups (Baver and Lynch 2006). The presence of grassroots organizations is reported all across the region, from Chile and Argentina to Mexico and the Caribbean (Baver and Lynch 2006; Bebbington 2011a; Bebbington and Bury 2013; Carruthers 2008; Christen et al. 1998; Foyer and Dumoulin Kevran 2015; Gutiérrez and Isuani 2014).

Instead of non-touching or opposing forces, others see professional organizations and grassroots groups as forming part of a same alliance or coalition and emphasize how different types of actors work together around a specific environmental "conflict" or "struggle." Examples of this approach can be found in the struggle against military control of the Vieques Island in Puerto Rico (McCaffrey and Baver 2006), the defense of transhumance and ancestral lands in Northern Argentina (Domínguez 2008), the resistances to open pit mining across Latin America (Cisneros 2016), and the influence of environmental coalitions on Argentine environmental policymaking (Gutiérrez 2018).

Finally, some scholars also conceive non-governmental organizations and grassroots and community groups as mobilizing together but with an important difference. They contend that both types of actors are part of a same environmental movement, as in the cases of Brazil (Viola 1992), Puerto Rico (Valdés Pizzini 2006), Mexico (Foyer and Dumoulin Kevran 2015; Velázquez López Velarde, Somuano Ventura, and Ortega Ortiz 2018) and the local struggles against mining in Peru and Ecuador (Bebbington et al. 2011).

Seen as ideal types, elite organizations are private organizations officially recognized by the state; they tend to be professionalized, rely on paid staff, have office installations, and may be funded by international donors or through state programs (Baver and Lynch 2006; Lewis 2016). Grassroots groups are made up of individuals bound together for a common issue, their work is often precipitated by local challenges, their resource base relies on volunteer work, and they are independent from international funding (Lewis 2016). Social movements build around networks of different actors (either elite or grassroots groups) that share some common values or identity and frame their claims along multiple issues—environment, community development, indigenous rights, health, and so on (Svampa 2012; Viola 1992). They may combine the resources of grassroots groups and elite organizations.

Issues in Question and Frames Deployed

Environmental mobilization in Latin America and the Caribbean involves a great heterogeneity of issues and frames.[1] Nevertheless, it is possible to identify two general trends as regards the number of issues addressed: a single-issue versus a multi-issue approach.

The early environmental mobilizations in the region have been characterized by a single-issue approach. Different elitist environmental groups mostly pursued specific conservationist issues and were under the influence of international environmental organization. But single-issue approaches have also been present in more recent experiences. For instance, conservation, biodiversity, and the protection of virgin lands have been central issues of the early elite environmental mobilizations in Brazil, Costa Rica, and Venezuela (Christen et al. 1998), while the opposition to open pit mining and hydrocarbons extraction dominates many more recent struggles in the Andean countries (Bebbington 2011a; Bebbington and Bury 2013; Cisneros 2016).

From a grassroots perspective, some authors point to the existence of a specific link between a single issue and a given territory. That link usually revolves around the defense of a lifestyle closely connected to local livelihood and ancestral subsistence practices. Examples of this are the claims around the impacts of tourism in Martinique in the 1990s (Burac 2006) as well as the struggles for land tenure in Costa Rica (Cordero Ulate 2015) and the emergence of environmental movements opposing mining in specific areas of Peru and Ecuador at the turn of the twentieth century (Bebbington et al. 2011).

As already said, the multi-issue approach is typical of social movements. Although the literature on social movements tends to focus on issues related to the depletion of natural resources (Foyer and Dumoulin Kevran 2015; Svampa 2012; Valdés Pizzini 2006; Velázquez López Velarde, Somuano Ventura, and Ortega Ortiz 2018), other multi-issue studies pay more attention to urban problems and the access to public goods and services. Interconnected issues such as urban expansion, access to drinkable water, and waste management have been central, for instance, in El Salvador (Cartagena Cruz 2015), Argentina (Gutiérrez 2018; Merlinsky 2013), and Brazil (Lemos and Looye 2003).

Latin American and Caribbean environmental mobilization presents a wide variety as regards the framing of environmental issues. Despite that, a general distinction can be made between status quo frames and more radical frames. On the one hand, elite environmentalists typically make their claims from a perspective that holds that environment sustainability is compatible with, or does not contradict, economic development. Thus, their most recurrent framings reflect different approaches to sustainable development (Lewis 2016) and an "environment-economy" perspective that proposes environmental protection as way to secure natural resources-based development (Jácome 2006). On the other hand, scholars that focus on grassroots groups or environmental movements account for more critical or radical frames. Radical framing includes different environmental justice frames (Acselrad 2010; Carruthers 2008; Lynch 2006) as well as frames that dispute the bases of the current development model, such as popular ecologism and eco-resistance (Lewis 2016; Martínez-Alier, Baud, and Séjenovich 2016). These radical frames shape the struggles of different actors such as women movements, independent unions, and indigenous and peasant groups that call for environmental and nature rights, climate justice, or non-extractivist uses of natural resources (Carruthers 2008; Lewis 2016; Martínez-Alier, Baud, and Séjenovich 2016).

Different authors emphasize how wide and flexible frames, as well as reframing processes, favor the formation of alliances, coalitions, and networks of different types of actors. For instance, the reframing of local grievances from their economic nature to environmental justice focusing on health, environment, and human rights has been crucial in the Vieques struggle in Puerto Rico (McCaffrey and Baver 2006); the confluence of environmentalist and indigenous groups went hand in hand with the merging of the sustainable development language and collective rights discourses in Northern Argentina (Dominguez 2008); and the progressive transition towards a sustainable development frame marked the consolidation of Brazilian environmentalism (Viola 1992).

Modes of Action and Participation

The literature on environmental mobilization in Latin America and the Caribbean reproduces the classic distinction between contentious and institutional modes of action (cf. Christel and Gutiérrez 2017 on this distinction). As seen by the literature, some groups focus mostly on one mode of action while others usually combine contentious and institutional types of participation.

The institutional modes of participation are mostly used by elite organizations or groups that are highly institutionalized (Bull and Aguilar-Støen 2015) and usually engage in collaborative interactions with the state (Christen et al. 1998; Lewis 2016). Instead, according to some authors, grassroots groups and environmental movements mostly perform contentious actions and see the state in an adversarial way (Baver and Lynch 2006; Martínez-Alier, Baud, and Séjenovich 2016) or have a limited capacity (or interest) to influence state decisions (Bull and Aguilar-Støen 2015; Edwards and Roberts 2015).

Nevertheless, some studies claim that pro-environment alliances, coalitions, and networks can combine contentious and traditional or institutionalized modes of actions (Bebbington et al. 2011; Christel and Gutiérrez 2017; Domínguez 2008; Viola 1992). Demonstrations, marches, blockades, strikes, signed petitions, and the like combine with institutionalized venues such as legal actions in subnational struggles against mining in Argentina (Christel 2020), consultations and plebiscites over forest management in Costa Rica (Cordero Ulate 2015) and large-scale mining projects in several countries (Walter and Urkidi 2016), and lobbying in the Vieques Struggle in Puerto Rico (McCaffrey and Baver 2006).

Scales of Mobilization

Environmental mobilization occurs at different scales in Latin America and the Caribbean. The literature shows that environmental mobilization may take place at the local, national, regional, or international level. It also shows that a same mobilization may scale up through several levels (see Spalding, von Bülow in this volume).

Some studies emphasize that grassroots mobilization is place-based and locally restricted, as is the case of mining conflicts in Guatemala (Aguilar-Støen 2015) and the many experiences of popular ecologism across the region (Martínez-Alier, Baud, and Séjenovich 2016). Others show that elite organizations usually work at different levels within a country and may have links with international organizations and donors (Christen et al. 1998; Lewis 2016). Altogether, these studies suggest that the chances of scaling up tend to be higher for the elite organizations than for grassroots groups.

Other studies, instead, show that local conflict can grow from the local to the national level (or to the provincial/state level in federal countries like Argentina and Brazil) or even go global, as in the conflict over the Belo Monte dam in Brazil (Bratman 2015) or many mining conflicts across the different countries (Alvarado Merino 2008; Walter and Urikidi 2015). The literature on environmental movements also entails a multiple-scale analysis as it centers on the networking that takes place through different levels within a given country and also at the international level (Bebbington et al. 2011; Svampa 2012; Velázquez López Velarde, Somuano Ventura, and Ortega Ortiz 2018; Viola 1992). In many cases, international partners are extremely important because they provide not only political, economic, logistic, and knowledge support from abroad but also access to international arenas. Thanks to all these national and transnational networks, alliances and coalitions, grassroots groups, and/or professional organizations can transcend the kind of "particularism" of local conflicts pointed out by several studies.

Relations to the State

Although this dimension is not explicitly examined by many studies on environmental mobilization, we distinguish in the literature two main ways in which social actors interact with the state: adversarial versus collaborative interaction (see Annunziata and Goldfrank, Gurza Lavalle and Szwako in this volume).

On one side of the equation, some authors show that grassroots groups (Martínez-Alier, Baud, and Séjenovich 2016) and environmental movements (Bebbington et al.

2011; Svampa 2012; Valdes Pizzini 2006) typically engage in an adversarial relation to the state. On the opposite side, professional or elite organizations are supposed to build a more collaborative interaction with the state (Christen et al. 1998; Gutiérrez and Isuani 2014; Lewis 2016).

A more balanced view is rendered by studies that point to different cases of alliances and networks in which local or municipal governments and other state agents join or support grassroots groups, professional organizations, and other social actors (Cartagena Cruz 2015; Christel 2020; Cordero Ulate 2015; McCaffrey and Baver 2006). Local governments are crucial allies in the opposition to the central government. As highlighted by Walter and Urkidi (2015) in their study of struggles against mining in Argentina, Colombia, Ecuador, Guatemala, and Peru, local authorities bring formal legitimacy to the demands of an environmental coalition, especially through the implementation of bottom-up consultations and plebiscites. In the same vein, Viola (1992) contests the state-society divide that informs much of the social movement literature by arguing that the environmental movement grew across all sectors in Brazil: civil society, the state, business, and science. Viola (ibid.) also argues that Brazilian environmental organizations and groups underwent a progressive process of professionalization during the 1980s, with a consequent switch towards a more moderate relation to the state.

Influence of Political and Economic Contexts

The influence of political and economic contexts has received less attention than the previous dimensions of environmental mobilization. With a few exceptions, contextual factors are particularly considered by scholars that see environmental mobilization through the lenses of social movements. Nevertheless, a few studies properly trace the causal mechanisms linking contextual factors and environmental mobilization. Important exceptions can be found in Bebbington's (2011a) and Bebbington and Bury's (2013) edited volumes on mining and hydrocarbons in South America as well as McCaffrey and Baver's (2006) study on Puerto Rico.

As a general characterization, we can distinguish between some studies that focus on national conditions and others that mainly focus on the international context. On the one hand, Velázquez López Velarde, Somuano Ventura, and Ortega Ortiz (2018) focus on the impact of Mexican domestic political factors such as the political opportunity structure, political alliances and coalitions, state capacities, and public opinion. On the other, in their study of the Vieques struggle in Puerto Rico, McCaffrey and Baver (2006) show how changes in the political opportunity structure at the international level affect (both negatively and positively) the prospects of environmental mobilization. Instead, Svampa (2012) and Bebbington et al. (2011) pay more attention to the international economic context and holds that the reprimarization of domestic economies fuels the struggles over land and the environment. In an intermediate space, Viola (1992) refers to both the international context and the domestic opportunity structure as a general background of the Brazilian environmental movement.

The Notion of Social Movement

How appropriate is the concept of social movement to understand environmental mobilization in Latin America and the Caribbean? The term "movement" is as profusely as vaguely used by scholarly works on environmental mobilization in the region. Not surprisingly, this holds true for several studies centered on elite organizations, grassroots groups, or environmental coalitions that occasionally use the term movement. But, as we will discuss in this section, conceptual shortcomings are also present in most works that try to make a case for the existence of environmental movements in Latin America and the Caribbean.

The notion of movement is referred to in several studies that emphasize the distinction between elite organizations and grassroots groups but in most cases without any proper conceptual definition or discussion. For instance, in the volume edited by Baver and Lynch (2006), all chapters that talk about an "environmental movement" also deny its existence (with the partial exception of the piece by Valdés Pizzini on Puerto Rico) by saying that the movement is diverse, scattered, and fragmented, lacking any unity. It is not therefore clear what they mean by "movement." By and large, the term environmental movement is uncritically used in these works as synonymous of environmental mobilization or environmental organizations.

In her study of Ecuador, Lewis (2016) refers to an ongoing discussion about whether there is or not an Ecuadorian environmental movement but never defines environmental movement properly nor she establishes what the conditions for talking about an environmental movement are. Even though she says that the predominant view seems to be that there is not an Ecuadorian environmental movement, Lewis is not conclusive on this point. In any case, it is clear that the wide diversity of Ecuadorian environmental organizations and activists portrayed by Lewis would not pass the test of any standard definition of social movement such of those by Tarrow (2011) or Diani (1992).

This lack of precision in using and referring to the notion of social movement is not surprising as this dichotomic view digs a rift between elite/non-governmental organizations and grassroots/community groups. Besides this rift, two additional points impede the dichotomic view from pinpointing environmental mobilization in terms of social movement: (1) the limited geographical scope of grassroots mobilization and (2) the competence among elite organizations for international funding and the dominance of the environmental agenda.

In contrast to the dichotomic view, there are numerous works that pay special attention to alliances, coalitions, and networks between social actors of different sorts and between them and state actors without making a case for the existence of environmental movements (Alvarado Merino 2008; Bratman 2015; Cisneros 2016; Cordero Ulate 2015; Domínguez 2008; McCaffrey and Baver 2006; Merlinsky 2013). Environmental alliances, coalitions, or networks typically pursue common, territorially bounded goals and confront other alliances, coalitions, or networks with opposing goals. Nevertheless, a few of these works (e.g., Cordero Ulate 2015; Domínguez 2008; Merlinsky 2013) do refer to the notion of environmental movement as equivalent to environmental mobilization or organization.

Merlinsky (2013), for instance, speaks of socio-environmental or citizen movements in Argentina but without developing any conceptual discussion of the term "movement." Domínguez (2008) speaks of the "global environmental movement" as an opportunity structure for local mobilization in Northern Argentina, but there is no discussion of what such a movement means. In his analysis of the Costa Rican "environmental movement," Cordero Ulate (2015) vaguely defines a social movement as the combination of structures of mobilization and specific collective actions. Without pursuing a further discussion of the concepts of social movement and environmental movement, Cordero Ulate (ibid.) reaches a contradictory conclusion. He asserts that there is a Costa Rican environmental movement, but he also points out that this movement is fragmented and discontinuous, and it lacks a unifying project or a shared view. Therefore, as with some dichotomic works, it seems that what Cordero Ulate calls a Costa Rican environmental movement lacks the main characteristics of any canonic definition of social movement—such as common goal, shared identity, and structuring network.

As expected, the literature that emphasizes the existence of environmental movements engages in a deeper conceptual discussion of the notion of social movement. By and large, two elements are common in the definitions of environmental (social) movements found in the literature: network of actors and shared identities or visions. Velázquez López Velarde, Somuano Ventura, and Ortega Ortiz (2018) define environmental movement as a network of individuals and groups moved by a common identity or a shared environmental concern. Among all definitions here reviewed, this is the one closest to canonic definitions of social movement that include shared identity. But like other authors, Velázquez López Velarde, Somuano Ventura, and Ortega Ortiz (2018) hold that within a given country (i.e., Mexico) there are several environmental movements, each of them pursuing a single issue.

Close to Velázquez López Velarde, Somuano Ventura, and Ortega Ortiz's (2018) definition, Svampa (2012) holds that socio-environmental or socio-territorial movements are tantamount to new social movements. Centered on conflicts around the access to and control of natural resources (with focus on indigenous and peasant communities), socio-environmental movements provide common frameworks for collective action and, as such, are "producers of a collective subjectivity," that is, they have a common identity that makes disparate groups part of a same social movement. Nevertheless, Svampa (2012) does not show or discuss how such a collective subjectivity is built or how it works to support a socio-environmental movement.

Viola (1992) focuses on shared values rather than on common identity. He discusses both the concept of social movement and its distinction from what he calls a historical movement. The difference lies on the position towards capitalism: while social movements seek to transform the capitalist social structure, historical movements are reformist by definition and point to the embodiment of post-materialist values. Based upon this distinction, Viola (ibid.) defines the Brazilian environmental movement as a historical movement. The distinction between social movement and historical movement actually replicates the classical distinction between revolutionary and reformist social movements. Regardless of that distinction, Viola does not elaborate further on how post-materialist, environmentalist values build and operate to form the Brazilian environmental movement.

Bebbington (2011b) distinguishes between social movement and network and defines the former as collective action processes involving actors with an important overlapping of visions. More than anything else, it is the overlapping of visions (rather than identity) that sustains and gives coherence to the movement. But networks, understood as structures of social relations among visible actors, are also important. Preexistent networks bring forth and sustain social movements. In the end, social movements comprise overlapping visions and networks of actors.

Similar to Bebbington (2011b), Foyer and Dumoulin Kevran (2015) understand environmental movement as something between a mere network for exchanging information and a social movement based on shared identity and strategy. What unites an environmental movement are complementarity and division of labor plus a set of common values. Networks (or coalitions) are also important, but the authors conceive the Mexican environmental movement as composed of two distinctive networks with no clear connection: a sustainable community development network and an environmental resistance network. So, as with Velázquez López Velarde, Somuano Ventura, and Ortega Ortiz's (2018) work, the question remains open as to whether there is or not a Mexican environmental movement.

To sum up, we find that the notion of social movement is used by most authors in vague or contradictory ways. We also find that the three key components of a social movement—involvement in a given conflict, informal networks of interaction, and a common collective identity—are not necessarily all together, even in those few works that try to make a case for the existence of environmental movements.

To start with, only the involvement in an environmental conflict is common to all studies on environmental mobilization—and not only in those centered on environmental movements. There is no doubt about the multiplicity of issues addressed by the literature and the multiplication of environmental struggles in Latin America and the Caribbean over the past decades.

Second, the existence of a shared identity—a major concern for the social movement literature—is absent in most of the literature. Furthermore, identity is only important to a few social movement scholars, while others stress that environmental movements are built upon common values or overlapping visions rather than a shared identity. It follows that the presence of a shared collective identity is not a main feature of environmental mobilizations in Latin America and the Caribbean. Therefore, a concept of social movement based on shared identity does not seem appropriate to deal with the mobilization of a plurality of actors who pursue a common goal and/or are bound by common values or overlapping visions.

Third, the functioning of informal networks is addressed by most works reviewed, especially those with a greater emphasis in alliances, coalitions, and social movements.

Despite this, the analysis of networks is, by and large, methodologically weak as there is not a systematic effort to measure them in a way similar, for instance, to Diani's (1995) reconstruction of the Italian environmental movement. This poses a particular challenge to social movement scholars who should prove the existence of working networks beyond the narrative of specific environmental mobilizations and conflicts. In the meantime, a question remains open: to what extent can we say that environmental actors indeed develop regular and systematic exchanges—typical of social movements—or only engage in sporadic and intermittent interactions?

Based on these findings, we conclude that the concept of social movement is not the soundest one by which to grasp the singularities of Latin American and Caribbean environmentalism. Instead, we argue that the notion of environmental mobilization is more appropriate to deal with those singularities and propose a wide definition of the concept in order to include the variety of cases studied by the literature. As already said, we define environmental mobilization as a collective action aiming to influence (in either contentious or institutionalized ways) the decisions regarding the political and economic regulation of the interactions between human beings and their environment. This definition is flexible enough to capture the eminently complex scenarios in which disparate actors with different identities and visions converge on manifold environmental issues, operate at multiple scales, and resort to diverse modes of action in order to achieve a common goal. Most case studies show that what unites a bunch of multifold actors in a same mobilization process is the pursuit of a common goal (rather than a common identity or even a common vision) and that in most cases such a common goal is territorially bounded. We understand that our concept of environmental mobilization is better equipped than the notion of social movement to grasp the real-life of such experiences of environmental struggle.

Conclusion

Throughout this chapter we have seen that the notion of social movement either is not used or is vaguely used by most studies on Latin American and Caribbean environmentalism. We have also seen that those few works that make a case for the existence of environmental movements in the region use the concept in such different and even contradictory ways that it is impossible to derive from them any comprehensive understanding of what an environmental movement is and how it works. We argue that underlying this lack of precision is the complex real life of environmental mobilization which cannot be grasped by the concept of social movement. That is why we propose a more basic definition of environmental mobilization in order to deal with the various and reach environmental struggles that have expanded all across the region during the last decades, most of which have built on locally bounded, common goals rather than shared identities and multiple-issue networks.

But how to improve the conceptual analysis of environmental mobilization? In this closing section we offer some suggestions regarding each of the components of our definition of environmental mobilization: collective action, the search for political influence, political and economic decisions over the environment, and the interactions between humans and their environment.

First, a better conceptualization of the type of collective action involved in environmental mobilization is needed. Above all, any dichotomic analysis of actors and modes of action must be avoided. Studies centered on coalitions, networks, and social movements underline the increasing combination of contentious actions with institutional participation channels. This is key because actors rarely pursue their goals alone or act in a similar way—they learn, make strategic decisions, seek allies, and take opportunities to achieve their collective goals. We must therefore improve our knowledge of how networks and coalitions operate, intensifying our theoretical and methodological efforts to move forward with their empirical determination (see Spalding in this volume). When the focus is on specific territorial conflicts, networks can be identified through narrative and qualitative methods. But if we want to move beyond local sites and specific territorial conflicts, we need other tools to deal with networks. Furthermore, if we are to focus on networks and coalitions, we need to pay more attention to the interactive dynamics of coalitions by studying not only the "environmental" coalition but also the working of the coalition that opposes environmental regulation.

Second, we need to pay more attention to the search for political influence. Those who mobilize and build networks and coalitions with others typically do so to influence those in charge of political and economic decisions that affect the environment. The relation between mobilization goals and demands, on the one hand, and political and economic decisions, on the other, is troublesome. Mobilization can and does change political and economic decisions. But how do we know when mobilization actually has an impact on decision-making and what impact it has? In our review of the literature on Latin America and the Caribbean we notice that the impact of environmental mobilization has not been deeply examined (Christel and Gutiérrez 2021). A greater conceptualization and empirical research of political impacts is much needed, taking into account the distinction and relations between the desired impacts, the impacts achieved, and the undesired consequences.

Third, and closely connected to the previous point, we must increase our knowledge of the making of political and economic regulations over the environment. In doing so, we must be prevented from simplistic views according to which state and economic actors always reject higher environmental regulation and therefore oppose environmental mobilization. As shown by a large part of the literature and our own research, there are many cases in which certain state agents and/or economic actors engage in the defense of environmental protection. More attention to the bureaucratic working of state actors and the way they, as well as some economic actors, search for strategic allies is needed for a better understanding of environmental mobilization and its political impacts.

Finally, by looking more seriously to the interactions between humans and their environment we can unveil the multiple dimensions of environmental mobilization (see Halvorsen and Rossi in this volume). Either in very local struggles or in the advocacy of global issues, environmental mobilization is never just about preserving "nature" or "the environment." While ecological sustainability may be the common ground of environmental demands, all cases of environmental mobilization merge environmental concerns with concrete preoccupations with livelihood, habitat, wellbeing, and equality as well as political, social, and even religious values. Therefore, a deep analysis of environmental mobilization in Latin America and the Caribbean may shed light on the different ways in which humans interact with their environment.

Note

1. The term frame is used here in a wide sense, following Goffman's (1974: 21) classic definition: "schemata of interpretation that enable individuals to locate, perceive, identify, and label occurrences within their life space and the world at large. By rendering events or occurrences meaningful, frames function to organize experience and guide action, whether individual or collective." Under this definition, frames may embrace either worldviews or strategic interpretations.

References

Acselrad, Henri (2010), "Ambientalização das lutas sociais: O caso do movimento por justiça ambiental," *Estudos Avançados* 24(68), 103–19.

Aguilar-Støen, Mariel (2015), "Staying the Same: Transnational Elites, Mining and Environmental Governance in Guatemala," in Benedicte Bull and Mariel Aguilar-Støen (eds.), *Environmental Politics in Latin America: Elite Dynamics, the Left Tide and Sustainable Development*, 131–49 (London: Routledge).

Alvarado Merino, Gina (2008), "Políticas neoliberales en el manejo de los recursos naturales en Perú: El caso del conflicto agrominero de Tambogrande," in Gina Alvarado Merino, Carlo Delgado Ramos, Diego Domínguez, Cecília Campello do Amaral Mello, Iliana Monterroso, and Guillermo Wilde (eds.), *Gestión ambiental y conflicto social en América Latina*, 67–103 (Buenos Aires: CLACSO).

Baver, Sherrie L. and Barbara Deutsch Lynch (eds.) (2006), *Beyond Sun and Sand: Caribbean Environmentalisms* (New Brunswick, NJ: Rutgers University Press).

Bebbington, Anthony (ed.) (2011a), *Minería, movimientos sociales y respuestas campesinas: Una ecología política de transformaciones territoriales* (Lima: IEP-CEPES).

Bebbington, Anthony (2011b), "Elementos para una ecología política de los movimientos sociales y el desarrollo territorial en zonas mineras," in Anthony Bebbington (ed.), *Minería, movimientos sociales y respuestas campesinas: una ecología política de transformaciones territoriales*, 53–76 (Lima: IEP-CEPES).

Bebbington, Anthony, Jeffrey Bury, Denisse Humphreys Bebbington, Jeannet Lingán, Juan Pablo Muñoz, and Martín Scurrah (2011), "Movimientos sociales, lazos transnacionales y desarrollo territorial rural en zonas de influencia minera: Cajamarca-Perú y Cotacachi-Ecuador," in Anthony Bebbington (ed.), *Minería, movimientos sociales y respuestas campesinas: Una ecología política de transformaciones territoriales*, 193–260 (Lima: IEP-CEPES).

Bebbington, Anthony and Jeffrey Bury (eds.) (2013), *Subterranean Struggles: New Dynamics of Mining, Oil and Gas in Latin America* (Austin: University of Texas Press).

Bratman, Eve (2015), "Passive Revolution in the Green Economy: Activism and the Belo Monte Dam," *International Environmental Agreements: Politics, Law and Economics* 15(1), 61–77.

Bull, Benedicte and Mariel Aguilar-Støen (eds.) (2015), *Environmental Politics in Latin America: Elite Dynamics, the Left Tide and Sustainable Development* (London: Routledge).

Burac, Maurice (2006), "The Struggle for Sustainable Tourism in Martinique," in Sherrie L. Baver and Barbara Deutsch Lynch (eds.), *Beyond Sun and Sand: Caribbean Environmentalisms*, 65–74 (New Brunswick, NJ: Rutgers University Press).

Carruthers, David V. (ed.) (2008), *Environmental Justice in Latin America: Problems, Promise, and Practice* (Cambridge, MA: The MIT Press).

Cartagena Cruz, Rafael (2015), "Environmental Conflicts and Social Movements in Postwar El Salvador," In Paul Almeida and Allen Cordero Ulate (eds.), *Handbook of Social Movements across Latin America*, 237–54 (New York: Springer).

Christel, Lucas G. (2020), "Resistencias sociales y legislaciones mineras en las provincias argentinas: Los casos de Mendoza, Córdoba, Catamarca y San Juan (2003–2009)," *Política y Gobierno* 27(1), 1–24.

Christel, Lucas G. and Ricardo A. Gutiérrez (2017), "Making Rights Come Alive: Environmental Rights and Modes of Participation in Argentina," *Journal of Environment & Development* 26(3), 322–47.

Christel, Lucas G. and Ricardo A. Gutiérrez (2021), "The Political Impact of Environmental Mobilization: A Theoretical Discussion in the Light of the Argentine Case," *Journal of Latin American and Caribbean Studies* 46(1), 57–76, 322–47.

Christen, Catherine, Selene Herculano, Kathryn Hochstetler, Renae Prell, Marie Price, and J. Timmons Roberts (1998), "Latin American Environmentalism: Comparative Views," *Studies in Comparative International Development* 32(2), 58–87.

Cisneros, Paul (ed.) (2016), *Política minera y sociedad civil en América Latina* (Quito: Editorial IAEN).

Cordero Ulate, Allen (2015), "Forest, Water, and Struggle: Environmental Movements in Costa Rica," in Paul Almeida and Allen Cordero Ulate (eds.), *Handbook of Social Movements across Latin America*, 255–71 (New York: Springer).

Diani, Mario (1992), "The Concept of Social Movement," *The Sociological Review* 40(1), 1–25.

Diani, Mario (1995), *Green Networks: A Structural Analysis of the Italian Environmental Movement* (Edinburgh: Edinburgh University Press).

Domínguez, Diego (2008), "La transhumancia de los campesinos kollas: ¿Hacia un modelo de desarrollo sustentable?," in Gina Alvarado Merino, Carlo Delgado Ramos, Diego Domínguez, Cecília Campello do Amaral Mello, Iliana Monterroso, and Guillermo Wilde (eds.), *Gestión ambiental y conflicto social en América Latina*, 137–91 (Buenos Aires: CLACSO).

Edwards, Guy and J. Timmons Roberts (2015), *A Fragmented Continent: Latin America and the Global Politics of Climate Change* (Cambridge, MA: The MIT Press).

Foyer, Jean and David Dumoulin Kevran (2015), "The Environmentalism of NGOs versus Environmentalism of the Poor? Mexico's Social-Environmental Coalitions," in Paul Almeida and Allen Cordero Ulate (eds.), *Handbook of Social Movements across Latin America*, 223–35 (New York: Springer).

Goffman, Erving (1974), *Frame Analysis* (New York: Harper Colphon).
Gutiérrez, Ricardo A. (ed.) 2018, *Construir el ambiente: Sociedad, estado y políticas ambientales en Argentina* (Buenos Aires: Teseo).
Gutiérrez, Ricardo A., and Fernando J. Isuani (2014), "La emergencia del ambientalismo estatal y social en Argentina," *Revista de Administração Pública* 48(2), 295–322.
Jacome, Francine (2006), "Environmental movements in the Caribbean," in Sherrie L. Baver and Barbara Deutsch Lynch (eds.), *Beyond Sun and Sand: Caribbean Environmentalisms*, 17–34 (New Brunswick, NJ: Rutgers University Press).
Lemos, María C. and Johanna Looye (2003), "Looking for Sustainability: Environmental Coalitions across the State-Society Divide," *Bulletin of Latin American Research* 22(3), 350–370.
Lewis, Tammy L. (2016), *Ecuador's Environmental Revolutions: Ecoimperialists, Ecodependents, and Ecoresisters* (Cambridge, MA: The MIT Press).
Lynch, Barbara D. (2006), "Conclusion: Toward a Creole Environmentalism," in Sherrie L. Baver and Barbara Deutsch Lynch (eds.), *Beyond Sun and Sand: Caribbean Environmentalisms*, 158–70 (New Brunswick, NJ: Rutgers University Press).
Martínez-Alier, Joan, Michiel Baud, and Héctor Séjenovich (2016), "Origins and Perspectives of Latin American Environmentalism," in Fabio de Castro, Barbara Hogenboom, and Michiel Baud (eds.), *Environmental Governance in Latin America*, 29–56 (New York: Palgrave-Macmillan).
McCaffrey, Katherine T. and Sherrie L. Baver (2006), "'Ni Una Bomba Más': Reframing the Vieques Struggle," in Sherrie L. Baver and Barbara Deutsch Lynch (eds.), *Beyond Sun and Sand: Caribbean Environmentalisms*, 109–28 (New Brunswick: Rutgers University Press).
Merlinsky, Gabriela (ed.) (2013), *Cartografías del conflicto ambiental en Argentina* (Buenos Aires: CICCUS).
Svampa, Maristella (2012), "Consenso de los commodities, giro ecoterritorial y pensamiento crítico en América Latina," *Observatorio Social de América Latina* 13(32), 15–39.
Tarrow, Sidney (2011), *Power in Movement: Social Movements and Contentious Politics* (Cambridge: Cambridge University Press).
Tilly, Charles (1978), *From Mobilization to Revolution* (Reading, CT: Addison-Wesley).
Valdés Pizzini, Manuel (2006), "Historical Contentions and Future Trends in the Coastal Zones: The Environmental Movement in Puerto Rico," in Sherrie L. Baver and Barbara Deutsch Lynch (eds.), *Beyond Sun and Sand: Caribbean Environmentalisms*, 44–64 (New Brunswick, NJ: Rutgers University Press).
Velázquez López Velarde, Rodrigo, María Fernanda Somuano Ventura, and Reynaldo Yunuen Ortega Ortiz (2018), "David contra Goliat: ¿Cómo los movimientos ambientalistas se enfrentan a las grandes corporaciones?," *América Latina Hoy* 79, 41–58.
Viola, Eduardo J. (1992), "O movimento ambientalista no Brasil (1971–1991): Da denúncia e conscientização pública para a institucionalização e o desenvolvimento sustentável," in Mirian Golbenber (ed.), *Ecologia, ciência e política*, 49–75 (Rio de Janeiro: Revan).
Walter, Mariana and Leire Urkidi (2016). "Community Consultations: Local Responses to Large-Scale Mining in Latin America," in Fabio de Castro, Barbara Hogenboom, and Michiel Baud (eds.), *Environmental Governance in Latin America*, 287–325 (New York: Palgrave-Macmillan).

CHAPTER 27

URBAN SOCIAL MOVEMENTS AND THE POLITICS OF INCLUSION IN LATIN AMERICA

PHILIP OXHORN

Introduction

Although cities have been centers of social mobilization for centuries, it was only in the 1970s that Manuel Castells first identified *urban social movements* as a distinct form of social mobilization. His *magnum opus*, *The City and the Grassroots* (Castells 1983), brought together an impressive historical and geographic breadth of original research and challenged social movement scholars to rethink how they approached urban-based social mobilization. Most generally, urban social movements were associated with a more proactive understanding of citizenship and inclusion, what I characterize as *citizenship as agency*. Central to this conception of citizenship are the demands for improved collective consumption, respect for community culture, and political self-governance that urban social movements champion. In particular, Castells characterized urban social movements as a complex, multidimensional phenomenon that transcended more common analyses that focused on particular dimensions of social mobilization, such as social class, the politics of identity, and self-interested forms of collective political participation. It was also one of the few studies to attempt to situate the Latin American experience in a larger comparative perspective that included North America and Western Europe.

While Castell's unifying theoretical trope of an advanced capitalist world economy with interventionist states that require a revolutionary transformation seems dated in today's post-Cold War world that has been transformed by neoliberal policies, his comparative holistic approach is perhaps even more relevant. Theoretically, it can provide new insights into the relationship between identity-based social movements examined in the so-called New Social Movements literature (Garretón and Selamé, Fontana in this volume), and traditional social movements behaving in a strategic fashion in order to maximize achievement of their interests in competition with other movements and actors. Empirically, it allows for a more nuanced understanding of the potential for urban social movements to achieve their goals.

In what follows, the chapter first examines the unique nature of Latin America's urbanization during the post-World War II period and its implications for understanding urban social movements. It then explores the various factors contributing to an ascendancy of urban social movements that share key characteristics with identity-based New Social Movements and their potential contribution to greater social and political inclusion. The final section concludes with a discussion of the principal challenges urban social movements must overcome in order to ensure the resiliency of such contributions.

Social Class and the Challenge of Urban Social Mobilization in Post-World War II Latin America

Latin America experienced a generalized and very rapid process of urbanization during much of the post-World War II period. Closely linked to the region's highly unequal social structure, the particular pattern of urbanization that predominated was highly inhospitable for the emergence of urban social movements. Even Castells (1983) was surprised by the lack of socioeconomic inclusion and the inability of urban social movements to generate lasting change. The driving dynamic behind political participation in Latin America—and much of the world—after World War II was increasingly viewed as being determined by economic structure and social class. The Cold War served as an ideological backdrop for power struggles pitting those who benefitted from Latin America's extremes of inequality against the various social classes in pursuit of their own inclusion or seeking to overthrow capitalist economic system. Non-class identities, including that of "citizen" so closely linked to urban social movements, were at best viewed as marginal to political participation. At worst, they were seen to be part of the problem, rather than a source of solutions for achieving socioeconomic inclusion (Deutsch 1961; Lipset 1959).

Between 1940 and 1975, regional urbanization doubled, from 19.6% of the population to 40.5%, with a number of countries experiencing much higher rates of urbanization. This massive influx of migrants, mainly from rural areas, had important implications for popular sector inclusion. The sheer volume of urban migration combined with the state's unwillingness or inability to invest sufficiently in urban services to satisfy popular sector needs meant that the popular sectors ultimately assumed the responsibility for creating their own cities through various forms of self-help in the provision of housing and basic urban services. This required the creation of important networks within and across urban communities, but collective action remained locally focused with little autonomy to demand meaningful inclusion in the political realm (Castells 1983; Roberts 1981, 2005).

The catalyst for rapid urbanization was the region's new insertion in the international economy and the associated socioeconomic and political changes that accompanied it. The contraction of the international economic system due to the Great Depression and World War II led most countries to adopt an Import Substitution Industrialization (ISI) development model (see Rossi in this volume). The ensuing economic growth and ability of manufacturers to absorb labor costs due to the lack of external competition allowed for relatively higher wages and minimal social rights for growing segments of the population, particularly among the middle classes and workers in the formal sector (see Ramírez and Stoessel in this volume). Yet such gains were restricted to specific segments of the population, generally excluding the majority.

The new development model and changing international economic relations meant that virtually all Latin American countries underwent a process of social modernization between 1960 and 1980.[1] At the heart of this process of social modernization was a twenty-year period of strong and relatively sustained economic growth of 5% to 6% annually, which resulted in a doubling of per capita GDP in the region. Despite the disequilibria and inequalities associated with it, "this growth represented a true process of development" which affected the majority of people in practically every country of the region (CEPAL 1991: 22).

Throughout Latin America, there was a transfer of people from low productivity activities, especially in agriculture, to areas of greater productivity in manufacturing and the service sector in particular. In 1950, more than 50% of the economically active population (EAP) in three-quarters of the twenty countries included in the CEPAL study was engaged in agricultural activities, primarily in subsistence farming or traditional agriculture on low-productivity *latifundia*. By 1980, however, only three countries had populations that were primarily engaged in agricultural activities—El Salvador, Guatemala, and Haiti. In a number of countries, the EAP in agriculture had fallen by approximately 30% (CEPAL 1989: 51–54).

Increased investment in capital and improved skills in the work force allowed for the absorption of a growing proportion of the EAP in activities that were characterized not only by higher levels of productivity but also by higher incomes and social status. In particular, employment in the formal sector grew at a rate of 4% per year between 1950 and 1980 (Altimir 1998: 5) and real wages rose (Thorp 1998). One important consequence of these rapid socioeconomic changes was that 26% of the EAP experienced upward mobility in terms of their social status and incomes between 1960 and 1980 according to a CEPAL study of general "structural mobility" in ten countries at various levels of social modernization.[2]

Despite often remarkable and rapid socioeconomic change, the region remained among the most unequal in the world. The foundation for such endemic inequality was the region's highly asymmetrical, segmented class structure. In his comprehensive study of Latin American class structures, Portes (1985) defined classes in terms of three criteria: control over the means of production, control over the labor power of others, and mode of remuneration. On this basis, he identified five distinct social classes in Latin America: the dominant class, the bureaucratic-technical class (middle sectors), the formal proletariat, the informal petty bourgeoisie, and the informal proletariat.

What is most striking about Portes' findings is the extreme asymmetry of Latin America's class structure. The dominant and bureaucratic-technical classes together accounted for less than 10% of the EAP for all of Latin America in the 1970s. In no country did they exceed 15%, and only Venezuela and Panama came close to even that low percentage. Yet these same two classes on average received more than 45% of national income.

Portes (1985) found a similar pattern among the three subordinate social classes. The formal proletariat (which Portes classified as those workers who receive wages on a contractual basis and an indirect wage through social welfare programs prescribed by law) represented more than half of the EAP only in Argentina, Uruguay, and Chile. The weighted regional average in 1972 was just 22.4%, and in most countries it hovered at around 12%.

The flip side of this was the large informal sector of the economy found in most of Latin America at the beginning of the 1980s. The informal petty bourgeoisie accounted for approximately 10% of the regional EAP. As a social class, it links the informal proletariat to the modern sector of the economy by subcontracting out for firms in the formal sector to lower their costs and supplying low-cost wage goods for consumption by the formal proletariat. In all countries except Uruguay, the informal proletariat represented at least 20% of the EAP in 1980. For the region as a whole, it represented roughly 60% of the EAP, or 80% of all workers.

The region's class structure and the extremes of inequality that it undergirds go to the heart of Latin America's political conundrum. For many policymakers and politicians, the hope (if not expectation) during the postwar period was that the spread of market relations and urbanization would mimic a romanticized understanding of capitalist development in the West, leading to the emergence of secular, urban liberal democracies (Deutsch 1961; Lipset 1959). While capitalist development did lead to rapid urbanization, the empirical reality of high levels of poverty, democratic instability, and socioeconomic inequality that so-called modernization theory predicted would disappear seemed beyond doubt, generating sometimes heated debates as to why (Hirschman 1981). For some, the problem was the inability of market relations to actually penetrate—and modernize—large segments of Latin America. Based on the work of Vekemans and the Centro para el Desarrollo Económico y Social de América Latina (DESEAL) research institute in Chile which he headed, a theory of marginality offered socioeconomic policy prescriptions to foster such penetration and promote popular sector participation in the economy and politics (Vekemans and Silva Fuenzalida 1968). For others, the speed with which market relations penetrated society was seen as the root cause of Latin American populism (Germani 1978). This is because the forces of modernization destroyed traditional normative structures before they could be replaced by more modern ones, leaving the masses in a virtual state of anomie that opportunistic elites could take advantage of. People were mobilized by populist elites, but without the necessary autonomy to ensure a significant level of accountability and under the terms set by the self-interested populist leadership (Oxhorn 1998).

The problem with these perspectives is that they ignored the kind of market relations that were emerging in the region (Oxhorn and Ducatenzeiler 1998). Rather than the degree and speed of capitalist market penetration, the problem was in how markets affected class structure and the distribution of power (Cardoso and Faletto 1970; Dos Santos 1970; see Rossi, Webber in this volume). For example, marginality theory was challenged by empirical studies that demonstrated how the so-called marginal segments of society—the poor, those working in the informal sector—were in fact intimately intertwined with the modern economy (Castells 1983; Perlman 1976). Rather than being excluded from participating in the modern sectors of the economy, these studies showed how the modern sectors of the economy were dependent on the socioeconomic exclusion of the popular sectors through their employment in the informal sector. This is because they were a source of labor that could keep production costs down and the power of organized labor in check because of the willingness of workers in the informal sector to work for lower wages. At the same time, their role in the economy lowered the cost of living for workers, in both the formal and informal sectors, providing less expensive goods and services for workers. While such conflicting interests only made it more difficult to mobilize majorities in favor of socioeconomic change, if not a revolution, the extreme asymmetry between the dominant and middle classes, on the one hand, and the working classes, on the other, raised the stakes in struggles for political power. Even small redistributive policies would have a disproportionate impact on those benefiting from inequality, just as those living at the bottom of the socioeconomic pyramid have much to gain (Oxhorn 2011).

In this context, *controlled inclusion* became the dominant mode of interest intermediation, and *citizenship as cooptation* defined the contingent rather than universal nature of basic rights of citizenship (Oxhorn 2011). This extreme class-based inequality effectively ruled out the possibility of the kind of class compromise that led to the emergence of the modern welfare state in the West (Bresser Pereira and Nakano 1998). Instead, beginning with the middle classes in the first decades of the twentieth century, the expansion of political incorporation was partial and segmented by social class. Access to public services, such as education, healthcare, and even minimal civil rights, was far from universal. Instead, access to such "rights" was contingent: it was offered to specific groups as a way of buying their allegiance to the status quo, exacerbating divisions among the working classes and further undermining efforts to mobilize them. When such allegiance was in doubt, there was a growing danger of an authoritarian backlash as the dominant and middle classes threw their support behind violent military regimes in order to preserve the status quo, which benefitted them so handsomely (Garretón 1989; O'Donnell 1979).

If the working class was considered the primary mover of socio-political change during the postwar period in an economistic understanding of social mobilization based on social class, identity-based social mobilization was viewed as its antithesis (see Fontana in this volume). Whether from the perspective of conservative modernization theories or the more radical perspectives of their critics, there was a general distrust of identity movements that were not based on social class. Identity-based movements, including those based on gender, ethnicity, religion, and nationalism, among others, were seen as anachronistic holdovers from pre-modern eras and uncompromising. Ironically, both the Left and Right agreed that modern industrialized, urban societies would reflect their growing irrelevance. For the Right, this was because they were displaced by a modern, middle-class citizenry's concern with maximizing the many competing interests it had in the complex liberal democratic societies associated with capitalist development. For the Left, this was due to the commodification of work caused by capitalist development, which created the material basis for a revolution led by the proletariat that inevitably would erase all forms of difference in a utopian communist society. For both the Right and Left, the material basis of most demands from the working classes, including more radical Marxist variants (Przeworski 1985), gave them a unique kind of political agency (see Webber in this volume). Such agency reflected the objectivity of their demands in ways that other identity-based movements could not match given their more holistic perspectives and the belief that compromising ones' identity was tantamount to self-denial and therefore incompatible with the existence of complex modern societies (Calhoun 1991).

Urban Social Movements and the Rise of Citizenship as Agency

Castells' research on urban social movements was seminal, but at the same time it was also transitional. Theoretically, he looked at how economically and politically marginalized urban residents mobilized rather than the "working" or "middle" classes, emphasizing the uniqueness of Latin America's capitalist economy compared to more advanced capitalist economies and the ways this distorted the expected evolution of class struggle. Yet he retained a Marxist perspective that postulated the necessity of an anti-capitalist revolution to achieve social equality and meaningful democracy. Without such a revolution, reform efforts were seen as doomed from the start, and he lamented the absence of the kind of urban social movements that were both innovative, despite their promise (Chile in the late 1960s and before the 1973 coup that ousted Allende) and enduring (Mexico).

The latter point reflects another way in which Castell's research was transitional: it largely ended *before* the region became dominated by extremely violent authoritarian regimes, including the military regime in Chile. Somewhat paradoxically, the violence and new neoliberal economic model associated with those regimes contributed to the emergence of a growing number of urban social movements and a new focus on democratic politics and citizenship rights (Oxhorn 2001). Traditional social movements based on class no longer played as central a role in either social movement theory or the identity-based movements, including urban social movements, that emerged in the latter twentieth and early twenty-first centuries (Escobar and Alvarez 1992).[3]

This transition from class-based to identity based social mobilization in the region had its roots in the high levels of inequality, which only began to improve significantly in the early 2000s due largely to rising commodity prices and, to a lesser extent, new social policies (Oxhorn 2011). The breakdown of controlled inclusion and citizenship as cooptation that preceded the rise in violence underscored the threat posed by working class mobilization to the middle and upper classes, a threat that was often exaggerated in order to justify the violence on the part of the state (Garretón 1989). At the same time, that violence made continued working-class mobilization increasingly difficult given the destruction of workers' organization and the loss of leadership due to the repression. This unprecedented level of state violence, however, also led to a renewed appreciation of the importance of political democracy. This was particularly true for much of the Left, which had disproportionately suffered the violent consequences of the collapse democratic regimes (Roberts 1998). However flawed democratic regimes might be in practice, they effectively curtailed the political violence associated with the region's postwar authoritarian regimes and allowed for the possibility that progressive political actors could win competitive elections (Przeworski 1986). This also meant that in the 1980s and 1990s, as most countries in the region experienced transitions to democracy, there was also an understandable fear on the part of many that working class mobilization would undermine new democracies by inviting a backlash from more privileged segments of the population that further reinforced this trend (O'Donnell and Schmitter 1986).

This shift away from class-based mobilization in a context characterized by high levels of state violence and structural inequality was reinforced throughout much of Latin America by an unexpected actor: the Catholic Church. The timing for what would become a resurgence of civil society under authoritarian regimes was particularly propitious as a result of important changes in the Catholic Church. Following the important Vatican II reforms of the mid-1960s intended to reverse declining Church membership resulting from the growing secularization of "modern" West European societies, progressive elements within the Latin American national church structures began to assert a new social activism through the practice of liberation theology. Among other things, liberation theology stressed the structural causes of poverty and the role that everyone, particularly the poor, had to play in collectively organizing to promote social change. Its primary instrument, Comunidades Eclesiales de Base (CEBs) were, despite their religious foundations and direct ties to the Church, pioneers in the development of an autonomous civil society (Mackin in this volume).

It is important to emphasize, however, that the Church's contribution to the strengthening of civil society during this period was not limited to the practitioners of liberation theology. Given the unprecedented levels of repression in a number of countries, including Brazil, Chile, El Salvador, and Uruguay, even moderate elements within the traditional church began to assume a new role of "social critic" by publicly opposing government repression and other policies. Often somewhat reluctantly, especially after the elevation of John Paul II to the papacy, the Church frequently assumed an increasingly political role by seeking to mediate conflict, defend human rights, and generally shelter a variety of civil society organizations against state repression (Oxhorn 1995).

This unique confluence of a fundamentally repressive environment, the spread of liberation theology, and the enabling role for civil society that the Church began to play led to an extraordinary growth in autonomous civil society organizational activity throughout Latin America (Alvarez, Dagnino, and Escobar 1998; Eckstein and Merino 2001). The Catholic Church supported a myriad of non-class organizations, many of which had the same characteristics and demands that Castells discussed in terms of urban social movements. This included human rights groups, organizations of the victims of repression, community self-help organizations of various kinds, women's organizations, and, to a lesser extent compared to the late 1990s and later, indigenous groups and environmental organizations, to name but a few.

These trends were further reinforced in most Latin American countries as they experienced a different kind of transition founded on market-based economic policies that led to a new model of citizenship as consumption, and a new mode of interest mediation, *neopluralism* (Oxhorn 2011; Oxhorn and Ducatenzeiler 1998). In sharp contrast to the ideal of universal citizenship rights (Marshall 1950), only the right to vote is more-or-less universal. While the importance of this cannot be underestimated, access to what normally would be considered minimal rights of democratic citizenship (e.g., education, healthcare, social security pensions, and rule of law) is dependent on the ability of citizens to acquire them by spending their often-limited economic resources in a marketplace of privatized services and a minimalist state. It is important to note that this model of citizenship both reflects and contributes to a more marginal role for class-based social movements. Labor movements generally are more fragmented and represent smaller fractions of the economically active population than in earlier periods, due to large informal sectors, changes in industrial structures following the implementation of market-oriented or neoliberal reforms, and changes in national labor laws (Ramírez and Stoessel in this volume).

More generally, the marked authoritarianism of neopluralism distinguishes it from the more traditional pluralist model associated with democracy in the United States. It is this close association of authoritarianism with a normative belief in the value of competitive elections that is unique to the current period and defines neopluralism. Dominant economic interests, as well as unelected power holders such as the military, exercise control over key state decisions. It is "pluralist" because through democratic elections, neopluralism reaffirms the normative belief that the best balance of interests and values within a given polity is produced by some form (however limited) of free competition among individuals in the rational pursuit of their self-interest. Ultimate political authority is essentially decided upon through a free political market of votes.

Citizenship as agency offers a model of citizenship that is antithetical with citizenship as consumption (and citizenship as cooptation). Paradoxically, it is made possible by the association of citizenship as consumption and neopluralism with relatively free and fair elections based on universal suffrage. The importance of political democracy to citizenship as consumption and neopluralism creates a unique opportunity for social mobilization that favors the emergence of urban social movements demanding improved collective consumption, respect for community culture and political self-governance that urban social movements champion—the definition of urban social movements developed by Castells in his seminal work. Yet such movements also epitomize the kind of *self-limiting radicalism* that Cohen (1985) suggests is central to the emergence of a New Left in Europe, and which was far removed from the revolutionary radicalism undergirding Castells' perspective on Latin America.[4] Structural change in pursuit of more equal societies is still the goal, but it is one that no longer is seen as mutually exclusive with political democracy, which is now recognized as both an end in itself and an essential means for achieving that change. More post-Marxist than neo-Marxist, this new appreciation of the dual role of political democracy is often conceptualized in terms of democratic deepening (Roberts 1998). Urban social movements are, in turn, among its principal proponents.

Urban social movements play an important role in this context. While market criteria and technical expertise associated with neopluralism and citizenship as consumption can play an important role in defining the nature of citizenship rights, any such role is conditioned by negotiations between civil society actors and local state officials. The institutions associated with this alternative therefore provide non-market participatory mechanisms for priority-setting and service delivery (Annunziata and Goldfrank in this volume). Responsiveness is turned directly to the citizenry and not indirectly to consumers through the market, with urban social movements (and civil society more generally) playing a crucial role in holding officials accountable for their actions (Smulovitz and Peruzotti 2000).

Important examples of this type of urban social mobilization include the *piqueteros* in Argentina (Rossi 2017a) and—including rural actors—the Movimiento al Socialismo (MAS) in Bolivia (Centro de Documentación e Información 2008), as well as Chile's student movement (Oxhorn 2011; Donoso in this volume). While unfortunately far less successful, the various mobilizations against violence in Mexico should also be included (Oxhorn 2011), along with a number of mobilizations against corruption in many Latin American countries (Pereyra, Gold, and Gattoni in this volume).

The struggle for the right to a decent life at the city-level is central to urban movements. Very common across Latin America are squatter movements, such as those in Montevideo studied by Alvarez Rivadulla (2012). Many times, these urban dynamics scale up to national politics. The movement of popular and neighborhood assemblies in Buenos Aires during the 2001–2003 crisis was a massive example of an urban movement crucial for national politics (Rossi 2005, 2017b). And the growing organization of neighborhood politics with the 1989 Caracazo is central to explain Venezuelan politics since then (García-Guadilla 2018; Velasco 2015).

The experience of participatory budgeting (PB) in Brazil in many ways epitomizes the potential and limits of urban social movements under neopluralism (Avritzer 2002; Baiocchi 2002; Wampler and Avritzer 2004). It was first implemented in Porto Alegre in 1989, and its resounding success led to the adoption of similar programs in over 100 cities in Brazil, as well as many others throughout the world.

The impetus for PB came from the national level in Brazil, when the 1988 Constitution granted greater authority to local governments to design new policymaking processes and recognized the legitimacy of participatory institutions. This reflected a growing demand for new forms of participation, particularly among marginalized groups, as expressed in the Constituent Assembly that drafted the Constitution in which civil society actors were prominent (Wampler and Avritzer 2004). Several local factors heavily influenced the direction new reforms would take in Porto Alegre. Porto Alegre had enjoyed a particularly vibrant civil society, which grew in opposition to Brazil's military dictatorship (1964–1985). This experience was ultimately eclipsed in 1986 when the Partido Democratico Trabalhista (PDT), a left-wing populist party that demobilized civil society in order to re-impose a more traditional clientelistic government, won the municipal elections. The initial proposal for some form of participatory budgeting actually originated within civil society, in large part to allow civil society organizations to renew their own sagging legitimacy in the face of the pervasive clientelism of the PDT government.

When public repudiation of the PDT led to the left-wing Partido dos Trabalhadores (PT) victory in the 1988 municipal elections, the PT had yet to establish itself as a strong party in Porto Alegre and it made PB the cornerstone of its municipal policies. Central to this decision were the close relations between the PT and the various civil society actors demanding greater popular participation in municipal government.

Despite these favorable circumstances, PB got off to a rocky start. Participation was initially relatively low and actually declined during its first two years (Goldfrank 2003). The PT responded by working with civil society organizations, negotiating and perfecting the institutions of PB. Funding levels were increased along with the scope of PB, and by the late 1990s, 100% of all discretionary municipal expenditures were decided through PB.

The end result of PB has been "a profound transformation of civil society itself" (Baiocchi 2002). The level of public participation continually increased, from just 976 people in 1990 to 26,807 in 2000. Moreover, the number of social organizations that formed the backbone of the urban social movement increased markedly as a result of the PB process. Conservative estimates suggest that the number of neighborhood organizations increased from 180 in 1986 to 540 in 1998 (ibid.). The growing levels of participation and organization tended to concentrate in poorer areas, and people with lower incomes and levels of education predominated in the PB process. This, plus the fact that municipal expenditures were deliberately redistributed toward poorer areas of the city, underscores the empowerment PB offers for disadvantaged groups. Participation in what had effectively become one of the most important urban social movements in the region was seen as relevant to meeting pressing needs, even though the level of funds administered amounted to just over US$200 per capita and was limited largely to municipal capital expenditures (see Annunziata and Goldfrank in this volume).

Urban Social Movements and the Challenge of Resilience

The hope for a democratic renewal and more equal societies that was raised by the emergence of urban social movements in the 1980s and 1990s ultimately proved to be short lived. Like the Latin American urban social movements Castells studied in the 1960s and early 1970s, within a matter of years they seemed to retreat from the public sphere, if not disappear with little apparent legacy.[5] The ultimate fate of PB in Brazil, despite its remarkable success in cities like Porto Alegre, is telling. The shifting fortunes of the PT belied an autonomous movement with the organizational capacity to adapt to a changing political and economic landscape. In Porto Alegre, participation began to decline markedly when the PT was voted out of office in 2005, long before the national-level PT became ensconced in unprecedented political and economic crises with the end of the commodity boom in the second decade of the twenty-first century. The 2015–2016 social mobilization against corruption that brought tens of thousands of people into the streets across the country raised the possibility of a new urban social movement that would take the struggle for greater democratic participation and accountability to a new level, impacting national politics in a way that the PB could not (see Pereyra, Gold, and Gattoni, von Bülow in this volume). Yet events quickly swept aside what was at best a proto-movement as Brazilian political parties seemed to implode. The culmination of this was anything but a democratic resurgence. Instead, after more than a decade of PT rule, the far-Right presidential candidate, Jair Bolsonaro, won the 2018 presidential elections on a platform that was the antithesis of the kind of urban social movement theorized by Castells a half century earlier.

To a certain extent, this lack of resilience among urban social movements is an inevitable consequence of their close association with the communities in which they emerge. Successful urban social movements are able to tap into this. This is why the key to PB's success in Porto Alegre and elsewhere was directly linked to their ability to channel participation around local communities. At that level, people are more likely to see the value of their participation if it results in policy change or a better quality of life than could ever be the case for participation at the subnational or national levels. The immediacy of issues and physical proximity of decision makers conditions a unique set of incentives and opportunities that can be tapped into to open up new mechanisms for citizen participation. Dahl (1961), in his seminal work that helped define the pluralist model of interest mediation, recognized this.

Urban social movements will need to overcome at least two challenges in order to achieve the resiliency necessary for a lasting social, economic, and political impact. The first challenge is overcoming *participant fatigue*. Even under the best of circumstances, maintaining high levels of local participation is difficult (Mansbridge 1980). This is particularly true for marginalized groups, who must struggle to maintain even a minimally acceptable standard of living. As examples like PB in Porto Alegre clearly demonstrate, the poor will participate if they can perceive positive reasons for doing so. If they cannot, however, other priorities quickly become more important and participation declines (Annunziata and Goldfrank in this volume).

The second challenge is the need to overcome the *limits* of local government, both in terms of the scope of decision-making and limited resources available to local governments, particularly in poor localities. This can be problematic even within municipalities and one of the most impressive achievements of PB in Porto Alegre was the creation of an institutional structure that ultimately allowed for the aggregation of community demands at the level of the central municipal government.

More generally, one of the key insights from Castells' research was that the dependence of marginal urban groups comprising much of the urban population on state resources, including large swaths of the middle class lacking resources to secure adequate housing, made them vulnerable to elite manipulation through what he called "urban populism" (Castells 1983).

Today's context has changed significantly compared to the period when Castells carried out his seminal research, making resilience even more difficult to attain. Structural inequality has deepened, stemming from new sources of insecurity reflected in citizenship as consumption. These include growing levels of criminal violence and a de facto marketization of the rule of law, as well as educational systems that block social mobility and social security policies that further segment the "haves" from the "have-nots" (Oxhorn 2011). Moreover, the consolidation of neopluralist democratic regimes has meant that the fate of urban social movements is closely tied to the political fortunes of the national political parties that supported them (see Roberts in this volume), while its authoritarian aspects can lead the people who might be expected to benefit from urban social movements to instead join a growing chorus of people rejecting traditional political parties in search of outsiders like Brazil's Bolsonaro who are allegedly untainted by corruption. As the example of Bolsonaro reminds us, the problems that Castells saw as driving the urban social movements a half a century ago have not gone away, and in some respects may have only deepened, despite the positive change towards democratic governance under neopluralism.

From the neo-Marxist perspective of Castells to the post-Marxism of Cohen's self-limiting radicalism, the goal of finding lasting solutions to the region's problems of inequality and social exclusion remains important, yet elusive. Similarly, the role that urban social movements could potentially play in achieving it remains under appreciated, even if such movements sometimes appear to face insurmountable obstacles. Ultimately, the real challenge may be to institute the kinds of reforms that can help urban social movements succeed. Such reforms would involve changes to local and central governance institutions (Oxhorn 2004) that, at long last, would offer real prospects for achieving the kind of democratic structural change subordinate groups in the region have struggled to achieve for decades.

Conclusion

Future research on urban social movements should entail both empirical and theoretical dimensions. Empirically, there was an unprecedented level of institutional reform in the region over the last three decades with the principal goal of increasing democratic citizen participation (Oxhorn, Tulchin, and Selee 2004). Rather than culminate in a democratic revolution, it has dead-ended into something that would have been difficult to anticipate a decade ago. The richness of this experience, which spanned governments of the Left, Center, and Right, needs to be better understood in order to gain new insights into how to realize its democratic potential. More specifically, what was the impact of these reforms on the political outlook and interests of the civil society actors who participated in them? What, if any, role did they play in their apparent demise?

Theoretically, research needs to move away from frameworks based exclusively on ideal types. Such a focus is actually rather ironic since we are studying poor, marginalized groups who could be expected to face the greatest challenges in meeting the demands on their time and limited resources that participatory democracy can entail. This reliance on theoretical ideals is also ironic since much of the work on urban social movements, beginning with Castells, grew out of the researchers' concern for developing new theories that better reflected the empirical reality on the ground. Rather than question the realism of the ideals behind those theories, however, they sought new theoretical insights for achieving them. In other words, how should we realistically understand the democratic potential of participatory democracy in a region still marked by high levels of inequality and authoritarianism to significantly erode those inequalities?

Notes

1. The following discussion is based on a series of studies of social change in Latin America carried out by the United Nation's Comisión Económica para America Latina y el Caribe (CEPAL); see CEPAL (1989, 1991).
2. A re-assessment of the available data suggests that the original CEPAL study may have overstated the extent of this social mobility, but it is unclear by how much and does not affect the substance argument I am making here; see Gurrieri and Sáinz (2003).
3. Latin America's experience has many parallels with the emergence of so-called New Social Movements in the advanced market economies of Western Europe and the United States during the same period, particularly the importance of non-class identities for mobilizing people (see Cohen 1985; Melucci 1985; Garretón and Selamé in this volume). Regardless of any similarities, however, the emphasis here is generally on factors unique to the region.

4. It should be noted that Castells' views of urban social movements in the United States and Western Europe, where structural inequality was much less severe, were more similar to Cohen's ideal of self-limiting radicalism.
5. Bolivia may prove to be a major exception. The ability of the MAS under Evo Morales to maintain relative political and economic stability based on a more fluid relationship between the party apparatus and its largely urban social movement base have contributed to the consolidation of the 2009 Constitution and other institutional reforms largely consistent with citizenship as agency and greater social inclusion.

References

Altimir, Oscar (1998), "Inequality, Employment and Poverty in Latin America: An Overview," in Víctor Tokman and Guillermo O'Donnell (eds.), *Poverty, Inequality in Latin America: Issues and New Challenges*, 3–35 (Notre Dame: University of Notre Dame).

Alvarez, Sonia E., Evelina Dagnino, and Arturo Escobar (eds.) (1998), *Cultures of Politics, Politics of Cultures: Re-visioning Latin American Social Movements* (Boulder, CO: Westview Press).

Alvarez Rivadulla, María José (2012), "Clientelism or Something Else? Squatter Politics in Montevideo," *Latin American Politics and Society* 54(1), 37–63.

Avritzer, Leonardo (2002), *Democracy and the Public Space in Latin America* (Princeton, NJ: Princeton University Press).

Baiocchi, Gianpaolo (2002), "Synergizing Civil Society: State-Civil Society Regimes in Porto Alegre, Brazil," *Political Power and Social Theory* 15, 3–52.

Bresser Pereira, Luiz Carlos and Yoshiaki Nakano (1998), "The Missing Social Contract: Governability and Reform in Latin America," in Philip Oxhorn and Graciela Ducatenzeiler (eds.), *What Kind of Market? What Kind of Democracy? Latin America in the Age of Neoliberalism*, 21–42 (University Park, PA: Penn State University Press).

Calhoun, Craig (1991), "The Problem of Identity in Collective Action," in Joan Huber (ed.), *Macro-Micro Linkages in Sociology*, 51–75 (Newbury Park, CA: Sage Publications).

Cardoso, Fernando Enrique and Enzo Faletto (1970), *Dependency and Development in Latin America* (Berkeley and Los Angeles: University of California Press).

Castells, Manuel (1983), *The City and the Grassroots: A Cross-Cultural Theory of Urban Social Movements* (Berkeley and Los Angeles: University of California).

Centro de Documentación e Información—Bolivia (2008), *Movimientos sociales urbanos en América Latina y Bolivia: Memoria del encuentro realizado en la ciudad de La Paz, 7 y 8 de diciembre de 2007* (Cochabamba: Centro de Documentación e Informacion Bolivia).

CEPAL (1989), *Transformación Ocupacional y Crisis Social en América Latina* (Santiago: CEPAL).

CEPAL (1991), *Magnitud de la Pobreza en América Latina en los Años Ochenta* (Santiago: CEPAL-PNUD).

Cohen, Jean (1985), "Strategy or Identity: New Theoretical Paradigms and Contemporary Social Movements," *Social Research* 52(Winter), 663–716.

Dahl, Robert (1961), *Who Governs: Democracy and Power in an American City* (New Haven, CT: Yale University Press).

Deutsch, Karl Wolfgang (1961), "Social Mobilization and Political Development," *American Political Science Review* 55(September), 493–514.

Dos Santos, Theotonio (1970), "The Structure of Dependence," *The American Economic Review* 60(May), 231–36.

Eckstein (ed) (2001), *Power and Popular Protest: Latin American Social Movements, Expanded and Updated Edition* (Berkeley and Los Angeles: University of California Press).

Escobar, Arturo and Sonia E. Alvarez (eds.) (1992), *The Making of Social Movements in Latin America: Identity, Strategy, and Democracy* (Boulder, CO: Westview).

García-Guadilla, María Pilar (2018), "The Incorporation of Popular Sectors and Social Movements in Venezuelan Twenty-First-Century Socialism," in Eduardo Silva and Federico M. Rossi (eds.), *Reshaping the Political Arena in Latin America: From Resisting Neoliberalism to the Second Incorporation*, 60–77 (Pittsburgh, PA: University of Pittsburgh Press).

Garretón, Manuel Antonio (1989), *The Chilean Political Process* (Boston, MA: Unwin Hyman).

Germani, Gino (1978), *Authoritarianism, Facism, and National Populism* (New Brunswick, NJ: Transaction Books).

Goldfrank, Benjamin (2003), "Making Participation Work in Porto Alegre," in Gianpaolo Baiocchi (ed.), *Radicals in Power: The Workers' Party (PT) and Experiments in Urban Democracy in Brazil*, 27–52 (London: Zed).

Gurrieri, Adolfo and Pedro Sáinz (2003), "Empleo y movilidad estructural: Trayectoria de un tema prebischiano," *Revista de la CEPAL* 80(80), 141–64.

Hirschman, Albert (1981), "The Rise and Decline of Development Economics," in Albert Hirschman (ed.), *Essay in Trespassing: Economics to Politics and Beyond*, 1–24 (Cambridge: Cambridge University Press).

Lipset, Seymour Martin (1959), "Some Social Requisites of Democracy: Economic Development and Political Legitimacy," *American Political Science Review* 53(March), 69–105.

Mansbridge, Jane (1980), *Beyond Adversary Democracy* (New York: Basic Books).

Marshall, T.H. (1950), *Citizenship and Social Class and Other Essays* (Cambridge: Cambridge University Press).

Melucci, Alberto (1985), "The Symbolic Challenge of Contemporary Movements," *Social Research* 52(4), 789–816.

O'Donnell, Guillermo (1979), *Modernization and Bureaucratic Authoritarianism* (Berkeley and Los Angeles: University of California).

O'Donnell, Guillermo and Philippe C. Schmitter (1986), *Transitions from Authoritarian Rule: Tentative Conclusions about Uncertain Democracies* (Baltimore, MD: Johns Hopkins University Press).

Oxhorn, Philip (1995), *Organizing Civil Society: The Popular Sectors and the Struggle for Democracy in Chile* (University Park, PA: Penn State University Press).

Oxhorn, Philip (1998), "The Social Foundations of Latin America's Recurrent Populism: Problems of Class Formation and Collective Action," *Journal of Historical Sociology* 11(June), 212–46.

Oxhorn, Philip (2001), "From Human Rights to Citizenship Rights? Recent Trends in the Study of Latin American Social Movements," *Latin American Research Review* 36(3), 163–82.

Oxhorn, Philip (2004), "Introduction: Unraveling the Puzzle of Decentralization," in Philip Oxhorn, Joseph S. Tulchin, and Andrew D. Selee (eds.), *Decentralization, Civil Society, and Democratic Governance: Comparative Perspectives from Latin America, Africa, and Asia*, 3–30 (Washington, DC: Johns Hopkins University Press/Woodrow Wilson Center).

Oxhorn, Philip (2011), *Sustaining Civil Society: Economic Change, Democracy and the Social Construction of Citizenship in Latin America* (University Park, PA: Penn State University Press).

Oxhorn, Philip and Graciela Ducatenzeiler (1998a), *What Kind of Democracy? What Kind of Market? Latin America in the Age of Neoliberalism* (University Park, PA: Penn State University Press).

Oxhorn, Philip, Joseph S. Tulchin and Andrew D. Selee (2004), *Decentralization, Democratic Governance, and Civil Society in Comparative Perspective: Africa, Asia, and Latin America* (Washington, DC: Woodrow Wilson Center Press).

Perlman, Janice (1976), *The Myth of Marginality: Urban Poverty and Politics in Rio de Janeiro* (Berkeley and Los Angeles: University of California Press).

Portes, Alejandro (1985), "Latin American Class Structures: Their Composition and Change during the Last Decades," *Latin American Research Review* 20(3), 7–39.

Przeworski, Adam (1985), *Capitalism and Social Democracy* (Cambridge: Cambridge University Press).

Przeworski, Adam (1986), "Some Problems in the Study of the Transition to Democracy," in Guillermo O'Donnell, Philippe C. Schmitter, and Laurence Whitehead (eds.), *Transitions from Authoritarian Rule: Comparative Perspectives*, 47–63 (Baltimore, MD: Johns Hopkins University Press).

Roberts, Bryan R. (1981), *Cities of Peasants: The Political Economy of Urbanization in the Third World* (London: Edward Arnold).

Roberts, Bryan R. (2005), "Citizenship, Rights, and Social Policy," in Charles H. Wood and Bryan R. Roberts (eds.), *Rethinking Development in Latin America*, 137–58 (University Park, PA: Penn State University Press).

Roberts, Kenneth M. (1998), *Deepening Democracy? The Modern Left and Social Movements in Chile and Peru* (Stanford, CA: Stanford University Press).

Rossi, Federico M. (2005), "Crisis de la República Delegativa. La constitución de nuevos actores políticos en la Argentina (2001–2003): Las asambleas vecinales y populares," *América Latina Hoy* 39, 195–216.

Rossi, Federico M. (2017a), *The Poor's Struggle for Political Incorporation: The Piquetero Movement in Argentina* (New York: Cambridge University Press).

Rossi, Federico M. (2017b), "Compulsion Mechanisms: State-Movement Dynamics in Buenos Aires," *Social Movement Studies* 16(5), 578–94.

Smulovitz, Catalina and Enrique Peruzzotti (2000), "Societal Accountability in Latin America," *Journal of Democracy* 11(4), 147–58.

Thorp, Rosemary (1998), *Progress, Poverty and Exclusion: An Economic History of Latin America in the 20th Century* (Washington, DC: Inter-American Development Bank).

Vekemans, Roger and Ismael Silva Fuenzalida (1968), *Integración latinoamericana y solidaridad internacional* (Santiago: Centro para el Desarrollo Económico y Social de América Latina).

Velasco, Alejandro (2015), *Barrio Rising: Urban Popular Politics and the Making of Modern Venezuela* (Oakland: University of California Press).

Wampler, Brian and Leonardo Avritzer (2004), "Participatory Publics: Civil Society and New Institutions in Democratic Brazil," *Comparative Politics* 36(3), 291–312.

CHAPTER 28

ANTI-CORRUPTION SOCIAL MOBILIZATION IN LATIN AMERICA

SEBASTIÁN PEREYRA, TOMÁS GOLD, AND MARÍA SOLEDAD GATTONI

Introduction

This chapter explores the relationship between social mobilization and anti-corruption in Latin America. Corruption scandals, press allegations, impeachments, large-scale demonstrations, and, lately, judicial procedures against significant political players have all shaped the political landscape of Latin American democracies. Nevertheless, anti-corruption movements have yet to emerge and, as a result, the study of social movements has paid little attention to anti-corruption frames and critiques of politics. At the same time, anti-corruption research has not taken into account protest and social mobilization dynamics. This gap in scholarship is not limited to the Latin American context, but can be generalized to other regions as well (della Porta 2017).

Furthermore, analysts have recently argued that the link between anti-corruption and protest has become more prominent due to a new international wave of mobilizations that emerged after the economic crash of 2008. This contentious wave was driven by the effects of the crisis and the development of austerity policies across countries, representing an anti-corruption paradigm emerging from below, opposed to the dissemination of technocratic standards linked to the paradigm of transparency (Bringel and Pleyers 2017; della Porta 2017). However, this thesis has been barely discussed beyond North American and European contexts.

Our work assesses this argument by mapping recent anti-corruption mobilizations in Latin America. First, this chapter reconstructs the emergence and transnational diffusion of a strong anti-corruption and transparency consensus in the region during the

1990s. Then, it analyzes how corruption as a social problem was incorporated into the vocabulary of social mobilization (Trom 2001) and used as an element of criticism and confrontation with party politics. Finally, it develops a comparative analysis of some of the the most recent and important large-scale anti-government demonstrations in the region after 2010. The chapter claims that although perceptions of corruption did not directly translate into an anti-corruption movement, the anti-corruption vocabulary has become a frame for the spread of large-scale anti-government demonstrations in the region, generating (a) a challenge to presidential figures and relevant leaders, (b) a critique of institutional politics in moral terms, and (c) the settling of specific repertoires that link anti-corruption demands to large-scale contention.

The comparative analysis of protest waves shows that there is a continuity between the increasing social recognition of corruption as a public problem and the consolidation of a repertoire of confrontation grounded in anti-corruption vocabulary (see Almeida in this volume). This repertoire aims to challenge government performance and their capacity to confront and solve major social problems (see Wada in this volume). Moreover, the protests are related to previous political processes within each country and, in particular, to the political debates and neoliberal policies of the 1990s (see Rossi in this volume). Consequently, we argue that the repertoire has been highly modular, and can be appropriated by very diverse actors, functioning as a unifying element for protesters with different ideologies or programmatic objectives.

The Emergence of an Anti-corruption Consensus in Latin America

Since the mid-1990s, Latin America has been a global frontrunner in fostering an anti-corruption consensus. The Organization of the American States (OAS) was the first to adopt the Inter-American Convention Against Corruption (IACAC) in 1996, followed by the Organization for Economic Cooperation and Development (OECD) in 1997, and the United Nations in 2003. This widespread adoption of transparency and accountability reforms throughout the continent was strongly linked to what analysts have called an "anti-corruption consensus" (Krastev 2004; Pereyra 2013; Sampson 2015), this is, a coalition of global players that associated corruption with two important issues: the consolidation of democracy and the promotion of free market reforms.

Over the following decades, the idea that corruption served as an impediment to economic growth and government efficiency took a prominent role in regional development cooperation. An international network of experts disseminated and reinforced anti-corruption rhetoric within their own countries (Gattoni 2016) while at the same time corruption scandals involving political figures (presidents, former presidents, and high-ranked government officials) started to receive increased media coverage (Llanos and Marsteintredet 2010; Pérez-Liñán 2007). During the 1990s, incumbent presidents

Fernando Collor de Mello in Brazil and Carlos Andrés Pérez in Venezuela were criminally prosecuted for corrupt practices. Ecuador's president Abdalá Bucaram was removed from office by the Congress on grounds of alleged mental incapacity, though he was also charged with corruption. Peruvian president Alberto Fujimori declared a state of emergency in 1996 and dismissed almost half of the Supreme Court on counts of corruption; in Argentina, Carlos Menem's two terms (1989–1995 and 1995–1999) were marked by corruption scandals. He was accused and convicted for arms trafficking in 2013. In Bolivia, the President and the Deputy of the Supreme Court were sentenced on charges of acts of corruption; in Colombia, President Ernesto Samper underwent a judiciary process for receiving large donations from drug traffickers during his election campaign.

Both the press and political parties took up the anti-corruption banner after the epistemic community of experts (Haas 1992) introduced corruption as a public problem, and therefore anti-corruption started to be strategically used within national political arenas (Balán 2011; Pereyra 2012; Waisbord 2000). Thus, although the perception of corruption has not drastically increased in the region since the 1990s, protests framed as a struggle against corruption have become a relatively routine form of political participation.

Bridging Corruption and Social Mobilization

Since the 1980s, a growing literature on Latin American social movements has examined the relationship between macro processes of political change and contentious politics. Several studies have analyzed social movements, protests, and institutional change in the region, focusing on the nature of democratic transitions during the 1980s (see Inclán in this volume), the characteristics and implementation of neoliberal policies, the strong resistance experienced from below in the 1990s (see Almeida; Rossi in this volume), and the resurgence of Latin American Left-to-center governments and their wide basis of socio-political support in the early 2000s (see Ramírez and Stoessel, Roberts in this volume). Yet this literature has been largely organized around the analysis of specific cases and focused on national and subnational levels of analysis. Few studies analyze recurrent phenomena that cut across historical stages and national contexts (Almeida and Cordero Ulate 2015; Rossi and von Bülow 2015). This chapter addresses that gap by analyzing the most recent wave of mobilizations, particularly large-scale demonstrations that became widespread across the region over the last decade.

Large-scale anti-government demonstrations multiplied in Latin America since the beginning of the century (Marsteintredet 2014). This study examines four waves of protest that have taken place since 2010: Argentina (2012–2013), Brazil (2013–2016), Guatemala (2015–2018), and Peru (2017–2018). We selected these cases because they are representative of widely different political and economic contexts. Protests emerged in countries with periods of both economic expansion and retraction, with medium-high and low GDP per capita, different geographic regions (the Southern Cone, Central America and the Andes region), different types of democratic transitions and current administrations with varied political and ideological orientations (center-Left and center-Right).

We analyze each case focusing on: (a) the structure of political opportunities within which these demonstrations emerged (see Somma in this volume), (b) their morphology and repertoires, (c) the specific actors that took part in them, and (d) the different frames and demands mobilized by contentious actors. This format allows us to show that large-scale demonstrations are recurrent contentious expressions of discontent and criticism towards politicians—framed as an anti-corruption demand—that are fueled neither by particular ideological orientations in governmental policies, nor by phases of economic retraction, but rather by a growing regional sentiment of *malaise in political representation* (Joignant, Morales, and Fuentes 2017).

Argentina (2012–2013)

The vast protests staged against the government of Cristina Fernández de Kirchner after her electoral triumph in 2011 shared striking similarities with the other cases explored in this chapter. The protest cycle, made up of four massive mobilizations that took place between September 2012 and August 2013, demonstrated a prevailing and latent party disaffection among large portions of the population. Demonstrations were fueled by political polarization and characterized by an increase in the anti-government tenor of claims and expressive repertoires, as well as the exclusion of opposition parties from the streets. Despite their tone, there is no evidence that the protests generated an anti-corruption social movement. Corruption, however, served as a moralized vocabulary that helped to trigger mobilization, rather than an ideological and programmatic platform for the construction of collective action.

Mixing different ideological traditions ranging from autonomism to liberalism, a small network of activists without partisan allegiance who lacked a centralized organizational structure, spokespeople, or partisan insignias initiated the protests (Gold 2019). Contention gained traction when word of the events disseminated across social media platforms with a hashtag that designated the specific dates (e.g., #8N, November 8). News regarding government corruption scandals, clientelism, and controversial economic measures also circulated on social media.

Survey data collected during the protests showed that more than 80% of participants became involved based on information diffused online, and more than 90% found out about the event without an intermediary organization. Also, although the social composition of the marches was heterogeneous and varied geographically, participants reported unusually high levels of education and income compared to other mobilizations

(Gómez 2014), a characteristic also found in the urban protests in Brazil (2013–2016) analyzed later in this chapter.

The protests revitalized a repertoire used during the contentious events of the 1990s and the uprising of 2001, one grounded in a moral criticism of politics: the public banging of pots and pans. Since the beginning of Carlos Menem's presidency in the 1990s,[1] pot-banging had been closely coupled with complaints of poor political representation and associated with non-Peronist urban middle-class sectors. Protests against the Menem administration focused on the issue of corruption but also addressed economic reform and neoliberal policies. Contentious actors comprised union members and diverse left-wing social movements, including the unemployed (Pereyra, Pérez, and Schuster 2015).

Resembling some of the demonstrations of the 1990s,[2] these new marches accompanied the banging of pots and pans with a display of banners and performances, like singing the national hymn or insulting the President. These performances emphasized corruption scandals and mismanaged public policies.[3] Although a clear master frame is difficult to trace across protests, critiques of corruption and rejection of the President were expressed in morally-charged terms: "I didn't vote for you!," "Thief!," "STOP! We want to live in peace," "Argentina, Without Cristina!," "She Must Go!," "Return What You Have Stolen!," among many others.

The government's strategy in confronting the protestors was based on discrediting them, depicting them as *cipayos*[4] and coup-instigators. This helped to open a political opportunity for the partisan opposition, who began to meet with the activists to assess how to channel discontent into an electoral movement (Gold and Peña 2018). The protests ended up contributing to the triumph of the opposition, both by eroding the government's legitimacy and by boosting a new party coalition in the 2013 legislative elections. As in the case of FREPASO during the 1990s, anti-corruption was a potent component of the new coalition's program.

In conclusion, although we have seen increased concern about corruption in Argentina's mobilizations, this preoccupation did not crystallize in an articulated social movement. On the contrary, we find that the subject of corruption permeates and shapes repertoires and vocabularies that are used primarily against political elites. In the case of the most recent mobilizations, social media served as a tool to rapidly disseminate morally charged narratives about politicians in power, incentivizing opposition party elites to build on popular resentment.

Brazil (2013–2016)

Brazil witnessed a series of large-scale demonstrations between 2013 and 2016. These demonstrations gained national and international visibility as they took place alongside corruption scandals and a political-institutional crisis that resulted in the impeachment of President Dilma Rousseff (2011–2014, 2015–2016), which altered the political landscape of the country.

The size and scope of this wave of protests was exceptional when compared to other contentious cycles along Brazil's history. Analysts have pointed out that these demonstrations can only be compared with two other episodes in the country's recent past: protests during the period of democratic transition in 1984, and the large cycle of mobilizations staged against President Collor de Mello at the beginning of the 1990s (Alonso and Mische 2015; Saad-Filho 2013; Tatagiba 2014). In 1992, between 100,000 and 700,000 people assembled in different cities across the country to demand the dismissal of President Collor de Mello after breaking news of his involvement in a corruption scandal. The student movement, aligned at the time with the opposition to the government (and with the support of the Partido dos Trabalhadores [PT]), played a crucial role in the protests (Santos 2018: 110–11) along with traditional left-wing demonstrators that opposed Collor's neoliberal economic policy. Although the protest wave resulted in a heterogeneous social alliance that included unions and human rights organizations, the Movimento por la Etica Pública was framed as a campaign against the government and its economic policy. Calls of corruption played a prominent role by awakening the interest and indignation of large audiences and unifying demands of heterogeneous actors. Each of these protest waves implied breakdowns in Brazil's political life, and the latter would not be an exception.

In June 2013, the Movimento Passe Livre (MPL)[5] initiated a series of protests denouncing long-standing infrastructure and transportation issues, a demand that had been sustained for a decade within anti-globalization movements connected to the World Social Forum (see von Bülow in this volume). More broadly, contention also arose and spread as a response to public works plans launched by the government to prepare for several major sporting events held in Brazil in 2014 (Confederations Football Cup, FIFA World Cup, and Olympic Games), which would arguably affect the provision of public goods and quality of life of the population.

This first series of protests underwent a scale shift as a result of the violent police response. After virulent repression a major wave of mobilizations began, which included diverse actors representing a wide array of demands and boosting the sympathy of the media. The loosely organized and heterogeneous participants included the middle classes, which had, until then, a weak tradition of mobilization. The protestors presented claims that multiplied in an unorganized fashion and targeted both sides of the political spectrum. The unifying elements were a frontal criticism of the government of Dilma Rousseff and the denunciation of widespread corruption within the political system: "'Fora! Partidos! Vocês querem o povo dividido!', 'Mensaleiros!', 'Corruptos, vocês se preparem, vão cair um por um!'" (Alonso 2017: 52).

After the 2014 presidential elections—which resulted in Rousseff's reelection by a tight margin—the political opposition reorganized and infused the protests with new vigor. The claims of major opposition parties' were strongly linked to charges of corruption, particularly in connection to the "Lava Jato" scandal.[6] Mobilizations propelled an investigation into corruption charges by Judge Sergio Moro and made corruption a recurrent and salient topic of public debate. One interesting characteristic of these demonstrations is the fact that they were organized through social media, without links to social or political organizations. Supporters of Rousseff's impeachment started to use the hashtag #ForaDilma, which was reproduced by the main opposition fan-pages as well as the Partido da Social Democracia Brasileira (PSDB), Partido do Movimento Democrático Brasileiro (PMDB), and other minor opposition parties (such as the Partido Social Liberal [PSL], which would become Bolsonaro's party). By contrast, the President's supporters denounced an attempted coup d'état (#NãoVaiTerGolpe). "A cada pessoa um cartaz" logic[7] (Tatagiba 2014: 41) prevailed, rejecting any collective definition of demands. Social media was then the main platform for protestors' coordination and self-expression (Tatagiba 2014).

The cycle came to an end with Rousseff's impeachment in 2016. In addition to the size of the demonstrations—which counted with 500,000 to a million participants and took place across several cities— they presented intriguing characteristics in terms of repertoires and socio-demographic composition. First, despite an oppositional stance that targeted government coalition leaders (Alonso 2017: 56), the demonstrations were non-partisan. As in other cases analyzed in this chapter, leaders and parties were explicitly rejected as mobilization structures. Mobilizations were linked to a public expression of outrage and rejection raised by individuals, and not by political organizations (Holston 2014: 888).

Second, as in the cases of Argentina and Guatemala, large-scale demonstrations in Brazil convened large contingents of demonstrators with neither previous experience of activism nor clear partisan affiliations; this draws particular contrast to what we observe in the mobilizations of the 1990s, in which union and leftist activists were present (Mische 2008). In the recurrence of mobilizations and amid anti-partisan claims, new actors interested in producing certain political effects that channeled the mistrust and opposition to the government (Anderson 2019) began to emerge. This temporal unfolding had three successive phases (Alonso 2017): the first phase, in June 2013, represented a moment of eruption, diversification, and massification. Then, between March and April 2015, protests reactivated in connection to what Alonso (ibid.) has called the "patriotic" repertoire of mobilization. Finally, from December 2015 to March 2016, a new phase of large demonstrations accompanied the debates and conflicts that led to presidential impeachment (ibid.: 50). This type of unfolding echoes the Argentine case.

Finally, we can observe the cumulative and growing influence of anti-corruption as a frame for large-scale anti-government demonstration. Brazil is a paradigmatic case because mobilizations against Collor de Mello in the 1990s ended with his impeachment. Between this event and the more recent demonstrations, the anti-corruption frame switched sides on the ideological spectrum—from the left to the right. This was possible due to the absence of an anti-corruption movement. Nevertheless, the vocabulary of anti-corruption was a key rhetorical component that allowed for the unification of grievances during the protests.

Guatemala (2015–2018)

Social mobilization in Guatemala after the democratic transition has been shaped by the legacies of a restrictive civic space, violations of fundamental rights, and the historical marginalization of the indigenous population (Brett 2008; Brocket, Rice in this volume). Social movements gradually started to articulate platforms by the end of 1996, after the peace accords. These combined a human rights frame with socioeconomic, cultural, and gender-based demands (Brett 2016; see Wolff in this volume).

Nonetheless, in contrast with cases like Argentina or Brazil, Guatemala has traditionally exhibited repressive policing tactics in response to social protests, a deterrent for social mobilization. In fact, just one year before large-scale demonstrations triggered the resignation of President Otto Pérez Molina in 2015, the Congress issued Decree Number 08-2014 limiting the right of assembly and demonstration. This law was largely condemned by international human rights movements and the World Organization Against Torture, among others.

At the beginning of 2015, the prosecutors' office and the Commission Against Impunity in Guatemala (CICIG)[8] released an investigation which revealed a multi-million-dollar kickback scheme in the customs agency. The scandal involved high-ranking officials, including the private secretary of Former Vice-President Roxana Baldetti, who was arrested following the investigation (Casas-Zamora and Carter 2017). In May 2015, another scandal involving the Instituto de Seguridad Social of Guatemala implicated both Baldetti and President Pérez Molina.

Immediately after these scandals broke, citizens started to gather in the central square of Guatemala City each Saturday, using social media platforms and the hashtag #RenunciaYa to organize. As in the cases of Brazil and Argentina, online media networks played a very important role. A non-partisan group of urban youth with no previous experience in social movements organized the first protests, largely on Twitter and Facebook. The interplay of digital media with traditional media brought other groups—such as indigenous rights organizations, businessmen, and peasants—into the fold (Flores 2019).

Several factors characterized Guatemala's 2015 demonstrations. First, the anti-corruption frame generated citizen outrage and helped align different interests and demands toward a single goal: the resignation of high-ranked leaders. A diversity of actors and cross-sectoral alliances ended up participating in the demonstrations, including students from public and private universities, labor unions, businessmen, and peasants (Díaz Luna 2017). Additionally, protestors received the support of international actors, ranging from the CICIG to the United States Embassy (Cuevas-Molina 2016). Social media helped to amplify citizens' demands.

In 2015, more than 100,000 Guatemalans across 140 municipalities participated in the mobilizations (Beltrán 2018). Demonstrators demanded that the Vice-President and President resign. Anti-corruption rhetoric framed this demand, giving voice to popular indignation by unifying sectoral grievances under the discourse of change. These demonstrations were described as the largest protests in Guatemala's history (Casas-Zamora and Carter 2017), and the first of their kind in terms of bringing people together from different sectors—particularly notable was the participation of young people.

The main repertoire within these demonstrations was people peacefully linking their arms and walking together around the central square. As in the Brazilian and Peruvian cases, demonstrators did not have a clear partisan affiliation or previous experience protesting. This was somewhat different from Argentina, where middle-class involvement in demonstrations in the late 1990s and 2001 served as an important precedent.

It was not until the Guatemalan Supreme Court ruled in favor of allowing impeachment proceedings that Pérez Molina submitted his resignation, in September 2015. News of the president's resignation came six days after a massive general strike, when the Comité Coordinador de Asociaciones Agrícolas, Comerciales, Industriales y Financieras (CACIF)—the largest and most powerful employers' association in Guatemala—withdrew its support for the President. According to Díaz Luna (2017: 53), this situation allowed representatives in Congress to vote in favor of stripping the President of immunity the following week.

Under the slogan "neither corrupt, nor a thief," Jimmy Morales was elected as the new president of Guatemala in October 2015. Morales, a political outsider "with questionable ties and allegiances based on his affiliation with the Frente de Convergencia Nacional Party (made up of ex-military personnel from the Asociación de Veteranos Militares de Guatemala)," was best known for his comedy show "Moralejas," which he ran for fourteen years (Mitchell and Cameron 2015). Once in power, Morales implemented a series of transparency reforms, particularly in the areas of public contracting and election financing. However, as investigations conducted by the public prosecutor and the CICIG progressed, new corruption cases involving bankers, private corporations, and family members of a powerful and entrenched economic elite started to appear, "creating rifts among those who had originally supported the anti-corruption agenda" (Flores 2019: 47).

When in August 2017 the CICIG Commissioner Iván Velásquez announced that there was enough evidence to suggest that Morales might had accepted illicit funding in his 2015 election run, a confrontation began. After this public declaration, Morales decided not to renew Velásquez's mandate and ordered him to leave the country, declaring him "non grato" (Arnson 2018). This decision triggered a second wave of demonstrations in the country, which then unfolded into two different types of mobilizations: those in support of and against the government.

The second cycle of demonstrations was catalyzed by a confrontation between President Morales and the CICIG and exhibited some similarities and differences with the first cycle. First, anti-corruption rhetoric unified demands from different sectors against a government that did not represent the interest of the citizens. However, in addition to using the moral judgement rhetoric as an opposition strategy that demanded the resignation of Jimmy Morales, this new cycle of demonstrations included a clear call to support CICIG's efforts in the country.

Although we cannot strictly speak of an anti-corruption movement per se, unlike the cases of Brazil and Argentina, there was more organicity and continuity among the demonstrators and their repertoires. The core of students and citizens who used social media to organize the first cycle of demonstrations around the hashtag #RenunciaYa, changed their call to action to the hashtag #JusticiaYa. #JusticiaYa was a flexible and horizontal platform for citizen participation in the context of a strong disenchantment with representative politics, similar to other platforms in the region such as the Mexican #YoSoy132 (Welp 2015; Donoso in this volume) or "pot-banging" in Argentina. This platform helped to amplify the discontent against the government and the political and economic elite as a whole, and despite support for the anti-corruption measures taken by the CICIG and the Prosecutor's office, its organizational structure as a social movement remained loose.

At the same time, this second cycle showed the emergence of new factions. For example, young people began to organize around the #GuatemalaInmortal hashtag to protect liberty and private property, directly challenging what they perceived to be "a 'leftist' takeover of the 2015 civic protests" (Flores 2019). Unlike the case of Brazil, in Guatemala the demonstrators who used the anti-corruption rhetoric in the first cycle included progressive civil society groups and human rights movements, such as the indigenous' and peasants' Comité de Desarrollo Campesino (CODECA), as well as more conservative groups with religious, anti-abortion, anti-LGTBQ rights agendas.

Peru (2017–2018)

There is strong academic consensus on the existence and historical impact of corruption in Peru (Quiroz 2008). However, there is comparably little evidence for, or academic study of, anti-corruption mobilization. As in the other cases analyzed in this chapter, the vocabulary of anti-corruption served to gather and build weak solidarity among different actors in specific contexts. These demonstrations were triggered by corruption scandals, which did not result in the construction of a stable social movement. In the case of Peru, institutional weakness and the fragmentation of contentious actors contributed to a deepening of this general regional dynamic.

Peru, like Guatemala, has not typically seen the high levels of mobilization characteristic of the other countries. Since the 1970s, a combination of neoliberal policies, weak corporatist incorporation, and internal struggles between guerrilla groups and the military eroded the power of labor organizations and social movements to resist repression and labor flexibilization (Silva 2009). Furthermore, decades of decay in the Peruvian party system contributed to the proliferation of candidate-centered electoral machines. During the 1990s, these conditions wore down the opposition's capacity to build coalitions and mobilize collectively against the authoritarian government of Alberto Fujimori (Levitsky and Cameron 2003).

The first major wave of protest against corruption peaked after the Vladivideo scandal that initiated the collapse of the Fujimori government in 2000 (Cameron 2006). The release of a series of videos showing Vladimiro Montesinos—head of the National Intelligence Agency and Fujimori's right-hand man—bribing legislators who had switched from the main opposition party a few months prior, represented undeniable evidence of corruption across every sphere of the state. The scandal was a crucial turning point for Peruvian democracy, allowing the weak and scattered opposition to challenge Fujimori, who had already faced several massive protests opposing his third consecutive presidential campaign.

The massive Marcha de los Cuatro Suyos in July 2000, organized by Fujimori's opponent—and future president—Alejandro Toledo, gathered thousands of protesters nationwide in opposition to the inauguration of Fujimori's third term. The movement symbolized unity in the social opposition to the government. After Toledo's speech on the night of the march, protestors attacked numerous public buildings as a response to incidences of police repression. The Vladivideo scandal fueled this already growing wave of discontent, illustrated by a repertoire that consisted of a weekly "washing" of the Peruvian flag in public square fountains. The autonomous collective "Sociedad Civil" performed the repertoire every Friday in the main square in Lima. Its public impact was widespread, forcing the new transitional President Valentín Paniagua (2000–2001) to acknowledge and embrace the struggle against corruption. He embraced one of the flags in a public address and promised to be held accountable to the Peruvian citizenry (Ilizarbe 2017).

After the fall of Fujimori in 2000, the political liberalization of the regime represented a major shift in the political opportunity structure of protest, one that would significantly change the landscape of mobilization in the country (Arce 2015). In fact, annual levels of protest in Peru would soon skyrocket and reach figures similar to other highly mobilized countries in the region. However, this increase in mobilization followed patterns delineated by the Peruvian political landscape: the decentralization process undertaken during the Toledo administration in 2002 gave more autonomy to regional governments but was highly disorganized and improvised. Decentralization gave way to a process of increased regionalization and sub-nationalization of protests, fragmenting opportunities for building national social movement organizations –both vertically and horizontally (Grompone and Tanaka 2009).

Therefore, although citizens' perception of corruption remained high, those perceptions did not translate into a motivation for a national unified protest. Anti-corruption was instead used as a vocabulary to target local governments. In fact, since 2002, major arenas of contention have been those directly related to direct investment from foreign/transnational corporations, particularly in regards to the mining industry (Arce 2008; Ponce and McClintock 2014; Christel and Gutiérrez in this volume).

Although the moralized vocabulary against inefficient local bureaucracies was widespread during the 2000s, Peru did not witness another major anti-corruption mobilization until the year 2018, when a regional scandal involving major bribes from the Brazilian company Odebrecht began to cascade. News that the construction company arranged bribes with more than eleven governments throughout Latin America (and several more across Africa) had a major impact in Peru. The legitimacy of President Pedro Pablo Kuczynski (2016–2018) had already been called into question by accusations of illicit enrichment related to consultancy services for Odebrecht when he was a public servant. His lack of credibility deepened when the press released several videos showing him negotiating bribes with the opposition to avoid the second presidential impeachment in less than a year. The scandal finally led to his resignation. Public opinion considered Kuczynski to be the last in a long line of corrupt presidents, which included Fujimori, Toledo (2001–2006), Alan García (1985–1990, 2006–2011), and even Ollanta Humala (2011–2016).

This series of events, which in many ways resembled the Fujimori case in 2000, became even more critical in July when leaked conversations between high-court officials revealed a widespread network of corruption within the judiciary branch. Triggered by a local investigation on drug trafficking, the audio leak revealed corrupt networks within the Supreme Court, and even among some members of the National Magistrates Council, the institution in charge of designating federal judges. It came to light that high-ranking members of the Fujimorista party were taking a leading role on vote-buying within the Council, spurring an investigation that ended with an unprecedented order for the preventive imprisonment of Keiko Fujimori.

The strong evidence of widespread corruption across the Peruvian political system sparked public outrage. On July 19 and 27, thousands of people mobilized across the country in protest of corruption. The demonstrations resembled the repertoires and main frames of the 2001 crisis in Argentina. Word of these two main protest events quickly spread across social media platforms with the hashtag #QueSeVayanTodos; the protests displayed a widespread rejection of the major political parties and the judiciary power. Organized by trade unions, student organizations, human rights organizations, and some Anti-Fujimori autonomous collectives (such as the Facebook fanpages "No a Keiko" and "No a la Korrupción"), the protesters gathered at the Plaza San Martín and ultimately faced police repression.

As in the cases of Argentina and Brazil, national symbols were granted a prominent place in the protests. Demonstrators in Lima as well as several other minor cities and towns across the country engaged in the repertoire of the washing of the Peruvian flag. In Cuzco, a group of teachers washed the flag, in Juliaca, recent graduates from the military academy did the same, as did members of the main trade union, the Confederacion General de Trabajadores del Perú (CGTP) in Tumbes, Piura, Talara, and Lambayeque. A similar action was taken at other protests headed by the Sindicato Único de Trabajadores de la Educacion del Perú (SUTEP) and autonomously organized citizens (see Defensoría del Pueblo 2017). This repertoire, which symbolized the need for cleaning the country from corruption, was accompanied by the display of banners that expressed a high rejection of the main political leaders of the country.

Despite the apparent similarities with the anti-Fujimori protests of the early 2000s, the more recent wave of mobilizations took place in a context characterized by a long-standing disaffection towards the main party leaders and their performance both within and outside office. In this sense, the vocabulary of anti-corruption was not only used to confront and challenge President Kuczynski, but also evolved into a critique of party politics more broadly, a dynamic seen in Argentina during the 1990s, in Brazil after the 2010s and in Guatemala during the 2018 demonstrations.

Conclusion

The analysis of these four cases highlights the importance of anti-corruption frames for the study of social movements, showing a consistent pattern involving: (a) the recurrent use of anti-corruption frames in large-scale demonstrations, (b) a strong confrontation and challenge to presidential figures, and (c) a critique towards institutional politics in moral terms. In the last decade, a fourth additional characteristic has emerged: (d) the use of social media to assemble large audiences with weak or no political engagement or mobilization experience. A primary conclusion of this analysis is that anti-corruption claims have neither been translated into a single motivation for protest, nor given rise to a social movement in any of these countries. Yet the issue of corruption has been progressively incorporated into the vocabulary and repertoires of protest, becoming a significant element of criticism of, and confrontation with, institutional politics.

The large-scale demonstrations analyzed here are convergent with a global rise in outrage against institutional politics. They also exhibit three elements that figure as central features of a broader wave of global protests. First, they illustrate an important transformation in the traditional organizational patterns of social movements. Previously, social movement organizations played a key role in defining central aspects of the demonstrations (Fillieule and Tartakowsky 2015), like the design of posters or flags, the spatial distribution of protesters, and the itineraries and directions of marches. These are well-known elements in the cultures of protest. Conversely, in recent anti-government demonstrations the expression of indignation or rejection is more individualized, or even constructed in a lax collective sense (i.e., as an aggregation of individual expressions).

Second, organizational patterns in anti-corruption mobilizations reveal the central use of online platforms as an umbrella to unify different demands, which are symbolized by slogans or hashtags (Bennett and Segerberg 2013). We have shown that in recent decades, anti-corruption seems to have worked as a general theme of rejection of the political class, identifying anti-corruption with anti-establishment claims. The rejection of presidential figureheads—and in general of political elites—functions as a unifying element capable of awakening the interest of massive audiences, linking their outrage to collective action.

Third, spontaneity and emotional priming seem to be present in most of these protest events, with protesters attending individually and expressing their outrage through handmade banners or other visual elements. In all these cases, rejection, indignation, or fatigue of leadership and political elites came from different, individualized perceptions of the situation of a given country, eventually leading to violence. The objectives of critique and the demands varied significantly: claims of "authoritarianism" or criticism of presidential insensitivity, economic difficulties, the privileges of the political elite, police abuses, lack of guarantees of civil rights, freedom of expression, independence of the justice system, demands for constitutional reform, or rejections of it, and so on.

Rejection of, and indignation with, corruption thus included diverse, and sometimes contradictory claims. This observation is consistent with recent theories on spontaneity, which emphasize a connection between the lack of organizational leadership and a process of script dissolution over the course of a mobilization (Snow and Moss 2016). As anti-corruption movements are not leading the protests, events become more open to innovation in repertoires and frames, with some partisan actors taking advantage of this ambivalence once protests begin (evident in the Argentine and Brazilian cases).

Thus, an important factor for understanding these waves of protests is their ubiquity. As our cases show, the anti-corruption issue has been tied to protests against governments of different political orientations, including some promoting neoliberal policies and others more inclined to state intervention and income redistribution. Demonstrators mobilizing anti-corruption rhetoric can thus belong to different sides of the political and ideological spectrum. Still, a frontal critique of institutional politics that acquired relevance refers to the centrality of political leaders and prominent party figures (Pereyra and Marentes 2019). Although the rejection of traditional political parties appears to be a widespread element that cuts across cases, the large-scale demonstrations analyzed here tended to focus on presidents or the most popular political leaders. These expressions of personalized rejection did not represent, as far as we could observe, a source of direct challenge to the mechanisms of representative democracy or democratic regimes. Rather, the indignation seems to emanate from the performances of political and governmental figures, which are constantly under public scrutiny.

Notes

1. The gradual disclosure of corruption scandals during Carlos Menem's (1989–1995, 1995–1999) neoliberal administrations led to a conception of corruption bounded to party politics, which started to permeate the vocabulary of protest. This change was boosted by two types of actors: opposition political parties on the one side, and NGOs and think tanks on the other.
2. During the late 1990s, the first strong claims related to transparency in politics were mobilized by the recently created center-Left alliance Frente Pais Solidario (FREPASO) and the traditional Union Cívica Radical (UCR) during pot-banging protests in 1996 and 1997, denouncing Menem's corrupt management of public companies' privatization and scandals related to organized crime in a context marked by intra-government competition and tensions.
3. As in the case of Brazil, the list of grievances was wide. The most salient complaints included: the *Ciccone* scandal, where Kirchner's vice-president Amado Boudou was accused of attempting to buy the money-printing company *Ciccone* through a front business; the *Once* rail disaster in the City of Buenos Aires, which exposed the lack of accountability over the operating private transportation companies; rumors—fed also by cabinet members—that Cristina Kirchner would pursue a constitutional reform to run for a third term; a lack of counter-inflation measures; and the implementation of currency exchange controls.
4. *Cipayo* is a popular adjective within Argentine political culture that refers contemptuously to the local population who supports the United States and its political and societal model.
5. MPL is a movement created in Brazil in 2005 within the World Social Forum of Porto Alegre. Since then, the movement's main claim is free fare for public transportation.

6. The corruption scandal involved politicians from most of the political parties in Brazil. The case uncovered an extensive money laundering network stemming from political corruption.
7. The expression can be translated as "one banner for each person," denoting a lack of collective coordination and organization.
8. The CICIG was established in 2007 by the United Nations to help investigate and dismantle criminal networks in Guatemala.

References

Almeida, Paul and Allen Cordero Ulate (eds.) (2015), *Handbook of Social Movements across Latin America* (New York: Springer).

Alonso, Angela (2017), "A politica das ruas: Protestos em São Paulo de Dilma a Temer," *Novos Estudos*, special issue (June), 49–58.

Alonso, Angela, and Anne Mische (2015), "June Demonstrations in Brazil: Repertoires of Contention and Government's Response to Protest," Paper presented at the ESA Research Network on Social Movements Midterm Conference, February 19–20, 2015, Universidad Complutense de Madrid, Spain.

Anderson, Perry (2019), "Bolsonaro's Brazil," *London Review of Books* 41(3), 11–22.

Arce, Moisés (2008), "The Repoliticization of Collective Action after Neoliberalism in Peru," *Latin American Politics & Society* 50(3), 37–62.

Arce, Moises (2015), *Resource Extraction and Protest in Peru* (Pittsburgh, PA: University of Pittsburgh Press).

Arnson, Cynthia J. (ed.) (2018), *In the Age of Disruption: Latin America's Domestic and International Challenges*, Woodrow Wilson Center Reports on the Americas, vol. 38 (Washington DC: Woodrow Wilson International Center for Scholars).

Balán, Manuel (2011), "Competition by Denunciation: The Political Dynamics of Corruption Scandals in Argentina and Chile," *Comparative Politics* 43(4), 459–78.

Beltrán, Adriana (2018) "Is Guatemala's Fight against Corruption under Threat?' *Foreign Affairs*, June 6, https://www.foreignaffairs.com/articles/guatemala/2018-06-06/guatemalas-fight-against-corruption-under-threat.

Bennett, Lance W. and Alexandra Segerberg (2013), *The Logic of Connective Action* (New York: Cambridge University Press).

Bringel, Breno and Geoffrey Pleyers (eds.) (2017), *Protesta e indignación global: Los movimientos sociales en el nuevo orden mundial* (Buenos Aires: CLACSO).

Brett, Rody (2008), *Social Movements, Indigenous Politics and Democratisation in Guatemala: 1985–1996* (Leiden: Brill).

Brett, Rody (2016), *The Origins and Dynamics of Genocide: Political Violence in Guatemala* (New York: Springer).

Cameron, Maxwell A. (2006), "Endogenous Regime Breakdown: The Vladivideo and the Fall of Peru's Fujimori," in Julio Carrión (ed.), *The Fujimori Legacy: The Rise of Electoral Authoritarianism in Peru* (University Park, PA: Penn State University Press), 268-293.

Casas-Zamora, Kevin and Miguel Carter (eds.) (2017), *Beyond the Scandals: The Changing Context of Corruption in Latin America, Rule of Law Report* (Washington, DC: Inter-American Dialogue).

Cuevas-Molina, Rafael (2016), "Guatemala: Reflections on the Social Movement That Led to the Resignation of the President and Vice President in 2015," *Temas de Nuestra América* 32(59), 67–80.

Defensoría del Pueblo (2017), *Reporte de conflictos sociales 161* (Lima: Defensoría del Pueblo).

della Porta, Donatella (2017), "Anti-Corruption from Below: Social Movements against Corruption in Late Neoliberalism," *Partecipazione e Conflitto* 10(3), 661–92.

Díaz Luna, Sergio (2017), "#RenunciaYa: A Case Study of Social Mobilization in Guatemala," PhD diss., Haverford College.

Fillieule, Olivier and Danielle Tartakowsky (2015), *La Manifestación: Cuando la acción colectiva toma las calles* (Buenos Aires: Siglo XXI).

Flores, Walter (2019), "Youth-Led Anti-Corruption Movement in Post-Conflict Guatemala: 'Weaving the Future'?" *Institute of Development Studies Bulletin* 50(3), 37–71.

Gattoni, Maria Soledad (2016), "La apertura estatal como agenda global: Apuntes para el debate sobre la institucionalización de la participación y la transparencia en América Latina," *Iberoamericana* 16(62), 187–92.

Gold, Tomás (2019), "Tracing the Left Turn Crisis through Argentine Protests: The Anti-Kirchnerist Cycle of Mobilisation (2012–2013)," in Juan Pablo Ferrero, Ana Natalucci, and Luciana Tatagiba (eds.), *Socio-Political Dynamics Within the Crisis of the Left Turn in Argentina and Brazil* (Lanham, MD: Rowman & Littlefield), 117–140.

Gold, Tomás, and Alejandro M. Peña (2018), "Protests, Signaling, and Elections: Conceptualizing Opposition-Movement Interactions during Argentina's Anti-Government Protests (2012–2013)," *Social Movement Studies* 18(3), 1–22.

Gómez, Marcelo (2014), "Radiografía de los movilizados contra el kirchnerismo. Resultados de una encuesta a la concurrencia del 8N," *Sudamérica* 3, 75–100.

Grompone, Romeo and Martín Tanaka (2009), "Conclusiones: Las nuevas relaciones entre protestas sociales y política," in Romeo Grompone (ed.), *Entre el crecimiento económico y la insatisfacción social: Las protestas sociales en el Perú actual* (Lima: Instituto de Estudio Peruanos), 381–412.

Haas, Peter M. (1992). Introduction: Epistemic communities and international policy coordination. *International Organization*, 46(1), 1–35.

Holston, James (2014), "'Come to the Street!': Urban Protest, Brazil 2013," *Anthropological Quarterly* 87(3), 887–900.

Ilizarbe, Carmen (2017), "Hegemonic Struggles of the Democratic Imaginary: Street Protests and the Public Sphere in Peru (1997–2006)," PhD diss., The New School for Social Research.

Joignant, Alfredo, Mauricio Morales and Claudio Fuentes (eds.) (2017), *Malaise in Representation in Latin American Countries: Chile, Argentina, and Uruguay* (New York: Palgrave-Macmillan).

Krastev, Ivan (2004), *Shifting Obsessions: Three Essays on the Politics of Anticorruption* (Budapest: Central European University Press).

Levitsky, Steven and Maxwell A. Cameron (2003), "Democracy without Parties? Political Parties and Regime Change in Fujimori's Peru," *Latin American Politics and Society* 45(3), 1–13.

Llanos, Mariana and Leiv Marsteintredet (2010), *Presidential Breakdowns in Latin America: Causes and Outcomes of Executive Instability in Developing Democracies* (New York: Palgrave).

Marsteintredet, Leiv (2014), "Explaining Variation of Executive Instability in Presidential Regimes: Presidential Interruptions in Latin America," *International Political Science Review* 35(2), 173–94.

Mische, Ann (2008), *Partisan Publics: Communication and Contention across Brazilian Youth Activist Networks* (Princeton, NJ: Princeton University Press).

Mitchell, Robie and Mark Cameron (2015), *Oligarchy in Retreat: Guatemala's Election* (Washington, DC: Council on Hemispheric Affairs).

Pereyra, Sebastián (2012), "La política de los escándalos de corrupción desde los años 1990," *Desarrollo Económico* 52(206), 255–84.

Pereyra, Sebastián (2013), *Política y transparencia: la corrupción como problema público* (Buenos Aires: Siglo XXI).

Pereyra, Sebastián and Maximiliano Marentes (2019), "Distance and Familiarity in Political Talk in Argentina," in Claire Saunders and Bert Klandermans (eds.), *When Citizens Talk about Politics* (New York: Rouletdge), 173–191.

Pereyra, Sebastián, Germán J. Pérez, and Federico L. Schuster (2015), "Trends of Social Protest in Argentina: 1989-2007," in Paul Almeida and Allen Cordero Ulate (eds.), *Handbook of Social Movements across Latin America* (New York: Springer), 335–360.

Pérez-Liñán, Aníbal (2007), *Presidential Impeachment and the New Political Instability in Latin America* (Cambridge: Cambridge University Press).

Ponce, Aldo F. and Cynthia McClintock (2014), "The Explosive Combination of Inefficient Local Bureaucracies and Mining Production: Evidence from Localized Societal Protests in Peru," *Latin American Politics & Society* 56(3), 118–40.

Quiroz, Alfonso W. (2008), *Corrupt Circles: A History of Unbound Graft in Peru* (Washington, DC: Woodrow Wilson Center Press with Johns Hopkins University Press).

Rossi, Federico M., and Marisa von Bülow (2015), "Introduction. Theory-Building Beyond Borders," in Federico M. Rossi and Marisa von Bülow (eds.), *Social Movement Dynamics: New Perspectives on Theory and Research in Latin America* (London: Routledge), 1–14.

Saad-Filho, Alfredo (2013), "Mass Protests under 'Left Neoliberalism': Brazil, June–July 2013," *Critical Sociology* 39(5), 657–69.

Sampson, Steven (2015), "The Anticorruption Package," *Ephemera: Theory and Politics in Organization* 15(2), 115–23.

Santos, Jordana de Souza (2018), "O movimento estudantil na democratização: Crise da era Collor e neoliberalismo," PhD diss., São Paulo State University.

Silva, Eduardo (2009), *Challenging Neoliberalism in Latin America* (Cambridge: Cambridge University Press).

Snow, David A. and Dana M. Moss (2016), "Protest on the Fly: Toward a Theory of Spontaneity in the Dynamics of Protest and Social Movements," *American Sociological Review* 79(6), 1122–43.

Tatagiba, Luciana (2014), "1984, 1992 e 2013. Sobre ciclos de protestos e democracia no Brasil," *Política & Sociedade* 13(28), 35–62.

Trom, Danny (2001), "Grammaire de la mobilisation et vocabulaires de motifs," in Daniel Cefaï and Danny Trom (eds.), *Les formes de l'action collective: Mobilisations dans des arères publiques* (Paris: Editions de l'EHESS), 99–134.

Waisbord, Silvio (2000), *Watchdog Journalism in Latin America: News, Accountability, and Democracy* (New York: Columbia University Press).

Welp, Yanina (2015), "Cuando Todo Lo Sólido Se Desvanece En Twitter: Análisis Del Movimiento Social# Yosoy132," *POSTData: Revista de Reflexión y Análisis Político* 20(2), 417–39.

CHAPTER 29

CONSUMER (RIGHTS) MOVEMENTS IN LATIN AMERICA

SYBIL RHODES

INTRODUCTION

Consumption is an integral part of the human experience, at least as essential as production, but various academic disciplinary traditions have often overlooked or dismissed consumer mobilization. The prioritization of production over consumption is not illogical. People's role in production is usually the way they ensure they can consume. Thus, an increase in subway fares (as occurred in 2019 in Chile) or a reduction of fuel subsidies (as occurred in Ecuador the same year) may plausibly have a worse impact on a working-class family than higher food prices, because workers have to take public transportation to their jobs. And yet, consumption of physical material taken from the natural environment as well as goods and services provided by others is more necessary for human survival than production.

Recognition of the importance of consumption in all human societies is the key point that unifies scholarship on consumerist and consumer rights movements. This unity is not always explicit, as most authors focus on consumption in narrower senses, such as elite opulence, poor people's mobilization to satisfy their basic needs, or middle-class pressure for truth in advertising as a facet of the development of mass markets. Some authors expand the definition of consumption to include the entire life cycle of goods, emphasizing reuse and recycling as much as initial use.

Because all humans must consume, consumption as a phenomenon worthy of study is not limited to mass consumption societies or political democracies. That said, market capitalism emphasizes the idea of consumer sovereignty, and political democracy facilitates all types of social mobilization, so the social mobilization of people in their role as consumers is more common in market democracies than in other systems. Only people whose basic consumption needs like food and clean water are secure can afford to mobilize in favor of legal-regulatory regimes protecting less immediate rights such as transparency of labeling, ethical concerns about production chains, or the right to compensation for defective merchandise. Movements in favor of the legal codification of what might be called higher-order consumer protections such as these are, therefore, most prevalent in the wealthiest market-based democracies (Breen 2004; Cohen 2003; McKendrick, Brewer, and Plumb 1982). A fundamental unsettled question in the consumerist literature is the extent to which basic consumption guarantees and higher order consumer protections are compatible.

This chapter discusses how scholars from various disciplinary fields have characterized consumption as motivating themes for social, cultural, and political movements in Latin America. The literature on this subject in Latin America is sparser than in Western Europe and North America, but at least three "generations," loosely defined here as such mostly by the chronological and thematic focus of their studies (but also somewhat by the timing and sequence of their work) of scholars have made original arguments drawn from the context of the region. The first generation of scholars to study consumption in Latin American history emphasized negative aspects, often taking a dim view of "irrational" consumer behavior that might be bad for economic development. A second generation was more positive, taking consumers' interests, rational or not, as a phenomenon worthy of study, along with analysis of mobilization and struggles for consumers' legal rights in the context of countries of the region. A third generation has moved in a postmodern, interpretive direction, considering the interplay of consumption with identity, especially but not limited to gender and peoples' relationship with the natural environment. Recent developments such as social media, internet shopping, and big data-based consumer analytics present interesting challenges that are only beginning to be analyzed from multiple disciplinary angles.

Although they are relatively small in number, scholars from and of the Latin American region have contributed interesting perspectives on the core questions in an increasingly international and wide-ranging academic conversation about consumerism. Is it inevitable that consumer movements are segmented by social class? What is the role of consumption in economic development, especially in a globalized world? Does advertising provide consumers with useful information, or fill them with superfluous desires? How do decisions in the marketplace (predominant in the repertoire of consumer movements) differ from other types of political participation, such as voting? What is the true consumer interest, and what type of rights are consumer rights? Is consumer mobilization more fruitfully viewed as a top-down or bottom-up process? Under what conditions are consumerist concerns incorporated by political parties? Is consumer activism indicative of mistrust in traditional political institutions, or is it complementary to them? What is the content and repertoire of consumer movements? How does consumerism relate to the performance of aspects of personal identity, particularly gender? And, increasingly, can political consumerism lead to a more ethical and/or sustainable economy?

Empirically, much more is known about the larger and wealthier countries in Latin America. The theoretical approaches employed by analysts are diverse, sometimes mutually exclusive and contested, and sometimes overlapping and complementary. The rest of this chapter discusses the primary lines of argument, with emphasis on what makes the study of Latin American consumer movements distinct from traditions in other regions. It begins with an overview of the treatment of consumption by the first generation in Latin American development studies leading up to and during the period of import substitution industrialization, then discusses the two newer generations that emerged in the context of the 1980s economic crises and subsequent period of market-based reforms, before turning to more recent approaches to consumer rights and consumerism. All three of the generations are still alive in the sense that these literatures are considering new questions and, occasionally, beginning to dialogue with each other, making consumer movements a dynamic area of study in the region, with plenty of potential for growth.

Consumption and the Context of Latin American Development up to and through the ISI Period (1940–1990)

Historians have long analyzed consumption as a dimension of capitalist development, cultural modernization, and globalization (Trentmann and Otero-Cleves 2017). This emphasis on consumption in Europe and North America, combined with the obvious transnational dimension of Latin American development, led early analysts, particularly the structuralists associated with the Comisión Económica para América Latina y el Caribe, to emphasize the importance of elites' cravings for foreign goods, obtained through international trade (Franco 2018). Cultural and political leaders attempted to construct national identities by juxtaposing "foreign" consumption habits with local traditions and preferences (Varsavsky 1971).

Versions of this basic pattern of political and cultural appeals, which might be placed along an axis ranging from luxurious/foreign to popular/national continued through the twentieth and into the twenty-first century, although in recent work the dichotomy has occasionally been challenged. For instance, those influenced by the structuralist school often assumed that Latin American elites had always merely wished to reproduce European or North American patterns (Bauer 2001), but Otero Cleves (2017) addresses the development of new identity through clothing styles after independence. (Thus, here we have an example of what this chapter calls the third generation productively conversing with the first generation of scholars.) Only recently have scholars attempted to discuss early mobilizations by Latin American non-elites in specific relation to consumption. Santos (2014), for example, documented demonstrations related to hunger in Brazil in the nineteenth century.

An austere, nationalist take on the luxurious-foreign to popular-national poles held considerable sway in economic studies into the mid-twentieth century. Founding father of the structuralist school, Raúl Prebisch (1993, cited in Pryluka and Coviello 2018) criticized the advertising industry for creating disruptive "new tastes" that interfered with national capital accumulation, and suggested that the importation of "unnecessary articles" be prohibited. Ferrer (1956), a student of Prebisch, further developed the point high earners were responsible for consuming resources that could be used to invest. "Consumer sovereignty" was a problem for developing economies, he argued (ibid.: 91). This view of elite consumption patterns as inherently wasteful provided some initial justification for policies of import substitution industrialization (Franco 2018). Critiques of conspicuous consumption and advertising are certainly not limited to the Latin American context (see, for example, Veblen 2017), but their influence in important economic policy paradigms native to the region, such as dependency theory, is notable.

As development occurred, and economic policies moved towards import substitution industrialization, however, political leaders began to walk a delicate line between criticizing opulence and promoting mass consumption (Pryluka and Coviello 2018). For example, Juan Domingo Perón argued that consumption is "a factor for wealth . . . unlike what some . . . believe, nobody ever got rich by saving" (Perón, 1974, cited in Pryluka and Coviello 2018). This shift towards mass consumerism is comprehensively documented by historians of consumption in Argentina. Elena (2011) analyzes the deliberate consumerist turns in Peronist rhetoric and policy. Legal reforms of the time reflected the development of consumer rights; for example, the Argentine constitutional reform of 1949 included ideas of rights to happiness and leisure. Milanesio (2013) goes beyond political economy to discuss the wholesale creation of a new cultural category, the "worker-consumer," through populist political movements like Peronism. "Worker-consumers," who could now afford to buy household appliances, watch movies, and go on vacation, were alternately courted and patronized by "experts" (advertising agencies, middle and upper classes, and politicians), but also participated themselves in developing their new role. Milanesio's work further provides a gendered analysis, showing, for example, how Perón called on housewives to discipline retailers who engaged in supposedly abusive practices.

The expansion of mass consumption and its gendered dimensions (see Johnson and Sempol in this volume) were, of course, also present in North American cases as well. The works by Elena and Milanesio cited above draw from, but do not merely mirror, accounts like Jacobs' *Pocketbook Politics* (2005), which depicted consumption as the foundation of civic identity in the United States. Perhaps the most crucial difference was the severity of the cleavage between opulent and international with patriotic austerity, which continued to hold sway into the second half of the twentieth century. Pryluka and Coviello (2018) discuss Argentina in the 1970s, during the third presidency of Perón. These authors identify a strategy by political elites of criticizing the consumption practices of elites, particularly the cultural emulation of foreign styles. Varsavsky (1971: 240) argued that basic necessities could be covered for the entire Argentine population with almost no need for imports if elites would only give up their opulence. Varsavsky also criticized the equivalence of "consumers" and "citizen" (Varsavsky 1971: 173), a debate which, as we shall see, continues to the present day.

In neighboring Brazil, meanwhile, the "cost of living movement," which emphasized the costs of basic goods and services, was perhaps the most important social movement of the 1960s and 1970s (Gohn 2003: 110–11). It was a direct manifestation of middle- and working-class people in their role as consumers (Doimo 1995). This popular movement, in combination with more directed activism by legal professionals, some of whom were influenced by the example of other countries, notably the United States, produced expanded protections even during the period of military rule in Brazil, and eventually led to the passage of the comprehensive Consumer Protection Code in 1990, as is well documented in Rios (1998).

It is worth pausing here to note a couple of interesting tendencies in the literature as discussed thus far. First, in the work of the Argentine authors cited earlier, politicians organize consumers from the top down, formally through labor unions, whereas in the Brazilian case, bottom-up mobilization by social classes and civil and professional organizations are key. Second, in the Argentine case, the production aspect of identity, that is, the *worker*-consumer, remains dominant. In the Brazilian case, as Santos (2014) argues, there was a popular consumer interest divided into two dimensions, one related to scarcity and hunger and another that sought to codify and enforce consumers' legal rights. This differentiation may be viewed as a class distinction, in the sense that people's first priority in consumption is purely material. As legal scholars have demonstrated, the better off are more likely than the poor to assert their legal rights in general (see Schmitz 2012; Willis 2015).

The legal rights movement progressed in tandem with private sector development, even under political dictatorship but especially after democratization in Brazil. At the same time that progressive activists worked to implement state protection of consumers, private businesses began to publicize the idea of customer service, creating public relations departments, consumer hotlines, and ombudsmen. In 1989, twenty professionals formed the Associação Nacional de Profissionais de Serviços ao Consumidor. Its membership reached 220 in four years. In 1979 there were fifty businesses with Consumer Relations departments, and by 1985, the number had reached 1,500 and was rising (Rios 1998). Similar developments occurred in other countries, but in no other Latin American country was the movement for consumers' legal rights as comprehensive or as well-documented as in Brazil.

Once legal rights were achieved, Santos (2014) argues, the need for consumer rights movements disappeared. Although the point that the establishment of consumer rights as legal rights is fundamental, it should also be kept in mind that consumers benefitted from economic development per se, in the sense of having access to more and a greater variety of goods and services than from the accompanying legal protection regime. Legal rights continue to evolve with economic developments such as online commerce, as we shall see.

Further, once democracy returned, Santos (2014) continues, the "popular perspective" and the "scarcity" issue were absorbed by political parties. Although there is some truth to these points about the Brazilian case, as we also shall see, occasionally Brazilian consumers have mobilized around consumption-related rights even in the New Republic (1985–present). Indeed, Latin American history provides ample evidence that consumers mobilize under democracy. Most dramatically, protest of rising prices has played a role in the overturn of several democratic governments in the region. In one example, Tinsman (2014) shows how middle-class women's worries about shortages and inflation, and how these would affect their families' consumption, led them to take to the streets and discredit the Salvador Allende government in Chile and, ultimately, led to support for the 1973 *coup d'état*. The mass protests, and eventually riots, sparked by the subway hikes of 2019, which were met with repression by the democratically elected government is now leading to concerns about the viability of market-based democracy in Chile, a country that quite a few scholars have viewed as a Latin American success story.

Thus far, we have seen that in Latin America, like in other regions, social mobilization based on consumers' experience with the marketplace and their demand for legal rights may have significant effects. A few authors have further shown that consumption and consumerism are gendered in the region, as they are elsewhere. Consumption, consumer rights, and consumerism are useful terms for categorizing some of these forms of mobilization. Finally, we have seen that structural and geopolitical context have often been linked with consumption, especially luxury and elite cultural consumption. The perceived linkage between consumerism and support for authoritarianism may also have contributed both to lack of interest in consumerism and to the predominance of critical approaches in recent decades (Barbosa 2006; Echegaray 2015). However, as the next section shows, interesting empirical work in diverse disciplines is making debates about Latin American consumption richer and more nuanced.

CONSUMPTION AND CONSUMERISM IN THE 1990S AND BEYOND

Scholars of the political and economic reforms carried out in numerous Latin American countries in the 1990s took the analysis of consumption issues in various new directions. Even as certain debates about the best way to fulfill people's rights in consumers in fair and/or inclusive ways remain contentious, the arguments are based on greater empirical knowledge and increasing interdisciplinary dialogue. Economic analysts who viewed the pro-consumer language of the Washington Consensus (which criticized protectionist trade polices as "rent-seeking" that benefitted workers of favored industries and hurt the general, consuming, public) favorably nonetheless did not usually study consumer mobilization. Rather, they tended to assume consumers face a classic collective action problem and therefore never mobilize (Olson 1965). The "rational apathy" of consumers, who are reluctance to pay the cost of legal action most of the time, is, in fact, well-documented by legal and business scholars (Landes and Posner 1975; van den

Bergh and Visscher 2008). Most dissatisfied consumers do not complain directly to private firms either (Schiffman and Wisenblit 2015; Vorhees, Brady, and Horowitch 2006). Indeed, most consumers do not even take the time to read contracts that explain their rights (Ayres and Schwartx 2014).

In Latin America, the compatibility of democratic politics and economic reform was one of the most important debates in political science in the 1990s. Perhaps for this reason, it was mostly political scientists who have analyzed the rhetoric of the Washington Consensus and its effects on public support for reforms such as more open trade, financial stabilization, and privatization of state-owned enterprises.

Although economic theory implies that consumers benefit from open trade, public opinion is often apprehensive about liberalization. Indeed, some students of Latin American trade debates showed that the Costa Rican public did not pay much attention to politicians' arguments about the consumer welfare benefits of the Central American Free Trade Agreement (Frajman 2004). Baker (2009) shows that Latin American publics could be receptive to political messages about consumers' gains from trade, however. Tinsman (2014) points out that greater trade openness allowed Chilean consumers, particularly women, to purchase durable goods that improved their lives. Studies of macroeconomic policy also incorporated a consumer perspective, even if they did not always specify it in those terms. For example, Armijo and Foucher (2004) showed that in a mass democracy, voting publics would demand price stabilization, and numerous authors argued that the record at the polls showed public support for liberal economic policies in general (Gervasoni 1999).

Like trade, the privatization of state-owned enterprises was also theorized to benefit consumers, but the initial studies of privatization focused on production. As for the case of trade, this emphasis was not illogical: consumers were, after all, the quintessential group of dispersed interests facing a collective action problem (Olson 1965). Rhodes (2006) describes how the combination of reforms such as privatization and democratization created a favorable opportunity structure for political entrepreneurs to mobilize consumers in some countries. Her study of the telecommunications sector showed that Brazil—the country with the most developed consumer legislation and the most significant consumer use of the legal system, which privatized under democractic rule—saw more organized consumer mobilization than Argentina or Chile. Rhodes further argues that Brazilian officials' attention to consumers' views produced a better regulatory outcome.

Rhodes (2012a) draws from existing work in the growing field of consumer studies in North America to develop a more complete analysis of consumerist frames used by Brazilian politicians to legitimate policies of trade liberalization, price stabilization, and privatization. She uses a tri-dimensional conceptualization of the consumer interest that incorporates the various motivations discussed in the international and regional literatures. The "competition dimension" corresponds to Cohen's (2003) "purchasing consumer" and the benefits she obtains from competitive markets. The "protection dimension" corresponds to Cohen's "purchaser as citizen," helping enforce national priorities and values; the "protection dimension" was also inspired by the efforts of Latin

American presidents, including Argentina's Perón, as mentioned earlier, and Brazil's José Sarney (O'Dougherty 2002), to enlist consumers, women in particular, to help keep shopkeepers from raising prices. Sarney's appeal was a part of the heterodox Cruzado Plan, which relied on price controls to stop hyperinflation in 1986. Rhodes concludes that the eventual failure of the Cruzado Plan had the result of disaccrediting the "protection" dimension of consumerism, paving the way for the more market-oriented "competition" dimension. Consumer legal advocates thus began framing their messages in pro-competition terms. This may be considered a kind of cultural shift, as analyzed by the third generation of scholars of consumer movements.

Finally, the "social action dimension" involves consumers' active use of their market power as agents to bring about broader social or political change, incorporated the strain of analysis devoted to "ethical" or "critical" consumption (Yates 2011). "Ethical" decisions by individual consumers to change their purchasing behavior is perhaps not a traditional social mobilization, but it is a kind of coordinated action that has social meaning. The meaning of consumer actions and culture are affected by a broader context: Rhodes (2012b) developed a database of media attention to the three frames in Brazil throughout 1985–2005, showing that the passage of the Consumer Protection Code in 1990 corresponded with more messages about "protection" from markets, whereas "competition" frames increased during political debates about liberal economic reforms.

Other analysts took a more critical approach to the idea of the "purchasing consumer" or "competition dimension." For example, some observers of the privation of some public utilities, particularly water, noted unjust outcomes, often objecting to the very idea of using a market system for, and particularly allowing multinational firms to participate in, the distribution of a critical substance for human needs (Olivera 2001; Spronk and Crespo 2008). When the authoritarian government of Augusto Pinochet implemented water privatization in Chile, the policy established standards for private management and no human right to access to water. Protests around water privatization in Bolivia (known as the Bolivian Water Wars) eventually led firms to exit the country and caused Bolivia to become an iconic example of the argument that access to water is a human right that should not be subject to market criteria.

Some scholars further argued more generally that the pro-consumer rhetoric that accompanied neoliberal reforms was reducing citizens to consumers, a presumably inferior category (García Canclini 2001; Oxhorn 2010 and in this volume). Several important studies of social movements identified perceived dangers of reducing state responsibility and moving issues into the private sphere. Indeed, some authors have considered individualized consumer tactics to be evidence that true social movements lack influence (Alvarez, Dagnino, and Escobar 1998: 22). Two sources of tension between more positive and more negative assessments concern the degree to which consumer mobilization is an individual activity or a truly collective, or social, movement, and the degree to which consumer mobilization is an essentially private, rather than public, activity. As Hirschman (1970) and others (Day and Landon Jr. 1977) argued, in competitive markets consumers can individually express displeasure by "exiting." As mentioned above, consumers rarely use "voice" to complain, and even if they do, such complaints are often purely individual ones, directed at private firms. This may plausibly be seen by some as a negative shift away from public concerns. However, scholars of business and marketing have developed a body of literature about consumer complaints. It shows that a small number of vociferous consumers can help solve the collective action problem for others by making their complaints public (Bolfing 1989). Published reviews are useful to consumers as a class, as is media coverage of seemingly oddballs who opt to exercise their right to complain despite the costs, both because they provide information, and because firms may feel pressured to respond.

Eckstein (2006) argues that framing of protest changed from production to consumption as a result of "neoliberalism." However, she emphasizes a return to issues related to the cost of living. She focuses on declining labor-based protests and increases in urban protests of rising food prices and protests against the decline of subsidies for public services.

Eckstein (2006) also mentions the solidarity-based "ethical consumption" activism of "northern" consumers, especially in the textile industry. She is somewhat skeptical that it can have an important impact on workers' rights, an argument borne out by the research of some movements in that sector (Armbruster 2004; Traub-Werner and Cravey 2002). Other sectors in which ethical or critical consumerism has been important for international consumers of Latin American goods are in "fair trade" or "social justice" coffee (Simpson and Rapone 2000) and organic foods.

Some aspects of the "ethical" consumerism to which Eckstein (2006) refers are also present in wealthier Latin American countries. As in other parts of the world, the analysis of consumption and consumer issues in Latin America has also incorporated concerns about the environment, and not just in the new generation—for example, in Argentina there were participants on both sides of the debate about the projections about the Club of Rome. The environmental arguments sometimes became intertwined with the familiar poles of luxurious-foreign and popular-national, as may be seen in the writings of the Fundación Bariloche (a prestigious research institution in the south of Argentina) in 1973, which argued that "the destructive and irrational use of natural resources and the deterioration of the natural environment" were a result of the increase in "consumption by developed countries and privileged minorities in developing countries . . . the result of an intrinsically destructive value system" (cited in Pryluka and Coviello 2018: 7; see Christel and Gutiérrez in this volume).

It is in Brazil where an emphasis on sustainable consumption as ethical consumption has received the most attention since the 1990s (Fontenelle 2006; Harrison, Newholm, and Shaw 2005; Jacobi 1999; Portilho 2005). The most prominent campaign related to these concerns in that decade was the Movimento para um Brasil Livre de Transgênicos, which persuaded the justice system to use consumer protection legislation to impose a restriction on genetically modified soy for years in the face of massive opposition from the powerful agribusiness sector. Whatever its merits, this case captured the attention of international environmental activists, but their legal victories were only possible because of the prior work of the Brazilian consumer rights movement (Rhodes 2012b).

Fair trade or worker-solidarity still do not figure as prominently in analyses of Latin American consumerism as in studies of other regions (but see Balladares 2008). The framing of sustainable consumption as a specific "buy local" preference is also not present, perhaps surprisingly given the historical prominence of criticisms of luxury imports. However, there is a trend towards studies of the impact of globalization on particular places and cultures as Kerssen (2015) does for quinoa. There is an emerging studies of food preparation and consumption, which is usually gendered (Pite 2013). In very recent years, animal rights and veganism have become mobilizing factors, especially for young people, so future studies will surely incorporate those themes.

Returning to the question of tension between consumerism and citizenship, the drive towards greater consumerism and emphasis on private actions seemed to coincide with growing public mistrust of public institutions. But was there really a causal relationship between these two trends in Latin America? The most comprehensive academic study of consumerism after the 1990s is that carried out by Echegaray (2015) in Argentina, Brazil, and Mexico in the 2008–2009 period, on the basis of commercial survey data of boycotting and "buycotting." Echegaray used public opinion studies in Argentina, Brazil, and Mexico to determine whether the argument that consumerism is incompatible with citizenship is supported empirically. He found no evidence that individuals who participate in political consumerism feel alienated by traditional politics. Rather, the opposite holds true: people who are active in party politics are more likely than others to participate in consumer activism. In contrast to Alvarez, Dagnino, and Escobar (1998), Echegaray (2015) has a different take on the expression of concerns to private firms, arguing that because such firms produce many public goods it is important for democracy that consumers exercise voice in the private arena.

Scholars of Latin American movements during the neoliberal reform period recognize the different manifestations of consumption as an area for mobilization. Is the rise of political consumerism a cause for worry, an indication of the vulnerability of labor as per Eckstein, or an indication of alienation from public life as per Oxhorn; or are the perspectives of Echegaray, Baker, and Rhodes warranted? Recall from the introduction to this chapter that this is the most basic tension in the consumerist literature worldwide. These and other questions may never be answered fully, but the debate is enriched when authors with different perspectives, and from diverse disciplines, acknowledge the multidimensional nature of consumer preferences. The latter part of this chapter discusses pending areas where analysts of Latin American consumer movements might continue to make important contributions.

POLITICAL AND CULTURAL STUDIES

Although economic studies have documented the expansion of spending power in various countries during the 2000s, the field lacks a prominent analysis of political and cultural frames regarding consumption during this period and beyond, which might provide meaning for social mobilization of consumers. Did politicians continue to emphasize the "worker-consumer" identity, and did people see themselves this way? How have changing patterns of international trade affected attitudes towards consumption of imports? This latter suggestion could draw from the work of Rocchi (2003), which documents the Americanization, or adoption of North American cultural tastes, of the consumption of imports, via marketing, in Argentina from 1920 to 1945.

By the late 2010s, economic outlooks in much of the region were more negative. As mentioned earlier, in 2019 subway fare hikes in Chile sparked mass protests, led at least at first by students, and rioting. Chileans were also discontent with the pension and education systems, and in general fed up with perceived unfairness. Protests in Ecuador in the same year began as a reaction to the end of fuel subsidies. These movements seem, at least at first glance, to be similar to the "cost of living" movements seen earlier in the region, but there is still much to be unpacked and analyzed about their causes. For example, it is possible that social media has played a role in harnessing consumers' dissatisfaction, by magnifying conspicuous consumption and making inequalities more immediately visible. We may be due a return of some of the themes emphasized by the first generation of scholarly comment on consumerism mentioned in this chapter.

Legal Studies, Class Action, and Multilateral Cooperation

By the 2000s, most Latin American countries had national consumer rights protection legislation. Although Santos (2014) might be right that in Brazil the implementation of the consumer protection code eliminated the need for a movement to legalize consumer rights at the national level (as explained above), the legal arena remains a dynamic area for the study of consumer issues in other Latin American countries. In the legal arena the question of whether consumer mobilization is an individual or collective phenomenon is closely related to the question of individual judicial actions versus class actions, or individual versus collective redress, as legal remedies for large classes of consumers are more commonly referred to nowadays. In most countries of the region these remain a contested issue (in some cases nationally, and sometimes even multilaterally). The regional multilateral debate about collective redress reflects in some ways the "decentering" of the US model (but also could be a partial result of the decline of the "class action" mechanism in the United States itself). In the 1990s some states in the region began to experiment with "class actions"; for example, the 1994 constitutional reform in Argentina specified consumers' formal rights to file suits based on collective interests for the first time. However, the Argentine Supreme Court has interpreted these actions in a strict way.

By the early 2000s, in Argentina and other places, the terminology had given way to "collective redress," which can refer to a hodgepodge of measures ranging from formal to informal and public to private. Some argue that the rise of internet commerce and the sharing economy are pushing collective redress in a private direction (Thierer, Hobson, and Kuiper 2015). However, globalization issues of legal protection often require international cooperation, particularly in such new areas as privacy protection (Dixon and Gorman 2014). Debates in the Organization of American States (OAS) about the harmonization of consumer law were among the most crucial issues in international trade talks in the region in the 2000s (Fernandez Arroyo 2009). States in the region are dealing with how to regulate consumer protection in e-commerce. It is not surprising that Brazil, the pioneer in Consumer Protection Law, has played a leading role in such negotiations (ibid.). As was the case with environmental questions, there is much to be learned from the Latin American experience.

Business Studies and Corporate Social Responsibility

As Echegaray (2015) argues, consumption politics reflects the optimistic belief that consumers may influence firms to produce public goods. This conviction reveals that people understand the power of business in society, as well as states' failure to carry out public responsibilities. This conviction is consistent with the belief that corporate social responsibility is a promising way to promote the collective good. The new generation of scholarship about ethical consumerism overlaps with growing emphasis in business and legal studies on corporate social responsibility and codes of conduct (Carvalho et al. 2010; Haslam 2004). Often these codes are the result of "ethical" consumer activism, as commented on above.

In Latin America there is tension between the US approach to corporate social responsibility as private and unenforceable and the European approach, which favors making it legally enforceable. Corporate social responsibility and the different ways it might be implemented are talked about a great deal in business school and civil society organizations.

The importance of business in Latin American political systems in the 2000s and 2010s is generally recognized. Barndt (2002) has suggested that one reaction to increasing power of business in Latin American politics might be a political shift to a party-based cleavage between producers and consumers. We saw earlier that Santos identified the absorption of "scarcity" movement concerns into the Brazilian party system. It could be productive in future work to inquire into the dynamics of the incorporation of consumers' concerns into party systems, or even other organizations for citizen representation, such as labor unions.

Social Movement Analysis: Performance and Social Media

Some Latin American scholars view social movements through the lens of "cultural production" (Caldeira 2015), and often a gendered one (Caldeira 1990). Within the cultural approach, there has been a turn towards performance studies. Consumerism lends itself to self-expression, such as via street art (Ryan 2016), making consumer movements would seem to be an ideal arena for study in this area. Treré's (2015) study shows that collective identity can be performed or expressed via digital social movements. However, with the exception of buycotts and boycotts discussed in Echgaray (2015) thus far there is little to no specific analysis of political consumerism in Latin America that focuses on performance tactics. There would appear to be numerous opportunities to explore existing questions combining performance and social media. For example, can the individual complainers referenced above be more effective at solving collective action problems if they employ innovative performance tactics? Are certain tactics more effective when the objects of protest are private firms as opposed to state officials? How does performance spill over into the relationship between consumers and political parties?

Conclusion

We have seen that the earliest analysis of consumption in Latin America emphasized derivations from ideally rational behavior and the effects of such behavior on development. What might be loosely called a second generation emphasized the development of legal rights and the complexity of the consumer interest. A third generation of scholarship emphasizes the importance of consumerism for expressing identity, especially but not limited to gender, and new values, particularly environmentalism, and working conditions and other ethical issues along the production chain. As happened in the case of North American consumer movements, analysts of consumption in Latin America have found that the lens of gender provides a crucial perspective; however, in this arena particularly there is much more terrain to be explored. Across the generations, many scholars from and of the region have maintained a focus on the fundamental problem of consumption differences between haves and have-nots. This basic tension continues in the current era, even as social media and globalization are reshaping the possibilities for collective action and the legal-regulatory regime for consumption.

Trentmann and Otero-Cleves (2017) state that there is a tendency not to acknowledge the autonomous development of consumerism in other regions, but also state that there has been a "decentering" of the US case. As Yates (2011) shows for Europe, and several of the authors mentioned earlier (the works by Baker, Echegaray, Rhodes) also show for Latin America, comparative studies reveal differences within regions as well.

There would appear to be ample opportunity for additional comparative and international analysis.

References

Alvarez, Sonia E., Evelina Dagnino, and Arturo Escobar (eds.) (1998), *Cultures of Politics/Politics of Cultures: Re-visioning Latin American Social Movements* (Boulder, CO: Westview).

Armbruster-Sandoval, Ralph (2004), *Globalization and Cross-Border Solidarity in the Americas: The Sweatshop Movement and the Struggle for Social Justice* (New York: Routledge).

Armijo, Leslie Elliot and Philippe Faucher (2002), "We Have a Consensus: Explaining Political Support for Market Reforms in Latin America," *Latin American Politics and Society* 44(2), 1–40.

Ayres, Ian and Alan Schwartz (2014), "The No-Reading Problem in Consumer Contract Law," *Stanford Law Review* 6(3), 545–609.

Baker, Andy (2009), *The Market and the Masses in Latin America: Policy Reform and Consumption in Liberalizing Economies* (New York: Cambridge University Press).

Balladares, Carina (2008), "Justicia y solidaridad en el comercio. Escalas transnacionales de acción y conceptualización," in Alejandro Grimson and Sebastián Pereyra (eds.), *Conflictos globales, voces locales. Movilización y activismo en clave transnacional*, 189–229 (Buenos Aires: Prometeo-UNRISD).

Barbosa, Lívia (2006), "O consumo nas ciências sociais," in Lívia Barbosa and Colin Campbell (eds.), *Cultura, consumo e identidade*, 21–46 (Rio de Janeiro: Fundação Getúlio Vargas).

Barndt, William T. (2002), "Corporation-Based Parties: The Present and Future of Business Politics in Latin America," *Latin American Politics and Society* 52(1), 1–22.

Bauer, Arnold J. (2001), *Goods, Power and History: Latin America's Material Culture* (Cambridge: Cambridge University Press).

Bolfing, Claire P. (1989), "How Do Customers Express Dissatisfaction and What Can Service Marketers Do About It?" *Journal of Services Marketing* 3(2), 5–23.

Breen, T. H. (2004), *The Marketplace of Revolution: How Consumer Politics Shaped American Independence* (New York: Oxford University Press).

Caldeira, Teresa (2015), "Social Movements, Cultural Production, and Protests. São Paulo's Shifting Political Landscape," *Current Anthropology* 56, S11–S136.

Caldeira, Teresa (1990), "Women, Daily Life, and Politics," in Elizabeth Jelin, (ed.), *Women and Social Change in Latin America*, 47–78 (London: UNRISD/Zed).

Carvalho, Sérgio W., Sankar Sen, Márcio de Oliveira Mota, and Renata Carneiro de Lima (2010), "Consumer Reactions to CSR: A Brazilian Perspective," *Journal of Business Ethics* 91(2), 291–310.

Cohen, Lizabeth (2003), *A Consumers' Republic* (New York: Alfred A. Knopf).

Day, Ralph L. and E. Laird Landon Jr. (1977), "Toward a Theory of Consumer Complaining Behavior," *Foundations of Consumer and Industrial Buying Behavior* 95(1), 425–37.

Dixon, Pam and Robert Gellman (2014), "The Scoring of America: How Secret Consumer Scores Threaten Your Privacy and Your Future," *World Privacy Forum*, https://wdf. https://www.worldprivacyforum.org/2014/04/wpf-report-the-scoring-of-america-how-secret-consumer-scores-threaten-your-privacy-and-your-future/

Doimo, Ana Maria (1995), *A vez e a voz do popular: movimentos sociais e participação política no Brasil pós-70* (Rio de Janeiro: Relume-Dumará).

Echegaray, Fabián (2015), "Voting at the Marketplace: Political Consumerism in Latin America," *Latin American Research Review* 50(2), 176–99.

Eckstein, Susan (2006), "Urban Resistance to Neoliberal Democracy in Latin America," *Colombia Internacional* 63, 12–39.

Elena, Eduardo (2011), *Dignifying Argentina: Peronism, Citizenship, and Mass Consumption* (Pittsburgh, PA: University of Pittsburgh Press).

Fernandez Arroyo, Diego (2009), "Current Approaches Towards Harmonization of Consumer Private International Law in the Americas," *International and Comparative Law Quarterly* 58, 411–25.

Ferrer, Aldo (1956). *El estado y el desarrollo económico* (Buenos Aires: Raigal).

Fontenelle, Isleide A. (2006), "Consumo ético: Construção de um novo fazer político?' *Revista Psicologia Política* 6(12), 1–21.

Frajman, Eduardo (2004), "Rational Calculation, Emotional Reactions, and Political Protests: Costa Rica in 2000," Paper presented at the 2004 Meeting of the American Political Science Association, Chicago, August, 28–31.

Franko, Patrice. (2018). The puzzle of Latin American economic development. Rowman & Littlefield.

Fundación Bariloche (1973), *Modelo mundial latinoamericano: Informe preliminar* (Bariloche: Fundación Bariloche).

García Canclini, Néstor (2001), *Consumers and Citizens: Globalization and Multicultural Conflicts* (Minneapolis: University of Minnesota Press).

Gervasoni, Carlos (1999), "El impacto electoral de las reformas económicas en América Latina (1982–1995)," *América Latina Hoy* 22, 93–110.

Gohn, Maria da Glória (2003), *História dos movimentos e lutas sociais: A construção da cidadania dos brasileiros* (São Paulo: Loyola).

Harrison, Rob, Terry Newholm & Deidre Shaw, eds. (2005) The Ethnical Consumer (London: Sage).

Haslam, Paul Alexander (2004), *The Corporate Social Responsibility System in Latin America and the Caribbean* (Ottawa: Canadian Foundation for the Americas).

Hirschman, Albert O. (1970), *Exit, Voice, and Loyalty* (Cambridge: Harvard University Press).

Jacobi, Pedro Roberto (1999). Meio ambiente e sustentabilidade. In *O município no século XXI: cenários e perspectivas*. São Paulo: CEPAM.

Jacobs, Meg (2005), *Pocketbook Politics: Economic Citizenship in Twentieth-Century America* (Princeton, NJ: Princeton University Press).

McKendrick, Neil John Brewer, and J. H. Plumb (1982), *The Birth of a Consumer Society: The Commercialization of Eighteenth-century England* (Bloomington: University of Indiana Press).

Kerssen, Tanya M. (2015), "Food Sovereignty and the Quinoa Boom: Challenges to Sustainable Re-Peasantisation in the Southern Altiplano of Bolivia," *Third World Quarterly* 36(3), 489–507.

Landes, William M. and Richard A. Posner (1975), "The Private Enforcement of Law," *Journal of Legal Studies* 4(1), 1–46.

Milanesio, Natalia (2013), *Workers Go Shopping in Argentina: The Rise of Popular Consumer Culture* (Albuquerque: University of New Mexico Press).

O'Dougherty, Maureen (2002), *Consumption Intensified: The Politics of Middle-Class Daily Life in Brazil* (Durham, NC: Duke University Press).

Olivera, Oscar (2001), "The Fight for Water and Democracy: An Interview with Olivera Oscar," *Journal of Public Health Policy* 22(2), 226–34.

Olson, Mancur (1965), *The Logic of Collective Action* (Cambridge, MA: Harvard University Press).

Otero-Cleves, Ana María (2017), "Foreign Machetes and Cheap Cotton Cloth: Popular Consumers and Imported Commodities in Nineteenth-Century Colombia," *Hispanic American Historical Review* 97(3), 423–56.

Oxhorn, Philip (2010), "Citizenship as Consumption or Citizenship as Agency: Comparing Democratizing Reforms in Bolivia and Brazil," *Sociologias* 12(24), 18–43.

Perón, Juan Domingo (1974), "Discurso en la CGT, pronunciado en la CGT el 13 de diciembre de 1973," in Juan Domingo Perón, *Juan Perón en la Argentina, 1973: Sus discursos, sus diálogos, sus conferencias* (Buenos Aires: Vespa Ediciones).

Pite, Rebekah (2013), *Creating a Common Table in Twentieth-Century Argentina: Doña Petrona, Women and Food* (Chapel Hill: University of North Carolina Press).

Portilho, Fátima (2005), *Sustentabilidade ambiental, consumo e cidadania* (São Paulo: Cortez).

Prebisch, Raúl (1993), "El coeficiente de expansión," in Raúl Prebisch, *Obras 1919–1949*, 350–70 (Buenos Aires: Fundación Raúl Prebisch).

Pryluka, Pablo F. (2015), "Growing Consumer Rights in Neoliberal Times: The Top-down Origins of Consumer Organizations in Argentina between 1978 and 1993," *Journal of Historical Research in Marketing* 7(3), 373–88.

Pryluka, Pablo F. and Ramiro Coviello (2018), "Consumo y desarrollo en el tercer gobierno peronista," *América Latina en la historia económica* 25(1), 98–135.

Rhodes, Sybil (2006), *Social Movements and Free-Market Capitalism in Latin America. Telecommunications Privatization and the Rise of Consumer Protest* (Albany: State University of New York Press).

Rhodes, Sybil (2012a), *Political Communication and Economic Reform: The Use of Consumerist Frames in Brazil, 1985–2005*, CEMA Working Papers, Serie Documentos de Trabajo no. 482 (Buenos Aires: Universidad del CEMA).

Rhodes, Sybil (2012b), "South American Adopters: Argentina, Brazil," in Stuart J. Smythe, David Castle, and Peter W. B. Phillips (eds.), *Handbook on Agriculture, Biotechnology and Development*, 86–98 (Northampton: Edward Elgar).

Rios, Josue (1998), *A defesa do consumidor e o direito como instrumento de mobilização social* (Rio de Janeiro: Mauad).

Rocchi, Fernando (2003), "La americanización del consumo: Las batallas por el mercado argentino, 1920–1945," in María I. Barbero and Andrés M. Regalsky (eds.), *Americanización: Estados Unidos y América Latina en el siglo XX: Transferencias económicas, tecnológicas y culturales*, 131–90 (Buenos Aires: EDUNTREF).

Ryan, Holly Eva (2016), *Political Street Art: Communication, Culture and Resistance in Latin America* (Routledge: 2016).

Santos, Dejalma Eudes dos (2014), "Sobre as possibilidades de ação política na esfera do consumo," *Psicologia & Sociedade* 26, 201–11.

Schiffman, Leon G. and Joseph L. Wisenblit (2015), "Research Indicates That Only a Few Unsatisfied Customers Actually Complain," in Leon G. Schiffman and Joseph L. Wisenblit (eds.), *Consumer Behavior*, 11th ed., 426 (London: Pearson).

Schmitz, Amy J. (2012), "Access to Consumer Remedies in the Squeaky Wheel System," *Pepperdine Law Review* 39, 279–366.

Simpson, Charles R. and Anita Rapone (2000), "Community Development from the Ground Up: Social-justice Coffee," *Human Ecology Review* 7(1), 46–57.

Spronk, Susan and Carlos Crespo (2008), "Water, National Sovereignty and Social Resistance: Bilateral Investment Treaties and the Struggles against Multinational Water Companies in Cochabamba and El Alto, Bolivia," *Law, Social Justice and Global Development* 1, 1–14.

Thierer, Adam, Christopher Koopman, Anne Hobson, and Chris Kuiper (2015), "The Internet, the Sharing Economy, and Reputational Feedback Mechanisms Solve the Lemons Problem," *University of Miami Law Review* 70(3), 830–78.

Tinsman, Heidi (2014), *Buying into the Regime: Grapes and Consumption in Cold War Chile and the United States* (Durham, NC: Duke University Press).

Traub-Werner, Marion and Altha J. Cravey (2002), "Spatiality, Sweatshops and Solidarity in Guatemala," *Social & Cultural Geography* 3(4), 383–401.

Trentmann, Frank and Ana María Otero-Cleves (2017), "Presentation. Paths, Detours, and Connections: Consumption and Its Contribution to Latin American History," *Historia Crítica* 65, 13–28.

Treré, Emiliano (2015), "Reclaiming, Proclaiming, and Maintaining Collective Identity in the #YoSoy132 Movement in Mexico: An Examination of Digital Frontstage and Backstage Activism through Social Media and Instant Messaging Platforms," *Information, Communication & Society* 18(8), 901–15.

Varsavsky, Oscar (1971), *Proyectos nacionales: Planteo y estudios de viabilidad* (Buenos Aires: Periferia).

Veblen, Thorstein (2017), *The Theory of the Leisure Class* (New York: Routledge).

Vergara, Sylvia Helena Constant (2003), *Impacto dos direitos dos consumidores nas práticas empresariais* (Rio de Janeiro: Editora FGV).

van den Bergh, Roger and Louis T. Visscher (2008), "The Preventive Function of Collective Actions for Damages in Consumer Law," *Erasmus Law Review* 1(2), 5–30.

Voorhees, Clay M., Michael K. Brady, and David M. Horowitz (2006), "A Voice from the Silent Masses: An Exploratory and Comparative Analysis of Noncomplainers," *Journal of the Academy of Marketing Sciences* 34(4), 514–57.

Willis, Lauren E. (2015), "Performance-Based Consumer Law," *University of Chicago Law Review* 82, 1309–26.

Yates, Lukes S. (2011), "Critical Consumption: Boycotting and Buycotting in Europe," *European Societies* 13(2), 191–217.

CHAPTER 30

AUTONOMIST MOVEMENTS IN LATIN AMERICA

MARCELO LOPES DE SOUZA

Introduction

From agroecology to *sem-teto/sin-techo* activism to some social movements well known internationally but specifically Latin American (such as the Mexican Zapatistas), the word "autonomy" has been present with an impressive frequency in the discourse of the social struggles of the last twenty or thirty years in Latin America. This, by itself, already seems to justify a strong interest for the term in question. For a researcher like myself, who has been inspired by the "*projet d'autonomy*" ("autonomy project") discussed brilliantly and in depth by Graeco-French philosopher Cornelius Castoriadis (1922–1997) since the 1970s (Castoriadis 1975, 1983, 1990, 1996), the interest is even bigger. However, much caution is needed, since the use of the same *word* does not mean that we are all using the same *concept*.

In fact, although "autonomy" has become a key term for several Latin American social movements (as well as for some movements outside Latin America), the meanings are still disparate and heterogeneous—and partly controversial. In the academic world itself, it is not uncommon for the word "autonomy" to be used without great rigor, just as it is frequent that researchers take this word in a banal sense when they hear or read it somewhere. The fact that "autonomy" is an everyday word, used in the most different situations, surely contributes to such polysemy. Of course, there is a kind of "kernel of meaning" that is common to most different discourses, and that has to do with the nature of autonomy as the *freedom or independence to do something*. But to say this is to say very little, and it is obvious that this "kernel of meaning" lends itself to many appropriations and interpretations. This is not a "defect" of the term, since many other key terms of political life—freedom, equity, justice, and so on—have also been interpreted in varying ways throughout history. At each moment, and regarding each term, what matters, first of all, is to check what contents it covers, trying to examine the potentialities and limitations (and possible contradictions) of the contents and their uses.

From a strongly political and philosophical point of view, we can say that the key ideas in relation to *autonomy* are surely *freedom* and *(social) justice*. But that is still too vague, as many political philosophies (from classical liberalism to Marxism to anarchism) could claim they are committed to "autonomy." What is "autonomy," then, from the specific standpoint of "autonomist" movements and thought?

The problem is even more complicated, as in the context of political philosophy, not only "autonomy" but also "autonomism" are already far from being monosemic terms, as the spectrum of possibilities ranges from a radical, left-libertarian alternative to both liberalism/capitalism and Marxism (as exemplified by Cornelius Castoriadis) to a kind of neo-Marxism (e.g., Antonio Negri and John Holloway)—not to mention Immanuel Kant's classical, individualist interpretation. If we focus only on the post-World War II European political and intellectual debate, which is the one that has influenced the Latin American political and intellectual landscape (and in turn has been influenced by it in the last two decades), we can distinguish between two different politico-philosophical sources, in terms of valuing the idea of "autonomy" from a critical and radical point of view:

1) *Left-libertarian autonomism*: The key representative of this strand is Cornelius Castoriadis, a Marxist thinker in his youth, but who first broke with Leninism in the late 1940s and, in the 1960s, abandoned Marxism altogether—which exacerbated the internal tensions of the famous *Socialisme or Barbarie* group, of which he was the leading exponent—as he considered that in Marx's own works there were already unacceptably heteronomous (i.e., authoritarian and centralization-oriented) elements, as well as a clear economistic, rationalistic, and deterministic bias.

2) *Neo-Marxist autonomism*: unlike Castoriadis, Italian intellectuals such as Antonio Negri have followed a different path: while distancing themselves from Leninism and Bolshevik-style political parties and adopting a perspective of social emancipation based on an understanding of the autonomous role of the working class, they did not explicitly or completely break with Marx's legacy. Instead, they preferred to bet on a re-reading of Marx, combined with the reassessment of other thinkers (in Negri's case, especially Spinoza [see, e.g., Negri 1999]), so as to try to fit the Marxist tradition while taking various challenges seriously, such as radicalizing the critique of Stalinist totalitarianism and of political centralism/bureaucratism in general, as well as an appreciation of the relevance of new social actors and movements beyond the working class in its conventional sense. John Holloway, inspired mainly by Latin American sources such as Zapatism, is another author who, more recently, has sought to make Marxism more identified with principles such as self-management and horizontality than with political parties and state-centrism (Holloway 2005).

Although very distinct from each other and, to a large extent, even opposite, these two sources interrelated in a complex way—and in fact, more often than usually admitted. Negri (and other intellectuals and activists who helped shape Italian "workerism"/

"autonomism" in the 1960s and 1970s), for example, was heavily influenced by the journal *Socialisme or Barbarie*, published by the namesake group between 1949 and 1965; indeed, what may be Negri's most profound book, *Insurgencies: Constituent Power and the Modern State* (Negri 1999), unquestionably reverberates Castoriadian themes and ideas, such as that of *instituting society*. As far as Holloway is concerned, he usually does not give any credit, neither to the anarchists—who since the nineteenth century have represented precisely the formula contained in the title of his best-known book, *Change the World Without Taking Power* (Holloway 2005)—nor to a non-anarchist left-libertarian such as Castoriadis (interestingly, Castoriadis himself never valued any systematic dialogue with the anarchist tradition). In any case, since the 1980s and 1990s, European social movements such as the German *Autonomen* have been drinking from both sources simultaneously (regarding the case of the *Autonomen*, see Katsiaficas 2006), as well as valuing anarchism directly, this way promoting a "political/theoretical hybridity" of varying consistency.

In the context of Latin American praxis, heterogeneity has been even more marked than in Europe, as there is a myriad of organizations, movements, and ideological streams whose theoretical sources of inspiration and local and regional political/cultural influences are highly variable (see, for instance, Souza 2016, 2017b). At the same time, in Latin America, probably more than in other continents, "autonomy" has been a key political term in the parlance of many activists and movements for the last two or three decades. Some of these movements have been explicitly identified as "autonomist." What do they understand under this label? Which parameters do they explicitly or implicitly use for defining "autonomy"? Are there any substantive political differences between these movements? Can we find internal discursive or practical contradictions? Where lie the potentialities, and where lie the limits of these movements?

The aim of the chapter is to offer an exploratory answer to these questions. An extensive though not exhaustive balance sheet of achievements, potentialities, and problems will be offered in the first section. Thereafter, a specific but nevertheless crucial problem will be explored in the second section in order to illustrate autonomism's potential relevance: the synergy between the struggle for autonomy and the struggle around ecology and environmental justice (a synergy that has seldom happened so far, however). Finally, in the Conclusion, I will briefly turn back to the question about the heterogeneity of Latin American "autonomism," in order to summarize what we can or should expect from "autonomist" movements.

A Tale of Unity in Diversity? Potentialities and Promises, Limits and Contradictions

As already seen, the word "autonomy" itself evokes a plethora of possible meanings. In fact, it can mean different things for different people, and above all it seems to imply different theoretical or political positions. In the light of the existing diversity of interpretations, it would be too rigid and positivistic to offer a simple or absolute "definition" in relation to which reality should be "assessed" or "judged" (Souza 2017b). Nevertheless, it is important to pay attention to the etymology of the term. Cornelius Castoriadis can help us exploring the deep implications that arise when we take the word's etymology seriously:

> Autonomy: *autos-nomos*, (to give oneself) one's own laws. . . . . In what sense can an individual be autonomous? . . . The autonomy of the individual consists of another relationship which is established between the reflexive instance and the other psychic instances, as well as between one's present and the history in the course of which one has made oneself as one is, allowing one's escape from the servitude of repetition, to reflect about oneself, about the reasons of one's thoughts and the motives of one's actions, guided by the intention of truth and the elucidation of one's desire. . . . Can I say that I put down my own law—if I necessarily live under the law of society? Yes, in one case: if I can say, reflexively and lucidly, that *this is also my law*. For me to be able to say that, it is not necessary that I approve it: it is enough to have had the real possibility of participating actively in the proposing and implementation of the law. The possibility of participating: if I accept the idea of self-government *as such* (not only because it is "good for me"), which, evidently, no "demonstration" can oblige me to do, and neither can it oblige me to choose my words according to my actions, the indefinite plurality of individuals belonging to society conducts immediately to democracy, as the actual possibility of equal participation of all, in the instituting activities as well as in the explicit power (Castoriadis 1990: 131–34).

If we consider the standards established by Castoriadis's "*projet d'autonomie*," we can easily arrive at the conclusion that real praxis (be it in Latin America or elsewhere) is not seldom far away from a certain "ideal" deepness, coherence, and radicality. Indeed, "autonomy" is often reduced, for example, to the immediate financial or economic autonomy of a social movement organization, without taking into account or perceiving the *multiscalarity* and the *economic and political complexity* of the processes of exploitation and subalternization (that is, of heteronomy).

This situation forces us to face an apparent dilemma, from which we are only able to free ourselves with some difficulty. On the one hand, according to Castoriadis, who sharply criticized the traditional understanding of "theory" (see Castoriadis 1975), a theory that limits itself to "judge" praxis instead of developing a dialogue with it (and ultimately learning from it), is by no means an example of emancipatory knowledge. On the other hand, it would also be obscurantist or naive to ignore a whole legacy of politico-philosophical reflections (from Kant to Castoriadis) in the name of some kind of *vox populi, vox Dei* approach to the social construction of knowledge and "truth." Therefore, a more dialectical way of dealing with social problems must be envisaged.

Let us pay attention to the following remarks made in a publication by Chile's *pobladores* movement:[1]

> As shown by the experience of the *pobladores* movement in the past eleven years, the core of the struggles of the twenty-first century corresponds to the search for autonomy. The latter expresses itself in a way so that the forms of action of some movements show a variegated set of measures that range from traditional demands and claims addressed to the state apparatus to self-managed alternatives that arise from the territories [themselves] (Movimiento de Pobladores en Lucha 2011: 18).

Considering this quote, one could think that "autonomy" is a central notion in *pobladores*' discourse. Moreover, this centrality seems to be embedded in a deep valuation of spatiality or, more specifically, territoriality (Davis and Davey, Fernandes and Welch in this volume). At the same time, however, *pobladores*' discourse typically reduces self-management (*autogestión*) to the movement's management of fiscal funds obtained from the state apparatus. It is in light of this that we can understand their approach to *autonomía*. Considering the narrow meaning ascribed to *autogestión*, it becomes evident that the meaning of autonomy itself cannot be as radical as one could perhaps expect. In terms of distance from political parties, too, the experience of *pobladores* seems to be ambiguous, to say the least, as this movement was deeply involved in the founding of a new political party, called Partido Igualdad. Actually, this latter circumstance is perhaps unsurprising if we take into account that several party activists have already come from other parties (e.g., the Communist Party of Chile). Nonetheless, it is legitimate to ask whether founding or entering a political party constitutes the best way to achieve more influence and effectiveness in terms of fostering self-management and horizontal, non-authoritarian, and fair social relations across society. After all, even if some kind of institutional struggle (in the sense of taking part in so-called "participatory" channels and councils) can be seen sometimes as useful or perhaps unavoidable and therefore as a supplement to direct action, though essentially subordinated to the latter (see Annunziata and Goldfrank in this volume), political parties do not seem to be a particularly fertile soil where seeds of self-management and horizontality (that is, of autonomy in a strong political sense) can adequately grow (see Roberts in this volume).

Symptomatically, as the examples of Chilean *pobladores* but also of a large part of Argentine *piqueteros*[2] show, "*autonomía*" has been often interpreted narrowly as autonomy from the state apparatus and political parties—an aspect that is obviously important but rather insufficient from a radical perspective. Undoubtedly, we can see a remarkable but often implicit political depth in the projects and actions embedded in the movements' own prefigurative politics. However, it is interesting that the aspect praised first and foremost by an observer such as Mabel Thwaites Rey is that the movements are "autonomous from the state apparatus, from the unions and from the traditional political parties" (Thwaites Rey 2013: 10), while the very core of autonomy *as an alternative both to liberalism and Marxism or to capitalist and "socialist" practices*—such as conceived in Castoriadis's radical "project of autonomy"—is not really discussed, and often not even mentioned. To a large extent, this is because this kind of radicality is more often than not present only in a diffuse and not programmatically explicit way in the praxis of such movements.

A further illustration of the widespread use of the term "autonomy" in Latin America is provided by some representatives of the "*movimientos indígenas*." However, for their representatives and spokespersons, expressions such as "*autonomía regional*" and "*autonomía territorial*" do not necessarily or always relate to values and principles such as self-management and horizontality or, in other words, for the overcoming of a hierarchical society. In fact, the territorially expressed right to self-determination in the face of power sources, social groups, and societies foreign to the considered local/regional group is often accompanied by a reinvention or reinvigoration of traditional institutions, which sometimes appear as more or less *heteronomous* from a radical, Western/Westernized point of view: "elders' councils," for instance, cannot be seen as the ultimate instance of horizontality and self-management. At the same time, there are other elements that are similar to (or reminiscent of) direct democracy sometimes, even if they owe much to ancient indigenous traditions that are supplemented or enriched here and there by Western influences, as is the case with assemblies and *cabildos populares* (people's councils). Be that as it may, in all these cases the term "autonomy" does not fully or automatically correspond to genuine internal autonomy, in the sense of a deep questioning of vertical forms of organization and the absence of any kind of oppression or structural asymmetry (see Díaz-Polanco 1998, 1999). Patriarchy or male dominance, for instance, is frequently not challenged in a persuasive way in such traditional contexts, as Zibechi (2006) let us see in relation to the Aymaras of the city of El Alto, Bolivia (see Rice in this volume).

In order to offer a systematic (though not exhaustive) account of the features—including the problems and contradictions—of the concrete uses of "autonomy" in contemporary Latin America, I would like to stress six points.

▪ The sources and their tensions

The sources of inspiration for autonomist activism have been heterogeneous, both in terms of politico-philosophical/theoretical sources—(neo-)Marxism, anarchism, indigenism, Magonism[3], Italian workerism [*operaismo*], Situationism...—and in relation to the influences of local and regional cultures (for instance, it is easy to imagine that Buenos Aires's autonomist *piqueteros* have a repertoire of tactics, strategies, and narratives that is very different from that of the Zapatistas of the Selva Lacandona in Chiapas). It is important to make it clear that I am not just saying that different social movements have different sources of philosophical/theoretical inspiration sometimes, but that a single movement is often eclectic in that sense—we can call it "political/theoretical hybridity," as I have already done in my introduction. This kind of hybridity can present some advantages, such as an immunization against dogmatism (in the style "Marxism versus anarchism," for example), but there are also risks, such as obscuring deep differences in terms of orientation and incompatibilities between political concepts and objects (see Souza 2017b on the strengths and risks of "political/theoretical hybridity").

Autonomy from the state apparatus

What does this goal *actually* mean? It is not difficult to see that the paths of different social movements have been highly diverse. Let us take the case of the Mexican Zapatistas as a first example. Their approach to the idea of self-government, guided by consistently applied principles such as "*mandar obedeciendo*" ("we obey while we command"), shows that it is not just a matter of "territorial corporatism," that is, of seeking greater independence from the central government (in this case, the Mexican state) for the sake of merely reproducing, on a small scale, the same hierarchical and vertical patterns of the exercise of power. In contrast to the Zapatistas, the case of Chilean *pobladores* makes it clear how "independence from the state apparatus' can be interpreted in a limited, fragile way. Incidentally, it is important to ask (as I have done in Souza 2006, 2017a, and 2017b, for instance) to what extent actions that are independent from the government (synthesized by me through the formula "*despite* the state" [Souza, 2006]) also and coherently represent a radical criticism of the state apparatus ("*against* the state"): seeking to remain as far as possible independent from state funding sources does not automatically mean *cultivating a radically critical view of the capitalist state*. Furthermore, the use of a radical rhetoric does not automatically imply that the actors are truly or consistently committed to revolutionary instead of reformist goals. Sometimes, even the problem of funding—which is a decisive aspect—is underestimated: in fact, even the *piqueteros*, very often seen as a particularly militant universe of activists, being radical and even aggressive in terms of theirs methods, have typically demanded government welfare or unemployment subsidies and struggled to control access to them (sure, the *piquetero* movement has always been highly heterogeneous and presented internal tensions, with the influences ranging from Maoism to Guevarism to Situationism and above all to Peronism, but in most cases the control over subsidies has been seen as if it could as such be understood as an important element of *autonomía*[4]).

In truth, beyond idealization and romanticism, it is necessary to understand the deep fragility of Latin American workers that has occurred in the wake of neo-liberalism's emergence (Gallegos and Stoessel in this volume). For the counterculture-influenced youth of the 1960s and 1970s (and even for the German *Autonomen* and many squatters in Europe and the United States during subsequent decades), a substantial part of the political and cultural struggle was motivated by the refusal of consumerist society, while for the poor workers in Latin America, in spite of politicized rhetoric and radical analysis, the motivation is ultimately a desire to be (re)incorporated into the formal job market but also and ultimately into the polity or political arena, as Rossi (2015) illustrates with the Argentine case. For this reason, contradictions and limits can be observed among several movements, and perhaps a more consistent critical attitude towards the state apparatus is shown precisely by those movements—particularly the Zapatistas—where the struggle for a higher level of formal employment (at the end of the day a "fight to be exploited") and the dependence from political arrangements with parties and governments is for more or less obvious reasons, both of socio-spatial nature (like the difference between peasants and urban workers) and by virtue of specifically political factors (strong influence of populist parties and trade-unions, such as in the *piqueteros*' case), not relevant (see Oikonomakis in this volume).

▪ What about the capitalist market?

As we have already seen, "independence from the state apparatus" (as well as from trade-unions and parties) should not be a *non plus ultra* in terms of autonomy, if we really want to build some kind of prefigurative politics aiming at an overcoming of heteronomous *status quo*. At this juncture, we should ask: and what about the *capitalist market*? Let us consider, for instance, the lessons we can draw from the movement of companies recovered by workers (*empresas recuperadas*) in Argentina. Zibechi (2007: 95ff) provides a useful description of the virtues and potentialities of this movement, which was particularly important in the 2000s; however, as I personally observed during fieldwork carried out in Buenos Aires in 2007, many recovered companies could already then be taken as examples of how contradictions and the "infrapower" of the capitalist imaginary can undermine even a great potential for resistance. While some companies (mainly factories) "appropriated" by workers still represented a commitment to self-management and radical social (or rather socio-spatial) change, the cooperative members who ran several recovered companies had then explicitly abandoned any critical discourse as well as the solidarity which they had often demonstrated in the past towards *piqueteros* and other activists and unemployed workers in general in favor of a "pragmatic" style of management: basically concerned about the success of their own companies, the workers of these recovered companies who were interviewed by me did not show an interest in promoting what has been called "conscious consumption," that is, critical information for consumers about the degree of social justice and concern for the environmental protection involved in the production and marketing conditions (see Rhodes in this volume). On the contrary, what shocked me, and was even clearly admitted by some people I interviewed, was an exclusive concern with the acceptance of the products by a traditional clientele, which resulted in very conventional marketing strategies (see Souza 2017a: 410).[5]

▪ The role of space

It has been often noted that "new geographies," that is, the bottom-up politicization of geographical space (see Davis and Davey, Halvorsen and Rossi in this volume), has been a crucial factor for contemporary social movements in Latin America, including those for which "autonomy" has played the role of a key political term (see for instance Chatterton 2005; Souza 2017a). In fact, "spatial politics" has been a very important feature of autonomist movements (as well as of some other movements) across Latin America. The interesting and almost untranslatable notion of "*trabajo territorial*" (literally "territorial work"), developed and used by the most clearly self-management-oriented portion of the *piquetero* movement seems to synthesize much of it:

> Indeed, "territorial work" contains in itself its own political definition. Performing territorial work does not only mean, in this case, strengthening the collective's work in the local space, but above all, attributing social change skills to these community activities. In the first place, work in the territory is proposed as the production of new values of solidarity that reconstitute the interpersonal ties and people's existential dimensions broken by unemployment, poverty and forms of authoritarianism that have, under different modalities, penetrated society. Second, this community construction aims at the production of a new society, which does not directly antagonize the places of the instituted power to impose itself, but rather projects itself and affirms itself as "non-state sovereignty" (Delamata 2004: 48).

In Argentina's emblematic situation, the neighborhood obviously pre-exists—as an intersubjectively shared geographical reference, that is, as a "lived space" or *place* in a strong sense—the social movement. However, socio-spatial identities are reinforced throughout the mobilization; in other words, *throughout the struggle*. In part, therefore, the neighborhood is, as a densely politicized place and as a territory that is (re)appropriated in a bottom-up style, somewhat produced by and through the social movement. "Territorial work" is thus represented in a case such as the MTD of Solano, for instance—which "takes as constitutive principles of the movement autonomy, horizontality and direct democracy" (Delamata 2004: 47)—as well as, with less emphasis, in the case of some other *piqueteros* organizations, a true guiding principle of the construction of "*autonomía*." The criticism that this sector of the movement received from those sectors linked to leftist parties or organized according to a party logic, such as the Movimiento Teresa Rodríguez (MTR), is that the autonomists' perspective would be too "light" (that was the word used by a prominent MTR militant interviewed by me in Buenos Aires in 2007)—which is certainly explained by the fact that the "autonomist" *piqueteros* are not concerned with or interested in seizing power, which is the strategic goal of any revolutionary organization committed to Marxist-Leninist thought. On the other hand, it is undoubtedly impossible to build up an autonomous society (in a strong sense) only by "moving away" from the state apparatus as much as possible, without directly and systematically confronting and fighting it. To a large extent, and regardless of its various interesting and promising aspects (like the stronger potential connection between production, consumption/reproduction and everyday life at the [micro-]local level), the "territorial turn" was also the expression of a *defensive* moment in the face of neo-liberalism, and sometimes also an adaptive strategy used by the workers in their struggle for reincorporation (see Rossi [2015] on the paradigmatic case of the *piqueteros*).

▪ Constraints imposed by the capitalist world-system

Almost all experiences built up by movements and organizations that claim "autonomy" as an essential political principle, even when they exist on a non-negligible time scale (at least several years), have been limited to the creation of "dissident territories" at a small, intraurban spatial level such as a neighborhood or even a single occupied and territorialized building or plot of land. The *Territorio Zapatista* in Chiapas is clearly an exception to this rule. Obviously, any state apparatus will do everything in its power to eradicate any socio-spatial experiment that poses a threat or represents an affront to the capitalist, heteronomous socio-spatial order. But this is not just a matter of repression on the part of nation-states: the capitalist world-system itself acts in various possible ways, both through its economic dynamics and the production of subjectivity (ideological level), to prevent the emergence of (or suppress) any significant challenge to the *status quo*. On the one hand, the globalization of the last four decades has brought with it a whole host of supporting technologies that, although clearly repressive or military in some cases (closed circuit TV cameras, drones, etc.), in other cases have a much wider spectrum of use, like the internet (which made social networks such as Facebook possible); the importance of modern communication technologies for certain contemporary protests and mobilizations has been extensively studied and sometimes even exaggerated (Treré and Harlow in this volume). On the other hand, this greater potential ease of communication and dissemination of information among activists goes hand-in-hand with an increasing fragmentation of the working class and, last but not least, with an increasing ability of the state apparatus and private companies to spy upon, track, and control the lives of citizens, thereby making repression much more efficient. This means, among other things, that while privacy spaces remain indispensable for workers' political organizing tasks, gaining the sympathy of a significant portion of society becomes a perhaps more crucial task than ever before—although at the same time, society has not only been increasingly subjected to ideological brainwashing and cultural influence by mass media such as television and the corporate press in general, but also depoliticized by the predominantly alienating uses of cell phones and the internet, hence proving itself often unable to demonstrate a critical view of the world.

▪ Achievements and legacy

Development of a "politics of scale," practice of transnational activism, the decisive test of improving the quality of life and the perception of justice of the people on the ground, and so on: from Mexican Zapatistas to the self-managed *ocupações* in Rio de Janeiro,[6] there have been in Latin America a plethora of achievements directly or indirectly related to the struggles of movements that reclaim "autonomy" as a key political concept. Some of these experiences emerged amidst a confrontation against sharply conservative governments: that was the case of the Zapatistas, who became known worldwide after the 1994 rebellion against the North American Free Trade Agreement (NAFTA) and the neoliberal policies of the Mexican government (see Oikonomakis, Inclán in this volume). In other cases, experiences flourished as social problems worsened in the wake of a political and institutional turmoil, such as the *piqueteros, asambleas barriales,* and *empresas recuperadas* in Argentina in the early 2000s. Finally, in some situations the experiences arose not in a context of crisis or extreme political conservatism, but within a political framework of "left" neo-populism, as occurred with the autonomous *ocupações* of the *sem-teto* movement in Rio de Janeiro between the mid-2000s and mid-2010s.

The most radical and challenging (from the statist/capitalist perspective) among these experiences, particularly the Zapatistas, have been able to survive to a large extent by virtue of a consistent practice of "politics of scale" and with help of transnational activists from several parts of the world: given that the conflict between the Zapatistas and the Mexican government did not end in 2000 as President Vicente Fox had promised, the Mexican state and also paramilitaries began to guard the borders of indigenous lands, controlling the entry of activists and tourists into the Zapatista Territory. The conflict did not escalate continuously thanks to the presence in indigenous areas of international support organizations such as Global Exchange, Chiapas Coalition 98, and Chiapas Peace House Project (United States); Chiapas Human Rights Observer Project (Canada); TM Crew (Italy); Solidarity Collective with the Zapatista Rebelión (Spain); and several others.

But what about the various movements and organizations that, because they lack the means to exercise territorial control over vast areas and because they are not as internationally visible as the Zapatistas, have had little or no international support at all? In such cases, the duration of socio-spatial experiments has often been much shorter, until a mixture of repression and co-optation determines the end or at least the clear weakening of a particular social movement or organization. It is obvious that, in most cases, one cannot realistically expect that, in the absence of a cycle of protest or revolutionary conjuncture, any decisive, long-term victory can be achieved; however, the question is: to what extent are the various movements, even after their weakening (such as the *piqueteros* in the last ten-fifteen years) or virtual disappearance (such as the autonomous *ocupações* of Rio de Janeiro's harbor area) capable of leave a *lasting legacy* in terms of protest repertoire and inspiring narratives? Even this is not very clear, and it certainly needs to be analyzed on a case-by-case basis.

From Disconnection to Synergy: "Autonomist" Activism and the Struggle around "Ecology" and Environmental Justice

The relevance of geographical space mentioned in the previous section has not prevented an important and widespread kind of silence: the relative neglect of space as *environment* in many cases (see Halvorsen and Rossi in this volume).

For several reasons, the "ecological" dimension—in a political sense, the links between (first) nature and society, or the *socio-natural metabolism*—has assumed an increasingly relevant role in many contemporary social struggles, including those that take place in large cities. From fighting the socio-ecologically negative impacts of building large hydroelectric dams to the fight of indigenous peoples and peasants for land (or, more broadly, for *territory*) to counteracting the effects of the neo-extractive paradigm that has thrived in Latin America to the struggle against situations of environmental injustice (for example, the creation of "sacrifice zones" on the outskirts of large cities in the wake of the installation of highly polluting industries), the "environmental issue" has gradually ceased to be reduced to an environmentally preservationist or "deep green" perspective, instead giving increasing rise to (or being embraced by) movements whose agendas gravitate around the interrelationship between human rights (housing, basic sanitation, maintenance of traditional lifestyles and cultures) and ecological problems (land degradation, environmental contamination, and so on).

It should also be noted at this point that Cornelius Castoriadis, probably the most notable political thinker to devote his attention to the idea of autonomy from a radical point of view, underlined on several occasions since the 1980s (see, e.g., Castoriadis and Cohn-Bendit 2014) what he saw as a crucial interdependence: that between autonomy and ecology.

In the light of all this, it might perhaps be expected that the "autonomist" movements in Latin America would also pay due attention to this relationship. However, this is often *not* what happens. On the one hand, there are numerous movements and organizations that could be viewed as "*socio-environmentalism without autonomism*"; on the other hand, there are a number of movements that represent what we might call "*autonomism without socio-environmentalism.*"

Although Latin-American "socio-environmentalism" represents an approach to "ecology" beyond conventional ecologism and "green activism," as well as environmental protection beyond middle-class environmentalism, many (to my best knowledge, probably most) movements and organizations developed around environmental justice and related questions do not reclaim "autonomy" as a key political principle. Many of them have been basically organized according to traditional, more often than not traditional principles and values; male domination, for instance, is seldom a relevant issue, and everyday practices show the persistence of this and other aspects of political verticality. Moreover, hierarchical organizational structures often also show the influence of political parties and/or of vertical leftism (particularly of Marxism-Leninism).

In contrast to "*socio-environmentalism without autonomism*," many autonomist movements represent the opposite problem: lack of explicit concern about the "ecological" dimension of social relations and the production of space (see Christel and Gutiérrez in this volume). A kind of "ecological blindness" and the lack of articulation between demands such as housing, infra-structure, and so on, on the one hand, and environmental justice (or more broadly socio-environmental concerns), on the other, seems to characterize a large part of "autonomist" movements. In Argentina, for instance, the available literature shows a gap between important instances of socio-environmental activism (see, e.g., Merlinsky 2017), from which any significant debate around "autonomy" seems to be absent, and a movement such as the *piqueteros*, whose links with the "ecological" or "environmental" question are usually not visible. In light of the "territorial turn" and the multiple connections between immediate demands and aspects of a socio-environmental agenda (such as the environmental impacts of *empresas recuperadas* and the problems of sanitation in the slums, to mention only two examples), this gap is pretty curious; it seems to indicate the persistence of a traditional difficulty in articulating economic and social demands with environmental concerns, even if the latter are to be considered from a radical and emancipatory viewpoint.

In relation to the abovementioned gap, the Zapatistas have been by far the most important exception. They have always shown a strong ecological sensitivity, articulated with other elements (both material and political) in the context of their demands and proposals regarding justice and dignity. Subcomandante Insurgente Marcos, for example, has repeatedly used elements of critical socio-environmentalism and even an aesthetic full of conservationist message amidst a strongly emancipatory discourse (Marcos 2008 and 2011). At the same time, however, Zapatistas have often explicitly opposed to conventional conservationism, as exemplified by the controversy around the Montes Azules Biosphere Reserve, where they sharply criticized the environmental NGO Conservation International for simplistically depicting the local indigenous populations as a threat to biodiversity (Crocker 2006). In fact, Zapatistas could be seen as representatives of "counter-hegemonic positions" as opposed to Conservation International as "environmental managers," to use Gudynas's (1992) terms, or as representatives of an "environmentalism of the poor" in contrast to a "bourgeois environmentalism," to use Vitz's (2018) terms. Be that as it may, Zapatistas' approach to conservation is deeply embedded in indigenous cultural values and identity, so that their demands and positions in this regard are primarily linked with the needs and way of living of local and regional groups in Chiapas, notwithstanding the cosmopolitan aspects of their emancipatory message (expressions of a "rooted cosmopolitanism," one could say). In the Zapatistas' case, we can find a synergy between "ecological" and radical social discourse, instead of the usual disconnection. Could it be a fruitful lesson for other movements?

Conclusion

The socio-political landscape around "autonomism" is far less homogeneous than one could perhaps expect, especially considering some academic tendencies to deal with disparate histories and geographies as if they would constitute a single, coherent pattern or "paradigm." At this point, I would try to answer the question that gives the first section of this chapter its title: yes, there is, to some extent, some unity behind the incredible diversity of situations; *but this unity is quite loose, because the differences are enormous.*

Nonetheless, surely there are several common elements behind that heterogeneous landscape. This circumstance is not an accident, as different people at different places have reacted (even if in part differently reacted) to more or less general trends and processes, from the crisis of Marxism-Leninism to the rise of neo-liberalism to the reinvigoration/rediscovering of left-libertarian ideas and tactics such as self-management, horizontality, and decentralization.

Any honest balance sheet inevitably demonstrates that "autonomist" movements have shown interesting and promising characteristics as well as achieved important things in terms of social justice and collective dignity. Such a balance cannot ignore, however, the many internal weaknesses and contradictions and external threats these movements have faced. Among the internal problems, we could probably mention a persistent neglect of the ecological dimension of social emancipation, particularly (but not exclusively) in the form of environmental justice. In a world where the articulation of traditional struggle agendas (from the housing question to the struggle for land) with elements of a critical socio-environmental agenda is increasingly a factor of strategic enrichment and political legitimation, overcoming this limitation seems to be an important task.

What can we expect from "autonomist" movements in the future? Will at least some of them be able to continuously reinvent themselves in the long run, in order to face new challenges and new conjunctures?

Notes

1. The word *poblador* has a number of meanings, from "settler' to "inhabitant." In the present case, it has been used in Chile as a synonym for "slum dweller." Access to housing has been the basic challenge the *pobladores* have faced since they emerged as a social movement in the 1960s and 1970s.
2. The word *piquetero* is a neologism that comes from *piquete*, a term that originally means a form of protest where a group of workers, within the context of a strike, tries to prevent other workers from going to work. In the parlance or Argentine's social movements, a *piquetero* is an unemployed worker who belongs to a group that has blocked a street with the purpose of protesting and calling attention over a specific demand or issue. Between their emergence in the mid-1990s and the beginning of the 2000s, the *piqueteros* became one of the most famous Latin American social movements along with Mexican Zapatistas and Brazilian *sem-terra*, although fragmentation and co-optation have significantly weakened them politically in the last fifteen years.
3. "Magonism' (in Spanish, *magonismo*) refers to the kind of anarchism associated with the legacy of Mexican revolutionary Ricardo Flores Magón (1874–1922), strongly influenced by indigenous thought.
4. I am *not* suggesting that social movements organizations should never try to exercise control over welfare subsidies, once they exist; I am only underlining the obvious fact that such an attempt does not have anything to do with direct action (the autonomist strategy *par excellence*), corresponding instead to a form of institutional struggle—hence the possibility of co-optation and "domestication." Incidentally, it should be noted that "autonomist"

piqueteros in a more or less strong sense, represented for instance by Movimiento de Trabajadores Desocupados (MTD) of Solano and some intellectual initiatives like the famous "grassroots think tank" of militant research Colectivo Situaciones (see, for instance, Colectivo Situaciones 2002; MTD of Solano and Colectivo Situaciones 2002), have in fact been nothing but a minority of activists and supporters, a circumstance that has become increasingly evident after the mid-2000s.
5. On the contradictions of this movement, other authors have pointed to problems besides those that I witnessed myself. Rebón and Saavedra (2006), for instance, have offered a balanced account of the achievements and setbacks of the movement, discussing, among other problems: the presence of a mentality that sanctions some capitalist criteria of profit sharing, notably the differentiation of remuneration according to the workers' qualifications; other types of prejudice, such as racism, xenophobia, and homophobia; the survival of forms of control over workers in the typical "discipline and punish" style—which not infrequently includes methods like the time card, punishment for absences and even stop-and-search of workers with the purpose of inhibiting thefts.
6. *Ocupações* are the "abandoned' or vacant buildings or plots of land territorialized by so-called *sem-teto* activists—who are invariably poor people, who used to live in *favelas* or even as primary homeless on the streets, from where they wanted to escape because of violence and other factors. *Ocupações* in Brazilian cities are organized and managed by several different social movement organizations, but they are generally not properly or consistently governed by principles such as horizontality and self-management. For around ten years (approximately between 2005 and 2015), Rio de Janeiro was a notable exception, because in that city several informally and loosely federated *ocupações* arose, which were internally managed in a manner significantly guided by autonomist values. The so-called "revitalization" project Porto Maravilha, which started in 2011 and aims at the gentrification of the city's harbor area, played a decisive role in the weakening and ultimate disappearance of these *ocupações*.

References

Castoriadis, Cornelius (1975), *L'institution imaginaire de la société* (Seuil: Paris).
Castoriadis, Cornelius (1983 [1979]), "Introdução: socialismo e sociedade autônoma," in Cornelius Castoriadis, *Socialismo ou barbárie: O conteúdo do socialismo*, 11–34 (Brasiliense: São Paulo).
Castoriadis, Cornelius (1990 [1988]), "Pouvoir, politique, autonomie," in Cornelius Castoriadis, *Le monde morcelé : Les carrefours du labyrinthe III*, 113–39 (Seuil: Paris).
Castoriadis, Cornelius (1996 [1994]), "La démocratie comme procédure et comme régime," in Cornelius Castoriadis, *La montée de l'insignifiance : Les carrefours du labyrinthe IV*, 221–41 (Seuil: Paris).
Castoriadis, Cornelius, Daniel Cohn-Bendit (2014 [1981]), *De l'écologie à l'autonomie* (Paris: Éditions Le Bord del'Eau).
Chatterton, Paul (2005), "Making Autonomous Geographies: Argentina's Popular Uprising and the 'Movimiento de Trabajadores Desocupados' (Unemployed Workers Movement)," *Geoforum* 36(5), 545–61.
Colectivo Situaciones (2002), *19 y 20: Apuntes Para el Nuevo Protagonismo Social* (Buenos Aires: De Mano en Mano).

Crocker, Adam (2006), "Identity and Environmentalism in Zapatista Public Discourse on the Montes Azules Biosphere Reserve," Master's thesis, University of Saskatchewan, Saskatoon.

Delamata, Gabriela (2004), *Los barrios desbordados: Las organizaciones de desocupados del Gran Buenos Aires* (Buenos Aires: EUDEBA).

Díaz-Polanco, Héctor (1998 [1997]), *La rebelión zapatista y la autonomía* (Madrid: Siglo XXI).

Díaz-Polanco, Héctor (1999 [1991]), *Autonomía regional: La autodeterminación de los pueblos indios* (Madrid: Siglo XXI).

Gudynas, Eduardo (1992), "Los múltiples verdes del ambientalismo latinoamericano," *Nueva Sociedad* 122, 104–15.

Holloway, John (2005 [2002]), *Cambiar el mundo sin tomar el poder: El significado de la revolución hoy* (Buenos Aires: Ediciones Herramienta and Benemérita Universidad Autónoma de Puebla).

Katsiaficas, George (2006 [1997]), *The Subversion of Politics: European Autonomous Social Movements and the Decolonization of Everyday Life* (Edinburgh: AK Press).

Marcos [Subcomandante Insurgente] (2008), *En algún lugar de la Selva Lacandona: Aventuras y desventuras de Don Durito*, (Iztapalapa: Eón).

Marcos [Subcomandante Insurgente] (2011) *Relatos del Viejo Antonio: Textos del Subcomandante Insurgente Marcos* (Chiapas: Ediciones Rebeldía).

Merlinsky, María G. (2017), "Conflictos ambientales y arenas públicas de deliberación en torno a la cuestión ambiental en Argentina," *Ambiente & Sociedade* 20(2), 123–40.

Movimiento de Pobladores en Lucha (2011), *Siete y cuatro: El retorno de los pobladores* (Santiago: Editorial Quimantú).

MTD of Solano and Colectivo Situaciones (2002), *La Hipótesis 891: Más Allá de los Piquetes* (Buenos Aires: De Mano en Mano).

Negri, Antonio (1999 [1992]), *Insurgencies: Constituent Power and the Modern State* (Minneapolis: University of Minnesota Press).

Rebón, Julián and Ignacio Saavedra (2006), *Empresas recuperadas: La autogestión de los trabajadores* (Buenos Aires: Capital Intelectual).

Rossi, Federico M. (2015), "The Second Wave of Incorporation in Latin America: A Conceptualization of the Quest for Inclusion Applied to Argentina," *Latin American Politics and Society* 57(1), 1–28.

Souza, Marcelo Lopes de (2006), "*Together with* the State, *Despite* the State, *Against* the State: Social Movements as "Critical Urban Planning" Agents," *City* 10(3), 327–42.

Souza, Marcelo Lopes de (2016), "Lessons from Praxis: Autonomy and Spatiality in Contemporary Latin American Social Movements," *Antipode* 48(5), 1292–316.

Souza, Marcelo Lopes de (2017a), *Por uma Geografia libertária* (Rio de Janeiro: Consequência).

Souza, Marcelo Lopes de (2017b), "What Is 'Autonomy,' and How Can We Make It Possible? Reflecting on Concrete Experiences from Latin America," *Community Development Journal* 52(3), 436–53.

Thwaites Rey, Mabel (2013), "Prólogo: La búsqueda de la autonomía," in Ana Cecilia Dinerstein (ed.), *Movimientos sociales y autonomía colectiva: La política de la esperanza en América Latina*, 9–18 (Buenos Aires: Capital Intelectual).

Vitz, Matthew (2018), *A City on a Lake: Urban Political Ecology and the Growth of Mexico City* (Durham, NC: Duke University Press).

Zibechi, Raúl (2006), *Dispersar el poder: Los movimientos como poderes antiestatales* (Buenos Aires: Tinta Limón).

Zibechi, Raúl (2007), *Autonomías y emancipaciones: América Latina en movimiento* (Lima: Universidad Nacional Mayor de San Marcos).

CHAPTER 31

TRANSNATIONAL SOCIAL MOVEMENTS IN LATIN AMERICA

MARISA VON BÜLOW

Introduction

On November 25, 2019, dozens of Chilean women made a performance on the streets of Santiago to celebrate the International Day for the Elimination of Violence Against Women. With a black blindfold around their eyes, they danced and chanted "And the blame was not mine, nor where I was, nor how I dressed," and "The rapist is you! (The rapist is) the state, the judges, the President . . . ."[1] They denounced the failure of the justice system and of the police to protect women, as well as the victim blaming that so often comes after a rape.

The call to participate in this performance was launched on social media by the group "Lastesistas," a feminist collective created by four Chilean activists. A week later, videos of the performance had become viral globally, and similar flash mobs had happened in at least ten countries around the world, including Argentina, Brazil, Colombia, and Mexico.[2] Following the path of previous antiviolence feminist campaigns in Latin America, such as #NiUnaMenos and #MeuPrimeiroAssedio, internet users shared videos of heartbreaking testimonials of abuse. They created an online network that was linked through the use of the hashtags #ElVioladorErestu and #ElVioladorenTuCamino (or their equivalent in various languages).

These mobilizations showcase the importance of Latin America as cradle for transnational social movements and campaigns. As this chapter argues, the region has historically yielded innovative and impactful instances of transnational collective action. The rapid diffusion of the Chilean performance also points to important characteristics of contemporary transnationalism that are not specific to the region. Through the use of new digital technologies and smartphones, ties among activists from different countries form and transform quickly, creating networks with fluid boundaries that often overlap with other networks and initiatives. At the same time, the important role played by the Lastesistas group also reminds us of the continuing importance of organizations and leaders in launching, framing, and coordinating action.

Transnational collective action is not, however, a new phenomenon. This chapter reviews the literature that analyzes the origins of regional transnational collective action and the impacts of its pioneers. It puts greater emphasis, however, on debating the post-2000 period.

Transnational collective action is defined as "the process through which individuals, nonstate groups, and/or organizations mobilize jointly around issues, goals, and targets that link the domestic and international arenas" (von Bülow 2010: 5). TSMs are a subset of this phenomenon, characterized by sustained and collective mobilization efforts of individuals, nonstate groups and/or organizations around issues, goals, and targets across multiple national territories.

This chapter is divided into seven parts. The first presents a brief overview of the pioneers of transnational collective action in the region, followed by three sections that summarize key debates that motivated research on the topic between the 1990s and 2010s. The fifth part presents two empirical examples of Latin American transnationalism: the case of trade networks and the experience of the World Social Forum. The last two parts discuss the research agenda of the new millennium. They emphasize the importance of better understanding the role of conservative or right-wing transnational movements, and the impacts of the incorporation of digital repertoires on transnational collective action.

Pioneering Transnationalists

The literature on Latin American social movements shows that transnational actors have played key roles in regional and global politics since the 1990s, having had important impacts in domestic and international negotiations and norms (for example, Keck and Sikkink 1998; von Bülow 2019). Less well known are the historical precursors to the region's transnationalism and their early consequences. The feminist movement provides a good example. The feminist performance mentioned above has deep historical roots. From the 1910s onward, Latin American feminists engaged in regular cross border meetings and collaboration. As Marino (2019) argues, many of these feminists contributed to debates about women's rights by pioneering a broader view of feminism than what was sponsored by their United States and European counterparts. In the interwar years, they incorporated labor concerns with equal rights demands and anti-imperialist and antifascist ideas, including but going well beyond demands for civil and political rights (ibid.: 5; see Ewig and Friedman in this volume).

The activism of these pioneering feminists had consequences not only on domestic legislation but also on regional and global forums and decision-making processes. They lobbied the International Conferences of the Organization of American States and, in 1928, some of them became delegates to the first inter-governmental body in charge of discussing women's issues: the Inter-American Commission of Women (CIM). According to the official history of the Commission, "The creation of CIM was the product of emerging women's movements throughout the hemisphere and reflected growing cooperation between the women of North, Central and South America."[3] In 1934, Mexican feminist Margarita Robles de Mendoza launched the Unión de Mujeres Americanas (UMA), which used Spanish as its official language and, by October of 1935, had thirty-nine affiliated groups (Marino 2019: 117–18; Soto 1986: 22–23). These Latin American activists joined other civil society actors in the global antifascist mobilizations of the mid-1930s (Marino 2019: 121). In this same decade, they successfully lobbied the International Labor Organization in favor of equal rights and maternity leave (ibid.: 132–33), and afterwards they influenced the language of the United Nations' Universal Declaration on Human Rights (ibid.: 223–24).

These key accomplishments are even more important if we consider that early transnational ties were fraught with disagreements and accusations of imperialism that hindered collaboration not only between Latin Americans and United States activists, but also among Latin American feminists themselves (Marino 2019). As the literature on contemporary transnationalism shows, power asymmetries across North and South and ideological differences among actors continued to resonate throughout the twentieth century, as key obstacles for effective transnationalism in the Americas (for example, Keck and Sikkink 1998; von Bülow 2010).

In spite of the evidence of the historical impacts of transnational actors, scholars were late in recognizing the importance of civil society activism across national borders. Only in the 1970s did international relations researchers begin to seriously consider the role of non-state actors. Even then, the issue was approached from a narrow empirical perspective in what remained for the most part a state-centric discipline.[4] As Risse-Kappen (1995a: 7) argues in his review of this early literature, it focused empirically mostly on cases of multinational corporations and then withered away in the 1980s. It was in the 1990s, in the context of transitions to democracy in South America and the end of the Cold War, that social movement and international relations scholars launched a systematic research agenda on the phenomenon. This was a global enterprise, but one to which Latin American scholars and activists contributed decisively, as shown in the next section.

Latin American Transnational Networks: A Multidisciplinary Research Agenda

Margaret Keck and Kathryn Sikkink contributed to launching a new research agenda on transnational civil society action in Latin America with their 1998 book, *Activists beyond Borders: Advocacy Networks in International Politics*. It was the first comparative analysis of the region's transnational advocacy networks across issue areas: women, human rights, and environmental networks. Keck and Sikkink's volume, alongside other publications that came out around the same time (for example, Risse-Kappen 1995b; Smith, Chatfield, and Pagnucco 1997), provided evidence of the increasing growth and influence of transnational networks in both domestic and international politics.

In their empirical analysis about the relevance of non-state actors and their transnational collaboration, Keck and Sikkink highlighted the potential effectiveness of the strategy of the "boomerang pattern." Actors launch the boomerang in the specific context of the blocking of domestic political opportunities. In such a context, "domestic NGOs bypass their state and directly search out international allies to try to bring pressure on their states from outside" (Keck and Sikkink 1998: 12). As part of these transnational efforts, networks of actors engage in four types of tactics: information politics (to quickly and credibly generate politically usable information and move it to where it will have the most impact); symbolic politics (to call upon symbols or stories that make sense of a situation); leverage politics (to call upon powerful actors to affect a situation); and accountability politics (to hold powerful actors to their previously stated policies or principles) (ibid.: 16).

One of the clearest examples of the effective use of the boomerang pattern is the case of the transnational advocacy network that linked Brazilian local actors in the Amazon region and activists in the United States in the 1980s. Unable to change the federal government's policies for the region at the domestic level, local groups allied with United States actors to lobby the Congress in that country to put pressure on the World Bank, which was giving loans to the Brazilian government to fund development projects in the Amazon region. The United States' political and economic clout on the World Bank meant that it was vulnerable to that type of pressure. In 1985, for the first time in its history, the World Bank temporarily suspended disbursements on the grounds that the Brazilian government was violating loan conditions on protecting natural and indigenous areas (Keck and Sikkink 1998: 139). As Keck and Sikkink (ibid.: 160–62) argue, because of the campaigns launched by this network throughout the 1980s, the ways governments and international organizations discussed tropical forest issues changed, both in terms of the actors being involved in them (with new seats on the table for local organizations and groups) and of the ways environmental assessment policies were included in projects funded by international banks.

Subsequent literature on Latin America has contributed to debates about the emergence and the impacts of transnational collective action in two key ways. First, by proposing a multilevel and dynamic analysis of the closing and opening of political opportunity structures to explain the emergence or the absence of collective action. Second, by studying transnational movements as defensive responses to threats. These contributions built on different theoretical frameworks, ranging from constructivist approaches that emphasized the agency and contingency of transnational phenomena, to structuralist theories that lay stress upon neoliberal globalization in explaining the emergence of transnational resistance movements in the region. The next sections review these contributions, focusing on some of the key examples of transnational movements from the region.

Beyond the Boomerang

In a book chapter published seven years after "Activists Beyond Borders," Sikkink proposed to expand on the idea of the boomerang pattern by differentiating among patterns of interactions between domestic and international opportunity structures (Sikkink 2005: 156–57). The variation in the degree of openness to civil society of institutions at these two levels, Sikkink argued, yields four types of domestic-international interaction.

The first, "diminished opportunities for activism" (closed domestic and international opportunity structures), refers not to the absence of activism, but to the expectation that action will face greater obstacles. A good example is the campaign in favor of abortion in Latin America in the 1990s, which faced a lot of resistance both at the domestic and at the international levels (Sikkink 2005: 160). The second type of interaction, the "boomerang and spirals" (closed domestic opportunity structures but open international opportunity structures), is exemplified by Sikkink with the case of the arrest of former dictator Augusto Pinochet in Britain, in 1998. Whereas it had been impossible for Chilean actors to successfully try Pinochet in local courts, they were more effective using international institutions and foreign actors (ibid.: 162).

The third type of interaction, "democratic deficit and defensive transnationalization" (open domestic opportunity structures but closed international opportunity structures), relates to cases in which activists perceive that they have to work internationally, "to minimize losses rather than to seek gains" (Sikkink 2005: 164). Good examples are the campaigns against free trade agreement negotiations in the Americas in the 1990s and 2000s, which were perceived by activists as threats that required mobilization (von Bülow 2010). Finally, the fourth type of interaction, "insider-outsider coalitions" (open domestic and international opportunity structures), refers to "coalitions that emerge when activists operate in open domestic and international opportunity structures" (Sikkink 2005: 165). This is exemplified by Sikkink with the case of groups working on the issue of transitional justice in Argentina. Local groups changed their strategy, from the boomerang pattern in the 1970s and 1980s to insider-outsider coalitions after the country's transition to democracy. It differs from the case of Pinochet because in Argentina activists perceived that there was a greater opening of the judicial system. Thus, they launched a series of domestic legal initiatives while at the same time working with international allies to denounce human rights violations of the military dictatorship period (ibid.: 165–71).

This typology helps understand how and when actors decide to "scale shift" upwards—from the domestic to the international arena—as well as downward—from the international to the domestic arena. Instead of analyzing the rise in transnational collective action as a linear process whereby social movements grow steadily and become more and more globalized, it is more fruitful to think in terms of the variety of pathways taken by actors across domestic and international arenas. These pathways to transnationality may vary significantly, in terms of actors' degrees of internationalization and their actions' endurance through time (von Bülow 2010: 32–33), depending on the multilevel opportunity structure interactions.

However, as Sikkink (2005) and other social movement scholars have argued (for example, Goodwin and Jasper 1999), political opportunity structures are dynamic and are not readily evaluated in the same ways by all actors (see also Somma, Wada, Almeida in this volume). The Latin American literature on transnational social movements provides ample evidence of how actors perceive such opportunity structures differently, in light of changes in the political context at the domestic and international levels. For instance, there were acute disagreements among participants in the Campaign Against the Free Trade Agreement of the Americas (FTAA) about the meanings of the election, in 2002, of Luiz Inácio Lula da Silva as President in Brazil. Because of the close ties between Lula's political party and many of the most active organizations in that Campaign, for some this meant that the new administration would endorse its demands. For others, however, Lula's administration was based on a broad coalition of actors, consisting of both allies and foes, and thus presented a much more restricted influence space for the Campaign than the first group perceived (von Bülow 2010: 186–87, 2013a).

Thus, the emergence of transnational collective action is not predetermined by the opening or closing of political opportunity structures, either at the national or at the international level. Furthermore, from this perspective opportunities are not only given, but also actively constructed by actors. In the first decade of the 2000s, under the center-Left administrations in countries such as Brazil, Venezuela, Argentina, and Bolivia, both national and foreign activists actively worked to empower their allies within governments and push for their agendas (von Bülow 2010: 186–89). And, as shown in the next section, actors have also worked to open closed opportunity structures, when threats become forces driving collective action.

Threats and Mobilization

In a region riddled with high economic inequality and poverty, scholars argue that it is important to "recognize how much collective action is driven by various forms of threat" (Almeida and Pérez Martín 2020), and not only by the opening of political opportunity structures the literature has mostly focused on. This is not a new debate. In the 1970s, social movement scholar Charles Tilly had pointed to both opportunities and threats as forces driving collective action. Threats were defined by Tilly as the "extent to which other groups are threatening to make claims which would, if successful, reduce the contender's realization of its interests" (Tilly 1978: 133). Building on this definition and on the empirical analysis of Central American cases, Paul Almeida (2005) proposed a typology of core forms of threat: state repression, state-attributed economic problems, and environmental harms.

State repression "involves acts by government and government-linked agents that attempt to suppress dissent within a population" (Almeida 2005: 107). The threats of state repression do not, by themselves, create collective action. As explained by Almeida, organizational infrastructure is also relevant, and periods of political liberalization prior to democratization allow for the formation of organizations (ibid.: 109). This helps explain the emergence and radicalization of collective action in Central America in the 1970s and 1980s (ibid.: 110).

State-attributed economic threats relate to the neoliberal policies enacted by states in Latin America in the late twentieth and early twenty-first centuries. These are, according to Almeida (2005: 112), "the most pressing state-attributed economic problem inducing large-scale protest campaigns" against economic liberalization and privatization initiatives. Transnational campaigns against free trade agreements in the Americas represent a good example. As Spalding (2014: 97) has put it, free trade agreement negotiations served as "a major catalyst for cross-regional organizing."

Finally, environmental threats became, in the 2010s, the driving force behind "the largest campaigns in contemporary Central America" (Almeida 2005: 116). In fact, Latin America as a whole has witnessed an increase in so-called socio-environmental conflicts, associated with the boom in exports of commodities from the region (Martí i Puig and de la Maza 2018; Christel and Gutiérrez in this volume). More often than not, these conflicts are multi-scale, involving a broad array of community-based, national, and international actors, targets, and strategies (Martí i Puig and de la Maza 2018: 5). The case of the campaign against the HydroAysén dam complex, in the Chilean Patagonia, is a good example. The civil society coalition Patagonia Sin Represas gathered over eighty local, national, and international organizations, and organized massive protests in 2011 both in Chile and in several other countries around the world (Schaeffer 2017: 131–32). Other cases also show that environmental threats can lead to transnational collaboration among civil society actors. As Albó (2011: 161) argues, threats from natural resources exploitation initiatives were an important incentive for the creation of new forms of transnational organization and collaboration among indigenous peoples from the Andean countries from the 1990s onward.

However, Latin American transnational social movements of the 1990s–2010s not only launched reactive campaigns to counter threats but also actively built new civil society forums to think about alternative agendas and policies. Two relevant examples are the creation of the Hemispheric Social Alliance, at the Inter-American level, and the World Social Forum meetings, the creation of which has important roots in Latin America.

Alternatives for the Americas and for the World

Throughout the 1990s and the first decade of the 2000s, a wave of bilateral and multilateral trade agreements proposed broad policy changes, which went well beyond tariff cuts. They also entailed extensive domestic reforms in investment rules, intellectual property, agriculture, and migration policies. These agreements became a major focus of contention, especially in the case of the highly asymmetrical negotiations between Latin American countries and the United States, which triggered multisectoral transnational campaigns that mobilized a broad range of actors from the mid-1990s onward.

Participants in trade networks sometimes operated only at the domestic level, while others had much deeper international commitments and built stronger ties with allies in other countries; their strategies also varied in time span, from short-term, to intermittent, to more sustainable collective action efforts (von Bülow 2010: 25–34). Based on an analysis of transnationalism in Central America, Spalding (2015) contributed to further specifying these pathways across scales by differentiating among three mobilization processes across borders: the "domestic loop," the "deleveraging hook," and "lateral transnationalism." Spalding defines domestic loop processes as "the intersection between domestic coalition partners and their . . . transnational allies as they construct discourse, frames, and strategies to address local problems of international origin" (ibid.: 184). The second, the deleveraging hook, refers to "the way in which domestic coalitions propel themselves into the international arena, frequently in an attempt to pry open unresponsive institutions and reduce external pressure on their domestic sphere" (ibid.: 184). Finally, lateral transnationalism maps processes of "frame construction and resource flows that emerge through exchanges between activists in most similar, and frequently neighboring, countries" (ibid.: 185).

As a result of these mobilizations, a new organizational infrastructure for transnational civil society collaboration was created in the Americas throughout the 1990s. National multisectoral alliances brought together nongovernmental organizations, social movement organizations, small business organizations, and faith-based initiatives. In Mexico, the Red Mexicana de Acción Frente al Libre Comercio (RMALC) was created in 1991 as a meeting space for a broad spectrum of civil society organizations to influence the North American Free Trade Agreement (NAFTA) negotiations among Mexico, the United States, and Canada. Similar national coalitions were created in subsequent years in other countries, such as the Alianza Chilena por un Comercio Justo y Responsable (ACJR) and the Rede Brasileira pela Integração dos Povos (Rebrip). At the same time, regional organizations were created, such as the Iniciativa Mesoamericana de Comercio, Integración y Desarrollo (Iniciativa CID), and issue-based coalitions, such as Mujer a Mujer, which brought together women's organizations to denounce the impacts of the NAFTA on women workers, especially those working in the maquila zone in Northern Mexico (Hale and Wills 2007: 460–61).

Many of these actors, in turn, met at the hemispheric level under the umbrella of the Hemispheric Social Alliance (HSA), which was created in 1997 in the context of the Free Trade Area of the Americas (FTAA) negotiations. The hemispheric—not only Latin American—character of the Alliance was a novelty in terms of coalition building in the region, as was its breadth of membership, which ranged from nongovernmental organizations to domestic and international social movement organizations. Although the HSA was defined by its members as an "open space," not every social movement could participate. It presented itself as a "forum of progressive social movements and organizations of the Americas, created to exchange information, define strategies and promote common actions, directed at finding an alternative and democratic development model" (von Bülow 2010: 124–25). Thus, having an HSA membership implied sharing a critical stance toward multilateral trade agreements and an interest in influencing Latin American regional integration processes.

As in past instances of North–South collaboration, such as the ties among feminists mentioned earlier in this chapter, historical tensions and power disputes remained important obstacles for long-term coalition-building. These were most clearly visible when actors discussed alternatives to liberalization policies. Although the HSA was initially created as a way of coordinating resistance to the FTAA negotiations, its members also sought to agree on proposals for trade governance. Between 1998 and 2005, HSA members produced five successive editions of the document "Alternatives for the Americas," in which they presented proposals for international regulation in the issue areas covered by trade agreements (von Bülow 2010: ch. 9).

The process of elaboration of "Alternatives for the Americas" within this heterogeneous coalition was fraught with tensions and disagreements alongside what Anner and Evans (2004) termed the "double divide"—between NGOs and social movements, and between North and South. While Southern-based actors denounced United States imperialism and framed trade agreement negotiations as part of the long history of United States dominance in the region, such claims were downplayed by actors in the North (von Bülow 2010: 165–65). Provisional agreements were reached, however, on a wide set of issues, including, for instance, labor rights (Anner and Evans 2004). HSA members agreed on the proposal to include a social clause in free trade agreements, but whether labor rights clauses should be or not enforceable through sanctions remained a source of contention. For Latin American actors, sanctions could lead to negative effects in terms of loss of investment and employment (von Bülow 2010: 166–67). As the FTAA negotiations stalled and in early 2000s new Center-Left governments were elected in various South American countries, the HSA progressively lost its convening power. However, the efforts at building common ground across different actors helped structure some of the key debates in global civil society arenas, such as the World Social Forum (WSF).

In 2001, around twenty thousand participants from 117 countries assembled in the city of Porto Alegre, Brazil, for the first WSF. Its optimistic motto, "Another World is Possible," summarized the goal of building alternatives to neoliberal globalization from below, that is, from the perspective of grassroots civil society organizations. It was also a call for actors to move away from resistance campaigns and to collaborate in designing concrete policy alternatives. It initially stood as a challenge to the gathering of political and economic elites at the World Economic Forum (WEF), held at the same time of the first WSF meeting in Davos, Switzerland. In 2005, the WSF held its largest meeting, with around 150 thousand participants, from 149 countries (von Bülow 2013b: 9). The WSF process also generated a long series of thematic, regional, and local meetings, thereby creating a flexible way of combining participation across scales and issues such as migration, racism, and gender.

As in the case of the HSA, not all of civil society was welcomed at the WSF. Shortly after its first meeting, the WSF International Council agreed to issue a Charter of Principles, which set the basic goals and participation rules (WSF 2001). It defined itself as a process of construction of alternatives to neoliberal policies, and it denied participation to armed movements (von Bülow 2013b: 10). Contrary to the HSA, WSF participants did not engage in a process of creating unified proposals. Meetings ended without a final document or declaration. No binding decisions on how to move forward were put to vote. This absence was, paradoxically, the result of a general decision made at the beginning of the process (WSF 2001). It remained, however, a key topic of disagreement.

As Santos (2005: 96) put it, this disagreement was related to the definition of the nature of the process. For some, the WSF should be a movement, or a movement of movements, that is, a political actor that puts forward a specific set of demands around which to mobilize. For others, the WSF should remain nondeliberative, an inclusive meeting arena—a "public square," according to Chico Whitaker (2005), one of the early participants and organizers. While Whitaker's position predominated throughout the first two decades of the 2000s, this debate has remained a matter of contention. As one member of the WSF International Committee criticized,

> resistance to collective political action relegated the WSF to a self-referential place of debate, rather than a body capable of taking real action in the international arena . . . As a result, the WSF has become akin to a personal growth retreat where participants come away with renewed individual strength, but without any impact on the world. (Savio 2019)

This debate disseminated to the discussions of thematic and regional forums, and in fact has remained an open debate. In preparation for the Eighth World Social Forum on Migrations, held in 2018 in Mexico City, a document released by the organizers identified the dichotomy event or process as one of the key debates.[5]

Notwithstanding critiques about its lack of impact, the WSF became a springboard for new transnational mobilizations and campaigns. In 2002, during a WSF meeting, actors launched the Continental Campaign Against the FTAA, which included but went beyond the HSA membership. That same year, the European Social Forum called for protests against the Iraq War, and in 2003 the WSF played an important role in organizing a global day of action against the war (Savio 2019).

The future of experiences such as the WSF process and the HSA became more uncertain in the 2010s, in part because of the disagreements mentioned above, and in part because of the changes in the political context in the region. The rise of new right-wing actors and their election to governments in countries such as Brazil (in 2018) simultaneously shifted the national and international political opportunity structures. While the literature on transnational social movements in the region had made great strides in understanding progressive actors, much less had been written on conservative or right-wing civil society actors and their transnational activism.

The Rise of Right-wing Transnational Actors

The Latin American literature on transnational social movements has primarily focused on resistance movements and on those that seek to promote progressive changes (such as the ones mentioned in the previous sections). In fact, as Almeida and Chase-Dunn (2018: 190) argue, this is a bias that characterizes the social movement literature in general, and not only that of Latin America (see also Bob 2013; Payne in this volume).[6]

This selective approach to TSMs in the literature began to change in the context of the late 2010s turn to the right in key countries of the region such as Brazil, after the demise of the so-called pink tide of center-Left governments of the first decade of the 2000s (Ferrero, Natalucci, and Tatagiba 2019; Luna and Rovira 2014). There has been a growing effort, for instance, to map the ties among right-wing actors in Latin America and their counterparts in the United States, in the case of women's movements (Power 2012), student movement organizations (Gobbi 2016), and gun control campaigns (Bob 2012).

In the context of the twenty-two months of the campaign for the impeachment of Brazilian President Dilma Rousseff (2014–2016), Latin American activists not only followed events closely but also participated in online networks, broadcasting protest events and using the campaign to fuel anti-leftist feelings in the region. As von Bülow and Dias (2019: 24) show in their analysis of pro-impeachment networks on Twitter, some of the most retweeted messages in the context of street protests were written in Spanish, originating from actors that also mobilized against governments in Venezuela and Cuba.

It is important to note, however, that conservative and right-wing transnational collective action is not new (Payne in this volume). While right-wing transnational civil society ties have not been as visible as leftist ones, they are not a recent phenomenon in the region. Furthermore, as in the case of the transnational Left, it is often intertwined with religious networks (see Mackin in this volume). For instance, conservative Catholic groups in the region have been highly critical of the WSF since its first meetings, calling it "a neorevolution based on anarchical ideology," and denouncing it as a "dangerous leftist international network" that challenges Christian civilization and its values (Penha 2002: 10–19). In spite of this, South–South ties among right-wing and religious actors remain understudied in the literature.

Digital Transnationalism

From activists' use of email and websites in the 1990s to social media platforms and messaging apps in the 2000s, digital technologies have offered new possibilities for political activism in general and for mobilization across borders in particular (for example,

Almeida and Lichbach 2003; Castells 2012; Treré and Summer in this volume). One of the earliest examples of successful use of digital technologies by social movements is what Inclán (2018: 102) calls "transnational Zapatismo." In the context of the uprising of the Ejército Zapatista de Liberación Nacional, in 1994 in the Southern state of Chiapas, Mexico, a global solidarity network emerged (Olesen 2008; see Oikonomakis in this volume). In the years that followed, transnational actors travelled to Chiapas and extensively used the digital tools available at the time—websites and email lists—to diffuse the insurgents' demands and pressure the Mexican government to open negotiations. In April of 1996, the Zapatistas organized the First Continental Encounter for Humanity and Against Neoliberalism, in which the group's demands were portrayed as global causes to thousands of national and international participants (Inclán 2018: 103–04).

In the 2010s digital activism had become part of the routine repertoire of social movements, be they preexisting ones that incorporate digital activist practices, such as the Chilean student movement (for example, von Bülow 2018), or new ones, such as the feminist hashtag campaigns against violence (for example, Friedman and Tabbush 2016). Such developments have important consequences in the debates about the emergence and characteristics of transnational social movements.

This is true across the ideological spectrum, as both right and left-wing actors use digital technologies for activism. Much of this collective action produces "transnational political hashtag networks" that are less bounded and sustainable than traditional offline social movements. Transnational political hashtag networks are "delimited digital platform ties, created by internauts and/or by automation mechanisms, based on the tagging of an issue, position or political goal, in a specific context" (von Bülow and Dias 2019: 6). The feminist hashtag campaigns, such as #NiUnaMenos, have been particularly visible in Latin America (see Ewig and Friedman in this volume). Less studied are the transnational ties among right-wing actors mentioned above, which connected actors who used the hashtags #ForaDilma in the context of the mobilization in favor of the impeachment of President Rousseff in Brazil (von Bülow and Dias 2019: 17–18).

The possibilities provided by new digital technologies have opened a debate about their impacts on democracy in general, and on collective action in particular. These technologies have a dual impact: at the same time that their affordances allow for new and exciting possibilities for actors to find like-minded peers across the world and voice their messages with great speed (for example, see Castells 2012), their use can deepen power asymmetries among actors (for example, see von Bülow 2018), and have been a powerful repression tool in the hands of authoritarian governments. Despite this duality, the use of new digital technologies has contributed to further blurring the distinctions among scales of activism.

Conclusion

Much of the literature on transnational social movements has focused on cases of the Global North. However, as this chapter shows, Latin American TSMs have been key actors in global governance debates and initiatives. The literature produced about these cases has made important contributions to broader debates about how and why social movements move across national borders, as well as their consequences. It has also helped reach a more precise understanding of the agency of actors faced with similar structural constraints. This chapter also reviewed some of the gaps in the literature, most importantly the need to do more research on right-wing transnational movements and on transformations of transnational collective action due to the appropriation of digital technologies.

In spite of all that has been accomplished by the literature on transnationalism, in general, Latin American scholars still tend to think of mobilization and the impacts of social movements in national terms. Take, for example, the much-discussed cycle of protests that became known as the "June Protest Cycle" in Brazil in 2013. Few scholars have mapped its ties to other cases of mobilization overseas. One is Canavarro (2015), who shows that the Turkish Taksim Gezi Park mobilizations, which began a few weeks before June of 2013, were an inspiration to Brazilian protestors' framing strategies. Protestors remixed a popular soccer cheering song to yell that "Love is over, this will become Turkey," held Turkish flags alongside the Brazilian ones, and produced memes and messages linking the movements in Brazil and Turkey on social media (ibid.: 7–9).

Another good example is that of the Chilean student movement. Its influence on other movements around the world remains understudied. And yet, in 2015, when Brazilian students occupied hundreds of public high schools in the state of São Paulo, their strategies were impacted by a Chilean textbook on how to organize school occupations (Catini and Mello 2016: 1179). They also chanted "This will become Chile," relocating geographically the 2013 song.

From this perspective, the most urgent challenge for the literature in transnational social movements in Latin America remains the same as it was in the 1990s: to change the ontological approach to social movements. We still need to broaden the methodological and theoretical lenses through which we view social movements and protests to include the key roles of transnational processes and mechanisms.

Notes

1. There are many online videos available. This one is of the November 25 performance in Santiago, Chile: https://www.youtube.com/watch?v=yJGE9zqgna8.
2. This is a rough estimation, based on a hashtag search conducted on Twitter, Facebook, and Instagram on December 2, 2019.
3. https://www.oas.org/en/cim/history.asp.
4. Among the most important works of this earlier debate are Keohane and Nye (1977); Nye and Keohane (1971); Rosenau (1969).
5. See the call for the Eighth World Social Forum on Migrations here: https://fsmm2018.org/8to-foro-social-mundial-mundial-las-migraciones-mexico-2018/.
6. An important exception is the pioneering work by Payne on a subset of right-wing actors, which she called "uncivil movements" in Brazil, Venezuela, and Nicaragua, defined as "political groups within democracies that employ both civil and uncivil political action to promote exclusionary policies" (Payne 2000: 1).

References

Albó, Xavier (2011), "Hacia el poder indígena en Ecuador, Perú y Bolivia," in Ana Cecilia Betancur (ed.), *Movimientos indígenas en América Latina: Resistencia y nuevos modelos de integración*, 133–67 (Copenhagen: Grupo Internacional de Trabajo sobre Derechos Indígenas).

Almeida, Paul (2005), "The Role of Threats in Popular Mobilization in Central America," in Federico M. Rossi and Marisa von Bülow (eds.), *Social Movement Dynamics: New Perspectives on Theory and Research from Latin America*, 105–25 (Farnham: Ashgate).

Almeida, Paul and Amalia Pérez Martín (2020), "Economic Globalization and Social Movements in Latin America," in Xóchitl Bada and Liliana Rivera-Sánchez (eds.), *The Oxford Handbook of the Sociology of Latin America*, 390–411 (Oxford: Oxford University Press).

Almeida, Paul and Chris Chase-Dunn (2018), "Globalization and Social Movements," *Annual Review of Sociology* 44, 189–211.

Almeida, Paul and Mark Lichbach (2003), "To the Internet, from the Internet: Comparative Media Coverage of Transnational Protests," *Mobilization* 8 (3), 249–72.

Anner, Mark and Peter Evans (2004), "Building Bridges across a Double Divide: Alliances Between the US and Latin American Labour and NGOs," *Development in Practice* 14(1/2), 34–47.

Bob, Clifford (2012), *The Global Right Wing and the Clash of World Politics* (Cambridge: Cambridge University Press).

Bob, Clifford (2013), "The Global Right Wing and Theories of Transnational Advocacy," *The International Spectator* 48(4), 71–85.

Canavarro, Marcela (2015), "Technopolitics and Emotional Contagion: The Inspiration from Turkey and Spain to Uprisings in Brazil in and after 2013," Paper presented at the Mediated Communication, Public Opinion & Society Section at the IAMCR 2015 Conference in Montreal, Canada, July 12–19.

Castells, Manuel (2012), *Networks of Outrage and Hope: Social Movements in the Internet Age* (Malden: Polity).

Catini, Carolina and Gustavo Mello (2016), "Escolas de luta, educação política," *Education and Society* 37(137): 1177–202.

Ferrero, Juan Pablo, Ana Natalucci, and Luciana Tatagiba (2019) (eds.), *Socio-Political Dynamics within the Crisis of the Left: Argentina and Brazil* (Lanham, MD: Rowman & Littlefield).

Friedman, Elisabeth Jay and Constanza Tabbush (2016), "#NiUnaMenos: Not One Woman Less, Not One More Death!," *NACLA*, November 1, https://nacla.org/news/2016/11/01/niunamenos-not-one-woman-less-not-one-more-death.

Gobbi, Danniel (2016), "Identidade em ambiente virtual: uma análise da Rede Estudantes Pela Liberdade," Masters' thesis, University of Brasília, Brasília.

Goodwin, Jeff and James Jasper (1999), "Caught in a Winding, Snarling Vine: The Structural Bias of Political Process Theory," *Sociological Forum* 14(1), 27–54.

Hale, Angela and Jane Wills (2007), "Women Working Worldwide: Transnational Networks, Corporate Social Responsibility and Action Research," *Global Networks* 7(4), 453–76.

Inclán, Maria (2018), *The Zapatista Movement and Mexico's Democratic Transition* (Oxford: Oxford University Press).

Keck, Margaret and Kathryn Sikkink (1998), *Activists Beyond Borders: Advocacy Networks in International Politics* (Ithaca, NY: Cornell University Press).

Keohane, Robert and Joseph S. Nye (1977), *Power and Interdependence* (Boston, MA: Little, Brown & Co).

Luna, Juan Pablo and Cristóbal Rovira Kaltwasser (eds.) (2014), *The Resilience of the Latin American Right* (Baltimore, MD: Johns Hopkins University Press).

Marino, Katherine (2019), *Feminism for the Americas: The Making of an International Human Rights Movement* (Chapel Hill: The University of North Carolina Press).

Martí i Puig, Salvador and Gonzalo Delamaza (2018), "Presentación," *América Latina Hoy* 79, 3–8.

Nye, Joseph and Robert O. Keohane (1971), "Transnational Relations and World Politics: An Introduction," *International Organizations* 25(3), 329–49.

Olesen, Thomas (2008), "Globalising the Zapatistas: from Third World Solidarity to Global Solidarity?," *Third World Quarterly* 25(1), 255–67.

Payne, Leigh A. (2000), *Uncivil Movements: The Armed Right Wing and Democracy in Latin America* (Baltimore, MD: The Johns Hopkins University Press).

Penha, Guilherme da (2002), "A pretexto do combate à globalização renasce a luta de classes: Fórum Social Mundial de Porto Alegre, berço de uma neo-revolução anárquica," *Catolicismo* 614, 10–19 February.

Power, Margaret (2012), "Transnational Connections among Right-Wing Women: Brazil, Chile, and the United States," in Kathleen Blee and Sandra McGee Deutsch (eds.), *Women of the Right: Comparisons and Interplay across Borders*, 21–35 (University Park: Penn State University Press).

Risse-Kappen, Thomas (1995a), "Bringing Transnational Relations Back in: Introduction," in Thomas Risse-Kappen (ed.), *Bringing Transnational Relations Back in: Non-State Actors, Domestic Structures and International Institutions*, 3–33 (Cambridge: Cambridge University Press).

Risse-Kappen, Thomas (ed.) (1995b), *Bringing Transnational Relations Non-State Actors, Domestic Structures and International Institutions* (Cambridge: Cambridge University Press).

Rosenau, James N. (1969), *Linkage Politics* (New York: Free Press).

Santos, Boaventura de Sousa (2005), *O Fórum Social Mundial: manual de uso* (Porto Alegre: Edições Afrontamento).

Savio, Roberto (2019), "Farewell to the World Social Forum?," *Common Dreams*, November 4, https://www.commondreams.org/views/2019/11/04/farewell-world-social-forum.

Schaeffer, Colombina (2017), "Democratizing the Flows of Democracy: Patagonia Sin Represas in the Awakening of Chile's Civil Society," in Sofía Donoso and Marisa von Bülow (eds.), *Social Movements in Chile: Organization, Trajectories and Political Consequences*, 131–59 (New York: Palgrave-Macmillan).

Sikkink, Kathryn (2005), "Patterns of Dynamic Multilevel Governance and the Insider-Outsider Coalition," in Donatella della Porta and Sidney Tarrow (eds.), *Transnational Protest and Global Activism*, 151–73 (Lanham, MD: Rowman & Littlefield).

Soto, Shirlene (1986), "Women in the Revolution," in W. Dirk Raat and William H. Beezley (eds.), *Twentieth-Century Mexico*, 17–32 (Lincoln: University of Nebraska Press).

Spalding, Rose (2014), *Contesting Trade in Central America: Market Reform and Resistance* (Austin: University of Texas Press).

Spalding, Rose (2015), "Domestic Loops and Deleveraging Hooks: Transnational Social Movements and the Politics of Scale Shift," in Federico M. Rossi and Marisa von Bülow (eds), *Social Movement Dynamics: New Perspectives on Theory and Research from Latin America*, 181–211 (Farnham, MD: Ashgate).

Tarrow, Sidney (2005), *The New Transnational Activism* (Cambridge: Cambridge University Press).

von Bülow, Marisa (2010), *Building Transnational Networks: Civil Society and the Politics of Trade in the Americas* (Cambridge: Cambridge University Press).

von Bülow, Marisa (2013a), "The Politics of Scale Shift and Coalition Building: the Case of the Brazilian Network for the Integration of the Peoples," in Eduardo Silva (ed.), *Transnational Activism and National Movements in Latin America: Bridging the Divide*, 72–95 (New York: Routledge).

von Bülow, Marisa (ed.) (2013b), *Fórum Social Mundial: a transnacionalização da sociedade civil brasileira* (Brasília: Editorial Universidade de Brasília).

von Bülow, Marisa (2018), "The Survival of Leaders and Organizations in the Digital Age: Lessons from the Chilean Student Movement," *Mobilization* 23(1), 45–64.

von Bülow, Marisa and Tayrine Dias (2019), "O ativismo de hashtags contra e a favor do impeachment de Dilma Rousseff," *Revista Crítica de Ciências Sociais* 120, 5–32.

Whitaker, Chico (2005), *O desafio do Fórum Social Mundial: um modo de ver* (São Paulo, Fundação Perseu Abramo/Edições Loyola).

WSF (2001), "Charter of Principles of the World Social Forum," São Paulo, April 9, https://fsmm2018.org/principles-of-the-world-social-forum/?lang=en.

CHAPTER 32

RIGHT-WING MOVEMENTS IN LATIN AMERICA

LEIGH A. PAYNE

Introduction

The vast enterprise of studies on right-wing movements in Western Europe only rarely travels outside a few national boundaries. Eastern Europe and the United States are occasionally included. Right-wing movements in other regions—such as Latin America—are not considered comparable. Sometimes the reason for excluding Latin America, such as its distinct political history, is expressly stated. Roger Griffin, for example, contends that, "[c]onsiderations of traditionalist forces operating outside Europeanized societies in a non-parliamentary context, such as Islamic fundamentalism, or of ideologically vacuous dictatorships, whether military or personal [such as those in Latin America], . . . need not detain us" (Griffin 2017: 16). Alternatively, Latin America's right-wing movements are seen as irrelevant to political or social life, as Meyer and Staggenborg (1996: 1630) suggest: "In Central America, movements of the Left and Right often engage in combat in which the state is at most a marginal player." Latin America is thus excluded from comparative analysis because of misunderstanding and misinterpretation of right-wing movements as trapped in the authoritarian past and inconsequential to contemporary social and political life.

This chapter contends that the problem of comparison is not the distinctiveness or irrelevance of Latin America's right-wing movements but the poverty and parochialism of the existing analytical frameworks. A great deal of variation exists among right-wing movements on the European continent without inhibiting scholars from attempting comparison. Similarly, those differences should not prevent finding comparison with Latin American right-wing movements. Moreover, decades since the end of the region's dictatorships, new, powerful right-wing movements have emerged that resemble those in Europe and the United States. Incorporating these new right-wing movements contributes to building analytical frameworks capable of traveling across continents to understand the broader global phenomenon.[1]

Defining Right-Wing Movements

The first step in building such a framework is developing a good definition of right-wing movements. Scholars have struggled in this effort, with some focusing on the conservative nature of such movements to preserve the status quo, resulting in a "backlash" or "roll-back" of the Left and its victories. Others focus on an economic, or neoliberal Right that proactively engages in state-shrinking while advancing unfettered trade and deregulation. A third category of a so-called moral Right defends conventional values perceived as under attack, such as the family, heteronormativity, and traditional gender and sexual norms. A fourth "nostalgic" Right idealizes authoritarian or fascist pasts and their systems of security and order. A nativist category is xenophobic, nationalist, and racist, threatened by immigration and "foreign" values and interests. Can a definition of right-wing movements capture this breadth and diversity?

Castro Rea's (2018) definition of Latin American right-wing movement offers a possibility. He emphasizes ideology. The political Right focuses on rights bestowed on those who deserve or prove their worthiness as rights-seekers. The Left, in contrast, recognize rights based on the intrinsic equality of individuals and groups, their worth as humans. Such a definition encompasses a full range of categories of right-wing movements. It distinguishes definition from origins, objectives, framing, and tactics.

The *movement* aspect of right-wing movements also requires definition. Scholars often find the social movement framework incompatible with exclusionary movements on the Right. In defense of that enterprise, Blee and Creasap (2016: 201) agree that, "[r]ightist movements fit awkwardly into the theoretical templates of social movements. . . . Such progressive movements [that make claims on behalf of the disadvantaged] . . . fare poor models for movements of privileged groups." Yet these authors, and others, recognize shared characteristics: "how rightist movements originate with movement entrepreneurs, frame their messages, respond to external political opportunities, forge collective identity, develop strategies and tactics, and serve as a source of vision and voice (however destructive) for their adherents" (ibid.). Moreover, characterization of right-wing groups as "privileged" or elite ignores those groups—largely religious or moral ones—that draw from the same social classes as social movements. Indeed, when a right-wing movement comprises members with diverse social and economic backgrounds, they lack social movement's coherence. Nonetheless, how they forge their identity, strategies, and tactics differentiates these groups on the Right from right-wing parties, interest groups, and lobbies.

Mudde (2017: 3–4) has attempted to sharpen the conceptual framework for right-wing movements, rescuing it from a "terminological quagmire." In Mudde's reader alone, right-wing, radical Right, extreme Right, conservative, and other terms are used interchangeably for such movements. Mudde finds fifty-nine defining characteristics of right-wing movements that he distills into three: nativism, authoritarianism, and populism.

While applauding Mudde's efforts at conceptual sharpening, these three core features do not travel well to Latin America. Yet the types of right-wing movements in contemporary Latin America are not that distinct from their European and United States' counterparts. Considering three new types of extreme Right radical opposition groups—*counter-movements, uncivil movements,* and *radical neoliberal movements*— that emerge in Latin America enhance comparative analysis and analytical precision in the study of right-wing movements.

Counter-movements are perhaps the most pervasive in Latin America. They are defined as "an organized response to a social movement, with the purpose of blocking the movement's activities, resisting change, and presenting alternative points of view" (*Dictionary of Sociology* 2018; Meyer and Staggenborg 1996; Mottl 1980). In Latin America, as in Europe and the United States, these movements emerge to oppose, counter, or roll back, the social, economic, political, and cultural rights claims and advances of social movements in the region. These movements are strongly associated with the "fundamentalist" or "religious right" in the United States that aim to reverse gains made by LGBT+ and reproductive rights movements. Indeed, Sutton and Borland (2013: 200 and 232, note 21) claim that United States-based groups, such as Human Life International and other Christian Right organizations, have stimulated and sustained pro-life anti-reproductive rights movements in Argentina.

Not all right-wing movements are counter-movements whose origin depends on pre-existing social movement successes. Like left-wing movements, the Right also directly confronts the state to defend or promote their rights. These include radical neoliberal movements. An extreme variant is "uncivil movements," which employ civil and democratic forms of political actions alongside uncivil violent practices to promote exclusionary outcomes (Payne 2000: 1).

These types of extreme right-wing movements tend to be overlooked in Latin America in favor of institutionalized conservative or neoliberal political parties (Luna and Rovira Kaltwasser 2014; Middlebrook 2000). As Bob (2012: 9–11) claims, however, institutionalized right-wing parties often depend on extremists for votes. By attracting and courting extremist counter-movements, uncivil movements, and militarized neoliberal movements, the right-wing alliance can threaten democratic procedures, values, and practice.

In sum, the study of Latin American right-wing movements offers a parsimonious definition and typology that travels across time and region. It separates defining characteristics of movements from explanations for their emergence and success in achieving their political objectives.

Right-Wing Mobilization

Defining movements is distinct from analyzing when, how, and why right-wing movements mobilize. Regarding "when," political moments do not necessarily catalyze movements to emerge, but these moments open up opportunities to broaden their base of support and increase their power (Caiani and della Porta 2011; Caiani, della Porta, and Wagemann 2012). Political opportunities, moreover, shape how right-wing movements mobilize: their framing processes (Benford and Snow 2000), their use of repertoires of collective action (Tilly 1978), their counter-mobilization to social movements, and the legitimating myths and coded language they use to appeal to civil society sectors. These moments shape the tactics employed by right-wing movements and their impact. The conceptual framework for analyzing right-wing movements in Latin America thus considers what political, economic, or social conditions (political opportunities) are exploited by right-wing movements, how they mobilize behind them (framing and tactics), and with what outcomes.

Political Opportunity

Studies of Europe concur that political instability and economic downturn are two conditions most commonly associated with the rise of right-wing mobilization. At these times, right-wing movements find the competitive space, the issue areas, and constituencies to mobilize. Latin America is not distinct from Europe in that regard. The political instability and economic downturn of the 1960s and 1970s is one such historical moment. While the constituencies of right-wing movements—business, military, politicians, middle class, and foreign allies—already existed, political instability united and catalyzed mobilization among otherwise disparate groups. Prior to this time, and after—particularly during the authoritarian regimes that they helped implant—the logic of unity and mobilization evaporated. With an ideological partnership in political power, their influence operated within, rather than outside, regimes. In contemporary Latin America, and in the wake of the so-called "pink tide" governments, right-wing movements have blamed left-leaning governments for economic decline and rampant corruption. Political and economic instability has thus opened up new opportunities in the region to catalyze support for right-wing movements.

Right-wing movements do not only respond to crises; they sometimes create them. Movements can transform particular events, or sets of events—changes or attempted changes in legislation or policy, electoral campaigns, mass political rallies—into catastrophes. The notion of threat, or "moral panic" (Cohen 2011), considered to be critical to the rise of right-wing movements in the European literature, is sometimes manufactured by right-wing movements themselves. They are not always successful:

> [E]ven very dramatic shifts can fail to produce political movements if agents prove incapable of framing them in ways that generate collective action. Similarly, very moderate proposals for political reform can generate dramatic political movements if agents frame these reforms in ways that mobilize groups. Successful framing involves depicting contemporary events in ways that resonate with individuals' personal experiences or their perspectives on the world. (Payne 2000: 22)

Thus, political and economic crises are neither insignificant to, nor determinative of, right-wing mobilization. Skillful right-wing movements can exploit nearly any political and economic moment to catalyze support through framing and tactics.

Framing

Framing by right-wing movements involves naming, blaming, aiming, and claiming (Payne 2000: 22–24). Naming the grievance, using a vernacular of threat or crisis, unites a broad constituency behind political action. Blaming a clear set of actors for that threat or crisis provides an identifiable culprit for the problems. In addition, right-wing movements take aim at a political system that has excluded them from power or decision-making. Yet they also need to claim the possibility of victory over those adversaries to present themselves as a viable alternative capable of implementing the desired change. Cataclysms are not necessary to mobilize; effective framing devices are.

"To frame political threats and opportunities successfully, [right-wing] movements tend to draw on a stock of cultural symbols that 'cue up' the movement with recognizable movements from the past, either domestic or foreign" (Payne 2000: 24). In their effort at naming the problem, these movements evoke the memory of past threats and the necessity of mobilizing to prevent them. They draw on, and blame, "cultural villains," use "vitriolic language and symbols" to provoke rage, and demonize their opponents (ibid.: 24–27). They do not faithfully adhere to past languages, symbols, or mobilizations, and instead adapt them to current needs (Tilly 1978: 154–56). In this way, right-wing movements play out "old ideas in new ways, but also new ideas in old ways" (Payne 2000: 27). Culture constitutes "usefully manipulatable tools" (Lancaster 1992: 90).

In their framing efforts, right-wing movements often confront contradictions in the movements' identity, objectives, and action. For example, a movement might condemn foreign intervention in an opposing group, while accepting foreign support for its own. Or a movement may claim to be oriented towards values such as "pro-life," while failing to condemn killing of criminals or other perceived "deviants." The notion of "legitimating myths" behind right-wing movements trades on "conflicting, and even contradictory, understandings of the movement and its goals" (Payne 2000: 30). Right-wing movements generate images and stories that can appeal to different constituencies. Pragmatic, economically oriented members seek reasons to disregard claims about movements' uncivil side. Movements prove those reasons by denying uncivil activity and presenting themselves in a different light. A common legitimating myth is movements' "anti-politics" orientation. "They can present themselves as political mavericks, unbeholden to any 'special interest group' and thus able to find nonpolitical solutions to national problems. They portray themselves as the authentic and 'democratic' representatives of excluded voices" (ibid.: 33), while also—by definition—advancing an exclusionary agenda. Legitimating myths also provide the means to draw on cultural cues from past crises to depict current crises, while also distancing themselves from the stigma associated with violent and discredited past right-wing movements.

Legitimating myths and cultural cues are framing devices used particularly when right-wing movements are associated with violent or uncivil forms of mobilizing. Right-wing movements "can easily spin myths about their civility by highlighting their work within the political system to show that they are significant political actors" (Payne 2000: 33). The contradiction between civil and uncivil political action can be exploited by movements to their advantage to sustain support among militant and pragmatic constituencies. They use denial of wrongdoing—blaming enemies for lies about them—to appeal to pragmatic constituencies, while at the same time embracing their tough image to appeal to militant members. These seemingly contradictory messages involve particular uses of language such as: relative-weight defense of uncivil acts (e.g., violence to end greater violence), civil disobedience (e.g., opposing unjust policies or practices), rotten apples (e.g., blaming some unrepresentative members for uncivil acts), just-war analogies (e.g., "soldiers sacrificing their personal security to fight a brutal and demonic enemy for the greater good of the nation" [ibid.: 34]), and traditional gendered ideals (e.g., hypermasculinity in defense of endangered women and children). Right-wing movements construct "these myths largely by drawing on cultural symbols but transforming them to fit a contemporary context" (ibid.: 36).

Where movements are associated with historical violent right-wing mobilizations, they confront unique challenges. Those past movements may continue to hold appeal for extreme groups. The right-wing movement itself may also lack imagination about how to reframe their movement to continue to appeal to supporters of past movements and to attract those who hope to distance themselves from those movements. In these cases, "movements do not break with past patterns but adopt and adapt them" to the current situation (Payne 2000: xxiv). Alternatively, these movements avoid their past and focus instead on their social movement counterparts, demonizing them. Bob (2012: 30) refers to this process as "framejacking," or appropriating and distorting social movement language and issues to catalyze a counter-movement.

In sum, framing involves not only mobilizing by exploiting a particular moment; it benefits from linking that moment to a recognizable past or national cultural trope. Naming, blaming, aiming, and claiming thus fits within a local cultural or historical repertoire: a recognizable threat, an identifiable source of that threat to be targeted and held responsible, and a successful set of solutions to be drawn on to resolve that threat.

Tactics

Latin American right-wing movements adopt a set of mobilization tactics that resemble or even mimic left-wing movements. These include double militancy, disruptive acts, transnational alliances, information politics, and movement entrepreneurs.

"Double militancy" (Alenda 2019; Alvarez 1990) entails working within and outside formal political institutions. Right-wing movements, like their social movement counterparts, use standard tactics of engaging with like-minded political parties, lobbying, campaigning, and running for elected office, as ways to influence political outcomes within the system. But they also retain their autonomy from political parties to exist as movements outside the formal institutional structure. Indeed, this is one of the contradictions within the movement, but not necessarily unique to it: the desire to appear as untainted outsiders while simultaneously working within it to affect change.

Right-wing movements use the common anti-system tactic of disruption. Taking to the streets in mobilizations with provocative signs, banners, and slogans indicates that these movements are not part of a stayed political elite but represent popular mobilization. Unconventional street politics also capture media attention. That attention can make the movement appear much stronger, more representative, and more powerful, belying its actual numbers.

Media attention also assists in achieving transnational linkages with similar movements outside the country. While the right-wing movement struggles are very local, about specific policies and practices in the country, these movements have established global linkages, not unlike transnational advocacy networks (TANs), to bolster support outside the country in order to pressure within (Keck and Sikkink 1998; see von Bülow in this volume). As Bob (2012: 74–76) shows, right-wing movements can build their own transnational advocacy networks to amplify their demands and to enhance their power and influence.

Right-wing movements have also engaged in "information politics" to advance their objectives (Alenda, Gartenlaub, and Fischer 2019; Castro Rea 2018). The links to think tanks and the media have facilitated the promotion of particular sets of views in the public sphere (Cannon 2016). Such linkages also potentially provide an air of legitimacy for movement campaigns, seemingly scientific or pseudo-academic studies that play on emotions and disguise fearmongering. As one report stated, these think tanks are "oriented less on developing genuinely new policy proposals [their typical role], and more on establishing political organizations that carry the credibility of academic institutions, making them an effective organ for winning hearts and minds" (Fang 2017). Right-wing think tanks in Latin America, moreover, are sustained by substantial financial support from think tanks abroad as well as corporations and governments (Cannon 2016; Fang 2017).

Framing and movement tactics are designed by "movement entrepreneurs" who "envision a movement-product that they can sell" in the political marketplace (Payne 2000: 31). "They package that movement, using the frames and cuing discussed above. They create both the movement-product and consumer demand for that product" (ibid.: 31). The European literature on right-wing movements emphasizes charismatic leaders over movement entrepreneurs. Charismatic leaders are less visible in Latin American counter-movements and radical neoliberal movements. When they emerge in uncivil movements, they become the identifiable face of the movement and play a crucial role in its appeal and expansion; they embody the movement's framing, contradictions and all.

Movement entrepreneurs, whether charismatic or not, generate the legitimating myths that allow constituents to deny, filter out, or justify aspects of the movement that they do not want to acknowledge or interrogate too thoroughly. They provide the means to bring together different individuals who share some, but not necessarily all, of the movement's tactics and ideas. They provide justification for individuals who might not otherwise join an overtly armed, right-wing, movement. They build on the vulnerability felt by certain sectors of the population, urging them to engage in collective action to end an urgent threat. They propose a possible solution to that threat that is recognizably similar to, but also distinct from, past . . . solutions. They create a new identity that unites individuals with different views. And they broaden the appeal of the movement by casting it in terms of democratic, collective, and national goals rather than authoritarian, self-, or class interests. (Payne 2000: 36)

While movement entrepreneurs generate these myths, those who join the movement "make sense" of them. Cohen describes this process as people finding "common currency in behavior whilst still tailoring it subjectively (and interpretively) to their *own* needs" (Cohen 1985: 17).

The face of the movement thus becomes part of the legitimating myths, the cultural cues, the very symbols that expand the movement from a small fringe group to a broader constituency, that overcome individuals' reluctance to join, even if they do so in hiding.

In sum, the analysis of contemporary Latin America suggests that charismatic leadership is not entirely necessary to right-wing movements, but movement entrepreneurs are. Those entrepreneurs do the work of developing framing and tactics (double-militancy, disruption, and information politics) to build movements' constituency. In the process, they employ and subvert left-wing social movement strategies and tactics to forge a shared identity, culture, and sense of empowerment at the service of halting progress on social issues, and to "disempower" popular movements (Payne 2000: 18).

Impact

The impact of contemporary right-wing movements in Latin America, despite their historic role during the coups and authoritarian regimes of the 1960s–1980s, is not supplanting democratic systems. Instead, they intend to influence and shape democratic institutions, discourse, and practices. In the process, they threaten the democratic nature of those systems by advancing exclusionary, rather than inclusionary, policies and practices.

The power of right-wing movements varies tremendously, however. They tend to be small fringe movements, unlikely to win mass support, or even support among elite political groups. Yet at key moments, and with effective framing and tactics, these groups have proved capable of allying with forces in the state and society to catalyze change. Attempting to control the impact of such movements on democracy proves difficult. The more extreme and violent they are, the more difficult they are to track. Their followers seem to be largely hidden, unwilling to openly admit to their adherence to extremist, exclusionary, or violent language and tactics. Open right-wing movements, in contrast, tend not to express extreme viewpoints, either in their image or framing. They thus hide any potential threat to the democratic rights of marginalized groups. Their small size and their location on the fringes of mainstream politics further indicate that they pose little threat to democratic values. Over time and without detection, however, these movements sometimes expand their base of support, through disruptive tactics that attract media coverage, generate substantial financial resources within and outside the country, and advance an exclusionary and anti-rights agenda that threatens democratic policies and practices.

Some inherent characteristics of right-wing movements further limit their power, specifically demobilization resulting from outcomes, internal dynamics, and institutionalization. Regarding outcomes, paradoxically failures and victories weaken the movement. Rational choice scholars explain that individuals are less likely to join unsuccessful political movements if they perceive that the cost of action outweighs the benefits. The stigma attached to right-wing movements, particularly extremist ones, is likely to limit potential membership, particularly when losing policy initiatives means that the cost of joining outweighs the benefits. Victory may also result in demobilization for different reasons. Success may transform the movement into a political party, thus reducing the appeal for anti-system members. Demobilization may also result from victory if there is movement burn-out related to high intensity mobilization. If victory is achieved, the movement may become "latent," no longer an active mobilization, but part of the cultural stock or collective action repertoire upon which future movements may rely.

In addition to outcomes, the internal dynamics of right-wing movements may lead to their demise. This may especially result from movements with charismatic leaders who form an emotional bond to the constituency. Charismatic leaders seem to plant the seeds of their own destruction. A host of events—succession crises, power-seeking leaders and competitors, instability, moderation, and contradictions—undermine the long-term capacity of movements to sustain themselves over time. These internal and leadership weaknesses often emerge with efforts to institutionalize the movement and transform it into a coherent political party. Because these movements derive much of their support from their anti-politics, anti-system position, becoming part of the mainstream can lead to a loss of support from those who view the shift as selling out the movement (Payne 2000: 44).

This demise may come very late, however, and after the sets of democratic rights for previously marginalized groups are dismantled. How democratic governments can check the power of right-wing movements depends on the existence of counter-information campaigns, investigation into uncivil activities, prosecution, and negotiation. In terms of counter-information, the falsehoods generated by these movements that instill fear and catalyze action can be refuted through investigative journalism and widespread campaigns. Nonetheless, these counter-information campaigns do not always succeed and may even reinforce right-wing movements' claims of "fake news." Uncivil activities carried out by movement leaders and members—particularly violent threats, inciting violence, or engaging in violence—can lead to judicial investigations and, potentially, prosecutions, reinforcing democratic rule of law. Credible investigations and prosecutions into leaders' own corrupt activities can point to hypocrisy in the movement. Such investigations, and a shift in the movement towards extremism, may result in moderate members abandoning and denouncing the movement, separating the movement from the militant hardcore, and reducing the power of anti-democratic and anti-system forces (Payne 2000: 45–49).

Case Studies

To apply the analytical framework set out above, this chapter focuses on one example for each of the three types of right-wing movements in the region: counter-movements, uncivil movements, and radical neoliberal movements. The case studies do not represent the only, or even necessarily the best, example of each type of right-wing movement. Instead, they attempt to show the variety of forms right-wing movements take across the region, the political opportunities that they seize, their framing and mobilization tactics, and their impact. The cases are El Salvador's anti-abortion counter-movement, Brazil's anti-LGBT+ uncivil movement, and Colombia's radical neoliberal movement.

El Salvador's Anti-abortion Counter-movement

Viterna (2012: 250) claims that mobilization in El Salvador against abortion began in 1992 with the election of the Frente Farabundo Martí de Liberación Nacional (FMLN) party to the presidency. Up to that point, and under the right-wing Alianza Republicana Nacionalista (ARENA) party, the Right had tolerated liberal and unenforced legislation on reproductive rights. The election catalyzed a broad coalition on the Right, uniting political and religious opposition to the FMLN. The pro-life movement became the face of the mobilization. In this sense, the FMLN's electoral success offered a political opportunity for the movement.

A second political opportunity opened up when the FMLN government passed legislation in 1995 that partially liberalized the country's abortion ban. Anti-abortion forces redoubled their efforts. They succeeded in winning a total ban on abortion in 1997.[2] In 1999 they fought for and won a constitutional amendment to protect life from the moment of conception.

The result is the most stringent and enforced anti-abortion ban in the world.[3] El Salvador criminalizes abortion with a two- to eight-year prison sentence for the woman, six to twelve years for abortion practitioners, and two- to five-year sentences for "accomplices." If a viable fetus is terminated, the abortion penalty can be converted to aggravated homicide with a thirty- to fifty-year sentence. Viterna documented twenty cases of women facing criminal sentences for abortion, and fifty-one cases of aggravated homicide, including when evidence of a miscarriage or stillbirth existed (Nicholasen 2018).

The success of the anti-abortion movement is linked to its capacity to catalyze support from a broad coalition of right-wing forces in the country, using anti-FMLN vitriol. Abortion rights foes demonize the "socialist" mission to advance atheism and undermine the family. The socialist agenda would, according to these forces, "legalize the slaughter of innocent unborn children, which is clearly against the laws of the Catholic Church, God, and Salvadoran values" (Viterna 2012: 252). The movement linked the abortion issue to the FMLN's historic use of violence in the Salvadoran civil war and its support for Cuba and Venezuelan leader Hugo Chávez. It professed a mission to defeat "socialist" and "international" influences over the country, beginning with abortion legislation. Broadcast and print media outlets reported on the movement's street mobilizations, drawn in by dramatic language and images, especially posters of bloody babies.

At the same time, the movement spun legitimating myths. Vida SV ("Si a la Vida") created a high-profile website (vidasv.org) and Facebook page (Escúchanos SV) that claimed neutrality and distance from specific religious and political affiliations. Contradicting that view, the organizational support listed in its social media included specific religious and political organizations, including ARENA party candidate in the 2019 presidential elections, Carlos Calleja.

The extreme position that the group holds with regard to abortion may not represent the majority of the right-wing in the country, but rather a powerful fringe movement. For example, the movement insists on criminalization of abortion, requiring it to ignore or discount as untrue the claims that the aggravated homicide law has been applied to cases of stillborn births and natural miscarriages. In the 2013 nationally and internationally known case of "Beatriz," the movement contends that medical intervention could have saved the mother without losing the child.[4] This contradicts even the conservative Salvadoran Supreme Court's decision to prohibit an abortion but allow an emergency Caesarean section to save "Beatriz's" life, given her medical condition of lupus and loss of kidney function. As medical professionals expected, the fetus died of anencephaly only a few hours later (Taylor 2017).

In contrast to the extreme position taken by the movement, its spokesperson Sara Larín presents herself as young, reasonable, and unemotional in her legal and medical defense of the total ban of abortion. She thus acts more as a movement entrepreneur— uniting a fragmented right-wing—than a charismatic leader. Such a position has not cost the movement its support from the extreme Right, and it may garner more support from a moderate Right. The contradictions in the movement coexist: its religious and political neutrality with strong support from the Archbishop of El Salvador and the ARENA party; its condemnation of international influence on the Left without a similar position on international support from United States-based groups, such as Human Life International. The movement's stated singular focus on abortion belies a broader right-wing framework to advance other traditional values, especially "gender ideology" concerns (see below).

This counter-movement did not originate with, but certainly thrived in the face of, domestic and international pro-choice mobilization. The movement took advantage of the uncertainty felt by the Right when the FMLN won the presidential elections. The fear of the Left catalyzed the movement and became part of the framing devices used to unite the Right and support the movement's goals of a hardline on abortion. The movement drew on a cultural stock of Catholic pro-family values and socialist demons. It used legitimating myths to name the problem as violence against the innocent, blaming the Left for disregarding life, and aiming its strategies against the FMLN and the pro-choice movement. It claimed victories along the way with its increasingly restrictive criminal law. It engaged in double militancy through disruptive tactics in the streets and political work within the ARENA party and the legislature. Using such tactics, the movement could elide the contradictions in its position, particularly the legal violence committed by a law that targeted poor young women vulnerable to sexual assault.

Brazil's Anti-LGBT+ Uncivil Movement

Violence against, and intolerance towards, the LGBT+ community in Brazil is what constitutes this uncivil movement. It illustrates how a relatively fringe movement can gain power taking advantage of a particular political and economic moment to unite a loose coalition of forces, and even win the presidency. Key to the movement's strength was the election of its charismatic leader, and the embodiment of the anti-LGBT+ mobilization, Jair Bolsonaro (2019–2022), referred to as the "Far-right Trump of the Tropics."

Bolsonaro's homophobic remarks catalyzed a movement from a previously diffuse set of individuals and groups around the country. During Bolsonaro's campaign and presidency, they no longer felt alone, isolated, or a minority fringe. Who Bolsonaro was and how open he was about anti-LGBT+ politics united, legitimized, and brought into the mainstream views that had been once taboo. As Bolsonaro stated, "Yes, I'm homophobic—and proud of it." Opinions that British actor Stephen Fry identified as "chilling" became everyday expressions. Bolsonaro claimed, for example, that "homosexual fundamentalists" were brainwashing heterosexual children to "become gays and lesbians to satisfy them sexually in the future," adding "Brazilian society doesn't like homosexuals." He has advocated parents beating gay children and proclaimed that he would prefer a dead son to a gay one.

With these words, one LGBT+ activist, Beto de Jesus, warned that Bolsonaro was not acting alone, but had forged a violent movement. As he stated, "the gates of hell have been opened... [it's] as if hunting season has been declared."[5]

This is not because anti-LGBT+ violence is new to Brazil. Indeed, it is so well-known and well-documented that the term "homocaust" has been used to describe it. Anti-LBGT+ acts of violence corresponded to legislative gains for civil unions and same-sex marriage, doubling since 2003 according to one of the world's oldest gay-rights associations, Grupo Gay da Bahia. To have a presidential candidate elected who spewed such violent rhetoric is what is different. Bolsonaro's words are associated with the violent attacks; news stories just days before his presidential election recounted the use of candidate Bolsonaro's name in the murder of a transgender woman and a drag queen.[6]

A fragmented group of forces coalesced behind the movement's charismatic leadership. Before Bolsonaro, anti-LGBT+ mobilizations mainly involved Evangelicals who use "their megachurches as the main venues in which to spread their venom against gay people" (Encarnación 2016: 201–02). A related Escola Sem Partido (School without Party) group attacked what they saw as promotion of "gender ideology" through the use of a "gay kit" to indoctrinate homosexuality and promiscuity among children.

Yet the movement also included unlikely alliances, such as the Movimento Brasil Livre (MBL), originally an economic conservative group, with the Christian Right. The MBL joined Liga Cristã and other groups to block the "Queermuseu" exhibition in Rio in 2018.[7] Such alliances also violently confronted United States philosophy professor, Judith Butler, when she attended a conference in São Paulo, accusing her of promoting gender ideology. This LGBT+ coalition of traditional, moral, religious, rural, and neoliberal movements enhanced the electoral power of extreme right-wing groups. In addition, they seemed to receive financial resources from foreign think tanks (Atlas) and funders (Koch brothers) (Schmitt and Roxo 2019).

The anti-LGBT+ movement achieved success by electing their charismatic leader to the presidency. Contradictions typical of right-wing movements began to present tensions after Bolsonaro's election. The conservative economic groups, including within the MBL, felt betrayed by the president's nationalist and protectionist stance. His rhetoric inciting violence against the LGBT+ community also contradicted his law and order campaign, aimed at curbing such extra-institutional violence. His open adoration of the military regime and its repressive apparatus created tensions with the democratic right-wing. It also contradicted his anti-corruption position, given known information about corruption during the military regime (Fogel 2019). Indeed, Bolsonaro and his supporters have allegedly engaged in the same corruption schemes that befell their predecessors. Finally, Bolsonaro's image as a "new" leader, outside the political establishment, with new ideas and solutions, is belied by his twenty-seven years in the legislature spouting right-wing, authoritarian, and anti-LGBT+ rhetoric.

In sum, the anti-LGBT+ movement capitalized on a political moment. It formed part of a broad set of forces that opposed the Partido dos Trabalhadores (PT), corruption, criminal violence, and the loss of traditional authority. According to Brandimarte (2018), this coalition even included LGBT+ voters themselves. They were willing to overlook their adversaries within the movement to vote for Bolsonaro as the lesser evil. He hints that the anti-PT views focused on corruption, but some also saw the PT as betraying the LGBT+ community by passing protective hate crime legislation when LGBT+ violence erupted.

The anti-LGBT+ movement swept in a candidate, but it was too weak to do so alone. Instead, it piggy-backed onto acceptable, legitimate, and widespread concern over corruption, loss of traditional values, and threats to the economy and security. While the anti-LGBT+ position was loud, visible, and violent, it was a relatively small part of a larger coalition of extreme Right, liberal economic Right, and traditional Right views, mixed with centrists. It was a fragile coalition (von Bülow 2018) that lost even more support after the leader seemed to turn his back on some of the core economic liberal issues (Schmitt and Roxo 2019) and democratic political institutions. In the meantime, however, the anti-LGBT+ community had won the presidency for their charismatic leader.

Colombia's Right-wing "Militarized Neoliberal" Movement

In 2016 the referendum on the peace process in Colombia was surprisingly defeated. None of the polls had predicted that outcome after over fifty years of armed conflict in the country. The vote also followed what had been widely viewed as a salutary and successful set of negotiations between the government and the Fuerzas Armadas Revolucionarias de Colombia (FARC). The international community's endorsement of the process was made evident in the awarding of the 2018 Nobel Peace Prize to the leader of the negotiations, and president at that time, Juan Manuel Santos.

No single factor fully explains the confounding outcome of the referendum (Álvarez and Garzón 2016). Yet analyses converge around a crucial component: right-wing mobilization. The right-wing ran a successful No Campaign that narrowly defeated (50.2 to 49.8) the October 2016 referendum. That right-wing mobilization did not dissolve after the referendum vote, however. Right-wing forces remained mobilized to act as veto players over the efforts to eventually pass a peace process in the legislature. In addition, they sustained their slight electoral majority to elect the post-referendum candidate on the Right, President Iván Duque (2018–2022). Who comprises this right-wing mobilization and how they mobilize to have such a powerful impact on the politics of the country is the focus of this case study.

The label "militarized neoliberalism" (Motta 2014) captures the broad coalition within this Colombian right-wing movement. Its undisputed leader—former president Álvaro Uribe Vélez (2002–2006, 2006–2010)—embodies both the "militarized" and "neoliberal" dimension of the movement. He is a charismatic leader, having created a powerful national bond uniting disparate forces on the Right. More importantly, however, he is a movement entrepreneur capable of holding together a fragile coalition of forces inherently divided by class, region, and religion. That entrepreneurship is evident in his choice of a successor. Constitutionally barred from seeking an additional presidential term, he handpicked then-Senator Duque to run in his place. Duque ran on the Centro Democrático (CD) party ticket, the party Uribe had created in 2014. Duque lacked Uribe's command over, and bond with the "militarized" and extremist right-wing factions among the landholding, rural, and regional factions associated with his military solution to armed conflict. On the other, he maintained Uribe's connection to "neoliberalism" of the Center-Right and Right by promoting private sector initiatives, free trade, deregulations, and market-based development policies.

The Duque government exposes the difficulty of holding together a coalition fragmented by its role in the armed conflict past (the "militarized" faction) and its potential role in the post-peace present (the "neoliberal" faction). The "militarized" faction is comprised of cattle ranchers, regional elites, landed estate owners, right-wing politicians, paramilitaries, and the armed forces that aimed to militarily defeat the armed Left. During the conflict, that political aim was connected to violent right-wing economic projects in resource extraction, land seizures and forced displacement, and control over rural labor. Uribe's landed elite background, his alleged connection to paramilitaries, and his military policies towards the guerrilla solidified his leadership of this "militarized" faction. Within the No Campaign, this faction saw the peace process as a capitulation to guerrillas and to Communism. They rejected it in favor of a military solution to the armed conflict.

The social conservative "neoliberal" dimension of the right-wing movement includes, in contrast, the urban business sector, conservative politicians, and conservative religious groups. These were also Uribe supporters. Duque represented this group as a young (40s), market-oriented, pro-business, technocrat, traditional Catholic, right-wing democrat. The group shares the concern over too many concessions to the armed Left in the peace process, particularly state-run redistribution programs of land and private property and institutionalizing a FARC political party to compete in elections.

Colombia's "militarized neoliberal" right-wing movement is not solely political and economic, it is deeply rooted in conservative religious values. Uribe and Duque embody these movement characteristics. These values played an important role in the No Campaign, moreover. The Evangelical Protestant and Catholic campaign against the referendum is well-documented. That campaign portrayed the peace process as capitulating to "terrorists" and turning the country over to FARC and "Castro-Chavista" Communist forces. Fearmongering and "misinformation campaigns" took the form of "intimidating text messages, threatening pamphlets and ominous posts on social media."[8] Responding to "moral panic," the No Campaign even linked the "Yes" vote to promoting "gender ideology" and homosexuality in the schools.

The "gender-ideology" component emerged from an earlier moral and Christian campaign run by the "militarized neoliberal" right-wing movement. That campaign targeted the Minister of Education, Gina Parody. Parody had responded to a teen suicide resulting from homophobic bullying by advancing education reforms—"Ambientes Escolares Libres de Discriminación"—to promote tolerance. Catholic and Evangelical protestant members of the right-wing movement carried out street protests in fourteen cities against the reforms. Leaders of the subsequent No Campaign—Uribe, who had previously mentored Parody, and former Attorney General Alejandro Ordóñez, a well-known leader of the Catholic Right—openly opposed the curriculum reforms. These reforms were seen as promoting "gender ideology" and homosexuality in the schools, a cry that was subsequently linked to the No Campaign and the FARC's threats to conservative religious values.

The movement thus encompassed a cultural, economic, and political right-wing project. That coalition alone did not seal Duque's election. It also depended on political opportunity. Duque's fiercest political opponent in the elections was left-wing leader Gustavo Petro. Their economic plans could not have been more opposite, with Petro advancing a welfare state, free education and health care, and environmental protections. Politically, they were also on opposite extremes with Petro, a demobilized (M-19) guerrilla himself, campaigning on the promise to extend the peace agreement to an active Ejército de Liberación Nacional (ELN) guerrilla group. This united the militarized faction behind Duque who already had support among a socially conservative neoliberal right-wing and the religious Right. Duque could even skim off support from practical and ideological voters who opposed Petro for any number of reasons but might have proved reluctant to cast their vote for a member of the militarized faction of the right-wing. Duque thus brought the extreme Right back into power, by partially disguising the militarized faction behind socially conservative neoliberalism. Petro, however, won the presidency against the radical neoliberal right in 2022.

Conclusion

The focus on Latin American progressive social movements often ignores the threat counter-movements, uncivil movements, and the radical neoliberal Right pose to civil society gains. Few scholars wish to study such movements in the region. And yet in Europe such studies abound with a proliferation of readers, handbooks, monographs, and edited volumes. By focusing only on Europe, those studies have limited analytical utility off the continent. This chapter has attempted to connect European approaches to right-wing movements in Latin America. In the process, it has endeavored to offer a broader conceptual framework that allows for cross-regional comparison of the phenomenon. It uses Latin American variants of those movements to advance a more comparative way of defining these movements, identifying a typology that travels across regions, explores the mobilization capacity of political opportunities, framing, and tactics, to understand the impact these movements can have on contemporary democracies.

Notes

1. A lengthier version of this chapter will be available in Payne (forthcoming).
2. In an interview, Viterna added the detail of the 1994 United Nations International Conference on Population and Development in Cairo. The Vatican responded negatively to the Conference's focus on advancing global education and family planning, and improving reproductive health. It highlighted those countries—such as El Salvador—that banned abortion, thereby further stimulating the movement against abortion in the country (Nicholasen 2018).
3. "El Salvador Court Frees Woman Jailed under Anti-abortion Laws," *BBC News*, December 18, 2018; Elisabeth Malkin, "They were jailed for Miscarriages. Now Campaign Aims to End Abortion Ban," *New York Times*, April 9, 2018.

4. See the statement made by ARENA presidential candidate Carlos Calleja: https://vidasv.org/2019/01/18/carlos-calleja/.
5. Tom Phillips, 'Brazil's fearful LGBT community prepares for a "proud homophobe," *The Guardian*, October 27, 2018.
6. Zoe Sullivan, "LGBTQ Brazilians on Edge after Self-described 'Homophobic' Lawmaker Elected President," *NBC News*, October 29, 2018, https://www.nbcnews.com/feature/nbc-out/lgbtq-brazilians-edge-after-self-described-homophobic-lawmaker-elected-president-n925726.
7. Renata Batista, "Exposição Queermuseu abre no Rio com protestos do MBL e da Liga Cristã," *Exame*, August 18, 2018.
8. Annette Idler, "Why the Real Test for Colombia's Peace Process Begins after the Demobilization Process," *Monkey Cage*, September 8, 2016.

References

Alenda, Stéphanie, Andrea Gartenlaub, and Karin Fischer (2019), "Ganar la batalla de ideas: el rol de los think tanks en la reconfiguración de la centro-derecha chilena," in Stéphanie Alenda (ed.), *Anatomía de la centro-derecha chilena: Nuevos y viejos protagonistas*, 119–156 (Santiago: FCE).

Alenda, Stéphanie (ed.) (2019), *Anatomía de la centro-derecha chilena: Nuevos y viejos protagonistas* (Santiago: FCE).

Alvarez, Sonia (1990), *Engendering Democracy in Brazil: Women's Movements in Transition Politics* (Princeton, NJ: Princeton University Press).

Álvarez Vanegas, Eduardo and Juan Carlos Garzón Vergara (2016), "Votando por la paz: Entendiendo la ventaja del 'No,'" *Fundación Ideas para la Paz*, October 6.

Benford, Robert D. and David A. Snow (2000), "Framing Processes and Social Movements: An Overview and Assessment," *Annual Review of Sociology* 26, 611–39.

Blee, Kathleen M. and Kimberly A. Creasap (2017), "Conservative and Right-Wing Movements," in Cas Mudde (ed.), *The Populist Radical Right: A Reader*, 200–18 (London: Routledge).

Bob, Clifford (2012), *The Global Right Wing and the Clash of World Politics* (Cambridge: Cambridge University Press).

Brandimart, Walter (2018), "Why Many of Brazil's Gay Voters Overlook Bolsonaro's Homophobic Rants," *Bloomberg*, October 25, https://www.bloomberg.com/news/articles/2018-10-27/gays-for-bolsonaro-why-many-will-overlook-his-homophobic-rants#xj4y7vzkg.

Caiani, Manuela and Donatella della Porta (2011), "The Elitist Populism of the Extreme Right: A Frame Analysis of Extreme Right-Wing Discourses in Italy and Germany," *Acta Politica* 46(2), 180–202.

Caiani, Manuela, Donatella della Porta, and Claudius Wagemann (2012), *Mobilizing on the Extreme Right: Germany, Italy, and the United States* (Oxford: Oxford University Press).

Cannon, Barry (2016), *The Right in Latin America: Elite Power, Hegemony and the Struggle for the State* (New York: Routledge).

Castro Rea, Julián (2018), "Right-Wing Think Tank Networks in Latin America: The Mexican Connection," *Perspectives on Global Development and Technology* 17(1–2), 89–102.

Cohen, Anthony P. (1985), *The Symbolic Construction of Community* (London: Routledge).

Cohen, Stanley (2011), *Folk Devils and Moral Panics* (London: Routledge).
Encarnación, Omar G. (2016), *Out in the Periphery: Latin America's Gay Rights Revolution* (Oxford: Oxford University Press).
Fang, Lee (2017), "Sphere of Influence: How American Libertarians are Remaking Latin American Politics," *The Intercept*, August 9, https://theintercept.com/2017/08/09/atlas-network-alejandro-chafuen-libertarian-think-tank-latin-america-brazil/.
Fogel, Benjamin (2019), "Brazil: Corruption as a Mode of Rule," *NACLA*, June 17, https://nacla.org/news/2019/06/17/brazil-corruption-mode-rule.
Griffin, Roger (2017), "Interregnum or Endgame? The Radical Right in the 'Post-Fascist' Era," in Cas Mudde (ed.), *The Populist Radical Right: A Reader*, 15–27 (London: Routledge).
Keck, Margaret E. and Kathryn Sikkink (1998), *Activists Beyond Borders: Advocacy Networks in International Politics* (Ithaca, NY: Cornell University Press).
Lancaster, Roger N. (1992), *Life is Hard: Machismo, Danger and the Intimacy of Power in Nicaragua* (Berkeley and Los Angeles: University of California Press).
Luna, Juan Pablo and Cristóbal Rovira Kaltwasser (eds.) (2014), *The Resilience of the Latin American Right* (Baltimore, MD: Johns Hopkins University Press).
Meyer, David S. and Suzanne Staggenborg (1996), "Movements, Countermovements, and the Structure of Political Opportunity," *American Journal of Sociology* 101(6), 1628–60.
Middlebrook, Kevin J. (2000), *Conservative Parties, the Right, and Democracy in Latin America* (Baltimore, MD: The Johns Hopkins University Press).
Motta, Sara C. (2014), "Militarized Neoliberalism in Colombia: Disarticulating Dissent and Articulating Consent to Neoliberal Epistemologies, Pedagogies, and Ways of Life," in Sara C. Motta and Mike Cole (eds.), *Constructing Twenty-first Century Socialism in Latin America*, 19–41 (Basingstoke: Palgrave-Macmillan).
Mottl, Tahi L. (1980), "The Analysis of Countermovements," *Social Problems* 27(5), 620–35.
Mudde, Cas (2017), "Introduction to the Populist Radical Right," in Cas Mudde (ed.), *The Populist Radical Right: A Reader*, 1–13 (London: Routledge).
Nicholasen, Michelle (2018), "Sociologist Explores Cultural and Transnational Forces behind such an Extreme Response," *Weatherhead Center Communications*, October 31, https://news.harvard.edu/gazette/story/2018/10/how-the-pro-life-movement-became-entrenched-in-el-salvador/.
Payne, Leigh A. (2000), *Uncivil Movements: The Armed Right Wing and Democracy in Latin America* (Baltimore, MD: The Johns Hopkins University Press).
Payne, Leigh A. (forthcoming), "The Right-Against-Rights in Latin America: An Analytical Framework," in Simón Escoffier, Leigh A. Payne, and Julia Zulver (eds.), *The Right Against Rights in Latin America* (Oxford: Oxford University Press).
Schmitt, Gustavo and Sérgio Roxo (2019), "O que pensa a direita que se tornou anti-Bolsonaro," *Epoca-Globo*, May 16, https://oglobo.globo.com/epoca/o-que-pensa-direita-que-se-tornou-anti-bolsonaro-23669904.
Sutton, Barbara and Elizabeth Borland (2013), "Framing Abortion Rights in Argentina's Encuentros Nacionales de Mujeres," *Feminist Studies* 39(1), 194–234.
Taylor, Sarah (2017), "El Salvador Should Decriminalize Abortion," *Human Rights Watch*, February 2, https://www.hrw.org/news/2017/02/16/el-salvador-should-decriminalize-abortion.

Tilly, Charles (1978), *From Mobilization to Revolution* (Reading, CT: Addison-Wesley).
Viterna, Jocelyn (2012), "The Left and 'Life' in El Salvador," *Politics and Gender* 8(2), 248–54.
von Bülow, Marisa (2018), "The Empowerment of Conservative Civil Society in Brazil," in Richard Youngs (ed.), *The Mobilization of Conservative Civil Society*, 13–18 (Washington, DC: Carnegie Endowment for International Peace).

CHAPTER 33

REVOLUTIONARY MOVEMENTS AND GUERRILLAS IN LATIN AMERICA

From Revolutions to revolutions

LEONIDAS OIKONOMAKIS

INTRODUCTION

At times they took the world by surprise, coming out of the Chiapan mist on New Year's Day 1994, "encapuchadas/encapuchados" like ghosts from an era considered long gone. Other times, they even pre-announced(!) their outbreak, setting thus a date for their *bras de fer* with the authorities: Francisco Madero had famously announced that his rebellion against the *Porfiriato* would begin at 6 p.m. *sharp* on November 20, 1910 (Easterling 2013: 67). Sometimes, guerrillas had been formed in order to liberate their countries from (normally United States-backed) dictatorial army Generals, as in the case of Nicaragua in 1979; some others the military had to intervene in a *coup d'état* fashion in order to bring down unpopular governments, as in the case of Guatemala's October Revolution, or in the case of Hugo Chávez's failed coup attempt in 1992. No matter how diverse and how heterogeneous they have been, though, Latin American Revolutions have always managed to catch the world's attention, to fascinate our hearts and minds, producing legendary revolutionaries like Fidel Castro, Augusto César Sandino, Che Guevara, Emiliano Zapata, and Subcomandante Marcos.[1] Often, whole revolutionary movements were named after such fallen revolutionaries, in order both to commemorate their name, but also to appear as the legitimate successors of their political and moral legacy (Jansen 2007: 954); as is the case with the Zapatistas, the Sandinistas, the Tupamaros, the Frente Farabundo Martí para la Liberación Nacional, and many others. But what exactly are we talking about when we refer to Latin American Revolutions? Revolutions are certainly rare, yet in many ways transformative (della Porta 2011: 30) events. They are also concepts that are normally easier to understand intuitively but rather more difficult to define analytically, and there has been no commonly accepted definition of what a Revolution actually is in academia. That is the first challenge this chapter has to overcome: before moving on to the analysis of guerrillas and revolutionary movements, we need to comprehend their diversity and characteristics, and agree that no commonly accepted definition can capture them all. Studying the actors of Latin American Revolutions, in this chapter I try to locate how the latter have changed in time, and—I argue—that maybe we should reconsider the meaning of revolution enriching our analyses with the relevant *political processes* and not just the *political events*.

SMALL R AND BIG R REVOLUTIONS

Building on Tilly's (1993) definition of "revolutionary situations," Goodwin (2001: 10) defines as *revolutionary* those social movements that "advance exclusive competing claims to control of the state, or some segment of it." For that definition to be valid therefore, there must exist a kind of dual power situation (or double sovereignty), and at least two contenders, one of which is necessarily the state. Normally, it is considered that we can talk of the *political event* of a Revolution when a revolutionary movement manages to grasp state power through irregular, normally violent, and extra-constitutional means. In the case now that this revolutionary movement promotes radical, transformative, social change after gaining state power, then we can talk of *social* revolutions (Goodwin 2001: 8). For Skocpol (1979) as well, revolutions are rapid, radical transformations within a given state and class structure and they are normally accompanied by, or are a product of, class-based revolts from below. Huntington (1968) defines revolutions as bringing about radical, violent, and fundamental changes in a society including its political institutions, its social structures, and its leadership. For Foran (2005: 5), *successful revolutions* are those that come to power and hold it long enough to bring about radical social transformations (see Martí i Puig and Álvarez in this volume).

Kruijt (2008: 30) defines the "guerrilla" in the Latin American context as follows: "In Latin America 'guerrilla' generally indicates the existence of so-called 'politico-military organizations' with an ideology characterized by the following features: intense nationalism, anti-imperialism or anti-colonialism; the prospect of a socialist utopia; and overt preparation for social revolution by means of armed struggle." According to Becker (2017: 25), the factors required to make a successful revolution are ideology (such as anti-imperialism, socialism, anticapitalism, or a combination of these), the presence of charismatic *vanguard leadership*, significant organizational and material *resources*, and all the above are normally mobilized against a discredited previous government, when all other avenues for change are closed.

We could therefore distinguish between the *political event* of a Revolution, which leads to the grasp of state power and regime change through irregular means (that is, *not* through elections); and the *political process* of a revolution which is related to bringing about radical social change after that regime has changed. Therefore, while the concept of *revolutionary social movements* is useful in defining movements that target the control of the state or a segment of it, at the same time it can be confusing because those movements do not always have a *revolutionary character*, in the sense of changing the regime through *revolutionary means* (irregular, extra-constitutional and/or violent means). Moreover, even if those movements manage to grasp power through *revolutionary* means, they do not always implement *revolutionary*, radical, social transformations within a given territory afterwards. In addition, while sometimes it is necessary to grasp state/regional power in order to bring about social change within a given social structure, that is not always the case. There have been cases of movements, with the Zapatistas (Oikonomakis 2019) being the most prominent yet not the only example,[2] in which movements do bring about radical social transformations outside the realm yet inside the territory of one or various states, *without* grasping state/regional power. They rather act in an autonomous way, prefiguring new social, political, and economic institutions, based on direct-democratic, communitarian, rotatory decision-making modes, instead of just occupying already existing structures.

To make matters even more complicated, while Revolutions *can* be related to violent, extra-constitutional, and rapid regime change, that is *not always* the case. And while Revolutions can at times bring about rapid, radical changes within a given social structure, this does *not always* happen either. Radical social transformations can also be *gradual, slow*, processes that have to do more with a shift in the socio-political consciousness and culture of the people and that do not happen overnight necessarily, or as a result of regime change only. In this sense I have found rather useful Holloway's (1996) distinction between Revolutions with capital "R" and revolutions with small "r." Revolution refers to the political event of the conquest of state power through irregular and—usually—violent means, an event that—if successful—necessarily leads to regime change but not necessarily to radical social transformations within the social structure of the territory in which it occurs. Instead, revolution is "humbler"; it refers to the gradual social transformation within a given society; a transformation that does not necessarily pass through the conquest of state power and the political event of the Revolution, nor is necessarily rapid or violent. I therefore argue that Revolution with capital "R" refers to the *political event* of regime change, while revolution with small "r" refers to the *political process* of radical social transformation. These two can at times be combined, yet not necessarily so. That distinction is a key one if we wish to understand revolutions in general, and Latin American revolutionary movements and guerrillas more specifically, and this is the main contribution of this chapter to the relevant literature: the suggestion of viewing Revolution as a *political event*, and revolution as a *political process*, which may or may not be combined. The *political event* of a Revolution necessarily leads to regime change through extra-constitutional and—sometimes—violent meant but not necessarily to radical social transformation, while the *political process* of the revolution leads to radical social change yet not necessarily through the grasp of state power via the armed struggle.

THE REVOLUTIONARIES

But who are the Latin American revolutionaries? What have been their political, gender, age, and class characteristics? Taking the cases of the Latin American revolutionaries of the twentieth century, successful or not, we notice the presence of a wide range of social classes: we notice *campesinos* like Emiliano Zapata, petty thieves like Pancho Villa, students and urban middle- and upper-class professionals like Fidel Castro, Che Guevara, or some of the leading Sandinistas like Tomás Borge or Carlos Fonseca, military men like Jacobo Árbenz and Hugo Chávez, priests like Camilo Torres, rural teachers like Lucio Cabañas and Arturo Gámiz, and of course anonymous working class people like the miners who played a protagonist role in the Bolivian 1952 Revolution. We also notice indigenous peoples like the Zapatistas, or the majority of the members of various other Latin American guerrillas. One characteristic they all share, however, is that at least in the forefront we see mostly men, not women; even though the latter are of course not absent and play key roles in Latin American revolutions. From the *Adelitas*, or *soldaderas*,[3] of the Mexican Revolution to the Sandinista guerrilleras, or the charismatic Comandantas Ramona and Elisa of the Zapatistas, women have always been present in Latin American revolutions, even though they have normally been overshadowed by their male compañeros. Wickham-Crowley distinguishes between two periods in the genealogy of Latin American guerrillas: the guerrillas of the 1960s–1970s and those of the 1970s–1990s.[4] Regarding the gender of the revolutionaries, Wickham-Crowley argues that women, especially in the 1960s—either by imposition or by own initiative—are normally relegated to secondary roles, in short to the job of "making the coffee" (Wickham-Crowley 1993: 22). That fact changes in the second wave of Latin American revolutions studied by the author (those of the 1970s onwards), especially so with the Sandinista Revolution in Nicaragua and the Frente Farabundo Martí para la Liberación Nacional (FMLN) in El Salvador, in which women gradually get more prominent roles (Kampwirth 2002). Women formed one third of the Sandinista militants and 40% of FMLN members, while half of the almost 18,000 FARC guerrilleras/guerrilleros were women. The same is the case for the Zapatista Comité Clandestino Revolucionario Indígena (CCRI): 50% are women. However, despite those feats, generally speaking women never become the *vanguard leaders* of Revolutions. Those roles remain predominantly male.

Regarding age and class, Latin American revolutionaries are mostly young, in their early twenties, and—especially those of the 1960s—come from middle- and upper-class backgrounds, and they are mostly urban (Kruijt 2008: 67). They are highly educated, and they move to the countryside from the cities (urban-rural transition[5]). When that happens those who become the rank-and-file members of the organizations are mostly peasants or students (Wickham-Crowley 1993: 23).

Summing up, Latin American revolutionaries have been mostly male, highly educated, and from middle- and upper-class backgrounds. They are normally radicalized in universities and when they make the urban-rural transition they usually recruit peasants and workers—without much success when it comes to indigenous peoples, with the notable exceptions of 1970s Peru and Guatemala.

Unlikely Radicals: Priests, Nuns, Military Men, and Poets

Any overview of Latin American revolutionary movements would be incomplete without making a special reference to the most unlikely of the revolutionaries: the priests, the nuns, the poets, and the military men who championed questions of social justice in the region throughout the twentieth century. Despite the fact that the Catholic Church and the army have normally been associated with reactionary politics, conservative cosmologies, and collaboration with dictatorships and United States' interests in the region—which is very often the case (see Payne in this volume)—there have been some notable exceptions coming from those who sided with the poor and exploited and very often paid for it with their lives.

Due to the impact of Liberation Theology in the region, especially during the 1970s, we witnessed an impressive number of religious people siding with revolutionary movements or becoming revolutionaries themselves (Mackin in this volume). Archbishop Óscar Romero, Ernesto Cardenal, and Camilo Torres are only some of the most characteristic such cases. Liberation Theology is a Catholic current that interpreted the Bible and the gospel in a rather radical way: for liberation theologists the Church should not just show compassion to the poor and exploited but also take practical action on their side (Lowy 1996; see also Mackin in this volume). Latin American bishops' conferences in Medellin in 1968 and Puebla in 1979 played a significant role in expanding liberation theology's influence in the region, and as a result numerous Christian Base Communities were created throughout Latin America, which in theory were discussing religious matters but also national and international politics (Kruijt 2017: 73). Such communities played and extremely important role in the radicalization of peasants in El Salvador, and Nicaragua, while many of the early indigenous Chiapanecos that became Zapatistas in Mexico were local catechists. As other forms of political and social organizing were normally banned—especially under authoritarian regimes—Christian Base Communities became the covert political-religious groups that challenged taken-for-granted positions of exploitation and social injustice. Very often, religious communities acted as the first step in the radicalization of their members (peasants, students, workers), where they would also discuss Marxism apart from the Bible, with the next step being their direct integration in revolutionary movements.

On the other hand, there have been currents within the army in several Latin American countries (Venezuela readily comes to mind but it is not the only case) (Ciccariello-Maher 2013) which were either influenced by the fascination that followed the Cuban revolution, or were unwilling to become pawns of US imperialism in the region and changed sides to work for the revolutionary ideal.[6] Kruijt (2017: 67) writes: "Before the Salvadoran and the Guatemalan armies were transformed into counterinsurgency machines, a certain proclivity to rebellion had existed among the young cadets and junior officers from the mid-1940s to the late 1950s." A product of that current has been Jacobo Árbenz, while Hugo Chávez has also been influenced by similar currents in the Venezuelan military this time, which explains the failed 1992 coup. It is for the military's long involvement in political life that Latin America has been called "the continent of political soldiers and military politicians" (Kruijt 2017c). Those political soldiers and military politicians came both from the Left and from the Right (see Payne in this volume), yet it is the former that interests us in this chapter. Their ideological reasoning, based on the tradition of the regions' nineteenth-century liberators, many of whom had been military men, could be summarized in general terms as follows: there should be a unity of the people and the army within the nation, against the oligarchies who work for and with US imperialism, therefore the army should act in favor of the least privileged for the homeland's honor and good. In general, military men of the Left in Latin America have been less radical than the guerrilleros/guerrilleras, promoting rather reformist—yet transformative—policies such as nationalizations of state assets, and land redistributions, as in the case of Jacobo Árbenz (1951–1954) in Guatemala and Omar Torrijos in Panama (1968–1981), to name just two examples.

Other—not so unlikely yet unusual—Latin American revolutionaries have come from the ranks of artists and poets, or have become poets during the Revolution itself. Rigoberto López Pérez, the Nicaraguan poet who assassinated the dictator Anastasio Somoza García in 1956 is one of the most characteristic cases. In El Salvador poet Roque Dalton's case has also been legendary. Roque Dalton became a member of El Salvador's communist party, was exiled to Cuba for his political activism, received training there, and later joined the Ejército Revolucionario del Pueblo (ERP). He met a tragic death due to an internal dispute within the ERP, which eventually led to his execution. Nicaraguan Ernesto Cardenal's poetry was also influenced greatly by his participation in the struggle, and his understanding of Liberation Theology as well as Marxism. Of course, despite him not being primarily a poet, one cannot help but noting the importance of Subcomandante Marcos' poetic texts in the diffusion of the Zapatista cause.

The Strategies

While earlier revolutions have been rather spontaneous and not so well prepared and planned, the most influential case when it comes to revolutionary strategizing in the region has been without doubt the experience of Cuba, and especially the *foco guerrillero* strategy. The theory of *foquismo*, or *foco guerrillero*, derives from Che Guevara's (1961) narration and praxis of how guerrilla warfare should be conducted, as well as of Debray's (1966) theorization of it. In short, it maintains that it is not necessary for the objective conditions for a revolution to take place to be fulfilled. Instead, a well-prepared vanguardist group can start the revolution and create itself the conditions for it to succeed. Guevara then identifies the countryside as the ideal location for such a group to start its revolutionary activities. *Foquismo* is also known as the *Guevara-Debray theory of revolution*. Unfortunately, while the *foco guerrillero* theory became extremely popular amongst Latin American revolutionaries mainly due to the immense popularity of Che Guevara and the Cuban *barbudos*, it did not lead to any victory anywhere else other than Cuba (see Martí i Puig and Álvarez in this volume). It rather led to numerous tragic failures. Years later, and after his own failed coup, at the World Social Forum of Porto Alegre Hugo Chávez would summarize Latin American revolutionaries' criticism towards *foco guerrillero* as follows:

> Although I admire Che Guevara very much, his thesis was not viable. His guerrilla unit, perhaps 100 men in a mountain, that may have been valid in Cuba, but the conditions elsewhere were different, and that's why Che died in Bolivia, a Quixotic figure. History showed that his thesis of *one, two, three Vietnams* did not work. Today, the situation does not involve guerrilla cells, that can be surrounded by the Rangers or the Marines in a mountain, as they did to Che Guevara, they were only maybe 50 men against 500, now we are millions, how are they going to surround us? Be careful, we might be the ones doing the surrounding... (Chávez 2005)

Tragic trial and error, therefore, has been the main reason that led Latin American guerrillas from the 1970s onwards to abandon *foquismo* in order to adopt a rather different theory of revolution that is known as *guerra popular prolongada* (prolonged people's war—GPP/PPL) (Wickham-Crowley 1993: 313). The concept of prolonged people's war, which is a Maoist one, promotes the long preparation of the population in the countryside, having as its focus the peasant populations, which can prepare and provide with both people and resources a rebel army that can fight and eventually beat the state's military and grasp state power. Indeed it took the Sandinistas eighteen years of political organizing and recruitment from the moment they established the Frente Sandinista de Liberación Nacional (FSLN) in 1961 until they eventually beat Somoza's regime in 1979. The same was the case for the Ejército Zapatista de Liberación Nacional (EZLN), and their mother organization the Fuerzas de Liberación Nacional (FLN): it took them more than ten years in the Chiapan mountains and jungles (if we do not count the FLN history since it was actually established in 1969) from the moment they set the first rebel camp in Chiapas in 1983 until they started their rebellion on January 1, 1994. While the GPP/PPL has born better fruits than *foquismo*, at least in the case of the Sandinistas,[7] the Fuerzas Armadas Revolucionarias de Colombia (FARC), and the initial years of the EZLN in Mexico, it has not exactly led to a multitude of successful revolutions either.

After Salvador Allende's and Unidad Popular's electoral victory in Chile in the 1970 elections, one more political strategy—institutional this time—appeared to be gaining ground amongst revolutionary movements in Latin America: that of participating in electoral competitions with their own parties, winning them, and trying to introduce radical social transformations through parliamentary means. Based on the Chilean experience this road to social change was known as the *Chilean Road to Socialism*. The initial excitement did not last too long though, since Augusto Pinochet's *coup d'état* came to shatter such a possibility, at least for some time (see Brockett in this volume). As the Fuerzas de Liberación Nacional (FLN) summarize in one of their internal documents shortly after Allende's fall: "The military coup in Chile had shown once more the necessity for revolution in order to form and consolidate the apparatuses of popular power" (FLN 1980: 6). The political disturbance that came with the failure of the Allende path, was translated into the radicalization of many militants (Oikonomakis 2019: 106). Later on, the Chilean road to socialism through electoral means would be reproduced (or at least, tried to) by the so-called *pink tide*, or *progressive*, governments of Chávez in Venezuela and Evo Morales in Bolivia among others, in processes that were self-called as the *Bolivarian Revolution*, or the *Process of Change*, respectively. In Ecuador, Rafael Correa called his own political process of change *Citizens' Revolution*.

A more contemporary stream of revolutionary movements should also not be ignored, one that rejects the state power road to social change, whether that comes through elections or Revolution. Influenced by an ideological stream that runs all the way from anarchism to Rosa Luxemburg, contemporary revolutionary social movements seem to be less susceptible to vanguardism and to the grasp of state power than earlier ones (see Souza in this volume). The Zapatistas are the most prominent case, however, there have been other such instances in contemporary Latin American history such as the experience of the Coordinadora por la Defensa del Agua y la Vida of Cochabamba, or certain streams of the *piqueteros* in Argentina. The reasoning of these movements, as well as the criticism they make to the state-power road to social change can be summarized in John Holloway's words:

> if we manage to become powerful, by building a party, or taking up arms, or winning an election, then we shall be no different from all the other powerful in history ... The problem of the armed struggle is that it accepts from the beginning that it is necessary to adopt the methods of the enemy in order to defeat the enemy: but, even on the unlikely event of military victory, it is capitalist socialist relations that have triumphed. (Holloway 2002: 213)

Such a reasoning led some contemporary revolutionary movements in Latin America to leave aside the issue of taking power, opting for creating alternative, autonomous, counter-power structures, and institutions instead. That's the revolutionary stream of *autonomy* that constitutes a small r revolutionary political process (Souza in this volume).

Revolutionary Political Strategizing

In his excellent book on Latin American Revolutions, Becker (2017) maintains that one of the factors that makes a successful revolution is the presence of a discredited government and the lack of other opportunities for social change. This also happens to be Goodwin's (2001) central argument: that social movements think of armed struggle when all other roads to power and social change are closed. The argument is reasonable, and is in line with political opportunities structure (POS), which argues that when political opportunities in a given political environment are open (new favorable electoral laws, alliances with opposition, access to resources), movements are expected to take a more reformist institutional path, while when they are closed (as under authoritarian regimes) movements are expected to be more radical and more revolutionary (see Goodwin and Jasper 1999; Kriesi 2004; Somma in this volume). However, social movements do not always behave *reasonably*, and that is one of the capabilities that normally can give an advantage to the movements: their creativity and unpredictability that can surprise their opponents. That is exactly why, I argue, the POS does not do justice to movements: it places disproportionate emphasis on their *external environment*, on the political context around them, presenting them as simply reacting to external stimuli in an almost instinctive, predictable manner. At least from my own research experience the political opportunities structure can't always explain the mechanisms through which political strategies are decided upon. At times it may be able to explain the timing of mobilization, and the form it eventually takes once people mobilize; however it cannot explain what happens earlier: how their political strategies are actually decided upon.

It is beyond the scope of this chapter to make a thorough analysis of revolutionary movements' political strategizing; however, as I have analyzed thoroughly elsewhere (Oikonomakis 2019), more focus should be placed on internal to the movements processes such as (a) the resonance of other political experiences at home or abroad, synchronically or not, (b) the internal struggles for ideological hegemony in which the protagonists are normally the movements'—organic or not—intellectuals, and (c) the process of internalizing those political experiences (and the strategies that accompany them) within the movements' political culture, which eventually becomes a way of politically forming the movements' grassroots. Earlier on in this chapter I analyzed the role of political experiences and strategies such as the Guevarist *foco guerrillero*, the Chilean road to socialism, and the Zapatista autonomy as resonant political strategies for revolutionary movements throughout the twentieth century. Just to give an example of my reasoning, it was not just because there was "no other way out" that the Zapatistas (the FLN at the time) chose to stick with their plan to start a Revolution in Mexico throughout the 1970s and 1980s. Actually, there had been an opening in political opportunities (Echeveria's 1974 electoral reform that reduced the electoral threshold to 1.5% and the Amnesty Law of 1978 for the members of the post-68 guerrillas), which the FLN rejected, exactly because they *did not believe in* the electoral road to social change, especially after seeing the fate of Allende and Unidad Popular, which showed the limits of the electoral road. So, while the POS would have predicted them to demobilize (as most of other Mexican guerrillas actually did), they actually behaved unpredictably. A similar case is that of the *Tupamaros* in Uruguay: despite living under a rather liberal democracy, they eventually opted for armed struggle, contrary to what the POS would have predicted. Generally speaking, revolutionary movements' political strategizing is a rather dynamic process, which is very much affected by the success or failure of relevant experiences at home or abroad, which become role models and tendencies for contemporary or future revolutionary movements' strategizing. Cuba has played the role of the model for a big part of the twentieth century, while Unidad Popular's experience has also been a case that shifted revolutionary tendencies towards electoral participation at least for a while; a strategy that was later on recuperated by *pink tide* governments. Hugo Chávez's Venezuela has been a particularly important case in this respect, largely replacing Cuba's central role in Latin American revolutionary politics both in terms of resource provision and in terms of inspiration and political coverage. And *Zapatismo* has also become a rather unconventional role model for those currents of the Left and Anarchism that are in favor of "changing the world without taking power" (see Souza in this volume).

Of course, when it comes to resonance, an additional special reference should be made to Cuba however, because when it comes to Latin American revolutionary movements, its importance has been largely disproportionate to the island's (rather small) size.

THE RESONANCE AND INTERNATIONAL ASSISTANCE

When it comes to Latin American revolutionary movements, especially those of the twentieth century, the case of Cuba is central, not only because it has enjoyed a tremendous resonance amongst Latin American revolutionaries, but also because postrevolutionary Cuba has actively tried to assist other revolutionaries in the region, through training, financing, and direct interventions. Che Guevara's failed revolutionary campaign, which also led to his death in Bolivia, is the most well-known, yet not the only, example. Eric Selbin (2009) argues that the triumph of the Cuban (and later Nicaraguan) Revolution provoked a process of mimesis (not *mimicry*, he emphasizes) amongst Latin American revolutionaries. The reasoning was simple: "if they can do it there, we can do it here" (ibid.: 69). Wickham-Crowley (1993: 32) agrees: "The thought processes of future guerillas were probably remarkably neat: if Cuba can carry out a socialist revolution under the very nose, and against the resistance, of *yanqui* imperialism then why not here as well?" Thus, hundreds of young revolutionaries set out to organize guerrillas in the whole of Latin America, both urban and rural, in an effort to follow Fidel Castro's and Che Guevara's steps and example. In Mexico alone, especially after

1968 Tlatelolco massacre, there were more than thirty-two urban and rural guerrillas according to Castellanos (2007).

Cuba, after the Revolution, became something like the Holy Land for Latin American revolutionaries. The island would receive inspired youths, exiled politicians, intellectuals, and revolutionaries, while it would also become a safe haven in which health services would be generously offered to guerrilleros and guerrilleras in need. Soon after the Revolution, it also established the Departamento América, a liaison instrument with Latin American and Caribbean insurgencies according to Kruijt (2016, 2017a, 2017b) whose role was to support, train, and build contacts with guerrillas and receive exiles from the aforementioned regions. It was run by Fidel's personal friend Manuel Piñeiro Lozada, and its role was possibly twofold: to support revolutions elsewhere in an effort to multiply socialist governments all over the world; and to relieve the pressure Cuba itself was experiencing on behalf of the United States, distracting the attention of the superpower away from the island. Of course, whatever support Cuba was offering to Latin American and Caribbean guerrillas was dependent on the diplomatic ties it had at each given time with the states in which the insurgencies would take place. The cases of Argentina and Mexico are characteristic: while Cuba initially supported the ERP, after 1976—maintaining its diplomatic ties with the Argentine dictatorship for the flow of goods from Argentina—led to eventually withholding any kind of support for the guerrilla. "Donde se come no se caga—where you eat you don't shit" was Fidel Castro's reply to Luis Mattini, the last ERP leader according to Kruijt (2017b: 39). The same rule applied to Cuba's relations with Mexico ever since the Cuban Revolution, despite the massive number of guerrillas active there and their endless efforts to establish connections with the island: Mexico was Cuba's main umbilical cord with the rest of the world after the United States imposed its embargo. It was from Mexico's coasts that *Granma* had set sail and this relationship would never be disturbed despite the Partido Revolucionario Institucional's (PRI) authoritarian grasp over Mexico for seventy years. There were also ideological preferences that Cuba was taking into account: Maoist and Trotskyist guerrillas were not normally supported (ibid.).

Generally speaking Cuba's support to revolutionary movements throughout the continent went through three phases according to Kruijt (2017b). From 1959 till 1970, excited by the post-revolutionary fervor, radical youth from all over Latin America would come to Cuba for various reasons. Some, in a revolutionary pilgrimage, some others exiled from their own countries, and others in order to seek political assistance, training, or resources. Cuba, inspired by Che Guevara's passionate internationalism, would rarely refuse any kind of assistance, whether that was direct military training or Cuba-led commando missions to the region, or military or political advice from experienced revolutionaries. From 1970 onwards, deeply affected by Che Guevara's tragic death in Bolivia, as well as by the failure to spark *focos guerrilleros* elsewhere, Cuba—under United States-imposed international isolation—changed its strategy. In this period, Cuba focused on re-establishing diplomatic and commercial relations with the members of the Organization of American States and became very careful in its internationalism and revolutionary assistance. It mostly tried to deter revolutionary organizations from radicalization, encouraging electoral participation instead. The third phase Cuba entered in began roughly in the early 1980s when it was becoming obvious that the Soviet Union (on which the island had become heavily dependent in terms of commercial and political relations) was imploding. For Cuba that meant limited resources and even more limited political backing. Therefore, when it comes to its internationalism the island now promotes more political than military solutions in the region, becoming a key player in international negotiations between guerrillas and states. It has also become very active in humanitarian assistance all over the globe: Cuban doctors are regularly sent to Latin American and African countries, while Cuban educators are also assisting in literacy programs of countries in need (Nicaragua and Angola are two such examples). With the coming to power of the pink tide governments in the early 2000s, Cuba has formed alliances with the Alianza Bolivariana para los Pueblos de Nuestra América countries[8] and become dependent on them for resources and political coverage. Slowly, Cuba's central position in Latin America started giving way to Chávez's reputation, popularity, and resources.

Summing up, while Cuba's support to revolutionary movements all over Latin America can be said to be ideological, it was also very pragmatic and passed through various phases, depending on the internal and international challenges the Revolution was facing.

Conclusion

In this chapter I have analyzed the main characteristics of Latin American revolutionary movements of the twentieth century. Based on the literature of revolutions I have argued that there is no generally accepted definition of what a Revolution really is. Sometimes, when scholars and militants talk of Revolution they refer to the extra-constitutional, irregular regime change that is sometimes rapid and violent but often not. Often, when talking about revolution one refers to the process of radical social transformation within a given territory, which sometimes is following regime change and other times not. At the same time, that process is at times rapid, but often it is rather gradual and slow, and it may or may not be accompanied by the grasp of state power. The relevant literature refers to the first process as *Revolution*, and—in case it is accompanied by radical social transformations—it talks of *social revolution*. I found useful John Holloway's distinction between capital R and small r revolutions, and put forward the concepts of the *political event*, and the *political process* of revolution that can at times be combined, yet not necessarily always.

After analyzing the social and political characteristics of twentieth century Latin American revolutionaries (male, mostly urban, educated, socialist, middle and upper class), and after presenting some of the most unlikely revolutionaries of the continent throughout the twentieth century (military men, priests, nuns, poets), I analyzed the most prominent revolutionary strategies and tactics employed by them. I explained how the Guevara-Debray theory of Revolution gained prominence throughout the region, and how—through trial and error—it was gradually abandoned for the tactic of the prolonged people's war. I also referred to the rise of the electoral strategy towards social change, mainly thanks to the short-lived experience of the Chilean road to socialism, which however was revived years later by several *pink tide* (or so-called progressive) governments in the region. The mechanisms through which revolutionary social movements form their political strategies were briefly analyzed, and a special reference was made to the impact of Cuba (not only as a point of reference and resonance for Latin American guerrillas but also as a country actively supporting other insurgent efforts in Latin America, the Caribbean, and beyond). This impact was depending on Cuba's own diplomatic interests at every given time period.

To conclude, while it is an undeniable fact that with the 2016 Colombian state-FARC peace deal it seems that the age of Latin American Revolutions as we used to know them at least seems to be coming to an end, we cannot exclude the possibility of the concept of Revolution changing meaning either. The resonance of the Zapatista movement, which is based on autonomy, anti-hierarchy, and direct democracy, and which does not claim state power but builds alternative political and community-based structures instead, cannot be ignored. The Zapatistas are a reference point for various revolutionary movements, in Latin America and beyond, and the reproduction of such experiences elsewhere may be the way forward for Latin American revolutions. Yet what is sure is that they will not be as we used to know them: from Revolutions with capital R, we may be passing to revolutions with small r; from the *political events* of Revolutions, we may be shifting towards the *political processes*. However, that remains to be seen, because as we have seen in this chapter Latin American—and not only Latin American—revolutionary politics, and their role models, are and have always been dynamic processes, deeply affected by the success or failure of other revolutionary experiences at home or abroad, contemporary or historical.

Notes

1. I am mentioning mostly men on purpose. There's a certain male chauvinism and male gender dimension when it comes to the leadership of Latin American revolutions historically.
2. The case of Rojava is also characteristic in this case. Rojava, or the Autonomous Administration of North and East Syria, is a de facto autonomous region in Syria. It consists of a number of sub-regions that gained their de facto autonomy in 2012.
3. The word *soldadera* refers to the use of soldiers' pay (*soldada*) in order to employ women assistants-servants. "La Adelita" is one of the most famous *corridos* of the Mexican revolution that has one of those *soldaderas* as its topic.
4. To this author's best knowledge we don't have much detailed and comparable data on that aspect of earlier Latin American guerrillas.
5. For an analysis of such urban-rural transitions, see O'Connor and Oikonomakis (2015).

6. For a detailed analysis of the political role of the military in Latin America, see Kruijt (2017c).
7. Here we should note that the Sandinistas eventually split into three tendencies in 1975–1976: those who favored an orthodox Marxist organizing of the urban proletariat into a politico-military organization, those who favored the GPP/PPL strategy, and the *terceristas*, who combined both strategies with a more open tendency to social-democratic organizations. Eventually the *tercerista* position became hegemonic.
8. Full members: Antigua and Barbuda, Bolivia, Cuba, Dominica, Ecuador (until 2018), Grenada, Nicaragua, Saint Kitts and Nevis, St. Vincent and the Grenadines, Santa Lucia, Venezuela.

References

Becker, Marc (2017), *Twentieth-Century Latin American Revolutions* (Lanham, MD: Rowman & Littlefield).
Ciccariello-Maher, George (2013), *We Created Chávez: A People's History of the Venezuelan Revolution* (Durham, NC: Duke University Press).
Castellanos, Laura (2007), *México armado 1943–1981* (Mexico: Ediciones Era).
Chávez, Hugo (2005), "Capitalism is Savagery," Speech at the World Social Forum, Porto Alegre, April 10. https://zcomm.org/znetarticle/capitalism-is-savagery-by-hugo-chavez/.
Debray, Regis (1966), *Revolution in the Revolution* (New York: Grove Press).
della Porta, Donatella (2011), "Eventful Protest, Global Conflicts: Social Mechanisms in the Reproduction of Protest," in James M. Jasper and Jeff Goodwin (eds.), *Contention in Context: Political Opportunities and the Emergence of Protest*, 256–76 (Stanford, CA: Stanford University Press).
Easterling, Stuart (2013), *The Mexican Revolution: A Short History 1910–1920* (Chicago: Haymarket).
FLN (1980), "Nuestra Historia," *Nepantla*, June 10 1980.
Foran, John (2005), *Taking Power: On the Origins of Third World Revolutions* (Cambridge: Cambridge University Press).
Jansen, Robert S. (2007), "Resurrection and Appropriation: Reputational Trajectories, Memory, Work, and the Political Use of Historical Figures," *American Journal of Sociology* 112(4), 953–1007.
Goodwin, Jeff (2001), *No Other Way Out: States and Revolutionary Movements, 1945–1991* (Cambridge: Cambridge University Press).
Goodwin, Jeff and James M. Jasper (1999), "Caught in a Winding, Snarling Vine: The Structural Bias of Political Process Theory," *Sociological Forum* 14(1), 27–54.
Guevara, Ernesto Che (1961), *Guerrilla Warfare* (New York: Monthly Review Press).
Holloway, John (1996), "The Concept of Power and the Zapatistas," *Common Sense* 19, 20–27.
Holloway, John (2002), *Change the World Without Taking Power: The Meaning of Revolution Today* (London: Pluto).
Huntington, Samuel (1968), *Political Order in Changing Societies*. (Yale: Yale University Press).
Kampwirth, Karen (2002), *Women and Guerrilla Movements: Nicaragua, El Salvador, Chiapas, Cuba* (University Park, PA: Penn State University Press).
Kruijt, Dirk (2008), *Guerrillas: War and Peace in Central America* (London: Zed).

Kruijt, Dirk (2016), "The Cuban Connection: The Departamento América and the Latin American Revolutions," in Alberto Martín Álvarez and Eduardo Rey Tristán (eds.), *Revolutionary Violence and the New Left: Transnational Perspectives*, 67–88 (London: Routledge).

Kruijt, Dirk (2017a), *Cuba and Revolutionary Latin America* (London: Zed).

Kruijt, Dirk (2017b), "Cuba and the Latin American Left: 1959—Present," *Estudios Interdisciplinarios de América Latina y El Caribe* 28(2), 30–53.

Kruijt, Dirk (2017c), "The Political Influence of the Latin American Military," Working Paper No. 30, Cuadernos del CEDLA (Amsterdam: CEDLA).

Kriesi, Hanspeter (2004), "Political Context and Opportunity," in David A. Snow, Sarah A. Soule, and Hanspeter Kriesi (eds.), *The Blackwell Companion to Social Movements*, 67–90 (Oxford: Blackwell).

Lowy, Michael (1996), *The War of Gods: Religion and Politics in Latin America* (London: Verso).

O'Connor, Francis Patrick and Leonidas Oikonomakis (2015), "Preconflict Mobilization Strategies and Urban-Rural Transition: The Cases of the PKK and the FLN/EZLN," *Mobilization: An International Quarterly* 20(3), 379–99.

Oikonomakis, Leonidas (2019), *Political Strategies and Social Movements in Latin America: The Zapatistas and Bolivian Cocaleros* (London: Palgrave-Macmillan).

Selbin, Eric (2009), *Revolution, Rebellion, Resistance: The Power of Story* (London: Zed).

Skocpol, Theda (1979), *States and Social Revolutions: A Comparative Analysis of France, Russia, and China* (Cambridge: Cambridge University Press).

Tilly, Charles (1993), *European Revolutions, 1492–1992* (Oxford: Blackwell).

Wickham-Crowley, Timothy P. (1993), *Guerrillas and Revolution in Latin America: A Comparative Study of Insurgents and Regimes since 1956* (Princeton, NJ: Princeton University Press).

PART IV

IDEATIONAL AND STRATEGIC DIMENSIONS OF SOCIAL MOVEMENTS

CHAPTER 34

SOCIAL MOVEMENTS IN LATIN AMERICA

The Cultural Dimension

TON SALMAN

Introduction

"Culture . . . many times I've wished I'd never heard the damned word," historian Raymond Williams (1979: 54) once stated. His lamentation indicates that "culture," even if we often use it inattentively and thoughtlessly, indeed brings along serious conceptual problems. In reflecting upon the cultural dimensions of social movements' vicissitudes in Latin America, we encounter the same combination: a loose mention of the obvious importance of the cultural perspective, and at the same time a clear problem in deciphering the precise role and presence of such cultural features in social movements' moves.

Two aspects can be distinguished here: on the one hand the impossibility to define, circumscribe or convincingly operationalize the meaning of "culture" in social movement analyses, and, on the other, the function it often quite thoughtless is given in all sorts of assertions: as the *explanans* for developments or stagnation, for events, for reactions, and for emotions prompted by slogans, by defying acts or by opponents' retaliation. In other words, we see here the "linear approaches to culture that measured attitudes, beliefs, opinions, or frame content as causes of movement participation" (Fenollosa and Johnston 2015: 62).

The first aspect points at the impossibility of ever *directly* connecting cultural features to societal developments or the shape dissidence takes, like in the case of social movements (Assies, Calderón, and Salman 2005: 9). There is near consensus that culture matters in social movement developments, but it turns out almost impossible to actually demonstrate a connecting effect. The other aspect reminds us that, in cases in which culture is presented as explanation, inevitably "culture" is reified, homogenized, and traditionalized (Breidenbach and Nyíri 2009; Cowan, Dembour, and Wilson 2001; Eriksen 2001; Kuper 2000). This idea, common in popularizing thought, today is often criticized for its elusiveness and simplicity. Kuper (2000: xi), for instance, doubts that culture could explain *any* phenomenon social sciences try to understand. He insists that "unless we separate out the various processes that are lumped together under the heading of culture, and then look beyond the field of culture to other processes, we will not get far in understanding any of it" (ibid.: 247).

Culture should not be presented as a variable or "cause" of anything. Culture is too multi-layered, multiscale, cacophonic, diverse, inconsistent, and elusive, and apart from that also too much present *before*, *in*, and *after* the explanandum, to serve as "demonstrable factor" in explaining any social development, event, or behavior. As Norton (2004: 2) reminds us: "Culture is not a 'dependent' or 'independent' variable. Culture is not a variable at all."

This makes culture both a complicated and a promising dimension in theorizing social movements. Complicated, because of the many and the mediated—and therefore ambivalent—ways in which it becomes manifest in social movement performances, and promising because it is one of the key issues at stake in social movement developments, discourses, demands, and actions. Culture typifies the socio-political world in which both movements and political establishments operate. But at the same time, cultural features might be precisely the contested meanings of the formative and performative processes that constitute the social movement's built-up, of the internal and external dynamics, and of its demands (Brysk 2000; Quintanilla 1996). As Polletta (2008: 82) remarked, we need to look both at "the cultural developments that served as triggers to protest and the cultural changes that were movements' aims and impacts." And as Chabal and Daloz (2006: 37) remind us, "the cultural environment in which we live influences our perception, understanding and organization of the world that surrounds us.... cultural systems have a *deep influence* on how we live" (italics in original; see also Fominaya 2014).

That brings us to three possible manifestations of culture in social movement dynamics. The first manifestation refers to the fact that cultural features of the world in which people are raised will be inscribed in people's perceptions of their position, their expectations of what is realistic, and their entitlements, also in the case they are facing the option of joining—or not—a social movement. Here, culture is the shared, overarching universe of "that complex whole which includes knowledge, beliefs, arts, morals, law, customs, and any other capabilities and habits acquired by [a human] as a member of society" (as Edward B. Tylor's still often cited definition of culture of 1871 goes; see Tylor 1871: 1).

The second manifestation is the one in which specific societal cultural patterns or arrangements become the target of social movement actions. The feminist movements, worldwide, denouncing the normalcy of female subalternity in many social realms, may be the exemplary illustration here.

The third feature we need to study is the one through which the social movement tries to recruit and mobilize followers by embodying an internal, proper culture that appeals to prospective and actual participants. The reciprocity and mutual help discourses of the members of the Movimento dos Trabalhadores Rurais Sem Terra (MST) in Brazil (Santos Nascimento 2017) may serve as an example here. The aspects of internal movement culture include things as diverse as internal sphere and vocabularies, and admiration of and devotion to historical heroes or specific chants, icons, or dresses.

In the three upcoming sections we will first address the overarching nature of culture, impacting both movements and the establishment; we will then elaborate on the ways culture becomes part of the contentious politics movements trigger; and finally we will reflect upon the ways social movements attempt to embody alternative cultures that might attract membership.

Culture as "The Complex Whole"

Culture, to cite Kuper once again, cannot be a "hyper-reference" (Kuper 2000: x), a sort of final backdrop against which social phenomena make sense. And yet, to account for social phenomena, culture matters. Societies, and the ways their political mores work, do not only depend on institutionalized systems, legislation, procedures, and the like. Culture, and—according to some—specifically *political* culture, is also important. According to a classical definition it is about "attitudes, feelings and value orientation towards politics that are present in a given society at a given moment" (Power and Clark 2001: 52). But in addressing such phenomena, we should avoid cultural casuistry: to explain the historical events through the data-source of culture; or in other words: to elucidate the *acts* referring to the cultural "*facts*."

Such a way of reasoning may be found in a book by Glen Dealy, of 1992: *The Latin Americans—Spirit and Ethos*. In it, the continent's culture is portrayed as "caudillista."[1] Institutional robustness is lacking. Therefore, the "relationist" code, an interaction pattern based on one's contacts and relations, will always prevail over the representationist or impersonal code, or over patterns based on formal institutions. Trust is never given to just "any other" or to a function, but only to a "specific other." Thus, any relation with politics is "a relation with someone, not with something" (Bustamante 1997: 63). Such a cultural feature would a priori restrict and condition chances for social movements— for *any* social movement. If trust and commitment cannot be based on shared ideals or goals, but only on particular, specific relations, then organizations or movements cannot be based on joint ideas. And ideas, about injustice, about causes of inequalities, and about ways to protest and change things, are a key component of social movement formation. Such a way of reasoning makes social movements an unlikely phenomenon in Latin America. Culture, in such a scheme, is guilty of history.

The Dealy type of reasoning (see also Smith 1994: 121;[2] Wiarda 2001), basically pretends to explain many, if not all, political features and notorious problems of Latin America: a cultural package of attributes, presented as static and given, accounts for its generalized injustices, the impunity, the clientelism and the absence of awareness about such a thing as citizen rights, without referring to concrete contexts, contingencies, people's motivations, aspirations, or anything else. The "Latin spirit" explains the event even before it occurs.

And yet—even if that is not the way we want to give culture a place in our analytical work on social movements—cultural features *do* have an important bearing on how social movements emerge, recruit, consolidate and design actions, and on how authorities, media, or other societal sectors will react. One can fruitfully study how culture resonates in institutions, meaning-schemes, and political repertoires present in a specific society, and how such echoes shape the way people believe that for instance petitioning, contestation, mobilization, and negotiation "should be done" (Assies, Calderón, and Salman 2005: 9–12; Touraine 1985; Zapata 2006). This being a truism obliges scholars to nuance and detail such an assertion. Reminders here are that culture does not prescribe decisions, actions, and strategies. It only affects things indirectly. It is about "shared mental worlds and their physical embodiments. . . [providing] a collection of discrete beliefs, images, feelings, values, and categories" (Jasper 1999: 12). Basic assumptions, distinctions, categories, routines, and values will be shared by both challengers and establishments.

For these reasons, culture, in a way, sits uneasy with the study of social movements. Whereas culture often is assumed to be mainly about longitudinal, largely unintentional, and largely shared features of social formations, as Tylor in his definition suggested, the study of social movements is about specific deliberate acts, often in relatively short episodes, strategic and goal-focused, and group-based. The translation of long-term, partially non-intentional and sub-conscious processes and dimensions—in other words "culture"—into a short-term sequence of often strategically triggered events, in other words, the adventures of social movements, can of course not be a one-dimensional one.

And yet, observing patterns of the development of conflicts in specific countries, specific regions or between specific opponents, the suggestion is strong that transversal cultural features shape both contesters and representatives of the status quo. Examples could be Chile's traditional urban and student mobilizations and movements' need to "take the Alameda"[3]; or Bolivia's rural, ethnic and trade-unionist call-ups (Lazar 2008) and sometimes histrionic acts by militants[4]; and finally the authorities' standard responses to all these forms of protest and rallying. All these things are not contingent phenomena. They emerge because they are telling, illuminating, and enlightening in specific constellations of meaning-giving by people sharing certain understandings. In that sense, they are culture.

Social Movements Challenging Cultures

But culture reveals itself also in other ways than as regularities or schemes comprising all mobilizations and all responses. Cultures are also self-awarenesses, ranging from submissive to assertive, that characterize the "constituencies" from which social movement initiators and leaders draw their members.

Cognizance of cultural patterns are here transformed into movement features. A telling example might be the way in which Peruvian peasants founded and developed *rondas campesinas*, in the 1970s and 1980s. Starn (1999) tells the story of how these local initiatives, originally founded to prevent cattle theft, ended up assuming tasks of communal administration of justice, like in cases of local land conflicts and even domestic violence. The shapes and attributes of the nightly patrolling and of the communal court cases revealed traditional, "popular" features like the community-broad deliberations, but also features borrowed from the larger society like military jargon and attire and judicial books, folios, and the Bible on the table behind which the locally appointed "judges" and the "registrar" sat—providing legitimacy to the event. The *rondas*, in turn, launched new creations of local popular culture: songs and ballads, annual celebrations of the founding date, and pride in the ability to evade the deficient and often humiliating official justice institutions. The *rondas* here *mix* the endogenous with elements from elsewhere.

The idea is similar to the ones developed by García Canclini (1990) in his *Culturas híbridas: Estrategias para entrar y salir de la modernidad*. Consumerism is culture, García Canclini argued. Cultural features cannot be split in the ones favorable and the ones detrimental to the movement's cause. Culture's role is as important as thorny and attempts to clarify that role in, for instance, terms of assets, or blockades, or framing, should be done with much caution and reticence. Shakow (2014: 180), talking about the amalgam of social movements supporting Evo Morales and his Movimiento al Socialismo (MAS) party in Bolivia, beautifully expresses this when stating that for many supporters the "ideal of a pure political life in a new society of prosperity for all, free of clientelism, clashed with the need to get a job, to support others who needed jobs, and the moral imperative to attain and maintain a middle-class lifestyle." In other words, Evo's supporters faced contradicting impulses, and different strategies to bring those dreams to reality. Shakow focuses on the emergent, also indigenous, middle classes and suggests that *ambiguity* may be the most adequate term to portray people's reactions and strategies: people wavered between sympathy for the MAS's modernizing and industrializing ambitions, their doubts about the equality-goal, and their "individual dreams for the attainment of middle class status" (ibid.: 72).

The type of reasoning is reminiscent of the new social movement theorizing that gained ground in the 1980s (see Garretón and Selamé in this volume). In this tradition (Evers 1984; Jelin 1985; Melucci 1985), it was argued that the "new" social movements operated in the socio-cultural, more than in the political realm. The debate on the "cultural quintessence" versus the political *raison d'être* of social movements initially tended to polarize too much. Moreover, it was complicated by the controversies about how "new" such movements—like the urban ones, no longer being only class-based—actually were, and how well the notion matched with what happened in Latin America— as opposed to the squatters, peace movements, feminist movements, or ecological movements in Europe and the United States.

But those disputes aside, scholars doubting the new social movements' approach argued that, in the case of social movements, it is and remains primarily the explicitly conflictual and manifestly political levels at which changes are fought over and achieved, and that the sociocultural domain is no more than the background, "neutral" as far as the conflict issue is concerned. Social movements, in this view, are about rational and strategically operating actors (Adler Hellman 1990: 11; Amenta, Caren, Chiarello and Su 2010; Aya 1984). Others, contrary to this view, argued that the real, profound changes at stake were about the daily, sociocultural, interrelational, and cultural-ideological realms (Evers 1984; Jelin 1985). Without the optimism about creating new democratic and equality-cultures, authors like Schelling (2001) and García Canclini (1990) were inspired by this cultural focus.

In later scholarly work, controversies about cultural versus political priorities of social movement's actions were largely overcome (Foweraker 1995; McAdam, McCarthy, and Zald 1996), and cases were presented to account for the simultaneous cultural and political, identity and strategic, and autonomous and institutionally embedded dimensions of the actions of social movements (Tan and Snow 2015). Various researchers have also done empirical work to illustrate the point (Andolina, Laurie, and Radcliffe 2009; Assies 1992; Burgwal 1995; Downs and Solimano 1988).

Other examples are Lucero (2008), in his analysis of how indigenous movements emerged in Latin America. He stresses "the imbrications of politics and culture [in which] social movements seek to question the narrow limits of political society by politicizing identities previously seen as nonpolitical" (ibid.: 47). And Chabal and Daloz (2006: 27) remind about the importance to "integrate a cultural approach—that is, not just pay lip service to a few self-evidently important cultural factors, like ethnicity or language, but to disentangle the relevant webs of significance that impinge on political action."

Another aspect of how culture trickles through in the forms social movements assume is in the way such movements echo changing cultural worlds. Such worlds, for instance contemporary dominating political discourses emphasizing human equality, freedom, and individual responsibility, are likely to result in individual self-awareness in which dreams about upward mobility, or self-blame in case of poverty, are strong. Analyzing developments of the last four decades, various authors (e.g., Schild 2013; Silva 2009) have pointed at the neoliberal onslaught to account for such socio-cultural patterns in various Latin-American countries. Neoliberalism also manages to produce a generalized feeling of living in and being submitted to "a truly meritocratic, impersonal mechanism by which individuals and communities could leverage their capital (financial, cultural, social, and creative resources) to promote their self-defined interests and priorities" (Lawn and Prentice 2015: 9). Neoliberalism here becomes invisible as a deliberately created and ideologically inspired social, political, and economic formation (ibid.). What is at stake here is illustrated by an analysis of changes in health care provisions inspired by neoliberal reforms, taking as examples Greece and Chile:

> Neoliberal policies have led to an individualization of the right to health and a reconceptualization of "health care ... as a private good for sale rather than a public good paid for with tax dollars" [McGregor 2001: 84]. This relocation of care from

the welfare state to the free market has a detrimental effect on access to healthcare services for groups that are already experiencing difficulties, such as people with disabilities. Evidence from Chile shows that neoliberal reforms have produced long-lasting, negative effects on health, disproportionately affecting the most vulnerable parts of the population. (Sakellariou and Rotarou 2017: 501)

It is not hard to see how such policies lead to the internalization of low expectations with regards to stated obligations, which in turn constitutes an extra barrier to transform feelings of frustration into political action.

Similarly, cultural worlds in which internal homogeneity, the need for internal loyalty, and the threat of an (imagined) enemy are propagated (like in dictatorial Chile and Argentina, "threatened by communism," and also Venezuela in 2019, "threatened by the United States of America"), are prone to lead to a different in-group fabric and collective identity-awareness than in cases where such discourses are absent. Various authors have, for instance, observed that indigenous peoples struggling for rights or an expansion of autonomy are less tolerant towards internal dissidence or allegedly "alien" ideas on female equality (Canessa 2010; Jackson and Warren 2005; Salman 2011). Hence, homogeneity, either enforced or "spontaneous," does influence the mobilization ability of social movement initiatives.

But to study such phenomena, we need studies ethnographically delving into the messiness, cacophony, disharmony, inconsistencies, subconscious routines, and unpredictability of assumed cultural "basics," instead of global depictions. One of the foci in such ethnographic studies often is to highlight how (collective) memories, life histories, skills, and socio-cultural (in)capacities become embodied in the actors who mobilize—or decide not to, as the case may be. Brunnegger and Faulk (2016) compiled a collection that focuses on how popular "senses of justice" manifest much more than notions of "justice" the law articulates. These and similar studies address that and how movements' emergence, development, shapes, and makeups are connected to local, ethnic, class, gender, political, religious, and other cultures.

An attempt some anthropologists may have doubts about, to operationalize culture as "institutional schemas," is visible in the work of sociologists of culture like Polletta (2008). In this approach, culture is conceptualized as "models, schemas, recipes, and rules of thumb that people rely on" (ibid.: 84) in their dealings with all sorts of institutions (including the less formal ones like "obstetrics and race relations"; ibid.). The becoming problematic of such schemas is both a trigger and a stake for social movements. Cultural or conceptual changes bring institutional routines under scrutiny. The transposition of specific schemas, like the moral idiom of Catholicism to the institution of repression and torture in Augusto Pinochet's Chile,[5] turned out to be one of the mechanisms through which schemas began to slide.

Closely connected to such an approach is the idea of *framing*. Benford and Snow (2000: 614) add to the idea of schemas the "interactive, constructionist character of movement framing," as process in which "movement adherents negotiate a shared understanding of some problematic condition or situation they define as in need of change, make attributions regarding who or what is to blame, articulate an alternative set of arrangements, and urge others to act in concert to affect change" (ibid.: 615). But their emphasis might lead to a neglect of the overarching dimensions of cultural arrangements—as elaborated above. Their conceptualization of culture, therefore, may lose some of its depth when they define it as a "stock of meanings, beliefs, ideologies, practices, values, myths, narratives, and the like" (ibid.: 629). The dimensions of culture that are not "accessible" for strategizing may not receive the attention they deserve here.

Additionally, current studies often involve a focus on social media use, as it changed the landscape substantially in recent decades (see Treré and Harlow in this volume). Sierra and Gravante (2018: 18) remark that "the massive spread of low-cost technologies and the broad experience built up since the 1970s in the region in community-based, grassroots communication aided the empowerment processes of the new media and digital culture for protests and in all aspects of social life." Social media is a very peculiar vehicle and mediator of culturally charged messages and is often highlighted as infrastructures democratizing and enabling mobilization as well as framing practices. But cultural patterns on the ground shape media use and effects as much as media use transforms cultural routines of movement's features. On the role of social media in building current protest, building protest cultures, studies are burgeoning. Salzman's (2016) work on the relationship between social media use and protest behavior in eight contiguous Latin American countries concluded that "online communication via social networks allows the organizers to frame the grievances inspiring the protest and update information about participation levels which increases individual-level confidence in the efficacy of protest participation" (ibid.: 81).

Creating an Alternative Movement Culture

Culture can also be a *component* of the struggles of social movements in the sense that the movement attempts to *embody*, and not only advocate, the cultural transition it strives for. Positive discrimination for women or minorities, far-reaching internal democracy, the abolition of private property, reducing the group's own CO2 emission, and the like, could be elements of such a counter-cultural proposal. In such cases, movements will develop a *proper* cultural narrative and practice, not only to justify their case and recruit supporters but also to demonstrate and exemplify the advantages and benefits of the changes they pursue. The idea recalls Antonio Gramsci's thinking in which he focused on the way that quotidian cultures might contribute to the reproduction of power hierarchies. In daily society, bourgeois "hegemony" was reproduced in cultural life through the media, universities, and religious institutions to build acquiescence and legitimacy. The movement, in its very makeup, could therefore reveal how this works and counter the "normalcy" of existing inequality or injustice.

Movements' own "alternative culture" can also be about aspects like the recognition and articulation of collective identities; the revitalization or invention of collective—combative—memories; and the allusion to appealing historical examples, heroes, and icons as integral features of movements' trajectories (Lash and Featherstone 2002; Roy 2010). These are the elements social movements will often bring in, to question the existing cultural "arrangements" that legitimize and uphold established political, religious (Althoff 2014), social, and gendered inequalities (Alvarez, Dagnino and Escobar 1998). And these are the elements they will try to realize internally, to strengthen their case and attract followers they believe would be sensitive to such alternatives.

Movements in recent decades have, for instance, questioned the tacit changes in the contents of the concepts of "citizenship" (Salmond 2012), "civil obligations," "free markets," "deregulation," and "governability." Resisting neoliberalism (I referred to it above, see also Stahler-Sholk 2007), Dagnino (2006) discussed how a "redefinition of citizenship that underlay its emergence in Latin America, linked to the democratizing processes in the last decades" took place, thus questioning the way the state often failed to deliver citizenship rights. Postero (2009) elaborates on the creation of a new, indigenous citizenship in Bolivia. The practical impacts of such re-significations have come under scrutiny in movements' accusations regarding the concealing effects of the meanings attached to these terms by hegemonic politics, (religious) authorities (Althoff 2014), or neoliberal spokespersons and discourses. In this realm, then, *meaning* is the stake of social movements' actions and of their composition and structure. It is about new cultures of communication, decision-making, self-valuation, deliberation, and mobilization that the movements consciously construct (including symbols, ceremonies, rituals, and codes). Which means bringing in elements like socio-cultural learning processes, consistencies in message and form, and new ethnic (Madrid 2012), gender, or religious identities being converted into a source of pride. In Melucci's (1985: 801, italics in original) terms: "The new organizational form of contemporary movements is not just "instrumental" for their goals. It is a goal in itself.... the *form* of the movement is a message.... People are offered the possibility of another experience of time, space, interpersonal relations, which opposes operational rationality of apparatuses."

One important aspect of this creation of a new internal culture is the making of a (strong) collective identity (see Fontana in this volume). Living a different cultural code confirms internal "sameness" vis à vis "the other." From Barth's (1969) work on ethnic boundaries, anthropologists are aware of the dynamic character of such distinguishing and separating processes and have sought to critically assess them, pointing at the constant processes of reorganization and redefinition without which movements and, for that matter, their constituencies cannot survive (Albro 2010; De la Peña 2006; Madrid 2012; Postero 2009; Razeto et al. 1990; Vélez-Ibañez 1983; Zuñiga 2000). In such analyses, the ongoing search for the appealing identitarian distinction emerges like a key component of movement formation. De Munter and Salman for instance, studying Aymara-dominated movements in Bolivia in the years before Morales' election, discuss how these movements "refer to qualities by which they themselves compensate for their material poverty: 'We are poor, but at least we are honest and *we care actively* for each other". What people express is a wish that politicians would be like 'humble people': honest, straightforward, heedful and caring" (De Munter and Salman 2009: 449, italics in original). Whenever people are confronted with, or pointed at, situations they reject and will protest against, and when they enrage because of injustice being done (Eckstein and Wickham-Crowley 2003), or when they are called upon to rally or organize, they also are "called into" an identity, a collective distinctiveness (Molineux 2001) that can, apart from other means, be sustained by (the suggestion of) the creation of a different culture. However, the internal and external visibility of this difference can, and often will, coincide with quite a bit of actual divergence within the movement.

Hence, the cultural "layer" of such movements will often turn out to be multi-interpretable. In an important article, Rubin (2004) elaborates on this idea of simultaneous "strong unity" and internal diversity. He argues that social movements (and states, for that matter) need to be analyzed in their historical and cultural dimensions, rather than as merely political phenomena. The internal dynamics and tensions constitute the movement just as well as does its external presence and actions. The risk of taking actors like social movements as unified agents or "pre-existing subjects" (ibid.: 108) or simply "rational actors"(ibid.: 137) is large, if one does not take into account "the diverse pieces of representation and meaning that come together in political actors" (ibid.: 136). The point is illustrated by referring to movements such as the largely indigenous Coalición Obrero Campesino Estudiantil del Istmo (COCEI) in southern Mexico, the Zapatistas, and the Pan-Maya movement in Guatemala.

A more specific point highlighted by Rubin (2004) about the role of the cultural dimensions of, in this case in particular, gender, beauty, and sexuality is illustrated by referring to the Afro-Reggae Cultural Group in Brazil (see Dixon and Caldwell in this volume). A movements' appeal, Rubin stresses, does not only stem from the "adequate" wording of a political or livelihood problem or the "convincing" strategy to solve these problems. A movement also needs to be attractive and promise, one way or the other, rewards, even "pleasure," and it does so by (re)signifying the cultural components of its make-up. Finally, Rubin stresses that movements inevitable essentialize, to be able to represent and make claims. He adds, however, that this does not mean all participants endorse these "essential" features: peoples' beliefs and experiences might very well differ from these prescripts. Such tensions between unison mottos and slogans and internal vagueness on the exact goals, Rubin (ibid.: 128) asserts, are the "ambiguities and contradictions inherent in cultures and movements."

Many social movements refer to icons and (historical) heroes to strengthen their case. In such maneuvers too, a recurrence to culturally significant phenomena shows. In Bolivia, for instance, Tupac Katari, the leader of an indigenous siege on the city of La Paz in 1871, was used on a poster showing both him and Evo Morales in a similar pose, by Bolivia's "political party-movement" MAS, which brought the country's first indigenous president to power (De Munter and Salman 2009). Other examples abound. The names of Emiliano Zapata, Augusto César Sandino, Ernesto "Che" Guevara, and many more have even become more famous due to movements that later acted in their names or individuals that honored them in songs, clothing, novels, and oral storytelling.

In heroes, movements find stimuluses for their discourses and legitimacy for their cause—and cultural inspiration. His or her words often still arouse enthusiasm and incite people to fight. A hero can help a group identify with a cause, with the group as such, and can help to clarify the need to fight the adversary. Cultural politics are, in this sense, part and parcel of social movements. Environmentalist movements have sometimes also heavily relied on representations of local, even "ancestral" ways of life that can and should be reproduced in new economies (Gudynas 2011), and even more urgently, in the movements that fights for such new economies (see Rossi in this volume).

Culture can serve social movements in other ways. Women, stressing their role as mothers, have been in the forefront of human rights movements in the struggle against Latin American dictatorships. The silent protests of the Madres de Plaza de Mayo in Buenos Aires (Navarro 2001; Pereyra 2015), who demanded the "alive reappearance" of the disappeared are perhaps the best-known example. Initially, they were regarded by many as crazy for demanding the impossible. But the fact that they were women, and as such made a social movement that had a completely different culture, not defiant in the field of power but denouncing *being vulnerable*, made it difficult to repress their manifestations, even for one of the cruelest military regimes. Their continuing protests when democracy was restored and even after the military had been granted an amnesty, which made further protests seem hopeless, have against all odds eventually contributed to the reopening of processes against the perpetrators (see Wolff in this volume).

A final aspect of the cultural features of social movements to be mentioned is the importance of ritual. Rituals in which leadership is installed and reaffirmed is one example: on January 21, 2006 and in most subsequent instalments, Evo Morales was ritually invested as Bolivia's new president during a colorful ceremony in Tiwanaku, an archaeological site which is a powerful symbol of the expanding indigenous presence in Bolivia's public and political realm. Morales' investiture as *mallku*—"condor" or indigenous "governor"—at that particular site is symbol-saturated. The political apparatus revitalized, and partly reinvented, instauration protocols, symbols, and wordings to highlight something unprecedented in the continent: an indigenous president who was accredited and paid tribute to, by "his people," in an act neither acknowledged by the nation's political code of rules nor enacted since colonization. The uniqueness of the event was underscored by precisely this highly ritualized act.

Conclusion

The culturally imbued or symbolically significant events, personae, or artefacts accompanying the emergence, development, and articulations of grievances and demands of social movements can support social movements—and can also hamper them. The findings of this chapter remind us of the enormous importance of culture, not only *in* but also as backdrop for social movement actions. In line with Rubin's (2004) argument, it looks like a good idea to move away from an entrance focusing on "the movement" as a stand-alone phenomenon, and instead opt for a contextualization of the organizations' and movements' activities in the light of overreaching and culturally embedded themes such as identities, ethnicity, gender relations, moral, ecological concerns, or broader political issues like democracy and citizenship (see Spanakos and Romo; Inclán in this volume). Social movements are not insulated machines for political change; they echo *and* they challenge culturally tacit and culturally controversial customs and patterns—like the ones on the governing routines in a community or nation-state, and the concomitant inclusions and exclusions. Often, the demand for inclusion is not only a demand for political reform, it is also a demand for a rupture of habitual, culturally sanctioned, or condoned bars and bans. The very movement meetings may in such cases attempt to foreshadow a broader and more inclusive democratic procedure. Social movements have, at times, been interpreted as "practice grounds for democracy" (Assies 1990: 82). In optimistic accounts, the participation in local organizations like neighborhood associations or councils, or social movements, was seen as a trajectory and learning process towards an increased political consciousness and increased social and political cohesion among the poor (Valdés 1986), and as an escape from dependency and fatalism (Levine 1990). Other studies suggested that such a unilineal logic does not exist (Schönwalder 2002; Shakow 2014 Vélez Ibañez 1983. Whereas on the one hand important learning processes should be highlighted, on the other hand there is an enormous ability of governments and powerful groups to reproduce structures of inequalities and exclusionary politics in the society at large. For movements, it is often hard to counter these hegemonies (Langman 2015).

People participating in movements become more articulate, learn how to express their viewpoints in public, and learn how to seek consensus on priorities and strategies. Cultural learning, with all its "slowness" and distortions, does indeed take place. "Slowness" here refers to the fact, stressed in this chapter, that changes in cultural patterns and routines take time and are often piecemeal; that is, hardly ever will one routine "instantly" be replaced by another one. But acquiring informal technical qualifications such as learning to speak up, to negotiate, and to take minutes of a meeting, often boosts people's self-confidence (Abers 2000). In this sense, movement participation can be a key learning school for citizenship, even if it competes with the heavy-weighing experiences outside these movements. Which is why, often, no radically and totally new, suddenly fully politically skilled people will emerge out of movement participation. Changes will often go slower than the movements would have hoped for and faster than powerholders would have wished for. The cultural encircling and interwovenness of movement's actions and authorities' responses may well help to account for these contrasting perceptions of the speed and depth of the changes the movements strive for.

Notes

1. "Caudillos" are powerful and charismatic leaders, and "caudillismo" refers to a political system that is not based on ideas or laws, but on individuals and their personal authority, usually in a specific region, but also in a country.

2. Where Smith (1994) speaks of "societies characterized by authoritarianism, clientelism, elitism, patrimonialism, familianism, hierarchy, caudillismo, machismo, and much more."
3. "The Alameda" is the main avenue of Santiago, Chile's capital. "Taking the Alameda" has become the expression referring to becoming a successful, prominent, nationally exposed social protest movement.
4. In Bolivia, acts like (albeit symbolic) crucifixion or sewing one's lips together have been part of protests.
5. The archbishopric of Santiago founded the *Vicaría de la Solidaridad*, a Church-based institution supporting and coaching families of detained (and afterwards often "disappeared") persons and denouncing the violations of human rights—that same Catholic Church defended the taboo on divorce and on an abortion law in Chile, issues many Catholic Chileans heading to the *Vicaría* for help, criticized the church for (Mackin in this volume).

References

Abers, Rebecca (2000), *Inventing Local Democracy* (Boulder, CO: Lynne Rienner).
Adler Hellman, Judith (1990), "The Study of New Social Movements in Latin America and the Question of Autonomy," *LASA Forum* 21(2), 7–12.
Albro, Robert (2010), "Confounding Cultural Citizenship and Constitutional Reform in Bolivia," *Latin American Perspectives* 37(3), 71–90.
Althoff, Andrea (2014), *Divided by Faith and Ethnicity; Religious Pluralism and the Problem of Race in Guatemala* (Berlin: Gruyter).
Alvarez, Sonia E., Evelina Dagnino, and Arturo Escobar (eds.) (1998), *Cultures of Politics/Politics of Culture: Re-visioning Latin American Social Movements* (Boulder, CO: Westview Press).
Amenta, Edwin, Neal Caren, Elizabeth Chiarello, and Yang Su (2010), "The Political Consequences of Social Movements," *Annual Review of Sociology* 36, 287–307.
Andolina, Robero, Nina Laurie, and Sarah A. Radcliffe (2009), *Indigenous Development in the Andes: Culture, Power, and Transnationalism* (Durham, NC: Duke University Press).
Assies, Willem (1990), "Of Structured Moves and Moving Structures", in Willem Assies, Gerrit Burgwal and Ton Salman, *Structures of Power, Movements of Resistance, An Introduction to the Theories of Urban Movements in Latin America* (Amsterdam: CEDLA, 9-98.
Assies, Willem (1992), *To Get Out of the Mud: Neighbourhood Associativism in Recife 1964–1988* (Amsterdam: CEDLA).
Assies, Willem, Marco Calderón, and Ton Salman (2005), "Citizenship, Political Culture and State Reform in Latin America," in Willem Assies, Marco Calderón, and Ton Salman (eds.), *Citizenship, Political Culture and State Transformation in Latin America*, 3–26 (Amsterdam: Dutch University Press).
Barth, F. (1969). *Ethnic groups and boundaries: The social organization of culture difference.* Long Grove, Illinois: Waveland Press.
Benford, Robert D. and David A. Snow (2000), "Framing Processes and Social Movements: An Overview and Assessment," *Annual Review of Sociology* 26, 611–39.
Breidenbach, Joana and Pál Nyíri (2009), *Seeing Culture Everywhere: From Genocide to Consumer Habits* (Seattle: University of Washington Press).
Brunnegger, Sandra and Karen Ann Faulk (eds.) (2016), *A Sense of Justice: Legal Knowledge and Lived Experience in Latin America* (Stanford, CA: Stanford University Press).
Brysk, Alison (2000), *From Tribal Village to Global Village: Indian Rights and International Relations in Latin America* (Stanford, CA: Stanford University Press).

Burgwal, Gerrit (1995), *Struggle of the Poor: Neighborhood Organization and Clientelist Practices in a Quito Squatter Settlement* (Amsterdam: CEDLA).
Bustamante, Fernando (1997), "¿Qué democracia? Una aproximación a los problemas de la gobernabilidad y la democracia en el Ecuador de fin del milenio," *Ecuador Debate* 42, 53–64.
Canessa, Andrew (2010), "Dreaming of Fathers: Fausto Reinaga and Indigenous Masculinism," *Latin American and Caribbean Ethnic Studies* 5, 175–87.
Chabal, Patrick and Jean-Pascal Daloz (2006), *Culture Troubles: Politics and the Interpretation of Meaning* (London: Hurst & Company).
Cowan, Jane, Marie-Bénédicte Dembour, and Richard Wilson (eds.) (2001), *Culture and Rights: Anthropological Perspectives* (Cambridge: Cambridge University Press).
Dagnino, Evelina (2006), "Meanings of Citizenship in Latin America," *Canadian Journal of Latin American and Caribbean Studies* 31(62), 15–51.
De Munter, Koen and Ton Salman (2009), "Extending Political Participation and Citizenship: Pluricultural Civil Practices in Contemporary Bolivia," *Journal of Latin American and Caribbean Anthropology* 14(2), 432–56.
Dealy, Glen (1992), *The Latin Americans: Spirit and Ethos* (Boulder, CO: Westview Press).
Downs, Charles and Giorgio Solimano (1988), "Alternative Social Policies from the Grassroots: Implications of Recent NGO Experience in Chile," *Community Development Journal* 23(2), 63–72.
De la Peña, Guillermo (2006), "A New Mexican Nationalism? Indigenous Rights, Constitutional Reform and the Conflicting Meanings of Multiculturalism," *Nations and Nationalism* (12)2, 279–302.
Eckstein, Susan and Timothy P. Wickham-Crowley (eds.) (2003), *Struggles for Social Rights in Latin America* (London: Routledge).
Eriksen, Thomas Hylland (2001), "Ethnic Identity, National Identity and Intergroup Conflict: The Significance Of Personal Experiences," in Richard D. Ashmore, Lee Jussim, and David Wilder (eds.), *Social Identity, Intergroup Conflict, and Conflict Reduction*, 42–70 (Oxford: Oxford University Press).
Evers, Tilman (1984), "Identity, the Hidden Side of New Social Movements in Latin America," in David Slater (ed.), *New Social Movements and the State* 43–71 (Amsterdam: CEDLA).
Fenollosa, L., Johnston, H. (2015). Protest Artifacts in the Mexican Social Movement Sector: Reflections on the "Stepchild" of Cultural Analysis. In: Almeida, P., Cordero Ulate, A. (eds) Handbook of Social Movements across Latin America. Handbooks of Sociology and Social Research. Springer, Dordrecht. https://doi-org.vu-nl.idm.oclc.org/10.1007/978-94-017-9912-6_5
Fominaya, Christina Flesher (2014), "Movement Culture as Habit(us): Resistance to Change in the Routinized Practices of Resistance," in Britta Baumgarten, Priska Daphi, and Peter Ullrich (eds.), *Conceptualizing Culture in Social Movement Research*, 186–205 (London: Palgrave-Macmillan).
Foweraker, Joe (1995), *Theorizing Social Movements* (London: Pluto).
García Canclini, Nestor (1990), *Culturas híbridas: Estrategias para entrar y salir de la modernidad* (Mexico: Grijalbo).
Gudynas, Eduardo (2011), "Buen Vivir: Today's Tomorrow," *Development* 54(4), 441–47.
Jackson, Jean E. and Kay B. Warren (2005), "Indigenous Movements in Latin America, 1992–2004: Controversies, Ironies, New Directions," *Annual Review of Anthropology* 34, 549–73.
Jasper, James M. (1999), *The Art of Moral Protest: Culture, Biography, and Creativity in Social Movements* (Chicago: University of Chicago Press).

Jelin, Elizabeth (1985), *Los nuevos movimientos sociales*, vols. 1 and 2 (Buenos Aires: CEAL).

Kuper, Adam (2000), *Culture: The Anthropologists' Account* (Cambridge: Harvard University Press).

Langman, Lauren (2015), "An Overview: Hegemony, Ideology and the Reproduction of Domination," *Critical Sociology* 41(3), 425–32.

Lash, S. and Featherstone, M. (eds.) (2002), *Recognition and Difference* (London: Sage).

Lawn, Jennifer and Chris Prentice (2015), "Neoliberal Culture/The Cultures of Neoliberalism," *Sites* 12(10), 1–29.

Lazar, Sian (2008), *El Alto, Rebel City: Self and Citizenship in Andean Bolivia* (Durham, NC: Duke University Press).

Levine, D. (1990). "Popular Groups, Popular Culture, and Popular Religion", *Comparative Studies in Society and History*, 32(4), 718–764.

Lucero, José Antonio (2008), *Struggles of Voice: The Politics of Indigenous Representation in the Andes* (Pittsburgh, PA: Pittsburgh University Press).

Madrid, Raúl L. (2012), *The Rise of Ethnic Politics in Latin America* (Cambridge: Cambridge University Press).

McAdam, Doug, John D. McCarthy, and Mayer N. Zald (eds.) (1996), *Comparative Perspectives on Social Movements: Political Opportunities, Mobilizing Structures, and Cultural Framings* (Cambridge: Cambridge University Press).

McGregor, Sue (2001), "Neoliberalism and Health Care," *International Journal of Consumer Studies* 25(2), 82–89.

Melucci, Alberto (1985), "The Symbolic Challenge of Contemporary Movements," *Social Research* 52(4), 789–816.

Molineux, Maxine (2001), "Analysing Women's Movements," in Maxine Molineux (ed.), *Women's Movements in International Perspective*, 140–62 (Houndmills: Palgrave).

Navarro, Marysa (2001), "The Personal is Political: Las Madres de Plaza de Mayo," in Susan Eckstein (ed.), *Power and Popular Protest: Latin American Social Movements*, 241–58 (Berkeley and Los Angeles: University of California Press).

Norton, Anne (2004), *95 Theses on Politics, Culture and Method* (New Haven, CT: Yale University Press).

Pereira Condinanza, Mariana (2015), *Memoria, trauma e identidad: rupturas y reencuentros*, Montevideo, Universidad de la República (Uruguay). Facultad de Psicología.

Polletta, Francesca (2008), "Culture and Movement," *Annals of the American Academy of Political and Social Science* 619(1), 78–96.

Postero, Nancy (2009), *Ahora somos ciudadanos* (La Paz: Muela del Diablo).

Power, Timothy J. and Mary A. Clark (2001), "Does Trust Matter? Interpersonal Trust and Democratic Values in Chile, Costa Rica, and Mexico," in Roderick Ai Camp (ed.), *Citizen Views of Democracy in Latin America*, 51–70 (Pittsburgh, PA: University of Pittsburgh Press).

Quintanilla, María Soledad (1996), "La historia local vista por sus protagonistas: Un eje para comprender la organización comunitaria," *Proposiciones* 27, 174–85.

Razeto, Luis, Arno Klenner, Apolonia Ramírez, and Roberto Urmeneta (1990), *Las organizaciones económicas populares 1973–1990* (Santiago: PET).

Roy, William G. (2010), "How Social Movements do Culture," *International Journal of Politics, Culture, and Society* 23(2–3), 85–98.

Rubin, Jeffrey (2004), "Meanings and Mobilizations: A Cultural Politics Approach to Social Movements and States," *Latin American Research Review* 39(3), 106–42.

Sakellariou, Dikaios and Elena S. Rotarou (2017), "The Effects of Neoliberal Policies on Access to Healthcare for People with Disabilities," *International Journal for Equity in Health* 16, 199.

Salman, Ton (2011), "Customary Law in Search for Balance: Bolivia's Quest for a New Concept of 'Rights' and the Construction of Ethnicity," *Canadian Journal of Latin American and Caribbean Studies* 36(72), 111–43.

Salmond, Anne (2012), "Ontological Quarrels: Indigeneity, Exclusion and Citizenship in a Relational World," *Anthropological Theory* 12(2), 115–41.

Salzman, Ryan (2016), "Exploring Social Media Use and Protest Participation in Latin America," *Journal of Latin American Communication Research* 5(2), 72–85.

Santos Nascimento, Jamil (2017), *The Struggle Goes On! Sustained Participation and Disengagement of the MST Activists* (Amsterdam: VUA Dissertation).

Schelling, Vivian (2001), "Reflections on the Experience of Modernity in Latin America," in Vivian Schelling (ed.), *Through the Kaleidoscope: The Experience of Modernity in Latin America*, 1–33 (London: Verso).

Schönwalder, Gerd (2002), *Linking Civil Society and the State – Urban Popular Movements, the Left, and Local Government in Peru, 1980-1992* (University Park, PA: The Pennsylvania State University Press).

Schild, Veronika (2013), "Care and Punishment in Latin America: The Gendered Neoliberalization of the Chilean State," in Mark Goodale and Nancy Postero (eds.), *Neoliberalism, Interrupted: Social Change and Contested Governance in Contemporary Latin America*, 195–223 (Stanford, CA: Stanford University Press).

Shakow, Miriam (2014), *Along the Bolivian Highway: Social Mobility and Political Culture in a New Middle Class* (Philadelphia: University of Pennsylvania Press).

Sierra Caballero, Francisco and Tommaso Gravante (2018), "Digital Media Practices and Social Movements: A Theoretical Framework from Latin America," in Francisco Sierra Caballero and Tommaso Gravante (eds.), *Networks, Movements and Technopolitics in Latin America: Critical Analyses and Current Challenges*, 17–38 (London: Palgrave-Macmillan).

Silva, Eduardo (2009), *Challenging Neoliberalism in Latin America* (Cambridge: Cambridge University Press).

Smith, Christian (1994), "The Spirit and Democracy: Base Communities, Protestantism, and Democratization in Latin America," in William Swatos (ed.), *Religion and Democracy in Latin America*, 1–26 (New Brunswick: Transaction Publishers).

Stahler-Sholk, Richard (2007), "Resisting Neoliberal Homogenization: The Zapatista Autonomy Movement," *Latin American Perspectives* 34(2), 48–63.

Starn, Orin (1999), *Nightwatch: The Politics of Protest in the Andes* (Durham, NC: Duke University Press).

Tan, Anne E. and David A. Snow (2015), "Cultural Conflicts and Social Movements," in Donatella Della Porta and Mario Diani (eds.), *The Oxford Handbook of Social Movements*, 513–33 (Oxford: Oxford University Press).

Touraine, Alain (1985), "An Introduction to the Study of Social Movements," *Social Research* 52(4), 749–87.

Tylor, Edward Burnett (1871), *Primitive Culture: Researches into the Development of Mythology, Philosophy, Religion, Language, Art, and Custom* (London: John Murray).

Valdés, Teresa (1986), *El movimiento poblacional: la recomposición de las solidaridades sociales* (Santiago: FLACSO Documento de Trabajo).

Vélez-Ibañez, Carlos (1983), *Rituals of Marginality: Politics, Process, and Culture Change in Central Urban Mexico, 1969–1974* (Berkeley and Los Angeles: University of California Press).

Wiarda, Howard J. (2001), *The Soul of Latin America: The Cultural and Political Tradition* (New Haven, CT: Yale University Press).

Williams, Raymond (1979), *Politics and Letters, Interviews with New Left Review* (London: New Left Books).

Zapata, Álvaro (2006), *Ciudadanía, clase y etnicidad: un estudio sociológico sobre la acción colectiva en Bolivia a comienzos del siglo XXI* (La Paz: Ediciones Yachaywasi).

Zúñiga, Gerardo (2000), "la dimensión discursiva de las luchas étnicas. Acerca de un artículo de María Teresa Sierra", *Alteridades* 10(19): 55–67.

CHAPTER 35

IDENTITY IN LATIN AMERICAN SOCIAL MOVEMENTS

LORENZA B. FONTANA

Introduction

Since the 1970s, identity has become an increasingly popular concept by which to describe contemporary social movements and underpin new theories of collective mobilization. The post-World War II era opened a new international scenario. Decolonization and democratization processes represented substantial qualitative changes for social and political relationships both between and within states. Following a turn towards post-industrialization and a period of intense economic growth that granted to millions of people the access to a middle-class status, the increasing differentiation of social movements and a qualitative change in collective action became evident across Western countries. New issues entered the social agenda, from civil rights to feminist and gender claims, from students' demands to environmental concerns, and from global peace to counter-globalization. In the Global South, decolonization struggles contributed to strengthening nationalist and ethnic-based movements, while patchy but significant economic development and urbanization gave relevance to a broader set of social demands.

Few areas of the world exemplify these changes more compellingly than Latin America. The wave of democratization processes following the overturn of dictatorial regimes that swept the region since the mid-1980s opened the doors to a growing social effervescence (Inclán 2018; Inclán in this volume). At the same time, the overwhelming impact of neoliberal economic policies throughout the 1990s contributed to fragment and limit the power of social actors, while triggering a new wave of struggles for social reincorporation of popular sectors across the region (Rossi 2017; Svampa 2006). It was indeed amid democratization and the wave of reaction against neoliberal reforms that a new generation of social movements with highly diversified sets of claims emerged in most Latin American countries.

One of the overarching characteristics of this qualitative shift in social demands was the new emphasis put on collective identities and cultural cleavages (Melucci 1980). Gender, sexuality, race, ethnicity, cultural traditions, and lifestyles rose as catalysts of social mobilization. It soon became evident that neither the social composition of these collective actors nor their key concerns could be adequately understood with exclusive recourse to class differences (Pakulski 1995). In this context, identity went from being a "peripheral concern in social and political theory" (Muro 2015: 185) to being a new dominant paradigm (Calderón and Jelin 1987; Slater 1985; Touraine 2005).

As Escobar and Alvarez (1992) note in a collection of essays on Latin American social movements that has become a reference since its publication, from the late 1980s, a sense of "newness" embedded in the significant transformation of both reality and its forms of analysis was shared by social movements scholars. The "old" was represented by traditional actors, particularly the working class and the revolutionary vanguards, struggling for the control of the state and characterized by strong socioeconomic or ideological codes. Society was conceived as a solid structure marked by class relationships that can be altered only through structural changes such as in-depth development reforms or revolutionary upheavals. Forms of collective participation were highly institutionalized through pyramidal organizations and emphasis on centralism. In contrast, the "new" became mainly about autonomy and identity: a multiplicity of social actors with very low degree of institutionalization organize around horizontal, decentralized, and flexible networks, establishing their presence and sphere of autonomy in a fragmented socio-political space (Habermas 1987). In this context, change is driven by the transformation of individual attitudes rather than through structural shifts (Escobar and Alvarez 1992; Rodríguez 2013; see Garretón and Selamé, Webber, Spanakos and Romo in this volume).

One of the key features of this "newness" is the centrality of social actors' collective identity. This has been defined as a "perception of a shared status or relation, which may be imagined rather than experienced directly, and it is distinct from personal identities, although it may form part of a personal identity" (Polletta and Jasper 2001: 285). Actors are now engaged, not only in political struggles to access power, but in struggles for recognition of their different identities and specific rights as well as against discrimination (Jelin 1990; Langlois 2015). Their objectives include denouncing injustice towards minorities, encouraging the generation of culturally-sensitive public policies, and obtaining greater institutional control—a demand that sometimes goes as far as self-government. Identity-centered theories emphasizing "the process by which social actors constitute collective identities as a means to create democratic spaces for more autonomous action" (Escobar and Alvarez 1992: 5) became incredibly popular in Latin America. In this context, collective identities came to be understood as "essential for any theory, utopia, or project for change" (Calderón, Piscitelli, and Reyna 1992: 27).

Identity movements form a wide and rather diverse universe of social actors. In the *International Encyclopedia of the Social & Behavioral Sciences*, Langlois (2015) distinguishes four main types of actors:

(1) *National identity movements*: these are movements formed by culturally distinct national minorities that are mobilizing to challenge the dominant national reference in their respective countries and to claim for greater autonomy and, in certain cases, self-determination.
(2) *Aboriginal identity movements* (also commonly referred to as indigenous or ethnic movements): these movements gather populations that suffered from colonization and conquest and that have nevertheless maintained or managed to revitalize a differentiated culture and sense of collective belonging. As national minorities, they usually demand institutional reforms and some degree of autonomy, although this rarely goes as far as secession.
(3) *Particularistic identity movements* (including feminist and civil rights movements): these movements aim to improve the rightful participation of specific groups of individuals that have historically suffered widespread discrimination based mainly on some aspects of their identity (e.g., gender, race, language). They advocate for institutional changes to introduce modes of participation suited to their particular characteristics.
(4) *Normative identity movements* (including movements based on sexual orientation and disability): these actors mobilize for the symbolic acceptance of their differences and to change social stereotypes. These differences are of a sexual, intellectual, or physical nature, such as the visible characteristics of certain immigrants. They also push for institutional reforms to improve their fair and equal recognition within society.

Relying on Langlois's categorization, I will examine in the rest of this chapter how the different movement types unfolded in the Latin American context. In particular, I will focus on three main examples of identity movements: indigenous peoples, feminist, and LGBT+ movements. Indeed, the "national identity movements" category does not fully apply to Latin America. Although nationalist discourses linked to ethnicity have been on the rise across the region (Fontana 2022), it is hard to identify ethnic minorities of both immigrants or autochthonous populations other than those generally labelled as indigenous peoples. I will therefore subsume the discussion about national minorities into the one about indigenous peoples' movements.

Indigenous Movements

Since the 1980s, the proliferation of indigenous organizations constituted one of the most compelling examples of the rise and mobilization of ethno-cultural identities into domestic and international public spheres. The new categories of "indigenous," "indigenism," and "indigenous peoples" suddenly acquired new meanings not only as specialized legal terms, but as expressions of identity for social actors and reminiscent of exotic realms for lay audiences across the world. "Indigenous people" is now a "marker of global identity, associated with mainly positive ideas about cultural wisdom and integrity and with politically significant claims to self-determination" (Niezen 2003: 217). Like most post-colonial societies, Latin American states had been ruled by political oligarchies of white or *mestizo* origin. The people of indigenous origins (descendants of pre-Columbian populations) suffered a state of subordination and marginalization, less institutionalized than in colonial times, but nevertheless extremely effective in preventing social mobility. These groups, the majority of whom inhabited rural and remote areas, were traditionally organized in communities and, since the 1950s, became the reserve of peasant unions, political parties, churches, and revolutionaries, which tried to forge class, partisan, religious, and/or revolutionary identities, often against ethnic ones (Yashar 1998). Indeed, for a long time, ethnicity had been considered a relatively marginal and weak category for social and political organizing.

This situation started to change in the 1980s, when the crisis and reconfiguration of peasant movements across the region coincided with the rise of a new generation of social movements with strong ethnic connotations. On the one hand, the peasant weakening was interpreted as the evidence that "class as an axis of political mobilization had lost much of its power" (Lucero 2008: 88) in the context of the wave of neoliberal reforms, economic austerity, and conservative politics. On the other hand, the vacuum left by the retreat of peasant organizations and a new attention of international and academic elites (especially anthropologists and development cooperation agents) towards the ethnic question opened new spaces to voice cultural and identity-based claims (see Salman, Rice in this volume).

Given the novelty represented by the indigenous rise, it is not surprising that culture and identity suddenly became central concerns for activists, scholars, and practitioners alike. Ethnic cleavages could not be ignored or reduced to class cleavages anymore. Although they may greatly overlap in practice, they started to be perceived as "qualitatively different" (Orlove and Custred 1980: 167). This differentiation had two interpretative implications on the understanding of the rural poor as political actors: on the one hand, the rural poor went from being reactors to being progressive vanguards of social change; on the other hand, the material differences that were used as traditional markers of social boundaries were assimilated into cultural and identity cleavages, blurring the distinctions between poverty, class, and ethnicity (Fontana 2022).

Indigenous movements inspired a countless series of scholarly works, especially within the "New Social Movements" paradigm. Emphasizing the newness, rather than the continuity, of ethnic-based social mobilization, scholars begun to understand indigenous movements as crucial emancipatory and progressive forces for social and political change (Le Bot 2009; Pallares 2002; Postero 2007; Stavenhagen 2002). Ethnicity as a collective identity was for the first time put at the center of social mobilization theories. Yet this new focus on the movements' formation and mobilization around a common identity, grounded in a long-standing past of marginalization and repression, had also the effect of crystallizing and reifying this very identity as immutable and somehow given.

Other scholars have tried to counter-balance this trend by focusing on the conditions that can explain the rise of indigenous movements, such as the opening of the political context, the availability of resources, and new transnational networks and legal frameworks favorable to the indigenous cause. Identity in this context is understood mainly as a strategic tool and a social construct. Inspired by transnational advocacy network theory (Keck and Sikkink 1998; von Bülow in this volume), authors have noted how indigenous organizations have borrowed a new language and discourse from the encounter with rising transnational movements (De la Cadena 2000), learning from the experience of other ethnic groups and gaining strength from the contemporary process of formalization of indigenous rights in international law (Engle 2010). Mediators in this process were anthropologists and international cooperation agents ready to put expertise and financial resources at the service of the indigenous cause (Andolina, Laurie, and Radcliffe 2009; Brysk 2000; Jackson 1995). At the same time, national endogenous dynamics also were identified as key variables to explain the success of indigenous movements. Yashar (2005) suggests that indigenous identities have the chance of becoming politically relevant when indigenous movements are not only embedded in strong organizational networks but also take advantage of structural changes linked to political liberalization and shifts in citizenship regimes to push political elites to include their rights in the democratizing pacts.

Taking advantage of the opportunities offered by the new political contexts, indigenous movements increasingly engaged in political activism, particularly after the late 1990s. The example of the paradigmatic Zapatista rebellion started in Chiapas, Mexico, in 1994, and the non-partisan stand of its leaders was not followed by indigenous movements in other countries (Oikonomakis in this volume). Empowered by decentralization reforms, which allowed local leaders to access formal political posts for the first time, and by the political training offered by NGOs and cooperation programs, indigenous activists soon made their way into national politics, either through the creation of indigenous and popular parties or through alliances with existing political forces. Less than three decades after the foundation of the first national indigenous organizations in Latin America, two countries in the region are governed by parties with relatively strong indigenous presence, at least during the first period of their mandates (Alianza PAIS in Ecuador and Movimiento Al Socialismo in Bolivia), and indigenous leaders such as Rigoberta Menchú and Berta Cáceres became prominent figures orienting social movements' agendas beyond Latin America. In recent years, the example of indigenous movements has been followed by other Latin American collective actors, and particularly Afro-descendent communities, which have started to claim recognition and rights based on their distinct cultural identity (Greene 2007; Hooker 2005; Paschel 2016; Dixon and Caldwell in this volume).

Women's Movements

Across Latin America, the democratization period saw an increase in the participation of women in social movements. In the 1980s, a distinction was established between women's movements (i.e., movements integrated exclusively or mainly by women) and feminist movements (i.e., movements whose claims are related to women's rights, etc.); later in the 1990s feminist movements would become more massive and transversal (see Ewig and Friedman in this volume). Feminist movements in this early phase were certainly influenced by previous movements that led crucial struggles particularly for women's political rights. Yet in the early 1990s, scholars started to focus mainly on the peculiarities of this new generation of women's and feminist movements. In this context, identity became a key variable to understand the "newness" of late twentieth-century Latin American feminism. In contrast with the middle-class feminists of the past, these new movements were formed by poor women struggling for basic survival and against state repression. They focused their demands on the state, rather than the market, and insisted upon distinct forms of incorporation that reaffirm their identity as women, and particularly as wives and mothers, rather than as members of subordinated classes (Di Marco 2011; Jaquette 1989; Jelin 1987). Examples of these new movements are the organizations of housewives in squatter settlements fighting for social reproduction or the associations of mothers defending human rights against state repression. In contrast with Western movements that have tended towards a gender-neutral participation in the public sphere, Latin American women emphasized in this phase their private roles as a way of legitimizing their claims against a state that was interfering with their ability to perform domestic tasks, killing or imprisoning their children, and raising the cost of living so that it became impossible to adequately feed their families (Safa 1990).

The most iconic and studied example of this new generation of women's movements with strong private identities is the one of the Madres de Plaza de Mayo, an association of Argentine mothers whose children disappeared during the military dictatorship that ruled the country between 1976 and 1983. The movement takes the name from the seat of the presidential palace, the Plaza de Mayo, where this group of women with no previous political experience have marched every Thursday wearing white kerchiefs and carrying photographs of their missing children and grandchildren (Bosco 2006; Gorini 2017a, 2017b, Taylor 1994). Following the example of the Madres, other women's human rights groups also arose in other countries, including Brazil, Chile, El Salvador, Guatemala, Honduras, and Uruguay (Wolff in this volume).

Feminist scholars have been polarized in their assessment of women's movements primarily defined by private identities and domestic roles and their potential to trigger broader social transformation. These tensions between private and public spheres are highlighted in Molyneux's (1985) conceptualization of practical versus strategic gender interests. The former are a response to an immediate perceived need and, although they are linked to a condition of subordination, they do not in themselves challenge it. The latter are the result of a reasoned identification of alternatives to subordination, which concretize in strategic objectives to overcome it. They generally include political and institutional measures. Critical voices tend to highlight how the new generation of women's movements mobilizing as mothers and housewives do not challenge the traditional division of labor and the unequal burden of social reproduction, therefore limiting their potential for structural change and overall improvement of women's conditions. In other words, collective mobilization remains driven by practical interests. Other scholars have been more optimistic about the potential of these movements to trigger social transformation, arguing that the collectivization of private tasks and their public display is indeed changing women's roles, even when this is not explicitly undertaken as a challenge to gender subordination. As practical gender interests are collectivized and politicized, they lead to a greater consciousness of gender subordination and to the formation of strategic gender interests (Safa 1990). This second group of scholars have tended to focus on those cases where women's movements not only claimed for their rights, but managed to become key political actors, particularly in the phase of democratic transition, and, ultimately, to transform the political sphere (Montecinos 2003). Indeed, "gaining access to decision-making power has been a central objective of women's movements in Latin America" (Htun and Jones 2002: 32). A key mechanism that favored the political engagement of women was the introduction of gender quotas. In 1991, Argentina was the first country in the region to implement a statutory gender quota for legislative offices, setting an example for the whole region (Piscopo 2015). Recent studies have confirmed the positive impact of well-designed quota legislations on the election of women across different electoral systems (Jones 2009).

Another way women managed to gain broader political influence in this phase has been by forging alliances with other identity-driven causes that have, over the last decades, acquired an unprecedented level of visibility and power. A telling example is the proliferation of female indigenous and Afro-descendent organizations, whose agenda combines ethnic and gender claims, stressing the linkages between different forms of subordination and marginalization based on identity (Viveros Vigoya 2018; Dixon and Caldwell in this volume). Examples of these movements are the organization of indigenous women from the Amazon Wanaaleru in Venezuela, the Organización Nacional de Mujeres Indígenas Andinas y Amazónicas del Perú (ONAMIAP), and the Asociación Integral Guatemalteca de Mujeres Indígenas (AIGMIM). In some cases, a common gender denominator has been used to build rather unusual trans-sectorial alliances, as it is the case of perhaps the most ecumenical Latin American feminist movement ever created: the Federación Nacional de Mujeres Campesinas, Artesanas, Indígenas, Nativas y Asalariadas del Perú (FENMUCARINAP).

As for indigenous movements, especially since the 2000s, a body of literature has developed focusing on the transnational dimension of Latin American feminism, as one of the defining characteristics of this new generation of social activism. Scholars have pointed out how the regional and global levels became privileged spaces for the formation of new meanings, identities, transgressive practices, and political networks. Some examples of these transnational spaces are the Latin American and Caribbean Feminist Meetings, at the regional level, and the World Social Forum at the global level (Alvarez 2003). At the same time, Latin American movements have developed cooperation networks with Western-based feminist organizations, albeit with mixed results in terms of inter-regional solidarity (Churchill 2009). Some scholars have leveraged the importance of the transnational sphere as a window of political opportunity for women's movements to criticize the primary focus on identity. "Concepts of networks, alliances and coalitions are more helpful in an analysis of feminist politics than those of identity or difference because they foreground the practice of recognizing differences and commonalities simultaneously" (Walby 2002: 547). Phillips and Cole (2009), for example, describe how feminist movements have deliberately engaged with more or less institutionalized and top-down international networks and organizations, from the United Nations to the World Social Forum, as well as with state agencies, advisory councils, and ministries as a "strategic politics of presence," in order to exercise some control and surveillance on national agendas for implementing gender equality. Whether through lobbing or social protest, Latin American women's movements have had a great impact in influencing public debates and political agendas, while new and old challenges keep the movement in constant transformation. The fight against gender-based violence, for example, have resurfaced in recent years and generated a fresh young movement through globally connected social media campaigns such as #NiUnaMenos in Argentina and #VivasNosQueremos in Mexico (Rovetto 2015), which embody the new transglobal identity of digital feminist activism (Mendes et al. 2018; see Treré and Harlow in this volume). At the same time, longstanding issues such as reproductive health and rights still remain highly controversial in many countries, while in others legal and policy reforms have been revoked—such as in the Dominican Republic, El Salvador, and Nicaragua, where abortion is now entirely banned—signalling a still long way to go for women's movements across the region.

LGBT Movements

Although LGBT groups have not been central actors in any Latin America democratic transition (Inclán 2018), democratic regimes created new opportunities for these movements. Indeed, what Encarnación (2011: 104) calls the "Latin America's gay rights revolution" did not happen until democracies were institutionalized across the region. Moreover, the rise of neoliberalism, while aggravating the situation of marginalized groups in many ways, was also accompanied by a new discourse on modernity that has, in certain cases, created the conditions for the incorporation of LGBT groups (McGee and Kampwirth 2015; Pecheny 2003; see Díez in this volume). At the same time, the AIDS crisis and its responses brought the issue of sexual minorities at the forefront of the international agenda and favored the consolidation of sexual rights across the globe (Pecheny 2013). It is not that LGBT movements did not exist before the 1980s in Latin America, but it was only since the 1990s that they were able to conduct an innovative and effective campaign to overcome the organizational weakness of traditional gay-liberation collectives and to reinvent the nature of the movement itself. The "old" gay collectives created in the 1960s were formed around a "unitarian identity" (as homosexual subject) and maintained strong ties with unions and workers' movements. An example is Nuestro Mundo, a collective founded in Buenos Aires in 1967 that became the first group publicly constituted with a homosexual orientation in South America (Figari 2010). For more than a decade, these groups tried to build political alliances, constantly clashing with the subordinate space where their struggles were relegated within the classist, materialist rhetoric of the Left (Green Facchini 2005; 2001; see Díez in this volume).

Since the mid-1980s, the numerous LGBT movements that mushroomed across the region after the collapse of most dictatorial regimes were significantly different than their predecessors. More autonomous from political dynamics, some of the most active organizations such as the Grupo Gay de Bahía and the Triángulo Rosa in Río de Janeiro put forward "integrationist" goals to fight stigmatization and expand the rights of sexual minorities. "It was no longer the fight against capitalism that was at play, but a better way of living integrated in modern societies, starting from the politics of 'recognition'" (Figari 2010: 230). In other countries that have traditionally pioneered the regional path of mobilization of sexual minorities, such as Argentina, the newly formed Comunidad Homosexual Argentina (CHA) self-identified in the early 1980s as a human rights organization, following the example of rising women's movements such as the Madres. Its motto was "the free exercise of sexuality is a human right," and its discourse emphasised the idea of a "minority identity" as both cause of discrimination and answer to marginalization (Bellucci and Rapisardi 1999; Leal Reyes 2016). This represented a key moment for the reframing of the LGBT struggle around an identity-centered agenda.

Not only the discourse on a "minority identity" became central, but, throughout the 1990s, gay movements also underwent a process of fragmentation and pluralization of that very identity: first the homosexual subject was replaced by the lesbian and gay subjects (Seidman 1996) and, more recently, by a growing plurality of identities including transvestites, transsexuals, bisexuals, and intersex. In Argentina, for example, the Gay-Lesbian Pride Marches, key moments within the politics of visibilization of sexual rights, were replaced by the Lesbian-Gay-Transvestite-Transsexual-Bisexual Pride Marches (Bellucci and Rapisardi 1999). New identities developed around new autochthonous and imported labels: "barbies" or "muscu-locas" (creasy-muscles, particularly fit gay men), "osos" (bears, hairy and fat gays), "cross-dressers" (hetero or homosexual men dressed like women), "S/M" (sadomasochists), "butch lesbians" (masculine women), and "drag-queens" and "drag-kings" (transsexual artists), among others (Figari 2010). This fragmentation coincided with the weakening of the link with political claims and a growing emphasis on lifestyles and shared tastes, preferences, and patterns of consumption. It was also reflected in a theoretical innovation in the field of gender and LGBT studies marked by the rise of queer theory. This new approach, which put at its core the deconstruction of social norms and taxonomies, emphasizing how identities are always complex, multiple, unstable, and arbitrary (Abelove, Aina Barale, and Halperin 1993; Bellucci and Rapisardi 1999), took in Latin America a vernacular form to emphasize the collective and "populist" dimension of sexual politics (De la Dehesa 2010; see Johnson and Sempol in this volume).

Indeed questions around the political dimension of these movements and the potential and outcomes of LGBT mobilization have constantly been under scrutiny (Corrales and Pecheny 2010; Díez 2015). The struggle for LGBT rights is now considered a "permanent and public fixture of politics in Latin America and the Caribbean, both in countries that have made strides as well as in countries that are moving slowly" (Corrales 2015: 60). LGBT groups have often been able to forge alliances with political parties and state authorities to amend legislations and introduce antidiscrimination norms (Inclán 2018). The support of the newly created network of transnational LGBT organizations, both at the global and regional level (the International Lesbian and Gay Association, ILGA, and the International Lesbian, Gay, Bisexual, Trans and Intersex Association for Latin America and the Caribbean, ILGALAC, respectively), has also been fundamental in this process. Overall, LGBT movements have been less successful than feminist groups in improving issues of representation both in politics and in the business sector (Corrales 2015). In contrast, establishing political alliances and convincing governments and courts to approve ground-breaking reforms have proven easier for LGBT movements than for feminist movements. Among the most important are the introduction of same-sex marriages and civil unions and gender identity laws that allow to change one's name and gender on official documents. This difference can be at least partially explained by the willingness of LGBT groups to adopt a more conservative discourse (e.g., LGBT rights are functional to social stability and market expansion) that allowed them to forge broader political alliances, especially during the neoliberal apogee.

In certain countries, the implementation of neoliberal politics opened up new opportunities for the political incorporation of sexual minorities, while acting as a demobilizing force for traditional social movements such as workers and peasants. Mexico is a telling example of this process and its contradictions. In the 1990s, Mexican LGBT groups have enjoyed more success than their counterparts in other Latin American countries in terms of institutionalization of new rights frameworks; yet in this process, they have also found themselves co-opted and demobilized as an unintended consequence of their efforts to establish alliances with powerful actors, including the state and international donors. McGee and Kampwirth (2015) offer an in-depth analysis of this process in the state of Oaxaca. This case also provides an interesting example of a movement, the *Muxe*, characterized by two overlapping marginal identities—one sexual and one ethnic—and mobilizing for both sexual minority rights and preservation of cultural authenticity. *Muxe* is an indigenous Zapotec adaptation of the Spanish *"mujer"* (woman). It refers to male-bodied Zapotec people who fulfil the passive role in sex with heterosexual men and perform jobs that are usually reserved for women in Zapotec culture, such as making artisanal crafts and working at the local market. In this sense, "Muxe selfhood lies in a crucial intersection of identities and imagined communities" (ibid.: 57), combining ethnic authenticity, femininity, and rural origins. On the one hand, the *Muxe* community embodies profoundly Mexican identities—those of indigenous peoples and rural workers—whose core struggle has traditionally been for group rights. On the other hand, following the example of most other LGBT movements, it has increasingly adopted the globalized discourse of individual rights. This emphasis on individual rather than collective identities and rights allowed to establish bridges with the hegemonic neoliberal discourse, triggering at the same time a process of political recognition and social deradicalization.

Identity Politics of Inclusion and Exclusion

The "turn towards identity" in social movements studies was one of the major disciplinary shifts over the past few decades and was certainly crucial to overcome limitations of rigid class-based analysis and to shed light on new social actors. As Escobar and Alvarez wrote (1992: 8): "to deny ... that there is anything new in today's collective action—in relation, say, to the earlier part of the [twentieth] century—is to negate the changing character of the world and its history." This novelty includes both the rise and proliferation of new movements, such as indigenous movements, as well as the substantial changes in the ideological and symbolic contents and in the modes of action and strategies of existing movements such as those for women and LGBT people. While it is misleading to consider collective identity a brand new feature of social movements (after all, traditional movements such as workers and peasants also had strong collective identities), the way in which identity is visibilized and portrayed in this latest phase by both social actors and scholars attributes to it an unprecedented importance and makes of it one of the key traits in the taxonomy of difference between "new" and "old" movements. In particular, this "newness" rests in a number of shared features of contemporary social movements' collective identities, namely: their fragmented and plural nature; their links with trasnational, transregional, and global identities; their hybridity and cross-contamination (e.g., gender/ethnic); and the tensions they embody between being constitutive of collective subjects by definition while, at the same time, privileging an individualistic approach to social transformation.

Identity-centered approaches are not without problems, however. Some scholars have been critical of the emergence of "tribalization" effects and the rise of sectarian and parcelized social communities. This process has been conceptualized as the result of the crisis of the classic narratives of emancipation and social cohesion and the emergence of market-driven neoliberal narratives. In certain cases, the emphasis on narratives of difference and fragmented identities is interpreted as a deliberate neoliberal strategy to neutralize social movements' potential for social and political transformation (Bellucci and Rapisardi 1999; Hale 2005; McGee and Kampwirth 2015). Other scholars, however, have been more optimistic about the capacity of social actors to adapt and reconstitute themselves under new shapes and identities without losing their transformative capacity, but shifting their *locus operandi* to more intimate, localized spaces (Jelin 1987; Safa 1990).

The second problematic aspect of identity-centered approaches is that, while they generally ascribe to socio-constructivist assumptions, the way in which they conceptualize and empirically study identity is in fact quite rigid. They ultimately introduce a certain degree of essentialization of collective actors and their identities, which constitutes a limitation when trying to answer questions about why certain social movements emerge in given historical moments. Further, the performative effects of policies, legal frameworks, and the very process of knowledge production on collective identities are downplayed. This has been particularly problematic in the case of indigenous movements, whose ethnic identities and cultural authenticity claims have been particularly prone to essentialized interpretations. In recent years, this performative dimension of norms on collective identities and self-identification preferences has been explored particularly by constructivist scholars interested in ethnic politics, showing how identities can be endogenous to the reform process: they can, in other words, be the result rather than the starting point of institutional changes. Indeed, taxonomies of human belonging do not exclusively work one way; they also work to create new human realities (Niezen 2010). In particular, constructivist approaches have highlighted how ethnic identities and boundaries are often the product of political and economic changes, rather than key variables that explain those changes (Chandra 2012; Fontana 2014 and 2022; Fontana and Sparti 2012; Singh and Vom Hau 2016; Wimmer 2013). The potential of these interpretative lenses has still to be fully explored, however, in the field of social movements studies.

Finally, if on the one hand, the focus on identity has contributed to broaden up the plethora of social movements that became object of scholarly attention, on the other hand, the case selection has tended to systematically exclude those movements that became associated with out-dated class politics: workers, peasants, unions, guerrillas, and so on. The empirical shift towards certain movements introduced some important biases at the moment of framing a broader all-encompassing picture of social actors in Latin America. In fact, "old" actors have not taken their last breath as yet (some research even found that labor-related conflicts are still the most numerous across the region, Calderón et al. 2012), but they have progressively shifted out of the radar of social movements scholars (but see Ramírez and Stoessel, Welch, Oikonomakis in this volume). This should not be understood only as an empirical problem: it reflects the construction of powerful narratives of inclusion (and exclusion). The invisibilization of certain social movements can also contribute to explaining why some traditionally class-based actors have started to deliberately generate a stronger identity and cultural discourse in the effort to gain attention in a context clearly biased towards identity-centered movements. This is the case, for example, of peasant groups across the Andean region that have recently engaged in the crafting of a new peasant identity, which goes beyond economic and class dimensions and focuses instead on cultural uniqueness. This uniqueness is rooted in a universe of value, a special relationship with the territory, long-standing traditions, and the historical role peasants played in the nation-building process (e.g., they were those that in practice occupied and pushed the countries' wilderness frontiers). A claim for recognition is now explicit in the discourse of Colombian peasants, while in Peru peasant organizations are in the process of pursuing ethnicization campaigns of their grassroots in the hope to gain visibility and a voice in the political arena. Ethnicization has proved an effective strategy to gain recognition. The shift of the peasantry towards culture and identity is rooted in their perceived marginalization within the existing social order, as well as in an effort to bridge the judicial disadvantage that national legislations have introduced with the recognition of new rights for indigenous peoples but not for peasant communities (Fontana 2022).

Without denying specificities and uniqueness of the contemporary historical moment, a broader analytical understanding of identity in social movement studies would encourage a more inclusive empirical look at social struggles, while being more open to explore multiple dimensions and their intersectionality, including class, gender, and ethnicity. Overcoming the apparent contradictions between identity-based and class-based movements would also have the merit of shedding light on struggles that have shifted to the background of social science research, as in the case of labor and peasant movements (Fontana 2022; Rossi 2017). In this sense, there is a value in understanding identity as a broader heuristic tool applicable to the analysis of any social movement and not only of those with a more explicit identity-based discourse, while recognition should be considered a need for any collective actor.

References

Abelove, Henry, Michèle Aina Barale, and David M. Halperin (1993), *The Lesbian and Gay Studies Reader* (New York: Routledge).

Alvarez, Sonia E. (2003), "Um outro mundo (também feminista . . .) é possível: Construindo espaços transnacionais e alternativas globais a partir dos movimentos," *Revista Estudos Feministas* 11(2), 533–40.

Andolina, Robert, Nina Laurie, and Sarah A. Radcliffe (2009), *Indigenous Development in the Andes: Culture, Power and Transnationalism* (Durham, NC: Duke University Press).

Bellucci, Mabel and Flavio Rapisardi (1999), "Alrededor de la identidad: Las luchas políticas del presente," *Nueva Sociedad* 162, 40–53.

Bosco, Fernando J. (2006), "The Madres de Plaza de Mayo and Three Decades of Human Rights' Activism: Embeddedness, Emotions, and Social Movements," *Annals of the Association of American Geographers* 96(2), 342–65.

Brysk, Alison (2000), *From Tribal Village to Global Village: Indian Rights and International Relations in Latin America* (Palo Alto, CA: Stanford University Press).

Calderón Gutiérrez, Fernando, Lorenza B. Fontana, M. Isabel Nava, and Huáscar Pacheco (2012), *La protesta social en América Latina* (Buenos Aires: Siglo XXI/UNDP).

Calderón, Fernando, Alejandro Piscitelli, and José Luis Reyna (1992), "Social Movements: Actors, Theories, Expectations," in Arturo Escobar and Sonia E. Alvarez (eds.), *The Making of Social Movements in Latin America: Identity, Strategy, and Democracy* (Boulder, CO: Westview Press), 19–36.

Calderón, Fernando and Elizabeth Jelin (1987), *Clases y movimientos sociales en América Latina: perspectivas y realidades* (Buenos Aires: CEDES).

Chandra, Kanchan (ed.) (2012), *Constructivist Theories of Ethnic Politics* (Oxford: Oxford University Press).

Churchill, Lindsey (2009), "Transnational Alliances: Radical US Feminist Solidarity and Contention with Latin America, 1970–1989," *Latin American Perspectives* 36(6), 10–26.

Corrales, Javier and Mario Pecheny (eds.) (2010), *The Politics of Sexuality in Latin America: A Reader on Lesbian, Gay, Bisexual, and Transgender Rights* (Pittsburgh, PA: University of Pittsburgh Press).

Corrales, Javier (2015), "The Politics of LGBT Rights in Latin America and the Caribbean: Research Agendas," *European Review of Latin American and Caribbean Studies* 100, 53–62.

De la Cadena, Marisol (2000), *Indigenous Mestizos* (Durham, NC: Duke University Press).

De la Dehesa, Rafael (2010), *Queering the public sphere in Mexico and Brazil: Sexual rights movements in emerging democracies* (Durham: Duke University Press).

Díez, Jordi (2015), *The Politics of Gay Marriage in Latin America: Argentina, Chile, and Mexico* (New York: Cambridge University Press).

Di Marco, Graciela (2011), *El pueblo feminista: Movimientos sociales y lucha de las mujeres en torno a la ciudadanía* (Buenos Aires: Editorial Biblos).

Encarnación, Omar G. (2011), "Latin America's Gay Rights Revolution," *Journal of Democracy* 22(2), 104–18.

Engle, Karen (2010), *The Elusive Promise of Indigenous Development: Rights, Culture, Strategy* (Durham, NC: Duke University Press).

Escobar, Arturo and Sonia E. Alvarez (1992), "Introduction: Theory and Protest in Latin America Today," in Arturo Escobar and Sonia E. Alvarez (eds.), *The Making of Social Movements in Latin America* (Boulder, CO: Westview Press), 1–16.

Facchini, Regina (2005), *Sopa de letrinhas? Movimento homossexual e produção de identidades coletivas nos anos 90* (Rio de Janeiro: Garamond).

Figari, Carlos (2010), "El movimiento LGBT en América Latina: Institucionalizaciones oblicuas," in Ernesto Villanueva and Marcelo Gómez (eds.), *Movilizaciones, protestas e identidades colectivas en la Argentina del bicentenario*, 225–40 (Buenos Aires: Nueva Trilce).

Fontana, Lorenza B. and Davide Sparti (2012), "Identità indotte: L'uso politico del riconoscimento in Bolivia," *Studi Culturali* 9(2), 175–200.

Fontana, Lorenza B. (2022), *Recognition Politics: Indigenous Rights and Ethnic Conflict in the Andes*. New York: Cambridge University Press.

Fontana, Lorenza B. (2014), "Indigenous Peoples vs. Peasant Unions: Land Conflicts and Rural Movements in Plurinational Bolivia," *Journal of Peasant Studies* 41(3), 297–319.

Gorini, Ulises (2017a), *La Rebelión de las Madres. Historia de las Madres de Plaza de Mayo*, vol 1, *1976–1983* (Buenos Aires: Norma).

Gorini, Ulises (2017b), *La otra lucha: Historia de las Madres de Plaza de Mayo*, vol. 2, *1983–1986* (Buenos Aires: Norma).

Green, James N. (2001), *Beyond carnival: Male homosexuality in twentieth-century Brazil* (Chicago: University of Chicago Press).

Greene, Shane (2007), "Introduction: On Race, Roots/Routes, and Sovereignty in Latin America's Afro-Indigenous Multiculturalisms," *Journal of Latin American and Caribbean Anthropology* 12(2), 329–55.

Habermas, Jürgen (1987), *The Theory of Communicative Action*, vol. 2, *Lifeworld and System: A Critique of Functionalist Reason* (Boston, MA: Beacon Press).

Hale, Charles (2005), "Neoliberal Multiculturalism: The Remaking of Cultural Rights and Racial Dominance in Central America," *Political and Legal Anthropology Review* 28, 10–28.

Hooker, Juliet (2005), "Indigenous Inclusion/Black Exclusion: Race, Ethnicity and Multicultural Citizenship in Latin America," *Journal of Latin American Studies* 37(2), 285–310.

Htun Mala N. and Mark P. Jones (2002), 'Engendering the Right to Participate in Decision-making: Electoral Quotas and Women's Leadership in Latin America.' In Craske Nikki, Molyneux Maxine (eds) *Gender and the Politics of Rights and Democracy in Latin America* (London: Palgrave Macmillan), 32–56.

Inclán, María (2018), "Latin America, a Continent in Movement but Where To? A Review of Social Movements' Studies in the Region," *Annual Review of Sociology* 44(1), 535–51.

Jackson, Jean (1995), "Culture, Genuine and Spurious: The Politics of Indianness in the Vaupés, Colombia," *American Ethnologist* 22(1), 3–27.

Jaquette, Jane S. (ed.) (1991), *The Women's Movement in Latin America Feminism and the Transition to Democracy* (Boulder: Westview Press).

Jelin, Elizabeth (ed.) (1987), *Ciudadania e identidad: Las mujeres en lo movimientos sociales Latinoamericanos* (Geneva: UNRISD).

Jelin, Elizabeth (1990), "Citizenship and Identity: Final Reflections," in Silke Staab and Shahra Razavi (eds.), *Gendered Dimensions of Development*, 249–70 (Geneva: UNRISD).

Jones, Mark P. (2009), 'Gender quotas, electoral laws, and the election of women: Evidence from the Latin American vanguard.' *Comparative political studies* 42(1), 56–81.

Keck, Margaret E. and Kathryn Sikkink (1998), *Activists Beyond Borders: Advocacy Networks in International Politics* (Ithaca, NY: Cornell University Press).

Langlois, Simon (2015), "Identity Movements," *International Encyclopedia of the Social & Behavioral Sciences* 66(1), 543–46.

Le Bot, Yvon (2009), *La grande révolte indienne* (Paris: Éditions Robert Laffont).

Leal Reyes, Carlos Alberto (2016), "Sobre las dimensiones del pensamiento queer en latinoamérica: Teoría y política," *Aposta. Revista de Ciencias Sociales* 70, 170–86.

Lucero, José Antonio (2008), *Struggles of Voice: The Politics of Indigenous Representation in the Andes* (Pittsburgh, PA: University of Pittsburgh Press).

McGee, Marcus J. and Karen Kampwirth (2015), "The Co-optation of LGBT Movements in Mexico and Nicaragua: Modernizing Clientelism?" *Latin American Politics and Society* 57(4), 51–73.

Melucci, Alberto (1980), "The New Social Movements: A Theoretical Approach," *Social Science Information* 19(2), 199–226.

Mendes, Kaitlynn, Jessica Ringrose, and Jessalynn Keller (2018), "# MeToo and the promise and pitfalls of challenging rape culture through digital feminist activism." *European Journal of Women's Studies* 25(2): 236–246.

Molyneux, Maxine (1985), "Mobilization without Emancipation? Women's Interests, the State, and Revolution in Nicaragua," *Feminist Studies* 11(2), 227–54.

Montecinos, Verónica (2003), "Feministas e tecnocratas na democratização da América Latina," *Estudos Feministas* 11(2), 351–80.

Muro, Diego (2015), "Ethnicity, Nationalism, and Social Movements," in Donatella della Porta and Mario Diani (eds.), *The Oxford Handbook of Social Movements*, 185–99 (Oxford: Oxford University Press).

Niezen, Ronald (2003), *The Origins of Indigenism* (Berkeley and Los Angeles: University of California Press).

Niezen, Ronald (2010), *Public Justice and the Anthropology of Law* (Cambridge: Cambridge University Press).

Orlove, Benjamin S. and Glynn Custred (eds.) (1980), *Land and Power in Latin America: Agrarian Economies and Social Processes in the Andes* (New York: Holmes and Meir).

Pakulski, Jan (1995), "Social Movements and Class," in Louis Maheu (ed.), *Social Movements and Social Classes*, 55–86 (Thousand Oaks, CA: Sage).
Pallares, Amalia (2002), *From Peasant Struggles to Indian Resistance: The Ecuadorian Andes in the Late Twentieth Century* (Norman: University of Oklahoma Press).
Paschel, Tianna S. (2016), *Becoming Black Political Subjects: Movements and Ethno-Racial Rights in Colombia and Brazil* (Princeton, NJ: Princeton University Press).
Pecheny, Mario (2003), 'Sexual Orientation, AIDS, and Human Rights in Argentina: The Paradox of Social Advance amid health crisis', in Susan E. Eckstein and Timothy P. Wickham-Crowley (eds.) *Struggles for social rights in Latin America*. (New York: Routledge) 262.
Pecheny, Mario (2013), 'Sexual politics and post-neoliberalism in Latin America'. *Scholar & Feminist Online* 11.1-11.2.
Phillips, Lynne and Sally Cole (2009), "Feminist Flows, Feminist Fault Lines: Women's Machineries and Women's Movements in Latin America," *Signs: Journal of Women in Culture and Society* 35(1), 185–211.
Piscopo, Jennifer M. (2015), 'States as gender equality activists: The evolution of quota laws in Latin America', *Latin American Politics and Society* 57(3), 27–49
Polletta, Francesca and James M. Jasper (2001), "Collective Identity and Social Movements," *Annual Review of Sociology* 27(1), 283–305.
Postero, Nancy G. (2007), *Now We Are Citizens: Indigenous Politics in Postmulticultural Bolivia* (Stanford, CA: Stanford University Press).
Rodríguez, Ernesto (2013), "Movimientos juveniles en América Latina: Entre la tradición y la innovación," in Ernesto Rodríguez (ed.) *Movimientos juveniles en América Latina y el Caribe: entre la tradición y la innovación*, 19–37 (Montevideo: CELAJU).
Rossi, Federico M. (2017), *The Poor's Struggle for Political Incorporation: The Piquetero Movement in Argentina* (Cambridge: Cambridge University Press).
Safa, Helen I. (1990), "Women's Social Movements in Latin America," *Gender & Society* 4(3), 354–69.
Seidman, Stevan (1996), *Queer Theory/Sociology* (Oxford: Blackwell Publishers).
Singh, Prerna and Matthias vom Hau (2016), "Ethnicity in Time: Politics, History, and the Relationship between Ethnic Diversity and Public Goods Provision," *Comparative Political Studies* 49(10), 1303–40.
Slater, David (1985), *New Social Movements and the State in Latin America*, vol. 29 (Amsterdam: CEDLA).
Stavenhagen, Rodolfo (2002), "Indigenous Peoples and the State in Latin America: An Ongoing Debate," in Rachel Sider (ed.), *Multiculturalism in Latin America*, 24–44 (London: Palgrave-Macmillan).
Svampa, Maristella (2006), "Movimientos sociales y nuevo escenario regional: Las inflexiones del paradigma neoliberal en América Latina," *Sociohistórica* 19–20, 141–55.
Taylor, Diana (1994), "Performing Gender: Las Madres de la Plaza de Mayo," in Diana Taylor and Juan Villegas (eds.), *Negotiating Performance: Gender, Sexuality, and Theatricality in Latino America*, 275–305 (Durham, NC: Duke University Press).
Touraine, Alain (2005), *Un nouveau paradigme pour comprendre le monde d'aujourd'hui* (Paris: Fayard).
Viveros Vigoya, Mara (2018), 'Race, Indigeneity and Gender: Colombian Feminism Learning, Lessons for Global Feminism', in James W Messerschmidt et al., *Gender Reckonings. New Social Theory and Research* (New York: New York University Press) 90–110.

Walby, Sylvia (2002), "Feminism in a Global era," *Economy and Society* 31(4), 533–57.

Wimmer, Andreas (2013), *Ethnic Boundary Making, Institutions, Power, Networks* (New York: Oxford University Press).

Yashar, Deborah J. (1998), "Contesting Citizenship: Indigenous Movements and Democracy in Latin America," *Comparative Politics* 31(1), 23–42.

Yashar, Deborah J. (2005), *Contesting Citizenship in Latin America: The Rise of Indigenous Movements and the Postliberal Challenge* (Cambridge: Cambridge University Press).

CHAPTER 36

IDEAS, IDEOLOGY, AND CITIZENSHIP OF SOCIAL MOVEMENTS

ANTHONY PETROS SPANAKOS AND MISHELLA ROMO RIVAS

Introduction

Social movements are the result of sustained collectivization of claims in a polity for greater political inclusion, social recognition, and material redistribution. The social movements that emerged during the end of the twentieth and early twenty-first century in Latin America responded to the neoliberal era of state withdrawal and conditions of austerity, what Rossi (2015: 8) calls a period of disincorporation. In their responses, social movements promoted a thick, social citizenship that seeks reincorporation into a newly reinvigorated state, consistent with broader trends in the region towards a post-neoliberal governmentality (Burbach, Fox, and Fuentes 2013; Grugel and Riggirozzi 2012; Spanakos and Pantoulas 2017).

Scholarship on social movements and citizenship assumes that democracy is improved and social movements successful when popular actors receive greater recognition from the state and their claims have more impact in politics. These literatures have focused primarily on the strategic action, tactics, and organizational capacity of movements; how governments and states have responded; and how institutional structures enable, foreclose, and/or respond to such political actions (see della Porta and Diani 2006; McAdam, Tarrow and Tilly 2001; Rossi 2017; Wampler 2015; Yashar 2005, 2007). The valuable insights derived from these literatures can be improved by giving greater consideration to the role of ideas and ideology. This chapter examines four cases of left-wing social movements in Latin America that have resisted neoliberalism, promoted popular sovereignty, and aimed at thickening citizenship and "democratizing

Table 36.1 Concepts of popular sovereignty held by social movements

	Reform	Transformation
National	*Piqueteros* (Argentina)	Indigenous groups (Venezuela)
Local	Zapatistas (Mexico)	*Colectivos* (Venezuela)

democracy" (see Inclán in this volume).[1] These groups might be distinguished based on their tactics (political or bureaucratic) and orientations (bottom-up or top-down; see Silva and Rossi 2018: 13) or by their relationship to institutions (reformist or radical; see Weyland, Madrid, and Hunter 2010). Examining ideology and ideas about popular sovereignty, however, highlights important nuances between movements that might otherwise be grouped together.

The typology introduced here identifies social movements in terms of two core elements of popular sovereignty: (1) the location of the primary space for political activity, and (2) how much transformation of the state and existing political apparatus is sought. Accordingly, the *piqueteros* (picketers) of Argentina see the core of their political struggle occurring at the national level for the sake of restoration of an earlier system of political-economic corporatism while indigenous groups in Venezuela similarly look primarily to national politics but they participate in a broader, more radical effort to transform the state. The Zapatistas in Mexico and *colectivos* (urban collectives) in Venezuela fiercely defend their autonomy over local territory but have different levels of engagement and promotion of political change at the level of the state (see Table 36.1).

Understanding these distinct positions helps explain actions that might otherwise make little sense, such as: why did the Zapatistas not use the massive political and symbolic capital they had in 1994 to push for national level change; why are Venezuelan *colectivos* who share the Zapatistas' zealous defense of the local such fundamental participants in radical state-level change; why are Venezuelan indigenous groups less grounded in local, spatial politics than indigenous groups in other Andean countries; and why do the *piqueteros* operate, despite very distinct tactics, largely in the tradition of Peronism and labor/class-based protests of the past.

SOCIAL MOVEMENTS AND CITIZENSHIP

Social Movements

Social movements are "collective challenges, based on common purposes and social solidarities, in sustained interaction with elites, opponents, and authorities" (Tarrow 1994: 2). Scholars studying social movements have given special consideration to their tactical use of contentious politics (McAdam, Tarrow, and Tilly 2009) to advance claims are often made by marginalized communities for whom regular and formal channels prove inhospitable and, therefore, an alternative means of grievances is sought to achieve political change.

Change, of course, is rare and scholars of social movements ask under what conditions populations with structural political, economic, social, and legal disadvantages vis-à-vis a political system are able to marshal sufficient resources to make successful bids (McAdam 1982; McCarthy and Zald 1977; Meyer and Lupo 2010). Tilly (1978, 1994, 2006) refers to a social movement's Worthiness, Unity, Numbers, and Commitment (WUNC) as critical to its success, and grievance theory (Geschwender 1968; Snow and Soule 2010) speaks of the importance of a claim on/against/for. The emphasis here is on the strategic action of a group in a particular structural situation. Other approaches give more emphasis to identity and framing. Some consider the relationship between identity and symbols to strategies and success (della Porta and Diani 2006: 5–6), while others consider how issues are framed and presented rhetorically (Lindekilde 2014; Snow and Benford 1988; Snow, Vliegenhart, and Ketelaars 2019). Lakoff's (2004) widely cited work on framing and rhetoric in politics encourages the consideration of framing as conjunctural strategic decisions made by leaders rather than as a persistent set of values which may shift in priority or emphasis on specific issues or at particular moments. That is, it lacks the ability to explain long-term perception and action in the way that ideology does. Like the political opportunity and resource mobilization literature, this scholarship gives little attention to ideas and ideology (see Somma, Salman in this volume).

Citizenship and Democracy

Scholars studying citizenship in the context of democratization emphasize overcoming inequalities as a way of building citizenship, especially for marginalized peoples (Diamond 1999; Forment 2013; Hagopian 2007; O'Donnell 2004). This task is paramount in Latin America, where deep-seated inequalities undermine citizenship as a shared set of rights and obligations that are universally enjoyed (Marshall 1963), fostering, instead, the notion that citizenship is thin and "relational" (Da Matta 1987), the result of one's proximity to persons, offices, and resources that confer power and status. Citizenship is critical because it defines "*who* has political membership, *which* rights they possess, and *how* interest intermediation with the state is structured" (Yashar 2005: 6). By logical extension, the depth and breadth of citizenship evidences the amount and quality of democracy in a polity (Diamond 1999).

Arguments on behalf of deepening democracy and enabling a robust citizenship rest heavily on case studies drawn directly from social movements or actions in which social movements figure as primary actors (Alvarez, Dagnino, and Escobar 1998). This scholarship considers how actions challenge entrenched power interests, demonstrate practical deployment of citizenship as a set of practices, and compel institutional bodies to recognize expansion of citizenship either in terms of new rights or groups claiming them (ibid.; Silva 2009; Van Cott 2003). This research gives greater attention to the role played by institutions and political parties in coordinating, enabling, and foreclosing success than is found among social movement studies (Ondetti 2008; Pereira 2012; Roberts 2015; Wampler 2015). Yet, even a volume which deliberately avoids privileging institutions vis-à-vis analysis of grassroots activity (Tulchin and Ruthenberg 2007), fails to evaluate more closely the role of ideas and ideology in shaping those involved in the struggles studied.[2]

Political ethnographies give greater attention to the beliefs and values of popular actors who engage in contentious politics (Azzellini 2018; Ciccariello-Maher 2013; Fernandes 2010; Ferrero 2014; Mora 2015; Pahnke 2018; Postero 2007; Stahler-Sholk 2014; Valencia 2015; Velasco 2011, 2015). As is the case in social movement literature, these scholars emphasize how political actors accomplish social change, particularly when they move "from the streets to the state" (see Gray 2018).

Ideas and Ideology

Ideology is a set of mental concepts that serves as a lens for what one observes and a guide for how one should act (Geertz 1964). It is a space wherein ideas develop, compete, and persuade (or not). The concept fell into disuse since it is associated with irrational behavior and/or slavish devotion to party or cause; analytically, the assumption that ideologies provide "blueprints for revolutionary outcomes" is seen as reducing the roles of agency, institutional structures, and contingency (Skocpol 1979: 170–71). Freeden's (1988) reconceptualization of ideology from a sense of beliefs to a semantic space that changes over time is particularly helpful. It recognizes that ideologies have core and peripheral concepts allowing the same issue to be understood differently by two groups or it could have a similar value but be more core to one and peripheral to another. This notion allows greater space for ambiguity, flexibility, and change, which is particularly helpful in investigating political actors who seem to occupy a very similar space in a simplistic partisan mapping.

Panizza (2009, 2015) shows how changes in ideas can replace a "there is no alternative" argument in favor of one set of policies (such as neoliberalism) with an alternative which is similarly presented as the "only viable option" (also Panizza and Philip 2014). Similarly, Caldeira's (2000) exploration of public tolerance of extra-legal violence against citizens helps explain the lack of will for police reform in democratic Brazil. More recently, Spanakos (2016) examines how ideas on citizenship explain political action and institutional change in Bolivarian Venezuela (see also Spanakos 2008). To argue that ideas matter does not downplay the political maneuvering and tactics pursued by their exponents nor the institutional structure in which such struggles took place (see Gurza Lavalle and Szwako in this volume). Nevertheless, the ideas espoused offered a critical window into what sort of crisis was being experienced and how actors responded (Rueschemeyer 2006).

While the left-wing social movements referred to in this chapter all pursue accomplishing popular sovereignty as the core of democracy, they understand the component parts of popular sovereignty—where rule takes place and how—quite differently. Some groups see it as the direct exercise of governance over a specific territory and others a national government in which the "people" exercise increasing space vis-à-vis a perceived entrenched elite class. Similarly, some see popular sovereignty as being a matter of recognition and redistribution whereas others insist on a much more complete transformation of the state edifice. These differences in ideological positions and concepts about democracy and popular sovereignty render what appear to be similar movements different and these differences, illustrated in the case studies below, are striking and important.

Case Studies

The Zapatistas

The Ejército Zapatista de Liberación Nacional (EZLN), an indigenous movement in Southern Mexico, commenced a rebellion in Chiapas in response to the dismantling of price supports for coffee, official termination of land distribution and reform, and the materialization of the North American Free Trade Agreement (NAFTA) which threatened established social rights for the Indigenous (see Mattiace 2012; Ross 1994; Yashar 2005: 19; Oikonomakis, Rice in this volume). The "traditional guerilla objective of taking state power" (Mora 2007: 65) was short-lived and the government and EZLN signed the San Andrés accords in 1996, which went beyond decentralization and involved "recognizing community-based rights to organize governance as they saw fit through *usos y costumbres* (practices and customs)" (Stahler Sholk 2014: 192). Yet after the Accords were signed, the government took little action to implement them, and the Zapatistas decided to implement the Accords on their own and avoid future involvement with the Mexican government.

The Zapatistas, building on claims of authentic rights on their land, began to design mechanisms for governance. Such claims present a radical statement about who is entitled to participate in rule. A 1995 communique explains:

> [t]hose who plunder or sell off the nation (the PRI, Salinas, etc.) are "foreigners" estranged from their purported motherland, while the indigenous peoples and their supporters are Mexicans, and the EZLN is the only true Mexican army—"Here the only Mexican army is the EZLN. The other is an armed group at the service of the powerful, with neither military honor or shame for serving falsehood." (Máiz 2010: 262, citing EZLN 1995: 41)

So stark was the notion of the "foreigner," that the Zapatistas decided that the civic-political governance of communities within the EZLN itself would not be dependent on the military decisions of the EZLN army but rather on "democratically elected authorities within the villages" (Sixth Declaration of the Selva Lacandona, Section II, para. 3). Moreover, they established *Juntas de Buen Gobierno* to oversee the five municipalities particularly in matters involving conflict resolution and resource distribution (Khasnabish 2010: 155–56). Only members of each community can participate in the governance of same. Governing by obeying (*mandar obedeciendo*) rests on this stark concept of who is part of the community.

The development of inclusion of community members to the exclusion of the Mexican government represents a radical local autonomism and participatory framework (Souza in this volume). This has been and remains the core of the Zapatista political experience. They have eschewed traditional politics to concentrate on establishing governance over the territories they administer in Chiapas and nearby jungle areas (Khasnabish 2010). In negative terms, this has meant "impeding the presence of functionaries and rejecting government development projects, while simultaneously exercising self-government through diverse social programs, such as education, health, and agricultural production" (Mora 2015: 88). In positive terms, the Zapatistas developed unique political administrative organs and processes which did not correspond nor were *de facto* bound by formal constitutional and informal political practices elsewhere in Mexico. They were not absent in national political discussions but, even in periodic marches, celebrations of national indigenous days, or dialogues with leftist and/or indigenous groups in Mexico and beyond, their aim is primarily to maintain and defend the space occupied, as opposed to changing the state structure in Mexico. As Stahler-Sholk (2014: 204) notes, the Zapatistas were reluctant to engage even with the Latin American Left, declining to "send a representative to the inauguration of Bolivia's first Indigenous president."

After more than two decades, unlike most leftist, grassroots groups that emerged in opposition to neoliberalism and privatization, the Zapatistas have not sought to restore the state to its developmentalist structure (Silva and Rossi 2018) nor have they been part of a broad revolutionary agenda. Rather, their goal was autonomy *from* the political economic structure of the state, which was very radical but also unexpectedly territorially limited.

Colectivos in Venezuela

The *colectivos* in Venezuela have demonstrated a preference for collective decision-making and local autonomy while being leading voices in terms of radical change of the state. They emerged in Caracas during the mid-1980s in an effort to address various unmet democratic needs of the densely populated urban barrios. With the decline of the distributional largesse of the Venezuelan petrostate, the urban poor endured the steady growth of inflation, unemployment, poor public service provision, and human insecurity. Residents created *barrio*-based[3] collectives to advance their decision-making role in local politics. The *La Piedrita* collective was involved in reclaiming spaces where drug traffickers operated, cleaning public areas for community use, and assembling brigades to paint murals as a form of political and social protest (Fernandes 2010: 61; Martinez, Fox and Farrell 2010).

Although the 1998 election of Hugo Chávez opened the possibility for many left-leaning local organized and non-organized peoples to cohere into more politically salient bodies which would be viewed favorably vis-à-vis state recognition (Spanakos 2008), members of *colectivos* regularly remind themselves, visiting academics, and politicians that they are "rebels" (Velasco 2011) and that they were "Chavistas before Chávez." The narrative of pre-Chávez Bolivarianism functions like a myth of a social contract, analytically difficult to falsify, yet meaningful because it gives the *colectivos* and their goals legitimacy prior to Chávez. Thus, they can claim "We created Chávez" (Ciccariello-Maher 2013). This language was not simply a response to opposition narratives which saw followers of duped by Chávez's populist rhetoric, but also as an occasional warning to politicians within the *Proceso* (the Bolivarian Revolutionary "Process") that they were and remained independent even of electoral movements and parties which had delivered substantial material and non-material goods to them. This autonomy remains a fundamental element of *colectivo* discourse and action, and it is evidenced by their periodic lukewarm support or unexpected silence for Chavista and Nicolás Maduro's proposals (such as the tepid support of the *colectivos* for the Constitutional Reform Referendum of 2007).

Colectivos have been known not only to occupy and take over government offices run by opposition figures (Valencia 2015) but also to close off or deny entry to political figures who want to visit "their" *barrio*. The message is clear: "Here, La Piedrita gives the orders and the government obeys" (Ciccariello-Maher 2013: 3). In 2005, the *Coordinadora Simón Bolívar* ousted the Metropolitan Police from the *barrio* noting that the force was unable to protect the community due to its involvement in repression and drug trade. In October of 2014, the *5 de Marzo Colectivo* planned a rally to the Attorney General's to demand the removal of sitting Minister of the Interior, Miguel Rodríguez, who the group accused of being responsible for an operation led by an investigative police unit which left one of its leaders dead. Yet, abruptly, the scheduled march was canceled and by the following day, the public official had been publicly dismissed by President Maduro. Smilde and Pérez Hernáiz (2014) considered this event as telling of the tenuous state monopoly on violence. The other side of the state's lack of monopoly is the effort of the collective to monopolize local political space even to the exclusion of political officials of sympathetic parties.

The idea of the government serving the people is not atypical among democratic discourses, but the particular way in which it is tied to an activist notion of a people working out and through their constituent power is (Dussel 2006). Indeed, many *colectivos* display ideological tendencies which understand popular sovereignty as the enacting of constituent power so as to render constituted power irrelevant. This creates a potential problem, as the same actors who champion a nationwide movement to root out elites and privileged sectors (in government office and elsewhere) require government power to challenge elites and materially and politically empower the *colectivos* in the first place. The *colectivos* have limited resources, and only limited voice without a government that advocates on their behalf. And yet, they are very clear that the government cannot expect uncritical support.

The *colectivos* share core notions of radical, left-populist notions of democracy and class struggle promoted by Chávez, Maduro, and the leadership of the Bolivarian process. But these notions have been leveraged to support a more core notion of autonomy which renders popular sovereignty something intensely local. While there is significant criticism about how much the state has co-sponsored Bolivarianism, it is difficult to overlook how Bolivarian ideas have absorbed notions surrounding the practice of *poder popular*, which resists the non-neutral capitalist logic of the state (see Azzellini 2018). This process along with the election of Chávez has yielded "new political ontologies" that have made politics and citizenship ubiquitous and ambitious (Spanakos 2008; Spanakos and Pantoulas 2017: 45). As in the case of the Zapatistas, this process is wide-ranging and deep on local issues and seeks to squeeze out any presence of a competing political body within the territory it occupies. However, unlike the Zapatistas, the *colectivos* are critical actors in a national process of radical change.

Piqueteros

The Argentine *piqueteros* challenge to the political, legal, and economic order is based on claims of recognition and *re*-integration into a nation-state mediated corporate structure, evidencing "a Peronist, nostalgic, national–populist social matrix" (Rossi 2013; Svampa and Pereyra 2003: 195–96). The movement first surfaced during the 1990s in conjunction with other "broader-based popular movements, organized against local governments and corporations in the context of a growing economic crisis" (Sitrin 2014: 212) and their moniker derived from their blocking of roads (*piquetes*). Though the initial scope of the *piqueteros* was local, it quickly expanded and eventually coalesced a multitude of social movement organizations with a variety of ideological orientations and goals. However diverse the goals, this reincorporation movement has core categories (disincorporation of the 1970s, their "claims for inclusion," opposition to neoliberalism) and "non-central categories" (mode of protest, leadership, organization format, and perception of democracy) (Rossi 2015: 4–5).

Piqueteros responded to the unemployment resulting from the large-scale privatization programs of President Carlos Menem by organizing roadblocks (Silva 2009). While neoliberal reforms were attempting to instill a "provincialization of politics" by shifting the "locus of protest to provincial governments" (Rossi 2018: 82), the *piqueteros* blocked highways in Buenos Aires in 2001, thereby nationalizing their grievances and becoming the new interlocutor between the unemployed and the national government (Wolff 2007: 8). The widespread media coverage of the blockades revealed how the movement had "replac[ed] the traditional Argentine means of working-class action, the strike" (Prevost 2012: 24–25) and encouraged other instances of collective action. According to Wolff (2007: 6) "in 1997 there were already 170 piquetes across the country, escalating year on year to 252 (1999), 514 (2000), 1,383 (2001) and 2,336 (2002) roadblocks."

The unrest led to the resignation of President Fernando de la Rúa (1999–2001) and then a period of acute government crisis which forced the state to recognize the movement. An initial truce and then collaboration with the Néstor Kirchner government (2003–2005) led to a "reincorporation process" (Rossi 2015: 15). Yet this had its costs. Though many *piqueteros* were popularly elected to executive and legislative positions since 2005, as well as occupied posts in the ministries and provincial deputy positions, they were not "allowed" to "occupy an agency in the trade union–controlled Ministry of Labor" and there was "the impossibility of transcending the PJ [Peronist *Partido Justicialista*] structure of horizontally and vertically uncoordinated informal, individualized, and territorialized links" thereby positioning the *piqueteros* as "secondary actors" (ibid.: 16). This had repercussions since it gave way to schisms within the movement between outsiders and insiders. The former found itself confronting limited resources and the latter with the inherent structural constraints involved in joining the state or "dancing with dynamite" (Dangl 2010).

Ultimately, the movement contributed to national politics in terms of accountability (through the resignation of various presidents) and recognition (from newly elected ones) and received concrete responses to their grievances (amongst these, employment programs). They engaged in innovative strategies which seemed radical but their ultimate claims upon the system were reformist. Moreover, they saw popular sovereignty as a matter of inclusion in the national corporatist state machinery not as governing local territories, as is the case for the Zapatistas and Venezuelan *colectivos*.

Indigenous in Venezuela

Popular sovereignty for the indigenous in Venezuela involves recognition, self-representation, and a state that promotes and supports cultural rights, diametrically opposed to a monocultural, liberal, political model that existed prior to 1999. Prior to then, indigenous policy was scant, and the national census did not include "indigenous" as a category (Angosto-Ferrández 2015: 58). Indigenous political efforts between the 1970s and 1990s were largely reactive and episodic, and this was even after the creation of the Consejo Nacional Indio de Venezuela (CONIVE) in 1989. Given the limited institutionalized recognition of indigenous communities and the small, dispersed indigenous population, Venezuela was considered by close observers to be a "least likely case of marginalized groups obtaining constitutional rights" (Van Cott 2003: 50). Since 1999, however, the Venezuelan indigenous movements have operated within a multiculturalist framework which recognizes the indigenous as part of a "multiethnic and pluricultural state" (Bello 2005; Ramirez and Maisley 2016; Tushnet 2017: 134; Van Cott 2003: 65). Quickly, the CONIVE became the recognized "interlocutor with state organs" and "a pivotal organization in the selection of candidates for seats allocated for indigenous representations at the national level" (Angosto-Ferrández 2015: 74).

Following the promulgation of the new constitution, CONIVE remained in politics and produced candidates for electoral contests with a small number of victories in national parliamentary elections over the past fifteen years. And, as Van Cott (2003) noted, the 1999 Constitution, as well as subsequent public declarations (such as the 2014 declaration of a day of the indigenous) and distributions of land to indigenous groups, represent important changes vis-à-vis indigenous politics. Yet the establishment of the new constitutional order, however, has neither prioritized indigenous agency in decision-making nor corresponded to territorial control which are elements typically found in indigenous-driven movements elsewhere (Angosto-Ferrández 2015, Augsburger and Haber 2018; see Fernandes Mançano in this volume).

The perception that the previous regime did not recognize the indigenous facilitates a willingness to support radical change particularly as a national revolutionary agenda presented itself. These tendencies encourage the absorption of CONIVE's pursuit of popular sovereignty into a broader, cleavage-crossing revolutionary movement as recognition of indigenous claims are grounded in broader rights to be recognized which it shares (ideologically and in organizational/activist performance) with Afro-Venezuelans, Women's Groups, and many other very diverse groups (Herrera Salas 2005).[4] Even the least pliant groups that try to make claims over territory and its resources understand that the national political space is central to political decision-making, so much so that Fernandes (2010) conceptualizes their rebellions as a form of "coalitional politics."

Like other Bolivarian movements, indigenous groups in Venezuela have, by and large demonstrated strong support for an activist and revolutionary state which plays a central role in socioeconomic inclusion in the arenas of education, health, and access to information. Many indigenous communal councils were created through the support of the Ministry of Popular Power (MIMPI)[5] and, more generally speaking, indigenous groups have been direct beneficiaries of the government's national projects of development (which have an anti-neoliberal connotation and orientation). Many of these benefits and forms of inclusion were enabled by the legal changes following the Bolivarian process. Given the Bolivarian movements' role in fomenting the positioning of indigenous groups in national politics, organizations such as CONIVE are quick to embrace the discourse of constitutionalism to both assert and defend its popular sovereignty, especially when it is threatened.

The danger of a return to the Constitutional framework of 1961, which was essentially the "hemisphere's least-modern regime of indigenous rights" (Van Cott 2003: 51), is one of the core motivators of the movement. For instance, during the briefly successful coup of 2002, CONIVE publicly declared the illegitimacy of Chavez's successor due to the extra-legal nature of his self-proclamation (Consejo Nacional Indio de Venezuela 2002; Herrera Salas 2005). This response is connected to a particular feature of Neo-Indigenismo, which sees recognition as so fundamental that any return to a prior a political order is unacceptable. Consequently, indigenous populations have since 1999 seen institutions and the state as a venue which will not only activate participation and self-representation, but which should continue to maintain a "regime of separate cultural rights, recognition, and autonomy" (Aguilar Rivera 2013: 598; Herrera Salas 2005).

Taking together the historical marginalization and decentralized organization of indigenous groups in Venezuela (vis-à-vis other ethnic movements in the region) pre-1999 with the core ideas of Neo-Indigenismo, it becomes clear why CONIVE consistently locates sovereignty within the institutional framework of the state. Noelí Pocaterra, the most recognizable politician associated with CONIVE when elected to the Constituent Assembly in 2017, insisted that this new body would not change the rights established with the 1999 Charter claiming that "The Bolivarian Revolution continues to take us into account" (Agencia Venezolana de Noticias 2017). This is much different from claims made by the candidate and leader of the *La Piedrita colectivo*, Valentin Santana, who explicitly asserted that his priority was to "deepen the [Bolivarian] Revolution" (El Tiempo 2017: para. 16). The former engaged in promoting the protection of multicultural citizenship (that secures the legal status quo) through a constituent assembly while the latter is driven by a revolutionary insurgent citizenship that aims to reorient and radicalize the state. But the continuation of the Bolivarian Revolution is seen as a precondition for the maintenance of recognition in national politics.

Conclusion

This chapter has focused on four social movements which share left-wing roots, antineoliberal politics, and make demands for recognition of marginal groups as part of a process of a thick form of citizenship. While all emphasize popular sovereignty, they differ considerably on how and where they rule. These differences can be tied to the ideological positions which flesh out "popular sovereignty" for the different movements. Specifically, CONIVE and the *colectivos* seek to transform the state, the *piqueteros* to restore an earlier corporatist model, and the Zapatistas are relatively quietist vis-à-vis the state. This is not to say that *piqueteros* and Zapatistas are not radical. The Zapatistas, like the *colectivos*, have pursued a deep form of political autonomy that is audacious in its efforts at both self-governance and exclusion of "outsiders." For CONIVE and the *piqueteros*, popular rule has meant supporting governments that are more inclusive and which invite their leaders to participate in ministries and decision-making.

Ultimately, each group occupies space but the primary spaces (local vs. national) of politics as well as the scope of change sought in the national political, economic, and legal framework differ profoundly. As a result, so do the goals, tactics, and outcomes of these groups. The outcomes can be examined through study of tactics or through interaction between movements and institutions, as is common in the social movement and citizenship literatures respectively. But the former would suggest that the *piqueteros* are more radical than would be expected given their ultimate political aims while the latter is likely to conflate CONIVE and the *colectivos* because they both support a state transformation project. Beginning from the motivating ideas and the ideology of the movements, however, allows for greater nuance and better explains the different tactics and outcomes of social movements.

Acknowledgements

The authors are very grateful to Federico Rossi for his excellent comments on earlier drafts of this chapter.

Notes

1. Clearly, not all social movements, nor anti-neoliberal nor democratizing politics, are on the political left. The aim here is not to show the diversity of possibilities for all social movements but to demonstrate the importance of ideology and ideas through selection of cases that seem to operate in the same space (Seawright and Gerring 2008).
2. The valuable frameworks of Holston (2007) and Armony (2007) are scholarly explanations of what is happening rather than an explanation of how actors involved perceive their actions.
3. *Barrio* normally translates as "neighborhood" but, in Venezuela, it refers to a poor neighborhood and/or shanty-town. *Urbanización* is used for a middle class or wealthy neighborhood.
4. Of course, this conscious trade-off is not one endorsed by all indigenous movements. For instance, the Yukpa movement in the northwest of Venezuela, has been a notable exception since it has been deliberately reluctant to trust party politics and the state-sponsored indigenous groups. The Yukpa movement saw government projects involving mining as a direct threat to their existence. Still, even this movement cannot be not fully "anti-statist" or autonomous as it benefits from state presence in their regions economically (as evidenced by the funding they receive and rely on from communal councils) and from the state's security (from paramilitary activity in their regions) and so on (Angosto-Ferrández 2015: 199).
5. This organization "prioritizes the creation of indigenous communal councils and communes at the expense of the ideals of strong autonomous territorialization envisaged by the 1999 Constitution . . . In fact, [former] minister Nicia Maldonado declared on several occasions that the creations of communes was an alternative route to the demarcation of indigenous lands" (Angosto-Ferrández 2015: 175).

References

Agencia Venezolana de Noticias (2017), "Noelí Pocaterra: La Revolución Bolivariana sigue tomando en cuenta a los pueblos indígenas," www.avn.info.ve/contenido/noelí-pocaterra-revolución-bolivariana-sigue-tomando-cuenta-pueblos-indígenas.

Aguilar Rivera, José Antonio (2013), "Latin American Political Ideologies," in Michael Freeden and Marc Stears (ed.), *The Oxford Handbook of Political Ideologies*, 583–606 (Oxford University Press).

Angosto-Ferrández, Luis F. (eds.), *Venezuela Reframed: Bolivarianism, Indigenous Peoples and Socialisms of the Twenty-first Century* (London: Zed).

Alvarez, Sonia E., Evelina Dagnino, and Arturo Escobar (1998), *Cultures of Politics/Politics of Cultures: Re-visioning Latin American Social Movements* (Boulder, CO: Westview Press).

Armony, Ariel C. (2007), "Fields of Citizenship," in Joseph S. Tulchin and Meg Ruthenburg (eds.), *Citizenship in Latin America*, 95–110 (Boulder, CO: Lynne Rienner).

Augsburger, Aaron and Paul Haber (2018), "Constructing Indigenous Autonomy in Plurinational Bolivia: Possibilities and Ambiguities," *Latin American Perspectives* 45(6), 53–67.

Azzellini, Dario (2018), *Communes and Workers' Control in Venezuela: Building 21st Century Socialism from Below* (Chicago: Haymarket).

Bello, Luis Jesús (2005), *Derechos de los pueblos indígenas en el nuevo ordenamiento jurídico venezolano* (Copenhagen: IWGIA).

Benford, Robert D. and David A. Snow (2000), "Framing Processes and Social Movements: An Overview and Assessment," *Annual Review of Sociology* 26, 611–39.

Betances, Emelio and Carlos Figueroa Ibarra (eds.) (2016), *Popular Sovereignty and Constituent Power in Latin America* (New York: Palgrave-Macmillan).

Burbach, Roger, Michael Fox, and Federico Fuentes (2013), *Latin America's Turbulent Transitions: The Future of Twenty-First Century Socialism* (London: Zed).

Caldeira, Teresa P. (2000), *City of Walls: Crime, Segregation, and Citizenship in São Paulo* (Berkeley and Los Angeles: University of California Press).

Ciccariello-Maher, George (2013), *We Created Chávez: A People's History of the Venezuelan Revolution* (Durham, NC: Duke University Press).

Ciccariello-Maher, George (2014), "Venezuela: Bolivarianism and the Commune," in Richard Stahler-Sholk, Harry E. Vanden, and Marc Becker (eds.), *Rethinking Latin American Social Movements Radical Action from Below* (London: Rowman & Littlefield), 209–32.

CONIVE (2002), *Declaración del Consejo Nacional Indio de Venezuela, Abril 2002*, http://www memoriacommx/160/Declaracionhtm.

Da Matta, Roberto (1987), "The Quest for Citizenship in a Relational Universe," in John Wirth, Edson de Oliveira Nunes, and Thomas Bogenschild (eds.), *State and Society in Brazil*, 307–35 (Stanford, CA: Stanford University Press).

Dangl, Benjamin (2010), *Dancing with Dynamite: Social Movements and States in Latin America* (Oakland, CA: AK Press).

della Porta, Donatella, and Mario Diani (2006), Social Movements: An Introduction. (Malden, MA: Blackwell Publishing).

Diamond, Larry (1999), *Developing Democracy: Toward Consolidation* (Baltimore, MD: Johns Hopkins University Press).

Dussel, Enrique (2006), *Twenty Theses on Politics* (Durham, NC: Duke University Press).

El Tiempo (2017), "Las Propuestas de los Candidatos a la Constituyente de Maduro," *El Tiempo*, July 23, https://www.eltiempo.com/mundo/latinoamerica/propuestas-de-candidatos-a-la-constituyente-de-venezuela-112056.

Escobar, Arturo and Sonia E. Alvarez (eds.) (1992), The Making of Social Movements in Latin America: Identity, Strategy, and Democracy (Boulder, CO: Westview Press).

EZLN (1995), "Comunicado sobre el festejo de la independencia," in *Documentos y Comunicados 2*, 41–45 (Ciudad de México: Era).

EZLN (2005), "Sixth Declaration of the Selva Lacandona," *Enlace Zapatista*, https://enlacezapatista.ezln.org.mx/sdsl-en/.

Fernandes, Sujatha (2010), *Who Can Stop the Drums? Urban Social Movements in Chávez's Venezuela* (Durham, NC: Duke University Press).

Ferrero, Juan Pablo (2014), *Democracy Against Neoliberalism in Argentina and Brazil: A Move to the Left* (New York: Palgrave-Macmillan).

Forment, Carlos, A. (2013), "Argentina's Recuperated Factory Movement and Citizenship: An Arendtian Perspective," in Mario Sznajder, Luis Roniger, and Carlos Forment (eds.), *Shifting Frontiers of Citizenship: The Latin American Experience*, 187–218 (Leiden: Brill).

Freeden, Michael (1998), *Ideologies and Political Theory: A Conceptual Approach* (Oxford: Oxford University Press).

Geertz, Clifford (1964), "Ideology as a Cultural System," in David Ernest Apter (ed.), *Ideology and Discontent*, 47–76 (New York: Free Press of Glencoe).

Geschwender, James (1968), "Explorations in the Theory of Social Movements and Revolutions Social Forces," *Social Forces* 47(2), 127–35.

Gottberg, Luis Duno (2011), "The Color of Mobs Racial Politics, Ethnopopulism, and Representation in the Chávez Era," in Daniel Hellinger and David Smilde (eds.), *Venezuela's Bolivarian Democracy: Participation, Politics and Culture under Chávez*, 273–94 (Durham, NC: Duke University Press).

Gray, Paul Christopher (eds.) (2018), *From the Streets to the State: Changing the World by Taking Power* (New York: SUNY Press).

Grugel, Jean and Pia Riggirozzi (2012), "Post-Neoliberalism in Latin America: Rebuilding and Reclaiming the State after Crisis," *Development and Change* 43(1), 1–21.

Hagopian, Frances (2007), "Latin American Citizenship and Democratic Theory," in Joseph Tulchin and Margaret Ruthenburg (eds.), *Analyzing Citizenship in Latin American Democracies*, 11–56 (Boulder, CO: Lynne Rienner).

Herrera Salas, Jesús María (2005), "Ethnicity and Revolution: The Political Economy of Racism in Venezuela," *Latin American Perspectives* 32(2), 72–91.

Hochstetler, Kathryn (2000), "Democratizing Pressures from Below? Social Movements in the New Brazilian Democracy," in Peter R. Kingstone and Timothy J. Power, (eds.), *Democratic Brazil: Actors, Institutions, and Processes*, 167–82 (Pittsburgh, PA: University of Pittsburgh Press).

Holloway, John (2002), *Change the World Without Taking Power* (New York: Pluto).

Holloway, John (2011), *'Zapatismo' seminario subjetividad y teoría crítica*, wwwjohnhollowaycommx/2011/07/30/zapatismo/.

Holston, James (2007), "Citizenship in Disjunctive Democracies," in Joseph S. Tulchin and Meg Ruthenburg (eds.), *Citizenship in Latin America*, 75–94 (Boulder, CO: Lynne Rienner).

Khasnabish, Alex (2010), *Zapatistas: Rebellion from the Grassroots to the Global* (London: Zed).

Lakoff, George (2004), *Don't Think of an Elephant! Know Your Values and Frame the Debate The Essential Guide for Progressives* (White River Junction: Chelsea Green Publishing).

Lindekilde, Lasse (2014), "Discourse and Frame Analysis: In-Depth Analysis of Qualitative Data in Social Movement Studies," in Donatella della Porta (ed.), *Methodological Practices in Social Movement Research*, 195–227 (Oxford: Oxford University Press).

Máiz, Ramón (2010), "The Indian Heart of the Nation: The Evolution of the Political Discourse of the EZLN in Mexico (1993–2009)," *Latin American and Caribbean Ethnic Studies* 5(3), 245–72.

Marshall, Thomas H. (1963), *Sociology at the Crossroads* (London: Heinemann).

Martinez, Carlos, Michael Fox, and JoJo Farrell (2010), *Venezuela Speaks! Voices from the Grassroots* (Oakland, CA: PM Press).

Mattiace, Shannan (2012), "Social and Indigenous Movements in Mexico's Transition to Democracy," in Roderic Ai Camp (eds.), *The Oxford Handbook of Mexican Politics*, 1–29 (Oxford: Oxford University Press).

McAdam, Doug (1982), *Political Process and the Development of Black Insurgency, 1930–1970* (Chicago: University of Chicago Press).

McAdam, Doug, Sidney Tarrow, and Charles Tilly (2001), *Dynamics of Contention* (Cambridge: Cambridge University Press).

McAdam, Doug, Sidney Tarrow, and Charles Tilly (2009), "Comparative Perspectives on Contentious Politics," in Mark Irving Lichbach and Alan S Zuckerman (eds.), *Comparative Politics: Rationality, Culture, and Structure*, 260–90 (Cambridge: Cambridge University Press).

McCarthy, John D. and Mayer N. Zald (1977), "Resource Mobilization and Social Movements: A Partial Theory," *American Journal of Sociology* 82(6), 1212–41.

Meyer, David S. and Lindsey Lupo (2010), "Assessing the Politics of Protest Political Science and the Study of Social Movements," in Conny Roggeband and Bert Klandermans (eds.), *The Handbook of Social Movements Across Disciplines*, 111–56 (New York: Springer).

Mora, Mariana (2007), "Zapatista Anticapitalist Politics and the 'Other Campaign': Learning from the Struggle for Indigenous Rights and Autonomy," *Latin American Perspectives* 34(2), 64–77.

Mora, Mariana (2015), "The Politics of Justice: Zapatista Autonomy at the Margins of the Neoliberal Mexican State," *Latin American and Caribbean Ethnic Studies* 10(1), 87–106.

O'Donnell, Guillermo (2004), "Why the Rule of Law Matters," *Journal of Democracy* 15(4), 32–46.

Ondetti, Gabriel A. (2008), *Land Protest and Politics: The Landless Movement and the Struggle for Agrarian Reform in Brazil* (University Park: Penn State University Press).

Pahnke, Anthony (2018), *Brazil's Long Revolution: Radical Achievements of the Landless Workers Movement* (Tucson: Arizona University Press).

Panizza, Francisco (2005), *Populism and the Mirror of Democracy* (London: Verso).

Panizza, Francisco (2009), *Contemporary Latin America: Development and Democracy Beyond the Washington Consensus* (London: Zed).

Panizza, Francisco (2015), "Populism, Social Democracy and the Tale of the 'Two Lefts' in Latin America," in Anthony Petros Spanakos and Francisco Panizza (eds.), *Conceptualising Comparative Politics*, 192–214 (New York: Routledge).

Panizza, Francisco and George Philip (eds.) (2014), *Moments of Truth: The Politics of Financial Crises in Comparative Perspective* (London: Routledge).

Pereira, Anthony (2012), "Human Rights and Military Abuses," in Peter Kingstone and Deborah J. Yashar (eds.), *The Routledge Handbook of Latin American Politics*, 114–30 (New York: Routledge).

Postero, Nancy G. (2007), *Now We are Citizens: Indigenous Politics in Postmulticultural Bolivia* (Stanford, CA: Stanford University Press).

Prevost, Gary (2012), "Argentina's Social Movements: Confrontation and Co-optation," in Gary Prevost, Carlos Oliva Camps, and Harry E. Vanden (eds.), *Social Movements and Leftist Governments in Latin America Confrontation or Co-optation?*, 22–33 (New York: Zed).

Ramirez, Silvina and Nahuel Maisley (2016), "The Protection of the Rights of Indigenous Peoples," in *The Latin American Casebook: Courts, Rights, and the Constitution* (eds.), Roberto Gargarella and Juan Gonzalez, 189–208 (London: Routledge).

Roberts, Kenneth M. (2015), "Populism, Social Movements, and Popular Subjectivity," in Donatella della Porta and Mario Diani (eds.), *The Oxford Handbook of Social Movements*, 681–95 (Oxford: Oxford University Press).

Ross, John (1994), *Rebellion from the Roots: Indian Uprising in Chiapas* (Monroe, ME: Common Courage Press).

Rossi, Federico M. (2013), "Piqueteros (workers/unemployment movement in Argentina)," in David A. Snow, Donatella della Porta, Bert Klandermans, and Doug McAdam (eds.), *The Wiley-Blackwell Encyclopedia of Social and Political Movements*, 929–32 (Oxford: Wiley-Blackwell).

Rossi, Federico M. (2015), "The Second Wave of Incorporation in Latin America: A Conceptualization of the Quest for Inclusion Applied to Argentina," *Latin American Politics and Society* 57(1), 1–28.

Rossi, Federico M. (2017), *The Poor's Struggle for Political Incorporation: The Piquetero Movement in Argentina* (Cambridge: Cambridge University Press).

Rossi, Federico M. (2018), "Social Movements, the New 'Social Question,' and the Second Incorporation of the Popular Sectors in Argentina and Brazil," in Eduardo Silva and Federico M. Rossi (eds.), *Reshaping the Political Arena in Latin America: From Resisting Neoliberalism to the Second Incorporation*, 78–112 (Pittsburgh, PA: University of Pittsburgh Press).

Rueschemeyer, Dietrich (2006), "Why and How Ideas Matter," in Robert Goodin and Charles Tilly (eds.), *The Oxford Handbook of Contextual and Political Analysis*, 227–51 (New York: Oxford University Press).

Seawright, Jason and John Gerring (2008), "Case Selection Techniques in Case Study Research: A Menu of Qualitative and Quantitative Options," *Political Research Quarterly* 61(2), 294–308.

Silva, Eduardo (2009), *Challenging Neoliberalism in Latin America* (Cambridge: Cambridge University Press).

Silva, Eduardo and Federico M. Rossi (eds.) (2018), *Reshaping the Political Arena in Latin America: From Resisting Neoliberalism to the Second Incorporation* (Pittsburgh, PA: University of Pittsburgh Press).

Sitrin Marina (2014), "Argentina Against and Beyond the State," in Richard Stahler-Sholk, Harry E. Vanden, and Marc Becker (eds), *Rethinking Latin American Social Movements Radical Action from Below*, 209–32 (London: Rowman & Littlefield).

Skocpol, Theda (1979), *States and Social Revolutions: A Comparative Analysis of France, Russia, and China* (New York: Cambridge University Press).

Smilde, David and Hugo Pérez Hernáiz (2014), "Removal of Minister Reveals Tenuous State Monopoly on Violence," *Venezuelan Politics and Human Rights Blog*, Washington Office on Latin America (WOLA), October 27, https://venezuelablogorg/removal-of-minister-reveals-tenuous-state-monopoly/.

Snow, David A. and Robert D. Benford (1988), "Ideology, Frame Resonance, and Participant Mobilization," in Bert Klandermans, Hanspeter Kriesi, and Sidney G. Tarrow (eds.), *From*

Structure on Action: Comparing Social Movement Across Cultures, 197–217 (Greenwich, CT: JAI Press).

Snow, David A. and Sarah A. Soule, (2010), *A Primer on Social Movements: Contemporary Societies* (New York: W. W. Norton).

Snow, David A., Rens Vliegenhart, and Pauline Ketelaars (2019), "The Framing Perspective on Social Movements: Its Conceptual Roots and Architecture," in David A. Snow, Sarah A. Soule, Hanspeter Kriesi, and Holly J McCammon (eds.), *The Wiley-Blackwell Companion to Social Movements*, 392–410 (Oxford: Wiley-Blackwell).

Spanakos, Anthony Petros (2008), "New Wine, Old Bottles, Flamboyant Sommelier: Chávez, Citizenship, and Populism," *New Political Science* 30(4), 521–44.

Spanakos, Anthony Petros (2016), "Institutionalism and Political Change in Bolivarian Venezuela," in Anthony Petros Spanakos and Francisco Panizza (eds.), *Conceptualising Comparative Politics*, 215–241 (New York: Routledge).

Spanakos, Anthony Petros and Dimitris Pantoulas (2017), "The Contribution of Hugo Chávez to an Understanding of Post-Neoliberalism," *Latin American Perspectives* 44(1), 37–53.

Stahler-Sholk, Richard (2014), "Mexico: Autonomy, Collective Identity, and the Zapatista Social Movement," in Richard Stahler-Sholk, Harry E. Vanden, and Marc Becker (eds.), *Rethinking Latin American Social Movements Radical Action from Below*, 187–207 (London: Rowman & Littlefield).

Svampa, Maristella and Sebastián Pereyra (2003), *Entre la ruta y el barrio: La experiencia de las organizaciones piqueteras* (Buenos Aires: Biblos).

Tarrow, Sidney (1994), *Power in Movement: Social Movements and Contentious Politics* (Cambridge: Cambridge University Press).

Tilly, Charles (1978), *From Mobilization to Revolution* (New York: McGraw-Hill).

Tilly, Charles (1994), "Social Movements as Historically Specific Clusters of Political Performances," *Berkeley Journal of Sociology* 38, 1–30.

Tilly, Charles (1995), *Popular Contention in Great Britain 1758–1834* (Cambridge, MA: Harvard University Press).

Tilly, Charles (2006), *Regimes and Repertoires* (Chicago: Chicago University Press).

Tulchin, Joseph S. and Meg Ruthenburg (2007), *Citizenship in Latin America* (Boulder, CO: Lynne Rienner).

Tushnet, Mark (2017), "The New 'Bolivarian' Constitutions: A Textual Analysis," in Rosalind Dixon and Tom Ginsburg (eds.) (2017), *Comparative Constitutional Law in Latin America*, 126–52 (Northampton: Edward Elgar).

Valencia, Cristóbal (2015), *We Are the State! Barrio Activism in Venezuela's Bolivarian Revolution* (Tucson: University of Arizona Press).

Van Cott, Donna Lee (2003), "Andean Indigenous Movements and Constitutional Transformation: Venezuela in Comparative Perspective," *Latin American Perspectives* 30(1), 49–69.

Velasco, Alejandro (2011), "We Are Still Rebels: The Challenge of Popular History in Bolivarian Venezuela," in David Smilde and Daniel Hellinger (eds.), *Venezuela's Bolivarian Democracy: Participation, Politics, and Culture Under Chavez*, 157–85 (Durham, NC: Duke University Press).

Velasco, Alejandro (2015), *Barrio Rising: Urban Popular Politics and the Making of Modern Venezuela* (Berkeley and Los Angeles: University of California Press).

Villalón, Roberta (2007), "Neoliberalism, Corruption, and Legacies of Contention: Argentina's Social Movements, 1993–2006," *Latin American Perspectives* 34(2), 139–56.

Wampler, Brian (2015), *Activating Democracy in Brazil: Popular Participation, Social Justice, and Interlocking Institutions* (Notre Dame, IN: University of Notre Dame).

Weyland, Kurt, Raul L. Madrid, and Wendy Hunter (eds.) (2010), *Leftist Governments in Latin America: Successes and Shortcomings* (New York: Cambridge University Press).

Wolff, Jonas (2007), "(De-)Mobilising the Marginalised: A Comparison of the Argentine Piqueteros and Ecuador's Indigenous Movement," *Journal of Latin American Studies* 39(1), 1–29.

Yashar, Deborah J. (2005), *Contesting Citizenship in Latin America: The Rise of Indigenous Movements and the Postliberal Challenge* (New York: Cambridge University Press).

Yashar, Deborah J. (2007), "Citizenship Regimes, the State, and Ethnic Cleavages," in Joseph S. Tulchin and Meg Ruthenburg (eds.), *Citizenship in Latin America*, 59–74 (Boulder, CO: Lynne Rienner).

CHAPTER 37

RELIGIOUS GROUPS AND SOCIAL MOVEMENTS IN LATIN AMERICA

ROBERT SEAN MACKIN

Introduction

Religious organizations have been the crucibles of social movements from across the political spectrum in Latin America (Zald and McCarthy 2017 [1987]). Scholars have analyzed indigenous movements, political parties, gender, and LGBT equality movements, and in each case religious organizations and individuals have often played important roles. In some cases, movements retain their religious character, but in others, they appear secular, even if composed of religious individuals (Mackin 2015). For this chapter, our focus will be on social movements in religious groups and how they impact the public sphere.

The 1960s were a turning point: a period of dramatic religious innovation and experimentation in Latin American religion. From 1962–1965, Roman Catholic bishops and cardinals gathered in Rome for the Second Vatican Council. The reforms from that council continue to influence Catholicism in Latin America and around the world. At the same time, Latin American Evangelical Protestants, especially Pentecostals, initiated a wave of evangelization which transformed the character of belief and practice in the region. Research on the Latin American religious field reveals an area undergoing rapid change. A brief sketch of those changes would include the following.

There is a scholarly consensus that the Catholic Church's hegemony in Latin America has ended and instead we have seen the emergence and consolidation of religious pluralism in many parts of Latin America. Several movements trace their origins or saw key turning points in the 1960s. Catholic lay activists were inspired by the reforms of the Second Vatican Council (Vatican II) from 1962–1965 and the second meeting of the Conferencia General del Episcopado Latinoamericano (CELAM II) in Medellín, Colombia. Some scholars (Casanova 2018; Martin 1990) suggest the reforms from Vatican II and Medellín amounted to the voluntary disestablishment of Roman

Catholicism across the region, creating new opportunities for movements of the laity, including but not limited to the liberation theology movement (Smith 1991) and the Catholic Charismatic Renewal movement (Cleary 2011). These reforms within Catholicism coincided with new forms of Protestantism, including Evangelicalism and Pentecostalism (Martin 1990; Stoll 1990), new forms of indigenous religious movements (Garrard-Burnet 2004), and religious movements which trace their roots to Africa (Burdick 1998; Chesnut 2003).

Early scholars portrayed Catholic and Protestant movements in adversarial terms. However, over time it became clear that these movements were learning from and adapting to each other. For example, the Catholic Charismatic Renewal movement which currently is the most significant Catholic lay movement in Latin America adopted practices such as speaking in tongues and divine healing which are more common in Pentecostal congregations. As a result, scholars (Chesnut 1997; Steigenga 2002, 2007) suggest we are witnessing the Pentecostalization of religion in Latin America.

Increasingly, scholars find that not only is religion in Latin America pluralistic, but also there is considerable variation within Latin American Catholicism and Latin American Protestantism as well. Scholars have observed conservative Christians (Catholic and Protestant) recognizing common ground and working together to address so-called morality issues (Corrales and Pecheny 2010; Haas 1999). Conversely, progressive Christians (Catholic and Protestant, including Pentecostals) often work together on a variety of social justice issues. This chapter seeks to address some of the key themes and findings of religious change in Latin America.

This chapter is organized in the following way. First, we conceptualize the intersection of religion and social movements in Latin America, delineating the scope of the present work. Then, given the historical importance of the Catholic Church in Latin America, we explore reform movements, that is, social Catholic movements, from the late nineteenth and early twentieth century. The third part describes the origins of liberation theology, its roots in social Catholic movements, the role of church elites and the laity, and its long-term consequences for gender and LGBT equality movements (see Díez in this volume). Then we discuss the Catholic Charismatic Renewal movement, which many observers initially saw—incorrectly—as an attempt to undermine liberation theology by conservatives. The next part explores Protestantism in Latin America and the dramatic growth of Pentecostalism. Like the Catholic Charismatic Renewal, new Evangelical and Pentecostal churches were regarded by many observers as a rejection of liberation theology. However, over time this was shown to be a simplification. The final section of the chapter discusses new directions in the field.

Social Movements in the Catholic Church: Reform and Revitalization

In the late nineteenth and early twentieth century leaders in the Catholic Church created "sponsored" lay movements, Catholic Action and later Specialized Catholic Action, which were first adopted in Europe and later promoted around the world (Mackin 2012; Poggi 1967). These movements were conceived as part of the "lay apostolate," a novel way to "turn nominal Catholics into practicing ones by bringing religion into their daily lives through secular activities within the context of religious study, and by drawing them into the structure of the Church as lay apostles" (Levinson Estrada 1994: 81–82). Leaders in the Italian Catholic Church also saw Catholic Action as a way to mobilize the laity to defend the church's interests vis-à-vis a secular state that increasingly sought to curtail church influence (Poggi 1967).

While Catholic Action and other lay movements seemed to enjoy limited success among the middle classes, the working class appeared to be something of a lost cause (de la Bedoyere 1958). Either due to indifference, or the new influence of socialism and communism, the church was losing the working class. In the late 1920s, a Belgian priest and later Cardinal, Joseph Cardijn, saw this trend and vowed to save the working class by designing what he called the Jeunesse Ouvriere Chrétienne (Young Christian Workers or YCW). The YCW eventually won the endorsement of the Vatican and Cardijn embarked on a massive tour—interrupted by World War II—to promote YCW around the world (de la Bedoyere 1958). Soon the YCW model was used to mobilize other groups, including students, rural workers, professionals, and others under the name Specialized Catholic Action (Mackin 2012).

On the surface, the Catholic Action and Specialized Catholic Action movements bear little resemblance to one another. Unlike Catholic Action, which separated participants by age and sex, the YCW organized the laity based on their membership in the working class. Priests dominated Catholic Action, such that when they gave them less attention the groups quickly folded.

The YCW, on the other hand, was organized as a movement of Catholic workers, led by Catholic workers. Cardijn called for "like on like" organizing, viz., a cadre of workers trained by the local priest would recruit and train other workers (de la Bedoyere 1958). After that, a YCW movement would operate with some degree of autonomy from church officials.

Another innovation of Cardijn was the "See-Judge-Act" methodology which was designed to remind the members of the YCW, of the link between activism and faith. Militants were encouraged to see their condition and that of their fellow workers; to judge their status in light of God's teachings; and, then, lastly, to act to change the world, making it closer to the ideals described in the gospels. Base Christian Communities (known as CEBs from the acronym derived from the Spanish, *comunidades eclesiales de base*)—closely associated with liberation theology in later decades—were small groups usually composed of neighbors who gather on a weekly basis to read and discuss the Bible. Later CEBs successfully adopted the YCW methodology, in part, because members were exposed to it when they were in the YCW and other specialized Catholic Action movements inspired by Cardijn's vision (Mackin 2012).

Over time, the YCW and the movements inspired by it came into conflict with local priests and bishops over questions of autonomy and use of church resources. In some places, the YCW took radical stands, for example, joining communists and other workers on strike. This often led activists to see they had more in common with their fellow workers than they did with church leaders (see Mackin 2012). In some places, these conflicts led to formal separation from the church while elsewhere, activists elected to remain (Tahar Chaouch 2007).

Catholic Action and YCW were early attempts by church leaders to reform the church in light of Catholic social teaching (Mackin 2012; O'Brien and Shannon 1992). However, the 1960s were a turning point. Church reformers learned from the experience of Catholic Action and YCW but led the church in new directions, one of which would be the liberation theology movement (Smith 1991). Two events are central: the Second Vatican Council (1962–1965) and the second meeting of the CELAM which took place in Medellín in 1968.

With Vatican II, Pope John XXIII sought to revise the church's relationship to the world. First, he proclaimed Vatican II would be carried out in a spirit of openness with the objective of *aggiornamento*—or bringing the church up to date. This involved an embrace of modernity, including democracy, and ecumenism.

The pope also sought to decentralize authority in the church, for example, he asked that the council be carried out in a spirit of "collegiality." For Pope John XXIII, this meant that the participating bishops at the conference should feel equal to other participants, be they from the Vatican or other parts of the world. At the heart of Pope John XXIII's proposal was a desire to decentralize the church, to put more power in the hands of local bishops and by extension their priests, religious women, and lay people. One of the chief means by which he did this was through the promotion of regional bishops' councils, for example CELAM in Latin America.

Pope John XXIII died during Vatican II and was succeeded by Paul VI, who oversaw the completion of the council. In the end, "Vatican II replaced the juridical, hierarchical definition of the church with more biblical and symbolic images and clearly articulated a sense of the church as taking its form and function from its relationship to the kingdom of God" (O'Brien and Shannon 1992: 163).

When Catholic bishops met at CELAM II, the objective was to apply the lessons of Vatican II to Latin America. However, conference attendees took the church in a direction more progressive than Vatican II. Medellín was a turning point for the liberation theology movement (Smith 1991). At Medellín, the bishops encouraged the formation of small [Base Ecclesial] communities, "grass-roots organizations and [collaboration] . . . with non-Catholic Christian Churches and institutions dedicated to the task of restoring justice in human relations," as a strategy to fight "structural sins," such as the dependence of under-developed countries on developed ones (quoted in ibid.: 19).

It was at Medellín that many observers suggest liberation theology was born. Smith (1991) argued liberation theology was a revitalization movement, led by progressive bishops, priests, and theologians. He documents how liberationists formed a critical mass in the church though rarely a majority in a particular national church, except perhaps in Brazil and Chile. Despite their size, liberationists encouraged priests and bishops to implement the reforms of Medellín, especially the promotion of CEBs. Smith (ibid.: 189) notes that conservative and moderate Catholic critics quickly formed a counter-movement, successfully limiting the influence of liberation theology in several places. However, despite these efforts, the primary objectives of liberation theology were confirmed at the third meeting of CELAM in Puebla, Mexico in 1979. For Smith (ibid.) liberation theology was instigated by church elites, including bishops, priests and theologians; however, liberation theology flourished among the laity in a variety of movements both formally tied to and independent of the church, including transnational indigenous movements, landless movement in Brazil, among many others (see Desmarais 2009; Mackin 2015).

While Smith (1991) emphasized the role of elites in the liberation theology movement, other writers, such as Berryman (1984), suggested it was a mass movement, a result of pressure from marginalized and exploited groups who inspired by their faith organized to protest poor and deteriorating socio-economic conditions. In the 1970s, CEBs were seen by many mass mobilization scholars as a revolutionary force in Latin American church and society. Berryman's classic work documented the role of radical Christians, predominately Catholics, in the revolutionary movements of Nicaragua, El Salvador, and Guatemala. However, Christian participation in revolutionary movements was the exception and not the rule (see Martí i Puig and Álvarez, Oikonomakis, Wolff in this volume).

The Evolution of Liberation Theology: Gender and LGBT Equality

Scholars have been interested in studying not only the emergence, maintenance, and decline of the liberation theology movement (Cousineau 2020; Drogus and Stewart-Gambino 2005; Smith 1991) but also how the movement has influenced, or "spilled over" into other movements (Meyer and Whittier 1994). This part of the chapter explores research on the relationship between liberation theology and gender and LGBT equality movements.

For many years feminism, women's movements, and sexuality movement issues were absent from the published statements of liberation theologians. Early scholarly studies of liberation theology also omitted these topics (Althaus-Reid 2006; Burdick 2004; Drogus 1997). Feminist liberationist critiques of liberation theology were slow to be acknowledged but have, over the years, come to be taken seriously by many. It is only recently that we have seen the small but growing influence of scholars who are developing a critical and systematic rethinking of liberation theology in light of the oppression and marginalization of populations based on gender and sexuality, that is, one's identity as LGBT (Althaus-Reid 2006; Petrella 2006).

While these debates on gender and sexuality among liberation theologians have continued to evolve, scholars have also documented the changing beliefs and practices among the laity. These scholars found that liberationist movements, especially CEBs, were crucial in the development of feminist consciousness among participants. Adriance (1995), for example, found that participation in CEBs in rural Brazil played an essential role in the development of feminist consciousness among women participants who developed leadership and communication skills through their shared reading and analyzing of the Bible. Burdick (2004) argues that one of the legacies of liberation theology in Brazil is the dramatic increase in attention given by the church to gender equality, including concerns about sexual and physical abuse of women and minors at home.

Despite the observed positive effect for women that comes from participating in CEBs, it would be wrong to conclude all or most participants in CEBs are feminists (Drogus 1997). This is striking because most CEB participants are women (Hewitt 1991). Instead, there is considerable variation among CEB activists in terms of their views on gender equality and politics more generally (Drogus 1997). Also, while liberationists and progressive Catholics more generally embrace gender equality, many do not identify as feminist. If we factor in views on access to birth control and legal abortion, there is even less consensus among Latin American Catholics (Maier and Lebon 2010). For many Latin American women, the term "feminism" implies a set of views and practices with roots in North America or Western Europe than in Latin America. This perspective can be seen, for example, in the contemporary debates among activists and scholars on feminism, womanism and female consciousness (see Kaplan 1982; Peña 1995; Ewig and Friedman in this volume). Where we do see some consensus is on opposition to the rights of the LGBT community. Liberationist Catholics have been slow to defend LGBT movements, but in general, the Catholic hierarchy has spoken forcefully against equal rights for sexual minorities, lobbying to prevent legislation recognizing same-gender unions, for example (Díez in this volume).

Beyond Liberation Theology: Catholic Charismatic Renewal

In the midst of this open conflict between liberationists and their critics, a new movement emerged, Catholic Charismatic Renewal (CCR). Like liberation theology, the reforms of Vatican II also inspired the CCR (Cleary 2011). It along with CEBs signaled that the Catholic laity would play more prominent roles in the church. For years, the CCR was relatively overlooked by scholars even though it had more adherents among the laity than liberation theology (or Pentecostalism). What is more, for most of its history it has received little support from the Catholic hierarchy.

Instead, the CCR most closely resembles a mass movement. Cleary (2011: 23) states,

> [A]t its inception, the hierarchy of the Catholic Church neither mandated the movement nor initially sponsored the movement . . . Rather [it] began from the mid-level workforce (priests and nuns) and the grassroots. Priests, sisters, and laypersons working in Latin America picked up the core ideas and practices in the United States or Canada and communicated what they knew to small groups in Latin America whose members, in turn, recruited others.

In its early years, the CCR bore a resemblance to CEBs. Both CEBs and CCR groups emphasize small gatherings of the laity who meet weekly and reflect on the Bible. However, that is where they diverge. While many CEBs included an analysis of social conditions in their reflections with an emphasis on achieving social justice, charismatic groups are much less likely to address politics. Rather, they are more likely to be consistent with the "Pentecostalization" of religion in Latin America; that is, worship services emphasizing a spirit-filled experience where social concerns are less important than addressing the individual's relationship with God (Chesnut 1997; Steigenga 2002, 2007). That being said, scholars have described how relatively apolitical Pentecostal groups have taken up practical political concerns (see Mackin 2012).

In the 1970s, the CCR was initially regarded by many as part of an effort by critics of liberation theology to undermine the movement (see Cleary 2011). However, scholars demonstrated that the CCR succeeded despite the lack of support from both progressive and conservative members of the hierarchy. By the early 1990s, and after a lengthy vetting process, the CCR was formally recognized by the Vatican, cementing it as part of the Catholic mainstream. Currently, Charismatic Catholic groups are present across Latin America, with about 75% found in Argentina, Brazil, Colombia, and Mexico (ibid.: 26).

Systematic examinations of CEBs and Charismatic Catholic groups reveals many counter-intuitive findings. First, early analysts portrayed CEBs and CCR as involved in a zero-sum game competition for members. Since then, scholars have demonstrated that while the dynamics of the two groups are usually different, in some places the differences are more a matter of "style than content" (de Theije 1999: 122). Furthermore, network analysis in communities reveals that it is common for individuals to participate in both groups (Cleary 2011; Steigenga 2007). In a related discovery, Burdick (2004) found that among those who only participate in a CEB or CCR there was less tension than one would have expected among groups that were competing for members.

PROTESTANTISM IN LATIN AMERICA: PLURALISM IN A GROWING CHURCH

Latin American Protestantism has historically been small and linked to immigrant communities. The first denominations, referred to as Historical Protestantism, included mission denominations of Presbyterians, Methodists, and Baptists (Freston 2008). These communities emerged in the nineteenth century and were quickly inserted into ongoing debates between conservatives who wished to maintain the status quo of Catholic hegemony and anti-clerical liberals who sought separation of church and state, a more laissez-faire state, and a more modern economy. Protestantism, then, was seen as part of a broader liberal plan to modernize the region (Freston 2008). It was in this context Protestants experienced repression from states allied with the Catholic Church and from lay Catholics who sanctioned any challenge to Catholic hegemony in the region (Hartch 2014).

In the early twentieth century, foreign Pentecostal missionaries began evangelizing in Latin America, but with little success. Freston (2008) suggests that by the 1950s and 1960s Pentecostal foreign missionaries were leaving the region and being replaced by Latin Americans. Soon after that, evangelical Protestant churches spread rapidly.

By the 1960s and 1970s new forms of Protestantism, especially Evangelicalism (including Pentecostalism), began to proliferate. In addition, other smaller Christian groups such as the Church of Jesus Christ of Latter-Day Saints and Jehovah's Witnesses also expanded.

Our discussion will mainly focus on Pentecostalism since this is the fastest growing movement within Latin American Protestantism. Before continuing, a brief caveat is necessary. Discussing Protestantism in Latin America poses a problem: Latin American Protestants do not, in general, adopt the same nomenclature as their counterparts in other parts of the world. As Freston (2008) points out, most Latin American Protestants describe themselves as *evangélicos*. It is important to underscore that most Latin American evangelical Protestants share many characteristics with North American evangelicals, such as the following: "conversionism (emphasis on the need for a change of life); activism (emphasis on evangelistic and missionary efforts); biblicism (that is, the importance of the Bible, but not necessarily the fundamentalist concept of 'inerrancy'); and crucicentrism (emphasis on centrality of Christ's sacrifice on the cross)" (ibid.: 5). While Latin American evangelicals share these characteristics, they differ in many ways from their North American counterparts (ibid.).

Scholars such as Freston (2008) note that Latin American Protestantism is much more pluralistic than Protestantism in the United States. For example, Latin American evangelicals might agree with their North American evangelicals on so-called morality issues (e.g., abortion, homosexuality, same-gender unions), but differ on US foreign policy and domestic policy, including the need for government assistance to the poor (Freston 2013).

In addition, we have also seen distinctions between Pentecostals and non-Pentecostal evangelicals. Two observers note that,

> [i]n sharp contrast to what takes place in traditional Catholic or Protestant worship, almost anyone accepted by the Pentecostal community is allowed to interpret Scripture during worship, to moralize about the conditions of life, to preach about the changes needed in personal conduct, to pray spontaneously, to offer suggestions for the community's response to an evil world, and to vote on questions of importance such as large expenditures of community assets. (Cleary and Stewart-Gambino 1997: 7)

While Pentecostal practices are different from mainline Protestantism and most evangelical Protestantism, all share beliefs and practices which are "deeply rooted in Protestant traditions such as interpretation of Scripture by ordinary Christians, the priesthood of all believers, and the priority of practice over dogma" (Cleary and Stewart-Gambino 1997: 7).

Increasingly scholars distinguish Pentecostals from so-called Neo-Pentecostals (who are also referred to as charismatics). In contrast to Pentecostals, Neo-Pentecostals tend to be wealthier, with large congregations (often mega-churches), eschew asceticism, and embrace the prosperity gospel (Steigenga 2002). Edward Cleary (1997) observes: "[t]hey noisily entered politics, preached an ethos of consumerism, and supported or emulated the showmanship of North America's religious-right figures Jerry Falwell and Pat Robertson" (Cleary and Stewart-Gambino 1997: 9). Neo-Pentecostals have enjoyed success in Central America, especially in Guatemala.

By the 1980s and 1990s the expansion of evangelical Protestantism, especially Pentecostalism, was so fast that Stoll (1990) provocatively asked, "Is Latin America Turning Protestant?" In a recent study, Freston (2008) reported that about 12% of Latin America is Protestant. However, this glosses over the variation in Protestantism's strength in Latin America. As a region, Central America has the highest percentage of Protestants, including about 50% of Guatemalans identifying as Protestant; then come countries in South America (Brazil, Chile, and Peru) with moderately sized Protestant communities, and lastly countries with small Protestant communities, including Argentina, Mexico, and Uruguay.

Explanations for the Rapid Growth of Pentecostalism in Latin America

Early explanations for the appeal and rapid growth of Pentecostalism in Latin America emphasized social strain. In a classic text examining the cases of Pentecostalism in Chile and Brazil, Willems (1967) argued that Pentecostalism appealed to the poor in countries experiencing industrialization and urbanization. Willems suggested that the value of self-reliance (i.e., a Protestant work ethic) emphasized by Pentecostal churches would help the poor achieve social mobility.

In another widely read study on the case of Chile, Lalive D' Epinay (1969) also argued that the growth of Pentecostalism was a result of the rapid structural changes. Lalive D' Epinay (1969) was more critical of the new development than Willems (1967), suggesting Pentecostalism provided a "Haven for the Masses," that is, a way for the poor to maintain traditional folk Catholic practices—with a pastor replacing the priest as authority figure—in a new setting. What is more, Lalive D' Epinay (1969) suggested Pentecostalism reinforced passivity and dependence, which could lead to support for authoritarian regimes.

These early studies continue to be read and cited by contemporary scholars. However, by the late 1970s and 1980s, Latin America had changed considerably. On the one hand, Protestantism in Latin America was growing at a faster pace than in the 1960s. The Southern Cone was in the midst of the long night of military-bureaucratic authoritarian regimes. Meanwhile, in Central America, the Sandinistas defeated the Somoza regime in 1979 while the fighting continued in El Salvador and Guatemala. The wars in Central America featured authoritarian regimes who were backed by the US government fighting Marxist revolutionary movements, many of whose fighters were inspired by their Christian faith. What is more, in each country priests and in some places religious nuns died at the hands of the military. Critical analyses of the role of the United States government in Latin America abounded (see Martí i Puig and Álvarez, Brockett in this volume).

Increasingly, the links between conservative North American Christians, the US government under President Ronald Reagan (1981–1985, 1985–1989), and Latin American Protestants became a focus of analysis. Some scholars suggested that the rapid growth of Latin American Protestantism was a result of US imperialism (Bastian 1990). This is seen in the overt support by US conservatives for General Ríos Montt (1982–1983) in Guatemala.

The regime of self-professed conservative Christian Efraín Ríos Montt is especially noteworthy. His regime crystalized the thinking of many: "The image of a self-professing Christian general presiding over a genocidal military in a poor Central American country victimized by military aid from the "colossus of the north' fed directly into stereotypical interpretations of a monolithically conservative Protestantism invading Latin America as an agent of cultural and political imperialism" (Samson 2008: 65). The later administration of Jorge Serrano (1991–1993) further enforced the idea that there was a relationship between conservative politicians, Latin American Protestantism, the US government, and conservative Christians in the United States. What is more, both Ríos Montt and Serrano "left office under clouds related to human rights violations and corruption" (ibid.: 70), undermining expectations that Evangelical political leaders would be more ethical than their predecessors while in office.

Scholars such as Stoll (1990) found some support for the position that evangelical success in Latin America was due to United States imperialism. He noted that for years the Central Intelligence Agency had used and funded Protestant missionaries to simultaneously gather information on local dynamics and promote projects that made North American culture more appealing to the local population, and ultimately yield a more favorable view of the United States in the region (ibid.). While the US government sought to influence Protestantism and politics in the region, Stoll (ibid.) concluded, it would be incorrect to see evangelical Protestantism, including Pentecostalism, as anything but an indigenous movement, that is, a grassroots movement led by Latin Americans, usually the poor.

Others soon came to similar conclusions. On the one hand, the example of Guatemala was not representative of the entire region, nor, for that matter, did the explanation of Protestant growth as a result of US imperialism accurately describe dynamics in Guatemala (Samson 2008; Steigenga 2007). Instead, scholars suggest the importance of networks, including family, friends, and acquaintances, as offering more powerful explanations of why and how people convert to Protestantism (Smilde 2007). As Martin

(1990) notes, Latin American Pentecostalism is led by the poor and funded by the poor, and evangelization occurs through networks and ties among the poor.

While Latin America was quickly turning Protestant, scholars sought to explain variation in Pentecostalism's appeal. Martin (1990) argued that in the 1960s there was a dramatic change in church–state structures such that the Catholic Church underwent a process of voluntary disestablishment. This change created an opportunity structure which allowed the emergence of Pentecostalism. Where the Catholic Church enjoyed autonomy from the state, but the populace was not severely secularized, then Pentecostalism would spread dramatically. This pattern obtained in Central America, Brazil, Chile, and Peru. However, where the church was not autonomous (e.g., Argentina, Colombia) or where the inhabitants were secularized (e.g., Uruguay) Pentecostalism was much less successful. Martin's work continues to spark debate about the growth of Protestantism in Latin America (see Casanova 2018).

Recent Research on Protestantism in Latin America: Gender and Sexuality

The rise of conservative religious movements often leads to what Bernice Martin (2001) calls a gender paradox: the formal re-assertion of patriarchal authority combined with the informal "domestication" of men and increased opportunities for women. During the early industrial period, Methodism in England and Wales fit this pattern (ibid.: 52). A similar dynamic obtains in Latin America where, with the rise of Pentecostalism several scholars have identified more egalitarian relations in church and family (Brusco 1995; Drogus 1997; Martin 2001).

It is useful to contrast traditional Latin American patriarchal norms with these new more egalitarian ones. Drogus (1997) summarizes the differences. Traditional Latin American gender norms are "highly patriarchal, legitimating male power over females generally and especially within families. It has traditionally divided the world into two spheres: the house (private) and the street (public). Men dominate both spheres. Ideally, men alone move in the public sphere of the street. Within the house, they have the ultimate authority" (ibid.: 56).

Formally, Pentecostalism is an orthodox interpretation of Christianity, which maintains that women are subordinate to men both at church and at home. In practice, many Pentecostal churches grant significant roles to women; what is more, while Pentecostals believe in male headship among other things that seem to enshrine male authority, informally Pentecostal couples are usually more egalitarian than non-Pentecostal couples. This is likely due to the shared beliefs among Pentecostals, which are more egalitarian, including equality before God. This is seen, for example, in the "priesthood of all believers" (Willems 1967) and in what Steigenga (2002) calls spiritual equality, that is, where anyone who is "touched by the Holy Spirit" may participate fully in the worship service. This may or may not involve speaking in tongues, or divine healing through touch. These egalitarian principles are clearly in tension with the traditional norms described above.

It is worthwhile noting that there is considerable variation in Latin American Pentecostalism (Drogus 1997; Steigenga 2002). Most Pentecostal groups adopt a more conservative reading of the Bible and restrict women's roles in public and private spheres. However, while Pentecostal groups formally adopt these conservative positions, in practice women's roles are changing quite dramatically. For example, a congregation may hold that only a man can be a pastor, yet a woman may take on many of the same responsibilities as a pastor (Drogus 1997). As a result, scholars emphasize the importance of comparing formal beliefs with the practices adopted in Pentecostal congregations (Steigenga 2002; Steigenga and Smilde 1999).

Since some Pentecostal women seem to achieve some degree of autonomy and agency in their churches and enjoy something approaching egalitarian relations at home, can we conclude that Pentecostal women are proto-feminists? Scholars such as Mariz and Campos Machado (1997) emphasize that while the practices of Pentecostal women (and men) appear consistent with feminist principles, in fact there are several differences which would likely prevent Pentecostals from embracing Western-style feminism without reservation.

One key difference between Pentecostalism and feminism concerns individualism. Both movements emphasize individualism, but they do so from very different perspectives (Mariz and Campos Machado 1997). For Pentecostals, all individuals are equal before God. To be a moral person one must have a modest lifestyle (be ascetic), be humble, including about one's faith, and forgive others. However, Pentecostals maintain that the devil is real and is the source of evil on earth. Therefore, forgiving others is paramount, including an alcoholic spouse or one prone to womanizing because, ultimately, it is the devil who is to blame for those sins.

A Western feminist is less likely to attribute such failings to the devil. They would not only more likely blame the transgressor but also interrogate a culture which encourages men to cheat on their wives and abuse alcohol as part of some essentialized identity. Mariz and Campos Machado (1999: 49–50) note that if we examine Pentecostal women with

> a western feminist lens, [they appear to be] . . . alienated because they accept self-limitation. However, for Pentecostal women, the only oppressor is the devil, therefore to be free is to be able to disobey the devil's will. Asceticism proves that one is free [not alienated]. Freedom [for Pentecostals, therefore] is not the absence of restrictions but resisting temptation and remaining faithful to the values and responsibilities one has assumed.

As a result, Mariz and Campos Machado suggest that while Pentecostalism for many women means new opportunities in society and church and a transformed relationship with their spouse, it does not mean they are proto-feminists. The authors note,

"Pentecostal women no longer see men as masters they must obey. Nor, however, do they view them as oppressors they must rebel against" (Mariz and Campos Machado 1999: 52).

Whether or not Pentecostals are feminists is less critical to Brusco (1995), because Pentecostalism is revolutionizing gender relations in the communities she studied in Colombia. Like other scholars, Brusco (ibid.) notes that formally Pentecostalism reinforces patriarchy in public and private lives, but informally is much more egalitarian. Brusco (ibid.) argues that with conversion, we see a dramatic change:

> Aggression, violence pride, self-indulgence, and an individualistic orientation [among men] in the public sphere are replaced by peace-seeking, humility, self-restraint, and a collective orientation and identity with the church and the home. [As a result,] ... the boundaries of public (male) life and private (female) life are redrawn, and the spheres themselves are redefined. (Brusco 1995: 137)

Similarly, other scholars have noted that while Protestant and Pentecostal churches formally encouraged congregants to adopt traditional gender roles, they also, unintentionally, encouraged women and men to see each other as equals (Steigenga and Smilde 1999). What is more, though Protestant and Pentecostal (but also many Catholic) men and women are hesitant to self-identify as feminist, their views on equality overlap considerably with mainstream feminism (ibid.).

Critics, such as Martin (2001), are less sanguine than Brusco (1995) about Pentecostalism's capacity to transform gender relations along more egalitarian lines. Martin acknowledges that Brusco's findings regarding the "domestication" of men based on fieldwork in Colombia are similar to findings on Pentecostalism in other parts of the developing world. However, Martin (2001) emphasizes that such changes are often precarious. Many men backslide, leaving their partners and congregation behind. This results in Pentecostal women finding themselves without partners in congregations composed of mostly fellow women (ibid.).

In general, Pentecostals oppose recognizing the rights of LGBT individuals. For example, recent research by Fediakova and Parker (2009: 61) confirms that more than 75% of Chilean Pentecostals oppose equal marriage rights for LGBT individuals. There are exceptions, however. Corrales and Pecheny (2010) note that in Brazil, a couple of prominent Pentecostals in the Partido dos Trabalhadores have publicly defended LGBT rights but inconsistently. Instead, Pentecostals have usually lobbied to prevent the extension of rights to the LGBT community. Scholars have noted that on occasions the Catholic hierarchy has joined with Pentecostals to oppose access to abortion, divorce and the extension of rights to LGBT individuals (Corrales and Pecheny 2010; Haas 1999). Despite this opposition, LGBT individuals have been extended rights in some countries, such as Argentina, Brazil, and Uruguay and in some cities including Mexico City, Bogotá, and Santiago (Payne, Díez in this volume).

NEW DIRECTIONS: RELIGIOUS ECONOMIES AND FIELD THEORY

Scholars in the religious economy paradigm have made several significant contributions to the field. They treat religion as similar to a market, where firms (e.g., churches) compete to obtain customers (members). Then they employ theories derived from economics to understand the actions of individuals and organizations. For example, Gill (1998) found national councils of Catholic bishops in Latin America were more likely to oppose dictators when Protestant (especially Pentecostal) churches were expanding in the area. Gill (ibid.) argued that bishops are "parishioner-maximizers" who challenged authoritarian regimes to prevent defections to competing Protestant churches. Where Protestantism was weaker, bishops were less likely to challenge dictators.

Similarly, Trejo (2009) explained variation in the Mexican bishops' responses to indigenous communities as a result of Protestant competition. Also, over several studies, Chesnut (1997, 2003) has examined religious markets in Brazil, including Pentecostal churches, Catholic churches, and the African-Brazilian religion of Umbanda among others as competitors in a religious marketplace. While the religious economy paradigm has received a fair amount of criticism (see Mackin 2003; also Steigenga 2007: 19–20), it has successfully directed attention to competition between religious organizations.

Field theory is another promising direction for the study of religion in Latin America. A key exemplar is the work of Tahar Chaouch (2007). Drawing on Pierre Bourdieu's work, Tahar Chaouch challenges three key ways the liberation theology movement has been portrayed: as Latin American in origins, as popular (of the poor), and as a movement. Regarding origins, Tahar Chaouch (ibid.) underscores that many key actors—both liberationists and their critics—received training in Europe. As a result, it makes more sense to describe the movement as transnational, reflecting both European and Latin American roots. What is more, he notes that in the 1960s and 1970s liberation theology was composed of a variety of networks, including intellectuals, bishops, priests, students, and the poor. It would be incorrect, Tahar Chaouch (ibid.) suggests, to claim liberation theology was a popular movement when the poor were one of many networks grouped in the category of liberation theology.

Lastly, these networks were often in conflict with one another over what it meant to be Catholic. In some cases, networks elected to break with the hierarchy. This part of Tahar Chaouch's analysis reflects Bourdieu's understanding, where "every field is the site of a more or less overt struggle over the definition of the legitimate principles of the division of the field" (Bourdieu 1985: 734). Tahar Chaouch (2007) recounts how Catholic students elected to sever formal ties to the Catholic Church in light of the episcopacy's effort to control and direct the movement. This dynamic occurred in other networks as well. As a result, the author suggests the variety of networks undermines the claim that liberation theology can be described as a unified movement. Mackin (2010) also acknowledges the variation within the movement but suggests that the networks within liberation theology bear a "family resemblance" to one another. In sum, Tahar Chaouch (2007)'s contribution is noteworthy and will likely inspire others in their analysis of the Latin American religious field.

Conclusion

Religious groups are crucibles for social movements (Zald and McCarthy 2017 [1987]). Informed by resource mobilization theory, Zald and McCarthy (ibid.) explicate the myriad ways religious groups are both ideal settings for social movement mobilization and to be influenced by social movements. Zald and McCarthy (ibid.) focused on social movements in the United States. However, research on religion and social movements in Latin America since the 1960s demonstrates a similar dynamic: Roman Catholic and Pentecostal churches have launched movements that shape the beliefs and practices of individuals. However, Catholic and Pentecostal groups have also been affected by other social movements (Mackin 2015). What is more, the movements discussed in this chapter also seek to influence the public sphere. This is perhaps most evident in the discussion of LGBT equality, and the changing role of Pentecostal women in families, churches, and society.

In recent years, scholars of social movements and religion have sought to go beyond the resource mobilization (and political process) paradigms which informed Zald and McCarthy (2017 [1987]) and dominated the field for decades (Yukich 2012). As scholars do so, Latin America will continue to be an important site of study.

References

Althaus-Reid, Marcella (2006). "Let Them Talk . . . Doing Liberation Theology from Latin American Closets," in Marcella Althaus-Reid (ed.), *Liberation Theology and Sexuality*, 5–17 (Burlington, VT: Ashgate).
Adriance, Madeleine (1995), *Promised Land: Base Christian Communities and the Struggle for the Amazon* (Albany: State University of New York Press).
Bastian, Jean-Pierre (1990), *Historia del protestantismo en América Latina* (Mexico: Casa Unida de Publicaciones).
Berryman, Phillip (1984), *The Religious Roots of Rebellion: Christians in Central American Revolutions* (Maryknoll, NY: Orbis).
Bourdieu, Pierre (1985), "The Social Space and the Genesis of Groups," *Theory and Society* 14(6), 723–44.
Burdick, John (1998), *Blessed Anastácia: Women, Race, and Popular Christianity in Brazil* (New York: Routledge).
Burdick, John (2004), *Legacies of Liberation: The Progressive Catholic Church in Brazil at the Start of a New Millennium* (Burlington, VT: Ashgate).
Brusco, Elizabeth E. (1995), *The Reformation of Machismo: Evangelical Conversion and Gender in Colombia* (Austin: University of Texas Press).

Casanova, José (2018), "Parallel Reformations in Latin America: A Critical Review of David Martin's Interpretation of the Pentecostal Revolution," in Hans Joas (ed.), *David Martin and the Sociology of Religion*, 85–106 (New York: Routledge).
Chesnut, R. Andrew (1997), *Born Again in Brazil: The Pentecostal Boom and the Pathogens of Poverty* (New Brunswick, NJ: Rutgers University Press).
Chesnut, R. Andrew (2003), *Competitive Spirits: Latin America's New Religious Economy* (New York: Oxford University Press).
Cleary, Edward (2011), *The Rise of Charismatic Catholicism in Latin America* (Gainesville: University Press of Florida).
Cleary, Edward and Hannah Stewart-Gambino (1997), *Power, Politics, and Pentecostals in Latin America* (Boulder, CO: Westview).
Corrales, Javier and Mario Pecheny (2010), *The Politics of Sexuality in Latin America* (Pittsburgh, PA: University of Pittsburgh Press).
Cousineau, Madeleine (2020), "Still Opting for the Poor: The Brazilian Catholic Church and the National Movement of the Street Population," *Journal for the Scientific Study of Religion* 59(4), 586–605.
de la Bedoyere, Michael (1958), *The Cardijn Story* (New York: Longman).
Desmarais, Anette Aurélie (2009), "La Via Campesina: Globalizing Peasants," in Carmen D. Deere and Frederick S. Royce (eds.), *Rural Social Movements in Latin America: Organizing for Sustainable Livelihoods*, 33–54 (Gainesville: University Press of Florida).
de Theije, Marjo (1999), "CEBs and Catholic Charismatics in Brazil," in Christian Smith and Joshua Prokopy (eds.), *Latin American Religion in Motion*, 111–24 (New York: Routledge).
Drogus, Carol Ann (1997), "Pentecostalism, Base Communities, and Gender," in Edward L. Cleary and Hannah Stewart-Gambino (eds.), *Power, Politics, and Pentecostals in Latin America*, 55–76 (Boulder, CO: Westview).
Drogus, Carol Ann and Hannah Stewart-Gambino (2005), *Activist Faith: Grassroots Women in Democratic Brazil and Chile* (University Park, PA: Penn State University Press).
Fediakova, Euguenia and Cristian Parker (2009), "Evangélicos en Chile Democrático (1990–2008): Radiografía al centésimo aniversario," *Cultura y Religión* 3(2), 43–69.
Freston, Paul (2008), "Introduction: The Many Faces of Evangelical Politics in Latin America," in Paul Freston (ed.), *Evangelical Christianity and Democracy in Latin America*, 3–36 (New York: Oxford University Press).
Freston, Paul (2013), "Pentecostals and Politics in Latin America," in Donald E. Miller, Kimon H. Sargeant, and Richard Flory (eds.), *Spirit and Power: The Growth and Global Impact of Pentecostalism*, 101–18 (New York: Oxford University Press).
Garrard-Burnett, Virginia (2004), "God was Already Here When Columbus Arrived: Inculturation Theology and the Mayan Movement in Guatemala," in Timothy J. Steigenga and Edward L. Cleary (eds.), *Conversion of a Continent: Contemporary Religious Change in Latin America*, 125–53 (New Brunswick, NJ: Rutgers University Press).
Gill, Anthony (1998), *Rendering unto Caesar: The Catholic Church and the State in Latin America* (Chicago: University of Chicago Press).
Hartch, Todd (2014), *The Rebirth of Latin American Christianity* (New York: Oxford University Press).
Haas, Liesl (1999), "The Catholic Church in Chile: New Political Alliances," in Christian Smith and Joshua Prokopy (eds.), *Latin American Religion in Motion*, 43–66 (New York: Routledge).

Hewitt, Warren Eduard (1991), *Base Christian Communities and Social Change in Brazil* (Lincoln: University of Nebraska Press).

Kaplan, Temma (1982), "Female Consciousness and Collective Action: The Case of Barcelona, 1910–1918," *Signs: Journal of Women in Culture and Society* 7(3), 545–66.

Lalive d'Epinay, Christian (1969), *Haven of the Masses: A Study of the Pentecostal Movement in Chile* (London: Lutterworth).

Levenson-Estrada, Deborah (1994), *Trade Unionists Against Terror: Guatemala City, 1954–1985* (Chapel Hill: University of North Carolina Press).

Mackin, Robert Sean (2003), "Becoming the Red Bishop of Cuernavaca: Rethinking Gill's Religious Competition Model," *Sociology of Religion* 64(4), 499–514.

Mackin, Robert Sean (2010), "In Word and Deed: Assessing the Strength of Progressive Catholicism in Latin America, 1960–1970s," *Sociology of Religion* 71(2), 216–42.

Mackin, Robert Sean (2012), "Liberation Theology: the Radicalization of Social Catholic Movements," *Politics, Religion & Ideology* 13(3), 333–51.

Mackin, Robert Sean (2015), "Liberation Theology and Social Movements," in Paul Almeida and Allen Cordero Ulate (eds.), *Handbook of Social Movements across Latin America*, 101–16 (New York: Springer).

Maier, Elizabeth and Nathalie Lebon (2010), *Women's Activism in Latin America and the Caribbean: Engendering Social Justice, Democratizing Citizenship* (New Brunswick, NJ: Rutgers University Press).

Mariz, Cecilia Loreto and María das Dores Campos Machado (1997), "Pentecostalism and Women in Brazil," in Edward L. Cleary and Hannah Stewart-Gambino (eds.), *Power, Politics, and Pentecostals in Latin America*, 41–54 (Boulder, CO: Westview).

Martin, Bernice (2001), "The Pentecostal Gender Paradox: a Cautionary Tale for the Sociology of Religion," in Richard K. Fenn (ed.), *The Blackwell Companion to Sociology of Religion*, 52–66 (Malden: Blackwell).

Martin, David (1990), *Tongues of Fire: The Explosion of Protestantism in Latin America* (Cambridge: Basil Blackwell).

Meyer, David S. and Nancy Whittier (1994), "Social Movement Spillover," *Social Problems* 41(2), 277–98.

O'Brien, David A. and Thomas J. Shannon (1992), *Catholic Social Teaching: The Documentary Heritage* (Maryknoll, NY: Orbis).

Peña, Milagros (1995), "Feminist Christian Women in Latin America: Other Voices, Other Visions," *Journal of Feminist Studies in Religion* 11(1), 81–94.

Petrella, Ivan (2006), "Queer Eye for the Straight Guy: Making Over Liberation Theology," in Marcella Althaus-Reid (ed.), *Liberation Theology and Sexuality*, 41–66 (Burlington, VT: Ashgate).

Poggi, Gianfranco (1967), *Catholic Action in Italy: The Sociology of a Sponsored Organization* (Stanford, CA: Stanford University Press).

Samson, C. Matthews (2008), "From War to Reconciliation: Guatemalan Evangelicals and the Transition to Democracy, 1982–2001," in Paul Freston (ed.), *Evangelical Christianity and Democracy in Latin America*, 63–96 (New York: Oxford University Press).

Smilde, David (2007), *Reason to Believe: Cultural Agency in Latin American Evangelicalism* (Berkeley and Los Angeles: University of California Press).

Smith, Christian (1991), *The Emergence of Liberation Theology* (Chicago: University of Chicago Press).

Steigenga, Timothy J. (2002), *The Politics of the Spirit: The Political Implications of Pentecostalized Religion in Costa Rica and Guatemala* (New York: Lexington).

Steigenga, Timothy J. (2007), "The Politics of Pentecostalized Religion: Conversion as Pentecostalization in Guatemala," in Timothy J. Steigenga and Edward L. Cleary (eds.), *Conversion of a Continent: Contemporary Religious Change in Latin America*, 256–80 (New Brunswick, NJ: Rutgers University Press).

Steigenga, Timothy J. and David Smilde (1999), "Wrapped in the Holy Shawl: The Strange Case of Conservative Christians and Gender Equality in Latin America," in Christian Smith and Joshua Prokopy (eds.), *Latin American Religion in Motion*, 173–86 (New York: Routledge).

Stoll, David (1990), *Is Latin America Turning Protestant?* (Berkeley and Los Angeles: University of California Press).

Tahar Chaouch, Malik (2007), "La teología de la liberación en América Latina: una relectura sociológica," *Revista Mexicana de Sociología* 69(3), 427–56.

Trejo, Guillermo (2009), "Religious Competition and Ethnic Mobilization in Latin America: Why the Catholic Church Promotes Indigenous Movements in Mexico," *American Political Science Review* 103(3), 323–42.

Willems, Emilio (1967), *Followers of the New Faith: Culture Change and the Rise of Protestantism in Brazil and Chile* (Nashville, TN: Vanderbilt University Press).

Yukich, Grace (2012), "Beyond Religion as Resource," *Mobilizing Ideas*, November 1, https://mobilizingideas.wordpress.com/2012/11/01/beyond-religion-as-resource/#more-4139.

Zald, Mayer N. and D. McCarthy John (2017 [1987]), "Religious Groups as Crucibles of Social Movements," in Mayer N. Zald and John McCarthy (eds.), *Social Movements in An Organizational Society*, 67–96 (New York: Routledge).

CHAPTER 38

EDUCATION, PEDAGOGY, AND SOCIAL MOVEMENTS IN LATIN AMERICA

REBECCA TARLAU

Introduction

Education is a central component of Latin American social movements. This education takes three forms: informal, non-formal, and formal. Perhaps most importantly, being part of a social movement in Latin America is itself an educational experience, shaping people's worldviews and understanding of power and politics. Social movement leaders in Latin America are often intentional about the informal learning happening within their movements, and therefore, might promote more collective organizational forms, gender equity in decision-making bodies, or cultural symbols of struggle in movement spaces—in order to teach participants about the values of the movement. Throughout Latin America, social movements have also developed non-formal educational offerings, known as popular education or *formación*. These educational programs are intentional and well-organized but are non-formal in the sense of not being recognized by the state as official spaces of schooling. Non-formal education can range from study groups of socialist newspapers to theatre projects, peer-to-peer agroecological trainings, or month-long courses on political theory. Finally, social movements in Latin America have also concerned themselves with schooling, taking part in the implementation of literacy and adult basic education programs, as well as the co-governance of public schools and university courses. This requires a contentious process of negotiation and conflict with national and subnational governments, as well ongoing relationships with teachers, administrators, parents, and students. Over the past century, these informal, non-formal, and formal educational processes have created uniquely Latin American pedagogies, which although different across regions and movements, share the common characteristic of helping to disrupt traditional forms of knowledge transfer, and instead, create an approach to learning, study, and analysis that reinforces the broader goals that these movements seek to achieve.

Socialism, Anarchism, and Political Education in Early and Mid-Twentieth-century Latin America

During the early twentieth century, workers' strikes began to erupt throughout Latin America, but especially in the rapidly industrializing Southern Cone countries such as Argentina, Brazil, Chile, and Uruguay. Communist and anarchist organizers played a central role instigating this unrest, and political education was often a tool of this agitation. According to some scholars (e.g., Kane 2001), the first critiques of mainstream education in Latin America were during this period, within the variety of movements for socialism, anarchism, radical liberalism, and popular nationalism. The organizations that formed, including unions and political parties, participated in and developed alternative educational programs. Some examples in the early twentieth century include the popular universities in El Salvador, the educational sector that Augusto César Sandino's guerrilla army developed in Nicaragua, and the educational programs promoted by Luis Recabarren within working-class organizations in Chile (Arnove 1986: 7; Kane 2001: 26; Rueda 2021).

Brazil offers a useful lens through which to explore the early dynamics of anarchist and communist organizing, as the most rapidly industrializing country in South America. As Dulles (1973) notes, by the year 1900, approximately 90% of São Paulo's industrial work force was foreign, and many of these immigrant workers had become followers of anarchism and socialism before leaving Europe. Socialists and anarchists often worked together, organizing the first May Day observance in Brazil in 1895. Illustrating an early focus on formal education, during the Second Brazilian Socialist Congress in 1902 the thirty-six point program included a demand for free and obligatory education for everyone under fourteen (ibid.: 11–12; see Ramírez Gallegos and Stoessel, Spanakos and Romo Rivas in this volume).

However, the demand for formal education was not the primary pedagogical tool of the anarchist and communist organizers. Most significantly, a vibrant "proletarian press" flourished in Rio de Janeiro and São Paulo, with newspapers of both ideological leanings distributed among workers, carrying news of domestic and international political events (Dulles 1973). Although illiteracy was high among the industrialized workforce, literate workers read these newspapers to their co-workers in informal study groups. In the cultural realm, anarchists in the early twentieth century were particularly active, organizing grassroots theatre projects known as "teatro operário" (Hardman 1983). Anarchists were also critical of the government-funded public schools and created their own "escolas modernas" that emphasized autonomy and self-organization (Luizetto 1986). According to Dore (2009), the combination of anarchists' rejection of formal schooling and the Brazilian communists' lack of a cultural agenda meant that no socialist proposal for the public school system developed, until the return to democracy in the 1980s. Nonetheless, informal and non-formal education was a central part of these early movements through socialist study groups and anarchist community schools, as well as socialist theatre and newspaper distribution.

In 1922, a group of anarchists left their movement and helped to found the Partido Comunista do Brasil (PCB). The PCB was a powerful force both in urban and rural organizing efforts for the next four decades, despite different periods of legality and illegality. In urban slums the PCB developed its base through Comitês Populares Democráticos (CPDs). This sometimes meant a tension between party activists attempting to "instill in residents some consciousness of the broader socioeconomic structures that shaped their misery ... [versus] concrete action on critical community issues" (Fischer 2014: 15). Nonetheless, CPDs functioned as important spaces of political education for local residents. The PCB also took leadership in the cultural realm, assuming direction of the União Geral das Escolas de Samba (UGES) in Rio de Janeiro (ibid.).

The most significant social movements in Brazil during the first half of the twentieth century were the Ligas Camponesas and rural unions, emerging most strongly in the Northeastern part of the country but also influencing São Paulo and other regions (Fernandes Mançano and Welch in this volume). What is important to note here is the role of education within these movements. Most significantly, the Movimento de Educação de Base (MEB) became an expansive educational program during the 1960s, led by the Conferência Nacional dos Bispos do Brasil and supported by the Federal Ministry of Education and Culture (MEC) (Dore 2009). The MEB focused on rural literacy while also emphasizing consciousness-raising, reaching tens of thousands of workers. However, these non-formal educational programs were also part of an overall national developmentalist approach, an explicit attempt to curb communist influence in rural regions (and indeed, were often funded by the United States government's Alliance for Progress). The literacy programs facilitated the growth of church-led rural unions in direct competition with the PCB-led Ligas Camponesas. Formal education was also used as a tool to subvert rural organizing.

These developmentalist interventions, however, did not succeed in subduing the peasant protests. On the contrary, the threat of rural mobilizations became a primary justification for the 1964 coup. Thus, in Brazil we can characterize the educational and pedagogical interventions of social movements during the first half of the twentieth century as widespread, involving primarily informal and non-formal education, and organized by a diverse group of anarchists, communists, and progressive priests all working with popular movements despite very different goals.

In Mexico, the early twentieth-century educational history of grassroots movements took a different, more formal turn. As Vaughan (1997: 4) documents, after the Mexican revolution in 1921 authorities created the Secretary of Public Education (SEP). In 1932 a left-wing group took power in the SEP, closely aligned with the ideals of the revolution. They wrote a Six-Year plan for a "Socialist Education," which would guide educational policy for the next decade, becoming especially influential after Lázaro Cárdenas was elected in 1934.[1] Socialist education "depicted workers and peasants as oppressed social classes, the protagonists of Mexican history, the makers and heirs of the revolution of 1910 . . . The multiethnic elements of popular culture, indigenous, mestizos, folkloric— were celebrated and packaged as national culture" (ibid.: 50).

Although these changes were driven by the state, Socialist Education led to a grassroots movement of educators attempting to uphold the ideals of the revolution. This was not simply a top-down attempt at incorporation, but rather, a moment of dialogue between the state and society around this educational project; the relative *incapacity* of the state meant that "the school became the arena for intense, often violent negotiations over power, culture, knowledge, and rights" (Vaughan 1997: 7). Socialist Education was contradictory, valorizing and empowering peasant communities while also serving as a project of state integration by helping in the formation of national organizations of workers, *campesinos*, and teachers that became part of the ruling party. Furthermore, there was a tension between some teachers who wanted to "rescue" *campesino* customs and transform them into a national culture, versus others who saw their role as transforming peasants into modern producers (Palacios 1998: 310). Nonetheless, for this brief decade, Mexican schools embodied many social movement ideals and became a sphere of negotiation over the future of Mexican society.

Finally, in a very different revolutionary context, the Cuban government also transformed education into a grassroots social movement. On September 26, 1960, less than two years after Fulgencio Batista (1952–1959) fled Cuba, Fidel Castro declared to the General Assembly of the United Nations that "our people intend to fight the great battle of illiteracy, with the ambitious goal of teaching every single inhabitant of the country to read and write in one year" (Kozol 1978: 342). This launched the most expansive and successful literacy campaign in Latin American history, involving more than 250,000 volunteers, including 100,000 urban school-aged children, who taught 707,212 illiterate adults to read and write and reduced the illiteracy rate from 25% to 4% in just eight months (Leiner 1987: 176). The Castro government meticulously planned and coordinated the campaign, closing down schools from April to December to allow for participation. Over a period of five months, the government offered eight days of training to the 100,000 young students, or *brigadistas* (ibid.: 180–81). The literacy campaign transformed the lives of both literacy trainers and adult students, teaching them the real meaning of revolution.

In terms of literacy methods, in 1961 the Brazilian educational theorist Paulo Freire was already leading literacy circles in Northeast Brazil; however, he was not connected to the 1961 Cuban campaign and he would not publish his influential *Pedagogy of the Oppressed* until 1968.[2] Nonetheless, the Cuban Ministry for Adult Education, with the leadership of Raúl Ferrer, developed a literacy method uncannily similar to what would become globally renowned as a "Freirean approach" in the coming decades.

For example, the literacy workbooks included generative words that allowed for the teaching of literacy as well as discussion of Cuban political and social life, such as the "Organization of American States" and the "National Institute of Agrarian Reform." The *brigadistas* also used pictures to initiate conversations with the adult learners, for example, depicting a fisherman holding up the catch from a day's work to illustrate "the cooperative" and a man walking home with groceries from "the People's Store" (Kozol 1978: 350). *Brigadistas* were also advised to avoid giving orders and to establish themselves as equals with their students.

Thus, in this Cuban revolutionary context, an education approach developed that emphasized equality, used photographs to stimulate dialogue, and focused on generative themes about the broader social and political context. Similar to the Brazilian anarchists and communists and the Mexican teachers, this was not simply a form of education imported from Europe. Party and movement leaders drew on international experiences but produced their own Latin American blend of education and social change. These Cuban experiences influenced other governments and movements, illustrating the importance of literacy for social equality and, twenty years later, directly inspiring Nicaragua's national literacy campaign (1980–1981). Importantly, all of these pedagogies developed before the "Freirean moment", which I discuss in the next section.

Educating under Authoritarianism: Paulo Freire and Liberation Theology's Impact

During the second half of the twentieth century, vibrant socialist mobilizations throughout Latin America gave way to dictatorships. This was when Paulo Freire's pedagogical ideas spread, reshaping Latin American social movement pedagogy as *popular education*.

In the 1950s, even before the height of liberation theology, some Catholic priests in Brazil engaged in literacy efforts in poor communities. Through the Catholic Action movement, Freire became familiar with the incipient progressive current that would become liberation theology (see Mackin in this volume). In 1960 Freire founded Recife's Movimento de Cultura Popular (MCP) and the following year he was appointed director of Culture and Recreation. At this moment in Latin America, adult education was typically a replication of the contents and methods used to educate children. Freire began to develop an approach that was particular to adults, not simply transmitting information but rather drawing on the experiences that adults brought with them into the classroom. In 1962, Freire had a first opportunity to implement these ideas in Rio Grande do Norte, teaching 300 sugarcane workers to read and write in forty-five days (Schugurensky 2011: 20–22). Following Freire's success, President João Goulart (1961–1964) invited him to develop a national literacy program that would organize twenty thousand "cultural circles" to teach two million illiterate adults how to read.

"Cultural circles" are a central part of Freire's literacy programs, an "educational approach aimed at liberation that combined study circles ... lived experience, work pedagogy, and politics" (Schugurensky 2011: 21). Before they are set up, several educators first go into the community with a tape recorder and notebook, noting all of the words, phrases, expressions, composition of verses, and characteristic ways of speaking. It is from this preliminary research that educators choose the generative themes put into the curriculum. In the process of teaching community members how to read and write, educators and members of the cultural circles both *codify* and *decodify* the themes together. For example, in the "codification" process they could talk about the word "farmer" and what the word represents, perhaps making a visual representation of a "farmer." Later on, questions are asked to "decodify" the word: What does it mean to be a farmer? How much money do they earn, how much time do they work? Do farmers choose their professions? Do farmers control their own destiny? In this way, the cultural circles are set up to teach people how to read and write words, while also *to read the world*. Freire's national literacy efforts were cut short with the 1964 coup, when Freire was designated a "subversive" and exiled from Brazil for fifteen years (ibid.; Torres 2014).

After a short stay in Bolivia, Freire moved to Chile, where he lived for five years (1964–1969). This was during Eduardo Frei's (1964–1970) United States-supported Christian democratic administration, which sought to modernize the country by eradicating illiteracy and promoting land reform (Holst 2006: 253). Freire worked for the Training Institute for Agrarian Reform, setting up literacy projects similar to the ones in Brazil. Importantly, as Holst (ibid.) describes, Freire's politics radicalized during this period. Agrarian reform under Frei failed to change power relations and the peasantry began to join unions affiliated with left-wing parties. The progressive members of the agrarian reform agency also split with Frei's party and joined the Unidad Popular or the Movimiento de Izquierda Revolucionaria (MIR). "Freire began to realize that his earlier humanistic analysis insufficiently explained movements that were clearly of a class nature" (ibid.: 260). Thus, it was in Chile that Freire became a Marxist humanist, directly shaping the *Pedagogy of the Oppressed*.

Importantly, during the late-1960s, some Catholic priests also began to take a more radical stance. The Second Vatican Council (1962–1965) called for a modernization of the church, and many clergy in Latin America interpreted this call as demanding an identification with the cause of the poor and a transformation in the church's teachings and practices (Hammond 1998: 26). As Berryman (1987: 15) outlines, clergy had previously supported "charity projects", but were not supposed to be involved in "political projects". Clergy began developing a theology of liberation, based on what became known as a "preferential option for the poor." In 1968, at a conference sponsored by progressive priests in Peru, Gustavo Gutiérrez (1973) gave the presentation "A Theology of Liberation". A few months later, Latin American Bishops met at Medellín to discuss how to apply the Vatican II to the region. In their conclusion statement they endorsed the main ideas of liberation theology, as well as a statement on education that called for a "liberating" education, reflecting Freire's early influence (Consejo Episcopal Latinoamericano 1979; Hammond 1998: 26; Mackin in this volume).

Catholic clergy began setting up Comunidades Eclesiales de Base (CEBs) all over Latin America, which were Bible study groups based on Freire's theory of *consciousness-raising*. The Bible study sessions began by discussing peoples' personal experiences, and then progressed to more macro discussions about structural inequalities, the political economy, and electoral politics (Berryman 1987: 36). In Brazil, 80,000 CEBs existed around the country by 1981 (Moreira 1985: 177). These CEBs became a force within Latin American communities, spurring the rise of oppositional union movements as well as women's, black, and landless movements throughout the continent (see Mackin in this volume).

El Salvador offers a critical example of the role of liberation theology and popular education under authoritarianism. During the 1970s, liberation theology-inspired clergy began forming CEBs in rural areas to promote social and political consciousness (Hammond 1998: 25–51). These priests were part of a "new left" who rejected the electoral and reformist politics of communist organizers and instead created guerrilla groups and social movements to fight the authoritarian regime (Chávez 2017; see Martí i Puig and Álvarez, Oikonomakis in this volume). This left included university students and faculty, Catholic intellectuals, teachers, peasant leaders, and poets. An alliance emerged between urban activists and peasant leaders, through what Chávez (2017) calls the "pedagogy of the revolution"—rural cooperative training, literacy programs, and workshops on Catholic doctrine. Clergy sponsored radio schools, which were daily radio broadcasts of primary school lessons that also included the formation of local political study groups (ibid.: 5). Then, after the start of the civil war in 1980, communities organized similar popular education programs and community schools in zones controlled by the Frente Farabundo Martí para la Liberación Nacional (FMLN), as well as in contested zones, cities, and in prisons and refugee camps. These programs were explicitly based on Freire's concept of consciousness-raising, helping to reduce illiteracy while also developing the political consciousness of rural peasants throughout the country who became the base of the insurgency (Hammond 1998).

Another important example of Freire's influence is the Nicaraguan Sandinista revolution (see Martí i Puig and Álvarez; Brockett in this volume). Similarly to El Salvador, in the 1970s university students started engaging in community organizing and grassroots educational efforts against the Somoza dictatorship (1967–1979). Fifteen days after the Frente Sandinista de Liberación Nacional (FSLN) came to power, in July 1979, the FSLN announced the launching of a national literacy campaign. Freire visited Nicaragua for a nine-day period, consulting with the team designing the campaign (Arnove 1986: 41). Liberation theology clergy were also actively involved, setting up "popular churches" directly tied to the literacy campaign (Berryman 1987: 146). In total, the literacy campaign succeeded in teaching 406,000 people how to read and write, lowering the illiteracy rate from 50.3% to under 15% in one year. After the campaign, the Sandinista government invested in ongoing adult basic education, popular health and communications programs, and the expansion of formal schooling at all levels (ibid.; Barndt 1990).

In summary, during a period of authoritarianism and dictatorship, grassroots education became a primary means of cultivating political struggle. Liberation theology transformed churches and Bible study groups into incubators of social critique. These popular education efforts were influenced by the previous era of socialist organizing, but they also represented a qualitatively different bottom-up approach to education and leadership. As Kane (2001: 248) states, "Above all, rather than an academic theory, popular education in Latin America is understood as the intellectual property of grassroots movements in which the notion of people as 'subjects' of change has a real meaning."

An Educational Moment: Social Movements in Contemporary Latin America

Over the past four decades, there has been an eruption of social movement organizing throughout Latin America and, simultaneously, a deepening and expansion of educational initiatives within, by, and for these movements. Paulo Freire was finally allowed to return to Brazil in 1980. At this moment, popular education was in its heyday in Latin America. Kane (2001) refers to three levels of popular education. First, there are thousands of activists at the grassroots level, organizing around local issues such as water, health, and housing, who incorporate popular education into their efforts. Second, there are the intermediate organizations, independent from the state and often funded by NGOs or third parties that aid grassroots organizations, for example the Instituto Mexicano para el Desarrollo Comunitario (IMDEC) and Brazil's Instituto Paulo Freire (IPF). Finally, there are the popular education networks, through which educators and centers come together to share expertise and resources. Among the largest are the Consejo de Educación Popular de América Latina y el Caribe (CEAAL), a network of 250 centers involved in popular education around Latin America, and the Centro de Estudios y Publicaciones Alforja (CEP Alforja), a network of popular education centers in Central America and Mexico. Educators in these networks collaborate directly with grassroots movements to promote popular education practices. These efforts have also led to a focus on more participatory action research in the region (Fals-Borda and Rahman 1991). Kane (2001: 260–61) argues that popular education in Latin America, although enacted differently in each country and between movements, maintains three common characteristics: (1) the curriculum comes out of the material interests of people in resistance and struggle, (2) the pedagogy is collective, and (3) the goal is to forge a direct link between education and social action

Another form of social movement pedagogy continues to be adult education and literacy programs, sometimes organized by the state and at other times through NGOs and international organizations. In Brazil, the Partido dos Trabalhadores (PT) won the municipal election in São Paulo in 1989 and Freire became the Secretary of Education, implementing a massive adult education program, the Movimento de Alfabetização de Jovens e Adultos (MOVA). A feature of the program was "the strong role of grassroots organizations in the design and implementation" (Stromquist 1997: 32). Social movement leaders worked *with* the government but not *for* the government, choosing their own curriculum and activities inside and outside of the classroom that supported both literacy and the movements' broader goals (Stromquist 1997: 170).

Similarly, in the 1990s, the Movimento dos Trabalhadores Rurais Sem Terra (MST) worked directly with the United Nations Educational, Scientific, and Cultural Organization (UNESCO) to run literacy programs in their occupied encampments and agrarian reform settlements. Freire attended the opening day of one of these literacy campaigns in 1991, in an MST settlement in the far south of Rio Grande do Sul. There, Freire commended the MST's educational efforts: "This afternoon begins something that already started, that started the very first moment of your struggle . . . the right to knowledge, the right to know that you already know, and the right to know what you do not yet know" (MST 2003: 8). Freire's participation in this program offered the MST's still nascent educational initiatives national recognition.

In the early 2000s, Cuban educator Leonela Relys Díaz, through the Cuban Ministry of Education's Instituto Pedagógico Latinoamericano y Caribeño (IPLAC), developed "¡Yo, Sí Puedo!" an alphanumeric literacy method that uses audio-visual technology, inspired by the 1961 literacy campaign and a Cuban radio literacy program developed in Haiti in the late 1990s. The Cuban government has implemented "¡Yo, Sí Puedo!" throughout Latin America and globally, as a form of "developmental internationalism" (Muhr 2015: 129), as Cuban illiteracy has already been eradicated. It is implemented across the Latin American region through inter-governmental cooperation and transnationally through partnerships with subnational governments and nonstate actors. For example, in 2005 the Cuban government worked with the Nicaraguan Asociación de Educación Popular Carlos Fonseca Amador (AEPCFA) and progressive municipal governments, sending six Cuban advisors and resources for 5,000 literacy locations, with TV sets, video players, and so on. The videos were adapted for the local context with constant references to anti-colonial and anti-imperialist leaders. In 2007, "¡Yo, Sí Puedo!" became a national campaign in Nicaragua, supported by 57,631 volunteers (Muhr 2015). Cuba has also helped implement "¡Yo, Sí Puedo!" programs in more than twenty other Latin American and Caribbean countries, as well as dozens of locations globally (ibid.). Importantly, Cuba also develops and implements post-literacy programs, and within Cuba, the government has opened up its own higher education institutions, including its famous Escuela Latinoamericana de Medicina, to thousands of social movement activists throughout the region.

Social movements have also developed their own informal and non-formal education programs, independent of NGOs, popular education centers, and socialist governments, to promote learning within their movements. Informally, factory occupations (Jaramillo, McLaren, and Lázaro 2011), road blockades (Harley 2014), and other social movement actions provide powerful pedagogical experiences—"fostering the conditions of possibility for the emergence of a new popular political subject" (Motta 2017: 9). Similarly, MST leader Rosali Caldart (2004: 331) argues that the pedagogy of the MST is not its educational programs, but rather, the movement's daily organizational and political practices, which help participants form a new identity as *sem terra* (landless people). In terms of non-formal education, social movements have also developed "movement schools" to promote the *formación* (political training and human development) of their activists. For example, the Colectivo de Mujeres Pazificas de Calí, Colombia coordinated a Political School that "nurtures new pedagogical practice that enable a collective and critical reading of the world and women's experiences of oppression, violence and displacement" (Motta and Cole 2013: 15).

Peasant and farmer movements have been particularly important innovators in developing "movement schools" that mold "values of the new woman and new man for egalitarian, cooperative social relations in the construction of a 'new society,'" while also providing for the "socialization of agroecological knowledges and senses" (McCune et al. 2016: 354). One of these movement-led programs is Campesino-a-Campesino (CaC), which started in Central America and spread to Mexico, eventually having its biggest impact in Cuba (Holtz-Giménez 2006; McCune and Sánchez 2018). Rather than taking place in a classroom, this program focuses on peer-to-peer agroecological learning, "based on the radical premise that peasants are the best teachers of peasants" (McCune and Sánchez 2018: 8).

The first CaC initiatives began in the 1970s in Guatemala, organized by Catholic Action and funded by an international NGO. Rather than drawing on Freire, the philosophical basis of the program "was the Mayan concept of seeing and feeling the land as a sacred being that must be taking care of" (McCune and Sánchez 2018: 6). The program drew on "inductive horizontalism," moving from simple to complex, the empirical to the systematic (ibid.: 6). The program, however, was cut short with the military repression of the 1980s. Participants fled to Mexico, Honduras, and Nicaragua, starting similar CaC programs. In Nicaragua, the Unión Nacional de Agricultores y Ganaderos de Nicaragua (UNAG) took over the program under the Sandinistas. Then, ironically, after the Sandinistas were voted out of office in 1990 a Swiss NGO began funding CaC, expanding the program into a mass-action, peasant-led, movement form of agroecology—but in the context of a period of privatization and co-optation of revolutionary processes (ibid.: 7). In 1996 a leader in the Cuban Asociación Nacional de Agricultores Pequeños (ANAP) came to Nicaragua and became familiar with the program. ANAP took the program on as its own in 2001, and CaC became a national, grassroots movement in Cuba, "the fundamental tool for transforming isolated experiences by diligent ecological farmers into widespread, massive, agroecological learning processes with strong social momentum" (ibid.: 8).

In contrast to this peer-to-peer learning model, the Brazilian MST developed non-formal political education programs that drew on Freirean popular education as well as Soviet pedagogues, including Anton Makarenko and Moisey Pistrak.[3] The five pillars of this approach include collectivity, work, culture, historical memory, and social struggle

(Caldart 2004). The MST's educational approach is a unique synthesis of popular education and socialist pedagogy, promoting dialogue and drawing on communities' local knowledge and context, while also incorporating the movement's cultural practices, agroecology, manual labor as an educational process, and student self-governance (Mariano, Hilário, and Tarlau 2016). This pedagogy is exemplified by the MST's Escola Nacional Florestan Fernandes in São Paulo, where thousands of activists from Brazil, Latin America, and other regions around the world study each year. The MST also oversees dozens of other similar *escolas de formacão* throughout the country. Other peasant groups, such as the Nicaraguan Asociación de Trabajadores del Campo (ATC), have set up similar networks of movement schools for internal political education (McCune et al. 2017).

In 2005, Venezuelan President Hugo Chávez (1999–2001, 2001–2007, 2007–2013, 2013) signed an agreement with the international peasant organization La Vía Campesina to create the first international peasant university, the Instituto Universitario Latinoamericano de Agroecología Paulo Freire (IALA-PF). The IALA-PF brings together young and old members of farmer organizations for periods of four to five years to be trained in both farming and the political-organizational aspects of collective struggle for food sovereignty, leading to a state-recognized degree. This model of movement agroecology quickly spread, and as of January 2018 IALAs had also been established in Argentina, Brazil, Chile, Colombia, Ecuador, Nicaragua, and Paraguay (McCune and Sánchez 2018). Although the schools have their own particularities (e.g., in Nicaragua IALA Mesoamérica integrates peer-to-peer learning; see McCune, Reardon, and Rosset 2014), all of the IALAs are highly influenced by the MST's educational approach.

Finally, in Mexico, the Ejército Zapatista de Liberación Nacional (EZLN) has developed its own autonomous education program, outside of the state realm. Hundreds of autonomous education promoters in their teens and twenties teach Zapatista children and adults in their communities. In return for their unpaid labor, community members fulfill the agricultural work and domestic responsibilities of these teachers. In each autonomous community an education collective elected by the local assembly supervises the curricular and pedagogical approaches that these education promoters employ (Baronnet 2008: 116). The autonomous communities also receive pedagogical and financial support from outside solidarity groups and volunteers (Vergara-Camus 2014: 151). Although not explicitly based in Freirean theory, it is reminiscent of this pedagogical tradition as local cultures, histories, and languages are prioritized. The central principles of the Zapatista schools are Autonomy and Rebellion (Pinheiro Barbosa 2015). In December 2012 the EZLN announced the creation of the Escuelita Zapatista, which is not a school for Zapatista students but rather a process for Mexican civil society and international supporters to study about Zapatista thought and action. The first school included a group of 1,700 students that lived in Zapatista homes and studied about the autonomous government, women's participation, and resistance (ibid.). Thus, the EZLN exemplifies both the challenges and possibilities of constructing an education program outside of and in parallel to the state, as well as the importance of education and learning with transnational allies.

Movements, Unions, and Students Organizing around and through Schools

Although Latin American social movements have demanded educational access for over a century, it is primarily since the 1980s that participation in and transformation of the formal public school system has become an explicit goal. This is part of a broader shift across Latin America, from social movements only engaging in confrontational struggle to other forms of civic engagement. Social movement activists are not only making demands for more public services but are also demanding the right to participate in the public sphere (Rossi 2017). This is in part due to the influential role of Gramscian theory among social movement activists, which represented a fundamental rupture with previous theories of the state as the locus of domination (Webber in this volume). "Gramsci served as a vehicle, a catalyst, and a pretext for a renovating discussion within the Left... [about] the very notion of power, understood by Gramsci not as an institution, a 'thing' to be seized, but as a relationship among social forces that must be transformed" (Dagnino 1998: 37).

The Brazilian MST is representative of this Gramscian shift towards the "long march through the institutions." MST activists have been involved in educational provisions since the start of their agrarian reform struggle, organizing educational activities for children in occupied encampments and developing adult literacy programs. In the early 1990s the MST National Education Sector began to develop teacher training programs in order to influence the public schools. Among the many consequences, this educational focus helped increase gender equity within the movement. By the late-1990s, the MST activists had developed a comprehensive educational program for the Brazilian countryside, known as Educação do Campo (Arroyo, Caldart, and Molina 2004). The movement has been able to implement this educational proposal in hundreds of public schools and universities across the country, often in coordination with other rural movements (Tarlau 2019).

The MST is only one of the many Brazilian movements that has made participation in educational provision a core demand. During the 1980s, Black leaders demanded the inclusion of Afro-Brazilian history in the curriculum and pressured the government to pass policies that addressed racial inequality in schools (Paschel 2016; Dixon and Caldwell in this volume). Indigenous groups in Brazil fought for the right to govern their own schools in the 1980s and 1990s, and in 1996 the federal government passed a law guaranteeing indigenous communities' right to a differentiated education. While schools in indigenous territories in Brazil are part of the public school system, communities appoint their own teachers who teach in their local language and incorporate the histories of their nations into the curriculum.

In the broader Latin American context, a well-known example of social movements transforming public education is in Ecuador. In 1988 the Confederación de

Nacionalidades Indígenas del Ecuardor (CONAIE) won the right to administer a new bilingual intercultural education program for thirteen indigenous nationalities, which meant that indigenous leaders coordinated teacher trainings and curriculum development, created standard orthography for indigenous languages, and oversaw the regional implementation of the program (Oviedo and Wildemeersch 2008). Similarly, indigenous movements in Bolivia under Evo Morales' leadership passed legislation that promoted the "decolonization" of public education (Lopes Cardozo 2011), and in Colombia both indigenous and black movements self-govern public schools in their respective territories (Walsh 2018). In Argentina, workers occupying factories in the late 1990s established secondary schools, shaping their curriculum and pedagogy (Jaramillo, McLaren, and Lázaro 2011). In Chile the student movement, from the "penguin" rebellions of 2006 to the university protests of 2011, as well as the feminist movements of 2018, have also demanded a radical transformation of their neoliberal-inspired school system (Atria 2015; Campos-Martínez and Olavarría 2020; Donoso in this volume).

In other parts of Latin America, teachers' unions have been protagonists demanding teachers' and communities' right to participate in educational governance (Gindin 2013). In Mexico in the late 1970s dissident groups of teachers separated from the official teachers' union to form the Coordinadora Nacional de Trabajadores de la Educación (CNTE), which has been an important mobilizing force throughout southern Mexico (Cook 1996). In 2006, police repression against CNTE led to a state-wide uprising, with teachers playing a leading role in the creation of the Asamblea Popular de los Pueblos de Oaxaca (APPO) (Stephen 2007). In 2010, Oaxacan teachers won the right to implement their own "Plan para la Transformación de la Educación de Oaxaca (PTEO)," which included community-centered cultural programs. Teachers from CNTE unions in other states have implemented similar pedagogical alternatives in their schools. Indeed, across Latin America teachers' unions frequently shift between narrowly defending the employment interests of teachers and developing concrete pedagogical proposals linked to social movements and broader visions of societal transformation.

In summary, across Latin America, grassroots movements have engaged in both contentious actions and political negotiation to transform their school systems and take part in the contentious co-governance (Tarlau 2019) of public education. Importantly, these formal educational struggles have served to resist global education reform efforts (Sahlberg 2016) that have prioritized teacher meritocracy, standardized testing, and market-based solutions to educational provision.

Conclusion

There are three broad lessons that emerge from these histories of social movements and education in Latin America. First, while Latin American social movement activists have always been influenced by transnational movements, including anarchist, socialist, agrarian, religious, women's, LGBTQ, and Black movements, the types of educational approaches that these movements have developed are uniquely Latin American. In other words, Latin American activists have drawn on the experiences of working-class movements around the globe and integrated these experiences into their local knowledge, customs, and practices.

Second, during periods of authoritarianism, grassroots educational programs became vital spaces for developing critical consciousness and stimulating counterhegemonic movements. Liberation theology, a Latin American blend of social Catholic thought, Freirean educational philosophy, and socialist practice, became the most important vehicle for the development and practice of popular education during this repressive era. CEBs spread like wildfire throughout Latin America, stimulating the emergence of hundreds of social movements.

Third and finally, since the 1980s and 1990s social movements in Latin America have been among the strongest and most vibrant globally. This strength is connected to the priority Latin American movements have put on education, pedagogy, and study. Freire became the global figurehead of Latin American popular education, but the force of his ideas was through their uptake in grassroots movements throughout the continent. Many movements have taken these innovative non-formal practices and attempted to implement them in public schools.

Education has long been a priority for Latin American social movements, helping them expand and diversify their membership, increase activists' technical and political capacity, and garner power. Given the resurgence of right-wing, authoritarian governments throughout the region, this educational and pedagogical focus will be of the utmost importance for activists to continue developing a shared analysis of the current political context, strategize about how to defend and grow their movements, and prefigure in the current world, the social, political, and economic practices they hope to build in the future.

Notes

1. There are several book-length accounts of Socialist Education, including Bremauntz (1943) and Lerner (1979).
2. Freire's first visit to Cuba was in 1987 for a Sociology Congress (Pérez 2010).
3. Makarenko and Pistrak were both involved in developing Soviet educational policy and practice immediately after the Bolshevik Revolution (see Tarlau 2019).

References

Arnove, Robert F. (1986), *Education and Revolution in Nicaragua* (New York: Praeger).
Arroyo, Miguel G., Rosali Salete Caldart, and Monica Castagna Molina (2004), *Por uma Educação do Campo* (Petrópolis: Editora Vozes).
Atria, Fernando (2015), *La mala educación: Ideas que inspiran al movimiento estudiantil de Chile* (Santiago: Catalonia).

Barndt, Deborah (1990), *To Change This House: Popular Education Under the Sandinistas* (Toronto: Between the Lines).

Baronnet, Bruno (2008), "Rebel Youth and Zapatista Autonomous Education," *Latin American Perspectives* 35(4), 112–24.

Berryman, Phillip. (1987), *Liberation Theology: Education at Empire's End.* (New York: Pantheon Books).

Bremauntz, Alberto (1943), *La educación socialista en México: Antecedentes y fundamentos de la reforma de 1934* (Mexico: Imprenta Rivadeneyra).

Caldart, Rosali Salete (2004), *Pedagogia do Movimento Sem Terra* (São Paulo: Expressão Popular).

Campos-Martínez, Javier and Dayana Olvarría (2020), "Learning from Chile's Student Movement: Youth Organising and Neoliberal Reaction," in Aziz Choudry and Salim Vally (eds.), *The University and Social Justice*, 98–115 (London: Pluto).

Chávez, Joaquín M (2017), *Poets and Prophets of the Resistance: Intellectuals and the Origins of El Salvador's Civil War* (Oxford: Oxford University Press).

Consejo Episcopal Latinoamericano (1979), *Medellín: Conclusiones* (Bogotá: Secretariado General del CELAM).

Cook, Maria Lorena (1996), *Organizing Dissent: Unions, the State, and the Democratic Teachers' Movement in Mexico* (University Park, PA: Penn State University Press).

Dagnino, Evelina (1998), "Culture, Citizenship, and Democracy: Changing Discourses and Practices of the Latin American Left," in Sonia Alvarez, Evelina Dagnino, and Escobar, Arturo (eds.), *Cultures of Politics, Politics of Culture: Re-Visioning Latin American Social Movements*, 33–63 (Boulder, CO: Westview Press).

Dore, Rosemary (2009), "Gramscian Thought and Brazilian Education," *Educational Philosophy and Theory* 41(6), 712–31.

Dulles, John W (1973), *Anarchists and Communists in Brazil, 1900–1935* (Austin: University of Texas Press).

Fals-Borda, Orlando and Mohammad Anisur Rahman (1991), *Action and Knowledge: Breaking the Monopoly with Participatory Action Research* (Lanham, MD: Rowman & Littlefield).

Fischer, Brodwyn (2014), "The Red Menace Reconsidered: A Forgotten History of Communist Mobilization in Rio de Janeiro's Favelas, 1945–1964," *Hispanic American Historical Review* 94(1), 1–33.

Gindin, Julián (2013), "Sindicalismo dos trabalhadores em educação: Tendências políticas e organizacionais (1978–2011)," *Educar em Revista* 48, 75–92.

Gutiérrez, Gustavo (1973), *Theology of Liberation* (New York: Orbis Books).

Hammond, John L. (1998), *Fighting to Learn: Popular Education and Guerrilla War in El Salvador* (New Brunswick, NJ: Rutgers University Press).

Hardman, Francisco Foot (1983), *Nem pátria, nem patrão: Vida operária e cultura anarquista no Brasil* (São Paulo: Brasiliense).

Harley, Anne (2014), "The Pedagogy of Road Blockades," *Interface: A Journal for and about Social Movements* 6(1), 266–96.

Holst, John D. (2006), "Paulo Freire in Chile, 1964–1969: Pedagogy of the Oppressed in Its Sociopolitical Economic Context," *Harvard Educational Review* 76(2), 243–70.

Holtz-Giménez, Eric (2006), *Campesino a Campesino: Voices from Latin America's Farmer to Farmer Movement for Sustainable Agriculture* (Oakland, CA: Food First Books).

Jaramillo, Nathalia E., Peter McLaren, and Fernando Lázaro (2011), "A Critical Pedagogy of Recuperation," *Policy Futures in Education* 9(6), 747–58.

Kane, Liam (2001), *Popular Education and Social Change in Latin America* (London: Latin America Bureau).
Kozol, Jonathan (1978) "A New Look at the Literacy Campaign in Cuba," *Harvard Educational Review* 48(3), 341–77.
Leiner, Marvin (1987), "The 1961 National Cuban Literacy Campaign," in Robert F. Arnove and Harvey J. Graff (eds.), *National Literacy Campaigns and Movements: Historical and Comparative Perspectives*, 173–96 (New York: Springer).
Lerner, Victoria (1979), *La educación socialista* (Mexico: El Colegio de México).
Lopes Cardozo, Mieke T. A. (2011), *Future Teachers and Social Change in Bolivia: Between Decolonisation and Demonstration* (Utrecht: Eburon).
Luizetto, Flavio (1986), "O movimento anarquista em São Paulo: A experiência da escola moderna," *Revista Educação & Sociedade* 24, 18–47.
Mariano, Alessandro, Erivan Hilário, and Rebecca Tarlau (2016), "Pedagogies of Struggle and Collective Organization: The Educational Practices of the Brazilian Landless Workers Movement," *Interface: A Journal for and about Social Movements* 8(2), 211–42.
McCune, Nils, Juan Reardon, and Peter Rosset (2014), "Agroecological Formación in Rural Social Movements," *Radical Teachers: A Socialist, Feminist, and Anti-Racist Journal on the Theory and Practice of Teaching* 94, 31–37.
McCune, Nils, Peter Rosset, Tania Cruz Salazar, Helda Morales, and Antonio Saldívar Moreno. (2017), "The Long Road: Rural Youth, Farming and Agroecological Formación in Central America," *Mind, Culture, and Activity* 24(3), 183–98.
McCune, Nils, Peter Rosset, Tania Cruz Salazar, Antonio Saldívar Moreno, and Helda Morales (2016), "Mediated Territoriality: Rural Workers and the Efforts to Scale out Agroecology in Nicaragua," *Journal of Peasant Studies* 44(2), 354–76.
McCune, Nils and Marlen Sánchez (2018) "Teaching the Territory: Agroecological Pedagogy and Popular Movements," *Agriculture and Human Values* 36(3), 595–610.
Moreira, Maria Helena Alves (1985), *State and Opposition in Military Brazil* (Austin: University of Texas Press).
Motta, Sara C. (2017), "Emancipation in Latin America: On the Pedagogical Turn," *Bulletin of Latin American Research* 36(1), 5–20.
Motta, Sara C. and Mike Cole (2013), *Education and Social Change in Latin America* (New York: Palgrave-Macmillan).
MST (2003), *Caderno de Educação N$_0$11: Educação de Jovens e Adultos. Sempre é tempo de aprender* (Veranópolis: Instituto Técnico de Capacitação e Pesquisa da Reforma Agrária).
Muhr, Thomas (2015), "South–South Cooperation in Education and Development: The ¡Yo, SíPuedo! Literacy Method," *International Journal of Educational Development* 43, 126–33.
Oviedo, Alexis and Danny Wildemeersch (2008), "Intercultural Education and Curricular Diversification: The Case of the Ecuadorian Intercultural Bilingual Education Model (MOSEIB)," *Compare* 38(4), 455–70.
Palacios, Guillermo (1998), "Postrevolutionary Intellectuals, Rural Readings and the Shaping of the 'Peasant Problem' in Mexico: El Maestro Rural, 1932–34," *Journal of Latin American Studies* 30(2), 309–39.
Paschel, Tianna S. (2016), *Becoming Black Political Subjects: Movements and Ethno-Racial Rights in Colombia and Brazil* (Princeton, NJ: Princeton University Press).
Pérez, Esther (2010), "Freire, Cuban Style," in Tom Wilson, Peter Park, and Anaida Colón-Muñiz (eds.), *Memories of Paulo*, 125–32 (Rotterdam: Sense Publishers).

Pinheiro Barbosa, Lia (2015), "El principio de la autonomía y la práxis de la libertad en la educación rebelde autónoma Zapatista," *CISMA. Revista Del Centro Telúrico de Investigaciones Teóricas* 6(3), 1–36.

Rossi, Federico M. (2017), *The Poor's Struggle for Political Incorporation: The Piquetero Movement in Argentina* (Cambridge: Cambridge University Press).

Rueda, Maria Alicia (2021), *The Educational Philosophy of Luis Emilio Recabarren: Pioneering Working Class Education in Latin America* (Abingdon: Routledge).

Sahlberg, Pasi (2016), "Global Educational Reform Movement and Its Impact on Schooling," in Karen Mundy, Andy Green, Robert Lingard, and Antoni Verger (eds.), *The Handbook of Global Education Policy*, 128–44 (Malden: Wiley-Blackwell).

Schugurensky, Daniel (2011), *Paulo Freire* (New York: Continuum).

Stephen, Lynn (2007), "'We Are Brown, We Are Short, We Are Fat . . . We Are the Face of Oaxaca': Women Leaders in the Oaxaca Rebellion," *Socialism and Democracy* 21(2), 97–112.

Stromquist, Nelly P. (1997), *Literacy for Citizenship: Gender and Grassroots Dynamics in Brazil* (New York: State University of New York Press).

Tarlau, Rebecca (2019), *Occupying Schools, Occupying Land: How the Landless Workers Movement Transformed Brazilian Education* (Oxford: Oxford University Press).

Torres, Carlos Alberto (2014), *First Freire: Early Writings in Social Justice Education* (New York: Teachers College Press).

Vaughan, Mary Kay (1997), *Cultural Politics in Revolution: Teachers, Peasants, and Schools in Mexico, 1930–1940* (Tucsan: University of Arizona Press).

Vergara-Camus, Leandro (2014), *Land and Freedom: The MST, the Zapatistas and Peasant Alternatives to Neoliberalism* (London: Zed).

Walsh, Catherine E. (2018), "Decoloniality in/as Praxis," in Walter D. Mignolo and Catherine E. Walsh (eds.), *On Decoloniality: Concepts, Analytics, Praxis*, 15–103 (Durham, NC: Duke University Press).

CHAPTER 39

REPERTOIRES OF CONTENTION ACROSS LATIN AMERICA

TAKESHI WADA

INTRODUCTION

The concept of repertoires of contention has become popular in the study of contentious politics and social movements. This chapter will give an overview of some of the recent studies on repertoires of contention across Latin America and assess their theoretical contributions to the literature beyond the region.

A repertoire of contention is defined by Charles Tilly as:

> a limited set of routines that are learned, shared, and acted out through a relatively deliberate process of choice. Repertoires are learned cultural creations, but they do not descend from abstract philosophy or take shape as a result of political propaganda; they emerge from struggle. People learn to break windows in protest, attack pilloried prisoners, tear down dishonored houses, stage public marches, petition, hold formal meetings, organize special-interest associations. At any particular point in history, however, they learn only a rather small number of alternative ways to act collectively. (Tilly 1995: 42)

To illustrate this idea of Charles Tilly's in the Latin American context, Figure 39.1 displays "alternative ways to act collectively" or tactical selections by country. The graph shows the proportions of different forms of contention—conventional, protest, and violent—employed by social actors between 2000 and 2004 based on the "10 Million International Dyadic Events," a database of worldwide political events (King and Lowe 2008).

Figure 39.1 reveals a lot about the repertoires of contention in these countries and generates plenty of interesting questions. We find that, for instance, violent forms were used at very high rates in some countries (Colombia and Haiti), while conventional

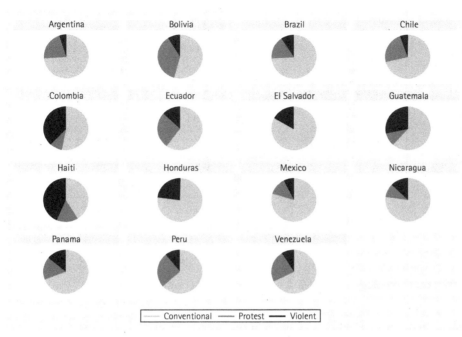

FIGURE 39.1 Tactical selections by Latin American country, 2000–2004

Source: King and Lowe (2008)

forms were more common in others (Argentina, Brazil, and Mexico). In some places, such as Bolivia, Ecuador, Peru, and Venezuela, the proportion of non-violent protest was much greater than in other societies.[1] Why were the ways of acting collectively so drastically different among the countries? The question of tactical choice is one of the principal issues addressed in the literature of repertoires of contention. The first part of this chapter presents recent studies dealing with this topic in Latin American contexts.

A focal point of debate in this chapter is the strengths and weaknesses of repertoire studies in Latin America. What insights can these studies on Latin America add to the general literature of repertoires of contention? What explains cross-national variations in Latin America? What causal factors influence tactical choices in Latin America? This chapter does not intend to provide an exhaustive review of the literature. Instead it explores theoretical advances and limitations as manifested in a selection of recent contributions.

Tactical Choice and Innovation

Potential factors that might influence tactical choices, according to the existing literature (della Porta and Diani 2006; Taylor and Van Dyke 2004), are classified into four

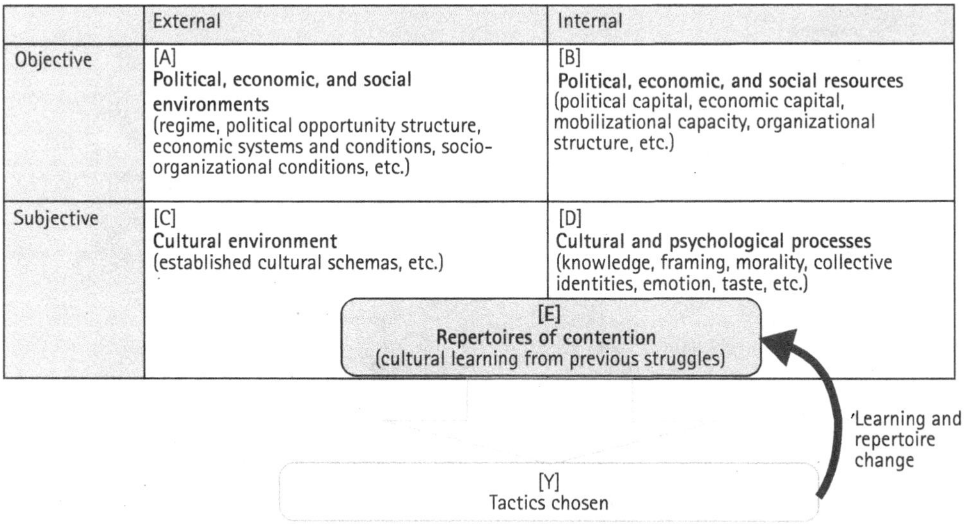

	External	Internal
Objective	[A] Political, economic, and social environments (regime, political opportunity structure, economic systems and conditions, socio-organizational conditions, etc.)	[B] Political, economic, and social resources (political capital, economic capital, mobilizational capacity, organizational structure, etc.)
Subjective	[C] Cultural environment (established cultural schemas, etc.)	[D] Cultural and psychological processes (knowledge, framing, morality, collective identities, emotion, taste, etc.)

[E] Repertoires of contention (cultural learning from previous struggles)

[Y] Tactics chosen

'Learning and repertoire change

FIGURE 39.2 Typology of causal factors in repertoires of contention

types (labeled A to D in Figure 39.2). Some factors (A and C) are "external" to challenging actors and therefore difficult for the actors to change. These include durable structures of politics, economy, society, and culture.

The other factors (B and D) are "internal" to challenging groups, which means that the actors can exercise more control over these factors. Factors internal to challenging actors are usually about political, economic, and social resources, and cultural and psychological processes.

The objective factors (A and B), such as political regime and material resources, are usually observable not only by insiders in a challenging group but also by outsiders. The subjective factors (C and D), such as cultural schemas, group morality, and collective identities, are harder to understand for outside observers who do not belong to a challenging group (D) or a broader society (C). The following section discusses which of these factors are relevant in repertoire studies in Latin America. For the moment we shall set aside the notion of "repertoires of contention," area E, which falls under the subjective factor category.

A: Objective and External Factors

Echoing Tilly's (2006) emphasis on the importance of regime characteristics in shaping tactical choices, some scholars on Latin American contention have addressed the relevance of structural factors (Franklin 2013; Kerrissey and Schofer 2018). Franklin (2013) examines whether choices of tactics—including protest, strikes, and rebellion—are explained by macro-structural regime characteristics, such as democracy, state capacity, and the generalized level of repression, or by dynamic–situational "micro-repression," meaning that when challengers have encountered governmental repression in using a specific tactic, they are likely to change the tactic to a new one.

Franklin used a cross-national large-N comparison approach and compiled 1,319 political events in seven randomly chosen Latin American countries—Argentina, Brazil, Chile, Guatemala, Mexico, Nicaragua, and Venezuela—between 1981 and 1995, drawing the data from several full-text news wire services (ibid.: 180–81). Applying multinomial logit regression, he found that the prevalence of the three types of tactic depends more on regime characteristics than on previous experiences of repression in using particular tactics.

Objective and external factors thus matter in the selection of tactics in Latin America, and scholars have used cross-national comparative approaches to identify the factors determining them.

B: Objective and Internal Factors

As it turns out, there are not many recent studies on Latin American contention that deal with objective and internal factors explicitly. For this reason, Medel Sierralta and Somma González's (2016: 163–64, 173) study on Chilean protests is valuable. Using a dataset of 2,342 protest events in Chile between 2000 and 2012, they explore the determinants of the adoption of thirty-seven specific tactics categorized into four types: "conventional" (demonstrations, public gathering of signatures or money, public declarations addressed to the authorities, etc.), "cultural" (theater or artistic representations, "bicycle rides", vigils, etc.), "disruptive" (civil disobedience, labor or student strikes, occupying buildings, blocking routes, etc.), and "violent" (setting fire to vehicles, properties, or buildings, destroying public or private property, looting, etc.).

Medel Sierralta and Somma González's multivariate regression models show the relevance of observable factors internal to challengers such as political and economic resources, formal organizations, and mobilizing capacity ("numerical resources") in tactical selection. Thus, resource-rich groups like workers (high in economic resources and political capital) prefer disruptive tactics but avoid violent ones because, the authors argue, the adoption of violence would undermine their political capital. In contrast, resource-poor groups such as indigenous groups (primarily Mapuche) would opt more for violent tactics (but only in the presence of radical demands) (Medel Sierralta and Somma González 2016: 186). While the presence of formal organizations in protest decreases disruptive and violent tactics, smaller protests in terms of the number of people mobilized are more likely to becoming disruptive and violent.

Their study reveals that even after controlling, to a degree, for the effects of objective and external factors (such as regime characteristics) in employing a single-country research design, considerable variation in tactical choice remains to be explained, and objective and internal factors should not be ignored.

C: Subjective and External Factors

The third set of the studies deals with subjective and external factors—broad cultural features—that are largely beyond the control of challenging groups. Echegaray (2015) and Barbosa and colleagues (2014) witness the rise of "political consumerism" in Latin America in the age of neoliberal economic reforms and globalization (see Rhodes in this volume). Political consumerism is "the act of influencing producers or choosing products on the basis of their ethical or socio-environmental credentials, to bring about change in power relations or in the distribution of public goods" (Echegaray 2015: 176). The tactic of political consumerism, such as boycotts and buycotts,[2] is considered new because it is largely individuals rather than groups who engage in the tactic and because it is exercised in the sphere of the market rather than in that of politics. The impact of this new tactic can be seen in the increases in consumption and market share of certified organic, eco-labeled, and fair-trade products (ibid.: 179).

What explains the emergence of these new individual tactics of contention in the markets? Major factors, according to Echegaray, include the structural shift to a market-centered economy (an objective and external factor) and the discursive change associated with this shift (a subjective and external factor). From the 1980s, neoliberal economic reforms were justified by employing pro-consumer language. The mechanisms to protect consumer rights legally were institutionalized through corporate social responsibility (CSR) regulations and policies and codes of conduct. "In all likelihood, these processes educated Latin Americans to connect seemingly private consumer issues to wider public affairs and to vote with their wallets to influence corporate policies" (Echegaray 2015: 182). Using survey data on urban populations in Argentina and Mexico, the author demonstrates the effect of subjective and external factors by showing a positive association between interest in CSR and use of political consumerism. The effect may not be universal, however, as the association is not statistically significant in the case of Brazil.

Barbosa and colleagues (2014) asked why involvement in political consumerism among young people in Brazil is lower than among the youth in Europe or in the United States. Based on a survey of young people in Rio de Janeiro and São Paulo, the authors found that the cultural influence of the family is the primary explanatory factor. In Brazilian culture, young people remain under the influence of the family much longer than is customary in European and North American societies. As a result, they are not economically independent, their involvement as consumers is reduced, and a sense of responsibility and individuality is formed late.

In sum, cultural codes, discourses, and values in a society—the subjective and external factors—are influential in the processes of tactical selection in Latin American contexts.

D: Subjective and Internal Factors

Some scholars argue that causal paths between objective factors and tactical choice are not direct and automatic, and, therefore, the subjective processes in between should not be ignored (Prieto 2016). Structural factors such as political opportunity and threat are not objectively assessed, nor do they automatically inspire protest (see Somma, Almeida in this volume). It is crucial to understand the way organizers and activists perceive and attribute opportunity and threat. The focus of the fourth set of studies lies on the subjective dimensions of challenging groups (internal factors).

Jansen (2016) analyzed a process of emergence of populism in Latin America through a study of the 1931 Peruvian presidential election. In their electoral campaigns, two frontrunner candidates—the conservative Luis Miguel Sánchez Cerro and the leftist Víctor Raúl Haya de la Torre—employed innovative "populist mobilization practices," defined as the mobilization of "ordinarily marginalized social sectors into publically visible and contentious political action, while articulating an anti-elite, nationalist rhetoric that valorizes ordinary people" (Jansen 2011: 82). This tactic had never been practiced in a sustained way at a national scale to secure elected office in Latin America prior to 1931 (Jansen 2016: 321).

Why did populism as a new form of contention emerge? For Jansen, *creative human actions* situated within dynamics of critical events at a historical moment were important. The new tactic emerged only because collective political actors

> had the broad experience necessary to develop *savvy understandings* of how changing conditions were unsettling their political routines and to *cobble together novel packages of ideas and tactics that were appropriate to the new context of action*. Through these processes, strikingly different actors ended up converging to elaborate a new mode of political practice in Peru in 1931. Once demonstrably successful, this mode of practice became increasingly routinized in Peru and was subsequently available to other Latin American political actors facing comparable conditions. (Jansen 2016: 352, italics in original)

Itzigsohn and Rebón (2015) examine the emergence of a unique form of struggle in Argentina: the appropriation of bankrupt enterprises by their workers. The new tactic emerged in the context of profound social dislocation triggered by the economic crisis beginning in 1998. From the late 1990s up to the time of their study, 286 enterprises were appropriated by their workers and transformed into self-managed cooperatives (Itzigsohn and Rebón 2015: 178). Based on a combination of a survey, in-depth interviews, and participant observation, Itzigsohn and Rebón (ibid.) argued that while the economic crisis and social dislocation (objective and external factors) forced the workers to respond and take defensive action, the crisis did not generate the new tactic of enterprise recuperation. The most important factor in its emergence was the presence of a *class culture* or the "identities and self-understandings of the Argentine working class and the emotional value attached to wage labor" (ibid.: 193), which help to explain the decisions to recuperate enterprises and the social legitimacy of this form of contentious politics.

These studies call for the examination of the subjective and internal factors of cultural interpretation, framing, identity formation, pride and value, and morality in the study of tactical choices.

E: Cultural Aspect of Repertoire

I have so far avoided the term *repertoire*. While most of the cited studies on tactical choice use the language of repertoire in one way or another, the cultural element of the repertoire concept is largely missed (with some important exceptions). As Tilly's definition of the repertoire concept at the beginning of this chapter indicates, the cultural aspect of repertoire—knowledge and learning—is fundamental. Repertoires "are handed down, reproduced over time, because they are what people know how to do . . . The forms of action used in one protest campaign tend to be recycled in subsequent ones" (della Porta and Diani 2006: 182). As with any process of learning, what people can learn at a time is limited. Even when a tactic is strategically the most effective one, people cannot choose the tactic if they do not know how to carry it out. This is because "in its theatrical variant, a repertoire of contention is constrained in both time and space. In any given period, knowledge concerning 'what is to be done' to protest is limited" (della Porta 2013: 1081). Thus, repertoires of contention are a sort of "cultural tool kit" (Swidler 1986) from which people select actual tactics to be used. In this sense, repertoires of contention are both "resources" facilitating people to employ particular well-known tactics and "constraints" preventing them from adopting unfamiliar ones.

If we take seriously the cultural aspect of repertoires of contention, we should distinguish conceptually repertoires of contention (E in Figure 39.2) from tactical choices (Y in Figure 39.2). This analytic distinction is important, although it is not easy to maintain in actual analyses because once a tactic is chosen and used, this experience of using the tactic becomes a learning process for the participants in contention and, as a result, the tactic will become a part of their repertoire (their cultural tool kit) for the next round of contention (curved arrow in Figure 39.2).

In fact, the above-mentioned studies (Itzigsohn and Rebón 2015; Jansen 2016) both point to the trial-and-error processes of applying old cultural tools to new contexts before ending up with new innovative tactics such as populist mobilization practices and factory recuperation. For example, facing the threat of social dislocation, the Argentine workers first tried the old and familiar repertoire of camping out in front of the factory demanding unpaid wages and severance packages (Itzigsohn and Rebón 2015: 193). When they realized these were not going to work, they looked in new directions.

Once we make the analytical distinction between tactical choices in a moment of contention and repertoires of contention as products of previous contentious struggles from which tactics are chosen, the time dimension becomes crucial to distinguish between the two, and it is thus logical to employ historical approaches. Edelman and León (2013) take the lead in this line of research. They underscore the importance of conceiving of the present as an outcome of past processes of contention. To give an example of their historical approach, they examine a massive wave of land recuperations after the 1998 Hurricane Mitch in the Bajo Aguán region of Honduras, a center of agrarian reform in the 1950s and of the scene of a powerful peasant movement during the 1970s. A large part of the land the peasants had obtained over time was lost due to subsequent counter-agrarian reform; between 1990 and 1994 over 70% of the land distributed during the agrarian reform was sold (ibid.: 1710). On May 14, 2000, some 700 families from Aguán's peasant movement peacefully occupied the former Regional Center for Military Training (CREM) and created the community of Guadalupe Carney. The CREM was a United States base created in 1983 to train Central American militaries and the Nicaraguan "contras."

The authors find that memories of previous cycles of contention clearly informed the actions and tactics of the occupants. First, their model was the national peasant movement of the 1970s: "bringing together this landless peasantry triggered memories of resistance, connecting new struggles with those of the great 1954 banana plantation strike and the 'golden age' of the peasant movement during the 1970s" (Edelman and Leon 2013: 1711). Second, peasant movements in Honduras have always used the tactic of recuperating public land, which is in stark contrast with other Central American countries where peasants target private property (ibid.: 1716). The 2000 occupation of the CREM followed the same pattern. Third, the movements required not only that those joining new peasant enterprises meet the agrarian law's criteria for reform beneficiaries but also that they must not have sold their land during the counter-reform. This requirement for taking part in land recuperations was a reflection of historical memories of the negative effects of the counter-reform in the 1990s and of the positive pride of the original cooperatives of the agrarian reform (ibid.: 1711). In sum, to understand why a group of people adopts a specific way of struggle, historical roots and antecedents of struggle must not be ignored (see Halvorsen and Rossi in this volume).

Alonso and Mische (2017) identified three historical roots of struggle in the June 2013 wave of political protests in Brazil. Demonstrations that began as a mobilization against public transportation fare increases quickly turned into a cycle of protest involving heterogeneous actors, many of them young students, making a myriad of claims. At the peak of the cycle on June 20, "the mainstream media reported a million people in the streets in over 100 cities" (ibid.: 149). Using newspaper event mapping, social media analysis, and interviews with members of groups active in the São Paulo protests in the immediate aftermath of the June events, the authors identified three different historical and cultural sources—the socialist, autonomist, and patriotic repertoires of contention—from which the heterogeneous groups made up what the authors call "hybrid performances."

The well-known socialist repertoire consisted of "highly committed activist communities, public displays of organisational membership (such as red flags and banners, party badges and T-shirts with party or movement symbols), centralised and hierarchical organisation, and high leadership visibility" (Alonso and Mische 2017: 151). This repertoire had characterized the previous protest cycles of the 1980s and the 1990s, shared by the student, popular, labor, and land reform movements.

The autonomist repertoire was composed of conventional non-violent marches, confrontational direct action (such as sit-ins and occupations), and violent displays of resistance such as black bloc tactics, the burning of objects, and the damaging of symbols of state and economic power. The repertoire had its roots in the nineteenth and early-twentieth-century anarchist forms of horizontal organizing rejecting centralized leadership and authority. It gained worldwide attention during the 1999 Seattle protests and came to dominate the global justice movement, with strong expression at the World Social Forums since 2001 and in popular and indigenous protests in Latin America (see Rice, von Bülow in this volume). Thus, the movements employing this repertoire often reject the goal of seizing the state power and instead seek to generate alternative sources of power outside of the state (Alonso and Mische 2017: 151–52).

The patriotic repertoire invoked nationalist sentiments, which had historical and situational meanings specific to the country. The Brazilian patriotic repertoire of huge demonstrations, marches, and strikes, the use of national symbols and slogans (the anthem, flag, and national colors), and hierarchical organizational models "received its content from a local political tradition built up during two previous waves of nationwide protest" (Alonso and Mische 2017: 152). The first wave was the Diretas Já movement during the 1984 campaign for direct presidential elections during the transition from authoritarianism to democracy. The second wave was the 1992 anti-corruption protest cycle against the government of President Fernando Collor de Melo (1990–1992) (see Pereyra, Gold, and Gattoni in this volume).

Both Alonso and Mische (2017) and Edelman and Leon (2013) highlight the importance of analyzing the historical roots and antecedents of the struggles of interest. Cultural and historical dimensions of repertoires of contention should not be overlooked.

A selective review of the recent literature in this section indicates that the idea of repertoires of contention has become an integral part of the study of contentious politics and social movements in Latin America. Scholars have confirmed that some of the explanatory factors suggested in the general literature of repertoires of contention are also important in explaining Latin American cases. The theories of repertoires of contention have indeed contributed to the literature of contentious politics in Latin America. What would be the contributions the other way around? What are the genuine theoretical breakthroughs of the studies on Latin American repertoires? This is the topic of the next section.

THEORETICAL CONTRIBUTIONS

Most studies on Latin American repertoires have contributed theoretically to the general literature *by presenting additional empirical cases from Latin America* which (usually) support some of the existing theories. To confirm the applicability of the theories to new cases is certainly a valuable scientific endeavor. The degree of theoretical contribution to the general literature, however, is limited in this way. This is because most studies are interested more in explaining cases at hand than in improving the theories of repertoires of contention. They borrow ideas from the repertoire literature to explain why new innovative forms of contention emerge.

However, I do find in the Latin American literature some genuine theoretical breakthroughs that might transform the ideas and theories of repertoires of contention in the general literature. I summarize these potential breakthroughs into three possible directions for contributing to the general literature, with some pioneering examples from Latin America.

Develop a Research Design Including Multiple Factors

The first direction is to develop a research design that can compare the effects of more than one factor. There is a rough correspondence between the main causal factors of interest and the research approaches adopted. Scholars interested in the effects of political regimes on tactical choices tend to employ a cross-national research design (Franklin 2013; Kerrissey and Schofer 2018: 427). Those who believe that subjective interpretations, framing, emotions, morality, or identities are crucial prefer interview and ethnographic approaches to examine contemporary contentions (Itzigsohn and Rebón 2015). Scholars who are concerned about the effects of a broad culture within society have a tendency to use survey methods (Barbosa et al. 2014; Echegaray 2015). And finally, scholars interested in the processes of cultural learning from earlier struggles are more likely to employ historical approaches (Edelman and Leon 2013; Schneider Marques 2017).

What is unclear, after reading these excellent empirical studies, is whether their findings are contradictory or complementary. Therefore, as a possible line of future research, scholars are encouraged to pick two or more types of causal factors (A, B, C, D, and E in Figure 39.2) at a time and develop a research design that can evaluate which of these factors is more important or what combination of factors explains tactical choice and innovation.

One of the drawbacks of the multiple-approach design—for instance, a cross-national comparative approach to capture the effect of regime structure (A) combined with an ethnographic approach to understand the processes of collective identity formation (D)—is a corresponding increase in research cost. This is where scholars need to be inventive. To take an example, Wada, Koo, and Hoshino (2016) attempt to account for the variation in the selection of violence, non-violent protests, and conventional forms of contention introduced in Figure 39.1 at the beginning of this chapter. Using a cross-national large-N approach, they explore which of the two factors (among many others) is more influential, state capacity (state strength) (A) or repertoires of contention (E). While a cross-national design is a common way to study objective and external factors such as state capacity, their invention is to obtain an approximate measure of repertoires of contention quantitatively from the cross-national event data. They calculate the degree of "repertoire familiarity" based on annual counts of each form of contention over the past ten years, as illustrated in Table 39.1. The table shows the annual counts of the

Table 39.1 Constructing repertoire familiarity scores (an illustrative example)

Forms	1990	1991	1992	1993	1994	1995	1996	1997	1998	1999	Weighted Sum	Repertoire Familiarity
Conventional	34	52	44	12	67	98	109	62	112	90	441	73%
Protest	21	12	10	5	11	21	6	23	42	11	99	16%
Violent	3	2	6	8	13	19	4	10	22	8	62	10%
Weights	.1	.2	.3	.4	.5	.6	.7	.8	.9	1.0	602	100%

conventional, protest, and violent forms of contention employed by an actor category of a country during a ten-year period from 1990 to 1999. The weighted sum of conventional forms in 2000 is computed as follows: 34 × .1 + 52 × .2 + ... + 90 × 1.0 = 441. The familiarity score is then calculated as 73% (=441÷602). The weights reflect the idea that people remember recent actions better than ones from the more remote past. Actors in this category are more familiar with conventional forms than with protest or violent forms. The repertoire familiarity scores are then used in the multilevel multinomial logit models to predict the actors' selection of conventional, protest, and violent forms from 2000 to 2004.

Figure 39.3 displays the predicted probabilities of each of the three forms by state capacity and by familiarity with nonviolent protest. Although both variables are statistically significant, the substantive effect of state capacity is quite limited. In comparison with the weakest state, the strongest state can reduce the probability of violent eruption by about 1% and that of protest by 2.5%. In contrast, the groups that are most familiar with protests have a more than 40% chance of choosing protest tactics while the groups least familiar with protests have almost no chance of employing them. While the repertoire familiarity measure used in this study needs to be refined, an advantage of an analysis like this is to be able to compare the effects of different causal factors.

Thinking of Repertoires as a Variable

The literature tends to pay more attention to specific tactics in a repertoire rather than to the repertoire (as a set of tactics) itself. The second line of future research this chapter suggests is to put more focus on the characteristics of the repertoire per se and conceive of the repertoire as a variable. One way of doing this is to think of the degree of rigidity and flexibility of the repertoire, as shown in Tilly's "strong repertoire hypothesis." The hypothesis assumes the limited variety of tactical forms employed by popular actors because, as Tilly's definition at the beginning of this chapter suggests, people can learn only a rather small number of alternative ways to act collectively at any particular point in history (Tilly 1995: 42). Tilly (2006) lamented that this strong repertoire hypothesis

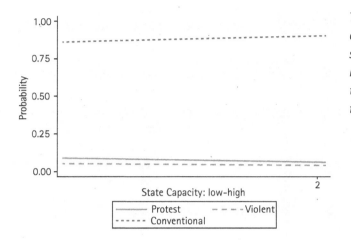

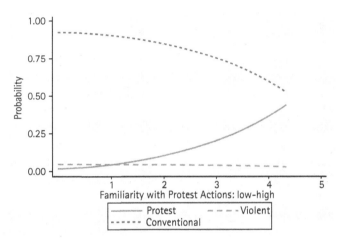

FIGURE 39.3 Predicted probabilities of violent, protest, and conventional forms of contention by state capacity and familiarity with protest, 2000–2004

was never empirically examined, although some attempts to address the issue of repertoire variation, breath, rigidity, and flexibility have recently emerged (Wada 2016).

In the Latin American literature, Franklin's (2013: 178) study mentioned above tries to fill this gap. Using an original dataset of 1,319 political events in Latin America, Franklin developed a measure of repertoire variation or "tactical fractionalization."[3] The measure shows, for example, that civil war—as it happened in places such as Guatemala and Nicaragua—"crowd out" the wide variety of public protest tactics, leading to a more limited and rigid repertoire. The scores change little over years, indicating the consistent clustering of the tactics employed, which is further evidence, according to the author, of the strong repertoire.

It is important to measure the degree of rigidity and flexibility of a repertoire not only because we can evaluate the relevance of Tilly's hypothesis but also because it might be related to movement success (Hughes 2010). Pousadela's (2016) study of the women's movement in Uruguay suggests that the reason for the success of the movement in getting abortion legalized lies primarily in its ability to harness a broad repertoire of contention. In a context of a "cultural war" against a "pro-life" countermovement organized in defense of the status quo, the women's "pro-legalization" movement accomplished its goal due to its ability to induce a deep transformation in the prevailing common sense of Uruguayan citizens (ibid.: 143). Such a transformation is linked to the breadth of the movement's repertoire, progressively expanded to include various tactics.

> Blending the old and the new, the Uruguayan women's repertoire of contention . . . encompasses classic street campaigning, demonstrations and rallies as well as online mobilization, e-mail petitions, the activation of social networks, and a wide variety of colorful cultural expressions—including dance, percussion, street performances, art installations, the use of costumes, masks, painted faces, humoristic placards, and high doses of spontaneity and irony." (ibid.)

Centered on their strong moral vision, the movement's core activists broadened the movement repertoire, through trial and error, by identifying and incorporating new forms of protest that would increase the visibility of the movement's demands and therefore its chances of being heard.

While repertoires are usually very limited, as Tilly hypothesizes, if challengers can broaden their repertoire and select tactics more flexibly out of a wider array of options, then, these studies claim, they are more likely to obtain a successful outcome. By treating repertoires as a variable, we can start to think about interesting hypotheses and research themes. The issue of modularity and transferability of repertoire is another interesting aspect of repertoires of contention that can be thought of as a variable (Steuer 2018; Tarrow 1993; Wada 2012). Firchow (2015) makes a valuable contribution on this front based on his historical analysis of resistance after the Argentinazo (a period of country-wide unrest in 2001–2002).

Refining the Repertoire Concept

The third direction for future research starts from the refinement of the repertoire concept in terms of its "components" (what kind of things should constitute a repertoire?) and "ownership" (what kind of people should share a repertoire?). Tilly's definition of repertoires, presented at the beginning of the chapter, as a limited set of *routines* or alternative *ways to act collectively* is still vague and open to broad interpretation and application.

Thus, while this chapter has consistently used "tactics" to describe repertoire components to avoid any confusion, the term repertoire is sometimes used to describe a stock of organizational forms (Shoshan 2018), discursive varieties (Borland 2014), performances (Tilly 2008), collective action (Schneider Marques 2017), political practices (Jansen 2016), and so on. To make matters more complicated, the level of abstraction of the repertoire components varies by study. Some studies analyze at a very concrete level, such as recuperating public lands (Edelman and Leon 2013), recuperation of bankrupt factories (Itzigsohn and Rebón 2015), or boycotts and buycotts (Barbosa et al. 2014; Echegaray 2015). Others aggregate specific forms of contention into more abstract categories, such as protest, strike, and rebellion (Franklin 2013), "institutional mobilization and extra-institutional political acts" (Kerrissey and Schofer 2018: 427), or conventional, cultural, disruptive, and violent tactics (Medel Sierralta and Somma González 2016).

My point here is not that everybody should adopt the same definition of repertoire components; every scholar should decide on their own definition given their questions and purposes. What I argue is that we should recognize that there are a variety of definitions and operationalizations under the same concept of repertoire, something that makes the comparison of findings from different studies complicated. A refined definitional framework enabling comparisons across different studies would be extremely helpful. From the Latin American literature, Rossi (2015) and Alonso-Fradejas (2015) attempt to offer such a useful framework.

In his study of the *piqueteros* (picketers) or unemployed workers' movement of Argentina, Rossi presents his analytical framework to capture the "full picture of the strategic dynamics of interaction of social movements with the state, allies, and antagonists" (Rossi 2015: 17). His framework is innovative on three fronts. First, it makes an important distinction between tactics as "the means and plan to win a single campaign (one battle)" and strategy as "the plan of how to win the struggle (the war)" (ibid.: 16). Second, Rossi proposes the analytical separation of the cultural knowledge about contention learned from the past history of struggle ("[E] repertoires of contention" in Figure 39.2, which Rossi calls "stock of legacies") from actual choices of action in the current round of struggle ("[Y] tactical choice," which Rossi calls "repertoires of strategies").

Third, relevant to our discussion of repertoire component is that Rossi's idea of "repertoire of strategies" broadens the conceptualization of "[Y] tactical choice" to include not only public contentious tactics but also a variety of semi-public contentious and non-contentious actions (evolving across specific groups) and private arenas. By applying this framework, Rossi finds that all social movement organizations (SMOs) within the *piquetero* movement employ the same public and contentious tactics of roadblocks, marches, and encampments (thus demonstrating the strong repertoire theory), whereas there is great variation in their semi-public contentious and non-contentious actions (multi-class popular front, insurrectional alliance, trade unionist, NGO-ization, and so on) which goes unnoticed if researchers look at public contentious tactics alone

(Rossi 2015: 23–24). Alonso-Fradejas (2015) presents a framework similar to Rossi's in his analysis of peasant resistance to the agrarian extractivist projects in Guatemala.

The second definitional issue is that of ownership of a repertoire. There is no clear agreement in the literature as to the appropriate unit of the holders of a repertoire of contention (for lack of a better term, I use "repertoire owner" and "ownership" here). If repertoires of contention are about people's cultural understandings of political struggle, then the owners must share some cultural knowledge about ways of making claims. What would be the appropriate unit to use in thinking about such cultural groups?

Studies in the existing literature rarely explicitly specify the repertoire owners. It appears that the following types of owner are implied: individual activists (Schneider Marques 2017), young people (Barbosa et al. 2014), workers (Itzigsohn and Rebón 2015), labor unions (Kerrissey and Schofer 2018: 427), movements (Edelman and Leon 2013), organizations (Rossi 2015), and societies or countries (Echegaray 2015).

Each of these studies makes sense on its own without worrying about the issue of repertoire ownership. The issue becomes important when one starts to think about the comparability of the empirical findings and theoretical implications from these studies. This is not a minor point. Returning to Figure 39.2, we can see that the rectangular block "(E) repertoires of contention" is placed over both the external (C) and internal (D) regions of the subjective factor, reflecting the ambiguity of the repertoire ownership definition. If we believe that the appropriate owner unit is that of the challenging groups such as workers, labor unions, movements, organizations, and so on, then we are presupposing that the block of repertoires of contention should belong to the region of subjective–internal factors (D). If we define that the owner unit is a broad society, then the block falls into the subjective–external region (C). While repertoires of a society would be difficult to change, as such a change would likely require a shift in cultural understandings of most people in that society, repertoires of a challenging group can be modified and innovated relatively easily.

Franklin (2013) is the only study, to my knowledge, that compares repertoire features between different ownership levels, one at the level of challenging groups (D) and the other at the level of country (C). Franklin explores whether Tilly's original idea of repertoires of contention as a limited variety of tactical forms (strong repertoire hypothesis) is validated more at a narrow and concrete level of ownership (campaign participants) or at a broad and abstract level of ownership (country). He concludes that the narrow and concrete ownership level would be the appropriate unit in terms of Tilly's theory. Franklin's brilliant piece has definitively improved the general literature of repertoires of contention.

Finally, there is more to the issue of repertoire ownership. While many studies presuppose that repertoires belong to the actors in contention, a few studies imply that repertoires are contingent on the target in contention (Walker, Martin, and McCarthy 2008). In Chile, protests against the state elicit conventional tactics, while protests against private companies elicit disruptive and violent tactics (Medel Sierralta and

Somma González 2016). In Ecuador and Peru, when young activists target civil society to advance sexual health policies, their tactics—responding to adult allies, carrying out social advocacy among youth, building organizations, carrying out political advocacy, developing themselves as activists, and so on—are different from protest tactics directed at the state (Coe et al. 2015).

Tilly (2006: 35) believed that the answer to the ownership problem lies not just in the actor or the target but in the actor–target pairs. His notion of performances constituting a repertoire "is congruent with the idea that collective action involves not only what people know how to do, but also what those on the receiving end would expect and understand" (Alimi 2014: 1). Only a few studies have so far applied such a dyadic owner unit in actual empirical studies (ibid.; Franzosi 1999; Tilly 2008; Wada 2005). This line of research will enrich our understanding of repertoires of contention in Latin America.

Conclusion

The first part of this chapter has documented recent progress in the study of repertoires of contention in Latin America and examined which causal factors—objective versus subjective, and external versus internal—influence tactical choices in Latin America. While we learn that some of the explanatory factors suggested in the general literature of repertoires of contention are important in explaining Latin American cases, the theoretical contributions of the Latin American literature are often limited because most studies are more focused on explaining cases at hand than on improving the theories of repertoires of contention.

The second part of the chapter has suggested three possible future directions to make genuine theoretical contributions: (1) develop a research design comparing the relative importance of different causal factors, (2) think repertoires as a variable, and (3) refine the repertoire concept by specifying components and ownership of a repertoire. I believe that there is plenty of room for theoretical and empirical improvement in this field. We shall look forward to new innovations in the actual repertoires of contention in Latin America as well as to new breakthroughs in scholarly research on repertoires.

Notes

1. The issue of media attention and bias in selecting and describing political events for publication is an important point but not a central one for the purposes of this chapter.
2. Buycott is the act of purchasing from particular companies to reward favorable ethical or socio-environmental behavior (Echegaray 2015: 177). See Rhodes in this volume.
3. Franklin (2013: 183–84) used the Herfindahl-Hirschman concentration index, which is commonly used to measure ethno-linguistic fractionalization, to build an innovative measure of tactical concentration–fractionalization.

References

Alimi, Eitan Y. (2014), "Repertoires of Contention," in Donatella della Porta and Mario Diani (eds.), *The Oxford Handbook of Social Movements*, 410–22 (Oxford: Oxford University Press).

Alonso, Angela and Ann Mische (2017), "Changing Repertoires and Partisan Ambivalence in the New Brazilian Protests," *Bulletin of Latin American Research* 36(2), 144–59.

Alonso-Fradejas, Alberto (2015), "Anything but a Story Foretold: Multiple Politics of Resistance to the Agrarian Extractivist Project in Guatemala," *Journal of Peasant Studies* 42(3/4), 489–515.

Barbosa, Livia, Fátima Portilho, John Wilkinson, and Veranise Dubeux (2014), "Trust, Participation and Political Consumerism among Brazilian Youth," *Journal of Cleaner Production* 63, 93–101.

Borland, Elizabeth (2014), "Storytelling, Identity, and Strategy: Perceiving Shifting Obstacles in the Fight for Abortion Rights in Argentina," *Sociological Perspectives* 57(4), 488–505.

Coe, Anna-Britt, Isabel Goicolea, Anna Karin Hurtig, and Miguel San Sebastian (2015), "Understanding How Young People Do Activism: Youth Strategies on Sexual Health in Ecuador and Peru," *Youth & Society* 47(1), 3–28.

della Porta, Donatella (2013), "Repertoires of Contention," in David A. Snow, Donatella della Porta, Bert Klandermans, and Doug McAdam (eds.), *The Wiley-Blackwell Encyclopedia of Social and Political Movements*, 1081–83 (Malden: Wiley).

della Porta, Donatella and Mario Diani (2006), *Social Movements: An Introduction* (Malden: Blackwell).

Echegaray, Fabián (2015), "Voting at the Marketplace: Consumerism in Latin America," *Latin American Research Review* 50(2), 176–99.

Edelman, Marc and Andrés León (2013), "Cycles of Land Grabbing in Central America: An Argument for History and a Case Study in the Bajo Aguán, Honduras," *Third World Quarterly* 34(9), 1697–722.

Firchow, Pamina (2015), "Power and Resistance in the Shaping of Argentine Domestic Policy," *Latin American Perspectives* 42(1), 74–83.

Franklin, James C. (2013), "Repertoires of Contention and Tactical Choice in Latin America, 1981–1995," *Research in Social Movements, Conflicts and Change* 35, 175–208.

Franzosi, Roberto (1999), "The Return of the Actor: Interaction Networks among Social Actors during Periods of High Mobilization (Italy, 1919–22)," *Mobilization* 4(2), 131–49.

Hughes, Neil (2010), "Indigenous Protest in Peru: The "Orchard Dog" Bites Back," *Social Movement Studies* 9(1), 85–90.

Itzigsohn, José and Julián Rebón (2015), "The Recuperation of Enterprises: Defending Workers' Lifeworld, Creating New Tools of Contention," *Latin American Research Review* 50(4), 178–96.

Jansen, Robert S. (2011), "Populist Mobilization: A New Theoretical Approach to Populism," *Sociological Theory* 29(2), 75–96.

Jansen, Robert S. (2016), "Situated Political Innovation: Explaining the Historical Emergence of New Modes of Political Practice," *Theory and Society* 45(4), 319–60.

Kerrissey, Jasmine and Evan Schofer (2018), "Labor Unions and Political Participation in Comparative Perspective," *Social Forces* 97(1), 427–63.

King, Gary and Will Lowe (2008), "10 Million International Dyadic Events," Harvard Dataverse Network, V5, https://dataverse.harvard.edu/dataset.xhtml?persistentId=hdl:1902.1/FYXLAWZRIA, retrieved June 14, 2011.

Medel Sierralta, Rodrigo Miguel and Nicolás Manuel Somma González (2016), "Demonstrations, Occupations or Roadblocks? Exploring the Determinants of Protest Tactics in Chile," *Política y Gobierno* 23(1), 163–99.

Pousadela, Inés M. (2016), "Social Mobilization and Political Representation: The Women's Movement's Struggle for Legal Abortion in Uruguay," *Voluntas* 27(1), 125–45.

Prieto, Greg (2016), "Opportunity, Threat, and Tactics: Collaboration and Confrontation by Latino Immigrant Challengers," in Landon E. Hancock (ed.), *Narratives of Identity in Social Movements, Conflicts and Change*, 123–54 (Bingley: Emerald).

Rossi, Federico M. (2015), "Conceptualizing Strategy Making in a Historical and Collective Perspective," in Federico M. Rossi and Marisa von Bülow (eds.), *Social Movement Dynamics: New Perspectives on Theory and Research from Latin America*, 15–41 (Farnham: Ashgate).

Schneider Marques, Teresa Cristina (2017), "O exílio e as transformações de repertórios de ação coletiva: A esquerda brasileira no Chile e na França (1968-1978)," *Dados* 60(1), 239–79.

Shoshan, Aya (2018), "Habitus and Social Movements: How Militarism Affects Organizational Repertoires," *Social Movement Studies* 17(2), 144–58.

Steuer, Clément (2018), "The Modularity of the "Revolutionary" Repertoire of Action in Egypt: Origins and Appropriation by Different Players," *Social Movement Studies* 17(1), 113–18.

Swidler, Ann (1986), "Culture in Action: Symbols and Strategies," *American Sociological Review* 51(2), 273–86.

Tarrow, Sidney (1993), "Modular Collective Action and the Rise of the Social Movement: Why the French Revolution Was Not Enough," *Politics & Society* 21(1), 647–70.

Taylor, Verta and Nella Van Dyke (2004), "'Get up, Stand up': Tactical Repertoires of Social Movements," in David A. Snow, Sarah A. Soule, and Hanspeter Kriesi (eds.), *The Blackwell Companion to Social Movements*, 262–93 (Malden: Blackwell).

Tilly, Charles (1995), *Popular Contention in Great Britain, 1758-1834* (Cambridge, MA: Harvard University Press).

Tilly, Charles (2006), *Regimes and Repertoires* (Chicago: University of Chicago Press).

Tilly, Charles (2008), *Contentious Performances* (Cambridge: Cambridge University Press).

Wada, Takeshi (2005), "Civil Society in Mexico: Popular Protest amid Economic and Political Liberalization," *International Journal of Sociology and Social Policy* 25(1/2), 87–117.

Wada, Takeshi (2012), "Modularity and Transferability of Repertoires of Contention," *Social Problems* 59(4), 544–71.

Wada, Takeshi (2016), "Rigidity and Flexibility of Repertoires of Contention," *Mobilization* 21(4), 449–68.

Wada, Takeshi, Yoojin Koo, and Kayo Hoshino (2016), "A Cross-National Comparison of the Patterns of Civic Participation: Worldwide Convergence, National Divergence, or Enduring Influences of Cultural Repertoires?," Presentation at the Third ISA Forum of Sociology, International Sociological Association, July 10–14, University of Vienna.

Walker, Edward T., Andrew W. Martin, and John D. McCarthy (2008), "Confronting the State, the Corporation, and the Academy: The Influence of Institutional Targets on Social Movement Repertoires," *American Journal of Sociology* 114(1), 35–76.

CHAPTER 40

SHIFTING GEOGRAPHIES OF ACTIVISM AND THE SPATIAL LOGICS OF LATIN AMERICAN SOCIAL MOVEMENTS

DIANE E. DAVIS AND TAYLOR DAVEY

Introduction

Social movements have played a central role in guiding political developments across Latin America for decades. Throughout Latin American history, the issues of poverty, marginality, social exclusion, and inequality have defined movement activism. Yet which particular groups have led the struggle, with what mobilization strategies or aims, and in which territorial spaces or geographies, have shifted over time. In contrast to the period between the 1970s and 1990s, when cities hosted a preponderance of social movements in Latin America, by the 2000s the region hosted a resurgence of mobilization in rural locations to match the urban. When democratization produced new political institutions for claim-making, movements began to use decentralized participatory processes to demand services, infrastructure, and public goods—although the spatial scale and target of such claims can vary between urban and rural movements (see Annunziata and Goldfrank, Welch, Oxhorn in this volume). Such differences owed partly to the fact that in certain territorial locations public goods are now more likely to be provided by the private sector. Finally, as movements focus less on regime change and more on the protest of everyday conditions, new forms of contestation emerge. Increasingly, activists are adopting spatial tactics to challenge or disrupt conditions, using these strategies as symbolic expressions of dissatisfaction as much as a means for demanding remedial action from the state. Our aim in this chapter is to document and account for these changes in movement activism. We identify new geographic and spatial repertoires of mobilization, link them to changing social, political, and economic conditions, and assess the significance of these shifts for both the theory and practice of social mobilization in contemporary Latin America.

It goes without saying that Latin America is a very diverse continent holding significant differences within and across its countries. This is especially so with respect to the precise temporality of shifting trends and how widespread they have been regionally. Each country's politics and history will directly inform social movement activism. Yet precisely because of country by country differences, much of the recent scholarship on social movements—with some notable exceptions (Almeida 2014; Rossi and von Bülow 2015; Silva 2009)—has explored activism through case study analysis, picking a single social movement in a given country for examination in greater detail. Such a methodology allows a more precise understanding of how and why a movement may or may not be successful. But it also can prevent a more comprehensive, generalized understanding of the shifting nature and structural dynamics of social movement activism in the region as a whole. To remedy this, we highlight general trends of social movement activism across Latin America, without privileging any particular country. After identifying general social movement trends across the region, we seek to link them to temporally shifting political and economic arrangements as well as to highlight the "geography" of these developments.

The latter term is intended to call attention to the territorial and spatial correlates of changing movement activism: their rural versus urban location, the spatial scales of mobilization (i.e., street, neighborhood, city, nation), and the adoption of space-based strategies and tactics to achieve movement aims. By inserting geography into social movement theory, and conceiving of space as a target and not merely a terrain of struggle, we seek to move beyond the preoccupation with resource mobilization/political opportunity structure and identity politics frameworks that dominated scholarship from the 1970s–1990s (Davis 2004; Guidry 2003; Nicholls 2007; see Garretón and Selamé, Fontana, Somma in this volume). With a better appreciation of how movements operate *in*, *through*, and *with* space, we arrive at a new epistemological reference point for theorizing when, how, and why Latin American social movements do what they do.

The Turn to Spatial Strategies and Tactics in Social Movement Theory and Practice

The emerging interest in the spatial and territorial dynamics of Latin American social movements can be traced partly to the increasing importance of scholarship by geographers in this field of inquiry. In recent years, the discipline of geography has taken up the mantle of activist research to claim the mandate originally associated with sociology and political science. While the latter disciplines preoccupied themselves with questions of social solidarity and regime change in the study of movement activism, the question that compels geographers is not necessarily what the nature of citizen claims *are* in a given period, or who they are directed towards, but *how space is used* to advance claims and whether geographic location impacts movement dynamics.

Scholars have advanced this line of thinking by exploring the ways that physical space (*territorio*) was important for rural movements in the 1990s (Agnew and Oslender 2013; Blank 2016; Clare, Habermehl, and Mason-Deese 2017; Lopes de Souza 2016; Mason-Deese 2012; Zibechi 2012 [2009]). The selection of the term *territorio* to frame the study of rural movements is informed by a counter-hegemonic discourse, which recognizes that in the context of early neoliberal development policies "territorial" development was widespread within state, NGO, and private sector vocabularies, often to justify occupation of peoples and lands that lay outside the modernist project. In this sense, deployment of the term *territorio* should be understood as purposefully subversive, paralleling in academic writings its use by such groups as the Zapatistas, the MST, indigenous movements in Ecuador and Bolivia, and Afro-groups in Colombia (Sandoval, Robertsdotter, and Paredes 2017; Halvorsen and Rossi, Souza in this volume).

Whatever its origins, a concern with the production of territory through social activism provides a new epistemological lens to interconnect citizen mobilization to spatial formation. Scholars argue that social movements produce *territorio* not just by making claims but also by exerting force *over* space in order to disrupt flows (usually capitalist ones) and power assemblages. Such acts are often intended to assert a claim to political autonomy that is grounded in notions of alternative (i.e., non-state) forms of territorial sovereignty. Sandoval, Robertsdotter, and Paredes (2017: 44), for example, see *territorio* as an "arena of dispute" primarily "concerned with power relationships in space, particularly those triggered by the confrontation between global forces on the one hand and local, place-based 'territorially anchored' groups on the other."

Such arguments are also consistent with scholarship highlighting how urban social movements use "'other' ways of constructing territory from below" by engaging different forms of power: from an exclusive concept of territorial power as *poder* (power *over*) to one that includes *potencia* (power *to*) (Clare, Habermehl, and Mason-Deese 2017: 7). The urban social movement perhaps most recognized for deploying this has been the *piqueteros* in Argentina. Though the *piquetero* movement began with picketing for jobs following the nation's economic collapse, the group subsequently turned attention to the occupation of neighborhoods, becoming an urban territorial movement that sought to address everyday problems of the unemployed, with the slogan: "*the neighborhood is the new factory.*" The *piqueteros* frequently use roadblocks as a means of disruption—a tactical action that, amongst others, conceptually unites a movement that is in fact internally heterogeneous in terms of long-term strategies and demands (Rossi 2015).

Piqueteros are frequently cited as an example of *territorio* not only for their choice of disruptive tactics but also because despite their urban location they also seek to establish autonomy, and thus separation from the state. Zibechi (2012 [2009]) notoriously declared the *piqueteros* to be the first instance of an urban movement displaying similar claims for territorial autonomy that drove many of the rural and indigenous movements of the preceding decades (see Rice, Souza in this volume). Lopes de Souza (2016: 1297) likewise states that for such Argentine urban social movements in the twenty-first century: "[A]utonomía means above all the building of *poder popular* ('people's power') independently of and despite the state apparatus." However, Rossi (2019) has recently questioned scholarship that emphasizes the *piqueteros*' claims for autonomy, claiming instead that the "goal of the *piquetero* movement is to reduce the distance of the state vis-à-vis the movement's constituency of marginalized people in the quest for being reincorporated as citizens and wage-earners" (ibid.: 823). In this struggle, territory remains a central cleavage nonetheless.

The growing focus on *territorio* and *autonomía* among contemporary scholars of rural and urban mobilization has also generated calls for more active theorization of these space-based tactics within the broader social movement literature. Bryan (2012: 223), for example, suggests that scholars need to generate "greater analytical clarity about the work that territory does," including "how it comes into being and why." Given this admonition, the question arises as to whether these conceptual frameworks suggest a new theory and praxis, or whether their discursive deployment in the study of social movements merely reproduces findings that have been well established in the study of social movement formation, strategies, and tactics.

Micro-Geographies of Disruption: Old Wine in New Bottles or Fundamental Shift in Praxis?

A cursory overview of social movement literature suggests that, to a great degree, scholars who adopt the notion of *territorio* are in dialogue with prior sociological and political scholarship on the relationship between social movement strategies and state actions, but they provide new analytical pathways for coming to these conclusions. For example, Rossi uses the case of Argentina to argues that both neoliberal reforms and the persistence of quasi-authoritarian regimes—political conditions long the subject of social movement scholarship—have shifted the locus of struggle, such that territory emerges as a central cleavage because "neo-corporatist arrangements for the resolution of socio-political conflicts in society" have either been weakened or dissolved (Rossi 2019: 817). Decades ago, questions about whether space is the subject or object of movement struggle also appeared in the writings of Manuel Castells (1978), whose path-breaking work on urban social movements reverberated across Latin America (see Oxhorn in this volume). Likewise, current scholarship on the strategic deployment of territory to mobilize citizens echoes prior sociological work that examined how space structurally mediates citizens' relationship to the state, often in ways that bring citizens *close to* or *far from* centers of power (Davis 1999). In that work "distance from the state" is not merely about territory, however, but understood to be determined by a four-fold axis that includes, geography, economy, culture, and institutions.

In addition, contemporary writings on how mobilization unfolds differently in urban and rural territories are usually grounded in the study of social and political inclusion or exclusion, a topic long studied by sociologists, political scientists, and historians of Latin America. This is particularly clear in recent work that links exclusion to both state neglect and territorial practice. When "activists feel that they have no true representation in the formal institutions of the state, they attempt to bring about change by getting involved in noninstitutionalized practices, such as the coordinated blocking of roads and massive mobilization of peasants in the streets" (Bosco 2008: 179). In many ways, such tactics can be considered "weapons of the weak," to draw on James Scott's (1985) classic notion.

As such, when contemporary scholars highlight protests and movements that deploy acts of spatial disruption, such as road blockades or shutting down commercial areas, they are adopting conceptual frameworks established in earlier literature on movement activism. Implicitly, at least, they are acknowledging the role that state neglect has played in pushing isolated or politically marginalized groups to forge an alternative spatial praxis for opposition or claim-making. The state's longstanding failure to respond to citizens' concerns is what makes it possible, meaningful, and urgent for them to deploy disruptive strategies, given the absence of other local mechanisms for participation (Yashar 1998: 31). Once the state enters the analytical picture, it also becomes evident why disruptive strategies and tactics may predominate in rural areas, but can also materialize in cities, and why they are not entirely new. Indeed, acts of spatial disruption can challenge the formal sociopolitical order, and they have a long history in cities. The hijackings of Mexico City buses in the 1970s and early 1980s, for example, demonstrated dissatisfaction with the urban transport services (Davis 1994: 237). Similar sentiments were also clear in the São Paulo building occupations of the late 1990s, a movement that drew on strategies of the Brazilian Movimento dos Trabalhadores Sem Terra (MST) to claim housing for the city's homeless by occupying abandoned inner-city buildings (Earle 2012; see Fernandes and Welch in this volume). More recently, protesting students in Santiago used space-based tactical measures to disrupt the flow of everyday life and call attention to the *invisibility of their grievances* in a larger neoliberal and democratic setting where politics as usual left little room for putting their concerns on the agenda (see Donoso in this volume).

The fact that acts of disruptive protest are wielded by populations who are excluded from institutionalized political mechanisms for expressing grievances may help explain why such tactics emerge in certain countries or locations more than others. But it also begs the question as to whether and why micro-geographies of disruption are becoming a common form of social activism in the contemporary era. In order to understand why this might be the case, it is helpful to return to the political and economic transitions that have occurred in Latin America since the 1970s, and chart changes in both state actions and citizen responses. Doing so will not only help shed light on the historical origins of contemporary movement dynamics that in previously classifications were seen as mere disruption (see Oxhorn in this volume). It will also help us historically ground an understanding of movement "micro-geographies" in the political, economic, and spatial conditions that preceded them, showing how the successes of prior social movements changed the territorial terrain and strategic focus of activism, thus laying the groundwork for the deployment of new spatial strategies and tactics. In what follows we chart the shifting dynamics of social movements in light of the changing political geographies of states and markets in Latin America, focusing broadly on three periods: 1970–1990, 1990–2000, and 2001–2015. By so doing, we show how and why the geography of social movements has shifted between city and countryside, and why micro-geographic disruption and other spatial strategies and tactics are now more common than demands for regime change among social movement activists.

From Old to New Social Movements, 1970–1990: Cities as Preferred Sites of Democratic Struggle

In twentieth-century Latin America, the adoption of macroeconomic policies that favored an alliance between capital and labor around rapid industrialization disadvantaged agriculture and helped intensify rural-urban migration. Yet the formal incorporation of labor into governing pacts also undermined autonomous worker-based social movements of the former period. By the 1970s, rapid urbanization had produced a whole array of social and spatial problems in cities that could not be addressed by workplace mobilization, such as inadequate housing, faulty infrastructure, and insufficient urban employment for the large numbers of new migrants. States, for their part, failed to develop robust welfare state policies, in no small part because the domestic and international forces who hitched their wagon to the predominant economic model also proved willing to support the state's strong-arm tactics and limited democratic participation if such arrangements allowed steady industrial growth. This combination of conditions inspired the emergence of new social movements undertaken by both popular and middle classes who were excluded from governance arrangements and the direct employment or income benefits that privileged corporatist worker organizations. They were often joined by students and independent or leftist labor movements who also decried the top-down control of labor under corporatism. Issues that united all these forces were the fight against authoritarianism and the struggle for democracy, justice, and greater government accountability (see Inclán in this volume).

A large number of these movements found their broadest political support in cities because of the concentration of class and social forces willing to join together in protest against the state (Castells 1973; Holston 2009). The fact that governing authorities frequently responded oppressively, with unrestrained use of violence to squelch dissent, further strengthened the calls for democratization and widened the class bases of urban mobilization beyond the poor and working-class to include the middle classes. In their study of this period, scholars documented the dialectic relationship between state abuse of power and intensified citizen mobilization, much of which unfolded at the seat of state and/or industrial power in a country's capital or largest cities (Collier and Mahoney 1997).

In theoretical terms, this period was identified as one in which so-called new social movements—built on culture, ethnicity, and even gender claims for political recognition and inclusion—began to replace older forms of mobilization associated with working-class claims about the power of capital and the exploitation of labor (see Garretón and Selamé in this volume), thus driving a more moderate form of social activism. These social mobilizations were theorized as producing an entirely different governance context in Latin America, in which the embrace of democracy served as a backdrop for state downsizing, a decentralization of decision-making in certain urban policy domains, and the adoption of neoliberal economic policies—the latter of which further damaged the corporatist pacts generated by earlier political arrangements, thus driving home the declining power of labor and reinforcing the ascendance of other social forces and identity-based movements (see Roberts; Rossi in this volume).

By the late-1980s, these changed conditions had produced new concerns for social movement scholars. Although a few went so far as to argue that the early 1990s saw a decline in protest activity (Archila 2011: 61), the general view was that the nature and objects of mobilization were in fact transforming, as formerly antagonistic protesters began to actively engage with new democratic institutions, thus leading to both mobilization and demobilization (Friendly 2017). Arce (2008: 38), for example, argues that decentralization and democratization have "shifted important decision-making downward in the political system, so that the appropriate locus of protest activity is likely to have changed." In that sense, he argues that this has re-territorialized contention rather than necessarily eliminating it. This was particularly the case in the cities, where an array of political reforms associated with decentralization produced a range of exploratory new mechanisms for asserting emancipatory social agendas at the municipal or neighborhood scale (Goldfrank and Schrank 2009). Yet these shifts also brought greater citizen attention to urban problems, and how to achieve social or other equity agendas through urban policy changes, leading to engagement with more conventional political institutions for claim-making. In particular, the embrace of participatory budgeting (Baiocchi 2004; Wampler and Avritzer 2004) and the electoral ascendance of leftist governments at the city level (Davis and Alvarado 1999) undermined independent social movement activism by bringing citizens directly into urban governance in a more direct fashion (see Annunziata and Goldfrank in this volume).

Some scholars have suggested that protests increased following democratization, in resistance to economic liberalization policies, thus challenging the assumption that contentious protests would diminish with the consolidation of democracy and neoliberalizing reforms (Bellinger and Arce 2011). Yet others have found that many of the institutional changes associated with democratic deepening served to erode civil society, turning citizens into regime participants more than regime protestors, particularly in cities (Friendly 2017; Oxhorn in this volume). Part of the explanation for this may be demographic. In recent decades, Latin American cities have hosted higher percentages of educated, formally employed, socially connected individuals than any other time; and in nations with well-functioning institutions, participants are more likely to channel energies through formal modes of political participation. However, it is also true that increased protest engagement is more likely in Latin American nations demonstrating weak political institutions with ineffective democratic representation (Moseley 2015). Given all these complexities, further attention to the urban versus rural location of protest is illuminating, since even with democratization the demographic and institutional contexts of governance will vary over space, even within the same nation.

POST-DEMOCRATIZATION, 1990–2000: INSTITUTIONALIZED POLITICS AND THE TERRITORIAL RESCALING OF SOCIAL MOVEMENT ACTIVISM

Precisely because of the uneven spatial roll-out of "actually existing" democratic transitions in Latin America, in which even the most radical of programs and governance arrangements could not fully eliminate or reverse fundamental socio-spatial and economic inequities, social movement activists did not disappear. But they did alter their strategies and tactics for change. Biekart (2005) argues that, since the 1990s, Latin American social movements have risen again and put themselves at the forefront of social protest; yet in contrast to the earlier period, this "'newest' generation of Latin American social movements (emerging after the Zapatista revolt) is not really interested in conquering the state" (ibid.: 91). Yet Biekart further suggests that, despite their unwillingness to seek state power, many of these recent movements have "shown more talent and dedication for social mobilization and toppling presidents . . . and thus have been closer to actually occupying the national palaces than any of their predecessors" (ibid.: 91).

In this transitional political terrain, as many countries began moving away from former authoritarian rule, democratization often worked as a Janus-faced sword, both strengthening and undermining autonomous social movements depending on their location and the institutional context of governance. In many countries, newly democratized institutions responded to the urban social movements of the 1980s, incentivizing more pragmatic claim-making. Such was the case of Brazil, whose 1988 constitution defined new social rights relating to public participation, thus leading urban social movements to fade away in the 1990s, though their original agendas went on to shape public policies (Caldeira 2015: S129). In rural areas, by comparison, where the new institutional mechanisms for citizen participation associated with decentralization and democratization were less likely to be developed, we see a resurgence of social movements in the 1990s (Bebbington, Abramovay, and Chiriboga 2008; Yashar 1999). In this sense, the countryside became the territorial site for some of the more oppositional social movements, particularly when contrasted with the city where citizens often turned to formal political institutions for making claims. With different grievances than their urban counterparts, very few rural movements built on alliances with urban partners.

The degree to which social movements were willing to engage in formal party politics varied on a case-by-case basis across the region (Bull 2013; Ventura 2007; see Roberts in this volume), largely depending on whether more radical parties had a chance at power as well as on historical allegiances, governance traditions, and perhaps most important, location. Indeed, although many social movements helped to bring "pink tide" governments to power across urban Latin America in the 1990s (Petras and Veltmeyer 2005), as was famously the case across major cities in Brazil, many others did not. In 1994, Mexico's Zapatistas drew the worldwide attention of observers and scholars alike by fully rejecting any formal interaction with the state, for instance, building their claims around regional identity, subaltern politics, and a visceral repudiation of decades of one-party rule (see Oikonomakis in this volume). By comparison, indigenous movements such as the Aymara movement in Bolivia or the *Pachakutik* movement in Ecuador established more serious attempts to enter the political arena, though this was done in efforts to rally for a plurinational state or mandates for autonomy and self-government (Biekart 2005: 91). The Afro-Colombian movement demonstrated similar political intent, mobilizing around ethnic identity claims in the debate over the 1991 constitution, thus tacitly participating in formal political processes and recognizing the legitimacy of the Colombian state over territorial land struggles (Agnew and Oslender 2013). Such struggles over political recognition and land rights did not involve urban populations and were framed around very unique local concerns that did not generate cross-territorial support or national impact.

In contrast, other rural-based social movements actively worked with urban allies to engage formal political institutions in the struggle to achieve larger political aims. In Bolivia, Evo Morales and the Movimiento al Socialismo (MAS) grew strength by mobilizing around water, a resource in short supply for both urban and rural populations (Anria 2013). Movement leaders joined with aspiring politicians to bring together territorially diverse populations, transcending urban-rural boundaries in movement composition and claim-making. The conscious effort to build a social movement with both rural and urban constituents departed somewhat from dominant practices in the 1990s, when most movements were likely to be either urban *or* rural by virtue of their targeting of specific localized conditions (Silva 2009). Yet having a responsive state willing to accommodate a cross-territorial mobilization with national aspirations often helped produce positive policy outcomes, thus keeping movement dynamics alive by showing that organized resistance can in fact generate change. Such cross-territorial support and national impact was achieved by reframing rural concerns and mobilization strategies to appeal to urban populations (see Fernandes and Welch, Dixon and Caldwell in this volume).

The point here is that the spatial scale of protest often affects a social movement's likelihood of bringing about fundamental change, with movements that remain isolated and rural showing less success in achieving transformative aims than those engaging populations across rural and urban territories. In regionally remote rural settings, where state accountability is often harder to ensure, rural movements were more readily repressed or stymied by longstanding regional caudillos, despite national moves toward democratization and decentralization, and even when rural protesters demanded a state response. In the case of Colombia, in particular, the spatially isolated Afro-Colombian movement was challenged by transnational corporations as well as drug traffickers, both of whom rejected any potential synergies between the movement leadership and governing authorities (Oslender 2016). Yet the divergent political contexts of Colombia and Brazil may also explain the variation in strategies, if only because decades of violence in Colombia had fragmented political parties in ways that brought very little connection between rural and urban constituencies. Differences in the national political context also mattered. In Brazil, leftist parties emergent from social movement activism were key players in regional and national politics, and any pathway to electoral success required alliance building across the city and countryside (see Roberts in this volume).

One reason it makes sense to assess the relationships between democratization, the territorial geographies of mobilization, and movement success is that a more spatially sensitive analysis can help reconcile some of the contradictory claims in the literature on social movements (see Halvorsen and Rossi in this volume). As noted above, while some authors have argued that democratization undermined social movements (Almeida 2014: 4; Archila 2011: 61), others have identified an increase in protests beginning in the 1990s (Biekart 2005). These divergent views can be explained partly by which countries were being examined and by the array of socio-spatial and political conditions that enabled or constrained the incorporation of social movements into progressive party politics in those settings. However, these outcomes were also contingent on a movement's location in rural versus urban settings, with the latter also determined by each country's agricultural versus urban-industrial economic model and the ways that democratization changed the geography of economic growth (Fernandes and Welch in this volume).

RESISTING NEOLIBERALIZATION, 2000–2015: FROM INFRASTRUCTURE AND SERVICES TO TERRITORY AND RESOURCES AS OBJECTS OF STRUGGLE

Once one identifies how economic changes set in motion by democratization impact social movements, and vice versa, it becomes clear that the advent and deepening of neoliberalization has been just as important as democratic transition in altering and even re-territorializing movement dynamics (Arce 2008). Although the embrace of new territorial strategies and spatial tactics may or may not be a direct product of neoliberal times, their proliferation in the post-2000 period suggests they can be seen as a response to the ways that both political and economic conditions have changed. As neoliberalization has intensified and conquered more locations across territory and within the spaces of everyday life, it brings new forms and locations of dissatisfaction and opposition.

For example, in his study of intensified social protests in Central America since 2000, Almeida (2014) links patterns of contention to the impacts of economic globalization on local contexts, particularly as mediated by the geographical pattern of state institutions and infrastructure needs determined during pre-economic globalization development priorities. He shows that beginning in 2000, protesters mobilized around a range of unwanted neoliberal economic policies such as privatization, free trade, labor flexibility, or price hikes. He further argues that, in contrast to more circumscribed protests of the past, these mobilizations were more inclusive, taking advantage of social sectors such as opposition political parties, women's collectives, NGOs, high school and university students, new social movements, and community-based groups (ibid.: 154). Directly contradicting claims that democratization would lead to pacification or formal co-optation by the state, Almeida argues that mobilizations in Latin America today are likely to involve a range of "calculated medium and long-term strategies such as strikes, rallies, marches, boycotts, sit-ins, and traffic obstruction" that are critical in helping advance movement success (ibid.: 7).

Of course, neoliberalization peeked its head in Latin America long before 2000. But studies have shown that the deepening of neoliberal economic reforms in the decades after democratization generated new locations and tactics of social activism (Almeida 2007). For example, Silva's (2009) survey of early anti-neoliberal contention in 1990s Latin America provides evidence of a rise in protest campaigns both in rural and urban areas, a finding consistent with Almeida's (2007: 129) study of the same period. Silva argues, however, that many of these protests were limited to individual policies by protestors who sought specific reforms, often in a localized manner. It was not until the early 2000s, he suggests, that protest waves assumed more coherent frames of mobilization in response to neoliberalization. Moreover, these frames helped anti-neoliberal protests in Latin American cities to become much more sustained social movements, thus propelling left-wing governments to power with an anti-neoliberal platform (Silva and Rossi 2018). This definitely was the case with Venezuela's Hugo Chávez in 1998, Argentina's Néstor Kirchner in 2003, and Bolivia's Evo Morales in 2005. As such, perhaps one of the most important impacts of deepening neoliberalization has been its capacity to give movement leaders opportunities to link local political struggles to national economic agendas, a strategy that offers new possibilities for territorial rescaling of protest. Natural resources that previously laid under the purview of national state authorities like water, gas, and electricity often lay at the center of the struggles, particularly as neoliberal regimes began selling off sovereign management authority in the wake of privatization. We see this starting in the late 1990s and early 2000s, with the result being a new geography of mobilization that linked citizens across localities and regions in networked opposition to the national state, because of growing concerns over a loss of national patrimony in the face of neoliberal economic reform.

A particularly instructive case is Bolivia's Water Wars (2000) and its later Gas Wars (2003), both of which brought the mobilization of citizens—the former in the regional outpost of Cochabamba and the latter in El Alto before its rapid geographic expansion—to clamor for economic justice after the advent of water privatization in June 1999. The Water Wars emerged in response to contractual terms of privatization, which allowed private firm access to water of the municipal water system as well as to water collected through private and communal wells. Tens of thousands of protestors used marches and road blockades, shutting down the center of the city and closing the regional airport and two major highways in and out of the city—a form of tactical disruption that came to dominate forms of social protest in Bolivia during the post-2000 era (Laserna and Ortego 2003). The success of the Water Wars in reversing the sale and renationalizing the water utility lay in the movement's ability to unite geographically dispersed citizens around a single issue, overcoming the type of territorial fragmentation that neoliberal reforms had begun to produce in Bolivia (Kohl 2002). Likewise, Bolivia's post-2000 Gas Wars mobilized against the uneven distribution of natural resources under neoliberalized environmental governance. This period of political unrest was responsible for the removal of two presidents and, according to Anria (2013), opened a new space for the MAS to grow into a national party as it expanded within the urban vacuum left by former party networks.

Similarly, in Peru, the sale of two state-owned electricity companies in the province of Arequipa in 2002 provoked mass outrage. Unlike many other countries in the region, anti-neoliberal contention was largely absent in the 1990s owing to a highly centralized and repressive authoritarian government under Alberto Fujimori (Silva 2009). The transition to Alejandro Toledo's government in 2000 promised a more democratic model of governance with an initial program of decentralization going forward, picking up on the nation's earlier decentralization plans that had been abandoned following Fujimori's election in 1990. Despite the haphazard and often chaotic process of decentralization, Arce (2008: 43) claims it created a much more conducive environment for contentious mobilization. Thus, when Toledo reversed his campaign promise to maintain the electric company's public ownership in 2002, outraged citizens in Arequipa demonstrated with the largest wave of mobilization to erupt during Toledo's tenure. Protests were known for their unique strategies and tactics— road blockades, seizure of public buildings, and marches (ibid.: 41). And by adopting common tactics, protestors in various cities were also able to create horizontal linkages with each other, including in the nation's capital, Lima.

What these movements show, first of all, is the critical role that state efforts to privatize natural resources have played in generating contemporary social movements, and in potentially linking rural and urban actors in ways that increase their strength if not impact. To be sure, electricity and water have always been of great concern to all populations no matter their location. Yet the fact that challenges to water and electricity distribution were being decided by market rather than solely state actors diverted the locus of struggle away from the state, thus explaining why rural and urban fates became more closely tied to each other when privatization undermined the national state's capacity to manage their supply and distribution. In this sense, neoliberalism offered opportunities to overcome territorial fragmentation among social movement organizations, allowing unification across issues and territorial scales of activism.

Second, these movements reveal that the capacity to find a unifying frame to link activists together across territory, even when natural resources are not the issues under contention, is the key to success. Neoliberalism and the discontents generated by the embrace of privatization and economic globalization have become that frame. One further example is seen in the widespread 2004 mobilization against the plans for a new Mexico City airport, proposed by national authorities to streamline the globalization of the economy (Flores Dewey and Davis 2013). Although opposition to the project began with local farmers from the rural village of Texcoco located outside the expanding Mexico City footprint, who were protesting the appropriation of their lands, it soon grew to include citizens in Mexico City along with its leftist Mayor, as well as Zapatistas in the far regions of Mexico, ultimately capturing the imagination and support of citizens worldwide (Davis and Rosan 2004). The use of social media helped generate global support for the Texcoco mobilization, creating a locally-nationally-globally-networked movement of protesters that spanned the Mexican territory and beyond, a mobilization strategy that helped lead to the cancellation of the project.

Third, these movements suggest the post-2000 emergence of new spatial strategies and tactics that focus attention on market dynamics related to the unequal social and spatial distribution of goods and services in both cities and countryside. In addition to the Bolivian and Peruvian examples noted above, we see evidence of this in the 2007 *Tortillazo* protests in Mexico City, which brought civil society together to shut down Mexico City thoroughfares. Protestors expressed opposition to rising corn prices and corn imports, with the symbolic space of the Mexican *home*—a "critical site for the production and reproduction of national belonging" (Simmons 2016: 158)—becoming a site of perceived vulnerability through the threat to affordable corn-based staples that were a central fixture in the traditional diet. Similar tactics can also be seen in Argentina with the rise of road blockades on provincial or national routes (Auyero 2002), and in Venezuela with increases in "illegal protest activity" (Arce 2008: 41) such as highway blockades, land invasions, and occupations of buildings, public plazas, and streetscapes.

That such protests and occupations were classified as illegal underscores yet one final aspect of change: the ways in which economic neoliberalization has transformed practically all urban and rural land into market commodities in ways that were not the case in earlier periods, when informality and uneven distribution of private property rights was more likely to be tolerated across rural and urban spaces in Latin America. When the private market becomes the main source of everyday reproduction, claims on the state reduce and citizens often have little recourse but to turn to disruptive protests to express grievances. In Latin America today, the primordial role of the market in organizing everyday life, and how it translates into a preference for acting in, through, and on space, is even clear in the behavior of criminal organizations seeking to assert a parallel political power to the state. In Mexico, Brazil, and much of Central America, where levels of drug trafficking and everyday violence are skyrocketing, the battle between citizens, governing authorities, and criminal organizations often unfolds around the struggle to control both micro and macro-territories, particularly key urban nodes in larger transnational criminal or capital networks (Davis 2010).

Although the rise of illicit trade and the proliferation of violence are not usually studied through the lens of social movement activism, this may be because they pose a challenge to collective action. Neither traditional grassroots mobilizations nor disruptive spatial tactics can readily empower citizens in the struggle against the perpetrators of crime and violence. Paradoxically, however, this may be due to the fact that organized criminal groups are themselves embracing the praxis of *territorio* and *autonomía*, struggling to cement spatial control over nodes and networks of illicit market activities in ways that strengthen their autonomy vis-à-vis the state and its sovereign power (Davis 2010).

Conclusion

In contemporary Latin America, social movement activism continues but manifests itself differently than in previous decades. Since 2000, micro-geographies of disruption are more common than the massive mobilizations for regime change that characterized the period from 1970–1990. Both democratization and neoliberalization help explain these shifts, precisely because they have transformed the institutional terrain of state action, reducing the state's responsibility for the provision of public goods and strengthening formal political institutions for expressing grievances, including the ballot box and decentralized institutions for claim-making (see Rossi in this volume). To the extent that these new dynamics have unfolded unevenly in space, with democratization initially bringing more opportunities for urban than rural residents, the geographic site for social mobilization shifted from city to countryside as the democratic transition unfolded.

As democracy deepened in formal terms, the neoliberal market dynamics of Latin American economic development also intensified, further privileging conditions in the city over the countryside. In this context, rural populations were doubly disadvantaged, seeing their livelihoods undermined by agrarian decline and their communities negatively impacted by increasing resource extraction and environmental degradation (see Christel and Gutiérrez in this volume). These trends not only reinforced a geographic shift of movement activism from city to countryside, they also laid the groundwork for the adoption of new spatial strategies and tactics that emphasized the struggle for territory and autonomy and that focused attention on protesting everyday conditions, and the market actors that produced them, more than petitioning the state.

With resource extraction and high levels of urbanization the twin pillars of neoliberalization, many Latin American countries now face a looming environmental crisis. In the current era the state seems incapable of responding to the urgency of climate disaster; and if this continues, one might expect to see the deployment of spatial strategies and tactics that bypass the state and focus on revealing the negative consequences on everyday life, particularly in rural areas where mining, deforestation, and water scarcities hit hard. Whether the disruptive spatial tactics deployed in the last several years will be seen as making a difference in the battle against looming environmental catastrophe remains to be seen. Yet the fact that the environmental impacts of climate change know no borders might also help incentivize the proliferation of cross-territorial movements, thus strengthening citizens' capacities to make a difference through social activism. But the question is to whom will these protests be directed? Maybe in the next phase of activism the state and its environmental policies will be on the agenda as the object of struggle, thus bringing full circle the social movement transformations discussed here.

References

Agnew, John and Ulrich Oslender (2013), "Overlapping Territorialities, Sovereignty in Dispute: Empirical Lessons from Latin America," in Walter Nicholls, Byron Miller, and Justin Beaumont (eds.), *Spaces of Contention: Spatialities and Social Movements*, 121–40 (New York: Routledge).

Almeida, Paul (2007), "Defensive Mobilization: Popular Movements against Economic Adjustment Politics in Latin America," *Latin American Perspectives* 154(34), 123–39.

Almeida, Paul (2014), *Mobilizing Democracy: Globalization and Citizen Protest* (Baltimore, MD: John Hopkins University Press).

Anria, Santiago (2013), "Social Movements, Party Organization, and Populism: Insights from Bolivian MAS," *Latin American Politics and Society* 55(3), 19–46.

Arce, Moisés (2008), "The Repoliticization of Collective Action after Neoliberalism in Peru," *Latin American Politics and Society* 50(3), 37–62.

Archila, Mauricio (2011), "Latin American Social Movements at the Start of the Twenty-First Century," *Labor* 8(1), 57–75.

Auyero, Javier (2002), "Los cambios en el repertorio de la protesta social en la Argentina," *Desarrollo Económico* 42(166), 187–210.

Baiocchi, Gianpaolo (2004), "Porto Alegre: the Dynamism of the Unorganized," in Daniel Chavez and Benjamin Goldfrank (eds.), *The Left in the City: Participatory Local Governments in Latin America*, 37–67 (London: Latin American Bureau).

Bebbington, Anthony, Ricardo Abramovay, and Manuel Chiriboga (2008), "Social Movements and the Dynamics of Rural Territorial Development in Latin America," *World Development* 36(12), 2847–87.

Bellinger, Paul T. and Moisés Arce (2011), "Protest and Democracy in Latin America's Market Era," *Political Research Quarterly* 64(3), 688–704.

Biekart, Kees (2005), "Seven Theses on Latin America Social Movements and Political Change: A Tribute to André Gunder Frank (1929-2005)," *European Review of Latin American and Caribbean Studies* 79, 85-94.

Blank, Martina (2016), "De-Fetishizing the Analysis of Social Movements Strategies: Polymorphy and Trabajo Territorial in Argentina," *Political Geography* 50, 1-9.

Bosco, Fernando J. (2008), "The Geographies of Latin American Social Movements," in Edward L. Jackiewicz and Fernando J. Bosco (eds.), *Placing Latin America: Contemporary Themes in Human Geography*, 177-90 (Lanham, MD: Rowman & Littlefield).

Bryan, Joe (2012), "Rethinking Territory: Social Justice and Neoliberalism in Latin America's Territorial Turn," *Geography Compass* 6(4), 215-26.

Bull, Benedicte (2013), "Social Movements and "Pink Tide" Governments in Latin America: Transformation, inclusion, and rejection," in Kristian Stokke and Olle Törnquist (eds.), *Democratization in the Global South: The Importance of Transformative Politics*, 75-99 (New York: Palgrave-Macmillan).

Caldeira, Teresa (2015), "Social Movements, Cultural Production, and Protests: São Paulo's Shifting Political Landscape," *Current Anthropology* 56 (S11), S126-36.

Castells, Manuel (1978), *City, Class, Power* (New York: Macmillan).

Castells, Manuel (1973), *The City and the Grassroots: A Cross-Cultural Theory of Urban Social Movements* (Berkeley and Los Angeles: University of California Press).

Clare, Nick, Victoria Habermehl, and Liz Mason-Deese (2017), "Territories in Contestation: Relational Power in Latin America," *Territory, Politics, Governance* 6(3), 1-20.

Collier, Ruth Berins and James Mahoney (1997), "Adding Collective Actors to Collective Outcomes: Labor and Recent Democratization in South America and Southern Europe," *Comparative Politics* 29(3), 285-303.

Davis, Diane E. (1994), *Urban Leviathan: Mexico City in the Twentieth Century* (Philadelphia, PA: Temple University Press).

Davis, Diane E. (1999), "The Power of Distance: Re-theorizing Social Movements in Latin America," *Theory & Society* 28, 585-638.

Davis, Diane E. (2004), *Discipline and Development: Middle Class and Prosperity in East Asia and Latin America* (Cambridge: Cambridge University Press).

Davis, Diane E. (2010), "Irregular Armed Forces, Shifting Patterns of Commitment, and Fragmented Sovereignty in the Developing World," *Theory & Society* 39, 397-413.

Davis, Diane E. and Arturo Alvarado (1999), "Descent into Chaos? Liberalization, Public Insecurity, and Deteriorating Rule of Law in Mexico City," *Working Papers in Local Governance and Democracy* 1, 95-197.

Davis, Diane E. and Christina Rosan (2004), "Social Movements in the Mexico City Airport Controversy: Globalization, Democracy, and the Power of Distance," *Mobilization: An International Quarterly* 9(3), 279-93.

Earle, Lucy (2012), "From Insurgent to Transgressive Citizenship: Housing, Social Movements, and the Politics of Rights in São Paolo," *Mobilization: An International Quarterly* 2(2), 129-47.

Flores Dewey, Onesimo and Diane E. Davis (2013), "Planning, Politics, and Urban Mega-Projects in Development Contest: Lessons from Mexico City's Airport Controversy," *Journal of Urban Affairs* 35(5), 531-51.

Friendly, Abigail (2017), "Urban Policy, Social Movements, and the Right to the City in Brazil," *Latin American Perspectives* 35(5), 531-51.

Goldfrank, Benjamin and Andrew Shrank (2009), "Municipal Neoliberalism and Municipal Socialism: Urban Political Economy in Latin America," *IJURR* 33(2), 443–62.

Guidry, John (2003), "Trial by Space: The Spatial Politics of Citizenship and Social Movements in Urban Brazil," *Mobilization: An International Quarterly* 8(2), 189–204.

Holston, James (2009), *Insurgent Citizenship: Disjunctions of Democracy and Modernity in Brazil* (Princeton, NJ: Princeton University Press).

Kohl, Benjamin (2002), "Stabilizing Neoliberalism in Bolivia: Popular Participation and Privatization," *Political Geography* 21(4), 449–72.

Laserna, Roberto and Jesús Ortego (2003), "Reflexiones sobre violencia, conflict, y diálogo social en Bolivia," *Boletín 8* (Cochabamba: Centro de Estudios de la Realidad Económica y Social).

Lopes de Souza, Marcelo (2016), "Lessons from Praxis: Autonomy and Spatiality in Contemporary Latin American Social Movements," *Antipode* 48(5), 1292–316.

Mason-Deese, Liz (2012), "The Neighborhood is the New Factory," *Viewpoint Magazine*, September 10, https://www.viewpointmag.com/2012/09/10/the-neighborhood-is-the-new-factory/.

Moseley, Mason W. (2015), "Contentious Engagement: Understanding Protest Participation in Latin American Democracies," *Journal of Politics in Latin America* 7(3), 3–48.

Nicholls, Walter (2007), "The Geographies of Social Movements," *Geography Compass* 1(3), 607–22.

Oslender, Ulrich (2016), *The Geographies of Social Movements: Afro-Colombian Mobilization and the Aquatic Space* (Durham, NC: Duke University Press).

Petras, James and Henry Veltmeyer (2005), *Social Movements and State Power: Argentina, Brazil, Bolivia and Ecuador* (London: Pluto).

Rossi, Federico M. (2015), "Conceptualizing Strategy Making in a Historical and Collective Perspective," in Federico M. Rossi and Marisa von Bülow (eds.), *Social Movement Dynamics: New Perspectives on Theory and Research from Latin America*, 11–22 (Farnham: Ashgate).

Rossi, Federico M. (2019), "Conceptualising and Tracing the Increased Territorialisation of Politics: Insights from Argentina," *Third World Quarterly* 40(4), 815–37.

Rossi, Federico M. and Marisa von Bülow (eds.) (2015), *Social Movement Dynamics: New Perspectives on Theory and Research from Latin America* (Farnham: Ashgate).

Sandoval, López Maria F., Andrea Robertsdotter, and Myriam Paredes (2017), "Space, Power, and Locality: The Contemporary use of Territorio in Latin American Geography," *Journal of Latin American Geography* 16(1), 43–67.

Scott, James C. (1985), *Weapons of the Weak: Everyday Forms of Peasant Resistance* (New Haven, CT: Yale University Press).

Silva, Eduardo (2009), *Challenging Neoliberalism in Latin America* (New York: Cambridge University Press).

Silva, Eduardo and Federico M. Rossi (2018), *Reshaping the Political Arena in Latin America: From Resisting Neoliberalism to the Second Incorporation* (Pittsburgh, PA: University of Pittsburgh Press).

Simmons, Erica S. (2016), *Meaningful Resistance: Market Reforms and the Roots of Social Protest in Latin America* (Cambridge: Cambridge University Press).

Ventura, Fernanda Somuano (2007), "Movimientos sociales y partidos políticos en América Latina," *Política y Cultura* 27, 31–53.

Wampler, Brian and Leonardo Avritzer (2004), "Participatory Publics: Civil Society and New Institutions in Democratic Brazil," *Comparative Politics* 36(3), 291–312.

Yashar, Deborah J. (1998), "Contesting Citizenship: Indigenous Movements and Democracy in Latin America," *Comparative Politics* 31(1), 23–42.

Yashar, Deborah J. (1999), "Democracy, Indigenous Movements, and the Postliberal Challenge in Latin America," *World Politics* 53(1), 76–104.

Zibechi, Raúl (2012) [2009], *Territories in Resistance: A Cartography of Latin American Social Movements* (Oakland, CA: AK Press).

CHAPTER 41

STRENGTHS AND BLIND SPOTS OF DIGITAL ACTIVISM IN LATIN AMERICA

Mapping Actors, Tools, and Theories

EMILIANO TRERÉ AND SUMMER HARLOW

INTRODUCTION

Latin America represents a particularly rich region in terms of experiences of media production and citizen participation, with an established and vivid tradition of community and Indigenous radios and citizens' media. The many difficulties that marginalized and oppressed groups face in order to penetrate the rigid boundaries of highly concentrated hegemonic media systems, along with the immense cultural diversity of the region (Caballero and Gravante 2018), have spurred a scenario of multiple media projects and uses in several Latin American countries, generating a vibrant, critical tradition of participatory communication for social change and transformation. The Mexican Zapatista uprising in the 1990s epitomized the possibilities and the challenges of the internet to support social struggles, and the massive spread of low-cost technologies, along with the technological expertise acquired since the 1970s by community-based and grassroots groups, paved the way for the subsequent forms of digital activism and protest of the 2000s, such as the student protests in Chile, the #YoSoy132 movement in Mexico, the media projects in the context of armed conflicts in Colombia, and the Cuban blogosphere, among others.

A few years ago, a special issue of the *International Journal of Communication* (Treré and Magallanes-Blanco 2015)—to which both the authors of this chapter contributed—made a strong call for developing research on digital activism and resistance in Latin America. The richness and diversity of episodes of digital contention in the region were highlighted, as well as the challenges of the literature, including the tendency towards fragmentation and the scarcity of research published in English. Considering the continual evolution of digital tools and their ever-increasing use for activism, we wondered, since then, had the situation changed? The analysis we provide in this chapter shows that it has significantly evolved and expanded, with an increasing number of publications in English by a substantial number of Latin American scholars that document and explore various manifestations of digital activism in the region. However, some of the challenges inherent in researching Latin American digital activism that were pointed out in the 2015 issue persist, even as others have emerged, as this chapter will illustrate. For example, studies often borrow theoretical frameworks from outside Latin America, tend to rely on country-specific case studies, and disregard any synthesis of the common and divergent dynamics of movements across the region. Identifying the strengths and blind spots in English-, Spanish-, and Portuguese-language scholarship, this chapter provides a much-needed critical meta-analysis of the literature—produced both within and outside the region—on social movements and digital activism in Latin America.[1] The chapter starts by assessing the actors, tools, and theories that constitute digital activism in Latin America. Then, it identifies some of the blind spots and challenges of research, conceiving them as factors that hinder the development of more general accounts of digital activism in the region. These include: the propensity to adopt conceptual lenses from the Global North and the resulting lack of South–North and North–South dialogue, the adoption of ahistorical approaches that disregard the legacy of previous protest events, the tendency to focus on just one medium/platform, the limitations of emerging computational methods, the emergence of digital agnosticism and a general uncritical stance towards digital media platforms. Finally, we illustrate the complexities of digital activism in the region with case studies of Guatemala and Mexico. Based on the insights of the chapter, we then provide future directions and areas of study in need of further scrutiny.

Actors, Tools, and Theories in Latin American Digital Activism

Actors

Studies of digital activism in Latin America have explored the appropriations of several digital technologies by a wide range of individual and collective actors, including social movements, civil society organizations, and activist collectives. For example, research has analyzed how digital media have been used in the struggles related to public education and within student movements, such as the so-called Penguin Revolution of 2006 in Chile (Bacallao-Pino 2016), the #YoSoy132 movement that emerged in 2012 in Mexico (Reguillo 2017; Rovira 2013; Treré 2015), and the #OcupaEscola uprisings of 2015 in Brazil. Further, scholars have studied how activists in environmental movements use digital technologies in their struggles against mining and aggressive extractivism in the region (Paredes 2016; Parra 2015). Researchers also have focused on the integration of digital platforms into the practices of indigenous peoples (Cadavid et al. 2017; Lupien et al. 2019; Magallanes-Blanco 2011; Salazar 2003) and examined cyber-feminist initiatives and actions in several Latin American countries (Benítez-Eyzaguirre 2019; Bentes 2017; Binder 2019; Matos 2017). Some scholars have looked at the development and characteristics of alternative media online (Harlow 2016, 2017), assessing the "alternativeness" of online-native media (Harlow 2021; Harlow and Salaverría 2016). Others have studied forms of "artivism" in the region and the manifold connections between artistic expressions such as music, poetry, and performative arts and digital activism (Chacón 2018). This has included reflecting on the creative innovations in the rich field of Latin American cyber-culture and cyber-literature (Pitman 2007). Another strand of studies has centered on the digital strategies of movements that fight against the growing violence in the region, often related to drug-trafficking and interwoven with issues of corruption and impunity as in the case of the Ayotnizapa protests (Gravante and Poma 2019; Meneses and Castillo González 2018), the Barrio Nómada Collective (Treré 2019a), and the Movimiento por la Paz con Justicia y Dignidad (MPJD) in contemporary Mexico (Treré and Cargnelutti 2014). Some scholars have devoted attention to how different social movements and civil society organizations are able to shape media policy (see in particular Segura and Waisbord 2016 and their conceptualization of "media movements") and legislation of radio and television broadcasting, also through the effective use of digital tactics (Gómez 2018; Gómez and Treré 2014). Issues of democratic governance and politics and their relation with the diffusion of digital technologies have also received the attention of academic scrutiny (Breuer and Welp 2014). More recently, attention has turned to diverse experiences of data activism (Chenou and Cepeda-Másmela 2019; Milan and Gutiérrez 2015; Ricaurte 2019), focusing on how citizens can appropriate data to promote social change and studying how this intersects with more traditional forms of digital activism across the region.

It is worthwhile to note that much of the research on Latin American digital activism focuses on movements initiated post-Arab Spring, despite the fact that the Mexican Zapatista resistance in 1994 and its use of the internet to spread communiqués and videos marked one of the world's first examples of online activism (Castells 2004). Further, most studies are focused on movements in Mexico and South America—Brazil and Chile especially—while activism in Central America is largely ignored. In some studies, there is a tendency to disregard the region's long history of digital activism. This at times can risk generating an incomplete, fragmented understanding of how different movements in diverse countries throughout time influence today's activists' use of technologies. An ahistorical approach that neglects activism in half of the region's countries prohibits cross-country dialogue that could serve not only to better refine our definition of Latin American digital activism, but also to create the scholarly foundation necessary for more theoretical development.

Tools

While the first explorations of online activism—such as the emblematic Zapatista movement (see later in this chapter)—were mainly focused on mailing lists, forums, and web pages, in recent years, when considering the specific tools, technologies, and platforms that scholars consider to be part of "digital activism," there has been a strong bend towards research examining social media platforms like Twitter, Facebook, and YouTube (among the many contributions, see: Bacallao-Pino 2016; Gómez and Treré 2014; Halpern, Rosenberg, and Arriagada 2013; Harlow and Harp 2012; Valenzuela, Arriagada, and Scherman 2012). That being said, studies have also looked at the role of blogs (Hind 2018; Matos 2017), immigrant tools (Delgado Moya 2018), WhatsApp (Milan and Barbosa 2020), Instagram, bots (Savage, Monroy-Hernandez, and Höllerer 2016), and various forms of video activism (Sierra and Montero 2015), often adopting the somewhat vague label of "information and communication technologies" (ICTs) in activism. In other words, within studies of digital activism in Latin America, definitions of what comprised "digital" included anything connected to the internet, whether a part of the online platform itself or a tool that could connect to the internet. Moreover, most research focuses on the role of just one particular online platform or tool. Relatedly, there is a tendency to define digital activism as activism carried out mostly on or through digital technologies, somehow disregarding the way digital technologies work in conjunction with analog media, such as newspapers, community radio, or television. We view this restricted focus on just one tool or technological manifestation of digital activism as a sign of the one-medium fallacy (Treré 2019b) that to a large extent defines most of the literature on social movements and digital protest. This stands in contrast to new research in the field of social movements and alternative media (Harlow 2016, 2017, 2021; Treré and Barranquero 2018) that highlights the need to look at the complexity and hybridity of the broader media ecology within which activists interact.

Theories

In terms of theory, research on digital activism in the region has also been significantly varied. Many studies apply theoretical frameworks from the Global North, mainly Europe and the United States (see for example: Halpern, Rosenberg, and Arriagada 2013; Valenzuela, Arriagada, and Scherman 2012). Other scholars adopt an approach that privileges activists' processes of social appropriation of digital technologies, in line with the critical Latin American tradition of communication for social change. These scholars employ conceptual frameworks from the region and other parts of the Global South, such as Martín Barbero's concept of mediation (Bacallao-Pino 2016; Sierra and Gravante 2017; Sierra and Gravante 2018), along with the notions of technopolitics (for a review of its application, see Treré and Barranquero 2018), mestizaje (Harlow 2017, 2021), and hybridity (Treré 2019a, 2019b). This strand of research has also been attentive to the dynamics of knowledge production (Sartoretto and Custodio 2019; Stephansen 2019), pedagogical practices (Barbas 2019) and decolonizing efforts (Loustauau 2018) within social movements and digital cultures, building important theoretical connections between the Global North and the Global South. However, this research that erects conceptual bridges between theories and concepts from the North and the South is still underdeveloped, even if the recognition of the need to de-Westernize communications studies has a long history in the region. Recent scholarly endeavors have illustrated (Harlow 2017; Treré and Barranquero 2018) how digital activism in Latin America could benefit from this kind of South–North cross-fertilization, as applying exclusively literature from the North may risk creating limited understandings of digital activism in the region: since research, definitions, and findings from the United States and Europe do not necessarily apply to Latin America. Another issue of the scholarly literature is that most research is constituted by case studies showing how existing theories apply to specific contexts, with less attention devoted to the construction of typologies, models, or some other form of conceptual development. In order to foster conceptual advancement and innovation, digital activism studies in Latin America would benefit from providing more analytical accounts and comparative works able to explore the communicative complexity of activism across actors, movements, and countries.

The Limits of Computational Methods

While most research on digital activism in the region relies on qualitative methods—such as semi-structured interviews and participant observation—a small, seemingly increasing branch of the literature focuses exclusively on big data collected from Google Trends or social media (Cadena et al. 2015; Sathappan et al. 2016). These studies use social movements and social unrest to test computational analytics and predict the possibility of future bouts of collective action. The use of large sets of data and sophisticated visualization techniques can allow for longitudinal overviews of social media coverage across the duration of different social movements, with the possibility of comparing behaviors, activities, and practices across movements. However, most of these studies profess a quasi-religious reliance on quantitative "big data" analysis that glosses over the understanding of the cultural, social, and political contexts where protest develops (Rodríguez, Ferrón, and Shamas 2014). This new field of study presents several challenges, such as the political dangers that could arise from using activists' tweets to predict and subsequently quash any social unrest. Such research also neglects the crucial question of why people protest and how activists can use technology to further their cause and push for social justice. While big data are useful, we urge caution not to focus merely on the creation and testing of formulas, and thereby abandon the "social" side of social science research. Rather, these massive datasets should also be used to help predict and explain what is needed to get people to take to the streets, and to provoke systemic social and policy changes.

The Issue of Digital Agnosticism

Generally, previous research on digital activism has been lumped into one of three camps: optimistic ("It was a Twitter revolution"), realistic/ambivalent (moderate changes depending on the use) or pessimistic ("clicktivism" hinders real activism) (Waisbord 2015). A substantial portion of research into digital activism in Latin America presents a realistic balance of the pros and cons of digital technologies in the region, showing scholars do not automatically assume that region-wide digital inequalities prohibit any democratic uses of digital tools. However, our review also sheds light on studies exhibiting what we are calling *digital agnosticism*. Digitally agnostic studies are those that fail to engage with the question of whether, or in what way, activists' use of new digital tools might benefit or harm efforts for social justice. Studies in political communication and political science are more likely to be digitally agnostic, as they often disregard the political economy implications of social platforms and the question of who was using these tools and for what purposes. These accounts of digital activism stand in contrast to the tradition of Latin American communication and alternative/community/citizen media studies that urge scholars not to separate their scholarship from their active engagement in the fight against oppression in Latin America, one of the most unequal regions in the world.

Digital Activism Complexities on the Ground: Guatemala and Mexico

In the next section, we chart the complexity of digital activism in the contexts of Guatemala and Mexico. Through these two snapshots, we show that digital activism taking place on the ground throughout the region is much more complex, technologically savvy, and reliant on digital *and* analog communication tools than the research would have you expect.

Hence, we depict two images of activism that build theory, are Global South-centric, avoid the one-platform fallacy, acknowledge the digital timeline of the region, and are digitally critical. Our aim is to advance a unified understanding of digital activism throughout the region that, by melding the fragments, can make a larger impact on scholarship worldwide and help open up more of a South–North dialogue.

Guatemala

While Central America's activist and rebel media of the 1980s have received significant scholarly attention, the same cannot be said of the region's digital activism. With some notable exceptions (e.g., García-Ruano, Pacheco, and Suazo 2013; Harlow 2012, 2015,

2016, 2017; Loustaunau 2018), most studies on digital activism neglect Central America. With this in mind, this portion of the chapter focuses specifically on Guatemala, which has witnessed various social media and hashtag-centric movements. For example, in 2009 a few concerned citizens and activists turned to Facebook to mobilize 50,000 protesters demanding the resignation of then-president Álvaro Colom (2008–2012), demonstrating the emerging potential of social media for mobilizing action online and offline (Harlow 2012). It is worth noting that Guatemala's Facebook-driven protests preceded the Arab Spring. And while the 2009 protests did not overthrow a president or prompt a revolution, they offered an early glimpse of the power of social media in the region's activism.

In April of 2015, a similar scenario played out when a 33-year-old small-business entrepreneur, Gabriel Wer, posted a message to his Facebook page grumbling about governmental corruption. A family friend saw it and added him as one of the organizers for an upcoming demonstration to demand the resignation of then-vice president Roxana Baldetti. His first order of business, Wer told one of the authors of this chapter (Harlow) during an interview in 2018, was to come up with a name for the event that could also serve as a hashtag on social media. He landed on "Renuncia Ya"—catchy and easy to remember. Wer, who said he did not consider himself an activist at the time, remarked that he and the other organizers thought maybe fifty or so of their friends would attend the event. To their shock, an estimated 30,000 showed up. Local news media publicized the event. During the coming weeks, demonstrations continued, Baldetti resigned, and "Renuncia Ya" morphed into "Justicia Ya." Eventually, the movement culminated in a general strike and 100,000 protesters converged on the main square of the capital, using the hashtag #NoTengoPresidente. President Otto Pérez Molina (2012–2015) resigned in disgrace, and a warrant was issued for his arrest.

Unlike most collective action in Guatemala, these protests were not limited to one social movement or advocacy organization. Instead, what made these protests unique, various activists said, was that they were inclusive: students, workers, Indigenous groups, LGBTQ+ groups, feminist groups, and more all came out to participate. The organizers also made an effort to keep the protests free of the influence of political parties. What is more, the protests united various socioeconomic classes, and the bulk of protesters were members of Guatemala's middle class—a segment of society that traditionally does not protest. Further, typically there is a sharp divide between rural and urban protests, but in this case, people from the interior, rural part of the country who could not make it to the capital to protest started organizing their own demonstrations on Facebook. Guatemalans abroad also joined in via social media and held their own events in Europe and the United States. The hashtags, like #JusticiaYa, even spread to anti-corruption street protests in neighboring Honduras.

Activists acknowledged that social media alone did not prompt the resignations, but they helped fan the flame, and bring together diverse groups of people. Activists also pointed out that the protests demonstrated the breadth of what digital activism can look like in Guatemala: liking a cause and writing to officials on Facebook or Twitter pushed people to take to the streets. At the same time, they recognized that the mass media, and online, independent news sites in particular, were key. As such, the people involved with organizing the 2015 protests regularly published press releases and contacted journalists to help them spread word of the demonstrations, especially to people without internet or social media.

These urban activists also said they recognize that their digital dependency can be limiting in a country where only about 57% of the population (Internet World Stats 2019) has internet access. Still, they argue, in the capital city most people have internet and smartphones, and for the youth, particularly the politically active youth they are trying to reach, social media are a part of their way of life.

In contrast, digital activism in the country's rural interior looks somewhat different. While rural women's, Indigenous, and anti-mining groups use social media, social platforms play less of a central role than they did for the 2015 hashtag protests. While social media are good for spreading information about Indigenous communities to the capital or outside Guatemala, text messages and cell phones are more useful for announcing community events, sending emergency warnings, and transmitting live from community meetings to the local community radio station (García-Ruano, Pacheco, and Suazo 2013). Because mainstream media tend to marginalize or altogether ignore Indigenous causes and demands, mobile phones offer an easy way to transmit news and information. In rural areas where electricity and internet access are limited, mobile phones are more accessible and thus more useful than the internet for mobilizing and informing. Further, mobile phones do not necessarily come with the same level of surveillance as social media. Several Indigenous activists pointed out that too often their messages are distorted on social media and turned into campaigns used against them. As such, in the last year or so various Indigenous groups and activists have distanced themselves from social media. Further, many activists argued that hosting press conferences and calling for road blockades and marches are still the most efficient ways for them to raise awareness about their causes.

At the same time, however, many young Indigenous activists have recognized the need for updated digital tactics, such as the creation of an online television channel, Tz'ikin TeVé. According to the group's website (https://realizadorestzikin.org/), the goal was to "decentralize, democratize and decolonize audiovisual production media." The program launched in 2015, transmitting via a website, YouTube, and local community TV stations.

Mexico

Condensing the long and intricate history of Mexican activism in the brief space of a chapter's section is an impossible task, but some general tendencies and challenges regarding the evolution of digital activism in this Latin American country can be fruitfully outlined. The Zapatista movement emerged in 1994 as a local rebellion of a group of farmers and Indigenous people in the highlands of Chiapas, but soon went global thanks to an international network of alliances united against neoliberal globalization

(Oikonomakis in this volume). The Ejército Zapatista de Liberación Nacional (EZLN) was fighting in part against Mexico's participation in the North American Free Trade Agreement (NAFTA), pointing out its negative implications on local communities (Inclán in this volume). The internet played an important role in the Zapatista uprisings, especially in the global diffusion of the protest and in the construction of multiple solidarity networks to the point that Manuel Castells (2004) celebrated them as the "first information guerrilla movement" and Harry Cleaver (1998) defined it as an "electronic fabric of struggle." Digital technologies were involved in various dynamics of the movement. First, solidarity networks organized under the principle (expressed by EZLN) to articulate their struggle with others in the world. Second, supporters did not act individually, but appropriated digital technologies to interact and collaborate in multiple ways. Finally, the people who got involved in the networks to support the Zapatista movement were related to different social struggles at a local level that were performed offline. Hence, online technologies allowed for more efficient communication among people and groups, facilitating the access to fragmented information and reducing the power of concealment exerted by traditional mainstream media.

While the Zapatista insurrection has seemingly turned into a prototype of digital resistance, the role of online communication inside this insurrection was often mythologized (Pitman 2007; Wolfson 2014), as was the figure of Subcomandante Marcos (Russell 2005). Indeed, the EZLN insurrection was marked by the striking importance of physical marches and meetings, which had a tremendous impact on public opinion, especially at the symbolic level, conveying the image that Zapatistas were legitimate emanations of the fight against global neoliberalism. Further, the Mexican newspaper *La Jornada* played a fundamental role in spreading the Subcomandante's messages (Hellman 2000), and local community radios contributed to the diffusion of his speeches, strengthening local ties and helping in the coordination of protests. The EZLN prompted the uprising of different experiences of free/community/citizen media (Magallanes-Blanco 2011; Rovira 2014), and represented a crucial point in the history of third-sector media in Mexico with their fight for access of Indigenous communities to broadcasting licenses without government intermediation, along with their push to achieve balance in the unequal and concentrated media sector as a condition for expanding Mexican democracy (Gómez 2018). While attention to the Zapatista uprisings faded over time, in 2005 and 2006 the Zapatista movement led "The other campaign," an initiative of participation towards social change from below. More recently, they made headlines during the 2018 Mexican elections, putting forward an Indigenous woman as a presidential candidate (see Inclán in this volume).

Following the Zapatistas, the 2000s saw a multiplication of digitally enabled contentions in Mexico. In 2006, a popular revolt in Oaxaca erupted when the local teachers' union went on strike to demand attention to a range of problems connected to their working conditions. Under the lead of state governor Ulises Ruiz Ortiz, teachers were brutally repressed, with several activists killed and detained by the police, giving birth to the APPO movement (Asamblea Popular de los Pueblos de Oaxaca) that went on to occupy the capital city for several months. The creation of alternative media, along with reflections around the democratization of communication and the Mexican mainstream media, played a pivotal role in the Oaxaca uprisings, including the appropriation of several local radio stations and Oaxaca's public broadcasting television channels. Further, as Cravey (2010) documented, during the protests, dispatches from local radios merged with images of posters and graffiti and a fast-selling DVD documenting protest repression was sold in the markets of Oaxaca to locals and tourists. These were complemented by vibrant activity online with the creation of more than 20 internet platforms giving voice to the oppressed and marginalized citizens of Oaxaca. In particular, the hybrid-digital radio stations Radio Escopeta and Radio Disturbio, as well as online portals Revolucionemos Oaxaca and Frida Guerrera, played a key role in the protests (Gravante 2016).

In 2009, Alejandro Pisanty, who represented the Internet Society in Mexico (an international non-governmental organization advocating for a free and open internet) created the Twitter hashtag #InternetNecesario to criticize a government proposal aimed at imposing new taxes on telecom services such as internet, cell-phone subscriptions, and pay TV. Pisanty tweeted the first message the morning of October 19, and within seven hours people had tweeted around 52,000 times using the hashtag (Torres Nabel 2009), while by midnight there were about 100,000 tweets. This was labeled as the Internet Necesario cyberprotest, seen as the first example of activism generated and carried out exclusively in an online environment in Mexico. Two days later, mainstream media picked up the story, publishing interviews and reports about the campaign. The protest had a political impact: it pushed the Mexican Congress to organize a hearing with NGOs and academics to discuss the situation and in the end the government's proposal was rejected.

Since then, digital media have continued to play a major role in several Mexican protests and movements, including the movements #YoSoy132, Movimiento 5 de Junio, and the MPJD; the No+Sangre, Gato Morris, and El Bronco campaigns; and the mobilizations for Wirikuta and Ayotzinapa. #YoSoy132 emerged in 2012 after the participation of then-presidential candidate of the Partido Revolucionario Institucional (PRI) Enrique Peña Nieto (2012–2018) in a university forum. The students protested against him, while the Mexican mainstream media presented misleading information about his achievements and demonized the protesters. In response, the students created the video "131 estudiantes de la Ibero [Iberoamerican University] responden." Students of other universities quickly expressed their solidarity, igniting the movement #YoSoy132, first online through hashtags and later in the streets, with demonstrations across the country and abroad. #Yosoy132 embodied the perfect example of a communicative movement (Reguillo 2017; Treré 2019b). Originated within a combination of social media platforms (media as genesis), it fought against the Mexican media system, reclaiming media democratization and pluralism (media as addressee). It also unleashed the full potential of digital technologies and social media including Twitter, Facebook, YouTube, and WhatsApp to spread its messages, organize, and build counter-hegemonic spaces and transnational connections (media as resources) (see Donoso in this volume).

However, it also showcased problematic aspects of social media (Treré 2015, 2019a), with everyday frictions and struggles among activists, together with issues of exploitation, surveillance, control, and intents of delegitimization that contributed to depict a controversial image of digital activism in Mexico. #YoSoy132 was caught in an "algorithmic trap" when an infiltrated agent of the Mexican Secret Services was able to appropriate the movement's main online platform to steal data, monitor protest activities, and discredit the movement's reputation (Treré 2016). The dark side of digital politics in Mexico has recently (and especially since 2014) unfolded several times in the increasingly more sophisticated digital strategies of Mexican politicians and the state, who have been able to bend social media algorithms to spread propaganda, enact repression, and generate paranoia. In the Mexican context, strategies of algorithmic repression have progressively become more treacherous, broadly deployed to limit, silence, confuse, defame, threaten, and attack activists, civil society actors, and news workers.

Discussion

The practices of activists in Guatemala and Mexico help refine our definition of digital activism, pointing to the importance of digital tools working in collaboration with traditional communications tactics, such as sending out press releases, calling press conferences, and contacting alternative, community, and mainstream media. Unlike research, digital activism on the ground in Guatemala and Mexico does not fall prey to the one-medium fallacy or problem of digital agnosticism, but rather represents a hybrid blending of the digital and analog and a recognition of the importance—and limitations—of both. Manifold digital and social media technologies are used in collaboration with traditional tactics and media outlets, composing a hybrid geography where the digital and the analog not only combine but often clash, as activists create alternative media outlets because their voice is systematically silenced by highly concentrated and biased conventional media.

In Guatemala, there emerges a clear divide between urban and rural activists that mirrors the country's digital inequalities. Unsurprisingly, the digital-dependent activists in urban areas tend to focus on the benefits of social media, somewhat discounting the limitations of an online activism that inherently leaves out much of the country's population. In rural areas, activists seemingly are more overtly conscious of the strengths and weaknesses of using digital tools in activism. It is important to note, though, that they do not dismiss digital tools out of hand simply because of any disparities in access or use. Rather, they have found ways to incorporate digital tools into a mostly analog toolbox, creating a hybrid form of activism unique to the resources and needs of each community. In Mexico, the rural/urban divide is also key to understanding digital activism, as the experience of two of the most prominent movements testify (the Zapatistas in Chiapas and the APPO in Oaxaca, two of the poorest regions in the country), while the movements of the last years have mainly emerged in urban contexts and in connection to the middle and upper classes (e.g., students from private universities). Future research needs to explore this urban-rural divide further, and critically analyze how perspectives about and uses of digital tools might reflect historic divisions of race and class.

It is also important to highlight that while the #RenunciaYa and #JusticiaYa movements in Guatemala and #YoSoy132 in Mexico showcase the use of social media and hashtags for large protest movements, more research is needed into the everyday actions of activists using WhatsApp, mobile phones, online video, and other digital tools. Focusing more on how digital tools are changing the practices and tactics for Indigenous rights or anti-mining activists would help address the lack of scholarly attention paid to forms of mediated activism beyond isolated episodes of protest actions (Waisbord 2018). Further, exploring how hashtags like #JusticiaYa spread from Guatemala to Honduras, or how various Ayotzinapa-related hashtags spread from Mexico to the United States and beyond, and examining the way digital tools were used to bring together protesters from diverse movements and socioeconomic backgrounds, could overcome the limited understandings of the multidimensional and longitudinal impact of networked citizenship (Waisbord 2018). Thus, Guatemala and Mexico offer an opportunity for researchers to advance our understanding of digital activism in Latin America, paying scholarly attention not just to the "trendy" bouts of hashtag activism, but also to the daily, lived experiences of activists working across movements and borders to develop best practices for incorporating digital tools into their work in counterhegemonic ways. Additionally, by making the connection between which digital tools activists in Guatemala and Mexico use in what ways with practices of activists throughout Latin America as well as the Global North, researchers will make an important step towards creating South–North dialogue that will not only better explain what is or is not unique about digital activism in different countries, but also contribute to the de-Westernization of research and of our perceptions about what kinds of social change digital tools can or cannot help accomplish.

Finally, the Guatemalan and Mexican cases testify to the dangers and risks inherent in the use of social media and the possibilities for spreading propaganda and misinformation, and for intimidating and repressing activist voices. This demonstrates the need to critically interrogate the use of these computational tools when analyzing protest movements, reflecting on how these sophisticated techniques are being used by governments and political and business elites to hinder Latin American activism.

Conclusion

Through a critical meta-analysis of scholarly articles, this chapter assessed the actors, tools, and theories that constitute research into digital activism in Latin America, and identified the strengths and blind spots of research that contribute to either a fragmented or a more unified region-wide understanding of this phenomenon. Further, we contrasted the limited picture of digital activism provided by the literature with complex, on-the-ground illustrations of digital protests in Guatemala and

Mexico. Importantly, we recognized in the literature tendencies to import theoretical frameworks from outside Latin America, to over-rely on country-specific case studies centered on a handful of countries, and to forego synthesizing the common and divergent dynamics of movements across the region. In particular, we identified within research factors hindering the conceptual development of a unified understanding of digital activism in Latin America, including the propensity to adopt conceptual lenses from the Global North, the lack of South–North dialogue, the tendency to focus on just one medium/platform, ahistorical approaches that disregard the legacy of previous protest events, the limitations of emerging computational methods, and the emergence of digital agnosticism.

Based on the findings and reflections of this chapter, we argue that bridging the gap between theory and practice will require a move on the part of researchers towards a more unified approach that overcomes the limitations of descriptive, Global North-centric, one-platform focused, ahistorical, digitally agnostic studies. It also will require investigations that look into how digital activism is inserted into broader dynamics of social change. Moreover, in light of the massive use of dangerous forms of computational propaganda in many Latin American countries, we see an urgency to explore how big data are reshaping the practice of digital activism in the region. Finally, scholars need to devote attention to several manifestations of right-wing digital activism (Waisbord 2018), since now research appears disproportionately weighted towards the analysis of progressive, left-wing social movements.

Note

1. We performed a meta-analysis of English, Spanish, and Portuguese-language research articles published between 1994 and 2018. The year 1994 was chosen as the start date since this marks the uprising of the Zapatistas in Mexico and the region's first instance of internet activism. We limited our analysis to articles published in the following journals and databases: *Chasqui, Com y Sociedad, Cuadernos.info, Intercom Revista de Comunicação, Journal of Latin American Communication Research, Matrizes, Palabra Clave, Signo y Pensamiento,* SCOPUS, and Web of Science. These sources were chosen as they represent the leading peer-reviewed academic journals published in or about Latin America, and the databases include indexed-journals with high-quality standards and quantitative and qualitative research. A series of search terms were employed in English, Spanish, and Portuguese. To provide a more balanced assessment, in our discussion we also include key books and monographs published in the last two decades that address forms of digital activism, politics, culture, and governance in Latin America.

References

Bacallao-Pino, Lázaro M. (2016), "Redes sociales, acción colectiva y elecciones: los usos de Facebook por el movimiento estudiantil chileno durante la campaña electoral de 2013," *Palabra Clave* 19(3), 810–37.

Barbas, Ángel (2019), "Educommunication for Social Change: Contributions to the Construction of a Theory of Activist Media Practices," in Hilde Stephansen and Emiliano Treré (eds.), *Citizen Media and Practice: Currents, Connections, Challenges. Critical Perspectives on Citizen Media*, 73–87 (London: Routledge).

Benítez-Eyzaguirre, Lucia (2019), "Ciberfeminismo y apropiación tecnológica en América Latina," *Virtualis* 10(18), 1–15.

Bentes, Ivana (2017), "Feminist Biopolitics and Subversive Aesthetics," *Matrizes* 11(2), 93–109.

Binder, Inés, (2019), Identidad y agencia colectiva del movimiento ciberfeminista en América Latina. El caso de [ciberfeministaslatam]. *Dígitos. Revista de Comunicación Digital*, (5), 210-233.

Breuer, Anita and Yanina Welp (2014), *Digital Technologies for Democratic Governance in Latin America: Opportunities and Risks* (London: Routledge).

Cadavid, Amparo, Eliana Herrera, David Fayad and Jair Vega (2017), "Apropiación de TIC, pueblos indígenas y procesos politicos de resistencia en Colombia: el caso del Tejido de Comunicación," in Francisco Sierra and Tommaso Gravante (eds.), *Tecnopolítica en América Latina y el Caribe*, 145–65 (Quito: Comunicación Social).

Cadena, Jose, Gizem Korkmaz, Chris Kuhlman, Achla Marathe, Naren Ramakrishnan, and Anil Vullikanti (2015), "Forecasting Social Unrest Using Activity Cascades," *PloS one* 10(6), 1–27.

Castells, Manuel (2004), *The Power of Identity*, 2nd ed. (Malden: Blackwell).

Chacón, Hilda (ed.) (2019), *Online Activism in Latin America* (London: Routledge).

Chenou, Jean-Marie and Carolina Cepeda-Másmela (2019), "#NiUnaMenos: Data Activism from the Global South," *Television & New Media* 20(4), 396–411.

Cleaver, Harry M. Jr. (1998), "The Zapatista Effect: The Internet and the Rise of an Alternative Political Fabric," *Journal of International Affairs* 51(2), 621–40.

Cravey, Altha (2010), "Media Geographies in the Oaxacan Uprising," *Aether: The Journal of Media Geography* 6, 10–13.

Delgado Moya, Sergio (2018), "A Theater of Displacement: Staging Activism, Poetry, and Migration through a Transborder Immigrant Tool," in Hilda Chacón (ed.), *Online Activism in Latin America*, 33–57 (London: Routledge).

García-Ruano, Karina J., Alejandro Pacheco, and Dessiree Suazo (2013), "The Use of Digital Media for Social Mobilization in Marginalized Communities: The Case of a Mayan Socioenvironmental Movement in Guatemala," *International Journal of Communication* 7, 1878–91.

Gómez, Rodrigo (2018), "The Mexican Third Sector of the Media: The Long Run to Democratise the Mexican Communication System," *tripleC: Communication, Capitalism & Critique. Journal for a Global Sustainable Information Society* 16(1), 332–52.

Gravante, Tommaso (2016), *Cuando la gente toma la palabra: Medios digitales y cambio social en la insurgencia de Oaxaca* (Quito: Ediciones Ciespal).

Gómez, Rodrigo and Emiliano Treré (2014), "The #YoSoy132 Movement and the Struggle for Media Democratization in Mexico," *Convergence* 20(4), 496–510.

Gravante, Tommaso and Alice Poma (2019), "Emociones, trauma cultural y movilización social: el movimiento por las víctimas de Ayotzinapa en México," *Perfiles latinoamericanos* 27(53), 1–23.

Halpern, Daniel, Andrés Rosenberg, and Eduardo Arraiagada (2013), "Who Are Those Green Guys? Understanding Online Activism in Chile from a Communicational Perspective," *Palabra Clave* 16(3), 729–59.

Harlow, Summer (2012), "Social Media and Social Movements: Facebook and an Online Guatemalan Justice Movement that Moved Offline," *New Media & Society* 14(2), 225–43.

Harlow, Summer (2015), "Twitterati as Instruments of Change? Reappropriating Social Media for Dialogue and Action via El Salvador's Citizen Debate Site Política Stereo," *International Journal of Communication* 9, 3721–40.

Harlow, Summer (2016), "Reconfiguring and Remediating Social Media as Alternative Media: Exploring Youth Activists' Digital Media Ecology in El Salvador," *Palabra Clave* 19(4), 997–1026.

Harlow, Summer (2017), *Liberation Technology in El Salvador: Re-appropriating Social Media Among Alternative Media Projects* (Cham: Palgrave-Macmillan).

Harlow, Summer (2021), "A New People's Press? Understanding Digital-Native News Sites in Latin America as Alternative Media," *Digital Journalism*, DOI: 10.1080/21670811.2021.1907204.

Harlow, Summer and Dustin Harp (2012), "Collective Action on the Web: A Cross-cultural Study of Social Networking Sites and Online and Offline Activism in the United States and Latin America," *Information, Communication & Society* 15(2), 196–216.

Harlow, Summer and Ramón Salaverría (2016), "Regenerating Journalism: Exploring the "Alternativeness" and "Digital-ness" of Online-native Media in Latin America," *Digital Journalism* 4(8), 1001–19.

Hellman, Judith Adler (2000), "Real and Virtual Chiapas: Magic Realism and the Left," *Socialist Register* 36, 161–86.

Hind, Emily (2018), "On Pirates and Tourists: Ambivalent Approaches to El Blog del Narco," in Hilda Chacón (ed.) *Online Activism in Latin America*, 113–27 (London: Routledge).

Internet World Stats (2019), "Central America Internet Usage and Population Statistics," available at https://www.internetworldstats.com/stats12.htm#central.

Loustaunau, Esteban (2018), "Decolonizing Youth Culture: Guatemalan Hip-Hop Dissidents in Cyberspace," in Hilda Chacón (ed.), *Online Activism in Latin America*, 68–85 (New York: Routledge).

Lupien, Pascal and Gabriel Chiriboga (2019), "Use of Information and Communications Technologies by Indigenous Civil Society Organizations in Ecuador," *Information, Communication & Society* 22(8), 1029–43.

Magallanes-Blanco, Claudia (2011), "Zapatista Media (Mexico)," in John Downing (ed.), *Encyclopedia of Social Movement Media*, 563–65 (Los Angeles: Sage).

Matos, Carolina (2017), "New Brazilian Feminisms and Online Networks: Cyberfeminism, Protest and the Female "Arab Spring"," *International Sociology* 32(3), 417–34.

Meneses, María Elena and María Concepción Castillo-González (2018), "Digital Storytelling and the Dispute over Representation in the Ayotzinapa Case," *Latin American Perspectives* 45(3), 266–83.

Milan, Stefania and Miren Gutiérrez (2015), "Citizens' Media Meets Big Data: The Emergence of Data Activism," *Mediaciones* 11(14), 120–33.

Milan, Stefania and Sergio Barbosa (2020), "Enter the WhatsApper: Reinventing Digital Activism at the Time of Chat Apps," *First Monday* 25(12), https://journals.uic.edu/ojs/index.php/fm/article/view/10414.

Muthiah, Sathappan, Bert Huang, Jaime Arredondo, David Mares, Lise Getoor, Graham Katz, and Naren Ramakrishnan (2016), "Capturing Planned Protests from Open Source Indicators," *Ai Magazine* 37(2), 63–75.

Paredes, Maritza (2016), "The Glocalization of Mining Conflict: Cases from Peru," *The Extractive Industries and Society* 3(4), 1046–57.

Parra, Daniela (2015), "Alternative Media in Latin American Grassroots Integration: Building Networks and New Agendas," *International Journal of Communication* 9, 3680–701.

Pitman, Thea (2007), "Latin American Cyberprotest: Before and After the Zapatistas," in Clara Taylor and Thea Pitman (eds.), *Latin American Cyberculture and Cyberliterature*, 86–110 (Liverpool: Liverpool University Press).

Reguillo, Rossana (2017), *Paisajes insurrectos: Jóvenes, redes y revueltas en el otoño civilizatorio* (Barcelona: NED Ediciones).

Ricaurte, Paola (2019), "Data Epistemologies, the Coloniality of Power, and Resistance," *Television & New Media* 20(4), 350–65.

Rodríguez, Clemencia, Benjamin Ferron and Kristin Shamas (2014), "Four Challenges in the Field of Alternative, Radical and Citizens' Media Research," *Media, Culture & Society* 36(2), 150–66.

Rovira, Guiomar (2014), *Zapatistas sin fronteras: Las redes de solidaridad con Chiapas y el altermundismo* (Mexico: Ediciones Era).

Rovira, Guiomar (2013), "México, #yosoy132: ¡no había nadie haciendo el movimiento más que nosotros!," *Anuario Del Conflicto Social* (2), 423–448.

Russell, Adrienne (2005), "Myth and the Zapatista Movement: Exploring a Network Identity," *New Media & Society* 7(4), 559–77.

Salazar, Juan Francisco (2003), "Articulating an Activist Imaginary: Internet as Counter Public Sphere in the Mapuche Movement, 1997/2002," *Media International Australia* 107(1), 19–30.

Sartoretto, Paola and Leonardo Custódio (2019), "The Production of Knowledge in Brazilian Social Movement Families," *Journal of Alternative and Community Media* 4(2), 60–73.

Savage, Saiph, Andres Monroy-Hernandez, and Tobias Höllerer (2016), "Botivist: Calling Volunteers to Action using Online Bots," *Proceedings of the 19th ACM Conference on Computer-Supported Cooperative Work & Social Computing*, 813–22 (New York, NY: Association for Computing Machinery).

Segura, María Soledad and Silvio Waisbord (2016), *Media Movements: Civil Society and Media Policy Reform in Latin America* (London: Zed).

Sierra, Francisco and David Montero Sánchez (2015), *Videoactivismo y movimientos sociales: Teoría y praxis de las multitudes conectadas* (Barcelona: Gedisa).

Sierra Caballero, Francisco and Tommaso Gravante (eds.) (2017), *Tecnopolítica en América Latina y el Caribe* (Quito: Ediciones CIESPAL).

Sierra Caballero, Francisco and Tommaso Gravante (eds.) (2018), *Networks, Movements and Technopolitics in Latin America* (Cham: Palgrave-Macmillan).

Stephansen, Hilde (2019), "Conceptualizing the Role of Knowledge in Acting on Media," in Hilde Stephansen and Emiliano Treré (eds.) *Citizen Media and Practice: Currents, Connections, Challenges. Critical Perspectives on Citizen Media*, 189–203 (London: Routledge).

Torres Nabel, Luis César (2009), "Ciberprotestas y consecuencias políticas: Reflexiones sobre el caso de internet necesario en México," *Razón y palabra* 14(70), 1–14.

Treré, Emiliano and Claudia Magallanes-Blanco (eds.) (2015), "Latin American Struggles and Digital Media Resistance," *International Journal of Communication* 9 (2015), 3652–661.

Treré, Emiliano (2015), "The Struggle Within: Discord, Conflict and Paranoia in Social Media Protest," in Lina Dencik and Olivier Leistert (eds.), *Critical Perspectives on Social Media and Protest: Between Control and Emancipation*, 163–80 (London: Rowman and Littlefield).

Treré, Emiliano (2016), "The Dark Side of Digital Politics: Understanding the Algorithmic Manufacturing of Consent and the Hindering of Online Dissidence," *IDS Bulletin* 41(1), 127–38.

Treré, Emiliano (2019a), "Nomads of Cyber-urban Space: Media Hybridity as Resistance," in Mette Mortensen, Cristina Neumayer, and Thomas Poell (eds.), *Social Media Materialities and Protest: Critical Reflections. Critical Perspectives on Citizen Media*, 42–56 (London: Routledge).

Treré, Emiliano and Daniele Cargnelutti (2014), "Movimientos sociales, redes sociales y Web 2.0: El caso del Movimiento por la Paz con Justicia y Dignidad," *Communication & Society/Comunicación y Sociedad* 27(1), 183–203.

Treré Emiliano and Alejandro Barranquero Carretero (2018), "Tracing the Roots of Technopolitics: towards a North-South Dialogue," in Francisco Sierra Caballero and Tommaso Gravante (eds.), *Networks, Movements and Technopolitics in Latin America*, 43–63 (Cham: Palgrave-Macmillan).

Treré, Emiliano (2019b), *Hybrid Media Activism: Ecologies, Imaginaries, Algorithms* (London: Routledge).

Valenzuela, Sebastián, Arturo Arriagada, and Andrés Scherman (2012), "The Social Media Basis of Youth Protest Behavior: The Case of Chile," *Journal of Communication* 62(2), 299–314.

Waisbord, Silvio (2015), "El optimismo digi-activista y sus problemas," in Adriana Amado and Omar Rincón (eds.), *La comunicación en mutación, remix de discursos*, 75–87 (Bogotá: Fundación Ebert).

Waisbord, Silvio (2018), "Revisiting Mediated Activism," *Sociology Compass* 12(6), 1–9.

Wolfson, Todd (2014), *Digital Rebellion: The Birth of the Cyber Left* (Champaign: University of Illinois Press).

PART V
INSTITUTIONAL POLITICS AND SOCIAL MOVEMENTS

CHAPTER 42

SOCIAL MOVEMENTS AND PARTY POLITICS

Popular Mobilization and the Reciprocal Structuring of Political Representation in Latin America

KENNETH M. ROBERTS

Introduction

Social movements and party politics are often studied in isolation from each other, giving the impression that they belong to separate and distinct "fields" of scholarship—what McAdam and Tarrow (2013: 325) have characterized as a "stark disciplinary divide" in the study of politics. Increasingly, however, social scientists have come to see this divide as both artificial and counterproductive, as it impedes scholarly progress in both areas of specialization. The disciplinary divide is artificial in the sense that parties and movements are both collective actors that offer citizens "voice" in the public sphere. That is, both parties and movements aggregate individual citizens and provide opportunities for those aggregations—for citizens working in concert—to express collective interests, preferences, identities, grievances, and demands. Moreover, as Goldstone (2003: 2) notes, the boundaries between these alternative forms of collective action, or between institutionalized and noninstitutionalized politics in general, are "fuzzy and permeable," since points of intersection and overlapping are commonly found. Indeed, in many—though not necessarily all—political contexts, parties and movements mutually condition each other and shape the patterns of political mobilization with which each is associated.

If movements and parties are "mutually constitutive," as McAdam and Tarrow (2013: 325) suggest, scholars are hard-pressed to understand one set of collective actors in isolation from the other. Political dynamics in Latin America are a case in point, as the region provides ample evidence of the mutual constitution of parties and movements and the ways in which they interact to reciprocally structure, and sometimes de-structure, mass political representation. Historically, patterns of social mobilization and protest in the region have been heavily conditioned by deficiencies in institutionalized, party-based forms of political representation—deficiencies that have left important social actors largely devoid of institutionalized "voice" and thus inclined to express their demands through extra-institutional forms of political mobilization or "contentious politics" (Arce and Rice 2019: 8; Roberts 2014). As Tarrow argues, contentious forms of collective action are intrinsically related to such failures of political representation, as they are typically employed by people "who lack regular access to representative institutions" and "act in the name of new or unaccepted claims" (Tarrow 2011: 7).

Parties can also shape patterns of social mobilization more directly, strengthening social movements or protest activities in some contexts, while suppressing them in others. Parties and their grassroots activists are sometimes embedded in the social networks that mobilize behind protest activities, making parties "force multipliers" that activate and link together otherwise disconnected social collectivities. In other contexts, however, partisan and electoral politics may demobilize movement networks by diverting social activists into formal institutional roles, splitting them into rival political camps, or making strategic choices to avoid "rocking the boat" by supporting socio-political mobilization outside formal institutional channels (see Mische 2008; Oxhorn 1995; Gurza Lavalle and Szwako, Lapegna, Paredes, and Motta, Combes and Quirós in this volume).

In turn, mass protest movements have often exerted a transformative effect on more institutionalized patterns of partisan and electoral representation in Latin America. Mass protest has been instrumental in weakening the hold of established parties on popular constituencies in a large number of countries, and in some countries—such as Ecuador, Argentina, and Bolivia at the turn of the twenty-first century—it has even induced the downfall of elected governments. More directly, social movements have sometimes spawned new partisan vehicles that have realigned and reconfigured national party systems, making them more broadly representative of previously excluded popular constituencies. Protest movements have been a major source of partisan and electoral volatility, and, in some countries, they have been a cornerstone for the restructuring of partisan representation.

This reciprocal structuring of parties and social movements calls for more explicit efforts to borrow insights from both fields of study and cross-fertilize across the subfield divide. Such cross-fertilization could enhance the conceptual, theoretical, and empirical integration of the study of political representation, while providing it with more secure sociological foundations. This chapter seeks to advance this integration along two principal fronts. First, I will analyze how party systems and different types of partisan alignments can be considered part of the "political opportunity structure" that shapes cyclical patterns of social mobilization and demobilization (see Somma in this volume). This section builds on the basic insight that social movements typically emerge to "politicize" issues or interests that have been largely excluded from consideration by mainstream parties and representative institutions. If widespread social protest is generally a response to flawed or failed forms of political representation, then these failures heavily condition the identity of the collective actors who engage in social mobilization, the specific content of their claims, and the repertoires of contention they employ (see Wada in this volume).

Second, if party politics structure social movements, it must be recognized that the causal arrow can also point in the opposite direction: social movements can structure or restructure party politics by influencing the composition and competitive alignments of national party systems. Social movements place new issues and claims on the policymaking agenda that established parties may be forced to address, and they mobilize new constituencies to which parties are pressured to respond. As such, movements are capable of transforming the social bases and programmatic content of partisan competition. Established parties that fail to respond may pay a severe price at the ballot box; indeed, mass protest was a prelude to the partial or complete collapse of national party systems in a number of Latin American countries in recent decades. More fundamentally, perhaps, some social movements enter the electoral arena directly by forming their own political parties to advance their claims in formal representative and policymaking institutions. Indeed, national party systems have been largely reconfigured around a competitive axis structured by the rise of movement-based parties in countries like Bolivia (the Movimiento al Socialismo, MAS), Brazil (the Partido dos Trabalhadores, PT), El Salvador (the Frente Farabundo Martí para la Liberación Nacional, FMLN), and Uruguay (the Frente Amplio, FA) (see Anria 2019).

In short, the reciprocal structuring of movements and parties has heavily conditioned the ways in which mass constituencies articulate their "voice" in the political arena, achieve representation, or protest their exclusion from formal institutions. This intersection of parties and movements has been integral to both the "first" and "second" historical stages of popular sector political incorporation in Latin America—that is, the period of labor incorporation during the early stages of industrialization in the first half of the twentieth century (Collier and Collier 1991), and the more recent phase of mass incorporation associated with the region's "Left turn" in the aftermath to neoliberal reform at the turn of the century (Roberts 2008; Rossi 2017; Silva and Rossi 2018). This paper will analyze how the interaction between movements and parties shaped both of these historical processes of popular incorporation, paying particular attention to societal resistance to market-based economic restructuring during the critical juncture of neoliberal reform.

Parties and the Political Structuring of Social Movements

Movements and parties may both give "voice" to social collectivities in the public sphere, but they are conventionally understood to be alternative *types* of collective actors that operate in different spheres of politics, perform divergent functional roles, and employ distinct collective action repertoires. Parties are widely conceived as teams of elite political entrepreneurs that seek access to public office by means of competitive elections (see, for example, Aldrich 2011: 5; Downs 1957: 25). Social movements, on the other hand, are understood to be loosely structured networks of social activists that engage in confrontational interactions with elites or authorities and "use protest . . . to present themselves in the public arena" (Rossi 2017: 21fn). Mainstream parties are "insiders" that operate in formal electoral, legislative, and policymaking institutions, whereas movements are seen as "outsiders" that mobilize in extra-institutional public spheres, often "in the streets," worksites, or public squares. Since parties must win elections to access public office, exercise public authority, and implement their policy platforms, they engage in collective action primarily for the purposes of electoral mobilization. Movements, by contrast, engage in contentious forms of collective action outside the electoral arena to protest against authorities or their policies, place new issues or claims on the policymaking agenda, or disrupt the everyday workings of the economy or polity.

Such neat conceptual divides between parties and movements, however, or between institutionalized and non-institutionalized politics, are difficult to sustain in the analysis of many real-world political contexts. As McAdam, Tarrow, and Tilly (2001: 7) argue, "Boundaries between institutionalized and non-institutionalized politics are hard to draw with precision," as "the two sorts of politics interact incessantly and involve similar causal processes." Not all parties, for example, are insiders; indeed, new parties often emerge from protest movements and reject the party label even after entering the electoral arena and sponsoring candidates for public office. Such "parties" may see electoral participation itself as a mode of protest or "contention by other means," transplanting their collective energies "from the streets" to the ballot box. The Bolivian MAS, at its genesis, was a paradigmatic example, a "hybrid" organization founded by coca grower union activists who sought a "political instrument" to advance the "self-representation of the masses." As Anria (2019: 62fn) states, union leaders rejected the party designation because they associated parties "with institutions that divide rather than unite popular forces," and they saw their role as "spokespeople, or messengers, for their constituencies, as opposed to their representatives."

Furthermore, as McAdam, Tilly, and Tarrow (2001: 7–8) argue, patterns of contention vary in the extent to which they transgress established institutions or operate within or alongside their formal channels and modes of political interaction. In some political contexts, established parties may serve as brokers that channel or mediate movement claims in conventional institutional and policymaking arenas. Indeed, parties may at times opt to mobilize their constituencies or broader activist networks to create social pressure as a form of political leverage in intra-governmental legislative or policymaking disputes. They may also resort to mobilizational strategies to assist with the implementation of specific social reforms. As Mische (2008) suggests, the early PT in Brazil—like the Bolivian MAS, a party founded by dissident labor and social movements—performed a "bridging function" for a plethora a local community activist groups, "knitting people together across the particularities of neighborhoods, movements, age groups, and community loyalists" (ibid.: 4). Similarly, in his study of anti-neoliberal and anti-globalization protest movements in Central America, Almeida (2014: 24) argues that opposition parties can "unify various groups and supporters in multiple localities across a country." Indeed, "social movement partyism" can arise "when an opposition party aligns with civil society associations and deploys its organizational membership to engage in mass actions such as street demonstrations, rallies, and blockades" (ibid.: 24). As Spalding (2014: 3) states, "interwoven networks" of anti-globalization activists in Central America "connected to left-wing political parties and electoral campaigns, eventually gaining traction."

Kathleen Bruhn observed a similar dynamic in her analysis of urban popular protest in both Brazil and Mexico, and found that the synergistic relationship between parties and movements was not contingent on a party's opposition status. According to Bruhn (2008: 170), "Organizations allied with political parties—particularly Left-leaning political parties—are if anything more likely to protest than independent organizations. And they routinely challenge even their friends in power." Kriesi (2015: 670) also recognizes that "parties can become important allies of social movements," as parties may benefit from the capacity of movements to expand the public issue agenda by crystallizing and framing new social grievances. Garay's (2016) research on the expansion of social programs to labor market "outsiders" in Latin America provides evidence of this dynamic, as political alliances between parties and movements were central to the adoption of more inclusionary social policies in countries like Brazil and Argentina. Such alignments, it should be noted, are not the exclusive preserve of the partisan Left; as Gold and Peña (2018) suggest, opposition protests against Cristina Fernández de Kirchner's government in Argentina played a major role in shaping the formation and the issue agenda of a conservative alliance in the national elections of 2015.

Even forms of contention that are highly transgressive—such as the 2001 Argentine food riots studied by Javier Auyero—may sometimes incorporate "insider" parties. As Auyero (2007: 20–21) states, "Party activists . . . may accept (and sometimes encourage and direct) collective violence" such as looting and rioting, creating a "gray zone" between institutionalized and non-institutionalized politics where clandestine connections shape political activity. In Auyero's account, protest dynamics in modern Argentina can hardly be understood without taking into consideration the "the power of disruption wielded by sectors of the Peronist Party" (Auyero 2007: 157). Likewise, Rossi's (2017) analysis of the Argentine *piqueteros* (unemployed workers) movement in the late 1990s and early 2000s provides ample evidence of the roles played by leftist party militants—and, at times, Peronist militants—in the groundswell of social protest that toppled the government of Fernando de la Rúa (1999–2001) and, eventually, ushered the Peronists back into power.

So conceived, political parties—especially, though not exclusively, those not in power—may well be considered part of the "political opportunity structure" that incentivizes social protest (Bruhn 2008: 6). Parties, in short, can be an institutional form of the "elite allies" that social movement scholars identify as a critical component of a favorable political opportunity structure (McAdam 1996: 27). Nevertheless, parties are hardly a uniform "force multiplier" for social movements; the Latin American experience is rife with examples of contexts where parties have coopted movements, transformed them into instruments of partisan control, or demobilized movements in the pursuit of more short-term institutional and electoral objectives. As Oxhorn (1995) argued, leftist parties in Chile that supported mass protests against the Augusto Pinochet military dictatorship in the early 1980s actively discouraged them once the regime opened political space for electoral contestation later in the decade (see also Roberts 1998). More recently, Wolff (2007) suggests that mass movements like the Argentine *piqueteros* and Ecuador's indigenous movement—the latter at the forefront of regional indigenous mobilization in the 1990s (Madrid 2012; Yashar 2005)—split and demobilized after entering into alliances with governing parties or elected officials.

Similarly, numerous studies have documented the transformation of party-movement relations between the PT and its affiliated civic networks in Brazil as the party shifted from local to national forms of electoral contestation and executive responsibility over the course of the 1990s and early 2000s (see, for example, Gómez Bruera 2013; Hunter 2010; Mische 2008). Although the PT retained linkages to civil society organizations, the "synergistic" effects that Mische identified in the 1980s, when "partisanship and popular mobilization... went hand in hand" (Mische 2008: 104), diminished over time. Indeed, they were largely replaced by more transactional or "reward-based linkages in the form of state subsidies and jobs in the state apparatus" as the party assumed responsibility for ensuring "governability" at the national level (Gómez Bruera 2013: 5). Along the way, a party founded as a classic "movement party" (Kitschelt 2006) was transformed into a more institutionalized "professional-electoral" organization that prioritized broad electoral appeal, access to public office, and the construction of ideologically diffuse governing alliances (Hunter 2010; Panebianco 1988).

Rather than synergistic effects, then, the recognition that there may be "an inverse relationship between electoral and protest politics" (Hutter and Kriesi 2013: 283) helps to account for the widespread emphasis on movement autonomy in many forms of popular mobilization in recent decades in Latin America (see Souza in this volume). This emphasis is only buttressed by long traditions of partisan instrumentalization of popular movements, a generalized distrust of party organizations, and the weakness or ineffectiveness of partisan forms of interest representation in much of the region. For these reasons, Fals Borda (1992: 306) argued that social movements were increasingly displacing traditional parties as "major political alternatives" and, in the process, "marking out a greater area of democratic participation." This was especially the case where parties had become "a dead weight impeding change when they take hierarchization and verticality to extremes, are reduced to defending the vested interests of certain groups or social classes... or allow manipulation and debasement to fester" (ibid.: 306).

These considerations point to a very different way of thinking about parties and political opportunity structures for social movements in Latin America. Rather than parties as elite, institutional allies or promoters of movements, the inverse could be true, at least in certain contexts: protest movements might find their most favorable opportunity structures where partisan forms of representation are weak, discredited, or otherwise in crisis. Lacking effective institutional channels to articulate myriad grievances and claims, citizens may be more inclined to express such claims in extra-partisan protest arenas. Arce and Rice (2019: 8), for example, argue that strong and well-institutionalized party systems induce social actors to adopt "assimilative strategies," working through established institutions that "offer multiple points of access to shape policies." In so doing, they exert "downward pressure on the scale and intensity" of social mobilization (ibid.: 8). By contrast, weak or inchoate party systems "do not serve as effective transmission belts to connect citizens with the state," creating a "representation gap" that "encourages disruptive, confrontational strategies" (ibid.: 8).

The social movements that helped shape Latin America's two major historical phases of mass political incorporation emerged in such contexts of severe representation gaps. These gaps, however, were not necessarily a function of party system weakness or inchoateness; they could also emerge where parties were reasonably strong but exclusionary, given their failure to represent important social constituencies. In the seminal work of Collier and Collier (1991), the "critical juncture" of labor incorporation was a political response by states and ruling parties to the social conflicts and economic disruptions caused by the rise of labor movements during the early stages of industrialization in the first half of the twentieth century. Prior to this incorporation, labor unions routinely engaged in transgressive forms of contentious politics, in particular strikes, at a time when suffrage rights were often severely restricted and party systems represented rival factions of agricultural and commercial elites. The exclusion of urban labor and popular constituencies from any form of institutionalized representation encouraged unions to express their grievances over wages, hours, and benefits through strikes and mass protest, whether oligarchic party systems were weak, as in Argentina, or well-organized, as in Chile. And it was largely in response to such militant and transgressive forms of popular mobilization that states and parties passed new legislation to institutionalize labor relations and, often, subject organized labor to top-down forms of corporatist control (see Gallegos and Stoessel, Rossi in this volume).

Likewise, Latin America's second historical phase of mass political incorporation— and the scope and intensity of anti-neoliberal social protest that preceded it—were heavily conditioned by varying levels of popular exclusion from partisan channels of representation during the transition from state-led development to neoliberalism in the 1980s and early 1990s. Widespread social protest—such as Venezuela's 1989 Caracazo (urban riots); Ecuador's cycles of indigenous and popular uprisings throughout the 1990s and early 2000s; Argentina's *piquetero* movement, food riots, and popular assemblies at the turn of the century; and Bolivia's water and gas wars in the early 2000s (Silva 2009; Almeida in this volume)—occurred in countries with relatively well-institutionalized party systems (Venezuela and Argentina), as well as those with more fluid and inchoate party systems (Ecuador and Bolivia). As such, what distinguished these countries from others with more localized or fragmented patterns of social mobilization was not the relative strength of party systems, but rather the programmatic alignment or dealignment of party systems during the "critical juncture" of neoliberal reform (Roberts 2014).

Simply put, where conservative actors led the process of neoliberal reform and major parties of the Left offered principled opposition, party systems were programmatically aligned in accordance with ideological preferences. Such alignment allowed societal opposition to market orthodoxy to find expression within established party systems, tempering the levels of extra-institutional social mobilization and protest in countries like Brazil, Chile, and Uruguay. Conversely, where historic labor-based or center-Left parties played a leading role in the adoption of market reforms—as in Argentina, Bolivia, Ecuador, and Venezuela—voters were left without an institutionalized channel of dissent from neoliberal orthodoxy. The resulting convergence of major parties around variants of the neoliberal model dealigned party systems programmatically and left them uniquely susceptible to mass social protest, as social groups opposed to neoliberal reforms mobilized outside and against established institutions. Indeed, mass social protest served as a prelude to mass electoral protest, as voters rejected traditional parties (with the partial exception of Argentina) and threw their support to anti-neoliberal populist figures (Hugo Chávez in Venezuela and Rafael Correa in Ecuador) or new "movement parties" (the MAS in Bolivia) that outflanked established parties on the Left.

The social movements that set the stage for these two historical phases of mass political incorporation clearly demonstrate the importance of the institutional terrain for shaping movement dynamics, as political opportunity structure approaches emphasize. They also suggest, however, that it is important to look beyond the presence or absence of elite allies to consider how patterns of inclusion or exclusion in partisan representation condition the scope and intensity of social mobilization. Failures of representation that leave large blocs of citizens on the margins of party systems are a standard recipe for the articulation of grievances and demands in extra-institutional protest arenas (Tarrow 2011: 7). Parties—or, perhaps better put, their shortcomings—can thus play a critical role in the structuring of social protest.

These two historical phases of mass political incorporation in Latin America, however, also provide ample evidence of the reciprocal effects—that is, of the myriad ways in which social movements can structure or transform party systems. As explained below, social movements can play a critical role in constituting and cleaving party systems, shaping their competitive alignments, and defining their issue agendas. These effects are analyzed in the section below.

Social Movements, Political Conflict, and their Party System Effects

Conceptualizing social movements as forms of "contentious politics" makes conflict an analytical cornerstone of the field of study (McAdam, Tarrow, and Tilly 2001). Likewise, socio-political conflict is front and center in the analysis of partisan representation and competition. Rarely, however, have social movements received systematic attention as central actors in the process of translating social conflicts into institutionalized forms of partisan contestation. In the classic work of Lipset and Rokkan (1967), party systems are understood to be grounded in deeply-rooted social conflicts, or cleavages, associated with nation-building and economic modernization (see also Bartolini and Mair 1990). Although these authors recognized that social mobilization and protest could be integral to the process of cleavage formation, too often the translation of class, religious, center-periphery, or other social cleavages into partisan organizations is treated as an analytical black hole, something that occurs naturally or inevitably as social blocs articulate their interests and identities in the political arena. Recent work in the sociological tradition assigns a prominent role to party leaders and activists themselves in "suturing" together social groups and constructing social cleavages (de Leon, Desai, and Tuğal 2015). What remains poorly understood is the role of social movements in articulating underlying conflicts, shaping the socio-political cleavages that form around them, and knitting together the organizational networks upon which parties are often built.

The generative role of social movements in structuring party systems may be especially important in Latin America, as recent scholarship has highlighted the centrality of political conflict in successful party-building endeavors in a region where stable party systems are few and far between. According to Levitsky, Loxton, and Van Dyck (2016: 14–15), "it is not the ordinary politics of democratic competition but rather extraordinary times, marked by intense—and often violent—conflict, that create the most favorable conditions for party-building." Intense conflict, they argue, mobilizes activists, encourages organization-building, strengthens partisan attachments, and reinforces organizational cohesion (ibid.: 15–16). So conceived, social movements that articulate and crystallize political conflicts may well provide building blocs for party-building efforts. They may also serve to align or realign the axes of socio-political competition in national party systems.

These party system effects are readily apparent in both of the aforementioned historical phases of mass political incorporation in Latin America. Oligarchic party systems were thoroughly transformed in much of the region by the social and political conflicts associated with labor mobilization and the formation of union movements. Although labor movements did not necessarily found new parties directly, labor and political activists with strong ties to unions forged new, mass-based populist and leftist parties across much of the region, especially in countries with large mining and industrial sectors (Collier and Collier 1991). Such labor-incorporating party-building ventures wholly or partially reconstituted national party systems, and they thoroughly realigned the competitive axes of these party systems. Partisan competition that previously reflected intra-oligarchic rivalries over commercial interests and church-state relations was displaced by new conflicts over workers' rights, union representation, and the role of the state in fostering industrialization, providing social welfare, and mediating class conflict. Labor movements and, in Mexico and Venezuela, peasant movements provided social foundations for the first true mass party organizations in many countries, such as the Partido Revolucionario Institucional (PRI) in Mexico, Acción Democrática (AD) in Venezuela, the Partido Justicialista (PJ) in Argentina, the Alianza Popular

Revolucionaria Americana (APRA) in Peru, and the Partido Comunista de Chile (PCCh) and Partido Socialista de Chile (PSCh) (see ibid.; Middlebrook 1995; Roberts 2014). These party-movement linkages were also instrumental in the construction of corporatist patterns of interest representation in the region, which allowed unions to engage in collective bargaining over wages and benefits, albeit often under the control of allied parties and states. Along multiple dimensions, then, labor movements were central actors in the region's transition from oligarchic to mass politics over the first half of the twentieth century.

Social movements also exerted transformative effects on party systems during the second phase of mass incorporation at the dawn of the twenty-first century, following decades of mass exclusion under the military dictatorships of the 1960s and 1970s and the neoliberal austerity and structural adjustment programs of the 1980s and 1990s (Silva and Rossi 2018). Social protest or insurgent movements partially reconstituted national party systems in a number of countries during periods of democratic transition in the 1980s and 1990s, most prominently in Brazil, El Salvador, and Uruguay, where the PT, El Salvador's FMLN, and the Uruguayan FA emerged as major leftist rivals to more traditional conservative parties. All of these parties incorporated social movement and activist networks that had mobilized against exclusionary authoritarian regimes, and all acquired municipal-level governing experience before ascending to national executive power during the first decade of the twenty-first century.

In other countries, mass protest emerged as part of a Polanyian "double movement" of societal resistance to market insecurities in response to neoliberal structural adjustment (Polanyi 1944; Silva 2009). Massive uprisings in Argentina, Bolivia, Ecuador, and Venezuela posed formidable challenges to traditional party systems in which all the major actors had converged in their support of neoliberal reform. Indeed, social protest was quickly channeled into anti-establishment electoral protest, leading to the virtual collapse of entire party systems in Bolivia, Ecuador, and Venezuela and the steep decline of the anti-Peronist side of the spectrum in Argentina. In each case, party systems were reconfigured around new populist or leftist alternatives with varied linkages to the social movements that had rocked the partisan establishment.

The most direct linkages were forged in Bolivia, where the MAS emerged organically as a movement-based party from the mobilization of coca growers in the Chapare region of Cochabamba (Anria 2019; Madrid 2012). Coca-grower union activists led by Evo Morales formed the party in the late 1990s, and then incorporated within its ranks many of the indigenous, peasant, and urban community-based movement networks that were mobilized during the massive protests over water privatization and natural gas exports after 2000 (Simmons 2016; Van Cott 2005). These protests forced two presidents to resign and thoroughly undermined traditional parties, paving the way toward the election of Morales and the MAS to national office in 2005 and, subsequently, the convocation of a national constituent assembly to refound Bolivia's democratic regime.

In the other three countries, Left-populist alternatives emerged in the wake of mass anti-neoliberal protests, but movements themselves did not directly forge the parties and leaderships that rose to power. Ecuador's powerful indigenous movement united highlands and lowlands groups in a single national confederation, anchoring waves of popular protest that toppled three consecutive presidents at the turn of the century. In contrast to the MAS in Bolivia, however, the party founded by Ecuador's indigenous movement, Pachakutik, was never able to compete on its own for political power at the national level (Van Cott 2005; Yashar 2005). Instead, it typically endorsed one or another independent populist figure in national presidential campaigns; those who won elections quickly abandoned their indigenous allies after taking office. Relations were especially tenuous between popular movements and Rafael Correa (2007–2009, 2009–2013, 2013–2017), a former economist who was elected president as a Left-populist outsider in 2006. Correa used state power, ample export revenues, and redistributive social programs to generate broad electoral support and build a new governing party. This party, however, emerged from technocratic circles rather than social movements, and the Correa government's autocratic tendencies led to repeated conflicts with independently organized labor, indigenous, and environmental groups (de la Torre 2013). As stated by Conaghan (2011: 274), Correa "took a dim view of all organized interests," and he "regarded Ecuador's turbulent and intrusive civil society as an obstacle, not a building block, for his revolution." Consequently, Ecuador's once-vibrant popular movements divided and demobilized in response to Correa's blending of technocratic redistribution with strategies to either coopt or exclude organized societal interests.

In Venezuela as well, a movement-based leftist party with strong ties to labor and community organizations, La Causa R, was thoroughly eclipsed and largely absorbed by the rise of Hugo Chávez (1999–2001, 2001–2007, 2007–2013, 2013) as a Left-populist outsider. Chávez, backed by a clandestine insurrectionary current within the Venezuelan army, first captured the public's imagination as the daring leader of an ill-fated military coup in 1992. After being pardoned and released from prison, he founded the first in a series of new party organizations by fusing together the scattered remnants of his military conspiracy with varied strands of Left party and community activists (including, eventually, much of La Causa R; see Ciccariello-Maher 2013 and Fernandes 2010). Capitalizing on the demise of the traditional party system, Chávez won national elections in 1998, then used plebiscitary forms of popular mobilization to convoke a constituent assembly and ratify a new constitution with heightened executive powers. He subsequently used state power, oil revenues, and charismatic authority to expand his leftist governing party and mobilize its affiliated grassroots networks around a wide range of social "missions" and community-based participatory councils (Hawkins 2010; López Maya 2011), albeit it under an increasingly autocratic mode of political authority that severely compromised Venezuela's democratic institutions.

The Argentine case provides yet another variant of the Left-populist pattern of reincorporation, as the *piquetero* and assembly movements of the early 2000s did not produce a major new party organization. Instead, they were partially incorporated within the traditional Peronist party, the Partido Justicialista (PJ), and a broader, "transversal" Left-populist front known as the Frente para la Victoria (FPV) that Néstor Kirchner grafted onto the PJ during his 2003 presidential campaign. Alone in the region, the PJ led the process of neoliberal reform in the late 1980s and early 1990s, then channeled much of the backlash against it after a new cycle of financial crisis triggered a popular uprising against de la Rúa's anti-Peronist coalition government in December 2001. Following de la Rúa's resignation, a series of Peronist successors—first Eduardo Duhalde (2002–2003), then Néstor Kirchner (2003–2007) and Cristina Fernández de Kirchner (2007–2011, 2011–2015)—used social policies and government appointment powers to address protestors' material demands, earn the political loyalty of leading protest organizations, and marginalize and demobilize the more militant, radical Left activist groups that declined to enter the Peronist/FPV fold. The post-2001 Peronist governments launched major public works and employment programs, provided new support for micro-enterprises, public pensions, and income support programs, reconstructed the Peronist alliance with national labor confederations, and brought leaders of the major *piquetero* organizations into legislative positions and the public administration of social programs (Etchemendy and Garay 2011; Ostiguy and Schneider 2018; Rossi 2017).

In these four countries, mass social protest was integral to processes of party system transformation in the aftermath of neoliberal reform. Anti-neoliberal protest movements led to the eclipse of one or more major traditional parties in all four countries; they generated new conflicts that redrew the cleavage lines of partisan and electoral competition; and they either directly constituted new movement-based party organizations, or cleaned the slate for the rise of more personalistic Left-populist alternatives. Even where mass protest did not itself reconstitute national party systems, it restructured partisan and electoral competition along a Left–Right programmatic axis that was a radical departure from the "neoliberal convergence" of the 1990s (Roberts 2014). It also played a central role in defining the two different pathways found in Latin America's post-1998 "left turn," distinguishing a more moderate and institutionalized "social democratic" path in countries like Brazil, Chile, and Uruguay from a more radical populist or "Bolivarian" path traveled by Bolivia, Ecuador, Venezuela, and (more partially) Argentina (see Levitsky and Roberts 2011; Madrid 2009; Weyland, Madrid, and Hunter 2010).

Close attention to party-movement relations, however, suggests that this conventional line of demarcation may obscure more than it reveals. The scope and intensity of social protest, on their own, tell us little about the nature and strength of party-movement bonds. On both sides of the divide between social democratic and populist (or Bolivarian) Lefts in Latin America, examples could be found of parties with strong ties to social movements, as well as parties with relatively weak ties. With the "Left turn" on the defensive after the death of Hugo Chávez in 2013, the end of a decade-long commodity boom, and the spread of corrosive corruption scandals, the cases from each camp with the strongest ties between parties and movements—Uruguay on the social democratic side, and Bolivia in the populist or Bolivarian camp—proved to be the most politically resilient. Even in these latter two cases, however, movement-backed parties were eventually (if briefly, in the Bolivian case) turned out of office by the end of the 2010s, as conservative forces challenged the reach and staying power of Latin America's second incorporation period.

Conclusion

The reversal of Latin America's "Left turn" over the second decade of the twenty-first century offered a number of instructive lessons regarding party-movement relations. As Anria (2019) suggests, close ties between parties and strong but relatively autonomous social movements—that is, movements that retain a capacity for independent social and political mobilization—provide a number of mechanisms by which social actors can hold political leaders and party organizations accountable to popular constituencies. In the absence of such accountability, governing leftist parties are prone to a wide range of deviations and deformities. As those in Chile and Brazil progressively detached from the movements they once nurtured, for example, parties became increasingly molded by the political orders they had set out to transform. Brazil's PT internalized the rent-seeking logic of a patronage-riddled political order and was driven from office in the midst of a systemic corruption scandal that eventually opened the door for a far-right alternative, Jair Bolsonaro. Chile's Socialists, on the other hand, largely reproduced Latin America's most vaunted neoliberal economy and were eventually outflanked on the left by a massive student rebellion against market society. By 2019 this student rebellion had been transformed into a generalized societal uprising against the post-Pinochet political and economic order, including the traditional parties that were linchpins of that order.

Meanwhile, governing Left-populist parties in Venezuela and Ecuador—as Panebianco (1988) surely would have predicted—never overcame their autocratic birth defects, remaining closely tethered to the personal interests and political whims of their dominant personalities. Ecuador's ruling party was eventually split by personal rivalries, while that in Venezuela resorted to increasingly authoritarian measures to hold onto power in the midst of a deepening economic crisis. Even in Bolivia—where the MAS had much deeper roots in social movements—tensions existed between the grassroots logic of popular constituencies that retained a capacity for autonomous collective action and the hierarchical logic of a dominant populist leader, Evo Morales. Indeed, Morales' autocratic tendencies contributed to his downfall in 2019: his unwillingness to adhere to constitutional term limits and a popular referendum against an additional term in office, his failure to prepare for leadership succession, and his government's manipulation of the electoral process all played into the hands of a conservative opposition that was determined to roll back the MAS's empowerment of indigenous and popular constituencies.

In short, the mutually constitutive character of party-movement relations can easily become unbalanced or severed, as the Latin American experience has amply shown. But the region also suggests that a delicate balance can sometimes be found, with potentially far-reaching political effects. That balance has no standard recipe or predetermined pathway. It is, ultimately, a political construct—a contingent product of reciprocal interactions and alternative, if overlapping, mobilizational patterns in different political and institutional domains. Such political constructs can only be understood where the study of parties and movements is mutually enriching.

REFERENCES

Aldrich, John H. (2011), *Why Parties? A Second Look,* 2nd ed. (Chicago: University of Chicago Press).

Almeida, Paul (2014), *Mobilizing Democracy: Globalization and Citizen Protest* (Baltimore, MD: Johns Hopkins University Press).

Anria, Santiago (2019), *When Movements Become Parties: The Bolivian MAS in Comparative Perspective* (New York: Cambridge University Press).

Arce, Moisés and Roberta Rice (2019), "The Political Consequences of Protest," in Moisés Arce and Roberta Rice (eds.), *Protest and Democracy,* 1–21 (Calgary: University of Calgary Press).

Auyero, Javier (2007), *Routine Politics and Violence in Argentina: The Gray Zone of State Power* (New York: Cambridge University Press).

Bartolini, Stefano and Peter Mair (1990), *Identity, Competition, and Electoral Availability: The Stabilisation of European Electorates, 1885–1985* (Cambridge: Cambridge University Press).

Bruhn, Kathleen (2008), *Urban Protest in Mexico and Brazil* (New York: Cambridge University Press).

Ciccariello-Maher, George (2013), *We Created Chávez: A People's History of the Venezuelan Revolution* (Durham, NC: Duke University Press).

Collier, Ruth Berins and David Collier (1991), *Shaping the Political Arena: Critical Junctures, the Labor Movement, and Regime Dynamics in Latin America* (Princeton, NJ: Princeton University Press).

Conaghan, Catherine M. (2011), "Ecuador: Rafael Correa and the Citizens' Revolution," in Steven Levitsky and Kenneth M. Roberts (eds.), *The Resurgence of the Latin American Left,* 260–82 (Baltimore, MD: Johns Hopkins University Press).

de la Torre, Carlos (2013), "Technocratic Populism in Ecuador," *Journal of Democracy* 24(3), 33–46.

De Leon, Cedric, Manali Desai, and Cihan Tuğal (2015), *Building Blocs: How Parties Organize Society* (Stanford, CA: Stanford University Press).

della Porta, Donatella, Joseba Fernandez, Hara Kouki, and Lorenzo Mosca (2017), *Movement Parties against Austerity* (London: Polity).

Downs, Anthony (1957), *An Economic Theory of Democracy* (New York: Harper and Row).

Etchemendy, Sebastián and Candelaria Garay (2011), "Argentina: Left Populism in Comparative Perspective, 2003–2009," in Steven Levitsky and Kenneth M. Roberts (eds.), *The Resurgence of the Latin American Left,* 283–305 (Baltimore, MD: Johns Hopkins University Press).

Fals Borda, Orlando (1992), "Social Movements and Political Power in Latin America," in Arturo Escobar and Sonia E. Alvarez (eds.), *The Making of Social Movements in Latin America: Identity, Strategy, and Democracy,* 303–16 (Boulder, CO: Westview Press).

Fernandes, Sujatha (2010), *Who Can Stop the Drums? Urban Social Movements in Chávez's Venezuela* (Durham, NC: Duke University Press).

Garay, Candelaria (2016), *Social Policy Expansion in Latin America* (New York: Cambridge University Press).

Gold, Tomás and Alejandro M. Peña (2018), "Protest, Signaling, and Elections: Conceptualizing Opposition-Movement Interactions during Argentina's Anti-Government Protests (2012–2013)," *Social Movement Studies* 13(3), 324–45.

Goldstone, Jack A. (2003), 'Introduction: Bridging Institutionalized and Noninstitutionalized Politics,' in Jack A. Goldstone (ed.), *States, Parties, and Social Movements*, 1–24 (New York: Cambridge University Press).

Gómez Bruera, Hernán F. (2013), *Lula, the Workers' Party and the Governability Dilemma in Brazil* (London: Routledge).

Hawkins, Kirk (2010), *Venezuela's Chavismo and Populism in Comparative Perspective* (New York: Cambridge University Press).

Hunter, Wendy (2010), *The Transformation of the Workers' Party in Brazil, 1989–2009* (New York: Cambridge University Press).

Hutter, Sven and Hanspeter Kriesi (2013), "Movements of the Left, Movements of the Right Reconsidered," in Jacquelien van Stekelenburg, Conny Roggeband, and Bert Klandermans (eds.), *The Future of Social Movement Research: Dynamics, Mechanisms, and Processes*, 281–98 (Minneapolis: University of Minnesota Press).

Kitschelt, Herbert (2006), "Movement Parties," in Richard S. Katz and William Crotty (eds.), *Handbook of Party Politics*, 278–90 (London: Sage).

Kriesi, Hanspeter (2015), 'Party Systems, Electoral Systems, and Social Movements,' in Donatella Della Porta and Mario Diani (eds.), *The Oxford Handbook of Social Movements*, 667–680 (Oxford: Oxford University Press).

Levitsky, Steven, James Loxton, and Brandon Van Dyck (2016), "Introduction: Challenges of Party-Building in Latin America," in Steven Levitsky, James Loxton, Brandon Van Dyck, and Jorge I. Domínguez (eds.), *Challenges of Party-Building in Latin America*, 1–48 (New York: Cambridge University Press).

Levitsky, Steven and Kenneth M. Roberts (eds.) (2011), *The Resurgence of the Latin American Left* (Baltimore, MD: Johns Hopkins University Press).

Lipset, Seymour Martin and Stein Rokkan (1967), "Cleavage Structures, Party Systems, and Voter Alignments: An Introduction," in Seymour Martin Lipset and Stein Rokkan (eds.), *Party Systems and Voter Alignments: Cross-National Perspectives*, 1–64 (New York: Free Press).

López Maya, Margarita (2011), "Venezuela: Hugo Chávez and the Populist Left," in Steven Levitsky and Kenneth M. Roberts (eds.), *The Resurgence of the Latin American Left*, 213–38 (Baltimore, MD: Johns Hopkins University Press).

Madrid, Raúl (2009), "The Origins of the Two Lefts in Latin America," *Political Science Quarterly* 125(4), 1–23.

Madrid, Raúl (2012), *The Rise of Ethnic Politics in Latin America* (New York: Cambridge University Press).

McAdam, Doug (1996), "Conceptual Origins, Current Problems, Future Directions," in Doug McAdam, John D. McCarthy, and Mayer N. Zald (eds.), *Comparative Perspectives on Social Movements: Political Opportunities, Mobilizing Structures, and Cultural Framings*, 23–40 (New York: Cambridge University Press).

McAdam, Doug and Sidney Tarrow (2013), "Social Movements and Elections: Toward a Broader Understanding of the Political Context of Contention," in Jacquelien van Stekelenburg, Conny Roggeband, and Bert Klandermans (eds.), *The Future of Social Movement Research: Dynamics, Mechanisms, and Processes*, 325–46 (Minneapolis: University of Minnesota Press).

McAdam, Doug, Sidney Tarrow, and Charles Tilly (2001), *Dynamics of Contention* (New York: Cambridge University Press).

Middlebrook, Kevin (1995), *The Paradox of Revolution: Labor, the State, and Authoritarianism in Mexico* (Baltimore, MD: Johns Hopkins University Press).

Mische, Ann (2008), *Partisan Publics: Communication and Contention across Brazilian Youth Activist Networks* (Princeton, NJ: Princeton University Press).

Ostiguy, Pierre and Aaron Schneider (2018), "The Politics of Incorporation: Party Systems, Political Leaders, and the State in Argentina and Brazil," in Eduardo Silva and Federico M. Rossi (eds.), *Reshaping the Political Arena*, 275–308 (Pittsburgh, PA: University of Pittsburgh Press).

Oxhorn, Philip (1995), *Organizing Civil Society: The Popular Sectors and the Struggle for Democracy in Chile* (University Park, PA: Penn State University Press).

Panebianco, Angelo (1988), *Political Parties: Organization and Power* (Cambridge: Cambridge University Press).

Polanyi, Karl (1944), *The Great Transformation* (New York: Farrar and Rinehart).

Roberts, Kenneth M. (1998), *Deepening Democracy? The Modern Left and Social Movements in Chile and Peru* (Stanford, CA: Stanford University Press).

Roberts, Kenneth M. (2008), "The Mobilization of Opposition to Economic Liberalization," in Margaret Levi, Simon Jackman, and Nancy Rosenblum (eds.), *Annual Review of Political Science*, 11, 327–49.

Roberts, Kenneth M. (2014), *Changing Course in Latin America: Party Systems in the Neoliberal Era* (New York: Cambridge University Press).

Rossi, Federico M. (2017), *The Poor's Struggle for Political Incorporation: The Piquetero Movement in Argentina* (New York: Cambridge University Press).

Silva, Eduardo (2009), *Challenging Neoliberalism in Latin America* (New York: Cambridge University Press).

Silva, Eduardo and Federico M. Rossi (eds.) (2018), *Reshaping the Political Arena in Latin America: From Resisting Neoliberalism to the Second Incorporation* (Pittsburgh, PA: University of Pittsburgh Press).

Simmons, Erica S. (2016), *Meaningful Resistance: Market Reforms and the Roots of Social Protest in Latin America* (New York: Cambridge University Press).

Spalding, Rose J. (2014), *Contesting Trade in Central America: Market Reform and Resistance* (Austin: University of Texas Press).

Tarrow, Sidney G. (2011), *Power in Movement: Social Movements and Contentious Politics* (New York: Cambridge University Press).

Van Cott, Donna Lee (2005), *From Movements to Parties in Latin America: The Evolution of Ethnic Politics* (New York: Cambridge University Press).

Weyland, Kurt, Raúl L. Madrid, and Wendy Hunter (eds.) (2010), *Leftist Governments in Latin America: Successes and Shortcomings* (New York: Cambridge University Press).

Wolff, Jonas (2007), "(De-)Mobilising the Marginalised: A Comparison of the Argentine *Piqueteros* and Ecuador's Indigenous Movement," *Journal of Latin American Studies* 39(1), 1–29.

Yashar, Deborah (2005), *Contesting Citizenship in Latin America: The Rise of Indigenous Movements and the Postliberal Challenge* (New York: Cambridge University Press).

CHAPTER 43

SOCIAL MOVEMENT ACTIVISM, INFORMAL POLITICS, AND CLIENTELISM IN LATIN AMERICA

HÉLÈNE COMBES AND JULIETA QUIRÓS

Introduction

In the past two decades, the social sciences have gained ground in consolidating relational approaches aimed at overcoming compartmentalized strategies of observing political activism and accounting for the interdependencies between contentious politics and institutional politics (Auyero, Lapegna, and Page 2009; Combes 2011; Goldstone 2003; Quirós 2011; Rossi 2017). Revisiting this perspective, this chapter analyzes the framework underlying the contentious politics of Latin American working-class sectors, informal party politics, and the dispute over state resources. In particular, we examine the daily dynamics generated by a set of relations and practices of political intermediation that involve social movements, political parties, and certain state agencies. Both lay and academic common sense tend to conceptualize—and denounce—such relationships as "clientelistic" (Combes and Vommaro 2016).

Using a comparative dialogue among long-term empirical studies in different countries of the region, we posit the following idea: recently in much of Latin America, the nature and dynamics of social movements have been shaped by an inseparable relationship between politicization and the reproduction of life of the working-class sectors that were either progressively excluded from salaried employment and relegated to growing poverty and precariousness (Auyero 2001; Merklen 2003; Munck 2013), or never had formal employment. Based on a medium-term analysis focused on contentious experiences in Argentina, Brazil, and Mexico (and Chile as a counterexample to the trends we identify in the rest of the region), we show how this interaction between politicization and reproduction of life has shaped certain specificities. We focus on (1) how social movements have become a "front-line desk" of the state at the local level; (2) how the territorial dimension of these movements has garnered political centrality; and (3) the place that moral economies (Thompson 1993) have earned in political participation in the daily dynamics of contentious action. Further, we show that the analysis of these phenomena is inseparable from the interpretations that the social and academic realms have of them. Thus, our overview concludes by analyzing how discussions—and category struggles (Bourdieu 2001)—undertaken in the academic world influence the debates within the general public and the media, having performative effects on how grassroots movements themselves problematize and negotiate their day-to-day mobilization practices.

The Relational Nature of Contentious, Party, and State Politics in Latin America

If analyzing the contentious interactions between anti-establishment actors and institutional politics has become a common practice in the sociology of social movements (McAdam, Tarrow, and Tilly 2001), it has not been so common in Latin America (with few exceptions, for example Eckstein 1989). The region's authoritarian nature favored a type of political organization in which "autonomy" vis-à-vis the state and party politics was the only way to achieve greater democratization. This led social scientists to analyze these experiences by tapping into the theories of new social movements (see Garretón and Selamé in this volume) and collective action (see Somma in this volume), despite the fundamental differences in context that exist between European and Latin American movements (Goirand 2015). These approaches (see, among others, Álvarez, Dagnino, and Escobar 1998; Álvarez and Escobar 1992) left the relationship with institutional politics in the background, both in its formal and informal aspects (Freidenberg and Levitsky 2007), even after the return of formal democracy and political pluralism. As Wickham-Crowley and Eckstein (2015) argue, the pertinence of such a framework for the study of Latin America has been in doubt since the 1990s. The growing interactions among social organizations—arising from the institutionalization of mobilization activity—and the formal and informal structures of the state and political parties that were resurrected or founded after authoritarian regimes, faded from the purview of mainstream sociology. Or they were denounced as clientelist, instead of being addressed as a *sui generis* political process. This is our point of departure for the analysis undertaken herein.

Accordingly, it is important to address the historicity of these interactions in each national context and analyze how they were studied. An outline of the "sociology of sociological studies" of the Latin American social movements would contend that "honeymoon" periods are followed by periods of "disenchantment," in which students thereof denounce the transformation and decay of mobilizations based on clientelism (see, among others, Álvarez, Dagnino and Escobar 1998 Álvarez and Escobar 1992).

Argentina is a good example. Unemployed people formed movements in large cities and other areas of the country in the 1990s as the main response of the working classes to the effects of disintegration (Merklen 2006; Svampa and Pereyra 2003) or disincorporation (Rossi 2017) by neoliberal policies that were more vigorously applied at that time. The working classes' growing precariousness derived from unemployment and labor informality was not addressed by the trade union organizations that existed then. The organized labor movement (Levitsky 2003) did not represent the unemployed and a novel form of territorially based and collective associations filled that vacuum, that is, the movements of unemployed workers. The main activities of these organizations centered on contentious politics: the *picketing* (blocking and occupation) of streets and roads around the country. Consequently, they grew in popularity as *piquetero* organizations or movements. Made up mostly of progressive and leftwing social leaders, the *piquetero* movement depicted itself since its inception as an alternative to the vices of authoritarianism and clientelism of traditional party politics, especially that embodied by the hegemonic grassroots movement of Argentina, that is, Peronism. As we noted earlier, by tapping into the theories of new social movements and collective action, the intellectual and academic world was an active participant in the social production of this depiction. Within mainstream sociological thought, a moral image gradually took hold that was "split off" from grassroots politics (Quirós 2011: 17). On the one hand contentious and resistance politics, embodied by *piquetero* organizations; on the other, the established politics of clientelism exemplified by Peronism; on the one hand, good social leaders, on the other, the *punteros* (informal party brokers) and the "political use" of poverty.

Although this academic view was politically beneficial for the initial legitimization of the *piquetero* organizations, before long the routinization of mobilization brought certain analytical difficulties. As some studies identified early on (Manzano 2013: 126; Quirós 2008), for the *piquetero* movement contentious politics was not only a means to start a public conversation about unemployment as a social issue. It was also an effective tool to struggle for basic state resources (mainly unemployment programs and food assistance programs) for the reproduction of life by grassroots sectors living in precarious conditions. The important role that these resources played in ongoing protest dynamics became a disturbing factor—an excess of "materialism" perhaps—from the mainstream social and sociological perspective. The latter was firmly grounded in approaches that gave greater weight to the autonomy of movements, vis-à-vis the state and the political potential of the so-called post-material struggles, among the principal features and values of contentious politics. The excess of "economism" that seemed to be a part of contentious politics was then reflected in debates about the danger of growing clientelism, cooptation, and bureaucratization of social organizations (see, among others, Campione and Rajland 2006; Rajland 2008; Svampa 2011). These controversies were exacerbated during the 2000s, when a significant portion of the *piquetero* movement reined in its contentious activities after it was included in the political institutions of the progressive governments of Néstor Kirchner (2003–2007) and Cristina Fernández de Kirchner (2007–2011, 2011–2015) (Rossi 2017).

Mexico City offers another example of the relationship between contentious politics, informal party politics, and struggles over state resource. Starting in the 1960s, the city and its suburbs grew in size as rural immigrants claimed land and built informal housing (Adler de Lomnitz 1975). In most cases, these were collective invasions led by neighborhood leaders (Adler Hellman 1994), some of whom were linked to the popular sector of the (then-hegemonic) Partido Revolucionario Institucional (PRI). Leaders of non-partisan left organizations, who sought to organize and politicize the popular sectors, led other invasions. In the former case, leaders negotiated with the state in order to access urban services; since they were linked to the PRI, they were scarcely studied by sociologists. In the latter case, organizations that sought to build autonomous spaces (Haber 2006) were often accompanied by sociologists who studied their progress. The 1985 earthquake was a watershed in various ways. Many local groups left the PRI and joined leftist organizations affiliated with the popular urban movement (MUP) (Serna 1997). Many people saw the state as being chiefly responsible for the extent of the disaster, thus becoming the main target of criticism. Accordingly, in less than a year the main demands shifted away from housing and moved toward political democratization of the city (Tavera Fenollosa 2015), as demonstrated by the quantitative analysis of the protests led by the main housing organization, the Asamblea de Barrios (Combes 2011: 109). The demands for social and political citizenship became very interconnected (Tamayo 1999). In Mexico until the late 1990s, analysts clearly distinguished between "good social organizations," with a left-leaning concern for democratic goals, and the "bad" organizations, linked to the PRI's corporate control. Sociologists' judgements about organizations and the disputes over legitimacy regarding the "good form" (Bourdieu 2001) of fulfilling a citizen's role in organizations, together with a migration of academic concepts into the social realm, facilitated by sociologists' activism, meant that being a "social movement," or not, became a part of the conflict and political dispute (Combes 2011: 16–22). In the 2000s, with the consolidation of the Partido de la Revolución Democrática (PRD, left-leaning) in Mexico City's local government (1997–2018), those social organizations that previously were labeled "democratic" were now also denounced as having a clientelist relationship (Tejera and Castañeda 2017).

Rural agrarian reform movements and urban housing movements in contemporary Brazil are another example of the complex framework underlying contentious politics, partisan politics, and disputes over state resources (see also Welch, Oxhorn in this volume). Since the late 1980s, these organizations were established in spaces where Brazilian popular sectors began to assert claims and dispute their right to (rural and urban) territory. They also made various redistributive demands regarding basic conditions of material reproduction: food assistance programs, urban and rural infrastructure, housing programs, and access to health care, among others. As in Argentina and Mexico, contentious politics—in this case, land occupations and setting up camps, marches, and occupation of public lands—became an effective method by which to transmit these demands (Sigaud 2005; Fernandes Mançano and Welch in this volume). Further, applying the "movement form" (Rosa 2012), non-unionized popular sectors could be organized and then recognized by the state as legitimate petitioners. As these and other empirical studies show (Fernandes Mançano 1998; Rangel Loera 2014; Wolford 2010), the "landless" or "homeless" cannot be viewed as pre-existing population groups or social identities that are "organized" into "movements." They are rather political categories with which people identify once they become members of organizations that uphold agrarian reform and the right to live in a city as demands that are in collective, political dispute. Those who participate in land occupations, for example, are not people who previously self-perceived as "landless," but are rather heterogeneous sectors of the rural and urban working classes. These classes find in such movements a commitment to seek a better life—the possibility of accessing a plot of land or a dwelling in the city—and spaces of collective belonging that guarantee access to resources, care, and welfare networks that are not covered by the informal economy in which they work (see Rossi in this volume).

Interestingly, in Brazil and Mexico, unlike in Argentina, the origin of these popular movements was closely linked to party structures. In Mexico, the organizations directly participated in the formation of the PRD at the territorial level, while playing a role in enlisting and politicizing the activists, particularly within the grassroots sectors (see Roberts in this volume). They were also a source of recruitment of candidates and party cadres in a context of very rapid growth. Eight years after its founding, the PRD became the second political force and won the Mexico City mayor's office (Combes 2011, 2015). In Brazil, movements have been a fundamental pillar behind the consolidation of the social base of the Partido dos Trabalhadores (PT) during the 1980s and 1990s. In that process, movements and party became part of collective-action networks (Levy 2012: 4). Initially, in the eyes of the activist and intellectual leftist circles, the movement-based PT represented a hope of building a non-clientelist, grassroots-power alternative (Gay 1998). However, this hope faded as the PT consolidated its position as a state party, first with access to administrative offices during the 1990s and then with the election of Luiz Inácio Lula da Silva as president in 2002. The growing involvement of social movements in institutional politics, through their filling of posts and self-transaction of resources and state programs (Abers, Serafim, and Tatagiba 2014; Rossi and Silva 2018), became problematic for both activists and academics. They saw a danger of "institutionalization" and "demobilization" of the movements. It was also a problem for the PT's political opponents, who soon voiced complaints of clientelism and corruption in the management of programs by social organizations (Levy 2012: 12). Although the identification of Brazilian academics with the PT gave an unusual nuance to the term "clientelism" in terms of the characterization or analysis of the relationships between social movements and formal politics (Goirand 2015), this does not mean that the movements' close relationship with the state was not disturbing and potentially "contaminating." Academic papers that discuss this matter emphasize the need for approaches that address movements and state relationships, in terms of reciprocal inter-dependencies (Nogueira 2017; Sigaud, Rosa, and Macedo 2008; Gurza Lavalle and Szwako in this volume).

Chile is an interesting counterexample. It is uninvolved in several aspects from the interaction between contentious politics and the reproduction of life that we identified in other countries and in Latin America as a whole. First, unlike Argentina, Brazil, and Mexico, which experienced important mobilizations throughout the 1980s and 1990s, Chile was an emblematic case of a transition to democracy with demobilization (Posner 2008). Breaking with the model of having links with social sectors during the pre-coup period (ibid.), the leftist parties that participated in the Concertación coalition actively discouraged direct participation in working-class neighborhoods. However, as Barozet (2005) notes, the country experienced a significant increase of social organizations in the fifteen years that followed the transition. Unlike other Latin American countries, these Chilean organizations were not the result of the institutionalization of social movements, but rather arose from community initiatives that hoped to influence local and national public policies that focused on certain sectors of the population (elderly, youth, women from vulnerable sectors, etc.). Aiming for inclusion in these programs, these initiatives led to the creation of neighborhood associations that established informal, interpersonal, and ongoing links with mayors and municipal agents (Luján-Verón and Pérez-Contreras 2018). Recent studies on the presence of political parties within municipalities—especially, but not limited to, right-wing parties—demonstrate the important intermediation role played by local leaders of these neighborhood organizations (Arriagada 2013; Luján-Verón and Pérez-Contreras 2018). These authors agree with the analysis undertaken in the mid-2000s by Barozet (2005: 8). Barozet holds that this intermediation was not accompanied by a recruitment of neighborhood activists by political parties, that is, intermediation did not lead to social organizations integrating into party structures; but it is interesting to note that it was not encouraged by contentious politics either. Could it be that these brokers played a role in the social upheavals of 2019, as was the case in Argentina in 2001 (Auyero, Lapegna, and Page 2009)? So far, reviewing the literature in this regard, we can say that, in Chile, neighborhood leaders operate as "solution intermediaries" who "cover a kind of information gap in the relationship between citizens and municipality" (Arriagada 2013: 25), without deploying the anti-establishment resource that we identified elsewhere in the region. Further, the intimate association between these organizations and social assistance programs was not subject to the social criticism of "clientelism" that was prevalent in other countries. Luján-Verón and Pérez-Contreras (2018: 240) argue that, until recently, analyses of the political relationships of the popular sectors in Chile had not focused on clientelism.

Contestation: A Way to Establish a Relationship with the State

The land occupations of Brazil, the occupation of land or public buildings in Mexico, and the roadblocks and picket mobilizations of Argentina can be characterized as collective contentious or "protest" actions ("against" the state and against political and/or economic power). When protests are viewed in perspective and in their day-to-day dynamics (how and when they began, who started them, against whom, how they dissolve, etc.), we observe that this characterization is insufficient, since it leaves out too much information. In the countries we have reviewed, as in others in the region, these actions and, generally, the contentious society, have gradually become one of the ways by which the precarious working classes can urge government representatives to meet demands, can exercise (part of) their social citizenship (Hurtado Arroba 2014), and can push for their socio-political (re)incorporation (Rossi 2017). In this sense, following Chatterjee (2011), we can say that contentious politics—both in its "transgressive" form or its routinized or "contained" form (McAdam, Tarrow, and Tilly 2001)—operate for the Latin American grassroots sectors as a way to produce and exercise effective rights that institutional politics virtually includes in its purview.

We should add some contextual elements behind this scenario. Starting in the 1990s, decentralization policies carried out by the state in many Latin American countries created additional levels of government and, consequently, the multiple possibilities of interpellation of the state (Combes and Vommaro 2016: 163) by anti-establishment actors. In addition, these policies were accompanied by the design and implementation of other neoliberal measures. The growing crisis of social and welfare policies that characterized the national populist period (Rossi and Silva 2018) of the 1930s to 1970s gave way to programs (Solidaridad in Mexico, Bolsa Família in Brazil, Plan Trabajar and Plan Jefas y Jefes de Hogar Desocupados in Argentina) that targeted sectors of the population perceived as socially vulnerable (Merklen 2003). The institutionalization of these programs led to a proliferation of intermediaries (Combes and Vommaro 2016), as well as mobilization practices aimed at attaining access to these programs.

How does this pragmatic contestation work? The first general principle is that, as studies that focused on the various national examples in this chapter show, mobilization is usually a call for dialogue with the authorities. Mobilizations make it imperative for state agents to "sit down and talk" (Quirós 2011: 165) and "make commitments" (Manzano 2013: 43). The action varies by how actors "approach" the state, either protesting (Combes 2000; Hurtado Arroba 2014) or petitioning, as in the Chilean case (Arriagada 2013; Luján-Verón and Pérez-Contreras 2018). Research regarding Argentina and Mexico indicates that it is common for the state itself to "wait" for mobilization. This is an example of how government agents can assess the magnitude of the demand and, therefore, the type of response that it merits. Thus, mobilization becomes a true gauge of (contending) forces. This brings us to the second principle: the number of mobilized people determines the type of attention that the state gives to demands and, among other things, the magnitude of public resources allocated to the population. The number of mobilized people is proof that the organizations in charge of the protest action represent a segment of the population. In Argentina, for example, the amount of people mobilized for a march determines how many employment programs or food rations will be allocated to the organizations that are protesting (Quirós 2011). In fact, the Mexico City government has a special service that interacts with protesters, gathers their demands, and channels them to relevant offices (Combes 2000). In Brazil, something similar happens with land occupations. As Rangel Loera (2014) reveals, the Ministry of Agrarian Reform prepares its records of petitioners of land based on the "barracks" (precarious housing) recorded in each camp. That same number is the basis for allocating other state resources, such as food baskets and drinking water and, in some cases, for determining enrollment in the Bolsa Família income-distribution program.

In Latin American then, popular neighborhoods, social movement activists, and organizations that have arisen from an institutionalization of diverse mobilizations have become a "front-line desk" of the state (Hurtado Arroba 2014). They have done so by becoming intermediaries in the implementation of specific social programs that involve both "finding" and/or "constructing" beneficiaries (Combes 2017), and "organizing" the needs of structurally precarious populations around collective rights and demands. This particularity of contentious politics leads us to focus special attention on the territory, that is, the space where a network links contentious politics, informal party politics, and disputes over state resources, in its daily and lived dimensions (see Davis and Davey, Mançano Fernandes and Welch, Halvorsen and Rossi in this volume).

A Daily Meeting Point: The Territory

Latin American social movements are circumscribed in a territory (Merklen 2006). They exist within a web of organizational relations. This shared territoriality implies having relationships of both opposition and competition among organizations (for state resources, for the enlistment and mobilization of grassroots sectors), as well as relationships of continuity, simultaneity, and cooperation that take place daily between social movements and political parties, and especially between movements and informal networks of party politics. In the first section, we mentioned that relations exist between movements and parties shaped "from above," that is, by formal and strategic alliances negotiated by the leaders of movements and political parties and/or governments with a background in "movement politics" (Pérez and Natalucci 2010). Examples of the latter are the PT of Brazil and its relationship with housing and land movements, or the case of Kirchnerism in Argentina and its alliance with some currents of the *piquetero* movement. This type of relationship "from above" translates into a growing participation of activists and leaders of social movements in spaces of institutional politics, both through their inclusion in elections and their work in public administrative posts (Rossi and Silva 2018). Our goal is to shed light on the informal modalities in which this relationship between movements and parties unfolds on a territorial level. Below, we differentiate these variations:

a) Party activists and leaders or activists of social movements who establish strategic local alliances or limited cooperation, who do not necessarily follow supralocal political and/or ideological alliances, according to studies focusing on Argentina (Ferraudi Curto 2014; Quirós 2011).
b) Activists who undergo political conversion: social movement activists become party activists and vice versa, as Mexico, Argentina, and Brazil demonstrate (Combes 2015).

c) The regular members of social movements that are linked to a number of political tendencies (Merklen 2006). Examples are the urban movement in Mexico City, whose members maintain simultaneous or consecutive participation in different political arenas of contentious and institutional politics (Combes 2011); or the Brazilian case, with "campers" of land occupations who maintain active links with local politicians and informal party brokers, giving support to the latter or, occasionally, "working" for them during elections (Rangel Loera 2014). These and other empirical studies reveal that Latin American popular sectors are not only in (social) movements, but are also *in movement* (Quirós 2008) through territorially situated organizational webs that interweave relations of contentious and routine politics.

The conversion of political parties allied to popular movements into government parties, that is, into the state (whether local, provincial, national), also has an impact on a territorial scale. In addition to consolidating and legitimizing their role as intermediaries, social activists begin to strengthen ties with the public administration in different ways. For example, by filling management and decision-making posts, establishing links of inter-knowledge and/or influence on government officials at different levels; in Mexico, working as legislative advisors or aides (a local deputy can have up to forty aides) (see Hurtado Arroba 2014). Likewise, in Argentina, activists can become the political base of certain governmental actors (deputies, ministers, party leaders) and thus operate, in practice, as part of informal organizations that promote party politics.

Interestingly, there are two characteristic features of these webs. On the one hand, leaders' functions and positions are always fluctuating in time and space. They occupy several roles in the sense that Goffman (1974) gives the term. Thus, for example, a leader can act as a representative of a municipality in a certain context, while in another he can serve as an activist of the housing organization he presides. Understanding the dynamics and versatility of these posts requires empirical studies that account for the effects of having different social roles (Combes and Vommaro 2016: 151–56). Furthermore, the proximity and/or participation of social activists in the state means they acquire administrative skills that have direct effects on the day-to-day capacity and functioning of organizations, as well as on their leaders' cultural and political capital (Manzano 2007, 2016). This increase in popular power is usually proportional to the increase in its resistance, that is, resistance by means of social criticism aimed at the "clientelistic use" of public resources by social organizations.

A Moral Economy of Territorial Involvement

A fundamental element in understanding the nature of Latin American popular movements and their interweaving with everyday formal and informal politics has to do with what organizations demand through contentious action. This includes not only public resources, but also the legitimate right to manage themselves collectively, that is, to distribute their allocation based on merit criteria (Combes 2017; Luján-Verón and Pérez-Contreras 2018; Manzano 2013; Quirós 2011).

The fact that the contentious action has been carried out on the street as a way to obtain state recognition and attention leads to a particular system of rights within the organizations. In brief, those who *participate*, that is, those who contribute with their presence to the social production of mobilizations deserve the benefits that are obtained thereof. In other words, contentious mobilization is a protest action but it is also a socially necessary work, and necessarily collective. This entails being part of a larger group in order to produce resources and have rights over them, for example, the right to food distribution, an unemployment allowance, a housing program, or a job in a work cooperative (Quirós 2011). This principle implies developing the collective creation of a systems of rights and obligations within the movements, which can be defined as a moral economy as outlined by Thompson (1993: 271). This type of economy, according to Thompson, is guided by criteria of justice and fairness. We can summarize it as follows, based on the cases we reviewed: being a leader who follows through; being an activist committed to the cause; being a fellow member who participates.

In Argentina, for example, empirical studies reveal that the movement of the unemployed have collectively registered and quantified the struggles, measured in terms of people attending mobilizations and other activities (assemblies, meetings, etc.) that (re)produce the movement as a collective actor. This data registry allows a distribution of resources based on merit, which are also moral determinations. In Brazil, in a "camp out" or land occupation, the possibility of access to a lot or public resources depends not only on "being camped out"—in essence living in provisional ramshackle housing—but also on how long one has "camped out" or participated in the struggle (number of days participating in mobilizations), all duly quantified (Rangel Loera 2014). In Mexico, the majority of housing organizations kept a record of members' participation in meetings, marches (Paladino Cupulo 2014), and party events (internal elections, rallies), scored with a point system. On several occasions, we observed how members themselves proposed or demanded that their participation be duly registered in order to establish order in the allocation of housing. "The keys will not fall from the heavens," one activist said at an assembly complaining of a "bad" leader from his point of view, for not taking role at the marches (Combes 2011: 191). In Viña del Mar, Chile, Lujan-Verón and Pérez-Contreras (2018: 250) reveal how inhabitants demanded that leaders disclose the guidelines for access to certain municipal resources. Similarly, leaders must balance how much "their people" contribute, to avoid demanding too much participation or fatiguing them (Combes 2017). What some analysts identify as the "collapse of networks" (Auyero, Lapegna, and Page 2009), or changes of "operators" (Tosoni 2007), demonstrates the crisis or the breakdown of the moral economy that regulates the relationship between intermediaries and neighbors (Vommaro and Quirós 2011).

Moral economies are not a given; they are the product of political and collective construction, negotiation, and consensus, which are not devoid of conflicts between contradictory principles of fairness within a framework of inter-knowledge relationships. People know who came to the march or was absent, who is no longer a "single mother" but still continues to apply for a program that supports this sector of the population, which fellow member "really needs" support and who does not, and who gets fully involved in the movement and who does only what is strictly necessary. Within movements, these moral economies are fraught with tension between the individual and the collective, as they argue whether participation is because of "need" or out of "commitment." In general, state social assistance resources are allocated individually. However, they are produced collectively in and through movements. This contradiction leads to frequent controversies in social organizations. To the unsuspecting eye, they may appear as mere "personal" conflicts, when in reality they often express the complexity of collectively building autonomous moral regulations, which often conflict with the criteria of merit that the state claims as legal.

For these reasons, moral economies of political participation generally must be permanently (re)validated vis-à-vis society and the state, and usually become the target of social criticism, not only of "clientelism," that is, "exchange" of public resources for political participation, but also of "coercion," "extortion," or exercise of political "violence" by territorial intermediaries. Academics have called for a sociological exploration of the interactions between contentious politics, clientelism, and relations of political violence (Auyero, Lapegna, and Page 2009). Long-term empirical studies in different countries of the region show, however, that in their daily expression, relations of intermediation are relations of domination (Combes and Vommaro 2016: 147) rather than of coercive power. The exercise of coercion and/or violence by intermediaries (be they social movements or party agents) on working-class people are an extreme and rather unusual event. In their ordinary and routine dimension, working-class politics operate through webs of interdependence rather than unilateral dependencies. These webs form through the multiplicity of intermediation networks in the same territory, which guarantees competition between them and the mobility of populations (see Hilgers 2012).

Conclusion

As Hélène Combes and Gabriel Vommaro (2016: 31) have proposed in their definition of clientelism, social actors (journalists, intellectuals, politicians) must be included in the analysis of this phenomenon. Through their complaints, these actors shape what is seen as clientelist in any given moment or situation (national or local), impacting on the ways certain relations or political spaces are interpreted in working-class neighborhoods. In Mexico, the "bad leader," criticized by an activist (see above), did not want to "take a head count" because he knew that doing so might bring accusations of clientelism from the press or other currents of his party (Combes 2011: 191–95). Accordingly, social leaders are also "bound" (Thompson 1993) by the same systems of reciprocity from which they want to distance themselves. Here, as in the experiences of Brazil and Argentina, we find social movement leaders concerned about not "reproducing" clientelistic relations or ensuring that self-management mechanisms are not "confused" with political "exchanges". To this end, organizations devise and deploy a whole repertoire of the moral economies at stake: "Don't thank us, comrades, you won this with your struggle," is a phrase often used by leaders with their bases.

Empirical studies also show that in the working-class neighborhoods of Latin America, their members are continuously questioning and negotiating the ways politics are practiced. Movements deploy collective processes of judgement, adjustment and reformulation, and/or creation of the criteria that stipulate members' obligations and rights (Quirós 2017). Far from the passivity or automatism of a so-called clientelist "culture" or "habitus", working-class politics are subjected to ongoing monitoring by their own members. Accusations of "clientelism" are not only hurled at popular organizations from "outside"; they are also used within the organizations as a regulatory mechanism of rules, relationships, and conflicts. Participants therein define and (re)negotiate their membership on a daily basis with criteria of what is fair or unfair, legitimate or illegitimate, within the framework of the moral economies that regulate all political spaces.

References

Abers, Rebecca, Lizandra Serafim, and Luciana Tatagiba (2014), "Repertórios de interação estado-sociedade em um estado heterogêneo: a experiência na Era Lula," *Dados* 57(2), 325–57.

Adler de Lomnitz, Lariza (1975), *Cómo sobreviven los marginados* (Mexico: Siglo XXI).

Adler Hellman, Judith (1994), "Mexican Popular Movements, Clientelism, and the Process of Democratization," *Latin American Perspectives* 31(2), 124–42.

Álvarez Sonia and Arturo Escobar (1992), *The Making of Social Movements in Latin America* (Boulder, CO: Westview Press).

Álvarez Sonia, Evelina Dagnino, and Arturo Escobar (1998), *Cultures of Politics, Politics Cultures: Re-visioning Latin American Social Movements* (Boulder, CO: Westview Press).

Arriagada, Evelyn (2013), "Clientelismo político y participación local: El rol de los dirigentes sociales en la articulación entre autoridades y ciudadanos en Santiago de Chile," *Polis* 12(36), 15–38.

Auyero, Javier (2001), *La política de los pobres* (Buenos Aires: Manantial).

Auyero, Javier, Pablo Lapegna, and Fernanda Page (2009), "Patronage Politics and Contentious Collective Action: A Recursive Relationship," *Latin American Politics and Society* 51(3), 1–31.

Barozet, Emmanuelle (2005), "Los nuevos patrones del clientelismo en las urbes chilenas: Reflexión acerca el uso político de las organizaciones comunitarias en Santiago Centro e Iquique," in José I. Porras and Vicente Espinoza (eds.), *Redes. Enfoques y aplicaciones del Análisis de Redes Sociales*, 361–400 (Santiago: Editorial Universidad Bolivariana).

Bourdieu, Pierre (2001), *Sciences de la science et réflexivité* (Paris: Le Seuil).

Campione, Daniel and Beatriz Rajland (2006), "Piqueteros y trabajadores ocupados en la Argentina de 2001 en adelante: Novedades y continuidades en su participación y organización en los conflictos," in Gerardo Caetano (ed.), *Sujetos sociales y nuevas formas de protesta en la historia reciente de América Latina*, 297–330 (Buenos Aires: CLACSO).

Chatterjee, Partha (2011), "La política de los gobernados," *Revista Colombiana de Antropología* 47(2), 199–231.

Combes, Hélène (2000), "El PRD y las manifestaciones callejeras (1998–1999)," *Anuario de Estudios Urbanos*, 309–35 (Mexico: Universidad Autónoma Metropolitana-Unidad Azcapotzalco).
Combes, Hélène (2011), *Faire parti: Trajectoires de gauche au Mexique* (Paris: Karthala).
Combes, Hélène (2015), "Politicals Parties and Legislators. A Latin American Perspective," in Jaspers James and Jan Willem Duyvendak (eds.), *Breaking Down the State: Protestors Engaged*, 53–74 (Amsterdam: Amsterdam University Press).
Combes, Hélène (2017), "Trabajo político territorial y (auto)clasificación del quehacer político," *Iconos* 60, 31–56.
Combes, Hélène and Vommaro, Gabriel (2016), *El clientelismo político* (Buenos Aires: Siglo XXI).
Das, Venna and Randeria, Shalini (2015), "Politics of the Urban Poor: Aesthetics, Ethics, Volatility, Precarity," *Current Anthropology* 56(11), 3–14.
Eckstein, Susan (ed.) (1989), *The Power and Popular Protest: Latin American Social Movements* (Berkeley and Los Angeles: California University Press).
Fernandes, Bernardo Mançano (1998), *Gênese e desenvolvimento do MST* (São Paulo: MST).
Ferraudi Curto, María Cecilia (2014), *Ni punteros ni piqueteros: Urbanización y política en una villa del conurbano* (Buenos Aires: Gorla).
Freidenberg, Flavia and Steven Levitsky (2007), "Organización informal de los partidos en América Latina," *Desarrollo Económico* 46(184), 539–68.
Gay, Robert (1998), "Rethinking Clientelism: Demands, Discourses and Practices in Contemporary Brazil," *European Review of Latin American and Caribbean Studies* 65, 7–24.
Goirand, Camille (2015), "Pensar las movilizaciones y la participación: Continuidad de perspectivas e imbricación de posiciones," in Hélène Combes, Sergio Tamayo, and Michael Voegtli (eds.), *Pensar y mirar la protesta*, 93–138 (Mexico: UAM Ediciones).
Goffman, Erving (1974), *Frame Analysis: An Essay on the Organization of Experience* (London: Harper and Row).
Goldstone, Jack (2003), "Bridging Institutionalized and Noninstitutionalized Politics," in Jack Goldstone (ed.), *States, Parties, and Social Movements*, 1–24 (New York: Cambridge University Press).
Haber, Paul Lawrence (2006), *Power from Experience* (University Park, PA: Penn State University Press).
Hilgers, Tina (2012), "Democratic Processes, Clientelistic Relationships, and the Material Goods Problem," in Tina Hilgers (ed.), *Clientelism in Everyday Latin American Politics*, 3–22 (New York: Palgrave-Macmillan).
Hurtado Arroba, Edison (2014), "Actores, escenarios y tiempos: Algunos desafíos para estudiar el acción colectiva en colonias populares," in Tarrès Barraza, María Luisa, Laura Montes de Oca Barrera, and Diana Silva Londoño (eds.), *Arenas de conflicto y experiencias colectivas: Horizontes utópicos y dominación*, 297–349 (Mexico: El Colegio de México).
Levitsky, Steven (2003), *Transforming Labor-Based Parties in Latin America: Argentine Peronism in Comparative Perspective* (New York: Cambridge University Press)
Levy, Charmain (2012), "Social Movements and Political Parties in Brazil: Expanding Democracy, the 'Struggle for the Possible' and the Reproduction of Power Structures," *Globalizations* 9(6), 783–98.
Luján-Verón, David and Aníbal Pérez-Contreras (2018), "Cercanía, favor, lealtad: Clientelismo en dos municipalidades chilenas," *Sociológica* 33(94), 235–68.

Manzano, Virginia (2013), *La política en movimiento: Movilizaciones colectivas y políticas estatales en la vida del Gran Buenos Aires* (Rosario: Protohistoria Ediciones).

Manzano, Virginia (2007), "Etnografía de la gestión colectiva de políticas estatales en organizaciones de desocupados de La Matanza-Gran Buenos Aires," *Runa* 28, 77–92.

Manzano, Virginia (2016), "Topografías variables del poder: Las relaciones entre movimientos sociales y el Estado argentino en dos tiempos," *Amnis* 15, http://journals.openedition.org/amnis/2762.

McAdam, Doug, Sidney Tarrow, and Charles Tilly (2001), *Dynamics of Contention* (Cambridge: Cambridge University Press).

Merklen, Denis (2003), "Du travailleur au pauvre. La question sociale en Amérique latine," *Études rurales*, 1-2 (165-166), 171–196.

Merklen, Denis (2006), "Une nouvelle politicité pour les classes populaires: Les piqueteros en Argentine," *Tumultes* 2(27), 173–97.

Munck, Ronaldo (2013), "The Precariat: A View from the South," *Third World Quarterly* 34(5), 747–62.

Nogueira, Aico Sipriano (2017), "Lulism and the Institutionalization of Social Movements in Brazil: Strengthening Democratic Inclusion and Perpetuating Hegemony," *Tempo Social* 29(3), 229–60.

Paladino Cupulo, Martín (2014), "El sentido de la acción: Interés y solidaridad en el movimiento urbano de la Ciudad de México," in María Luisa Tarrés Barraza, Laura B. Montes de Oca Barrera, and Diana A. Silva Londoño (eds.), *Arenas de conflicto y experiencias colectivas: Horizontes utópicos y dominación*, 211–56 (Mexico: El Colegio de México).

Pérez, Germán and Ana Natalucci (2010), "La matriz movimientista de acción colectiva en Argentina: La experiencia del espacio militante kirchnerista," *América Latina Hoy* 54, 97–112.

Posner, Paul W. (2008), *State, Market, and Democracy in Chile: The Constraint of Popular Participation* (London: Palgrave-Macmillan).

Quirós, Julieta (2008), "Politics and Economics in Collective Action: An Ethnographic Critique of Dichotomic Premises," *Mana* 15(1), 127–53.

Quirós, Julieta (2011), *El porqué de los que van. Peronistas y piqueteros en el Gran Buenos Aires (una antropología de la política vivida)* (Buenos Aires: Antropofagia).

Quirós, Julieta (2017), "Política y sectores populares: La investigación social ante una relación siempre vidriosa," *Ciencia Hoy* 27(157), 52–56.

Rajland, Beatriz (2008), "Movilización social y transformación política en Argentina: de autonomías, articulaciones, rupturas y cooptaciones," in Margarita López Maya, Nicolás Iñigo Carrera, and Pilar Calveiro (eds.), *Luchas contrahegemónicas y cambios políticos recientes de América Latina*, 339–63 (Buenos Aires: CLACSO).

Rangel Loera, Nashieli (2014), *Tempo de acampamento* (São Paulo: Editora UNESP).

Rosa, Marcelo Carvalho (2012), "Landless: Meanings and Transformations of a Collective Action Category in Brazil," *Agrarian South: Journal of Political Economy* 1(2), 205–31.

Rosa, Marcelo Carvalho (2015), "Beyond MST: the Impact on Brazilian Social Movements," in Miguel Carter (ed.), *Challenging Social Inequality: The Landless Rural Workers Movement and Agrarian Reform in Brazil*, 375–390 (Durham, NC: Duke University Press).

Rossi, Federico M. (2017), *The Poor's Struggle for Political Incorporation: The Piquetero Movement in Argentina* (New York: Cambridge University Press).

Rossi, Federico M. and Eduardo Silva (2018), "Reshaping the Political Arena in Latin America," in Eduardo Silva and Federico M. Rossi (eds.), *Reshaping the Political Arena in Latin*

America: From Resisting Neoliberalism to the Second Incorporation, 3–20 (Pittsburgh, PA: University of Pittsburgh Press).

Serna, Leslie (1997), ¿Quién es Quién en el MUP? (Mexico: Ediciones ¡UníoS!).

Sigaud, Lygia (2005), "As condições de possibilidade das ocupações de terra," Tempo Social 17(1), 255–79.

Sigaud, Lygia, Marcelo Rosa, and Marcelo Ernandez Macedo (2008), "Ocupações de terra, acampamentos e demandas ao estado: uma análise em perspectiva comparada," Dados 51(1), 107–42.

Svampa, Maristella and Sebastián Pereyra (2003), Entre la ruta y el barrio: La experiencia de las organizaciones piqueteras (Buenos Aires: Biblos).

Svampa, Maristella (2011), "Argentina, una década después: Del "que se vayan todos" a la exacerbación de lo nacional-popular," Nueva Sociedad 235, 17–34.

Tamayo, Sergio (1999), Los veinte octubres mexicanos, ciudadanías e identidades colectivas (Mexico: UAM).

Tavera Fenollosa, Ligia (2015), "Eventful Temporality and the Unintended Outcomes of Mexico's Earthquake Victims Movement," in Federico M. Rossi and Marisa von Bülow (eds.), Social Movement Dynamics: New Perspectives on Theory and Research from Latin America, 127–54 (Farnham: Ashgate).

Tejera Gaon, Héctor, Diana Castañeda (2017), « Estructura política, redes político-clientelares y oscilaciones electorales en la Ciudad de México », Perfiles Latinoamericanos, (50) 25, 227-246.).

Thompson, Edward P. (1993), Customs in Common (London: Penguin).

Tosoni, María Magdalena (2007), "Notas sobre clientelismo político en la Ciudad de México," Perfiles Latinoamericanos 29, 47–69.

Vommaro, Gabriel and Julieta Quirós (2011), "'Usted vino por su propia decisión': Repensar el clientelismo en clave etnográfica," Desacatos 36, 83–106.

Wickham-Crowley, Timothy P. and Susan Eckstein (2015), "The Persisting Relevance of Political Economy and Political Sociology in Latin American Social Movement Studies," Latin American Research Review 50(4), 3–25.

Wolford, Wendy (2010), This Land is Ours Now: Social Mobilization and the Meanings of Land in Brazil (Durham, NC: Duke University Press).

CHAPTER 44

LEGAL MOBILIZATION

Social Movements and the Judicial System across Latin America

ALBA RUIBAL

INTRODUCTION

The use of the law and courts for social transformation is one of the main innovations in the repertoire of collective action and in the interaction between social movements and the state since democratization processes in Latin America. It has taken place at a moment in which constitutional review and constitutional adjudication started to be relevant in the institutional and political landscape, generally after constitutional and judicial reforms that created new constitutional courts (or strengthened existing supreme courts with ultimate judicial review powers), incorporated new constitutional rights, and introduced new legal instruments for their defence across the region. Thus, the interaction of social movements with the judiciary is part of a larger process, which has involved the redefinition of the role of constitutional courts in Latin American political systems, with a strengthened and more activist role of judicial institutions. This has included the development, within some sectors of the legal community, of neo-constitutionalist perspectives, giving preeminence to human rights law and constitutional principles, away from the formalism of traditional legal positivism (see Couso and Hilbink 2011).

In this context, the rights discourse and the discourse on the rule of law set out to permeate political claims, social actors started framing their grievances and goals in terms of legal and constitutional rights, and there have been significant developments in the areas of strategic and public interest litigation in different countries across the region. As a consequence, the perception of the role of courts in Latin America has shifted from being seen as obstacles to social change, to being considered one of the possible venues for rights claims (Couso 2006). Social movements started to become, in this setting, relevant actors in constitutional politics, and legal mobilization has become part of their work and strategies. Here we assume a broad definition of legal mobilization as the articulation of a movement's aspirations and grievances into a claim that asserts legal rights (Zemans 1983: 700), although we focus on the relationship between movements and the judicial system and, in particular, on strategic litigation. This type of litigation seeks to achieve high social impact and changes for large social groups, through the judicialization of an emblematic situation of rights violation. These are incipient trends in the region, and more verifiable in some countries than in others, but they certainly entail a novelty in Latin America's social and institutional history.

This chapter presents an account of the main processes and events in the recent history of the interaction between social movements and the judicial system in Latin America. It first discusses analytical frameworks for the study of social movements and courts in the region. Secondly, it analyzes the role of social movements in the creation of new legal opportunities, through their influence in constitutional conventions and judicial reform. Third, it points out some of the main developments in the interaction of movements with the court system, including progressive judicialization as well as counter-legal mobilization. Finally, it addresses multi-level processes of legal mobilization, by pointing out the importance of studying international litigation as well as subnational legal mobilization and the impact of federalism.

Frameworks for the Study of Social Movements and Courts in Latin America

Legal mobilization, or the use of the rights discourse and legal institutions by social movements, in Latin America has involved changes along the three main dimensions of collective action, as defined by social movement theory, and applied by legal studies. Movements have created new framings, incorporating the language of legal rights; they have developed new organizational resources and support structures in order to carry out strategic litigation. They have also seized legal opportunities, and, in some cases, they have contributed to the creation of new institutional opportunities in the judicial systems.

The study of the recent relationship of social movements and the court system in Latin America—and arguably elsewhere—can thus benefit from the combination of three theoretical perspectives developed in separate fields of scholarship, which have analyzed the interaction of movements and the law, but are usually not connected: (1) social movement theory, generally—but not exclusively—developed in the field of sociology; (2) legal mobilization studies within the law and society tradition; and (3) the strand of constitutional theory known as democratic constitutionalism. Despite sharing a common interest in the interaction between social actors and the legal system, these three academic fields developed separately and remained for a long time fairly independent of each other (for an analysis of the lack of dialogue between legal and social movement scholarship, see Rubin 2001).

These theories and their analytical frameworks complement each other, and their integration can offer a more comprehensive understanding of the socio-legal processes involved in the interaction between movements and the court system, as each contributes a particular understanding of different aspects of that relationship. In the first place, democratic constitutionalism argues that social movements can be central actors in the generation of a discourse that begins from the bottom and that can influence the law officially sanctioned by the state (Pope 1996; Rubin 2001; Siegel 2006). From this perspective, not only are social movements constituted by law, as the law and society literature has remarked, but they can also have an impact on legal change. Furthermore, their influence may not only be related to exerting pressure and creating momentum for reform, but they can also contribute to shaping the content of norms. As Siegel (2006) has put it, by framing their claims in legal terms, social movements produce new constitutional understandings that under certain circumstances can be incorporated by courts into constitutional law. It should be observed, following Rubin (2001), that considering social movements as a source of law does not imply that they have a preeminent role with respect to the other factors that may influence legal change—in particular the political and economic spheres. But it is meant to acknowledge that the politics of legal change is not only constituted by special-interest groups or by hegemonic political powers, but also by the interests and aspirations of actors in civil society (ibid.).

However, with illustrious exceptions (most notably, Siegel 2006), constitutional theory does not take into account the collective action processes involved in the creation of legal concepts and discourses by social movements, or the organizational and contextual factors that affect movements' capacity to influence legal reform. The operationalization of the cultural, organizational, and contextual dimensions of social movements' work and their relationship to the legal field requires an integration into the analytical framework of the other two scholarly fields. In particular, social movement theoretical and empirical research, and its main approaches focusing on resources, framings, and opportunities (see Somma in this volume), offers a privileged perspective into the social construction of legal claims and arguments that reach the courts, as well as into the political and organizational dimensions of that process. For their part, drawing on the political opportunities and the resource mobilization frameworks, legal mobilization studies have developed, respectively, the influential concepts of "legal opportunities" (Hilson 2002) and "support structures for legal mobilization" (Epp 1998). Legal opportunities include relatively stable or structural components, mostly related to rules and conditions of access to courts, as well as more contingent aspects related to courts' receptivity towards the claims of social movements (Hilson 2002: 243–44). The conceptualization of support structures comprises the presence of public interest lawyers, rights advocacy organizations, and the availability of financing sources to sustain litigation (Epp 1998: 18).

While the study of recent legal mobilization processes in Latin America can benefit from the combination of these academic traditions, it also offers the opportunity to discuss and advance nuances concerning those theoretical perspectives, which were generally developed to account for social and legal processes in affluent industrialized nations. A context of scarce resources and uncertain legal opportunities, such as we can generally find in Latin America (where nonetheless we can observe important cases of legal mobilization), compels us to revise or adjust some of the assumptions of those perspectives. Furthermore, Latin American processes of legal mobilization are taking place in transitional contexts, that is, in settings in which social movements' participation in constitutional politics as well as a more activist role of courts in the protection of rights are still recent processes, and legal practices and institutions are being reconfigured, after constitutional and judicial reforms. Given the novelty of these processes in the region, their study allows us to more clearly and directly identify the changes that can take place both at the level of civil society and courts when movements, or some of their organizations, set out to pursue a legal strategy and to interact with the judicial system.

Movements and the Creation of New Legal Opportunities: Constitutional Conventions and Judicial Reform

Movements can modify political opportunities (Gamson and Meyer 1996), as well as legal opportunities, and in this way they can contribute to shape the institutional terrain of future struggles. One of the first significant interventions of social movements in the legal system since the democratic transitions in Latin America took place in the context of constitutional conventions, which took place mostly during the 1990s. In countries such as Argentina, Brazil, and Colombia, and they were instrumental in demanding the constitutional reform itself, in introducing key constitutional rights, or in resisting the incorporation of clauses that could limit the exercise of certain rights. In the Brazilian case, the *Movimento Sanitário* (health reform movement) presented one of the most thorough and influential proposals during the 1988 Constitutional Convention. Progressive health professionals and academics, who reacted against the privatization and structural inequality of the health care system promoted by the 1964–1985 military regime in Brazil (Weyland 1995), had created this movement in the mid-1970s. Its influence on the constituent process led to the incorporation of a fundamental right to health, and eventually to the creation of one of the few public health systems in Latin America to include universal coverage as well as embedded mechanisms of social participation and accountability as its main pillars (Lago 2004).

In Colombia, in the context of an alarming level of violence and armed conflict, the students' movement was a leading force in promoting the 1991 Constitutional Assembly as a path to achieving peace and justice, which brought about a highly progressive Constitution (Ramírez 2002). The 1991 constitutional text recognized the rights of different collectives in Colombia and established effective means for their protection and created the most emblematic Constitutional Court in the region in terms of its activist role in rights protection. In Argentina, in the context of the 1994 Constituent Assembly, more than 100 organizations formed the *Mujeres Autoconvocadas para Decidir en Libertad* (MADEL) coalition, in order to resist the incorporation of a clause on the right to life from conception (Gutiérrez 2000). Due to this mobilization, and to the relatively high presence of women at the Convention (there was a female representation of 26.4%, thanks to the country's 1991 vanguard gender quota law), who worked together on this issue across party lines, the government-promoted right to life provision was not incorporated into the constitutional text.

A key social actor in post-transition constitutional reform processes was the feminist movement (see Ewig and Friedman in this volume). The relatively high presence of women at the constitutional convention in Argentina contrasts with the low female representation at the constitutional assemblies in Brazil in 1988 and Colombia in 1991. However, in both the Brazilian and Colombian cases, women organized and mobilized around the constituent process, and obtained the recognition of most of their demands, including the introduction of a reproductive freedom clause, establishing that women can choose the number and spacing of their children (Lago 2004; Morgan and Alzate 1991). Also in both cases, women's organization inside and outside the Constitutional Convention successfully resisted the incorporation of a clause on the right to life from conception.

Later on, as part of a second wave of constitutional reforms since democratization processes in the region (see Inclán in this volume), this time under leftist governments that came to power in the region since 1998, countries such as Venezuela (2000), Bolivia (2008), and Ecuador (2008) enacted new Constitutions aimed at dismantling the neoliberal state. The drafting of new constitutions presented a critical juncture for social movements, which generally supported and participated in these processes, although not without contradictions and concerns about co-optation and representation (Becker 2011). The new constitutional texts declared the plurinational character of the state (Bolivia, Ecuador) and incorporated participatory mechanisms and new collective and individual rights long claimed by social actors, most prominently—especially in the cases of Ecuador and Bolivia—indigenous people's organizations (Barbosa, Moricz, and González 2009).

Beyond their role in constitutional conventions, the influence of social movements in the 2003 reform of the Argentine Supreme Court shows how social actors can have a direct impact in the generation of momentum as well as of technical proposals for the reform of judicial institutions. During the 2001–2002 economic and political crisis in this country, the Supreme Court was one of the most contested state powers and a main target of social protest, as it was indicated as a key responsible actor for the country's breakdown. The professional organization *Asociación de Abogados Laboralistas* (Labor Lawyers Association) headed massive protests against the Court, demanding the removal of Court members accused of corruption (see Rossi 2005). As part of their repertoire of action, protesters carried out symbolic "ethical trials" of the Court in the public space. At the same time, the crisis also propitiated the coordinated work of a group of NGOs, including some of the most important rights advocacy organizations in the country, which formed the coalition "Una Corte para la Democracia" and developed a comprehensive program for the Court's reform. These organizations were Centro de Estudios Sociales y Legales (CELS); Asociación por los Derechos Civiles (ADC); Poder Ciudadano; Instituto de Estudios Comparados en Ciencias Penales y Sociales (INECIPE); Fundación Ambiente y Recursos Naturales (FARN); and Unión de Usuarios y Consumidores. Their proposals included new mechanisms of transparency and participation of civil society in the nomination processes of new judges, a partial renewal of the Court and a reduction in its size, and a series of changes in the Court's functioning, including more transparency and public participation in its internal procedures (Ruibal 2009). Since 2003, the government and the Court itself implemented these reforms almost in their entirety. In terms of the effectiveness of social movements in judicial reform, and institutional change more generally, the Argentine case highlights the importance of the synergy between two different types of intervention in the public sphere. On the one hand, massive street protests demanding the renewal of the Court installed the demand of Court reform at the center of the public discussion. This type of collective action received the largest media attention and created momentum for reform. On the other hand, the technical work by a coalition of NGOs offered a plan of action to be implemented by governmental powers, which not only included the recommendation of removing corrupt judges but, most importantly, suggested the institutional way for achieving a more independent and legitimate Court. The case shows that in certain opportunities popular protest and the work of NGOs can complement and reinforce each other to effect change.

THE INTERACTION OF MOVEMENTS WITH THE COURT SYSTEM

Especially after constitutional and judicial reform processes, social movements set out to use the court system to advance their demands. Strategic litigation before constitutional courts, or supreme courts with ultimate constitutional review powers (here we use the term constitutional courts to refer to both), has been one of the most prominent tools in this regard. In these processes, there has been a dynamic interaction between social movements and new or reformed courts in different countries across the region. Movements started appealing to courts in search for long-pursued reforms and institutional responses they did not find through the political process. For their part, courts, which were in the process of building or redefining their institutional roles and legitimacy in the political system, in some emblematic cases started engaging in an unprecedented relationship with actors in civil society. These developments have taken place only in some countries and cases, and have generally met with strong resistances for enforcement and implementation (see Rodríguez-Garavito 2010), but they point to a new type of relationship between courts and civil society in the region, and a new role of social movements and courts in the pursuit of social change

Along their participation in these processes, Latin American social movements have developed new organizational means, or support structures for legal mobilization. In fact, the development of strategic litigation, and legal mobilization more generally, requires specific organizational resources, given the technical expertise normally required to interact with the legal field, and the requirements of legal standing to litigate collective rights claims in most judicial systems in the region, which require legal representation and legal personhood from litigants. Thus, in order to pursue legal strategies, social movements must count on professionalized and specific organizational resources, which means that, in general, the interaction of movements with the court system in Latin America, and usually elsewhere, is generally carried out by NGOs. These organizations can take a direct part in social movements, or share movement goals and lend them their technical expertise and organizational means. In transitional contexts, where social movements have not yet developed their own support structure and legal expertise, the decision by social actors to pursue a legal strategy can lead them to start building from the beginning their own resources for legal mobilization, for example by creating new organizations oriented to the legal defence of rights. This was the model adopted by Colombian feminist legal advocates in order to carry out strategic litigation for abortion rights, when they established the Colombian office of Women's Link Worldwide in 2005. In transitional settings, movements may also recourse to alliances with partners and allies in the legal profession, until they acquire their own resources. This was the initial strategy of the main organizations that led legal strategies for abortion rights in Mexico (GIRE, Grupo de Información en Reproducción Elegida, created in 1991) and Brazil (ANIS, Instituto de Bioética, Direitos Humanos e Gênero, founded in 1999). These organizations contacted male lawyers with expertise in public interest litigation, who assisted them in translating their claims into a legal strategy. After that first stage, both organizations developed their own resources for legal mobilization, and they have trained and incorporated young feminist lawyers. Nowadays they are key legal actors in the feminist camp, and in the area of public interest law more generally in their respective countries.

As part of the novel interaction between courts and social movements in the region, Courts also made changes in their way of functioning. In this process, constitutional courts have, for example, opened up their institutional procedures in order to facilitate the participation of social actors, mainly through the regulation and implementation of public hearings and amicus curiae briefs for the first time in their institutional history. The Argentinean Supreme Court did so as part of the reform process to its procedures initiated in 2003. The Mexican and Brazilian constitutional courts promoted public deliberation through the implementation of these mechanisms for social actors' participation when they had to decide on the highly controversial abortion rights issue, which judges at both Courts considered as the most important cases in the institutional history of their respective Courts (see Ruibal 2015).

These changes, both in social movements and courts, point to a synergy through which both types of actors redefined and built new forms of action and intervention, in a transitional context in which legal mobilization and judicial activism in the field of rights protection were novel processes.

In the landscape of strategic litigation before constitutional courts in the region, some cases stand out in terms of their impact on public opinion, as well as in terms of the role of courts in effecting relevant decisions and the type of court intervention and interaction with other actors in the political system, including social organizations. In the judicialization of rights before constitutional courts, social movements have had a key role as plaintiffs, or through participation in court proceedings through public hearings and amicus curiae briefs, as well as in monitoring commissions formed to oversee the implementation of court decisions in complex structural reform cases.

An illustrative example of interaction between social movements and courts involving all those dimensions can be found in Argentina, after the reform of the Supreme Court. A reference to these cases allows to see the dynamics between social movements and constitutional courts in a transitional moment, in which movements were attempting to create new legal opportunities for their participation in the judicial system, and the Court was in the process of redefining its institutional role in society. After the Court was renewed in 2003, it implemented a series of reforms to its own internal procedures that had been proposed by the coalition of NGOs, Una Corte para la Democracia. These institutional reforms created new opportunities for strategic litigation and for the intervention of civil society's organizations in the Court's decisional processes, mainly by regulating public hearings and amicus curiae submissions. As soon as the new procedures were in place, in 2004 key social actors that had promoted those institutional reforms submitted collective petitions in two emblematic cases before the Court, regarding the conditions of imprisonment in the Province of Buenos Aires (so-called *Verbitsky* case), and environmental damages due to pollution of a river basin (so-called *Mendoza* case). In both cases, the Court upheld collective petitions and intervened in structural reform or complex litigation.

The *Verbitsky* case, litigated by CELS, which is one of the most important human rights organizations in the country, is paradigmatic in terms of the implementation of innovative judicial procedures and the new interaction of the Supreme Court with social actors. The Court upheld for the first time a collective habeas corpus brief, it convoked several public hearings with participation of social movements, and accepted amicus curiae briefs for the first time, which were submitted by several social organizations, among them ADC and the NGOs *El Agora* and *Casa del Liberado*. Furthermore, the Court mandated the creation of a permanent discussion panel (*Mesa de Diálogo*) to define measures and supervise the development of this case, including provincial authorities and civil society's organizations. The *Mendoza* case was litigated by a group of neighbors from "Villa Inflamable," located in the province of Buenos Aires, accompanied by health professionals and supported by several NGOs that were included as third parties throughout the process—most prominently among them CELS and FARN. The Court held several public hearings with governmental authorities; businesses and social organizations such as Asociación de Vecinos de La Boca, CELS, FARN, and Greenpeace Argentina. As in the former case, in this one the Court did not establish the policies to be implemented but mandated the national Executive Power to develop a long-term plan and to create an institutional structure (the Matanza-Riachuelo Basin Authority) to supervise the process, which included the mentioned social organizations that participated in the judicial process.

The literature on courts and social change in Latin America has generally focused on social and economic rights, as the legal struggle and the judicial activism on these rights have been fundamental in the region (see Couso, Huneeus, and Sieder 2010; Gargarella, Domingo Villegas, and Roux 2006; Gauri and Brinks 2008). However, since the mid-2000s, reproductive rights, and abortion rights in particular, have become an important field of social movement litigation and participation in constitutional court proceedings, and courts have sided for the first time in the region with feminists' claims to decriminalize abortion in certain circumstances. Brazilian and Colombian feminist NGOs, with support from other feminist organizations in their respective countries, have carried out two of the most important cases of strategic litigation for abortion rights in Latin America. In 2004, the Brazilian feminist organization ANIS was the first one in the region to present a demand at the country's Supremo Tribunal Federal (STF), claiming the liberalization of the abortion law in cases of anencephaly, which was upheld by the Tribunal in 2012. More recently, in 2017, the same organization, accompanied by a wide range of feminist organizations working throughout the country, became the first feminist NGO in Latin America to demand the Court to legalize first trimester abortion. On both occasions, the STF convoked public hearings, in 2008 and 2018, respectively, eliciting unprecedented participation of social movements at the Court's proceedings, and the widest public debate on abortion at a state institution so far in Brazil. For its part, in 2005, the Colombian office of Women's Link Worldwide, with support by the *Mesa por la Vida y la Salud de las Mujeres*, which is the most important coalition for the defense of abortion rights in Colombia, filed a petition at the country's Constitutional Court, asking for the liberalization of country's highly restrictive abortion law. As a response, the Court issued the first sentence by a constitutional court to expand the abortion law in Latin America, and it did so through a groundbreaking argumentation, as it was the first decision by a constitutional court worldwide to review the constitutionality of abortion following a human rights framework (Undurraga and Cook 2009).

Counter-legal Mobilization and Courts

Social movement theory has shown that organized opposition is a normal consequence of the presence of relevant movements in the political landscape. It also argues that in contemporary societies this opposition increasingly takes the form of a social movement, or a counter-movement, which uses the same forms of mobilization (Meyer and

Staggenborg 1996). In Latin America, progressive institutional reforms that favored the use of the human rights framework as well as of new legal remedies by social actors, also promoted the development of conservative legal mobilization. Counter-legal mobilization processes have been most prominent in the region in the field of sexual and reproductive rights. Especially since the 1990s, and due to the advancement of women's movements in the international and national arenas, conservative religious sectors started organizing as a social movement, or counter-movement (Payne in this volume). In this process, they have developed a language more in keeping with the discourse of democracy and human rights (see Lemaitre 2012), and have leveraged the institutional means provided by the democratic structure and the new legal opportunity for legal mobilization and strategic litigation in the region.

Constitutional Courts, which in many cases have been a forum for progressive causes, have also been key actors in backlash processes in the field of reproductive rights, and have upheld the claims of counter-movements. Legal mobilization by conservative NGOs has been most noticeable in the Argentine case. Since the early 2000s, conservative NGOs such as Portal de Belén and its partner organization Mujeres por la Vida, have led the field of judicialization of reproductive rights in this country. In particular, in 2002 Portal de Belén was the first organization to use the progressive legal framework for social actors' claims created by the constitutional reform of 1994, in order to present a collective petition against emergency contraception pills, which was upheld by the Court on that year. This case was key for the Supreme Court's conservative jurisprudence in the field of reproductive rights until its landmark 2012 decision that liberalized the abortion law (so-called F., A.L. case). More recently, after the F., A.L. decision, Portal de Belén judicialized in 2012 the protocols for the attention of lawful abortions at subnational courts and obstructed the implementation of the Court's decision in some local jurisdictions.

MULTI-LEVEL PROCESSES OF LEGAL MOBILIZATION

Most of the literature on law and social change in Latin America has analyzed the interaction between social movements and legal institutions, particularly at the national level (see the volumes edited by Couso, Huneeus and Sieder 2010; Gargarella, Domingo Villegas, and Roux 2006; Gauri and Brinks 2008). This emphasis on national high courts is understandable, given the relevance of the recent creation or empowerment of constitutional courts for political systems across the region. However, the research agenda on legal mobilization in the region should also pay attention to international and subnational litigation, and the ways legal actions in different levels influence each other. This is so because movements have appealed, many times successfully, to international judicial and quasi-judicial bodies when national judicial processes were blocked to the advancement of their causes. Moreover, particularly in federal systems, most times the enforcement of citizen's rights is crucially defined at the subnational level.

International Litigation

Latin American social movements have appealed in the past decades to international and regional human rights courts and committees, and the legal opportunities at these jurisdictions have generally been favorable to Latin American social actors. Particularly important in this regard have been movements' legal actions before the Inter-American Human Rights system and the United Nations Human Rights Committee. Decisions by these organs have had strong symbolic significance; they have obliged states to comply with human rights provisions; and movements have used the pronouncements of international organs to support their claims at national courts (see von Bülow in this volume).

International litigation by human rights organizations has been a key component in the judicialization of the politics of accountability for past human rights violations during military dictatorships in countries such as Argentina, Chile, and Uruguay, when amnesty laws under democratic governments blocked domestic prosecutions of the military juntas and dictators (see Sikkink 2005; Wolff in this volume). In fact, the traditional litigation and decisions of international human rights organs centered on the violation of civic and political rights. However, in the two past decades movements have increasingly appealed to international organs to claim for economic, social, and cultural rights, including the rights to health, to water, to education, as well as labor rights (Leão and Zerbini 2010). In this context, international legal mobilization by organizations of indigenous peoples claiming for the defense of their territories and rights has posed—according to Rodríguez-Garavito and Arenas (2005)—some of the most significant challenges to current legal systems in the region. In particular, they have introduced a collective understanding of rights, which has contributed to transform national and international legal frameworks and to redefine liberal conceptions of human rights. Latin American contemporary indigenous movements, developed since the 1970s in countries such as Bolivia, Colombia, Ecuador, and Mexico and have developed transnational networks—such as the International Group on Indigenous Affairs and Survival International—and have pursued legal claims through alliances with environmentalist movements and other protest movements, combining national and international mobilization (see Rodríguez-Garavito and Arenas 2005).

In the field of reproductive rights, Latin American feminists have recurred to international organs in search of redress for injustices regarding access to abortion in their countries, and landmark cases have been successfully litigated by feminist organizations at different international human rights treaty bodies. The two most salient examples in this regard are the case known as *K.L. v. Peru* and the so-called *Paulina* case. The former case motivated the first abortion rights decision by the United Nations Human Rights Committee, which in 2005 condemned the Peruvian state to pay for reparations and confirmed a state's positive obligation to provide therapeutic abortion. The petition had been filed in 2002 by the Peruvian feminist NGOs Estudio para la Defensa de los Derechos de la Mujer (DEMUS) and Comité Latinoamericano y del Caribe para la Defensa de los Derechos de la Mujer (CLADEM), in partnership with the Center for Reproductive Rights, based in New York, on behalf of a young Peruvian girl who had been denied access to a lawful abortion in a case of anencephaly. For its part, the *Paulina* case was litigated by the leading Mexican feminist NGO GIRE and the Mexican organization Alaíde Foppa, in alliance with the Center for Reproductive Rights, before the Inter-American Commission on Human Rights, against the Mexican state for not providing access to abortion in case of rape to a young girl. In 2006, the case was settled at the Inter-American Commission of Human Rights, obliging the Mexican state to carry out a comprehensive program of reparations.

Subnational Legal Mobilization and Federalism

Finally, analysis of the interaction between social movements and courts in the region should consider the subnational dimension of this phenomenon, as the defense and implementation of the rights of large populations in the region is, to a great extent, defined at the subnational level. The four federations in Latin America—Argentina, Brazil, Mexico, and Venezuela—with their delegation of policy powers to subnational units, concentrate a majority of the population in the region. If we consider, following Smulovitz (2015), that federalism leads to the uneven protection of rights throughout national territories, we can expect further challenges for legal activists in federal countries, in a region already signed by the most unequal distribution of social and economic goods in the world. On the other hand, federal arrangements can also create opportunities for rights advocates working at subnational units. The federal architecture of the state, including judicial federalism, can promote a synergy between national and local factors, in both civil society and the state, which can favor subnational legal mobilization (Ruibal 2018). This can take place, for example, due to the creation of federal agencies for the protection of rights connected with parallel institutions at the local level, which has been a common development in Latin American federal countries, as part of the process of institution building after democratic transitions. The presence of institutional activists working within these state institutions at the local level can foster legal mobilization by social movements in subnational jurisdictions, by providing support to their causes. These features of Latin American political systems, particularly under federalism, point to the relevance of analyzing legal mobilization processes at the subnational level and considering the impact of federal arrangements on these processes.

Conclusion

The examination of the recent interaction between social movements and the court system across Latin America shows that movements and their organizations have become important actors in the reform of judicial institutions, as well as in the effective functioning and decision-making of courts in the region. Indeed, movements have been key actors in the configuration of new legal opportunities, through their participation in constitutional and judicial reform. Later on, they have used new legal instruments for the advancement of their causes, through strategic litigation and other forms of involvement in the judicial process, such as the participation public hearings and the presentation of amicus curiae briefs. In this process, movements have developed new organizational resources, or support structures for legal mobilization, and some of their organizations have become leading public interest litigators in their respective countries. As part of this recent dynamic, courts have also transformed their internal procedures, in order to facilitate their interaction with social actors, and have implemented new forms of decision-making, including social organizations as part of their innovative role in complex cases involving constitutional rights. Conservative actors have also seized the new legal opportunities in the region to develop counter-legal mobilization, particularly in the field of reproductive rights, and abortion rights in particular.

Finally, this chapter argues for the need to look at the relationship of movements with international and regional judicial institutions, since part of the legal actions by social actors in the region has a transnational dimension. It also highlights the importance of analyzing subnational processes of legal mobilization, particularly under federalism, given that in federal systems the rights of citizens are to a great extent defined at the local level, and the federal architecture of the state can create obstacles as well as advantages for Latin American legal activists.

REFERENCES

Barbosa, Leticia, Mariana Moricz, and Milena González (2009), "Los procesos de las Asambleas Constituyentes de Bolivia, Ecuador y Venezuela: La institucionalización de otros paradigmas," *Revista Latinoamericana de economía social y solidaria* 3(4), 174–95.

Becker, Marc (2011), "Correa, indigenous movements, and the writing of a new constitution in Ecuador," *Latin American Perspectives* 38(1), 47–62.

Courtis, Christian (2005), "El caso Verbitsky: ¿Nuevos rumbos en el control judicial de la actividad de los poderes políticos?," in CELS (ed.), *Temas para pensar la crisis: Colapso del sistema carcelario*, 91–120 (Buenos Aires: CELS/Siglo XXI).

Couso, Javier (2006), "The Changing Role of Law and Courts in Latin America," in Roberto Gargarella, Pilar Domingo Villegas, and Theunis Roux (eds.), *Courts and Social Transformation in New Democracies: An Institutional Voice for the Poor?*, 61–79 (Burlington, VT: Ashgate).

Couso, Javier and Lisa Hilbink (2011), "From Quietism to Incipient Activism," in Gretchen Helmke and Julio Ríos Figueroa (eds.), *Courts in Latin America*, 99–127 (New York: Cambridge University Press).

Couso, Javier, Alexandra Huneeus, and Rachel Sieder (eds.) (2010), *Cultures of Legality: Judicialization and Political Activism in Latin America* (New York: Cambridge University Press).

Epp, Charles (1998), *The Rights Revolution: Lawyers, Activists, and Supreme Courts in Comparative Perspective* (Chicago: The University of Chicago Press).
Gamson, William and David Meyer (1996), "Framing Political Opportunity," in Doug McAdam, John McCarthy, and Mayer Zald (eds.), *Comparative Perspectives on Social Movements, Political Opportunities, Mobilizing Structures, and Cultural Framings*, 275–90 (New York: Cambridge University Press).
Gargarella, Roberto, Pilar Domingo Villegas, and Theunis Roux (eds.) (2006), *Courts and Social Transformation in New Democracies: An Institutional Voice for the Poor?* (Burlington, VT: Ashgate).
Gauri, Varun and Daniel Brinks (eds.) (2008), *Courting Social Justice: Judicial Enforcement of Social and Economic Rights in the Developing World* (Cambridge: Cambridge University Press).
Gutiérrez, María Alicia (2000), "Mujeres para decidir en libertad (MADEL): La experiencia reciente del movimiento de mujeres," *Cuadernos del Foro* 2(3), 83–106.
Helmke, Gretchen and Jeffrey Staton (2011), "The Puzzling Judicial Politics of Latin America," in Gretchen Helmke and Julio Ríos Figueroa (eds.), *Courts in Latin America*, 306–31 (New York: Cambridge University Press).
Hilson, Chris (2002), "New Social Movements: The Role of Legal Opportunity," *Journal of European Public Policy* 9(2), 238–55.
Lago, Tania (2004), "La participación ciudadana en la toma de decisiones con respecto a la salud de la mujer en Brasil," in Ana Langer and Gustavo Nigenda (eds.), *Procesos de reforma del sector salud y programas de salud sexual y reproductiva en América Latina: Cinco estudios de caso*, 45–72 (Mexico: FUNSALUD).
Leão, Renato and Renato Zerbini (2010), "El rol de la sociedad civil organizada para el fortalecimiento de la protección de los derechos humanos en el siglo XXI: Un enfoque especial sobre los DESC," *Revista IIDH* 51, 249–71.
Lemaitre, Julieta (2012), "By Reason Alone: Catholicism, Constitutions, and Sex in the Americas," *International Journal of Constitutional Law* 10(2), 493–511.
Meyer, David and Suzanne Staggenborg (1996), "Movements, Counter-movements, and the Structure of Political Opportunity," *American Journal of Sociology* 101(6), 1628–60.
Morgan, Martha and Mónica Alzate (1991), "Constitution-making in a Time of Cholera: Women and the 1991 Colombian Constitution," *Yale Journal of Law and Feminism* 4, 353–413.
Pope, James (1996), "Labor's Constitution of Freedom," *Yale Law Journal* 106, 941–1031.
Ramírez, Óscar (2002), "Sociología e historia del movimiento estudiantil por la Asamblea Constituyente de 1991," *Revista colombiana de sociología* 7(2), 125–51.
Rodríguez-Garavito, César (2010), "Beyond the Courtroom: The Impact of Judicial Activism on Socioeconomic Rights in Latin America," *Texas Law Review* 89(7), 1698.
Rodríguez-Garavito, César and Luis Arenas (2005), "Indigenous Rights, Transnational Activism, and Legal Mobilization: The Struggle of the U'wa People in Colombia," in Boaventura de Sousa Santos and César Rodríguez-Garavito (eds.), *Law and Globalization From Below: Towards a Cosmopolitan Legality*, 241–66 (Cambridge: Cambridge University Press).
Rossi, Federico M. (2005), "Aparición, auge y declinación de un movimiento social: Las asambleas vecinales y populares de Buenos Aires, 2001–2003," *European Review of Latin American and Caribbean Studies* 78, 67–88.
Rubin, Edward (2001), "Passing through the Door: Social Movement Literature and Legal Scholarship," *University of Pennsylvania Law Review* 150(1), 1–83.

Ruibal, Alba (2009), "Judicial Reform and Self-Restraint: The Process of Supreme Court Independence in Argentina," *Latin American Politics and Society* 51(3), 59–86.

Ruibal, Alba (2015), "Social Movements and Constitutional Politics in Latin America: Reconfiguring Alliances, Framings and Legal Opportunities in the Judicialisation of Abortion Rights in Brazil," *Contemporary Social Science* 10(4), 375–85.

Ruibal, Alba (2018), "Federalism and Subnational Legal Mobilization: Feminist Litigation Strategies in Salta, Argentina," *Law and Society Review* 52(4), 928–59.

Siegel, Reva (2006), "Constitutional Culture, Social Movement Conflict and Constitutional Change: The Case of the de facto ERA," *California Law Review* 94, 1323–419.

Sikkink, Kathryn (2005), "The Transnational Dimension of the Judicialization of Politics in Latin America," in Rachel Sieder, Line Schjolden, and Alan Angell (eds.), *The Judicialization of Politics in Latin America*, 263–92 (New York: Palgrave-Macmillan).

Smulovitz, Catalina (2005), "Petitioning and Creating Rights: Judicialization in Argentina," in Rachel Sieder, Line Schjolden, and Alan Angell (eds.), *The Judicialization of Politics in Latin America*, 161–85 (New York: Palgrave-Macmillan).

Smulovitz, Catalina (2015), "Legal Inequality and Federalism: Domestic Violence Laws in the Argentine Provinces," *Latin American Politics and Society* 57(3), 1–26.

Undurraga, Verónica and Rebecca Cook (2009), "Constitutional Incorporation of International and Comparative Human Rights Law: the Colombian Constitutional Court Decision C-355/2006," in Susan Williams (ed.), *Constituting equality: Gender Equality and Comparative Constitutional Law*, 215–47 (New York: Cambridge University Press).

Weyland, Kurt (1995), "Social Movements and the State: The Politics of Health Reform in Brazil," *World Development* 23(10), 1699–712.

Zemans, Frances (1983), "Legal Mobilization: The Neglected Role of the Law in the Political System," *American Political Science Review* 77(3), 690–703.

CHAPTER 45

SOCIAL MOVEMENTS AND PARTICIPATORY INSTITUTIONS IN LATIN AMERICA

ROCÍO ANNUNZIATA AND BENJAMIN GOLDFRANK

Introduction

Research on social movements rarely pays attention to participatory institutions (PIs), since they tend to be introduced by government authorities from the top down and oriented towards consensus, rejecting openly contentious action. In fact, work in this field tends to understand participation in terms of advocacy, social protest, and struggle for rights, that is, repertoires of contention (Risley 2015; Rossi and von Bülow 2015; cf. Alvarez et al. 2017). Typically, the point of departure is a degree of autonomy of civil society that provides capacity to make demands on authorities outside of institutional frameworks.

On the other hand, the literature on PI often emphasizes social movements as the key promoters, supporters, or participants. In fact, some authors consider PIs to be products of demands from below, results of pressure from organized civil society (Alvarez et al 2017; Avritzer 2015; Cannon and Kirby 2012; Dagnino, Olvera and Panfichi 2006; Schneider and Welp 2011). In this perspective, social movements prevail over reluctant rulers or get articulated within left coalitions to multiply the arenas for citizen participation. Other authors identify a strong associative network as a crucial condition for the success of participatory policies. Preexisting associative density (Baiocchi et al. 2011) as well as cohesion and high social capital (Welp and Serdült 2012; Zaremberg et al. 2018) and capacity to resist instrumentalization (Bacqué et al. 2005) are often pointed out as performance determinants of PIs. In this perspective, only when there is true civil society autonomy is it possible to speak of "participatory democracy." Where civil society is weak, distorted forms of participation such as co-optation or clientelism often emerge (Zaremberg 2012; see Combes and Quirós in this volume). Although to a lesser extent, the literature on PI has also paid attention to the effects they can have on social movements. Some research finds that the adoption of PIs produces a strengthening of civil society by developing a sense of solidarity, increasing the number of organizations, expanding the range of their activities, and promoting new partnerships with governments (Baiocchi 2001; Touchton and Wampler 2014; Wampler et al. 2018: 3); other studies find that elite resistance to power-sharing or partisan politics within PIs can lead to frustration, disillusionment with collective action, and division within participating social movement organizations (Hanson 2018; Lima 2019).

Research in this field, then, has addressed social movements as both explanatory factors in the origins and success or failure of PI and as potential outcomes of PIs. This interest in social movements and civil society organizations is due to the fact that one of the most important issues that runs through research on PIs is who participates. Who is invited by authorities to participate? Who is their ideal participant? How do pre-existing social actors respond to the invitation made by the authorities? The links between PIs and social movements are quite diverse. As we will see later, there are mechanisms designed for the participation of organized civil society and others designed for the participation of non-organized individuals. Facing institutional processes controlled by government officials, social movements may prefer to appropriate the participatory tool in their favor, to opt for more contentious dynamics instead, or, in some cases, attempt to maintain a dual strategy of working both within the new PIs and mobilizing outside them as well.

This chapter aims to analyze the different relationships between participatory institutions and social movements in Latin America. We conceptualize four ideal types of PI focusing on the role that social movements play (or not) within them: (1) PIs promoting an interface between the state and organized civil society; (2) PIs promoting individual citizen participation; (3) PIs conceived for individual citizen voting but requiring campaigning by social movements; and (4) PIs promoting local-level popular organization and governance in competition with representative authorities rather than in concert. In the next section we define PIs and describe their origins and expansion in recent years in Latin America. The third section centers on who participates in different PIs, and particularly on the role of social movements. We describe each of our four types and then illustrate them with at least one key example: National Public Policy Conferences in Brazil, Participatory Budgeting in Argentina, Citizen-Initiated Popular Consultations in Uruguay, and Communal Councils in Venezuela. In the conclusion, we reflect on the advantages and limits of the different types, noting that the role of social movements is not always and not necessarily related to more inclusionary participation.

Latin America's Participatory Turn

Since the region's democratization wave in the 1980s, Latin America gradually gained renown as a center for experiments with participatory institutions. This experimentation has been uneven across countries, across different levels of government, and with respect to the degree of implementation. Nonetheless, a general increase in the number and importance of PIs is unmistakable up to the mid-2010s. According to Pogrebinschi's (2017) study of sixteen countries in the region, there were 1,889 "participatory innovations" between 1990 and 2015, making Latin America a global leader in creating such institutions as participatory budgeting, public policy conferences, deliberative councils, and citizen consultations. Social movement demands for the right to participate in public policy decisions and even, in some cases, for particular forms of participation often played important roles in the implementation of new institutions or the revival of older institutions following democratization, but not always (see Gurza Lavalle and Szwako in this volume). Their degree of influence depended not only on their own strength and strategy, but on whether their agendas converged with those of other key actors, such as international aid organizations and the political parties in power (Roberts in this volume), and on whether windows of political opportunity opened (Somma in this volume).

On the whole, the 1990s and 2000s provided a favorable context for social movements demanding PIs. International development organizations and aid agencies provided encouragement, technical support, and funding for governments to decentralize and to increase opportunities for citizen participation as part of poverty reduction strategies, in some cases to ease the pain of structural adjustment. The decentralization trend included the emergence or re-emergence of mayoral elections in municipalities across the region, even in national capitals that had indirectly elected or appointed chief executives in the past, facilitating experimentation with participation in major cities. First at the local level and later at the national level, many political parties and leaders on the Left or center-Left campaigned on the idea of deepening democracy through developing forms of popular participation beyond traditional representative institutions (see Oxhorn in this volume). Some centrist and more modern conservative governments showed an openness to PIs as tools to reduce corruption and increase efficiency, often as part of "second generation" reforms following the Washington Consensus. While some PIs thus emerged as a result of regular pluralistic democratic competition, pressure from social movements, and international inducements, other PIs came out of periods of political crisis, often culminating in constituent assemblies that provided unique opportunities for social movements to press for the right to participation. New PIs were introduced, at least on paper, in Colombia's constitutional re-writing in 1991 as part of negotiations to end the civil war, in Peru during the transition away from Fujimori in the 2000s, following the collapse of the party systems in Venezuela in the 1990s and in Bolivia and Ecuador in the mid-2000s, and after the Argentine economic and political meltdown at the turn of the millennium.

The region's participatory turn has had diverse origins, with social movement influence varying across countries and time periods. Undeniably, in the past few decades, millions of Latin Americans have had increased opportunities to take part in institutionalized forms of civic engagement beyond the occasional election of representatives. Broadly defined, participatory institutions directly involve citizens, individually or in groups, in (a) public decision-making processes, (b) project implementation, or (c) government oversight. Some PIs include just one of these mechanisms, while others, particularly at the neighborhood or local level, encompass two or more. A non-exhaustive list of recently created PIs prevalent across the region should include: oversight commissions and public audits; neighborhood or communal councils; participatory budgeting; public policy and planning councils, conferences, forums, citizen dialogues, and roundtables; indigenous self-governance institutions; and direct democracy mechanisms like recall referendums, prior consultations, citizen initiatives, and policy referendums. The types of PIs introduced vary widely depending on the country, emphasizing different levels of government and policy sectors and granting more or less power and resources to participants. One of the key differences across PIs is the role of social movements.

Who Participates: The Different Roles of Social Movements

PIs as Interfaces between the State and Organized Civil Society

One common type of participatory mechanism promotes regularized interactions between the state on one hand and organized social movements, civic associations, and non-governmental organizations on the other. These PIs are designed to provide forums where state officials can discuss public policy or resources with the leaders of civil society organizations. Typically, these PIs focus on specific sectors or issues rather than territories. Individual citizens may be allowed to participate in certain stages, but the target interlocutors for the state are members and especially leaders of organizations with specialized interests and knowledge relevant to the subject. Sometimes, participation is restricted to specific groups or the institutional design enables only officially registered civil society organizations to participate (and even quotas or proportions for participation of certain groups of actors are fixed). Participation criteria like these can bias the interface dynamic, accentuating corporatism and excluding the weakest actors in society. The Roundtables for the Fight Against Poverty (RFAP) in Peru illustrate this latter pattern (Goldfrank 2018), while Brazil's National Public Policy Conferences (BNPPCs) are paradigmatic examples of the more open design.

Public policy conferences in Brazil date back to the Getúlio Vargas era (1930–1954), well before the transition to democracy in the 1980s, but their regular use picked up dramatically during the Luiz Inácio Lula da Silva administration (2003–2006, 2007–2010). From 2003 to 2011, the government convened between fifty-eight and seventy-four BNPPCs, more than those held in all previous governments combined since the first in 1941 (Pogrebinschi and Samuels 2014: 320–21; cf. Avritzer 2012: 7–8). The BNPPCs are organized thematically, focused on issues such as healthcare, education, security, food and nutrition, human rights, the environment, and social assistance, and they are structured in a pyramidal way, with municipal- and state-level conferences preceding a final national conference. In this last stage, the participants gather and review the proceedings from the earlier stages and produce a report with a long list of policy proposals.[1] While concerned individual citizens do participate at the municipal-level, the majority of participants are members of civil society organizations, and to participate at the state- and national-level conferences, one must be selected at the municipal level to represent a particular group. State actors participate in large numbers as well, especially at the higher-level conferences. For example, at the VII National Conference on Social Assistance in 2009 it was established that 50% of the delegates would be representatives of the public sector and 50% would be civil society actors; and at the II National Conference on Policies for Women in 2007, the proportion was 40% government and 60% civil society (Faria, Petinelli, and Lins 2012: 271–73).[2] Roughly seven million Brazilians, or about 5% of the adult population, participated in the BNPPCs in the 2003–2011 period (Avritzer 2012: 11; Pogrebinschi and Samuels 2014: 321).

Given this relatively large number of participants and the wide range of public policies addressed, the BNPPCs have been characterized as "by far the world's largest experiment" with participatory democracy (Pogrebinschi and Samuels 2014: 321). Indeed, before the Partido dos Trabalhadores (PT) was stripped of power in Brazil in 2016 by forces hostile to participation, the BNPPCs did provide a venue for social movement organizations to put their policy proposals on the governing agenda. Studies by Petinelli (2014) and Pogrebinschi and Samuels (2014), among others, found that high percentages of policy proposals approved in the BNPPCs were later incorporated in the programs of the respective agencies or federal ministries, or in legislated or decreed public policies, illustrating the potential of these kinds of PIs as effective state-society interfaces (for a contrasting view, see Baiocchi 2017: 42). One disadvantage of this kind of sector-specific and organized civil society-focused PI is that non-affiliated individual citizens may perceive them to be far removed from their day-to-day concerns. This seems to have occurred to some degree in Brazil in the 2010s, when massive protests broke out over transit fare increases (Dagnino and Teixeira 2014: 59).

PIs that Favor Individual Citizen Participation

Some PIs are conceived for individual citizen participation. Members of civil society organizations can participate, but they do so in an individual capacity as citizens rather than as representatives of a movement. In these types of participatory mechanisms social movements tend not to play a relevant role. The ideal participant is a disaffiliated and depoliticized habitant concerned with micro-level local and neighborhood problems. Many participatory budgeting (PB) processes and neighborhood councils have this feature. They usually have a territorialized design in which participants never come into contact with the problems and concerns of their fellow citizens from other neighborhoods. This design promotes fragmentation in many small projects and discourages the development of redistributive strategies that might improve the life conditions of the most disadvantaged. Such designs are also associated with another crucial limit on effective participation processes: the small or even minuscule budget they usually have to execute projects selected by citizens.

PB in Argentina is perhaps an emblematic example of this dynamic. PB was first developed under that moniker in Porto Alegre, Brazil, in 1989, granting citizens the possibility to discuss and vote on municipal spending through deliberation in assemblies and selection of projects. It quickly expanded to other cities in Brazil and then to other cities in Latin America, leading to the emergence of cases in all countries in the region and on all continents, though designed differently in each country (Ganuza and Baiocchi 2012; Sintomer, Herzberg, and Röcke 2012). This accelerated worldwide expansion of PB was influenced both by the alter-globalization movements—particularly since Porto Alegre hosted the World Social Forum in 2001 (Oliveira 2017; Sintomer, Herzberg, and Röcke 2008)—and by international development organizations, particularly the World Bank (Goldfrank 2012). Despite the social justice principles of the original experience (Wampler 2012) and the emancipatory rhetoric that usually accompanies its adoption, the version of PB that is most widespread in the region and in the world is that of a technical and neutral instrument to improve administration (Ganuza and Baiocchi 2014), and sometimes it is no more than a label (Pateman 2012).

In Argentina, it was clearly a weak version of PB that was adopted most frequently. In Argentina it was only after the crisis of 2001 that the first experiences emerged, in the City of Buenos Aires and in Rosario. After 2008 there was an accelerated growth to reach fifty-nine experiences in fourteen provinces by 2013, declining to fifty-one in 2018 (Arena 2018: 126–27). It is estimated that 30% of the population lives in a municipality with PB (ibid.: 126). PB usually develops in four major stages. In the first stage citizens raise their ideas and concerns in neighborhood assemblies; in the second stage, the projects that arise from these ideas are elaborated in smaller assemblies to arrive at a definitive list that will be put to a vote; the third stage is the voting, which is usually open to the whole community; finally, the following year the municipal government executes the projects. Before the voting stage, the projects always undergo a "feasibility analysis," in which municipal officials filter the list established in the assemblies, defining which projects are technically feasible and which ones will be left out of the voting (Annunziata 2013). In almost half of the municipalities, participation rates are low, not even reaching 1.5% of the population and, on average, the municipalities that implement it allocate about 1.8% of their budget to this tool (Martínez and Arena 2013). The projects implemented with this mechanism are predominantly associated with low-cost urban infrastructure upgrading (street lights, improvements in squares, pruning, tree planting in public areas, removal of small garbage dumps, construction of wheelchair ramps, etc.) or "social" projects requiring a minimal budget and consisting mainly of courses offered by the municipality (art, dance, computers, etc.).

In addition to the small budget available through PB, the institutional design itself affects the narrow redistributive power of the mechanism. The proposals and projects are generated and selected in micro-local spaces, and the allocated budget is also distributed according to a predominantly territorial criterion. Other practices reinforce this tendency towards design-induced fragmentation. The motivations of citizens to participate are rooted in their daily experiences, in the problems or obstacles they suffer daily in their neighborhoods. When they participate, they do so by defending "my" project, competing with and compared to other citizens who have "their" projects in turn (Annunziata 2015), in a logic that can be characterized as similar to that of NIMBY ("not in my backyard") movements. This dynamic deters movements or organizations from proposing larger collective projects, since their members have to act as individuals and do not have any representative function. Even when movement members present themselves as non-organized actors, they are suspected of wanting to take advantage of a tool belonging to all neighbors for the benefit of their own organization.

It should be noted that the moment of expansion of PB in Argentina coincides with the consolidation of such important social movements as the *piqueteros*. Although a large part of their action strategies have been territorial (Rossi 2019), these movements did not participate in the mechanisms opened up "from above" by local governments. It could be said, rather, that the politicized vision of territorial representation held by the *piqueteros* had entered into competition with the depoliticized vision of the processes promoted by the authorities. The Argentinian case shows how participatory institutions and social movements can be paths that never cross.[3]

In general, the Argentinian design is similar to most but not all Latin American cases of PB. Most processes are conceived on a territorial basis, lack criteria of poverty or marginalization for distributing projects or resources, and involve individual citizen participation in open neighborhood assemblies followed by a voting stage for the selection of projects (Montecinos 2014). This institutional design, engaging individual citizens—which Wampler, McNulty, and Touchton (2018) call "open meetings"—may involve more people than other designs that restrict participation to civil society organizations, and has the advantage that it encourages participation of citizens who are less represented (Baiocchi 2001). At the same time, however, it promotes small, individual projects, and the election of projects at the end of the cycle can reverse the preferences of those who actively participated for several months during the assemblies, discouraging future activism.

PIs with Campaigning by Social Movements

There are other kinds of participatory institutions conceived for individual citizen voting but that in practice would never exist without the mobilization and campaigning of social movements. This is the case for some direct democracy mechanisms. The actual moment of participation in decision making is individual, but social movements play an indispensable role in activation of direct democracy mechanisms and in organizing political campaigns before the day of the election. Altman defines a mechanism of direct democracy (MDD) as "a publicly recognized institution wherein citizens decide or express their opinion on issues—other than through legislative and executive elections—directly at the ballot box through universal and secret vote" (Altman 2015: 3). Some MDDs are initiated by authorities—mandatory referendums and plebiscites proposed by the executive or legislative branches—and others are initiated from below by signature gathering. In these latter cases, popular consultations are activated when a threshold of collected signatures is reached. While for all mechanisms of direct democracy the campaigns prior to the electoral moment are fundamental for forming public opinion (Bernhard 2012; Welp and Lissidini 2016), in the case of mechanisms initiated by citizens, a double campaign is required: first to gather the signatures and trigger the mechanism, then to influence the vote. In this sense, MDDs, particularly the citizen-initiated ones, cannot be considered as instances of strictly individual participation because they demand significant societal mobilization.

The emblematic example of this third type of relationship between participatory institutions and social movements is the Citizen-Initiated Popular Consultation in Uruguay. Although in Latin America the use of mechanisms of direct democracy has multiplied during the last decades (Zovatto 2014), Uruguay stands out for the use of mechanisms activated "from below" by citizens (instead of by executive or legislative branches, or by the Constitution).[4] Uruguay is also the country with the strongest tradition of direct democracy experiences, since the introduction of these mechanisms dates from the beginning of the twentieth century and has more than double the impact of the regional average, according to the Direct Democracy Practical Potential index elaborated by Altman (2015). In the Uruguayan case, the threshold of signatures required to initiate a consultation is 10% of the electoral registry (Altman 2010), and the initiative may aim to propose laws or constitutional amendments or to revoke laws enacted by Congress.

Citizen-Initiated Popular Consultations in Uruguay have been used in reference to issues of great social, economic, and political impact. The role of these mechanisms to prevent privatization must be highlighted (Lissidini 2015). For example, in 1992, a referendum was activated to partially revoke the Privatization Law that had been approved in Congress and that enabled the Executive Power to privatize state-owned enterprises or services. The initiative was launched by the workers' unions of the public companies with the support of the political parties, particularly the Frente Amplio. In 2003, the unions also promoted—and won—a referendum against the law that had ended the monopoly of the state oil company Administración Nacional de Combustibles, Alcoholes y Portland (ANCAP). In 2004, businessmen, neighborhood associations, unions and environmental organizations met at the National Commission for the Defense of Water and Life to avoid the privatization of water services through a plebiscite. In addition to achieving this purpose, the citizens' initiative made it possible to declare that "access to potable water and to sanitation constitute fundamental human rights" (Lissidini 2015). Other policies of great social importance were approved through citizen initiatives, such as the regulations for the protection of retirees and pensioners' rights in 1994 (Altman 2011; Zovatto 2014). As we can see, the unions (especially those of employees of public companies) and organizations such as the Organización Nacional de Asociaciones de Jubilados y Pensionistas del Uruguay (ONAJPU) were essential actors in the campaigns for these initiatives. However, it should be noted that a key mobilizing force was the Frente Amplio, at that time an opposition party with which the social movements were allied (Altman 2010).[5]

As Bernhard (2012) shows, interest groups and social movement organizations play a crucial role during the campaigns because they provide the resources for mobilization. Mechanisms of direct democracy need a very strong and organized civil society, but even when this happens, political parties are often involved. The great demand for material, symbolic, and social resources (Lissidini 2015) supposed by MDDs—and especially by those initiated "from below"—before the day of the election, make the political parties their true protagonists to the extent that political use of such processes often distorts their original meaning (Welp and Serdült 2009, 2014). Nevertheless, the Uruguayan case reveals that direct democracy mechanisms can exercise much influence in politics even when they are not triggered, because the authorities take into account their existence, moderating their political decisions; this is what Matsusaka (2014) calls the "indirect effects" and Altman (2013) the "paradox" of direct democracy.

PIs Promoting Local Popular Organization

A fourth type of participatory institution encompasses those implemented to empower local civil society but in parallel to, separate from, and often in competition with existing local elected authorities. These local PIs are conceived as local popular organizations engaging in their own public decision-making processes, implementing the projects and policies they decide, and monitoring the results as well. The primary function of this type of PI is not as a state-society interface. Social movements here are not conceived to be co-governing with state officials or to be merely contributing to policy or budget decisions. Rather, the logic of this type of PI is that it can create local-level popular organization when and where it does not exist and can unite social movements where they do exist (though in practice they may replace existing movements rather than unite them). This type of PI is always territorially based, involving relatively small communities. The communitarian participation processes in some of the autonomous indigenous areas in Bolivia (Bazoberry Chali 2008; Mayorga 2014) and Venezuela's communal councils (Azzellini 2016) exemplify this type of PI.

In Bolivia, the processes of communitarian democracy in the frame of the so-called "Autonomías Indígenas Originarias Campesinas" (AIOC) have aimed at the recognition of traditional practices of indigenous peoples in terms of political organization and justice. The first autonomies emerged towards 2009 as in the case of Jesús de Machaca (Fernández 2018). In 2010, the Autonomies and Decentralization Framework Law, Number 031, was approved, which would regulate the conformation of the AIOC, the election of its authorities and forms of government according to their "uses and customs." In the 2010s some municipalities have approved autonomous statutes through referendums such as those of Charagua Iyambae, Uru Chipaya, and Raqaypampa, the only cases to have completed the entire process to become an AIOC (Tockman 2017).

Tomaselli (2015) points out that the procedure for creating autonomies is very complex, since it requires broad popular participation and at the same time presupposes homogeneous socio-cultural environments without providing mechanisms to resolve internal conflicts.

The experiments of this type involving the largest numbers of participants are Venezuela's communal councils (CCs). First appearing in the Bolivarian Constitution of 1999, the CCs can be created by between 150 and 400 families in urban areas and by a minimum of twenty families in rural areas and a minimum of ten families in indigenous areas (Goldfrank 2011: 177–82). The primary objectives of the CCs are to propose, implement, and monitor a community strategic plan, which can include projects and programs. The CCs operate through the citizens' assembly, which is supposed to gather together all who want to participate but particularly those activists who form part of the local *fuerzas vivas* or social movements. The citizens' assembly selects spokespeople to coordinate any number committees to address community issues ranging from health, housing, and water to security, gender equality, and alternative media. While in theory the CCs are conceived as a form of autonomous self-governance, and in fact typically bypass municipal governments, in practice they need to be registered with a national-level executive commission in order to receive funds. Indeed, by the late 2000s, official records indicated that more than 30,000 CCs had been created across Venezuela involving more than eight million participants, independent surveys suggested that about 35% of the adult population had attended at least one CC meeting, and the CCs had received roughly four billion dollars in order to carry out thousands of mostly small infrastructure projects as well as some housing and community development projects (Azzellini 2016: 102–03; Goldfrank 2011: 177–78).

Unlike the examples of the other three ideal types of PI presented earlier, all of which are envisioned to work in conjunction with and as complementary to existing representative institutions, the CCs are aimed at replacing and supplanting local and provincial elected authorities, which were starved of resources and responsibilities while the CCs received extensive funding (Eaton 2013: 433–35). Ultimately, the CCs in Venezuela were envisioned to link up together to form communes and eventually a communal state to replace the existing state and facilitate a transition to socialism (Ciccariello-Maher 2016: 20–21). The more movement-based *comuneros* viewed this through a "dual power" perspective in which the communes would maintain local control and autonomy, while government loyalists saw the process through a "vanguardist" lens as a way to help the ruling party consolidate power (Abbott and McCarthy 2019). With Venezuela's recent economic and political crisis, in practice the CCs have been starved of funds as the government has focused on distributing subsidized food baskets through new local organizations called Local Supply and Production Committees. While a few observers like Ciccariello-Maher (2016) and Azzellini (2016) continue to see advantages of the CCs and communes as empowering for subaltern social movements, most scholars highlight instead how the CCs have been used by the ruling party for clientelist purposes, which has only worsened with the CLAPs (García-Guadilla 2017). The experiences of the thousands of CCs certainly have varied, but significant disadvantages include the cooptation and subordination of previously autonomous social movements, the lack of internal pluralism, and the resulting sowing or deepening of distrust within communities (García-Guadilla 2018; Hanson 2018).

Conclusion

As we have seen, social movements can play different roles in participatory institutions. Each of these roles implies advantages and disadvantages and the nature of the role itself seems not to be a guarantee of more inclusive or meaningful participation. While some of the literature on PIs exalts one model above the rest, it is more useful to highlight the trade-offs between the diverse types of PI with regard to representativeness, inclusion, autonomy, and the ability to make an impact on social reality.

Institutions that favor the participation of social movements have greater potential to produce projects with more impact that allow for effective responses to demands for new rights, health issues, housing, public services, and the like, as we show with the examples of the BNPPCs, the CCs, and citizen-initiated MDDs. In these three types of social movement-oriented PIs, organized civil society is more involved than isolated individuals, and all three, in their own way, either in community concerns or at the national level, have had an impact on improving living conditions for the population. In contrast, their defect is that they tend to over-represent those already represented. These PIs can thus leave unaffiliated individual citizens, who are often far from politics and lacking the social and symbolic resources to participate, voiceless. The needs and concerns of a good part of the citizenry may thus be excluded. In turn, PIs that promote the participation of individual citizens better solve the problem of reaching those who do not have a voice, but at the same time they tend to produce projects that are so limited in scope that they fail to reduce inequalities or transform the living conditions of the most disadvantaged, as we observe in many PB experiences. The greater openness and inclusion with regard to who is entitled to participate seems to go hand in hand, paradoxically, with less inclusion in regard to the impact and scope of policies arising from participatory arenas.

Another significant trade-off between the types of PI has to do with the rate of participation and the autonomy of the participants from the state. PIs with greater openness to individual participants, without requirements of belonging to recognized civil society organizations, do not necessarily have higher participation rates. Citizens not affiliated with social movements or organizations are often reluctant to participate and their commitment is intermittent. The case of PB in Argentina, and in many other countries, demonstrates that not encouraging the protagonism of civil society organizations often leads to participatory spaces without participants. The three types of social movement-focused PIs tend to show higher rates of participation. On the other hand, stimulating the participation of organized civil society does not guarantee their autonomy with respect to the state or political actors in general. The BNPPCs and other mechanisms that establish participation quotas by social sector show the corporatist drift that many PIs can have. The citizen-initiated MDDs attest that social movements with greater capacity for mobilization are generally articulated in alliances with political parties. The CCs reveal another side of participation supported by community organizations: their strong potential for cooptation and instrumentalization by the government in office.

Since roughly the mid-2010s, the Latin American participatory boom has stalled. The causes of this stagnation—whether disenchantment with the ineffectiveness of PIs, the rise of right-wing governments in the region, or replacement by more administrative, technical, and less social movement friendly alternative paradigms such as Open Government, whose focus is on open data and transparency rather than participation—remain to be explored, but it is clear that the same has not happened with social movements. Citizen and trade-union street demonstrations, protests backed by social networks, women's marches, social and communitarian vetoes against extractive industry projects, petitions organized through online platforms for signature collection, and other forms of citizen intervention that are not institutionalized and not convened by governments could maintain the vitality of participation in the region. In these circumstances, the role of social movements will be as crucial as it was for the invention and expansion of PIs since the 1980s and 1990s.

Notes

1. One feature of the BNPPCs in Brazil which makes them unique among Latin American PIs is that they have allowed for an experiment with citizen participation that ascends progressively from the local scale until reaching the national level. Analyses of the BNPPCs suggest an increase of their deliberative potential at the higher levels (scaling up), particularly when arriving at the state and national levels. At the most local level, the informality of exchanges and more personal and narrative arguments predominate, with an important presence of "users knowledge," while at the highest levels it is possible to observe how even the same proposals are defended by using other kinds of arguments, with more technical, legal, and political information and a greater degree of generality (Avritzer 2015; Ramos 2013).
2. As Romão (2015) points out, in some cases workers in the public sector or businessmen have significant bargaining power.
3. While the origin of PB in cities like Buenos Aires and Rosario was in part a response to the assemblies' movement that emerged in the 2001–2002 crisis, very quickly the movement's members stopped participating. For the relationship between assemblies, the state, and PB, see Rossi (2017) and Ford (2013).
4. The MDDs initiated "from above" have revealed dubious results in the Latin American region: they have often been analyzed in terms of manipulation by plebiscitary leaders or, at least, of legitimization for the ruling elites (Altman 2010; Lissidini 2015); the same has been said about some of the MDDs initiated "from below" (Welp and Serdült 2012).
5. Altman (2011) even demonstrates that citizens vote in MMDs following party loyalty.

References

Abbott, Jared, and Michael McCarthy (2019), "Grassroots Participation in Defense of Dictatorship: Venezuela's Communal Councils and the Future of Participatory Democracy in Latin America," *The Fletcher Forum of World Affairs* 43(2), 95–116.

Altman, David (2010), "Plebiscitos, referendos e iniciativas populares en América Latina: ¿Mecanismos de control político o políticamente controlados?," *Perfiles Latinoamericanos* 35, 9–34.

Altman, David (2011), *Direct Democracy Worldwide* (New York: Cambridge University Press).

Altman, David (2013), "Bringing Direct Democracy Back In: Toward a Three-Dimensional Measure of Democracy," *Democratization* 20(4), 615–41.

Altman, David (2015), *Measuring the Potential of Direct Democracy Around the World (1900–2014)*, Working Paper Series no.17, The Varieties of Democracy Institute, University of Gothenburg.

Alvarez, Sonia, Gianpaolo Baiocchi, Agustín Laó-Montes, Jeffrey Rubin, and Millie Thayer (2017), "Interrogating the Civil Society Agenda, Reassessing Uncivic Political Activism," in Sonia E. Alvarez, Jeffrey W. Rubin, Millie Thayer, Gianpaolo Baiocchi, and Agustín Laó-Montes (eds.), *Beyond Civil Society: Activism, Participation, and Protest in Latin America*, 1–24 (Durham, NC: Duke University Press).

Annunziata, Rocío (2013), "Decisión y deliberación en las formas no electorales de participación en Argentina: El caso del Presupuesto Participativo," *Revista Estudios Políticos* 43, 115–35.

Annunziata, Rocío (2015), "Ciudadanía disminuida: la idea de la 'construcción de ciudadanía' en los dispositivos participativos contemporáneos," *Revista Temas y Debates* 30, 39–57.

Arena, Emiliano (2018), "Participatory Budgeting in Argentina (2002–2018): Advances and Setbacks in the Construction of a Participatory Agenda," in Nelson Dias (ed.), *Hope for Democracy: 30 years of Participatory Budgeting Worldwide*, 123–33 (Faro: Oficina).

Avritzer, Leonardo (2012), *Conferências Nacionais: Ampliando e redefinindo os padrões de participação social no Brasil*, IPEA Texto para discussão no. 1739, Rio de Janeiro: IPEA.

Avritzer, Leonardo (2015), *Los desafíos de la participación en América Latina* (Buenos Aires: Prometeo).

Azzellini, Dario (2016), *Communes and Workers' Control in Venezuela: Building 21st Century Socialism from Below* (Leiden: Brill).

Bacqué, Marie-Hélène, Henri Rey, and Yves Sintomer (2005), *Gestion de Proximité et Démocratie Participative. Une perspective comparative* (Paris: La Découverte).

Baiocchi, Gianpaolo (2001), "Participation, Activism and Politics: The Porto Alegre Experiment and Deliberative Democratic Theory," *Politics & Society* 29(1), 43–72.

Baiocchi, Gianpaolo (2017), "A Century of Councils: Participatory Budgeting and the Long History of Participation in Brazil," in Sonia E. Alvarez, Jeffrey W. Rubin, Millie Thayer, Gianpaolo Baiocchi, and Agustín Laó-Montes (eds.), *Beyond Civil Society: Activism, Participation, and Protest in Latin America*, 27–44 (Durham, NC: Duke University Press).

Baiocchi, Gianpaolo, Patrick Heller, and Marcelo Silva (2011), *Bootstrapping Democracy: Transforming Local Governance and Civil society in Brazil* (Stanford, CA: Stanford University Press).

Bazoberry Chali, Oscar (2008), *Participación, poder popular y desarrollo: Charagua y Moxos*, Cuadernos de Investigación CIPCA no. 68 (La Paz: CIPCA-U-PIEB).

Bernhard, Laurent (2012), *Campaign Strategy in Direct Democracy* (Basingstoke: Palgrave-Macmillan).

Cannon, Barry and Peadar Kirby (2012), "Civil Society-State Relations in Left-Led Latin America: Deepening Democratization?" in Cannon and Kirby, (eds.), *Civil Society and the State in Left-Led Latin America: Challenges and Limitations to Democratization*, 189–202 (London: Zed).

Ciccariello-Maher, George (2016), *Building the Commune: Radical Democracy in Venezuela* (London: Verso).

Dagnino, Evelina and Ana Cláudia Teixeira (2014), "The Participation of Civil Society in the Lula's Government," *Journal of Politics in Latin America* 6(3), 39–66.

Dagnino, Evelina, Alberto Olvera, and Aldo Panfichi (2006), "Para uma outra leitura da disputa pela construção democrática na América Latina," in Evelina Dagnino, Alberto Olvera, and Aldo Panfichi, (eds.), *A disputa pela construção democrática na América Latina*, 13–91 (São Paulo: Paz e Terra – Unicamp).

Eaton, Kent (2013), "The Centralism of 'Twenty-First-Century Socialism': Recentralising Politics in Venezuela, Ecuador and Bolivia," *Journal of Latin American Studies* 45(3), 421–50.

Faria, Cláudia Feres, Viviane Petinelli Silva, and Isabella Lourenço Lins (2012), "Conferências de políticas públicas: um sistema integrado de participação e deliberação?," *Revista Brasileira de Ciência Política* 7, 249–84.

Fernández, Francisca (2018), "Municipio, sistema de cargo y autonomía indígena en Bolivia: el caso de Jesús de Machaca, departamento de La Paz," *Journal of Latin American and Caribbean Anthropology* 23(3), 579–92.

Ford, Alberto (2013), *Experimentos democráticos: Asambleas barriales y Presupuesto Participativo en Rosario (2002-2005)* (Saarbrücken: Publicia).

Ganuza, Ernesto and Gianpaolo Baiocchi (2012), "The Power of Ambiguity: How Participatory Budgeting Travels the Globe," *Journal of Public Deliberation* 8 (2), Article 8.

Ganuza, Ernesto and Gianpaolo Baiocchi (2014), "Beyond the Line: The Participatory Budget as an Instrument," in Nelson Dias (ed.), *Hope for Democracy: 25 years of Participatory Budgeting Worldwide*, 65–74 (Sao Bras de Alportel: In Loco).

García-Guadilla, María Pilar (2017), "El socialismo petrolero venezolano en la encrucijada por su supervivencia: El soberano unívoco, la inclusión neoliberal y la participación leninista," *LASA Forum* 48(1), 43–47.

García-Guadilla, María Pilar (2018), "Exclusionary Inclusion: Post-Neoliberal Incorporation of Popular Sectors and Social Movements in New Left 21st Century Socialism: The Experience of Venezuela," in Eduardo Silva and Federico M. Rossi (eds.), *Reshaping the Political Arena in Latin America: From Resisting Neoliberalism to the Second Incorporation*, 72–89 (Pittsburgh, PA: University of Pittsburgh Press).

Goldfrank, Benjamin (2011), "The Left and Participatory Democracy: Brazil, Uruguay, and Venezuela," in Steven Levitsky and Kenneth Roberts (eds.), *The Resurgence of the Latin American Left*, 162–83 (Baltimore, MD: Johns Hopkins University Press).

Goldfrank, Benjamin (2012), "The World Bank and the Globalization of Participatory Budgeting," *Journal of Public Deliberation* 8(2), Article 7.

Goldfrank, Benjamin (2017), "Participatory Budgeting in Latin American Cities," in Thomas Angotti (ed.), *Urban Latin America: Inequalities and Neoliberal Reforms*, 113–28 (Lanham, MD: Rowman & Littlefield).

Goldfrank, Benjamin (2018), "Brazil's Participatory System in Comparative Context," *Latin American Studies Association Annual Meeting*, May 23–26, Barcelona.

Hanson, Rebecca (2018), "Deepening Distrust: Why Participatory Experiments Are Not Always Good for Democracy," *The Sociological Quarterly* 59(1), 145–67.

Lima, Valesca (2019), "The Limits of Participatory Democracy and the Inclusion of Social Movements in Local Government," *Social Movement Studies* 18(6), 667–81.

Lissidini, Alicia (2014), "Paradojas de la participación en América Latina: ¿Puede la democracia directa institucionalizar la protesta?" in Alicia Lissidini, Yanina Welp, and Daniel Zovatto (eds.), *Democracias en movimiento: Mecanismos de democracia directa y participativa en América Latina*, 71–106 (México: UNAM- IDEA).

Lissidini, Alicia (2015), "Democracia directa en América Latina: Avances, contradicciones y desafíos," in Anja Minnaert and Gustavo Endara (eds), *Democracia participativa e izquierdas: Logros, contradicciones, y desafíos*, 121–90 (Quito: Friedrich Ebert Stiftung).

Martínez, Carlos and Emiliano Arena (2013), *Experiencias y buenas prácticas en Presupuesto Participativo* (Buenos Aires: UNICEF).

Matsusaka, John (2014), "Disentangling the Direct and Indirect Effects of the Initiative Process," *Public Choice* 160(3–4), 345–66.

Mayorga, Fernando (2014), *Incertidumbres tácticas: Ensayos sobre democracia, populismo y ciudadanía* (La Paz: PIEB-Plural).

Montecinos, Egon (2014), "Diseño institucional y participación ciudadana en los presupuestos participativos: Los casos de Chile, Argentina, Perú, República Dominicana y Uruguay," *Política y Gobierno* 21(2), 351–78.

Oliveira, Osmany Porto de (2017), *International Policy Diffusion and Participatory Budgeting: Ambassadors of Participation, International Institutions, and Transnational Networks* (Cham: Palgrave-Macmillan).

Pateman, Carole (2012), "Participatory Democracy Revisited," *Perspectives on Politics* 10(1), 7–19.

Petinelli, Viviane (2014), "O impacto das conferências nas políticas nacionais e seus condicionantes: A 1ª conferência de aquicultura e pesca, de cidades, de meio ambiente, de esporte, de mulheres e de promoção da igualdade racial," *IX Encontro da Associação Brasileira da Ciência Política*, Brasília, August 4–7.

Pogrebinschi, Thamy (2017), "Democratic Innovation: Lessons from Beyond the West," in The Hertie School of Governance (ed.), *The Governance Report 2017*, 57–72 (Oxford: Oxford University Press).

Pogrebinschi, Thamy and David Samuels (2014), "The Impact of Participatory Democracy: Evidence from Brazil's National Public Policy Conferences," *Comparative Politics* 46(3), 313–32.

Ramos, Alfredo (2013), "Conferência Nacional de Política para as mulheres: interações discursivas e implicações para a legitimidade epistêmica," in Leonardo Avritzer and Clóvis Henrique Leite de Souza (eds.), *Conferências Nacionais: atores, dinâmicas participativas e efetividade*, 95–121 (Brasília: IPEA).

Risley, Amy (2015), *Civil Society Organizations, Advocacy, and Policy Making in Latin American Democracies: Pathways to Participation* (New York: Palgrave-Macmillan).

Romão, Wagner (2015), "Políticas públicas y democracia participativa: avances y límites de las conferencias nacionales en Brasil," in Anja Minnaert and Gustavo Endara (eds.), *Democracia participativa e izquierdas: logros, contradicciones y desafíos*, 239–94 (Quito: Friedrich-Ebert-Stiftung).

Rossi, Federico M. (2017), "Compulsion Mechanisms: State-Movement Dynamics in Buenos Aires," *Social Movement Studies* 16(5), 578–94.

Rossi, Federico M. (2019), "Conceptualising and Tracing the Increased Territorialisation of Politics: Insights·from Argentina," *Third World Quarterly* 40(4), 815–37.

Rossi, Federico M. and Marisa von Bülow (eds.) (2015), *Social Movement Dynamics: New Perspectives on Theory and Research from Latin America* (Farnham: Ashgate).

Schneider, Cecilia and Yanina Welp (2011), "¿Transformación democrática o control político? Análisis comparado de la participación ciudadana institucional en América del Sur," *Íconos: Revista de Ciencia Sociales* 40, 21–39.

Sintomer, Yves, Carsten Herzberg and Anja Röcke (2008), *Les budgets participatifs en Europe. Des services publics au service du public* (Paris: La Découverte).

Sintomer, Yves, Carsten Herzberg and Anja Röcke (2012), "Modelos transnacionais de participação cidadã: O caso do Orçamento Participativo," *Sociologias* 14(30), 70–116.

Tomaselli, Alexandra (2015), "Autogobierno Indígena: El caso de la autonomía indígena originaria campesina en Bolivia," *Política, Globalidad y Ciudadanía* 1(1), 73–97.

Tockman, Jason (2017), "The Hegemony of Representation: Democracy and Indigenous Self-Government in Bolivia," *Journal of Politics in Latin America* 9(2), 121–38.

Touchton, Michael and Brian Wampler (2014), "Improving Social Well-Being Through New Democratic Institutions," *Comparative Political Studies* 47(10), 1442–69.

Wampler, Brian (2012), "Participatory Budgeting: Core Principles and Key Impacts," *Journal of Public Deliberation* 8(2), Article 12.

Wampler, Brian, Stephanie McNulty, and Michael Touchton (2018), *Participatory Budgeting: Spreading Across the Globe*, Transparency Initiative, January, https://www.transparency-initiative.org/wp-content/uploads/2018/03/spreading-pb-across-the-globe_jan-2018.pdf.

Welp, Yanina and Alicia Lissidini (2016), "Democracia directa, poder y contrapoder. Análisis del referendo del 21 de febrero de 2016 en Bolivia," *Bolivian Studies Journal/Revista de Estudios Bolivianos* 22, 162–90.

Welp, Yanina and Uwe Serdült (eds.) (2009), *Armas de doble filo: La participación ciudadana en la encrucijada* (Buenos Aires: Prometeo).

Welp, Yanina and Uwe Serdült (2012), "Direct Democracy Upside Down," *Taiwan Journal of Democracy* 8(1), 69–92.

Welp, Yanina and Uwe Serdült (eds.) (2014), *La dosis hace el veneno. Análisis de la revocatoria del mandato en América Latina, Estados Unidos y Suiza* (Quito: Instituto de la Democracia).

Zaremberg, Gisela (2012), ""We're Either Burned or Frozen Out": Society and Party Systems in Latin American Municipal Development Councils (Nicaragua, Venezuela, Mexico, and Brazil)," in Maxwell Cameron, Eric Hershberg and Kenneth Sharpe (eds.), *New Institutions for Participatory Democracy in Latin America. Voice and Consequence* (New York: Palgrave-Macmillan), 21–51.

Zaremberg, Gisela, Marcela Torres Wong and Valeria Guarneros-Meza (2018), "Descifrando el desorden: Instituciones Participativas y conflictos en torno a megaproyectos en México," *América Latina Hoy*, 79, 81–102.

Zovatto, Daniel (2014), "Las instituciones de la democracia directa," in Alicia Lissidini, Yanina Welp and Daniel Zovatto (eds.), *Democracias en movimiento. Mecanismos de democracia directa y participativa en América Latina* (Mexico: UNAM- IDEA), 13–70.

CHAPTER 46

SOCIAL MOVEMENTS AND MODES OF INSTITUTIONALIZATION

ADRIAN GURZA LAVALLE AND JOSÉ SZWAKO

INTRODUCTION

Within most of the prominent analytical approaches that we have at our disposal today, social movements and institutionalization maintain, at best, an uneasy relationship to one another. Social mobilization and institutions are terms that have traditionally sat at opposite ends of the civil society/state divide, associated on the one hand with the correlated concepts of autonomy, social change and contestation, and with domination, status quo, and repression on the other.

For historical reasons, the field of social movements has been marked from the outset by the mobilization of "outsider" or "anti-system" actors engaged in the defense of civil rights and in emergent causes, such as environmentalism and the transformation of ways of life. These origins made the literature sensitive to the internal dynamics and transformative potential of the complex systems of collective action that we know, conceptually, as social movements. Yet this has also had a cognitive toll. It has limited our understanding of institutionalization processes, bestowing on them a negative valence flowing from their presumed connection to demobilization and movement bureaucratization (Giugni and Passy 1998; Goldstone 2003). Although the imagery emanating from the field of the study of social movements is still in thrall to the contentious politics of anti-systems actors (Tilly and Tarrow 2006), the current literature has developed a focus on the constitutive role that political institutions play in the success of social mobilization (Skocpol 1992), definitions of movements' action strategies (Amenta 1998; Banaszak 2005), and the conformation of organizational repertoires, as well as the impact of movements on the conformation of state administrative capacities (Clemens 1997). This focus, it is worth mentioning, does not privilege institutional dimensions in detriment to social movement dynamics. Rather, it opposes dualism and views institutional dimensions as constitutive of mobilization and, vice-versa—which means that movement actions are also conceived as constitutive of state capacities.

Analytical interest in the relevance of institutionalization for Latin American social movements is rooted in conjuncture. The electoral consecration of Left and center-Left parties throughout the sub-continent during the 2000s has awarded greater visibility to the fact that social movements and civil society organizations have functions or at least some role in the structuring and execution of public policies. Governments of the so-called "Pink Tide" in Latin America presented a challenge to our theoretical and political imagination, bearing the promise and wager to "open" the doors of the state and of social policy to "outsiders." This has certainly occurred with variation in pace, meanings and degrees of openness. In South America in particular, these processes have meant ample coalitions and political party fronts in which former "comrades" from different parties, trade unions and popular movements take part together in governments and bureaucratic machinery, complexifying and complicating state/civil society relations.

It is this set of circumstances which triggers the development of a new analytical focus on the relationship between social movements and institutionalization. After the neoliberal wave of the 1990s and throughout the period associated with the "Pink Tide," social movements came back on stage with a protagonism that was reminiscent of their influential performance within an earlier period of democratic transitions (see Inclán in this volume). Yet in reality, movements had never really abandoned political struggles (Dagnino, Olvera, and Panfichi 2006).

Interpellated by this new scenario, part of the social movement literature devoted to Latin America has become more focused on the forms and patterns of state/civil society interactions and their institutional effects. In criticizing earlier dichotomous assumptions, analyses have questioned how civil actors (namely, trade unions and social movements) shape and re-shape the political arena, generating effects such as the expansion of social policy and reincorporation of marginalized social groups (Collier and Collier 1991; Garay 2016; Rossi 2017; Silva and Rossi 2018). These critiques have worked to improve our understanding of social movements and their interactions, through new concepts. The notion of "political project," for example, brings out the transversality of alliances between parts of civil society and the state (Dagnino, Olvera, and Panfichi 2006), while emphasis on "practical authority" provides evidence of the creative consequences that the relations between state and social actors have on politics (Abers and Keck 2013). Furthermore, notions such as "repertoire of strategies" (Rossi 2017) and "domains of agency" (Gurza Lavalle et al. 2019) enable us to move beyond the implicit structuralism of the notion of contentious repertoires, highlighting the institutionalizing tactics and abilities of social actors in their relations with authorities. The progressive refinement of the new research agenda has meant rethinking how political system, parties, elected authorities, bureaucracies, and coalitions enter into analytical equations (Gurza Lavalle and Szwako 2015), with particular emphasis on social movements' agency as builders of "state capacities" and "institutional fits" capable of transforming policy permeability (Gurza Lavalle et al. 2019). An immense variety of empirical cases have been brought to bear, reflecting the relevance of state/civil society interactions around issues of institutional dynamics and moving far beyond the so-called "social question" and struggles for recognition (see Rossi; Fontana in this volume). To mention only two examples, over the last few decades Latin American social movement organizations have not only touched but also played significant roles in environmental governance, as well as in media reform policy (De Castro et al. 2016; Segura and Waisbord 2016; Zimmerer, 2011; Christel and Gutiérrez in this volume).

Inspired by historical institutionalism, our understanding of the processes, actors, and factors involved in institutionalization dynamics is relational and centered around the political system and state actors' interactions with movements and civil society organizations. Above all, our perspective rests on the premise of the mutual constitution of civil society and the state. Thus, when we speak of institutionalization, we are dealing with the state/society co-production of artifacts, instruments, knowledge, technologies, and capacities that become institutions *through* state and civil society interactions. This means relinquishing externalist or autonomist explanations which—explicitly or not—presume a dichotomous separation or opposition between social movements and actors they target in political and institutional positions. It means moving beyond the externalist forms of reasoning that are evident in judgements in which social movements are defined as operating "from below" (cf. Garay 2016: 29) or seen as gaining their efficacy in influencing public policy from their "autonomous" or isolated position in relation to the institutional world (cf. Htun and Weldon 2018).

In emphasizing dynamics of mutual constitution or co-determination, we assert that the actors and networks of civil society transform their demands, values, and resources for action within state institutions. This means they act not "from below," but via processes of interaction against, through, and from within the state, which may also lead to the strengthening and creation of state capacities (Gurza Lavalle et al. 2019). Similar understandings inspired by other analytical perspectives exist and we maintain a dialogue with them. Most notable in this regard are feminist approaches, especially as they develop notions such as that of "state feminism" (Mazur and McBride 2008; Johnson and Sempol in this volume) and demonstrate the role of "activists or organizations located within the State" (Banaszak 2005: 150). In fact, feminist literature has been successful in showing how feminist struggles have "raised public awareness about questions of gender, lobbied state officials, and worked *with or within* the state to help formulate state policy" (Htun 2003: 5 italics added).

Research agendas directed towards the institutionalization of social movement demands enjoy a wide scope and the list of possible case studies is very extensive. Our focus here is necessarily more limited and we do not intend to offer an encyclopedic list of specific examples. Rather, we examine the modes of institutionalization through which social movements demands have become public policy, and their occurrence within the context of social movements/state relations in Latin America during the period that spans the 1980s democratic transitions to the years of the leftward shift of the 2000s and 2010s. We propose four highly relevant modes of institutionalization based on our own research experience and cumulative knowledge. Thus, we identify

(1) programmatic, (2) symbolic, (3) practical, and (4) positional institutionalization as four modes for the institutionalization of social movement interests, values, and resources for action. We use these modes to analyze LGBT and family farmer (peasant) movements in different parts of the region, as well as other movements that may be pertinent to only one of these modes, becoming emblematic examples of institutionalization in these particular terms.

It is important to mention that we are speaking of "modes" rather than "models" or "ideal types." This means that we are referring to the recurrent ways in which institutionalization works, shaping the behavior of social and state actors, rather than signifying a mere stylization for the purposes of normative evaluation or for empirical evaluation based on pure types. In focusing on modes and contemplating their occurrence within a variety of social movements and policies, we relinquish a more thorough reconstruction of the processes and interactions that have led to the cases of institutionalization that we examine. Although institutionalization is a political construction and can only be understood case by case or comparatively, through the reconstruction of the processes that produce it, this is not a task we have chosen to take on here. Last, we do not discuss the effects of institutionalization, nor do we presume, a priori, that they are desirable or defensible.

Modes of Institutionalization

All of the movements that we examine here underwent notable experiences of institutionalization over the course of democratic transitions and, later, with the leftward turn, albeit individually marked by their own particular trajectory and dynamics. The gay movement experienced a moment of expansion in the region during the 1980s, in reaction to the expanding HIV/AIDS epidemic. It took on a crucial role in the development of policies in the health field, notwithstanding the severe stigmatization of the group it advocated for, subjects defined as a "risk group" (Pecheny and de la Dehesa 2011). In this context, there were growing demands for the recognition of transexual identities (LGBTT) which multiplied and contributed to the defense of diversity that was central to the 1990s. The movement was also vocal within struggles for the approval of anti-discrimination and identity-affirming legislation (Serrano-Amaya and Santos 2016; see Díez in this volume).

With the exception of Chile, institutionalization of policies for family farming on the continent occurred after the realization of wider processes of political redemocratization and economic stabilization. Under the leadership of actors from rural Brazil and the strong influence of initiatives such as MERCOSUL's "Specialized Meeting on Family Farming" (Sabourin et al. 2014), movements in support of family farming have found relevant fits and roles in processes of policy making. With the leverage received primarily from Pink Tide governments, family farming policies have generally been situated within a broader package of policies, such as food security and territorial and rural development (Schneider 2016). The movements that we devote our attention to here are merely a few of those that have to a greater or lesser extent followed the inflections wrought by democratization and the leftward turn. A key example can be found in the way indigenous or native peoples' movements became emergent actors in the region as of the 1990s. They gained singular protagonism during the constitutional processes that were encouraged by the governments of Rafael Correa in Ecuador and Evo Morales in Bolivia (Toledo 2005).

Programmatic Institutionalization

Programmatic institutionalization refers to the most visible, and often the most potent attempts to institutionalize the agendas and interpretative schemas of social movements. It consists of the creation of administrative organs, the definition of specific programs and policies, the approval of laws, and the creation of permanent channels of intermediation between state institutions and social actors (participatory institutions) (see Annunziata and Goldfrank in this volume). Cases can be considered to represent programmatic institutionalization insofar as they explicitly express the connection between movements and institutions, awarding a relatively stable influence to the former in making of public policies. Given its visibility and relevance, this mode of institutionalization is the most studied by the literature.

Argentina became noteworthy within Latin America for its recognition of LGBTT rights through legislative measures, and most significantly, through its Egalitarian Marriage (2010) and Gender Equality (2012) legislation. In both cases, a decisive role was played by the Instituto Nacional contra la Discriminación, la Xenofobia y el Racismo (INADI), which had been created a decade earlier, in 1995, as a privileged channel for interaction between the LGBTT movement and the state (Colling 2015).[1] In Brazil, programmatic institutionalization did not have its origin in legislative pathways. Rather, it began within the ambit of executive power, which was in fact a general tendency of institutionalization processes in this country in which participatory institutional arrangements implemented in trans-sectorial fields linked to social movement demands emerged as innovations in terms of influence on public policies (Isunza and Gurza Lavalle 2018). This was the case of the National Council to Combat Discrimination and for the Advancement of LGBT Rights and the National LGBT Conference, both with subnational versions at state and municipal levels. Perhaps the most emblematic case of programmatic institutionalization in relation to LGBTT movements and the state is the Brazil without Homophobia Program (2004), a sort of "metaprogram" which was very broad in scope and devoted to designing and implementing public policy programs and actions for the civil, political, and social rights of the LGBTT population. It included the introduction of education on sexual orientation into official national curriculum parameters, as well as policies to combat HIV/AIDS (de la Dehesa 2010; Feitosa 2017). In Mexico, in keeping with a focus on the national level, progress was more timid—the Federal Law to Prevent and End Discrimination (2003) and the creation of the National Day Against Homophobia, by executive decree (2014). In a sharper form than in Argentina, institutionalization in Mexico has been related to the mobilization of marginalized groups, rather than primarily through the LGBT movement. Campaigns against homophobia were conducted by the National Council for the Prevention of Discrimination (Salinas 2008).

Specificities aside, the trajectory that the institutionalization of public policies for family farming takes in Latin America reveals strong parallels and continuities between national cases. Particularly within the countries of the Southern Cone, "[from] 1995 until today, the emergence and dissemination of specific policies expressly directed towards family farming" (Sabourin et al. 2014: 22) are noteworthy. Countries such as Argentina, Brazil, Chile, Cuba, and Uruguay have maintained specific policies for that sector of society, while most of the other nations in the region sustain policies that have only indirect impact on family farming. A recurrent theme in existing analyses is the formation of advocacy coalitions, as well as the presence, within such coalitions, of militants who are members of rural movements and unions that "are able to build alliances with technical and academic segments" (Sabourin et al. 2014: 24). In all these cases, state action has been decisive in supporting family farming (Schneider 2016: 5). An equally influential factor in national cases of specific policies for family farming is the interaction with agencies such as the Food and Agriculture Organization (FAO). In Argentina, Brazil, and Uruguay, the establishment of specific programs unfolds through the institutionalization of the agenda of family farming within government ministries (establishing specific "secretariats" or "directorates"). It is no coincidence that in these three cases, there is noteworthy presence of significant rural peak associations that have built coalitions in defense of family farming and strategically aligned themselves with authorities and academic communities (cf. Sabourin et al. 2014; Nogueira et al. 2017).

Black movement organizations in Brazil are another good example of the programmatic mode of institutionalization (see Dixon and Caldwell in this volume). There, the issue of health emerged out of a generic demand for inclusion, taking on the state in the context of the military dictatorship. Slowly, over the course of thirty years, this demand evolved into the creation of a specific field of public policy, that is, the "health of the Black population," thereby converging with actions taken by the government organ for the promotion of racial equality, the Special Ministry for the Advancement of Racial Equality, which operated during the Lula administration (Lima 2010). Less fortunate than the aforementioned movements in terms of substantive effects of institutionalization, the uprising of the Ejército Zapatista de Liberación Nacional in Mexico was followed by the dismantling of indigenista ideology (Spanakos and Romo, Rice in this volume). This led to the extinction of the fifty-year old National Indigenist Institute, which symptomatically handed its assets and resources over to the government for the creation, in 2003, of the National Commission for the Development of Indigenous People (Saldívar 2011).

Symbolic Institutionalization

Symbolic institutionalization refers to the forging of categories of classification, that is, the ways of the naming and morally ordering the world that social movements use in articulating demands and making grievances known. Such categories can, on the one hand, be constructed in such a way as to ressignify earlier world views. This is illustrated by contemporary uses of the terms "race" and "queer," which tend to produce new positive content through activism and performance (see Johnson and Sempol; Dixon and Caldwell in this volume). On the other hand, categories used to classify the world, drawing attention to injustice and inequality, can be constructed in such a way as to create or express a *sui generis* characteristic that stands in contrast or in opposition to other categories. One way or another, it is through different historical mechanisms and processes of interaction between actors and state institutions, movements, and civil organizations that such categories come to shape the juridical and administrative language of the state and are utilized by bureaucrats, parties, and politicians in their conception and execution of public policies, producing effects on design and implementation of the latter. That is, through interactions with non-state actors, these symbolic categories become a central part of the ways in which the world is cognitively apprehended by political agents situated within state institutions and in the social world (see Szwako and Gurza Lavalle 2019). The constitutive effect of naming/classification is particularly visible insofar as it assumes the shape of a law, yet functions similarly when it becomes part of operation of policies through administrative rules of lower hierarchy.

Among all the experiences of social mobilization that span the 1970–2010 period, no other movement stands out as much as LGBTT activism has for its engagement—in defense of diversity—in the constructive labor of (self) naming (Fachini 2005).[2] Its categorization, however, moves beyond the internal redefinition of the movement, engaging in intense discursive negotiation over state systems of classification and creating "world-producing" effects through legislation and public policies. In Argentina, the Law on Egalitarian Marriage not only recognized transgender and homosexual affectivity and family arrangements as equal to those of heterosexually based families, but also awarded priority to the revision of criteria used to determine paternity, maternity, and kinship relations. Again privileging legislative forms of action, the LGBT movement engaged itself in the definition and promulgation of the new Civil and Comercial Code of Argentina, which adopted the concept of *"procreational will"* as a category awarding equal value to biological relations, adoption and assisted reproduction. In Brazil, the very adoption of the abbreviation "LGBT" responded to an agreement that was made during the First National Conference of Gays, Lesbians, Bisexuals, Travestis, Transgenders and Transexuals (as called by the federal executive), as official denomination approved with the endorsement of government representatives. With more evident implications, especially given its consequences for Family Law, the LGBT movement's engagement with the Ordem dos Advogados do Brasil and with the Judiciary Introduced a grammar of feeling and homoaffectivity (rather than sexuality or eroticism) as anchor in the defense of rights and constitutional review by Supreme Court (Nichnig 2014). Coming from a more hermetic political context marked by the mass presence of conservative lawmakers, the Mexican LGBT movement took steps forward at the level of local legislatures and through categories of translation that circumvented the lexicon of identity, yet carved a political space for negotiating the defense of its demands (de la Dehesa 2010). The Legislative Assembly of the Federal District presented its first bill on civil unions that were different from the heterosexual nuclear family. It was written up by a female lawmaker from the LGBT movement, promoting the category of "convivial societies" as a form of civil partnership tied neither to sex nor to marital status (ibid.: 268).

The institutionalization of the category of "family agriculture" through public policy is complex. It includes both the multiple forms of self-classification of rural and ethnic identities and state definition of criteria regarding the target population of family farming policy. Thus, although official national definitions vary, using "peasant agriculture," "small scale agriculture," or "small scale production" as terminology, family farming policies bring out a myriad of local identities, such as *colonos*, *ribeirinhos*, *éjidos*, *minifundistas*, and *chacareros*, to mention but a few. Furthermore, in addition to operating as an institutional fit, such policies also became an opportunity for demands of recognition and financing of identities, as in the cases of organic farmers, traditional fishermen, communities displaced by dam-building, and Afro-descendents (cf. Grisa and Schneider 2015). At the root of these transformations lay not only the mobilization of rural movements but also the advances in research that no longer saw these forms of rural life as synonyms of backwardness and poverty (Picolotto 2014). Incorporating such perspectives, international agencies and more recent policies on family farming now understand specific modes of the reproduction of life as the distinctive trait of their target population. They also consider the ways in which different populations conjugate and create their own hierarchies from the elements "family labor," "land size," and "productivity" (Schneider 2016). The Argentine "Law of Historical Reparation of the Family Farming" is a telling expression of this cognitive capacity, representing the legal consolidation of the category of "family farmer" while able to account for and benefit the above-mentioned variety of groups and symbolic designations it holds (see Welch in this volume).

An emblematic case of symbolic institutionalization can be found in the case of the ethnic movements of the Andean region and the category of "good living"—"buen vivir" or "vivir bien," in its Spanish versions.[3] At the height of the Pink Tide, the progressive governments of Evo Morales, in Bolivia, and Rafael Correa, in Ecuador, brought the concept of "good living" into their pluri-national constitutions. In the Bolivian case, "good living" appeared, alongside other indigenous categories, as one of the major values and moral and ethical principles promoted by the state, and a guiding principle of the economic model that the nation had adopted. In the Ecuadorian case, the category was written into its entire constitution, guiding the public policies implemented within a number of sectors and extending into environmental issues ("the rights of nature"), development regime, and defense of the country's economic sovereignty. Although each country institutionalized the notion of "good living" in its own way, the category, in addition to its internal diversity (Gudynas 2011), denotes a critical conception of the production and reproduction of life and an alternative to conventional (Western and capitalist) modes of development (Farah and Vasapollo 2011).

Practical Institutionalization

Practical institutionalization operates within an environment that is seen as "technical" and for this reason often goes unnoticed. Policies presuppose diagnostics of public problems and/or needs as well as solutions based on known forms of dealing with them. In order to operate, policies produce a range of *policy instruments* which are not merely technical apparatuses but have a life of their own, instigating actors to do certain things rather than others (Lascoumes and Le Galès 2007). Thus, we are dealing not only with diagnostics that select solutions and instruments, but also with the converse relationship in which the latter determine the way politics operate. Although political instruments may be taken for granted as "technical" resources, they may also become the object of intense dispute at the time of their institutionalization. Instruments can have their genesis in bureaucracy or the state but may also express a socio-genesis in which processes of interaction between institutions and movements make social techniques migrate to the domain of policy. Part of the way in which policies are made operational, such as in the case of community credit or the collective practices of home-building within the ambit of social housing policies, has its origin in social techniques developed by civil actors. In such cases, we are able to refer to a practical mode of institutionalization in which the "technical" dimension of state ways of operation and problem-solving are susceptible to "de-naturalizing" and coming to be understood as a result of the interactional dynamics of institutionalization.

Promoting the sexual and reproductive health of youth and combating prejudice through state-sponsored public education is a potent policy, given its capilarity and operation at the micro-level. Nonetheless, it begs the question of *how* to proceed with classroom discussions on the matter and *how* to train teachers to carry them out. In Brazil, LGBT movement organizations worked in collaboration with the Ministry of Health and the Ministry of Education for two years in putting together the *Adolescent and Youth Guidebook for Peer Education* and the *Kit for Combating Homophobia*, which unfortunately gained notoriety through its reframing by right-wing politicians as the "*gay toolkit.*" The former material was implemented and suspended, later, in the heat of the veto orchestrated by conservative factions within the House of Representatives (Oliveira Júnior and Maio 2015; Payne in this volume). Both sets of proposals were policy instruments, one an instrument for classroom use in promoting horizontal methods to aid in the struggle against prejudice (peer education) and the other, a vehicle for specific pertinent topics.

The relationship between education and sexual diversity is a sensitive matter which in Argentina galvanized public opinion when the publication of the "Law of Sexual Education," in 2006, and the Program for Integral Social Education developed as public policy responsible for bringing changes to fruition. In this case, the *Curriculum Guidelines* were conceived as an instrument to orient teachers' classroom work. Their implementation became possible due to concessions made to conservative sectors and written into the Guidelines text, allowing each school be able to adjust state-defined content according to its own community and institutional educational project (Esquivel 2013). In Mexico, where a religious party was among the prime forces within the party system, the doors to the dispute around the topic of sexual diversity in education remained closed to the LGBT movement. Nonetheless, the "Program for Sexual and Reproductive Health for Teens," created in 2006, was able to implement the country's first policy focusing on sexual (rather than merely reproductive) health. Movement organizations were engaged in the definition of materials for the dissemination of policy content outside the school milieu (Estrada 2013).

In the case of rural policies over the last few decades, there is a wide range of practical instruments that go beyond common lines of action such as credit, financing, and technical assistance. In the Uruguayan case, for example, the enforcement of the 2007 "Law for the Decentralization and Coordination of Agricultural Policies" found a concrete space for local participation in the *Rural Development Tables*. Even in countries such as Paraguay and Nicaragua, whose policy institutions are less friendly to family farming, *public purchases* or *crop insurance* are in place (Sabourin et al. 2014: 30). Argentina and Uruguay, in turn, keep a *record* in which the dimensions and beneficiaries of family farming policies are quantified. In Brazil, innovations in practical institutionalization have included forms of certification, with *seals* and *certification of capabilities* provided by associations that act as a sort of gatekeeper for seal prestige. Still within the rural world, a notable case of practical institutionalization can be found in Brazil's cisterns. Intermittent shortages of drinking water and long periods of drought are well-known facts of life in the semi-arid region that covers a large portion of the northeastern Brazilian interior. Through a partnership between the Ministry of Social Development and the Articulação Semiárido Brasileiro (ASA), the "One Million Cisterns Program" (P1MC) was conceived and developed. The program's major goal was the building of water storage cisterns for the families and communities of Brazil's semi-arid zone who suffer from lack of water suitable for human consumption. Within the ambit of the program's conception, ASA militants reframed the problem of drought, shifting the emphasis from the "struggle against" to ways of "living with" (Albuquerque 2010). Within this new framework, what is at stake is no longer the challenge to overcome or do away with drought but the provision of decent living conditions to those who must co-exist with it. For this policy problem, the socio-technical solution offered by the ASA has been the "*plate cistern*." Aligning government financing and the practical, accumulated knowledge of local organizations (a process not without its tensions) (Costa and Dias 2013), ASA militants, from within the P1MC, installed more than 500,000 cisterns, thereby providing a practical alternative to the Brazilian drought.

POSITIONAL INSTITUTIONALIZATION

Lastly, *positional institutionalization* refers to occupying positions within the state as a social movement action strategy. Paradoxically, in spite of its visibility, this mode has not received much attention. The institutional consolidation of positions inside the state administrative apparatus may take shape through the making of governments and holding of high-level office positions within them—appointments—or through regular civil service career positions. There are basically five routes to obtaining a post: as a career in the civil service, contingent upon competitive examination and demonstratation of abilities; through the electoral race; through the appointment of partisan or government coalition allies; through appointment of movement activists; or through the creation of positions that are earmarked for members of movements or particular social groups. Positional institutionalization is a mode that favors movement agendas and demands, clearing the way for other modes to then kick in.

Certainly, the operation of the "National Institute Against Discrimination, Xenophobia and Racism" in Argentina, the "Brazil without Homophobia" Program in Brazil, or the National Council to Prevent Discrimination in Mexico, is not unaffected by the profile of those who occupy positions of command, whether appointees or career civil servants. The presence of activists who have been trained by movements favors institutional performance that is in sync with movement demands, as was the case of LGBT sectors involved in disputes over guidelines and programs. Thus, rather than providing a roster of names and positions occupied, it is important to identify positional institutionalization patterns of LGBT movements.

In Mexico, the earliest attempts to occupy positions through the ballot took place in the 1970s, but it was not until the 1980s that a LGBT movement strategy in relation to political parties and the electoral arena was consolidated. Since the Mexican political party system was a closed one, the LGBT movement opted for an alliance with a small party of the radical Left, of Trotskyist leaning. In Brazil, the movement refused to make alliances with any political party and chose, instead, to work with different parties along the political spectrum and in the building of a multi-party alliance within Congress. In Argentina, alliances were also made with Trotskyists and with the Communist Party, but electoral politics were closed off (de la Dehesa 2010; Rapisardi 2008; Díez in this volume). The emergence of an epidemic of HIV/AIDS led movement organizations to engage not only in work of solidarity and prevention within the community but to explore other channels of relationship with the state, occupying positions within the policy sectors. Where legislative access was more restricted, such as in Mexico, positional institutionalization took on a more important role in the defense of an agenda for diversity that did not resonate within the congress (de la Dehesa 2010). Finally, the arrival of leftist governments gave rise to opportunities to occupy positions within offices and institutional spaces that were set up to combat discrimination and promote policies with similar goals.

In the case of family farming, the connection between the movement and rural unionism favored another pattern of positional institutionalization. Within the ambit of rural policies, the National Program for the Strengthening of Family Farming (PRONAF) was the first and continues to be the most consolidated public policy for Brazilian family farming. In direct dialogue with international organizations and scientific authorities, the PRONAF drew its most significant bureaucratic staff from civil society, namely the Confederação Nacional dos Trabalhadores Rurais Agricultores e Agricultoras Familiares (CONTAG), and the Departamento de Estudos Socioeconômicos Rurais.[4] In Argentina, the official creation of organizations such as Foro Nacional de la Agricultura Familiar (FoNAF) and the Foro de Políticas Públicas Rurales sealed the process of approximation between authorities and rural organizers. While in the early years of the institutionalization of family farming within the country, the Federación Agraria Argentina stood out for its actions in the field, the later emergence of the Federación de Organizaciones Nucleadas de la Agricultura Familiar has reconfigured and widened state-civil society connections around family farming (Nogueira et al. 2017).

Positional institutionalization pervades a variety of national cases. Militants and organizations of *piqueteros*, in Argentina, were able to win, both with and against other actors from hegemonic political parties, a distinguished policy domain of their own for the "*piquetero* question" (note, not framed as the "unemployment question") (Rossi 2017). Activists were appointed primarily to the Ministry of Social Development and the Ministry of Federal Planning and, in lesser numbers, to other ministries such as International Relations. However, feminisms extended their reach beyond specific national contexts and were able to occupy positions and institutions throughout Latin America and the world (Htun and Weldon, 2018). Among feminists, earlier polarization between those who defended autonomy and those who accepted positions within government institutions—a common division in contexts of dictatorships that were coming to an end—led to activists' entrance, largely but not exclusively, into the so-called *Women's Policy Agencies* (WPA), which are now present throughout the continent (Guzman and Montaño 2012). A product of feminist demands, the WPAs were institutionalized, particularly after international conferences, through the expertise of militants and civil society women's networks. More recently, as feminisms multiply, they have also multiplied at the oficial level and become "state feminisms" (Mazur and McBride 2008) or "participatory state feminism" (Matos and Alvarez 2018). It is worthwhile to note that, although state feminism is identified with the WPA, the holding of posts and positions extends beyond them, involving the (subnational) staff of "secondary mechanisms" that are similarly oriented by gender agendas (Fernós 2010).

Conclusion

Engaged in the defense of different causes, social movements institutionalize their demands, values, and resources for action through processes of contentious and cooperative action with the state. This is how they become relevant actors in public policy domains. A sensitive analysis of institutionalization processes leads us to observe that movements act not only outside the state, applying pressure against it at moments when policies or provision of public goods or services are defined but also they operate through, and from within the state, constituting state administrative capacities, as well as categories of classification and cognition within particular arenas. Likewise, neither are social movements entirely restricted to exercising pressure in moments in which laws are made or approved. Rather, they operate continuously, turning laws in regulations, rules into programs, and policies into instruments. Understanding the relationship between social movements and modes of institutionalization demands placing institutional intermediation at its core, thereby going beyond the opposition between the will and autonomy of movements and external institutional constraints, assuming and approach in which movements act simultaneously *against*, *through*, and *from within* the state.

The democratic transitions of the 1980s and 1990s and the leftward turn of the decade of 2000–2010 in Latin America defined a scenario in which state institutions became permeable to the demands and actions of movements that were traditionally conceptualized as outsiders. However, as a theoretical and empirical issue, institutionalization is not restricted to the leftward turn—although the latter certainly constitutes a time of extraordinary intensity and one in which a wide spectrum of actors, including some who were traditionally maintained on the sidelines, take part. In other scenarios, including periods of dictatorship, institutionalizations occur, yet are often ignored, largely because they are not visible through the analytical lens—and normative assumptions of the literature. During the years of the military dictatorship in Brazil, for instance, certain institutional positions were occupied by members of the *Movimento Sanitarista*, while in the countryside there was an unprecedented spread of unionism via the official category of "rural worker" (Dowbor 2012; Houtzager 2004). The observation of modes of practical and symbolic institutionalization, in the case of the LGBT movement, alongside the reaction and panic of countermovements, reveals intense dispute around apparently simple objects, such as a "toolkit" (cf. Leite 2019), a scenario largely neglected by dichotomous perspectives within social movement studies.

Acknowledgements

The authors would like to thank Gisela Zaremberg, Federico Rossi, Marisa von Büllow, Victoria Irisarri, Barbaro Bueno and Wagner Romao for helpful comments, as well as Miriam Adelman for her work on translating our text. Gurza Lavalle would like to thank the support of the Centre for Metropolitan Studies (CEM), grant number 2013/07616-7 provided by the *Fundação de Amparo à Pesquisa do Estado de São Paulo* (FAPESP). Szwako thanks the Prociencia Scholarship provided by the State University of Rio de Janeiro (UERJ).

Notes

1. Another relevant channel is the Grupo de Organismos del Estado Nacional para la Protección y Promoción de los Derechos de la Población LGTBI, yet it is made up of of a network of twenty-four organizations with lesser degress of institutionalization.
2. The abbreviation is not consensual, and may appear in longer or shorter forms, according to the country and in response to the demands of intersex (I) or assexual (A) communities, for example.
3. "Sumak kawsay" is the Quechua term for the Spanish "buen vivir"; "suma qamaña" is the Aymara term translated as "vivir bien." We adopt the translation of both of them into the English term "good living."
4. Analogous to family farming, the analysis of the technical team of the Ministério do Meio Ambiente also expresses connections, for environmental policy, between environmental movement organizations and the Brazilian state, between 2003 and 2013 (see Abers and Oliveira 2015).

References

Abers, Rebecca Neaera and Keck, Margaret (2013), *Practical Authority: Agency and Institutional Change in Brazilian Water Politics*. 1st. ed. (Oxford and New York: Oxford University Press).

Abers, Rebecca and Marilia Oliveira (2015), "Nomeações políticas no Ministério do Meio Ambiente (2003–2013): interconexões entre ONGs, partidos e governos," *Opinião Pública* 21(2), 336–64.

Albuquerque, Maria do Carmo (2010), "Novos paradigmas no Semiárido brasileiro: A experiência da ASA na construção de novas modalidades de políticas públicas," in Leandro Morais and Adriano Borges (eds.), *Novos paradigmas de produção e consumo: experiências inovadoras*,143–75 (São Paulo: Polis Institute).

Amenta, Edwin (1998), *Bold Relief: Institutional Politics and the Origins of Modern American Social Policy* (Princeton, NJ: Princeton University Press).

Banaszak, Lee (2005), "Inside and Outside the State: Movement Insider Status, Tactics, and Public Policy Achievements," in David Meyer, Valerie Jenness, and Helen Ingram (eds.), *Routing the Opposition: Social Movements, Public Policy, and Democracy*, 149–76 (Minneapolis: University of Minnesota Press).

Clemens, Elizabeth (1997), *The People's Lobby: Organizational Innovation and the Rise of Interest Group in the United States, 1890–1925* (Chicago: University of Chicago Press).

Collier, Ruth and David Collier (1991), *Shaping the Political Arena: Critical Junctures, the Labor Movement, and Regime Dynamics in Latin America* (Princeton, NJ: Princeton University Press).

Colling, Leandro (2015), *Que os outros sejam o normal: tensões entre movimento LGBT e ativismo queer* (Salvador: EDUFBA).

Costa, Adriano and Dias, Rafael (2013), "Estado e sociedade civil na implantação de políticas de cisternas," in Adriano Costa (ed.), *Tecnologia Social e Políticas Públicas*, 33–64 (São Paulo; Brasília: Polis Institute – Fundação Banco do Brasil).

Dagnino, Evelina, Alberto Olvera, and Aldo Panfichi (eds.) (2006), *A disputa pela construção democrática na América Latina* (Campinas: Paz e Terra – Unicamp).

Daniliauskas, Marcelo (2011), "Relações de gênero, diversidade sexual e políticas públicas de educação: Uma análise do programa Brasil sem homofobia," MA diss., Faculdade de Educação da Universidade de São Paulo.

De Castro, Fabio, Barabara Hogenboom, and Michiel Baud (eds.) (2016), *Environmental Governance in Latin America* (London: Palgrave).

de la Dehesa, Rafael (2010), *Queering the Public Sphere in Mexico and Brazil: Sexual Rights Movements in Emerging Democracies* (Durham, NC: Duke University Press).

Dowbor, Monika (2012), "A arte da institucionalização: Estratégias de mobilização dos sanitaristas (1974-2006)," PhD diss., Universidade de São Paulo.

Esquivel, Juan (2013), "Narrativas religiosas y políticas en la disputa por la educación sexual en Argentina," *Cultura y Religión* 7(1),140-63.

Estrada, Márquez F. (2013), "Implementación del Programa de Salud Sexual y Reproductiva para Adolescentes en México: Un análisis de governanza desde el enfoque de redes," PhD diss., FLACSO México.

Facchini, Regina (2005), *Sopa de letrinhas? Movimento homossexual e produção de identidades coletivas nos anos 1990* (Rio de Janeiro: Garamond).

Farah, Ivone and Vasapollo, Luciano (eds.) (2011), *Vivir Bien: ¿Paradigma No Capitalista?* (La Paz: cIdES-uMSA).

Feitosa, Cleyton (2017), *Políticas Públicas LGBT e Construção Democrática no Brasil* (Curitiba: Appris).

Fernós, Maria Dolores (2010), *National Mechanism for Gender and Empowerment of Women in Latin American and the Caribbean Region*, Mujer y Desarrollo, no. 102 (Santiago: CEPAL).

Garay, Candelaria (2016), *Social Policy Expansion in Latin America* (New York: Cambridge University Press).

Giugni, Mario and Florence Passy (1998), "Contentious Politics in Complex Societies: New Social Movements between Conflict and Cooperation," in Marco Giugni, Doug McAdam, and Charles Tilly (eds.), *From Contention to Democracy*, 81-107 (Lanham, MD: Rowman & Littlefield).

Goldstone, Jack (ed.) (2003), *States, Parties, and Social Movements* (Cambridge: Cambridge University Press).Grisa, Catia and Sergio Schneider (eds.) (2015), *Políticas públicas de desenvolvimento rural no Brasil* (Porto Alegre: UFRGS)

Gudynas, Eduardo (2011), "Buen Vivir: Today's Tomorrow," *Development* 54(S4), 441-47.

Gurza Lavalle, Adrian and José Szwako (2015), "Sociedade civil, Estado e autonomia: argumentos, contra-argumentos e avanços no debate," *Opinião Pública* 21 (1), 157-187.

Gurza Lavalle, Adrian, Euzeneia Carlos, Monika Dowbor and José Szwako (2019), "Movimentos sociais, institucionalização e domínios de agência," in Adrian Gurza Lavalle, Euzeneia Carlos, Monika Dowbor and José Szwako (eds.), *Movimentos sociais e institucionalização: Políticas sociais, raça e gênero no Brasil pós-transição*, 21-87 (Rio de Janeiro: IESP/EduERJ/CEM).

Guzmán, Virginia and Montaño, Sonia (2012), Políticas públicas e institucionalidad de género en América Latina (1985-2010), Mujer y Desarollo, no. 118 (Santiago: CEPAL).

Houtzager, Peter (2004), *Os últimos cidadãos: Conflito e modernização no Brasil rural (1964-1995)* (São Paulo: Globo).

Htun, Mala (2003), *Sex and the State: Abortion, Divorce, and the Family under Latin American Dictatorships and Democracies* (Cambridge: Cambridge University Press).

Htun, Mala and S. Laurel Weldon (2018), *The Logics of Gender Justice: State Action on Women's Rights around the World* (New York: Cambridge University Press).

Isunza, Ernesto and Gurza Lavalle, Adrián (eds.) (2018). *Controles democráticos no electorales y regímenes de rendición de cuentas en el Sur Global* (México, Colombia, Brasil, China y Sudáfrica, Oxford: Peter Lang Ltd, International Academic Publishers).

Lascoumes, Pierre and Le Galès, Patrick (2007), "Introduction: Understanding Public Policy through its Instruments," *Governance: An International Journal of Policy, Administration, and Institutions* 20(1), 1–21.

Leite, Vanessa (2019), "'Em defesa das crianças e da família': Refletindo sobre discursos acionados por atores religiosos 'conservadores' em controvérsias públicas envolvendo gênero e sexualidade," *Sexualidad, Salud y Sociedad* 32, 119–42.

Lima, Márcia (2010), "Desigualdades Raciais e Políticas Públicas," *Novos Estudos CEBRAP* 87, 77–95.

Matos, Marlise & Alvarez, Sonia (eds.) (2018), Quem são as mulheres das políticas para as mulheres no Brasil: o feminismo estatal participativo brasileiro. 01. ed. Porto Alegre: Editora Zouk,. v. 2. 276p.

Mazur, Amy and McBride, Dorothy (2008), "State Feminism," in Gary Goertz and Amy Mazur (eds.), *Politics, Gender, and Concepts: Theory and Methodology*, 244–69 (Cambridge: Cambridge University Press).

Nichnig, Claudia (2014), "Os conceitos têm história: Os usos e a historicidade dos conceitos utilizados em relação à conjugalidade entre pessoas do mesmo sexo no Brasil," *Revista Gênero & Direito* (1), 27–46.

Nogueira, Maria, Marcos Urcola, and Mario Latuatta (2017), "La gestión estatal del desarrollo rural y la agricultura familiar en argentina: Estilos de gestión y análisis de coyuntura 2004-2014 y 2015–2017," *Revista Latinoamericana de Estudios Rurales* 4, 25–59.

Oliveira Júnior, Isaias and Eliane Maio (2015), "Diversidade sexual e homofobia: A cultura do "desagendamento" nas políticas públicas educacionais," *Práxis Educativa* 10(1), 35–53.

Pecheny, Mario and Rafael de la Dehesa (2011), "Sexualidades y políticas en América Latina: un esbozo para la discusión," in Sonia Correa and Richard Parker (eds.), *Sexualidade e política na América Latina: Histórias, interseções e paradoxos*, 31–78 (Rio de Janeiro: ABIA).

Picolotto, Everton (2014), "Os Atores da Construção da Categoria Agricultura Familiar no Brasil," *Revista de Economia e Sociologia Rural* (52), 63–84.

Rapisardi, Flavio (2008), "Escritura y lucha política en la cultura argentina: Identidades y hegemonía en el movimiento de diversidades sexuales entre 1970 y 200," *Revista Iberoamericana* 74 (225), 973–95.

Rossi, Federico M. (2017), *The Poor's Struggle for Political Incorporation* (New York: Cambridge University Press).

Sabourin, Eric, Mario Samper, Jean Le Coq, Gilles Massardier, Octavio Sotomayor, and Jacques Marzin (2014), "Análisis transversal de las políticas sobre agricultura familiar en América Latina," in Eric Sabourin, Mario Samper, and Octavio Sotomayor (eds.), *Políticas públicas y agriculturas familiares en América Latina: Balance, desafíos y perspectivas*, 19–48 (Santiago: ECLAC – Red PPAL – IICA).

Saldívar, Emiko (2011), "Everyday Practices of Indigenismo: An Ethnography of Anthropology and the State in Mexico," *The Journal of Latin American and Caribbean Anthropology* 16(1), 67–89.

Salinas, Héctor M. (2008), *Políticas de disidencia sexual en México* (Mexico: Conapred).

Schneider, Sergio (2016), "Family Farming in Latin America and the Caribbean: Looking for New Paths of Rural Development and Food Security," *International Policy Centre for Inclusive Growth*, Working Paper 137 (New York: UNDP).

Segura, Maria and Silvio Waisbord (2016), *Media Movements: Civil Society and Media Policy Reform in Latin America* (London: Zed).

Serrano-Amaya, José and Gustavo Santos (2016), "LGBT Activism in Latin America," in Nancy A. Naples (ed.), *The Wiley-Blackwell Encyclopedia of Gender and Sexuality Studies*, 1–6 (Malden, MA: Wiley-Blackwell).

Silva, Eduardo and Federico M. Rossi (eds.) (2018), *Reshaping the Political Arena in Latin America: From Resisting Neoliberalism to the Second Incorporation* (Pittsburgh, PA: University of Pittsburgh Press).

Skocpol, Theda (1992), *Protecting Soldiers and Mothers: The Political Origins of Social Policy in the United States* (Boston, MA: Harvard University Press).

Straw, Cecilia (2017), "La visión socio-política de los derechos reproductivos en Argentina," *RJUAM* 35(1), 171–95.

Szwako, José and Adrian Gurza Lavalle (2019), "Seeing Like a Social Movement: Institucionalização simbólica e capacidades estatais cognitivas," *Novos Estudos CEBRAP* 38(2), 411–34.

Tilly, Charles and Sidney Tarrow (2006), *Contentious Politics* (Boulder, CO: Paradigm).

Toledo, Víctor (2005), "Políticas indígenas y derechos territoriales en América Latina: 1990–2004 ¿Las fronteras indígenas de la globalización?," in Pablo Dávalos (ed.), *Pueblos indígenas, Estado y democracia* 67–102 (Buenos Aires: CLACSO).

Zimmerer, Karl (2011), "'Conservation Booms' with Agricultural Growth? Sustainability and Shifting Environmental Governance in Latin America, 1985–2008 (Mexico, Costa Rica, Brazil, Peru, Bolivia)," *Latin American Research Review* 46, 82–114.

Index

For the benefit of digital users, indexed terms that span two pages (e.g., 52–53) may, on occasion, appear on only one of those pages.

Tables and figures are indicated by *t* and *f* following the page number

A

aboriginal identity movements, 592
abortion rights, 347, 752, 754
Acción Nacional Revolucionaria, 183–84
activism. *See also* digital activism; geographies of activism; politics of social movement activism
   androcentric visions of, 109
   anti-mining activists, 75, 92–93, 254, 362–63, 703
   autonomist movements and, 515–17
   Black women's activism, 288, 343, 377–80, 381–82
   domestic-based activism, 109
   global justice activism, 262, 667–68
   indigenous movements, 359–64
   LGBTIQ+ movements, 417–18, 418*t*
   by revolutionary movements, 307–10
   rights-oriented activism, 429
   of right-wing movements, 429
   sem-teto/sin-techo activism, 505
   social justice activists, 372–73
   state-directed activism, 417–18, 418*t*
   territorial activism, 77
   of territorial movements, 77
   urban poor activism, 73
   women's movements, 343–44
activist networks, 77–78, 89–90, 93, 718–19, 724
Activists beyond Borders: Advocacy Networks in International Politics (Keck, Sikkink), 523–24
Administración Nacional de Combustibles, Alcoholes y Portland (ANCAP), 768–69
advocacy organizations, 219–20, 221–22, 223, 426, 702, 748, 750–51
aesthetic-political experiences, 115
affirmative epistemology, 130
Afro-civil society, 373–78
Afro-Colombian movement, 686
Afro-descendant, defined, 381–82
Afro-descendant women activists, 114, 345–46
afro-descendente, defined, 381–82
afro-descendiente, defined, 381–82
Afro-diasporic thought, 124–25, 130
afro-epistemology, 130
Afro-Latin American movements
   addressing racism, 370–71, 380–83
   Afro-civil society, 373–78, 376*t*
   Black women's activism, 377–80
   feminism in, 380
   feminist movements and, 288
   historical antecedents, 371–72
   introduction to, 8, 370–71
   labor movements and, 238
   racism and, 370–71, 380–83
   regional and transnational mobilizations, 380–83
   rise of, 372–74
   social gains, 383
   summary of, 383–84
Afro-Reggae Cultural Group in Brazil, 582
agency
   citizenship as, 8–9, 455, 460–65
   demobilization and, 283
   domains of, 778–79
   in institutionalization process, 778–79
agnosticism and digital activism, 701

agrarian reform movements, 252, 270–71, 272–73, 306, 666–67, 734–35
agrarian social movements, 321, 329, 330, 332
agribusiness model, 266–67, 278–80
agricultural modernization, 269, 332–33
agroextractivism, 270–71, 277, 278
agro-monoculture and raw material export model was, 232–33
Agrupación Nacional Putos Peronistas, 73
Aguascalientes units, 190–91
Alcoholics Anonymous, 146
Alfonsín, Raúl, 44
Alianza Centroamericana Frente a la Minería (ACREFEMIN), 261
Alianza Chilena por un Comercio Justo y Responsable (ACJR), 528
Alianza Ciudadana contra la Privatización (ACCP), 147
Alianza Femenina, 340
Alianza Patriótica para el Cambio, 155
Alianza Popular Revolucionaria Americana (APRA), 20, 308
Alianza Republicana Nacionalista (ARENA), 546, 548
Allende, Salvador, 202–3, 308–9, 395–96, 492–93, 563
alliance behavior, 100, 419, 683
Almeida, Paul, 526
alternative movement culture, 580–83
alternative nationalisms, 168–69
Amazon Wanaaleru in Venezuela, 596
Amerafricanidade, 380
American Free Trade Agreement (NAFTA), 514–15
anarchy/anarchism, 10–11, 259–60, 306, 643–45
ancestral origin patriarchy, 130
androcentric processes of democracy, 8
androcentric visions of social activism, 109
anthropocentric ontology of social sciences, 80
anti-abortion counter movement, 546–48
anti-Americanism, 25–26
anti-capitalist movements, 262, 460
anti-colonialism, 127, 128–29, 134–35, 165–66, 359, 557, 651
anti-corruption social mobilization
Argentina, 472–73, 474–75, 477
Brazil, 472–73, 475–77
Colombia, 472–73
emergence of, 472–73
Guatemala, 477–80
introduction to, 471–72
Peru, 480–82
relationship between, 473–82
summary of, 483–84
anti-extractivist mobilizations, 78
anti-fascist feminist movements, 339–40
anti-globalization movements, 61
anti-imperialism, 20–21, 148–49, 182, 184, 308, 337–38, 339, 392, 557, 651
anti-LGBT+ uncivil movement, 45–46, 480, 548–50
anti-mining activists, 75, 92–93, 254, 362–63, 703
anti-neocolonialism, 152
anti-neoliberal protest movements, 94, 146, 152–54, 432–33
anti-sweatshop advocacy coalitions, 238–39
anti-terrorism laws, 286
APPO movement (Asamblea Popular de los Pueblos de Oaxaca), 704–5
Aquinas, Thomas, 407
Arab Spring, 217
Árbenz, Jacobo, 186, 204–5, 325–26, 559, 561
Argentina. See also *piquetero* movement in Argentina
addressing racism, 382
anti-corruption social mobilization, 472–73, 474–75, 477
autonomist movements, 509–10, 511–12, 513, 516–17
consumer mobilization, 491–92
contentious politics, 733–35, 736–37
Córdoba university reform, 390–93
coups in, 310–11
cultural dimension of social movements, 579
demobilization process in, 289–92
democratic transitions from above, 216–17, 290
environmental mobilization, 442, 448
feminist movements in, 261, 347–48
gay movement in, 117
grassroots social movements in, 290
human rights movements in, 424–25, 428
institutionalization of social movements, 781–82, 784, 786, 787, 788

labor legislation in, 305
land occupation conflict, 275–76
legal mobilization, 749–51, 752–53
LGBTIQ+ movements, 410, 411–12, 417
military dictatorships, 310–11, 595
military regimes, 200–4
moral economy and, 740
nationalism and, 168–69, 170
participatory institutions in, 765–67
party politics, 719–20, 721, 725–26
peasant movements in, 289–90
Peronists and, 242
protests against taxation, 240–41
repertoires of contention, 665
social protest, 200, 478, 719–20, 750–51
strikes in, 314
student movements in, 394–95
territorial movements, 738–39, 740
transnational collective action, 525
urban social movements, 458
worker-run factories, 261
workers mobilization and, 315–16
Argentine Supreme Court, 750–51, 752–53
Articulação Semiárido Brasileiro (ASA), 786
Asociación Cultural de Jóvenes Peruanos Negros, 374–75
Asociación de Abogados Laboralistas (Labor Lawyers Association), 750–51
Asociación de Educación Popular Carlos Fonseca Amador (AEPCFA), 651
Asociación de los Trabajadores del Campo (ATC), 329
Asociación de Trasvestis, Transexuales y Transgenérico, 416
Asociación Integral Guatemalteca de Mujeres Indígenas (AIGMIM), 596
Asociación Interétnica de Desarrollo de la Selva Peruana (AIDESEP), 131–32, 253
Asociación Nacional de Agricultores Pequeños (ANAP), 652
Asociación por la Identidad Trasvesti Transexual, 416
Asociación por los Derechos Civiles (ADC), 750–51, 753–54
Associação Nacional de Profissionais de Serviços ao Consumidor, 492
associational hubs, 75, 91

asymmetrical bargaining, 98
austerity, 237, 252, 312
authoritarianism. *See also* dictatorships; social movements under authoritarianism
Afro-social movements and, 375–76
Central America, 204–6
competitive authoritarianism, 6, 206–8
competitive authoritarian regimes, 206–8
democratic transitions from above, 215–17
dependency theory, 23
educational movements under, 647–50
introduction to, 6, 196, 197t
LGBTIQ+ movements under, 411–12
military regimes, 199–206
military regimes and, 6, 199–206
of neopluralism, 462
personal dictatorships, 197–99
proliferation of, 25–26
reaction to capitalism, 57
Southern Cone regime, 200–4
student movements and, 392–97
summary of, 208–9
totalitarian regimes, 196, 506
transnational networks, 95
women's movements and, 344
autonomía, defined, 680–81
Autonomías Indígena Originario Campesinas (AIOC), 769–70
autonomist movements
achievements and legacy of, 514–15
activism and, 515–17
Argentina, 509–10, 511–12, 513, 516–17
Brazil, 510–11
capitalist constraints, 513–14
capitalist markets, 512
Chile, 508–10, 511
communal councils and, 770–71
diversity and, 507–15
geographical space and, 512–13
globalization and, 513–14
introduction to, 9, 505–7
Mexico, 511
politics and, 733–34
sources and tensions, 510–11
state apparatus and, 511–12
Zapatista movement and, 514–15
autonomous municipalities, 190–91

autonomy/autonomism
  Afro-Latin American movements and, 371
  of civil society organizations, 761–62
  communal rebuilding and, 129–30
  decentralization and, 9, 98
  defined, 505–6
  development of consumerism, 500–1
  devoid in social movements, 125–26
  EZLN and, 612
  feminist movements, 340–41
  food autonomy, 133, 134
  indigenous movements and, 359–64
  left-libertarian autonomism, 506
  limits to Brazilian universities, 393
  Marxism and, 28, 29, 510–11, 518
  from nation-state, 129–30
  need of gaining, 37
  neo-Marxist autonomism, 506
  organizational autonomy, 99, 329–30, 393
  party politics and, 732
  peasant movements and, 329
  repertoires of contention, 667–68
  socio-environmentalism, 441, 516–17
  summary of, 517–18
Auyero, Javier, 719
Aymara people, 278
Ayotnizapa protests, 697–98
Aztec Empire, 166

B

Bachelet, Michel, 314
Baldetti, Roxana, 478
Ballet Folklórico Ñuca Trans project, 115
Bambirra, Vânia, 23
barrio-based collectives, 612–13
Barrio Nómada Collective, 697–98
Bartolina Sisa peasant women's organization, 345–46
Batista, Fulgencio, 183–84, 197
Bechtel Corporation, 253
behavioral approach to nationalism, 163–64
Berlin Wall, 190–92
Bickford, Louis, 433
bilateral trade agreements, 527–28
Black, defined, 374
Black consciousness, 8, 376–77
Black feminism, 130, 288, 377–78

Black identity, 373–75, 384
Blackness, defined, 370, 374, 379–80
Black Panther Party, 410
Black social movements, 370–75, 377, 378, 782. *See also* Afro-Latin American movements
Black women's activism, 288, 343, 377–80, 381–82
blockmodeling, 88–89
bloc recruitment, 90–91
Bloque Popular Revolucionario (BPR), 147
Bolivia
  coca growers in, 38
  cultural dimension of social movements, 577
  demobilization process in, 292–95
  educational movements, 648, 654–55
  feminist movements in, 345–46, 347
  geographies of activism, 686, 689
  indigenous movements in, 220–21, 321–22, 356, 362
  land occupation conflicts, 271–72
  Movimiento al Socialismo, 242
  party politics, 724
  Plurinational Legislative Assembly, 315
  popular militias in, 309–10
  revolutionary movements in, 182, 183, 184–85, 192
  social protest, 689, 721
  water privatization in, 495
  Water War of Cochabamba, 253, 313, 689
  workers mobilization and, 314, 315
Bolivian Revolution, 326–27
Bolsonaro, Jair, 348, 548–50
bonding ties in network mechanisms, 90–91
boomerang pattern strategy, 524
border-crossing movements, 261–62
boundary-making mechanisms, 113
Bourdieu, Pierre, 638
bourgeois hegemony, 29
Braig, Marianne, 433–34
Brazil
  addressing racism, 382
  Afro-Reggae Cultural Group in, 582
  anti-corruption social mobilization, 472–73, 475–77
  anti-LGBT+ uncivil movement, 548–50

INDEX 799

autonomist movements, 510–11
autonomy limits to Brazilian universities, 393
Belo Monte dam conflicts in, 445
Black women's activism, 378–79
consumer mobilization, 492, 494–95, 496–97
contentious politics, 734–36
criminalization of social movements in, 286, 288
demobilization process in, 286–89
educational movements, 644–45, 650–51, 652–53, 654
Eldorado dos Carajás massacre, 274
environmental mobilization, 448–49
feminist movements in, 340, 341, 342, 347–48
geographies of activism, 685–86, 690–91
globalized neoliberalism, 252
grassroots social movements in, 288
guerrilla movements, 202
indigenous movements in, 322–23, 326
institutionalization of social movements, 782, 785
June Protest Cycle in, 533
land occupation conflicts, 271–72
legal mobilization, 749, 752–53
LGBTIQ+ movements, 412, 417
military dictatorships, 208, 341, 464, 782, 789
military regimes, 200–4
OcupaEscola uprisings, 697–98
participatory budgeting in, 262, 464–65
participatory institutions in, 764–65, 766
Partido dos Trabalhadores, 240
party politics, 720
peasant movements in, 288–89
quilombos movement, 129–30, 131–32
repertoires of contention, 667–68
right-wing movements, 548–50
social protest, 478
Soul Movement in, 372–73
student movements in, 393–94, 396, 400–1
urban social movements, 464–65
workers mobilization and, 311
Brazil's National Public Policy Conferences (BNPPCs), 764–65, 771–72
bridging ties in network mechanisms, 90–91
brokerage ladder, 91
Bruhn, Kathleen, 719
Brysk, Alison, 425–26
Bucaram, Abdalá, 472–73
Buen Vivir/Vivir Bien, 241

C

Calleja, Carlos, 547
Campaign Against the Free Trade Agreement of the Americas, 526
campaigning by social movements, 767–69
Campanha da Mulher pela Democracia, 341
campesindio (indigenous peasants), 330, 331
Campesino-a-Campesino (CaC), 652
Canclini, García, 577
capitalism/capitalist development
    agro-monoculture and raw material export model was, 232–33
    anti-capitalist movements, 262, 460
    authoritarianism reaction to, 57
    cyclical crisis of, 239
    demise of, 152
    development of, 65
    grassroots social movements and, 235, 236
    integration of peasant movements, 323–26
    introduction to, 6–7, 229
    market-led development, 236–39
    Marxism and, 18–20, 230
    modernization of agriculture, 303
    neoliberalism and, 27, 250
    overview of, 231–43
    relations of production, 320
    social movement studies and, 230–31
    state-led development, 233–36
    summary of, 243
Caracoles units, 190–91
Cardenal, Ernesto, 560
Cárdenas, Félix, 355
Cárdenas, Lázaro, 308, 340–41
Cardoso, Fernando Henrique, 23
Carneiro, Sueli, 114, 381–82
Castañeda, Jorge, 206
Castells, Manuel, 455–56, 681–82, 703–4
Castoriadis, Cornelius, 505, 506, 507–8, 516
Castro, Fidel, 183–84, 327–28, 556–57, 646
catalyst movement, 185

800 INDEX

Catholic Action, 626–28
Catholic Charismatic Renewal (CCR) movement, 625–26, 630–31
Catholic Church, 202–3. *See also* religious groups and movements
   clergy, 92–93
   feminist organizations and, 342
   human rights movements and, 426, 427
   introduction to, 625–26
   land occupation conflict, 273, 274
   LGBTIQ+ movements and, 406–7, 414
   Nicaraguan Revolution and, 329
   Protestantism and, 631–37
   reform and revitalization, 626–31
   revolutionary movements and, 560
   social justice theology, 330
   social mobilization and, 461–62
   student movements and, 391, 394–95
   support for indigenous movements in Mexico, 92–93
Catholic Right, 551
Catholic Social Doctrine, 152–53
caudillos, 182–83, 687
Central America
   authoritarianism in, 204–6
   educational movements, 652
   geographies of activism, 688
   military regime, 204–6
   protest campaigns, 252
   social movements under authoritarianism, 204–6
   social protest, 688
   transnational collective action, 528
   urban workers in, 305
Central American Free Trade Agreement (CAFTA), 98–99, 155, 252, 494
Central Bolivariana Socialista de Trabajadores, 314
Central de Trabajadores de la Argentina (CTA), 147, 313
Central General dos Trabalhadores do Brasil, 311
Central Intelligence Agency (CIA), 309, 325–26
centralism, 506, 591, 667
Central Obrera Boliviana (COB), 309–10
Central Obrera Regional (COR), 295

Central Social Movement, 63
Central Única dos Trabalhadores (CUT), 287, 311
Centro de Estudios Panameños, 374–75
Centro de Estudios Sociales y Legales (CELS), 426, 750–51, 753–54
Centro de Estudios y Publicaciones Alforja (CEP Alforja), 650
Centro Democrático (CD), 550
Centro para el Desarrollo Económico y Social de América Latina (DESEAL), 458–59
César Sandino, Augusto, 556–57
Chaco War, 183
Change the World Without Taking Power (Holloway), 506–7
Chaouch, Tahar, 638–39
charismatic leaders, 543, 545
Chávez, Hugo, 207–8, 240, 314, 346–47, 396–97, 547, 556–57, 561, 613, 725, 726
Chiapas Zapatista movement, 58–59, 64, 262
child welfare, 337–38
Chile
   autonomist movements, 508–10, 511
   consumer mobilization, 494
   contentious politics, 736
   democratic transitions from above, 215–16
   educational movements, 644, 654–55
   feminist movements in, 348
   feminist organizations in, 340, 345
   human rights movements, 242
   human rights movements in, 424–25, 427, 428
   indigenous movements in, 325, 364
   institutionalization of social movements, 780–81
   labor legislation in, 305
   LGBTIQ+ movements, 411–12
   military dictatorships, 424, 719–20
   military regime in, 424, 460–61
   Penguin Revolution in, 697–98
   pobladores movement, 508–10, 511
   revolutionary movements, 563
   social explosion in, 242
   social media use, 100
   student movements in, 390, 392, 395–96, 397–98, 533
   transition to democracy, 238
   transnational collective action, 521–22, 527

urban social movements, 458–59
workers' movement, 304, 310–11, 314
Chilean Road to Socialism, 563
Chí'xi thought, 130
Christian Base Communities (Comunidades Eclesiales de Base) (CEBs), 152–53, 560, 627, 629–30, 649
Christian Right organizations, 539
Church-led ecologism, 92–93
Church of Jesus Christ of Latter-Day Saints, 632
cisgender heterosexuality, 112
Citizen-Initiated Popular Consultation in Uruguay, 768–69
citizen media, 99, 701, 704
citizenship
 as agency, 8–9, 455, 460–65
 case studies, 611–17
 colectivos (urban collectives) and, 608, 612–14
 as cooptation, 459
 democracy and, 609–10
 ideas and ideology, 610–11
 indigenous in Venezuela, 615–17
 introduction to, 607–8, 608t
 piquetero movement and, 608, 614–15, 617
 social movements and, 608–9
 summary of, 617–18
 Zapatista movement and, 608, 611–12, 617
citizenship rights, 8–9, 151, 416, 423–24, 430–31, 460–61, 462, 463, 581
The City and the Grassroots (Castells), 455
Civil Code reforms, 117
civil liberties, 215–17, 218, 413–14, 429, 431
civil rights, 61–62, 337–39, 397, 422, 425, 432–33, 459, 483–84, 590, 777–78
civil rights movement (US), 39, 91–92
civil society, 151, 361, 461–62, 748, 777–80
civil society groups, 370, 422, 480
civil society organizations, 40, 720, 761–62, 764–71
class-based mobilization, 18–20, 113–14, 459, 461, 498–99
class conciliation, 182
class culture, 665
Cleary, Edward, 424
clientelism, 575–76, 735–36, 741–42

close ties in network mechanisms, 90–91
Coalición Obrero Campesino Estudiantil del Istmo (COCEI), 582
cocalero organizations, 292–93, 295
Cochabamba "Water War" in Bolivia, 253, 313, 689
cognitive approach to nationalism, 164–65
colectivos (urban collectives) in Venezuela, 608, 612–14
collective action
 debates over, 64
 decision-making in, 111
 environmental mobilization and, 449, 451
 feminist and queer perspectives, 110, 111
 internal competition and, 98
 legal mobilization of, 746–47
 mutual support in, 290–91
 nationalism and, 163–64
 party politics and, 715
 social change through, 3
 use of law and courts, 12
 workers mobilization, 312–16
collective identity, 3, 72, 112–15, 440, 591
collective psychological terror, 25
collective subjectivity, 12, 448, 600
Collins, Patricia Hill, 378
Colombia
 Afro-Colombian movement, 686
 anti-corruption social mobilization, 472–73
 Black women's activism, 379
 demobilization process in, 293–94
 educational movements, 651–52
 feminist organizations in, 340
 geographies of activism, 686, 687
 identity culture, 601–2
 indigenous movements in, 220–21, 323, 328
 labor legislation in, 305
 land occupation conflict, 275–76
 legal mobilization, 749–50, 752
 Nasa peoples, 129–30
 participatory institutions in, 763
 right-wing movements, 550–52
 student movements in, 392, 396, 398–99
Colombian Unión Femenina, 340
colonialism, 3, 21, 152, 407–9. *See also* anti-colonialism; decolonizing approaches to social movements

coloniality of being, 130
coloniality of gender, 130
coloniality of power, 130
Comintern orthodoxy, 20
Comisión Económica para América Latina y el Caribe, 490
Comité Clandestino Revolucionario Indígena (CCRI), 559
Comité Coordinador de Asociaciones Agrícolas, Comerciales, Industriales y Financieras (CACIF), 479
Comité de Amas de Casa del Distro Minero Siglo XX, 342–43
Comité de Cooperación para la Paz en Chile, 203
Comité de Desarrollo Campesino (CODECA), 480
Comité de Unidad Campesina de Guatemala, 133
Comité Latinoamericano y del Caribe para la Defensa de los Derechos de la Mujer (CLADEM), 756–57
Comitês Populares Democráticos (CPDs), 645
Commission Against Impunity in Guatemala (CICIG), 478–80
communal councils (CCs), 770–72
communalizing practices and knowledge, 133–34
communal lands, 272–73
communal rebuilding, 129–30
communication flow directionality, 88–89
communism, 169, 305, 306, 323–26, 579
Communist International, 20, 306, 332
Communist Parties, 10–11, 20, 22, 23
communitarian democracy, 769–70
community *(ayllu)* proprietorship, 321–22
community-based water management initiatives, 133
community self-government, 276
competitive authoritarianism, 6, 206–8
compulsive control mechanisms, 75
compulsive support mechanisms, 75
Comunidades Eclesiales de Base (CEBs), 461
Comunidad Homosexual Argentina (CHA), 414
Confederação Nacional dos Trabalhadores Rurais Agricultores e Agricultoras Familiares (CONTAG), 326, 788

Confederación de Nacionalidades Indígenas del Ecuador (CONAIE), 26, 331, 361, 654–55
Confederación de Trabajadores de América Latina (CTAL), 308
Confederación de Trabajadores de Chile (CUT), 307
Confederación de Trabajadores de Colombia (CTC), 307
Confederación de Trabajadores de la Economía Popular (CTEP), 315–16
Confederación de Trabajadores de Venezuela (CTV), 312, 314
Confederación General del Trabajo (CGT), 307, 394–95
Confederacion General de Trabajadores del Perú (CGTP), 482
Conferência Nacional dos Bispos do Brasil, 645
Congresses on Black Culture in the Americas, 374–75
Consejo de Educación Popular de América Latina y el Caribe (CEAAL), 650
Consejo de Mujeres, 340–41
Consejo de Todas las Tierras (CTT), 364
Consejo Nacional Indio de Venezuela (CONIVE), 615–18
Constitutional Assembly (1991), 749–50
Constitutional Convention (1988), 749
constitutional theory, 167–68, 748
consumer mobilization
   after 1990, 493–97
   Argentina, 491–92
   Brazil, 492, 494–95, 496–97
   business studies on, 499
   Chile, 494
   class action and, 498–99
   corporate social responsibility, 499
   Costa Rica, 494
   ethical consumption, 496–97
   globalization and, 496–97
   introduction to, 9, 488–90
   legal studies on, 498–99
   mass consumption, 488–89
   multilateral cooperation in, 498–99
   during 1940-1990, 490–93
   performance and social media analyses, 500

political and cultural studies on, 497–98
  summary of, 500–1
consumer organizations, 38–39
Consumer Protection Code, 492, 495
consumer rights, 38, 488, 489–90, 491, 492, 493, 496–97, 498, 664
consumer sovereignty, 488–89, 491
contentious politics, 722–26, 731, 732–38
controlled inclusion, 459, 461
Coodinadora de las Organizaciones Indígenas de la Cuenca Amazónica (COICA), 363–64
cooperativism, 123
Coordinadora Andina de Organizaciones Indígenas (CAOI), 261
Coordinadora de Comunidades Mapuche Williche por la Defensa del Territorio Willi Lafken Weychan, 132–33
Coordinadora de Defensa del Agua y de la Vida, 253, 313
Coordinadora de Movimientos Sociales, 147, 313
Coordinadora Latinoamericana de Organizaciones, 133
Coordinadora Latinoamericana de Organizaciones del Campo (CLOC), 330, 332
Coordinadora Nacional de Comunidades Afectadas por la Minería, 131–32
Coordinadora Nacional de Resistencia Popular (CNRP), 147, 150
Coordinadora Nacional de Trabajadores de la Educación (CNTE), 655
Coordinadora Revolucionaria de las Masas (CRM), 147
Coordinadora Social in Nicaragua, 147
Córdoba university reform, 390–93
Cordobazo protest, 200, 208–9
corporate social responsibility (CSR), 499
Corpus Christi massacre, 207
Correa, Rafael, 361, 724–25
Correlates of War database, 171
Corriente Clasista Combativa (CCC), 147
corruption concerns, 9, 148, 400–1. *See also* anti-corruption social mobilization
Costa Rica
  consumer mobilization, 494
  environmental mobilization, 448
  labor legislation in, 305
  land occupation conflicts, 274–75

Costa Rican Communist Party, 151
Council for the Popular Economy and the Complementary Social Wage, 315–16
Council for the Production of Development, 307
counter-legal mobilization, 754–55
counter-movements, 9, 539
coup d'état, 241–42, 476–77, 492–93, 556–57, 563. *See also* military coups
court system in legal mobilization, 747–49, 751–55
Coutinho, Carlos Nelson, 24
COVID-19 pandemic, 242–43
creative human actions, 665
Creole patriotism, 166–67
criminalization of social movements in Brazil, 286, 288
Criola, 378–79
critical theories of modernity, 124–25
critic negotiators, 98–99
cross-border tourism, 249
cross-national alliances, 95
Cruzado Plan, 494–95
Cry *(El Grito)* of Alcorta, 307
Cuba
  barbudos in, 561–62
  educational movements, 646–47, 651
  feminist organizations in, 340
  revolutionary movements, 182, 183–90, 192, 561–62, 566–67
Cuban Communist Party, 151
Cuban Revolution, 22, 23, 24–25, 57, 326, 327–28, 372–73
cultural dimension of social movements
  alternative movement culture, 580–83
  Argentina, 579
  Bolivia, 577
  challenges to, 576–80
  culture, as complex whole, 575–76
  introduction to, 573–75
  Peru, 577
  summary of, 583–84
cultural identity, 113, 321, 377, 592–93, 594
cultural modernization, 168–69, 490
cultural movements, 55, 374–75
cultural production, 500
Culturas híbridas: Estrategias para entrar y salir de la modernidad (Canclini), 577

Cultures in Conflict: Social Movements and the State in Peru (Stokes), 24
cyborg feminism, 130–31

D

Dalton, Roque, 561
Davis, Angela, 378
Dealy, Glen, 575–76
Debray, Regis, 185–86
decentralization
    autonomists and, 9, 98
    democracy and, 684, 685–86, 687, 689
    EZLN and, 611
    fiscal policies of, 294
    market-led development and, 236, 237
    network concepts, 90
    political liberalization and, 481, 518, 594
    state policies of, 284–85, 737, 763
decolonial feminism, 115–17, 124–25
decolonizing approaches (DA) to social movements
    concepts and perspectives, 128–31
    contribution to debate on, 125–28
    introduction to, 5, 123–24
    nationalist and ethnic-based movements, 590
    overview of, 124–25
    to public education, 654–55
    research agenda summary, 134–35
    territorial struggles, 131–34
deconstructivism, 118
deforestation, 133, 692
deleveraging hook, 75, 98
de Mello, Collor, 476, 477
demobilization
    in Andean region, 292–95
    in Argentina, 289–92
    in Brazil, 286–89
    introduction to, 283
    mechanisms of, 284–86
    of right-wing movements, 545
    in South America, 286–95
    summary of, 295–96
    working class at the grassroots, 309
democracy
    androcentric processes of, 8
    citizenship and, 609–10
    communitarian democracy, 769–70
    decentralization and, 684, 685–86, 687, 689
    market-based democracies, 488–89, 492–93
    need for social movements, 59
    neoliberal democracy, 249–50, 263
    political institutions for claim-making, 678–79
    radical democracy, 114–15
    redemocratization, 45–46
    revalorization of, 58–59
    right-wing movements in, 545–46
    shape movements through, 43
    social movements within, 220–22
    transitions to, 12, 37, 43, 213–14, 220–24, 473–74, 685, 749, 757, 778, 779–80, 789
    women's movements and, 344–46
    workers mobilization and, 310–12
democratic deficit and defensive transnationalization, 525
democratic polity, 110
democratization
    Argentina, 216–17, 290
    cities, democratic struggle of, 683–85
    impact of, 590–91
    international trend toward, 152
    introduction to, 213–14
    labor movement role, 238
    liberal democratization, 9, 237–38
    of media, 396–97, 399–400
    Mexico, 704–5
    mixed development, 239–43
    protracted transitions, 218–20
    regional democratization, 6–7, 250, 256–57
    social movements within democracy, 220–22
    summary of, 222–24
    transitions from above, 215–17
    transitions from below, 217–18
    understanding transitions, 214–20
    of universities, 392–93, 395
Dependencia y desarrollo en América Latina (Cardoso, Faletto), 23
dependency theory, 22–24
dependentistas, 23
D'Epinay, Lalive, 633
destabilization stage, 115, 233, 239
deterritorialization process, 77–78, 278

Dialéctica de la dependencia (Marini), 23
Díaz, Porfirio, 182, 322
Díaz Herrera, Roberto, 198–99
dictatorships. *See also* authoritarianism
    foundational dimension of, 57–58
    Haiti, 198
    human rights movements, 56, 427–30
    military dictatorships, 37, 182–83, 375–76, 789
    Panama, 198–99
    personal dictatorships, 6, 197–99
    protest waves against, 149
    terroristic dictatorships, 25, 198
    workers' movement and, 310
diffusionism, 91
digital activism
    actors in, 697–98
    agnosticism and, 701
    discussion, 706–7
    Guatemala, 701–3, 706–7
    introduction to, 696–97
    limits of computational methods, 700
    Mexico, 697–98, 699, 703–7
    summary of, 707–8
    theories of, 699–700
    tools of, 699
    transnationalism and, 531–32
    Zapista movement and, 698, 699
Directorio Revolucionario 13 de Marzo, 184
disincorporation, 237, 238
domains of agency, 778–79
domestic-based activism, 109
domestic loops, 75, 528
dominant elites, 256–57, 323
Domitila Barrios de Chungara, 342–43
Dos Santos, Theotonio, 23
double militancy, 345–46, 542–43, 548
double movement, 724
dual pressure, 285, 287, 291, 294–95, 296
Duque, Iván, 550–52
Duvalier, François, 197, 198
Duvalier, Jean-Claude, 198

E

earthquake victims movement, 74
Echeverría, Luis, 207
ecodependents, 99
ecoentrepreneurs, 99
ecogenoethnocide, 130
ecological blindness, 516–17
economically active population (EAP), 457–58
Economic Commission for Latin America and the Caribbean (ECLAC), 233–34
economic dynamics, 6–7
economic elitism, 97
economic liberalism, 415–16
economic liberalization, 145–46, 147, 151, 155, 416, 527, 684–85
economic reprimarization, 439
economic theory and consumerism, 494
economic threats, 150–52
economism, 733–34
ecoresisters, 99
Ecuador
    constitutional reform processes, 347
    demobilization process in, 293, 294–95
    environmental mobilization, 447
    environmental movement in, 99
    indigenous movements in, 220–21, 356
    institutionalization of social movements, 784–85
    labor legislation in, 305
    Left Turn government, 361
    National Indigenous Uprising in, 356
    party politics, 724–25
educational movements
    anarchism and, 643–45
    under authoritarianism, 647–50
    Bolivia, 648, 654–55
    Brazil, 644–45, 650–51, 652–53, 654
    Central America, 652
    Chile, 644, 654–55
    Colombia, 651–52
    Cuba, 646–47, 651
    early and mid-twentieth century, 644–47
    EZLN and, 653
    grassroots social movements and, 650
    Guatemala, 652
    introduction to, 643–44
    Mexico, 645–46, 650, 652, 653
    organizing of, 654–55
    political education, 644–45
    socialism and, 644, 645–46
    social movement and, 650–53
    summary of, 655–56

education protest, 147
eigenvector centrality, 88–89
Ejército de Liberación Nacional (ELN), 187, 551–52
Ejército Revolucionario del Pueblo (ERP), 187, 561, 566
Ejército Zapatista de Liberación Nacional (EZLN)
　autonomist movements and, 514–15
　Chiapas Zapatista movement, 58–59, 64, 262
　citizenship and, 608, 611–12, 617
　democratization and, 45
　digital activism and, 698, 699
　educational movements and, 653
　elite-negotiated democratizing pacts, 213–14
　enactment of, 331
　formation of, 278
　geographies of activism, 686
　impact of, 40, 76–77
　neoliberalism and, 153, 260
　overview of, 190–92, 218–20, 331, 356
　within a protracted transition, 218–20
　rebel camp in Chiapas, 562
　revolutionary movements and, 563
　transnational collective action and, 531–32
　transnational development and, 258
　transnational networking, 96–97
　women's equality and, 343–44
El Aguila Mexicana journal, 338–39
Eldorado dos Carajás massacre, 274
Eliécer Gaitán, Jorge, 328
elite-based movements, 233, 235, 243
elite-negotiated democratizing pacts, 213–14
El Salvador
　anti-abortion counter movement, 546–48
　anti-mining activists, 254
　guerrilla movements, 18–19, 21–22, 92
　indigenous movements in, 324–25
　insurgent path to democracy, 213–14
　military regime, 204–6
　non-violent protest wave in, 145
　political liberation in, 148–49
　resistance by rural workers, 306–7
　revolutionary movements in, 189
　right-wing movements, 546–48
　transitions from below, 217–18
El Tambo, 125

emancipatory horizons of the European left, 124–25
encampments, 276, 651, 654, 673–74
Engels, Friedrich, 17–18
entanglement perspectives, 129–30
environmentalism, 253–54, 441, 443–44, 516–17
environmental justice, 287–88, 443–44, 507, 515–17, 518
environmental mobilization
　action and participation in, 444–45
　actors involved in, 442–43
　Argentina, 442, 448
　Brazil, 448–49
　collective action and, 449, 451
　Costa Rica, 448
　defined, 440
　general trends, 440–46
　grassroots social movements and, 441, 442, 445–46
　introduction to, 439–40
　issues in, 443–44
　Mexico, 449
　political and economic contexts, 446
　relations to state, 445–46
　scales of, 445
　as social movement, 447–50
　summary of, 450–52
environmental rights, 221, 241, 432
epistemic diversity, 130
epistemic pluriversity, 130
epistemic reductionism, 130, 131–32, 134–35
Escola Sem Partido, 549
e Silva, Costa, 393
Estado Mayor, 147
Estenoz, Evaristo, 372
Estudio para la Defensa de los Derechos de la Mujer (DEMUS), 756–57
ethical consumption, 496–97
ethnic rights, 5–7, 287–88
Eurocentrism, 25–26, 130
European immigration, 306
ex post facto theoretical, 185–86
extra-academic intellectual practices, 128
extractivism, 95, 129
extreme poverty, 223–24, 288–89
extreme right-wing movements, 118, 289, 538–39, 547, 549–50, 552

F

fake news, 545–46
Family Farming Food Acquisition Program, 289
Federación de Estudiantes de la Universidad de Chile (FECH), 395
Federación de Estudiantes Secundarios (FESES), 395
Federación de Juntas vecinales de la Paz (FEJUVE), 295
Federación Democrática de Mujeres Cubanas, 340
Federación de Organizaciones Nucleadas de la Agricultura Familiar, 788
Federación Ecuatoriana de Indios (FEI), 331
Federación Internacional de Estudiantes, 393
Federación Nacional de Mujeres Campesinas, Artesanas, Indígenas, Nativas y Asalariadas del Perú (FENMUCARINAP), 596
Federación Obrera Regional Uruguaya, 307
Federación Sindical de Trabajadores Mineros de Bolivia (FSTMB), 183
federalism, 322, 747, 757, 758
Federal Law to Prevent and End Discrimination, 781–82
Federal Ministry of Education and Culture (MEC), 645
feminism
　Afro-Latin feminism, 380
　Black feminism, 130, 288, 377–78
　cyborg feminism, 130–31
　legal mobilization and, 754
　lesbian feminists, 345–46
　LGBTIQ+ movements and, 412–13
　liberal feminists, 338
　participatory state feminism, 788
　Protestantism and, 635–37
Feminismo Americano, 337–38
feminist and queer perspectives. *See also* LGBTIQ+ movements
　challenges to mainstream theory, 108–11
　collective identity formation, 112–15
　decolonial feminism, 115–17, 124–25
　introduction to, 5, 107–8
　summary of, 118
feminist movements
　anti-fascist feminist movements, 339–40
　Argentina, 261
　Brazil, 340, 341, 342, 347–48
　demands of, 337–39
　identity culture in, 594–97
　introduction to, 336, 337–38
　Lastesistas, 521–22
　lesbian feminists, 345–46
　state feminism, 288
Ferrer, Raúl, 646–47
field theory, 638–39
fiesteras, in Buenos Aires, 409
First Conference of Latin American Communist Parties in Buenos Aires, 324
First Continental Encounter for Humanity and Against Neoliberalism, 531–32
First National Conference of Gays, Lesbians, Bisexuals, Travestis, Transgenders and Transexuals, 783–84
fiscal decentralization, 294
foco theory, 185–86
Food and Agriculture Organization (FAO), 782
food autonomy, 133, 134
foquismo/foco guerrillero, 561–62, 564–65, 566–67
Foro de Políticas Públicas Rurales, 788
Foro Indígena de Abya Yala, the Foro de Comunicación Indígena, 261
Foro Nacional de la Agricultura Familiar (FoNAF), 788
Fortuny, José Manuel, 325–26
Foucault, Michel, 109–10, 111, 413–14
fragmentation, 98–99, 237
framejacking, defined, 542
framing by right-wing movements, 541–42
fraud use by military regimes, 205
Free Trade Agreement of the Americas (FTAA), 526
free trade agreements, 38–39, 525, 527–28
Free Trade Area of the Americas (FTAA), 95–96, 98–99, 528–29, 530
Freire, Paulo, 646–50
Frente Amplio, 398
Frente de Acción Popular Unificado (FAPU), 147
Frente de Convergencia Nacional Party, 479

Frente de Liberación Homosexual, 412
Frente Farabundo Martí para la Liberación Nacional (FMLN), 92, 146–47, 189–90, 546–48, 559, 649
Frente Homosexual de Acción Revolucionaria (FHAR), 412–13
Frente Nacional de Defensa de los Bienes Públicos y el Patrimonio Nacional, 147
Frente Nacional de Lucha (FNL), 147
Frente Nacional de Resistencia Popular (FNRP), 147, 150
Frente Nacional por la Defensa de los Derechos Económicos y Sociales (Frenadeso), 147
Frente Negra Brasileira, 372–73
Frente País Solidario (FREPASO), 146–47, 475
Frente para la Victoria (FPV), 725–26
Frente Sandinista de Liberación Nacional (FSLN), 146–47, 186–87, 188–90, 192–93, 197–98, 328–29, 562, 649
Fry, Stephen, 548
Fuentes, Ydígoras, 186
fuero real, 407
Fuerzas Armadas de Liberación Nacional (FALN), 187
Fuerzas Armadas Rebeldes (FAR), 186
Fuerzas Armadas Revolucionarias de Colombia (FARC), 328, 550, 562
Fuerzas de Liberación Nacional (FLN), 562, 563, 564–65
Fujimori, Alberto, 472–73
Fundación Ambiente y Recursos Naturales (FARN), 750–51, 753–54
Fundación Colombiana para la Investigación de la Cultura Negra, 374–75
fundamentalist right, 539
FundeMujer, 379

G

Galvão, Patricia, 340
García, Alan, 44
García Bárcenas, Rafael, 183–84
Garvey, Marcus, 372–73
gay identity, 414
Gay-Lesbian Pride Marches, 415
Gay Liberation Movement, 410
gay marriage, 45
Geledés, 378–79

gender-based violence, 130
gender equality, 338, 346–47, 410–11, 412–13, 596–97, 629–30, 770, 781–82
gender ideology, 118, 419, 547, 549, 551
gender oppression, 18–19
General Agreement on Tariffs and Trade (GATT), 332
genocide, 143
geographical space, 512–13
geographies of activism
  Bolivia, 686, 689
  Brazil, 685–86, 690–91
  Central America, 688
  Colombia, 686, 687
  democratic struggle of cities, 683–85
  institutionalized politics, 685–87
  introduction to, 678–79
  Mexico, 690–91
  micro-geographies of disruption, 681–83, 691
  Peru, 689
  resistance to neoliberalism, 687–91
  spatial strategies in social movement theory, 679–81
  summary of, 691–92
geopolitical dimension of knowledge, 127
German *Autonomen,* 506–7, 511–12
global Depression, 150–51
globalization. *See also* neoliberal globalization
  autonomist movements and, 513–14
  border-crossing movements, 261–62
  consumer mobilization, 496–97
  defined, 249
  environmental challenges, 253–54
  introduction to, 6–7, 249–50
  Left organizations and, 259–61
  LGBTIQ+ movements and, 415–16
  modernity model and, 60
  new communication technologies, 258–59
  protest waves and, 251–52
  resource mobilization and, 39
  summary of, 263
global justice activism, 262, 667–68
global protest wave (2011-2012), C23P1. *See also* protest waves
glocalization, 285–86, 294
González, Clara, 338
Gonzalez, Lélia, 378–79, 380

Goulart, João, 341, 647–48
government corruption protest waves, 148
Gramsci, Antonio, 4, 22, 24, 580
grassroots social movements
    Argentina, 290
    Brazil, 288
    capitalism and, 235, 236
    Christian communities and, 329
    communication, 99
    educational movements and, 650
    environmental mobilization and, 441, 442, 445–46
    incorporation of, 304
    political liberalism and, 37
    water privatization by, 260
    workers mobilization and, 312–16
Great Depression, 233, 241–42
Griffin, Roger, 537–38
Grupo Gay de Bahía, 414, 415, 548–49
Grupo Latinoamericano de Estudio, Formación y Acción Feminista, 125
Guatemala
    anti-corruption social mobilization, 477–80
    democratic transitions from above, 216–17
    digital activism, 701–3, 706–7
    educational movements, 652
    guerrilla movements, 18–19
    indigenous movements in, 325–26
    Mayan peasant associations, 251–52
    military regime, 204–6
    mining conflicts in, 445
    Pan-Maya movement in, 582
    peasant movements, 205
    revolutionary movements in, 186, 189
Guatemalan National Police, 206
guerra popular prolongada (prolonged people's war-GPP/PPL), 562
guerrilla movements. *See also* revolutionary movements and guerrillas
    Brazil, 202
    El Salvador, 18–19, 21–22, 92
    Guatemala, 18–19
    guerrilla, defined, 557
    military regimes and, 204
    second-wave guerrilla groups, 188–89
    warfare by, 184, 185–86

Guevara, Che, 185–86, 187, 556–57, 561–62, 566–67
Guevara-Debray theory of revolution, 561–62
Gutiérrez, Gustavo, 648–49

H

hacendados, 322
Haitian dictatorships, 198
Haitian Revolution, 371–72
health care reforms, 578–79
Hemispheric Social Alliance (HSA), 528–29, 530
heteronormativity, 112, 113, 240, 538
History of Sexuality (Foucault), 413–14
HIV/AIDS crisis, 111, 414–15, 780, 781–82, 787
Ho-Chi Minh, 188
Holloway, John, 506–7
homosexuality rights, 406–7, 408–11, 412, 413–14, 415
Honduran Consejo Cívico de Organizaciones Populares e Indígenas, 133
Honduras, 145–46, 150, 666–67
horizontalism, 97, 100, 260–61, 372–73
Housewives Committees, 342–43
human rights claims, 56, 423, 430–31, 432–34
human rights groups, 200–1, 424–25, 427, 431, 433, 462, 595
human rights movements
    anti-corruption social mobilization, 480
    Argentina, 424–25, 428
    Catholic Church, 426, 427
    Chile, 242, 424–25, 427, 428
    citizenship rights and, 430–31
    dictatorships and, 56, 427–30
    emergence of, 424–25
    expansion of, 430–33
    introduction to, 8–9, 422–24
    key elements, 425–27
    Mexico, 59
    militant motherhood, 341–43
    military dictatorships and, 422–23, 424, 425
    non-governmental organizations and, 426, 427–28
    social rights and, 432–33
    summary of, 433–34
    women in, 583
human rights organizations (HROs), 218, 428, 433, 756

human rights violations, 43–44, 57–58, 223–24, 424, 427–29, 433–34, 525, 634

I

identity/identity movements
  aboriginal identity movements, 592
  Black identity, 373–75, 384
  Blackness in, 370, 374, 379–80
  collective identity, 3, 72, 112–15, 440, 591
  Colombia, 601–2
  cultural identity, 113, 321, 377, 592–93, 594
  exclusion/inclusion politics, 600–2
  gay identity, 414
  in indigenous movements, 592–94
  indigenous people and, 359–64
  intersectional identities, 93–94
  introduction to, 10, 590–92
  labor movements, 238
  LGBTIQ+ movements, 413–14, 597–99, 780
  minority identity, 598
  national identity movements, 592
  negro/a identity, 381–82
  normative identity movements, 592
  particularistic identity movements, 592
  Peru, 601–2
  sexual identity theory, 109–10
  shared identity, 440, 448, 449, 544
  in social mobilization, 10
  women and, 108–9
  in women's movements, 594–97
illegal protest activity, 690
immigrant rights, 221
immigration, 306
imperialism, 561, 634–35
import substitution industrialization, 491
impression management, 284
Inca Empire, 166
incorporation mechanisms, 75
Indigenous and Afro-diasporic trajectories, 124–25
indigenous communities, 96, 148–49, 277–78, 615–17
indigenous dipossession movements
  historical roots of, 355–56
  introduction to, 8, 354–55
  struggles of, 359–64
  summary of, 364–65
  theoretical explanations for, 356–59
indigenous movements. *See also* peasant movements
  autonomist movements and, 510
  Bolivia, 220–21, 321–22, 356, 362
  Brazil, 322–23, 326
  Chile, 325, 364
  Colombia, 220–21, 323, 328
  Ecuador, 220–21, 356
  El Salvador, 324–25
  environmentalization, 441
  geographical perspectives, 77
  globalization and, 259–60
  in Guatemala, 325–26
  identity and, 592–94
  introduction to, 8, 354–55
  liberation movements, 27–28
  Mexico, 92–93, 322, 323–24, 356
indigenous prior consultation (IPC), 293
indigenous rights, 287–88, 431, 432
indiscriminate repression, 149
indissolubility of systems, 76
industrialization, 182, 234, 304, 491
Indymedia, 40
inflection in decolonization, 124–25
information politics, 543
Iniciativa Mesoamericana de Comercio, Integración y Desarrollo (Iniciativa CID), 528
institutionalization of social movements
  Argentina, 781–82, 784, 786, 787, 788
  Brazil, 782, 785
  Chile, 780–81
  collective actions, 389
  Ecuador, 784–85
  introduction to, 12–13, 777–80
  Mexico, 782, 786, 787
  modes of, 780–81
  participation in, 288
  politics of, 11–13, 685–87, 718
  positional institutionalization, 787–88
  practical institutionalization, 785–86
  programmatic institutionalization, 781–82
  in revolution, 182
  socioterritorial movements and, 77–78
  summary, 788–89

symbolic institutionalization, 783–85
Uruguay, 786
workers' mobilization and, 308–9
institutional recognition, 284–85, 287, 296
institutional schemas, 579
Instituto de Pesquisas e Estudos Afro-Brasilieros, 374–75
Instituto Mexicano para el Desarrollo Comunitario (IMDEC), 650
Instituto Nacional contra la Discriminación, la Xenofobia y el Racismo (INADI), 781–82
Instituto Nacional de Tecnología Agropecuaria (INTA), 291–92
Instituto Paulo Freire (IPF), 650
Instituto Pedagógico Latinoamericano y Caribeño (IPLAC), 651
Instituto Universitario Latinoamericano de Agroecología Paulo Freire (IALA-PF), 653
insurgent elites, 6, 181
integration of peasant movements, 323–26
Inter-American Commission of Women (CIM), 339, 522–23
Inter-American Convention Against Corruption (IACAC), 472
Intercontinental Encounter for Humanity and against Neoliberalism, 190–91
internal competition in network mechanisms, 98–99
international aid chain, 258
International Day for the Elimination of Violence against Women, 348, 521
International Encyclopedia of the Social & Behavioral Sciences (Langlois), 592
International Feminist Congress in Buenos Aires, 338–39
International Journal of Communication, 696–97
International Labor Organization Convention 169 (ILO 169), 293
International Labor Organization (ILO), 364
international litigation, 756–57
International Monetary Fund (IMF), 150, 236
internet communicational technologies (ICTs), 147

Internet Society in Mexico, 705
inter-relational perspectives, 129–30
intersectionality, 72–73, 93–94, 112–13
irreversibility of time, 129
ISI economies, 236–37
issue-based coalitions, 528
itrofill mongen of diversity, 132–33

J

Jáuregui, Carlos, 413–14
Jehovah's Witnesses, 632
Jelin, Elizabeth, 427–28
Jeunesse Ouvrière Chrétienne (Young Christian Workers) (YCW), 627–28
Joaquín Chamorro, Pedro, 198
John XXIII, Pope, 628
jornais cariocas, in Rio de Janeiro, 409
June Protest Cycle in Brazil, 533
Juntas de Buen Gobierno (Good Government Boards), 190–91, 612
Juventud Ortodoxa, 183–84
Juventud Revolucionaria Nicaragüense (JRN), 186–87

K

Kant, Immanuel, 506
Katari, Tupac, 582
Keck, Margaret, 523–24
Kirchner, Cristina Fernández de, 289, 315–16, 474, 719, 725–26
Kirchner, Fernández de, 290
Kirchner, Néstor, 289, 290, 314, 725–26
Krenak, Ailton, 277
Kubitscheck, Juscelino, 340–41
kume felen (good living), 132–33

L

labor legislation, 305
labor movements, 7–8, 18–19, 235, 236, 238, 462, 723–24
La Causa R, 725
Lacerda, María, 340
Lame Chantre, Manuel Quintín, 323
Lampão da Esquina, 412–13
La Mujer journal, 338–39
landlessness, 239, 269, 271–72, 276

land occupation
　conflicts over, 266–71
　criminalization of, 273–74
　disputes and development, 278–80, 279*t*
　indigenous people and, 277–78
　introduction to, 266–68
　peasantry and, 275–77
　summary of, 280–81
　territorial conflicts and, 266–71
　territorialization, 277
　typology of, 271–75, 272*t*
land reform, 229, 269–70, 287–89, 325, 328, 648, 667
land reforms, 269–70, 356
La Piedrita collective, 612–13
Las Bambas mine in Apurimac, 253–54
Lastesistas, 521–22
lateral transnationalism, 97
latifundia, 269–70, 271–72, 457
Latin American Marxism (1870-1910). *See* Marxism
Latin American Security Operation, 328
The Latin Americans-Spirit and Ethos (Dealy), 575
Left Turn government, 361
left-wing social movements
　citizenship and, 611
　electoral triumphs, 143
　emancipatory horizons of the European left, 124–25
　globalization and, 259–61
　government rule and, 26
　indigenous movements and, 28
　left-libertarian autonomism, 506
　libertarian autonomism, 506
　oppositional leftist parties, 145
　populism and, 59, 339, 340–41
　women's movements, 339–41, 342
legal mobilization
　Argentina, 749–51, 752–53
　Brazil, 749, 752–53
　Colombia, 749–50, 752
　counter-legal mobilization, 754–55
　court system and, 747–49, 751–55
　federalism and, 757
　feminist organizations and, 754
　framework of, 747–49
　impact of, 749–51
　international litigation, 756–57
　introduction to, 746–47
　Mexico, 752–53
　multi-level processes of, 755–57
　subnational legal mobilization, 757
　summary of, 757–58
legal rights movement, 492
Lei Suplicy, 393
lesbian feminists, 345–46
Lesbian-Gay-Transvestite-Transsexual-Bisexual Pride Marches, 415
LGBTIQ+ movements
　anti-LGBT+ uncivil movement, 45–46, 480, 548–50
　under authoritarianism, 411–12
　claims for recognition, 73
　discrimination issues, 40–41
　early mobilization, 409–11
　feminism and, 107–8, 110, 111, 112, 114–17
　gay marriage, 45
　globalization and economic liberalism, 415–16
　historical and cultural context, 407–9
　HIV/AIDS crisis, 111, 414–15, 780, 781–82, 787
　homosexuality rights, 406–7, 408–11, 412, 413–14, 415
　identity culture of, 413–14, 597–99, 780
　institutionalization of, 781–82, 783–84, 786, 787
　introduction to, 8, 406–7
　lesbian feminists, 345–46
　liberation theology movement and, 629–30
　Mexico, 599
　Pentecostals and, 637
　political alliance building, 45
　political identities, 116–17
　role in democratization, 238
　same-sex marriage legalization, 116–17
　schisms in, 412–13
　state-directed activism, 417–18, 418*t*
　summary of, 418–19
LGBTQ rights, 221, 287, 431
Liberación de la Madre Tierra Project, 133
liberal democratization, 9, 237–38
liberal-elitist nationalism, 168

liberal feminists, 338
liberal model of development, 233
liberation theology movement, 152–53, 409–10, 560, 561, 629–30, 647–50
Libertad y Refundación (LIBRE), 146–47
Liga Cristã, 549
Liga da Mulher pela Democracia, 341
Liga Internacional de Mujeres Ibéricas e Hispanoamericanas, 339
Ligas Camponesas, 645
Ligas de Comunidades Agrarias, 323–24
living well *(buen vivir/vivir bien/sumak kawsay)*, 79
López Obrador, Andrés Manuel, 258–59
López Pérez, Rigoberto, 561
L'Ouverture, Toussaint, 371–72
Lozano, Betty Ruth, 379
Luisi, Paulina, 338
Lula da Silva, Luis Inácio, 286, 287–88, 313–14, 526
Luso-Hispanic colonial legacy, 3
Luxemburg, Rosa, 563

M
Machado, Gerardo, 151
Macri, Mauricio, 315–16
macroeconomic policy, 239, 494
macro-social projects, 55
Madero, Francisco I., 182, 556–57
Madres de Plaza de Mayo, 59, 72–73, 201, 341–42, 422, 426, 428
Maduro, Nicolás, 207–8, 397
Manuel Santos, Juan, 550
Mao Tse Tung, 188
Mapuche movement, 278, 325, 364
maquiladora industries, 315–16, 432
Marcha de los Cuatro Suyos, 481
Marcha de los Turbantes (March of the Turbaned Ones), 379
Marcha de Putas/Vadias, 347–48
marginalization, 93–94, 112, 170, 355, 374–75, 477–78, 593, 596, 598, 601–2, 629
Maria, José, 323
Mariátegui, José Carlos, 4, 20–22, 306, 324
Marini, Ruy Mauro, 23
market-based democracies, 488–89, 492–93
market-based economics, 9, 462, 717
market-led development, 236–39, 241
maroons, 267, 271–72, 277, 371–72
Márquez Mina, Francia, 379
Marx, Karl, 17–18, 74
Marxism
  capitalism and, 18–20, 230
  class and, 18–20
  collectivist society and, 306
  decolonization and, 123
  dependency theory, 22–24
  introduction to, 4, 17
  Liberation Theology and, 560, 561
  neoliberalism and, 24–29
  neo-Marxism, 241, 463, 466–67, 506
  opening phases, 20–22
  overview of, 17–18
  Stalinized Marxism, 24
  summary of, 29–30
  totality and, 18–20
Mayan indigenous struggles, 133
mechanism of direct democracy (MDD), 767–69, 771
media democratization, 396–97, 399–400
memory keeping strategies, 87–88
Menem, Carlos, 472–73, 475, 614–15
Mesa Amplia Nacional Estudiantil (MANE), 399
Mesa por la Vida y la Salud de las Mujeres, 754
mestizo (mixed race) culture, 356, 592–93
Mexican Revolution (1910), 20, 190, 305, 326, 393
Mexico. *See also* Ejército Zapatista de Liberación Nacional (EZLN)
  addressing racism, 382
  agrarian reform, 272–73
  authoritarian regimes in, 207
  autonomist movements, 511
  Aztec Empire, 166
  contentious politics, 734–36
  debt crisis, 237
  democratization in, 704–5
  digital activism, 697–98, 699, 703–7
  educational movements, 645–46, 650, 652, 653
  environmental mobilization, 449
  geographies of activism, 690–91
  human rights movements, 59

Mexico (*cont.*)
  indigenous movements in, 92–93, 322, 323–24, 356
  institutionalization of social movements, 782, 786, 787
  institutional politics, 114
  legal mobilization, 752–53
  LGBTIQ+ movements, 410, 412, 417
  muxe of Oaxaca, 408, 599
  NAFTA and, 279
  nationalism and, 168–69, 170
  revolutionary movements, 182–83, 184–85, 192, 563, 565–66
  student movements in, 393, 394, 396, 399–400
  Tlatelolco Plaza massacre, 207, 394, 565–66
  unionism in, 315
  workers mobilization and, 312
  YoSoy132 movement, 258–59, 390, 697–98
micro-geographies of disruption, 681–83, 691
militant motherhood, 341–43
militarized neoliberal movement, 539, 550–52
military coups, 23, 150, 241–42, 310, 324, 393–96, 424, 426, 563, 725
military dictatorships
  Argentina, 310–11, 595
  Black women's movements and, 378–79
  Brazil, 208, 341, 464, 782, 789
  Chile, 424, 719–20
  civilian rule after, 375–76
  gay and lesbian activism against, 411–12
  grassroot resistance to, 236
  human rights movements and, 422–23, 424, 425
  human rights violations during, 525, 724
  mass incorporation and, 724
  New Social Movements and, 54
  repression and, 46–47
  trade unions and, 235
  truth commissions and, 216–17
military regimes
  Afro-social movements and, 375–76
  authoritarianism and, 6, 199–206
  double militancy, 345–46, 542–43, 548
  repression against student movements, 393
  structural adjustment policies and, 310–11
  workers mobilization and, 310–11

militias, 21–22, 183–84, 278, 309–10, 326–27, 328
minimum wages, 314
Ministry for Agrarian Development (MAD), 289
Ministry of Indigenous and First Peoples Affairs (MAIPO), 362
Ministry of Popular Power (MIMPI), 616
minority identity, 598
MMG Limited, 253–54
mobilization dynamics, 72, 80, 233, 242–43, 471
Mobilizing for Human Rights in Latin America (Cleary), 431
mobilizing resources, 169–70, 171
modernity model, 60
modernization process, 29
Montesinos, Vladimiro, 480–81
moral economy, 739–41
Morales, Evo, 63–64, 292–93, 294–95, 314, 361, 362, 577, 582, 686
Morales, Jimmy, 479
moralizing campaigns, 305
moral panic, 414, 540, 551
moral Right, 538
MORENA party, 146–47
movement entrepreneurs, 36, 358, 538, 542, 543–44, 547, 550
movement exhaustion, 155
Movimento Brasil Livre (MBL), 549
Movimento de Alfabetização de Jovens e Adultos (MOVA), 650–51
Movimento de Cultura Popular (MCP), 647–48
Movimento de Educação de Base (MEB), 645
Movimento dos Trabalhadores Rurais Sem Terra (MST), 38, 44, 72, 252, 268–69, 287, 329–30, 574–75, 651, 652–53, 654, 682
Movimento Negro Unificado (MNU), 378–79
Movimento Passe Livre (MPL), 476
Movimento por la Etica Pública, 476
Movimento Sanitário (health reform movement), 749
Movimiento al Socialismo (MAS), 146–47, 242, 361, 577, 686
Movimiento de Izquierda Revolucionaria (MIR), 648
Movimiento 26 de Julio (M26J), 183–84
Movimiento de la Izquierda Revolucionaria (MIR), 187

Movimiento de Liberación Nacional Tupamaros, 187
Movimiento de los Trabajadores Rurales Sin Tierra of Bolivia (MST-B), 271–72
Movimiento de Resistencia-12 de Octubre, 147
Movimiento de Unidad Plurinacional Pachakutik-Nuevo País (MUPP-NP), 361
Movimiento Indígena Pachakuti (MIP), 146–47
Movimiento Nacional Campesino-Indígena (MNCI), 291–92
Movimiento Nacionalista Revolucionario (MNR), 183–84, 309–10
Movimiento Popular Unificado (MPU), 147
Movimiento por la Paz con Justicia y Dignidad (MPJD), 697–98
Movimiento pro Emancipación de la Mujer Chilena, 340
Movimiento Revolucionario 13 de Noviembre (MR13), 186
Movimiento Teresa Rodríguez (MTR), 513
Mujeres Autoconvocadas para Decidir en Libertad (MADEL) coalition, 749–50
Mulher, Maria, 378–79
multi-class movements, 308–9
multiculturalism, 6, 170, 173, 416
multilateral cooperation in consumer mobilization, 498–99
multilateral trade agreements, 527–29
multisectoralism, 75, 90, 91, 101
mutual aid societies, 303
mutualist societies, 304
muxe of Oaxaca, Mexico, 408, 599

N

Nacimiento, Abdias do, 374–75
Nasa peoples, 129–30, 133
Nascimento, Beatriz, 378–79
National Commission for the Defense of Water and Life, 768–69
National Commission for the Development of Indigenous People, 782
National Council for the Prevention of Racism in Mexico, 382
National Council to Combat Discrimination and for the Advancement of LGBT Rights, 781–82
National Council to Prevent Discrimination in Mexico, 787
National Day Against Homophobia, 781–82
National Democratic Convention, 190–91
national identity movements, 592
National Indigenous Uprising in Ecuador, 356
National Institute against Discrimination, Xenophobia, and Racism in Argentina, 382
National Intelligence Agency, 480–81
nationalism
 alternative nationalisms, 168
 conceptual and theoretical considerations, 163–65
 creation of, 165–67
 introduction to, 6, 162–63
 liberal-elitist nationalism, 168
 multicultural nationalism, 170
 rejection of, 169–71
 separatist mobilization, 171–73
 state-seeking, 171–73
 summary of, 173–74
 transformation of, 167–69
National LGBT Conference, 781–82
National Program for the Strengthening of Family Farming (PRONAF), 788
National Strike Council, 394
Natural Law ideas surrounding sexuality, 407–9
Negri, Antonio, 506
negro/a identity, 381–82
neo-developmentalism, 239, 315–16
neo-extractivism, 239–40, 516
Neo-Indigenismo, 616–17
neoliberal democracy, 249–50, 263
neoliberal globalization
 grievances and resistance, 250–55
 NGOs as political actors, 257–58
 political dimensions of, 60–62
 protestors against, 251–52
 regional democratization, 256–57
 transnational processes, 254–62, 263
neoliberalism
 adoption of, 173
 consumption and, 496
 countermovement against, 94
 demobilization and, 283, 290

neoliberalism (cont.)
  economic crisis of, 26–29, 94
  economic threats under, 145–46
  globalization of, 60–62
  health care reforms, 578–79
  indigenous dipossession and, 356
  introduction to, 6–7, 8
  Marxism and, 24–29
  militarized movements, 9
  militarized neoliberal movement, 550–52
  modernity model and, 60
  movements opposed to, 45–46
  protest waves and, 151
  protest waves during, 145–46
  radical neoliberal movements, 539
  resistance to, 687–91
  territorialization of agribusiness corporations, 280
  transition to, 230
  women's movements and, 344–46
  workers mobilization and, 310–12, 315
neo-Marxism, 241, 463, 466–67, 506
Neo-Pentecostals, 633
neopluralism, 462–64, 466
neo-Polanyist regimes, 155
neo-structuralism, 239–40
network mechanisms in social movements
  elements and arguments, 90–91
  fragmentation and internal competition in, 98–99
  introduction to, 87–90
  old vs. new movements, 93–95
  participation and recruitment, 91–93
  social media and, 99–100
  summary of, 100–1
  transnational networks, 95–98
new communication technologies, 258–59
New Social Movement (NSM) in Latin America (NSMLA)
  concept and debates, 57–60
  cultural interpretations of, 55
  democratic struggle of cities, 683–85
  dimensions of, 60–62
  indigenous claims, 130–31, 593
  introduction to, 54–57
  Marxism and, 18–19, 25
  network mechanisms, 93–95
  socio-political matrix, 62–64
  summary of, 64–66
  workers mobilization and, 312–16
new territoriality, 76, 267, 276, 687–88
Newton, Huey P., 410
NGOization of resistance, 257–58
Nguyen Giap, 188
Nicaragua
  anti-mining mobilization in, 92–93
  austerity programs, 252
  authoritarianism of, 348
  authoritarian regimes in, 207–8
  indigenous movements, 220–21
  repertoire of contention, 150
  revolutionary movements in, 186–87, 189, 192
  Sandinista Revolution in, 22, 559, 649
  Somoza family dynasty, 197–98
Nicaraguan Revolution, 24–25, 326, 328–29
NIMBY (not in my backyard) movements, 766–67
Non-Aligned Movement, 152
non-governmental organizations (NGOs)
  feminists and, 346
  in human rights movements, 426, 427–28
  judicialization strategies, 238–39
  legal mobilization, 750–51, 752, 753–54
  neoliberalism and, 146
  NGOization of resistance, 257–58
  as political actors, 257–58
non-institutionalized collective actions, 389
non-institutionalized politics, 718, 719
non-nationalist movements, 164
non-profit organizations, 38–39, 273
Noriega, Manuel, 198–99
normative identity movements, 592
North American Free Trade Agreement (NAFTA), 96, 279, 331, 356, 528
novo sindicalismo, 311
Nuestro Mundo, 410, 412–13, 414

O

occupation struggles, 269–70
OcupaEscola uprisings, 697–98
Ojo T poetry project, 115
old social movements networks, 93–95
oligarchization, 285, 305, 723–24

ollas comunes, 57–58
Onganía, Juan Carlos, 394–95
open regionalism, 239
oppositional leftist parties, 145
Ordóñez, Alejandro, 551
Organic Law of Labor, Men and Female Workers, 314
Organización Auténtica (OA), 184
Organización Latinoamerican de Solidaridad (OLAS), 328
Organización Nacional de Asociaciones de Jubilados y Pensionistas del Uruguay (ONAJPU), 768–69
Organización Nacional de Mujeres Indígenas Andinas y Amazónicas del Perú (ONAMIAP), 596
Organización Negra Centroamericana, 380–81
organizational autonomy, 99, 329–30, 393
organizational domestication, 97
organizational ecology theory, 41, 89
organizational interlayering, 94
Organization for Economic Cooperation and Development (OECD), 472
Organization of American States (OAS), 382, 472, 499, 522–23, 566–67
original entry occupations, 274
Orpheus and Power (Hanchard), 377
Ortega, Daniel, 150, 207–8
O Sexo Feminino journal, 338–39
Owen, Robert, 123
Oxhorn, Philip, 430–31

P

Pachakutik movement, 686
Pact of Pedrero, 184
País, Frank, 183–84
palenques, 376–77
Panama, 198–99, 458
Paniagua, Valentín, 481
Pan-Maya movement in Guatemala, 582
paradigm other, 124–25
Paraguay, 276–77
Parody, Gina, 551
participant fatigue, 465–66
participatory budgeting (PB), 262, 464–65, 765–67
participatory institutions (PI)
  Argentina, 765–67
  Brazil, 764–65, 766
  campaigning by social movements, 767–69
  civil society organizations and, 761–62, 764–71
  Colombia, 763
  defined, 763–64
  experimentation with, 762–64
  individual citizen participation, 765–67
  introduction to, 761–62
  local popular organization, 769–71
  Peru, 763, 764
  state officials and, 764–71
  summary of, 771–72
  Uruguay, 768–69
  Venezuela, 770–71
participatory state feminism, 788
particularistic identity movements, 592
Partido Comunista de Chile (PCCh), 325
Partido Comunista de Colombia (PCC), 328
Partido Comunista do Brasil (PCB), 271–72, 326, 645
Partido Comunista Salvadoreño (PCS), 324–25
Partido da Social Democracia Brasileira (PSDB), 476–77
Partido de la Revolución Democrática (PRD), 734, 735–36
Partido Democratico Trabalhista (PDT), 464
Partido do Movimento Democrático Brasileiro (PMDB), 476–77
Partido dos Trabalhadores (PT), 24, 149, 240, 286, 311, 346–47, 464–66, 476, 650–51, 735–36
Partido Ecologista Verde of Mexico, 399–400
Partido Guatemalteco del Trabajo (PGT communist), 186
Partido Independiente de Color (PIC), 372–73
Partido Justicialista (PJ), 725–26
Partido Nacional Feminista (National Feminist Party), 338
Partido Obrero Revolucionario (POR), 183
Partido Peronista Femenino, 340–41
Partido Revolucionario Institucional (PRI), 44, 193, 206–7, 394, 399–400, 566, 734
Partido Socialista, 323
Partido Socialista Popular (PSP), 184
Partido Socialista Unido de Venezuela, 346–47
Partido Social Liberal (PSL), 476–77

party politics
   Argentina, 719–20, 721, 725–26
   autonomy and, 732
   Bolivia, 724
   Brazil, 720
   contentious politics and, 722–26
   Ecuador, 724–25
   introduction to, 715–17
   neoliberal reform and, 721–22
   social movement partyism, 155
   structuring of social movements and, 717–22
   summary of, 727–28
   Venezuela, 725, 726
passion-driven protest, 90–91
patriarchal junction, 130
patrimonial praetorian regimes, 181
Paul VI, Pope, 628
Paz Estenssoro, Víctor, 183, 326–27
peak associations, 75, 91, 782
peasant movements
   in Argentina, 289–90
   in Brazil, 288–89
   ecologism, 92–93
   environmentalization, 441
   Guatemala, 205
   importance of, 7–8
   integration of, 323–26
   introduction to, 320–21
   people's power movements, 329–31
   restoration movements, 320–23
   revolution in, 326–29
   summary of, 332–33
peasantry and land occupation, 275–77
Pedagogy of the Oppressed (Freire), 646–47, 648
Pedro II, King, 323
peleguismo, 311
PEMEX privatization, 146–47
Peña Nieto, Enrique, 258–59, 399–400, 705
peñas, 57–58
Penguin Revolution in Chile, 697–98
Pentecostals/Pentacostalism, 10, 632–35
people's power movements, 329–31
people's war, 188–89
Pérez Molina, Otto, 478
performative governance, 284, 287–88, 293, 296
Perlongher, Néstor, 117

Perón, Juan Domingo, 200, 234, 308, 340–41, 491
personal dictatorships, 6, 197–99
Peru
   anti-corruption social mobilization, 480–82
   Creole patriotism, 166–67
   cultural dimension of social movements, 577
   demobilization process in, 292–95
   environmental conflicts, 253
   geographies of activism, 689
   identity culture, 601–2
   indigenous movements in, 362–63
   nationalism and, 170
   participatory institutions in, 763, 764
   student movements in, 392
Petro, Gustavo, 549
physical integrity rights, 431
Piñeiro Lozada, Manuel, 566
Piñera, Sebastián, 255
Pink Tide, 313–14, 346–48, 540, 563, 564–65, 784–85
Pinochet, Augusto, 47, 310–11, 341, 397–98, 525, 563, 579
piquetero movement in Argentina
   autonomist movements and, 512–13
   citizenship and, 608, 614–15, 617
   demobilization trends, 289, 290–91
   as mixed-gender movements, 113
   old-new movement divide, 94
   participatory budgeting and, 767
   party politics, 719–20, 721, 725–26
   positional institutionalization, 788
   repertoires of contention, 673–74
   struggle for reincorporation, 74, 239
   tactical actions, 680–81
   unemployment and, 733–34
   unionism and, 313
   urban social mobilization and, 463
Pisantry, Alejandro, 705
Plan Jefes y Jefas de Hogar Desocupados (PJJHD), 290, 291
Plurinational Legislative Assembly, 315
pluriverse, 78–79
pobladores movement, 508–10, 511
Pocketbook Politics (Jacobs), 491–92
Poder Ciudadano; Instituto de Estudios Comparados en Ciencias Penales y Sociales (INECIPE), 750–51

Polanyi, Karl, 251–52
polarization, 42, 75, 242–43, 289, 290, 295, 296, 474, 788
policy instruments of institutionalization, 785–86
political communication, 89–90, 109, 166, 701
political culture, 24, 43, 58, 114–15, 181, 507, 564–65, 575
political dynamics, 6–7, 43, 190–91, 598, 715–16
political education, 10–11, 644–47, 652–53
political event of a Revolution, 557, 558
political event of regime change, 558
political instability, 42, 43, 46, 220–21, 326, 540
political intervention projects, 124–25
political liberalism, 37
political liberalization, 144, 148–49, 153–54, 233, 357, 481, 527, 594
political modernization, 168–69
political movements, 6, 23, 167, 357–58, 360, 489, 491, 540, 545
political ontology, 78, 79, 80, 614
political opportunities structure (POS), 564–65
political pluralism, 196, 217, 732
political process theory (PPT)
    assumptions about, 43–44
    future research, 47–48
    influential allies, 45–46
    introduction to, 35–36
    openness or closure of polity, 44–45
    overview of, 42–48
    political instability, 46
    into relational mechanisms, 73–74
    repression, 46–47
    summary of, 48
political rights, 36–37, 166–67, 191, 201, 215–16, 218, 338–39, 406, 425, 432, 433, 522, 594–95, 756
politics of power, 361
politics of social movement activism
    contentious politics, 731, 732–38
    institutional politics, 731, 732
    introduction to, 731–32
    moral economy, 739–41
    political pluralism, 196, 217, 732
    state politics, 538–39

    summary of, 741–42
    territorial movements and, 738–41
popular protests, 208, 719, 725, 750–51
popular sovereignty, 10, 168, 607–8, 611, 613–14, 615–17
populism
    capitalism and, 458–59
    debates over, 24
    emergence of, 665
    leftist populism, 59, 339, 340–41
    nationalist populism, 356–57
    neo-populism, 515
    right-wing populism, 538–39
    urban populism, 466
    women's movements and, 339–41
    workers' mobilization, 308–9, 313–14, 316
Portal, Magda, 340–41
Portantiero, Juan Carlos, 24
Portugal, 256–57
positional institutionalization, 787–88
post-neoliberalism, 239
post-World War II urban social movements, 456–60
potencia (power *to*), 680
power blocks, 308
practical authority, 778–79
practical institutionalization, 785–86
praxis in decolonization, 124–25
Prebisch, Raúl, 491
precaristas, 327–28
Primer Congreso Internacional de Estudiantes, 393
Prison Notebooks (Gramsci), 29
privilege/power patterns, 112
problematique, defined, 59, 61–62, 64
procreational will, 783–84
Programa Social Agropecuario (PSA), 291–92
Program for Integral Social Education, 786
programmatic institutionalization, 781–82
progressive social movements, 118, 528–29, 552
progressivism, 315–16
projet d'autonomy (autonomy project), 505–6, 508
pro-legalization movement, 672
property rights, 217, 269, 337, 339, 690–91
protectionism, 233–34, 308, 493–94, 549
Protestantism, 37, 631–37

protest waves
    capitalism and, 236
    dynamics of, 143–44
    economic threats, 150–52
    education protest, 147
    facilitating conditions of, 144–54
    government corruption protest waves, 148
    by indigenous rural laborers, 21–22
    introduction to, 3, 6, 7, 143
    neoliberal globalization and, 251–52
    organizational infrastructures, 144–48
    outcomes of, 154–56
    party politics and, 716
    political liberation, 148–49
    state repression, 149–50
    summary of, 156
    unifying frames, 152–54, 154t
public health services, 337–38
Public Order Law, 204
punteros (informal party brokers), 733
pyramidal organizations, 591

Q

Quechua people, 278
queer perspectives/queer theory. *See* feminist and queer perspectives
Queer Theory, 416
quilombolas, 267, 270–71, 287–88
quilombos movement, 129–30, 131–32, 267, 371, 372, 376–77

R

racial destabilization, 115
racial discrimination, 306, 371, 372–74, 378, 380–83
Racial Equality Statute (Brazil), 288
racial justice, 8, 372–73, 374–77
racial oppression, 18–19, 370, 374, 376–77
racism
    addressing racism, 370–71, 380–83
    Afro-Latin American movements and, 370–71, 380–83
    Brazil, 382
    decolonizing approaches, 125
    intersection between sexism and, 112, 114, 340, 345–46
    Marxist reading of, 130
    Mexico, 382

radical democracy, 114–15
radicalization, 57, 75, 155–56, 186–87, 188, 204, 241, 308–9, 527, 560, 563, 566–67
radical neoliberal movements, 539, 543, 546, 551–52
radical Right, 538–39
Radio Caracas Televisión, 396–97
Ránquil revolt, 325
Rea, Castro, 538
Reagan, Ronald, 634
recognition mechanisms, 75
recruitment in network mechanisms, 91–93
recurring mobilization, 90–91
Red Andina de Organizaciones Afro, 380–81
Red Continental de Organizaciones Afroamericanas, 380–81
Red de Mujeres Afrolatinoamericanas, 380–81
Red de Mujeres Negras, 379, 380
Red de Mujeres Rurales of Costa Rica, 133
Red de Semillas Libres in Colombia, 133
Rede Brasileira pela Integração dos Povos (Rebrip), 528
redemocratization, 10–11, 45–46
Rede Povos da Floresta, 277
redistribution policies, 269–70, 295–96
Red Mexicana de Acción Frente al Libre Comercio (RMALC), 528
Red Nacional de Defensa de los Consumidores (RNDC), 147
redundant communication, 90
Regional Center for Military Training (CREM), 666–67
regional democratization, 6–7, 250, 256–57
relationality perspective
    ecological approaches, 78–80
    geographical approaches, 76–78
    historical approaches, 73–75
    intersectional approaches, 72–73
    introduction to, 4–5, 70–72, 71t
    social conflict and, 70–72
    summary of, 80–81
relational nature of territory, 132–33
relational worlds, 78–79
relief organizations, 304
religious groups and movements. *See also* Catholic Church

Catholic Charismatic Renewal movement, 625–26, 630–31
  economy paradigm and field theory, 638–39
  introduction to, 10, 625–26
  liberation theology movement, 152–53, 409–10, 560, 561, 629–30
  Pentecostals, 632–37
  Protestantism, 631–37
  reform and revitalization, 626–31
  revitalization of social movements, 203
  summary of, 639
religious right, 539, 551–52
Renta Dignidad, 295
repertoires of contention
  Argentina, 665
  Brazil, 667–68
  cultural aspect of, 666–68
  Honduras, 666–67
  introduction to, 11, 660–61, 662f
  objective and external factors, 662–63
  objective and internal factors, 663
  refining concept, 672–75
  research design for, 669–70, 670t
  subjective and external factors, 663–64
  subjective and internal factors, 664–65
  summary of, 675
  tactical choice and, 661f, 661–68
  theoretical contributions to, 668–75
  as variable, 670–72, 671f
repression
  indiscriminate repression, 149
  military dictatorships and, 46–47
  political process theory and, 46–47
  protest waves and, 149–50
  state repression, 149–50, 526–27
  against student movements, 393
reproductive rights, 109–10, 116, 343, 344, 346–47, 348, 419, 539, 546, 754–55, 756–58
resource mobilization theory (RMT)
  development of, 36–37
  introduction to, 35–36
  Marxism and, 18
  overview of, 36–42
  pending issues, 41–42
  into relational mechanisms, 73–74
  relevance of organizations, 39–40
  source of resources, 40–41

  summary of, 48
  types of activists/movements, 38–39
restoration movements, 320–23
Revista El Teje: Primer Periódico Travesti Latinoamericano, 115
revolutionary character, 558
revolutionary means, 558
revolutionary movements
  activism by, 307–10
  after fall of Berlin Wall, 190–92
  in Bolivia, 182, 183, 184–85, 192
  Cuba, 182, 183–90, 192
  in El Salvador, 189
  in Guatemala, 186, 189
  introduction to, 7, 9, 180–81
  Latin American traditions, 182–85
  in Mexico, 182–83, 184–85, 192
  mobilizations by, 143
  in Nicaragua, 186–87, 189, 192
  peasant movements and, 326–29
  revolutionary wave, 185f, 185–90
  social revolution, 180–81
  successful revolutions, 6, 181, 184–85, 188, 192, 557, 562, 564
  summary of, 192–93
revolutionary movements and guerrillas
  Chile, 563
  Cuba, 561–62, 566–67
  defined, 557–59, 567
  introduction to, 556–57
  Mexico, 563, 565–66
  resonance and international assistance, 565–67
  revolutionaries in, 559–60
  revolutionary situations, defined, 557
  strategies of, 561–65
  studies on, 181, 184
  summary of, 567–68
  unlikely radicals, 560–61
revolutionary radicalism, 463
revolutionary situations, defined, 557
revolutionary social movements, 558, 563, 567–68
revolutionary unionism, 308, 309–10
revolutionary women, 18–19, 343, 344
Reyes, Rafael, 392
Richard, Nelly, 117

right-wing movements
  activism of, 429
  anti-abortion counter movement, 546–48
  Brazil, 548–50
  case studies, 546–52
  Colombia, 550–52
  defined, 538–39
  El Salvador, 546–48
  extreme right-wing movements, 118, 289, 538–39, 547, 549–50, 552
  framing by, 541–42
  fundamentalist right, 539
  impact of, 544–46
  introduction to, 537–38
  mobilization by, 539–46
  political opportunity, 540–41
  populism and, 538–39
  summary of, 552
  tactics of, 542–44
  transnational collective action, 530, 531
  women's mobilization, 341
Ríos Montt, Efraín, 634
Rivadulla, Alvarez, 463
Rivera-Cusicanqui, Silvia, 124, 127
Robles de Mendoza, Margarita, 522–23
Roca, Blas, 184
Roman Catholicism. *See* Catholic Church
Romero, Óscar, 560
rondas campesinas, 577
Roundtables for the Fight Against Poverty (RFAP), 764
Rouseff, Dilma, 258–59
Rousseff, Dilma, 289, 475, 477
Royal Geographical Society, 125
rule-conforming collective actors, 98
rule-violating collective actors, 98
rural workers, 235, 306–7
Russian revolution (1917), 20

S

same-sex marriage legalization, 116–17
San Andres Accords, 191
Sandinista Revolution in Nicaragua, 22, 559, 649
Santizo, Felicia, 338
Santos, Juan Manuel, 398–99
Sarney, José, 494–95

Scott, James, 682
secessionist movements, 171–72
Second Vatican Council, 256–57, 625–26, 648–49
second-wave guerrilla groups, 188–89
Secretaría de Educación Pública (SEP), 169
Secretary of Rural Development and Family Farming (SRDFF), 292
See-Judge-Act methodology, 627
segmented corporatism, 315
self-governing collective practices, 28
self-limiting radicalism, 463, 466–67
sem-teto/sin-techo activism, 505
separatist mobilization, 171–73
Ser Mujer, 379
Serrano, Jorge, 634
Servicio de Paz y Justicia en América Latina (SERPAJ), 426–27
sex-gender relations, 112
sexism, 112, 114, 340, 343–44, 345–46, 378
sexual identity theory, 109–10
shared identity, 440, 448, 449, 544
Sikkink, Kathryn, 424, 427–28, 523–25
Siles Suazo, Hernán, 183
Silva, Marina, 287
Silva Henríquez, Raúl, 203
Simmel, Georg, 74
Sindicato Nacional de Trabajadores de la Educación, 312
Sindicato Único de Trabajadores de la Educacion del Perú (SUTEP), 482
Smaper, Ernesto, 472–73
social action, 256, 495, 650
social capital, 90, 181, 761–62
social citizenship, 146, 151, 250, 251–52, 607, 737
social class, 19–20, 54, 93, 113, 144, 149–50, 270, 280–81, 455, 456–60, 489, 492, 538, 559, 645–46, 720
social conflict, 4, 59, 70–72, 229–30, 237, 293, 721, 722–23
social conformism, 285, 288–89, 291, 294–95, 296
socialism, 259–60, 306, 644, 645–46, 770–71
social media, 99–100, 147
social movement organizations (SMOs), 38, 41, 72, 673–74
social movement partyism. *See* party politics
social movement unionism, 237

social network analysis, 72, 88–89
social positioning, 112–14
social protest
　anti-neoliberalism and, 721, 726
　Argentina, 200, 478, 719–20, 750–51
　Bolivia, 689, 721
　Brazil, 478
　Central America, 688
　democratization and, 685
　gender equality and, 596–97
　Indigenous political movements, 360
　military dictatorships, 724
　participatory institutions and, 761
　party politics and, 684–86
　political representation impact on, 716–17
　Venezuela, 612–13, 721–22
social revolution, 155–56, 180–81, 183, 557, 567.
　See also revolutionary movements
social security programs, 150, 288–89, 314
social welfare, 146, 251, 337, 458, 723–24
socio-ecological resistance, 27
socio-environmentalism, 287–88, 441, 448, 516–17
socio-historical movements, 126
sociology of absences, 130
socio-natural metabolism, 516
socionatural relations, 78
socio-political conflict, 6–7, 23, 27, 54–57, 62–64
socioterritorial movements, 77–78, 271–72, 273, 448
solidarity movements, 98, 181
Somos in Rio de Janeiro, 412
Somoza Debayle, Anastasio, 197–98
Somoza family dynasty, 197–98
Somoza García, Anastasio, 561
Sotillo, Sara, 338
Soul Movement in Brazil, 372–73
Sousa Santos, Boaventura de, 124
South America, 286–95
Southern Cone regime, 200–4
Southern Copper, 253–54
Soviet Union, 24–25, 238, 308
Spain, 256–57
spatial strategies in social movement theory, 679–81
Special Ministry for the Advancement of Racial Equality, 782

Special Secretariat for the Promotion of Racial Equality Policies in Brazil, 382
Stalinized Marxism, 24
state-led development, 145–46, 151, 233–36, 252, 255, 721
state politics, 538–39
state repression, 149–50, 526–27
state-seeking nationalism, 171–73
state-society relations, 7–8, 29, 62, 285, 287, 354, 356, 364–65
state terrorism, 196, 202, 205
status-based movements, 18–19
Stokes, Susan, 24
strain theories, 35, 38, 43
strategic capital, 94–95
strategy-oriented paradigm, 25–26
strikes, 236, 311, 314
structural adjustment policies, 252, 310–11
structural determination, 55–56
The Struggle for Human Rights in Latin America (Cleary), 424
student movements
　Argentina, 394–95
　authoritarianism and, 392–97
　Brazil, 393–94, 396, 400–1
　Catholic Church and, 391, 394–95
　Chile, 390, 392, 395–96, 397–98, 533
　Colombia, 392, 396, 398–99
　contemporary mobilizations, 396–401
　Córdoba university reform, 390–93
　introduction to, 8, 389–91
　Mexico, 393, 394, 396, 399–400
　military regimes and, 393
　Peru, 392
　revolutionary hopes of, 235
　summary of, 401–2
　Venezuela, 392–93, 396–97
students' rights, 221
subaltern political action, 18
Subdesarrollo y revolución (Marini), 23
sub-imperialism, 23
subjectivation, 60–62, 63–64, 66, 316
subnational legal mobilization, 747, 757
subnetworks, 96
successful revolutions, 6, 181, 184–85, 188, 192, 557, 562, 564
sui generis political process, 315–16, 732, 783

super-exploitation, 23
supportive mobilizations, 75, 290
Supremo Tribunal Federal (STF), 754
symbolic institutionalization, 783–85
symbolic interactionism, 123

T

tactical fractionalization, 671–72
taking sides, 285, 289, 290, 295, 296
Taller de Historia Oral Andina (Rivera-Cusicanqui), 124
Teatro Experimental do Negro, 372–73
tekohá, 268–69
Temer, Michel, 289
territorialization, 27, 237, 277
territorialization, deterritorialization and reterritorialization (TDR), 77–78
territorial movements
　activism of, 77
　autonomist movements and, 510
　indigenous movements and, 359–64
　moral economy, 739–41
　new territoriality, 76, 267, 276, 687–88
　politics of, 738–41
　resource mobilization and, 38
　socioterritorial movements, 77–78, 271–72, 273, 448
　struggles of, 131–34
territorio, defined, 679–82
terroristic dictatorships, 25, 198
Tía María copper mine, 253–54
Tilly, Charles, 526–27, 660, 670–72
TIPNIS indigenous groups, 295
Tlatelolco Plaza massacre, 207, 394, 565–66
Toldeo, Alejandro, 481
Torres, Camilo, 560
Torrijos, Omar, 198–99
totalitarian regimes, 196, 506. *See also* authoritarianism
totality and Marxism, 18–20
trabajo territorial, 512–13
trade corporations, 304
trade liberalization, 169–70, 239, 494–95
trade unions, 56, 94, 287, 309. *See also* unionism
transdisciplinary fields in decolonization, 124–25

transitional justice, 216–17, 422–23, 428–29, 430, 525
transnational advocacy networks (TANs), 426–27, 543
transnational collective action
　alternatives to, 527–30
　Argentina, 525
　Central America, 528
　Chile, 521–22, 527
　digital transnationalism, 531–32
　by feminists, 521–23
　introduction to, 521–22
　multidisciplinary research agenda on, 523–25
　patterns of interactions, 525–26
　pioneering of, 522–23
　right-wing actors, 530, 531
　summary of, 532–33
　threats and mobilization, 526–27
transnationalized bourgeoisie, 200
transnational labor organizing, 96
transnational movements, 95–98, 254–62, 285–86, 531–32
Triángulo Rosa in Río de Janeiro, 414, 415
tribalization effects, 600
Tri-Continental Conference (Prashad 2007), 152
Trujillo, Rafael, 197
Tupamaros in Uruguay, 564–65
Turkish Taksim Gezi Park mobilizations, 533
Twitter users, 100, 147
Tzul-Tzul, Glagys, 129–30

U

Ubico, Jorge, 149
Ubico Castañeda, Jorge, 325–26
Ulate, Cordero, 448
Una Corte para la Democracia, 753
uncivil movements, 9, 539, 545–46
unemployed organizations, 290–91
unemployed workers' movement, 27
unemployment, 312, 733
União de Lavradores e Trabalhadores Agrícolas do Brasil (ULTAB), 326
União Geral das Escolas de Samba (UGES), 645
União Metropolitana dos Estudantes and Dissidência, 393–94

União Nacional dos Estudantes (UNE), 392–93
Unidad Popular, 395, 563
Unión Cívica Radical Party, 392
Unión de los Trabajadores Rurales Sin Tierra of Argentina (UST), 271–72
Unión de Mujeres Americanas (UMA), 522–23
Unión de Usuarios y Consumidores, 750–51
unionism, 237, 308, 309–10, 313, 315
Unión Nacional de Trabajadores (UNT), 314
United Fruit Company, 325–26
United Nations, 321, 345, 363–64
United Nations Conferences, 284–85
United Nations Declaration on Human Rights, 522–23
United Nations Declaration on the Rights of Indigenous Peoples (UNDRIP), 364
United Nations Educational, Scientific, and Cultural Organization (UNESCO), 651
United Nations Human Rights Committee, 756–57
United Nations World Conference against Racism, Racial Discrimination, Xenophobia, and Related Forms of Intolerance, 380
United Nations World Conference on Population and Development, 380
United Nations World Conference on Women, 380
United States Agency for International Development (USAID), 328
Universal Declaration of Human Rights, 425–26
Universal Negro Improvement Association, 372–73
universal suffrage, 8–9, 183, 233, 235, 338, 463
Universidad Autónoma del Estado de Potosí, 393
Universidad de Chile, 392
Universidad de la Tierra de Oaxaca (Mexico), 125
Universidad Nacional de Córdoba (UNC). *See* Córdoba university reform
urbanization, 145, 168–69, 234, 243, 308, 409, 456–57, 458–59, 590, 633, 683, 692
urban poor activism, 73
urban social movements
  Brazil, 464–65
  challenge of resilience, 465–67
  citizenship as agency, 455, 460–65
  introduction to, 8–9, 455–56
  social class and, 456–60
  summary of, 467
  Venezuela, 463
Uribe Vélez, Álvaro, 550–51
Uruguay
  feminist movements, 114, 340
  institutionalization of social movements, 786
  LGBTIQ+ movements, 417
  Ojo T poetry project, 115
  participatory institutions in, 768–69
  Tupamaros in, 564–65
  urban social movements, 458
used territory, 76
utopian-revolutionary dialectic, 20

V

vanguardism, 97, 557, 559
Vargas, Getúlio, 234, 308, 340–41
Vatican II reforms, 152–53
Velandia, Manuel, 412
Venezuela
  authoritarianism of, 348
  authoritarian regimes in, 207–8
  Chávez, Hugo, 240
  colectivos (urban collectives) in, 608, 612–14
  constitutional reform processes, 347
  democratic path to socialism, 241
  indigenous in, 615–17
  participatory institutions in, 770–71
  party politics, 725, 726
  popular protests in, 208
  Radio Caracas Televisión, 396–97
  social protest, 612–13, 721–22
  student movements in, 392–93, 396–97
  urban social movements, 458, 463
Venezuelan Cecosesola Network, 133
Via Campesina peasant movement, 113
Vicaría de la Solidarida, 203
Vicente Gómez, Juan, 392–93
Vida SV ("Si a la Vida"), 547
Villa, Pancho, 182
Villarroel, Gualberto, 183
Virgin of Guadalupe, 166
voting rights of women, 338, 339

W

Wankavika Trans project, 115
Washington Consensus, 58–59, 493–94
water privatization, 260, 495
Water War of Cochabamba, 253, 689
Wer, Gabriel, 702
WhatsApp, 148
Williams, Raymond, 573
women and Protestantism, 635–37
women's international nongovernmental organizations (WINGOs), 97
women's movements
   activism of, 108–11, 343–44
   Black women's activism, 377–80
   democracy and neoliberalism, 344–46
   identity and, 594–97
   introduction to, 8, 336–37
   leftist consciousness of, 339–41
   left-wing social movements, 339–41, 342
   maternal demands, 337–39
   militant motherhood, 341–43
   Pink Tide, 346–48
   populism and, 339–41
   revolutionary women, 18–19, 343, 344
   summary of, 348–49
Women's Policy Agencies (WPA), 788
women's rights, 221, 337–39, 431, 432
workers mobilization
   collective action, 7–8
   democracy and neoliberalism, 310–12
   developmentalism, heteronomy, and revolution, 307–10
   emergence of workers, 304–7
   introduction to, 303–4
   neoliberalism and, 310–12, 315
   new organizational formats, 312–16
   summary of, 316
workers' rights, 7–8, 93, 315–16, 338, 496, 723–24
Working Group on Indigenous Populations (WGIP), 363–64
World Bank, 236, 270, 524
World Economic Forum (WEF), 262, 529–30
World Social Forum of Porto Alegre Hugo Chávez, 561–62
World Social Forum (WSF), 262, 529–30, 596–97
Worthiness, Unity, Numbers, and Commitment (WUNC), 609

Y

Yacimientos Petrolíferos Fiscales, 290
Yanomani people, 277
YoSoy132 movement, 258–59, 390, 697–98

Z

Zapata, Emiliano, 182, 322, 556–57
Zapata Olivella, Manual, 374–75
Zapatista movement in Mexico. *See* Ejército Zapatista de Liberación Nacional (EZLN)
Zárate Willka, Pablo, 322
Zuazo, Hernán Siles, 149
Zuleta, León, 412